The
Bowker
Annual

The Bowker Annual

Library and Book Trade Almanac™

2005 | 50th Edition

Editor Dave Bogart
Consultant Julia C. Blixrud

 Information Today, Inc.

Published by Information Today, Inc.

International Standard Book Number 1-57387-216-4
International Standard Serial Number 0068-0540
Library of Congress Catalog Card Number 55-12434

Information Today, Inc.
143 Old Marlton Pike
Medford, NJ   08055-8750
Phone: 800-300-9868 (customer service)
         800-409-4929 (editorial queries)
Fax: 609-654-4309
E-mail (orders): custserv@infotoday.com
Web Site: http://www.infotoday.com

Printed and bound in the United States of America

US $199

ISBN 1-57387-216-4

9 781573 872164   19900>

Contents

Part 1
Reports from the Field

International Reports

Special Reports

Part 2
Legislation, Funding, and Grants

Legislation

Funding Programs and Grant-Making Agencies

Part 3
Library/Information Science
Education, Placement, and Salaries

Part 4
Research and Statistics

Library Research and Statistics

Book Trade Research and Statistics

Part 5
Reference Information

Bibliographies

Ready Reference

Distinguished Books

Part 6
Directory of Organizations

Directory of Library and Related Organizations

Directory of Book Trade and Related Organizations

Preface

This milestone 50th edition of the *Bowker Annual* marks a half century of chronicling the worlds of librarianship and publishing.

The *Bowker Annual* traces its ancestry to the *American Library Annual* for 1955–1956, a 165-page compilation of reports and statistics on the nation's library and book trade organizations. As the "information industry" has evolved and expanded, so have we, keeping pace with developments year by year.

In a Foreword to this edition, Wayne A. Wiegand looks back at those 50 years and the many changes they have brought, both for those directly involved in librarianship and publishing and for the people they serve.

To mark this occasion, we have assembled six Special Reports on a broad variety of current issues:

- Trisha L. Davis takes a detailed look at the challenges posed as licensing increasingly takes the place of purchase of the electronic resources libraries now find indispensable.
- In a survey of the year in electronic publishing, Edward J. Valauskas and Nancy R. John examine the growing movement toward "open access" to scientific and other publications—a matter of great interest to both libraries and publishers.
- The growing role of institutional repositories in scholarly publishing is explored by Kimberly Douglas.
- Lisa Janicke Hinchliffe explains how libraries are playing a vital role in information literacy, guiding the public in learning to find, assess, and use information in the electronic age.
- An overview of library assessment and performance measures—how libraries assess how well they're doing their increasingly complex job—is presented by Julia C. Blixrud and Wanda Dole.
- Sarah K. Wiant discusses concerns about digital technologies and their importance in the constantly changing realm of copyright law.

Also in Part 1 are reports on the year's activities from federal agencies, federal libraries, and national and international library and publishing organizations.

The year's legislation and regulations affecting both libraries and publishing are examined in Part 2, along with the activities of grant-making and funding programs.

Part 3 contains professional information for librarians: guides to sources of scholarships and employment, our annual look at trends in library placements and salaries, and a list of 2004's major scholarship and award winners.

A wealth of research and statistics makes up Part 4, from descriptions of noteworthy research projects to detailed data on library acquisition expenditures, prices of materials, book title output, and the position of the United States in the international book trade.

Reference information in Part 5 ranges from lists of the year's bestselling books, top literary prizes, and recommended materials to such practical information as how to obtain an ISBN, SAN, or ISSN.

Part 6 contains our updated directory of library and book trade organizations at the state, national, and international levels. It is followed by detailed indexes and a calendar of information industry events.

The *Bowker Annual* is the work of many hands, and gratitude goes to all those who contributed articles, assembled reports, supplied statistics, and responded to our requests for information. Special thanks are due Consultant Editor Julia C. Blixrud and Contributing Editor Catherine Barr.

We believe you will find this edition a valuable and frequently used resource, and—as always—we welcome your comments and suggestions for future editions.

Dave Bogart
Editor

Foreword to the 50th Edition

American Librarianship During
Bowker Annual's First Half Century

Wayne A. Wiegand

"The best reading for the greatest number at the least cost." When Melvil Dewey convinced the American Library Association to adopt this as ALA's motto in 1879, he identified a set of priorities that have dominated the practice of librarianship ever since. And for 50 editions, the *Bowker Annual* has documented in various ways librarianship's efforts to identify "the best reading," to reach "the greatest number," and to deliver service "at the least cost."

Already in 1956, when the first *Bowker Annual* was published (originally as *American Library Annual*), debates about what constituted "best reading" preoccupied the profession. UCLA Director of Libraries Lawrence Clark Powell argued that "books are basic." To be effective professionals, he said, librarians primarily had to be readers. Many in the nation's library community agreed. For this "fundamentalist" view, however, Powell was heavily criticized by Jesse Shera, dean of Western Reserve's School of Library Science. Shera wanted librarianship to focus on "information"—a modern-day definition of "reading"—and to form links with a group of scientists evolving a community that was well placed to benefit from federal funding. Because these scientists generally agreed that traditional libraries had not been meeting their needs, they had begun to establish science information centers and initiate their own indexing and abstracting services to more rapidly retrieve the information they needed. Although many librarians worried that "information scientists" tended to ignore the larger populations most libraries served (i.e., "the greatest number"), they nonetheless maintained connections. Almost symbolically, Powell and Shera regularly exchanged pleasantries when they crossed paths at national conferences.

By the late 1950s, the infusion of federal funds into all sectors of the library community was having significant impact on American libraries. In 1956 President Dwight D. Eisenhower signed the Library Services Act (LSA), the first federal legislation intended to fund some library services. The act made it to his desk only because a group of state librarians from the South had managed to convince their congressmen and senators (many of whom held crucial congressional committee chairs) that passage of the act would not curtail states' rights because state library agencies would have the power to determine the distribution of the

Wayne A. Wiegand is F. William Summers Professor of Library and Information Studies and Professor of American Studies at Florida State University and co-editor of *Library Quarterly,* published by the University of Chicago Press.

funds. The issue of library services to African Americans was a constant subtext in librarians' lobbying efforts. LSA funds gave state library agencies a new source of power. To serve remote populations, many bought bookmobiles, which functioned as moving examples of "the best reading for the greatest number at the least cost."

Evaluating Materials

In 1960 ALA published *Standards for School Library Programs,* which acknowledged the value audiovisual materials held for school libraries (and thus expanded the definition of "reading"). Nine years later ALA published *Standards for School Media Programs,* which had been jointly developed by the American Association of School Librarians and the National Education Association's Division of Audio-Visual Instruction. Lyndon Johnson's 1960s Great Society legislation, including the Library Services and Construction Acts (1964, 1965), the Higher Education Act (1965), and, of particular importance to school libraries, the Elementary and Secondary Education Act (1965), significantly impacted library development in the United States. Influenced by funding from all three, the number of public schools with libraries increased from 50 percent of the total in 1958 (40,000) to 93 percent in 1985 (74,000). At the same time, the average size of book collections in public schools increased from 2,972 in 1958 to 8,466 in 1985.

To help identify "best reading," peer-reviewed academic journals and university presses, reputable and authoritative literary periodicals, and trade publishers worked together throughout the 20th century to evaluate newer materials and eventually form a consensus on a hierarchy classifying the rest. Since 1905 ALA had been screening these published professional reviews and from them selecting those identified as the best for citation in *Booklist*; most public libraries subscribed. In addition, the H. W. Wilson Company published *Fiction Catalog, Children's Catalog, Public Library Catalog,* and *Junior and Senior High School Library Catalog* in quinquennial editions (all citations contained therein were based on reviews in Wilson indexes), and updated them with annual supplements. Beginning in 1964 the Association of College and Research Libraries issued *Choice,* a monthly list of books recommended for purchase by academic libraries; in 1967 *Books for College Libraries,* a more comprehensive guide, appeared. Thus, librarians systemically built into their practice a reliance on outside authorities, and chose materials for their libraries from a pool whose boundaries had already been carefully defined by others.

Growth in Library-Related Publications

Multiple divisions, sections, and roundtables within ALA began issuing their own journals, some of which published applied research aimed at improving library services and management, including the Reference and Adult Services Division's *RQ* (now *Reference and User Services Quarterly*), the American Association of School Librarians' *Top of the News* (now the *Journal of Youth Services in Libraries*), the Association for Library Collections and Technical Services' *LRTS,* and the Association of College and Research Libraries' *College & Research Libraries.* The Wilson Company continued to publish *Reader's Guide* (begun in 1900) and an array of other indexes, all of which facilitated access to the "best reading" in particular subject fields. The R. R. Bowker Company, Scarecrow Press, Libraries Unlimited, and ALA (among others) also published numerous monographs, mostly to address librarians' practical needs. And each publisher also issued hundreds of new reference titles to improve essential library services. Thus, the vast majority of library literature and library research in the past half-century addressed "the best reading for the greatest number at the least cost." Not even research journals such as *Library Quarterly, Library Trends,* and *Library and Information Science Research* varied significantly from this pattern.

Professional Training, Intellectual Freedom

New professionals coming out of library schools in the 1960s had little reason to question these priorities. Before mid-century, entrance exams tested library school applicants' knowledge of current events, high-culture literature, and political (largely Western) history. After mid-century, library school applicants generally needed a liberal arts undergraduate degree from an accredited institution, where they had already been taught the "best reading" by academic experts. Once enrolled in library schools they took the core curriculum, usually consisting of cataloging and classification, reference, management, book selection, and often a generic "library in society" course. The first four addressed institution and expertise; the last was intended to socialize students to the "library spirit" and inculcate a "library faith" that as an institution the library was essential to a functioning democracy. In their "library and society" courses students were also to be exposed to the profession's position on ethics, which up to the 1970s had largely been treated as rules for professional behavior.

In 1967 ALA established an Office of Intellectual Freedom (OIF) to implement the policies of the Intellectual Freedom Committee and the ALA Council. In 1969 the Freedom to Read Foundation was incorporated as a separate entity to be coordinated by the OIF to provide financial and legal assistance to censorship challenges. And in 1973 several ALA members organized an Intellectual Freedom Round Table to provide an organization within the association through which individuals could express themselves on specific and general intellectual freedom issues. In 1976 and 1981 ALA issued statements of ethics that addressed principles governing intellectual freedom, professional relationships with colleagues and vendors, and service to library patrons, among others. However, like the Library Bill of Rights approved by ALA in 1939, the Statement of Ethics was unenforceable. No librarian ever suffered professional censure for violations of either.

Enter 'Information Scientists' and a New Social Focus

Beginning in the 1970s government and information scientists began to view the library as a site for "knowledge" research, and some library schools were quick to take advantage, although they seldom analyzed cultural biases built into the conventional definition of "knowledge." Soon "information scientists" began to populate library school faculties, and "schools of library science" began to change their names to "schools of library and information science" (and later "schools of information") and to produce their own information scientists. Library and information science research continued to experiment with social science methods ranging from cybernetics to operations research, and, with the arrival of computer-based bibliographic networks and utilities, the groundwork was laid for user studies based on library service models that encompassed online studies and reference work evaluation. Many—including a growing number of information scientists—touted the scientific method as the most appropriate way to investigate library problems.

Within librarianship, however, some criticized the profession's leaders for elitist attitudes that flavored efforts to reach "the greatest number." In the early 1970s Michael Harris extrapolated from conclusions of revisionist educational historians in his analysis of the origins of the Boston Public Library. Harris argued that the founders—all white, all male, and all from Boston's first families—set up the institution primarily as a means to exercise control of the city's new immigrants, especially the Irish. His conclusions struck at the heart of the library faith, but they also fit the times. ALA was experiencing a revolt occasioned by hundreds of its younger members who saw in the principle of "neutrality" most often advocated by veteran librarians (1) an excuse not to address inequities in library practice caused by racism, sexism, and homophobia; (2) a rationale not to confront a government bent on conducting an unjust war in Southeast Asia; and (3) a mechanism to give the Library Bill of Rights a strict construction that rendered it ineffective in the fight to include alternative perspectives in library collections. With the organization of the Social Responsibilities Round Table in 1969, these rebels found a home in ALA.

Revisionist library history also grounded other efforts to correct inequities in the library profession. At the ALA annual conference membership meeting in 1964, E. J. Josey rose to "vigorously protest" an award to the Mississippi Library Association. Josey pointed out that a decade earlier the association had withdrawn from ALA because it refused to integrate. He followed his protest with a motion to prohibit ALA officers and staff members from attending or speaking in any official capacity at state library associations that were not also a chapter of ALA. The motion passed by a wide margin. In 1970 Josey organized the Black Caucus to monitor ALA policy and practice concerning race and to give African Americans a more prominent voice in professional matters.

African Americans were not the only minority to protest their plight within ALA and the profession. In 1970 Israel Fishman and Janet Cooper organized an ALA Task Force on Gay Liberation (TFGL), the first openly gay and lesbian group established as part of a professional organization. Under Barbara Gittings's energetic leadership after 1971, TFGL sponsored the compilation of bibliographies of works by and about gays and lesbians, produced conference programs, protested discrimination (including the absence of coverage of gay and lesbian press titles in periodical indexes published by mainstream library press companies), and initiated a "best book" award that ALA did not officially endorse until 1986. At the 1971 annual conference in Dallas, TFGL organized a "Hug-a-Homosexual" kissing booth that drew much attention from the local press. But professional leaders learned slowly. A 1986 ALA publication titled

The Library Disaster Preparedness Handbook recommended that "librarians use the occasion of detecting persons in overt homosexual activity to spread the word about the library's hostility to this abuse of the facility. This is done through a humiliating interrogation and browbeating in a formal setting, like a security office."

Women (gay or straight) in the library profession also suffered sexist attitudes and practices from employers and patrons. In 1970 several women founded the Feminist Task Force of the Social Responsibilities Round Table within ALA. In a 1983 publication, Kathleen Heim pointed out that although men made up only 20 percent of all librarians in the United States, they accounted for 58 percent of library school faculty members, 47 percent of the work force at the Library of Congress, and 38 percent of academic librarians. Once identified, sexism in librarianship was more easily attacked, wherever it surfaced.

Management Evolves

But for most practicing librarians, eliminating racism, sexism, and homophobia in the profession seemed less compelling than other developments in library practice that addressed issues of "the least cost." When Donald Coney surveyed library administrators in 1952, he discovered that few were acquainted with management principles, and most believed management was intuitive. In subsequent decades, library management literature made frequent reference to theorists such as Peter Drucker. In 1969 the Association of Research Libraries (ARL) created a Committee on University Library Management. In 1970 the Council on Library Resources funded ARL's Office of Management Studies, which then contracted with Booz Allen & Hamilton to study the Columbia University Library to determine how library services might be improved. The resulting report, "Organization and Staffing of the Libraries of Columbia University" (1973), helped guide other university library managers striving to meet the demands that higher education and research were placing on their facilities. At the same time, however, the distribution of power in the organization of libraries did not shift significantly. Few chose to shake a system of hierarchy and departmentalization that had settled into library organization.

By that time financial support for libraries had also eroded (which in part explains why the Friends of Libraries USA organized in 1974), and—because inflation decreased purchasing power at the same time as the volume of publications increased and computerization of bibliographic records demanded heavy investments—"managing change" became the primary responsibility of administrators of large libraries. ARL's Office of Management Studies (OMS) undertook several initiatives, most of which were based primarily on human relations and nonquantitative approaches to management science. The office established the Management Review and Analysis Project (to help individual libraries review planning, control, organization development, and personnel practices), the Academic Library Development Program (to improve collection development, public services, and preservation at the small academic library), and the Consultant Training Program (to create a corps of OMS-trained professionals to develop further studies). At many institutions, library administrators adapted to the management systems initiated by parent institutions (e.g., management by objectives; zero-based budgeting; planning, programming, and budgeting systems [PPBS]; and total quality management [TQM]), but they tended to avoid tools of decision theorists such as operations research, economic analysis, and modeling.

Automation and Online Access

In 1967 the Ohio College Association founded the Ohio College Library Center. For the first four years, the center developed a systems architecture and provided catalog card production services. In 1971 it began online operation with its Cataloging Subsystem. Under Frederick Kilgour's visionary leadership, little more than a decade later the center had evolved from a local college network into a national bibliographic utility known as OCLC (Online Computer Library Center). It had also initiated a number of online subsystems, including Interlibrary Loan, Serials Control, Acquisitions, and EPIC (a subject access system). Because OCLC had also adopted MARC records (a standard format for machine-readable bibliographic records developed by the Library of Congress) on which many libraries depended, by the year 2000 thousands of libraries around the world were using its database for cooperative cataloging. OCLC also participated in national programs, including the ARL/NFAIS A&I Project (host system for the National Serials Data Project and Serials Cataloging for the Library of Congress), and the Linked Systems Project (host system for CONSER and the U.S. Newspapers Microforms Program). The CONSER Program established an ongoing effort between the national and major research libraries of North America and the OCLC network to create a large database of bibliographic records for serials.

By the turn of the century, thousands of libraries of all types had developed online public access catalogs, adopted packaged automated circulation systems, and incorporated use of CD-ROM products into the provision of traditional library services. Still, librarians could not seem to rid information retrieval systems of historic cultural biases. Not until 1972 did the Library of Congress remove "see also" references from "homosexuality" and "lesbianism" to "sexual perversion." Four years later, it introduced subject headings for "lesbians" and "homosexuals, male," which for the first time recognized them as classes of people. Yet in 1990 only 35 of the more than 270,000 records on RLIN's archival database contained some form of "lesbian" as a descriptor. By misidentifying or refusing to identify, librarians (often unknowingly) participated in hegemony's tendency to render whole classes of people invisible.

Adapting to Changing Populations, Priorities

Elsewhere in the library world, social changes brought other effects. As "white flight" drained cities in the 1960s, urban public library circulation decreased, in the largest communities by as much as 16 percent. Because those who stayed did not value the kind of printed cultural forms libraries routinely collected as much as those who left (they differed in their definitions of "best reading"), librarians had to alter traditional practices and devise new ways to address a different set of information needs. Information and referral became one approach, most evident in

Detroit Public Library's TIP (The Information Place) Program initiated in 1971. Librarians there developed card file systems listing social and county organizations and the services they provided, their hours, addresses, telephone numbers, and personnel. Many of these files were later converted to machine-readable databases. Elsewhere, public librarians took different approaches. One administrative approach to new circumstances was the evolution of federated library systems in which individually governed libraries volunteered to participate in joint efforts to purchase materials and share information and referral (I&R) services. Opportunities brought by improvement in electronic data processing accelerated the process.

Another change was the emergence of highly successful county library systems, most notably in places such as Broward County, Florida; Hennepin County, Minnesota; and Montgomery County, Maryland. All these developments were reflected in a set of recommendations detailed in *The Public Library Mission Statement and Its Imperative for Service,* issued by ALA's Public Library Association in 1979. Public libraries should step away from acculturation, the document argued, and instead become educational, cultural, information, and rehabilitative agencies that celebrate and serve the multicultural heritage of their communities in nontraditional ways. Another trend evident in the 1970s was the evolution of multitype systems that embraced more than one type of library in a cooperative network. Whereas 75 percent of library systems in the United States in 1975 were limited to public libraries, that number dropped to 62 percent a decade later.

Other efforts to prepare different futures met mixed results, some of which were reflected in the experiences of the Council on Library Resources (now the Council on Library and Information Resources), established by a Ford Foundation grant in 1956 to facilitate research that had potential for improving library services and collections. In the late 1960s, for example, the council began pouring millions of dollars into MIT's Information Transfer Experiment (INTREX) Project—up to that time the largest nonmilitary information research project ever undertaken—in order to reconfigure the research library of the future. Because it was designed primarily by engineers and emphasized the information they considered most valuable, the project ultimately failed to produce the prototypical all-purpose research library for which it was funded. In 1986, however, the council formed a Commission on Preservation and Access, produced a very effective film on the deterioration of paper with high acidity called *Slow Fires,* and joined with other higher education and scholarly agencies (for example, the Brittle Books Program of the National Endowment for the Humanities) to focus attention on a problem that affected the printed materials held by most libraries. All libraries now worry about conservation and preservation; many have formal programs to help protect their collections.

In the late 1950s the introduction of diffusion-transfer reversal (Thermofax) and electrostatic (Xerox) copying machines transformed library services, as students and patrons lined up to copy materials from library resources. Telefacsimile did not arrive until the late 1980s. The computer accelerated all these changes, and more. In 1972 the New York Public Library began a computer-produced book catalog for the Research Libraries Group. The University of South Carolina was the first to use a bar code and light pen to automate its circulation system. Computer Library Systems, Inc. (CSLI) pioneered online systems in the early 1970s, and by 1985 had captured a major share of the market. The evolution of these online public library catalogs (OPACs) also influenced classification systems, which were usually evaluated against the potential their notational schemes had as access points to the collections.

In the 1980s a machine-readable version of the Dewey Decimal Classification proved highly promising, and shortly thereafter multifunction systems incorporating classification schemes allowed libraries and their patrons not only to read all MARC information on items held, but also to identify whether any title in the library collection had been checked out or was on the shelf. Within a decade dial-in access systems enabled library patrons to check on the circulation status of individual items in library collections from remote sites, to request materials via electronic mail, and to "hold" materials already in circulation. They also enabled libraries themselves to better study use data to improve access and availability. Reference work was profoundly affected by "the online revolution," which greatly expanded (and rapidly increased the speed of) the reference librarian's literature searching ability, and also his or her status within the library profession. In many libraries, database librarians set up appointments with patrons to help them tailor their queries to terms the systems could most easily manipulate.

By 2000 the scores of consortia and networks that had developed to generate and centralize cataloging information had evolved into four major bibliographic utilities—OCLC, RLIN, WLN (initially called the Washington Library Network, and later Western Library Network), and UTLAS (for the University of Toronto Library Automated System, which developed it and later sold it to a commercial organization). All four maintained online databases of authorities and bibliographic information, functioned as a source of cataloging copy for libraries with online catalogs, and produced catalog cards for libraries without online catalogs.

In the last quarter of the 20th century, the Defense Department's Advanced Research Projects Agency established a computer network. When several years later the federal government sponsored a program to establish communication protocols to integrate multiple networks, the Internet was born. Ever since, librarians have both admired and feared it. Some argue that the Internet will replace libraries; others argue it will sediment into yet another means to carry out librarianship's traditional mission. If history provides any indication, the latter prediction is likely to be closest to reality.

Conclusion

Over the past half century, events in American librarianship described here—and documented in the hundreds of feature essays and reports and the thousands of statistics published in the first 50 editions of the *Bowker Annual*—mirror the professional priorities contained in the ALA motto—"the best reading for the greatest number at the least cost."

At the same time, however, the perspective applied to these priorities has largely been "user in the life of the library." Because American libraries are largely voluntary civic institutions that their publics do not need to use, those same publics have exercised substantial influence over the generations on the contours and parameters of library services. American library history convinces me that libraries have done three things exceptionally well in the past 150 years. They have (1) made information accessible to millions of people on many subjects; (2) provided tens of thousands of places where patrons have been able to meet informally as clubs or groups, or informally as citizens and students utilizing a civic institution and a cultural agency; and (3) furnished billions of reading materials to millions of patrons.

I have argued elsewhere that to deepen our understanding of the latter two, we have to develop another perspective. Rather than looking mostly at "the user in the life of the library," we have to look much more at the "library in the life of the user." Only by applying this second perspective can we move beyond the priorities manifest in the ALA motto and come to a deeper understanding of the roles that reading as an essential human behavior and the "library as place" play in the everyday lives of the millions of people. And for the past half-century library statistics on circulation and library visits show mostly steady growth, which suggests that the library of the future will probably be as important for its roles of facilitating reading and providing civic space as in the past it has been for providing information access. Hopefully, some of the next 50 editions of the *Bowker Annual* will contain essays that take this perspective, and address these questions.

Part 1
Reports from the Field

News of the Year

The Year in Public Libraries:
Budgets, Technology, Outreach

Kathy Dempsey

During 2004 the library world continued fighting budget battles and working on advocacy. It dealt with ever-increasing amounts of digital content, along with the technologies to store and access it. And once again the year's hot topics included threats to patron privacy, collaboration, library design, and the growing influence of Internet search engines. Libraries celebrated anniversaries and survived disasters, and librarians got involved in election-year politics.

Funding, Salaries, Jobs

Despite continued publicity and public relations campaigns, financial situations at many libraries are not good. Carol Brey-Casiano, American Library Association (ALA) 2004–2005 president, lamented that more than $80 million was cut from public library budgets during 2004. All sorts of librarians still find themselves fighting for funding and trying not to cut hours or staff.

In part because of the financial pinch, some libraries have resorted to using collection companies to recover overdue materials. A spokesperson for the Dayton (Ohio) Metro Library reported that more than 500 patrons each had $300 worth of items overdue, and that the library was losing up to $400,000 a year in materials. After hiring Unique Management Systems, a 10-year-old collection company specializing in libraries, 70 percent of the delinquent patrons contacted were reported to be cooperating with requests to return or to pay for their overdue materials. Those who didn't respond to Unique's "gentle persuasion" were being reported to credit agencies.

As for librarians' personal finances, the opening sentences of *Library Journal*'s annual Placements and Salaries Survey article gave this summary: "If the economy is rebounding, the library world has yet to feel it. The budget constraints of the last several years are now showing up in salary growth that lags behind inflation and in job searches that seem endless and are three times as long, on average . . ." It went on to report some troubling statistics. Men in library jobs continue to make higher average salaries, and while more minority librarians are getting master's degrees, they "lost significant ground in salary

Kathy Dempsey is editor-in-chief of *Computers in Libraries* and editor of *Marketing Library Services* newsletter, both published by Information Today, Inc.

parity" during the survey period, down about 6 percent from the previous year. Meanwhile, the average library job search took 4.5 months after graduation, and while 98.6 percent of responding graduates did find some sort of library job, for many the job was only part-time. On a bright note, the average salaries for professionals in school media centers rose slightly (by 1.02 percent) for the second year running. [For the complete report, see "Placements and Salaries 2003" in Part 4—*Ed.*]

Technology Marches On

Many librarians see new and improved technologies as both a blessing and a curse. Staying abreast of, evaluating, buying, learning to use, and maintaining the latest hardware, software, and databases is time-consuming, and the pace of technology didn't slow in 2004. Here are some of the tools that librarians had to deal with.

Open Access

Perhaps the biggest tech buzz-phrase of the year was "open access" or "OA." The OA movement is trying to make research simpler and faster for searchers, but it's not necessarily easy on librarians or vendors. The idea is to base more electronic information on the same standards so that people (search engines or crawlers, really) can search across many databases or platforms simultaneously. Vendors, once very protective of their expensive-to-produce data, are now scrambling to adhere to the standards that make such federated searching possible. Systems librarians themselves are doing the same, coding together their OPACs, their online databases, their serials lists, and their electronic journals, so that a user can type in one search, see what the library has on the topic (regardless of format and material type), and be linked to an appropriate copy of a document that's owned within the institution. Research gets easier, but system maintenance gets harder. Couple this with the continued proliferation of digital content—and the licensing and access details necessary to make it all work—and the challenges become apparent.

Electronic Resource Management

A new type of product aiming to help coordinate all this digital data is Electronic Resource Management (ERM) technology. Only a handful of vendors had ERM tools in 2004, but more were in development for 2005 release. ERM may help to simplify the management of a library's plethora of electronic resources, but it will be yet another tool that tech librarians will need to learn about, compare, buy, be trained to use, and then maintain.

OCLC (the Online Computer Library Center) acknowledged the growing difficulty of managing electronic content in the report *2004 Information Format Trends: Content, Not Containers.* It explained how information trends have forced librarians to organize more-complex resources, and concentrated on how content has been unbundled from traditional "containers" such as books. It covered, among other things, open-source publishing, e-learning, and blogs.

Blogs Proliferate

"Blog" (short for Web log) became a buzzword back in 2003, and library blogs proliferated during 2004. More and more libraries saw their usefulness and began employing them to rush news, alerts, and book lists to patrons. Since patrons could subscribe to blogs or RSS feeds (RSS stands for "Really Simple Syndication," an XML-based format for distributing and aggregating Web content such as news headlines), librarians didn't have to worry that outgoing e-mail to patrons would be mistaken for spam. An interesting year-end report emerged from two Pew Internet and American Life surveys saying that "By the end of 2004, blogs had established themselves as a key part of online culture." Blog readership jumped an estimated 58 percent in 2004, now includes more than a quarter of all Internet users, and about 12 percent of Internet users say they have posted to blogs. On the other hand, the Pew surveys also found that 62 percent of Internet users didn't know what a blog was.

Major Stride by Google

Library blogs may make library professionals look more "hip" and media-savvy, but in the meantime the major search engine Google continues to nearly out-library the librarians—in the public eye, anyway. Google went public, financially, in the summer of 2004, and made more news in mid-December when it announced an ambitious project to scan millions of texts from five major libraries and make them searchable online (in full text where copyright allows it). The project will involve Harvard University, Stanford University, Oxford University, the University of Michigan, and the New York Public Library. It has been estimated that the process could take more than a decade. And while the project will eventually help millions to access books and documents that formerly lived only in print, some librarians still worry that the commercial service will someday cut libraries out of the loop altogether.

Reaching Out

The Smartest Card

The Public Library Association (PLA), a division of ALA, took its turn pulling the advocacy bandwagon with the campaign "The Smartest Card Is @ your library." The goal was to reach out with the message that a library card could be the most valuable card in anyone's wallet. "Advocacy is a fundamental goal of the PLA Strategic Plan," the announcements declared. This major initiative was announced at PLA's National Conference in February. Over the following months, PLA created a downloadable Internet tool kit complete with sample public relations materials, posters, and electronic artwork, and the campaign was officially launched in September to coincide with National Library Card Sign-Up Month.

Also of note was the fact that this PLA National Conference, the organization's tenth, saw record-breaking attendance. Nearly 8,700 staff, exhibitors, authors, and guests gathered in the Washington State Convention and Trade Center in Seattle, and its exhibit hall of nearly 800 booths was sold out.

Serving Spanish-Speakers

Outreach efforts further embraced the growing Spanish-speaking population. ALA added a series of public service announcements in Spanish to its "@ your library" site. Additionally, the Library Video Network released a 24-minute video, "Bridging the Digital Divide in the Spanish-Speaking Community," that demonstrates ways in which libraries can welcome Spanish-speaking patrons, make the library an attractive destination for them, and ensure that they get quality services.

Trends and Topics

The trend toward personalization didn't seem to lose any momentum in 2004. Libraries are still catering to the "me generation" by using the word "my" in front of many services, resulting in catchy names like MyPortal or MyLibrary or MyState. The technology to do this has become commonplace, and the desire to use it doesn't seem to have slowed.

One word heard at information-industry conferences around the country during 2004 was "collaboration." Driven in part by tight budgets and big needs, many nonprofit organizations are working with libraries to achieve their goals. Librarians have always been sharers, but this level of cooperation with groups outside the field is unprecedented. These projects often also tie in with outreach, advocacy, and fund-raising ideals. For instance, at Vigo County (Indiana) Public Library, tech-savvy librarians create free Web sites for qualifying local nonprofit groups. To make the workload realistic, the library limits the size of the sites, uses templates to design them, and allows the organizations to send updates only once each quarter. But the nonprofits—with their lack of money, time, and expertise—are thrilled to be able to broaden their reach, and the community now has improved access to local information. Everyone wins; the Vigo library quietly proves its value to the community, and the community hopefully will respond when the library needs funding or favors. This type of collaboration is one way in which libraries are helping themselves (and other underfunded altruistic organizations) to stay afloat.

As people in the library field become more knowledgeable about marketing, they are starting to design their spaces differently. Some new libraries strive to be more "homey" and welcoming, adding fireplaces or reading areas with comfortable furniture. Others are turning more high-tech, adding computer labs, training rooms, or wireless zones. Another trend is toward the bookstore model, adopting retail stores' methods. Designers are working to keep the necessary functionality while losing some of the institutional feel. In many ways, the new ideal of "What do my patrons want?" is pushing aside the old ideal of "What do I think my patrons need?" This can only be a good thing. In addition to more comfortable furniture and surroundings, we see do-it-yourself checkout stations that save patrons time and systems where patrons can place their own holds, pay their fines via debit cards, and reserve time slots on Internet stations. Like the other efforts to personalize computer use, it's all about the "me" generation—and about good customer service.

Some less-pleasant topics of discussion are still with us, unfortunately. And privacy concerns, especially those surrounding the controversial USA Patriot Act, look as if they'll be with us for some time.

Disasters, Natural and Man-Made

The year saw many physical disasters affecting libraries, some natural and some man-made.

The damage caused by an earthquake that hit Iran on December 26, 2003, was still being assessed during much of 2004. The ancient city of Bam, where the 6.7-magnitude quake struck, had three public libraries. Two were buried under rubble, and 95 percent of the collection of the third was destroyed. Iranian authorities were still working on their first priority—restoring essential services—eight months after the disaster, and said that restoration of schools and libraries would be their second priority. Help came from many places. A South Korean nonprofit donated 20 portable libraries for schools, and other institutions and countries sent books and dollars by the thousands. Then, on August 16, another earthquake (4.2 magnitude) struck the area, and has left many books unrescued in the rubble.

In Iraq, as war and unrest continued throughout the year, many of the country's libraries were ravaged. In a rescue effort, the Harvard University library system announced a partnership with the Simmons Graduate School of Library and Information Science. They planned to help train Iraqi librarians and archivists, modernize some libraries, and try to address the shortage of librarians. Simmons and Harvard were awarded $100,000 by the National Endowment for the Humanities for the project.

A series of hurricanes that hit Florida and other East Coast states took a toll during the summer of 2004. Many suffered through the one-two punch of Hurricanes Charley and Frances, then watched nervously as Ivan spun across the sea, eventually hitting land as well. Others named Jeanne and Bonnie also stopped by. Florida State Librarian Judith Ring told *Library Journal* (October 15) that "there isn't a single county that wasn't affected" by at least one of the storms.

Another disaster of note was a major fire that swept through the Duchess Anna Amalia Library in Weimar, Germany, in early September, destroying many rare or unique volumes. The library was in a 16th-century palace that housed 120,000 volumes (only part of the million-volume collection). Luckily, workers were able to save thousands of books by passing them hand-to-hand in a human chain before they had to clear the building. Among the priceless works saved was a 1534 Bible once owned by Martin Luther. Damage was estimated in the tens of millions of euros. The collection itself was not insured for fire, since much of it could not be replaced.

On October 30 a flood hit the University of Hawaii at Manoa. According to reports, "a wall of water up to seven feet high swept through the library's ground floor." It knocked down walls and stacks, damaging government document and map collections as well as computers and servers in the tech services department.

The year's final disaster will be long remembered. The tsunami that followed a major earthquake in the Indian Ocean on December 26 left a death toll in the hundreds of thousands as well as millions of dollars in property damage. The world rushed to help, and library groups joined in.

Getting Out the Vote

Another of the year's major topics was politics. Librarians made an important contribution to the nationwide drive to get out the vote for the presidential election. ALA and Working Assets cosponsored a voter-registration Web page as part of the "Register to Vote @ Your Library" initiative. ALA also benefited because every registration made through the site generated a donation from Working Assets to ALA's advocacy programs. There were also grants available for the libraries that signed up the most voters through their sites.

California Project Wins Praise

It's not unusual for a school or academic library to share its space with a local public library to keep costs down and offer convenience, but in 2004 there was a much comment about San Jose State University in California and San Jose Public Libraries operating jointly in the new Dr. Martin Luther King, Jr. Library, the only co-managed city-academic library in the country. The public and the academic libraries shared the 2004 Library of the Year Award (from *Library Journal* and Thomson Gale), and the marketing campaign that preceded the opening won both a major award from the Public Relations Society of America and the 2004 John Cotton Dana Library Public Relations Award from ALA and H. W. Wilson.

Movie Librarian Causes a Stir

"The Librarian: Quest for the Spear," a made-for-TV movie on TNT, got the library industry's attention in December. The hero, a perennial college student who doesn't know what to do with his life, ends up becoming a librarian who then finds himself in charge of guarding a special collection that includes such treasures as Pandora's Box and the Ark of the Covenant. ALA made a point of alerting everyone to the film and then asking for comments to post online afterward. The listservs sizzled. Many were displeased because the librarian was made out to be a bumbling action hero who didn't even have an MLS. But it was a fun film. And if you believe that there is no such thing as bad publicity, this movie was a nice way to wrap up a librarian's year.

School Librarianship 2004:
Advocating for a Professional Identity

Walter Minkel

George W. Bush's re-election in November 2004 sent an emphatic message to educators: No Child Left Behind would continue to push the policies and bedevil the budgets of state departments of education and local school districts. Not only would states be subjecting elementary and middle school students to increasing numbers of standardized tests in reading and math, but federal requirements were planned to add science testing, and, soon after the election, Bush announced that he wanted high school students tested as well. The pressure on America's schools would only grow.

America's school librarians, however, had an additional predicament to worry about. The federal No Child Left Behind (NCLB) legislation, which the president had signed in January 2002, did not identify media specialists or school libraries as essential to a school's success. Although ensuring that classroom teachers were "highly qualified"—for example, that they had passed a degree program in the subjects they taught—was a cornerstone of NCLB, there was no such clause covering the qualifications of school library media specialists. Some states required certified librarians in at least their middle schools and high schools, but NCLB contained no such requirement.

State governments, suffering from decreased tax revenues, had been cutting their education budgets by millions of dollars each year since 2001. NCLB's lack of a mandate for qualified librarians sent many school librarians back to classroom teaching positions, or in some cases sent them to the unemployment line. In many districts, budgets for books, videos, and computer software were cut or eliminated.

Most state legislatures, if they focused on NCLB, concentrated on complaining to Rod Paige, then U.S. secretary of education. The legislatures of Utah, Alaska, and Virginia, for example, complained about the costs of the mandates for teacher training and tutoring students so they could pass the standardized tests. But funding school libraries didn't seem to rank high on legislators' priority lists.

School Librarians' 2004 Priorities

Members of the American Association of School Librarians (AASL) knew that action had to be taken. Throughout the second half of 2004, AASL President Dawn Vaughn, herself a school library media specialist in Colorado, distributed two questions to affiliated state associations with the request that they send them to as many school library media specialists as possible, both association members and nonmembers. The questions were

- What are the most important issues that you see facing school library media programs, library staff, and library associations over the next five to ten years?

Walter Minkel is supervising librarian at the Early Childhood Resources and Information Center at the New York Public Library and former technology editor of *School Library Journal*.

• What can a national association do to address these issues that a local school library media specialist, school district staff, state level staff, or a state association cannot do on its own?

The tally of responses was released during the American Library Association's Midwinter Meeting in January 2005. It gives a clear insight into the concerns of school librarians.

Staffing requirements and job security headed the list, followed by a need for advocacy and marketing action plans for state and district-level boards, for greater role recognition (e.g., having "teacher" be part of a school librarian's job title), for legislation and advocacy at the national level, and for fostering others' awareness of the roles a school librarian plays in education.

Other concerns cited by the respondents included a need for greater collaboration between media specialists and teachers, technology issues, reading instruction and testing issues, the question of flexible versus fixed scheduling, and student apathy toward using the library.

But here's a look at each of the top five concerns.

Staffing requirements and job security. The highest-ranked priority in the survey (mentioned by 36 percent of the respondents) might be renamed "What will be the role and importance of the school librarian over the next few decades?" Things didn't look good for the profession in 2004, and it appeared that the number of professionally trained and certified school librarians was on the wane. With education budgets squeezed by the demands of NCLB, many district administrators had to cut all but the absolutely essential positions and programs in schools; in other words, almost everyone is susceptible to staff cuts but the classroom teachers—the ones who teach the children to pass the standardized tests.

Whether school library media specialists are as "essential" as classroom teachers is one of the hottest topics in the profession. Many schools nationwide already have no art or music teachers, no school nurses, and "pay-to-play" sports teams in which parents must financially support basketball, baseball, and soccer. Having no school librarian may be a growing trend.

Most librarians, naturally, consider themselves essential. They point to the research studies published by Keith Curry Lance of Colorado State Library's Library Research Service. Lance and his research group have found that test scores rise in proportion to the number of print volumes in the library, the number of Internet-capable PCs linking libraries with classrooms, and—most importantly—to the number of hours that a certified librarian and support staff are available in the school library to assist students. "Test scores rise in both elementary and middle schools," says the second Colorado study (2000), "as library media specialists and teachers work together."

In addition to the 1993 and 2000 Colorado studies, Lance and his group conducted studies in Alaska, Iowa, Michigan, New Mexico, Oregon, and Pennsylvania that compare the quality of library services in a school and its students' scores on standardized tests; other researchers have run similar studies in Florida, Massachusetts, Minnesota, and Texas. The results have been the same in every study: the better the library and the more hours the library is staffed by certified personnel, the better the students do on standardized tests. However, even in Colorado, where Lance's work is well known among educators, the number of librarians with professional training has diminished.

Another problem his study cites is the high number of school librarian retirements expected within the next few years. Lance notes that "Retiring librarians who participated in this study are not optimistic about the future of their positions. Many expect their jobs to be downgraded, combined with other jobs, or outright eliminated," adding that "Almost one out of five expects to be succeeded by someone with less education." [For an in-depth look at the study, see "Retirement, Retention, and Recruitment: The Future of Librarianship in Colorado" in Part 4—*Ed.*]

Advocacy and marketing action plans for state and district-level boards. Professional media organizations such as AASL and the state school library associations have over the last decade realized how badly school libraries and school librarians need firm voices to explain their value to the public. The Lance studies, and the other statewide studies in a similar mold, have given school librarians the basic message: Better school libraries build students' information literacy skills and help them score higher on standardized tests. But this message needs to be delivered to a skeptical, impatient audience that may neither know nor care much what "information literacy skills" are. This audience is made up of parents, voters, teachers, administrators, and politicians—the people who can choose whether to support school libraries when budgets are tight and demand is strong for the same education dollars—dollars that fund everything from smaller class sizes to better bus service.

This is where advocacy comes in. AASL continues to refine and update its online package of advocacy materials (http://www.ala.org/ala/aasl/aaslproftools/toolkits/aasladvocacy.htm), which focuses on the slogan "Because Student Achievement IS the Bottom Line." Scholastic, a leading publisher for school libraries, released in 2004 *School Libraries Work* (http://www.scholasticlibrary.com/download/slw_04.pdf), an advocacy document that describes the significance of the various studies in the language teachers and administrators speak. It was designed for librarians to hand to skeptical teachers, administrators, and other education stakeholders.

Almost every state media association Web site contains articles, or links to articles, about advocacy. The New York Library Association School Library Media Section's Web page (http://www.nyla.org/index.php?page_id=52) included this message in early 2005: "Many School Library Media Specialists are finding their budgets being cut and their staff reduced. Some jobs are in danger of being eliminated because administrators do not appreciate the impact of the school library media program on learning. Do not assume that there is nothing you can do. Promote your library and libraries in general. Become an advocate!"

Role recognition. Many school librarians feel that their fellow teachers don't think of them as "teachers" because librarians aren't, in the end, accountable under NCLB for how their students do on standardized tests. Thus, the librarians often feel like second-class citizens; they want to be recognized as teachers—by the classroom teachers in their school, by their principal, and by other school staff and administrators.

Over the past few years there has been a push to recognize this by adding the word "teacher" to librarians' job titles. Some professional leaders, among them Michael Eisenberg, dean of the Information School at the University of Washington, favor "teacher librarian," the title school librarians take routinely in Canada and Australia but only rarely in the United States. The other title commonly used is "library media teacher," found particularly in California, a state in which 30 years of poor funding for education have decimated the ranks of school librarians (the average ratio of school librarians to students nationwide is 1:882; California's ratio is 1:5,342).

Legislation and advocacy on the national level. Advocacy on the national level is, of course, an extension of local advocacy. But specifically, it's two things. First, it's the struggle to get the federal government to recognize the value of school librarians as a key part of NCLB. So far, the only recognition in federal funding of the role school librarians play is the chronically underfunded "Improving Literacy Through School Libraries" program of the U.S. Department of Education (http://www.ed.gov/programs/lsl). The program is funded nationally at $19 million for fiscal year 2005, a decrease of $800,000 from the previous year.

Second, advocacy on the national level is any way that libraries can use the national media, the federal government, or nationwide foundation money to promote the role of school libraries and school librarians. The closest school libraries came to this kind of national focus was First Lady (and former school librarian) Laura Bush's 2002 White House Conference on School Libraries, an event that has not been repeated and doesn't seem to have brought about any changes in the nation's attitude toward school librarians.

Others' awareness of roles a school librarian plays in education. This restates the concerns of all the others, and also takes the form of advocacy. But it concentrates on internal advocacy; it ties into the need for teachers and administrators to recognize that a school librarian is a teacher. Part of the problem with internal advocacy is that AASL, state associations, and many in the library community themselves have come to see their primary role as teaching students information literacy skills. Anyone familiar with the literature of information literacy—including AASL's Information Power (http://www.ala.org/ala/aasl/aaslproftools/informationpower/informationpower.htm)—knows that these skills are extremely useful in the modern online world. How will students know how to buy insurance or get a loan without the skills to sort out complex legal language or to differentiate between competing claims, for example? How will they know the difference between a Web site that contains impartial, authoritative information and another written by flacks for a political party or a business association? But school librarians, after years of trying, still have not managed to convince many teachers, principals, or members of the public that teaching students information literacy skills is a good reason to pay librarians' salaries. Most students who need to do research are making only one stop these days—typing search terms into Google and accepting whatever comes up—and their teachers are largely accepting the material they find that way.

Unfortunately, when budgets are tight and choices must be made, librarians are still hearing that teaching children information literacy isn't teaching children to read or do math, and that mastering information literacy skills doesn't have much effect on test scores.

But librarians, after decades of reluctance to make a lot of noise about what they do and why it's important, are rising up in larger numbers to vigorously advocate for the profession. Advocacy has become an everyday part of work as a school librarian.

Politics Is Major Force in Election-Year Publishing

Jim Milliot

Senior Editor, Business and News, *Publishers Weekly*

The big story in book publishing in 2004 was—books. The presidential election and policies of the Bush administration produced dozens of books that generated headlines throughout the year not only in the trade press but in the mainstream media as well. Virtually every candidate who competed for the Democratic presidential nomination wrote a book that was released in 2004, while fans and foes of both President Bush and Democratic nominee John Kerry released works right up to the election.

Although books penned by the Democratic candidates were not big sellers, many other political titles sold in large numbers, making politics the hottest segment in the industry for most of 2004. The book that created the most media buzz and became the fastest-selling nonfiction book in recent history was former president Bill Clinton's *My Life*. Released in June, *My Life* sold 400,000 copies on its first day of sale, breaking records at bookstore chains and independent booksellers alike. Excitement about the book began to build in early June when the former president gave the keynote address at BookExpo America. The standing-room-only event drew waves of media coverage and stories regarding the book and its publication appeared almost daily in the press throughout the remainder of the spring and into the summer.

Publication of *My Life* went relatively smoothly, although there were a few bumps along the way. Unauthorized excerpts from the book appeared in a few newspapers before its release, and some booksellers ran out of copies as the tremendous early demand caught publisher Knopf a bit short of supply despite a first printing of 1.5 million copies that was quickly supplemented by an additional 1 million. Clinton's book tour also had some booksellers grumbling, particularly over the decision to have Clinton sign books at some non-bookstore outlets. Some independent booksellers were also angered that Clinton did an unofficial second tour in which he used the Barnes & Noble corporate jet to do signings only at B&N stores.

While *My Life* was one of the most popular books in 2004, a book on the other side of the political spectrum was one of the most controversial, and a good seller in its own right. *Unfit for Command* by John O'Neill and Jerome Corsi, which sharply criticized John Kerry's war record, was published in August by Regnery Publishing. A media blitz by its authors spurred intense interest in the book, and early demand outstripped supply. The book's unavailability in bookstores prompted some to charge that booksellers were not stocking the book because of a liberal bias. Regnery acknowledged, however, that it had underestimated demand, and boosted supply from an initial printing of 85,000 to 650,000.

Other books that drew lots of attention, and sales, in the months before the election were largely anti-Bush works. Among the most noteworthy were *The Price of Loyalty, Politics of Truth,* and *Against all Enemies.* A number of books about the Iraq war also made headlines, led by Bob Woodward's *Plan of Attack.* The most unusual bestselling book of 2004, however, was the official report of the Sept. 11 Commission. *The 9/11 Commission Report: Final Report of the National Commission on Terrorist Attacks Upon the United States* was published in the summer by W. W. Norton and the book and its conclusions generated widespread media coverage. Despite fears that the in-depth media coverage about its contents would limit sales, the book quickly hit bestseller lists, and Norton eventually had about 1 million copies of the $10 trade paperback in print. The book received more press attention when, despite the lack of a single author, it was nominated for a National Book Award. It lost out in the nonfiction category to *Arc of Justice* by Kevin Boyle.

President Bush's re-election gave rise to speculation about what type of political books would sell best in 2005. *What's Wrong with Kansas,* which analyzes weaknesses in the Democratic Party, was a bestseller immediately following the Bush victory, but interest in political works declined noticeably in the fall and holiday season. The one exception was the faux textbook *America (The Book)* by "The Daily Show" host Jon Stewart. The satirical look at politics was the bestselling book over the 2004 holiday season (and earned *Publishers Weekly*'s first "Book of the Year" award).

How books are sold to customers was another major issue for the publishing industry throughout 2004. Penguin got the debate rolling early in the year when it began offering visitors to its Web site the chance to buy titles directly from the site. While many smaller publishers sell titles directly to customers online, larger trade publishers have avoided the practice because of both economic (not worth it financially) and political (not wanting to offend retailers) reasons. But the decision by Barnes & Noble to increase its publishing program made publishers take another look at online sales. Penguin said that while online sales were small in 2004, it will continue to sell direct in 2005. At the end of 2004 Random House and Simon & Schuster both said they were exploring the possibility of selling their books directly from their Web sites.

The growing trend by consumers to use the Internet to buy books resulted in a boom of used-book sales online, to the dismay of most publishers and authors. Amazon, which began selling used books in a major way in 2003, continued the practice of placing used book "buttons" next to the icons to buy new books. The growth of used-book sales online was also seen by the expansion of Abebooks and Alibris, two of the largest online used book sites. Although Alibris withdrew plans for an initial public offering in the year, the company did report that sales grew 46 percent in 2003, to $45.4 million. Abebooks also reported record sales in 2003 and both companies began selling new books via their sites in the year.

Another online venture that caused a stir within the industry was the debut of Google Print at the Frankfurt Book Fair. Over a year in the testing phase, Google Print scans a book's content into Google's huge search engines. To entice publishers to participate in the program, which Google hopes will add reams of content to its databases, Google includes a link to e-retailers and bookstores that sell the book that appeared in the search. Publishers also will receive a portion of any advertising connected to the book. Although publishers expressed some piracy and copyright concerns, most supplied Google with enough titles to give the program a full test.

Google followed up its Google Print initiative with the announcement later in the year that it had reached an agreement with four major university libraries plus the New York Public Library to scan their book collections into its databases. Google will scan only portions of some libraries' collections, mostly out-of-print, rare, and public domain titles, but it will scan the entire works of Stanford and University of Michigan libraries. This initiative also raised some copyright concerns among publishers, at the same time calling into question the future role of libraries.

Issues

Political books were not the only publishing industry area to catch the eye of the media. In early July the National Endowment for the Arts (NEA) released "Reading at Risk," a study that documented a decline in the reading habits of Americans. The NEA survey found that 57 percent of adult Americans had read any type of book in the past year, down from 61 percent in 1992. The percentage of Americans who read any type of fiction, moreover, fell even more—down to 47 percent in 2002 from 54 percent in 1992 and 57 percent in 1982. NEA Chairman Dana Gioia observed that reading fell among nearly all groups surveyed, including the affluent and educated, the two groups most associated with buying and reading books. While the study did not detail reasons for the reading decline, it noted that the use of electronic media, ranging from the Internet to cell phones, dramatically increased in the 1992–2002 period. The release of the study prompted a debate about what can be done to reverse the reading decline, a debate that carried into 2005.

What Americans can read, and publish, was another major issue in 2004. Reacting to restrictions on what type of dealings publishers can have with countries that fall under the U.S. trade embargo, a group of publishing associations filed a lawsuit against the U.S. Treasury Department's Office of Foreign Control challenging rulings that limited publishers' access to foreign works. Just before the end of the year, the Treasury Department issued a new ruling that cleared the way for American publishers to publish works from writers in countries under the embargo.

In another First Amendment issue, the Supreme Court ruled against the Child Online Protection Act (COPA), which calls for heavy fines on Web operators who fail to monitor online materials.

The high price of textbooks drew the attention of the mainstream media in 2004 as well as the interest of Congress. To keep critics at bay, several college publishers began introducing lower-priced editions of some texts.

Barnes & Noble continued to expand its publishing throughout 2004. In addition to increasing the number of titles in its classics line, B&N added to its popular reference lists with such titles as *The Perfect Name* and *The Baseball Encyclopedia*.

B&N is not the only bookstore chain to publish its own titles. Books-A-Million has quietly expanded its publishing program through three methods: original publishing, usually with the help of packagers; special editions of titles; and co-publishing with British publishers.

Mergers and Acquisitions

With a few exceptions, niche acquisitions were again the rule in 2004. The biggest deal with an impact in the United States involved British-based Taylor & Francis, which merged with another British media company, Informa. Taylor & Francis has extensive professional publishing holdings in the United States. A financial firm, Mannheim Holdings, entered the publishing market in March 2004 with its purchase of Springer Publishing, the New York City professional publisher. In September, Mannheim added Demos Medical Publishing to its fold.

The most notable acquisition in the trade segment was British-based Bloomsbury's purchase of Walker Publishing just before the end of the year. The purchase, for $6.5 million, significantly expanded Bloomsbury's presence in the United States. Rockport Publishers, a division of the British-based Quarto Group, paid $10.8 million for the how-to imprints of Creative Publishing. Pet and animal book publisher BowTie, Inc. made two purchases in the year, acquiring Kennel Club Books in May and Doral Publishing in June. Among the niche acquisitions in the trade sector were Avalon Publishing Group's purchase of Four Walls Eight Windows and Amadeus Press's purchase of the performing arts publisher Limelight Editions. Another fine arts publisher, Applause Books, was bought by Hal Leonard Corp. Red Wheel/Weiser picked up two small publishers, Phanes Press and Belle Tress Books.

A merger of two boutique children's publishers saw Boyds Mills Press acquire the assets of Front Street, Inc. Another small deal in children's publishing involved the purchase of Nord-Sud Verlag, owner of North-South Books, by a group of Swiss and German investors.

The bankruptcy of Millbrook Press resulted in two sales. Henry Holt acquired Millbrook's Roaring Brook Press imprint for $4.7 million, while Lerner Publishing Group bought the publisher's Millbrook and Twenty-First Century imprints for $3.4 million. Another bankruptcy action, the liquidation of Weatherhill, resulted in the sale of its 150 titles to Shambhala Publications. In a third bankruptcy action, Disney bought the comics assets of graphic-novel publisher CrossGen.

School Specialty, Inc., which sells supplementary materials and equipment to schools, deepened its commitment to the supplementary content market with the $46 million purchase of McGraw-Hill Children's Publishing division, a unit that sells supplementary educational materials to retail channels through such companies as Instructional Fair and Frank Schaffer. In another significant purchase in the supplementary market, Harcourt, Inc. bought Saxon Publishers. Pearson Education added to its supplementary holdings with the purchase of Dominie Press. In a much smaller deal in the supplementary part of the market, Guideposts' Ideals Publications subsidiary acquired Williamson Publishing.

Test preparation for mandated school tests is becoming a major business and prompted Haights Cross Communications to pay $25 million for Buckle Down Publishing.

Highlighting the deals in the retail sector was Borders' purchase of Paperchase Products Ltd., a British stationery chain.

The wholesale market underwent some consolidation in 2004. Baker & Taylor made several purchases in the year with the biggest deal its acquisition of the STM (scientific, technical, and medical) wholesaler J. A. Majors. In addition,

Baker & Taylor added the British wholesaler Delta International Book Wholesalers and the Spanish wholesaler Libros Sin Fronteras. Brodart also increased its presence in the Spanish-language market with the purchase of the San Francisco-based Books on Wings.

The big purchase in Canada in 2004 was the acquisition of the highly regarded Key Porter Books by its distributor, H. B. Fenn and Co.

People

Executive changes began early in 2004 when David Steinberger, president of corporate strategy and international at HarperCollins, joined Perseus Book Group as president, succeeding Jack McKeown. A month after Steinberger's appointment, Buz Teacher, a cofounder of Perseus subsidiary Running Press, took on a part-time role and John Whalen was named publisher. Also at Running Press, associate publisher Carlo DeVito resigned to join Penguin Group USA. Back at Harper, Brian Murray was named president of the general books group, succeeding Cathy Hemming. Onetime president of Random House Erik Engstrom was appointed CEO of Elsevier. Ted Nardin resigned as group vice president of the McGraw-Hill Companies professional book group. In another top departure, Ken Quigley resigned as president of the American division of Continuum Publishing.

On February 1, 2004, Michael Hyatt was promoted to president and COO of Thomas Nelson Publishers. Charles Tillinghast succeeded Michael Nicita at Advanced Marketing Services (AMS) in April; in November, Tillinghast, an AMS cofounder, retired and was succeeded by Bruce Myers. Rodale appointed Giannia Crespi president of Rodale International. Michael Jacobs resigned as head of Scholastic's trade division in January, and turned up later in the year as president of Harry Abrams. At another art publisher, Phaidon, Chris North, COO of HarperCanada, was named managing director. Veteran reference publisher Gordon Macomber was named to replace Allen Paschal as president of Thomson Gale. Lynn Bond resigned from Kensington Publishing to become president of Book Club of America. Industry veteran Walter Weintz replaced the retiring Bruce Harris as COO of Workman Publishing. Also at Workman, Andrew Mandel was named to the new post of deputy publisher. In a third Workman appointment, Kristina Peterson was named director of international publishing. Tim Jarrell was appointed publisher of Fodor's Travel Publishing. David Rothenberg was promoted to president of legal publisher Nolo.

On the editorial side, Rick Horgan moved from Warner Books to Crown as vice president and executive editor. Greg Michaelson, who had formed one half of the literary publisher Blue Hen, joined Algonquin as editor-at-large. Geoff Shandler was promoted to editor-in-chief of Little, Brown, and Tracy Behar moved from Simon & Schuster to Little, Brown as executive editor. Rebecca Saletan moved from Farrar, Straus & Giroux, where she was editorial director of the North Point Press imprint, to join Harcourt as editor-in-chief of its adult trade imprint. Airie Stuart left John Wiley for Palgrave, where she was named editorial director of the trade division. Sterling Publishing named Julie Trelstad executive editor of acquisitions. Former editor and agent Gene Brissie was appointed editor-in-chief of Kensington's Citadel Press imprint.

Key changes in marketing and sales included the promotion of Josh Marwell to head the consolidated HarperCollins sales division. Chris Murphy moved from Scholastic to vice president of sales for Time Warner's diversified group. Linda Keene was named to replace longtime Scholastic marketing vice president Dick Spaulding. Jack Perry left Sourcebooks to be vice president of sales for Scholastic's trade division. Longtime Donnelley sales executive Kevin Spall left to join Lightning Source as vice president, sales.

In children's publishing, Kaylee Davis was named editor-in-chief of Children's Book-of-the-Month Club. Eileen Bishop Kreit was promoted to publisher of Puffin Books. Brenda Bowen left Simon & Schuster to become editor-in-chief of Hyperion Books for Children. Veteran children's publishing executive Vivian Antonangeli joined Brighter Child Interactive to oversee its launch into book publishing. Marc Aronson signed on with Candlewick to acquire young adult novels. Jean Reynolds, a cofounder of bankrupt Millbrook, joined Lerner Publishing as associate publisher. Jason Lee was promoted to publisher of Lee & Low.

At industry publications and institutions, Sam Tanenhaus was named editor of the *New York Times Book Review.* Brigid Hughes was appointed to the top spot of the *Paris Review,* succeeding George Plimpton who died earlier in 2004. Longtime *Publishers Weekly* editor John Baker retired from full-time duty, although he will continue to work for the magazine on a freelance basis. Also at *Publishers Weekly,* publisher Joe Tessitore resigned and was succeeded by Bill McGorry; Tessitore ended up at HarperCollins as head of a new reference group. And on the first business day of 2005, longtime *Publishers Weekly* editor-in-chief Nora Rawlinson resigned and was succeeded by publishing journalist Sara Nelson.

At the National Book Foundation, Neil Baldwin was succeeded by Harold Augenbraum as executive director. At BookExpo America, Chris McCabe was named to replace Greg Topalian as show manager. The Association of American Publishers appointed J. Bruce Hildebrand executive director of its higher education division. The board of the Frankfurt Book Fair announced just before last year's meeting that it was not renewing the contract of fair director Volker Neumann.

The major announcement in the retail sector was the appointment of Vin Altruda as president of Borders' U.S. stores. Altruda succeeded Tami Heim, who later in the year joined Thomas Nelson. Phil Ollila, vice president of marketing at Borders, left in the spring to head a new distribution division at Ingram. Also at Ingram, Jim Chandler, chief commercial officer, was promoted to president of Ingram Book Company. In another change at the top in wholesaling, Arthur Brody turned over the reins of Brodart to Joe Largen.

Changes in electronic publishing/new media were highlighted by the move of Keith Titan from Simon & Schuster to Random House, where he was named director of new media. Claire Israel succeeded Titan at Simon & Schuster Online. Giles Dana, one-time president of Simon & Schuster Audio, launched Gildan Media.

Downsizing and Upsizing

There were nearly as many people leaving publishing as starting new ventures in 2004. On the downside, Perseus Books reduced its staff by about 15 percent and closed the company's Westview office in Colorado. Oxford University Press eliminated 35 positions in a reorganization. In religion publishing, Multnomah Publishers cut 15 positions. In one of the few instances of outsourcing to affect publishing, the print-on-demand publisher Xlibris moved about 35 customer service jobs to the Philippines.

A few independent houses closed their doors in 2004. Creative Arts Books, a Berkeley, California, publisher of poetry and fiction, went bankrupt early in the year. New Millennium Enterprises, a book and spoken word audio publisher, filed for bankruptcy in the spring.

Penguin Group ended its experiment with television production, pulling the plug on Penguin Television.

The distribution and wholesaling segment took a few hits in the year. Bookpeople, the West Coast wholesaler, closed March 15. Efforts to save its Words Distribution division proved futile, and Words closed later in the year. Midwest Booksource said in the fall that it would exit the retail wholesale market by year end and close its year-old California office, affecting about 12 employees. Following the Booksource announcement, Bookazine, based in New Jersey, said it would expand its efforts in the Midwest. Riverside Distributors, which serves the evangelical Christian market, closed early in 2004. Brodart eliminated 20 jobs, about 2 percent of its staff.

In the education market, disappointing sales resulted in LeapFrog cutting its workforce by 100 jobs, 10 percent of its staff.

Among the independent retailers that closed in 2004 was the St. Paul, Minnesota, institution Ruminator Books. The venerable WordsWorth of Cambridge, Massachusetts, also closed its doors in 2004.

In a downsizing of facilities, both the American Booksellers Association (ABA) and Reader's Digest sold their headquarters during the year. Because of steady staff reductions, both ABA and Reader's Digest had more space than they needed. Both organizations signed lease agreements to remain in smaller quarters at their present locations.

An area where publishers saw room for growth in 2004 was graphic novels, and a number of companies announced initiatives in the year. Scholastic revealed plans to start the Graphix imprint, which will publish two to four projects a year. Shortly after acquiring Roaring Brook, Henry Holt said it planned to form a graphic-novel imprint under the Roaring Brook unit. Penguin's Puffin Books division announced plans to publish books in its Puffin Graphics line in summer 2005. Dallas Middaugh, director of Del Rey's manga publishing program, started Seven Seas Entertainment, specializing in manga for the international market. Capstone Press said it intended to start a graphic-library line in January 2005. Comics/graphic novel publishers that formed prose imprints were Dark Horse Comics, which formed M Press, and Marvel, which created Marvel Press.

Among the joint ventures and partnerships undertaken during the year was Random House's agreement with the South Korean publisher JoongAng Ilbo Publishers to form Random House JoongAng. The new company publishes Korean-language titles.

Pearson signed a deal with the University of Pennsylvania's Wharton School to launch a new business education imprint, Wharton School Publishing. Another high-profile signing involved a deal between Pearson and IBM to form IBS

Press. In another business book deal, Harvard Business School Press teamed up with Gartner, Inc. to copublish Gartner-branded titles. Later in the year, HBSP signed a three-year deal with Bejing-based Commercial Press to publish Chinese-language works. After its agreement with the Free Press expired, the Wall Street Journal inked a publishing deal with Crown Publishing. Gallup, which had partnered with various publishers to produce books with Gallup content, formed its own publishing division, Gallup Press.

Imprints that debuted in 2004 included Caliber, a military imprint from Penguin. Wizards of the Coast started the children's imprint Mirrorstone. Prometheus Books entered the fiction market with the launch of the science fiction imprint Pyr Books. Grove/Atlantic revived the Black Cat imprint to publish edgy fiction. Farrar, Straus & Giroux signed Sarah Crichton, who formed the nonfiction imprint Sarah Crichton Books. Thomas Nelson formed the Nelson Business imprint. Warner Books launched the Center Street imprint aimed at heartland America. New Age publisher Llewellyn created a new mystery imprint. Harlequin's Red Dress imprint launched a Spanish-language book line. In spoken word audio, Sound Room launched the nonfiction imprint Pocket University. London-based Nicholas Brealey Publishing expanded its U.S. presence by opening a Boston office.

To fill the growing need for test-preparation materials, book packaging veteran Fred Grayson founded Webster House Publishing. Another packager making the move to publisher was Melcher Media, which had a first list of seven titles.

Bestsellers

The years may have moved from 2003 to 2004, but the names on the bestseller list stayed much the same, particularly in fiction. Dan Brown was the dominant novelist in 2004 as his *The Da Vinci Code* topped the fiction charts for 31 weeks. His earlier books, *Angels & Demons, Deception Point,* and *Digital Fortress,* all spent long periods on the bestseller charts. Another 2003 bestseller that made a strong return in 2004 was Mitch Albom's *The Five People You Meet in Heaven,* with its sales given a boost by the release of the TV movie late in the year. The longest running title on *Publishers Weekly*'s bestseller list in 2004, *The Rule of Four,* had a *Da Vinci Code*-like historical conspiracy theme.

Political books drove the action in nonfiction, but a few old favorites also did well again in 2004 after strong sales in 2003. Rick Warren's *The Purpose-Driven Life,* for example, spent all of 2004 on the *Publishers Weekly* bestseller list. *The South Beach Diet* continued its strong run on the bestsellers list in 2004.

The number of books reaching the *Publishers Weekly* bestsellers lists remained steady for the third year in a row. A total of 421 books hit the lists for the first time in 2004, compared with 420 in 2003 and 422 in 2002. Random House, to no one's surprise, had the most bestsellers in 2004, publishing 75 hardcover bestsellers and 58 paperback bestsellers. Its share of the hardcover bestseller list held even at 28.4 percent in 2004. Simon & Schuster, helped by a number of political books, had the strongest rise on the hardcover charts, increasing its share of the hardcover list by 4.1 percent to 14.8 percent and jumping past Penguin USA and HarperCollins into second place behind Random. Penguin

USA had more books hit the hardcover bestseller list than Simon & Schuster—49 compared with 36—but its titles spent fewer weeks on the list, and its share fell 1.8 percent to 13.3 percent. HarperCollins had 34 books on the hardcover charts and its share rose 2.1 percent to 12.8 percent. The Time Warner Book Group had 26 hardcover bestsellers in 2004 and its share slipped 0.7 percent to 10 percent.

Random House lost a bit of its edge in paperback; 58 trade and mass market paperbacks hit the charts in 2004, dropping its share 3.9 percent to 25.1 percent. Penguin's share rose 3.5 percent in the year, helped by 51 bestsellers, and it had a 17.6 percent share of the paperback bestseller market. HarperCollins's share of the paperback bestseller list plunged 7.6 percent in 2004, to 5.9 percent, putting it behind Simon & Schuster, Time Warner, and the Von Holtzbrinck group in the paperback column.

Weak sales in September and October had many trade publishing members worried about sales heading into the all-important holiday season. But although gains fell short of the increase posted in the 2003 holiday season, the three major bookstore chains reported a 2.8 percent increase in sales in 2004. Independent retailers said sales were up very modestly in the 2004 holiday season. Amazon reported that holiday book sales hit record levels between Thanksgiving and New Year.

The lack of hot new fiction titles limited sales gains in 2004. *The Da Vinci Code* and *The Five People You Meet in Heaven,* bestsellers in 2003, topped the holiday charts again in 2004. A few fiction titles gained some traction late in the holiday season, led by *State of Fear* and *A Salty Piece of Land.* Weakness in fiction was offset by healthy gains in nonfiction. *America (The Book)* was the most popular gift book in 2004, while the cookbook, humor, and children's categories all had solid gains.

Federal Agency and
Federal Library Reports

Library of Congress

Washington, DC 20540
202-707-5000
World Wide Web http://www.loc.gov

Audrey Fischer
Public Affairs Specialist, Library of Congress

The Library of Congress was established in 1800 to serve the research needs of the U.S. Congress. For more than two centuries, the library has grown both in the size of its collection (now totaling more than 130 million items) and in its mission. As the largest library in the world and the oldest federal cultural institution in the nation, the Library of Congress serves not only Congress but also government agencies, libraries around the world, and scholars and citizens in the United States and abroad. At the forefront of technology, the library now serves patrons on-site in its three buildings located on Capitol Hill in Washington, D.C., and worldwide through its highly acclaimed Web site.

Highlights of the Year

- On September 30 the library awarded a total of $13.9 million to eight institutions to preserve historically important digital materials.
- On November 29 the library announced that the $1 million Kluge Prize for Lifetime Achievement in the Humanities was awarded to historian Jaroslav Pelikan and philosopher Paul Ricoeur.
- The library celebrated the 65th anniversary of the Hispanic Division with a panel discussion on the *Handbook of Latin American Studies,* the division's 60-volume guide to Latin American scholarship. Today the library's collection of Luso-Hispanic materials comprises some 11 million items.
- In October the library sponsored the fourth National Book Festival on the National Mall.
- On November 4, the library signed a memorandum of understanding with the National Library and Archives of the Islamic Republic of Iran for the exchange of materials. Signed during a visit by the Librarian of Congress

to Iran, the agreement will fill a 25-year gap in the library's collection of materials published in Persian and other languages of Iran.

Legislative Support to Congress

Serving Congress is the library's highest priority, particularly in the area of legislative support. During the year, the library provided Congress with the most current research and analysis relevant to the war on terrorism, homeland security, and many other issues of national and international concern.

Congressional Research Service

In 2004 the Congressional Research Service (CRS) delivered more than 899,000 research responses to members of Congress and committees. Upon release of "The 9/11 Commission Report: Final Report of the National Commission on Terrorist Attacks Upon the United States," a CRS interdisciplinary team assisted Congress by analyzing the report's recommendations and providing 70 written products about the report, the subjects it highlighted, and legislative response to the report's recommendations. These products were made accessible to members of Congress on the CRS Web page. In addition, continued enhancements were made to the Legislative Information System for Congress.

Law Library

During the year, Law Library staff produced 995 written reports for Congress— an increase of nearly 60 percent over the previous year. The Law Library also embarked on a major upgrade of the Global Legal Information Network (GLIN), a network of government agencies and international institutions that contribute official texts of laws and related legal materials to a database that is accessible over the Internet. Through the contributions of 25 countries and international institutions and the addition of laws for 23 other countries by the staff of the Law Library, GLIN provides timely access to the laws of 48 of the world's governing bodies. During the year, there were about 1.5 million transactions recorded on the GLIN database.

Copyright Office

The Copyright Office provided policy advice and technical assistance to Congress on important copyright laws and such related issues as the Digital Millennium Copyright Act (DMCA), the setting of royalty rates for Webcasting, distance education, and Copyright Arbitration Royalty Panel (CARP) reform. The Copyright Office also responded to numerous congressional inquiries about domestic and international copyright law and registration and about recordation of works of authorship.

Congressional Relations Office

In addition to assisting members of Congress and their staff in making use of the library's collections, services, and facilities, the Congressional Relations Office, along with other library offices, worked with member and committee offices on such current issues of legislative concern as the library's appropriations, the construction of a Capitol Visitor Center, the National Digital Information Infrastructure and Preservation Program, the Veterans History Project, and reauthorization of the National Film Preservation Program.

Security

With generous support from Congress, the library further developed its security in a climate of heightened alert while continuing to carry out its mission of sustaining, preserving, and making accessible its universal collections. In coordination with other agencies on Capitol Hill, the library continued upgrading its perimeter security, entrance and exit screening procedures, emergency preparedness capabilities, and internal controls safeguarding the library's priceless collections. The library's Office of Security and Emergency Preparedness moved forward on the security enhancement implementation plan while focusing on emergency preparedness.

To ensure the security and integrity of its computer systems, the library issued an information technology (IT) security plan based on the guidelines of federal security "best practices." Developed by representatives from throughout the library, the IT security plan will ensure the protection and safeguarding of IT data and systems in an increasingly complex environment.

During the year the library's Information Technology Services (ITS) office restructured the library's firewall and installed a new intrusion detection system. Having established an alternate computer facility in 2003, in 2004 ITS launched a continuity of operations plan (COOP) for survivability of the library's information technology infrastructure and the more than 200 applications that the infrastructure supports. COOP provides the foundation for a rigorous, well-documented, and repeatable set of procedures for accountable management of the library's IT resources.

Budget

The Library of Congress received a total of $559,299,548 in appropriations for fiscal year (FY) 2004 as the result of a series of legislative actions. These included Public Law 108-83, the Fiscal 2004 Legislative Branch Appropriations Bill (H.R. 2657), which the president signed into law on September 30, 2003; and Public Law 108-199, signed by the president on January 24, 2004, which called for a 0.59 percent rescission of federal agency budgets. The result was a final appropriation for the library of $559,299,548, including authority to spend $36,298,567 in receipts.

Development

During FY 2004 the library's fund-raising activities brought in a total of $11 million, representing 828 gifts from 713 donors. The donor categories included 543 individuals giving $4.3 million; 76 corporations giving $2.2 million; 36 associations, councils, and societies giving $2.6 million; and 42 foundations and 16 trusts and estates giving $1 million each. These gifts, including $612,000 received through the library's Planned Giving program, were made to 90 separate library funds and consisted of $6.6 million in cash gifts, $4.3 million in new pledges, and $62,000 in in-kind gifts. The library forged new partnerships with 300 first-time donors, including 230 individuals; 21 associations, councils, and societies; 31 corporations; 11 foundations; and 7 trusts, estates, and embassies. These new donors gave $4.1 million, representing 37 percent of the gifts received this year. Thirteen new gift and trust funds were established.

The James Madison Council—the library's first private-sector advisory group—continued to provide substantial support for a number of library initiatives. Gifts from members in FY 2004 totaled $5.9 million, bringing the council's total support since 1990 to $159.1 million. The contributions received this fiscal year provided support for numerous retrospective acquisitions, including various publications from Iraq, an 18th-century Hebrew and Spanish Bible, a Revolutionary War-era powder horn, and an original George Gershwin letter; seed money to support the future acquisition of South East Asian illustrated manuscripts from Thailand and the Archive of the St. Mark's Poetry Project; major support for the general collections; and support for the National Book Festival, the Veterans History Project, and the activities of the Phillips Society, a friends group of the Geography and Maps Division.

Collections

During 2004 the size of the library's collections grew to 130 million items, an increase of 2.5 million over the previous year. This figure included more than 29 million cataloged books and other print materials, 58 million manuscripts, 14 million microforms, 4.8 million maps, 5 million items in the music collection, nearly 14 million visual materials, 2.7 million audio materials, and more than 1 million items in miscellaneous formats.

Integrated Library System

The Library of Congress Integrated Library System (ILS) performs routine library functions such as circulation, acquisitions, and serials check-in. It also provides access to the library's online public access catalog (OPAC). During the year the OPAC function was upgraded to improve system accessibility. As a result, the system can accommodate 525 simultaneous users—up from 425 simultaneous users the previous year.

Arrearage Reduction/Cataloging

At year's end the arrearage in special formats was 19,034,859 items, a decrease of 46.6 percent since the library's arrearage census of September 1989. During the year the Cataloging Directorate and Serial Record Division cataloged a total of 294,510 bibliographic volumes. Production of full- and core-level original cataloging totaled 185,309 bibliographic records. Cataloging staff also created 24,392 inventory-level records for arrearage items, 46,363 copy cataloging records, and 23,872 minimal-level cataloging records.

With the library serving as the secretariat for the international Program for Cooperative Cataloging (PCC), member institutions created 146,645 new name authorities, 9,453 new series authorities, 2,558 subject authorities, and 71,661 bibliographic records for monographs. In addition, the library contributed 92,311 new name authorities, 8,770 new series authorities, and 6,393 subject authorities.

Secondary Storage

With support from Congress, the library continued to fill new storage units at Fort Meade, Maryland. During the year nearly 568,000 items were transferred to Fort Meade, bringing the total number of items transferred to Module 1 since the program's inception to 1.2 million, or 90 percent of the module's capacity. Construction of Module 2 began in December 2003 with completion expected in 2005.

Planning continued for the National Audio-Visual Conservation Center (NAVCC) in Culpeper, Virginia, scheduled to open in 2005. Funded by the Packard Humanities Institute and supported by Congress, the facility will eventually house the library's recorded sound, videotape, safety film, and nitrate film collections.

Important New Acquisitions

The library receives millions of items each year from copyright deposits, federal agencies, and purchases, exchanges, and gifts. Significant acquisitions made possible by the Madison Council during the year included a 1762 edition of the Old Testament in Hebrew and Spanish, retrospective Iraqi publications (previously unavailable due to sanctions that prevailed for 12 years), a powder horn from the American Revolution era, a George Gershwin letter, and 45 additional titles to reconstruct Thomas Jefferson's library. In addition, the library's Veterans History Project received more than 80,000 items documenting the experience of the nation's veterans and their families.

The library also acquired the following significant items and collections in 2004:

- The Jay I. Kislak collection of rare books, manuscripts, and maps and art of the Americas, including the first printed navigational chart of the world (Carta Marina), prepared by cartographer Martin Waldseemüller in 1516; manuscript documents by early explorers Hernando Cortes and Francisco Pizarro; and letters by and about the nation's founding fathers
- The Alan Lomax Collection, an unparalleled assemblage of ethnographic documentation collected by the folklorist over a period of 60 years, which—coupled with the material acquired by his father, John Lomax, during his tenure at the library's Archive of American Folk Song during the 1930s and 1940s—brings the entire Lomax collection together at the library for the first time

- Additions to the papers of political cartoonist Herbert Block, comprising 175,000 items of the cartoonist's manuscript (nongraphic) collection of correspondence, notes, drafts of writings, photographs, and other papers
- The papers of conductor/composer Isaac Stern, culminating a ten-year effort to bring Stern's papers to the library
- Two rare children's books, *ABCs of Great Negroes* by Charles C. Dawson (Dawson Publishers, 1933) and *The Alphabet Annotated for Youth and Adults* (Ackermann and Co., London, 1853)

Digital Projects and Planning

Strategic Planning

Established in FY 2001 and funded with an appropriation of $99.8 million from Congress, the library's Office of Strategic Initiatives continued planning for the development and implementation of a congressionally approved National Digital Library Information Infrastructure and Preservation Program (NDIIPP). The goal of NDIIPP is to encourage shared responsibility for the collection, selection, and organization of historically significant cultural materials regardless of evolving formats; the long-term storage, preservation, and authentication of those collections; and rights-protected access for the public to the digital heritage of the American people. On September 30, 2004, the library advanced this goal by awarding a total of $13.9 million to eight lead institutions and their partners to identify, collect, and preserve historically important digital materials. These awards from the library will be matched dollar-for-dollar by the winning institutions in the form of shared costs to execute the cooperative preservation program.

Internet Resources

The library continued to expand its electronic services to Congress and the nation through its award-winning Web site. During the year more than 3.3 billion transactions were recorded on all of the library's computer systems. The following are selected resources available on the Web site.

Online Catalog. The library continued to provide global access to its OPAC. The site recorded more than 436 million transactions during 2004—up 20 percent from the previous year.

American Memory. At year's end more than 9.2 million American historical items were available on the American Memory Web site. In 2004 three new multimedia historical collections were added to the site, bringing the total to 126. Eight existing collections were expanded with new content. These included the George Washington, Thomas Jefferson, and Alexander Graham Bell Family papers, which made these collections complete. Use of the American Memory Web site was up by more than 50 million hits during the year (from 564 million in 2003 to 617 million in 2004).

America's Library. Work continued to expand the content and features available on America's Library, an interactive Web site for children and families that draws upon the library's vast online resources. The site has won numerous awards and is one of the library's most popular online offerings. America's Library logged more than 218 million transactions during the year, compared with 184 million in 2003.

THOMAS. The public legislative information system known as THOMAS continued to be a popular resource, with 150 million transactions recorded in 2004.

Global Gateway. Work continued on the expansion of the Global Gateway Web site, a portal to the library's international collections and those of other major repositories worldwide through collaborative digitization projects. Redesign of the site began in FY 2004. New content was added to several existing Global Gateway presentations, including "Meeting of Frontiers: Siberia, Alaska, and the American West"; "The Atlantic World: America and the Netherlands"; and "United States and Brazil: Expanding Frontiers, Comparing Cultures." Additions in 2004 included selections from the Naxi Manuscript Collection, featuring ceremonial writings of the Naxi people of China's Yunnan Province; and an original scrapbook kept by children's author Lewis Carroll between the years 1855 and 1872.

Online Exhibitions. Seven new library exhibitions were added to the library's Web site in 2004, bringing the total to 54. This feature allows users to view many of the library's past and current exhibitions online.

Wise Guide. Since its inception in October 2002, this portal to the library's main Web site has been refreshed monthly, much like a magazine, with links to the best of the library's online resources.

Reference Service

In addition to serving Congress, the Library of Congress provides reference service to the public in its 21 reading rooms and through its Web site. During the year the library's staff handled more than 680,000 reference requests that were received in person, on the telephone, or through written and electronic correspondence. Nearly 1.3 million items were circulated for use within the library.

Digital Reference

The library is a leader in providing Web-based reference and information services. QuestionPoint, successor to the Collaborative Digital Reference Service initiated in 1999, has grown to a membership of more than 800 libraries around the world, providing around-the-clock reference service to patrons through their local libraries' Web sites. This service, which is available to libraries by subscription, is free for library patrons. During the year the library's digital reference team answered nearly 14,000 QuestionPoint inquiries.

The library also continued to operate the "Ask a Librarian" service, by which a question can be submitted and answered (within five business days) through an interactive form on the library's Web site. The service, which is supported by the QuestionPoint software, includes a live chat feature that allows researchers to consult a reference librarian in real time via e-mail. During the year the digital reference team conducted 1,130 live chat sessions.

Preservation

The library continued to play a leadership role in the preservation of materials in a variety of formats such as books, films, sound recordings, and items "born digital." The library also played an outreach role in the preservation of the nation's heritage through several oral history projects.

In 2004 the Preservation Directorate completed more than 10 million assessments, treatments, rehousings, and reformattings for books, codices, manuscripts, maps, cartoons, political posters, palm leaves, architectural drawings, photographs, newspapers, discs, films, magnetic tapes, and artifacts. A total of 4,132,284 items were repaired, mass deacidified, or microfilmed at a total cost of $18,367,801. The average cost per item was $4.44, representing a decrease of $2.05 per item from 2003. The library took action to preserve its collections by

- Deacidifying 299,064 books and 1,219,500 sheets of paper as part of its 30-year (one-generation) mass deacidification plan to stabilize more than 30 million general collection books and manuscripts in three decades (as of the end of 2004, the library had deacidified 1 million bound volumes and more than 2 million sheets of manuscript materials)
- Using a single-sheet treatment cylinder on-site at the library to deacidify paper-based nonbook materials that were too valuable to be transported to the mass deacidification vendor plant near Pittsburgh
- Providing conventional or highly customized preservation treatments for 289,401 general and special collection books, manuscripts, drawings, prints, and photographs
- Rehousing 630,269 documents, photographs, discs, films, and magnetic tape reels and cassettes
- Assessing 4,103,419 photographs, papers, and other collection materials for future preservation needs
- Converting 4,111,415 documents, newspaper pages, and motion picture reels to microfilm and digital format
- Stabilizing 31,663 items to allow scanning and mounting on the library's Web site
- Treating 1,372 items and matting 562 items for display in library exhibitions
- Treating 16,024 bound newspaper pages using a new technology for paper strengthening
- Preservation microfilming 2.3 million exposures (4 million pages)
- Working in partnership with other organizations to develop an NDIIPP to sort, acquire, describe, and preserve electronic materials

American Folklife Center

The American Folklife Center (AFC) continued its mandate to "preserve and present American folklife" through a number of outreach programs such as the Veterans History Project and "Save Our Sounds."

Established by Congress in 2000, the purpose of the Veterans History Project is to record and preserve first-person accounts of armed services personnel who served during wartime, including members of Congress. During the year project staff continued to gather veterans' stories and make them accessible on the project's Web site at www.loc.gov/folklife/vets. By the end of the year the project had collected more than 80,000 items from veterans and their families. On Memorial Day 2004 the project staff participated in the dedication of the World War II Memorial.

"Save Our Sounds," a joint program with the Smithsonian Institution and supported by the White House Millennium Council's "Save America's Treasures" program, seeks to preserve a priceless heritage of sound recordings housed at the two institutions. The program is now in its fourth year, and nearly all of the eight collections earmarked for preservation have been digitized and made accessible on the library's American Memory Web site. Several new collections have been identified for preservation as part of this continuing project.

National Film Registry

The library continued its commitment to preserving the nation's film heritage. The 25 films listed below were named to the registry in 2004, bringing the total to 400. The library works to ensure that the films listed on the registry are preserved either through its motion picture preservation program at Dayton, Ohio, or through collaborative ventures with other archives, motion picture studios, and independent film makers.

Ben-Hur (1959)

The Blue Bird (1918)

A Bronx Morning (1931)

Clash of the Wolves (1925)

The Court Jester (1956)

D.O.A. (1950)

Daughters of the Dust (1991)

Duck and Cover (1951)

Empire (1964)

Enter the Dragon (1973)

Eraserhead (1978)

Garlic Is As Good As Ten Mothers (1980)

Going My Way (1944)

Jailhouse Rock (1957)

Kannapolis, N.C. (1941)

Lady Helen's Escapade (1909)

The Nutty Professor (1963)

OffOn (1968)

Popeye the Sailor Meets Sindbad the Sailor (1936)

Pups Is Pups (Our Gang) (1930)
Schindler's List (1993)
Seven Brides for Seven Brothers (1954)
Swing Time (1936)
There It Is (1928)
Unforgiven (1992)

National Sound Registry

In March 2004 the Librarian of Congress announced the 2003 additions to the National Recording Registry. Under the terms of the National Recording Preservation Act of 2000, the librarian is responsible for selecting recordings annually that are "culturally, historically, or aesthetically significant." The following list recognizes many important firsts in the history of recording in America—technical, musical, and cultural achievements.

"The Lord's Prayer" and "Twinkle Twinkle Little Star," Emile Berliner (circa 1888)
"Honolulu Cake Walk," Vess Ossman (1898)
Victor Releases, Bert Williams and George Walker (1901)
"You're a Grand Old Rag," Billy Murray (1906)
Chippewa/Ojibwe Cylinder Collection, Frances Densmore (1907–1910)
The first Bubble Book (the first children's book bound with recordings) (1917)
"Cross of Gold" speech re-enactment by William Jennings Bryan (1921)
Cylinder recordings of African American music, Guy B. Johnson (1920s)
Okeh Laughing Record (1922)
"Adeste Fideles," Associated Glee Clubs of America (1925)
Cajun-Creole Columbia releases, Amade Ardoin and Dennis McGee (1929)
"Goodnight Irene," Leadbelly (1933)
"Every Man a King" speech by Huey P. Long (1935)
"He's Got the Whole World in His Hands," Marian Anderson (1936)
The Complete Recordings, Robert Johnson (1936–1937)
Interviews with Jelly Roll Morton conducted by Alan Lomax (1938)
"Carnegie Hall Jazz Concert," Benny Goodman (1938)
Complete Day of Radio Broadcasting, WJSV, Washington, D.C. (September 21, 1939)
"New San Antonio Rose," Bob Wills and his Texas Playboys (1940)
1941 World Series Game Four, New York Yankees vs. Brooklyn Dodgers
Bach "B-Minor Mass," Robert Shaw Chorale (1947)
Beethoven String Quartets, Budapest Quartet (1940–1950)
"Porgy and Bess," original cast, George Gershwin (1940, 1942)
"Oklahoma!" original cast, Rodgers and Hammerstein (1943)
"Othello," Paul Robeson, Uta Hagen, Jose Ferrer, and others (1943)

Vivaldi "Four Seasons," Louis Kaufman and the Concert Hall String Orchestra (1947)

Ives "Concord—Piano Sonata No. 2," John Kirkpatrick (1948)

Mussorgsky "Pictures at an Exhibition," Rafael Kubelik conducting the Chicago Symphony Orchestra (1951)

"Problems of the American Home," Rev. Billy Graham (1954)

Bach "Goldberg Variations," Glenn Gould (1955)

"Ella Fitzgerald Sings the Cole Porter Song Book" (1956)

"Roll Over Beethoven," Chuck Berry (1956)

"Brilliant Corners," Thelonius Monk (1956)

Steam Locomotive Recordings, O. Winston Link (6 vol., 1957–1977)

Richard Wagner "Complete Ring Cycle," Georg Solti and the Vienna Philharmonic Orchestra (1958–1965)

"Winds in Hi-Fi," Eastman Wind Ensemble with Frederick Fennell (1958)

"Mingus Ah-Um," Charles Mingus (1959)

"New York Taxi Driver," Tony Schwartz (1959)

"Crazy," Patsy Cline (1961)

Kennedy Inaugural Ceremony, John Fitzgerald Kennedy, Robert Frost, and others (1961)

"Judy at Carnegie Hall," Judy Garland (1961)

"I've Been Loving You Too Long (To Stop Now)," Otis Redding (1965)

"Sgt. Pepper's Lonely Hearts Club Band," The Beatles (1967)

"At Folsom Prison," Johnny Cash (1968)

Ali Akbar College of Music Archive Selections (1960s–1970s)

"What's Goin' On," Marvin Gaye (1971)

"Tapestry," Carole King (1971)

"A Prairie Home Companion," Garrison Keillor (first broadcast of the radio variety show, July 6, 1974)

"Born to Run," Bruce Springsteen (1975)

"Live at Yankee Stadium," Fania All-Stars (1975)

Copyright

During the year the Copyright Office received 614,235 new claims to copyright, which covered more than a million works. It registered 661,469 claims. The office received more than 23,000 full electronic claims for textual works and music, and recorded 14,979 documents covering more than 470,000 titles. The copyright public record, available for searching online, grew with the cataloging of 567,607 registrations and the indexing of thousands of parties and titles of works contained in documents recorded. The office also continued major initiatives to re-engineer its core business processes and use information technology to increase the efficiency of operations and the timeliness of public services.

The Americana collections of the Library of Congress have been created largely through the copyright system. The Copyright Office annually transfers to the library about 1 million deposit copies in all formats. In 2004 the Copyright Office forwarded 1,038,561 copies of works with a net worth of $36,456,888 to the library, including 523,743 items that were received from publishers under the mandatory-deposit provisions of the copyright law.

National Library Service for the Blind and Physically Handicapped

Established by an act of Congress in 1931, the National Library Service for the Blind and Physically Handicapped (NLS) has grown to a program that supplies 23 million recorded discs and braille materials to more than 500,000 readers through a network of nearly 140 cooperating libraries around the country. During the year work continued toward replacing outmoded analog audiotapes and cassette players with state-of-the-art digital talking books (DTBs).

Having completed the five-year development phase of the project, NLS began the conversion phase to implement the new DTBs and playback machines by 2008. During the year NLS issued several requests for proposals for equipment procurement and conversion of analog-recorded catalog titles to DTB format.

Now in its fifth year, the Internet-based Web-braille service continued to provide access to braille books, magazines, and music scores online at http://www.loc.gov/nls/braille. In addition to providing access to braille material to users with a special braille keyboard and screen, the system allows a library that has lost a braille volume to order a new embossed bound copy and put the title back in circulation. The Web-braille site is password-protected, and all files are in an electronic form of contracted braille, requiring the use of special equipment to gain access. Web-braille began with approximately 2,600 titles and only a few hundred registered users. At year's end the system offered 6,628 book titles, 582 music scores, 29 NLS-produced magazines, and six sports schedules to 3,554 users.

John W. Kluge Center

The John W. Kluge Center was established in the fall of 2000 with a gift of $60 million from John W. Kluge, Metromedia president and founding chairman of the James Madison Council. Located within the library's Office of Scholarly Programs, the center's goal is to bring the world's best thinkers to the Library of Congress where they can use the institution's resources and interact with public policymakers in Washington, D.C.

On November 29, the Librarian of Congress announced the award of the second John W. Kluge Prize for Lifetime Achievement in the Human Sciences to historian Jaroslav Pelikan of New Haven, Connecticut, and French philosopher Paul Ricoeur. The Kluge Prize of $1 million is awarded in areas of scholarship for which there are no Nobel Prizes.

Publications

The Publishing Office produced more than 30 books, calendars, and other products describing the library's collections in 2004, many in cooperation with trade publishers. Several publications accompanied library exhibitions with the same titles. These included *Humor's Edge: Cartoons by Ann Telnaes* (with Pomegranate Communications), *From Haven to Home: 350 Years of Jewish Life in America* (with George Braziller, Inc.), and *A Heavenly Craft: The Woodcut in Early Printed Books* (with George Braziller, Inc.).

In collaboration with National Geographic Books, the library published *Voices of War: Stories of Service from the Home Front and the Front Lines*. Released on Veterans Day, the book features the personal accounts of more than 70 veterans and civilians—from World War I to the Persian Gulf War—gathered by the library's congressionally mandated Veterans History Project.

Published in association with Harry N. Abrams, *Bound for Glory: America in Color, 1939–1943* is the first book to feature the color photography of the Farm Services Administration/Office of War Information Collection.

Old Glory: The Flag Unfurled is the first of several books to be published with Bunker Hill Publishing on American icons as seen through the collections of the Library of Congress. *Old Glory* describes the histories and myths surrounding the flag of the United States from its birth during the Revolutionary War to the present day. *Canals,* the second volume of the Norton/Library of Congress Visual Sourcebooks Architectural, Design and Engineering series, provides the largest single source of material for those interested in the history of America's first transportation network.

Published in association with Black Dog & Leventhal, *First Daughters: Letters Between U.S. Presidents and Their Daughters* chronicles the triumphs, hopes, tragedies, and daily lives of 21 presidents and their daughters as recorded in their private correspondence. The assemblage is drawn from the library's collection of 23 American presidents as well as from other repositories.

At year's end the library, in cooperation with Bernan Press, published the *Encyclopedia of the Library of Congress: For Congress, the Nation and the World,* an authoritative one-volume reference work describing the historical development of the collections, functions, and services of the world's largest library and research institution from its origin in 1800 through late 2004.

Exhibitions

Several of the library's major exhibitions in 2004 commemorated historic events. These included "'With an Even Hand': *Brown* v. *Board* at Fifty," which marked the 50th anniversary of the Supreme Court decision that brought an end to school segregation, and "From Haven to Home: 350 Years of Jewish Life in America," which commemorated the first Jewish settlement in New Amsterdam (later to become New York City) in 1654 and the subsequent assimilation of American Jewry over a period of nearly four centuries. A major library exhibition, "Churchill and the Great Republic," emphasized Sir Winston Churchill's lifelong connection to the United States and the pivotal role he played in shaping the events of World War II. An exhibition titled "Humor's Edge," featuring 60 original drawings by Pulitzer Prize-winning cartoonist Ann Telnaes, exemplified her pointed commentary on national and international issues.

In keeping with conservation and preservation standards, several rotational changes were made in the continuing "American Treasures of the Library of Congress" exhibition. These include an assemblage of materials and oral histories drawn from the Veterans History Project titled "From the Home Front to the Front Lines," and "'I Do Solemnly Swear . . .': Inaugural Materials from the Collections of the Library of Congress," which featured some 50 items from the inaugurations of 18 presidents.

Special Events

A variety of special events such as literary events, concerts, and symposia were held at the library throughout the year, many of which were cybercast on the library's Web site.

National Book Festival

The library organized and sponsored the 2004 National Book Festival, which was held in early October on the National Mall. Hosted once again by First Lady Laura Bush, the event drew the largest crowd yet, an estimated 85,000.

The event, which was free and open to the public, featured more than 70 award-winning authors, illustrators, poets, and storytellers, including children's book authors Kate DiCamillo (2004 Newbery Medal winner), Sonia Manzano ("Maria" from "Sesame Street"), and E. L. Konigsburg; illustrators Marc Brown and David Shannon; historians Douglas Brinkley and Nathaniel Philbrick; journalists Cokie Roberts and Juan Williams; mystery writers Clive Cussler, Sandra Brown, and Stephen Hunter; novelists Joyce Carol Oates, Anna Quindlen, and Barbara Taylor Bradford; poet laureate Ted Kooser; chef Patrick O'Connell; and home-improvement experts Tom Silva and Kevin O'Connor of the television series "This Old House." A new Science Fiction and Fantasy pavilion featured futurist Frederick Pohl and other masters of the genre including Ben Bova and Catherine Asaro. Basketball legend Kareem Abdul-Jabbar came to the festival to promote literacy (through the NBA's "Read to Achieve" program) and to discuss his new book, *Brothers in Arms: The Epic Story of the 761st Tank Battalion, WWII's Forgotten Heroes* (Broadway Books). In addition to author readings and book discussions, the festival featured book sales and signings and appearances by children's storybook characters.

Literary Events

Sponsored by the Center for the Book in the Library of Congress, the Books and Beyond lecture series centered on the importance of books and readings. [For more information on the center, see the following article, "Center for the Book"—Ed.]. In 2004 the series featured several new books about presidents, including *Dark Horse: The Surprise Election and Political Murder of President James A. Garfield* by Kenneth Ackerman, *Theodore Roosevelt: A Strenuous Life* by Kathleen Dalton, and *First Daughters: Letters Between U.S. Presidents and Their Daughters* by Gerald W. Gawalt of the library's Manuscript Division and his daughter Ann G. Gawalt.

In August Librarian of Congress James H. Billington announced the 2004–2005 appointment of Ted Kooser as the library's 13th Poet Laureate Consultant in Poetry. Kooser opened the library's fall literary season on October 7 with a reading of poems.

Concerts

The library's 2003–2004 concert season featured many classical performances in the Coolidge Auditorium by such ensembles as the Juilliard String Quartet, the Beaux Arts Trio, the Mendelssohn String Quartet, and the Kennedy Center Chamber Players. Robert Mann, the founder of the Juilliard String Quartet, was honored in a concert featuring the winners of the Walter W. Naumburg International Competitions in Chamber Music—the Biava String Quartet, violinist Frank Huang, and pianist Gilles Vonsattel.

Sponsored by the American Folklife Center, the outdoor concert series continued with performances by country musicians Norman and Nancy Blake; the Paschall Brothers; the Oinkari Basque Dancers from Boise, Idaho; the Phuong Nguyen Ensemble; and a performance of North Indian Kathak music and dance.

In April country singer and songwriter Dolly Parton was presented with the library's "Living Legend" award, followed by her performance for the library's Madison Council members and invited guests.

Lectures and Symposia

During the year the library sponsored a number of lectures and symposia in conjunction with its major exhibitions. These included "Churchill and Three Presidents" (Roosevelt, Truman, and Eisenhower) and a series of programs to commemorate the Supreme Court's *Brown* v. *Board of Education* decision and to celebrate 350 years of Jewish life in America.

George P. Shultz, secretary of state for eight years under President Ronald Reagan, delivered the third annual Henry A. Kissinger Lecture on "A Changed World." Chosen annually by the Librarian of Congress, the Kissinger lecturer is an individual who has achieved distinction in the field of foreign affairs.

Outreach

The library continued to share its treasures both nationally and internationally on its Web site, through its Learning Page for teachers, traveling exhibitions program, and other initiatives. During the year the library's exhibition "Rivers, Edens, Empires: Lewis and Clark and the Revealing of America" began a nationwide tour. After its presentation at the library (July 24–November 29, 2003), the exhibition traveled to the Joslyn Art Museum in Omaha, Nebraska, for viewing July 10–October 3, 2004.

Additional Sources of Information

Library of Congress telephone numbers for public information:

Main switchboard (with menu)	202-707-5000
Reading room hours and locations	202-707-6400
General reference	202-707-5522
	TTY 202-707-4210
Visitor information	202-707-8000
	TTY 202-707-6200
Exhibition hours	202-707-4604
Copyright information	202-707-3000
Copyright hotline (to order forms)	202-707-9100
Sales shop (credit card orders)	888-682-3557

Center for the Book

John Y. Cole
Director, Center for the Book
Library of Congress, Washington, DC 20540
World Wide Web http://www.loc.gov/cfbook

With its network of affiliated centers in 50 states and the District of Columbia and more than 80 organizations serving as national reading promotion partners, the Center for the Book is one of the Library of Congress's most dynamic and visible educational outreach programs. Since its creation in 1977 it has used the resources and prestige of the Library of Congress to stimulate public interest in books and reading and to encourage the study of books, reading, and the printed word. The Center for the Book is a successful public-private partnership. The Library of Congress supports its four full-time positions, but all of its activities are funded through contributions from individuals, corporations, and foundations, or by transfers of funds from other government agencies.

Highlights of 2004

- A study tour to South Africa, "A Journey to Promote Reading and Literacy"
- Major contributions to the fourth National Book Festival on October 9, specifically to the festival's author and reading promotion programs, including the Pavilion of the States
- Record-breaking participation by students in "Letters About Literature," the center's principal reading and writing promotion program
- The first "Reading Powers the Mind" family literacy workshop
- Completion of the *Encyclopedia of the Library of Congress: For Congress, the Nation and the World*
- Organization of the public memorial service for Librarian of Congress Emeritus Daniel J. Boorstin, the center's founder

Themes and Campaigns

The Center for the Book creates and publicizes national reading promotion themes that stimulate interest and support for reading and literacy projects that benefit all age groups. Used by affiliated state centers, national organizational partners, and schools and libraries across the nation, the themes remind Americans of the fundamental importance of books, reading, and libraries in today's world. The center's current national reading promotion theme, "Telling America's Stories," cosponsored with the library's American Folklife Center, is widely used; ideas are available in a Center for the Book brochure and on the center's Web site. Previous themes still promoted by the center and often used by its affiliates and partners include "Books Change Lives," "Books Make a Difference," "Building a Nation of Readers," "Read More About It!" and "Explore New Worlds—READ!"

State Centers for the Book

The state partnership affiliation program began in 1984 when the Florida Center for the Book, hosted by the Broward County Library, was approved as the first state center. Today there are affiliated centers in all 50 states and the District of Columbia. Most of them are hosted by state libraries, large public library systems, state humanities councils, or universities. Each works with the national center to promote books, reading, and libraries, as well as the state's own literary and intellectual heritage. Each also develops and funds its own operation and projects, making use of Library of Congress themes and assistance as appropriate. State centers must apply every three years to renew their affiliate status. In December 2004, renewal applications were approved from Hawaii, Iowa, Kentucky, Michigan, Montana, New Jersey, New York, North Carolina, Oklahoma, Oregon, South Dakota, Utah, Washington, Wisconsin, and Wyoming.

On May 3, 2004, state center representatives participated in an idea exchange session at the Library of Congress. It was marked by lively discussion about topics such as "one book" community reading and discussion projects, state book awards programs, state book festivals, and state center participation in the Pavilion of the States at the National Book Festival.

Nancy Pearl, coordinator of the Washington Center for the Book at the Seattle Public Library, described her successes as a spokesperson in the national media for books and reading promotion. In addition to creating the Washington Center for the Book's "If All Seattle Read the Same Book," the inspiration for hundreds of subsequent "one book" projects, she is the inspiration for the best-selling Nancy Pearl librarian action figure and the author of *Book Lust: Recommended Reading for Every Mood, Moment, and Reason* (Sasquatch Books, 2003).

Reading Promotion Partners

The Center for the Book is part of several reading, education, and literacy promotion networks, including the National Coalition for Literacy and the Department of Education's Federal Interagency Committee on Education. In addition, more than 80 civic, educational, and governmental organizations are "reading promotion partners" of the center, working with it to promote books, reading, literacy, and libraries in ways that are compatible with their own organizational goals.

On March 30, 2004, representatives from most of the partner organizations met at the Library of Congress to exchange information and promotion ideas. New Center for the Book partners in 2004 included the American Psychological Association, Family Literacy Partnership, Mortar Board, Mystery Writers of America, and Publishers Marketing Association.

Projects and Events

During the year the center hosted 15 "Books and Beyond" author talks at the Library of Congress, each featuring the author of a newly published book that was based on the library's collections or focused on a library project or program. Cosponsors within the library included the Hispanic, Humanities and Social Sciences, Manuscript, Music, and Prints and Photographs Divisions, the Law Library, and the Publishing Office.

The family literacy program that the Center for the Book administered from 1998 to 2003 was reorganized and given a new name: "Reading Powers the Mind." The new program, directed by Center for the Book consultant Virginia H. Mathews, was inaugurated at a July 21–23 workshop at the Library of Congress that introduced pilot family literacy projects in Alabama, Arizona, Arkansas, Georgia, Louisiana, Mississippi, New Mexico, Oklahoma, South Carolina, Tennessee, Texas, and West Virginia. U.S. Senator Jeff Bingaman (D-N.M.) was the keynote speaker. Like the earlier project, "Reading Powers the Mind" is funded by the Viburnum Foundation.

"Letters About Literature," a national reading and writing promotion program for children and young adults, had a record-breaking year in number of entries and involvement by state centers for the book. Under the leadership of Center for the Book consultant Catherine Gourley, more than 40,000 students wrote letters to their favorite authors, and state centers in 41 states and the District of Columbia honored state winners. Six national winners were selected from among the state winners, and Target Stores, the program's national retail sponsor, brought the six national winners, their parents, and one of their teachers to Washington, D.C., for the October 9 National Book Festival on the National Mall. There the six winners read their winning letters in the "Teens and Children" pavilion in a program moderated by Librarian of Congress James H. Billington. Target Stores also placed full-page color advertisements congratulating state and national "Letters About Literature" winners in their hometown newspapers.

Drawing on its extensive experience in dealing with authors and their publishers, the Center for the Book made a major contribution to the 2004 National Book Festival, which attracted a record-breaking crowd of more than 80,000. Center for the Book staff members coordinated the recruitment and selection of the 74 authors, illustrators, and poets who participated. The center also organized the Pavilion of the States, which highlighted the book, reading, and library promotion activities of the 50 states, the District of Columbia, and four U.S. territories.

International Activities

From May 25 to June 4, the Center for the Book led "South Africa: A Journey to Promote Reading and Literacy," a study tour and professional visit that focused on reading and literacy promotion efforts currently under way in schools, libraries, and educational institutions throughout South Africa. The visit was organized in cooperation with the South African Centre for the Book, part of the National Library of South Africa (Cape Town campus) and Alterra Global Educational Initiatives, an organization that specializes in educational exchanges between South Africa and the United States. Twenty-two teachers, librarians, and reading promoters participated in the visit, which was led by Center for the Book director John Y. Cole and Judith R. Casey, the cofounder of the Colorado and Wisconsin state centers. The delegation visited Cape Town (including the National Library and the South African Centre for the Book), Johannesburg (including the Johannesburg Public Library), and Pretoria, where they learned about the U.S. Embassy's literacy projects in South Africa and toured Sesame Street's South African branch, "Takalani Sesame Street." All but two of the 22 participants opted for an additional three days in the Bongani private game reserve in northeastern South Africa. A $200 tax deductible contribution to the Center for the Book was part of the cost of the trip.

On May 1, 2004, at the Library of Congress (in cooperation with the African and Middle Eastern Division; the African Studies Association; and Africa Access, one of its national reading promotion partners), the center hosted the annual Children's Africana Book Awards. At the Library on September 24 (in cooperation with the Hispanic Division and the Consortium of Latin American Studies Programs), the center hosted the 11th annual Americas Awards for Children's and Young Adult Literature, and on September 8 (in cooperation with the International Reading Association) the center hosted the official U.S. celebration of International Literacy Day, a program that included the announcement of the 2004 UNESCO International Literacy Prizes.

During 2004 groups of librarians from South Korea, Russia, Turkey, Ukraine, and Uzbekistan visited the Center for the Book for briefings about its reading promotion activities.

Outreach and Publications

The scope of the center's Web site continued to expand, along with its use. The site describes Center for the Book themes and projects, publications, and forthcoming events. It provides information about the center's national and international partnerships and describes book festivals and literary events taking place across the country. There is also a link to the National Book Festival Web site. The center's site also documents "One Book" reading initiatives throughout the nation.

Two online issues of the newsletter *Center for the Book News* were produced in 2004. The Library of Congress issued 23 press releases about the center's activities, and a two-page "News from the Center for the Book" appeared in each monthly issue of the *Library of Congress Information Bulletin.* Most of the center's "Books and Beyond" author talks were filmed and can be seen on the center's Web site. By the end of 2004, 45 Center for the Book public programs from 1998 through 2004 could be viewed.

In 2004 the director of the center completed a major project: the co-editing of the *Encyclopedia of the Library of Congress: For Congress, the Nation and the World,* an authoritative one-volume reference work. Scheduled for publication in 2005, it is 569 pages in length, contains more than 350 black-and-white photographs, and includes newly written essays, articles, and statistical appendices. The director also wrote "Ainsworth Rand Spofford and the New Library of Congress, 1871–1897," which was published in the Spring 2004 issue of the *Capitol Dome,* the newsletter of the U.S. Capitol Historical Society, and "In Memoriam: Daniel J. Boorstin, 1914–2004," in the September 2004 issue of *Perspectives,* the newsmagazine of the American Historical Association. As Librarian of Congress, in 1977 Boorstin established the Center for the Book. He died on February 28, 2004, and the center organized his April 27 public memorial service at the Library of Congress.

Federal Library and Information Center Committee

Library of Congress, Washington, DC 20540
202-707-4800
World Wide Web http://lcweb.loc.gov/flicc

Susan M. Tarr

Executive Director

Highlights of the Year

During fiscal year (FY) 2004 the Federal Library and Information Center Committee (FLICC) continued to carry out its mission "to foster excellence in federal library and information services through interagency cooperation and to provide guidance and direction for FEDLINK."

FLICC's annual information policy forum, "E-Competencies for E-Government: Changing Role of the Federal Information Professional," focused on the major information issues ushered in with the E-Government Act and identified the competencies needed to address developing trends in electronic content. The keynote speaker was Janice R. Lachance, executive director of the Special Libraries Association and former director of the U.S. Office of Personnel Management. Her talk was followed by a morning panel discussion on the e-competencies needed by federal information professionals, with commentary from Robert S. Martin, director of the Institute of Museum and Library Services; Artemis Kirk, university librarian, Georgetown University Libraries; Suzanne Grefsheim, chief, National Institutes of Health Library Branch; and Jane Dysart, principal and founder, Dysart & Jones Associates. Karen Evans, associate director for information technology and e-gov, Office of Management and Budget, began the afternoon session with the executive keynote address, which was followed by a panel discussion on federal e-gov programs and issues with Jonathan Womer, analyst, Office of Management and Budget (OMB); Oscar Morales, chair, Federal eRulemaking Initiative; Deanna Marcum, associate librarian for library services, Library of Congress; and Judy Russell, superintendent of documents, Government Printing Office (GPO). The final afternoon presentation looked at content rights management for electronic government, with Sarah Sully, associate attorney, Morrison & Foerster, LLP. Donna Scheeder of the Congressional Research Service concluded the forum with her perspective and summary of the day.

Working Groups

The FLICC working groups completed an ambitious agenda in FY 2004. Among their activities, the working groups

- Selected FLICC Awards recipients for 2003 and offered the sixth annual FLICC Awards to recognize the innovative ways in which federal libraries, librarians, and library technicians fulfill the information demands of government, business, scholarly communities, and the American public

- Assisted the Department of Homeland Security (DHS) in providing information services for its staff of 180,000 and in hiring a new library services director for the agency
- Implemented a leadership and management education series for current and potential federal library managers
- Addressed issues of cataloging, taxonomy, digital project management, preservation and binding, virtual reference, and other information science policy concerns.

Attorney-Librarian Meetings

FLICC also continued its collaboration with the general counsel of the Library of Congress on a series of meetings between federal agency legal counsels and agency librarians. Now in their sixth year, the forums grew out of the recognition that federal attorneys and librarians face many of the same questions in applying copyright, privacy, Freedom of Information Act, and other laws to their agencies' activities in the electronic age. These meetings have enhanced the relationship between agency attorneys and librarians and have helped them develop contacts with their counterparts at other agencies. The year's series featured discussions on assessing copyright and fair-use issues, and on rights management for access to research results funded by federal grants.

Federal Library Survey

Without an updated census of federal libraries and information centers by the National Center for Educational Statistics, FLICC endorsed membership participation for a second year in the annual Outsell survey of content-deploying functions in industry, academia, and the public sector. Nearly 300 federal librarians participated in the survey. According to Outsell, Inc., a research and advisory firm that focuses on the information-content industry, the survey showed that federal library government budgets were significantly lower in 2004 and that staffing levels had declined for the second consecutive year. Federal content managers identify themselves primarily as information professionals and librarians, managing externally procured content; however, content-related functions are amalgamating throughout every subset of government. The trend of reporting into administration and operations deepened during the year despite the fact that science, as well as research and development, is the most common mission of government content managers.

FEDLINK Operations

FLICC's cooperative network, FEDLINK, continued to enhance its fiscal operations while providing its members with $60.7 million in transfer-pay services, $7.7 million in direct-pay services, and an estimated $26.1 million in the new Direct Express services, saving federal agencies more than $10 million in vendor volume discounts and approximately $8.5 million more in cost avoidance.

To meet the requirements of the Fiscal Operations Improvement Act of 2000 (P.L. 106-481) that created new statutory authority for FEDLINK's fee-based activities, FEDLINK governing bodies and staff members developed a five-year business plan in FY 2002 that entered its third year in FY 2004. Program work in FY 2004 continued to take advantage of the increased opportunities of FEDLINK's authority as a revolving fund. Staff members made significant progress on goals relating to improving processes and expanding marketing initiatives.

FY 2004 also saw innovative educational initiatives, including workshops and seminars on Library of Congress subject headings, integrating resource and cartographic cataloging, virtual reference, and information retrieval and searching. Staff members sponsored 38 seminars and workshops for 1,557 participants and conducted 39 OCLC (Online Computer Library Center), Internet, and related training classes for 551 students.

FEDLINK also continued to customize and configure software and support services for electronic invoicing and to increase online access to financial information for member agencies and vendors. FEDLINK's continuing financial management efforts ensured that FEDLINK successfully passed the Library of Congress financial audit of FY 2003 transactions performed by Clifton Gunderson, LLP.

FLICC and FEDLINK programs continue to thrive in the Facilitative Leadership (FL) environment. The FL tools consistently provided approaches and techniques to involve FEDLINK staff members and customers in the planning process, resulting in streamlined, efficient, and cost-effective program actions.

FLICC Quarterly Membership Meetings

Beyond regular FLICC Working Group updates and reports from FLICC/ FEDLINK staff members, each FLICC quarterly meeting included a special focus on a new or developing trend in federal libraries or a guest speaker. The year's first quarterly meeting featured U.S. Public Printer Bruce James of GPO. The second included a federal information policy update by Jane Bortnick Griffith, assistant director, National Library of Medicine; Jeffrey Seifert, analyst in information science and technology policy, Library of Congress; and Jonathan Womer, policy analyst, OMB. The third meeting's focus was a presentation on the "Business Case for Information Services at the Environmental Protection Agency" by Richard Huffine, manager, National Library Network, Environmental Protection Agency. And the fourth meeting featured Walter Warnick, director, Office of Scientific and Technical Information, Department of Energy, on Science.gov, an Internet gateway to government science information provided by U.S. government science agencies.

FLICC Executive Board

The FLICC Executive Board (FEB) focused its efforts on a number of initiatives relating to competitive sourcing, e-government, fair use, and the renewal of the FLICC authorization. Early in the year the board selected the 2003 FLICC Awards winners; it later approved a recommendation from the Awards Working Group to clarify eligibility criteria for the Library Technician of the Year award. At the end of the year FEB also approved discontinuation of the ad hoc FLICC Working Group for the DHS Libraries.

FLICC Working Groups

Awards Working Group

To honor the innovative ways in which federal libraries, librarians, and library technicians fulfill the information demands of government, business, research, scholarly communities, and the American public, the Awards Working Group administered a series of national awards for federal librarianship.

The 2003 Federal Library/Information Center of the Year award, large library/information center category, went to the National Institute of Standards and Technology (NIST) Research Library in Gaithersburg, Maryland. The library was recognized for its technological innovations and comprehensive knowledge-management systems that provided the tools necessary to support new programs, superior customer service, and the agency mission. Library staff was commended for its work in 2003 on both the design and creation of the NIST Integrated Knowledge EditorialNet (NIKE), a project designed to ease the capture, organization, retrieval, and distribution of NIST publications; and for the Laboratory Liaison program, which promotes collaboration between researchers and the library and enhances collection development and access.

The award in the small library/information center category (for libraries or information centers with a staff of ten or fewer) went to the Library Services Department at the Naval Medical Center, Portsmouth, Virginia. The library was commended for its provision of knowledge-based resources that optimize military health care, promote research, and encourage professional growth.

The 2003 Federal Librarian of the Year award went to Lillian Woon Gassie, senior systems librarian, Dudley Knox Library, Naval Postgraduate School, Monterey, California, for her work during 2003 in articulating the needs of the library to faculty, policymakers, and information technology stakeholders. Gassie provided guidance and technical knowledge as the library developed wireless and remote proxy access to the campus network and implemented a knowledge portal and mobile education teams to support federal and state homeland security policy and strategy. Her extensive technical knowledge brought the highest level of visibility and credibility to the library as a builder of information systems and supported the overall mission of the agency.

Wilma Riley, library technician at the NIST Research Library in Gaithersburg was named Federal Library Technician of the Year for her dedication to service excellence in support of the mission of the library and the core values of the NIST Information Services Division. In 2003 Riley set up communications connections for telecommuting staff, ensured that the library wireless technology was current, and provided dynamic end-user training.

At the annual FLICC Forum on Federal Information Policies in March 2004, the Librarian of Congress presented the award winners with a framed certificate and an engraved crystal award in the shape of a book honoring their contributions to the field of federal library and information service.

Budget and Finance Working Group

The FLICC Budget and Finance Working Group developed the FY 2005 FEDLINK budget and fee structure in the winter quarter. The group produced an online budget questionnaire for FEDLINK members and used the results to verify assumptions for the budget for FY 2005. The final budget for FY 2005 kept membership fees for transfer-pay customers at FY 2004 levels: 7.75 percent on accounts up to $300,000 and 7 percent on amounts exceeding $300,000. Direct-pay fees also remained at FY 2004 levels, as did Direct Express fees of 0.75 percent for all participating commercial online information services vendors. Library officials approved the budget in August 2004.

Competitive Sourcing Working Group

In its first year, the Competitive Sourcing Working Group reviewed the competitive sourcing chapter of the online *Handbook of Federal Librarianship* and compiled competitive sourcing resources for the FLICC Web site.

Content Management Working Group

The Content Management Working Group sponsored four discussion series, on topic maps, taxonomy mapping projects, portals, and content syndication, as well as the 2004 information technology update program, "The E-Government Act of 2002: A Progress Report," for a total of 212 attendees. The group also collaborated with the General Services Administration on the Federal Webmasters Forums, a high-level group dealing with major library knowledge and content management issues, and worked with the CENDI (Commerce, Energy, NASA, Defense Information Managers Group) Copyright Task Force on its efforts to develop rights language for government information distribution.

DHS Libraries Working Group

The DHS Libraries Working Group addressed a number of procurement and management issues, including arranging for enterprise-wide licenses for commercial databases and initiating a pilot project for virtual reference services. It also helped to draft a position description for a DHS library services director; the agency filled the position by the end of the summer. The working group's subgroup on DHS Virtual Reference implemented an Ask-a-Federal-Librarian tool and planned a promotion campaign that included posters, conference giveaways, and an exhibit stand for internal and external outreach activities. After successfully completing its charge, the FLICC Executive Board voted in September to discontinue the ad hoc working group.

Education Working Group

During FY 2004 the FLICC Education Working Group sponsored a total of 24 seminars, workshops, and lunchtime discussions for 817 members of the federal library and information center community in the areas of cataloging, digital project management, XML, the USA Patriot Act, and leadership development. Included in that total were two FLICC orientations to national libraries and information centers and two brown-bag luncheon discussions.

The working group responded to the educational agenda developed by the FLICC membership in 2001 by continuing its seminar series from the American Management Association with a multi-day session on planning and management and a "mini-MBA" series for federal library directors. The working group also released its Web-based *Handbook of Federal Librarianship* and held an inaugural discussion series session on the handbook to promote its release and to begin to identify additional sections for future development.

Human Resources Working Group

The Human Resources Working Group (formerly the Personnel Working Group) began the year with an official name change, then renewed its work on the critical areas of core competencies, recruitment and retention of federal librarians, and professional development and advancement for federal librarians. The working group also developed a number of employment resources both for those seeking federal jobs and those hiring. These materials were the basis for a new Web page for the working group and are featured along with links to other educational resources and professional organizations. Ongoing projects include removing "librarian" as a category in the Department of Labor's Directory of Occupations under the Contracts Services Act and establishing a collection of existing classified librarian position descriptions. The working group also researched the Presidential Management Fellows Program as a potential recruitment tool for outstanding library and information science graduate students. In September FLICC e-mailed a notice to 44 accredited library schools, informing them of the program and encouraging them to nominate their best students.

Nominating Working Group

The FLICC Nominating Working Group oversaw the 2004 election process for FLICC rotating members, FLICC Executive Board members and the FEDLINK Advisory Council. Librarians representing a variety of federal agencies agreed to place their names in nomination for these positions.

Working Group on Federal Libraries/GPO Partnership

Early in the year, nine librarians on the ad hoc Working Group on Federal Libraries/GPO Partnership met with the Superintendent of Documents to discuss issues relating to the future of the depository program within the federal library context. In the succeeding months, the group received proposals from GPO via its closed listserv and commented on GPO plans from a federal library perspective.

Preservation and Binding Working Group

The Preservation and Binding Working Group completed its efforts on a "statement of work" for developing a standard federal conservation/preservation service contract that opened for bids in the spring. After members of the working group reviewed bidders' proposals for conservation and preservation services, Library of Congress contracts and grants management awarded basic ordering agreements to 13 preservation services vendors. The working group also held an informational session on the GPO binding contract.

Publications and Education Office

In FY 2004 FLICC's Publications and Education Office supported an ambitious publication schedule, producing six issues of *FEDLINK Technical Notes* and two issues of the *FLICC Quarterly Newsletter.*

FLICC revised mission-critical materials and developed targeted resources to support the FEDLINK program, including the electronic-only FY 2005 *FEDLINK Registration Pamphlet* and six FEDLINK Information Alerts. It also produced the minutes of the four FY 2004 FLICC Quarterly Meetings and six FLICC Executive Board meetings, as well as all FLICC Education Program promotional and support materials including the FLICC Forum announcement, forum attendee and speaker badges, press advisories, speeches and speaker remarks, and forum collateral materials. A total of 38 FLICC Meeting Announcements were produced to promote FLICC education programs, FEDLINK membership and OCLC users' meetings, brown-bag discussions, and education institutes, along with badges, programs, certificates of completion, and other supporting materials.

FLICC and FEDLINK staff members continued to manage, support, and update the FLICC/FEDLINK Web site, which has more than 1,000 pages of content, video, and resource links. Special Web projects during the year included the second edition of the online *Handbook of Federal Librarianship*; a FEDLINK authority page; password-protected vendor pricing pages; archives for newsletters, information alerts, meeting minutes, and meeting announcements; and revisions to the federal library resources site. Staff also upgraded the secondary pages of all sections of the Web site with enhanced graphics designed for better projection and added a link to the video library throughout the Web site. Staff members worked closely with the FLICC working groups and began work on a new Content Management Working Group page. FLICC staff members continued to convert all publications, newsletters, announcements, alerts, member materials, meeting minutes, and working group resources into HTML and PDF formats, uploading current materials within days of print publication. Staff completed an extensive initiative to update the many links throughout the Web site and continued to enhance and expand the site via an inter-unit Web team of content, design, editorial, and technical personnel.

FLICC also continued to build its distance-learning offerings by providing on-demand Web videos of both the fall and spring FEDLINK Membership Meetings, as well as the annual FLICC Information Policy Forum, the FLICC Awards Ceremony, and several events on taxonomy, e-government, and topic maps.

FLICC staff members recorded five educational programs to make the discussions and presentations at the FLICC quarterly membership meetings available for members at remote locations.

In collaboration with FEDLINK Network Operations staff members, FLICC publications staff continued to offer dynamic resources, including OCLC usage analysis reports and pricing data; many new documents, including the FY 2005 budget questionnaire and ballot; and a variety of training resources. Staff also worked with Library of Congress contracts and grants management staff to make electronic versions of FEDLINK's requests for proposals available online for prospective vendors.

Publications staff members continued to support the member services unit and their online registration/online interagency agreement (IAG) system. The online registration site also included an update screen regarding outstanding contracts and centralized all of the other resources customers need to manage their accounts on one Web page.

In conjunction with the working groups, FLICC offered seminars, workshops, and lunchtime discussions to members of the federal library and information center community. Multi-day institutes looked at cataloging integrated resources and electronic serials, planning and managing organizational change, and digital licensing; one-day sessions offered hands-on and theoretical knowledge on taxonomy, digital project management, XML, content management, QuestionPoint, portals, Library of Congress subject headings, and virtual reference. FLICC was also the host to three general counsel forums on rights management for access to research funded under federal contracts and grants and fair use, and three federal webmaster forums on emerging technology issues related to e-government initiatives. FLICC also collaborated with OCLC CAPCON on educational events by co-promoting programs and opening events up to each other's members when additional seats were available.

FLICC hosted a popular teleconference series, "Soaring to . . . Excellence," produced by the College of DuPage. Following the success of previous programs, FLICC held the eighth annual Federal Library Technicians Institute. The week-long summer institute again focused on orienting library technicians to the full array of library functions in the federal sector. Federal and academic librarians joined FLICC professionals to discuss various areas of librarianship, including acquisitions, cataloging, reference, and automation.

FLICC also provided organizational, promotional, and logistical support for FEDLINK meetings and events including the FEDLINK Fall and Spring Membership Meetings, two FEDLINK OCLC Users Group meetings, and 47 vendor presentations with 374 customers attending.

FEDLINK

During FY 2004 FEDLINK (Federal Library and Information Network) managers and professional staff members executed plans for the third year of the business plan under the revolving fund. They improved processes, increased marketing of the program to federal libraries and their partner contracting officers, and expanded the number and types of services that libraries and information centers can procure via the FEDLINK program. They also continued work to ameliorate the effects on federal libraries of the bankruptcy of a major serials subscription agent, Faxon/RoweCom, by working with the Library of Congress general counsel and the Department of Justice on the bankruptcy proceedings claim made by the U.S. government on behalf of the FEDLINK program.

FEDLINK continued to give federal agencies cost-effective access to an array of automated information retrieval services for online research, cataloging, and interlibrary loan. FEDLINK members also procured print serials, electronic journals, books and other publications, CD-ROMs, and document delivery via Library of Congress/FEDLINK contracts with more than 100 major vendors. The program obtained further discounts for customers through consortia and enterprise-wide licenses for journals, aggregated information retrieval services, and electronic books. FEDLINK awarded a new contract for ILL fee payment, and initiated the new area of preservation services with 13 companies in place to provide microfilming, duplication, and conservation of books, archival materials, and photographs and other flat materials, as well as tailored consultation on how best to preserve materials in federal collections. A number of national conferences highlighted FEDLINK programs, including the Special Libraries Association and Medical Library Association meetings.

The FEDLINK Advisory Council met eight times during the fiscal year. In addition to its general oversight activities, the council advised FEDLINK managers on priorities for the third year of the five-year business plan, provided insight into trends in the information industry, and supported adoption of the proposed FY 2005 budget. It also supplied feedback on the administration of consortial purchases and provided insight to FEDLINK staff members on customer requirements.

The annual Fall FEDLINK Membership Meeting featured an overview of Library of Congress Digital Archiving Programs presented by William LeFurgy of the Library of Congress Office of Strategic Initiatives. FEDLINK staff presented information about new services and a comparison of the advantages of the Direct Express and transfer-pay purchase options.

The Spring FEDLINK Membership Meeting featured Carol Bursik, chair of the FLICC Budget and Finance Working Group, who presented the proposed FY 2005 budget, and a presentation by Cathy De Rosa, OCLC vice president for corporate marketing, on the 2003 OCLC Environmental Scan: Pattern Recognition report that examines the significant issues and trends having an impact on OCLC, libraries, museums, archives, and other allied organizations.

FEDLINK/OCLC Network Activity

FEDLINK OCLC Users Group meetings in November and May provided in-depth presentations on OCLC's expanded Web services, including improved interfaces for cataloging, interlibrary loan, reference databases, and full text in FirstSearch and NetLibrary, and on QuestionPoint, the Library of Congress-OCLC cooperative digital reference system. During the May meeting, CAPCON members joined FEDLINK members for a regional QuestionPoint Users Group meeting at which OCLC outlined upcoming enhancements and current users described implementation plans, training materials, and online support.

FEDLINK staff members supplemented these biannual OCLC meetings with six "OCLC News" articles in *FEDLINK Technical Notes,* postings on electronic lists, extensive telephone consultations, and e-mail. Staff members visited 16 member libraries to provide in-depth demonstrations of OCLC services and to consult on work flow and best practices. They provided demonstrations and lectures at agency meetings, such as Navy and Air Force library meetings, the Military Librarians Workshop, and the Defense Technical Information Center Users Group meeting. Staff members also monitored OCLC usage, posted usage data monthly to FEDLINK's online account management system (ALIX-FS), and reduced deficits in OCLC accounts.

FEDLINK members Carol Bursik, assistant director for access and organization, Department of Justice Libraries, and Eleanor Frierson, deputy director, National Agricultural Library, represented federal libraries on the OCLC Membership Council, where they added a federal perspective to issues of librarianship and information science and contributed to plans to meet the cooperative needs of libraries.

Training Program

The 2004 FEDLINK training program included 26 on-site training classes for 367 students and 13 off-site programs for 184 participants. FEDLINK facilitated training by Library of Congress cataloging experts for Army libraries in Europe and taught OCLC workshops to Army and Air Force library staff members in Germany and Japan.

FEDLINK also promoted its training agreements with other OCLC networks so that FEDLINK customers could fund training accounts for workshops held by Amigos, BCR, CAPCON, Michigan Library Consortium, Missouri Library Network Corporation, NYLINK, OCLC Western, PALINET, and SOLINET. FED-LINK also brokered the Computers in Libraries conference at a discounted rate for 262 attendees, saving the government nearly $70,000.

Procurement Program

After a successful pilot of a new procurement method in FY 2003, FEDLINK established new contracts with vendors of online information services and incorporated the Direct Express option into 56 of the 62 contracts. Staff worked closely with Library of Congress Contracts and Grants Management to issue a request for proposal for serials subscription services and anticipate awards in FY 2005. FEDLINK also awarded new contracts for ILL fee payment and preservation. Thirteen companies will provide microfilming, duplication, and conservation of books, archival materials, and photographs and other flat materials, as well as tailored consultation on how best to preserve materials in federal collections. FED-LINK added training agreements with Missouri Library Network Corporation and SOLINET.

FEDLINK staff members continued to support consortial arrangements for services such as INSPEC, LexisNexis, and West. A Department of Defense group, with library representatives from all four services, pilot-tested various procurement options and selected the FEDLINK consortium as the most beneficial. They noted cost avoidance and savings of an estimated $19 million a year.

Faxon/RoweCom Bankruptcy

At the end of FY 2003, the Library of Congress requested a decision from the Government Accountability Office (GAO) regarding the issue of liability for federal agency funds lost in the bankruptcy of serials vendor RoweCom. The request posed "whether the revolving fund or the specific agencies on whose behalf the library had placed orders with the defaulting contractor should bear the cost of the losses associated with the default."

GAO determined that the "loss resulting from RoweCom's bankruptcy is related to the operation of the FEDLINK program, and is an appropriate expense of the revolving fund. . . . The Library should use FEDLINK's administrative reserve to cover this deficit. If the Library wishes to allocate the costs differently in the future, it should add a clause dealing with contractor defaults to the interagency agreements." Thus, the FEDLINK revolving fund, rather than the subscribing agency customers, will bear the financial loss associated with RoweCom.

Following the decision, FEDLINK managers, with guidance from the library's Office of General Counsel and the Department of Justice Bankruptcy Counsel, exchanged information with the debtor (i.e., the representatives of RoweCom) to establish the net amount of the loss after libraries had been credited for journals "graced" by the publishers (despite nonpayment by RoweCom). The amount of the Library of Congress claim included library losses from prepaid subscriptions, costs of reprocuring alternative subscriptions, costs of reprocuring alternative subscription agents service, and FEDLINK's administrative costs for satisfactorily resolving the contracts for more than 50 FEDLINK transfer-pay customers with RoweCom contracts in FY 2002 and FY 2003. At the close of FY 2004, FEDLINK had agreed with Library of Congress and Department of Justice counsel to submit a joint settlement agreement, in cooperation with the debtor, to the U.S. Bankruptcy Court, rather than pursue further litigation. Once the court approves the settlement agreement, FEDLINK will reimburse libraries for their losses as established under the settlement. The debtor will then pay the FEDLINK program with whatever proceeds from the estate accrue to the Library of Congress as an unsecured creditor.

FEDLINK Fiscal Operations

FEDLINK Vendor Services

Total FEDLINK vendor service dollars for FY 2004 comprised $60.7 million for transfer-pay customers, $7.7 million for direct-pay customers, and $26.1 million of estimated vendor billings to Direct Express customers. Database retrieval services, available only through the transfer-pay and Direct Express options, represented $25.2 million and $26.1 million, respectively. Within this service category, online services comprised the largest procurement for transfer-pay and Direct Express customers, representing $23.9 million and $25.0 million, respectively. Publication acquisition services, available only through the transfer-pay and standard direct-pay options, represented $27.5 million and $7.7 million, respectively. Within this service category, serials subscription services comprised the largest procurement for transfer-pay and direct-pay customers, representing $19.9 million and $7.5 million, respectively. Library support and other miscellaneous services, available only through the transfer-pay option, represented $8 million. Within this service category, bibliographic utilities constituted the largest procurement area, representing $5.3 million.

Accounts Receivable and Member Services

FEDLINK processed FY 2004 registrations from federal libraries, information centers, and other federal offices for a total of 529 signed IAGs. In addition, FEDLINK processed 1,733 IAG amendments (1,047 for FY 2004 and 686 for prior-year adjustments) for agencies that added, adjusted, or ended service funding. These IAGs and IAG amendments represented 6,258 individual service requests to begin, move, convert, or cancel service from FEDLINK vendors. FEDLINK executed service requests by generating 5,983 delivery orders that Contracts and Grants issued to vendors. For FY 2004 alone, FEDLINK processed $60.7 million in service dollars for 2,223 transfer-pay accounts and $7.7 million in service dollars for 29 direct-pay accounts. Included in the above member service transactions were 974 member requests to move prior-year (no-year and multi-year) funds across fiscal year boundaries. These no-year and multi-year service request transactions represented an additional contracting volume of $5.4 million.

The FEDLINK Fiscal Hotline responded to a variety of member questions ranging from routine queries about IAGs, delivery orders, and account balances to complicated questions regarding FEDLINK policies and operating procedures. In addition, the FLICC Web site and e-mail contacts continued to offer FEDLINK members and vendors 24-hour access to fiscal operations. Staff members continued to schedule appointments to discuss complicated account problems with FEDLINK member agencies and FEDLINK vendors while senior staff members concentrated on resolving complex current- and prior-year situations. The FLICC executive director, business manager, and systems unit head visited the program's largest customer to review their library procurement system and initiate dialogue on how best to support customer requirements for similar systems in the future.

FEDLINK's online financial service system, ALIX-FS, provided current- and prior-year transfer-pay account information in FY 2004 and continued to offer members early access to their monthly balance information throughout the fiscal year. FEDLINK prepared monthly mailings and e-mails that alerted individual members to unsigned IAG amendments, deficit accounts, rejected invoices, and delinquent accounts, and issued an advance year-end schedule for fiscal year IAG transactions.

Transfer-Pay Accounts Payable Services

For transfer-pay users, FEDLINK processed 51,419 invoices for payment during FY 2004 for both current-year and prior-year orders. Staff members efficiently processed vendor invoices and earned $6,919 in discounts in excess of interest payment penalties levied for the late payment of invoices to FEDLINK vendors. FEDLINK continued to maintain open accounts for three prior years to pay publications service invoices ("bill laters" and "back orders") for members using books and serials services. Staff members issued 88,082 statements to members (22,508 for the current year and 65,574 for prior years) and continued to generate current fiscal year statements for electronic information retrieval service accounts on the last working day of each month, and publications and acquisitions account statements on the 15th of each month. FEDLINK issued final FY 1999 statements in support of closing obligations for expired FY 1999 appropriations and quarterly statements for prior fiscal years while supporting the reconciliation of FY 2000 FEDLINK vendor services accounts. FEDLINK issued the final call for FY 2000 invoices to vendors in early December 2003.

Direct Express Services

At the beginning of the fiscal year, FEDLINK expanded the Direct Express program to include all 55 of its vendors offering database retrieval services. During FY 2003, just five vendors in this category were involved in the pilot program. The program was set up to provide customers procurement and payment options similar to GSA, in which the vendors pay a quarterly service fee to FEDLINK based on customer billings for usage. The advantage for the customers and the vendors is the elimination of the process steps for setting up an IAG for the direct purchase of online services citing FEDLINK contract terms and conditions. The Direct Express program, although successful, only generated 77 percent of the fee revenue initially anticipated in the budget for FY 2004. FEDLINK attributes the shortfall to a slow start-up during the pilot phase, associated with insufficient information required for customer and vendor awareness of program operations. It should be noted that Direct Express fee revenue contributions did exceed lowered forecast estimates as revised early in FY 2004.

Budget and Revenue

During FY 2004 FEDLINK revenue from signed IAGs was approximately 4.7 percent above FY 2003 levels, but was 1.7 percent less ($81,900) than budgeted. The budget difference in program fee revenue is attributed to the slow start-up of the Direct Express program. The program fee revenue exceeded FY 2004 expenditure obligations by $83,300, which is higher than the $23,700 anticipated surplus in the budget for FY 2004. Program expenditure obligations (net of training reimbursements) are expected to be approximately $283,600 less than the budget due to unexpected/ unplanned attrition and reassignment of senior staff.

The 4.7 percent increase in fee revenue over FY 2003 is directly attributed to an 8.9 percent increase in transfer-pay service dollars, which is the result of adding a new large federal agency to FEDLINK's customer base.

Reserves and Risks

At the close of FY 2004 FEDLINK reserve carryover is estimated to increase by approximately $80,000 from the FY 2003 balance of $1,369,000. During FY 2004, GAO rendered its decision affirming FEDLINK's liability for transfer-pay customer losses associated with the Faxon bankruptcy (see "Faxon/RoweCom Bankruptcy" above). FEDLINK will reduce its reserve position by approximately $350,000 to $400,000 in the first quarter of FY 2005 to absorb customer agency losses not covered by publisher gracing and settlement agreements.

Other Financial Management Accomplishments

FEDLINK successfully passed the Library of Congress financial audit of FY 2003 transactions and completed vulnerability assessments of program financial risks for Library Services, Office of the Inspector General (OIG), and the Planning, Management and Evaluation (PMED) audit review. As a follow-up requirement, staff members completed detail control reviews of program financial operations for Library Services, OIG, and PMED review. Support for these audits includes financial systems briefings, documented review and analysis of the financial system, testing and verification of account balances in the central and subsidiary financial system, financial statement preparation support, security briefings and reviews, and research and documented responses to follow up audit questions and findings.

FEDLINK continued to provide central accounting for customer agency account balances to meet Treasury Department reporting requirements. FEDLINK also implemented all aspects of revolving fund reporting, including preparation, review, and forecasting revenue and expenses for the accounting period.

In support of the Library of Congress's implementation of a new financial management system, FEDLINK staff members worked with staff members from the Office of the Chief Financial Officer on its conversion efforts. To accomplish this task, FEDLINK staff members worked with vendors to pay customer invoices in advance of "prompt pay" requirements, modified year-end schedules for IAG transactions, and supported interface testing and conversion of vendor records for FEDLINK customer agencies and FEDLINK service providers.

FLICC Systems Office

FLICC systems staff worked with other FLICC/FEDLINK units and the Library of Congress's contractors to determine if the library's new financial system would be a suitable replacement for FEDLINK's older financial management system. FLICC managers determined that the new system will work as a replacement, and efforts began with a plan to implement the new system for FEDLINK by spring 2005.

National Agricultural Library

U.S. Department of Agriculture, NAL Bldg., 10301 Baltimore Ave.,
Beltsville, MD 20705-2351
E-mail agref@nal.usda.gov
World Wide Web http://www.nal.usda.gov

Len Carey
Public Affairs Officer

The National Agricultural Library (NAL), established within the U.S. Department of Agriculture (USDA) when the department was created in 1862, is the primary resource in the United States for information about food, agriculture, and natural resources.

Congress assigned to the library the responsibilities to

- Acquire, preserve, and manage information resources on agriculture and allied sciences
- Organize agricultural information and information products and services
- Provide agricultural information and information products and services within the United States and internationally
- Plan, coordinate, and evaluate information and library needs relating to agricultural research and education
- Cooperate with and coordinate efforts toward development of a comprehensive agricultural library and information network
- Coordinate the development of specialized subject information services among the agricultural and library and information communities

NAL is located in Beltsville, Maryland, near Washington, D.C., on the grounds of USDA's Henry A. Wallace Beltsville Agricultural Research Center. The library's 15-story Abraham Lincoln Building is named in honor of the president who created the Department of Agriculture and signed many of the major laws affecting U.S. agriculture.

Today NAL employs about 170 librarians, information specialists, computer specialists, administrators, and clerical personnel, supplemented by about 80 contract staff, volunteers, and cooperators from NAL partnering organizations. The library's expert staff, leadership in delivering information services, collaborations with other U.S. and international agricultural research and information organizations, extensive collection of agricultural information, AGRICOLA bibliographic database of citations to the agricultural literature, and advanced information technology infrastructure make it the world's foremost agricultural library.

NAL is an electronic gateway to a widening array of scientific literature, printed text, and images. It maintains more than 40,000 Web pages and in 2004 delivered more than 50 million direct customer services throughout the world via its Web site (http://www.nal.usda.gov) and other Internet-based services. NAL also works with other agricultural libraries and institutions to advance open and democratic access to information about agriculture and the nation's agricultural knowledge. NAL is the U.S. node of the international agricultural information system, and therefore a way for the world to access U.S. agricultural libraries and information resources.

NAL's eight national information centers are specialized gateways to science-based information in key areas of agriculture, including alternative farming systems (see http://www.nal.usda.gov/afsic), animal welfare (http://www.nal.usda.gov/awic), food and nutrition (http://www.nal.usda.gov/fnic), food safety (http://www.nal.usda.gov/foodsafety), invasive species (http://www.invasivespecies.gov), rural revitalization (http://www.nal.usda.gov/ric), technology transfer (http://www.nal.usda.gov/ttic), and water quality (http://www.nal.usda.gov/wqic). These centers provide targeted information services in collaboration with other organizations throughout government to provide timely, accurate, comprehensive, and in-depth coverage within their subject areas.

The Collection

NAL manages an immense collection of information and databases about agriculture. The breadth, depth, size, and scope of the library's collection—more than 3.5 million items on 48 miles of shelves, dating from the 16th century to the present, covering all aspects of agriculture and related sciences and including special one-of-a-kind items not available elsewhere—make it an irreplaceable resource for agricultural researchers, policy makers, regulators, and scholars. The NAL collection includes the most extensive set of materials anywhere on the history of agriculture in the United States, and is the most complete repository of U.S. Department of Agriculture publications. The library acquires more than 19,900 serial titles, including licenses for more than 1,900 electronic serials, annually.

NAL is a member of the National Digital Strategy Advisory Board, which works with the Library of Congress to advance the National Digital Information and Infrastructure and Preservation Program to ensure that important digital works documenting American life and culture are preserved. NAL has digitized and preserved the highly popular *Home and Garden* publication series and has implemented its digital object registration system, which ensures that digital works have persistent identifiers to ensure continued public access to digital works on the Internet. NAL participated in testing the Stanford University LOCKSS (Lots of Copies Keeps Stuff Safe) digital preservation system.

NAL's AGRICOLA (AGRICultural OnLine Access) bibliographic database contains more than 4 million citations to agricultural literature with links to the full text of many publications. From AGRICOLA's Web site (http://agricola.nal.usda.gov), NAL provides a broad base of users with no-cost access to this information.

NAL is nationally known as a leader in preservation of publications in print, digital, and other formats to ensure long-term access to agricultural information, and has led development of policies and procedures for preserving Department of Agriculture digital publications. The library is known for its expertise in preservation of microforms.

NAL's technology leadership in partnership with others can be seen in the newly implemented distributed architecture for managing agricultural information through the Agriculture Network Information Center (AgNIC) alliance.

AgNIC (http://www.agnic.org) is a discipline-specific, distributed network on the Internet, providing quality agricultural information selected by an alliance involving NAL, land-grant universities, and other institutions.

Under NAL leadership, AgNIC was established by an alliance of agricultural organizations that included Cornell University, Iowa State University, the University of Arizona, and the University of Nebraska–Lincoln. In 1995 NAL established the AgNIC Web site with a calendar of events and a database of agriculture resources. During the following year AgNIC partners added subject-specific sites including agricultural statistics, animal science, plant science, range management, rural information, and food and nutrition. In 1997 online reference was added as a partner requirement for each subject. In 2003 AgNIC gained two new members, bringing the partnership to 42, and offered 44 subject-specific sites. Plans for AgNIC's future include expanded communication and emphasis on further developing a portal interface, developing content for each subject site, populating the new database, increasing subject coverage by increasing membership, continuing to expand coverage to include non-English languages, and locating funding resources.

Information Management

NAL is a national and international bibliographic authority on managing agricultural information, both nationally and internationally, and an authority on the development and use of controlled vocabulary for agriculture. In July 2003 NAL began using its new thesaurus for indexing, and the retrospective AGRICOLA database was converted to NAL Thesaurus terms. Its strong foundation and experience in collection development, implementation of bibliographic control standards, and systems for information retrieval uniquely position NAL to define and develop new models for identifying, organizing, preserving, and providing access to the vast quantities of agricultural information available digitally on the Internet and elsewhere. The collective expertise of the NAL staff and the vast array of print and digital information present in the national collection offer opportunity for collaboratively developing and testing innovative methods of creating and linking agricultural research information.

During the Year

Web-Based Products and Services

NAL continues to emphasize the expansion of its presence on the World Wide Web to provide broader access to information for its global clientele on an every-hour-of-every-day basis. Delivery of Web-based services and improved Web content was developed in key areas of customer interest.

DigiTop

In early 2004, a year after launching the pilot of DigiTop, the Digital Desktop Library for USDA, NAL moved the project into full implementation. DigiTop provides online access to the full text of thousands of journals, a number of citation databases, and hundreds of newspapers from around the world, as well as significant reference resources. DigiTop is available to all USDA employees and contractors worldwide—more than 110,000 people—24 hours a day. Comparing the cost of supplying full-text journal articles through DigiTop with the cost of providing the same number of articles through traditional document supply channels yields a remarkable return on investment.

NAL/MSU Pilot Demonstration Project

With the success of DigiTop, NAL extended the digital desktop library concept into a pilot demonstration project with Mississippi State University (MSU) in Starkville, Mississippi. NAL Director Peter R. Young and Mississippi State University President Charles Lee signed an agreement in January 2004 to launch the DigiTop PLUS Pilot Demonstration Project. The collaboration means MSU researchers, teachers, and students will have easier and faster access to the latest information in the agricultural sciences. The project will also give NAL the opportunity to test the feasibility, costs, and effectiveness of extending the digital desktop system to other colleges and universities with programs in agricultural sciences.

The first phase of the project enabled MSU faculty, staff, and students, as well as researchers at the Mississippi Agricultural and Forestry Experiment Stations and the Mississippi State Extension Service, to have NAL-facilitated access via the World Wide Web to science-based information in agriculture and related fields in about 70 select journals not previously available electronically through MSU libraries. These MSU DigiTop PLUS journals are tagged with a DigiTop PLUS icon and available through the electronic journals A-Z list maintained on the MSU libraries' Web site. MSU users can click on the MSU DigiTop PLUS icon, or on an article title, and be automatically linked to full-text articles licensed through NAL. The second phase of the project added journals and integrated these publications with access services, including reference and document delivery, provided by NAL.

Nutrition.gov

In December 2004 then-Agriculture Secretary Ann Veneman launched an NAL-developed nutrition Web site (http://www.nutrition.gov) designed to help people find answers to nutrition and food-related questions.

Nutrition.gov is a resource that includes databases, recipes, interactive tools, and specialized information for infants and children, adult men and women, and seniors. The Web site also links to information on the food pyramid, dietary guidelines, dietary supplements, fitness, and food safety. The site is a comprehensive source of information on nutrition and dietary guidance from multiple government agencies.

The site is maintained by a team of dietitians and nutrition information specialists at NAL's Food and Nutrition Information Center who work in cooperation with scientists and professionals at USDA's Agricultural Research Service, USDA Food and Nutrition Service, the U.S. Department of Health and Human Services, and other federal partners. The Web site is an important tool in developing food- and exercise-based strategies for obesity prevention and in coordinating with federal agencies in a national prevention effort.

Science.gov

NAL was involved in May 2004 in launching Science.gov Version 2.0 (http://www.science.gov) as an improved gateway to reliable information about science and technology from across federal government organizations. Science.gov 2.0 offers groundbreaking, user-friendly technology enhancements to the interagency science portal. While retaining the content and advances originally unveiled in December 2002 with the first version of Science.gov, Science.gov 2.0 sorts through the government's vast reservoirs of research and rapidly returns information in an order of relevancy more likely to meet patrons' needs. Science.gov is made possible through a collaboration of 12 major science agencies.

Science.gov is for the educational and library communities as well as business people, scientists, and anyone with an interest in science. The information is free of charge, and no registration is required. The Science.gov Web site provides the ability to search across 30 databases and more than 1,700 science Web sites. It currently accesses more than 47 million pages of government science information.

WIC Works Training Module

USDA made available in March 2004 a free Web-based training course for registered dietitians and others who work with USDA's Special Supplemental Nutrition Program for Women, Infants, and Children (WIC). The WIC Learning Online course was developed by NAL's Food and Nutrition Information Center in collaboration with the USDA Food and Nutrition Service.

The course is composed of 12 modules organized into four lessons. Each module provides a basic introduction and background on the topic as well as tips for practical application in the clinic setting. Each module requires less than 30 minutes for completion. The course includes an online tutorial, a bookmark feature that allows students to re-enter the course at the same point at which they stopped, and job aids that can be printed for future reference.

The online course provides WIC staff with a user-friendly and efficient tool for staff development and continuing education. The course has been approved as a self-study course by the American Dietetic Association's Commission on Dietetic Registration, meaning that completing the course counts toward the continuing professional education requirements for registered dietitians.

Anyone can take the course by logging onto the site and creating a unique username and password. A student who successfully completes the assessments at the end of each lesson with a score of 70 percent or better may print a personalized certificate of completion.

Conservation Effects Assessment Project Bibliographies

NAL published a series of bibliographies in October from a comprehensive review of the current literature covering conservation programs, including the research needed to improve practices. The bibliographies were prepared by NAL's Water Quality Information Center in support of the USDA Conservation

Effects Assessment Project (CEAP). Through CEAP, USDA is studying the environmental benefits of conservation practices implemented through various USDA conservation programs.

The bibliographies are available in four volumes, all on the Web. Together they offer more than 2,700 citations, with abstracts where available, and with URLs when the documents are freely available online.

Documenting the Long Journey of Corn

In June 2004 NAL made available on the Web (http://www.nal.usda.gov/ research/maize/introduction.shtml) a chronology of corn's migration from Mexico's Aztec civilization to the Silk Road to China. The story, prepared by NAL technical information specialist Susan McCarthy and Agricultural Research Service chemist Anne Desjardins, details corn's global travels, starting with the crop's only known center of domestication in Mesoamerica, a region composed of south-central Mexico and adjacent areas of Central America.

The authors' sources include Christopher Columbus, whose explorers were the first known Europeans to encounter corn, during the first of his four voyages. While in Cuba, Columbus is said to have logged an account in which ". . . [his party] had seen many fields . . . also of a grain like panic-grass that the Indians call maize. This grain has a very good taste when cooked, either roasted or ground and made into a gruel." The publication chronicles early events in corn's five-century journey from Mesoamerica to Europe, Africa, and Asia, with subsections providing historical context.

National Library of Medicine

8600 Rockville Pike, Bethesda, MD 20894
301-496-6308, 888-346-3656, fax 301-496-4450
E-mail publicinfo@nlm.nih.gov
World Wide Web http://www.nlm.nih.gov

Robert Mehnert
Director, Office of Communications and Public Liaison

The National Library of Medicine (NLM), a part of the U.S. Department of Health and Human Services' National Institutes of Health (NIH) in Bethesda, Maryland, is the world's largest library of the health sciences. NLM has two buildings with 420,000 total square feet. The older building (1962) houses the collection, public reading rooms, exhibition hall, and library staff and administrative offices. The adjacent 10-story Lister Hill Center Building (1980) contains the main computer room, auditorium, audiovisual facility, offices, and research laboratories.

The library, as a public institution, welcomes patrons of all kinds—students, scientists, health practitioners, and the general public—and offers many services and resources helpful in their search for health-related information. The library's collections today number almost 8 million books, journals, audiovisuals, and historical materials in many languages, and encompass all the health sciences. Holdings range from 900-year-old manuscripts to the latest medical materials whether on paper, film, disk, or database.

In 1994 NLM introduced its Web site—one of the federal government's first—and began a decade of rapid growth in the amount and variety of medical information it made available. The NLM home page was redesigned in 2004 to make this wealth of information more easily accessible. Today the library's Web service provides not only free access to Medline/PubMed, the largest database of published scientific medical information in the world, but NLM has also created information products designed specifically for patients, families, and the public.

To safeguard the library's extensive computer-based services, NLM in 2004 established the NIH Consolidated Collocation Site. This site, distant from Bethesda, Maryland, provides backup capability for both NLM and NIH.

The success of Medline/PubMed has led to the demise of one of the library's best-known products, the monthly printed *Index Medicus* bibliography. Started by John Shaw Billings in 1879 and published for 125 years, *Index Medicus* ended with the December 2004 issue. Once an indispensable tool for health professionals and librarians, it became a seldom-used alternative to Medline/PubMed and other Internet-based products that contain the database from which *Index Medicus* was generated.

Of special note to the medical library community in 2004 was the issuing of a completely updated Collection Development Manual of the National Library of Medicine (fourth edition). The revised manual reflects the complex and changing environment of health care and biomedical research. Sections on bioinformatics, molecular biology, plant science, toxicology, and biological sciences describe an increased emphasis on fundamental biological research in fields of biomedicine. The manual also elaborates on the library's collecting policy for many print and nonprint formats and literature types, such as journals, electronic resources, audiovisuals, digital images, and datasets. The manual is on the library's Web site at http://www.nlm.nih.gov/tsd/acquisitions/cdm.

Information Services for the Public

The library first seriously considered creating information services for the general public in 1997 when it became apparent that the Medline/PubMed database for scientific medical literature was in fact being used heavily by consumers. The following year the NLM Board of Regents formally recommended that the library expand its mandate to include serving the public. Since that time, NLM has created a series of highly successful information services aimed at consumers.

MedlinePlus

MedlinePlus, a Web-based service available in English and Spanish, provides integrated access to authoritative consumer health information. Launched in November 1998, MedlinePlus today is one of the most heavily trafficked Web sites containing health information for the public. As of late 2004 it was being consulted some 60 million times a month by 6 million unique visitors. MedlinePlus has more than 670 "health topics," containing, for example, overview information, pertinent clinical trials, alternative medicine, prevention, management, therapies, current research, and the latest news from the print media. In addition to the health topics, there are medical dictionaries, encyclopedias, directories of hospitals and providers, and interactive "tutorials" with images and sound. MedlinePlus in Spanish was introduced in 2002 and has grown to virtual parity with the English version. Both scored the highest marks of any federal Web site in a recent evaluation by the American Customer Satisfaction Index. A new aspect of MedlinePlus is "Go Local," which links users with community helping services near them. North Carolina and Missouri are the first MedlinePlus partners to "go local"; more states will be coming online soon.

Information Rx

Even with such heavy usage, the library actively seeks to promote the database. For example, since the fall of 2002 NLM has collaborated with the American College of Physicians (ACP) Foundation in "Information Rx," a project to encourage physicians to make information referrals to MedlinePlus. Because patients trust their physicians to recommend good health information, the idea is to promote MedlinePlus as "the Web site your doctor prescribes." The foundation sees this as an opportunity to help member physicians provide reliable health information for their patients. NLM has worked with the ACP governors in three states—Georgia, Iowa, and Virginia—to pilot the project. NLM provided a variety of information materials to the participating physicians, including posters and prescription pads. The Information Rx project was rolled out nationally in New Orleans at the ACP annual meeting in spring 2004. The project continues to be expanded and the results so far are encouraging—two thirds of the physicians ranked MedlinePlus as their first or second choice for referring patients.

ClinicalTrials.gov

ClinicalTrials.gov is another popular Web-based NLM database. This resource gives patients, families, and members of the public easy access to information about clinical studies. Each record includes the locations of a study, its design and purpose, criteria for participation, contact information, and further information about the disease and intervention under study. General information on clinical research written in lay language—including a glossary, answers to frequently asked questions, and links to resources—provides ways to place medical research into the context of medical care, essential for the patient or the healthy volunteer considering taking part in a trial. In November 2004 ClinicalTrials.gov contained 12,000 studies sponsored by the public and private sectors in more than 90 countries. It receives more than 2.5 million page views monthly and hosts up to 17,000 visitors in a single day. ClinicalTrials.gov was honored in 2004 by being named a recipient of Harvard University's prestigious "Oscar" of government awards, the Innovations in American Government Award.

Tox Town, TOXMAP

The library's Division of Specialized Information Services has introduced a number of Web-based information services for the general public: Tox Town, which has information about harmful substances found in every community; the Household Products Database, with information about the health effects of more than 4,000 common household products; and several information resources for specific populations such as Asian Americans and those living in the Arctic and far north. In 2004 the division introduced two new information resources: American Indian Health, which deals with the unique health needs of this population, and TOXMAP, which shows, on maps, the amount and location of certain toxic chemicals released into the environment in the United States. The TOXMAP site also links to NLM's extensive collection of toxicology and environmental health references, as well as to a rich resource of data on hazardous chemical substances in its TOXNET databases.

NLM's Lister Hill Center also sponsors several information resources for the general public. The Genetics Home Reference database provides simple and understandable information about diseases and disorders that run in families. The center also maintains Profiles in Science, a Web site that makes available to the public the archival collections of a growing number of pioneering biomedical scientists. The site (http://profiles.nlm.nih.gov) was launched in September 1998 and promotes the use of the Internet for research and teaching in the history of biomedical science. The collections contain published and unpublished items, including books, journal volumes, pamphlets, diaries, letters, manuscripts, photographs, audiotapes, video clips, and other materials. During 2004 the papers of former U.S. Surgeon General C. Everett Koop and those of Wilbur A. Sawyer, a key figure in preventive medicine and international public health, were added to Profiles in Science.

NIHSeniorHealth.gov

Another recent Web service for consumers is NIHSeniorHealth.gov, created by NLM in cooperation with the National Institute on Aging, which contains information on health-related subjects of interest to seniors in a format that is especially usable by them. For example, the site features large-print, easy-to-read segments of information repeated in a variety of formats—such as open-captioned videos and short quizzes—to increase the likelihood it will be remembered. NIHSeniorHealth.gov has a "talking" function, which allows users to read or listen to the text.

Serving Special Communities

With all these information resources, it becomes increasingly important for the library to engage in outreach to let potential users know what is available. The 5,000-member National Network of Libraries of Medicine is an important partner in these outreach endeavors. Many of the programs are directed at minority populations. For example, there are programs to assist in remedying the disparity in health opportunities experienced by African Americans, Latinos, Native Americans, senior citizens, and rural populations. One notable program is the Listening Circle, a Native American/Alaska Native concept that enables an open dialogue and exchange of perspectives and information between Native Americans and NLM in order to build mutual understanding and trust on which future collaborations can be based. It has proven to be an excellent means to identify needs and special opportunities for reducing health disparities, as defined by the actual people NLM intends to serve with its outreach programs. NLM has participated in Listening Circles in North Dakota, Alaska, and Hawaii.

Under a program with the Historically Black Colleges and Universities (HBCUs), NLM is helping to train people to use information resources in dealing with environmental and chemical hazards. The latest aspect of this outreach effort is NLM's collaboration with the United Negro College Fund Special Programs Corporation to work with the HBCUs to encourage the use of reliable electronic health information (such as that provided by NLM) by the public.

NLM also has been instrumental in reaching out to other countries to help improve their access to scientific medical information. The oldest such program is that involving formal partnerships with major institutions in 20 nations. NLM helps them obtain computerized access to the literature; the countries in turn help NLM receive the medical literature from other parts of the world. The library is also a key player in the Multilateral Initiative on Malaria, the multiagency effort to improve malaria research in African nations. NLM's role is to establish and maintain the first malaria research communications network, MIMCOM. There are now 19 research sites participating in nine countries, with full access via the Internet.

Information Services for the Scientific Community

Medline/PubMed is a free, Web-based resource. MEDLINE is NLM's database of indexed journal citations and abstracts now covering nearly 4,500 journals published in the United States and more than 70 other countries. New citations are added weekly and the database expands at the rate of more than half a million records a year. PubMed is the system that provides access not only to MEDLINE but to some out-of-scope citations, additional life science journals, and older materials. PubMed reached the milestone of 15 million records in 2004. The growth in usage of Medline/PubMed since its introduction in 1997 has been exceptional. In 2004 there were more than 670 million searches, with page views totaling 2.5 billion.

Improvements to PubMed continue to be introduced, and today the database offers a high degree of flexibility to users. For example, there are now Web links to more than 90 percent of the journals represented in Medline, allowing users to have access to the full text of articles referenced in the database. A user's view of PubMed can be customized to highlight electronic and print journals available through the local hospital or academic health sciences library with which he or she is affiliated. Where links to electronic full text are not available, the user may use PubMed to place an online order for an article directly from a library in the National Network of Libraries of Medicine.

An increasingly popular service for the professional community and the public is PubMedCentral. This is a rapidly growing digital archive of life sciences journal literature to which publishers electronically submit peer-reviewed research articles. NLM undertakes to guarantee free access to the material; copyright remains with the publisher or the author. Creating such "digital archives" to ensure that the world's biomedical literature—including research resulting from federally supported research and development—is properly recorded and available for future generations is an important NLM responsibility. In 2004 Britain's Wellcome Trust, an independent charity funding research to improve human and animal health, in partnership with the Joint Information Systems Committee and NLM, announced plans to digitize the complete backfiles of a number of important and historically significant medical journals for PubMedCentral. In addition to creating a digital copy of every page in the backfiles, the digitization process will also create a PDF file for every discrete item (article, editorial, letter, advertisement, and so forth) in the archive, and use optical-character-recognition technology to generate searchable text.

The NLM component that has played a major role in creating many of the information systems offered by the library is the National Center for Biotechnology Information (NCBI). Within the scientific community, NCBI is well known for GenBank, a database of all publicly available DNA sequences. GenBank now contains more than 32 million sequence entries totaling 37 billion base pairs from more than 140,000 species. The database, which is accessed by some 50,000 scientists daily, contains more than 100 complete genomes as well as protein product and other relevant genetic information.

Wireless Information System for Emergency Responders (WISER) is a new information system introduced by NLM in 2004. WISER employs a handheld PDA to provide on-the-spot information for first-responders about hazardous materials released into the environment. WISER offers mobile support, supplying emergency-situation responders with critical information where and when they need it. It features a wide range of information on hazardous substances, including chemical identification support, physical characteristics, human health data, and containment and suppression data. The system is currently designed to work in stand-alone mode; future versions will also operate in connected mode. WISER, created by NLM's Division of Specialized Information Services, can be downloaded at http://wiser.nlm.nih.gov.

Communications Research and Development

NLM's Lister Hill National Center for Biomedical Communications conducts and supports research and development in the dissemination of high-quality imagery, medical language processing, high-speed access to biomedical information, intelligent database systems development, multimedia visualization, knowledge management, data mining, and machine-assisted indexing.

One popular example is the Visible Human Project, which consists of two large (50 gigabytes) data sets of anatomical MRI, CT, and photographic cryosection images, one based on a male cadaver and one on a female. These data sets are available to individuals and institutions through a free license agreement. The demand for Visible Human anatomic images by medical researchers and educators has been steadily growing throughout the world. A new Web site, Anat-Quest, has been developed under Lister Hill Center auspices to meet this demand and to provide new and visually compelling ways to bring anatomic images to a broad range of users, including the public. The site offers users thumbnails of the cross-section, sagittal and coronal images of the Visible Male and Female, from which full resolution views are accessed. In addition, a few hundred three-dimensional anatomic structures are provided. Users can zoom in and out as they navigate through the images. The project has the potential to generate improvements in the state of the art that would benefit access to any image database, in the exploration of suitable models for linking term queries (and document text) to images, and in the development of system architectures for image processing and handling. NLM is now seeking ways to link the print library of functional-physiological knowledge with the image library of structural-anatomic knowledge, forming a single, unified resource for health information. This linking to anatomic images would add great value to text resources such as Medline/PubMed and MedlinePlus.

NLM's Extramural Programs are authorized by the Medical Library Assistance Act of 1965. The act, as amended and extended, authorizes the library to award grants for research, training and fellowships, medical library assistance, improving access to information, and publications. For more than 20 years NLM has supported the training of medical informaticians at universities across the United States. In the early years the program focused on training of informaticians for clinical care. Today the training programs have added opportunities for training in bioinformatics, the field of biomedical computing for the large data sets characteristic of modern research. NLM now provides 18 grants for biomedical informatics training at 26 universities, supporting 250 trainees. NLM also participates in NIH Roadmap activities, almost all of which have major emphasis on biomedical computing. For example, training is an important requirement of the National Centers for Biomedical Computing, an initiative for which NLM is one of the key leaders. Training as embedded in Roadmap activities is expected to become a significant complement to NLM's traditional support of informatics training.

In another area, the library can play an important role in bringing together the resources and people needed to create key components of a truly national health information technology infrastructure. One significant stumbling block has been the inability to share clinical data across systems, impeding clinical research and contributing to medical treatment errors. NLM has already made an important contribution in this area with its development of the Unified Medical Language System (UMLS) and the recent licensing of SNOMED CT (Systematized Nomenclature of Medicine—Clinical Terms), a standard clinical vocabulary available freely to all. The national licensing of SNOMED CT and its uniform distribution with other clinical and administrative standards within UMLS makes it possible for software vendors, healthcare providers, hospitals, insurance companies, public health departments, medical research facilities, and others to incorporate uniform terminology into their information systems much more readily. This is an important step toward establishing interoperable electronic health records that can be made available wherever and whenever patients need treatment. In addition to improving the safety and quality of health care, standard electronic health data will assist in detecting and responding to public health emergencies and provide one of the key building blocks for a cost-effective national research infrastructure.

Administration

The director of NLM, Donald A. B. Lindberg, M.D., is guided in matters of policy by a board of regents consisting of 10 appointed and 11 ex officio members. Appointed as regents in 2004 were Richard Chabrán, chairman of the California Technology Policy Group, and former U.S. Rep. Newt Gingrich (R-Ga.).

Table 1 / Selected NLM Statistics*

Library Operation	Volume
Collection (book and nonbook)	7,952,247
Items cataloged	21,238
Serial titles received	20,769
Articles indexed for MEDLINE	571,000
Circulation requests processed	640,000
For interlibrary loan	360,000
For on-site users	280,000
Computerized searches (Medline/PubMed)	678,000,000
Budget authority	$329,089,000
Staff	675

*For the year ending September 30, 2004

United States Government Printing Office

732 North Capitol St. N.W., Washington, DC 20401
202-512-0212
E-mail vmeter@gpo.gov
World Wide Web http://www.gpo.gov

Veronica Meter
Director, Office of Public Relations

The Government Printing Office (GPO) is part of the legislative branch of the federal government and operates under the authority of the public printing and documents chapters of Title 44 of the U.S. Code. Created primarily to satisfy the printing needs of Congress, today GPO is the focal point for printing, binding, and information dissemination for the entire federal community. In addition to Congress, approximately 130 federal departments and agencies, representing more than 6,000 government units, rely on GPO's services. Congressional documents, Supreme Court decisions, federal regulations and reports, IRS tax forms, and U.S. passports are all produced by or through GPO.

Traditionally, GPO's mission was accomplished through production and procurement of ink-on-paper printing. Today, after more than a generation of experience with electronic printing systems, GPO is at the forefront in providing government information through a wide range of formats, including digital presentation, DVD and CD, printing, and microfiche.

GPO's central office facility is located in Washington, D.C. Nationwide, GPO maintains 14 regional printing procurement offices, six satellite procurement facilities, a major distribution facility in Pueblo, Colorado, a bookstore in its Washington, D.C., facility, and a retail sales outlet at its publications warehouse in Laurel, Maryland.

This report focuses on GPO's role as the disseminator of government information in print and electronic formats.

Information Dissemination/Superintendent of Documents

GPO's documents activities, overseen by the Office of Information Dissemination/Superintendent of Documents (ID), disseminate one of the world's largest volumes of informational literature. In fiscal year (FY) 2004, GPO distributed 28,225,260 government publications in tangible formats. In addition, more than 1 million documents were downloaded from GPO Access each day, an average of approximately 34 million documents each month.

GPO Customer Contact Center

GPO's new Customer Contact Center is working to provide the highest-quality service to the public. The mission of the Contact Center is to deliver highly effective customer relationship management services designed to answer questions and serve needs relating to the ID program. Between its inception in August 2004 and February 2005, the Contact Center processed approximately 80,000 calls and 30,000 e-mails and generated more than 2,500 new frequently asked questions (FAQs). This new organization replaces GPO's Office of Electronic Information Dissemination Services and the former Order Division, serving as the agency's "voice to the customer and library communities," and centralizes all incoming e-mail and written correspondence for processing.

The center uses a state-of-the-art customer relationship management knowledge base, which is populated daily with answers to FAQs. Users can search or browse this knowledge base as a whole or by category/subcategory. Questions that cannot be answered by the knowledge base can be sent to GPO using the Ask a Question tab; they are then routed to the appropriate subject specialists within GPO. The Customer Contact Center is available via the Internet at http://www.gpoaccess.gov/help/index.html, by e-mail at contactcenter@gpo.gov, or by toll-free telephone at 866-512-1800 (in the Washington metropolitan area 202-512-1800), from 7:00 A.M. to 9:00 P.M. Eastern Time, Monday through Friday, except federal holidays.

Authentication/PKI

Since the completion of the operational "stand-up" of a public key infrastructure (PKI) and an external audit of operations, staff in the chief information officer's organization has been working on testing and evaluating several digital-signing tools using GPO's PKI. This may lead to the future application of digital signatures to GPO Access files, beginning with congressional bills. In parallel with this testing, steps are being taken to cross-certify GPO's PKI operations with the Federal Bridge Certification Authority (FBCA). GPO has been working closely with FBCA representatives to ensure that business, administrative, and technical processes relating to GPO's PKI match those of the bridge. FBCA is a fundamental element of the trust infrastructure that provides the basis for intergovernmental and cross-governmental secure communications. Once certification is completed, live signatures will be made available on GPO Access files.

eGovernment Act 2002

GPO has worked on several committees for the implementation of the eGovernment Act 2002. Section 207 deals with the categorization of government information. The Interagency Committee on Government Information, Categorization of Government Information, prepared a report with recommendations to the Office of Management and Budget (OMB) on definitions, search interoperability, searchable identifiers, and categorization. The report was submitted to OMB in December 2004.

GPO has also been co-chair with the General Services Administration (GSA) of a committee for the implementation of Sections 213 and 215 of the eGovernment Act, which have to do with the community technology centers (CTSs) and issues around the "digital divide." The first phase of the effort was completed in December 2004, with a follow-on phase that began in January 2005 and was scheduled to be completed in April 2005. The work product for this effort is a survey of the current state of the "digital divide" and the CTCs, with follow-on recommendations.

Federal Depository Library Program

Information Dissemination Implementation Plan

ID is compiling the Information Dissemination Implementation Plan, FY 2005–2006, which will reflect its plans for the full scope of programs and operations. To date, the plan's chapters include the latest versions of three plans previously issued separately: the National Bibliography, the National Collection (formerly Collection of Last Resort), and the Federal Depository Library Program (FDLP) Electronic Collection. Other new chapters will be added as they become available. The plan also includes a consolidated glossary, references, and a list of acronyms. This document will be available on GPO Access for review and comment.

Center for Research Libraries Decision Framework

GPO has contracted with the Center for Research Libraries to develop a decision framework for creating shared federal document repositories. The Federal Depository Library Council commented on the draft version of the framework and found it a reasonable initial draft for developing regional repositories for tangible federal government documents. Three related decision framework documents were developed for accessible, light, and dark archives, providing criteria for establishing such archives for the National Collection of U.S. Government Publications. The three documents were merged into a single document and released for public comment on September 20, 2004. The Decision Framework for Federal Document Repositories, prepared for GPO by the Center for Research Libraries, is available at http://www.access.gpo.gov/su_docs/fdlp/pubs/matrix_repository_type.pdf.

National Collection of U.S. Government Publications

GPO is developing the National Collection of U.S. Government Publications, which will provide permanent public access to U.S. government publications in all formats, past, present, and future. Multiple collections of tangible and digital publications will be located in multiple sites and operated with various partners within and beyond the U.S. government. Although publications produced solely for administrative or operational use are excluded by law from depository distribution, GPO, where possible, will acquire such publications for the National Bibliography of U.S. Government Publications and retain copies in the National Collection. The National Collection will also serve as a repository for products from future GPO initiatives.

In 2004 the National Collection continued to receive one copy of every tangible publication distributed through FDLP. In addition, there were a number of important acquisitions from depository and federal libraries during the year. GPO was able to acquire many long runs of series and serials from the Free Public Library and Cultural Center of Bayonne (New Jersey), including the *Foreign Relations of the United States* 1907–1957, the annual report of the American Historical Association (1906–1984), annual reports from the Departments of Labor, Transportation, and Treasury, the Library of Congress, the National Aeronautics and Space Administration, the Small Business Administration, and the Smithsonian Institution, as well as a number of bulletins from the Bureau of American Ethnology. Other acquisition highlights include

- 82 folios of the *Geologic Atlas of the United States*
- *Federal Reserve Bulletin* 1918–2002
- More than 50 years of reports from the U.S. Tax Court
- *Social Security Bulletin* 1939–1989
- Numerous U.S. Geological Survey Circulars

Digitization of the Legacy Collection

GPO is committed to creating a digital media services business unit, and a cross-functional team consisting of members of the various business areas of GPO is developing the digital media services plan. The plan focuses on converting printed legacy documents into digital content that meets FDLP standards. The digital media services unit will allow content to be added to the future digital content system as addressed in the "Concept of Operations for the Future Digital System." The complete document for the future digital system is found at http://www.access.gpo.gov/su_docs/fdlp/tools/Conops_1004.pdf. A three-page summary is at http://www.access.gpo.gov/su_docs/fdlp/tools/Conops_Summary.pdf.

The goal of digitizing a complete legacy collection of tangible U.S. government publications held in libraries participating in FDLP will be one of the first areas targeted by the new digital media services unit. To this end, GPO has been developing specifications for scanning and metadata that can be used not only for the conversion of the historical collection but also for inclusion of other content in the future digital system.

Scanning specifications and the "Report from the Meeting of Experts on Digital Preservation: Preservation Masters" can be seen at http://www.gpoaccess.gov/about/reports/preservation.html.

Print on Demand

A print-on-demand (POD) needs survey was issued in August/September 2004 to assess the ability of POD technology to improve FDLP. The most recent results can be viewed at http://www.gpoaccess.gov/pod/pod_stats.html. The survey showed considerable interest in a POD program, and GPO is working on a plan to implement a POD allowance program of $500 per library or $1,500 per regional library. GPO hopes to have a complete plan by the fourth quarter of FY 2005.

LOCKSS

GPO plans to use LOCKSS (Lots of Copies Keep Stuff Safe) technology and GPO's harvesting capabilities to develop a pilot that focuses on collecting, managing, disseminating, and preserving access to federal government e-journals. All e-journals selected for this pilot will be within the scope of FDLP and the International Exchange Service (IES). The pilot will be divided into two phases. In

Phase 1, GPO will establish and test a LOCKSS cache at GPO. In Phase 2, GPO will make e-journal content available to pilot federal depository libraries, the IES library, and LOCKSS partners.

ILS and Retrospective Conversion Projects Update

Implementation of the integrated library system (ILS) at GPO has progressed since the award of the contract to Progressive Technical Federal Systems (PTFS) in fall 2004. Systems librarians and key GPO personnel have completed training.

The data set of GPO-cataloged records dating from July 1976 to October 2004 has been loaded and is being tested and reviewed by GPO staff. Additional testing of the initial load is scheduled, and a "go live" gap load of records from October 2004 is being evaluated.

In preparation for "go live," GPO staff are working on many projects, including the customization of the out-of-the-box public interface, the development of training sessions for staff who will be using the system, ongoing authority control services, and the migration of the locate-libraries function to the new online public access catalog (OPAC).

The Office of Bibliographic Services has completed a statement of work for retrospective conversion services for the pre-1976 GPO historic shelf list.

ID Policy 72

ID Policy 72—which sets conditions for withdrawing, recalling, or restricting access to government documents available through GPO's information dissemination programs—is under review. The current ID 72 Policy Statement is available at http://www.access.gpo.gov/su_docs/fdlp/pubs/sod72_policy_rev.pdf.

FDLP Partnerships

GPO, the U.S. Census Bureau, and the university library of Case Western Reserve University have agreed to extend for an additional two years their partnership for making electronic government information products from the 2000 Census accessible under the auspices of FDLP.

GPO and the Institute of Education Sciences of the U.S. Department of Education are working together to modify the existing partnership agreement to provide permanent public access to in-scope federal publications from the Education Resources Information Center (ERIC) Program for the benefit of FDLP and its participants.

GPO and the Federal Reserve Bank of St. Louis are developing a partnership agreement to provide depository access to federal government information in the Federal Reserve Archival System for Economic Research (FRASER) service. GPO is also working on developing FDLP partnership agreements for permanent public access of the following digitization projects:

- University of Michigan, Harlan Hatcher Graduate Library, *Public Papers of the President* digital collection

- University of Wisconsin–Madison Libraries, Foreign Relations of the United States digital collection
- University of Maryland School of Law, Thurgood Marshall Law Library, Historical Publications of the United States Commission on Civil Rights
- Southern Methodist University, Central University Libraries, Historic Government Publications from World War II Digital Library collection

GPO Access

GPO Access (http://www.gpoaccess.gov) provides access to electronic information products from all three branches of the federal government, as established by the Government Printing Office Electronic Information Access Enhancement Act of 1993 (P.L. 103-40). GPO Access now contains nearly 3,000 separate databases in more than 100 applications. For FY 2004 the GPO Access collection totaled more than 285,000 titles—more than 172,000 titles on its servers and more than 112,000 titles through links to other federal government Web sites.

GPO Access Statistics

June 2004 marked the 10th anniversary of GPO Access. Since its inception, users have retrieved more than 2 billion documents. Usage has increased from an average of about 20,000 monthly retrievals in 1994 to an average of about 34 million a month in 2004.

By January 2005 GPO had disseminated a total of 10,080 online and tangible titles in various formats. When multiple formats of the same title are removed, approximately 94 percent of the new titles were electronic rather than tangible distributions.

Bound Congressional Record Now on GPO Access

The most requested title in the GPO digitization survey was the bound *Congressional Record,* which is the newest application on GPO Access. A full-text, searchable Vol. 145 (1999, first session of the 106th Congress) is available at http://www.gpoaccess.gov/crecordbound/index.html. Additional volumes will be added in the near future.

GPO also plans to release, for the first time, a *U.S. Reports* application, followed by a *Statutes At Large* application.

U.S. Government Online Bookstore

In January 2005 enhancements were made to the U.S. Government Online Bookstore, available through GPO Access at http://bookstore.gpo.gov. The bookstore is now running on a new server with modern software, and as a result the search facility has been greatly enhanced and the detailed publications information has been greatly expanded. More upgrades were anticipated during FY 2005. Once these enhancements are in place, customers will be able to ship to multiple addresses as well as foreign addresses. In addition, customers should be able to order publications using a new print-on-demand capability.

Finding Aids

GPO Access provides a number of free tools to assist users in browsing or searching for government information. In order to provide more visibility, the finding aids have been further integrated into the pages of the redesigned GPO Access. These tools act as a portal to information available on government Web sites. They can be used to conduct government-wide searches, locate government publications online and in print, and find agency Web sites based on broad subject areas. A complete list of finding aids can be found at http://www.gpoaccess.gov/branches.html#federal.

Ben's Guide to U.S. Government for Kids

Ben's Guide to U.S. Government for Kids (http://bensguide.gpo.gov) strives to introduce and explain the workings of all three branches of the federal government through the use of primary source materials, age-appropriate explanations, and a stimulating site design.

The site is broken down into four grade levels—K–2, 3–5, 6–8, and 9–12— and also provides an area for parents and educators. The material in each of these sections is specifically tailored to its intended audience. Ben's Guide includes historical documents and information on the legislative and regulatory processes, elections, and citizenship. The site also features learning activities and a list of federal Web sites designed for students, parents, and educators.

Training Classes, Demonstrations, and Trade Shows

The continuing rapid growth of GPO Access resulted in a number of requests for training classes, demonstrations, and trade shows to educate users about electronic products and services available through the Office of Information Dissemination/Superintendent of Documents. Recent sessions were conducted in Nashville, San Diego, Orlando, New York, San Antonio, Boston, Kansas City, Atlanta, and Chicago.

Section 508 Compliance

In 1998 the Workforce Investment Act amended Section 508 of the Rehabilitation Act of 1973 to include accessibility requirements for electronic and information technology. Section 508 now requires that electronic and information technology used by the federal government, including Web sites, be made as accessible for people with disabilities as it is for people without disabilities. GPO continues to ensure that pages under the gpoaccess.gov domain are Section 508-compliant.

Additions and Improvements to Web Pages and Applications

For each new year or session of Congress, new databases, such as the 2004 Federal Register, are added to existing applications on GPO Access. Several other new applications were made available in FY 2004, and improvements were made to the way users find and retrieve documents. The following is a list of significant enhancements to the Web site:

- *Report of the Select Committee on Intelligence on the U.S. Intelligence Community's Prewar Intelligence Assessments on Iraq* at http://www. gpoaccess.gov/serialset/creports/iraq.html. The report is intended to provide the Senate and the public with a substantial record of the facts underlying the committee's conclusions regarding the intelligence community's prewar assessments of Iraq's programs for weapons of mass destruction and its ties to terrorism. The Senate Select Committee on Intelligence oversees and makes continuing studies of government intelligence activities and programs.

- *The 9-11 Commission Report: Final Report of the National Commission on Terrorist Attacks Upon the United States,* official government edition. The commission's final report provides a complete account of the circumstances surrounding the September 11, 2001, terrorist attacks, including preparedness for such attacks and the immediate response to the attacks. It also includes recommendations designed to guard against future attacks.

- GPO Access has added a feature (http://www.gpoaccess.gov/chearings/ browse.html) that allows users to browse a current catalog of congressional hearings. Catalogs are available for the 105th Congress to the present. Links are included with each congressional hearing listed in the catalog that retrieve the text of the corresponding document as an ASCII text or PDF file. GPO Access continues to add hearings as they become available during each session of Congress. Congressional hearings not listed in the catalog are not currently available electronically via GPO Access. GPO Access also added a similar feature for congressional documents at http:// www.gpoaccess.gov/serialset/cdocuments/browse.html.

Selling Government Publications

The Superintendent of Documents' sales program currently offers for sale approximately 6,000 government publications on a wide array of subjects. These are sold principally via electronic, e-mail, telephone, fax, and mail orders. The program operates on a cost-recovery basis. Publications for sale include books, forms, posters, pamphlets, maps, CD-ROMs, computer diskettes, and magnetic tapes. Subscription services for both dated periodicals and basic-and-supplement services (involving an initial volume and supplemental issues) are also offered.

Express service, which includes priority handling and Federal Express delivery, is available for orders placed by telephone for domestic delivery. Orders placed before noon Eastern time for in-stock publications and single-copy subscriptions will be delivered within two working days. Some quantity restrictions apply. For more information, call the order desk at 866-512-1800 (toll free) or 202-512-1800 (in the Washington metropolitan area).

Consumer-oriented publications are also sold or distributed at no charge through the Federal Citizen Information Center in Pueblo, Colorado.

The GPO sales program continues to streamline its operations by reducing overhead. It has begun using print-on-demand technology to increase the long-term availability of publications and testing the capabilities of a number of vendors. The program is also engaged in bringing its bibliographic practices more in line with those of the commercial publishing sector by exploring ONIX (online information exchange), the publishing industry's standard electronic format for sharing product data with wholesale and retail booksellers, other publishers, and anyone else involved in the sale of books. ONIX will enable GPO to have government publications listed, promoted, and sold by commercial book dealers worldwide.

Product Information

The U.S. Government Online Bookstore (http://bookstore.gpo.gov) is the single point of access for all government information products available for sale from GPO. A search interface with the *Sales Product Catalog,* a guide to current government information products offered for sale through the Superintendent of Documents and updated every working day, is part of the main page interface. Advanced search options are also available. Another feature on the main page is a "pop-up box" that enables customers to "Browse a Topic." This list of topics is based upon the approximately 160 subject bibliographies available through the online bookstore. Customers can also browse special collections at the U.S. Government Online Bookstore, including CD-ROMs, Electronic Products, the Subscriptions Catalog, and the Federal Consumer Information Center. Special collections include a list of federal tax products, emergency response publications, and a catalog of regulatory and legal publications.

Items purchased from the U.S. Government Online Bookstore are now assigned a unique order number that customers can reference when contacting GPO's Order Division. A detailed transaction receipt is provided after each order submission, and a copy of the transaction receipt is sent to the customer's e-mail address if provided on the online order form. In addition, customers can now use American Express for payment, in addition to VISA, MasterCard, and Discover/ Novus.

Customers can also register to receive e-mail updates when new publications become available for sale from the Superintendent of Documents through the New Titles by Topic E-mail Alert Service, found at http://bookstore.gpo.gov/ alertservice.html.

The sales program also lists selected titles on Barnesandnoble.com, Amazon. com, and other online commercial book-selling sites.

National Technical Information Service

Technology Administration
U.S. Department of Commerce, Springfield, VA 22161
800-553-NTIS (6847) or 703-605-6000
World Wide Web http://www.ntis.gov

Linda Davis
Marketing Communications

The National Technical Information Service (NTIS) serves as the nation's largest central source and primary disseminator of scientific, technical, engineering, and business information produced or sponsored by U.S. and international government sources. NTIS is a federal agency within the Technology Administration of the U.S. Department of Commerce.

Since 1945 the NTIS mission has been to operate a central U.S. government access point for scientific and technical information useful to American industry and government. NTIS maintains a permanent archive of this declassified information for researchers, businesses, and the public to access quickly and easily. Release of the information is intended to promote American economic growth and development and to increase U.S. competitiveness in the world market.

The NTIS collection of approximately 3 million titles contains products available in various formats. Such information includes reports describing research conducted or sponsored by federal agencies and their contractors, statistical and business information, U.S. military publications, multimedia training programs, computer software and electronic databases developed by federal agencies, and technical reports prepared by research organizations worldwide. Approximately 60,000 new titles are added and indexed annually. NTIS maintains a permanent repository of its information products.

More than 200 U.S. government agencies contribute to the NTIS collection, including the National Aeronautics and Space Administration, Environmental Protection Agency, the departments of Agriculture, Commerce, Defense, Energy, Health and Human Services, Interior, Labor, Treasury, Veterans Affairs, Housing and Urban Development, Education, Transportation, and numerous other agencies. International contributors include Canada, Japan, Britain, and several European countries.

NTIS E-Government Virtual Library

NTIS offers Web-based access to the latest government scientific and technical research information products. Visitors to http://www.ntis.gov can search more than 600,000 NTIS database records dating back to 1990 free of charge. NTIS also provides access links to documents online at other government agency Web sites when available, downloading capability for many technical reports, and purchase of the publications on customized CD-ROMs.

NTIS Database

The NTIS Database (listings of information products acquired by NTIS since 1964) offers unparalleled bibliographic coverage of U.S. government and world-wide government-sponsored research. Its contents represent hundreds of billions of research dollars and cover a range of important topics including agriculture, biotechnology, business, communication, energy, engineering, the environment, health and safety, medicine, research and development, science, space, technology, transportation, and more.

Most records include abstracts. Database summaries describe technical reports, datafiles, multimedia/training programs, and software. These titles are often unique to NTIS and generally are difficult to locate from any other source. The complete NTIS Database provides instant access to more than 2 million records.

Free 30-day trials of the NTIS Database are available through the GOV. Research_Center (http://grc.ntis.gov). The NTIS Database can be leased directly from NTIS, and it can also be accessed through the following commercial services: Cambridge Scientific Abstracts, 800-843-7751, http://www.csa.com; DATA-STAR (DIALOG), 800-334-2564, http://www.dialog.com; EBSCO, 800-653-2726, http://www.epnet.com; Engineering Information (Ei), 800-221-1044, http://www.ei.org; Knowledge EXPRESS, 800-529-5337, http://www.knowledge express.com; NERAC, Inc., 860-872-7000, http://www.nerac.com; Ovid Technologies, Inc., 800-950-2035, http://www.ovid.com; SilverPlatter Information, Inc., 800-343-0064, http://www.silverplatter.com; and STN International/CAS, 800-848-6533, http://www.cas.org. For an updated list of organizations offering NTIS Database products, see http://www.ntis.gov/products/types/databases/commercial.asp.

To lease the NTIS Database directly from NTIS, contact the NTIS Subscriptions Department at 800-363-2068 or 703-605-6060. For more information, see http://www.ntis.gov/products/types/databases/ntisdb.asp

Other Databases Available from NTIS

NTIS offers several valuable research-oriented database products. To find out more about accessing the databases, visit http://www.ntis.gov/products/types/databases/data.asp.

FEDRIP

The Federal Research in Progress Database (FEDRIP) provides access to information about ongoing federally funded projects in the fields of the physical sciences, engineering, and life sciences. The ongoing research announced in FEDRIP is an important component of the technology transfer process in the United States; FEDRIP's uniqueness lies in its structure as a nonbibliographic information source of research in progress. Project descriptions generally include project title, keywords, start date, estimated completion date, principal investigator, performing and sponsoring organizations, summary, and progress report. Record content varies depending on the source agency.

There are many reasons to search FEDRIP. Among these are to avoid research duplication, locate sources of support, identify leads in the literature, stimulate ideas for planning, identify gaps in areas of investigation, and locate individuals with expertise. To access an updated list of organizations offering FEDRIP Database products, see http://www.ntis.gov/products/types/databases/fedrip.asp.

AGRICOLA

As one of the most comprehensive sources of U.S. agricultural and life sciences information, the Agricultural Online Access Database (AGRICOLA) contains bibliographic records for documents acquired by the National Agricultural Library (NAL) of the U.S. Department of Agriculture. The complete database dates from 1970 and contains more than 4 million citations to journal articles, monographs, theses, patents, software, audiovisual materials, and technical reports relating to agriculture. AGRICOLA serves as the document locator and bibliographic control system for the NAL collection. The extensive file provides comprehensive coverage of newly acquired worldwide publications in agriculture and related fields. AGRICOLA covers the field of agriculture in the broadest sense. Subjects include Agricultural Economics, Agricultural Education, Agricultural Products, Animal Science, Aquaculture, Biotechnology, Botany, Cytology, Energy, Engineering, Feed Science, Fertilizers, Fibers and Textiles, Food and Nutrition, Forestry, Horticulture, Human Ecology, Human Nutrition, Hydrology, Hydroponics, Microbiology, Natural Resources, Pesticides, Physiology, Plant and Animal, Plant Sciences, Public Health, Rural Sociology, Soil Sciences, Veterinary Medicine, Water Quality, and more. To access an updated list of organizations offering AGRICOLA Database products, see http://www.ntis.gov/products/types/databases/agricola.asp.

AGRIS

The International Information System for the Agricultural Science and Technology (AGRIS) Database is a cooperative system for collecting and disseminating information on the world's agricultural literature in which more than 100 national and multinational centers take part. References to citation for U.S. publications given coverage in the AGRICOLA Database are not included in AGRIS. A large number of citations in AGRIS are not found in any other database. Reference to nonconventional literature (documents not commercially available) contain a note about where a copy may be obtained. AGRIS can be used to find citations to agricultural information from around the world. Much of this information includes government documents, technical reports, and nonconventional literature that have their source in both developed and developing countries and that can be found nowhere else. To access an updated list of organizations offering AGRIS products, see http://www.ntis.gov/products/types/databases/agris.asp.

Energy Science and Technology

The Energy Science and Technology Database (EDB) is a multidisciplinary file containing worldwide references to basic and applied scientific and technical research literature. The information is collected for use by government managers, researchers at the national laboratories, and other research efforts sponsored by the U.S. Department of Energy, and the results of this research are transferred to the public. Abstracts are included for records from 1976 to the present. EDB also contains the Nuclear Science Abstracts, a comprehensive abstract and index collection for the international nuclear science and technology literature for the period 1948–1976. Included are scientific and technical reports of the U.S. Atomic Energy Commission, U.S. Energy Research and Development Administration and its contractors, other agencies, universities, and industrial and research organizations. Approximately 25 percent of the records in the file contain abstracts. Nuclear Science Abstracts contains more than 900,000 bibliographic records. The entire EDB contains more than 3 million bibliographic records. To access an updated list of organizations offering EDB products, see http://www.ntis.gov/ products/types/databases/engsci.asp.

Immediately Dangerous to Life or Health Concentrations Database

The NIOSH (National Institute for Occupational Safety and Health) documentation for the Immediately Dangerous to Life or Health Concentrations (IDLHs) Database contains air concentration values used by NIOSH as respirator-selection criteria. This compilation is the rationale and source of information used by NIOSH during the original determination of 387 IDLHs and their subsequent review and revision in 1994. Toxicologists, persons concerned with use of respirators, industrial hygienists, persons concerned with indoor air quality, and emergency response personnel will find this product beneficial. This database will enable users to compare NIOSH limits with other limits and will be an important resource for those concerned with acute chemical exposures. To access an updated list of organizations offering IDLHs Database products, see http://www.ntis. gov/products/types/databases/idlhs.asp.

NIOSH Manual of Analytical Methods Database

The NIOSH Manual of Analytical Methods (NMAM) Database is a compilation of methods for sampling and analysis of contaminants in workplace air and in the bodily fluids of workers who are occupationally exposed to that air. These methods have been developed specifically to have adequate sensitivity to detect the lowest concentrations and sufficient flexibility of range to detect concentrations exceeding safe levels of exposure, as regulated by the Occupational Safety and Health Administration and recommended by NIOSH. The Threshold Values and Biological Exposure Indices of the American Conference of Governmental Industrial Hygienists are also cited. To access an updated list of organizations offering NIOSH Manual of Analytical Methods Database products, see http:// www.ntis.gov/products/types/databases/nmam.asp.

NIOSH Pocket Guide to Chemical Hazards Database

The NIOSH Pocket Guide to Chemical Hazards (NPG) Database is intended as a source of general industrial hygiene information that is quick and convenient for workers, employers, and occupational health professionals. NPG presents in abbreviated tabular form key information and data on chemicals or substance groupings (e.g., cyanides, fluorides, manganese compounds) that are found in the work environment. The industrial hygiene information found in NPG should help users recognize and control occupational chemical hazards. The information in NPG includes chemical structures or formulas, identification codes, synonyms, exposure limits, chemical and physical properties, incompatibilities and reactivities, measurement methods, recommended respirator selections, signs and symptoms of exposure, and procedures for emergency treatment. Industrial hygienists, industrial hygiene technicians, safety professionals, occupational health physicians and nurses, and hazardous materials managers will find the database a versatile and indispensable tool in their work. For an updated list of organizations offering Pocket Guide to Chemical Hazards Database products, see http://www. ntis.gov/products/types/databases/npgfacts.asp.

NIOSHTIC

NIOSHTIC is a bibliographic database of literature in the field of occupational safety and health developed by NIOSH. Although the file has been static since 1998, it contains retrospective information, some dating back to the 19th century. Because NIOSH examines all aspects of adverse effects experienced by workers, much of the information contained in NIOSHTIC has been selected from sources that do not have a primary occupational safety and health orientation. NIOSHTIC subject coverage includes the behavioral sciences; biochemistry, physiology, and metabolism; biological hazards; chemistry; control technology; education and training; epidemiological studies of disease/disorders; ergonomics; hazardous waste; health physics; occupational medicine; pathology and histology; safety; toxicology; and more. To access an updated list of organizations offering NIOSHTIC products, visit http://www.ntis.gov/products/types/databases/nioshtic.asp.

Registry of Toxic Effects of Chemical Substances Database

The Registry of Toxic Effects of Chemical Substances (RTECS) is a database of toxicological information compiled, maintained, and updated by NIOSH. The program is mandated by the Occupational Safety and Health Act of 1970. The original edition, known as the Toxic Substances List, was published in June 1971 and included toxicological data for approximately 5,000 chemicals. Since that time, the list has continuously grown and been updated, and its name changed to the current title. RTECS now contains more than 133,000 chemicals as NIOSH strives to fulfill the mandate to list "all known toxic substances . . . and the concentrations at which . . . toxicity is known to occur."

RTECS is a compendium of data extracted from the open scientific literature. The data are recorded in the format developed by the RTECS staff and arranged in alphabetical order by prime chemical name. No attempt has been made to evaluate the studies cited in RTECS; the user has the responsibility of making such assessments. To access an updated list of organizations offering RTECS Database products, visit http://www.ntis.gov/products/types/databases/rtecs.asp.

Specialized Online Subscriptions

Those wishing to expand their access to subject-specific resources through use of the Internet are likely to benefit from the NTIS online options highlighted below. Online subscriptions offer quick, convenient online access to the most current information available.

Government Research Center

The GOV.Research_Center (GRC) is a collection of well-known government-sponsored research databases available on the World Wide Web via an online subscription service. Customers can subscribe to a single GRC Database product or to several databases. The following databases made available at the GOV. Research_Center by NTIS and the National Information Services Corporation (NISC) are searchable at the site using NISC's Biblioline search engine. These database subscription products include the NTIS Database, FEDRIP, NIOSHTIC, EDB, Nuclear Science Abstracts Database, AgroBase, AGRICOLA, and RTECS.

NTIS and NISC are constantly improving the content and features of GRC. Online ordering allows ordering of documents directly from the NTIS Database by using a credit card or NTIS deposit account; cross-database searching allows use of a single search query across all databases within a subscription plan. Limited day-pass access to the NTIS Database is available for a nominal fee.

For more information, visit the GOV.Research_Center at http://grc.ntis.gov.

World News Connection

World News Connection (WNC) is an NTIS online news service accessible only via the World Wide Web. WNC makes available English-language translations of time-sensitive news and information from thousands of non-U.S. media. Particularly effective in its coverage of local media, WNC provides the power to identify what is happening in a specific country or region. The information is obtained from speeches, television and radio broadcasts, newspaper articles, periodicals, and books. The subject matter focuses on socioeconomic, political, scientific, technical, and environmental issues and events.

The information in WNC is provided to NTIS by the Foreign Broadcast Information Service (FBIS), a U.S. government agency. For more than 60 years, analysts from FBIS's domestic and overseas bureaus have monitored timely and pertinent open-source material, including gray literature. Uniquely, WNC allows subscribers to take advantage of the intelligence-gathering experience of FBIS.

WNC is updated every government-business day. Generally, new information is available within 24 to 72 hours of the time of original publication or broadcast.

Subscribers can conduct unlimited interactive searches and have the ability to set up automated searches known as profiles. When a profile is created, a search is run against WNC's latest news feed to identify articles relevant to a subscriber's topic of interest. The results are automatically sent to the subscriber's e-mail address.

Access to WNC is available through Dialog Corporation. To use the service, complete the WNC form at http://www.dialog.com/contacts/forms/wnc.shtml.

U.S. Export Administration Regulations

U.S. Export Administration Regulations (EAR) provides the latest rules controlling the export of U.S. dual-use commodities, technology, and software. Step by step, EAR explains when an export license is necessary and when it is not, how to obtain an export license, policy changes as they are issued, new restrictions on exports to certain countries and of certain types of items, and where to obtain further help.

This information is now available through NTIS in looseleaf form, on CD-ROM, and online. An e-mail update notification service is also available.

For more information, see http://bxa.fedworld.gov.

Davis-Bacon Wage Determination Database

The Davis-Bacon Wage Determination Database subscription product contains wage determinations issued by the U.S. Department of Labor under the mandate of the Davis-Bacon Act and related legislation. The department determines prevailing wage rates for construction-related occupations in most counties in the United States. All federal government construction contracts and most contracts for federally assisted construction over $2,000 must abide by the wage structure as provided for in the Davis-Bacon wage determinations. This product offers such value-added features as electronic delivery of modified wage decisions directly to the user's desktop, the ability to access wage decisions issued earlier in the year, and extensive help desk support.

A variety of access plans are available. For more information, see http://davisbacon.fedworld.gov.

Service Contract Act Wage Determination Database

The Service Contract Act Wage Determination (SCA) Database contains unsigned copies of the latest wage determinations developed by the U.S. Department of Labor. These wage determinations, issued by the Wage and Hour Division in response to specific notices filed, set the minimum wage on federally funded service contracts. SCA is updated each Tuesday with all wage determinations that were added or revised by the preceding Thursday.

For federal agencies participating under a memorandum of understanding with the department's Wage and Hour Division, and meeting all of its requirements, SCA can be used in the procurement process. For all other users, the wage determinations are for information only. They are not considered official wage determinations for specific solicitations or contracts and are not to be used to set prevailing wage rates on federal service contracts, but these data form a convenient and accurate basis upon which rates can be compared by occupation and geography.

A variety of access plans are available. For more information, see http://servicecontract.fedworld.gov.

Special Subscription Services

NTIS Alerts

More than 1,000 new titles are added to the NTIS collection every week. NTIS Alerts were developed in response to requests from customers to search and tap into this newly obtained information. NTIS prepares a list of search criteria that is run against all new studies and R&D reports in 16 subject areas. An NTIS Alert provides a twice-monthly information briefing service covering a wide range of technology topics.

An NTIS Alert provides numerous benefits: efficient, economical, and timely access to the latest U.S. government technical studies; concise, easy-to-read summaries; information not readily available from any other source; contributions from more than 100 countries; and subheadings within each issue designed to identify essential information quickly.

For more information, call the NTIS Subscriptions Department at 703-605-6060 or see http://www.ntis.gov/new/alerts_printed.asp.

SRIM

Selected Research In Microfiche (SRIM) is an inexpensive, tailored information service that delivers full-text microfiche copies of technical reports based on a customer's needs. Customers choose from Standard SRIM Service (selecting one or more of the 320 existing subject areas) or use Custom SRIM Service, which creates a new subject area to meet their particular needs. Custom SRIM Service requires a one-time fee to cover the cost of strategy development and computer programming to set up a profile. Except for this fee, the cost of Custom SRIM is the same as the Standard SRIM. Through this ongoing subscription service, customers receive microfiche copies of new reports pertaining to their field(s) of interest, as NTIS obtains the reports.

The SRIM service is now available in CD-ROM format. Documents are digitized and stored in PDF format that can easily be viewed using free Adobe Acrobat Reader software. With S&T (Science and Technology) on CD, NTIS can provide more publications—those that cannot be rendered on microfiche, such as colorized illustrations or oversized formats.

For more information, see http://www.ntis.gov/products/srim.asp. To place an order for a SRIM subscription, call 800-363-2068 or 703-605-6060.

Also at NTIS

NTIS Homeland Security Information Center

NTIS is a valuable resource for scientific and technical information relating to homeland security. It provides a Web-based finding aid in the following homeland security categories: health and medicine, food and agriculture, biological and chemical warfare, preparedness and response, and safety training. For more information, see http://www.ntis.gov/hs.

NTIS FedWorld

Since 1992 NTIS FedWorld Information Technologies has served as the online locator service for a comprehensive inventory of information disseminated by the federal government. FedWorld assists federal agencies and the public in electronically locating federal government information, both information housed within the NTIS repository and information FedWorld makes accessible through an electronic gateway to other government agencies. FedWorld is currently meeting the information needs of tens of thousands of customers daily. Examples of electronic information available on FedWorld include EPA auto emissions information, federal job searches, and Supreme Court decisions. Visit FedWorld at http://www.fedworld.gov.

NTIS Customer Service

NTIS's automated systems keep it at the forefront when it comes to customer service. Shopping online at NTIS is safe and secure; its secure socket layer (SSL) software is among the best available today.

Electronic document storage is fully integrated with NTIS's order-taking process, allowing it to provide rapid reproduction for the most recent additions to the NTIS document collection. Most orders for shipment are filled and delivered anywhere in the United States in five to seven business days. Rush service is available for an additional fee.

Key NTIS Contacts for Ordering

Order by Phone

Sales Desk	800-553-6847
8:00 A.M.–6:00 P.M. Eastern time, Monday–Friday	or 703-605-6000
Subscriptions	800-363-2068
8:30 A.M.–5:00 P.M. Eastern time, Monday–Friday	or 703-605-6060
TDD (hearing impaired only)	703-487-4639
8:30 A.M.–5:00 P.M. Eastern time, Monday–Friday	

Order by Fax

24 hours a day, seven days a week	703-605-6900
To verify receipt of fax, call	703-605-6090
7:00 A.M.–5:00 P.M. Eastern Time Monday–Friday	

Order by Mail

National Technical Information Service
5285 Port Royal Road
Springfield, VA 22161

RUSH Service (available for an additional fee)   800-553-6847
                                                             or 703-605-6000
Note: If requesting RUSH Service, please do not mail your order

Order Via World Wide Web

Direct and secure online ordering   http://www.ntis.gov

Order Via E-Mail

24 hours a day   orders@ntis.gov.

For Internet security, customers placing an order by e-mail can register their credit card in advance. To do so, call 703-605-6070 between 7:00 A.M. and 5:00 P.M. Eastern time, Monday through Friday.

National Archives and Records Administration

8601 Adelphi Rd., College Park, MD 20740
301-837-2000, World Wide Web http://www.archives.gov

Ellen Fried
Policy and Communications Staff

The National Archives and Records Administration (NARA), an independent federal agency, ensures for the citizen, the public servant, the president, Congress, and the courts ready access to essential evidence that documents the rights of American citizens, the actions of federal officials, and the national experience.

NARA is singular among the world's archives as a unified federal institution that accessions and preserves materials from all three branches of government. NARA assists federal agencies in documenting their activities, administering records management programs, scheduling records, and retiring noncurrent records to federal records centers. The agency also manages the presidential libraries; assists the National Historical Publications and Records Commission in its grant program for state and local records and edited publications of the papers of prominent Americans; publishes the laws, regulations, presidential documents, and other official notices of the federal government; and oversees classification and declassification policy in the federal government through the Information Security Oversight Office. NARA constituents include the federal government, a history-minded public, the media, the archival community, and a broad spectrum of professional associations and researchers in such fields as history, political science, law, library and information services, and genealogy.

The size and breadth of NARA's holdings are staggering. Together, NARA's facilities hold more than 27 million cubic feet (equivalent to more than 81 billion pieces of paper) of original textual and nontextual materials from the executive, legislative, and judicial branches of the federal government. Its multimedia collections include more than 112,000 motion picture films; more than 6.4 million maps, charts, and architectural drawings; more than 236,000 sound and video recordings; more than 20 million aerial photographs; more than 19 million still pictures and posters; and more than 5.6 billion electronic records.

Strategic Directions

NARA's strategic priorities are laid out in *Ready Access to Essential Evidence: The Strategic Plan of the National Archives and Records Administration, 1997–2008,* revised in 2003. Success for the agency as envisioned in the plan will mean reaching five strategic goals:

- Essential evidence will be created, identified, appropriately scheduled, and managed for as long as needed.
- Electronic records will be controlled, preserved, and made accessible for as long as needed.

- Essential evidence will be easy to access, regardless of where it is or where users are, for as long as needed.
- All records will be preserved in an appropriate environment for use as long as needed.
- NARA will strategically manage and align staff, technology, and processes to achieve its mission.

The plan lays out strategies for reaching these goals, sets milestone targets for accomplishments through 2008, and identifies measurements for gauging progress. The targets and measurements are further delineated in NARA's Annual Performance Plans.

The Strategic Plan and NARA's Annual Performance Plans and Reports are available on the NARA Web site at http://www.archives.gov/about_us/index.html or by calling the Policy and Communications staff at 301-837-1850.

Records and Access

Internet

NARA's Web site provides the most widely available means of electronic access to information about NARA, including directions on how to contact the agency and do research at its facilities; descriptions of its holdings in an online catalog; direct access to certain archival electronic records; digital copies of selected archival documents; an online guide to researching family history in the 1930 census microfilm, including a searchable online database that helps locate specific rolls of microfilm to consult (at http://1930census.archives.gov); an Internet Web form (at http://www.archives.gov/global_pages/inquire_form.html) for customer questions, reference requests, comments, and complaints; electronic versions of *Federal Register* publications; online exhibits; and classroom resources for students and teachers. NARA is continually expanding the kinds and amount of information available on the Web site and evaluating and redesigning the site to make it easier to use. For example, veterans and the next-of-kin of deceased veterans may now submit requests for their service records through a Web-based, interactive inquiry program at http://www.archives.gov/research_room/vetrecs. Copies of military pension records from the American Revolution through World War I can now be ordered through "Order Online!" at http://www.archives.gov/research_room/orderonline.html.

NARA also plays a key role in a nationwide civics initiative called Our Documents, at http://www.ourdocuments.gov, which features 100 milestone documents drawn primarily from NARA's holdings. NARA has also established a Web site with access to federal rules and a mechanism for accepting comments from the public, at http://www.regulations.gov.

Electronic Access Project

As a result of NARA's Electronic Access Project, anyone, anywhere, with a computer connected to the Internet, can search descriptions of NARA's nationwide holdings and view digital copies of some of its most popular documents. This is a significant piece of NARA's electronic access strategy as outlined in its Strategic Plan. The centerpiece of the project is the Archival Research Catalog (ARC), an online catalog of all NARA holdings nationwide, that allows the public to use computers to search for information about NARA's vast holdings, including those in the regional archives and presidential libraries. Because of the extent of NARA holdings, it will take several years to complete the online catalog. At present, the catalog contains more than 586,000 descriptions of archival holdings and 124,000 digital copies of high-interest documents. This represents about 34 percent of NARA's growing holdings. The documents available online include many of the holdings highlighted in the Public Vaults, NARA's permanent interactive exhibition. The catalog is available on the Internet at http://www.archives.gov/research_room/arc.

Renovation and Re-encasement

In September 2003 NARA reopened the Rotunda for the Charters of Freedom at the National Archives Building in Washington, D.C. It had been closed for renovation since July 2001. Returned to display were the Declaration of Independence, the Constitution, and the Bill of Rights—known collectively as the Charters of Freedom—which had received conservation treatment and were placed in new state-of-the-art encasements. For the first time, all four pages of the Constitution are on permanent display, and all the documents are now displayed so that they are easier to view by young visitors and those using wheelchairs.

The reopening of the rotunda launched the National Archives Experience, a set of interconnected resources that provide a variety of ways of exploring the power and importance of America's records. The National Archives Experience is made possible by a public-private partnership between NARA and the Foundation for the National Archives.

The National Archives Experience continued to expand in 2004 with the opening of the William G. McGowan Theater, the unveiling of the Public Vaults, and the inauguration of the Lawrence F. O'Brien Gallery. The 290-seat McGowan Theater is a state-of-the-art showplace for NARA's extensive audiovisual holdings and serves as a forum for lectures and discussion. It is also home to the new Guggenheim Center for the Documentary Film. The Public Vaults is a 9,000-square-foot permanent exhibition that conveys the feeling of going beyond the walls of the rotunda and into the stacks and vaults of the working archives. Dozens of individual exhibits, many of them interactive, reveal the breadth and variety of NARA's holdings. Complementing the Public Vaults, the O'Brien Gallery hosts a changing array of topical exhibits based on National Archives records.

Future additions will include a learning center and a set of Web pages that will make the National Archives Experience available to people who are unable to travel to Washington. For more information, visit http://www.archives.gov/national_archives_experience/index.html.

In October 2003 the new National Archives Building Research Center was opened. It consolidates on the first floor many of the research services previously on upper floors and offers a number of new services for researchers. The building-wide renovation is expected to be completed in 2005.

Archives Library Information Center

The Archives Library Information Center (ALIC) provides access to information on ready reference, American history and government, archival administration, information management, and government documents. ALIC is physically located in two traditional libraries in the National Archives Building in Washington and the National Archives at College Park. Customers also can visit ALIC on the Internet at http://www.archives.gov/research_room/alic, where they will find "Reference at Your Desk" Internet links, staff-compiled bibliographies and publications, an online library catalog, and more. ALIC can be reached by telephone at 202-501-5415 in Washington and 301-837-3415 in College Park.

Government Documents

U.S. government publications are generally available to researchers at many of the 1,350 congressionally designated federal depository libraries throughout the United States. A record set of these publications also is part of NARA's archival holdings. Publications of the U.S. Government (Record Group 287) is a collection of selected publications of U.S. government agencies, arranged by the classification system (SuDoc System) devised by the Office of the Superintendent of Documents, Government Printing Office (GPO). The core of the collection is a library established in 1895 by GPO's Public Documents Division. By 1972, when NARA acquired the library, it included official publications dating from the early years of the federal government and selected publications produced for and by federal government agencies. Since 1972 the 28,000-cubic-foot collection has been augmented periodically with accessions of U.S. government publications selected by the Office of the Superintendent of Documents as a byproduct of its cataloging activity. As with the federal depository library collections, the holdings in NARA's Record Group 287 comprise only a portion of all U.S. government publications.

NARA Publications

NARA publishes guides and indexes to various portions of its archival holdings; catalogs of microfilmed records; informational leaflets and brochures; general interest books about NARA and its holdings that will appeal to anyone with an interest in U.S. history; more-specialized publications that will be useful to scholars, archivists, records managers, historians, researchers, and educators; facsimiles of certain documents; and *Prologue,* a scholarly journal published quarterly. Some NARA publications are available through the National Archives Fax-on-Demand System described below. Some are also available on NARA's Web site, at http://www.archives.gov/publications/online_publications.html. Many are available from NARA's Customer Service Center in College Park, Maryland, by calling 800-234-8861 or 866-272-6272 (in the Washington, D.C., area 301-837-2000) or faxing 301-837-0483. The NARA Web site's publications' home page, http://www.archives.gov/publications/index.html, provides detailed information about available publications and ordering.

Fax-on-Demand

NARA customers can request faxed copies of select informational materials at any time by calling NARA's interactive fax retrieval system at 301-837-0990. By following the voice-activated instructions, customers will receive by fax copies of the materials stored digitally on the hard drive of an agency computer. Among the materials available by fax are brochures regarding NARA internships, NARA and federal government employment, and the semiannual Modern Archives Institute; published general information leaflets, other fact sheets about various NARA holdings, programs, and facilities (especially those located in Washington, D.C., and College Park and Suitland, Maryland, and the National Personnel Records Center in St. Louis); instructions, forms, and vendor lists for ordering copies of records; and finding aids for some textual, audiovisual, and micrographic records. Instructions and a listing of currently available documents are found on NARA's Web site at http://www.archives.gov/publications/fax_on_demand/fax_on_demand.html. There are no charges for using this service other than the cost of long-distance telephone calls.

Federal Register

The *Federal Register* is the daily newspaper of the federal government and includes proposed and final regulations, agency notices, and presidential legal documents. The *Federal Register* is published by the Office of the Federal Register and printed and distributed by the Government Printing Office (GPO). The two agencies collaborate in the same way to produce the annual revisions of the *Code of Federal Regulations* (*CFR*). Free access to the full text of the electronic version of the *Federal Register* and *CFR* is available through the GPO Access service, on the Internet at http://www.access.gpo.gov. In addition to these publications, the full texts of other *Federal Register* publications are available through GPO Access, including the *Weekly Compilation of Presidential Documents, Public Papers of the President,* slip laws, *U.S. Statutes at Large,* and *United States Government Manual.* All of these publications also are maintained at all federal depository libraries. The *Electronic Code of Federal Regulations* (*eCFR*) is an unofficial, currently updated online publication also available through the GPO Access service. Public Law Electronic Notification Service is a free subscription e-mail service available for notification of recently enacted public laws. The Federal Register Table of Contents Service is a free e-mail service available for delivery of the daily table of contents from the *Federal Register* with direct links to documents. The Office of the Federal Register also publishes information about its ministerial responsibilities associated with the operation of the Electoral College and ratification of constitutional amendments and provides access to related records. Publication information concerning laws, regulations, and presidential documents and services is available from the Office of the Federal Register (telephone 202-741-6000). Information about and additional finding aids for *Federal Register* publications, the Electoral College, and constitutional amendments are also available through the Internet at http://www.archives.gov/federal_register. Publications also can be ordered from GPO by writing to: New Orders, Superintendent of Documents, P.O. Box 371954, Pittsburgh, PA 15250-7954.

Customer Service

Customers

NARA's Customer Service Standards, available free of charge in its research rooms nationwide and on its Web site at http://www.archives.gov/about_us/customer_service/customer_service_standards.html, lists the many types of customers NARA serves and describes NARA's standards for customer service. Few records repositories serve as many customers as NARA. In fiscal year (FY) 2004 there were nearly 170,000 research visits to NARA facilities nationwide, including archives, presidential libraries, and federal records centers. At the same time, more than 1 million customers requested archival information in writing. NARA also served the executive agencies of the federal government, the courts, and Congress by providing records storage, reference service, training, advice, and guidance on many issues relating to records management. Federal records centers replied to more than 10.8 million requests for information and records, including more than 800,000 requests for information from military and civilian government service records provided by the National Personnel Records Center in St. Louis. NARA also presented informative public programs at its various facilities for more than 223,000 people. Exhibits in the presidential library museums were visited by more than 1.4 million people. NARA's customer service accomplishments are detailed in its Annual Performance and Accountability Reports.

Customer Opinion

Among the specific strategies published in NARA's Strategic Plan is an explicit commitment to expanding the opportunities of its customers to inform NARA about information and services they need. In support of that strategy, NARA continues to survey, hold focus groups, and meet with customers to evaluate and constantly improve services. For example, the agency continuously surveys visitors to the Web site and users of military service records. NARA also maintains an Internet Web form (at http://www.archives.gov/global_pages/inquire_form.html) to facilitate continuous feedback from customers about what is most important to them and what NARA might do to better meet their needs.

Grants

The National Historical Publications and Records Commission (NHPRC) is the grant-making affiliate of NARA. The Archivist of the United States chairs the commission and makes grants on its recommendation. The commission's 14 other members represent the president of the United States (two appointees), the U.S. Supreme Court, the U.S. Senate and House of Representatives, the U.S. Departments of State and Defense, the Librarian of Congress, the American Association for State and Local History, the American Historical Association, the Association for Documentary Editing, the National Association of Government

Archives and Records Administrators, the Organization of American Historians, and the Society of American Archivists.

The commission carries out a statutory mission to ensure understanding of the nation's past by promoting nationwide the identification, preservation, and dissemination of essential historical documentation. The commission supports the creation and publication of documentary editions, including eight from America's founding era, and basic and applied research in the management and preservation of authentic electronic records, and it works in partnership with a national network of State Historical Records Advisory Boards to develop a national archival infrastructure. NHPRC grants help state and local governments, and archives, universities, historical societies, professional organizations, and other nonprofit organizations establish or strengthen archival programs, improve training and techniques, preserve and process records collections, and provide access to them through finding aids and documentary editions of the papers of significant historical figures and movements in American history. For more information about the commission, see http://www.archives.gov/nhprc.

Administration

NARA employs approximately 3,100 people, of whom about 2,700 are full-time permanent staff members. For FY 2005, NARA received a budget of $321,300,000, including $5,000,000 to support NHPRC.

National Center for Education Statistics
Library Statistics Program

U.S. Department of Education, Institute of Education Sciences
1990 K St. N.W., Washington, DC 20006

Adrienne Chute
Elementary/Secondary and Libraries Studies Division

In an effort to collect and disseminate more complete statistical information about libraries, the National Center for Education Statistics (NCES) initiated a formal library statistics program in 1989 that now includes surveys on academic libraries, public libraries, school library media centers, and state library agencies.* The Library Statistics Program (LSP) is administered and funded by NCES, under the leadership of Jeffrey Williams, program director. The U.S. National Commission on Libraries and Information Science (NCLIS) and the U.S. Bureau of the Census work cooperatively with NCES in implementing the program.

The four library surveys conducted by NCES are designed to provide comprehensive nationwide data on the status of libraries. Federal, state, and local officials, professional associations, and local practitioners use these surveys for planning, evaluating, making policy, and drawing samples for special surveys. These data are also available to researchers and educators.

The program's Web site (http://nces.ed.gov/surveys/libraries) links to data search tools, publications, data files, survey definitions, details of new information that is coming up, and a Researchers and Respondents Corner. This article describes the four library surveys.

Public Libraries

Descriptive statistics from more than 9,000 public libraries are collected and disseminated annually through a voluntary census, the Public Libraries Survey. The survey is conducted by NCES through the Federal-State Cooperative System (FSCS) for Public Library Data. In 2005 FSCS will complete its 17th data collection.

The Public Libraries Survey collects identifying information about public libraries and each of their service outlets, including street address, city, county, zip code, and telephone number. Additional identifying information includes Web address and mailing address. The survey collects material including data on staffing; type of legal basis; type of geographic boundary; type of administrative structure; type of interlibrary relationship; type and number of public service outlets; operating revenue and expenditures; capital revenue and expenditures; size of collection (including number of electronic books and databases); current serial subscriptions (including electronic); service measures such as number of reference transactions, interlibrary loans, circulation, public service hours, library vis-

---

*The authorization for the National Center for Education Statistics (NCES) to collect library statistics is included in the Education Sciences Reform Act of 2002 (P.L. 107-279), under Title I, Part C.

Note: Jeffrey Williams and Elaine Kroe of NCES contributed to this article.

its, circulation of children's materials, and children's program attendance; number of Internet terminals used by the general public; and number of users of electronic resources per year.

The survey also collects several data items about outlets, including the location of an outlet relative to a metropolitan area, number of books-by-mail-only outlets, number of bookmobiles by bookmobile outlet, and square footage of the outlet.

The 50 states and the District of Columbia participate in data collection. Beginning in 1993 the following outlying areas joined the FSCS for Public Library Data: Guam, Commonwealth of the Northern Mariana Islands, Republic of Palau, Puerto Rico, and the U.S. Virgin Islands. For the collection of fiscal year (FY) 2003 data, the respondents that provided publishable data were the more than 9,000 public libraries identified by state library agencies in the 50 states, the District of Columbia, and the U.S. Virgin Islands. The first release of Public Libraries Survey data occurs approximately five months after data collection with the release of the updated Compare Public Libraries Tool on the LSP Web site. The data used in this Web tool are final, but do not include imputations for missing data (imputation is a statistical means of providing an estimate for each missing data item). The next release is the public use data file, followed by the release of an E.D. Tabs (an NCES publication that presents data "highlights" followed by a succinct presentation of descriptive statistics, including tables) on the NCES Web site. [For a sampling of content from several recent E.D. Tabs, see "Highlights of NCES Surveys" in Part 4—Ed.]

Final imputed data files that contain FY 2002 data on more than 9,000 responding libraries and identifying information about their outlets were made available in June 2004 on the LSP Web site. The FY 2002 data were also aggregated to state and national levels in the E.D. Tabs *Public Libraries in the United States: Fiscal Year 2002* and released in spring 2005 on the LSP Web site. NCES expects to release FY 2003 data and an E.D. Tabs in summer 2005.

The Compare Public Libraries Tool and the Find Public Libraries Tool have been updated with FY 2002 data. FY 2003 data are expected to be available on these tools in 2005.

The FSCS for Public Library Data is an example of the synergy that results from combining federal/state cooperation with state-of-the-art technology. The Public Libraries Survey was the first national NCES data collection in which the respondents supplied the data electronically; all public libraries survey data collections are now electronic.

Descriptive data on public libraries are collected via Windows-based data-collection software called WinPLUS. WinPLUS also collects identifying information on all known public libraries and their service outlets. The resulting universe file has been a resource for use in drawing samples for special surveys on such topics as literacy, access for the disabled, and library construction. WinPLUS will be converted to a Web-based application beginning with the FY 2005 data collection cycle.

At the state level and in the outlying areas, data coordinators appointed by each state or outlying area's chief officer of the state library agency administer FSCS. FSCS is a working network. State data coordinators collect the requested data from public libraries and submit these data to NCES. NCES aggregates the data to provide state and national totals. An annual training conference is provided for the state data coordinators, and a steering committee that represents them is active in the development of the Public Libraries Survey and its data-collection software. Technical assistance to states is provided by state data coordinators, by NCES staff, by the Bureau of the Census, and by NCLIS. NCES also works cooperatively with NCLIS, the Bureau of the Census, the Institute for Museum and Library Service's Office of Library Programs, the Chief Officers of State Library Agencies (COSLA), the American Library Association (ALA), and the U.S. Department of Education's National Library of Education.

Recent Public Library Data Projects

A survey completed by NCES's Fast Response Survey System on the topic of public library programming for adults, including adults at risk, has been completed. The survey covered programming for adult literacy instruction, family literacy, adults with physical disabilities, limited English-speaking, elderly, and parents. The survey also asked about programming offered to adults using the Internet. Data were collected from a sample of outlets nationwide in 2000 and early 2001; the response rate was 97 percent. A report, *Programs for Adults in Public Library Outlets* (NCES-2003-010) by Laurie Lewis of Westat, Inc., was released on the NCES Web site and in print in November 2002.

LSP has also released on the Web site its redesigned Compare Public Libraries Tool (updated with FY 2002 data). With this tool, a user can select a library of interest and search for a peer group of libraries by selecting key characteristics to define it (such as all other libraries in the same state with similar total operating expenditures), then view customized reports of the comparison between the selected library of interest and its peers. To use this tool, visit http://nces.ed.gov/surveys/libraries/publicpeer.

Questions about public libraries have also been included as parts of other NCES surveys. For example, in fall 2002 questions about the purposes for which households use public libraries were included as part of a supplement to the Current Population Survey. NCES plans to release these data in 2005.

Additional information on public libraries data is available from Adrienne Chute, Elementary/Secondary and Libraries Studies Division, National Center for Education Statistics, Room 9091, 1990 K St. N.W., Washington, DC 20006 (telephone 202-502-7328, e-mail adrienne.chute@ed.gov).

Academic Libraries

The Academic Libraries Survey (ALS) provides descriptive statistics from approximately 3,700 academic libraries in the 50 states, the District of Columbia, and the outlying areas of the United States. NCES surveyed academic libraries on a three-year cycle between 1966 and 1988. From 1988 to 1998, ALS was a component of the Integrated Postsecondary Education Data System (IPEDS), and was on a two-year cycle. Beginning with FY 2000, ALS is no longer a component of IPEDS, but remains on a two-year cycle. IPEDS and ALS data can still be linked using the unit identification codes of the postsecondary education institutions. In aggregate, these data provide an overview of the status of academic libraries nationally and by state. ALS collects data on libraries in the entire universe of degree-granting postsecondary institutions, using a Web-based data collection system.

ALS has established a working group composed of representatives of the academic library community. Its mission is to improve data quality and the timeliness of data collection, processing, and release. NCES also works cooperatively with ALA, NCLIS, the Association of Research Libraries, the Association of College and Research Libraries, and academic libraries in the collection of ALS data.

ALS collects data on total library operating expenditures, full-time-equivalent (FTE) library staff, service outlets, collection size, number of documents digitized by library staff, circulation, interlibrary loans, public service hours, library visits, reference transactions, consortia services, number of presentations, attendance at presentations, and online services. Academic libraries are also asked whether they offer library reference services by e-mail, electronic document delivery to a patron's account-address, and technology for patrons with disabilities.

The E.D. Tabs *Academic Libraries: 2000* was released on the NCES Web site in November 2003. NCES has developed a Web-based peer analysis tool for ALS. It has a number of features similar to the Compare Public Libraries Tool, and has been updated with FY 2000 and FY 2002 unimputed data.

Additional information on academic library statistics is available from Jeffrey Williams, Elementary/Secondary and Libraries Studies Division, National Center for Education Statistics, Room 9026, 1990 K St. N.W., Washington, DC 20006 (telephone 202-502-7476, e-mail jeffrey.williams@ed.gov).

School Library Media Centers

National surveys of school library media centers in elementary and secondary schools in the United States were conducted in 1958, 1962, 1974, 1978, 1986, 1994, 2000, and 2004.

NCES, with the assistance of the Bureau of the Census, conducted the School Library Media Centers Survey as part of the 1999–2000 Schools and Staffing Survey (SASS), the nation's largest sample survey of K–12 public and private schools. Data from the school library media center questionnaire provide a national picture of school library staffing, collections, expenditures, technology, and services. *The Status of Public and Private School Library Media Centers in the United States: 1999–2000* (NCES 2004-313), a report based on the 1999–2000 SASS, can be downloaded from the NCES Web site and can be ordered from EDPubs. The report *Schools and Staffing Survey, 1999–2000: Overview of the Data for Public, Private, Public Charter, and Bureau of Indian Affairs Elementary and Secondary Schools* (NCES 2002-313) is also available from the NCES Web site. The restricted-use data file for this survey was released by NCES in January 2003. The 2003–2004 SASS included a Public School Library Media Center Survey, and the data were being processed at the time of this report.

NCES has included some library-oriented questions on the parent and the teacher instruments of its new Early Childhood Longitudinal Study. For more information, see http://nces.ed.gov/ecls.

NCES also included a questionnaire about high school library media centers in the National Education Longitudinal Study of 2002 (ELS: 2002). This survey collected data from tenth graders about their schools, their school library media centers, their communities, and their home life. Teachers, principals, and parents also completed questionnaires. The report *School Library Media Centers: Selected Results From the Education Longitudinal Study of 2002* (ELS: 2002) (NCES 2005-302) is available on the NCES Web site and can be ordered through EDPubs. For additional information about this survey, visit http://nces.ed.gov/surveys/els2002.

More information on school library media center statistics can be obtained from Barbara Holton, Elementary/Secondary and Libraries Studies Division, National Center for Education Statistics, Room 9030, 1990 K St. N.W., Washington, DC 20006 (telephone 202-219-7095, e-mail barbara.holton@ed.gov).

State Library Agencies

The State Library Agencies (StLA) Survey collects and disseminates information about the state library agencies in the 50 states and the District of Columbia. A state library agency is the official unit of state government charged with statewide library development and the administration of federal funds under the Library Services and Technology Act (LSTA). StLAs' administrative and developmental responsibilities affect the operation of thousands of public, academic, school, and special libraries. StLAs provide important reference and information services to state governments and some also provide services to the general public. StLAs often administer state library and special operations such as state archives and libraries for the blind and physically handicapped, and the state Center for the Book.

The StLA survey began in 1994 as a cooperative effort among NCES, COSLA, and NCLIS. The FY 2003 StLA survey collected data on the following areas: direct library services, adult literacy and family literacy, library development services, resources assigned to allied operations such as archive and records management, organizational and governance structure within which the agency operates, electronic networking, staffing, collections, and expenditures. These data are edited electronically, and prior to FY 1999 missing data were not imputed. Beginning with FY 1999 data, however, national totals included imputations for missing data. Another change is that beginning with FY 1999 data the StLA survey became a Web-based data-collection system. The most recent data available are for FY 2003. The survey database was released in September 2004 and the E.D. Tabs *State Library Agencies, Fiscal Year 2003* in December 2004. The E.D. Tabs was redesigned to include selected findings and eight tables of summary data for 50 states and the District of Columbia; 37 supplemental state tables were projected for release in spring 2005. Two FY 2002 data products were released on the Internet in March 2004 through the NCES Web site: the E.D. Tabs *State Library Agencies, Fiscal Year 2002*, with 37 tables for the 50 states and the District of Columbia, and the survey database. FY 2004 data were being processed at the time of this report.

More information on the StLA survey is available from Elaine Kroe, Elementary/Secondary and Libraries Studies Division, Room 9027, National Center for Education Statistics, 1990 K St. N.W., Washington, DC 20006 (telephone 202-502-7379, e-mail patricia.kroe@ed.gov).

How to Obtain Printed and Electronic Products

As a result of its library surveys, NCES regularly publishes E.D. Tabs that consist of tables presenting state and national totals, a survey description, and data highlights. NCES also publishes separate, more in-depth studies analyzing these data.

Internet Access

Many NCES publications (including out-of-print publications) and edited raw data files from the library surveys are available for viewing or downloading at no charge through the electronic catalog on NCES's Web site at http://nces.ed.gov/pubsearch.

Ordering Printed Products

Many NCES publications are also available in printed format. To order one free copy of recent NCES reports, contact the Education Publications Center (ED Pubs) at

Internet: http://www.edpubs.org
E-mail: customerservice@edpubs.org
Toll-free telephone: 877-4-ED-Pubs (877-433-7827)
TTY/TDD toll-free number: 877-576-7734
Fax: 301-470-1244
Mail: ED Pubs, P.O. Box 1398, Jessup, MD 20794-1398

Many publications are available through the Educational Resources Information Clearinghouse (ERIC) system in three formats: paper, electronic (PDF), and microfiche. Orders can be placed with the ERIC Document Reproduction Service (EDRS) by phone at 800-443-3742 or 703-440-1400, by fax at 703-440-1408, or by e-mail at service@edrs.com. For more information on services and products, visit the EDRS Web site, http://www.edrs.com.

Out-of-print publications and data files may be available through the NCES Electronic Catalog on NCES's Web site at http://nces.ed.gov/pubsearch or through one of the 1,400 federal depository libraries throughout the United States. Use the NCES publication number included in the citations for publications and data files to quickly locate items in the NCES Electronic Catalog. Use the GPO number to locate items in a federal depository library. Locate a federal depository library at http://www.gpoaccess.gov/libraries.html.

National Commission on Libraries and Information Science

1110 Vermont Ave. N.W., Suite 820, Washington, DC 20005-3552
202-606-9200, fax 202-606-9203, e-mail info@nclis.gov
World Wide Web http://www.nclis.gov

Trudi Bellardo Hahn
Executive Director

The National Commission on Libraries and Information Science (NCLIS) was established as a permanent, independent agency of the United States government with Public Law 91-345 (20 U.S.C. 1501 *et seq.*), signed July 20, 1970. The law includes the following statement of policy:

> The Congress hereby affirms that library and information services adequate to meet the needs of the people of the United States are essential to achieve national goals and to utilize most effectively the Nation's educational resources and that the Federal Government will cooperate with State and local governments and public and private agencies in assuring optimum provision of such services.

It is the commission's responsibility to develop and recommend plans that will enable the American people to have adequate library and information services. In carrying out this responsibility, the commission is directed to advise the president and Congress on the implementation of national policy with respect to libraries and information science.

The commission includes the Librarian of Congress, the director of the Institute of Museum and Library Services (IMLS), and 14 commissioners appointed by the president and confirmed by the Senate for terms not to exceed five years. The law requires that five of the appointees be librarians or information specialists. At least one commissioner must be "knowledgeable with respect to the technological aspects of library and information services and sciences" and one must be "knowledgeable with respect to the library and information service and science needs of the elderly."

From its beginnings, NCLIS has played a significant role in addressing the nation's library and information science needs. By its second year of operation, the commission had put forward a draft of a new national program of library and information services, culminating in the 1975 publication of *Toward a National Program for Library and Information Services: Goals for Action*. NCLIS published another seminal document soon after, *Library and Information Service Needs of the Nation*.

In following years, the commission played an influential role in addressing issues affecting library and information service delivery. It organized two White House conferences on library and information services and was responsible for numerous important studies. An overview of the commission's work makes clear the scale of the NCLIS mission. No other government agency, professional association, trade association, research and development organization, academic institution, or philanthropic organization has the statutory responsibility that is the commission's reason for being—to provide policy advice to the president and

Congress with respect to libraries and information science. Of course, such other organizations are involved in these matters, and these organizations are invited and encouraged to advise, partner with, and collaborate with the commission in developing the knowledge that informs NCLIS's recommendations to the president and Congress. All such organizations—U.S. and international—are solicited to join with NCLIS in sharing this knowledge in the larger society, since such knowledge development and knowledge sharing is for the common good. But only the commission has the statutory responsibility to provide policy advice.

The elements for success are there, and the commission's influence is or can be without bounds. Commission members, whose role and influence far exceeds that of library trustees, scholars, community leaders, and others who work with libraries, have the additional and distinctly advantageous connection to the larger construct of knowledge services. By its definition, the commission is expected to address issues that go beyond librarianship to connect to the larger and broader field of information science. In the 21st century's knowledge-based environment, librarianship, information management, knowledge management, and learning are intrinsically connected, and only NCLIS has been authorized to provide the advice and direction that leads to the establishment of policy for these interconnected disciplines.

Appointments Bring NCLIS to Full Strength

In 2004 President George W. Bush appointed and the U.S. Senate confirmed 12 new commissioners, bringing NCLIS to full strength for the first time in several years.

The new commissioners are José Antonio Aponte, executive director of the Pikes Peak Library District, Colorado Springs; Sandra Frances Ashworth, director of the Boundary County (Idaho) District Library; Edward Louis Bertorelli, member of the Massachusetts Board of Library Commissioners; Carol L. Diehl, retired school librarian and an instructor at the University of Wisconsin–Oshkosh; Allison Druin, assistant professor at the College of Information Studies, University of Maryland–College Park; Beth Fitzsimmons, president, Information Strategists, Ann Arbor, Michigan, and former chair of the Depository Library Council to the U.S. Public Printer; Patricia M. Hines, former chief of staff of domestic policy under President Ronald Reagan and assistant secretary of research and development in the Department of Education under President George H. W. Bush; Colleen Ellen Huebner, associate professor, University of Washington School of Public Health and Community Medicine; Stephen M. Kennedy, former official in several New Hampshire state administrations; Bridget L. Lamont, former director of policy and program development for Illinois Governor George Ryan and former director of the Illinois State Library; Mary H. "Mitzi" Perdue, former syndicated columnist on environmental matters and founder of Healthy U of Delmarva, a 6,000-member health-promotion organization; and Herman L. Totten, Regents professor of library and information sciences, University of North Texas School of Library and Information Sciences, Denton. The new commissioners join sitting NCLIS members Joan Challinor of Washington, D.C., and Jack Hightower of Austin, Texas.

Commissioner Fitzsimmons was designated chairman. In October 2004 Trudi Bellardo Hahn was named Interim Executive Director.

After their appointment and confirmation, the commissioners drew up a strategic plan to guide the commission's deliberations and actions. One consideration had to do with the role of the commission and the variety of expectations that are held, by people in many different walks of life and at all levels of society, about libraries and the role of libraries, information management, knowledge management, and learning in today's world.

At their first official meeting, in April 2004, the commissioners gave attention to NCLIS's vision, mission, and values. The vision statement, which for any organization is a description of what success will look like, is clearly spelled out; the legislation that created the commission states plainly what American policy with respect to libraries and information science is to be. With that policy statement in mind, a vision statement for the commission declares that ". . . library and information services adequate to meet the needs of the people of the United States" will be provided, and that "the Federal Government will cooperate with State and local governments and public and private agencies in assuring optimum provision of such services."

As for the commission's mission statement, describing why the commission exists and what it is to do, that language, too, is clearly stated in the legislation that created the commission:

> The Commission shall have the primary responsibility for developing or recommending overall plans for, and advising the appropriate governments and agencies on, the policy set forth in . . . section 2.

The commission's current mission statement, published on the NCLIS Web site, identifies NCLIS as "a permanent, independent agency of the Federal Government charged with advising the executive and legislative branches and other public and private organizations on national library and information policies and plans."

As for the commission's values, an organization's values statement or philosophy is usually thought of as those beliefs and principles that guide the organization's members as they do their work, the core values that inspire everything the organization does and how it is done. A statement of shared values for the successful realization of the NCLIS vision and the achievement of the NCLIS mission is

> The U.S. National Commission on Libraries and Information Science intends to serve the people of the United States efficiently and effectively while striving to achieve the highest levels of performance in an atmosphere of mutual trust, honesty, and integrity. These values are important to the present Commission as it seeks to fulfill the NCLIS vision and accomplish the NCLIS mission:
>
> • *Leadership*: Recognizing the Commission's statutory responsibilities, NCLIS plays a leading role in addressing the library and informational needs of the American people and ensuring that libraries and other information services organizations are able to support the intellectual and learning needs of Americans. In carrying out this leadership

responsibility, NCLIS is not aligned with any specific agenda put forward by any societal, political, or professional entities.

- *Collaboration and Strategic Partnering*: The Commission continually seeks opportunities to meet, communicate with, collaborate with, and partner with stakeholders in the knowledge services community (that is, all people working in the disciplines of librarianship, information management, knowledge management, and learning).
- *Communications, Visibility, and Ongoing Relevance*: The Commission's efforts are communicated within the larger societal framework so that its leadership role is visible to and understood by the American people, thus ensuring library and information services adequate to meet the needs of the people of the United States.
- *Innovation, Education, and Continuous Strategic Learning*: In addressing the library and informational needs of the American people, all NCLIS stakeholders—including Commissioners, staff, and all strategic partners—continuously strive to seek and share knowledge with others.
- *Superior Customer Service*: NCLIS provides the highest levels of service delivery, recognizing that the Commission's "customers" are the President and the Congress and through them (as NCLIS policy and advice are received and accepted by the President and the Congress), to the American people.[1]
- *Superior Product Delivery*: NCLIS conducts the highest caliber research studies, analyses, and appraisals of library and information services, recognizing that the Commission's "products" are policy advice and guidance provided to the President and Congress and, through them, to the American people.
- *Results and Accountability*: Recognizing its leadership role and the expectations of all parties for the highest standards of performance from the Commission, NCLIS delivers measurable results in all activities it undertakes, including the establishment of performance goals, the development of performance indicators, and the publishing of a benefits statement for each program affiliated with NCLIS.[2] The Commission and all NCLIS stakeholders—including Commissioners, staff, and all strategic partners—are expected to operate with the highest levels of ethics and honesty.

1. Executive Order No. 12862, September, 1994, and later documentation.
2. USC 1115, January 12, 2002.

The Strengthened Commission's Plans

With the appointment of the new commissioners, NCLIS has been considerably strengthened in the specialized qualifications required for enabling it to achieve its mission and to fulfill its statutory responsibility. NCLIS members now include two library managers, a former school librarian and school board member, a former state official and state librarian, a government executive who also serves as a library trustee, a historian, two scholars in library and information science, a scholar in public health and community medicine, two executives in the information services field, a retired judge and former U.S. Congressman, and a former syndicated columnist and community health leader.

The newly constituted commission adopted in principle a plan that describes NCLIS's goals and objectives and incorporates three complementary points of view: fulfilling the commission's statutory function, addressing presidential ini-

tiatives, and (because the commission is a federal agency) meeting the requirements of the President's Management Advisory Initiatives.

The commission's three goals are

- To appraise library and information services provided for the American
  people
- To strengthen the relevance of libraries and information science in the
  lives of the American people
- To promote research and development for extending and improving
  library and information services for the American people

To achieve these goals, the commissioners also set a number of objectives.
These will be accomplished through specific strategic initiatives, and each initiative, in turn, will result in specific policy advice to be delivered to the president
and to Congress as required by law. The initiatives chosen by the commissioners
for immediate attention are

- *Emergency preparedness and the role of libraries as community distribution centers for emergency preparedness and disaster response information.* This initiative seeks to identify how libraries can participate in
  disaster preparedness and serve as their communities' "knowledge nexus."
- *The role of libraries in distributing consumer health information and in
  promoting healthy lifestyles.* This initiative seeks to expand the role of
  libraries in addressing the public's health-information needs and, in doing
  so, to enable libraries to play a key role in encouraging the development
  of healthy lifestyles. The overarching objectives of the initiative are to
  identify methodologies and strategic partners for working with the commission to ensure that all libraries are empowered to respond to citizens'
  health-information needs. To determine how libraries are providing health
  communication products and services to their constituent user groups and
  to collect a body of best practices to be published, in 2004 the commission
  sponsored the NCLIS Blue Ribbon Consumer Health Information Recognition Award for Libraries. Nominees for the award, designed to recognize library programs that excel in offering health information to their
  users, were submitted by state library agencies. NCLIS provided overall
  direction and an NCLIS task force organized the process and judged the
  entries. Thirty-seven libraries were recognized for their efforts in health
  communication, and a best-practices report has been published for library
  managers who want to develop or enhance their own libraries' health
  information programs.
- *Adequacies and deficiencies of current library and information resources
  and services.* This initiative seeks to identify methodologies and to determine how to prepare a national assessment of America's library and information services. The law that created NCLIS specifically charges the
  commission to undertake such appraisals. A specific product of the initiative will be the development of a recommended statement of policy, probably delivered in several stages and over a period of time, providing an

assessment of U.S. libraries and recommending specific actions for improvement.

- *Information dissemination about the relationship—based on scientific research and evidence—between school libraries and educational achievement.* This initiative seeks to identify how school libraries affect learning and to disseminate this information to community organizations, school administrators, local funding authorities, the news media, the larger educational community, and all others who have an interest in the role of libraries in educational achievement. The purpose of the initiative is to raise the awareness of community leaders about the value of school libraries and to provide them with scientific evidence that can be used as they set funding priorities.

- *Library services for the aging.* This initiative, a specific statutory responsibility of the commission, seeks to identify opportunities for improving library services for the elderly. The initiative also seeks to identify how libraries might use the skills and experience of seniors as employees.

- *International library and information science issues.* Among its statutory responsibilities, the commission is expected to "promote research and development activities which will extend and improve the Nation's library and information-handling capability as essential links in the national and international communications and cooperative networks. . . ." The commission has participated in a number of international activities and expects to continue to do so. This NCLIS initiative looks at two areas. The first is the role of libraries in describing the United States to citizens of other countries. The second is the role of libraries and library-like organizations as distribution centers for HIV/AIDS information for people in developing countries.

Other subject areas of interest and concern include the following, which are being considered for attention and in-depth study when resources are available:

- Economic development, job creation, and the role of libraries in influencing economic development
- The current status of and an assessment of the Universal Services Telecommunication Act of 1996
- The role of libraries in digitized information
- Scholarly publishing and non-U.S. ownership of scientific/technical/medical (STM) research conducted in the United States and, related to this, open access to published STM research

The commissioners have determined that addressing these strategic initiatives is necessary if NCLIS is to achieve its goals, and all of these initiatives are being implemented through the commission's efforts. They have been chosen because they support objectives that will enable NCLIS to achieve its goals and because they address a number of important issues having to do with the nation's information needs.

Funding: A Major Concern

NCLIS has gone through a period of uncertainty, and much momentum in the effort to carry out its functions has been lost. These functions are described in the law, but the commission's ability to conduct business and provide for the delivery of services has been severely compromised. That particular danger appears to be now past; the commission, now strengthened with the appointment of a full roster of members, can begin its work again in earnest.

However the commission's present role is assessed, though, it is clear that funding will continue to be a major concern. In fiscal year (FY) 2001 the commission's appropriation was reduced by one third to $1 million, and has remained at that level since. Requests to increase the commission's appropriation have been made, but—at least through September 2005—the funding level will remain where it is.

NCLIS is therefore severely hampered in attempting to fund its operations. The commission's initiatives are unfunded, as there are no appropriated funds currently available to support them. As NCLIS attempts to carry out its work in the remainder of FY 2005 (through September 30, 2005), the grim reality is that none of these initiatives can be undertaken without an infusion of funds, and the commission's work is therefore limited to informal planning.

In the case of NCLIS, however, "nonappropriated" funds are acceptable to the federal government. In fact, such funding might have been in the minds of those who were involved in the creation of the commission, since the law states, under a section titled "Contributions":

> The Commission is authorized to solicit, accept, hold, administer, invest in the name of the United States, and utilize gifts, bequests, and devises of services or property, both real and personal, for the purpose of aiding or facilitating the work of the Commission.

So while NCLIS's programs and projects described in this report demonstrate a level of commitment to and interest in the nation's library and information needs, additional energies will be required for identifying and working with strategic partners, sponsors, collaborating organizations, and other government agencies to ensure that these ambitious initiatives are realized. Wider and more substantial collaboration with other organizations and the development of strategic partnerships will be a feature of NCLIS activity for the remainder of the current fiscal year and into FY 2006 and beyond. The commission desires to continue working toward fulfillment of the proactive leadership position envisioned in the NCLIS statute. Collaboration with partners, sponsors, and enthusiastic cooperative associates—recognized as critical characteristics in any successful organization—will become vital.

The appointment and confirmation of a full commission roster has stimulated a burst of enthusiasm about NCLIS and about what it can accomplish. This enthusiasm, and the commissioners' individual expertise, have well equipped NCLIS to continue its move forward in its role as the nation's principal advisory agency on policy with respect to library and information science. The advice provided to the president and Congress for the benefit of the people will continue to be sound, authoritative, and for the common good.

Defense Technical Information Center

Fort Belvoir, Virginia
World Wide Web http://www.dtic.mil

Sandy Schwalb
Public Affairs Officer

The Defense Technical Information Center (DTIC) has served the information needs of the defense community for 60 years. DTIC is the central facility for the collection, storage, retrieval, and dissemination of scientific and technical information for the Department of Defense (DOD). The center

- Provides controlled access to DOD information
- Is a vital link in the transfer of information among the defense-related government and civilian research and development communities
- Is a primary provider of Web services for organizations within the DOD

DTIC is located in the Andrew T. McNamara Headquarters Complex Building, Fort Belvoir, Virginia, and has four regional offices, whose addresses appear at the end of this article.

A Year of Change

In 2004 DTIC went through a number of organizational changes, which included a return to the defense acquisition, technology, and logistics community where DTIC had resided through a major portion of the 1990s. DTIC now reports to the Director, Defense Research and Engineering (DDR&E) and is a DOD field activity, one of several organizations whose work reaches across all segments of DOD.

The year 2004 also saw a change in leadership. Kurt N. Molholm, DTIC's administrator since 1985, retired in 2004, and Deputy Administrator R. Paul Ryan was named acting administrator in November.

Security of Information

While there is much publicly accessible material in the DTIC collection (nearly half of DOD's technical reports are publicly available the day they are published), some information is restricted by security classifications. The DOD's scientific and technical information is always categorized (or "marked" which is the term used in the defense community) by the office that originates the document. This marking determines how, and to whom, the information can be disseminated.

Some information is marked to protect national security. DTIC's databases contain such classified information, which may be marked "confidential" or "secret." DTIC's databases also contain information that, although not classified, is still sensitive for various reasons. These documents are marked to show why the information is sensitive and with whom the document can be shared. Such documents are considered "unclassified, limited." Information in DTIC's databases that is neither classified nor limited can be released to the public and is referred to as "unclassified, unlimited." The information in DTIC's collection is 41 percent "unclassified, unlimited," 51 percent "unclassified, limited," and 8 percent "classified."

Resources

DTIC's holdings include technical reports on completed research; research summaries of planned, ongoing, and completed work; independent research and development summaries; defense technology transfer agreements; DOD planning documents; DOD directives and instructions; conference proceedings; security classification guides; command histories; and special collections that date back to World War II.

DOD-funded researchers are required to search DTIC's collections to ensure that they do not "reinvent the wheel" and undertake unnecessary or redundant research.

The scope of DTIC's collection includes areas normally associated with defense research. DOD's interests are widespread, however, and include such areas as agriculture; atmospheric sciences; behavioral and social sciences; human factors engineering; information warfare; mathematic and computer sciences; nuclear science and technology; propulsion, engines and fuels; radiation studies; and virtual reality.

Registering for Services

DTIC offers its information services to a diverse population of the defense community. Because of the nature of the information that DTIC handles, users must qualify for services. To be eligible, a user must be

- An employee of a DOD organization, DOD contractor, or potential DOD contractor
- An employee of a U.S. federal government agency or U.S. government contractor
- Affiliated with a university or college funded by DOD or a U.S. federal government agency for research throughout the United States
- A Small Business Innovation Research/Small Business Technology Transfer (SBIR/STTR) Program participant
- A faculty or staff member or student of a Historically Black College and University (HBCU), Hispanic Serving Institution (HSU), Tribal College and University (TCU), or other Minority Institution (MI)

Everyone can search DTIC's publicly accessible collections and display or download such information. Descriptions of the various DTIC databases follow. Unless otherwise noted, the databases are available to the public. Registered users can order documents directly from DTIC. Individuals who are not eligible to register with DTIC can order "unclassified, unlimited" documents by contacting the National Technical Information Service (NTIS) at 800-553-6847 or by visiting http://www.ntis.gov. [A full report on NTIS appears earlier in Part 1— *Ed.*]

DTIC's Primary Collections

The *Technical Reports* database contains nearly 2 million reports in print and nonprint (software, datafiles, databases, and video recordings) formats conveying the results of defense-sponsored research, development, test and evaluation efforts. It includes journal articles, DOD-sponsored patent applications, studies, analyses, open-source literature from foreign countries, conference proceedings and theses. Between 30,000 to 35,000 new documents are added each year.

The *Research Summaries* (RS) database contains descriptions of DOD research that provide information on technical content, responsible individuals and organizations, principal investigators, and funding sources at the work-unit level. Available only to certain registered users, this collection is controlled by individual restrictions. The collection consists of approximately 300,000 active and inactive summaries from 1965 to the present.

The *Independent Research and Development* (IR&D) database contains more than 169,000 descriptions (dating back to the mid-1970s) of research and development projects initiated and conducted by defense contractors independent of DOD control and without direct DOD funding. More than $3 billion worth of IR&D projects are submitted to DTIC each year. The database includes basic and applied research, technology development efforts, and systems and concept formulation studies. Defense contractors and potential contractors are encouraged to submit project descriptions to the IR&D database. Accessible only to U.S. government organizations, the information is used to identify contractors with expertise in areas of interest to DOD and to avoid DOD duplication of industry R&D efforts.

The *Technical Reports Automated Information List* (TRAIL) is a free electronic mailing list that automatically disseminates citations to "unclassified, unlimited" technical reports recently added to the DTIC technical reports database. Subscribers can choose to receive their first bibliography via e-mail immediately after subscribing; TRAIL listings will follow every two weeks.

DTIC maintains the Defense Technology Transfer Information System (DTTIS) in cooperation with military and defense agencies. The DTTIS contains project information on DOD technology transfer activities, active Cooperative Research and Development Agreements (CRADAs), and active Patent License Agreements.

STINET Services

DTIC's Scientific and Technical Information Network (STINET) is one of DOD's largest repositories of scientific and technical information currently available. There are three versions of the database: Public STINET, Private STINET, and Classified STINET.

- Public STINET, available to the general public and free of charge, provides access to citations of "unclassified, unlimited" reports that describe the progress or results of research efforts and other scientific and technical information held by DTIC. Many of these documents are available in full text and can be downloaded.

- Private STINET is a password-protected, value-added service for individuals who have registered with DTIC. A homeland defense resource site was added in 2004. Other information available through Private STINET includes free online full-text versions of all "unclassified, unlimited" and "unclassified, limited" documents recently added to the TR database; the Research Summaries database; Systran Language Translator; free access to two international database services (Canada Institute for Scientific and Technical Information's CISTI Source and the British Library Document Supply Centre's "inside web"); information from the Interagency Gray Literature Working Group; and ProQuest Research Library Complete, an index to journal articles. (STINET MultiSearch is available in both Public STINET and Private STINET. A portal to the "deep Web" for government scientific and technical information, it searches content below the "surface" Web for information not accessible through commercial and government search engines.)

- Classified STINET went "live" in 2004 and is the latest addition to DTIC's offerings. Located on the Secret Internet Protocol Router Network (SIPRNET), this database contains the complete DTIC collection, including "unclassified, limited" reports and "classified" citations. In order to use this service one must be able to access the SIPRNET and register with DTIC.

Current Awareness Products

DTIC registered users can receive up-to-date information in their areas of research under the Current Awareness Bibliography (CAB) program. Customized bibliographies are disseminated twice a month to users who have established a subject profile. The bibliography provides the most recent information added to the DTIC technical reports collection and is available in a number of formats:

- CAB in paper provides abstracts to "unclassified, unlimited," "unclassified, limited," and "classified" citations according to user eligibility. There is a fee for this service.

- Electronic CAB (ECAB), provided electronically via e-mail, contains abstracts to "unclassified, unlimited" citations only. All "unclassified, limited" and "classified" citations appear without abstracts or identifiers. This service is free of charge.

- ECAB Documents (ECAB-DOCS) contain embedded links in each citation of the bibliography to the full text of the "unclassified, unlimited" and "unclassified, limited" documents. Abstracts are supplied for the "unclassified, unlimited" documents in the bibliography. The user is required to subscribe to Private STINET to access the full-text document links in this product. These are free of charge.

Training Opportunities

Training is offered free of charge to DTIC registered users at DTIC's Fort Belvoir, Virginia, headquarters and at four regional offices (the addresses of which appear below). Training is available off site if the instructor's travel costs are borne by the host organization/user. Arrangements can also be made to customize courses.

A three-day, hands-on class, "Searching DTIC Databases using Private STINET," covers methods for searching and retrieving scientific, research, and engineering information. The course also provides tools on how to search the various databases found within Private STINET.

DTIC offers a three-day course designed to acquaint scientific and technical information (STINFO) managers and other interested personnel with the requirements of the DOD Scientific and Technical Information Program. Marking documents and contract reporting requirements are covered. A one-day STINFO manager overview covers the highlights of the standard three-day class.

A class that examines the rationale and mechanics of marking technical documents is available by arrangement with the instructor.

Additional training information is available at http://www.dtic.mil/dtic/training.

Other DTIC Activities and Programs

Information Analysis Centers

DTIC manages and funds contractor-operated joint service-oriented Information Analysis Centers (IACs), which are research organizations. Chartered by DOD, IACs identify, analyze, and use scientific and technical information in specific technology areas. They also develop information and analysis products for the defense science and engineering communities and are staffed by experienced technical area scientists, engineers and information specialists. The DTIC-managed IACs are AMPTIAC (Advanced Materials and Processes Technology IAC), CBIAC (Chemical and Biological Defense IAC), CPIA (Chemical Propulsion In formation Agency), DACS (Data and Analysis Center for Software), HSIAC (Human Systems Information Analysis Center), IATAC (Information Assurance Technology Analysis Center), MTIAC (Manufacturing Technology IAC), NTIAC (NondestructiveTesting Information Analysis Center), RAC (Reliability Analysis Center), SENSIAC (Sensor Information Analysis Center), SURVIAC (Survivability/Vulnerability IAC), and WSTIAC (Weapon Systems Technology IAC).

Many of the products and services produced by the IACs are free of charge and include announcements of reports relevant to the particular IAC's field of interest, authoritative bibliographic search reports, the latest scientific and engineering information on specific technical subjects, consultation with or referral to world-recognized technical experts, and status of current technologies. For more information, visit http://iac.dtic.mil.

The Total Electronic Migration System (TEMS), a gateway to the IAC collection, is available online (http://tems-iac.dtic.mil). TEMS gives DTIC registered users the ability to perform full-text searches and retrieve mission-critical information.

QuestionPoint

DTIC is a participating member of QuestionPoint, a new virtual reference service developed jointly by the Library of Congress and OCLC (the Online Computer Library Center) and supported by cooperating institutions worldwide. This collaborative digital-reference service, available around the clock seven days a week, allows libraries and information centers to expand reference services with shared resources and subject specialists around the world. DTIC is part of two QuestionPoint cooperatives: Global Reference Network, a worldwide group of libraries and institutions committed to digital reference, and Defense Digital Library Research Service (DDLRS), an around-the-clock electronic reference assistance for DOD libraries. Questions submitted by patrons via this Web-based digital reference service can be referred to the Global Network or to the cooperatives of DOD or Department of Homeland Security libraries.

2004 Users Conference

Nearly 300 customers, exhibitors, and DTIC personnel took part in the 30th annual DTIC Users Meeting and Training Conference held March 29–April 1, 2004 in Alexandria, Virginia. The conference consisted of speakers, exhibits, and professional seminars. More than 30 topics were offered, including "Information Law in the Age of Terrorism," "Copyright and Government Rights: Impact on DOD Information Dissemination," "Wireless Technology: Beaming It to the User," and "NGA Today, an Overview of the National Geospatial-Intelligence Agency." A tour was offered of the addition to the National Air and Space Museum, the Udvar-Hazy Center, located in Chantilly, Virginia.

"Defense Research and Engineering: Turning Data into Knowledge" is the theme of the 2005 conference, scheduled for April 4–6.

Customer Surveys

DTIC has surveyed its registered customers since fiscal year 1999 in order to gauge the level of satisfaction among general users and identify possible areas for improving products and services. Web-based and e-mail surveys are the primary collection methods used. One-on-one telephone interviews gather contact information and, on occasion, are used to administer the survey. These multiple collection methods were selected not only to offer DTIC users a variety of survey response options, but also to increase response rates. Two surveys are conducted yearly: the Customer Satisfaction (CS) Survey, a complete sampling of all users, and the Top 200 Users Survey, which canvasses roughly 200 users of DTIC's products and services on the basis of dollar value of billing, number of documents ordered, and downloads from Private STINET.

The majority of the 2004 survey respondents were satisfied with DTIC services as a whole. DTIC continues to exceed the Federal Government American Customer Satisfaction Index (ACSI) baseline/benchmark score. The ACSI survey, conducted in December 2003, showed a customer satisfaction rating of 70.9 percent; DTIC's "score" was 76 percent.

Outreach

DTIC customers can host, at their location, a briefing or demonstration of DTIC's products and services tailored to the organization's schedule and information needs. For more information, contact DTIC by e-mail at bcporder@dtic.mil.

Tours and briefings are available at DTIC's headquarters on a quarterly basis. Visitors do not need a security clearance to attend. However, special arrangements are needed for foreign nationals and employees of foreign governments. For more information, visit http://www.dtic.mil/dtic/events/tours_brief.html.

Handle Service

Ensuring the permanent availability of information in the DTIC collection is a high priority. DTIC's Handle Service preserves access to electronic resources on the Web, guaranteeing their availability over time and changing formats. A "handle" is a permanent identifier, or permanent name, for a digital object regardless of where and how it is stored. It provides long-term access to a digital resource and allows for the reliable management of information on the Internet over long periods of time. Handles have been added to the public information on DTIC's Public and Private STINET services. These handles link directly to full-text PDF documents. Future plans are to extend handles to limited resources which DTIC registered users will be able to access from Private STINET. Handles offer several benefits; they do not change, unlike uniform resource locators (URLs), and ensure that information will be available over long periods of time; they act as a "seal of approval," created by publishers, that guarantees the authenticity of the resource; and they help in the creation of accurate, "live" links within bibliographies and other research papers.

Web Hosting Expertise

As a pioneer in Internet use for information dissemination, DTIC now hosts approximately 100 Web sites sponsored by components of the Office of the Secretary of Defense, military service headquarters organizations, and several defense agencies.

In 2004 DTIC worked on the Regional Air Movement Control Center (RAMCC) Web site. The RAMCC coordinates the movement of fixed-wing aircraft in support of military, humanitarian, and commercial air operations over Iraqi, Afghan, and Pakistani airfields. RAMCC promotes the safety and efficiency of military, peacekeeping, humanitarian assistance, and other operations in both Afghanistan and Iraq. The site was used quite heavily during the Afghan inauguration ceremonies in December 2004.

DTIC partnered with the Coalition Provisional Authority (CPA) for Iraq to develop and maintain its Web site in 2003. The site was created to inform news organizations, contractors, military personnel, and the general public of the reconstruction, humanitarian, and peacekeeping initiatives in the aftermath of Operation Iraqi Freedom. Following the dissolution of the CPA in June 2004, the responsibility for the site was transferred to the Department of State. For historical purposes, DTIC will provide access to the final June 2004 site (http://www. cpa-iraq.org) until June 30, 2005.

Publications

DTIC Digest, a Web-based newsletter, is produced quarterly and provides information about programs, initiatives, activities, issues and developments in the technical information arena. This publication is on DTIC's Web site (http://www. dtic.mil).

A second publication, the DTIC *Review,* includes the full text of selected technical reports and a bibliography of other references of interest. Each issue provides a sampling of documents from the DTIC collection on a specific topic of current interest. The *Review* is also available to DTIC registered users as a subscription product.

Cooperation and Collaboration

DTIC works with the information community through many partnerships and affiliations. They include

- Science.gov, a collaboration of 17 scientific and technical organizations in the federal government that is a free gateway to over 1,700 government information resources about science, including technical reports, journal citations, databases, federal Web sites, and fact sheets
- CENDI, an interagency working group of senior scientific and technical information managers from a number of U.S. federal departments and agencies, including Commerce, Energy, Defense, Interior, the National Aeronautics and Space Administration, and the Government Printing Office.
- NFAIS, the National Federation of Abstracting and Information Services
- FLICC, the Federal Library and Information Center Committee
- ASIDIC, Association of Information and Dissemination Centers
- SLA, the Special Libraries Association
- NISO, National Information Standards Organization

DTIC Regional Offices

Midwestern Regional Office
Wright-Patterson Air Force Base, Ohio
Tel. 937-255-7905, fax 937-656-7002
E-mail dayton@dtic.mil

Northeastern Regional Office
Hanscom Air Force Base, Massachusetts
Tel. 781-377-2413, fax 781-377-5627
E-mail boston@dtic.mil

Southwestern Regional Office
Kirtland Air Force Base, New Mexico
Tel. 505-846-6797, fax 505-846-6799
E-mail albuq@dtic.mil

Western Regional Office
El Segundo, California
Tel. 310-363-6642, fax 310-363-6705
E-mail losangel@dtic.mil

Note: DTIC and STINET are registered service marks of the Defense Technical Information Center.

National Library of Education

Institute of Education Sciences
U.S. Department of Education
400 Maryland Ave. S.W., Washington, DC 20202
800-424-1616, 202-205-4945, fax 202-401-0547
World Wide Web http://www.ed.gov/about/offices/list/ies/ncee/nle.html

Christina Dunn
Director, National Library of Education
202-219-1012
E-mail christina.dunn@ed.gov

The National Library of Education (NLE) operates two major programs: the Education Resources Information Center (ERIC) and the U.S. Department of Education (ED) Reference Center. The ERIC program is covered separately in the following article.

Responsibilities of NLE

Originally authorized under Public Law 103-227 (the Educational Research, Development, Dissemination, and Improvement Act of 1994, part of the Goals 2000: Educate America Act) and reauthorized under Title I of Public Law 107-279 (the Education Sciences Reform Act of 2002), NLE is part of the National Center for Education Evaluation and Regional Assistance in the Institute of Education Sciences. The national center is headed by a commissioner who, among other responsibilities, is charged with managing NLE. In turn, NLE is headed by a director qualified in library science.

The legislation charges NLE with four responsibilities:

- Collecting and archiving information, including products and publications developed through, or supported by, the Institute of Education Sciences, and other relevant and useful education-related research, statistics, and evaluation materials and other information, projects, and publications that are consistent with scientifically valid research or the priorities and mission of the institute, and developed by the department, other federal agencies, or entities
- Providing a central location within the federal government for information about education
- Providing comprehensive reference services on matters relating to education to employees of the Department of Education and its contractors and grantees, other federal employees, and members of the public
- Promoting greater cooperation and resource sharing among providers and repositories of education information in the United States

ERIC is primarily responsible for conducting activities to support the first and second charges, while the ED Reference Center has primary responsibility for the third. Promoting cooperation and resource sharing among U.S. providers and repositories of education information is handled by the office of the NLE director.

ED Reference Center

The ED Reference Center, housed in ED's headquarters building, has a staff of 11, organized into a single unit to allow for maximum flexibility, streamlined management, and easy and quick coordination to meet user needs.

Collections

The overall focus of the Reference Center's collection is education issues, research, and policy. It includes monographs in the field of education published since 1965, as well as related topics such as law, public policy, economics, urban affairs, sociology, history, philosophy, psychology, and library and information science. Current periodicals holdings number more than 800 English-language print and electronic journals, including most of the journals indexed by ERIC and other major education and psychology databases. It also holds a complete collection of ERIC microfiche; research reports supporting the work of the What Works Clearinghouse (http://www.whatworks.ed.gov), a project of the Institute of Education Sciences; and a collection of government documents, serving as a federal depository library under the Government Printing Office.

In addition, the Reference Center holds historical collections of Department of Education publications and documents spanning more than 100 years related to federal education legislation. Other historical collections include documents and archives of the former National Institute of Education and the former U.S. Office of Education, including reports, studies, manuals, statistical publications, speeches, and policy papers. Together, these collections represent a resource covering the history of the U.S. Department of Education and its predecessor agencies.

Services

The Reference Center provides general and legislative reference and statistical information services in response to inquiries from ED staff, contractors, and grantees; other federal agencies; other libraries; and the general public. More than 75 percent of Reference Center customers are from the general public; this includes referrals from the Library of Congress Virtual Reference Desk and the ERIC Help Desk. The remaining 25 percent are from ED staff and contractors (21 percent), other libraries (2.5 percent), and other government agencies (1.5 percent). Of the general public contacting the Reference Center in 2004, approximately 80 percent were K–12 educators, students in institutions of higher education, researchers, or parents. More than 90 percent of all customers accessed the Reference Center by telephone or e-mail; only about 10 percent visited the facility at department headquarters.

In 2004 the Reference Center responded to more than 12,000 inquiries, with most questions coming from the general public and pertaining to U.S. Department of Education programs and statistics and current education-related issues, such as the requirements of the No Child Left Behind Act, early reading, student achievement and testing, education reform, school and teacher quality, and evidence-based education. In addition, the center serves other libraries by lending books and other documents from its collection. During 2004 the Reference Center made available more than 1,600 items, mostly research reports, to institutions of higher education, federal and state agencies, and other libraries. This is almost double the number of interlibrary loans made in 2003. ED staff and contractors conducted more than 13,000 searches of the library's databases, and the Reference Center delivered more than 6,000 documents and journals articles to these customers. Of these items, nearly 800 were borrowed from other libraries.

During 2004 Reference Center staff continued to focus on improving information services to ED staff and contractors, increasing training on use of electronic resources available on the desktop, enhancing daily alert services on education research and federal policy, and redesigning its portal for ED staff. Also, it worked closely with the ERIC staff to identify agency and other resources for inclusion in the ERIC database. Reference staff continues to be available in program offices where they are directly accessible to researchers.

The ED Reference Center can be reached by e-mail at library@ed.gov or by telephone at 202-205-5015 or 202-205-5019 or toll-free at 800-424-1616. It is open from 9:00 A.M. to 5:00 P.M. weekdays, except federal holidays.

Cooperation and Resource Sharing

In its efforts to promote greater cooperation and resource sharing among providers and repositories of education information, NLE sponsors the National Education Network, a planning group of librarians from institutions of higher education and K–12 libraries. In cooperation with the Education and Behavioral Sciences Section of the Association of College and Research Libraries and the Education Division of the Special Libraries Association, NLE is planning its first national meeting of major education research libraries to discuss common concerns and interests.

Education Resources Information Center

ERIC Program Office
National Library of Education, Institute of Education Sciences
U.S. Department of Education
400 Maryland Ave. S.W., Washington, DC 20202
World Wide Web http://www.eric.ed.gov

Luna Levinson

Director, ERIC Program

A fundamental goal of the Education Resources Information Center (ERIC) is to increase the availability and quality of research and information for educators, researchers, and the general public by providing a database that is

- Comprehensive, consisting of journal articles and non-journal materials, including materials not published by commercial publishers, that are directly related to education
- Easy-to-use and searchable, allowing database users to find the information they need quickly and efficiently
- Electronic, making ERIC operations accessible to the maximum extent feasible and linking to publishers and commercial sources of journal articles
- Bibliographic and full-text, with bibliographic records conveying the information users need in a simple and straightforward manner, and whenever possible including full-text journal articles and non-journal materials free of charge

The public database resides on the ERIC Web site at http://www.eric.ed.gov and is also made available to commercial database vendors.

Recent Developments

In September 2004 ERIC launched a new Web site, a milestone in public access to the U.S. Department of Education's re-engineered database of education literature. With a new mission more sharply focused on the ERIC database and an operations plan promising to employ modern and sustainable technology, ERIC was transformed from a clearinghouse-developed collection with more than 30 related Web sites and four search engines to a single Web site with a single search engine.

While the former ERIC mission was broadly "to improve American education by increasing and facilitating the use of educational research and information to improve practice . . . ," the organization's new mission is to provide a "comprehensive, easy-to-use, searchable, Internet-based bibliographic and full-text database of education research and information." Realizing that mission requires re-examination of paper and digital processes developed during the ERIC clearinghouse era (1966–2003), followed by new developments in virtually every aspect of database acquisitions, processing, quality control, and Web site design and functionality.

Context for Change

The idea of modernizing ERIC had been under discussion since the late 1990s, but it was the authorizing legislation for the Institute of Education Sciences (Sec. 172(a)3 of Public Law 107-279, the Education Sciences Reform Act of 2002) that provided the context for changing ERIC. In the past, legislation had required the continuation of the clearinghouse structure, procedures, and products, but the new legislation envisioned the ERIC topics as part of the totality of enhanced information dissemination to be conducted by the Institute of Education Sciences.

More specifically, the act requires that the commissioner for education, evaluation, and regional assistance "make . . . information accessible in a user-friendly, timely, and efficient manner (including through the use of a searchable Internet-based online database)." Sec. 172 (b) of the act also requires the commissioner to "ensure that information [is] disseminated . . . in a cost-effective, non-duplicative manner." Shifting emphasis from traditional ERIC tasks and structure to the new requirements, the Department of Education issued a new statement of work for ERIC in 2003 and awarded a single contract for the operation of ERIC in March 2004.

To help ensure maintenance of a high-quality database and adherence to the performance metrics specified in the ERIC statement of work, the department awarded a separate ERIC quality-assurance contract in September 2004. Monitoring tasks for the third-party contractor include reviewing the ERIC database to determine whether journals are added to the database within one month of publication; decide whether indexing and Web links are accurate; and measuring the capacity, speed, interoperability, and other performance aspects of the online ERIC system.

Web Site Design

Simplicity is the driving principle of the new ERIC Web site, from interface design and features to search functionality. The initial release includes such popular Web site features as the capacity to save searches, narrow results, and display related documents. Three separate formative usability tests were conducted in 2004 during the iterative design development with teachers, librarians, and students serving as participants. The purpose of testing was to determine if the Web site was functional and useful for both experienced and inexperienced ERIC users and to learn what directions made site navigation easier. Suggestions and corrections were documented and adjustments were made to the interface views and navigation. Because most users enter simple queries, emphasis was placed on presenting a simple, basic search feature.

The basic search provides a drop-down menu to select materials by title, author, or ERIC document number, while the advanced search allows the designation of more specific criteria—publication type and date, ERIC Thesaurus terms, journal names, sponsoring organization, and other record fields. Continuing efforts to improve the search experience will focus on the Boolean search exposed through the advanced search feature. Refinements and modifications are announced on the Web site as specific tasks are tested and released.

Search results are enhanced by clicking a details button that leads to the full ERIC record with ERIC Thesaurus descriptors and a set of related ERIC documents. Additional searches can be launched through author links, descriptors, and up to five related items. Finally, the Web site allows users to voluntarily rate their experience using a scale of 1 to 5 and to enter comments.

ERIC Content

A pivotal component of the new vision for ERIC is access to full-text documents, either through electronic links to commercially available journal articles or free full-text, non-commercial materials. In October 2004 ERIC added more than 107,000 full-text non-journal documents (issued 1993–2004) that previously had been sold through the ERIC Document Reproduction Service (EDRS). Eliminating fee subscriptions for libraries, organizations, and individuals is arguably the most significant development in increasing public access to ERIC resources. Adding to this convenience was improved download performance of the image files.

Content accessioned into ERIC (materials published in 2004 and beyond) will meet the new ERIC selection policy. The ERIC collection will continue to be composed of journal and non-journal materials, and accession numbers will perpetuate the ED and EJ ERIC prefix model. The broad selection standard provides that all materials added to the ERIC database are directly related to the field of education. The collection scope includes early childhood education through higher education, vocational education, and special education; it includes teacher education, education administration, assessment and evaluation, counseling, information technology, and the academic areas of reading, mathematics, science, environmental education, languages, and social studies. In addition, the collection will also include resources addressing one of the three objectives identified in Section 172 of the Education Sciences Reform Act: closing the achievement gap, encouraging educational practices that improve academic achievement, and conducting education research.

Following that standard, there are three sets of specific criteria providing guidance for document selection. The quality criteria consist of five basic factors: completeness, integrity, objectivity, substantive merit, and utility/importance. Selection is further determined by sponsorship criteria, and preference for inclusion in ERIC is given to those resources with identified sponsorship (for example, professional societies and government agencies). Detailed editorial criteria also provide factors for consideration, especially with regard to journals considered for comprehensive indexing. The complete selection policy is provided on the ERIC Web site.

All submissions considered for selection must be in digital format and are accompanied by author permission for dissemination. For individual document submissions, authors (copyright holders) register through the ERIC Web site feature "My ERIC"; follow the steps to enter bibliographic information, abstract, and document file; and submit the electronic document release form authorizing

ERIC to disseminate the materials. Journal publishers, associations, and other entities with multiple documents also submit electronic content following guidance and instructions consistent with provider agreements provided by ERIC.

As the number of arrangements with content providers grows in the coming year, ERIC will continue to refine the technical architecture that enables the dissemination of education literature. ERIC remains committed to providing more content that is more easily accessible to the public; to informing understanding and implementation of education practices and policies; and to expanding knowledge and understanding of education research.

National Association and Organization Reports

American Library Association

50 E. Huron St., Chicago, IL 60611-2729
312-944-6780, 800-545-2433
World Wide Web http://www.ala.org

Carol A. Brey-Casiano
President, 2004–2005

The American Library Association (ALA), founded in 1876 in Philadelphia, is the oldest, largest, and most influential library association in the world. The association's membership of more than 64,000 includes not only librarians but also library trustees, publishers, and other interested people from every U.S. state and many nations. The association serves public, state, school, and academic libraries, plus special libraries for people working in government, commerce and industry, the arts, and the armed services or in hospitals, prisons, and other institutions. ALA added a new membership category for library support staff, effective September 1, 2004.

ALA's mission is "to provide leadership for the development, promotion, and improvement of library and information services and the profession of librarianship in order to enhance learning and ensure access to information for all."

ALA is governed by an elected council—its policy-making body—and an executive board, which acts for the council and administers policies and programs. These are proposed by standing committees, designated as committees of the association or of the council. ALA's operations are directed by an executive director and implemented by staff through a structure of programmatic offices and support units.

ALA has 11 membership divisions, each focused on a type of library or type of library function. They are the American Association of School Librarians (AASL), the Association for Library Collections and Technical Services (ALCTS), the Association for Library Service to Children (ALSC), the Association for Library Trustees and Advocates (ALTA), the Association of College and Research Libraries (ACRL), the Association of Specialized and Cooperative Library Agencies (ASCLA), the Library Administration and Management Association (LAMA), the Library and Information Technology Association (LITA), the Public Library Association (PLA), the Reference and User Services Association (RUSA), and the Young Adult Library Services Association (YALSA). ALA also hosts roundtables for members who share an interest that does not fall within the scope of any of the divisions. A network of affiliates, chapters, and other organizations enables ALA to reach a broad audience.

ALA's key action areas include diversity, education and continuous learning, equity of access, intellectual freedom, and 21st-century literacy.

ALA offices are units of the association that address broad interests of concern to ALA members; they track issues and provide information, services, and products for members and the general public. ALA offices are the Chapter Relations Office, the Development Office, the Governance Office, the International Relations Office, the Office for Accreditation, the Office for Diversity, the Office for Government Relations, the Office for Human Resource Development and Recruitment, the Office for Information Technology Policy, the Office for Intellectual Freedom, the Office for Literacy and Outreach Services, the Office for Research and Statistics, the Public Information Office, the Public Programs Office, and the Washington (D.C.) Office.

ALA headquarters is in Chicago; the Office for Government Relations and the Office for Information Technology Policy are located in the Washington Office. ALA also has an editorial office in Middletown, Connecticut, for *Choice,* a review journal for academic libraries.

ALA is a 501(c)(3) charitable and educational organization.

A Focus on Library Advocacy

During her presidential year, 2004–2005 ALA President Carol A. Brey-Casiano focused on library advocacy, which she defined as turning passive support into educated action by encouraging supporters to "stand up and speak out for libraries."

Brey-Casiano defined advocacy in a broad way that includes talking about libraries with everyone: coworkers, library board members, officials of all levels of government—and neighbors across the backyard fence. "We must ensure that we are all advocates on the grassroots level," she said.

She also pledged to continue the efforts of her immediate predecessors, Carla Hayden and Maurice "Mitch" Freedman, to promote equity of access and improve salaries within the profession. "We're the heart of the library," she said, "and we can't have effective libraries without well-paid, effective people who work in them."

Highlights of the Year

Fight for Fair Use Continues

ALA continued work through the year to fight for fair use of copyrighted material by working to increase cosponsorship of H.R. 107, the "Digital Media Consumers' Rights Act," the most significant proposed fair-use legislation in years. ALA also joined with ACRL, the Association of Research Libraries (ARL), the American Association of Law Libraries (AALL), the Medical Library Association, the Scholarly Publishing and Academic Resources Coalition (SPARC), and the Special Libraries Association (SLA) to form the Information Access Alliance, whose purpose is to promote greater scrutiny of proposed mergers of publishing firms. The coalition was formed over concerns that large commercial publishers are controlling more and more of the academic publishing arena, threatening scholarly and public access to research, and limiting the availability of important scientific, technical, and medical research. The Information Access Alliance (http://www.informationaccess.org) meets regularly to develop strategies for challenging publishing mergers.

Threats to fair use were at stake in several notable court cases, and libraries filed "friend-of-the-court" briefs involving copyright issues relating to peer-to-peer file-sharing networks (see http://www.ala.org/ala/washoff/WOissues/copyrightb/copyright.htm).

Copyright Guide for Librarians

Complete Copyright: An Everyday Guide for Librarians by Carrie Russell of the ALA Office for Information Technology Policy was released at the 2004 Annual Conference in Orlando and became ALA Editions' No. 1 seller. The 260-page handbook is unique in that it includes a substantive court-case analysis section and glossary, model copyright presentations for librarians to use at their home institutions, a fair-use advocacy section, and an interesting cast of library characters who encounter copyright dilemmas on the job. *Complete Copyright* uses a Creative Commons license called a "commons deed" to define how readers can use the book, modeling the more open access philosophy endorsed by librarians. Users are not required to seek prior permission from ALA to use the book for nonprofit educational purposes, and they may make derivative works based on the original work as long as the new works created also carry a "commons deed" license. A companion Web site (http://www.ala.org/ala/washoff/WOissues/copyrightb/completecopyright/completecopyright.htm) has been created to provide updates to the book as copyright law evolves. It includes PowerPoint presentations that librarians can download and use without permission.

Protecting Civil Liberties and Access to Information

ALA continued to play an active role in preventing restrictions on access to information.

On July 23, 2004, for example, it was announced that the Department of Justice had asked the Superintendent of Documents of the Government Printing Office to instruct depository libraries to remove and destroy all copies of five particular documents, two of which are texts of federal statutes, that the department deemed not "appropriate for external use." The topics addressed in the named documents include information on how citizens can retrieve items that may have been confiscated by the government during an investigation.

ALA immediately filed a Freedom of Information Act (FOIA) request for the documents, and on August 2 the Superintendent of Documents notified the Federal Depository Library Program that the Department of Justice had rescinded its request. ALA then withdrew its FOIA request. Sen. Patrick Leahy (D-Vt.) and Rep. John Conyers, Jr. (D-Mich.) followed up with a letter to U.S. Attorney General John D. Ashcroft suggesting that the Department of Justice action "was yet another attempt to erode the public's right to know."

Also in August, after almost two years of litigation, a settlement was reached with the Department of Justice that resulted in the disclosure of additional records, including a copy of the procedural rules of the Foreign Intelligence Surveillance Court. The settlement came in response to FOIA requests by the American Civil Liberties Union, the Freedom to Read Foundation, the Electronic Privacy Information Center, and the American Booksellers Foundation for Free Expression.

The USA Patriot Act of 2001 continued to generate heated controversy during the year over antiterrorism activities and their impact on civil liberties. The USA Patriot Act, passed in October 2001 in response to the terrorist attacks of September 11, is of particular interest to librarians because it led to changes in guidelines on FBI investigations and related activities that prompted serious concern about issues relating to library patron confidentiality. ALA has developed Web-based materials for librarians and others on both the USA Patriot Act (http://www.ala.org/ala/pio/mediarelations/patriotactmedia.htm) and the Children's Internet Protection Act (http://www.ala.org/Template.cfm?Section=cipa), which withstood a challenge before the U.S. Supreme Court in June 2003.

ALA worked both with specific legislators to secure their support of H.R. 1157, the Freedom to Read Protection Act, and with a broad group of organizations concerned with civil liberties to secure introduction of, and support for, legislation that addresses a broad range of privacy and liberty issues, including the concerns of libraries, in the USA Patriot Act. The ALA Washington Office also continued to work with AALL, ARL, and other public-interest organizations to encourage agencies to talk with their constituencies about the criteria they are using to review materials for dissemination on their Web sites and to restore access to these materials as quickly as possible.

ALA remains on guard against further encroachments, in both the executive and legislative branches, on the public's right to know. To learn more, visit the Washington Office's Government Information pages (http://www.ala.org/ala/washoff/washingtonoffice.htm) and click on "issues."

Legislative Day Draws More Than 500

National Library Legislative Day 2004 events brought more than 500 librarians, including 2003–2004 ALA President Carla Hayden, library trustees, board members and friends of libraries to Capitol Hill to speak with their representatives and senators about issues of concern to the library community. The event, cosponsored by the District of Columbia Library Association and ALA and held each May, drew participants from 49 states (all but South Dakota); Illinois topped the attendance list in 2004 with 60 delegates, followed by Maryland, Ohio, New York, and California. As part of the event, Friends of Libraries U.S.A. (FOLUSA) gives an annual public service award to a member of Congress who provides leadership on, and demonstrates commitment to, important library issues. In 2004 the FOLUSA award went to two recipients: Sen. Russ Feingold (D-Wis.) and Rep. Bernie Sanders (I-Vt.).

Banned Books Week

With the theme of "Elect to Read a Banned Book," ALA encouraged libraries nationwide to sponsor events, exhibits, and other activities during Banned Books

Week 2004, observed September 25–October 2, to call attention to the fact that books are challenged in the United States every day. Individuals and libraries marked the week in many ways. At the Enoch Pratt Free Library's central branch in Baltimore, a huge sign on a display table warned readers, "DO NOT READ—These BOOKS are BANNED." At the Des Plaines (Illinois) Public Library, readers had to peek at a similar display through slits in a large brown-paper shield. And "read-outs" from banned books were held nationwide.

The ALA Office for Intellectual Freedom (OIF) records hundreds of book challenges each year—about 9,000 since 1990. Each challenge is an effort to remove books from public or school library shelves or from school curricula.

Banned Books Week—Celebrating the Freedom to Read has been observed during the last week of September each year since 1982. It is sponsored by the American Booksellers Association, the American Booksellers Foundation for Free Expression, ALA, the American Society of Journalists and Authors, the Association of American Publishers, and the National Association of College Stores. It is endorsed by the Center for the Book of the Library of Congress. In 2005 Banned Books Week is set for September 24–October 1.

Lawyers for Libraries

OIF held three Lawyers for Libraries regional training institutes in 2004, in San Francisco, Dallas, and Boston, providing attendees with the background and tools to represent libraries within the context of their First Amendment obligations. The expert faculty addressed a range of issues, including the library as a public forum, unprotected speech, minimizing liability, and privacy and confidentiality.

Lawyers for Libraries is an ongoing OIF project designed to build a nationwide network of attorneys committed to the defense of the freedom to read and the application of constitutional law to library policies, principles, and problems. The Lawyers for Libraries network now includes more than 150 members. As OIF continues to sponsor regional institutes, more and more attorneys are learning about the intricacies of First Amendment law as applied to libraries.

Every Child Ready to Read Project

The multiyear Every Child Ready to Read project, a partnership between the PLA and ALSC, developed products, tools, and resources for libraries of all sizes to use in disseminating early childhood information to parents, child-care providers, early childhood educators, children's advocates, and political decision-makers. Results of research conducted in public libraries, ordering information and additional data about this project are available at the Every Child Ready to Read Web page (http://www.ala.org/ala/pla/plaissues/earlylit/earlyliteracy.htm).

ALSC's Great Web Sites for Kids (http://www.ala.org/greatsites) now allows users to search its pages and recommended links by keyword or age level. The search engine will help children, parents, teachers, and librarians find the Web resources that interest them much more quickly and easily.

Another new feature on the ALSC Web site grew out of the program booklet distributed at the 2003 ALSC Charlemae Rollins President's Program, "Boys Will Be . . . The Unique Reading and Development Needs of Boys in Libraries." This resource includes author tips to, and messages for, librarians, and highlights lists of recommended titles for boys, successful library programs for boys, and relevant Web sites. The booklet can be accessed by visiting the ALSC home page (http://www.ala.org/alsc) and clicking on "Resources," "For Librarians and Educators," and "Service to Boys."

Books to Caucasus

The International Relations Office (IRO) shipped $100,000 worth of donated books to the Caucasus in Central Asia as part of its project "Fostering Civil Society: Improving Access to Information in Academic Libraries in the South Caucasus," funded by a grant from the Carnegie Corporation of New York. IRO also coordinated the participation of 40 fellows from 23 countries in the IFLA World Library and Information Congress in Buenos Aires in August through the "Fellowship of the Americas" program sponsored by the IFLA (International Federation of Library Associations and Institutions) 2001 National Organizing Committee.

@ Your Library

In February 2004 PLA rolled out its own "@ your library" campaign, "The Smartest Card: Get It. Use It. @ your library," whose goal is to make the library card a valued card in every wallet. Campaign themes focus on the public library as a critical contributor to a vibrant and educated community, essential and indispensable for a free people, a place of opportunity, and a destination for a wide variety of valuable services.

School libraries and public libraries thus joined academic and research libraries in having their own @ your library campaigns, and the ACRL @ your library campaign continued with marketing programs hosted by ACRL at both the ALA Midwinter Meeting and Annual Conference.

Suspense Surrounds Teen Read Week

Horror, mystery, forensics, and genetics were the focus of libraries, schools, and bookstores nationwide as they celebrated the seventh annual Teen Read Week October 17–23, sponsored by the YALSA. The theme, "It's Alive @ your library," prepared thousands of youngsters (and adults) for a night of scary fun that was to follow a week later, on Halloween.

Campaign for the World's Libraries

ALA divisions are bringing the Campaign for the World's Libraries to libraries nationwide and abroad. More than 25 nations have joined the multiyear public education and advocacy effort cosponsored by ALA and IFLA.

Programs and Partners
We the People Bookshelf

ALA and the National Endowment for the Humanities partnered to present the inaugural We the People Bookshelf, which provided sets of 15 classic children's books on the theme of courage to 1,000 public and school (K–12) libraries in all 50 states. The initiative aims to encourage young people to read and understand great literature while exploring themes in American history. A second Bookshelf project, on the theme of freedom, will award grants to another 1,000 libraries in 2005.

Campaign Partnerships

The "Get on Board and Read @ your library" program, which encourages young adults to skateboard their way to libraries, borrow a book, and create an entry about how the book was meaningful to them, received a record 1,500 entries from teenagers nationwide following its launch in November 2003. Some 4,200 librarians registered for the program, which was sponsored by ALA and Dean Foods, marketer of Hershey's Milk. Three teenage boys from Maine were the grand prize winners for their video on how the book *Shoeless Joe* by W. P. Kinsella reflected their own community's efforts to raise money for a skate park. Their prize was a trip to meet skateboard legend and program spokesperson Tony Hawk.

Walgreens joined as the latest campaign "founding partner" in the "Be Well Informed @ your library" program, which was launched at the ALA Annual Conference in June 2004 and focuses on consumer health education. As part of the program, 16,400 public libraries received brochures about the new Medicare drug discount card and ten library systems received grants to host a series of health-literacy seminars that position librarians and pharmacists as expert information resources.

Another partnership saw continued success. The "Put It in Writing @ your library" program, sponsored by ALA and *Woman's Day* magazine, featured 15 libraries hosting workshops during National Library Week (April 18–24) on how aspiring writers can get published in a magazine. This was the third year of the program, but the first time that community college libraries, as well as public libraries, hosted the workshops, which were led by librarians and *Woman's Day* writers. The publication's online book club also evolved in its second year by featuring recommendations to parents and caregivers from members of ALSC, AASL, and YALSA.

The "Join the Major Leagues @ your library" program, which began its fourth year in 2004, continued to be a hit, with all-new baseball trivia questions developed by the librarians at the National Baseball Hall of Fame. Year four was cosponsored by PLA and was designed to complement summer reading programs. Librarians could access free promotional tools from a Web site that was available in both English and Spanish. By its second month, 1,400 libraries had registered for the program. An event to launch the program to the public was held at the St. Petersburg (Florida) Public Library in June during the ALA Annual Conference. "Join the Major Leagues @ your library" is sponsored by ALA, Major League Baseball, and the Major League Baseball Players Association.

The "Register to Vote @ your library" program, sponsored by ALA and the company Working Assets, continued the long tradition of libraries helping citizens register to vote. The program directed voters to a specific Web site where they could complete a voter-registration form. For each citizen who used the site to register or update his or her voter information, ALA received funds for library advocacy from Working Assets.

ALSC and the National Aeronautics and Space Administration (NASA) continued their collaboration on the "NASA @ your library" traveling exhibit. Three identical exhibits, designed for all ages and traveling simultaneously, were featured for at least four weeks in each of 12 libraries. The goals of the program are to encourage participation at public libraries, raise awareness and interest in science, encourage young people to pursue careers in science, and increase the visibility of NASA programs and many of their findings.

Conferences and Workshops

2004 Midwinter Meeting

"Equity of access is a core value of the library profession and the ALA," 2003–2004 President Carla Hayden said in announcing the President's Program at the Midwinter Meeting in San Diego January 9–14, 2004.

"We must be clear that installing filters that block access to safe and legal information deepens the digital divide between those who have Internet access at home, work, or school and those who 'have not,'" said Hayden.

Midwinter keynote speaker Richard Rodriguez, delivering the annual Arthur Curley Memorial Lecture, noted that "grandmothers and libraries know the true history of America." Rodriguez, the author of *Brown: The Last Discovery of America* (Viking, 2002), said Martin Luther King, Jr.'s dream of racial equality remained unfulfilled partly because the racial history of this country is a largely untold story retained in the memories of grandparents or waiting to be discovered in books. He described a nation in which conventional labels such as "black," "white," "Hispanic," and "Native American" are no longer adequate because people want to be free to be themselves instead of having to fit into predetermined categories.

The "@ your library" public awareness campaign conducted a daylong workshop, hosted by the Marketing Academic and Research Libraries Committee of ACRL. It featured tools and strategies for implementing the academic arm of the Campaign for America's Libraries.

Midwinter Meeting attendance was nearly 10,800.

2004 Annual Conference

More than 19,700 people attended ALA's 2004 Annual Conference in Orlando June 24–30. Featured speakers included author E. L. Doctorow and Richard W. Clarke, counter-terrorism expert under Presidents Bill Clinton and George W. Bush.

Although it occurred after 10 P.M. on a Sunday, a screening of Michael Moore's film *Fahrenheit 9/11* packed the auditorium with about 2,300 conference-goers who paid $10 each to see it. Proceeds went to ALA intellectual freedom programs.

At her inaugural banquet, 2004–2005 ALA President Brey-Casiano elaborated on her presidential theme of grassroots advocacy and urged supporters to "never, never give up." She said her goal was to "get each and every one of you fired up about advocacy for libraries and the people who work in them" and to "show how much we can accomplish by talking to our neighbors about libraries—whether those neighbors live next door or in the state capital."

Political issues from the past several years continued to surface at the conference. The ALA Washington Office announced plans to conduct a survey of libraries to determine the extent to which federal agents have used Section 215 of the USA Patriot Act to obtain library records. Section 215 allows the federal government to order any person or entity to turn over "any tangible things," as long as it specifies that the order is "for an authorized investigation . . . to protect against international terrorism or clandestine intelligence activities." Chris Hansen, senior staff counsel for the American Civil Liberties Union, told an Intellectual Freedom Round Table session to "anticipate that there will be additional litigation over filtering in public libraries and maybe even in public schools within the next year."

ALA Council, with little discussion and only one dissenting vote, accepted the report of the second Core Values Task Force, which was formed following the rejection four years ago of the original group's efforts. The values enumerated in the new list—access, confidentiality, privacy, democracy, diversity, education and lifelong learning, intellectual freedom, preservation, the public good, professionalism, service, and social responsibility—"reflect the history and ongoing development of the profession as portrayed in the ALA's policy statements," the council said.

The Public Programs Office presented the LIVE! @ your library Reading Stage, which included readings by 17 authors and poets, including Mary Kay Andrews (*Hissy Fit*), Christopher Bram (*Lives of the Circus Animals*), Andrei Codrescu (*Wakefield*), Bridgett M. Davis (*Shifting Through Neutral*), Andre Dubus, III (*House of Sand and Fog*), Patricia Henley (*In the River Sweet*), Khaled Hosseini (*The Kite Runner*), Edward P. Jones (*The Known World*), Susan Kinsolving (*The White Eyelash*), Dionisio D. Martinez (*Climbing Back*), and Jacqueline Winspear (*Maisie Dobbs*).

2005 Midwinter Meeting

A record-breaking 13,232 librarians, publishers, and others in the library and information industry gathered in Boston January 14–19 for the ALA 2005 Midwinter Meeting and to share information and ideas on the various challenges that face America's libraries.

Library funding cuts remained at the forefront of those challenges—nationally, more than $82 million had been cut from library budgets in the previous year. To address the issue, 2004–2005 President Brey-Casiano led the first-ever ALA Advocacy Institute, featuring a keynote address from Kerry Healey, Massachusetts lieutenant governor, who, as a member of the Friends of the Library in Beverly, Massachusetts, helped raise more than $1 million in private funds and grants to rebuild the library. The more than 250 institute participants were encouraged to share ideas on how to secure funds to support library services.

The ALA Midwinter President's Program, "Creating an Advocacy Epidemic," sponsored by Little, Brown and Company, drew a sellout crowd. Bestselling author Malcolm Gladwell delivered the keynote address for the program. Following Gladwell's remarks, Brey-Casiano and a panel of ALA leaders discussed how to mobilize individual grassroots advocacy efforts to create a nationwide advocacy "epidemic."

Attendees at the annual business meeting also discussed library funding and advocacy strategies, library users' privacy, and recruitment.

Midwinter also hosted the "Academy Awards of children's literature," ALA's Youth Media Awards.

Publishing

American Libraries

ALA members now have online access to whole issues of *American Libraries,* ALA's monthly magazine, before they arrive by mail. Leonard Kniffel, *American Libraries* editor and publisher, notes that this is especially important for ALA's international membership, since the print issue often takes weeks to reach foreign destinations.

Booklist

Continuing to honor its commitment to serve both collection development and reader adviser librarians, *Booklist* magazine published more than 8,000 reviews of new books and media in Vol. 100 (2003–2004) as well as features designed to help librarians assist patrons in deciding what to read next. Joyce Saricks, nationally known reader adviser expert and author of *Readers' Advisory Service in the Public Library,* has joined the *Booklist* roster of columnists; "At Leisure with Joyce Saricks" appears in every first-of-the-month issue and is devoted to "leisure reading." *Booklist* also participated in various reader adviser activities and programs at PLA's tenth National Conference in Seattle, culminating in a reception hosted by the magazine that honored the work of reader advisers across the nation. Finally, *Booklist* and ALSC published *60 Years of Notable Children's Books,* which includes many titles from ALSC's Children's Notable Lists, grouped by decade (1940–1999) and by theme.

CHOICE

CHOICE: Current Reviews for Academic Libraries, a publishing unit of ACRL, marked its 40th year of continuous publication with its March 2004 issue. *CHOICE* publishes 6,500 to 7,000 reviews a year of books and electronic and Internet resources; more than 105,000 reviews are available online at http://www.ala.org/ala/acrl/acrlpubs/choice/home.htm.

ALA Editions

ALA Editions continued to serve the needs of information professionals by publishing 31 new titles and collaborating with other ALA units. *From Outreach to Equity,* by Robin Osborne with a foreword by Carla Hayden, and the 35th anniversary edition of *The Coretta Scott King Awards* were both developed in partnership with the Office for Literacy and Outreach Services. Strong backlist sales were led by *Information Power: Building Partnerships for Learning* and *Complete Copyright: An Everyday Guide for Librarians* by ALA copyright expert Carrie Russell and *Fundamentals of Collection Development* by Peggy Johnson. Other key publications during the year included *Power Tools Recharged* by Joyce Valenza, and *Cataloging with AACR2 and MARC 21* by Deborah Fritz.

ALA Graphics

ALA Graphics introduced the ALA author poster series, which features such influential writers as Sherman Alexie, Neil Gaiman, Julia Alvarez, and Nancy Pearl. Children's and young-adult characters such as Batgirl, Nutbrown Hare from *Guess How Much I Love You,* and various figures from *Megatokyo* also have become themed posters for ALA. Other new products include a Dewey teacup produced with the cooperation of OCLC (Online Computer Library Center) and Dewey cat-and-dog collars to complement the growing line of Dewey products.

The best-selling Celebrity READ series has grown to include actor Orlando Bloom, soprano Renée Fleming, country music star Trace Adkins, and Animal Planet adventurer Jeff Corwin and is now available on CD to help library staff extend their reach quickly, easily, and affordably. ALA Graphics also focused on partnering within the association with such projects as National Library Week, Teen Read Week, Library Card Sign-up Month, and the "@ your library" campaign. And, recognizing that many states have drastically cut budgets for library services, ALA Graphics partnered with state and regional libraries and chapters to provide group-purchase discounts and new revenue opportunities through consignment sales.

Leadership

Carol A. Brey-Casiano, director of the El Paso (Texas) Public Library, was inaugurated as ALA president at the 2004 Annual Conference in Orlando.

Before working in El Paso, Brey-Casiano was director of the Thomas Branigan Memorial Library System in Las Cruces/Doña Ana County, New Mexico (1996–2000), and earlier was director of the Oak Park (Illinois) Public Library (1991–1995). She also has served as an adjunct professor at Dominican University in River Forest, Illinois, the University of Texas at Austin, and the Universidad Autónoma de Chihuahua in Chihuahua, Mexico.

Brey-Casiano holds a master's degree in library science from the University of Illinois and has continued her studies at the University of Texas at Austin. She also manages her own consulting firm, Visions.

Michael Gorman, dean of library services at California State University–Fresno's Madden Library, was elected ALA president-elect in the 2004 election and is to be inaugurated ALA president at the 2005 Annual Conference in Chicago. His presidential focus will be on library education, recruitment, accreditation, and certification.

Teri R. Switzer, associate dean, research, operations, and document delivery services at the University of Colorado at Denver and Health Sciences Center, Auraria Library, was elected to a full term (2004–2007) as ALA treasurer. Switzer had been elected to a one-year term as treasurer in the 2003 ALA election to fill a vacancy created by the resignation of ALA Treasurer Liz Bishoff.

Two new ALA Executive Board members were elected by the ALA Council in a vote taken at the 2004 ALA Midwinter Meeting in San Diego. Janet Swan Hill, professor and associate director for technical services at the University of Colorado Libraries in Boulder, and Nann Blaine Hilyard, director of the Zion-Benton Public Library in Zion, Illinois, are serving three-year terms that began in June 2004.

Grants and Contributions

The Institute of Museum and Library Services (IMLS) awarded the ALA Office for Diversity a grant of almost $940,000 in July 2004 to allow it to double the number of ALA Spectrum scholarship recipients over the next three years. The grant also will fund several programmatic diversity initiatives.

Established by ALA in 1997 to address the under-representation of minority librarians within the profession, the Spectrum program provides a one-year $5,000 scholarship and more than $1,500 in professional development opportunities to eligible recipients each year. The IMLS grant will match scholarships funded by ALA over the next three years, providing a total of up to 105 additional scholarships.

The estate of William C. Morris provided a donation of $800,000 to ALA. At Morris's request, the donation was divided equally between ALSC and YALSA for establishment of a named endowment in each division to support youth programming. Morris, a charter member of the ALA Legacy Society and a former HarperCollins Children's Books vice president and director of promotion, has been credited with developing the modern marketing of children's books. He received ALSC's first Distinguished Service Award in 1992 and was an ALA member for 21 years. He died on September 28, 2003, at age 71.

The ALA Public Programs Office (PPO) was awarded a grant from the National Endowment for the Humanities to present a sixth season of the award-winning "StoryLines America," focusing on New England literature. The series was broadcast on participating public radio stations in New England and nationwide in autumn 2004. Participating libraries received copies of the books that were highlighted in the series, discussion and promotional materials, and CDs of the series to present public programs for their patrons.

PPO also received a grant from the National Library of Medicine to organize "Changing the Face of Medicine: Celebrating America's Women Physicians," an exhibit that celebrates the lives and achievements of women in medicine since they first gained admission to American medical schools 150 years ago. It is based on a major multimedia exhibition that is to open at the National Library of Medicine in 2005. The traveling exhibition will visit 30 public, academic, and medical libraries between May 2005 and September 2008.

Major Awards and Honors

The 2004 Newbery Medal, awarded annually by ALSC to the author of the most distinguished contribution to American literature for children, went to Kate

DiCamillo for *The Tale of Despereaux: Being the Story of a Mouse, a Princess, Some Soup, and a Spool of Thread* (Candlewick Press). The Caldecott Medal for 2004 went to writer-illustrator Mordicai Gerstein for *The Man Who Walked Between the Towers* (Roaring Brook Press/Millbrook Press); this medal is awarded annually to the artist of the most distinguished American picture book for children.

The Coretta Scott King Awards are presented annually by the ALA Social Responsibilities Round Table to authors and illustrators of African descent whose distinguished books promote an understanding and appreciation of African American culture. The awards commemorate the life and work of Dr. Martin Luther King, Jr., and honor his widow, Coretta Scott King, for her courage and determination in continuing the work for peace and world brotherhood. The winners of the 2004 awards were Angela Johnson, author of *The First Part Last* (Simon & Schuster Books for Young Readers), and Ashley Bryan, illustrator and author of *Beautiful Blackbird* (Atheneum Books for Young Readers).

Angela Johnson's *The First Part Last* was also the winner of the 2004 Michael L. Printz Award, which honors a book that exemplifies literary excellence in young adult literature.

The Robert F. Sibert Informational Book Award, which is awarded annually by ALSC to the author of the most distinguished informational book published during the preceding year, went to Jim Murphy for *An American Plague: The True and Terrifying Story of the Yellow Fever Epidemic of 1793* (Clarion Books/ Houghton Mifflin).

Hope Anita Smith, author of *The Way a Door Closes,* was the Coretta Scott King/John Steptoe New Talent Author Award winner in 2004, and Elbrite Brown, illustrator of *My Family Plays Music,* was the Steptoe New Talent Illustrator Award winner.

Julia Alvarez won the 2004 Pura Belpré Medal for Narrative for *Before We Were Free* (Alfred A. Knopf, 2002), and Yuyi Morales was awarded the Belpré Medal for Illustration for *Just a Minute: A Trickster Tale and Counting Book* (Chronicle Books, 2003). The awards are cosponsored by ALSC and the National Association to Promote Library and Information Services to Latinos and the Spanish-Speaking (REFORMA), an ALA affiliate.

Honorary Members

ALA bestowed honorary membership, its highest honor, on two individuals in 2004. Sanford Berman, head cataloger at the Hennepin County (Minnesota) Library for 26 years, was honored "for his accomplishments as a cataloging theorist and practitioner and for his commitment to making catalog records accessible to library users. Using subject headings as a tool for social awareness, Berman has had a profound influence on the way librarians think and work." Norman Horrocks, professor emeritus at the School of Library and Information Science at Dalhousie University (Halifax, Nova Scotia, Canada) and editorial consultant for Scarecrow Press, was recognized "for his long and distinguished career in librarianship that spans several countries and six decades; his contributions as a library educator, parliamentarian, writer and publisher; and his influence as a mentor to generations of librarians."

Honorary membership can be conferred upon a living citizen of any country whose contribution to librarianship or a closely related field is so outstanding that it is of lasting importance to the advancement of the whole field of library service. Honorary members are elected for life by vote of the ALA Council upon recommendation of the ALA Executive Board.

Other Highlights

ACRL Strategic Plan

The new Strategic Plan of ACRL, which was approved by the ACRL Board of Directors at the ALA Annual Conference in June 2004, has three strategic areas (higher education and research, the profession, and the association). It also states ACRL's core purpose, core values, and "big audacious goal," which is to be "responsible and universally recognized for positioning academic and research librarians and libraries as indispensable in advancing learning and scholarship." The ACRL board also approved new Standards for Libraries in Higher Education.

ACRL's new user-friendly Information Literacy Web site (http://www.ala. org/ala/acrl/acrlissues/acrlinfolit/informationliteracy.htm) is both a gateway to resources and a gathering place for important initiatives, including ACRL's Institute for Information Literacy (and its Best Practices and Immersion programs). Included are links to biographies, examples of information literacy in action, and a standards tool kit for working through the information literacy competency standards for higher education.

New Accreditation Policies

The ALA Office for Accreditation (OA) published new accreditation policies and procedures that are helping to open the lines of communication between accredited library and information science programs and the Committee on Accreditation (COA). The OA also introduced a searchable online directory of ALA-accredited programs. It has been working with COA to make the goals and work of ALA accreditation more visible in the library and information science community and beyond, and to that end COA begun an aggressive program to share its message at state and regional conferences. The office also shepherded one program from conditional to full accreditation and added a new accredited program to its roster for the first time in 16 years.

National Library Workers Day

ALA-Allied Professional Association celebrated the first annual National Library Workers Day on April 20, 2004, to honor the "hard work, dedication, and expertise of library support staff and librarians." Buttons carried the slogan "Libraries Work Because We Do."

Association of American Publishers

71 Fifth Ave., New York, NY 10010
212-255-0200, fax 212-255-7007

50 F St. N.W., Washington, DC 20001
202-347-3375, fax 202-347-3690

http://www.publishers.org

Judith Platt
Director, Communications/Public Affairs

The Association of American Publishers (AAP) is the national trade association of the U.S. book publishing industry. The association was created in 1970 through the merger of the American Book Publishers Council, a trade publishing group, and the American Educational Publishers Institute, an organization of textbook publishers. AAP's more than 300 corporate members include most of the major commercial book publishers in the United States as well as smaller and medium-sized houses, not-for-profit publishers, university presses, and scholarly societies.

AAP members publish hardcover and paperback books in every field including general fiction and nonfiction; poetry; children's books; textbooks; Bibles and other religious works; reference works; scientific, medical, technical, professional, and scholarly books and journals; computer software; and a range of electronic products and services.

AAP also works closely with some 2,000 smaller regional publishers through formal affiliations with the Publishers Association of the West, the Publishers Association of the South, the Florida Publishers Association, the Small Publishers Association of North America, and the Evangelical Christian Publishers Association.

AAP policy is set by a board of directors elected by the membership for four-year terms, under a chair who serves for two years. There is an executive committee composed of the chair, vice chair, secretary, and treasurer and a minimum of two at-large members. Management of the association, within the guidelines set by the board, is the responsibility of AAP's president and CEO, Pat Schroeder.

AAP maintains two offices, in New York and Washington, D.C.

Highlights of 2004

Among the highlights of the year in publishing:

- AAP's 2004 Honors went to Emmy Award-winning television journalist Jorge Ramos for his work in promoting books and reading in the Latino community
- Scholastic's Jean Feiwel received the 28th Curtis Benjamin Award for Creative Publishing as the award ceremony returned to the AAP Annual Meeting
- The newly created Miriam Bass Independent Publishing Award went to McBooks Press President Alexander Scutt

- Book sales totaled $23.4 billion in 2003, a 4.6 percent increase over 2002, according to figures released by AAP in March
- HarperCollins CEO Jane Friedman began her second year as AAP chair
- AAP's Professional and Scholarly Publishing Division joined in a lawsuit against the government's Office of Foreign Assets Control over regulation of publishing activities
- The R. R. Hawkins Award for the outstanding professional, scholarly, or reference work published in 2003 went to Oxford University Press for Mary Jane West-Eberhard's *Developmental Plasticity and Evolution*
- Highlights of the sixth year of "Get Caught Reading" included the "Get Caught Reading at Sea" cruise
- J. Bruce Hildebrand was named to the newly created post of AAP executive director for higher education
- AAP stepped up its antipiracy campaign in Asia
- The second Jeri Laber International Freedom to Publish Prize went to Indonesian publisher Joesoef Isak
- AAP joined the American Library Association (ALA), PEN, and the American Booksellers Foundation for Free Expression (ABFFE) in sponsoring the "Campaign for Reader Privacy"
- AAP's School Division held another of its popular "summit" meetings in Washington, this year focusing on English-language learners
- The new AAP "Book Yourself a Career" campaign seeks to increase diversity in every area of publishing
- AAP partnered with the National Endowment for the Arts to raise awareness of a serious decline in literary readership
- The International Freedom to Publish (IFTP) Committee brought Iranian works in translation to U.S. publishers

Government Affairs

AAP's Washington office is the industry's front line on matters of federal legislation and government policy. The office keeps AAP members informed about developments on Capitol Hill and in the executive branch to enable the membership to develop consensus positions on national policy issues. AAP's government-affairs professionals serve as the industry's voice in advocating the views and concerns of American publishers on questions of national policy.

A separate report details legislation and regulatory actions affecting book publishers in 2004. [See "Legislation and Regulations Affecting Publishing in 2004" in Part 2—*Ed.*]

Communications/Public Affairs

The Communications and Public Affairs program is AAP's voice, informing the trade press and other media, the AAP membership, and the general public about AAP's work to promote the cause of American publishing and serving as the industry's spokesman on a host of issues. Through the program's regular publications, press releases and advisories, op-ed pieces, and other means, AAP expresses the industry's views and provides up-to-the-minute information on subjects of concern to its members. The program has primary responsibility for the AAP Web site.

AAP's public affairs activities include outreach and cooperative programs with such organizations as the Center for the Book in the Library of Congress, the Arts Advocacy Alliance (supporting the National Endowment for the Arts and other federal arts programs), PEN American Center and its International Freedom to Write program, and a host of literacy and reading-promotion efforts including the early childhood literacy initiative Reach Out and Read. The public affairs program also coordinates AAP's participation in the National Book Festival.

In 2004 the communications program initiated electronic distribution of the AAP newsletter, *AAP Monthly Report,* which is also published online.

BookExpo America

AAP is a cosponsor of BookExpo America (BEA), the premiere English-language book event. BookExpo 2004 was held in Chicago June 4–6. Among the highlights was a solo turn by comedian and author George Carlin to benefit the Book Industry Foundation, which supports the work of ABFFE and the "Get Caught Reading" campaign.

At BookExpo, AAP joined with ABFFE and the Freedom to Read Foundation in sponsoring a program featuring U.S. Sen. Richard Durbin (D-Ill.), who cosponsored the SAFE Act, legislation to amend the USA Patriot Act and restore federal judicial safeguards to Section 215 seizures of bookstore and library purchase or borrowing records. Durbin was presented with the first batch of "Campaign for Reader Privacy" petitions.

Get Caught Reading

AAP in 2004 continued its work to promote a love of reading with the "Get Caught Reading/¡Ajá, leyendo!" campaign. With the addition of celebrities including singer Alicia Keys, New York Yankees player Gary Sheffield, the cast of the movie *Friday Night Lights,* and others, the campaign extended its reach to a wider audience. A highlight in 2004 was the "Get Caught Reading at Sea" cruise, sponsored by AAP and facilitated by Levy Home Entertainment. Nine of the country's largest book publishers partnered to bring 23 popular and best-selling authors on the cruise, a Celebrity Line ship that sailed the Caribbean for eight days in October. With more than 600 "Get Caught Reading at Sea" passengers aboard, the trip was an overwhelming success and served as a reminder that reading is a social activity to be shared with friends.

AAP continued its partnership with the American Booksellers Association (ABA) in issuing Book Sense/Get Caught Reading recommended-reading lists around major holidays. A new Web site was launched in 2004, in addition to a quarterly e-newsletter. AAP also continued its partnership with the National Basketball Association. "Get Caught Reading" had a presence at the Harlem

Book Fair in July and at the Magazine Publishers of America annual conference in March.

Copyright

The AAP Copyright Committee coordinates efforts to protect and strengthen intellectual property rights and to enhance public awareness of the importance of copyright as an incentive to creativity. The committee monitors intellectual property legislation in the United States and abroad and serves as an advisory body to the board of directors in formulating AAP policy on legislation and compliance activities, including litigation. The committee coordinates AAP's efforts to promote understanding and compliance with U.S. copyright law on America's college and university campuses. Bob Bolick (McGraw-Hill) chaired the committee in 2004.

AAP participated in a number of amicus briefs in 2004 supporting the ability of copyright owners under the Digital Millennium Copyright Act (DMCA) to obtain user information from online service providers in cases involving online copyright infringement. Among the cases in which AAP provided amicus support were *Rossi* v. *MPAA* (8th Circuit), *RIAA* v. *Charter Communications* (8th Circuit), and *RIAA* v. *Verizon* (supporting a petition for certiorari to the U.S. Supreme Court).

AAP joined with a host of groups representing media and professional sports organizations whose members rely on effective copyright protection in an effort to get the U.S. Supreme Court to review and overturn a ruling by the 9th Circuit in *Metro-Goldwyn-Mayer Studios, Inc.* v. *Grokster, Ltd.* that would allow providers of peer-to-peer file-sharing services to avoid secondary liability for facilitating acts of copyright infringement simply by taking no action to eliminate or minimize the amount of online copyright infringement by users of their service. The brief points out that notwithstanding an earlier ruling by a separate panel of the 9th Circuit in the Napster case requiring that a peer-to-peer service do "everything feasible to block files from its system which contain noticed copyrighted works," the Grokster ruling held that "by simply switching from a centralized index of files to a decentralized index of files (a process invisible and meaningless to an Internet user)" the peer-to-peer service could duck all secondary liability. The brief points out that the Grokster decision "has the perverse effect of discouraging peer-to-peer services from acting responsibly." The case will be closely watched, as the court is expected to revisit its 1984 landmark ruling in the Betamax case, which upheld the right of viewers to record broadcast television programs for later ("time-shifted") viewing as a noninfringing fair use of the copyrighted television broadcast. In that ruling, a closely divided court established the principle that manufacturers and distributors of devices that can be used to infringe copyright, such as the videocassette recorders at issue in the case, cannot be held secondarily liable for infringements by their users as long as the devices are "capable of substantial noninfringing use." The case was to be argued before the Supreme Court in March 2005.

AAP joined in an amicus brief to the 2nd Circuit in *Faulkner* v. *National Geographic Society*, asking the appellate court to sustain a ruling by the U.S.

District Court for the Southern District of New York that runs counter to the disappointing outcome of the Greenberg case in the 11th Circuit. The New York court held that a CD-ROM compilation of *National Geographic* print magazines was a revision of a collective work under Section 201(c) of the Copyright Act and therefore that National Geographic was not required to obtain permission from the individual photographers whose work appeared in the original print editions.

AAP joined in an amicus brief opposing an appeal by Legg Mason of an $18 million jury award to Lowry's Reports for copyright infringement of its newsletter.

The Copyright Committee is looking at a possible amicus role for AAP in a high-profile patent infringement case involving print-on-demand (POD) technology, in which On Demand Machine Corporation won a jury verdict against Amazon.com, Lightning Source, and Ingram for violating its patent on the business method allowing customers to use a computer to enter an order for a publication and have the publication produced on demand. On Demand Machine Corp. is seeking to enjoin use of the method not only by the defendants but customers as well (including publishers) while the appeal is pending.

The Copyright Committee has been closely monitoring issues arising from the use of copyrighted works in digital formats on college campuses, including library e-reserves. The committee has been working with the Copyright Clearance Center, which—following substantial research on university and library views regarding "blanket licenses"—has implemented an "Electronic Course Content Service" to facilitate the authorized use of such materials.

The committee met with representatives of Australia's reprographic rights organization (CAL) to hear about a pilot project, being conducted with the cooperation of some AAP members, to look at print-on-demand coursepack delivery using digital object identifiers (DOIs).

The committee continues to focus attention on the issue of questionable document-delivery practices, particularly from European sources.

During 2004 the committee's Online Piracy Working Group was revitalized under the chairmanship of Keith Titan (Random House). The group is studying the extent and nature of online book-piracy activities.

In order to develop an AAP position on the handling of "orphan works" (where copyright owners cannot be located for purposes of obtaining permission to use the work), a subcommittee was created to look at various options including the Canadian model based on a compulsory licensing scheme, along with options based on "liability limitation."

The committee is also looking at the copyright implications of the Google Library Program announced late in 2004 that is intended to make information in library collections searchable online.

The Rights and Permissions Advisory Committee (RPAC), which operates under the aegis of the Copyright Committee, sponsors educational programs for rights and permissions professionals. Bonnie Beacher (McGraw-Hill) chaired the group in 2004. RPAC held a full-day conference in New York in May focusing on copyright basics, the Digital Media Consumers Act, parallel importation, issues confronting publishers in the digital age, and the No Child Left Behind Act. The committee also presented a one-day accessibility session. In November the committee conducted a half-day seminar on the No Child Left Behind and TEACH Acts.

Diversity/Recruit and Retain

AAP's Diversity/Recruit and Retain Committee (DRRC) continued in 2004 its mission to attract more talented, diverse voices to the book publishing industry with its "Book Yourself a Career" campaign. The committee was chaired in 2004 by Bridget Marmion (Houghton Mifflin).

The centerpiece of the campaign is the Bookjobs.com Web site (http://bookjobs.com), which serves as a comprehensive database of jobs and internships in the industry as well as a "one-stop shopping" resource for information about book publishing. The jobs database includes job and internship listings from nearly 300 book publishers of all types—large and small, consumer, professional, and educational. The Web site has a wealth of information covering types of publishers, individual companies, types of jobs in publishing, matches between college majors and particular job departments, publishing programs, and events in the industry.

DRRC launched a college outreach initiative in 2004 to publicize the Web site on college campuses, with a focus on schools that have a high academic standard and a diverse student population.

Education Program

AAP's education program is designed to provide educational opportunities for publishing industry personnel. The most popular of these is the intensive "Introduction to Publishing" course, held in October. Among the other educational programs in 2004 were "Finance for Editors" and AAP's tax seminar, which features speakers with experience in the area of finance and taxation.

Enabling Technologies

AAP's Enabling Technologies Committee (ETC) works to foster the development and implementation of technologies facilitating print and digital publishing. Companies from all segments of the industry (trade, educational, and professional and scholarly) participate in the committee's activity.

The committee continued its work on issues related to the expansion of the International Standard Book Number (ISBN) from 10 digits to a 13-digit standard, which is scheduled to go into effect on January 1, 2007. ETC formed an ISBN-13 Task Force to communicate with libraries, college bookstores, and K–12 school districts regarding the upcoming change, as well as to stay apprised of ISBN-13 efforts with the greater book-buying community.

In meetings with representatives of ALA and the National Association of College Stores (NACS), the ETC task force learned that technology vendors to the library and college-bookstore communities are expected to be well prepared to enable the system-wide handling of the 13-digit number. The task force was informed, however, that awareness of the new ISBN was not universal in the K–12 community, and that many school districts knowledgeable about the change reported that they would have problems dealing with it. In response, the task force partnered with two committees of the AAP School Division to engage in outreach to the districts and their textbook depositories. The school committees began preparing a notice on the change to the districts and meeting with officials from the depositories to study and address ISBN-13 implementation issues.

Related to the ISBN revision was a proposal by BISG that the industry standardize on using only the 13-digit, item-identifying "Bookland EAN" bar code on the back cover of all books. To accommodate general retailers, mass market paperbacks have historically featured a different bar code called the "price-point" UPC, a 12-digit code specifying the book's suggested retail price. (Decades ago, a number of nonbook retailers expressed a preference or requirement for using the UPC code.)

ETC members and AAP staff participated in, and made recommendations to, a BISG task force that conducted surveys to find out whether and when general retailers would be able to scan, store, and process the Bookland EAN. The surveys found that retailers accounting for more than 85 percent of mass market paperback wholesalers' volume would be ready to do so by July 1, 2005, and that most of the rest would be ready by the end of 2005. Consequently, the task force recommended that by the third quarter of 2005 the Bookland EAN be the only bar code printed on the back cover of all new books.

Freedom to Read

The mandate of the AAP Freedom to Read Committee is to protect the free marketplace of ideas for American publishers. The committee serves as the publishing industry's early-warning system on such issues as libel, privacy, school and library censorship, journalists' privilege and the right to protect confidential sources, Internet censorship, government regulation of protected speech, third-party liability for protected speech, and efforts to punish speech that "causes harm." The committee coordinates AAP participation in First Amendment cases, sponsors educational programs, plays an active role in Media Coalition (a trade association of business-oriented groups concerned with censorship issues), and works with groups within and beyond the book community to advance common interests in the area of intellectual freedom. Lisa Drew (Lisa Drew Books/Scribner) chaired the committee in 2004.

The USA Patriot Act and the Campaign for Reader Privacy

Section 215 of the USA Patriot Act, especially as it applies to library and bookstore records, continues to be a source of deep concern for publishers and for the larger book community. Over and above the issue of library and bookstore records, publishers have serious business concerns about Section 215. If, for example, the FBI were to become interested in a book about terrorism and wanted to pursue the author for more information, all of a publisher's records pertaining to the book—including editorial correspondence, proposals, drafts of the manuscript, marked-up proofs, and royalty statements—would be subject to a Section 215 seizure with virtually no judicial safeguards. Section 215 could also be used for "fishing expeditions," allowing the government to obtain, without showing probable cause, information about subscribers to various publications, notably scientific journals.

Building on successes the previous year in effecting introduction of House and Senate bills to restore judicial safeguards stripped away by Section 215, in 2004 AAP joined with ALA, ABA, and PEN American Center in sponsoring the "Campaign for Reader Privacy," the centerpiece of which is a nationwide petition drive supporting legislation to amend Section 215. Evidence that the plea was being heard on Capitol Hill came in a vote in the House on July 8 on an amendment denying Justice Department funds to carry out Section 215 searches of libraries and bookstores. Although the amendment went down to the narrowest defeat, the fight on the House floor reflected what one newspaper termed ". . . the growing consensus on Capitol Hill that too much liberty and privacy was given up under the Patriot Act."

At a press conference in the Capitol during the 2004 celebration of Banned Books Week, AAP President Schroeder joined with PEN President Salman Rushdie and officials of ALA and ABA to present members of Congress with campaign petitions containing 180,000 signatures collected in bookstores and libraries across the nation. Petitions and information on the campaign were circulated at the National Book Awards banquet in November. AAP continues to articulate the industry's concerns about Section 215, notably in an extensive piece by Schroeder that appeared in the December 2004 issue of *Playboy*. As the 109th Congress gets under way, with some provisions of the Patriot Act due to expire in December 2005, AAP is gearing up for a full-scale lobbying effort.

In the Courts

- The Freedom to Read Committee played a key role in a landmark First Amendment victory in Texas involving the right to satirize public officials without fear of defamation liability. In a unanimous ruling, the Texas Supreme Court dismissed a libel suit brought by two public officials against an alternative weekly newspaper, and in doing so strengthened free speech protections in the state. AAP organized and led a broad coalition of media and First Amendment groups in an amicus brief that asked the court to protect the use of "comic exaggeration to draw attention to . . . misuse of authority." The opinion handed down by the court indicated that close attention had been paid to the AAP brief. The court rejected the argument that the newspaper's admitted intent to ridicule the defendants could be taken as evidence of actual malice, ruling significantly that "actual malice concerns the defendant's attitude toward the truth, not toward the plaintiff."

- AAP joined in asking the U.S. Supreme Court to overturn a California court ruling in *Tory* v. *Cochran,* the first libel case to be heard by the high court in more than a decade. Challenging a permanent injunction that prevents a disgruntled former client of celebrity lawyer Johnnie Cochran from ever saying anything again in a public forum about Cochran or his law firm, the case involves the most serious type of First Amendment violation—a prior restraint of speech, justifiable only to protect the highest national security interests.

- Early in 2004 AAP took the lead for a second time in an amicus brief asking the U.S. Supreme Court to strike down the Children's Online Protection Act (COPA). The case went up three years ago on the narrow question of whether "community standards" can be applied to the Internet. Failing to strike COPA down solely on this ground, the high court sent the case back to the 3rd Circuit, which again held COPA unconstitutional, this time on broader First Amendment grounds. In June 2004 the Supreme Court, while upholding the preliminary injunction, ruled that the many legal and technological changes that have occurred in the five years since the case was first heard have changed the landscape enough to warrant a new trial. The case is once again before the district court with the burden on the government to prove that COPA is the least restrictive means of protecting minors from unsuitable material on the Internet.

- AAP joined U.S. and Canadian media organizations, Internet companies, journalist groups, and free-expression advocates as an "intervenor" (similar to an amicus or "friend of the court") in the Court of Appeal for Ontario in *Bangoura* v. *Washington Post,* a Canadian case with far-reaching implications for Internet speech. The case involves a troubling ruling by a lower court allowing a libel case against the *Washington Post* to proceed in Canada because the allegedly defamatory story, which still resides in the *Washington Post*'s online archives, can be downloaded in Ontario. The Canadian ruling cited a recent finding by an Australian court that publication takes place where an article is downloaded and read rather than where it originates. The Canadian case is particularly bizarre because the plaintiff was a United Nations official stationed in Kenya at the time the articles accusing him of malfeasance were published, had only resided in Ontario for a few years, and the archived item had only been downloaded once—by the plaintiff's attorney. However, the Canadian judge ruled that the newspaper "should have reasonably foreseen that the story would follow the plaintiff wherever he resided."

- AAP was one of the plaintiffs that, in spring 2003, brought a legal challenge to an Arkansas statute governing the display and accessibility of "harmful-to-minors" material. The challenge ended successfully in November 2004 when a federal district court held the statute to be an unconstitutional burden on adults' and older minors' ability to access material to which they are entitled.

Educational Programs

At BookExpo America in Chicago, AAP cosponsored a program featuring U.S. Senator Richard Durbin (D-Ill.), who spoke about the need to amend the USA Patriot Act and restore federal judicial oversight to the process of obtaining records, including library and bookstore records, under Section 215 of the act.

At the ALA Annual Conference in Orlando, AAP cosponsored "Censorship of the Written Word: Still Alive and Kickin'" featuring author Robie Harris, whose award-winning books including *It's Perfectly Normal: Changing Bodies, Growing Up, Sex and Sexual Health* are perennially among the most challenged and banned in the country. She was joined by Jerilynn Williams, director of the Montgomery County (Texas) Library System, who successfully rallied community members to fight off an attempt to remove Harris's books from the library.

Higher Education

AAP's Higher Education Committee serves the needs and interests of AAP members who publish for the postsecondary educational market. The Higher Education Executive Committee was chaired by John Isley (Pearson Education) in 2004.

Countering 'Ripoff 101' Accusations

The year 2004 will go down as the year of the battle over college textbook pricing. In January the California Public Interest Research Group (CALPIRG) issued the first of its "Ripoff 101" reports. Predicated on misunderstandings and selective data, the report asserted that college and university faculty did not have a high regard for textbooks, were opposed to new editions and supplemental learning materials, and that students were being "ripped off" by having to purchase these materials at inflated prices. Media response to the report was equally skewed and error-filled.

AAP and its higher education members countered with a series of steps designed to inform the media and give the public a more accurate picture of the industry. As an initial response, AAP President Schroeder sent a letter to PIRG noting that the study was "totally one-sided and fatally flawed." She subsequently met with PIRG representatives in California.

Public relations executives from member houses, working with AAP's director of communications and public affairs, produced a brochure titled *College Learning Materials: More than a Textbook* detailing the range, diversity, and value of today's higher education learning materials. The brochure was sent to college and university presidents, state and federal legislators and policy makers, student groups, the student press, and the media. The group also created a video—*Higher Education Goes High-Tech,* intended to educate people about technological advances in higher education publishing—that aired nationally on more than 200 stations.

Reflecting the commitment of member publishers to expand communications and government relations activities in the area of higher education publishing, Bruce Hildebrand joined AAP in July as executive director for higher education.

On July 20, at hearings before the House Subcommittee on 21st Century Competitiveness on the question of whether college textbooks are priced fairly, the answer from AAP was resoundingly affirmative. In the course of the testimony, presented by Higher Education Executive Committee Chairman John Isley (Pearson Higher Education, International and Professional Group), AAP outlined many of the ways in which the U.S. publishing industry is striving to adapt higher education textbooks to meet the significant teaching and learning changes that have taken place over the past decade. Isley noted that higher education textbooks and the digital resources that support them offer today's students and teachers not only quality and value but also a degree of flexibility that would have been hard to imagine even a few years ago. Also testifying were representatives of the National Association of College Stores (NACS), PIRG, and the University of Wisconsin–River Falls. Isley's testimony was the first opportunity for college publishers to comprehensively counter PIRG's charges on the public record.

Prompted by the PIRG report, several members of Congress signed a joint letter that was sent in March to the General Accountability Office (GAO) requesting a study of textbook pricing. In July, on the same day the House hearings were held, a separate meeting took place at AAP's offices in Washington between a team of analysts from GAO and executives from AAP's Higher Education Committee member houses. GAO was in the initial phases of developing a model for its research, and the meeting gave publishers an opportunity to provide memoranda and data on competitiveness and other complex industry issues. At the conclusion of the meeting, GAO's chief analyst indicated that its original concept for a model would have to be substantially altered to incorporate what GAO had learned. Individual publishers have since held one-on-one meetings with GAO staff to provide greater detail on the development and marketing of textbooks. GAO's report is expected in late summer 2005.

The start of the 2004–2005 academic year in September generated renewed interest in the PIRG report. To obtain solid data to answer PIRG's assertions, AAP's higher education publishers approved two surveys. The first was a study of U.S. college faculty members to determine their views on textbooks and instructional materials. The nationwide survey, carried out by Zogby International, surveyed faculty members at four-year and community colleges during December 2004. The results indicated overwhelming faculty support of textbooks and supplemental materials. Zogby was slated to release its findings in January 2005. The second study will analyze student attitudes toward textbooks and other instructional materials and will be released in 2005.

Accessibility Issues

The "accessibility" issue gained momentum in 2004 as legislatures accelerated efforts to pass legislation requiring publishers to provide instructional materials to postsecondary institutions in specified digital formats that would require the publishers to make expensive conversions. Ed McCoyd, AAP's director of digital policy, and the Critical Issues Task Force (CITF) worked with representatives of colleges, organizations for the disabled, and legislatures to determine the best ways to meet college students' accessibility needs while protecting publishers' rights.

In New York, McCoyd and CITF members worked with the State Department of Education to develop guidelines for the implementation of New York's Chapter 219, an accessible-files statute passed in 2003 and amended in 2004. CITF submitted proposed guidelines for implementation of SB 6501, a new postsecondary accessible-files law in Washington State; participated in the Higher Ed E-Text Working Group of the Open eBook Forum (OeBF) to develop solutions for the creation, distribution, tracking, security, and delivery of electronic text files to disabled students; and began drafting a piece of model legislation for possible use in states where legislation is being drafted.

CITF will continue to deal with these issues in 2005. Activities will include working with the New York State Education Department to hold training sessions to explain the requirements created by Chapter 219 and to discuss the implementation guidelines developed by the advisory group, being part of a panel at the Washington Association on Postsecondary Education and Disability meeting to discuss AAP's proposed implementation guidelines for Washington State's postsecondary accessible textbook files legislation, and participating in the OeBF working group's upcoming projects.

In October executives from member houses met in New York with the current and incoming presidents of NACS and that association's senior staff to discuss ways to bridge the communications gap that had been exacerbated by the PIRG report and subsequent media coverage. It was agreed at the meeting that the dialogue would continue between the two organizations, and there has been continuing communication.

International Committee

The International Committee represents a broad cross-section of the AAP membership with interests in overseas markets. Deborah Wiley (John Wiley & Sons) chaired the committee in 2004.

The committee's International Sales Subcommittee focuses on issues relating to the export of mass market paperbacks. Composed of export sales directors from AAP member houses and chaired in 2004 by David Wolfson (HarperCollins), the subcommittee's major concerns are piracy, on-line export, and distribution and currency issues associated with export sales to the U.S. military, overseas schools, hotels, bookstores, and airports. The group works to facilitate publisher/bookseller/distributor dialogue at major book fairs.

International Copyright Protection

AAP conducts a vigorous international program designed to combat the worldwide problem of copyright piracy, increase fair access to foreign markets, and strengthen foreign copyright law regimes. Deborah Wiley (John Wiley & Sons) chaired the International Copyright Protection Committee in 2004.

In carrying out its overseas antipiracy campaign, AAP and the regional representatives of member publishers work in close alliance and in cooperation with appropriate local government authorities. As a consequence, book pirates in six Asian countries felt the long reach of AAP's antipiracy campaign in a series of raids coordinated by the association and carried out from January through early May. AAP and its members are pursuing appropriate legal action growing out of the raids.

- In South Korea in March 2004 foreign and local publishers joined forces for the first time in years, conducting raids under the authority of the Korean Ministry of Culture and Tourism and the Korea Reprographic and Transmission Rights Center. The enforcement actions took place near 16 universities in Seoul and Kyunggi Province. AAP conducted more raids on March 8 in Suwon City, in conjunction with the Suwon Prosecutor's Office, targeting two copy shops on a university campus. The shop owners were arrested and 148 infringing copies of books were seized. The following week, AAP and authorities raided the manufacturing facility owned by the copy shop owner, resulting in the seizure of master computer files and some 1,000 illegal copies of books published by eight AAP members—Cambridge University Press, Elsevier, Thomson Learning, McGraw-Hill, Houghton Mifflin, Oxford University Press, Pearson Education, and John Wiley & Sons. South Korean enforcement continued in April with a raid, in conjunction with the Ansan Prosecutor's Office and local authorities, on a copy shop and a warehouse facility operated by the copy shop owner, who subsequently admitted to having copied more than 25,000 books over a two-year period. Seized were more than 5,000 infringing copies of titles belonging to Pearson Education, John Wiley & Sons, Elsevier, Thomson Learning, McGraw-Hill, Oxford University Press, and others.

- AAP worked with local authorities to raid two copy shops in the Philippines in May, resulting in the confiscation of 16 photocopying machines and the seizure of infringing copies, including titles published by McGraw-Hill and Elsevier.
- In Hong Kong, between February and April, the Hong Kong Customs and Excise Bureau carried out raids on seven copy shops with cooperation from AAP and its member companies. A total of more than 1,200 infringing copies, eight copy machines, and six binding machines were seized in the raids, and three arrests resulted.
- Coordinated raids on ten copy shops in five cities in Taiwan were undertaken in March in conjunction with the Ministry of Justice and local officials. More than 228 illegal books were seized.
- Raids were carried out in January on three copy shops in Malaysia, near Taylor's University in Subang Jaya. Undertaken in cooperation with officials from the Malaysian Ministry of Domestic Trade and Consumer Affairs and AAP local counsel, the raids resulted in the confiscation of eight copying machines and three binding machines and the seizure of 500 sets of infringing books.
- In Singapore, two copy shops were raided in January in conjunction with local authorities and counsel. One of the same facilities was raided again in April, along with two other operations, yielding 39 infringing copies and 30 original books being used for copying purposes.

Following the successful spring raids, the International Copyright Enforcement program kept up the pressure with a series of actions over the summer and into the fall of 2004.

- AAP continued its ongoing collaboration with the Hong Kong Reprographic Rights and Licensing Society and the Hong Kong Customs and Excise Department to raid establishments at the beginning of the 2004 fall academic term. Authorities raided 12 photocopy establishments throughout Hong Kong in September, seizing 404 infringing copies and eight photocopying machines worth more than $15,000.
- Working with local counsel and the Ministry of Domestic Trade and Consumer Affairs, AAP raided a Malaysian copy shop in July, seizing more than 30 infringing books.
- AAP continued to closely monitor China's preparations regarding commitments to open certain aspects of its market to foreign publishers (a prerequisite to China joining the World Trade Organization).

- With the cooperation of local counsel, the National Bureau of Investigation, and local police, AAP raided several photocopy establishments in the Philippines in July, targeting street stalls in Manila selling a wide variety of infringing books in both printed and CD-ROM format. Police seized hundreds of infringing titles owned by a number of AAP members. AAP also conducted a market survey in academically oriented Baguio City, 250 kilometers north of Manila, giving AAP members some insight into photocopying practices outside Manila's metropolitan area.

- Successes achieved earlier in the year in South Korea continued into September, as publishers greeted the new academic term with raids on two copy shops near Seoul. Authorities seized 124 copies of infringing books belonging to John Wiley & Sons, Thomson Learning, Pearson Education, McGraw-Hill, Elsevier, and a number of others. AAP also completed a comprehensive survey of students' photocopying habits in South Korea.

- Working with the Taiwan Book Publishers Association and the Ministry of Justice, AAP began the academic year with island-wide raids in October.

- AAP members prepared for more aggressive enforcement in Thailand, conducting extensive research on educational exemptions in the Thailand Copyright Act and carrying out market surveys with which to garner evidence of photocopying, print piracy, and illegal translations. The information obtained is useful to support lobbying efforts aimed at U.S. and Thai officials in conjunction with the ongoing U.S./Thailand Free Trade Agreement negotiations.

- The Office of the United States Trade Representative (USTR) released its annual Special 301 Report for 2004 on May 3, detailing the adequacy and effectiveness of intellectual property protection in selected countries worldwide. AAP, as a member of the International Intellectual Property Alliance (IIPA), had submitted specific recommendations to USTR on February 14 as part of the annual review. AAP members estimate annual losses of more than $500 million as a result of copyright piracy. The Special 301 process is one of several tools available to the U.S. government to help industries fight to improve legislative and enforcement efforts in key markets in an attempt to stem losses from copyright piracy.

International Freedom to Publish

AAP's International Freedom to Publish (IFTP) Committee defends and promotes freedom of written communication worldwide. The committee monitors human rights issues and provides moral support and practical assistance to publishers and authors outside the United States who are denied basic freedoms. The committee carries on its work in close cooperation with other human rights groups, including Human Rights Watch and PEN American Center, and maintains its own Web site at http://www.IFTPC.org. Hal Fessenden (Viking Penguin) assumed the chairmanship of the committee in 2004.

IFTP continued to provide Judith Krug, director of ALA's Office for Intellectual Freedom, with information on book censorship around the world. This listing of books that are banned in their own country but available in the United

States forms the new international section of the *Banned Books Week Resource Guide* published by ALA.

In spring 2003 IFTP established the Jeri Laber International Freedom to Publish Award, to be given annually to a book publisher outside the United States who has demonstrated courage in the face of political persecution. The award, which carries a $10,000 cash prize, is named in honor of human rights activist Jeri Laber, one of the committee's founding members, who continues to direct its work as a consultant to AAP. In spring 2004 the committee announced that the award would go to Joesoef Isak, an Indonesian publisher who, in the face of political obstacles and personal danger, continued to publish important works of literature, resisting attempts by the Indonesian government to suppress them. The award was presented on April 20 at the PEN gala in New York.

In December 2004, in an effort to encourage and increase the diversity of literary works being published in the United States, the committee offered U.S. publishers a unique opportunity to bring the work of three gifted Iranian authors to an American audience.

In consultation with a distinguished group of scholars and writers in the United States and Iran, IFTP selected three contemporary Iranian novels and commissioned partial translations and a precis of each. The novels are *The Drowned* by Moniru Ravanipur (translated by M. R. Ghanoonparvar), *The Empty Palace of Soluch* by Mahmoud Dawlatabadi (translated by Judith M. Wilks), and *Christine and Kid* by Houshang Golshiri (translated by Roxanne Zand). To support U.S. publication of the works, the committee secured funding to provide $10,000 to the U.S. publisher contracting for English-language rights for each work, half of which would be used for further costs of translation and half to be used for promotion and publicity. In making its announcement, the committee noted that despite the confusion over U.S. Treasury Department Office of Foreign Assets Control (OFAC) regulations regarding publishing involving Iran and other countries under the U.S. trade embargo, the revised regulations issued on December 15 seems to indicate that whatever the outcome of the lawsuit, U.S. publishers would not need to seek government permission to publish the Iranian novels offered.

IFTP members, at their own expense, undertake missions to meet with writers, publishers, human rights activists, and others in areas where freedom of expression is seriously threatened. Committee chairman Fessenden and member Wendy Wolfe (Viking Penguin) undertook such a mission to Turkey in late 2004. Accompanied by historian Joshua Brown and journalist Dawn Drzal, they spent five days in Istanbul meeting with a wide variety of book publishers, journalists, NGOs, and human rights activists. They found the mood to be generally optimistic but wary. While the crisis mode of a few years ago has abated, in large measure as a result of Turkey's determination to conform to guidelines to gain entrance into the European Union, publishers—especially those who deal with Kurdish issues—are still being detained, fined, and harassed, Wolfe reported.

Postal

AAP's Postal Committee coordinates activity in the area of postal rates and regulations, monitors developments at the U.S. Postal Service (USPS) and the independent Postal Rate Commission, and intervenes on the industry's behalf in formal proceedings before the commission. The committee also directs AAP lobbying activities on postal issues. Paul DeGuisti (McGraw Hill) chaired the committee in 2004.

On April 14 AAP submitted formal comments to Congress on the report of a special presidential commission on postal reform. In a letter to Rep. Tom Davis (R-Va.), chairman of the House Committee on Government Reform, AAP welcomed the opportunity to express the publishing industry's views on the findings and recommendations put forth in "Embracing the Future: Making the Tough Choices to Preserve Universal Mail Service," a report issued last summer by the President's Commission on the United States Postal Service.

The letter expressed strong support for the commission's recommendation that the postal service continue to focus on its "core value"—universal service. "Fundamentally, AAP believes that the Postal Service needs to adhere to its primary mission of providing universal service at affordable rates for all classes of mail," the letter stated. AAP also expressed full support for the commission's recommendation against privatizing the postal service.

While expressing concern over the commission's recommendations regarding the rate-making process, fearing that they will not produce "the relief long sought by mailers," AAP did voice general support for the recommendations regarding increased work-sharing and the use of negotiated service agreements, and agreed with the commission's conclusion that significant efforts must be made to reduce labor costs.

Leaders on postal matters in the House and Senate introduced similar comprehensive postal reform proposals. Both bills featured reforms that would (1) shift rate regulation from its current litigation model to one tied to the Consumer Price Index for market-dominant products while permitting flexible market pricing for competitive products, (2) define "postal services" and limit USPS offering of nonpostal products, and (3) give the renamed Postal Regulatory Commission subpoena power and broaden its regulatory and oversight functions.

The respective committees of jurisdiction in the House and Senate gave their approval to this legislation, but neither bill received floor consideration. While this was due, in part, to scheduling problems in an election year plagued by partisan gridlock and a limited calendar, it was also attributable to opposition from major postal unions and continuing concerns of the Bush administration regarding the cost of the legislation. Both bills would have transferred pension cost obligations connected with military service credit for postal employees from USPS to the Treasury, in addition to abolishing the 2006 escrow requirement in order to delay the need for a rate case. The administration also questioned whether the legislation went far enough in providing transparency to prevent cross-subsidization of competitive products with monopoly product revenue, as well as in providing flexibility to reduce high labor costs.

Professional/Scholarly Publishing

The Professional/Scholarly Publishing (PSP) Division is composed of AAP members who publish books, journals, looseleaf, and electronic products in technology, science, medicine, business, law, humanities, the behavioral sciences, and scholarly reference. Professional societies and university presses play an important role in the division. Marc Brodsky (American Institute of Physics) chaired the division in 2004.

The 2004 PSP Annual Conference, with the theme "Value in a Culture of Open Access," was held in Washington in February. Featured speakers were Hal Varian of the School of Information Management and Systems, University of California–Berkeley, and Robert L. Park of the American Physical Society, a professor at the University of Maryland and author of *Voodoo Science* (Oxford University Press). Prior to the opening of the meeting, the division's Electronic Information Committee sponsored a preconference seminar on "Financial and Organizational Impacts of Electronic Publishing."

The division sponsors an awards program, open only to AAP/PSP members, to acknowledge outstanding achievements in professional, scholarly, and reference publishing. At the 28th annual PSP awards, the R. R. Hawkins Award for the outstanding professional/scholarly work of the year went to Oxford University Press for *Developmental Plasticity and Evolution* by Mary Jane West-Eberhard. In addition, book awards were presented in more than 30 subject categories, in design and production, and in journal and electronic publishing.

Among the division's educational activities in 2004, the PSP Journals Committee sponsored two roundtable discussions, "Consortia and Site Licenses 101: Building and Maintaining a Relationship" and "Consortia and Site Licenses 102: What's In It for Me? A Librarian's Perspective." The PSP Books Committee created the first Books Boot Camp to educate people with less than three years' experience in professional, scholarly, and academic book publishing.

The PSP Public Issues Task Force has developed and maintains a PSP "issues glossary," an online reference and research tool for PSP members. The glossary is available through a new link on the home page of the PSP Web site (http://www.pspcentral.org).

The PSP Executive Council directs an ongoing campaign to improve relationships between the PSP communities and user and scholar communities. The campaign explains the role that PSP members play and the value they add to the dissemination of scholarly information. In 2004 the council established a Public Relations Committee, chaired by Susan Spilka (Wiley), and a Books Committee, chaired by Elizabeth Schacht (McGraw-Hill).

Opposing OFAC Rules

Calling the Treasury Department's continued attempts to exert control over publishing activities involving information and literature from countries under U.S. trade embargo a violation of the essential right of all Americans to learn about the world, PSP joined with the Association of American University Presses, PEN American Center, and Arcade Publishing in a lawsuit filed in September in U.S. District Court in New York against the department's Office of Foreign Assets Control (OFAC). The plaintiffs asked the court to strike down OFAC regulations that require publishers and authors to seek a license from the government to perform the routine activities necessary to publish in the United States foreign literature from embargoed countries such as Iran, Cuba, and Sudan. A series of OFAC rulings has created uncertainty and confusion among publishers fearful of incurring prison sentences of up to ten years or fines of up to $1 million per violation.

Those rulings and the regulations they interpret mandate that U.S. publishers (1) may not enter into transactions for works not yet fully completed, (2) may not provide "substantive or artistic alterations or enhancements" to the works, and (3) may not promote or market either new or previously existing works from the affected countries.

The regulations were challenged on the grounds that they violate the Trading with the Enemy Act (TWEA) and the International Emergency Economic Powers Act (IEEPA) as well as the First Amendment. TWEA and IEEPA were twice amended by Congress (in the Berman Amendment and the Free Trade in Ideas Amendment) to make clear that the statutes exempt transactions involving "information and informational materials" from trade embargoes. The complaint charges that the OFAC regulations directly contravene the statutes and threaten constitutionally protected rights of publishers, authors, and the public. A separate suit filed by Nobel laureate and human rights activist Shirin Ebadi was subsequently joined to the original challenge.

Despite the government's repeated assertions that it was not reacting to the lawsuit, the Treasury Department issued revised regulations on December 15, 2004, stipulating that U.S. publishers do not need to seek a specific license to engage in "all transactions necessary and ordinarily incident to the publishing and marketing of manuscripts, books, journals, and newspapers in paper or electronic format," with individuals in Cuba, Iran, and Sudan, but AAP believes this was done in an obvious attempt to defuse the legal challenge. According to the Treasury Department's announcement, "the new rule enables U.S. persons to freely engage in most ordinary publishing activities with persons in Cuba, Iran and Sudan, while maintaining restrictions on certain interactions with the governments, government officials, and people acting on behalf of the governments of those countries." Although acknowledged as a "step in the right direction," the revised regulations remain problematic for the plaintiffs and for U.S. Rep. Howard Berman (D-Calif.), the sponsor of the original "free trade in ideas" legislation. In a statement issued on December 16, Berman rejected the revised regulations "as a desperate attempt to head off mounting legal and political pressure" and not "a serious effort to rationalize an indefensible and counterproductive policy," taking strong exception to the fact that "the regulations continue to represent that the government has the inherent legal authority to regulate these activities." "In America, publishers do not need permission," he said. Berman also pointed out that the revised regulations apply only to publishing, and not to other creative works. "Why should it be okay for a publisher to commission a book from an Iranian dissident, but not for a film studio to work with a Sudanese filmmaker, or a recording studio to collaborate with a Cuban musician? This makes absolutely no sense." At the time this report was prepared, lawyers for the government and the plaintiffs were looking at the effect, if any, of the new regulations on the lawsuit.

Open Access

Another major issue for AAP's Professional/Scholarly Publishers in 2004 was the rise of the "open access" business model for scientific journal publications, a model espoused by some academic librarians and scholars and several user groups. Supporting open access, the National Institutes of Health (NIH) formally called for scientists who receive NIH grants to post their papers on NIH's PubMed Central Web site within six months of publication in a peer-reviewed journal, or sooner if the publisher agrees. PSP publishers and scientific societies argue that such a "one-size-fits-all" requirement would put many small scientific societies—particularly those that publish infrequently—out of business. PSP publishers also strongly object to a government-mandated, regulated open access model, preferring to let the marketplace determine what authors, readers, and users want and need. Publishers also point out that never has there been more access to more information, citing the page "How to Find Medical Information" on the PSP Web site. Rather than NIH posting the actual author manuscript, scholarly publishers want a link from the PubMed Central site to the publishers' Web sites, arguing that posting the manuscript would create confusion and impugn the scientific record, given that the author version would be different from the final version published in journals.

Resources for the Book Publishing Industry

AAP publishes a variety of resources for the book publishing industry, including *Survey on Compensation and Personnel Practices in the Book Publishing Industry,* which is widely regarded as a comprehensive and reliable source of data in this area. AAP's Compensation Committee, composed of senior compensation and human resources professionals, met throughout the year to create job descriptions and manage the survey process.

AAP also publishes industry statistics for all segments of book publishing, on a monthly and annual basis. Committees in the areas of consumer, trade, higher education, and professional publishing met throughout 2004 to revise the program and develop a seamless system for the distribution of electronic monthly reports.

School Division

The School Division is concerned with publishing for the elementary and secondary school (K–12) market. The division works to enhance the role of instructional materials in the education process, to maintain categorical funding for instructional materials and increase the funds available for the purchase of these materials, to simplify and rationalize the process of state adoptions for instructional materials, and to generally improve the climate in which education publishers do business. The division serves as a bridge between the publishing industry and the education community, promoting the cause of education at the national and state level, and working closely with an effective lobbying network in key adoption states. Kathryn Costello (Pearson Education) chaired the division in 2004.

In 2004 California was without question the state where education publishers faced their greatest problems but also where they achieved many important successes. As the year began, California continued to struggle with its budget crisis and a projected $17 billion deficit. Newly elected Governor Arnold Schwarzenegger struck a deal on the budget, which would have eliminated all categorical funding for instructional materials. In addition, AAP fought more than half a dozen pieces of legislation that, among other things, would have set price limits on textbooks, lengthened the book-adoption cycle from six to eight years, required publishers to sell classroom sets of textbooks at a 30 percent discount off the bid price, and required an electronic version of all adopted instructional materials—all of which would have serious negative consequences for member publishers. AAP worked with the California Department of Education to mitigate the most onerous requirements in adopting regulations to implement a new state law mandating weight limits on textbooks.

Intensive lobbying efforts by AAP and member companies succeeded in retaining categorical funding for instructional materials. In a significant funding victory for publishers, a total of $558 million was approved for instructional materials, including $138 million resulting from settlement of the *Williams* v. *State of California* lawsuit.

While AAP was not directly involved in *Williams* v. *State of California,* the School Division monitored it closely because of the critical role that the issue of instructional materials played in the lawsuit. The Williams plaintiffs claimed that the state of California had failed to provide students in some school districts with the essentials for the adequate education guaranteed by the state's constitution. Among the conditions cited by the plaintiffs were an absence of textbooks and other educationally necessary curricular materials, outdated or defaced textbooks, and inadequate supplies of textbooks and other instructional materials, all resulting in the inability of teachers to properly assign homework. The state of California ultimately settled the lawsuit, and as part of the settlement agreement gave $138 million in additional funds for textbooks and instructional materials to the neediest schools.

The case established good legal precedent to support claims that adequate supplies of up-to-date textbooks and instructional materials are essential in providing the opportunity for adequate education required by most state constitutions.

AAP members played a leading role in the U.S. Department of Education's Technical Advisory panel, which developed the National Instructional Materials Accessibility Standard (NIMAS) file specification. AAP will also be involved with the group charged with implementing and overseeing the NIMAS file format.

Also in 2004 AAP created a special task force to assist publishers and their customers in establishing uniform standards for ordering textbooks electronically. States and local districts are increasingly adopting electronic ordering systems for school supplies including textbooks and other instructional materials. AAP's goal is to ensure that such ordering systems can easily interact with publishers' order fulfillment systems.

Textbook publishers and their customers will face a challenge in 2007 as publishers move from 10- to 13-digit ISBN numbers. AAP has a task force to alert major customers to this pending change and help make the transition as smooth as possible (see the section on Enabling Technologies above).

In fall 2004 the School Division held another of its "summits" in Washington, D.C. Bringing together more than 140 publishers, educators, public officials, and academic experts, the 2004 summit focused on the issue of teaching students for whom English is a second language.

AAP lobbying efforts in Florida resulted in a number of major victories. Funding for instructional materials was increased by $7.5 million, 3.3 percent above the previous year. In order to achieve this, the division fought to restore a $35 million reduction in textbook funding by Florida's House Education Committee. AAP lobbying succeeded in getting the Florida Department of Education to extend from 30 to 45 days the time within which, once they receive an order from the depository, publishers must deliver instructional materials before a penalty for late delivery is imposed.

AAP was involved in the following additional state action:

- In Alabama AAP joined with the state depository to successfully lobby to increase textbook funding by $36.7 million from the year before.
- In New York AAP lobbyists were victorious in preserving categorical funding for instructional materials despite efforts by the speaker of the state Assembly to permit computer hardware and other technology equipment to be purchased with instructional-materials funds. New York also restored $187,000 in state aid for textbooks that was cut the year before.
- In Georgia AAP worked with the state Department of Education to get publishers more time to revise their textbooks after the State Board of Education made many last-minute changes in the state's social studies curriculum standards. AAP was also successful in heading off legislation in Georgia that would have required publishers to offer an electronic version of all adopted instructional materials.

Although the Texas legislature was not in session during 2004, the School Division was actively working there on a number of issues of importance to educational publishers. Both the state House and Senate education committees held hearings and reviewed the state's textbook adoption process, developing recommendations for changes to the system.

In addition, the Texas Education Agency was undergoing a "sunset" review by another legislative committee. This review also looked at the textbook adoption process and has recommended some potential changes to the process.

The Texas State Board of Education also reviewed and rewrote some of its rules related to textbooks and the adoption process.

Standardized Testing

Another area of interest to AAP members is standardized testing. The School Division Test Committee was active on a number of issues relating to implementation of the testing and accountability provisions of the No Child Left Behind Act (NCLB). This committee met with U.S. Department of Education officials on implementing the peer review process required for each state's testing and accountability plans to ensure compliance with NCLB.

The test committee also produced a publication titled *The War on Standardized Testing—Kill the Messenger* by Richard P. Phelps. This brochure, based on a book of the same name, was distributed to policymakers to help them better understand the growing debate about the use of standardized tests in the nation's schools.

Trade Publishing

AAP's Trade Publishing group is made up of publishers of fiction, general non-fiction, poetry, children's literature, religion, and reference publications, in hard-cover, paperback, and electronic formats. Robert Miller (Hyperion) chaired the committee in 2004.

The committee's major areas of attention in 2004 included the development of an Adopt-a-School Partnership with the New York City Department of Education, partnership with the National Endowment for the Arts (NEA) to encourage reading, promotion of books by and for Latinos, expanding the Get Caught Reading campaign, serving AAP's Smaller and Independent Publishers, and overseeing AAP's Diversity and Recruit and Retain initiative, including the Young to Publishing Group.

The New York Adopt-a-School program, which will be expanded in 2005 to include more schools, gives publishers the opportunity to support city schools by providing the specific resources that schools request through AAP, including books, guidance in developing literary publications and yearbooks, author visits and events, field trips to publishing houses, and participation in career fairs at schools.

The NEA partnership will help raise awareness and mobilize public action in the face of a decline in book readership, which NEA documented in a report released in July. The report, "Reading at Risk," points to an ongoing and significant drop in the number of readers in the United States, especially readers of fiction, poetry, and drama. As part of the partnership, AAP provided a $19,000 grant to NEA and participated in a nationwide series of "Reading at Risk" presentations at which professional NEA staff members discussed the study and its implications with groups of educators, policymakers, and scholars at meetings across the country. In 2005 AAP is working with NEA on a second phase of the initiative, to encourage and assist cities across the United States in implementing "city reads" programs, and to develop a series of literary events.

AAP formed the Publishing for Latinos Task Force in 2002 in response to the burgeoning market for books for Latinos. In 2004 the task force continued its efforts to heighten awareness and understanding, among consumers and within the publishing industry, of books published by and for Latinos. The task force published a brochure, *Publishing Latino Voices for America,* that highlights titles by Latino authors in English and Spanish. The task force launched Latino Books Month in June, and as part of that effort developed a recommended-reading list for children and adults that was published in *USA Today* and distributed to libraries, schools, and bookstores. The task force was also active at BookExpo America, with a panel discussion on the Spanish-language marketplace.

The Trade Publishing group also works on the AAP honors program, nominating and electing a candidate from outside the publishing industry to be honored at the AAP Annual Meeting for helping to promote U.S. books and authors. Selection of the 2004 honoree reflected the growing attention being paid to the Latino book. The honors went to television journalist Jorge Ramos for his work in promoting books, authors, and reading in the Latino community.

AAP's Smaller and Independent Publishing (SIP) Committee held a seminar in conjunction with the Annual Meeting, open to both AAP members and nonmembers, with a special session at the Library of Congress and panels addressing such topics as promotion, special sales, foreign rights, and increasing productivity. The SIP committee also held a conference in September in New York with panels on topics including the state of the industry, building a successful publishing house, Internet opportunities, library markets, and media strategies. This group met throughout 2004 to discuss issues pertaining to the smaller independent publishing house.

AAP also launched the Miriam Bass Award for Creativity in Independent Publishing in 2004 to honor her many contributions to the independent book publishing community. The award, which carries a $5,000 prize funded by Rowman & Littlefield and the National Book Network, was given to Alexander G. Skutt, President of McBooks Press, Inc.

Young to Publishing Group

The Young to Publishing Group (YPG) continued its expansion in 2004, growing to 700 members from publishing houses around the country. YPG satellite chapters in Boston and San Diego grew as well, and the brown bag lunch series in New York featured speakers from across the industry. The group hosted several social events in 2004 and continued to publish the popular *YPG Newsletter*.

2004 Annual Meeting

Corporate strategy guru Kosmo Kalliarekos was the keynote speaker at AAP's 2004 Annual Meeting at the Hyatt Regency Hotel in Washington, D.C. Kalliarekos, senior partner at the Parthenon Group, focused on the weaknesses and strengths of existing business models in three main areas of publishing—educational (K–12 and postsecondary), professional, and trade.

Other speakers included Lynne Cheney, author and wife of Vice President Dick Cheney, and U.S. Rep. George Miller (D-Calif.), the ranking Democrat on the House Education and Workforce Committee, who urged the industry not to look at expressions of concern over the cost of instructional materials as "an adversarial situation," but rather as an opportunity to expand the dialogue with faculty and students.

The 28th annual Curtis Benjamin Award for Creative Publishing was presented to Jean Feiwel, senior vice president of Scholastic, Inc., and editor-in-chief and publisher of Scholastic Books.

The membership approved an operating budget of $6,697,955 for fiscal year 2004–2005, with $4,439,930 allocated to Core (including the three committees serving the Trade, Higher Education, and International constituencies) and $2,258,025 to the two divisions ($1,443,725 for School Division and $814,300 for PSP).

American Booksellers Association

828 S. Broadway, Tarrytown, NY 10591
914-591-2665, e-mail info@bookweb.org
World Wide Web http://www.BookWeb.org

Jill Perlstein
Director of Marketing

Founded in 1900, the American Booksellers Association (ABA) is a not-for-profit trade organization devoted to meeting the needs of its core members—independently owned bookstores with storefront locations—by providing advocacy, opportunities for peer interaction, education, support services, and new business models. ABA actively supports free speech, literacy, and programs that encourage reading. The association, headquartered in Tarrytown, New York, also hosts the annual ABA Convention in conjunction with the BookExpo America (BEA) trade show each spring.

Although ABA provides programs and services to others in the bookselling industry, its primary focus is on its core members, which provide influential and vital links between authors, readers, publishers, and the community.

Key components of ABA's strategic plan, "Independent Bookselling: Competing in a Changing World," for the years 2003–2007 follow.

Goal 1—Provide independent professional booksellers with access to the education, information, and business services they need to succeed in a changing world.

To fulfill this goal, ABA organized a full day of educational programming at its 2004 annual convention. ABACUS (a financial benchmark study by and for independent booksellers) was completed, and—as part of its continuing efforts toward helping its members become better businesspeople—ABA offered budgeting and monitoring workshops. It sponsored a school for prospective and new booksellers at BEA and at other times during the year in conjunction with the bookstore training and consulting group Paz & Associates. The association also offered education programs at 10 regional trade shows and conducted 14 informational sessions on the new Book Sense gift card program.

Fifteen bookseller forums were organized and facilitated during the year in various regions of the country, drawing 293 booksellers from 195 stores.

ABA's Web site, BookWeb.org, continued to be the principal source for association news, services, and resources, in addition to providing networking opportunities via the online forums "Idea Exchange" and "Ask ABA." The Web site offers links to related industry organizations and companies as well as educational materials and professional development resources.

Bookselling This Week (*BTW*) offers weekly news dispatches e-mailed to more than 12,000 subscribers. *BTW* features breaking industry news, in-depth articles, the latest developments in ABA's Book Sense marketing program, and other association news. *BTW* is available at http://news.BookWeb.org.

The ABA *Book Buyer's Handbook,* available online to ABA members at BookWeb.org, is a prime source for publishers' discount schedules, return policies, trade terms, and more, including links to publishers' Web sites and e-mail addresses for ordering and general information. Fully searchable and continually updated, it also lists the latest information on publishers' special offers.

Goal II—Serve as the voice of professional independent booksellers and advocate on their behalf on such issues as free expression, trade practices, literacy, and community activism.

Along with the American Booksellers Foundation for Free Expression (ABFFE), ABA defended the public's right to read, leading the effort on the Freedom to Read Protection Act by working to repeal parts of the USA Patriot Act through the Campaign for Reader Privacy. It also joined forces with ABFFE in building coalitions with a wide range of companies and associations to promote free expression. Additional information on ABFFE and its activities is found later in this report.

ABA also maintained trade-practice vigilance through ongoing meetings with publishers, wholesalers, and others. The association worked with other industry leaders in the continued fight for sales tax equity. It also disseminated information on the positive economic impact of locally owned businesses and continued to build alliances with like-minded independent retailers in other fields. The report *Liveable City,* analyzing the economic effects of local merchants versus chain retailers, was prepared and disseminated with the cooperation of the Austin, Texas-based organization Liveable City, the American Independent Business Alliance (AMIBA), the economic analysis firm Civic Economics, Waterloo Records, and the independent Austin bookseller BookPeople.

In addition, ABA supported the following industry-wide observances: the Association of American Publishers' "Get Caught Reading" advertising campaign and Latino Book Month, the Audio Publishers Association's audiobook promotion, the National Book Festival, the American Library Association's Teen Read Week, the Children's Book Council's National Children's Book Week, the Academy of American Poets' National Poetry Month, the Small Press Center's Small Press Month, and ABFFE's Banned Books Week.

Goal III—Promote the value of independent booksellers as a group through Book Sense and other cooperative activities.

"Book Sense—Independent Bookstores for Independent Minds" is ABA's national branding and marketing program for independent bookstores. The program involves more than 1,200 participating locations in all 50 states and Bermuda, Puerto Rico, and the Virgin Islands.

The main components of the Book Sense program are

- Book Sense Picks (formerly the Book Sense 76), a monthly list of recommendations from booksellers across the country
- The Book Sense Bestseller List, compiled from nearly 500 reporting stores each week
- Book Sense Book of the Year Awards
- The Book Sense Gift Card Program, launched in October 2003, under which consumers can purchase and redeem gift cards in more than 300 locations in 46 states and on some bookstores' Web sites

- BookSense.com, an e-commerce Web site that allows participating stores to offer a secure shopping environment and now hosts more than 240 independent bookstores' Web sites

In celebration of Book Sense's fifth anniversary, a marketing campaign promoting the Best of Book Sense from the First Five Years was introduced. A Best Books ballot included 223 adult and 148 children's titles, culled from the Book Sense 76 lists of the past five years plus any additional Book Sense Book of the Year winners, was sent to members, and from those results a final list of ten adult fiction, five adult nonfiction, and ten children's titles were chosen as the Best of Book Sense.

The Best of Book Sense sparked an initiative by Newmarket Press, Book Sense Marketing Director Mark Nichols, and the Book Sense team to publish *Book Sense Best Books: 125 Favorite Books Recommended by Independent Booksellers.* The foreword was written by bestselling author Barbara Kingsolver and the introduction by ABA CEO Avin Mark Domnitz.

Goal IV—Foster development of new and enhanced business models, systems, and services.

ABA continued to offer Business Management Services to its members. These include LIBRIS, which offers casualty and property insurance for booksellers and liability insurance for publishers; FedEx Ground and FedEx Express service, shipping small and large packages; CDW Computer Centers, providing member access to computer hardware at reduced prices; and Bank of America, offering members competitive rates for credit card processing.

American Booksellers Foundation for Free Expression

The American Booksellers Foundation for Free Expression (ABFFE), the bookseller's voice in the fight against censorship, is active in defense of the privacy of bookstore customers. In early 2004 it coordinated the release of a statement by more than 40 organizations and 80 companies in the book and library community demanding that Congress restore protections for the privacy of bookstore and library records that were eliminated by the USA Patriot Act. In July a majority of the members of the U.S. House of Representatives voted to cut funding for bookstore and library records searches under the act (the effort failed, however, when a number of representatives were persuaded to switch their votes). ABFFE also filed an amicus brief in an American Civil Liberties Union case challenging a provision of the USA Patriot Act that gives the FBI virtually unlimited power to search Internet records, including bookstore and library records, in national-security investigations. A district court struck down the provision, but the government has appealed.

ABFFE spoke out on two other federal issues. It joined the protest over the growth of secrecy in the federal government by filing an amicus brief in a case involving U.S. Vice President Dick Cheney's effort to keep secret the names of the members of an "energy task force" that he formed soon after he took office. ABFFE also issued a statement condemning the Treasury Department's Office of

Foreign Asset Control (OFAC) for asserting that publishers must obtain a government license to publish works by authors living in countries that are the subject of an American trade embargo. Publishers and writers have filed suit in an effort to overturn this policy.

ABFFE challenged efforts in three states to ban the display of First Amendment-protected books and magazines in bookstores. With support from ABFFE, the Mountains and Plains Booksellers Association and Colorado booksellers defeated a bill in the Colorado legislature that could have forced booksellers to segregate "harmful to minors" material in a section of their stores inaccessible to minors. ABFFE also participated in two legal challenges to state laws passed in 2003 that regulate the display of "harmful" material. In September a Michigan judge ruled that the new law there would not apply to the kind of books that are found in most bookstores; in November a judge declared an Arkansas display law unconstitutional (the state of Arkansas was appealing the decision).

ABFFE was also a plaintiff in two cases that vindicated the First Amendment rights of booksellers in cyberspace. In July the U.S. Supreme Court upheld an injunction barring the enforcement of the Child Online Protection Act (COPA), a federal law that bans the display of "harmful" sexual material on commercial Internet sites. However, a final decision on the constitutionality of COPA may be several years away because the court also ordered further research on one of the issues in the case. Meanwhile, acting in a case filed by ABFFE and others, a federal judge struck down a similar restriction that had been passed by the Vermont legislature.

ABFFE has its headquarters at 139 Fulton St., Suite 302, New York, NY 10038. Chris Finan is its president. The telephone number is 212-587-4025 and the organization's Web address is http://www.abffe.org.

Association of Research Libraries

21 Dupont Circle N.W., Washington, DC 20036
202-296-2296, e-mail arlhq@arl.org
World Wide Web http://www.arl.org

Duane E. Webster
Executive Director

The Association of Research Libraries (ARL) represents 123 principal research libraries serving major research institutions in the United States and Canada. ARL influences the changing environment of scholarly communication and the public policies that affect research libraries and the communities they serve. ARL pursues this mission by advancing the goals of its member research libraries, providing leadership in public and information policy to the scholarly and higher education communities, fostering the exchange of ideas and expertise, and shaping a future environment that leverages its interests with those of allied organizations.

ARL fulfills its mission and builds its programs through a set of strategic objectives. Each February the ARL Board of Directors identifies the priorities that the association staff and standing committees will address in the coming year. To guide ARL programs in 2004, the board adopted the following priorities:

- *Positioning ARL for the Future.* Initiate a strategic planning process for ARL that comprehends a review and discussion of the future agendas of its member libraries and articulates a vision of how the association can support and advance those agendas; based on the findings, review ARL's current mission, objectives, and governance structure to determine if changes are appropriate for repositioning the ARL agenda.

- *Information Policies.* Provide leadership in advocacy and educational efforts within the North American and international research and educational communities to influence legislation, institutional policies, and individual practices in the areas of intellectual property, copyright, privacy and other individual rights, and other information policies.

- *Scholarly Communication.* Encourage and support development of and access to discipline- and institution-based repositories for the work of scholars and explore other strategies that could lead to more cost-effective models for managing scholarly communication in a global environment, including open access publishing models.

- *Collections, Access, Preservation, and Technology.* Promote tools, policies, and programs to ensure enduring, cost-effective, and integrated access to research materials from all parts of the world, in all formats, for readers working both near and at a distance from those resources and, to the greatest extent possible, support delivery of these resources and related services to the user's desktop.

- *Staffing and Management.* Develop effective strategies to assist member libraries in recruiting, retaining, and developing talented staff in a changing demographic and economic environment.

• *Performance Measures.* Develop new approaches and models for measuring and improving library service effectiveness, diversity, and leadership.

In November 2004 the ARL Board of Directors approved a new Strategic Plan for 2005–2009 that named the three top priorities—scholarly communication; information policies; and teaching, learning, and research—that will provide the conceptual framework for the association's future programmatic efforts.

Scholarly Communication

The Office of Scholarly Communication (OSC) undertakes activities to understand and influence the forces affecting the production, dissemination, and use of scholarly and scientific information. OSC seeks to promote innovative, creative, and affordable ways of sharing scholarly findings, particularly through championing evolving electronic techniques for recording and disseminating academic and research scholarship.

To this end, ARL has been a strong supporter of the National Institutes of Health (NIH) initiative to provide free public access to research articles resulting from NIH-funded research and has written letters of support to both NIH and Congress. ARL also worked with other organizations to establish the Alliance for Taxpayer Access, a broad-based coalition that supports reforms to make publicly funded biomedical research accessible to the public.

To build a better understanding of the evolving publishing environment, OSC tracks mergers and acquisitions in the scholarly publishing arena and works with antitrust authorities to raise awareness of library concerns about the increased consolidation of the publishing industry. The Information Access Alliance (IAA), formed by ARL and six other library organizations, continues to push for a revised analysis of publisher mergers. The June 2004 issue of *College & Research Libraries News* (*C&RL News*) featured "Information Access Alliance: Challenging Anticompetitive Behavior in Academic Publishing" (see http://www.ala.org/ala/acrl/acrlpubs/crlnews/backissues2004/june04/iaa.htm) and an invitational workshop on antitrust issues in academic publishing was planned for early 2005.

The August 2004 issue of *ARL: A Bimonthly Report* reported on the results of two recent surveys of ARL members' subscriptions to electronic journals. ARL undertook these surveys in 2002 and 2003 to better understand the issues libraries are facing in ensuring the effective use of electronic resources and in dealing with e-journal licensing. The paper focuses on the seven commercial and seven nonprofit publishers whose electronic titles were most subscribed to by the responding libraries. It confirms that libraries need to be tough when negotiating uses of the resources they need and notes that support from others on campus has been critical to the ability to cancel journal bundles and/or negotiate better terms with publishers.

In celebration of the Year of the University Press, ARL and the Association of American University Presses (AAUP) encouraged their members to highlight the important role presses play in the scholarly communications process. The ARL Scholarly Communication Committee held a briefing at the May Membership Meeting in which participants shared ideas for successful local programming. In addition, the April issue of *ARL: A Bimonthly Report* featured the article "Learning to Work Together—The Libraries and the University Press at Penn State."

Federal Relations and Information Policy

ARL's Federal Relations and Information Policy program monitors activities resulting from the legislative, regulatory, or operating practices of international and domestic government agencies and other relevant bodies on matters of concern to research libraries. The program analyzes and responds to federal information policies and influences federal action on issues relating to research libraries. It examines issues of importance to the development of research libraries and develops ARL positions on issues that reflect the needs and interests of members. Through the Canadian Association of Research Libraries (CARL), the program monitors Canadian policies on copyright, intellectual property, and access to government information.

As part of ARL's interest in raising awareness of issues associated with copyright and intellectual property management, the federal relations program joined with others in the public and private sectors during 2004 in filing a number of friend-of-the-court briefs. On the legislative front, the program worked to overcome the current prohibitions in the 1998 Digital Millennium Copyright Act that impair the ability of libraries to make fair use of digital materials, preserve digital content, and take full advantage of other library exemptions under federal copyright law. ARL has actively supported H.R. 107, the Digital Media Consumers' Rights Act, which aims to restore the proper balance in copyright law between the rights of copyright users and the rights of copyright owners.

The U.S. House of Representatives Committee on Appropriations recommended that NIH implement a policy of making research articles available to the public free of charge on PubMedCentral within six months of publication in a peer-reviewed scientific journal. At the October ARL Membership Meeting, the federal relations program convened a panel to discuss "Enhanced Public Access to NIH Research." David Lipman, director of the National Center for Biotechnology Information (National Library of Medicine, NIH) spoke about the issues involved in the NIH proposal and Heather Joseph, president and chief operating officer of BioOne, talked about the concerns that scholarly publishers have about the impact of the NIH proposal on their budgets.

ARL, along with the Government Printing Office and others in the library community, is re-examining the role of the Federal Depository Library Program in the networked environment. The ARL Information Policies Committee proposed no-fee, public domain, and perpetual online access to historical documents via a national, cooperative, digitization initiative. More than 50 ARL libraries expressed interest in participating in the U.S. Government Document Digitization Program and a number of ARL institutions are engaged in pilot projects testing various aspects of the initiative.

Collections

The ARL collections capability pursues initiatives to assist in developing the collections of ARL libraries and enhancing access to scholarly resources, regardless of their location. The focus is both local and collaborative, covering a variety of strategies, including access to digital resources, and collaborating with other organizations in collections-related projects, both within North America and internationally.

Discussions on revising the annual ARL Statistics survey unearthed differing opinions regarding the way collections can and should be described in an environment in which multiple formats abound, collaborations flourish, and electronic content offers new ways of doing business. Representatives of three ARL standing committees (Statistics and Measurement, Collections and Access, and Membership) formed the Task Force on Measuring Collections to define the issues and propose solutions for measuring research library collections.

The ARL Special Collections Task Force's white paper "Education and Training for Careers in Special Collections" found a pressing need for recruitment, education, and training of special collections professionals at all career levels. It calls for the articulation of professional competencies needed for positions in special collections, the development of a shared culture among librarians and archivists, and encouragement of the provision of opportunities for development and professional growth for mid-career practitioners. The white paper is available at http://www.arl.org/collect/spcoll/SCTF.ED.pdf.

The October 2004 Status Report of the Special Collections Task Force summarizes progress in exposing hidden collections, education and training, developing assessment tools, and outreach work (see http://www.arl.org/collect/spcoll/tforce/status0904.html). One of the major recommendations issuing from the "Exposing Hidden Collections" conference was the identification and promotion of a shared commitment to certain themes and subjects to encourage cooperative action among libraries and archives to process this material. The follow-up survey elicited descriptions of 466 discrete collections held by 99 institutions with interest in working cooperatively to process these special collections (see http://db.arl.org/SCsurvey/search.html).

Access Services

The ARL Access capability undertakes activities to support resource sharing among research libraries in the electronic environment and to improve access to research information resources while minimizing costs for libraries. This capability works to strengthen interlibrary loan and document delivery performance (ILL/DD), interoperability among library systems, cooperative cataloging programs, and policies that increase user access to information both on site and remotely.

The Assessing ILL/DD Services Study was ARL's third effort in the past decade to measure the performance of interlibrary loan operations in North American libraries. The study tracked the performance of mediated and user-initiated ILL/DD operations in 72 research, academic, and special libraries, including unit cost, fill rate, and turnaround time. The final report of the study, "Assessing ILL/DD Services: New Cost-Effective Alternatives," confirmed that, in general, user-initiated services have lower unit costs, higher fill rates, and faster turnaround times than mediated ILL/DD services. The report also identified high-performing borrowing and lending operations and laid out strategies for libraries seeking to improve local services. Key findings are available at http://www.arl.org/arl/pr/ill_dd_study.html.

The ARL Portal Applications Working Group completed its work by issuing a report, "The Current State of Portal Applications in ARL Libraries," that summarizes the survey of ARL members on the application of search engines and other resource integration tools and services (http://www.arl.org/access/portal/PAWGfinalrpt.pdf). Seven ARL member institutions collaborating with Fretwell-Downing, Inc. completed the first phase of the project and have either released the software campuswide or are starting with limited releases.

The Association of American Universities/ARL Global Resources Network (GRN) Advisory Committee, composed of leaders from both libraries and the academy, endorsed the "Goals and Outcomes, 2004–2007" (http://www.arl.org/collect/grp/GRNgoals.html), approved a five-year transition budget, approved the "GRN Roles and Responsibilities," and agreed on the "Principles for Participation and Fees." At the May 2004 ARL Business Meeting, members reviewed the May 2004 Update Report and discussed the options for a 2005 financial strategy for the GRN. On June 1 ARL transferred to the Center for Research Libraries (CRL) the responsibility for overseeing the administrative functions for the German Resources Project and the Latin Americanist Research Resources Project. An agreement, approved by the ARL and CRL boards, provides ARL funding to CRL for oversight and operational support for GRN projects that choose such support.

Preservation

ARL's Preservation capability pursues initiatives that support member libraries' efforts to provide enduring access to their research collections. Strategies include encouraging and strengthening broad-based participation in national preservation efforts in the United States and Canada, supporting development of preservation programs within member libraries, supporting effective bibliographic control of preservation-related processes, encouraging development of preservation information resources, and monitoring technological developments that may have an impact on preservation goals.

The ARL Board endorsed digitization as an acceptable preservation reformatting option and released the paper "Recognizing Digitization as a Preservation Reformatting Method" (see http://www.arl.org/preserv/digit_final.html) as a first step in building community support and facilitating the development of policies, standards, guidelines, and best practices. The Council on Library and Information Resources, the Coalition for Networked Information (CNI), OCLC (the Online Computer Library Center), and RLG (formerly the Research Libraries Group) have joined ARL in supporting digitization as a viable preservation reformatting strategy. To reach out to the preservation community, Bill Gosling (university librarian, Michigan), Sherry Byrne (preservation librarian, Chicago), and Carla Montori (preservation librarian, Michigan) led a panel discussion on the ARL digitization paper at the ALA PARS (Preservation and Reformatting section) meeting in June and presented a briefing session on digitization as a reformatting strategy at the CNI task force meeting in December. The fall issue of *Microform & Imaging Review* was devoted to the ARL digitization paper, with comments from a number of preservation experts.

Sound Savings: Preserving Audio Collections presents the papers and recommendations from the 2003 conference held at the University of Texas at Austin. The two-and-a-half day program featured talks by experts on topics ranging from assessing the preservation needs of audio collections to creating, preserving, and making publicly available digitally reformatted audio recordings. Conference attendees—critical stakeholders of the future of audio preservation—articulated seven areas for future action to move the field effectively forward.

Diversity

The ARL Diversity Program supports and extends efforts within member institutions to promote and develop library staff and leaders who are representative of a diverse population. These efforts include the recruitment and retention of library personnel from a variety of backgrounds, particularly from groups traditionally under-represented in the academic and research library work force, and the creation of professional development opportunities and networks that help promote diverse leadership.

The Initiative to Recruit a Diverse Workforce grants stipends to students from minority backgrounds to assist in the completion of a master's degree in library science (MLS). The initiative is funded by a $413,000 grant from the Institute of Museum and Library Services (IMLS) and by contributions from 59 ARL member libraries. Recipients agree to a minimum two-year working relationship with an ARL library upon graduation. Fifteen participants were selected for the 2004–2006 program, which offers a two-year stipend of $10,000, a mentoring relationship, and leadership training for MLS candidates from under-represented groups.

The Diversity program also administers the Leadership and Career Development Program to prepare talented mid-career minority librarians for leadership roles in the research library community. Twenty-two celebrated the completion of their program at the ALA Annual Conference in June 2004. This class, Intentional Visionaries, was the fourth set of minority librarians to participate in the program. Eighty librarians have taken part in the program since its inception in 1997. In December 2003 the ARL Diversity program launched the MLS Graduate Student Résumé Database and as of fall 2004 the database had 180 active candidates. Library administrators and human resource specialists are encouraged to visit the database to view resumes for vacant positions (http://db.arl.org/careers/res/submit.html).

To encourage minority undergraduates to consider a career in library sciences, ARL and Washington University in St. Louis developed a pilot program that brought minority undergraduate students from Lincoln University to intern in the John M. Olin Library at Washington University for ten weeks during summer 2004.

ARL and the National Association for the Advancement of Colored People (NAACP) collaborated to commemorate the 50th anniversary of the landmark civil rights case *Brown* v. *Board of Education.* ARL librarians created an annotated bibliography for the NAACP's national programmatic tool kit (http://www.arl.org/diversity/naacp.html).

Office of Leadership and Management Services

Over the past 30 years, the Office of Leadership and Management Services (OLMS) has designed and facilitated effective and well-attended library staff development programs. OLMS offers services that help research libraries serve their clientele through the training and strategic deployment of talented individuals.

In 2004 ARL developed two pilot projects to recruit and train librarians at an advanced level. With funding from IMLS, ARL is piloting "ARL Academy: Careers in Academic and Research Libraries" in partnership with three library schools—Catholic University of America, University of North Carolina at Chapel Hill, and Simmons College. The goal is to recruit, educate, and train 45 master's-level students who already have an advanced degree in another profession or discipline. Another major OLMS initiative is the Research Library Leadership Fellows (RLLF) Program, designed to meet the increasing demands for succession planning at very large research libraries. This pilot executive leadership program—sponsored by five ARL member libraries: University of California, Los Angeles; Columbia University; University of Illinois at Urbana-Champaign; University of Texas at Austin; and University of Washington—offers a dramatically new approach to preparing the next generation of directors of research libraries. Twenty-one individuals, representing a broad array of ARL institutions, were selected to participate in the 2004–2006 RLLF Program.

The ARL/OLMS Online Lyceum provides affordable and innovative professional development opportunities via distance learning technology, bringing together core topics and current issues to keep participants up to date on recent trends and practices in libraries. In 2004 OLMS and the Medical Library Association began offering reciprocal membership benefits for Web-based continuing education courses. In addition, the Online Lyceum hosted a number of webcasts, including a popular live, interactive Web presentation on institutional repositories and their increasing importance to scholarly communication cosponsored by the Scholarly Publishing and Academic Resources Coalition and CARL. In conjunction with the Statistics and Measurement Program, two webcasts were produced to educate library staff about the importance of networked library statistics (e-metrics) and to inform viewers about the ARL Statistics Data Collection process.

OLMS publishes current information on library operating practices and policies in its SPEC Kit series. These important resources serve as guides for libraries as they face ever-changing management problems. Recent publications include *SP285 Library Services in Non-Library Spaces, SP284 Security in*

Special Collections, SP283 Grant Coordination, SP282 Managing Electronic Resources, SP281 The Information Commons, and *SP280 Library User Surveys*.

Statistics and Measurement

The ARL Statistics and Measurement program seeks to describe and measure the performance of research libraries and their contributions to teaching, research, scholarship, and community service. The program also includes the New Measures Initiative, a series of projects and services to develop new approaches for describing and evaluating library service effectiveness, diversity, and leadership.

The program publishes a series of annual publications that describe salary compensation and institutional trends for research libraries, including the *ARL Annual Salary Survey, ARL Statistics, ARL Academic Law Library Statistics, ARL Academic Health Sciences Library Statistics*, and the *ARL Preservation Statistics*. The ARL Interactive Statistics, hosted at the Geostat Center of the University of Virginia, continues to be one of the most popular ways of accessing the annual data collected by ARL. The ranked lists allow users to pick from a list of more than 30 variables for data reports (see http://fisher.lib.virginia.edu/arl/index.html).

Through a variety of New Measures Initiatives, ARL continues to develop new assessment methods for understanding changes in user behavior. The LibQUAL+ survey, now in its fifth year, measures user perceptions of, and satisfaction with, library services. More than 200 libraries participated in the survey in 2004 and more than 112,000 responses were gathered and analyzed (see http://www.libqual.org). Kent State University Libraries and ARL are cosponsoring the Project for Standardized Assessment of Information Literacy Skills (SAILS), designed to develop an instrument for programmatic-level assessment of information literacy skills that is valid and credible to university administrators and other academic personnel. Seventy-six North American libraries of all types registered to participate in Phase III from August 2004 through July 2005 (http://sails.lms.kent.edu).

In addition to trying to understand library-user behavior in the familiar library environment, developmental work is under way for understanding user demographics, purpose of use, perceptions, and expectations in the digital library environment. DigiQUAL, partially supported by a grant from the National Science Foundation, National Science Digital Library (NSF/NSDL), is developing an instrument to assess the dimensions of library service quality in the digital environment. An item bank for survey testing purposes at different digital library settings is being developed. MINES (Measuring the Impact of Networked Electronic Services) is a protocol for evaluating purpose of use and collecting user demographics for specific uses of electronic resources through a pop-up survey. ARL has contracted with the Ontario Council of University Libraries (OCUL) to implement the protocol and analyze the data collected from June 2004 to May 2005.

"Mainstreaming New Measures," a special double issue of *ARL: A Bimonthly Report* (October–December 2003), documents a rich and varied set of new measures projects undertaken by ARL in recent years. The publication *Libraries Act on their LibQUAL+ Findings: From Data to Action* highlights the continued efforts of participating libraries to use the LibQUAL+ survey data to assess and evaluate their service quality, resource allocations, staffing, technology, and policies.

Office of Research and Development

The ARL Office of Research and Development (ORD) consolidates the administration of grants and grant-supported projects administered by ARL. The major goal within this capability is to identify and match ARL projects that support the research library community's mission with sources of external funding. Another initiative of ORD is the ARL Visiting Program Officer (VPO) program that provides an opportunity for a staff member in an ARL member library to assume responsibility for carrying out part or all of a project for ARL. It provides a very visible professional development opportunity for an outstanding staff member and serves the membership as a whole by extending the capacity of ARL to undertake additional activities. VPOs for 2004 included Evelyn Frangakis (New York Public Library), Dan Hazen (Harvard College), Eudora Loh (UCLA), Carla Montori (University of Michigan), Judith Panitch (North Carolina, Chapel Hill), Jill Thomas (Boston College), Steve Hiller (University of Washington), and Jim Self (University of Virginia).

Communications, External Relations, and Publications

The Communications, External Relations, and Publications capabilities are engaged in many activities that support ARL's objectives. These include acquainting ARL members with current, important developments of interest to research libraries; influencing policy and decision makers within the higher education, research, and scholarly communities; educating academic communities about issues relating to scholarly communication and research libraries; and providing the library community with information about activities in which research libraries are engaged. Using print and electronic media as well as direct outreach, the communications program disseminates information about ARL to the higher education and scholarly communities, as well as to ARL member institutions. The publications program offers a full range of timely, accurate, and informative resources to assist library and higher education communities in their efforts to improve the delivery of scholarly communication. ARL makes many of its titles available electronically via the World Wide Web; some are available in excerpted form for preview before purchase and others are available in their entirety. News about ARL activities and publications is available through the arl-announce listserv, distributed widely to the library and higher education communities. To subscribe, visit http://www.arl.org/arl/pr/subscription.html.

Association Governance and Membership Activities

Representatives of 110 ARL libraries met in Tucson at ARL's 144th Membership Meeting in May to consider systemic changes in research institutions. The meeting, hosted by the University of Arizona, focused on new concepts of teaching, learning, and research that are now possible through the creative application of information technologies.

A total of 111 member institutions were represented at ARL's 145th Membership Meeting, held in Washington, D.C., in October. The meeting focused on governance review and the new strategic plan for the association. Diana Oblinger, vice-president of EDUCAUSE, gave the keynote address on "Library Roles in the National Learning Infrastructure Initiative." On October 14, Ann Wolpert (MIT) began her term as ARL president. The board elected Brian E. C. Schottlaender as vice-president/president-elect and the membership elected three new board members: Joyce Garnett (Western Ontario), Tom Leonard (California, Berkeley), and Suzanne Thorin (Indiana).

SPARC

21 Dupont Circle N.W., Suite 800
Washington, DC 20036
202-296-2296, e-mail sparc@arl.org
World Wide Web http://www.arl.org/sparc

Richard Johnson
SPARC Enterprise Director

SPARC (the Scholarly Publishing and Academic Resources Coalition) is an initiative begun in 1997 by the Association of Research Libraries (ARL) to correct market dysfunctions in the scholarly publishing system. It is now a worldwide alliance of more than 200 research institutions, libraries, and organizations. SPARC Europe, a partner initiative, shares SPARC's goals and focuses on European actions and interests; it has a membership of 111 institutions and organizations.

Market failures have helped drive the cost of scholarly journals (especially in science, technology, and medicine) to insupportably high levels that inhibit the advancement of scholarship. SPARC is a catalyst for action intended to stimulate the emergence of new systems that expand dissemination of research and reduce financial pressures on libraries. Working in concert with other stakeholders, SPARC encourages use of the networked digital environment to serve scholarship. SPARC recognizes that the central functions of scholarly publishing (registration, certification, dissemination, archiving, and rewarding), traditionally aggregated in printed journals, can become increasingly disaggregated in the digital networked environment, enabling performance of the functions to be distributed among multiple agents. The availability of technical standards, protocols, or legal instruments ensures that information can be shared across the network and offers the possibility of breaking the monopoly on control of research content that is the source of much of the dysfunction in the current system. As a practical matter, SPARC program activity also recognizes that, in some areas, the interests of academe may be best served in the near term by affordable subscription-supported publishing solutions.

SPARC's strategies seek to reduce the economic barriers to access, sharing, and use of scholarship and, in particular, scientific research. The focus of SPARC's activities has been on science, although not to the exclusion of the social sciences and humanities. Rising STM (scientific, technical, and medical) journal prices have had a serious negative impact on library operations and scientific research. Through its projects and educational work, SPARC has been able to demonstrate that it is possible to develop high-quality, affordable competitors to high-price commercial journals. Through its advocacy work, SPARC has also encouraged motivated editors and authors to be their own agents of change.

To stimulate change, SPARC tries to

- Educate stakeholders about the problems facing scholarly communication and the opportunities for change
- Advocate policy changes that support the potential of the digital networked environment to advance scholarly communication and that recog-

nize that dissemination is an essential, inseparable component of the scientific research process
- Incubate real-world demonstrations of business and publishing models that benefit scholarship and academe

Since 2002 SPARC's highest priority has been to promote the goal of open access. As defined by the Budapest Open Access Initiative (http://www.soros.org/openaccess), open access refers to "works that are created with no expectation of direct monetary return and made available at no cost to the reader on the public Internet for purposes of education and research." The initiative stated that open access would "permit users to read, download, copy, distribute, print, search, or link to the full texts of works, crawl them for indexing, pass them as data to software, or use them for any other lawful purpose, without financial, legal, or technical barriers other than those inseparable from gaining access to the Internet itself. Open access does not apply to materials for which the authors expect to generate revenue." There are two complementary strategies for achieving open access:

- Self-archiving—scholars depositing their refereed journal articles in open electronic archives
- Open access journals—charging no subscription fees, these journals provide barrier-free access to scholarly articles

Through its education, advocacy, and incubation activities, SPARC promotes both strategies.

Key Activities in 2004

SPARC's priorities for 2004 were raising the public policy profile of scholarly communication issues, promoting open access strategies for research dissemination, and advancing community control of scholarly publishing.

Public Policy

To address its highest priority—public policy—SPARC developed a working plan for the SPARC-organized Open Access Working Group (OAWG)[1] to advocate for open access to federally funded scientific research. This plan included public relations activities and working with federal agencies and Congress to educate key individuals about the need for National Institutes of Health (NIH) investigators to deposit an electronic version of the author's final manuscript of NIH-funded research in PubMed Central, NIH's digital repository. The concomitant benefits and the legal foundation were also emphasized. To address

1. Organizations represented in OAWG are the American Association of Law Libraries, the Association of Academic Health Sciences Libraries, the Association of College and Research Libraries, the American Library Association, the Association of Research Libraries, Creative Commons, the Medical Library Association, the Open Society Institute, Public Knowledge, the Public Library of Science, and SPARC. The Special Libraries Association joins with OAWG in support of selected matters.

OAWG's major advocacy initiative in support of taxpayer access to research funded by NIH, SPARC facilitated the creation of the Alliance for Taxpayer Access (http://www.taxpayeraccess.org) as a collective voice for patient organizations, libraries, and others. The effort yielded extensive press coverage of open access issues and of the NIH proposal, including articles in *USA Today,* the *Washington Post,* the *Baltimore Sun,* United Press International, the *Economist,* and a range of industry periodicals. In addition, a group of 25 Nobel Prize winners wrote an open letter of support for open access to NIH research that received significant press coverage. The issue was also featured as part of an "NBC Nightly News" segment, "Fleecing of America." SPARC generated a number of public statements on the issue, including one to the British House of Commons inquiry into scientific publishing; an early 2004 letter to the NIH director urging NIH to support publishing in open access journals as part of its research grants; and a response to the "Washington DC Principles for Free Access to Science" (http://www.dcprinciples.org).

Institutional Repositories

To continue to promote interest in institutional repositories as a tool for scholars to deposit their research, SPARC joined with ARL's Office of Leadership and Management Services (ARL/OLMS) and the Canadian Association of Research Libraries (CARL) to present a webcast on institutional repositories. SPARC and SPARC Europe then organized a highly successful institutional repository conference in November 2004. Nearly 300 participants from 11 countries attended the two-day event, which featured a combination of presentations and discussions.

Copyright

Working with Professor Michael Carroll of Villanova law school and Creative Commons, SPARC drafted two model addenda to publishers' copyright agreements with authors of articles. They are designed to reserve rights for authors and users of the articles. The addenda were the basis for a workshop on copyright at Kent State University in October 2004 and will be the basis of a national webcast in 2005.

Publishing Collaborations

With its publisher partner programs, SPARC supports partners that introduce price and service competition. The SPARC Alternative Program encourages and supports projects that represent a direct and strong competitive alternative to existing high-priced titles in important established STM fields. The Leading Edge program encourages and supports projects that represent a paradigm shift in technology use, introduce an innovative business model, and/or meet the scholarly and research information needs of an emerging or fast-growing field. Scientific Communities partnerships recognize the importance of building new outlets for scientific communication around the broad information needs of the communities of users they serve. The program supports development of nonprofit information aggregations or portals that serve specified scientific communities by providing high-quality, reasonably priced access to peer-reviewed research and other needed content from a variety of sources or publishers. In 2004 several titles reported increased content, higher impact factors, and positive reviews, all of which confirm that high-quality journals can be produced cost-effectively.

SPARC developed and formalized several publisher partnerships in 2004. With the International Coalition of Library Consortia (ICOLC) and the Southeastern Library Network (SOLINET), SPARC is encouraging library support for long-term open access to the *Stanford Encyclopedia of Philosophy* (*SEP*). The initiative aims to build an endowment sufficient to cover *SEP*'s continuing operating costs and to sustain its free accessibility on the public Internet. SPARC designated *SEP* a SPARC publisher partner and is encouraging its members to use funds allocated from their SPARC purchase commitments to help build the *SEP* endowment. The new partnership between SPARC and *SEP* allows SPARC to broaden its support for open access publication and continue to reach into the humanities.

Optics Express, published by the Optical Society of America (OSA), has been selected as a SPARC Leading Edge partner. The partnership is intended to call attention to the potential for open access publishing in the society-publishing environment. Ranked in the top ten optics journals by ISI, *Optics Express* was among the first peer-reviewed open access journals in the marketplace and has played an increasingly important role for the society since the journal's founding in 1997. From the beginning, *Optics Express* has been an "author-centric" journal. Its online peer-review process and rapid turnaround from submission to publication—averaging 47 days—were groundbreaking steps. Free publication of color figures and acceptance of all kinds of multimedia also helped advance the journal's standing among authors. Its early commitment to electronic-only publication was a bold step to keep operating costs down.

The E-print Network, a free service of the U.S. Department of Energy (DOE) Office of Scientific and Technical Information (OSTI), was chosen as a SPARC Scientific Communities publisher partner. The E-print Network reveals research mainly in physics, but also in chemistry, biology and life sciences, materials science, nuclear sciences and engineering, energy research, computer and information technologies, and other disciplines. The E-print Network provides deep Web search capability that combines full-text searching through PDF documents residing on Web sites with a distributed search across e-print databases. Users of the E-print Network, which was first launched as PrePRINT Network in January 2000, can perform full-text searches on more than 16,000 Web sites and in 39 major databases of e-prints from around the world. Close to 20 million pages of full text are available to users at no charge, and the network offers a weekly alert service that provides patron notification of new documents as well as links to 2,300 scientific societies.

Academic Serials in Communication—Unified System (ASCUS) was designated a SPARC Leading Edge publishing partner in 2004. ASCUS will be a comprehensive database and online portal for journals and other research and reference publications in the communication field, published by leading academic societies and associations. Digital content will include current and back issues of journals and over the long term may grow to include other types of valuable publications and resources. The enterprise will be operated by a not-for-profit organization governed by officials from the University at Albany, the Communication Institute for Online Scholarship (CIOS), ARL, SPARC, and representatives of participating scholarly and professional societies.

Labor: Studies in Working-Class History of the Americas is the first humanities journal endorsed by SPARC. The inaugural issue became available in 2004 and was created by the walkout of the entire editorial board of *Labor History*. The journal expands the field's scope beyond traditional labor history scholarship and its primary focus on social movements and institutions. The journal gives equal attention to other critical labor systems (agricultural work, slavery, unpaid and domestic labor, the informal sector, the professions, and so forth) and social contexts (race, gender, class, ethnicity, and so forth) in the United States and Latin America.

Several other publishing partners made strides in 2004.

- Lund University Libraries launched the second phase of the Directory of Open Access Journals (DOAJ), a Leading Edge partner. The new version includes records at the article level and a search functionality that allows users to search articles in open access journals. More than 1,400 journals are in the database and more than 350 can be searched at the article level. DOAJ is also Open URL-compliant, the metadata is freely available for downloading, and the service supports the OAI protocol for metadata harvesting (OAI-PMH).

- The Public Library of Science launched its open access medical journal, *PLoS Medicine,* in October 2004. This Leading Edge publisher also designed an institutional membership program for individual libraries, universities, companies, and other institutions, as well as consortia.

- BioOne, a SPARC Scientific Community, reported that for 2004 it saw a large increase in Web traffic—up 190 percent from 2003. There was strong growth in the number of institutions that support BioOne, both in the United States and internationally. BioOne also developed or enhanced programs with JSTOR, CrossRef, LOCKSS, National Science Digital Library, Cambridge Scientific Abstracts, OAIster, and a number of regional OCLC (Online Computer Library Center) consortia networks. It expanded programs for less-developed countries through HINARI, eIFL, and AGORA. Through its advisory groups and meetings, BioOne facilitated communication among publishers and librarians.

- Finland was the first country to make a nationwide commitment to support open access publishing with BioMed Central, a SPARC Leading Edge partner.

- Another Leading Edge partner, *New Journal of Physics* (*NJP*), finalized an agreement with Britain's Joint Information Systems Committee (JISC) to ensure that all British-university-affiliated researchers can publish in the journal free of charge.

- The Scientific Communities partner eScholarship provided University of California faculty with open access to peer-reviewed series and journals online by making available a new peer-review capability.

- Eight new journals joined the SPARC Scientific Communities partner Project Euclid Prime collection, bringing the total number of titles in the aggregation to 18. In addition, Project Euclid and Duke University Press introduced DMJ 100, the online digital archive of the *Duke Mathematical Journal,* Vols. 1–100.

SPARC also provides business consulting services and advice to numerous journal editors seeking alternative publishing channels and faculty seeking to launch new journals. Marketing support for publishing partners is provided through SPARC publications and through exhibit space at library events.

Education and Advocacy

SPARC publishes *SPARC E-news,* an electronic newsletter that appears several times a year and provides information on current SPARC activities, open access news highlights, publishing partner information, an industry roundup, workshop and conference information, and recent articles of interest.

SPARC continued support for Peter Suber's popular monthly *SPARC Open Access Newsletter* and the associated Open Access News blog (http://www.earlham.edu/~peters/fos/fosblog.html). It contains news and analysis of open access and has become a major source of information about the movement. Two important brochures were made available in 2004—a major revision and reformatting of the *Create Change* brochure and a new brochure for use on campuses to educate faculty about the benefits of open access. SPARC staff made presentations at dozens of conferences, meetings, and campus symposia and prepared papers for major scientific and humanities conferences.

The recurring SPARC/ACRL (Association of College and Research Libraries) forums were held at American Library Association (ALA) meetings. The ALA Midwinter Meeting featured Helen Doyle (Public Library of Science), Henry Hagedorn (*Journal of Insect Science*), and Joe Branin (Ohio State University) addressing "Open Access: Getting From Here to There." The ALA Annual Conference program "Scholarly Communication in the Humanities: Does Open Access Apply?" included speakers John Unsworth (University of Illinois at Urbana-Champaign), James Niessen (H-Net: Humanities and Social Science OnLine), and Edward Zalta (*Stanford Encyclopedia of Philosophy*).

Priorities for 2005

Given the rapidly increasing pace of changes in scholarly communication, particularly in the area of open access, SPARC will be continuing its focus on advancing the acceptance of open access publishing models in 2005. The program activities will attempt to build a broader understanding of the opportunities open access will provide. Key program strategies will again focus on public policy issues through increased advocacy activities by building on the NIH experience. SPARC will again lead and manage the policy advocacy work of the Open Access Working Group and serve as the organizational focal point for the Alliance for Taxpayer Access. This activity in 2005 will focus on ensuring that the NIH policy results in a satisfactory outcome, and that the policy is extended to other U.S. Department of Health and Human Service agencies. SPARC will also support adoption of government-wide policies on public access to published results of publicly funded research.

Industry concentration results in rapid escalation of the price of information in schools and universities and negative effects from publisher bundling practices. With other members of the Information Access Alliance (an organization composed of several key U.S. library associations), SPARC will work to help increase understanding of antitrust issues in journal publishing.

Based on preliminary work done in 2004, SPARC will introduce a promotional brochure and publicity surrounding a model contract addendum that journal article authors can append to publishers' copyright agreements to assert key rights, including deposit in institutional repositories.

Since so many of the changes in scholarly communication and the debate on open access publishing affect societies, SPARC will develop a white paper that offers a clearer understanding of the challenges currently facing society publishers and the adequacy or inadequacy of the prevalent publishing model to respond to those challenges for various types of society publishers. This analysis will provide the context for an evaluation of alternative publisher models available to society publishers and the benefits those models offer publishing societies, their members, and other academic community stakeholders. It will also form the basis for stimulating a broader community discussion of the future of societies.

SPARC will continue its campus education and grassroots advocacy efforts by cosponsoring the Create Change program and Web site (http://www.create change.org) and by collaborating with ACRL and other organizations.

Governance

The initiative's activities are guided by the SPARC Steering Committee, with representatives elected annually for staggered terms by SPARC's voting membership. The committee meets regularly at ALA conferences and by conference call. Three new members were elected to serve three-year terms (January 2005–December 2007): Nancy Baker (University of Iowa), Gwendolyn Ebbett (University of Windsor), and Joyce Ogburn (University of Washington). In addition, the SPARC voting members re-elected Deborah Carver (University of Oregon) for another term. Two individuals accepted appointments for three-year terms: Carolynne Presser (University of Manitoba), representing the Canadian Association of Research Libraries, and J. S. M ("Bas") Savenije (University of Utrecht), representing SPARC Europe. Steering Committee members whose terms concluded in December were Cynthia Archer (York University), Ross Atkinson (Cornell University), and Ken Frazier (University of Wisconsin–Madison). Other Steering Committee members include James Neal (Columbia University, chair), Sherrie Bergman (Bowdoin College), Sam Demas (Carleton College), Ray English (Oberlin College), Sarah Michalak (University of North Carolina at Chapel Hill), and MacKenzie Smith (MIT).

SPARC Europe was formally incorporated as Stichting SPARC Europe in the Netherlands. It is led by David Prosser, director. Its board consists of members representing many countries within the European library community: Chris Bailey (Britain), Raymond Bérard (France), Raf Dekeyser (Belgium), Rick Johnson (SPARC U.S.A.), Bulent Karasozen (Turkey), Elmar Mittler (Germany), Erland Kolding Nielsen (Denmark), Bas Savenije (Netherlands), and Paul Sheehan (Ireland).

Council on Library and Information Resources

1755 Massachusetts Ave. N.W., Suite 500, Washington, DC 20036-2124
202-939-4754, fax 202-939-4765
World Wide Web http://www.clir.org

Kathlin Smith
Director of Communications

The Council on Library and Information Resources (CLIR) is an independent, nonprofit organization dedicated to improving the management of information for research, teaching, and learning. CLIR's mission is to expand access to information, however recorded and preserved, as a public good.

CLIR pursues three primary goals in support of its mission:

- To foster new approaches to the management of digital and nondigital information resources so that they will be available in the future
- To expand leadership capacity in the information professions
- To analyze changes in the information landscape and help practitioners prepare for them

CLIR's program staff develops projects, programs, and publications to advance these goals.

CLIR is supported by fees from sponsoring institutions, grants from public and private foundations, contracts with federal agencies, and donations from individuals. CLIR's board establishes policy, oversees the investment of funds, sets goals, and approves strategies for their achievement.

In 2004 Nancy Davenport was appointed CLIR president, succeeding interim directors Richard Detweiler and Sally Sinn. Davenport previously was with the Library of Congress, most recently serving as its director of acquisitions.

CLIR's current activities are represented in six program areas: resources for scholarship, preservation awareness, digital libraries, economics of information, leadership, and international developments.

Resources for Scholarship

New forms of scholarship and publishing are radically changing the relationships among those who create, store, and distribute information. In the digital realm, scholars and librarians are forming new intellectual partnerships. Creators and publishers of scholarly resources are seeing how their decisions—not just those of libraries and archives—influence access to information resources now and in the future. Through a variety of activities, CLIR aims to inform and support new partnerships in scholarly communication.

Survey of the State of Audio Collections in Academic Libraries

In 2004 CLIR published a report of a survey of original audio collections in academic libraries. The libraries surveyed included members of the Association of

Research Libraries and smaller research libraries at liberal arts colleges that are members of the Oberlin Group. The purposes of the survey were to identify audio recordings of historic importance that exist on university and college campuses, to assess their state of preservation and accessibility, and to highlight barriers to access. The report cites several things that are needed to help ensure the preservation of most of the rare and historically important audio collections on campus. They include new approaches to intellectual and inventory control, new technologies for audio-signal capture and automatic metadata extraction, new programs of education and training, and more aggressive access policies under the fair-use exemption of the copyright law for education. The report also recommends that a cadre of librarians and archivists with expertise in recorded-sound formats and genres be developed and supported.

Cyberinfrastructure Commission

Digital technologies are no longer merely tools that enhance established research methodologies; rather, they are the foundation for new infrastructures for knowledge creation. A recent National Science Foundation (NSF) report, *Revolutionizing Science and Engineering Through Cyberinfrastructure,* argues for large-scale investments across all disciplines to develop the shared technology infrastructure that will support expanded capacities. It is crucial for humanists and social scientists to join scientists and engineers in defining and building this infrastructure so that it meets the needs and incorporates the contributions of all disciplines.

In March 2004 the American Council of Learned Societies (ACLS) formed a commission to investigate and report on the development of a cyberinfrastructure for the humanities and social sciences—specifically, what potential the cyberinfrastructure described in the NSF report has to advance the humanities and social sciences and how these domains can contribute to it. CLIR Program Director Abby Smith has been working with the commission and will serve as editor of its report, which will be published in 2005.

Scholarly Communication Institute

In July 2004 CLIR and the University of Virginia hosted the second Scholarly Communication Institute (SCI). The institute was established to provide a forum for discussion and collaboration among scholars, librarians, publishers, technologists, and academic officers. It grew from the recognition that a changing system of scholarly communication is enabling new approaches to scholarship and is presenting the creators, keepers, and distributors of information with new roles and opportunities. The focal point of discussions at this year's SCI was the field of practical ethics. As a new field that draws on deep humanistic roots in philosophy and religious studies, yet is not firmly entrenched within the university department structure, practical ethics touches on many disciplines. This makes it an ideal basis for SCI participants to study a wide range of possible initiatives wrought by information technology.

Mellon Dissertation Fellowships for Research in Original Sources

Now in its third year, the Mellon Dissertation Fellowship program supports original-source doctoral research in libraries and archives, without regard to the location or the format of those sources. Thirteen fellows were selected in 2004 from more than 350 candidates. As in the past, the fellows represent a wide range of repositories, ranging from municipal archives in Siberia to the Louisiana State Museum. Their topics of study were similarly broad in scope.

At the beginning of their fellowship year, the fellows convened at the Library of Congress for a one-day workshop on research in archives and special collections. This year also saw the program's first post-fellowship seminar. All first-year fellows came together for this event, which was also held at the Library of Congress, to discuss what they had learned about the research experience.

Preservation Awareness

In April 2004 CLIR published *Access in the Future Tense,* based on the meeting "Rethinking Preservation in the 21st Century" held in 2003. *Access in the Future Tense* concludes that the ways in which we have defined the problems of preservation in the print-on-paper domain, as well as the solutions we have developed to address them, are largely irrelevant to other media and formats. In fact, the challenges facing preservationists today extend far beyond those associated with the physical preservation of media. The primary obstacles are economic and legal. In 2004 CLIR continued to work with key preservation stakeholders—creators, distributors, librarians, archivists, and users of information resources in all formats and media—to identify what is at stake and recommend effective responses.

Legal and Technical Issues Surrounding Audio Recordings

Legal and technical challenges pose serious hurdles in preserving audio recordings. In response to the mandate set forth in the National Recording Preservation Act of 2000, the Library of Congress asked CLIR to develop and implement the first phase of a national preservation-planning strategy for audio resources. To this end, in 2004 CLIR commissioned June Besek of Columbia Law School to conduct studies to assess copyright issues relating to the preservation of and access to (1) commercial sound recordings made before 1972, and (2) unpublished audio recordings. CLIR also commissioned Tim Brooks, executive vice president of research at Lifetime Cable Networks, to undertake a study of the reissue practices under current U.S. copyright law, looking at all pre-1965 recordings. CLIR will publish the results of these three studies in 2005.

In January 2004 CLIR convened a group of experts in the preservation reformatting of analog audio and in digital-sound engineering to map an agenda for work on analog-to-digital preservation. A summary of findings from the technical experts' meeting will be presented to the National Recording Preservation Board in 2005, and CLIR will publish a report summarizing the recommendations.

National Digital Information Infrastructure and Preservation Program

In 2004 CLIR again provided technical support and other services to help the Library of Congress coordinate the work of the National Digital Information Infrastructure and Preservation Program (NDIIPP). The NDIIPP legislation, passed in December 2000, called for a phased approach to building an infrastructure of cooperating institutions to help ensure the long-term preservation of digital content. As part of this work, CLIR, in cooperation with the National Endowment for the Humanities and NSF, organized the processes by which applications for NDIIPP funding are evaluated. In addition, CLIR staff continued to participate in communication and outreach activities designed to raise awareness of digital preservation needs among stakeholder communities in education, research, business, and government.

Digital Libraries

CLIR's work at the intersection of libraries, scholarship, and technology is enhanced by the activities of the Digital Library Federation (DLF). Housed at CLIR, DLF is a consortium of 33 members and 5 allied organizations that are pioneering the use of electronic information technologies to extend library collections and services. In 2004 DLF welcomed its first international member, the British Library, and its first overseas ally, Britain's Joint Information Systems Committee (JISC).

DLF focused in 2004 on a range of initiatives that cut across traditional areas of DLF activity—preservation, production, metadata, management, usability, and architecture—and that will contribute to the creation of a distributed digital library.

Sharable Metadata

Creating sharable, interoperable metadata is a central challenge in building a distributed library. DLF is working with metadata experts to build records that can be harvested en masse and are interoperable. The payoff will be a first-generation multi-institutional finding system for digital library objects that is quicker and more comprehensive than any currently available system. This work builds on past DLF investments in the development of the Open Archives Initiative protocol for metadata harvesting.

In June 2004 DLF convened a group of scholars working on digital projects, editions, and archives to serve as an advisory panel on this issue and other matters relating to resource discovery and reuse, academic credit for digital work, institutional repositories, and the need for new tools for new scholarship. Facilitating this level of service is a fundamental challenge in building a distributed digital library, and one in which DLF will continue to work.

Registry of Digital Masters Library

Developed by DLF in collaboration with OCLC (the Online Computer Library Center), the Registry of Digital Masters is a list of digitized books and journals that exist in a page-image format and have been created in accordance with preservation standards set forth in DLF's Benchmarks for Digital Reproductions. The Digital Registry Phase One Implementation Guidelines were completed in 2004 and are now being tested by several institutions.

Production Workflow Good Practices

In spring 2004 DLF assembled a team of designers and managers who are sharing their expertise about design workflow, file-naming choices, lessons learned, and management software used or developed. The goal is to articulate a set of needed workflow practices.

E-Resources Management Initiative

The E-Resources Management Initiative (ERMI) is developing a common, sharable, XML database record for expressing the content of license agreements, related administrative information, and internal processes associated with collections of licensed electronic resources. ERMI has created a list of data fields that will be tested on vendors, aggregators, publishing-standards bodies, and publishers. A report of DLF's Electronic Resource Management Initiative was published in August 2004 (http://www.diglib.org/pubs/dlfermi0408).

Interoperation of Learning-Management and Library Information Systems

The growth of learning-management systems (courseware) in higher education has been accompanied by an explosion of Internet-accessible collections of use to teachers and students. Although course Web sites are increasingly produced through formal learning-management systems, these systems rarely provide for interactions with external repositories and discovery systems. To help resolve this issue, the Andrew W. Mellon Foundation funded a DLF study group that examined the interaction between digital libraries and learning-management systems. The group issued a report of its findings in June 2004 (http://www.diglib.org/pubs/cmsdl0407) that provides a basis for further DLF activity in this area.

Economics of Information

The transformation of the information environment has placed new organizational, technical, and financial demands on libraries. CLIR is supporting a project to help libraries explore ways to respond to these demands.

Work-Redesign Project

Libraries are challenged to offer new services, such as information literacy training and digital-asset management, while maintaining traditional functions, often with unchanging budgets. In 2003 CLIR initiated a project, with support from the Andrew W. Mellon Foundation, to explore whether there are ways to gain efficiencies in traditional areas so that staff can be deployed to new responsibilities. In early 2004 six directors of consortial libraries undertook a one-year redesign project at their home institutions. The projects focus on how to rethink work in both public and technical services. The directors will complete their projects in 2005. CLIR will make a report of their work available to other libraries.

Leadership

In 2004 CLIR continued several programs designed to address evolving leadership needs in the information profession and introduced a new fellowship to build collaboration among scholars, librarians, and information technologists.

Fellowship in Scholarly Information Resources

CLIR launched a new fellowship program in 2004 that will enable recent Ph.D.'s in the humanities to spend extended periods of time in academic libraries. The fellowship is intended to educate new scholars about the opportunities created by new forms of scholarly research and the traditional and digital information resources that support them. Eleven scholars were awarded fellowships in the program's first year. Each is working 12 to 24 months in one of ten academic institutions participating in the program. A two-week seminar at Bryn Mawr College prepared fellows for their internships. Throughout their internships, fellows are "meeting" monthly in a virtual classroom, developed by the University of Illinois Graduate School of Library and Information Science, to hear lectures and engage in discussions.

Frye Leadership Institute

The Frye Leadership Institute, created to develop leaders who can guide and transform academic information services for higher education, marked its fifth anniversary in 2004. The institute was held June 6–28 at the Emory Conference Center in Atlanta. The class of 43 information technologists, librarians, and faculty members was selected from among more than 200 applicants. Class members came from public and private institutions of all sizes and included representatives from Ireland, Britain, and Australia as well as the United States. Deanna Marcum and Richard Detweiler served as deans, and presenters included leaders in higher education and industry, members of the CLIR Board, and several Frye graduates.

Academic Librarians Advisory Committee

In 2004 the Academic Librarians Advisory Committee (ALAC), which advises CLIR on issues of interest to liberal arts colleges and small research libraries, began planning a workshop on digital-asset management for library and information technology directors in small libraries. The workshop, held in February 2005, was cosponsored by DLF with partial support from the Andrew W. Mellon Foundation.

Chief Information Officers of Liberal Arts Colleges

CLIR's Chief Information Officers (CIO) Group is composed of 28 directors of organizations that have merged their library and technology units on liberal arts college campuses. In 2004 three CIO members collaborated to write an article identifying issues that campuses should consider when planning to merge their information services. Titled "Greater Than the Sum of Its Parts: The Integrated IT/Library Organization," the article appeared in the May/June 2004 *EDUCAUSE Review*. The group continues to explore the extent to which institutions are merging functional units and staff, what has changed in these organizations at the working level as a result of such mergers, and what benefits have accrued from them.

A. R. Zipf Fellowship in Information Management

Joan A. Smith, a doctoral student in computer science at Old Dominion University in Norfolk, Virginia, received the A. R. Zipf Fellowship in Information Management for 2004. She is the eighth recipient of the fellowship, which was established in 1997 to recognize a graduate student who shows exceptional promise for leadership and technical achievement in information management. Smith worked in information management for private industry for 12 years before embarking on her doctorate. Her research focuses on access to and preservation of digital library resources.

International Developments

CLIR Named to U.S. National Commission to UNESCO

In November 2004 CLIR was named to the U.S. National Commission for the United Nations Educational, Scientific, and Cultural Organization (UNESCO). Fifty nongovernmental members and 38 federal, state and local, and at-large members currently make up the commission, whose purpose is to advise the State Department on issues relating to education, science, communications, and culture, and the formulation and implementation of U.S. policy toward UNESCO.

Bill and Melinda Gates Foundation Access to Learning Award

China's Evergreen Rural Library Service and Denmark's Aarhus Public Libraries were joint recipients of the Bill and Melinda Gates Foundation Access to Learning Award for 2004. Each library system was recognized for its outstanding efforts to improve free public access to information technology, particularly to underserved communities.

In China, Evergreen is placing computers in rural public high schools in the three western provinces of Qinghai, Gansu, and Shaanxi and in the northern province of Jiangsu. The computers are used not only by students but also by their parents and other residents of these rural areas. To meet the information needs of Denmark's rapidly growing immigrant population, Aarhus has developed innovative library-based outreach programs, including provision of computer training in immigrants' languages and of electronic and print resources in multiple languages.

The Access to Learning Award, which totals $1 million, is given annually to public libraries or similar kinds of organizations outside the United States for innovative programs giving the public free access to information technology. The award is intended to inspire others to expand access to information, particularly for the poor, disabled, and minorities. CLIR has managed the award program for the past three years.

Rovelstad Scholarship

The Rovelstad Scholarship in International Librarianship is awarded annually to encourage students who have an interest in international library work and help enable them to participate in the activities of the International Federation of Library Associations and Institutions (IFLA) early in their careers. Kathleen Marie Smith, a graduate student in information science at the University of Texas at Austin, was named the second recipient. The award, which CLIR administers through the generosity of Mathilde and Howard Rovelstad, provides travel funds for a student of library and information science to attend the World Library and Information Congress, IFLA's annual meeting.

CLIR Publications

In 2004 CLIR published the following:

Bishoff, Liz, and Nancy Allen. *Business Planning for Cultural Heritage Institutions* (January 2004).

Council on Library and Information Resources. *Access in the Future Tense* (April 2004).

Schonfeld, Roger C., Donald W. King, Ann Okerson, and Eileen Gifford Fenton. *The Nonsubscription Side of Periodicals: Changes in Library Operations and Costs between Print and Electronic Formats* (June 2004).

Smith, Abby, David Randal Allen, and Karen Allen. *Survey of the State of Audio Collections in Academic Libraries* (August 2004).

Valentine, Susan. *E-Powering the People: South Africa's Smart Cape Access Project* (March 2004).

Newsletters

CLIR Issues, nos. 37–42.

Association for Library and Information Science Education

1009 Commerce Park Drive, Suite 150, Oak Ridge, TN 37831-4219
Tel. 865-425-0155. fax 865-481-0390, e-mail contact@alise.org
World Wide Web http://www.alise.org

Louise S. Robbins
President, 2003–2004

The Association for Library and Information Science Education (ALISE) is an independent, nonprofit professional association whose mission is to promote excellence in research, teaching, and service for library and information science (LIS) education through leadership, collaboration, advocacy, and dissemination of research.

The association grew out of a series of informal meetings of library school instructors at American Library Association (ALA) conferences. The Round Table of Library School Instructors, as it called itself, voted in 1915 to form a permanent organization and to be identified as the Association of American Library Schools. The association, for the past 90 years, has provided a forum for library educators to share ideas, to discuss issues, and to seek solutions to common problems. In 1983 the association changed its name to its present form to reflect more accurately its mission, goals, and membership.

ALISE is now both an institutional and individual membership association. Its institutional members are units within universities—whether departments, programs, or schools—that provide courses and programs designed to educate professionals for libraries and other information agencies. Its personal members are both instructors in the member programs and those who have an interest in education for the library and information professions. While the majority of its institutional members are programs accredited by ALA's Committee on Accreditation, membership is not limited to those programs, and an effort is currently under way to increase its other institutional memberships. In addition, while it is chiefly North American, with a preponderance of its membership drawn from the United States and Canada, ALISE does have international institutional affiliates and personal members. Dues from institutional and personal members are the single largest source of operating funds for the association.

The association also publishes a journal, the *Journal of Education for Library and Information Science,* edited for many years by Joseph Mika of Wayne State University, Detroit, and newly under the joint editorship of Cheryl Knott Malone and Anita Sandaram Coleman of the University of Arizona. Other publications include a membership directory and *Library and Information Science Education Statistical Report,* a statistical compendium published in cooperation with ALA's Committee on Accreditation, which gathers statistics for accreditation purposes. These publications are available for purchase through ALISE.

The business of the association is carried out by a board of directors elected by the membership. The board—which establishes policy, sets goals and strategic directions, and provides oversight for association management—consists of a president, vice-president/president-elect, past president, secretary/treasurer, and three board members elected on a rotating basis. Each year's slate includes nominees for one board position and for president-elect. Every third year the slate also includes candidates for secretary/treasurer. Thus all board members generally serve three-year terms. The current officers are Ken Haycock (University of British Columbia), president; John Budd (University of Missouri–Columbia), president-elect; Louise S. Robbins (University of Wisconsin–Madison), past president; James Benson (St. John's University), secretary/treasurer; and board members Linda Smith (University of Illinois at Urbana-Champaign), Gloria Leckie (University of Western Ontario), and Heidi Julien (University of Alberta).

After a number of difficult years, the association in 2003 fired its management firm and issued a request for proposals for a new management group. It was fortunate to be able to hire a management team from Information International Associates (IIa): Deborah York is executive director, Susanne Dupes is assistant director, and Lance Vowell is in charge of membership and publications. The board is pleased with the progress the association has made to date in carrying out its activities.

Annual Conference

The major activity of the association, in addition to its publications, is its annual conference, currently held immediately prior to the ALA Midwinter Meeting. The conference not only serves as a venue for sharing scholarship related especially—although not exclusively—to teaching and learning in information and library science, but also as the major opportunity for programs to meet and interview prospective faculty members. A doctoral poster session, which in 2005 featured approximately 90 exhibitors, allows established faculty to see the work of doctoral students. In addition, the association distributes applicant résumés and provides space for interviewing candidates.

Each year two students are honored with Doctoral Students to ALISE awards on the basis of a short essay and the recommendation of their program head. This award provides free registration and a $500 stipend to defray the selected students' conference expenses.

ALISE's special interest groups (SIGs) also meet at the conference, sometimes in informal discussion groups, but more often in order to present panels or papers on topics of interest. SIGs provide a means for individuals to become involved in a relatively small group of people with similar research or teaching interests. ALISE is currently evaluating its SIGs in order to eliminate those no longer pertinent and to add new areas of interest. The list of SIGs can be found on the ALISE Web site.

Another means of involvement in ALISE is participation in one of its committees, which also meet at the conference. The committees are established by the board to meet the needs of the association. The committee structure is currently under review with an eye to providing additional opportunities for participation and streamlining the association's structure.

Research Awards

One of the busiest committees is the Research Committee, which determines the winners of the association's several research awards. Awards are announced and award-winning papers are presented at the Annual Conference. The ALISE Web site contains full details concerning the following research awards:

- The Eugene Garfield Doctoral Dissertation Award, funded by the Eugene Garfield Foundation. Up to two outstanding dissertations completed between December 15, 2003, and July 15, 2005, will be selected. Each winner will receive $500, plus 2006 conference registration and personal membership in ALISE for 2006. Winners of the Dissertation Competition will present a summary of their work at the 2006 conference. Doctoral students who have recently graduated in any field of study, or who will have completed their dissertations by the July 15, 2005, deadline, are invited to submit two complete copies of their dissertation. Dissertations must deal with substantive issues related to library and information science, but applicants may be from within or outside LIS programs.
- The Bohdan S. Wynar Research Paper Award, funded by Greenwood Press/Libraries Unlimited. The purpose of this award is to further stimulate the communication of research at ALISE annual meetings. Research papers concerning any aspect of library and information science are eligible, not just those pertaining to LIS education. Any research methodology is acceptable. Up to two winning papers may be selected; an honorarium of $2,500 will be awarded to the author(s) of each paper. In cases of joint authorship, one honorarium will be awarded for the paper. At least one applicant in a group must be a personal member of ALISE as of the deadline date.
- A Methodology Paper Award. Like the Wynar Award, this competition is intended to encourage the communication of excellent research—especially of innovative approaches to research methodologies. Any research methodology may be entered. Papers must be limited to description and discussion of a research method or a technique associated with a particular research method; for example, papers may address such areas as sampling, grounded theory, historical methods, or statistical methods. Papers must explain the particular method/technique, including methodological implications for library and information science. Examples to illustrate its value can come from LIS-related published studies, proposed studies, and works-in-progress. One winning paper will be selected. An honorarium of $500 will be awarded to the author(s). In cases of joint authorship, one honorarium will be awarded for the paper. Methodology papers prepared by joint authors are eligible for entry, but at least one author must be a personal member of ALISE as of the deadline date.
- A Research Grant Award. An award of one or more grants totaling $5,000 may be made to support research broadly related to LIS education. The

award cannot be used to support a doctoral dissertation. At least one applicant in a group submitting a proposal must be a personal member of ALISE as of the deadline date.

- The OCLC/ALISE Library and Information Science Research Grant (LISRG) Awards. OCLC (the Online Computer Library Center) and OCLC Research, in collaboration with ALISE, in order to recognize the importance of research to the advancement of librarianship and information science, provide one or more grant awards of up to $15,000 to promote independent research that helps librarians integrate new technologies into areas of traditional competence and contributes to a better understanding of the library environment. When possible, priority is given to proposals from junior faculty and applicants who have not previously received LISRG funds. Additional details on this award can be found at the ALISE Web site or at http://www.oclc.org/research/grants.

Service Awards and Honors

Each year the ALISE Awards Committee presents awards at the annual conference to members nominated in various categories representing various kinds of sustained contributions to the field or the association. The following awards are presented:

- Service to ALISE. This award is presented to a member who has provided regular and sustained service to ALISE through holding various offices and positions within the organization or accomplishing specific responsibilities for the organization; through participating in activities that have enhanced the association's stature, reputation, and overall strength; or through representing ALISE to other appropriate organizations, institutions, or governmental agencies.
- Teaching Excellence. This award is presented to a member who has demonstrated evidence of regular and sustained excellence in teaching library and information science; has contributed to curriculum design that demonstrates subject expertise and the ability to integrate new developments in the field; and has mentored students, alumni, and/or practicing professionals outside the classroom; as well as using effective and innovative teaching methods.
- Professional Contribution to Library and Information Science Education. The winner of this award has demonstrated regular and sustained service that promotes and strengthens the broad area of LIS education through the holding of appropriate offices and positions within the profession; through promoting and enhancing the status of LIS education; and through leadership and initiative in dealing with issues relating to LIS education.
- Pratt-Severn Faculty Innovation. Established in 1996, this $1,000 cash award (sponsored by the Pratt Institute School of Information and Library Science on behalf of the late David Severn, a 1968 Pratt alumnus) is designed to identify innovation by full-time faculty members, or a group

of full-time faculty members, in incorporating evolving information technologies in the curricula of accredited master's degree programs in library and information studies.

Council of Deans, Directors, and Program Chairs

The only entity of ALISE other than the board that is established by the bylaws is an organization made up of the executive officers of institutional members. The group meets at least annually, at the conference, but may meet at other times as well. Often many members of the group also meet in conjunction with the American Society for Information Science and Technology (ASIS&T). It provides a venue for the program chiefs to discuss common concerns such as faculty shortages, accreditation, and international interests. Recently the council has begun to try to address the issue of developing leadership within faculties, as nearly every program has had at least one new director in the past decade and a number of positions remain open or will be opening in the next few years.

The ALISE Landscape

As alluded to above, ALISE has come through a difficult decade. Managed by a single individual for most of its existence, the association—with its publications, conference, and other activities—became too complex and large for one person to handle. In an attempt to find an excellent replacement for its historically good management, the association had several less-than-optimum management situations during the decade ending in mid-2003. During the same time period, LIS education was regrouping and rapidly changing following a flurry of school closings and in the face of changes in the higher education environment. The management situation diverted the volunteer elected leaders from what might have been an opportunity to lead ALISE to an even greater role in helping to reshape education for librarians and other information professionals.

One major effort to identify the new directions LIS education was taking was the KALIPER-Kellogg-ALISE Information Professions Education Renewal project, "the most extensive examination of the library and information science curriculum since the 1923 Williamson report" (KALIPER, p. 1). The two-year research study, headed by Joan Durrance of the University of Michigan School of Information (a winner of ALISE's award for professional contributions to the field), revealed that LIS programs were addressing broad-based information problems through a user-centered research and curricular core, and that they are investing heavily in technology and using it in innovative ways to deliver courses in many formats and structures. They are developing different configurations to allow specializations and are expanding their programs to provide undergraduate, doctoral, and related degree programs in addition to the ALA-accredited master's degree.

Of course, in a changing environment, differences among programs may widen according to the focus of the program and its location within its host university. Thus, while the ALISE member institutions have many similarities, they increasingly exhibit differences in numbers and types of students (whether they have undergraduate students, for example). They also differ in the sizes and composition of their faculties, with well-resourced, stand-alone schools generally expanding and hiring more people whose research is not grounded in the institution of the library, while those situated within another college or that are less well-resourced have not gained or have gained more slowly and thus have hired people more closely related to traditional library-related research. Some schools reach hundreds of students half a continent away, while others concentrate on delivering face-to-face education. Some run large research and consulting enterprises, while others are mainly teaching institutions.

These differences have forced ALISE and its members to deal with perceptions that LIS education is far removed from the professional practice of librarianship. It has challenged ALISE officers to develop familiarity with and to represent the full range of the association's members. During the past two years, a considerable effort has been made—which will continue into the future—to focus on ALISE members' commonalities and to communicate the robustness of the various programs and their commitment to educating forward-looking and proactive librarians and other information professionals.

Specific actions ALISE has taken in this regard in the past two years have included thanking First Lady Laura Bush for her support of LIS education, which has been followed by increasing appropriations for "Librarians for the 21st Century" grants; speaking out against the educational and gender stereotypes suggested by former Attorney General John Ashcroft's characterization of librarians who oppose the USA Patriot Act as "hysteric"; writing letters in support of retaining Clark Atlanta University's library education program (which is scheduled to close in 2005); finding new editors for the *Journal*; resuming the strategic planning process that was impossible to maintain under previous management—a process that will reach fruition under incoming president Ken Haycock's leadership; and working to cooperate with ALA and our institutions to increase diversity within the field.

The Future

The fortunate coincidence of the ALA 2005–2006 presidency of Michael Gorman, who wishes to focus on library education during his presidential year, and the renewed vigor of ALISE, now under the leadership of Haycock and an excellent management team, bodes well for continuing improvement in communication around LIS education issues. Major renewal and reorganization of the internal structure of ALISE should enable the association to respond more quickly and effectively, always a challenge for a volunteer organization. A new strategic plan will focus the association on its strengths and allow it to expand its membership and continue to prosper.

International Reports

International Federation of Library Associations and Institutions

P.O. Box 95312, 2509 CH The Hague, Netherlands
Tel. 31-70-314-0884, fax 31-70-383-4827, e-mail ifla@ifla.org
World Wide Web http://www.ifla.org

Beacher Wiggins
Director for Acquisitions and Bibliographic Access, Library of Congress
Library of Congress Representative to the Standing Committee of the
IFLA Section on Bibliography

The International Federation of Library Associations and Institutions (IFLA) is the preeminent international organization representing librarians, other information professionals, and library users. During 2004 IFLA protected the world's cultural and documentary heritage from the ravages of war and natural disaster; broadened participation in its activities by countries with developing economies; expanded the theory and practice of bibliographic control; adopted a new operational model for the federation; and promoted equitable access to information without regard to barriers of poverty, handicap, or geographical isolation.

World Library and Information Conference

More than 3,800 librarians, publishers, and exhibitors from 121 countries traveled to Buenos Aires in late August 2004 to attend the second World Library and Information Conference, which was also the 70th IFLA General Conference and Council and the first General Conference ever held in South America. The theme of the August 22–27 conference, "Libraries: Tools for Education and Development," expressed IFLA President Kay Raseroka's vision of libraries as core infrastructure for national development. Argentine novelist and journalist Tomás Eloy Martínez, distinguished professor and director of the Latin American Studies Program and the Center for Hemispheric Studies at Rutgers University, presented the keynote address, "The Book in Globalization Times." IFLA President-Elect Alex Byrne led an all-day special planning session to consider how to carry out his presidential theme of "Partnership." Discussion focused on how IFLA and its member associations can help each other during his presidency, which will begin in August 2005.

Satellite meetings in several South American venues offered more-specialized discussions. The Library and Research Services for Parliaments Section organized a satellite meeting in Valparaiso, Chile, on "Clients, Commitments, and Trust" August 18–19 to explore "What Legislators Expect from Their Libraries." The Marketing and Management Section's satellite meeting in São Paulo, Brazil, "Improving Virtual Customer Relationships in the Information Environment," attracted 250 participants. The Conference of Directors of National Libraries held its annual gathering in conjunction with IFLA, meeting at the National Library of Argentina. A workshop at the Goethe Institut, Buenos Aires, titled "Reaching Further: Telecentres and Libraries Working Together to Create the Shared Knowledge Society," promoted better understanding of challenges faced by both libraries and "telecentres," or learning centers that focus on Internet-based information.

Response to War and Natural Disaster

The international library community's concern for the preservation of cultural heritage was demonstrated as never before in 2004. In 1996 IFLA joined with three other organizations—the International Council on Archives, the International Council on Monuments and Sites, and the International Council of Museums—to found the International Committee of the Blue Shield (ICBS) to protect cultural property in the event of natural and human disasters. Throughout 2004 ICBS worked with the United Nations Educational, Scientific and Cultural Organization (UNESCO) and the International Criminal Police Organization (INTERPOL) to mitigate damage to cultural and documentary heritage caused by the war in Iraq and the massive earthquake that occurred in Bam, Iran, on December 27, 2003. ICBS continued to work toward full international adoption of the 1954 Hague Convention—the Convention for the Protection of Cultural Property in the Event of Armed Conflict—and the two additional Protocols of 1954 and 1999. These protocols define "cultural war crimes" and would give ICBS a formal advisory role in the protection of cultural property during armed conflicts.

With the Association of Caribbean University, Research, and Institutional Libraries, the IFLA Core Activity for Preservation and Conservation (PAC) presented a workshop on "Mitigating the Consequences of Natural Disasters for Caribbean Libraries and Archives" May 21–22, 2004, at the National Library Building, Port-of-Spain, Trinidad and Tobago. The workshop discussed the risks of hurricanes and other natural disasters, preventive measures, and recovery measures. Almost immediately after the earthquake and tsunami that devastated parts of South and Southeast Asia on December 26, 2004, IFLA began fund raising and other efforts to restore some of the hundreds of libraries that were destroyed, particularly in Sri Lanka. Rescue work for Sri Lankan and other South Asian libraries will continue for years to come.

Bibliographic Control

The federation has worked steadily over the decades to improve bibliographic control, through practical workshops, support of the International Standard Bibliographic Description, and research that seeks to establish basic principles of bibliographic control and to identify areas where cataloging practice in different cultures can be harmonized to make library catalogs less expensive to produce and easier for patrons to use.

The IFLA Governing Board in 2003 joined with six national libraries—the British Library, Die Deutsche Bibliothek, the Library of Congress, the National Library of Australia, the Biblioteca Nacional de Portugal, and the Koninklijke Bibliotheek (Netherlands)—and the Conference of Directors of National Libraries (CDNL) to form the IFLA-CDNL Alliance for Bibliographic Standards (ICABS). In addition to general issues of bibliographic control, ICABS works to advance the understanding of issues relating to long-term archiving of electronic resources. The first ICABS program took place at the Buenos Aires conference.

The second International Meeting of Experts on an International Cataloging Code (IME ICC) was also held in Buenos Aires, where Latin American and Caribbean experts met prior to the IFLA General Conference. The IME ICC meetings are a series of five regional invitational conferences sponsored by IFLA to explore similarities and differences in current national and regional cataloging rules in an attempt to clarify where variations for languages and cultural differences may be needed and where rules might be the same. The first meeting was held in Frankfurt in 2003, for experts from Europe and North America. The goal is to increase the ability to share cataloging information worldwide by promoting standards for the content of bibliographic and authority records used in library catalogs.

Rare Books

The IFLA Rare Books and Manuscripts Section is revitalized and beginning to take fairly direct action in terms of establishing standards for exhibition loans of rare materials and for collaborations. Standards for collaborative digitization projects are necessary to prevent duplication of efforts by multiple libraries. The section is creating a central Web site for listing available antiquarian books, raising the issue of standards for how such information is represented on the Web. Explorations also began in 2004 into compiling a catalog of all Latin American works printed before 1815. The Rare Books and Manuscripts Section showed great energy in its work despite the disparity of resources between Third World and First World libraries.

Grants and Awards

IFLA continues to collaborate with corporate partners and national libraries to maintain programs and opportunities that would otherwise not be possible, especially for librarians and libraries in developing countries.

The IFLA/OCLC (Online Computer Library Center) Early Career Development Fellowships bring to the United States, for four weeks of intensive experience in librarianship, library and information science professionals from countries with developing economies who are in the early stages of their careers. In 2004 the fellows were from Ghana, Rwanda, Pakistan, and Sri Lanka. Announced at the Buenos Aires conference, the 2005 awards went to applicants from China, Colombia, Georgia, Jamaica, and Malawi.

The Frederic Thorpe Award was established in 2003 and is administered by the IFLA Libraries for the Blind Section and the Ulverscroft Foundation of Leicester, England, which Thorpe founded. Travel stipends were awarded to three individuals in 2004: Wendy Patricia Ling of the South African Library for the Blind; Ademike Olorundore, librarian at the Anglo-Nigerian Welfare Association for the Blind; and Sarah Home, operations and development manager at the National Library for the Blind of the United Kingdom.

The Bill and Melinda Gates Foundation Access to Learning Award was presented during the Buenos Aires conference to the Århus Public Library in Denmark, and the China Evergreen Network, which serves rural libraries in China. This annual award, managed by the Council on Library and Information Resources, presents up to $1 million to libraries, library agencies, or comparable organizations outside the United States that have been innovative in providing free public access to information.

The IFLA/3M International Marketing Awards were presented in 2004 to three organizations that promoted library service and generated widespread visibility and support for libraries through their strategic approach to marketing communications. The first place award went to the Australian Islamic College, Kewdale, Western Australia, for using its school library resources to promote reading and computer literacy among 300 refugee children from Afghanistan, Iraq, and Somalia. The Krasheninnikov Regional Research Library, Kamchatka, Russia, won second place for its marketing campaign "Remedy for the Soul," aimed at the elderly and disabled. The African Rice Center in Abidjan, Ivory Coast, received the third place award for its outreach to agricultural researchers.

Membership

IFLA has approximately 1,700 members in 150 countries. Initially established at a conference in Edinburgh, Scotland, in 1927, it has been registered in the Netherlands since 1971 and has headquarters facilities at the Koninklijke Bibliotheek (Royal Library) in The Hague. Although IFLA did not hold a General Conference outside Europe and North America until 1980, there has since been steadily increasing participation from Asia, Africa, South America, and Australia. The federation now maintains regional offices for Africa (in Dakar); Asia and Oceania (in Bangkok); and Latin America and the Caribbean (in Rio de Janeiro). The organization has five working languages—English, French, German, Russian, and Spanish—and offers six membership categories: international library associations, national library associations, other associations, institutions, personal affiliates, and student affiliates. Association and institution members have voting rights in the IFLA General Council and may nominate candidates for IFLA offices; personal affiliates have no voting rights but may run for any office. In 2001, for a four-year trial period, IFLA began offering student affiliate memberships at reduced rates, with the aim of broadening participation and enhancing the stability and continuity of the organization by attracting affiliate members early in their careers. In addition, approximately 30 corporations in the information industry have formed working relationships with IFLA as corporate partners, providing financial and "in kind" support. At the 2004 conference in Buenos

Aires, the federation announced the new category of "other association" membership, intended to enable regional or specialized library associations to participate as members. UNESCO has given IFLA formal associate relations status, the highest level of relationship accorded to nongovernmental organizations by UNESCO.

Personnel, Structure, and Governance

Ross Shimmon, the secretary general of IFLA since May 1999, retired in May 2004. Ramachandran Rasu served as secretary general from April through November, and Sjoerd M. J. Koopman, coordinator of professional activities, an IFLA headquarters position, then served as acting secretary general until Peter Lor assumed that role on a permanent basis on February 15, 2005.

The current president of IFLA is Kay Raseroka, director of library services at the University of Botswana, who began her two-year term in August 2003. She is the first president of IFLA from a developing country and the first to have served as president-elect before becoming president. Raseroka chose as the theme for her presidency "Libraries for Lifelong Literacy," reaffirming IFLA's core values of freedom and equity of access to information while recognizing the impact of the speed of change and the penetration of new technologies and spheres of knowledge. Alex Byrne, university librarian of the University of Technology, Sydney, Australia, is the president-elect. Ingrid Parent, assistant deputy minister for documentary heritage collection, Library and Archives Canada, is the treasurer for 2003–2005.

Under revised statutes that took effect in 2001, IFLA's former Executive Board and Professional Board were combined in a new Governing Board. The 21-member board (plus the secretary general, ex officio) is responsible for the federation's general policies, management and finance, and external communications. The current members, in addition to Raseroka, Byrne, Parent, and Lor, are Evgeniy Kuzmin (Russian Federation), Claudia Lux (Germany), Sissel Nilsen (Norway), Ana Maria Peruchena Zimmermann (Argentina), Vinyet Panyella (Spain), Shawky Salem (Egypt), Ellen Tise (South Africa), Tiiu Valm (Estonia), and Jianzhong Wu (China), plus the chair and members of the IFLA Professional Committee, named below. In addition, Keith Michael Fiels, executive director of the American Library Association, and Gary Strong, university librarian, University of California, Los Angeles, were co-opted to the IFLA Governing Board for one year ending August 2005.

The governing board delegates responsibility for overseeing the direction of IFLA between board meetings, within the policies established by the board, to the IFLA Executive Committee. The executive committee includes the president, president-elect, treasurer, chair of the professional committee, two members of the governing board (elected every two years by members of the board from among its elected members), and IFLA's secretary general, ex officio. The current elected governing board members of the executive committee are Tise and Cristóbal Pasadas Ureña, who is a member of both the board and the professional committee.

The IFLA Professional Committee monitors the planning and programming of professional activities carried out by IFLA's two types of bodies: professional groups (eight divisions, more than 50 sections, and discussion groups) and core activities (formerly called core programs). The professional committee is composed of one elected officer from each division plus a chair elected by the incoming members; the president-elect and the coordinator of professional activities; and two elected members of the governing board, currently Nilsen and Panyella. Ia C. McIlwaine, director of the School of Library, Archive and Information Studies, University of London, chairs the professional committee.

The eight divisions of IFLA and their representatives on the professional committee are General Research Libraries (Cristóbal Pasadas Ureña, Spain), Special Libraries (John Meriton, United Kingdom), Libraries Serving the General Public (Torny Kjekstad, Norway), Bibliographic Control (Barbara Tillett, United States), Collections and Services (Edward Swanson, United States), Management and Technology (Nancy E. Gwinn, United States), Education and Research (Marian Koren, Netherlands), and Regional Activities (Jacinta Were, Kenya). Each division has interest sections such as statistics and evaluation, library theory and research, and management and marketing; other sections focus on particular types of libraries or parts of the world.

The six core activities are Advancement of Librarianship (ALP), Preservation and Conservation (PAC), IFLA-CDNL Alliance for Bibliographic Standards (ICABS), IFLA UNIMARC Programme (UP), Committee on Free Access to Information and Freedom of Expression (FAIFE), and Committee on Copyright and Other Legal Matters (CLM).

IFLA's Three Pillars: Society, Members, and Profession

In December 2004 the IFLA Governing Board endorsed a new operational model for IFLA based on three pillars: society, membership, and professional matters. A review of IFLA's core activities, conducted in 2003 and 2004, showed that all of the federation's core functions were related to three strategic factors: the societal contexts in which libraries and information services operate, the membership of the federation, and the library profession.

Although the three pillars and the infrastructure of IFLA are interdependent, they can be roughly analyzed as follows: The society pillar focuses on the role and impact of libraries and information services in society. Activities supported by the society pillar include FAIFE, CLM, Blue Shield, and IFLA's presence at the World Summit on the Information Society. The profession pillar focuses on the activities covered by IFLA's sections and divisions and its core activities ALP, ICABS, PAC, and UNIMARC. The members pillar includes IFLA's member services, conferences, and publications. The federation's operational infrastructure—consisting of IFLA Headquarters, the IFLANET Web site, and the IFLA governance structure—support and receive strategic direction from these three pillars.

Within the framework of the three pillars, the president and governing board positioned IFLA for significant change. In the short term, the governing board charged working parties to focus in 2005 on the society pillar, to improve the

IFLANET Web site, and to articulate a new approach to budget management with a view toward developing a business plan based on the framework of the three pillars. The business plan is a critical concern because the federation ended 2004 with a budget deficit of nearly 116,000 euros, although it has a reserve fund of approximately 490,000 euros. The budget for 2005 calls for 1,035,900 euros in revenue and 1,029,000 euros in expenditures. President Raseroka and the board laid preparations for a strong advocacy role for libraries at the second World Summit on the Information Society, to be held in Tunis, Tunisia, in November 2005. The summit is sponsored by the International Telecommunications Union, a United Nations organization separate from UNESCO, and IFLA is concerned that, without substantial input from the library community, the summit will address only a technical and corporate agenda. The federation's major periodical publication, *IFLA Journal,* will be published by Sage Publications beginning in January 2005; it had been published by K. G. Saur since 1978. Beyond these immediate changes, the three pillars will provide a focus for IFLA's future budgets and management decisions.

Special Libraries Association

331 South Patrick St., Alexandria, VA 22314
703-647-4900, fax 703-647-4901
E-mail sla@sla.org
World Wide Web http://www.sla.org

Janice R. Lachance
Executive Director

Founded in 1909 and headquartered in Alexandria, Virginia, the Special Libraries Association (SLA) is an international professional association that represents thousands of information experts in 83 countries who collect, analyze, evaluate, package, and disseminate information to facilitate strategic decision making. SLA members work for corporations, private companies, government agencies, not-for-profit organizations, technical and academic institutions, museums, law firms, and medical facilities. SLA promotes and strengthens its members through learning, advocacy, and networking initiatives.

SLA's core values are

- *Leadership*: Strengthening members' roles as information leaders in their organizations and communities, including shaping information policy
- *Service*: Responding to clients' needs, adding qualitative and quantitative value to information services and products
- *Innovation and continuous learning*: Embracing innovative solutions for the enhancement of services and intellectual advancement within the profession
- *Results and accountability*: Delivering measurable results in the information economy and members' organizations; the association and its members are expected to operate with the highest level of ethics and honesty
- *Collaboration and partnering*: Providing opportunities to meet, communicate, collaborate, and partner within the information industry and the business community

As of December 2004, SLA had 59 regional chapters in the United States, Canada, Europe, Asia, and the Middle East; 25 divisions representing a variety of industries; and 11 special-interest caucuses. Its divisions include Advertising and Marketing; Biomedical and Life Sciences; Business and Finance; Chemistry; Competitive Intelligence; Education; Engineering; Environmental and Resource Management; Food, Agriculture, and Nutrition; Geography and Map; Information Technology; Government Information; Insurance and Employee Benefits; Legal Library Management; Materials Research and Manufacturing; Military Librarians; Museums, Arts, and Humanities; News; Petroleum and Energy Resources; Pharmaceutical and Health Technology; Physics/Astronomy/ Mathematics; Science-Technology; Social Sciences; Solo Librarians; and Transportation. Membership totals about 12,000.

Programs and Services

Advocacy. SLA serves the profession by advocating publicly on the value and values of the profession. Whether by communicating with executives and hiring professionals on the important role information professionals play in the workplace or sharing the views and opinions of the membership with government officials worldwide, SLA exists to represent the profession and perpetuate its existence.

Conference and Exhibits. SLA's yearly conference brings together more than 6,000 information professionals and provides a forum for discussion on issues shaping the information industry. The conference offers more than 400 events, programs, panel discussions, and seminars, and includes an exhibit hall with more than 300 participating companies.

Consultation Service. SLA offers a free consultation service that assists members and nonmembers in defining their organizations' information requirements. It also maintains a database of SLA member consultants at http://www.sla.org/consultonline.

Employment and Career Services. The association provides a variety of services to meet the career needs of its members. Career Connection, at the annual conference, offers members an opportunity to meet privately with employers.

Information Center. The SLA Web site offers links to resources relevant to the operation and management of special libraries, from information portals to research and surveys.

Professional and Student Networks. SLA's student groups are located throughout the world and are affiliated with accredited graduate schools of library and information science. Through membership in SLA, students gain valuable professional experience and make important industry contacts.

Professional Development. The mission of SLA's Professional Development Center is to help information professionals become more capable learners, more capable professionals, and more capable people. Its goal is to set the standards for learning and development throughout the global community of information professionals. SLA aims to provide learning experiences through live and virtual events that will transform the profession's value.

Publications. SLA's monthly magazine, *Information Outlook,* provides news, features, and evaluation of trends in information management.

Research. SLA funds surveys and projects, endowment fund grants, and research studies related to all aspects of information management.

Scholarships and Awards Program. SLA scholarships consist of awards for graduate study leading to a master's degree, graduate study leading to a Ph.D., and for post-MLS study. The program honors individuals for their achievements and contributions to SLA and to the information profession.

Virtual Community. SLA's online community offers allows members to access the association's services and to network globally and equitably at any time.

Annual Conference

Approximately 4,700 information professionals attended SLA's 95th Annual Conference in June 2004 in Nashville.

Guest speakers included Carl Ledbetter, an expert on information security, and Bill Ivy, director of the Curb Center for Art, Enterprise, and Public Policy at Vanderbilt University and former chairman of the National Endowment for the Arts.

Leadership Development Institute

The Leadership Development Institute, sponsored by Dialog, focused on preparing leaders for a time of change. SLA's chapter, division, and caucus leaders were introduced to the association's top leaders, newly approved candidates for the SLA Board of Directors, and Executive Director Janice Lachance. Each leader was given the opportunity to participate in one or more roundtable discussions on 33 leadership topics.

Awards Reception

The 2004 SLA awards reception, held as part of the Annual Conference, took place at the Parthenon in Nashville. The ceremony recognized and acknowledged the accomplishments and achievements of 25 individual award winners. SLA sponsors and conference major partners were also acknowledged for their continued support of various SLA activities and events. [Major SLA awards are listed in "Library Scholarship and Award Recipients, 2004" in Part 3—*Ed.*]

Canada's Libraries in 2004:
Access, Funding, Policy Among Top Issues

Karen G. Adams

Director of Library Services and Information Resources,
University of Alberta Libraries

A June 2004 federal election saw Prime Minister Paul Martin returning as head of a minority government, the first in nearly 25 years. His October 5 Speech from the Throne focused on seven major themes: a strong economy; the health of Canadians; children, caregivers, and seniors; aboriginal Canadians; Canada's cities and communities; the environment; and a role of pride and influence for the nation. On the economic side, the target is a reduction in the debt-to-GDP ratio to 25 percent over the next 10 years.

Canada's GDP rose 3.2 percent from November 2003 to November 2004 with increases in all sectors except "arts, entertainment, and recreation"; the decrease in that sector is attributed to the lockout within the National Hockey League. Early in 2004 Statistics Canada released its analysis of government spending on culture over the decade 1990–1991 to 2001–2002. For 2001–2002, it identified a total of C$6.8 billion contributed by all three levels of government, a 7.6 percent increase over 2000–2001 and the fourth year in a row of steady increases. The increase in federal government spending was 8.9 percent; the provinces and territories spent 2.6 percent more, and municipalities 9.3 percent more. The figure approximates expenditures of C$217 for each Canadian. Libraries received C$768.5 million (up 4.2 percent) from the provinces and municipalities. Indeed, the major portion of municipal spending on culture, approximately 75 percent, goes to libraries. Municipal spending on culture fell only in Manitoba and the Yukon, with the largest increases in Prince Edward Island, Ontario, and British Columbia.[1, 2]

More recent figures for the 2004–2005 fiscal year indicate that the trend to increases in library funding continues. The provinces of Saskatchewan (1 percent), British Columbia (5 percent), Nova Scotia (9.7 percent from both levels of government), and New Brunswick (2 percent) all report increases in provincial funding, with Newfoundland and Alberta both reporting funding levels remaining the same, but with special funding added; in the case of Newfoundland, C$1 million for collections, and in Alberta, C$800,000 to enable libraries to meet the standards of the province's broadband network, SuperNet.

The stronger Canadian dollar contributed to improving the buying power of collections budgets in academic libraries. The Canadian Association of Research Libraries (CARL), in an analysis of its most recent statistical compilation, noted an increase in spending on electronic journals from an average of C$1.01 million in 2000–2001 to an average of C$1.4 million in 2001–2002—an increase of 38.6 percent. The University of Waterloo was the first Canadian library to spend more on electronic serials than on print.[3]

International and National Information Policy Issues

The Canadian Library Association (CLA) released independent trade researcher Ellen Gould's *Update on the GATS Negotiations and Their Implications for Public Sector Libraries* in June. The study concludes that "there have been explicit requests for liberalization of library and archive services. These requests are being made against a backdrop of pressure to treat the cultural sector generally as no more sensitive than any other. Countries like Canada that have said they will not make cultural service commitments are being criticized on the grounds that they are not following the official negotiating guidelines to have all service sectors on the negotiating table." [4]

The library community continued to have concerns about access to published government information through the federal Depository Services Program (DSP). As one consequence of the "sponsorship scandal," the DSP's host department, Communication Canada, was disbanded on March 31, 2004. DSP was transferred to Public Works and Government Services Canada, and changed its supplier for the provision of warehousing and distribution services so that the physical inventory had to be moved. Service delays resulted. The library community continued to work with Library and Archives Canada (LAC) toward having DSP moved under the jurisdiction of LAC. DSP is also responsible for two other agreements affecting libraries: one makes the 15 journals published by the National Research Council Press available at no cost to all Canadians; the other provides topographic data from Natural Resources Canada to the research community. In recognition of the fact that government publishing also takes place in the provinces and territories, CARL initiated a survey of library activities to collect and preserve electronic publications from that level of government. [5, 6]

Copyright

On the federal scene, the course of copyright reform was altered when Parliament was prorogued in December 2003 due to the retirement of Prime Minister Jean Chrétien. Bill C-36 was stalled, effectively changing government's intent to extend copyright protection for unpublished works ("The Lucy Maud Montgomery provisions") and effectively ending perpetual copyright for unpublished works. In March the departments responsible for copyright (Industry and Canadian Heritage) issued their report on copyright legislation to the Standing Committee on Canadian Heritage. The departments identified issues where they believed consensus on the approach to be taken had been reached and areas where further investigation of the options was desired. CLA and CARL both responded to the report. In May, following two weeks of hearings, the standing committee tabled its interim report on copyright reform, urging legislative amendments that would have expanded licensing regimes to include such matters as interlibrary loans to the desktop and educational use of material on the Web. Of course, committee membership and ministerial portfolios changed after the federal election, with the result that the Standing Committee on Canadian Heritage had only two of its former members, and 8 of 12 members were new members of Parliament. In keeping with the minority status of the government, the Liberal Party that had formed the previous government had only 5 of 12 members on the standing committee. This made it difficult for it to continue its pre-election agenda on copyright reform, which had included the notion of forming a licensing collective for use of materials on the public Internet. However, the library community has continued its necessary vigilance, including meetings of federal officials and CLA, CARL, and the Association pour l'Avancement des Sciences et des Techniques de la Documentation (ASTED). Many letters have been written, with provincial library associations also engaged in the campaign to connect with members of Parliament and improve their understanding of the issues surrounding copyright and user rights.[7]

Part of the copyright landscape in Canada is the absence of relevant case law to help interpret the Copyright Act. The year 2004 saw three major court decisions that supported the importance of the rights of the user. The first, in March, dealt with library photocopying at the Law Society of Upper Canada, under an action begun in 1993 by legal publisher CCH Canadian. The Law Society Great Library operates a photocopying service on a cost-recovery basis under a policy that includes limitations such as making only a single copy. The Supreme Court ruled that the Law Society's dealings with the works of three legal publishers through its custom photocopy service were "research-based and fair." The landmark decision enables members of the legal profession to access copies of court decisions and other legal materials in the Great Library without fear of copyright infringement. Because the Law Society did not have a license with the collective Access Copyright, the decision is viewed as both a clarification of the concept of fair dealing and a step forward in clarifying users' rights under the Copyright Act.[8]

On March 31 the Federal Court ruled against motions filed by the Canadian Recording Industry Association (CRIA) seeking disclosure by five Canadian high-speed Internet service providers (ISPs) of the names of 29 individuals accused of distributing music files illegally over peer-to-peer networks. The court ruled that there was insufficient evidence that making music files available for others to access constitutes copyright infringement under Canadian law; placing files in a shared directory does not constitute distribution or authorization of their reproduction. CRIA filed its appeal on April 13.[9, 10]

Since 1997 it has been legal in Canada to make private copies of recorded music, with the Canadian Private Copying Collective established to propose rates to the Copyright Board to be levied on blank recording media and to distribute the levies collected to rights-holders and performers. The Federal Court of Appeal ruled that MP3 players and iPods are not subject to the levy because they are devices rather than media.[11]

Digital Divide Funding

Industry Canada has traditionally led the federal government's initiatives to address the digital divide with a wide range of programs intended to support ubiquitous connectivity. In the 2004–2005 fiscal year, the government announced that its showcase programs, Community Access (CAP) and SchoolNet, would receive reduced funding, down to C$50 million over two fiscal years for both grants and program operation, with C$15 million each year directed to First Nations SchoolNet. LibraryNet was discontinued. At its annual meeting, CLA adopted a resolution opposing the reduction of the CAP/LibraryNet program.[12]

In support of Industry Canada's decision to reduce funding to the more well-developed regions of Canada, an Ipsos-Reid survey found that 60 percent of

Canadians 55 and older are now online, compared with 48 percent a year ago. Similarly, Statistics Canada found that in the 2003–2004 school year 98 percent of schools had at least one Internet-connected computer, with the average number of computers being 71.6. Older Canadians and elementary and secondary students had been target audiences for funding programs under earlier Industry Canada programs. While the CAP and SchoolNet programs have been reduced, digital divide communities continue to receive funding through the Broadband for Rural and Northern Development Program and the National Satellite Initiative. The two programs had up to C$35 million to bring broadband to aboriginal communities, and approximately C$20 million to bring broadband access via satellite to 52 remote communities in British Columbia, Manitoba, Ontario, and Quebec.[13, 14, 15]

Events

On May 21 the Library and Archives of Canada Act came into force, finalizing the process of merging two national institutions. With the retirement of National Librarian Roch Carrier, former National Archivist Ian Wilson became Librarian and Archivist of Canada in September. During the transition, the objectives of the new institution were announced as being

- To preserve the documentary heritage of Canada for the benefit of present and future generations
- To serve as a source of enduring knowledge accessible to all, contributing to the cultural, social, and economic advancement of Canada as a free and democratic society
- To facilitate in Canada cooperation among the communities involved in the acquisition, preservation, and diffusion of knowledge
- To serve as the continuing memory of the government of Canada and its institutions

The new Library and Archives Canada (LAC) has noted the interest of other countries in the Canadian model. One of the challenges of the new institution is facilities; LAC has been cited by Auditor General Sheila Fraser because some 90 percent of its collections are housed in buildings that do not meet temperature and humidity standards.[16]

One of the special projects completed by LAC during the year was Project Naming, an initiative launched in 2001 that involved youth traveling across Nunavut showing elders photographs on laptops of Inuit people photographed between the 1920s and 1950s, so that Nunavut residents and their stories could be identified and recorded.[17]

Presidential Visit

During their November visit to Canada, U.S. President George W. Bush and the First Lady, accompanied by U.S. Ambassador Paul Celluci and Mrs. Celluci, visited Library and Archives Canada. Minister of Canadian Heritage Liza Frulla used the opportunity to thank Mrs. Celluci for her role in promoting libraries, especially research libraries, during her time in Canada.[18]

Consolidation in Quebec

The Bibliothèque Nationale du Québec began to consolidate its collections from four former locations, in preparation for the spring 2005 opening of the Grande Bibliothèque, whose programs and services will be available to everyone in the province.[19]

School Library Day

Teacher-librarians across Canada celebrated International/National School Library Day on October 25. In British Columbia, teachers urged government to undo its damage to literacy programs and restore funding for school libraries as individual schools celebrated reading and libraries. The Manitoba minister of education proclaimed the day with a theme of "Linking Libraries, Literacy and Learning."[20, 21, 22]

Honors for Halifax

Halifax (Nova Scotia) Public Libraries won the American Library Association's 2004 John Cotton Dana Library Public Relations Award, for the second year in a row, for its promotion of the 2003 Summer Reading Program, "Summer Reading Quest." The libraries made a special effort with a public relations campaign to achieve balanced participation across the area, including inner-city libraries.[23]

Linked Search Service

The Coquitlam and Port Moody Public Libraries in British Columbia won the Web Junction Award for Innovative Content and Use of Technology for their combined service, Two Libraries: Search Service. The service integrates the libraries' Web sites within a new structure supported by both municipalities and linked to a new portal at http://www.citysoup.ca. It offers a common search interface that allows community members to search the catalogs of both libraries, other library catalogues in the province, as well as disparate subscription databases (many of which offer electronic full-text articles and encyclopedias), all from the same screen.[24]

Firebombed Library Reborn

The library of the United Talmud Torah School in Montreal was destroyed by firebombing on April 5. Three men were charged in the case. Using donations of books and money received from people across Canada and other countries, the library reopened on December 7, coinciding with the start of Hanukkah. It occupies approximately double its original space.[25]

Collection Lost in Flood

Peterborough (Ontario) Public Library was the hardest-hit facility when a flood caused the city to be declared a disaster area in July. Books were lost when the basement flooded, and the loss included the irreplaceable Peterborough Collection of historical documents and periodicals.[26]

Regina Forestalls Closures

Regina (Saskatchewan) Public Library announced its intention not to close three branches and its art gallery. The 2003 announcement of the proposed closures—prompted by budget restraints—saw a challenge mounted by a friends-of-the-library group. In the end, the revenue shortfall was covered through delays in filling library positions and reductions in all discretionary expenditures.[27]

Toronto Opens 99th Branch

In October Toronto Public Library opened its 99th branch, in St. Jamestown, a high-rise community of extraordinary density and a high number of low-income families. Ten language groups, including Tamil, Russian, and Korean, are featured at the new branch. Toronto Public Library is North America's busiest public library system. More than 300,000 people visit its 99 branches every week and borrow more than half a million items.[28]

Merger in Alberta

The University of Alberta libraries gained a library with the merger of the University and Augustana University College in Camrose. Post-merger plans include the construction of a new library to serve the Augustana faculty.[29]

Innovations and Initiatives

Research Knowledge Network Forms

The Canadian Research Knowledge Network was established as an incorporated body on April 1, 2004, having begun as the Canadian National Site Licensing Project that was initially formed with federal grant support to license electronic journals for 64 universities. The goals of the organization remain the same, and licensing of electronic resources continues to be the focus of its activities, with an expanded membership of post-secondary institutions.[30]

Audio Books Go Digital

The Canadian National Institute for the Blind (CNIB) Library announced a move to producing audio books exclusively in digital format. The announcement followed an agreement with Random House that will see the publisher supplying electronic source files at the same time that the book is being printed for the general reader.[31]

Human Resource Study

In March the "8Rs Study" released *The Future of Heritage Work in Canada,* the results of a survey of museums, archives, and libraries providing a snapshot of human resource issues. The results of the library portion of the study confirm that issues of recruitment, retirement, retention, education, training, and human resource practices are important to the sector. An analysis of the difference between the number of librarian hires and departures revealed a librarian human resource growth rate of 2.4 percent in 2002. The report supported a national summit across the library, archives, and museums sector in Ottawa.[32]

National Digitization Project

The Canadian Initiative on Digital Libraries (CIDL) endorsed a new national digitization project initiated by Simon Fraser University, the University of Calgary, Vancouver Public Library, and other community partners, including the Chinese Freemason Society of Canada and the Multicultural History Society of Ontario. The goal of the project is "to promote greater learning, understanding, and communication among and within the cultural groups that have built Canada."[33]

School Groups Merge

The Association for Teacher Librarianship in Canada (ATLC) and the Canadian School Library Association (CSLA) merged in June to form the Canadian Association for School Libraries, a division of the Canadian Library Association. ATLC was formed 15 years ago when a membership motion to dissolve CSLA as a division of CLA was defeated by a single vote.[34]

Summer Reading Club

Library and Archives Canada (LAC) and the TD Financial Group sponsored the TD Summer Reading Club in nine provinces/territories over the summer. The club was founded by Toronto Public Library with English-language materials developed there; Ottawa Public Library and LAC prepared the French version.[35]

Knowledge Dissemination Study

The Social Sciences and Humanities Research Council–Canadian Association of Research Libraries' study of research knowledge dissemination was completed. Work during the year included expert presentations on the six issues most likely to affect the dissemination of scholarly knowledge in Canada, followed by a two-day consensus panel later in the year during which the issues were turned into five research themes: knowledge systems, knowledge/data storage and retrieval, knowledge production and the social contract, power and infrastructure within the academy, and copyright and intellectual property. The study looked at the current state of scholarly communication in Canada, and asked about the role of external drivers in transforming knowledge dissemination and about the need for a national research strategy to facilitate the adaptation of the scholarly communication system to the new environment. The final report, *Towards an Integrated Knowledge Ecosystem: A Canadian Research Strategy,* includes recommendations on a national strategy and research program.[36, 37]

Open Access Archive

The Universities of Toronto and Ottawa and McMaster University have committed to putting their books in an open access archive, using the Internet Archive, as part of an international project designed to support the goal of universal access to all knowledge. Part of the University of Toronto's participation involves testing use of a robotic scanner to digitize items and then turn them back into print.[38]

Libraries Without Walls

British Columbia has completed a new strategic-planning document, *Libraries Without Walls: The World within Your Reach; A Vision for Public Libraries for British Columbia.* Under the plan, Premier Gordon Campbell announced increased funding for libraries. Starting in 2005–2006, an additional C$12 million will be invested over three years to provide broadband in every community library, increase access to online journals, and establish a provincewide "one-card system" and a virtual reference desk to serve the entire province.[39]

Books for First Nations Communities

Ontario Lieutenant Governor James Bartleman completed his campaign to get books to 33 First Nations (aboriginal) communities in northern Ontario by announcing that more than 500,000 books were collected. The Lieutenant Governor's Book Program is part of Bartleman's broader effort to encourage aboriginal students to pursue reading and education.[40]

Storytelling Week

Storytelling Week, organized by the Library Services for Saskatchewan Aboriginal Peoples' Committee and the Parkland Regional Library, took place in 18 communities in February, the traditional time for storytelling. Some 3,000 people participated, in spite of winter weather intervening in some locations. The organizers plan to make it an annual event.[41]

New Programs in Ontario

Ontario introduced two programs in October to improve public library services. The first provides a 20 percent discount for public libraries that order small arts and literary magazines from members of the Canadian Magazine Publishers Association; the second offers francophones more online reference services in French through the Virtual Reference Library.[42]

Fines Campaign Bears Fruit

For the first time in the history of their province's library service, Prince Edward Islanders are being charged fines for overdue materials because of the high incidence of books not being returned on time; early results indicated that the number of overdue books had decreased by 60 percent.[43]

'IsleAsk' Online Reference

Residents of Prince Edward Island have access to a new service: IsleAsk, a project of Holland College, the University of Prince Edward Island, and the PEI Provincial Library Service. Questions are submitted online and answered by reference librarians in one of the three institutions, usually within 24 hours. The initiative won the Community and Technical College Libraries' Innovation Achievement Award for 2004.[44]

'Ask a Librarian Live'

In September the University of Saskatchewan Library announced its new "Ask a Librarian Live" service, an online, real-time service that connects the client directly to a librarian. The service is open to everyone in the province, although licensing agreements may limit the resources used to answer questions from the public.[45]

Digital Herbarium

Acadia University launched its E. C. Smith Digital Herbarium. The actual herbarium, established in 1910, contains many rare and endangered species of Nova Scotia plants; these are the basis for the digital project. The Digital Herbarium is the first of its kind in Canada, and one of 12 worldwide.[46]

Online Book Club

Edmonton Public Library launched its first online book club for adults, with contests, reading lists, and a discussion forum on the Web site.[47]

Wireless Internet Access

Blackfalds (Alberta) Public Library is the first rural library in the province to offer wireless Internet access for patrons with laptops.[48]

Winnipeg Fund Drive Advances

The Winnipeg Library Foundation's Millennium Community Campaign reported that transformation of the 30-year-old main library was under way, with the C$18 million fund-raising campaign 95 percent complete.[49]

Conclusion

Access to information continues to be a strong local value, with communities across Canada investing in their libraries and innovative services, including a wide variety of Web sites designed to make community information and history accessible. Continuing, if uneven, provincial and local funding for libraries of all types enables an ongoing sense of growth and progress. However, those most engaged with libraries remain concerned about Canada's gaps in information policy, notably copyright and access to government information.

Notes

1. http://www.statcan.ca/Daily/English/050131/d050131a.htm.
2. http://www.statcan.ca/Daily/English/040107/d040107a.htm.
3. http://www.carl-abrc.ca/projects/stats/news_release-0104-e.htm.
4. http://www.cla.ca/issues/gats_update_gould.pdf.
5. http://dsp-psd.pwgsc.gc.ca/new-e.html.
6. http://www.carl-abrc.ca/frames_index.htm.

7. http://www.pch.gc.ca/progs/ac-ca/progs/pda-cpb/reform/index_e.cfm.
8. http://library.lsuc.on.ca/GL/news_alert.htm.
9. http://www.cirpa.ca.
10. http://www.cria.ca.
11. http://www.cpcc.ca.
12. http://ihab-transition-dgaai.ic.gc.ca/pub/index.html?iin.lang=en.
13. http://www.ipsos-na.com/news/pressrelease.cfm?id=2374.
14. http://www.statcan.ca/Daily/English/040610/d040610b.htm.
15. http://www.ic.gc.ca/cmb/welcomeic.nsf/ICPages/NewsReleases.
16. http://www.tbs-sct.gc.ca/est-pre/20042005/NLNAC-BNANC/NLNAC-BNANCr4501_e.asp.
17. http://www.collectionscanada.ca/whats-new/013-203-e.html.
18. http://www.collectionscanada.ca/whats-new/013-216-e.html.
19. http://passerelle2.bnquebec.ca; http://portail2.bnquebec.ca/portal/dt/a_propos_bnq/
    communiques/courants/com_2004_11_11.htm.
20. http://www.nsld.ca.
21. http://www.bctf.bc.ca/publications/newsreleases/archive/2004/2004-10-html.
22. http://www.edu.gov.mb.ca/ks4/iru/schoolib/proclamation.pdf.
23. http://halifaxpubliclibraries.ca/awards.html.
24. http://webjunction.org/do/DisplayContent;jsessionid=C7A1C995E8ADEC831DD2785
    E52D864CB?id=8210.
25. http://www.ctv.ca/servlet/ArticleNews/story/CTVNews/1102444768932_45?hub=Canada.
26. http://www.peacefulcommunities.ca/2004/July/July23.htm.
27. http://www.reginalibrary.ca/news_archives.html.
28. http://www.torontopubliclibrary.ca/new_arc_04oct14_st_james_town.jsp.
29. http://www.uofaweb.ualberta.ca/govrel/nav02.cfm?nav02=25140&nav01=22977.
30. http://www.cnslp.ca.
31. http://www.cnib.ca/library.
32. http://www.ls.ualberta.ca/8rs/FutureofHeritageFinalReport.pdf.
33. http://www.multiculturalcanada.ca/background.htm.
34. http://www.cla.ca/top/whatsnew/wnjn2404_2.htm.
35. http://www.collectionscanada.ca/tdclub/index-e.html.
36. http://www.kdstudy.ca/news.html.
37. http://www.kdstudy.ca/results.html.
38. http://www.archive.org/iathreads/post-view.php?id=25361.
39. http://www.mcaws.gov.bc.ca/lgd/public_libraries/plplan/library_strategic_plan.pdf.
40. http://www.lt.gov.on.ca/book_program.html.
41. http://www.parkland.lib.sk.ca/links/garden.htm#Information_about_2004_Aboriginal.
42. http://ogov.newswire.ca/ontario/GPOE/2004/10/22/c3484.html?lang=_e.html.
43. http://www.gov.pe.ca/news/getrelease.php3?number=3782&PHPSESSID=5a0fc6f59191b.
44. http://islandlibraries.ca/isleask_policies-pls.php.
45. http://library.usask.ca/uask.
46. http://luxor.acadiau.ca/library/Herbarium.
47. http://www.epl.ca/BigChill.
48. http://www.blackfaldslibrary.com/services.htm.
49. http://www.millenniumlibrary.com/community.html.

Canadian Library Association

328 Frank St., Ottawa, ON K2P 0X8
613-232-9625, fax 613-563-9895
E-mail info@cla.ca
World Wide Web http://www.cla.ca

Don Butcher
Executive Director

The Canadian Library Association (CLA) is Canada's national professional and sector association for the library and information community. Its mission: "CLA is my advocate and public voice, educator and network. We build the Canadian library and information community and advance its information professionals."

Membership—now at more than 2,350—is composed both of individuals (librarians and other information professionals, library board trustees) and of institutions (mainly libraries, but also encompassing suppliers to the library and information community). It is predominantly English-language, with selected activities also in French.

CLA's activities are driven by its values:

- We believe that libraries and the principles of intellectual freedom and free universal access to information are key components of an open and democratic society.
- Diversity is a major strength of our association.
- An informed and knowledgeable membership is central in achieving library and information policy goals.
- Effective advocacy is based upon understanding the social, cultural, political, and historical contexts in which libraries and information services function.

Founded in 1946, CLA is a federally incorporated not-for-profit organization. It is governed by an 11-person executive council, which is advised by 14 standing committees and as-needed task forces.

Much of CLA's work is done through its five divisions:

- Canadian Association of College and University Libraries (CACUL), including the Community and Technical College Libraries (CTCL) section
- Canadian Association of Public Libraries (CAPL), including the Canadian Association of Children's Librarians (CACL) section
- Canadian Library Trustees Association
- Canadian Association for School Libraries
- Canadian Association of Special Libraries and Information Services (CASLIS), which has geographic chapters in Calgary, Edmonton, Manitoba, Ottawa, Toronto, and Atlantic Canada

In 2004 each of the six English-language library and information science (LIS) university-level schools in Canada had a CLA student chapter, as did the city of Montreal.

To facilitate sharing of information on specific areas of interest, CLA has 21 interest groups on topics as diverse as access to government information, action for literacy, library and information needs of native people, new librarians and information professionals, and rural and remote libraries.

Governance

In June 2004 CLA inaugurated as its president Stephen Abram, vice president, innovation, at Sirsi Corporation. A librarian with a wide range of experience in the community, Abram's theme for the year is to reignite the passion of librarians by encouraging them to rediscover the library movement that brought them to the profession in the first place. He succeeded Madeleine Lefebvre, university librarian, Saint Mary's University of Halifax, Nova Scotia.

Also serving as officers for 2004–2005 are Barbara Clubb, vice president; A. A. ("Sandy") Cameron, treasurer; and Don Butcher, executive director.

Major Activities

Two major activities dominated CLA activity during 2004.

CLA completed a year-long exercise to reconsider and revise its strategic planning, and, from that, took on new activities and enhanced long-standing ones.

Building on its 2001 Writing the Future Commission, and with the financial support of the Canadian government through the Department of Canadian Heritage, CLA in 2003 undertook an extensive revision of its strategic plan with the aim of enhancing its capacity to serve its members and to support Canada's cultural, social, and economic life. After drafting a new mission and potential objectives, CLA took these core strategic planning elements to its members in a survey in March 2004. The members provided extensive and valuable feedback that led later in the year to the adoption of three core initiatives and one support initiative.

Advocacy

Based on the preliminary results of the member research, CLA undertook an extensive effort to advocate for libraries during Canada's 2004 federal election. Using the expertise of senior library and information leaders from across the country, a foundation advocacy position document was created. From this, key messages were transmitted to political candidates and their support staff through a grassroots advocacy campaign involving local librarians and information professionals, supported by direct CLA national office communication to all candidates from all parties in all ridings.

Advocacy continued in central areas: potential revisions to the Copyright Act, culminating in a public advocacy campaign; research and a draft position paper on privacy and the impact of the USA Patriot Act in Canada; a call for reinstatement of funding for access to the Internet via public libraries; a push for an enhanced role for Library and Archives Canada (the successor organization to the National Library of Canada) in the dissemination of government documents; and continued work on the provision of a nationwide network of equitable library service for the print-disabled.

Continuing Professional Development

CLA's Annual Conference was held jointly with the British Columbia Library Association in Victoria, B.C. Delegate and exhibitor attendance was excellent, allowing financial results to exceed expectations. Major conference highlights included the keynote speeches. Michael Gorman, dean of library services at the Henry Madden Library, California State University, and president-elect of the American Library Association, spoke on the crucial importance of core values in the library community. Bill Richardson, a Canadian radio personality, author, and former children's librarian, challenged and entertained with his speech "Becoming Bunny Watson" (Bunny Watson, played by Katharine Hepburn, was the librarian star of the 1957 movie *Desk Set*).

CLA furthered its commitment to expanding continuing professional development for its members by hiring a staff person specifically for that purpose.

During 2004 one CLA division, the Canadian School Library Association (CSLA), and a similar organization, the Association of Teacher-Librarians of Canada (ATLC), were both disbanded to facilitate the creation of a new CLA division, the Canadian Association for School Libraries. The new division creates a stronger voice for school libraries and teacher-librarians as they advance child and youth literacy.

International Activities

CLA modestly expanded its international activities in 2004 through leadership in Canadian participation in the International Federation of Library Associations and Institutions (IFLA), including chairing the Canadian caucus and supporting l'Association pour l'Avancement des Sciences et des Techniques de la Documentation (ASTED) as it prepares to host the World Library and Information Congress in Quebec City in 2008.

Member Communications

As information professionals, Canadian librarians depend on timely and attractive publications from their professional association.

CLA's bimonthly publication *Feliciter* continued to explore core themes in the library community: management and human resources, media literacy and democracy, buildings and library space, and exploring how libraries interact with and lead their communities. Each issue had a guest editor.

Current LIS community news is now captured in an electronic membership newsletter, *CLA Digest,* and the CLA Web site (http://www.cla.ca) was used to a much greater extent for current member and public communication, as well as retaining its role as a repository of historical and long-lived information.

Awards and Honors

As always, the strength and power of any community comes down to its people. CLA recognized a few special individuals from the Canadian library and information community with awards and honors in 2004.

CLA's highest honor, the Outstanding Services to Librarianship Award, went to Wendy Newman of Hamilton, Ontario. Newman—a former academic, special, and, most recently, public librarian—is currently librarian-in-residence at the University of Toronto, Ontario. The reasons for honoring her are many. Among them are her role in advancing public libraries in Ontario and internationally through UNESCO, her active participation on a Canadian government task force on broadband access and at a government summit on innovation, her role in Internet literacy for children through the Media Awareness Network, and her leadership of CLA through the ALA/CLA Conference in Toronto.

The CLA/Information Today award for Innovative Technology was presented to the Windsor (Ontario) Public Library for its project Geographic Information Systems (GIS) Applications in Health.

Jannah McCarville of McGill University won the CLA Student Article Contest for her article "Balancing Access and Privacy in Archives."

The CLA Award for the Advancement of Intellectual Freedom was presented to Monique Désormeaux, a manager at the Ottawa Public Library, for her leadership and courage in guiding the library through a challenge to its Internet access policy.

The W. Kaye Lamb Award for Service to Seniors was awarded by CLA and the Ex Libris Association to Toronto Public Library for ongoing service to seniors.

Conclusion

After a challenging year in 2003, 2004 proved to be a return to the basics for CLA: listening to members, strategic planning, and undertaking activities to meet members' expressed needs and wants. A modest increase in membership numbers in the latter part of the year, and balanced financial results, suggest that CLA is on a solid course as it provides leadership to the Canadian library and information community.

Special Reports

Licensing of Electronic Resources: Resources for Dealing with the Challenge

Trisha L. Davis

Evolution to Date

In the mid-1990s the library and publishing world began to acknowledge that licensing of electronic resources was replacing the purchase of products distributed and accessed in digital format. The now ubiquitous license agreement at first appeared only when the larger research libraries were actually buying data on physical media that was to be mounted and served by the library. The traditional purchase order form from the vendor included use terms and restrictions along with the price and product details. Librarians frequently interpreted their signature on the form as a purchase approval rather than a signature binding the institution to a legal contract. With the advent of distribution via CD-ROM, even smaller libraries were confronted with a shrink-wrapped form of agreement and accepted the contractual terms without much consideration as part of the acquisition process. By the time information providers began the shift to online access, libraries were dealing with shrink-wrapped, click-on, and formal license agreements with virtually every purchase of an electronic resource.

Publishers, aggregators, and librarians shared a common learning curve as lawyers appeared on the scene to take charge of the licensing process. At first, trusting their publishers to understand their needs and support them as they always had, librarians simply accepted the shrink-wrapped legalese, clicked on the "I agree" buttons, and signed legally binding agreements with at best a minimal understanding of the process or the commitment. Most libraries had no access to lawyers or copyright specialists and failed to realize that their assumed rights as granted by the copyright law were not included in the license agreement. Many failed to realize that they could actually negotiate the terms of the license to include these rights. However, a few of the larger libraries with unique requirements began to realize that these standardized licenses would not apply to their situation or did not grant the rights they needed to adequately access and use the product in their environment. At this point, librarians turned to their own

Trisha Davis is an associate professor and head of serials and electronic resources at the Ohio State University Libraries. She has worked for the Association of Research Libraries since 1997 and is a course designer and instructor for ARL's introductory and advanced workshops on licensing electronic resources and its Online Lyceum course "Licensing Review and Negotiation."

lawyers and began the lengthy, often tedious learning curve of contract law and its implications for their libraries.

By the time the Digital Millennium Copyright Act (DMCA) of 1998 took effect, the majority of parties involved in the process realized that they had become antagonists rather than partners in the process of acquisition. The publishers defaulted to their lawyers' advice and insisted on protecting their rights via contract rather than depending on the new copyright law, which failed to address many library use issues and had never been tested. Many librarians and most library patrons continued to assume that the "fair use" rights of the 1976 Copyright Act, including its amendments and exceptions, continued to apply in the digital realm. Meanwhile, the Uniform Computer Information Transactions Act (UCITA) widened the gulf even further as libraries were threatened with terms that were truly non-negotiable and frequently not acceptable.

By the late 1990s professional associations, universities, and consultants began writing licensing principles, drafting their own versions of model licenses, building Web sites, and eventually publishing a few good guides. While there is currently no industry standard for license agreements, the wording of many terms in these guides appears repeatedly in today's licenses, indicating that standardization is desirable to both parties. Thanks to these seminal documents, librarians have guidance in negotiations and publishers have a guide to what libraries desire in a license agreement.

Licensing Principles

In July 1997 a working group from six national library associations[1] issued the final draft of *Principles for Licensing Electronic Resources.*[2] The very first sentences of the introduction state:

> License agreements are a fact of life in conducting business in the electronic environment. Providers of electronic information resources are employing licenses as a legal means of controlling the use of their products.

This draft was the first document issued by a national organization to declare that licensing was replacing purchase as the preferred form of acquisition for electronic products, that the terms of a license agreement could supplant the traditional fair uses assumed under copyright, and that librarians needed guidelines for negotiating these agreements. In drafting this document, the working group studied similar documents from the National Humanities Alliance (NHA)[3] and the University of California Libraries' Collection Development Committee.[4] The 15 licensing principles were widely distributed and discussed throughout the six organizations, resulting in many groups either adopting them or writing their own versions. Regardless of content, the fact that model guidelines were being developed alerted librarians throughout the world that they could no longer avoid dealing with these agreements.

There are five primary sets of principles available today. In addition to the AALL/ALA/AAHSL/ARL/MLA/SLA Licensing Principles noted above, California Digital Libraries (CDL) has issued multiple guidelines documents. The International Coalition of Library Consortia (ICOLC) issued its "Statement of Current Perspective and Preferred Practices for the Selection and Purchase of Electronic Information" in March 1998.[5] The Canadian Research Knowledge Network (CRKN) issued its "Principles for Licensing Electronic Resources" in May 2000.[6] The International Federation of Library Associations and Institutions (IFLA) issued its "Licensing Principles" in March 2001. In Britain, the Joint Information Systems Committee (JISC) Committee for Content Services established its own set of "General Principles"[7] based primarily on those from ICOLC and model licenses developed by several library associations.

These principles documents have many elements in common. The more salient points are

1 Licensing has now become an accepted part of the acquisition process for electronic resources.

2 A license agreement should ask each party to respect the intellectual property rights of the other, as is expected under copyright law.

3 License terms should balance the rights and responsibilities of both parties.

4 All license terms, including price, should be clearly stated and negotiable.

5 Both parties, the licensor and the licensee, should expect contractual obligations to be explicitly stated in the agreement and should establish internal policies to enforce these obligations.

6 License agreements should include the well-established fair-use rights for noncommercial, educational use by authorized users. Such rights should include access, search, download, printing, and copying rights assumed by library users in the print environment.

7 The definition of authorized user should not prohibit the library's registered patrons and traditional users from access, including remote access from any location. The definition also should include nonaffiliated walk-in patrons at public workstations within library buildings.

8 A license agreement should not ask the library to assume responsibility for use of the resource by the end user. The library as licensee, however, should take responsibility for alerting end users to the license terms and should make reasonable efforts to prevent misuse and assure the security and integrity of the licensed product.

9 Archival rights are important to libraries. When perpetual access or permanent use is acquired, the licensor should include license terms that assure the licensee may take appropriate action to make a usable electronic preservation or archival copy or, if license terms preclude that option, should accept responsibility for the provision of such a copy.

10 The right to gather statistics and measure use belongs to both parties. The licensor should be expected to gather and share data with the licensee while at the same time protecting the anonymity and confidentiality of individual users and their use activity. Such information should never be disclosed to third parties for any purpose other than marketing or purchase analysis.

11 Pricing models should be affordable in relation to print prices, should offer unbundled print, online, and consortia options, and should not place the burden of funding the shift to the electronic format solely on the licensee.

Model Licenses

Soon after the development of licensing principles, librarians realized the need for additional help in reviewing, revising, and negotiating the complex terms found in license agreements. This need was met by standardized license language found in model licenses developed by various library organizations. The "Joint Information Systems Committee and Publishers Association Working Party Proposed 'Model Licence' Between UK Universities and Publishers" draft issued in July 1997 was developed collaboratively by a working party of British publishers and university librarians.[8] It quickly became the standard from which additional models evolved. The U.K. National Electronic Site License Initiative, NESLI, extended the initial JISC draft into the "Model NESLi2 Licence for Journals."[9] This model license currently is used by JISC staff or its agents in negotiations with journal publishers.

At the American Library Association (ALA) Annual Conference in June 1999, a set of four model licenses was developed by a team of librarians and representatives of four major international subscription agents,[10] led by John Cox Associates, a British international publishing consultancy specializing in licensing and content management. Based on the PA/JISC model, the four model licenses are for single academic institutions, academic consortia, public libraries, and corporate and other special libraries. The revised versions were released in 2000.[11]

In March 2000 the Committee on Institutional Cooperation (CIC), a consortium of 12 major U.S. research universities, developed a Statement on Standardized Agreement Language[12] for members of the consortium to use in negotiating with vendors. This statement is not a complete model license, but provides model language to address the license terms that have proven most problematic in previous negotiations. In a similar fashion, the Canadian National Site Licensing Project (CNSLP), a national effort by a consortium of 64 Canadian university libraries to provide access to full-text electronic journals, released its CNSLP License Agreement to accompany its "Principles for Licensing Electronic Resources," released in May 2000.

In spring 2001 the Liblicense Standard Licensing Agreement—sponsored by the Council on Library and Information Resources (CLIR), the Digital Library Federation (DLF), and Yale University Library—was made available to the public via the Yale University Web site. Created by college and university librarians, lawyers, and other university officials responsible for licensing, with significant input from the academic publishing community, this effort represents a singular viewpoint: the American academic library community's needs.[13]

Top-Notch Advice on Handling License Agreements

The review, revision, and negotiation of license agreements continues to be a difficult and time-consuming process because of the lack of formal standards and inexperience on the part of both the library and the publisher. Most of the published literature discusses licensing in terms of copyright law, handling the negotiation process, pricing, and consortia relations. For information on how to handle agreements, there are few choices.

Two excellent guides to the licensing process have been published in the last decade.

The first was Arlene Bielefield and Lawrence Cheeseman's *Interpreting and Negotiating Licensing Agreements: A Guidebook for the Library, Research, and Teaching Professions,* published by Neal-Schuman in 1999. Both authors are MLS-degreed librarians, and Bielefield also holds a law degree. They have collaborated on several books relating to library processes and the law that have been reviewed and recommended by key library journals. Although the book is now a bit dated, the content is highly valuable and the organization quite helpful for those needing a clear explanation of common legal clauses. In 2002 ALA published *Licensing Digital Content: A Practical Guide for Librarians* by Lesley Ellen Harris, a Canadian lawyer who specializes in copyright and licensing issues. This book is written for the librarian, from the perspective of working one's way through a license agreement, and includes excellent definitions, great tips for the negotiation process, and answers to common questions.

Harris also offers one of two highly popular Web-based courses on licensing. Her Digital Licensing Online[14] course is available on a regularly scheduled basis and consists of three e-mail lessons for nine weeks and access to a course listserv for questions and discussions. The Association of Research Libraries (ARL) offers a five-week course, Licensing Review and Negotiation,[15] as part of its Online Lyceum series. The course is run on an interactive Web format and includes five content modules, individual journals, exercises with feedback from instructors, and scheduled chat sessions. Similar to the Harris course, the ARL course is offered several times a year.

Finally, two extensive Web resources are available to assist with the licensing process. Best known is the Yale University Library Liblicense[16] site, the first to offer in-depth discussion and information on the licensing process. The ARL Web site includes a section on "Issues in Scholarly Communication" that includes a page devoted to licensing issues[17] and serves as an excellent directory to other sites. Many universities have mounted Web sites to assist their staff in dealing with copyright issues, but few have licensing guidelines available to the public.

Key License Terms

Just as publishers' license agreements vary widely, each of the model licenses has a unique set of terms. Examined in their entirety, many of the model license terms fall into common categories: definitions critical to the library as licensee; rights desired by the library as licensee; the library's obligations as licensee; the publisher's obligations as licensor; and standard contractual terms. A summary of the key terms in each category follows.

Definitions Critical to the Library as Licensee

Authorized Users: Consistently defined as any employee, student, registered patron, or other persons approved to use the library or authorized to access the product on-site or via remote access regardless of their location, including nonaffiliated walk-in users on the premises. The proper definition of authorized users is essential to the value of the license. In the print environment, libraries could assume their resources could be made available to any person, at any time, and for any purpose. A license's standard definition of authorized user has the potential to exclude certain classes of users. The library must build its own definition based on the expected users of the product in question and assure the definition meets those criteria, or revise the definition to do so.

Authorized Uses: Unlimited access, search, retrieval, downloading, and display of licensed content; printing, copying in print or electronic format, and storing temporarily in print or electronic format a reasonable amount of content for the purposes of research, education, personal, or other noncommercial uses consistent with fair-use provisions of the U.S. and other copyright laws. In a similar but much broader manner, the definition of authorized uses also is essential to the value of the license. In the print environment, the library was not held responsible for the user's intent or actions. A license's standard definition of authorized uses may deny or limit common usage by either the library or the end user. The library must determine which uses are key to the product in question and assure that those rights are included in the definition or elsewhere in the license.

Rights Desired by the Library as Licensee

Archival/Backup Copying: The right to make one copy of the licensed content in digital form to be maintained as backup or archival copy. Backup and/or replacement rights are common when the license applies to content supplied on physical media that can be damaged or destroyed. Yet some standard licenses fail to address this problem, and backup rights must be added by the library. However, ownership of the digital content and use rights in perpetuity is the only way to assure an archival copy. When the digital content is accessed via an external server, archival rights are more difficult to obtain. Only on rare occasion will a standard license grant the right to copy and store the entire content of the product. Frequently the publisher will refuse archival rights because they simply want continued income for the right to access the content perpetually. Even when archival access is granted, the future promise of a digital copy in an unknown format of the future remains a risk.

Course Packs: The right to use a reasonable portion of the licensed content in print or digital form for sale and/or distribution to authorized users as part of course packs relating to classroom instruction. The standard publisher license often fails to address this right; if important to the library, a clearly written definition added to the agreement is frequently accepted by the publisher.

Course Reserves: The right to include a reasonable portion of the licensed content as part of course reserves in print or digital form for use by authorized users relating to classroom instruction. Like course pack rights, the standard publisher license often fails to address course reserves; if important to the library, a clearly written definition added to the agreement is frequently accepted by the publisher.

Electronic Links: The right to provide electronic links to the licensed content from library or course Web sites in order to increase accessibility and usage of the licensed content. Again, the standard publisher license often fails to address this right; if important to the library, a clearly written definition added to the agreement is frequently accepted by the publisher.

Interlibrary Loan: The right to use of a reasonable portion of the licensed content to fulfill interlibrary loan requests in print or digital form in accordance with the Interlibrary Loan Provision of section 108 of the U.S. Copyright Law and the CONTU (National Commission on New Technological Uses of Copyright Works) Guidelines. In the last decade, interlibrary loan rights have become standard in license agreements for electronic journals. Should a license fail to address this right, the library should not hesitate to add language from one of the standard licenses and expect that it will be accepted. There normally is no need for interlibrary loan rights in a license agreement for a database product unless it includes full-text articles. In that case, the standard language should be modified to indicate that the library wishes to lend only the full-text articles, not other content. The database owner, however, may not have the right to grant that permission.

Scholarly Sharing: The authorized users' right to share a limited amount of the licensed content in print or digital form with a colleague who is not defined as an authorized user for the purpose of scholarly, educational, or personal research only. The standard publisher license will not include this right; if important to the library, a clearly written definition added to the agreement is often, but not always, accepted by the publisher. Once the content is shared with someone who is not a party to the license agreement, the terms of use no longer apply and the publisher has lost the ability to control use.

The Library's Obligations as Licensee

Breach: The obligation to investigate or to assist in the investigation of a suspected or known breach of the terms of the agreement and to take reasonable action to assure that such activity ceases. Most libraries with significant digital resources have been alerted to suspected or proven breaches. The most common breach is high-volume downloading. The important issue when dealing with breaches is that the publisher alert the library to the breach with sufficient evidence and sufficient time to investigate and remedy the breach. It is unreasonable to accept terms that allow the publisher to terminate access immediately and/or without notice due to a suspected breach. The standard licenses include excellent language regarding suspected breaches and how they should be handled.

Commercial Use: The obligation to not knowingly permit and to take reasonable action to prevent use of the licensed content for commercial purposes. The key concept here is the ignorance of use purpose by the library. If and when the library learns that a known user is copying or distributing content for a commercial purpose, specific steps should be taken to halt such activity or even deny access to those involved.

Copyright Notice: The obligation to not knowingly permit and to take reasonable action to prevent copying of licensed content in a manner that would remove, obscure, or modify the author's name or any copyright notice included in the licensed content. It is unimaginable that any library would provide content in a manner that would remove, obscure, or modify copyright statements. However, some licenses state that the library is obliged to assure that copyright notice is printed on all copies with no mention of their own responsibility for its presence in the content.

It is not the library's responsibility to assure the addition of a copyright statement if it is not present in the licensed content as it is copied or printed by the user.

Redistribution: The obligation to not knowingly permit and to take reasonable action to prevent mounting and redistribution of licensed content on any electronic network, the Internet, or Web-based course management systems, other than for the agreed-upon use for interlibrary loan, course packs, and course reserves. Again, the key concept here is the library's ignorance of the user's illegal actions. If and when the library learns that a known user is distributing content for any unapproved purpose, specific steps should be taken to halt such activity or even deny access to those involved.

Systematic Copying: The obligation to not knowingly permit and to take reasonable action to prevent systematic printing or copying of license content for any purpose other than production of an agreed-upon archival or backup copy. As with previous terms, the key concept here is the library's ignorance of the illegal activity. If and when the library learns that a known user is systematically copying content for any unapproved purpose, specific steps should be taken to halt such activity or even deny access to those involved.

Unauthorized Users: The obligation to not knowingly permit and to take reasonable action to prevent unauthorized users remote access to the licensed content. This obligation relates to the integrity of the library's proxy server or other access control mechanisms. When alerted by the publisher to any suspected remote activity by unauthorized users, specific steps should be taken to halt such activity or even deny access to those involved.

The Publisher's Obligations as Licensor

Availability of Licensed Content: The obligation to make reasonable efforts to assure the continuous (around-the-clock) availability of the licensed content to the authorized users and to schedule down time for maintenance at an agreed-upon time to minimize inconvenience. The standard licenses provide excellent language to define availability in terms of hours available, speed of system response, and the product's ability to sustain high volume of use.

Changes to Licensed Content: The obligation to refund a prorated amount of the license fee to the library and terminate the license agreement should the publisher/content provider make any significant additions, deletions, or modifications to the licensed content that render the product unacceptable to the authorized users. Many libraries have been discouraged to learn that rights to important content were lost by the content- or database-provider and the product has lost its usefulness. This language should be present in all licenses for products that include content not owned by the provider, but licensed from a third party.

Changes to Licensed Software: The obligation to refund a prorated amount of the license fee to the library and terminate the license agreement should the publisher make any significant changes to the licensed software that renders use of the product unacceptable to the authorized users. In a similar fashion, many libraries have been discouraged to learn that the search or display software has been changed to the extent that the product can no longer be accessed and used from some locations. This language should be present in all licenses for all Internet-based products not controlled and served by the library.

Confidentiality of Use Data: The obligation to assure the confidentiality of any data relating to the use of the licensed content by authorized users. This has become a critical issue for online products. The publisher or provider has full capability to capture use statistics that could reveal identity, search terms, content retrieved, and even patterns of use. Any license should include language that protects the privacy of the user, and the standard licenses provide excellent terms that may be added to any license.

Notification: The obligation to give prompt notice of any significant changes to the licensed content or the licensed software. The obligation obviously ties in directly to the publisher's obligation to refund a prorated amount of the license fee should such changes result in a material loss of use. For many reasons, the publisher should be required to give notice, in advance if possible, of significant changes, especially if the opportunity to terminate the license is limited to a specified time period after such a change.

Standard Contractual Terms

Contract law varies from state to state and frequently mimics the federal Uniform Commercial Code in its content. Only a lawyer, or someone who has studied contract law, is qualified to interpret what are known as "boilerplate" terms of a standard license agreement. The following terms are just a few of the clauses that might be modified by the library's legal counsel. However, these are the terms most commonly negotiated by the library and should be considered in advance of review by legal counsel when the license is not acceptable as written.

Governing Law: Should be assigned to a jurisdiction convenient to both parties or left unassigned. The standard contract will state the governing law as the state in which the content owner does its primary business. Libraries in state institutions often must change this language in order to abide by their state law. Most libraries follow one of two options: change the governing law to the state of the library, or remove the language altogether.

Indemnities: Should either be mutual or nonexistent. Licenses frequently ask the library to indemnify the content provider from any claims of third parties and ask the library to pay any expenses to defend the publisher if necessary. There is no reason to accept such language. Some libraries will accept indemnity clauses if the protection is mutual. Most libraries, and libraries in state institutions, will simply remove the language from the contract.

Desired Terms Not Yet Addressed in the Model Licenses

Even as publishers and librarians use terms from the model licenses in drafting, revising, and negotiating license language, new issues arise regularly. These are among the most recent terms to be added to licenses:

ADA Compliance: The publisher's Web site should meet the requirements of the Americans with Disabilities Act Section 508.[18] Although information providers normally will not agree to these requirements because of the high cost of compliance, it is important that libraries make the request.

LOCKSS Compliance: LOCKSS[19] (Lots Of Copies Keep Stuff Safe) is free software used to capture, preserve, and provide access to acquired Web-based content. Libraries that participate in the LOCKSS system request the right to archive data in this manner.

Project COUNTER Compliance: Project COUNTER (Counting Online Usage of NeTworked Electronic Resources)[20] is an international standard for measuring use of electronic resources. The statistics collected and reported to libraries should follow the COUNTER Code of Practice.

A Glimpse into the Future

The current handwriting on the wall says that licensing is here to stay. The Digital Millennium Copyright Act[21] (DMCA) has failed to assure the digital rights and exemptions granted in print environment by the 1976 Copyright Act.[22] The good news is that DMCA continues to be analyzed, developed, debated, tested, and hopefully will recognize and expand fair-use rights in the next decade. In the meantime, libraries need to approach licensing as any good negotiator would. The library's representative must understand the publisher's position, rights, fears, and the value of its commodity. At the same time, the librarian must analyze and know the library's own requirements, request the rights the library must have, refuse the obligations it cannot meet, and be reasonable. The library needs a product, the publisher needs a sale; with research, education, practice, and preparation, the licensing process can be a win-win situation.

Notes

1. American Association of Law Libraries (AALL), American Library Association (ALA), Association of Academic Health Sciences Libraries (AAHSL), Association of Research Libraries (ARL), Medical Library Association (MLA), and Special Libraries Association (SLA).
2. The Principles are available at http://www.arl.org/scomm/licensing/principles.html.
3. National Humanities Alliance. "Basic Principles for Managing Intellectual Property in the Digital Environment," March 24, 1997 (http://www.nhalliance.org/ip/ip_principles_1997.html).
4. University of California Libraries, Collection Development Committee. "Principles for Acquiring and Licensing Information in Digital Formats," May 22, 1996 (http://www.cdlib.org/inside/collect/framework.html).
5. The ICOLC statement is available at http://www.library.yale.edu/consortia/statement.html.
6. The CRKN principles are available at http://www.cnslp.ca/about/principles.

7. The JISC general principles are available at http://www.jisc.ac.uk/index.cfm? name=collections_licensing_principles.

8. The PA/JISC model license is available at http://www.ukoln.ac.uk/services/elib/papers/pa/licence.

9. The Model NESLi2 Licence is available at http://www.nesli.ac.uk/model.htm.

10. EBSCO, Harrassowitz, RoweCom, and Swets Blackwell.

11. The second versions are available at http://www.licensingmodels.com.

12. The most recent version of the CIC Standardized Agreement Language is available at http://www.cic.uiuc.edu/programs/CLIConsortialAgreementProgram/archive/BestPractice/Stand ardizedAgreementLanguageDec02.pdf.

13. Version 2.0 of the CLIR/DLF Model License is available at http://www.library.yale.edu/~llicense/modlic.shtml.

14. Registration information for this course is available at http://copyrightlaws.com/index2.html.

15. Registration information for this course is available at http://arl.org/training/licensing.html

16. See http://www.library.yale.edu/~llicense.

17. See http://www.arl.org/scomm/licensing.

18. For additional information on Section 508 compliance, see http://www.section508.gov.

19. For additional information on LOCKSS, see http://lockss.stanford.edu.

20. For additional information on Project COUNTER's Code of Practice, see http://www.projectcounter.org.

21. DMCA is available at http://www.copyright.gov/legislation/dmca.pdf. ARL's excellent analysis with comments on the status of the legislation is available at http://www.arl.org/info/frn/copy/dmca.html.

22. The 1976 Copyright Act is available at http://www.copyright.gov/title17.

Information Policies and Open Access:
Internet Publishing Makes Headlines in 2004

Edward J. Valauskas

Follett Chair, Graduate School of Library and Information Science, Dominican University
Chief Editor, *First Monday* (http://firstmonday.org)

Nancy R. John

Assistant University Librarian, University of Illinois at Chicago

The interests of the research community, the taxpayer and the publishing industry (whether commercial or not for profit) are closely intertwined. The continuation of widely disseminated, accessible top quality peer-review research, produced efficiently and at competitive prices, is in everyone's interests.

—House of Commons Science and Technology Committee[1]

Open content and open access emerged in 2004 as serious and highly contentious information policy issues. Government agencies in several countries and international organizations decreed support for open access. Eventually, some agencies scaled back their support for open access and open content under the pressure of intense lobbying. Scholars responded with a variety of organizational tactics, including a letter from Nobel laureates to the U.S. Congress on the matter. Because data form the basis of many papers in journals and magazines, an incredible tug-of-war is going on over how this information will be made available.

The year opened with a pivotal meeting in Paris of the Organization for Economic Cooperation and Development (OECD) on scientific and technological policies. At the conclusion of the session in late January 2004 an impressive array of signatories of 34 countries, including Britain and the United States, agreed to a "Declaration on access to research data from public funding." This declaration recognized that "open source will maximise the value derived from public investments in data collection." All parties agreed to balance "the interests of open access . . . to increase the quality and efficiency of research and innovation with the need for restriction of access . . . to protect social, scientific and economic interests."[2]

Open access was certainly on the minds of the ministers in Paris. Maria van der Hoeven, Dutch minister of education, culture, and science, explained her support of open access in this way:

One of our researchers, he is a logician, has characterised information as the only resource that will grow by its use. Information and data resources will not be depleted by use . . . You can have your cake and eat it as well, again and again. The same data can be used over and over again by many people at many different times and places and this will only increase their value.
It is obvious that Open Access will be a necessary condition to realise the potential of research data as the *floating capital of global science*"[3] [emphasis original].

These proceedings actually were in character for the international information policymaking community. There was, in a sense, considerable momentum to support open access at a policy level going into 2004. In December 2003 the

World Summit on the Information Society released a "Declaration of Principles" and "Plan of Action." In the declaration it was clearly stated that "The ability for all to access and contribute information, ideas and knowledge is essential in an inclusive Information Society." [4] In the plan of action, there were encouraging words for advocates of open access. Governments and other "stakeholders" were asked to "promote electronic publishing, differential pricing and open access initiatives to make scientific information affordable and accessible." [5]

We might trace the lineage of these weighty remarks to supportive acts by other parties, such as the collective support of German research organizations in October 2003. Their resulting document, the "Berlin Declaration on Open Access to Knowledge in the Sciences and Humanities," clearly supports open access and the use of the Internet "as a fundamental instrument for a global scientific base and human reflection." [6] There are nearly 60 signatories to the Berlin Declaration. [7]

These policy moves were further blessed with data presented in February 2004 at Stevan Harnad's EPrints.org-supported conference at Britain's Southampton University. As might be expected, the one-day event brought together Harnadian-minded scholars. [8] One of the few Americans presenting at the conference, Michael J. Kurtz of the Harvard-Smithsonian Center for Astrophysics, provided some preliminary information on the use of astronomical data. He found that restrictive access dramatically affected the "reading behavior of working researchers." [9]

Restrictive access certainly influences the ways in which instructors use information found in journals in their classes. In a study reported in the pages of *BMC Medical Education,* Michele Langlois and her team at the University of Manchester reported enormous difficulties in accessing online content for Web-based classes. They warned that problems in securing permission to use some literature as readings would lead to biases in medical education. [10]

Cost Considerations

Clearly, the true meaning of "access" was one issue on the table in 2004. The cost of open access was another contentious topic. In February 2004 the editors of the *Proceedings of the National Academy of Sciences* (*PNAS*) conducted an informal survey to test financial models. A little over 600 authors of papers in *PNAS* were asked to participate in the survey; 210 responded. Of those 210, about half (49.5 percent) supported open access upon publication. But about 80 percent of those supporting open access would only pay a fee of $500, or about a quarter of the publication costs in the absence of subscription income. The National Academy of Sciences already has made *PNAS* available without cost globally six months after publication and immediately upon publication for more than 130 developing countries. The editors of *PNAS* commented obliquely on the survey by remarking that they "will continue to weigh the comments and concerns" of their readers and contributors "as well as the effect on our finances." [11]

These comments were echoed in the remarks of Catherine DeAngelis and Robert Musacchio in the pages of the *Journal of the American Medical Association* (*JAMA*), where they noted that "the true cost of scientific publishing has not yet been determined." [12] *JAMA,* like *PNAS,* is treating open access experimentally, providing free access to major articles and editorials six months after publication and free access to selected countries in the developing world.

PLoS Biology noted in an April 2004 editorial the significance of a financial model based on publication fees, and the findings of the National Academy of Sciences survey. *PloS Biology*'s editorial noted that "nearly 90 percent of those who submit manuscripts do not request a fee waiver, and the few who do still offer to pay some portion of the fee."[13] The fee itself has no influence on the peer-review process as a firewall prevents editors and reviewers from knowing who has paid a fee and who has not.

All of these questions about open access truly revolved around the larger issue of sustainability. Jan Velterop of BioMed Central pointed out that these questions were truly red herrings. Velterop wrote:

> The issue is not "Open Access or not" anymore. That's a station we've already passed. . . .
> Any business that can deliver what customers need or want, at a price that they are willing to pay, is sustainable. The crux of the matter lies in the phrase "the price customers are willing to pay" for the "value" or "added-value" of a product or service. The Open Access model is sustainable as long as its customers are prepared to pay for the service they receive. The traditional model is the one that is unsustainable, precisely because its customers are no longer prepared to pay the asking price.[14]

Open access gained notable support in the summer of 2004 from two significant sources, the British House of Commons Science and Technology Committee and the U.S. National Institutes of Health (NIH). Given the prelude of open access support, at a variety of levels, in the first six months of 2004, these recommendations for open access by important government bodies might not be surprising.

After months of testimony, the Science and Technology Committee saw open access as a "viable" alternative that needed both support and continued experimentation.[15] The committee recommended that researchers funded by the British government make their works available online, and that "author-pays" models of open access needed further investigation. (Under an author-pays system, a publication charges authors a fee to have their work published online in lieu of charging readers to access articles.)[16]

These recommendations flew in the face of remarks made by some publishers before the committee. Elsevier warned that "by introducing an author-pays model, Open Access risks undermining public trust in the integrity and quality of scientific publications that has been established over hundreds of years."[17]

Unfortunately for supporters of Open Access and experimentation in Internet publishing, the British government elected not to take action on the committee report, because the government was "not aware that there are major problems in accessing scientific information."[18] For members of the committee, this response was disappointing. The committee remarked that "The debate about scientific publications is still evolving, and the Committee will be pursuing the issues in a variety of ways. We are disappointed that the Government has missed the opportunity to take more decisive action in response to our Report."[19] An opportunity for broader experimentation in Britain with Open Access and Internet publishing indeed was lost. But given the global nature of the Internet and Open Access, opportunities may appear elsewhere.

NIH Move Causes Stir

A parallel experience occurred across the Atlantic, with the release in September of an NIH plan that would require NIH-funded researchers to post their papers at NIH's PubMed Central within six months of publication.[20] NIH received both considerable praise for this plan and serious criticism from publishers. For example, the Association of Learned and Professional Society Publishers remarked:

> ... to embark on a course of action which could lead either to journals being destroyed, or to precipitate adoption of an untried alternative business model which might be no better at ensuring their survival, is—we believe—not helpful to the scholarly research endeavour. We believe that it would be far preferable to recommend, rather than mandating, self-archiving; to allow publishers to determine the delay after publication; or, indeed, both.[21]

Hence, it is not surprising that NIH back-pedaled, with a final report in February 2005 that recommended (not required) posting papers at PubMed within up to 12 months rather than 6. Many on Open Access side saw this "retreat" as "unjustified and regrettable."[22]

Nevertheless, the issues are far from dead. Twenty-five Nobel Prize laureates sent a letter to the U.S. Congress in support of NIH's initial plan, remarking that "open access truly expands shared knowledge across scientific fields—it is the best path for accelerating multi-disciplinary breakthroughs in research."[23] In addition, major independent funding bodies, among them Britain's Wellcome Trust, are strongly supporting open access and Internet publishing.[24]

"Open" motives are spreading to other disciplines, with biologists' genetic information available via a "protected technology commons."[25] Open software, such as Bram Cohen's BitTorrent, is already causing new headaches for media giants.[26] The "open" genie[27] is certainly out of the bottle and shows incredible reluctance to return.

The traditional publishers (if one can still use that nomenclature), meaning those publishers that have a long history in paper and electronic formats, and who sell their content at prices designed to make for good business, were both visible in public forums and hard at work on reshaped business plans and product development strategies. The past decade has seen most, if not all, journal publishers develop robust business environments for creating and managing formerly paper journals for electronic access. More recently, publishers have retrofitted these systems to meet standards that have emerged, e.g., OpenURL. However, the delivery of this content had remained pretty much unchanged—creating a functional Web site that allows searching for specific articles, browsing issues, or mining the site for articles by a particular author or on a particular topic. While features had been added—such as "hot" or linked references and citations in articles or stable bookmarks (permanent URLs) to provide for standard citations— these journal Web sites were fundamentally the same as when they premiered in the mid-1990s. With the processes for creating, delivering, and retrospectively converting content in place and Web sites functioning, journal publishers began to deploy new businesses in 2004.

It is important to understand what is driving the development of these new businesses. Like so many other industries, the journal-publishing sector is finding out what its new role will be in a networked online environment. Challenged by user arguments that lower costs for production should lead to lower journal costs, pressed by movements such as Taxpayer Alliance that encourage authors to place articles in open repositories, and aware of emerging competition such as Google Scholar, these publishers are now trying to responding to the question "What (new) value do you add?" It has become clear that the value that publishers provided when communication was difficult and paper documentation was essential for scholarship is being questioned. Despite studies that show how much inaccurate information is available on the Web and how difficult it can be to find information on the Web, many users are not buying the arguments of the value of the traditional publishing chain, and libraries can no longer afford to buy such quality unquestioningly. In this environment, the publishers are developing new services and products that respond to a changed marketplace.

These products and services are being built for the most part upon the infrastructure created to perform the functions of delivering the content. There's an interesting conundrum at work. One original argument for maintaining paper-based subscription costs was to allow the publishers the capital to develop the infrastructure to provide high-quality electronic delivery. That infrastructure is now being sold as a new product.

Another observation is that these services are taking the publishers into roles that were formerly filled by journal aggregators and abstract and indexing services. This has resulted in some surprising alliances among the product developers. Among the leading new products was Elsevier's Scopus, which leverages Elsevier's search infrastructure with citations of Elsevier and other STM (scientific, technical, and medical) publishers, creating what http://www.scopus.com modestly calls "The world's largest abstract database of scientific literature . . . " enhanced with information about citations and cited-by's. Meanwhile Blackwell's announced its Online Open, a place where "authors who wish to publish their research in a Blackwell journal [are given] the opportunity to ensure that their article is immediately made freely available for all to access online." The cost of "freely available" during the trial is $2,500. Thomson ISI significantly expanded its ability to link-out to other publishers including 200 open access journals. These are only three of the various approaches that the journal-publishing industry is pursuing in the face of open access, Google, and government reports and policies.

With the next World Summit on the Information Society scheduled for November 2005 in Tunis, Internet publishing, and especially open access, will be avidly debated and discussed. In the meantime, experimentation will continue, while analysis of operational Internet journals will become a new focal point for research; 2005 will be open to many surprises.

Notes

1. United Kingdom Parliament, House of Commons Science and Technology Committee, 2004. Responses to the Committee's Tenth Report, Session 2003-04, "Scientific Publications: Free for All?" Fourteenth Report of Session 2003-04 (1 November). London: Stationery Office, p. 10, at http://www.publications.parliament.uk/pa/cm200304/cmselect/cmsctech/1200/120002.htm.

2. OECD, 2004. "Science, Technology and Innovation for the 21st Century. Meeting of the OECD Committee for Scientific and Technological Policy at Ministerial Level, 29–30 January 2004—Final Communique," at http://www.oecd.org.

3. OECD, 2004. "Statement by Dutch Minister of Education, Culture and Science on Access to Research Data from Public Funding," at http://www.oecd. org.

4. World Summit on the Information Society, 2003. "Declaration of Principles. Building the Information Society: A Global Challenge in the New Millennium," Document WSIS-03/GENEVA/DOC/4-E (12 December), at http://www.itu.int/wsis.

5. World Summit on the Information Society, 2003. "Plan of Action," (12 December), at http://www.itu.int/wsis.

6. Max-Planck-Gesellschaft, 2003. "Berlin Declaration on Open Access to Knowledge in the Sciences and Humanities," at http://www.zim.mpg.de/openaccess-berlin/berlindeclaration.html.

7. Mac-Planck-Gesellschaft, 2003. "Signatories," (9 February) at http://www.zim.mpg.de/open access-berlin/signatories.html.

8. http://opcit.eprints.org/feb19prog.html.

9. See Michael J. Kurtz, 2004. "Restrictive Access Policies Cut Readership of Electronic Research Journal Articles By a Factor of Two," at http://opcit.eprints.org/feb19oa/kurtz.pdf, and Michael J. Kurtz, Guenther Eichhorn, Alberto Accomazzi, Carolyn Grant, Markus Demleitner, and Stephen S. Murray, 2005. "Worldwide Use and Impact of the NASA Astrophysics Data System Digital Library," *Journal of the American Society for Information Science and Technology,* vol. 56, no. 1, pp. 36–45.

10. Michele Langlois, Richard F. Heller, Richard Edwards, Georgios Lyratzopoulos, and John Sandars, 2004. "Restrictions Impeding Web-Based Courses: A Survey of Publishers' Variation in Authorising Access to High Quality Online Literature," *BMC Medical Education,* vol. 4, at http://www.biomedcentral.com/1472-6920/4/7.

11. Nicholas R. Cozzarelli, Kenneth R. Fulton, and Diane M. Sullenberger, 2004. "Results of a PNAS Author Survey on an Open Access Option for Publication," *Proceedings of the National Academy of Sciences* (U.S.), vol. 101, no. 5 (3 February), p. 1111.

12. One would assume that some publishers actually have a reasonable idea about the true cost of scientific publishing. In any case, see Catherine D. DeAngelis and Robert A. Musacchio, 2004. "Access to JAMA," *Journal of the American Medical Association*, vol. 291, no. 3 (21 January), pp. 370–371.

13. Helen Doyle, Andy Gass, and Rebecca Kennison, 2004. "Who Pays for Open Access?" *PLoS Biology,* vol. 2, no. 4 (April), pp. 0409–0410, at http://biology.plosjournals.org.

14. Jan Velterop, 2005. "The Myth of 'Unsustainable' Open Access Journals," *Nature* Web (12 February), at http://www.nature.com/nature/focus/accessdebate/10.html.

15. United Kingdom Parliament, House of Commons Science and Technology Committee, 2004. "Scientific Publications: Free for All?" (20 July), at http://www.publications.parliament.uk/pa/cm200304/cmselect/cmsctech/399/39902.htm.

16. Delcan Butler, 2004. "Britain Decides 'Open Access' Is Still an Open Issue," *Nature*, vol. 430, no. 6998 (22 July), p. 390.

17. Reed Elsevier, 2004. "Responses to Questions Posed by the Science and Technology Committee" (February), at http://www.publications.parliament.uk/pa/cm200304/cmselect/cmsctech/399/399we57.htm.

18. United Kingdom Parliament, House of Commons Science and Technology Committee, 2004. "Response from the Government" (8 November), at http://www.publications.parliament.uk/pa/cm200304/cmselect/cmsctech/1200/120006.htm#a1.

19. United Kingdom Parliament, House of Commons Science and Technology Committee, 2004. "Scientific Publications: Free for All? The Government Response" (8 November), at http://www.publications.parliament.uk/pa/cm200304/cmselect/cmsctech/1200/120003.htm.

20. Geoff Brumfiel, 2004. "National Institutes of Health to Publish Papers Online," news@nature.com (8 September), at http://www.nature.com/news/2004/040906/pf/431115a_pf.html.

21. http://www.alpsp.org/2004pdfs/NIHALPSPresponse.pdf.

22. Erika Check, 2005. "NIH Open-Access Plans Draw Fire from Both Sides," *Nature*, vol. 433, no. 7026 (10 February), p. 561.

23. "An Open Letter to the U.S. Congress Signed by 25 Nobel Prize Winners" (26 August), at http://www.fas.org/news/2004/08/nobel082604.pdf.

24. Jim Giles, 2004. "Trust Gives Warm Welcome to Open Access," *Nature*, vol. 432, no. 7014 (11 November), p. 134. The support for open access by the Wellcome Trust, the largest non-governmental source of research funds in Britain, is not surprising. In April 2004 the trust issued a report titled "Costs and Business Models in Scientific Research Publishing" that concluded that there would be major savings in publishing costs if scientific results were made available on the Internet. The report is available at http://www.wellcome.ac.uk/doc_WTD003185.html.

25. For example, this "protected technology commons" is noted in Wim Broothaerts, Heidi J. Mitchell, Brian Weir, Sarah Kaines, Leon M. A. Smith, Wei Yang, Jorge E. Mayer, Carolina Roa-Rodriguez, and Richard A. Jefferson, 2005. "Gene Transfer to Plants by Diverse Species of Bacteria," *Nature*, vol. 433, no. 7026 (10 February), pp. 629–633.

26. Daren Fonda, 2005. "Downloading Hollywood," *Time*, vol. 165, no. 7 (14 February), p. 43.

27. "The Proverbial Genie Is Out of the Bottle." From Jan Velterop, 2005. "The Myth of 'Unsustainable' Open Access Journals," *Nature* Web (12 February), at http://www.nature.com/nature/focus/accessdebate/10.html.

Institutional Repositories:
A Growing Force in Scholarship

Kimberly Douglas

University Librarian, California Institute of Technology

The use of the term *institutional repository* (IR) to describe organization-specific digital works management has not yet entered the mainstream of library operations or of the scholarly world, much less that of the public at large. Yet it is a force within research libraries that is capturing the imagination and energy of staff as a vision for the future. Whether the IR label will endure is not known. It is, however, the contemporary term for newly cast activities in academic libraries born of digital technologies and the economic upheaval in the scholarly publishing world.

I. Where Did Institutional Repositories Come From?

A few years after the launch of the National Center for Supercomputing Applications' World Wide Web client, Mosaic, in 1994, there began a series of meetings on the topic of scholarly publishing in the electronic environment. Economists, librarians, publishers, and faculty recognized the opportunities that this new technology offered, and there was much discussion about electronic publishing and the fate of scholarly journals and libraries.[1]

Principles forming the foundation IRs hark back to many of those meetings, among which was the 1997 Conference on the Future of Scholarly Communication held at Caltech, an invitational meeting attended by many university librarians, provosts, and scholarly society directors. The unique format of this meeting, organized around working groups on specific topics, resulted in a critical and specific conclusion: "that the certification of scholarly articles through peer review could be 'decoupled' from the rest of the publishing process."[2] In addition, there were strong feelings that because the peer review process was already supported by the universities whose faculty serve as editors, members of editorial boards, and referees, it would be possible to create a certification system separate from the distribution mechanism. This conclusion provided a publishing model conceptually compatible with the "Subversive Proposal" advanced by Stevan Harnad of the University of Southampton in 1994,[3] which argued for the public posting of all faculty preprints, a recommendation that was intended to significantly hasten the transition to fully electronic publishing and provide unblocked access to the scholarly record.

Following on these discussions, the Open Archives Initiative (OAI) was launched at a meeting in 1999, often called the Santa Fe Convention, at which Paul Ginsparg, Rick Luce, and Herbert Van de Sompel led a group in developing technical solutions to enable the goal of open access among scholarly e-print archives.[4] The following year, Harnad established the EPrints project at the University of Southampton and in November of that year, version 1.0 of that open source application was released. It supported the posting or self-archiving of papers in an OAI 0.2-compliant database management environment. Since then all institutional repository software has complied with the OAI protocols. It is an expected—if not formally required—feature, especially within nonprofit research organizations.

Around the same time, several seminal papers and news articles on the high pricing of journals appeared in highly visible and respected places.[5] This was not new information for librarians, who had been documenting and addressing the high prices for commercial scholarly journals for some time. These articles led, however, to greater shared awareness, activity, and concern within broad academic circles. In this way, the technical tools and the political mandate for action became more aligned and a host of repository projects followed. A few university libraries undertook the task of loading the EPrints software from the University of Southampton, with the conviction that faculty output would be forthcoming. The University of Nottingham[6] was among the first institutions to do this, and Caltech—in developing its repository for computer science technical reports, having first worked with the Dienst software developed at Cornell—switched to the EPrints system in 2000. However, the majority of EPrints sites developed were subject-specific repositories similar to Cogprints, Harnad's own cognitive sciences site.

Definition and Growth of Support

The designation *institutional repository* is a fairly recently coined phrase and appears to have evolved in 2001 from combining the word *institutional* from Harnad's description of scholarly self-archiving objectives with the word *repository* instead of *archive* to provide a technical context that was not overly burdened with the inherent connotations of the word *archive*.[7] *Digital* came to be commonly added as a further qualifying descriptor, especially outside the United States.[8]

In all cases, the term as used in this report designates an online site where digital materials are stored. The term *institutional* defines the scope: The materials stored there are under the control of, or are issued from and with authorization of, an institutional body such as a university, society, or company. The meaning of the word *repository* in this context is much more difficult to define. As Clifford Lynch pointed out in mid-2003,[9] the term *repository* can be used in a very technical way by certain groups, such as those that manage interactive learning objects, while in other cases it may simply designate a collection of materials that are stored passively on an online site.

Some institutions, especially in Britain, use the term *archive* rather than *repository*. Harnad, for example, uses the term *institutional archives* to describe his EPrints effort, and, according to the EPrints site, there are currently 240 *archives* available on the Internet.[10] Over half of these use the EPrints software and are defined as containing institutionally or departmentally maintained research content.

One might ask why this term—rather than just *digital library* as in *institutional digital library* —should be used. The differences between an IR and a digital library are twofold. In terms of content, the scope of the former is defined as restricted to specific output from that institution. Thus an institutional repository can be a subset of a digital library, where the scope is usually discipline- or sub-ject-based and is not restricted to any specific institution's output. The IR, having been born out of the OAI activity, primarily plays the data provider role and may or may not include a data service function. The digital library, by comparison, in virtually all cases includes tools along with content, and such content is typically much broader in scope than that of an IR.

The term *institutional repository* gained formality, acceptance, and promi-nence with the conference "Institutional Repositories: A Workshop on Creating an Infrastructure for Faculty-Library Partnerships" held by SPARC (the Scholarly Publishing and Academic Resources Coalition) in October 2002, which was timed to immediately precede MIT's release of its DSpace open source IR software in early November of that year. Two years earlier, MIT Libraries had been awarded a $1.8 million grant by Hewlett Packard to build a stable and sus-tainable long-term open source digital repository system and to explore, through the development of this system, the issues surrounding access control, rights management, versioning, retrieval, community feedback, and flexible publishing capabilities.[11] DSpace is intended to serve as a system and template for other uni-versities to establish content repositories for their faculty output.

In 2003 and 2004 a plethora of workshops and conferences on IRs occurred all around the world, in Asia, Europe, and North America. Perhaps the most exhilarating aspect of this effort is the extent to which and speed with which international communities have been motivated to embrace this concept. Of course, the open access movement has also been internationally recognized dur-ing this period, and two of the defining meetings were held outside the United States.[12] The rapidly growing support for the open access movement has stimulat-ed the IR movement, and vice versa. The speed with which both of these move-ments have developed over the last two years is evidence of the powerful influence of Internet technology and the empowerment it delivers.

Each year, starting in 2002, summary papers on the status of IRs have appeared. The first, by Raym Crow, was commissioned by SPARC in preparation for the 2002 conference mentioned above. Crow exhaustively interviewed IR managers to compile and organize details on the issues involved in implementing and developing an IR. His guide[13] remains a worthwhile source for anyone con-sidering such an implementation.

Crow's results formally defined an IR as having four characteristics:

• Institutional in authority and scope of content
• Scholarly in level of content
• Cumulative and perpetual in purpose
• Open and interoperable in design

Crow also found among the practitioners of the time that there were two pri-mary reasons for launching institutional repositories:

• An IR is a feasible and appropriate platform from which to change schol-arly publishing by providing an alternative distribution mechanism for tra-ditional peer-reviewed papers.

• An IR presents an opportunity for an institution to make its scholarly contributions more globally visible.

Clifford Lynch attended the 2002 SPARC conference and in the final presentation of the program outlined some of his concerns. In his 2003 paper[14] he emphasized the importance of institutional commitment as a necessary requirement for responsible stewardship over time and he saw a danger that the rush to implement IRs could go the way of most fads. He also had concerns that the overarching goal of effecting changes in scholarly publishing practices as found and summarized by Crow could lead to overbearing and restrictive policies regarding the kinds of content that would be accepted and the conditions under which an IR would accept works. In short, Lynch argued that while the technical infrastructure needs to be rigorously maintained and supported, there also needs to be sufficient flexibility in content policies so that innovative solutions and different approaches by faculty incorporating the full capability of computer networks would not be excluded. Lynch articulates these issues as cautions, but also formulates this definition for an IR: "a set of services that a university offers to the members of its community for the management and dissemination of digital materials created by the institution and its community members."[15]

At the end of 2003, participants in an executive roundtable discussion of the Coalition of Networked Information repeated these concerns, but added specific challenges particularly relevant to library decision-makers:

• Can a specially funded bottom-up pilot project successfully transition to a robust infrastructure for whatever digital content the faculty may devise and find productive? Or is it better to transition existing operations and funds in a manner that reflects the library's continuing core responsibilities?

• Is the context of an IR too confining, and does it therefore inherently create risks that the design and capabilities will not serve a wide range of digital-asset-management needs as they evolve across a campus?

• While IRs are by definition not discipline-based, it is acknowledged that new subject-specific needs will develop and must be integrated into the service. This is particularly the case as the cyber-infrastructure environment evolves. How will an IR be both institutionally based and responsive to the represented disciplines? How will the institution coordinate its content with external subject domains, for example by establishing links between internal and external content?

• How will a university manage the boundaries between institutional marketing, public relations, and presentation, and the intellectual freedom of the faculty in scholarly publishing, particularly as it might relate to a wide range of legal issues? How will faculty mobility from one university to another be handled in this context?

These questions could not be resolved before further action in the field. In 2004 another force gained traction and had considerable impact on the increasing visibility of the IR movement. It started when Mark Walport, director of Britain's

Wellcome Trust,[16] was taken aback upon discovering that he could not electronically access a peer-reviewed paper published as part of a Wellcome-funded project. What could be a more compelling illustration of the need for change in the present scholarly commercial publishing system than the specter of disgruntled funding agencies and their directors when they are blocked from getting to the results their resources had made possible?

In 2004 more than one funding agency issued statements and policies proposing that public access to the scholarly papers and research they had funded was to be guaranteed. In October the Wellcome Trust issued a research report and a supportive policy position on open access to scholarly information. Since then other funding or public agency groups, including the U.S. National Institutes of Health and Britain's House of Commons Science and Technology Committee, as well as Danish, German, and other continental European agencies and the National Scholarly Communications Forum in Australia, have all, in one way or another, announced that the results of publicly funded research for which they are responsible must be made openly available to the public. A quick scan of Peter Suber's *Open Access Newsletter*[17] certainly makes the volume and visibility of this recent political activity very clear.

Finally, also in 2004, two comprehensive reports on IRs appeared. Mark Ware, a consultant, was engaged by the Joint Information Systems Committee of the United Kingdom to report on IRs,[18] and Susan Gibbons's report "Establishing an Institutional Repository"[19] was published as a *Library Technology Report*. By this time, IRs had been actively promoted by a formal SPARC effort for more than a year. Publishers were beginning to take notice as investment analysts evaluated this movement as a threat to the traditional scholarly publishing business model.[20] Grant agencies, like libraries, were looking at alternative mechanisms to ensure public access to research. However, Ware concluded that the IRs are more complementary than competitive to current publication models, largely due to both faculty indifference and their inertia in mounting their own publications in an open access environment.

Nevertheless the IR is a phenomenon whose time has come. The fundamentally disruptive and empowering nature of the Internet and Web has allowed everyone to mount content of all kinds and make it accessible to the world while Google and the OAI protocols have ensured that much of this material will be discoverable. This new and open environment comes with its own built-in distribution mechanism and requires no traditional publisher.

At the same time, there is growing unrest regarding the sustainability of legacy scholarly journal publishing models. In particular, the underlying economic system has become difficult to support as for-profit commercial publishers continue to raise prices at rates wildly exceeding inflation. Meanwhile, society publishers are grappling for a new model that will allow them to survive as the behavior of their members also changes, many of them begin dropping societal subscriptions and depending on institutional subscriptions for access to the society's publications.

The open access movement rests on the opportunity that the IR movement promises. And vice versa—the hope of the IR effort is based on the motivations and values of the open access movement. These two dynamics, one based on a building economic crisis and growing frustration with the rapid escalation of journal prices and the other driven by a rapidly evolving technical environment of alternatives, have finally reached the point that all members of the scholarly community can join forces and, buttressed by the open source movement, begin to free scholarly content from the access barrier generated by the high prices. University libraries, emboldened by their positive experience with electronic theses and other digital collections, now envision a role in providing an alternative model for management and distribution of scholarly works in which the costs of publication will be more accountable and sustainable.

The open access movement and IRs create a synergy that agencies and governments have come to recognize.[21] At their peril, commercial publishers continue to dismiss and avoid constructively engaging with this trend.

II. Why and How Should an Institutional Repository Be Created?

Who will do the work? How will it affect other library functions? How will the IR operations be funded? Much depends on how a library strategically positions the IR. Such an undertaking, with a commitment of resources and staff, will take funding, so the institution must be willing to commit adequate long-term support. As Susan Gibbons points out, "A . . . core feature is that the IR has institutional support."[22]

The IR environment is new; it has emerged from a convergence of the previously separated functions of publishing, indexing, and archiving and therefore bears study and analysis in each organization regarding the type and levels of service it will provide, and how those services will be deployed, supported, marketed, and funded. In short, one could say that the IR business model analysis is one of recasting or rearticulating the research library's role and benefit in the university as it specifically pertains to the intellectual output of the institution.

For this reason, a well-articulated role for the IR in the institution should be clearly defined from the outset. Support and funding models will vary according to whether the IR is an entrepreneurial experiment on the part of the library and/or computer center or is devised to formally support faculty publishing activities, much like a university press. In some institutions, the IR may function as part of the general environment the university provides to support the activities of the faculty and students. This may be provided wholly or in part, similar to the old interlibrary loan model under which the institution provides the mechanism or infrastructure to create the loan but the requester pays the incurred use fees. Certainly comprehensive research libraries that retain extensive legacy print resources and maintain collection development standards, and already have considerable costs in preservation and conservation, cannot easily divert funds. Institutions that have less long-term commitment to print archives are likely to envision a transition model in which resources are redirected over time. Therefore, whether it is developed as an operations model that is completely subsumed as infrastructure or is treated as a business that generates revenue, or is some combination of the two, the understanding of the conditions under which the IR will be supported and sustained must be defined at the outset.

Two institutions are currently working on formal understandings of how the IR will be positioned. In addition to their unique software development and distribution objectives, the MIT DSpace Business Plan report[23] cites four other key areas of targeted planning:

- Service distribution or differentiation
- Service delivery or operations
- Building awareness and driving adoption or marketing
- Financial models or cost and revenue flows

Cambridge University is also working on the analysis and articulation of how the IR fits into current library operations.[24] The MIT report was concluded in 2002, although evolution continues within that organization; the Cambridge study project is scheduled for completion in December 2005.

Of importance in the establishment of IRs is the recognition that each organization will differ economically, culturally, and also politically, so the final profile of each IR will be unique to each institution. These differences will lead to different decisions and prioritization of the necessary components in each implementation, and each one will have a different growth and maintenance plan.

Fundamentally, the IR endeavor must emerge from a market analysis in each organization, but one that can evolve as the scholarly communication environment changes. The DSpace report expresses the fluid nature of contemporary action: ". . . the importance of dedicated business and operational planning conducted in parallel with the research and development process is paramount."[25] While many questions can be asked, the answers are not immediately forthcoming and concrete responses will emerge only after some trials and experience have demonstrated the practical issues and problems associated with each institution's IR instantiation. The Cambridge perspective adds that these analyses activities are, of necessity, iterative. Specifically, the Cambridge project intends to provide techniques and strategies for continual data gathering of user behavior, effectiveness and impact, and costs, leading to continual evaluation that a library may follow to make initial decisions and adaptations as the future reveals itself.

In the absence of these forthcoming quantitative metrics, IR implementers look for windows of opportunity within their organizations. The reasons and degree to which an institution may support a repository infrastructure depend on its anticipated benefits. Gibbons outlines five purposes[26] that may resonate with an institution's administration:

- Stewardship—reliable management of digital documents of enduring value
- Efficiencies—economies of scale through centralization of content management
- Showcase—opportunity to highlight the aggregate output of the institution by positioning content for greatest visibility and discoverability
- Wider distribution—fulfillment of faculty desire to extend the reach of their papers to the widest possible audience
- Scholarly communication crisis—action to challenge the abuse of the inelastic market by the for-profit commercial scholarly publishing sector

In general, the more centrally controlled and administered an organization is, the more likely it is that such arguments will resonate with the administration's interests and may result in additional or special funding. More-decentralized organizations are less able to agree on a single set of common priorities, and there is a greater inclination to test the efficacy of innovations with a revenue center model—the logic being that if units, or individuals, will contribute from their resources for either better service or to achieve greater savings, then the service is worthwhile for the organization. However, for such an approach to be effective with faculty, the proposed change must be extremely compelling and immediately advantageous.

The administration can be positively inclined to an IR but typically have little desire to exert power from above on an issue so tightly linked to the individual faculty member's research habits and values. Gibbons reports working with an anthropologist[27] who established unequivocally that individual faculty are not as motivated as the central organization to the goals and importance of an IR and therefore are not willing to make any extra effort, contribute funds, or otherwise change their behavior in order to support its implementation. The MIT business plan took these issues into account and defined services as *core* (those that are basic and part of the university's infrastructure) or *premium* (those that are determined to be special and additional). In this way, the plan allowed the library to charge for certain services, thus equipping it to respond to the probable special needs of unique and unpredictable situations in a manner that would be financially sustainable.

A clear description of the core services also serves as a marketing function by educating the community about the complexity of the infrastructure involved. Offering it free of charge serves to communicate the organization's priorities and encourages local participation and early adoption by individual faculty. The marketing plan established at MIT was designed to attract the faculty by promoting the "compelling value"[28] of the MIT libraries' trusted management of the content, which supports diverse file formats, guaranteed long-term preservation, and sophisticated search and retrieval capabilities. It is these added services that are most likely to capture interest for an IR among an otherwise frequently distracted faculty.

Cost Considerations

Crow, in his SPARC report in 2002, made considerable effort to identify the specific cost categories and appropriate benchmark figures surrounding the establishment of a typical IR. He found that they could not be definitively quantified since the funding practices already in place at the polled institutions varied greatly. There was no reliable applied methodology for separating out technical infrastructure costs such as security, back-up procedures, and network software by application in diverse environments. By contrast, it is relatively straightforward to predict the direct cost of the hardware and software, and one can gain insight into systems support requirements based on the experience of others running the same application.[29] If an organization is unwilling and unable to support a sophisticated computing infrastructure, then it is not going to be able to support a locally mounted IR. On the other hand, if an organization has all the elements of a well-supported and up-to-date computing system in place, then adding an IR can be done for a relatively nominal initial cost of a server and the allocation of some part-time IT and librarian expertise.

IRs differ from digital libraries in that this initial technical barrier for entry can be quite low. Most digital library efforts are grant funded and include original development of innovative digital tools for either research or education, often of an interactive nature, along with appropriately prepared content objects. The IR software, EPrints, however, is LAMP- (Linux, Apache, MySQL, Perl) based and anyone willing to maintain a standard Linux server can load the application and begin to work with it, even on a basic personal computer. Metadata is also kept to a very simple set of seven Dublin Core fields. This is a strong point for easy adoption but also a potential weakness in its simplification and incomplete indexing of potentially complex materials. At the very least, an IR additionally requires a policy and implementation of persistent identifiers, a function not specifically supported by EPrints. Therein lies an example of why some IR implementations may not endure in the long run. Without sufficient contemporary knowledge and attention to requirements and standards, and continuing investment in that expertise for each repository, digital content is easily lost.[30]

Yet there is more to an IR than the server. The undeniable focus on needed technology tends to slight the human context. This is especially true when behavior is expected to automatically change over time as tools and contexts evolve. The technical infrastructure cost of an IR is not a complete measure of all the support the community may need. Each institution's culture and implementation plan will dictate how much effort needs to be expended on content recruitment and support and to aid authors in the preparation of their submissions. These activities require staff time to proselytize, educate, plan submission flow, train, support, troubleshoot, and do almost anything else that can come up. This cost is, by far, the largest and most difficult to control, given the range of an IR's impact on differing operations and the differing sizes of faculties. It is for this reason that an operations plan is needed at the outset to help define the service and thus constrain user choices based on what the organization intends as an outcome and how much it is willing to invest to achieve it.

Especially in the open source IR environment, there should be a plan to contribute time and expertise to the group endeavor. An alternative to open source that is gaining prominence is the use of third-party commercial packages. At this time, the California Digital Library uses Berkeley Electronic Press for eScholarship, and Proquest has developed and is marketing a package named Digital Commons that performs such functions. There are other commercial systems under development. Depending on the contract, some of the support for end-user use and troubleshooting of the IR and development objectives can be met by the vendor instead of by in-house staff and thus contain institutional costs while still achieving the goals. Nevertheless, such contracts can be inflexible and therefore may not perform for the organization over time. Much depends on how the library wishes to present itself to the faculty and administration. Experience is limited; just as libraries learned to establish exit strategies in the integrated library system environment, the same kind of plan is needed with an IR vendor.

Susan Gibbons makes the case for special attention to the costs of ensuring the permanence of digital content. Aside from standard back-up requirements with off-site data storage, she adds the need to build in redundancy with additional servers and/or mirror sites to guarantee "zero-tolerance policy for IR content loss."[31] However, future preservation costs are largely unknown, although per-unit costs will surely decrease as storage and capture technology matures. Gibbons suggests the creation of dedicated escrow accounts to prepare for eventual expenditures, but it is unlikely that such accounts will be established as long as downstream costs remain unpredictable. It may be more realistic to establish that the content of an IR is so critical to the mission of the university that risk of its loss is unacceptable. Digital theses, for example, certainly claim a high-profile role. In the future, when the costs are better known, support can be more realistically acquired.

Of the two primary categories of cost—hardware and staff—the figure needed will ultimately be determined by the goals and timeline, and the effort required to meet them.

- Direct costs include line-item identifiable charges for necessary hardware and possibly software and the provision of sufficient technical support to install and configure the software. Depending on the volume of content expected, the disk space could start with as little as a couple of terabytes or as much as 50 terabytes. Once the system is running, further direct staffing costs will be incurred, depending on how much effort is dedicated to further system development and customization, to the education and liaison with faculty, and to user support of the system. Choosing an open source application saves licensing and maintenance fees but such IR projects then need the commitment of high-level technical expertise.

- Organizational costs include percentage of time of designated staff in IR supportive roles or actions. This may include library administration liaison, reference staff, document delivery staff, and high-level technical services staff, all of whom are necessary to contribute ancillary services such as proxy submission, digitization, and/or metadata enhancements. Additional training or travel may also be needed. Even in situations where there is dedicated IR staff, the presence and effort required of an IR affect all positions.

- Fundamentally, the necessary implementation plan defines the institutional commitment, resources, degree, and speed with which the university wants to implement the IR facility. Alternatively, an institution may decide to engage a third party to provide the necessary operational support, leaving regular staff free to focus on community development.

The conditions needed to launch an IR are straightforward. The continued success of the IR over time will be a measure of the thoroughness and execution of the business plan.

III. What Content Does an Institutional Repository Contain?

IRs suffer the same limitations as other breakthrough technological innovations. Social and legal constraints and conventions prevent immediate full deployment and use; no repository can exist without content, yet acquiring or recruiting content—particularly peer-reviewed content—is contentious and problematic. There are two reasons for this.

Copyright ties the legal issue of permission to print constructs and legacy processes. Scholarly publishing usually involves the transfer of copyright from the author to the publisher. While some faculty members have taken steps to retain copyright when publishing their papers, such awareness and action is very limited at this time. The authors' focus is quite rightly on getting published. Faculty members have come to view the copyright form as a paperwork necessity and nuisance to dispense with as expeditiously as possible. Most professors cannot find any of the agreements they have signed over the years, and, often, neither can the publishers. So there is little documentation available on which to base a decision.

The managers of an IR therefore cannot be sure of the rights of a file sent their way. If an author provides the file, it is inferred that he has the right to pass on the document and his signed assurance to this effect is considered sufficient. However, even if the right to post a document is accepted by the IR manager, identifying and processing content into the repository may require individual interaction with each author and individual analysis and manipulation of each paper. Such requirements add to the ad hoc nature of a repository and make sustainable and continuing repository processes difficult to maintain in an efficient and effective manner.

Faculty behavior and habits, in a general sense, present a second difficulty. First, the faculty is very busy and focused on research activities. Overall, the process of submitting articles to journals via the peer-review process, and the acknowledgement through promotion and tenure process this provides, is not broken—though it is not perfect, either. In this chain, only the pricing model of the for-profit commercial publishers is badly in need of repair and can no longer be financially supported by the academy. The collections-development and budget processes used by libraries insulate the faculty from these prices and the difficulties they cause and they therefore do not perceive an acute and tangible imperative to change.

Repository managers have to cajole and convince faculty to participate by proselytizing the long-term benefits of the IR in broadening the world's access to the individual's research, in guaranteed archiving of the individual's papers over time, and, clearly, in addressing the journal pricing issue.

Therefore a very large hurdle for a library instituting an IR is to define under what circumstances and with which mechanisms the library will identify appropriate material, establish sufficient permissions and rights, and acquire the content in compliance with the purpose of the IR. The business plan must address how much and what level of staff time will be afforded this activity. Such commitment varies among universities.

The gold standard for content in the IR is peer-reviewed papers. Yet, in the most recent survey of IR content, Ware[32] found that most current IR content consists of gray literature along with theses and dissertations. It is worth noting that as long as ownership of content remains within the academy, permission seems to be readily and easily acquired. The author, a department head, or a conference convener can typically be contacted to establish such rights fairly definitively.

Peer-reviewed papers, however, are the result of the publisher-managed process, which usually includes editorial and formatting improvements to the original manuscript. Not all authors prepare their own presentation version of a paper with all text and graphics well integrated, and many prefer the appearance of the publisher's formatted version. For these reasons, therefore, authors, depending on the field, may not desire any version but the final published paper to be distributed. In 2004 the open access movement gained sufficient visibility to persuade publishers to include among the rights returned to authors[33] the right to mount a "postprint" of a paper in open archives of their choosing. A postprint generally means that version of the paper that captures the changes resulting from peer review but not necessarily those from copy editing. In general, the publishers acknowledge that the intellectual content, the research, can be made openly available. It is the post-refereeing formatting, the "as published" appearance, that cannot. Nonetheless, even in the postprint-version scenario the ultimate copyright and source of the final version by the publisher are to be noted.

Some scholarly publishers couple the peer-review service with an exclusive news business model to enhance the importance and value of their journal. This is particularly the case with *Science, Nature,* and some medical journals such as the *New England Journal of Medicine* and the *Journal of the American Medical Association.* Scholars whose work fits the selection criteria for those journals reap the rewards of recognition by agreeing not to release a preprint or early version of their paper. Such early distribution is determined to be prior publication and eliminates the paper from consideration by these journals. Many editors of the American Chemical Society journals have similar policies. Such restrictive publishing practices have a dampening effect on content recruitment for IRs. (To help authors and librarians understand the conditions under which material may be used, Britain's Joint Information Systems Committee, through the University of Nottingham, maintains a Web site with a database of publishers' copyright policies.)[34]

Successful strategies for content recruitment may relate more closely to characteristics of the faculty members than to the type of content. Gibbons[35] provides a succinct description of different marketing messages targeting different faculty groups by discipline and by generation. Groups operate in different cultures and face different problems at the various career stages. Subject-specialist and faculty-liaison librarians have the kind of access to, and knowledge of, the faculty to properly act on these differences. A single convinced and committed early-adopter faculty member in each discipline may be the most effective change agent.

In general, the content genres for which author permissions are currently most easily gained include

- Theses and dissertations
- Gray literature (preprints, technical reports, working papers)
- Conference papers if not published elsewhere
- Out-of-print works for which the author gains rights back
- Any content that has not yet been published

In addition, other types of information should not be discounted:

• Presentations
• Videos
• Sound recordings
• Syllabi and other teaching aids

A few repositories are working on systematic approaches to acquiring content. The California Digital Library is launching an automated identification and permission-requesting system to acquire postprints of papers.[36] The Hong Kong University of Science and Technology developed a hierarchical comprehensive approach for one-on-one interactions with each faculty member.[37] Nevertheless, the content identification and recruitment process is in its infancy and is evolving as the issues around scholarly communication are changing.

Aside from the author changing his own behavior because of altruistic or progressive inclinations, other incentives for change rest among those in a leverage position, especially the research funding agencies. University administrations are unlikely to dictate or set rules for faculty that seek to govern or control their publishing behavior, given the latter's either explicit or implicit understanding of intellectual freedom. Rather, it is the funding agencies and governments that are taking up this challenge. In general, their argument is that they are funding research for the public good and the public therefore should be able to have access. While the agencies do not specify in what manner a paper may be made publicly available, IRs are such a potential avenue. This was clearly stated in a report released by the British House of Commons Science and Technology Committee, *Scientific Publications: Free for All?*[38] in which many of the 82 recommendations made there were many specific to IRs. Peter Suber selects these two as the most important:[39]

• The government should provide funds for all British universities to launch open access institutional repositories.
• Government funding agencies should require faculty receiving research grants to deposit copies of their articles in their institutional repositories.

However, before the year was out, Britain's Department of Trade and Industry responded to the recommendations saying that there was no need for government action. As this report was being written, the community awaited further announcement from the U.S. National Institutes of Health regarding its proposal to require authors to make their papers available in open access at some point after publication. While the lack of specific mandate from either of these government agencies sustains the ambiguity, it is important to keep in mind how much has changed in just a few years. In 1999 no publisher would have signed off on preprints, much less on postprints, and no publisher would have given a second thought to the possibility of open access causing it even the slightest inconvenience. The now firmly established trend toward a general revision of copyright practices in scholarly publishing bodes well for the open access movement in the long term, though challenges remain.

Over the years, researchers in engineering and physics seem to have functioned quite successfully in the establishment of a system that allows the wide-scale distribution of preprints and technical reports, both of which are early forms of formal papers. It has not been possible to establish the same practice in biology and chemistry, however, because of the difficulty of constructing an adequately trusted gatekeeping function for guaranteeing the quality of such papers, which, for example, have practical application in medicine and medical treatments. The problem of potential liability has been one of the hurdles that has kept a preprint archive for biomedical literature from being established.

In all cases, however, identifying the bona fide peer-reviewed content so that it can be read, properly cited, and reliably tracked and retrieved over time is of concern, and in biology and chemistry, especially, is of paramount concern. Each discipline has slightly different practices that challenge any single policy that an IR might attempt to establish and thus warrants the organization of content separately. DSpace, for example, is structured to allow each department or unit on a campus to devise its own approach to many of these policy questions.

Differences across disciplines may also affect version control policies and practices and the use of some type of uniform identifier, whether it is a Corporation for National Research Initiatives (CNRI) handle, a digital-object identifier (DOI), or a locally applied unique and resolvable syntax. Also, what does an IR do when a faculty member leaves an institution and wants to "take" his content with him? Is it removed from the IR? Or is the content simply duplicated in the IR at the new home university? How confusing and counterproductive would such redundancy be? These are all issues that have yet to be consistently addressed on an inter-institutional basis.

These controversial issues around both the content and the challenges that IR managers face in acquiring it stem from the inherent conflicts in transitioning from print to electronic information. These conflicts and controversies are built into the reality that the solutions that work in the print environment and make the print model succeed are not necessarily designed for the global digital network. The problem in large part is that the legal framework is based on the fixed expression, a long-established environment in which the role of a publisher in copy editing and formatting and in providing peer review and other gatekeeping functions is well defined and has been perfected by more than a century of trial and error. In the new digital environment, the structure of these legacy relationships and responsibilities is being questioned. Yet viable economic plans that can sustain an entirely digital system have proven difficult to invent and are far from being perfected. This is an unavoidable and very contemporary dilemma. The academy must struggle through this transition by making changes and adjustments as they become necessary. At some point, print will be bypassed for most academic information creation and dissemination scenarios, and a new framework will emerge specifically for the digital world.

IV. What Is the Future for Institutional Repositories?

Projecting the future is a risky business. However, if one adheres to documented emerging themes and principles and refrains from specifics, there is some chance of credibility over time.

The advances in network technology and trends in human behavior as they relate to it have led to the following uncontested observations:

- Network technology leads to greater access and greater sharing of information; that's for better, as in easy discovery and retrieval, or for worse, as in loss of privacy.

- Legacy print-based linear processes developed over the centuries to package and distribute information are collapsing. They are being replaced by digital applications and tools that support more efficient and faster concurrent processes, from peer review to publication and distribution.

- Principles of intellectual property and how they interact with the scholarly enterprise are changing and becoming more fluid and less well defined, largely because of the ease of duplication and dissemination of digital media.

The Pew Internet and American Life Project reports[40] provide ample evidence of the spread of such behaviors as self-posting and publication of information that has led to ever-increasing volume of searches for this material and consequent downloading of files on the Web. The numbers are so high compared to known activity in the print world that there is hardly a reliable order-of-magnitude multiplier.[41] It is simply a very different environment and market. What used to require a secretary, a graphic artist, a copy editor, and a layout specialist can in fact be done by one properly equipped individual.

Copyright practices in the scholarly environment are changing rapidly as the research community begins to leverage its primary-producer role. Digital rights management models designed to maintain print-era-based controls and intermediaries have failed through presenting too much of a barrier to users, and the restrictions they impose are too rigid to make sense in the highly volatile and mutable online environment. The sample licenses of the Creative Commons[42] demonstrate that it is not necessary to change the laws; it is only necessary to change the way business is conducted so that the network can be used to fullest advantage.

The capabilities of the network—coupled with the value and necessity of sharing in research, the collapsing of processes, and, finally, alternative approaches to handling intellectual property—will ultimately result in a very different knowledge environment. The clearest trend or need at this time to reach the next level of utility is for richer standardized data and content formats, and visualization and authoring tools. These will form the basis for a different approach to how information is gathered and used for research.

Whether an IR or a digital library, there is increasing understanding by faculty, grant administrators, university administrators, and librarians that the underlying contextual structure of information objects needs to be formalized to create sophisticated and appropriate tools for quicker and more sophisticated discovery, harvesting, manipulation, and reuse of information. It is not enough to provide a static presentation view, the ultimate output in the print era. There have to be methods and standards that establish open paths to research results that are appropriate for each discipline and enable computational tools to be reliably deployed across the Web.

As early as 1997 these issues were being looked at in the National Science Foundation (NSF)/Defense Advanced Research Projects Agency (DARPA) project Flexible Extensible Digital Object and Repository Architecture (FEDORA) at Cornell.[43] Its very name communicates refinement and differentiation of tagged content with the intent to support research tools and repurposing of data elements. In 1999 the University of Virginia took up the developed framework to prototype its digital library. Based on its success, in 2001 Cornell and the University of Virginia acquired Mellon Foundation funding to continue the work, and in May 2003 Fedora 1.0 was released.[44] This was a large undertaking, as evidenced by the span of time.

In 2001 Tim Berners Lee[45] introduced the Semantic Web, a vision of captured context and meaning in data bits across all activities of human information exchange. Meanwhile, the World Wide Web Consortium (W3C) has been working on the data modeling structures necessary for the needed content ontologies and taxonomies, but with a special view toward business applications on the Web.

Scientific disciplines are also currently addressing or coping with their digital information needs. The astrophysicists are so far along in managing shared data sets that they agitate the government to create an advanced global technical infrastructure that supports real-time access to and manipulation of data around the world. Other fields are not quite so well integrated and their behaviors differ. Biologists, in particular, have a great need to manage shared genetic databases, yet the funding patterns and culture of competing laboratories and discrete projects present a hindrance. Nevertheless, the need for consistent, in-depth data management to make sharing of research results more timely and productive recently became a national program.

NSF's new unit[46] delves into this issue and has begun to work within certain subject areas. This has import for IRs. They may be institutional in scope, but must become more tightly linked to subject-specific developments so that new so-called knowledge communities can arise. In fact, the coined phrase "cyberinfrastructure-enabled knowledge communities" (CKC), is the newly described distant objective.

That term, though unfortunately cumbersome, does foreshadow ever more sophisticated convergence and reordering of legacy steps in research and scholarly communication. The technology can deliver it; the question is how and when the cultural, behavioral, and funding constructs will evolve to create and sustain the new structures.

University libraries are well positioned within their organizations to contribute to the development and implementation of important and essential standards that facilitate IRs. Librarians understand well-structured content and the need for standards and, even more importantly, they have a deeply engrained professional commitment to maintaining such standards consistently over time. Their culture and practice have required this. While in the print era those standards allowed for consistent description, and therefore transferable intelligence, to ensure exact identification of specific items in disparate collections, in the digital era the same attention to standards must serve real-time navigation, interoperability, and reuse of content elements among disparate services.[47]

Therefore libraries must chart a course that closely integrates their work with faculty information-processing needs. The University of Rochester is developing "researcher tools" to augment the IR service so that a faculty member can group research and information elements in a manner that relates to his or her research and display this information to the public as the individual's own Web page although it is derived from the IR. MIT has a number of developing tools among which is a project of collaboration with W3C and others on semantic Web techniques.[48] Through such innovations, libraries running IRs are potentially positioned to capture contextual relationships at the grass-roots level where the creative work originates.

In 2003 Eric Miller of W3C suggested that the research agenda in digital libraries could aid the development of the next level of information-structuring techniques by engaging in projects related to identifying and describing taxonomies, vocabulary, and social context and data access rules.[49] MIT's DSpace is positioned for such infrastructure development because of its growing critical mass of content in many fields and because DSpace is open source and structured for sharing code. A large number of institutions participate in DSpace.[50] It is entirely possible for IRs, particularly multiple IRs with complementary content, to take on disciplinary investigations.

Ultimately, there will be convergence among these technical developments to respond to researchers' needs around the world. Meanwhile, Google appears bent on testing the limits of "good enough" with its purely computational approach, exercising little concern for well-structured content and standardized descriptive metadata. Of course, such developments will improve Google capabilities just as the OAI-PMH (Open Access Initiative—Protocol for Metadata Harvesting) has already done.[51] But the Google developers are not waiting.

The viability of the institution-specific repository will, in the long run, be a result of the success with which the IR developers are able to integrate, support, and augment disciplinary relationships and context for both the specialists in the field and for interdisciplinary repurposing. As Lynch noted, this requires institutional commitment, openness to emerging content formats, staying abreast of disciplinary trends, and digital library developments.

In conclusion, the IR effort sits prominently on the continuum of change in scholarly communication. It is not a be-all or end-all solution. It has, however, a definite role in careful and thoughtful experimentation comprising the inevitable exploration necessary to equip scholars to embrace the new technologies and to influence how their social and cultural conventions will adapt to the new functions.

Notes

1. Andrew Odlyzko, Michael Lesk, Ann Peterson Bishop, Ann Okerson, Malcom Getz, Don King, and Carol Tenopir are among the early writers. Early articles include "The Crisis in Scholarly Communication" by Sanford G. Thatcher, *Chronicle of Higher Education,* March 3, 1995, and *Untangling the Web. Proceedings of the Conference Sponsored by the Librarians Association of the University of California, Santa Barbara, and Friends of the UCSB Library,* April 26, 1996, at University of California, Santa Barbara.

2. Anne Buck, Rick Flagan, and Betsy Coles, "Scholars' Forum: A New Model for Scholarly Communication" (California Institute of Technology, 1999).

3. Harnad wrote his proposal in June 1994 and published it a year later. Stevan Harnad, "Universal FTP Archives for Esoteric Science and Scholarship: A Subversive Proposal," in *Scholarly Journals at the Crossroads; a Subversive Proposal for Electronic Publishing,* ed. by Ann Okerson and James O'Donnell (Association of Research Libraries, 1995).

4. Herbert Van de Sompel, and Carl Lagoze, "The Santa Fe Convention of the Open Archives Initiative," D-Lib 6, no. 2 (2000).

5. Joseph J. Branin, and Mary Case, "Reforming Scholarly Publishing in the Sciences: A Librarian Perspective," Notices of the American Mathematical Society, April (1998); "To Publish and Perish," *Policy Perspectives* 7, no. 4 (1998); Maarten Cornet and Ben Vollard, "Tackling the Scientific Journal Crisis," in CPB Netherlands Bureau for Economic Policy Analysis Working Paper (2000), and articles in the *Chronicle of Higher Education* and the *New York Times.*

6. See Stephen Pinfield's papers in the University of Nottingham's Institutional Repository. http://eprints.nottingham.ac.uk/view/subjects/Gen2.html.

7. Mark Ware, "Pathfinder Research on Web-Based Repositories, London: Publisher and Library/Learning Solutions (Pals)," (2004), p. 5. Ware claims that "repository" has become preferred to avoid the complications that the term "archive" implies.

8. SPARC specifically does not use "digital."

9. "Check out the New Library [Interview with Clifford Lynch]," *Ubiquity* 4, no. 23 (2003).

10. http://archives.eprints.org/ under the heading "Institutional Archives Registry—Analysis as of 11/18/2004."

11. Margret L. Branschofsky, "DSpace Project," *MIT Faculty Newsletter* 12, no. 4 (2000).

12. In 2003 open access meetings were held in Berlin, Budapest, and Bethesda, Maryland.

13. Raym Crow, "SPARC Institutional Repository Checklist & Resource Guide," (SPARC, 2002).

14. Clifford A. Lynch, "Institutional Repositories: Essential Infrastructure for Scholarship in the Digital Age," in *ARL Bimonthly* 226 (February 2003).

15. Ibid.

16. Geoff Watts, "Crusaders for a Truly Free Flow of Ideas," *Times Higher Education Supplement,* January 5, 2004. Excerpted by Peter Suber in *SPARC Newsletter for Open Access,* January 10, 2004. http://www.earlham.edu/~peters/fos/2004_01_04_fosblogarchive. html.

17. Peter Suber. *SPARC Open Access Newsletter* http://www.earlham.edu/~peters/fos.

18. Mark Ware "Pathfinder Research on Web-Based Repositories, London: Publisher and Library/Learning Solutions (Pals)."

19. Susan Gibbons, "Establishing an Institutional Repository," *Library Technology Reports* 40, no. 4 (2004).

20. Leigh Watson Healy, et al., "Competitor Assessment: STM: Revolution in the Land of the Giants," (Outsell, 2004) and subsequent investor reports refer to the Open Access and IR movement as threats.

21. The British government decided to allow the merger of Springer and Kluwer. See: European Commission, "Conditional Clearance for Acquisition of Joint Control by Candover and Cinven of German Publisher Bertelsmann Springer" (Brussels: 2003). Financial analysts report that open access can exert serious competitive pressure on commercial publishers. See report by Sami Kassab for BNP Paribas in October 2003. Summarized by Peter Suber in *SPARC Open Access Newsletter,* November 2, 2003.

22. Gibbons, "Establishing an Institutional Repository." p. 6.

23. Mary R. Barton and Julia Harford Walker, "MIT's Dspace Business Plan Project: Final Report to the Andrew Mellon Foundation," (Massachusetts Institute of Technology, 2002).

24. Presentations: Peter Morgan and Julie Walker, "DSpace Impact Factor: Measuring Progress in Developing and Institutional Repository" (paper presented at the DSpace User Group Meeting, March 10–14, 2004); Peter Morgan, "Developing a Business Plan for DSpace@ Cambridge" (paper presented at "Institutional Repositories: The Next Stage," Washington, D.C., November 18–19, 2004); Peter Morgan, "Dspace@Cambridge: An Institutional Repository for Cambridge University" (paper presented at the "International Conference on Developing Digital Institutional Repositories: Experiences and Challenges," Hong Kong, December 10–11, 2004).

25. Barton, "MIT's Dspace Business Plan Project: Final Report to the Andrew Mellon Foundation," p. 22

26. Gibbons, "Establishing an Institutional Repository," p. 11ff.

27. Ibid. p. 11.

28. Barton, "MIT's DSpace Business Plan Project: Final Report to the Andrew Mellon Foundation," p. 15f.

29. See *A Guide to Institutional Repository Software V 3.0,* 3rd ed. (Open Society Institute, 2004).

30. Refer to the comprehensive reports by Crow, Gibbons, and Ware and the Ibid. for the state of the art as of December 2004.

31. Gibbons, "Establishing an Institutional Repository," p. 55.

32. Ware, "Pathfinder Research on Web-Based Repositories, London: Publisher and Library/ Learning Solutions (Pals)."

33. A common practice is for the author to transfer copyright for a paper to the publisher and the publisher grants certain rights back to the author, such as the right to duplicate for personal teaching and research and to reuse in another work.

34. http://www.sherpa.ac.uk/romeo.php, SHERPA/RoMEO Publishers' Copyright Listings.

35. "Self-Archiving and Institutional Repositories," p. 58f.

36. See http://repositories.cdlib.org/postprints/about.html.

37. Diana L. H. Chan, "Managing the Challenges: Acquiring Content for the Hkust Institutional Repository" (Hong Kong University of Science and Technology, 2004).

38. "Scientific Publications: Free for All?" (United Kingdom Parliament, House of Commons Science and Technology Committee, 2004). See Chapter six and the recommendations at the end of the report. More than 20 recommendations address institutional repositories.

39. Peter Suber. *SPARC Open Access Newsletter.* August 2, 2004. http://www.earlham.edu/ ~peters/fos/newsletter/08-02-04.htm#Ukreport.

40. See "Pew Internet and American Life Project," http://www.pewinternet.org.

41. Data regarding the use of print theses versus downloading of electronic theses are particularly illustrative. See Virginia Tech University Libraries, "Some Facts About VT ETDs" (Virginia Tech). http://scholar.lib.vt.edu/theses/data/somefacts.html.

42. The Creative Commons, established in 2001at Stanford University, has "the aim [. . .] to make access to that material cheaper and easier. To this end, Creative Commons will create metadata that can be used to associate creative works with their public domain or license status in a machine-readable way." A Creative Commons license allows the creator of original work to specify up front how it can be used. In other words, mechanisms of communicating are being recast for the digital environment. See http://creativecommons.org.

43. More detail is available at http://www.fedora.info/about.

44. Fedora 2.0 was released on January 31, 2005.

45. Tim Berners-Lee, James Hendler, and Ora Lassila, "The Semantic Web," Scientific American, no. 5 (2001).

46. The Division of Shared Cyberinfrastructure within the Directorate of Computer and Information Science and Engineering of the National Science Foundation. http://www.cise.nsf.gov/sci.

47. James J. Duderstadt, Daniel E. Atkins, Douglas Van Houweling, *Higher Education in the Digital Age: Technology Issues and Strategies for American Colleges and Universities* (Praeger, 2002). P. 11 describes the library as "more a center for knowledge navigation," and on p. 72 sees the library as "assisting scholars to navigate a vast array of digital knowledge resources scattered through cyberspace."

48. Simile Project. See http://simile.mit.edu.

49. Eric Miller, "Enabling the Semantic Web for Scientific Research and Collaboration," in *Wave of the Future: Post Digital Library Futures Workshop* (2003).

50. There were 72 worldwide listed in the DSpace Wikipedia (http://wiki.dspace.org/Dspace Instances) as of January 2005.

51. OAIster, Google Scholar, DP9 come to mind, not to mention the positive effect it has had for ISI's Web of Science and Elsevier's Scopus developments.

Sources

"Check out the New Library" [Interview with Clifford Lynch]. *Ubiquity* 4, no. 23 (2003). http://www.acm.org/ubiquity/interviews/c_lynch_1.html (accessed January 5, 2005).

A Guide to Institutional Repository Software V 3.0. 3rd ed: Open Society Institute, 2004. http://www.soros.org/openaccess/software (accessed January 25, 2005).

Scientific Publications: Free for All? United Kingdom Parliament, House of Commons, Science and Technology Committee, 2004. http://www.publications.parliament.uk/pa/cm200304/cmselect/cmsctech/399/39902.htm (accessed January 25, 2005).

"Self-Archiving and Institutional Repositories." http://www.sparceurope.org/Repositories (accessed January 25, 2005).

"To Publish and Perish." *Policy Perspectives* 7, no. 4 (1998). http://www.the learningalliance.info/Docs/Jun2003/DOC-2003Jun13.1055537929.pdf (accessed January 7, 2005).

Barton, Mary R. and Julia Harford Walker. "MIT's DSpace Business Plan Project: Final Report to the Andrew Mellon Foundation." 33. Massachusetts Institute of Technology, 2002. http://libraries.mit.edu/dspace-mit/mit/mellon.pdf (accessed December 15, 2004).

Berners-Lee, Tim and James Hendler and Ora Lassila. "The Semantic Web." *Scientific American,* no. 5 (2001). http://www.sciam.com/article.cfm?articleID=00048144-10D2-1C70-84A9809EC588EF21&ref=sciam (accessed January 25, 2005).

Branin, Joseph J., and Mary Case. "Reforming Scholarly Publishing in the Sciences: A Librarian Perspective." *Notices of the American Mathematical Society,* no. April (1998): 475–486. http://www.ams.org/notices/199804/branin.pdf (accessed January 28, 2005).

Branschofsky, Margret L. "DSpace Project." *MIT Faculty Newsletter* 12, no. 4 (2000): 1. http://www.dspace.org/news/articles/dspace-project.html (accessed January 25, 2005).

Buck, Anne, Rick Flagan and Betsy Coles. "Scholars Forum: A New Model for Scholarly Communication." California Institute of Technology, 1999. http://resolver.caltech.edu/CaltechLIB:1999.001 (accessed January 5, 2005).

Chan, Diana L. H. "Managing the Challenges: Acquiring Content for the Hkust Institutional Repository." Hong Kong University of Science and Technology, 2004. http://hdl.handle.net/1783.1/1973 (accessed January 28, 2005).

Cornet, Maarten, and Ben Vollard. "Tackling the Scientific Journal Crisis." In CPB Netherlands Bureau for Economic Policy Analysis Working Paper, 2000. http://www.cpb.nl/eng/pub/werkdoc/121 (accessed January 25, 2005).

Crow, Raym. "SPARC Institutional Repository Checklist & Resource Guide." SPARC, 2002. http://www.arl.org/sparc/IR/IR_Guide.html (accessed January 28, 3005).

Duderstadt, James J., Daniel E. Atkins, Douglas Van Houweling. *Higher Education in the Digital Age: Technology Issues and Strategies for American Colleges and Universities.* Praeger, 2002.

European Commission. "Conditional Clearance for Acquisition of Joint Control by Candover and Cinven of German Publisher Bertelsmann Springer." 2003. http://europa.eu.int/rapid/pressReleasesAction.do?reference=IP/03/1130&format=HTML&aged=0&language=EN&guiLanguage=en (accessed January 24, 2005).

Gibbons, Susan. "Establishing an Institutional Repository." *Library Technology Reports* 40, no. 4 (2004).

Harnad, Stevan. "Universal ftp Archives for Esoteric Science and Scholarship: A Subversive Proposal." In *Scholarly Journals at the Crossroads; a Subversive Proposal for Electronic Publishing,* ed. by Ann Okerson and James O'Donnell. Association of Research Libraries, 1995. http://www.arl.org/scomm/subversive/toc.html (accessed January 25, 2005).

Healy, Leigh Watson, et al. "Competitor Assessment: STM: Revolution in the Land of the Giants." 36: Outsell, 2004. http://content.outsellinc.com/coms2/summary_0245-709_ITM (abstract accessed January 25, 2005).

Lynch, Clifford A. "Institutional Repositories: Essential Infrastructure for Scholarship in the Digital Age." In *ARL Bimonthly* 226, February 2003. http://www.arl.org/newsltr/226/ir.html (accessed January 25, 2005).

Miller, Eric. "Enabling the Semantic Web for Scientific Research and Collaboration." In *Wave of the Future: Post Digital Library Futures Workshop.* 2003. http://www.sis.pitt.edu/~dlwkshop/paper_miller.pdf (accessed January 24, 2005).

Morgan, Peter. "Developing a Business Plan for DSpace@Cambridge." Paper presented at "Institutional Repositories: The Next Stage," Washington, D.C., November 18–19, 2004. http://www.arl.org/sparc/meetings/ir04/presentations/morgan_files/morgan.ppt (accessed January 25, 2005).

———. "DSpace@Cambridge: An Institutional Repository for Cambridge University." Paper presented at the International Conference on Developing Digital Institutional Repositories: Experiences and Challenges, Hong Kong, December 10–11 2004. http://library.ust.hk/conference2004/papers/morgan-paper.ppt (accessed January 25, 2005).

Morgan, Peter, and Julie Walker. "DSpace Impact Factor: Measuring Progress in Developing and Institutional Repository." Paper presented at the DSpace User Group Meeting, March 10–14 2004. http://www.dspace.org/conference/presentations/cambridge-mit.ppt#403,1,Slide 1 (accessed January 25, 2005).

Van de Sompel, Herbert, and Carl Lagoze. "The Santa Fe Convention of the Open Archives Initiative." *D-Lib* 6, no. 2 (2000). http://www.dlib.org/dlib/february00/vandesompel-oai/02vandesompel-oai.html (accessed January 28, 2005).

Virginia Tech University Libraries. "Some Facts About VT ETDs." Virginia Tech. http://scholar.lib.vt.edu/theses/data/somefacts.html (accessed January 25, 2005).

Ware, Mark. "Pathfinder Research on Web-Based Repositories, London: Publisher and Library/Learning Solutions (Pals)." (2004).

http://www.palsgroup.org.uk/palsweb/palsweb.nsf/0/8c43ce800a9c67cd80256e370051e88a?OpenDocument (accessed January 5, 2005).

Developments in Information Literacy

Lisa Janicke Hinchliffe

Information literacy is currently receiving a great deal of attention in the library and information science literature, at conferences, and in everyday discussions in libraries of all types. The volume of information about information literacy has grown rapidly in the last 25 years, ranging from empirical investigations to rhetorical essays to case studies of library practice. Even before *information literacy* became a common term, the literature and library practice showed attention to the skills and abilities of library users and related library programs. In the face of such growing emphasis, it is worth exploring the contours of the concept of information literacy.

"Information literacy" is used to describe both the characteristic of an individual person and one or more initiatives aimed at helping individuals attain that characteristic. A full understanding of the current state of information literacy involves understanding both of these uses and how they inform each other. This report will consider first the individual characteristic and then present a discussion of library initiatives in various types of libraries and institutions.

The Information Literate Individual

The final report of the American Library Association's Presidential Committee on Information Literacy included what has become the touchstone definition of the information literate individual:

> To be information literate, a person must be able to recognize when information is needed and have the ability to locate, evaluate, and use effectively the needed information . . . Ultimately, information literate people are those who have learned how to learn. They know how to learn because they know how knowledge is organized, how to find information, and how to use information in such a way that others can learn from them. They are people prepared for life-long learning, because they can always find the information needed for any task or decision at hand.[1]

The idea of information literacy as an individual characteristic is expressed in many information literacy learning standards documents. This focus is particularly obvious in the Information Literacy Competency Standards for Higher Education,[2] which were developed by a committee led by the Association of College and Research Libraries (ACRL) and which reflect closely the definition given in the final report:

Standard 1. The information literate student determines the nature and extent of the information needed.

Lisa Janicke Hinchliffe is coordinator for information literacy services and instruction and an associate professor of library administration at the University of Illinois at Urbana-Champaign. She is also a member of ACRL's Institute for Information Literacy immersion program faculty and has taught both library school instruction and undergraduate courses in critical thinking. She is editor of *Research Strategies,* an information literacy and library instruction journal focusing primarily on higher education settings, and the author of the *Neal-Schuman Electronic Classroom Handbook* (2001).

Standard 2. The information literate student accesses needed information effectively and efficiently.

Standard 3. The information literate student evaluates information and its sources critically and incorporates selected information into his or her knowledge base and value system.

Standard 4. The information literate student, individually or as a member of a group, uses information effectively to accomplish a specific purpose.

Standard 5. The information literate student understands many of the economic, legal, and social issues surrounding the use of information and accesses and uses information ethically and legally.

The Information Literacy Standards for Student Learning[3] created by the American Association of School Librarians (AASL) and the Association for Educational Communications and Technology also focus on the individual, but offer a richer set of standards reflecting not only the definition in the final report but also contextualizing the concept with notions of independent learning and social responsibility:

Standard 1. The student who is information literate accesses information efficiently and effectively.

Standard 2. The student who is information literate evaluates information critically and competently.

Standard 3. The student who is information literate uses information accurately and creatively.

Standard 4. The student who is an independent learner is information literate and pursues information related to personal interests.

Standard 5. The student who is an independent learner is information literate and appreciates literature and other creative expressions of information.

Standard 6. The student who is an independent learner is information literate and strives for excellence in information seeking and knowledge generation.

Standard 7. The student who contributes positively to the learning community and to society is information literate and recognizes the importance of information to a democratic society.

Standard 8. The student who contributes positively to the learning community and to society is information literate and practices ethical behavior in regard to information and information technology.

Standard 9. The student who contributes positively to the learning community and to society is information literate and participates effectively in groups to pursue and generate information.

This focus on information literacy as an individual characteristic is not only found in the United States. For example, SCONUL (the Society of College, National and University Libraries) of the United Kingdom and Ireland has articulated an information-skills model that includes Seven Pillars of Information Literacy:[4]

1 The ability to recognise a need for information
2 The ability to distinguish ways in which the information "gap" may be addressed

3 The ability to construct strategies for locating information

4 The ability to locate and access information

5 The ability to compare and evaluate information obtained from different sources

6 The ability to organise, apply, and communicate information to others in ways appropriate

7 The ability to synthesise and build upon existing information, contributing to the creation of new knowledge

Similarly, the Australian and New Zealand Information Literacy Framework[5] promulgated by the Australian and New Zealand Institute for Information Literacy focuses on the individual:

1 The information literate person recognises the need for information and determines the nature and extent of the information needed

2 The information literate person finds needed information effectively and efficiently

3 The information literate person critically evaluates information and the information-seeking process

4 The information literate person manages information collected or generated

5 The information literate person applies prior and new information to construct new concepts or create new understandings

6 The information literate person uses information with understanding and acknowledges cultural, ethical, economic, legal, and social issues surrounding the use of information

It is interesting to note, however, that—although derived from the Information Literacy Competency Standards for Higher Education—these standards use "person" rather than "student"—perhaps reflecting a subtle shift from an emphasis on information literacy as learned to information literacy as lived. This may reflect a newer approach to defining information literacy, deriving a definition or understanding of information literacy as perceived by those who are information literate or who, perhaps more accurately stated, have engaged in acts of information literacy. Christine Bruce's "Seven Faces of Information Literacy in Higher Education"[6] is perhaps the most widely known document in this approach. The "seven faces" are particularly interesting because they represent a diversity of ways of understanding information literacy rather than an attempt to create a single comprehensive and normative statement:

1 Information literacy is seen as using information technology for information retrieval and communication

2 Information literacy is seen as finding information located in information sources

3 Information literacy is seen as executing a process

4 Information literacy is seen as controlling information

5 Information literacy is seen as building up a personal knowledge base in a new area of interest

6 Information literacy is seen as working with knowledge and personal perspectives adopted in such a way that novel insights are gained

7 Information literacy is seen as using information wisely for the benefit of others

Continuing in this vein is Sheila Webber and Bill Johnston's project "UK Academics' Conceptions of, and Pedagogy for, Information Literacy,"[7] which is particularly interesting in its research into whether there are disciplinary differences in how information literacy is understood in higher education.

Information Literacy as a Component of Literacies

The documents referenced above primarily aim to define or describe information literacy as a specific characteristic, or set of characteristics, of individuals. In addition, information literacy is often included as a component of the larger set of characteristics or abilities needed for full participation in an information society. The notion of multiple literacies is very broadly discussed in the "White Paper of the 21st Century Literacy Summit,"[8] which puts forth the following components as challenges for education, workplace skills, and civic engagement:

Technology Literacy. The ability to use new media such as the Internet to effectively access and communicate information.

Information Literacy. The ability to use new media such as the Internet to effectively access and communicate information based on the results.

Media Creativity. The growing capacity of individuals everywhere to produce and distribute content to audiences of all sizes.

Social Competence and Responsibility. The competence to consider the social consequences of an online publication and the responsibility vis-à-vis children.

Likewise, the enGauge 21st Century Skills[9] framework offers four skill clusters—Digital-Age Literacy, Inventive Thinking, Effective Communication, and High Productivity—each of which is broken down into skill sets. Digital-Age Literacy encompasses basic, scientific, economic, and technological literacies; visual and information literacies; and multicultural literacy and global awareness skills.

The American Library Association's 21st Century Literacy initiative[10] takes a more generalized approach and discusses information literacy under the umbrella of literacy generally conceived rather than attempting to separate out all of the various types of literacies.

Information Literacy as Educational Initiative

Although individuals can become information literate independent of formal instruction, librarians today advocate for systematic instruction to support and encourage development of information literacy. Many of the documents presented above that define or describe information literacy are foundational to an information literacy curriculum broadly conceived. In addition to formal instruction activities, almost the entire range of services and resources offered by a library can be conceptualized as contributing to information literacy if they encourage and support the development of information literacy as an individual characteristic. It is useful to examine those activities aimed specifically at information literacy, but it is helpful to keep in mind this more holistic viewpoint as different libraries will necessarily support information literacy in different ways because of their different missions and resources.

Information Literacy and School Library Media Centers

School library media centers focus perhaps more than any other libraries on the development of information literacy. Collaboration among teachers and school library media specialists, collection building, student programming, and library space design are all pursued in the context of promoting and enhancing student learning. The focus of the school library media specialist, sometimes called the teacher-librarian, on instruction and student learning is primary and can be seen in all four roles—teacher, instructional partner, information specialist, and program administrator—detailed in *Information Power: Building Partnerships for Learning*.[11] Particularly important are efforts to connect information literacy standards with other content knowledge standards and to understand developing levels of proficiency in information literacy.

Information Power specifically provides details for understanding the Information Literacy Standards for Student Learning in relation to levels of proficiencies and content area standards. Possible learning activities are offered for four sets of grade ranges for each standard, representing a range of curriculum areas. Examples of content area standards that can be linked to each information literacy standard are identified. In addition, performance indicators are given for each standard and three levels of proficiency—basic, proficient, and exemplary—are defined for each indicator. In addition to content area standards that are promulgated by various educational associations, school librarians are also likely to be concerned with standards outlined by a state's education department.

Process models for information literacy learning are also widely used in school libraries. Perhaps the best-known is the Big6 information problem-solving model,[12] which posits six steps—each with two sub-steps—for approaching any information-based question:

1. Task Definition
   1.1 Define the information problem
   1.2 Identify information needed
2. Information Seeking Strategies
   2.1 Determine all possible sources
   2.2 Select the best sources
3. Location and Access
   3.1 Locate sources (intellectually and physically)
   3.2 Find information within sources
4. Use of Information

4.1 Engage (e.g., read, hear, view, touch)
4.2 Extract relevant information
5. Synthesis
  5.1 Organize from multiple sources
  5.2 Present the information
6. Evaluation
  6.1 Judge the product (effectiveness)
  6.2 Judge the process (efficiency)

Such process models complement the standards that describe the characteristics of an information literate student by offering a series of tasks through which students can both learn and demonstrate their information literacy abilities. The process models can also serve as a framework for lesson planning for teachers and librarians.

Information Literacy and Academic Libraries

Like school library media centers, academic libraries are connected to larger educational institutions and thus have concerns about instruction and student learning. Academic libraries, however, vary in the degree to which information literacy is a primary focus of activity, just as colleges and universities vary in the degree to which teaching and learning are a primary focus as balanced against research- and scholarship-related activities.

Academic libraries often employ a coordinator or head of information literacy with formal responsibility for leading and developing information literacy and library instruction efforts. These coordinators may or may not supervise other instruction librarians. In addition, reference librarians and bibliographers are likely to have formal instruction activities among their responsibilities, and technical services librarians may be expected to participate in formal instruction programs as well.

Information Literacy Competency Standards for Higher Education serves as the program framework for many academic libraries. However, some libraries use locally developed standards and others continue to use the "Model Statement of Objectives for Academic Bibliographic Instruction"[13] because of that document's emphasis on how experts understand and use information resources, which is particularly relevant in exploring information literacy in a disciplinary context. Though many information literacy efforts in higher education have been integrated into general education programs, and particularly into composition courses, attention to information literacy in the disciplines is increasing.

Instruction programs in academic libraries can also draw guidance from ACRL's "Characteristics of Programs of Information Literacy That Illustrate Best Practices: A Guideline"[14] and "Guidelines for Instruction Programs in Academic Libraries."[15]

Many academic librarians have also been inspired by Jeremy J. Shapiro and Shelley K. Hughes, who stated that

> information literacy should in fact be conceived more broadly as a new liberal art that extends from knowing how to use computers and access information to critical reflection on the nature of information itself, its technical infrastructure, and its social, cultural and even philosophical

context and impact—as essential to the mental framework of the educated information-age citizen as the trivium of basic liberal arts (grammar, logic, and rhetoric) was to the educated person in medieval society.[16]

Unfortunately, though inspired, very few have been able to achieve the kind of curriculum that Shapiro and Hughes outline.

In addition to formal in-person instruction sessions, academic librarians have also developed a variety of Web-based tutorials and resources to instruct students in information literacy skills. Collaboration among faculty and librarians, student-group outreach activities, and advocacy in the realm of curriculum development and reform are popular strategies for integrating information literacy into campus curricula and student learning experiences.

Information Literacy and Public Libraries

Though not explicitly linked with a larger educational institution, public libraries have long aimed to assist their users in improving their skills and abilities. The information literacy activities of a public library are usually not tied to a particular curricular framework, and lifelong learning is likely to be the framework for the range of programs that are offered. Programs are often developed in response to recognized community needs or to user requests. Activities include formal teaching sessions, often highlighting technology-based resources and strategies, as well as traditional one-to-one consultation at the reference desk and library tours. Perhaps most unique to the public library setting is the emphasis on reading for its own sake and the concomitant programming, including reader's advisory, book talks, bibliographies, exhibits, and displays that encourage reading per se and support users in making their reading decisions.

Public libraries are traditionally very actively involved in literacy programming, both for children and adults. For example, the Every Child Ready to Read Project[17] focuses on early literacy development, and the ALA Office of Literacy and Outreach Services[18] offers a variety of literacy-related information, including a number of adult literary resources. Computer and technology literacy are also receiving increasing attention in many public libraries.

Some public libraries or public library systems employ a training coordinator, but developing and offering various programs is often incorporated into the responsibilities of children's, young adult, and adult reference services librarians.

Information Literacy and Special Libraries

The information literacy efforts of special libraries are necessarily as broad and varied as the missions of special libraries. Some special libraries are also academic libraries and pursue activities similar to those outlined above. Others have missions that parallel those of public libraries and thus have parallel information literacy activities. The information literacy activities that have not yet been discussed and that are unique to some special libraries often relate to the concepts of knowledge management and workplace skills and are undertaken in corporate or nonprofit organizational settings. As a specific example, Tom W. Goad presents a model of information literacy in the workplace that details a 16-step information process and discusses communication, thinking and decision making, creativity, innovation and risk taking, computer literacy, and subject matter literacy as necessary skills.[19]

Strategies used by special libraries in supporting the development of knowledge management or other skills relating to information literacy are varied and may reflect the culture of the larger organization. Such strategies include formal seminars and workshops, brown-bag lunches, organization-wide e-mail messages and newsletters, and participation in new-employee orientation and other professional development initiatives.

The Competencies for Information Professionals of the 21st Century[20] promulgated by the Special Libraries Association includes an applied scenario that highlights the instructional role:

> Develops, delivers and manages curricula educating clients in information literacy, Internet usage, and locating and interpreting information sources.

The specifics of these curricula will reflect the diversity of goals, sizes, and audiences of particular special libraries.

Information Literacy and Collaboration

Academic and school librarians often seek to establish collaborative relationships with the other educators in their institutions, including instructors, technology specialists, professional development staff, and administrators. Relationships with instructors are particularly important to incorporating information literacy instruction throughout the curriculum and communicating its importance to learners, perhaps through the school or higher education institution highlighting information literacy as a priority learning outcome for all students. Public and special librarians may also have opportunities to establish partnerships for various information literacy activities.

While information literacy is often addressed in the context of a particular library or by a community of librarians who work in the same type of library, efforts have also been made to connect information literacy initiatives across the boundaries of traditional library types. The AASL/ACRL Blueprint for Collaboration[21] recommended a variety of joint activities related to the educational role of librarians for school and academic libraries and their respective associations. Among the outcomes of the Blueprint for Collaboration was the creation of the AASL/ACRL Interdivisional Committee on Information Literacy as a standing committee aimed at preparing K–20 students to be information literate and providing an ongoing channel of communication for the two organizations on the topic of information literacy and library instruction.

Community partnerships for information literacy[22] are another way of conceptualizing information literacy collaborations. These collaborations focus on information literacy development activities in a particular geographic area or community and often involve other organizations as well as libraries. The specific programming activities of these community partnerships reflect national trends, but are developed to respond specifically to local needs and circumstances.

Information Literacy Assessment and Research

Systematic investigation into information literacy as individual characteristic and as educational initiative is crucial for continuing to enhance understanding of what it is to be an information literate individual and how library activities impact the skills and abilities of individuals. Such investigation can take many forms and occur at a variety of levels.

Assessment

In the context of formal instruction, librarians pursue classroom assessment of student learning. What is being learned, how well, and through what mechanisms are the primary areas of concern. Though tests and quizzes are used for classroom assessment, performance-based assessments—in which learners are asked to demonstrate information literacy abilities through authentic, real-world tasks—are often viewed as more useful because they provide a richer set of data to examine in judging student achievement. Assessment results are used to give feedback to students about their learning, improve the existing instructional activities, or enhance instruction in future instructional settings.

In addition to classroom assessment, many librarians are also seeking a standardized information literacy assessment instrument that can be used in a variety of educational settings and for a range of learners. Such an instrument would aim to assess individuals' information literacy, whether as a separate characteristic or as a component of a larger literacies concept, more generally, without regard to any particular instructional programs or learning activities. Such a test remains somewhat elusive. Currently, the Educational Testing Service is developing an ICT (Information and Communication Technology) Literacy test[23] and the Association of Research Libraries is sponsoring SAILS (Standardized Assessment of Information Literacy Skills)[24] as one component of its New Measures Initiative.[25] Though these still-developing tests are attractive as standardized approaches to assessing individuals' information literacy, it is difficult to judge their ultimate utility and the degree to which they can substitute for more performance-based, authentic assessment approaches.

Beyond assessing student learning, librarians may also be concerned with assessment of instructional effectiveness and program assessment. Assessment of instructional effectiveness investigates issues as wide-ranging as instructor preparedness, presentation and classroom management abilities, content knowledge expertise, and pedagogical repertoire. Student and supervisor assessments are common but self-assessment mechanisms such as portfolios and reflective journals are also useful mechanisms. Program assessment investigates the overall effectiveness and efficiency of the administration and implementation of a set of instructional activities. Data from classroom assessments, standardized tests, and instructional effectiveness assessments are likely to be incorporated into program assessment, which will also likely use benchmarking relative to other institutions or professional or accreditation standards.

Research

The nexus between information literacy as an individual characteristic and information literacy as initiative is most often seen in writings and presentations about
information literacy, particularly as librarians seek to show a connection between
their efforts and the abilities of their libraries' users. Articles, books, and conference presentations abound, but the empirical or investigative base underlying
claims about the importance of information literacy and the effectiveness of
library activities is not robust. In attempting to remedy this gap, the profession
offers guidance for those interested in contributing to the scholarly conversation
in a systematic way.

The Research Agenda for Library Instruction and Information Literacy[26] promulgated by ACRL's Instruction Section outlines general areas of inquiry and
specific research questions about the following topics:

I   Learners—Audiences, Skills, Learning Styles
II   Teaching—Pedagogy, Design and Implementation, Methods of In-
     struction, Library Teaching, and Continuing Education
III Organizational Context—Relationship within the Library Organiza-
     tional Structure, Relationship to the Larger Institutional Environment,
     Relationship with Faculty
IV   Assessment—Evaluation of Instructors and Programs, Assessment of
     Learning Outcomes, Transferability

The research agenda includes such thought-provoking questions as

- What impact does the relationship between students' actual and perceived
  library and search skill levels have on their information-seeking behaviors?
- Can effective, scalable instruction be developed for institutions of all
  sizes?
- What are the most effective ways for a librarian who has previously done
  little or no teaching to learn fundamental methodologies and pedagogies?
- How does instruction as a function overlap with, and what is its impact
  on, other services in the library such as reference, distance education, and
  Web development?
- Do the different ways in which librarians and teaching faculty perceive
  research have an effect on how students learn research skills?
- How can assessment of information literacy be integrated into other institutional assessment measurements?

Similarly, though not focused exclusively on information literacy, Delia
Neuman offers a research agenda for school library media that outlines these
broad questions:

1 What are the contributions of library media programs to student achievement?

2 What are the roles of the library media specialist in today's schools?
3 How do students use electronic information resources for learning?
4 What has been the impact of the information literacy standards for student learning on library media programs?[27]

Conclusion

As the information landscape continues to change and develop and societies become increasingly focused on information exchange and use in education, work, and civic settings, the importance of information literacy will only continue to grow. Libraries must, and by all indicators will, continue to focus attention and effort on the information literacy abilities of their users and seek to develop information literacy programming to best support and encourage their users in becoming information literate.

Notes

1. *Presidential Committee on Information Literacy, Final Report* (American Library Association, 1989), http://www.ala.org/ala/acrl/acrlpubs/whitepapers/presidential.htm (accessed February 24, 2005).

2. Information Literacy Competency Standards for Higher Education (American Library Association, 2000), http://www.ala.org/acrl/ilcomstan.html (accessed February 24, 2005).

3. American Association of School Librarians and Association for Educational Communications and Technology, Information Literacy Standards for Student Learning: Standards and Indicators, http://www.ala.org/ala/aasl/aaslproftools/informationpower/InformationLiteracy Standards_final.pdf (accessed February 24, 2005).

4. Information Skills in Higher Education: A SCONUL Position Paper, http://www.sconul.ac. uk/activities/inf_lit/papers/Seven_pillars.html (accessed February 24, 2005).

5. *Australian and New Zealand Information Literacy Framework: Principles, Standards and Practice,* ed. by Alan Bundy (Australian and New Zealand Institute for Information Literacy, 2004), http://www.anziil.org/resources/Info%20lit%202nd%20edition.pdf (accessed February 24, 2005).

6. Christine Bruce, "Seven Faces of Information Literacy in Higher Education," 1997, http://sky.fit.qut.edu.au/~bruce/inflit/faces/faces1.php (accessed February 24, 2005).

7. Sheila Webber and Bill Johnston, "UK Academics' Conceptions of, and Pedagogy for, Information Literacy," 2004, http://dis.shef.ac.uk/literacy/project (accessed February 24, 2005).

8. 21st Century Literacy Summit, White Paper: 21st Century Literacy in a Convergent Media World (Berlin, 2002). Original Web site no longer online; document can be accessed through the Internet Archive at http://web.archive.org/web/20030405070437/www.21st centuryliteracy.org/white/WhitePaperEnglish.pdf (accessed February 25, 2005).

9. Learning Point Associates, 21st Century Skills, http://www.ncrel.org/engauge/skills/skill21. htm (accessed February 25, 2005).

10. American Library Association, 21st Century Literacy @ your library, http://www.ala.org/ ala/proftools/21centurylit/21stcenturyliteracy.htm (accessed February 25, 2005).

11. American Association of School Librarians and Association for Educational Communications and Technology, *Information Power: Building Partnerships for Learning* (American Library Association, 1998), 4–5.

12. Big6 Associates, "Big 6: An Information Problem-Solving Process," http://www.big6.com (accessed February 24, 2005).

13. ACRL/BIS Task Force on Model Statement of Objectives, "Model Statement of Objectives for Academic Bibliographic Instruction," in *Read This First! An Owner's Guide to the New Model Statement of Objectives for Academic Bibliographic Instruction,* ed. by Carolyn Dusenbury (Association of College and Research Libraries, 1991), 5–15.

14. Association of College and Research Libraries, "Characteristics of Programs of Information Literacy that Illustrate Best Practices: A Guideline," 2003, http://www.ala.org/ala/acrl/acrlstandards/characteristics.htm (accessed February 24, 2005).

15. Association of College and Research Libraries, "Guidelines for Instruction Programs in Academic Libraries, 2003," http://www.ala.org/ala/acrl/acrlstandards/guidelinesinstruction.htm (accessed February 25, 2005).

16. Jeremy J. Shapiro and Shelley K. Hughes, "Information Literacy as a Liberal Art: Enlightenment Proposals for a New Curriculum," *Educom Review,* 31(March/April 1996), http://www.educause.edu/pub/er/review/reviewArticles/31231.html (accessed February 24, 2005).

17. Public Library Association and Association for Library Service to Children, Every Child Ready to Read Project, http://www.ala.org/ala/pla/plaissues/earlylit/earlyliteracy.htm (accessed February 24, 2005).

18. American Library Association, Office for Literacy and Outreach Services, http://www.ala.org/Template.cfm?Section=olos (accessed February 24, 2005).

19. Tom W. Goad, *Information Literacy and Workplace Performance* (Quorum Books, 2002).

20. Special Libraries Association, Competencies for Information Professionals of the 21st Century, 2003, http://www.sla.org/content/learn/comp2003/index.cfm (accessed February 24, 2005).

21. AASL/ACRL Task Force on the Educational Role of Libraries, Blueprint for Collaboration, 2000, http://www.ala.org/acrl/blueprint.html (accessed February 25, 2005).

22. Presidential Initiative: Information Literacy Community Partnerships Initiative, http://www.ala.org/ala/ourassociation/governanceb/pastpresidents/nancykranich/informationliteracy.htm (accessed February 24, 2005).

23. Information and Communication Technology: Assessing Literacy for Today and Tomorrow, Educational Testing Service, http://www.ets.org/ictliteracy (accessed February 24, 2005).

24. Project SAILS, http://sails.lms.kent.edu/index.php (accessed February 24, 2005).

25. Association of Research Libraries, ARL New Measures Initiatives, http://www.arl.org/stats/newmeas/index.html (accessed February 24, 2005).

26. Instruction Section, Association of College and Research Libraries, Research Agenda for Library Instruction and Information Literacy, http://www.ala.org/ala/acrlbucket/is/iscommittees/webpages/research/researchagendalibrary.htm (accessed February 25, 2005).

27. Delia Neuman, "Research in School Library Media for the Next Decade: Polishing the Diamond," *Library Trends* 51 (Spring 2003): 503–524.

Library Assessment and Performance Measures: An Overview

Julia C. Blixrud
Association of Research Libraries

Wanda Dole
Washburn University

Statistics are no substitute for judgment.

—Henry Clay

The last few years have been marked by a dramatic increase in assessment activities and by a shift from just plain descriptive library statistics (input and output measures) to a search for quantitative and qualitative performance measures for services, value, and cost effectiveness. This shift occurred in all types of libraries and library organizations throughout the world.

One indication of this is the change in name and scope of committees and sections of library organizations. The Statistics Section of the American Library Association's Library Administration and Management Association (LAMA) changed its name to the Measurement, Assessment and Evaluation Section (MAES); the Statistics Section of the International Federation of Library Associations and Institutions (IFLA) changed its name to Statistics and Evaluation Section. Another indication is the proliferation of conferences and training events devoted to assessment in general or to specific assessment tools such as LibQUAL+ and Balanced Scorecard.

The reasons for the rise in assessment include increased demands for accountability, the sluggish economy (which requires managers to do more with less and to concentrate on core activities), the volatility of e-publishing and scholarly communication, and government legislation such as "No Child Left Behind." Libraries throughout the world are being asked by funding and accrediting bodies to demonstrate their impact on the user community by employing a series of metrics that are outcomes- and data-based. In Britain, for example, public library funding is linked to meeting standards established by the government.[1]

Developing a "culture of assessment" has become a goal for many libraries. Amos Lakos writes that an organization with a culture of assessment is one "in which decisions are based on facts, research and analysis, and where services are planned and delivered in ways that maximize positive outcomes and impacts for library clients. A Culture of Assessment exists in organizations where staff care to know what results they produce and how those results relate to customer expectations."[2] In a study for the Digital Library Federation (DLF) about digital library usage to inform future planning, Denise Troll Covey noted the challenges identified by DLF participants regarding assessing the usability of digital collections and services during a time in which there is a multiplicity of assessment methods but not enough time or resources to take advantage of all of them. DLF respondents indicated that it is important to focus efforts on collecting meaningful, purposeful data; to develop the skills to gather, analyze, interpret, present, and use data; to develop comprehensive assessment plans; to organize assessment as a core activity; to compile and manage assessment data; and to acquire sufficient information about the environment to understand trends in library use.[3]

This overview provides a summary of library assessment activities in the last few years and the movement from descriptive statistics to performance measures.

Descriptive Statistics

Library performance often has been based on descriptive statistics. Libraries often benchmark their own data against that collected for similar institutions. Data for libraries in the United States are collected by the National Center for Education Statistics (NCES), an agency within the U.S. Department of Education and the Institute of Education Sciences charged with the collection and analysis of data relating to education in the United States and other nations. NCES initiated a formal library statistics program in 1989 and works cooperatively with the U.S. National Commission on Libraries and Information Science and the Bureau of the Census to implement the Library Statistics Program. It reports on its programs each year in the *Bowker Annual* [See "National Center for Education Statistics Library Statistics Program" earlier in Part 1—*Ed.*]

The longest-running series of annual statistics is produced for the members of the Association of Research Libraries (ARL) and describes collections, expenditures, staffing, and service activities. Statistics have been collected and published annually since 1961–1962. ARL also collects descriptive data for salary information, health and law libraries, and preservation. A test bed for new variables is conducted through its supplementary survey and, occasionally, new data are added to the main statistics. Data are now collected through a Web-based interface and interactive statistics are available for member and other library use.

The NCES Academic Library Survey (ALS) asks for data on total library operating expenditures, full-time-equivalent (FTE) library staff, service outlets, total volumes held at the end of the academic year, circulation, interlibrary loans, public service hours, patron count, reference transactions per typical week, and online services. Beginning in 1996, libraries were asked whether they offered the following electronic services: an electronic catalog that includes the library's holdings, electronic full-text periodicals, Internet access, library reference services by e-mail, and electronic document delivery to patron's account-address. Beginning with the fiscal year (FY) 2000 survey, questions about consortial services were added. In FY 2000 ALS changed to a Web-based data collection. The FY 2002 data collection closed March 2003.

The Association of College and Research Libraries (ACRL) also collects descriptive data and publishes *Academic Library Trends and Statistics,* a compilation of data consisting of five major categories: collections, expenditures, personnel and public services, institutional academic information, and trends. These data are also collected electronically and made available for searching, selecting peer institutions, establishing comparison criteria, and displaying or downloading data.

Similarly, nationwide descriptive statistics on public libraries are collected through a voluntary census, the Public Libraries Survey. The survey is conducted by NCES through the Federal-State Cooperative System for public library data (FSCS). Statistics are collected from more than 9,000 public libraries. Data are available for individual public libraries and are also aggregated to state and national levels. The American Library Association (ALA) publishes the *Public Library Data Service Statistical Report,* which also includes information on a current hot topic. *Hennen's American Public Library Ratings* (http://www. haplr-index.com) uses the data to rate, score, and rank public libraries on 15 input and output measures such as per capita expenditures, collection turnover, and circulation per visit.

NCES collects state library data yearly and school library data less often (data surveys were conducted in 1958, 1962, 1974, 1978, 1986, 1994, 2000, and 2004); however, the Library Research Service in Colorado (http://www.lrs.org) collects school library data annually.

In Canada, the National Core Library Statistics Program (NCLSP) collects national statistics on Canadian libraries (public, academic, and special libraries, but not school libraries) for more than 25 library-specific variables. LISU, a research and information center for library and information services in the Department of Information Science at Loughborough University, collects descriptive statistics for libraries in Britain and conducts a range of research projects (http://www.lboro.ac.uk/departments/dis/lisu/list03/list03.html). Australian and New Zealand academic library statistics are collected by CAVAL (Cooperative Action among Victorian Academic Libraries) under the auspices of the Council of Australian University Librarians. The Australian Bureau of Statistics collects library statistics from national, state, and local governments. LibEcon, a project funded by the European Commission DG Information Society (http://www. cordis.lu/ist/ka3/digicult/home.html), was established to collect statistical data on libraries of all types to obtain data aggregated at the national level. These data are intended to provide interpretations, comparisons, and trend information on library activities in the nearly 30 countries that are currently participating.

While sometimes thought of as unfashionable, descriptive information can provide useful trend data for managing library operations or benchmarking library services. Many of the data-gathering organizations now provide some means for interactive analysis and display of the data, enabling libraries to customize inquiries and incorporate results into local reports. Coupled with data-mining techniques from other library service data, descriptive information can provide a useful picture about a library's performance.

Assessing Library Collections

To evaluate how well library collections serve their constituencies, libraries have used the information from local and national surveys on collection size, types of materials, and expenditures for collections in order to develop benchmarking data. For several years, libraries used the RLG Conspectus, which was an inventory for research libraries to identify their collection strengths and collecting intensity. It was adopted by ARL for the North American Collections Inventory Project and spread to other countries. The Western Library Network (WLN) developed PC-based software for libraries to maintain a local collection assessment database. OCLC (Online Computer Library Center) has recently introduced a WorldCat Collection Analysis service that will allow libraries to compare their collection holdings with other libraries for purposes of collection management.

Circulation of materials has been an important measure of use of a collection and remains an important measure, especially for public libraries. While book volumes still form a major part of public, academic, and school libraries, other media are becoming an increasingly larger component of library collections. It is not enough to gather descriptive data about collections, however. Academic libraries have seen circulation statistics decrease as more electronic resources are provided and users access those resources from their offices, residence halls, or homes. Developing the best measures to track electronic usage trends has been of increasing interest.

Since the late 1990s, an increasing percentage of library budgets has been directed to the purchase of electronic resources. Members of ARL began to discuss at a retreat in 2000 what new measures would be needed to determine whether the significant investment in these resources was of benefit to their library users. The three-phase ARL E-Metrics project began in May 2000 and was completed in December 2001. Project deliverables included a summary of current data-collection practices, a set of recommended statistics and measures, a data-collection manual of procedures, an instructional module, and papers that address potential linkages between library measures and institutional outcomes. One of the major priorities for ARL's Statistics and Measurement Program in 2004 was the incorporation of metrics that describe the character and nature of electronic resources that a library is making available. Several new variables are now a part of the annual data-gathering process.

Libraries of all types have struggled in recent years to find ways to take advantage of usage data from electronic information sources.[4] During ARL's E-Metrics project, it became clear that to get useful data for electronic resources, libraries needed to partner with the vendors who produced or supplied the products and services. Several organizations, including ARL, joined together to form COUNTER (Counting Online Usage of NeTworked Electronic Resources), a multi-agency project with the objective of developing a single, internationally accepted code of practice that would allow usage of online information products to be measured more effectively. COUNTER goals include

- Developing, reviewing, disseminating, and gaining support for an internationally agreed code of practice governing the recording and exchange of online usage data and other appropriate codes of practice relating to online publications
- Developing an organizational framework for implementation of and compliance with such codes of practice
- Contributing to the public, commercial, and professional understanding of online information use

The releases of COUNTER's codes have been successfully implemented by several publishers and aggregators, and *Release 2 of the Code of Practice for*

Journals and Databases was scheduled for publication in spring 2005 (http://www.projectcounter.org).

Service Quality and Satisfaction

LIBQUAL+

New models for measurement and evaluation not only address issues of describing electronic resources, but also address issues of service quality. One of the major successes in the ARL New Measures Initiative has been a project known as LibQUAL+, which quickly matured into an established service operation. It is a suite of services that libraries use to solicit, track, understand, and act upon users' opinions of service quality. LibQUAL+ had been implemented in more than 500 libraries as of spring 2004. Results have been used to develop a better understanding of perceptions of library service quality, to interpret user feedback systematically over time, and to identify best practices across institutions. It has been documented extensively in the literature.[5]

The LibQUAL+ protocol was developed as an interdisciplinary research and service project involving faculty from the Texas A&M University (TAMU) Libraries (Colleen Cook, Wright professor of library science, and Fred Heath, formerly Evans professor of library science, now at the University of Texas), the TAMU College of Education and Human Development (Yvonna Lincoln, distinguished professor and Harrington professor of educational leadership, and Bruce Thompson, professor), and ARL.

Starting as a pilot project with 12 ARL libraries in 2000, LibQUAL+ has grown to a multilingual, multinational program. This pilot project initially tested the feasibility of using the SERVQUAL survey instrument to measure user satisfaction in libraries. (SERVQUAL was originally developed for the for-profit sector and is based on the gap theory of quality.) The results were then presented at an international symposium on performance measures sponsored by ARL in Washington, D.C., in October 2000 and at the fourth Northumbria Conference on Performance Measures in Pittsburgh in August 2001.

In 2004 more than 200 libraries in North America, Britain, Europe, and the Middle East participated. In addition to ARL libraries, North American libraries of all sizes and types and several library consortia have joined the project. In 2003, libraries in four countries (the United States, Canada, Britain, and the Netherlands) administered the instrument, and the survey was translated into languages other than American English: a British English version was used in 20 British universities, a Dutch English version in one institution in the Netherlands, and a Canadian French version in two universities in Canada. In 2004 the European Business Schools Library Group (EBSLG) and the American Universities in Cairo, Egypt, and Sharjah, United Arab Emirates, participated, and the survey was made available in Swedish, Dutch, and Continental French. Data have been collected from more than 300,000 users. The current survey instrument is available in eight language variations.

The LibQUAL+ survey has evolved over time, from a 41-item instrument in 2000 that measured five dimensions of library survey quality to today's 22-item format measuring three dimensions: Service Affect, Library as Place, and Information Control. Service Affect is the human dimension of library service quality. Questions in this dimension relate to the extent to which library employees are courteous, knowledgeable, helpful, and reliable. The Library as Place dimension includes questions covering such issues as the usefulness of space, the symbolic value of the library, and the library as a refuge for work or study. The third dimension, Information Control, measures how users want to interact with the modern library, and whether the information they need is delivered in the format, location, and time of their choosing.

The growing LibQUAL+ community of participants and its extensive dataset are rich resources for improving library services and have made important contributions to the study of library service quality. The survey's Web-based instrument makes little demand of local resources, while compiling a robust dataset from all participants. In addition, the grounded questions yield data that are sufficiently granular to be of local use, while normative data enable the comparison of results across cohort groups. The survey has also helped to identify "best practices" that may benefit other libraries.

DigiQUAL and MINES

In addition to the descriptive data elements that ARL is institutionalizing into an annual data collection, questions about the perceived value of electronic resources, the demographics of the people who use a library's virtual resources, and their purposes of use are important areas of investigation that supplement descriptive data elements.

The most recent development in the LibQUAL+ project is DigiQUAL, an adaptation of the survey to the digital library environment. Partially supported by a grant from the National Science Foundation, National Science Digital Library (NSF/NSDL), the goal of e-QUAL is the development of a digital library service quality assessment process that "enhances student learning by permitting the allocation of resources to areas of user-identified need." The objectives include the development of a tool for measuring user perceptions and expectations of digital library service quality across NSDL digital library contexts and the establishment of a digital library service quality assessment program as part of the library service quality assessment program at ARL. The DigiQUAL project developed and tested a set of survey questions in late 2003 and again in spring 2004.

In order to learn more about the individuals who use electronic resources, ARL also has adopted MINES (Measuring the Impact of Networked Electronic Services). Developed by Brinley Franklin (University of Connecticut) and Terry Plum (Simmons College), MINES is a Web-based survey and sampling plan that measures who is using electronic resources, where they are using them, and the purpose of their use. It has been conducted in several main academic and health science libraries and was one component of a cost-analysis study that was linking sponsored research costs to electronic resource use. The study is being conducted with Canada's Ontario Council of University Libraries in 2004–2005. This study is attempting to answer the questions of how extensively researchers use electronic resources and what methodology works best.

JUBILEE

The JUBILEE (JISC User Behaviour in Information Seeking; Longitudinal Evaluation of EIS) has completed its fourth year. The project is focused on monitoring and evaluating user information behavior in relation to EIS (Electronic Information Services) and is funded by the Joint Information Systems Committee in Britain. Project staff are developing a tool kit, and different disciplines are color-coded for easy implementation. The research project is putting user interactions into context and attempting to conduct longitudinal tracking of users to determine information-seeking success criteria from the users' point of view.

Surveys

Libraries continue to conduct regular user surveys to measure service quality. Steve Hiller reports on the University of Washington's triennial surveys and compares the method and results of these with LibQUAL+.[6] Sarah K. McCord and Mary M. Nofsinger also compared the results of traditional surveys (1996, 2000) to those of LibQUAL+.[7]

Rowena Cullen provides a useful overview of user satisfaction surveys.[8] She notes that as libraries face increasing competition for their services, they must improve or they will not survive. User surveys are one way of gathering information about what expectations users have for their library services and their perspectives about the experience once it has occurred. Cullen also discusses the research surrounding the relationship between service quality and user satisfaction. A user's experience for one particular encounter may not be directly related to the satisfaction. More research needs to be done to understand user behavior.

Peter Hernon and colleagues have done considerable investigation into service quality and user satisfaction. He notes that because traditional measures do not assess a library's performance in terms of what's important to customers, libraries should measure on a much broader scale in order to get the best picture of how well the library is performing.[9]

Surveys are being conducted using paper, the Web, and other technologies. In 2001 at the Boston IFLA conference, Keith Curry Lance of Library Research Service reported on an Institute of Museum and Library Services (IMLS) grant project called "Counting on Results."[10] The project developed customized Pendragon Forms software for Palm Digital Assistants to facilitate data collection on observed user activities in the library as well as standardized user outcome questionnaires for selected Planning for Results service responses (in both Web and postcard format).

Efficiency and Effectiveness of Library Operations

Methods for evaluating libraries have been adapted from industry, and as libraries continue to seek ways to present information on their performance, especially through data, it is likely that more use of industry tools will be made. One library assessment method undertaken at some international and a few U.S. libraries comes from the business world. The balanced scorecard is a framework that looks at the performance of an organization from four perspectives:[11]

- How do our customers see us?
- How do we look to those responsible for our finances?
- How well do we perform our internal processes?
- How can our staff continue to grow and learn?

Using this tool requires a significant effort on the part of the library since it is designed for strategic management and requires the institution to think differently about the type of data it collects and how those data are presented. Examples of the decision to use the scorecard, and of its use, can be found at the University and Regional Library of Münster (Germany),[12] the University of Virginia (http://www.lib.virginia.edu/bsc), and Deakin University Library in Australia (http://www.deakin.edu.au/library/staff/publications/helen/BSCIQPC.html).

Cost analysis for specific library operations is another way libraries work toward improving their performance. To examine the cost-effectiveness of interlibrary loan and document delivery operations, ARL undertook its third study of the performance of ILL/DD in North American libraries and collected data on the 2001–2002 performance of mediated and user-initiated ILL/DD operations in 72 research, academic, and special libraries. This was the first analysis of user-initiated or unmediated ILL services (i.e., those that are initiated without staff involvement and received directly by a potential supplier). When the cost data were combined with data on turnaround time and fill rate, it was possible to identify the characteristics of the most cost-effective operations. The results provided useful benchmarking information for other libraries seeking to improve their performance.

The Chronos Group, with Notre Dame and Vanderbilt Universities, has been studying how staff time and costs are allocated across the library. The TCA DecisionBase methodology and software is being used to collect and analyze data in order to understand time and costs at the macro—or center—level and time data at the task level. The methodology combines a longitudinal approach and time sampling, and reports can be generated for any defined administrative unit. The background for this project is from time studies conducted several years ago in the technical services divisions at Iowa State University.[13] Other recent activity-based costing projects have been conducted at Oxford University Library and at the University of Newcastle in Australia.

The Normative Data Project for Libraries (NDP) (http://www.library normativedata.info) is a cooperative effort among hundreds of libraries in North America, the GeoLib Program research program at Florida State University, and Sirsi Corporation to compile and link transaction-level data with geographic and demographic data on communities served by libraries. This is an example of how libraries can combine regularly collected use data in conjunction with other data to help in decision making.

Outcomes and Performance Measures

Outcome measures are the most compelling and yet the most difficult to derive. The importance of libraries to their communities can be characterized in direct or indirect measures, tangible or intangible benefits. There are many projects under way to take advantage of data already gathered by libraries and to find new data that will address the value a library provides to its users and its parent organizations. While efficiency measures speak to how well the library provides its services, outcome measures ask whether the services provided are the right ones for its users. In particular, libraries look to ways to align themselves with the overall organizational mission and to provide evidence that their performance is contributing to the success of that mission.

How does a library add value? Special libraries have always had an interest in communicating the value of the library to the larger organization for purposes of resource allocation. Joe Matthews discusses how special libraries can determine and communicate their value in ways that will help them justify their existence.[14] Similarly, the Special Libraries Association (SLA) often addresses how libraries can measure impact. Matthews covers the same ground for public libraries by focusing on their mission and constituencies.[15]

In California, community colleges have begun to address new measures in a concerted way. Library and learning resources program administrators have selected a set of output measures they feel are the most valuable for measuring their programs.

The impact of school libraries and librarians on academic achievement has been studied by the Library Research Service in Colorado since 1990 and it has evidence that school libraries do indeed improve test scores.[16] It is collecting similar information from other states.

There is considerable interest surrounding studies of how to assess library outcomes within the higher education environment. Peter Hernon and Robert Dugan edited a recent publication that includes perspectives from a number of organizations that address overall philosophy toward case study and tools.[17] Higher education itself is looking for ways in which it can demonstrate its value to its communities and funding authorities. This has become an opportunity for libraries to work with administrations to find new ways to articulate value. Bonnie Gratch-Lindauer has written on the importance of libraries integrating their planning activities with the broader campus.[18]

Much work on outcomes is being done in Britain. One example is Outcomes and Measures, an 18-month project funded by the HEFCE (Higher Education Funding Council for England) Fund for Good Management Practice that is being conducted by evidence base at the University of Central England. This project aims to investigate

- How the contribution of library services to institutional outcomes is measured
- How the library's contribution is perceived by other parts of the organization
- How the library's contribution is perceived internally
- How libraries might make a greater contribution to the higher education agenda by aligning themselves more closely with institutional outcomes at all levels

A component of the project, eVALUEd, is looking at the evaluation of electronic information systems and developing a tool kit as a ready source of information on good practice. It includes model questions, evaluation themes, case studies, and practical advice on how to conduct evaluations with staff, students, and academic faculty.

Academic libraries are also looking at how they meet the needs of researchers. Efforts here are linked to the ability to communicate with the researcher about whether the library is meeting his or her needs. Projects such as MINES and JUBILEE are likely to be more successful methods of evaluating library performance, particularly as the library tries to reach those researchers who work primarily with electronic information.

One of the critical areas of attention for higher education and libraries is that of student learning. Cecilia López provides a brief overview, from her perspective as a staff member in one of the accrediting agencies, of some of the challenges identified and strategies institutions can pursue.[19] Outcomes at the student-learning level involve determining if there has been a change that occurs within the student, rather than in what the instructor does. Learning outcomes are "a level of knowledge, skills, abilities that a student has obtained."[20] Similarly, for libraries, a behavior change by the student should be as a result of using library resources or services. This is a complex area for investigation and requires that libraries work with faculty and the broader campus community to help define "learning" in their environment.

Accreditation in the United States is a driving force for change in how libraries look at performance measures. Gratch-Lindauer conducted a content analysis of the standards and supplemental documentation of the six U.S. regional accrediting commissions of higher education. It identified the overall trends in accreditation and how they affected libraries by comparing how user and institutional outcomes are represented in the standards. The report described how electronic and networked services are referenced in the standards and emphasized the need for libraries to show the connection between those services and fulfillment of the higher education institution's mission. And finally, Gratch-Lindauer provided some observations and recommendations for libraries based on her analysis.[21]

In Britain, the accreditation scheme for libraries in the health sector, originally produced by the LinC Health Panel, has been published in a second revised edition.[22] The checklist includes a set of assessment criteria with explanatory notes, along with guidelines for assessment teams. It is accompanied by a workbook customized for use by assessment teams and by library managers who are preparing for assessment. This document places emphasis on the need for library services to be integrated into the life of the organizations they serve.

Discipline-specific documents also serve as an additional source of information on learning outcomes. At the national level, the American Chemical Society, the American Psychological Association, and the Accreditation Board for Engineering and Technology have all developed statements to address what they expect to see in graduates from professional programs. These documents undergo periodic revision, and libraries can contribute to the development of new standards.

A 1995 report from the U.S. Department of Education, Office of Educational Research and Improvement, "National Assessment of College Student Learning: Identifying College Graduates' Essential Skills in Writing, Speech and Listening, and Critical Thinking: Final Project Report,"[23] describes analyzing, locating, and evaluating information as dimensions of critical thinking.

An indirect measure that is being used by some institutions is the College Student Experiences Questionnaire (CSEQ). This survey asks students to indicate the amount of time they spend engaged in various activities that affect learning. It includes questions regarding library use, and some modifications are expected to those questions. Although self-reported data, analysis of the response indicates that "focused library activities" have a "significant" impact on critical thinking.[24] However, other researchers find that the library does not contribute directly to gains in information literacy and other desirable outcomes and suggest that the lack of baseline measures and a variety of college experiences contribute to gains and satisfaction.[25]

With the development of the Information Literacy Competency Standards for Higher Education (http://www.ala.org/ala/acrl/acrlstandards/information literacycompetency.htm) and the associated tool kit that lists the outcomes for each standard (http://www.ala.org/ala/acrl/acrlstandards/objectivesinformation. htm), libraries are looking for ways to evaluate the success of their information literacy programs. One activity is Project SAILS (Standardized Assessment for Information Literacy Skills), conducted by Kent State University in conjunction with ARL. Funded by an IMLS grant, this research project is testing whether an instrument can collect data from students for programmatic level assessment. The project is being conducted in three phases; the final phase was to be completed in spring 2005. Nearly 90 libraries participated over the life of the project. If successful, this tool will be a way for libraries to compare information literacy skills with other academic achievement scores and to benchmark against like institutions. ACRL collaborates with the Teaching, Learning, and Technology (TLT) Group on an online seminar series in which library staff develop local information literacy program assessment plans.

Information literacy is a popular international topic. On the agenda of a working group of the Council of Australian University Librarians (CAUL) is the development of an assessment instrument for information literacy and the establishment of appropriate measures to evaluate information literacy programs within university libraries. The Australian and New Zealand Institute for Information Literacy (ANZIL) and CAUL have published a second edition of the *Australian and New Zealand Information Literacy Framework: Principles, Standards and Practices* (http://www.caul.edu.au/info-literacy/InfoLiteracyFramework.pdf). They have also published a best-practices document and an information skills survey (http://www.caul.edu.au/info-literacy/publications.html).

Recently the Educational Testing Service (ETS), in conjunction with several colleges and universities, has developed the ICT Literacy Assessment. This interactive Web-based tool is intended to measure a student's proficiency in information and communication technology. Partners include the California Community College System, the California State University System, Miami Dade College, Oklahoma State University, University of California–Los Angeles, University of Louisville, University of Memphis, University of North Alabama, University of Texas System, and University of Washington. The test is intended to evaluate whether students have the ability to use technology as a tool to research, organize, evaluate, and communicate information. A pilot was planned for spring 2005. This is intended to be a large-scale testing activity that could be conducted with all beginning classes.

In addition to looking at overall library performance, some libraries are assessing specific services to see if they are meeting user needs. Evaluating reference services currently has been done since the mid-1980s using the Wisconsin-Ohio Reference Evaluation Program (WOREP). This tool assesses in-person reference transactions by collecting data from both the patron and staff. Currently managed from Kent State University, the program is easy to implement and has been used by both academic and public libraries (http://worep.library.kent.edu). In Australia, the CAVAL Reference Interest Group Working Party on Performance Measures for Reference Service encouraged colleagues to take advantage of the ASK (Attributes, Support, Knowledge) model and its associated performance at the national level. At that time, libraries were just becoming aware of the difficulties of determining measures for service performance.

Performance measures activities are not limited to North America, Western Europe, or Australasia. At the fourth Northumbria Conference on Performance Measures, Anu Nuut and others reported on performance measures in Estonia. Nuut gave an overview of Estonia library surveys from the late 1990s to early 2000s, describing two large projects: the Estonian Science Foundation's project Performance Measurement and Evaluation of Research Libraries in Estonia (January 2000–December 31, 2002) and the survey Library Performance Measurement and Benchmarking Methods in Estonian Research Libraries, 1995–2000. At the fifth Northumbria Conference, Luiza Batista Melo and Maria Sampaio provided a view from Portugal and Brazil.

Standards

Descriptive statistics, both in the United States and internationally, rely on standards. The U.S. Library Statistics Standard, ANSI/NISO Z39.7-1995, was first released in 1968 and revised in 1983 and again in 1995. The 1995 revision committee acknowledged at that time that the standard did not address the emerging areas of the measurement of electronic resources and performance measures and recommended that they be examined at the next five-year review point. NISO held a Forum on Performance Measures and Statistics for Libraries in February 2001 (http://www.niso.org/news/reports/stats-rpt.html). Recommendations from the forum resulted in the development of a revision to the standard that was released as a "draft standard for trial use." At the end of the trial period, the standard was balloted successfully and NISO Z39.7-2002 Information Services and Use: Metrics and Statistics for Libraries and Information Providers—Data Dictionary was approved. Upon establishment of a maintenance agency and process, the standard will be ready for promotion, although many agencies have already begun to use the new definitions.

The two major international standards for performance measures and library statistics come from the International Standards Organization, Technical Committee 46, Subcommittee 8, Working Group 2. ISO 2789, Information and Documentation—International Library Statistics is under revision and expected to be published in 2006. Like the NISO standard, ISO is also addressing electronic resources, and Information and Documentation—Statistics for the Use of Electronic Library Services is in development. ISO 11620, Information and Documentation—Library Performance Indicators is being revised, also with a publication target date of 2006. As libraries move ever more into electronic information, the standards for defining and collecting data about that information must change as well.

EQUINOX (http://equinox.dcu.ie/index.html) was a project funded under the Telematics for Libraries Programme of the European Commission. It was intended to address the needs of libraries to develop and use performance measures in the networked electronic information environment. The organizers were interested in developing existing agreements about performance measures and in developing useful tools for library managers. They came up with an extensive list of measures that were included in the discussion of the ISO standards process and software that could be successfully implemented.

ACRL revised its Standards for Libraries in Higher Education in 2004 to take into consideration the movement from input-driven measures to outputs and outcomes (http://www.ala.org/ala/acrl/acrlstandards/standardslibraries.htm).

The standards refer to other guidelines and standards such as the Information Literacy Competency Standards for Higher Education and the *ACRL Task Force on Academic Library Outcomes Assessment Report*. As accrediting agencies themselves move to a more outcomes-based approach, ACRL responded in kind.

Professional Development

The need for a conceptual understanding of the importance of using data for decision making and developing a culture of assessment that encourages staff to make use of gathered data cannot be overstated. Library organizations are stepping up to help staff to develop the necessary skills to work in an environment that demands understanding of evidence, analysis, and data-driven decisions. Examples can be found at any national or international library meeting. Every other year, Britain's School of Information Studies, University of Northumbria at Newcastle, coordinates an international conference on performance measures, drawing an increasingly larger set of individuals who are interested in sharing information about issues, projects, and tools that libraries can use to develop local measures for success.

In a survey of library administrators, Susan Beck noted that administrators were using more data to make decisions for a range of planning and organizational issues.[26] The University of Arizona has promoted its institutional culture of assessment and touted its value in helping the university to respond quickly to changes in its environment.[27] With support for data-driven decisions coming from the top of the organization, libraries are establishing staff positions or committees to address performance measures and library assessment. This institutional commitment is ensuring continued attention to the importance of assessment and measurement activities throughout the library.

Summary

In the past, libraries could rely primarily on descriptive statistics to provide information about their value to their communities. The extent of collections, the size of budgets, and the number of staff were usually sufficient to tell how well a library could serve its constituency. These input measures described the resources allocated to the library by a parent organization. In many cases, more meant better. In the early 1990s, more of an emphasis was placed on output measures. These measures indicated how much a library did (e.g., books circulated, reference questions answered, instruction sessions taught). In addition, libraries began to promote measures that demonstrated how cost-effective they were. Those measures included ratios for input and output as well as time and cost studies for work processes. Libraries could then illustrate their ability to run efficient operations. Most recently, libraries have looked for ways to characterize their contributions to their communities. These outcome measures are intended to indicate the impact or benefit that the library and its services have on its community. Librarians have examined and tested new methodologies and assessment tools to communicate their ability to meet expectations. Performance measures, once usually a theoretical exercise, are now often a required part of every library's operating plan. This is a reflection of the environment in which all types of libraries operate—one of increased accountability, demonstrated ability, and articulated strategy. And the library community, both nationally and internationally, has worked collectively to develop measures that are meaningful within the context of outcomes and performance.

Notes

1. Claire Creaser and John W. Sumsion, "Affluence and Public Library Use: The DoE Index of Local Conditions and Library Use in London and the Metropolitan Districts of England," *Library Management* 15, no. 6 (1995): 3–15.

2. Amos Lakos, "Culture of Assessment As a Catalyst for Organizational Change in Libraries," *Proceedings of the 4th Northumbria International Conference on Performance Measurement in Libraries and Information Services, August 12 to 16, 2001.* Association of Research Libraries, p. 311.

3. Denise Troll Covey, *Usage and Usability Assessment: Library Practices and Concerns.* Digital Library Federation and Council on Library and Information Resources, 2002, p. 2.

4. Colleen C. Cook, *A Mixed Methods Approach to the Identification and Measurement of Academic Library Service Quality Constructs, LibQUAL+.* Doctoral dissertation, Texas A&M University, 2001; Colleen Cook and Fred Heath, "The Association of Research Libraries LibQUAL+ Project: An Update," *ARL Newsletter: A Bimonthly Report on Research Library Issues and Actions from ARL, CNI and SPARC,* 211 (August 2000): 12–14; Colleen Cook and Fred Heath, "Users' Perceptions of Library Service Quality: A LibQUAL+ Qualitative Interview Study," *Library Trends* 49, no. 4 (2001): 548–584; Colleen Cook, Fred Heath, Martha Kyrillidou, and Duane Webster, "The Forging of Consensus: A Methodological Approach to Service Quality Assessment in Research Libraries— The LibQUAL+ Experience." In Joan Stein, Martha Kyrillidou, and Denise Davis (eds.), *Proceedings of the 4th Northumbria International Conference on Performance Measurement in Libraries and Information Services* (Association of Research Libraries, 2002): 93–104; Colleen Cook, Fred Heath, and Bruce Thompson, "Users' Hierarchical Perspectives on Library Service Quality: A LibQUAL+ Study," *College and Research Libraries* 62 (2001): 147–153; Colleen Cook, Fred Heath, and Bruce Thompson, "Score Norms for Improving Library Service Quality: A LibQUAL+ Study," *Portal: Libraries and the Academy* 2, no. 1 (January 2002): 13–26; Colleen Cook and Bruce Thompson, "Scaling for

the LibQUAL+ Instrument: A Comparison of Desired, Perceived and Minimum Expectation Responses Versus Perceived Only." In Joan Stein, Martha Kyrillidou, and Denise Davis (eds.), *Proceedings of the 4th Northumbria International Conference on Performance Measurement in Libraries and Information Services* (Association of Research Libraries, 2002): 211–214; Colleen Cook, Fred Heath, Bruce Thompson, and R. L. Thompson, "The Search for New Measures: The ARL LibQUAL+ Study—A Preliminary Report," *portal: Libraries and the Academy* 1 (2001): 103–112; Colleen Cook, Fred Heath, R. L. Thompson, and Bruce Thompson, "Score Reliability in Web- or Internet-Based Surveys: Unnumbered Graphic Rating Scales Versus Likert-Type Scales," *Educational and Psychological Measurement* 61 (2001): 697–706; Colleen Cook and Bruce Thompson, "Higher-order Factor Analytic Perspectives on Users' Perceptions of Library Service Quality" *Library Information Science Research* 22 (2000): 393–404; Colleen Cook and Bruce Thompson, "Reliability and Validity of SERVQUAL Scores Used to Evaluate Perceptions of Library Service Quality," *Journal of Academic Librarianship* 26, 248–258; Colleen Cook and Bruce Thompson, "Psychometric Properties of Scores from the Web-Based LibQUAL+ Study of Perceptions of Library Service Quality," *Library Trends* 49, no. 4 (2001): 585–604; Fred Heath, Colleen Cook, Martha Kyrillidou, and Bruce Thompson, "ARL Index and Other Validity Correlates of LibQUAL+ Scores" *portal: Libraries and the Academy* 2, no. 1 (January 2002): 27–42; Bruce Thompson, "Representativeness Versus Response Rate: It Ain't the Response Rate!" Paper presented at the Association of Research Libraries (ARL) Measuring Service Quality Symposium on the New Culture of Assessment: Measuring Service Quality, Washington D.C. (October 2000); Bruce Thompson, Colleen Cook, and Fred Heath, "The LibQUAL+ Gap Measurement Model: The Bad, the Ugly and the Good of Gap Measurement." *Performance Measurement and Metrics* 1 (2000): 165–178; "How Many Dimensions Does it Take to Measure Users' Perceptions of Libraries? A LibQUAL+ Study," *portal: Libraries and the Academy* 1 (2001): 129–138; Bruce Thompson, Colleen Cook, and R. L. Thompson, "Reliability and Structure of LibQUAL+ Scores," *portal: Libraries and the Academy* 2, no. 1: 3–12. An updated bibliography is also available at http://www.libqual.org/Publications/index.cfm.

5. John McDonald, "Electronic Use Statistics: A Panacea or Just a Problem?" *Against the Grain* 15, no. 6 (December 2003/January 2004): 1, 18.

6. Steve Hiller, "Assessing User Needs, Satisfaction and Library Performance at the University of Washington Libraries," *Library Trends*, vol. 49, no. 4 [Spring 2001], 605–625). Cf. Steve Hiller, "But What Does It Mean? Using Statistical Data for Decision Making in Academic Libraries," *Statistics in Practice—Measuring and Managing: Proceedings of IFLA Satellite Conference, Loughborough, August 2002*. LISU, 2003, pp.10–23.

7. Sarah K. McCord and Mary M. Nofsinger, "Continuous Assessment at Washington State University Libraries: A Case Study," *Performance Measurement and Metrics*, vol. 3, no. 2 (2003), 68–73.

8. Rowena Cullen, "Perspectives on User Satisfaction Surveys," *Library Trends* 49, no. 4 (Spring 2001): 662–686.

9. Peter Hernon and Ellen Altman, *Assessing Service Quality: Satisfying the Expectations of Library Customers*. American Library Association, 1998, p. 9.

10. Keith Curry Lance, et al. *Counting on Results: New Tools for Outcome-Based Evaluation of Public Libraries*. Library Research Service and Geo-Marketing International for BCR, Nov. 2001.

11. Robert S. Kaplan and David P. Norton, "The Balanced Scorecard—Measures That Drive Performance," *Harvard Business Review* 70 (January/February 1992): 71–79.

12. Roswitha Poll, "Managing Service Quality with the Balanced Scorecard," in *Advances in Library Administration and Organization*, vol. 20, ed. by Edward D. Garten and Delmus W. Williams. Elsevier Science, 2003.

13. Dilys Morris, "Time and Cost Analysis: Staff Allocations Project," *ARL Bimonthly Report 230/231* (October/December 2003): 23.

14. Joseph R. Matthews. *The Bottom Line: Determining and Communicating the Value of the Special Library,* Libraries Unlimited, 2002.

15. Joseph R. Matthews. *Measuring for Results: The Dimensions of Public Library Effectiveness,* Libraries Unlimited, 2004.

16. Keith Curry Lance, "Libraries and Student Achievement," *Threshold* (Winter 2004): 8–9.

17. Peter Hernon and Robert E. Dugan, eds. *Outcomes Assessment in Higher Education: Views and Perspectives,* Libraries Unlimited, 2004.

18. Bonnie Gratch-Lindauer, "Defining and Measuring the Library's Impact on Campuswide Outcomes," *College & Research Libraries* 59, no. 6 (November 1998): 546–570.

19. Cecilia L. López, "Assessment of Student Learning: Challenges and Strategies," *Journal of Academic Librarianship* 28, no. 6 (November 2002): 356–357.

20. "Student Learning Outcomes Workshop," *CHEA Chronicle* 5, no. 2 (May 2002) (http:// www.chea.org/Chronicle/vol5/no2/Chron-vol5-no-2.pdf).

21. Bonnie Gratch-Lindauer, "Comparing the Regional Accreditation Standards: Outcomes Assessment and Other Trends," *Journal of Academic Librarianship* 28, nos. 1 and 2 (January/February 2002): 14–25.

22. *Accreditation of Library and Information Services in the Health Sector: A Checklist to Support Assessment,* 2nd ed., compiled by Chris Fowler and Val Trinder. Health Libraries & Information Confederation—Helicon, October 2002 (http://www.nelh.nhs.uk/librarian/ accreditation.asp).

23. Elizabeth A. Jones, et al., *National Assessment of College Student Learning: Identifying College Graduates' Essential Skills in Writing, Speech and Listening, and Critical Thinking: Final Project Report.* National Center for Education Statistics, U.S. Department of Education, Office of Educational Research and Improvement, 1995.

24. Ethelene Whitmire, "Development of Critical Thinking Skills: An Analysis of Academic Library Experiences and Other Measures," *College & Research Libraries* 59 (1998): 266–273.

25. Geroge D. Kuh and Robert M. Gonyea, "The Role of the Academic Library in Promoting Student Engagement in Learning," *College & Research Libraries* 64, no. 4 (2003): 256–282.

26. Susan J. Beck "Data-Informed Decision Making," *ARL Bimonthly Report 230/231* (October/December 2003): 30.

27. Shelley E. Phipps, "Performance Measurement as a Methodology for Assessing Team and Individual Performance: The University of Arizona Library Experience." *Proceedings of the 3rd Northumbria International Conference on Performance Measurement in Libraries and Information Services* (2000): 113–117 (http://www.dizzy.library.arizona.edu/library/teams/ fast/sphipps.pdf).

Bibliography

Assessment in College Library Instruction Programs, comp. by Lawrie H. Merz and Beth L. Mark. (CLIP Note no. 32.) (Association of College and Research Libraries, 2002).

Avery, Elisabeth Fuseler, ed. *Assessing Student Learning Outcomes for Information Literacy Instruction in Academic Institutions* (Association of College and Research Libraries, 2003).

Bertot, John Carlo, and Charles R. McClure. "Outcomes Assessment in the Networked Environment: Research Questions, Issues, Considerations, and Moving Forward," *Library Trends* 51, no. 4 (Spring 2003): 590–613.

Bertot, John Carlo, Charles R. McClure, and Joe Ryan. *Statistics and Performance Measures for Public Library Networked Services.* (American Library Association, 2001).

Gratch-Lindauer, Bonnie. *Measuring What Matters: A Library/LRC Outcomes Assessment Manual,* Rev. ed. [s.l.]. Learning Resources Association of California Community Colleges, 2004.

Hernon, Peter, and John R. Whitman. *Delivering Satisfaction and Service Quality: A Customer-Based Approach for Libraries.* American Library Association, 2001.

Hernon, Peter, and Robert E. Dugan. *An Action Plan for Outcomes Assessment in Your Library.* American Library Association, 2002.

Hiller, Steve, and James Self. "From Measurement to Management: Using Data Wisely for Planning and Decision-Making," *Library Trends* 53, no. 1 (Summer 2004): 129–155.

Iannuzzi, Patricia. "We are Teaching, But Are They Learning? Accountability, Productivity, and Assessment," *Journal of Academic Librarianship* 25, no. 4 (1999): 304–305.

Maki, Petty L. "Developing an Assessment Plan to Learn About Student Learning," *Journal of Academic Librarianship* 28, nos. 1 and 2 (January/March 2002): 8–13.

"Measuring Service Quality." Ed. by Martha Kyrillidou and Fred M. Heath. *Library Trends* 49, no. 4 (Spring 2001): 541–799.

Peters, Thomas A., ed. "Assessing Digital Library Services" *Library Trends* 49, no. 2 (Fall 2000): 221–390.

Poll, Roswitha. "The House that Jack Built: The Consequences of Measuring," *Performance Measurement and Metrics* sample issue (August 1999): 31–44.

Proceedings of the 1st Northumbria International Conference on Performance Measurement in Libraries and Information Services, August 31–September 4, 1995, ed. by Pat Wressel. Information North for the Department of Information and Library Management, University of Northumbria at Newcastle, 1995.

Proceedings of the 2nd Northumbria International Conference on Performance Measurement in Libraries and Information Services, September 7–11, 1997, ed. by Pat Wressel. Information North for the Department of Information and Library Management, University of Northumbria at Newcastle, 1998.

Proceedings of the 3rd Northumbria International Conference on Performance Measurement in Libraries and Information Services, August 27–31, 1999, ed. by Pat Wressel Associates. Information North for the School of Information Studies, University of Northumbria at Newcastle, 1999.

Proceedings of the 4th Northumbria International Conference on Performance Measurement in Libraries and Information Services, August 12–16, 2001, ed. by Joan Stein, Martha Kyrillidou, and Denise Davis. Association of Research Libraries, 2002.

Proceedings of the 5th Northumbria International Conference on Performance Measurement in Libraries and Information Services, July 28–31, 2003. Emerald Publishing Group, 2004.

Special Issue: Outcomes Assessment in Higher Education. *Journal of Academic Librarianship* 28, nos. 1 and 2 (January/March 2002).

Special Issue on New Measures. *ARL Bimonthly Report 230/231* (October/December 2003) (http://www.arl.org/newsltr/230).

Statistics in Practice—Measuring & Managing: Proceeedings of IFLA Satellite Conference, Loughborough, August 2002, ed. by Claire Creaser (LISU Occasional Paper no, 32): LISU, Department of Information Science, Loughborough University, May 2003.

Thebridge, Stella, et al "*e*VALUE*d* The Evaluation of Electronic Information Services: Outcomes Assessment" (Project Paper 2) [s.l.]: Centre for Information Research, University of Central England in Birmingham, October 2002.

Van House, Nancy A., Beth T. Weil, and Charles R. McClure. *Measuring Academic Library Performance: A Practical Approach.* American Library Association, 1990.

Whitmire, Ethelene. "Academic Library Performance Measures and Undergraduates' Library Use and Educational Outcomes." *Library & Information Science Research* 24 (2002): 107–128.

Zweizig, Douglas, et al. *The TELL IT! Manual: The Complete Program for Evaluating Library Performance.* American Library Association, 1996.

Digital Technologies Lead Copyright Concerns

Sarah K. Wiant

Law Librarian and Professor of Law, Washington and Lee University

WIPO Development Agenda

The General Assembly of the World Intellectual Property Organization (WIPO) met during the fall of 2004 to re-evaluate the direction it has taken in recent years. The American Association of Law Libraries (AALL), the American Library Association, the Association of Research Libraries, and the Special Libraries Association all endorsed the resulting Geneva Declaration on the Future of the World Intellectual Property Organization, which calls for the recognition of intellectual property for the "future of humanity" and stresses the need to balance law and policies. Among the concerns of library organizations are the lengthening of the term of copyright protection that delays the entry of works into the public domain, the development of technological measures that prevent circumvention done for lawful purposes, and the development of proposals for the protection of databases containing public-domain information.

The International Federation of Library Associations and Institutions (IFLA) joined with hundreds of nongovernmental organizations and endorsed the Geneva Declaration supporting the preamble of the WIPO Copyright Treaty, which stresses "the need to maintain a balance between the rights of authors and the larger public interest, particularly education, research and access to information, as reflected in the Berne Convention." However, IFLA and others believe the balance has become distorted and the public domain is shrinking. Restrictive rules and technological protection measures have led to this imbalance, causing, among other things, a digital divide between advanced countries and developing countries. Many countries are imposing, through free-trade agreements, stricter copyright protections than are required by the World Trade Organization's TRIPS (Trade-Related Aspects of Intellectual Property Rights) Agreement.

The library and information associations encourage WIPO to move beyond the protectionist approach by allowing works to enter the public domain after a reasonable period of commercial exploitation by copyright holders, and to permit reasonable uses of copyrighted works for legitimate purposes, thereby encouraging international growth and development.[1]

UCITA

The Uniform Computer Information Transactions Act (UCITA)[2] began as a proposed revision to the Uniform Commercial Code (UCC). The UCC is generally considered the most influential source of contract law in the United States, and most states have adopted it or some version of it. It is drafted by two groups: the American Law Institute (ALI),[3] composed of some 3,000 elected judges, law professors, and lawyers; and the National Conference of Commissioners on Uniform State Laws (NCCUSL),[4] an organization composed of approximately 300 lawyers, judges, and law professors appointed by states as commissioners. If both organizations approve a revision, it is then often reviewed by the American Bar Association (ABA) before being submitted to each state government for adoption. Each state then enacts the proposed section or selected provisions, and those enactments become the law of that state.

UCITA is an attempt to conform state law relating to software and information licensing to a uniform national standard. Specifically, the legislation was drafted to address the problem of "shrink-wrap" software licenses, which bind consumers to their tenets as a condition of use. Often this term generically encompasses "click-through" and "active click wrap" licenses, which accompany much of the information found online. Unlike shrink-wrap licenses, which take their name from the plastic they are often printed on, click-through and active click wrap licenses exist only electronically. They typically appear on the computer monitor as a condition of accessing information or installing software. Most users agree to these conditions as a matter of course, without stopping to read or consider their restrictions. Although such licenses have become commonplace, some courts have hesitated to enforce them. Disparate judicial treatment of these agreements led to an attempt to standardize the law relating to them.

For more than ten years, the two groups debated the merits of various proposals to cover the licensing of software and information, including the most recent proposal, UCC 2B, but were unable to agree on a solution. Current law is based on transactions of tangible goods. Both sides saw a need for clear uniform rules for transactions involving software and information. In May 1999 ALI withdrew its support after concluding that the UCC 2B approach was flawed.[5] Despite opposition from ALI and dozens of educational, library, and consumer groups, NCCUSL ratified the model legislation in July 1999, renamed it the Uniform Computer Information Transactions Act (UCITA), and sent it to the states for enactment without either the endorsement of ALI or a review by ABA.

By 2001 the model legislation had been studied or introduced in 27 state legislatures, but only Virginia[6] and Maryland[7] passed this legislation. A number of state attorneys general signed a letter to NCCUSL expressing reservations about the proposed legislation,[8] and the debate has been spirited on both sides. Under a UCITA contract, the licensor may designate the forum (generally the state in which the software producer is located) in which any issues would be litigated, making it inconvenient if not impossible for the licensee to resolve the issue. In other cases the licensor may not designate the state where the issues will be litigated, but may designate the body of law—Virginia or Maryland—that the court must consider.[9]

This controversial legislation could have a profound effect on library operations because the definitions of information and computer information include most information a library acquires, although UCITA excludes traditional written forms such as books. UCITA enables authors and other content providers to contract around the important public uses guaranteed by copyright law. The statute would validate shrink-wrap and click-through licenses that would restrict uses by libraries allowed by the federal copyright law. Libraries rely on section 109 of the Copyright Act, which establishes the first-sale doctrine that allows libraries to lend, sell, or otherwise distribute materials they have purchased; section 107 permits fair use of materials; and section 108 provides for preservation, lending, and interlibrary loan. Because UCITA would allow authors and publishers to license their works instead of selling them, no sale occurs and the protections afforded under the first-sale doctrine never ripen. Libraries fear that clauses in a UCITA contract would allow vendors to dictate limitations or rights otherwise available to them to conduct business.

UCITA will affect more than copyright law. It will fundamentally change the way consumers interact with software and information vendors because buyers will often lack the opportunity to review the terms of a license and because vendors could unilaterally modify the terms of a contract during its operation.[10]

Proponents of UCITA intended to seek an endorsement from the House of Delegates at the ABA meeting, but in view of the response from the library community and some members of the business community, the resolution was withdrawn.

Some states have enacted "bomb shelter" bills allowing a state to protect its residents and business from the choice of law and choice of forum provisions of UCITA. While UCITA activities have been dormant, Americans for Fair Electronic Commerce Transactions (AFFECT), an organization in opposition to the model act, continues its watch and has developed "12 Principles for Fair Commerce in Software and Other Digital Products" that will be posted on the Web at http://www.fairterms.org.

Databases

Cases

In *New York Times Co., Inc.* v. *Tasini,*[11] the U.S. Supreme Court upheld freelance writers' rights to separate compensation for electronic copies of their works. Freelance writers argued that their contracts with the print newspapers *New York Times* and *Newsday* and the magazine *Sports Illustrated,* owned by Time Inc., did not relinquish their copyrights in their articles, nor did they grant permission for the electronic reproduction and distribution of their works in any database, with or without compensation. Neither print nor electronic publishers sought permission from the authors. The databases reproduce each author's entire article and each article is individually searchable and retrievable, but—unlike microfilm reproductions—not the entire issue.

In deciding that a freelancer should be able to benefit from the demand for a single article, the court looked to 17 U.S.C. § 201(c), a section addressing collective works, and concluded that database publishers do not reproduce and distribute articles as part of a collective work privileged under section 201(c). Although the court could have issued an injunction against the inclusion of the articles, it instead remanded the case to the lower court to address the remedies. Initially the trial court, later reversed, held for the publishers, finding no cause of action.

Some publishers threatened to remove unauthorized reproductions from the electronic record. For the future, publishers and writers will likely agree to track uses of copyrighted works going forward. This decision did not affect archival microfilm collections that reproduce the entire edition of works such as periodicals.

Faulkner v. *National Geographic Society*[12] was on appeal in early 2005 to the U.S. Court of Appeals for the Second Circuit. The District Court held that

Section 201(c) of the Copyright Act permits National Geographic to reproduce and distribute the copyrighted works of freelance contributors as part of a CD-ROM product, *The Complete National Geographic*. Faulkner relies on *Greenberg* v. *National Geographic Society*,[13] which held that it was unlawful to convert intact periodicals from one medium to another because the product combined digital facsimiles of entire collective works with software that enables users to search and perceive them with the aid of a machine or device. The lower court in *Faulkner* rejected this reasoning, finding this product similar to the microfilm collection that the Supreme Court found permissible in *Tasini*.

Some publishers place their hope in Congress, expecting it to determine the nature and scope of the problem by passing database legislation that would provide an appropriate licensing remedy.

Legislation

After having negotiated database bills since 2001, the House Energy and Commerce Committee and the House Judiciary Committee have been unable to reach agreement. One approach would grant new "sweat-of-the-brow" protections to facts and data outside copyright law. The library associations supported bills that were more balanced and that would not overturn the *Feist*[14] decision, which held that originality, not "sweat of the brow," is required for copyright protection. AALL and other information associations believe that current laws would protect databases from piracy. Publisher efforts to revive versions of database legislation, which the library community opposes, have been unsuccessful.

TEACH Act

The Technology, Education and Copyright Harmonization Act of 2002 (TEACH Act)[15] amends the Copyright Act of 1976 by rewriting Section 110(2) and adding a new Section 112(f) to provide new exemptions for the asynchronous use of digital resources in distance education. These sections permit instructors at accredited nonprofit educational institutions using interactive digital networks to use, under limited circumstances, copyrighted works in classes offered to distance-education students enrolled in courses wherever they are located without seeking permission. Under the act, teachers may transmit digitally entire nondramatic literary or musical works and reasonable and limited portions of other performances, including those incorporated in audiovisual works. Instructors are permitted to digitally transmit displays of protected works in amounts comparable to displays in face-to-face classes. The act limits the use of works produced primarily for the education market, works not lawfully acquired, and student course materials purchased for the class. Moreover, the performance or display remotely of digital works must be part of systematic "mediated instructional activities" and be directly related to the teaching content of the course. The act's many technical provisions are addressed in "The TEACH Tool Kit, An Online Resource for Understanding Copyright and Distance Education."[16]

The TEACH Act is not a replacement of fair use. Even if a use is not permitted under the TEACH Act, it might still be permitted as a fair use.

Copyright Clearance Center

In July 2004 the Copyright Clearance Center (CCC), a large licensing agent for text-reproduction rights, launched a Web site for business professionals called *Guide to Copyright Compliance*.[17] It is intended to help businesses concerned about their ability to comply with copyright law to implement corporate best practices and to educate their employees in lawfully using copyrighted content. In addition to an overview of best practices for developing and implementing a corporate copyright policy, the site includes a copyright primer for the use of digital content, an explanation of fair use, an interactive quiz, and a guide to obtaining permission to use copyright works.

In January 2005 CCC and Innovative Interfaces (III), provider of a leading integrated library management system, announced a partnership to streamline compliance for electronic reserves when required.[18] Direct access to CCC's rights database from III's electronic reserves module will provide for efficient copyright permissions when necessary.

Copyright Term Extension Act

On January 15, 2003, the U.S. Supreme Court ruled that the Sonny Bono Copyright Term Extension Act[19] (CTEA) was constitutional in the landmark decision *Eldred* v. *Ashcroft*.[20] The court held that Congress has the authority to determine the "limited times" for which copyright protection will be available as provided in the U.S. Constitution.

CTEA, signed into law on October 27, 1998, extended the term of copyright from life of the author plus 50 years to life plus 70 years. On appeal, *Eldred* raised two issues: the retroactivity of term extension and whether a statute that extends protection beyond the term of copyright is immune from First Amendment challenges. The case did not challenge the term extension for new works, but rather focused on the retroactive protection that applies to all works still protected by copyright. As a result of this decision, only works published prior to 1923 are in the public domain and no new works—presuming no further extensions—will enter the public domain until 2018.

Eric Eldred, owner of the Eldritch Press, digitizes works in the public domain and makes them available on his Web site. Although he was the named plaintiff, other plaintiffs included a distributor of rare books, a sheet music distributor, a choir director, and a film preservation company. The lower court ruled against Eldred and upheld the constitutionality of term extension. He lost on appeal to the U.S. Court of Appeals for the District of Columbia and appealed to the U.S. Supreme Court. The library associations developed an amicus brief on the side of Eldred.

The majority opined that Congress had acted properly by voting to extend the term of protection, even retroactively, because it had done so on several occasions in the past. The term of copyright has been extended legally several times since 1790, when the term of protection was 14 years, to life plus 50 years when the Copyright Act of 1976 became effective. Terms are still "limited," even though they have been extended. The court was clear that it was not determining the merits of extending the term of copyright protection but rather whether Congress had the power to do so.

The court refused to apply "strict scrutiny" (the highest-level test) or even heightened scrutiny to the First Amendment claims, finding that the appeals court had spoken too broadly when it declared that copyrights were "categorically immune from challenge under the First Amendment."

Justice John Paul Stevens strongly dissented, finding that Congress had exceeded its authority in enacting CTEA because of policies that favor the public domain. Justice Stephen Breyer disagreed with the majority, believing that CTEA should be reviewed using heightened scrutiny. He found no justification for the extension because the benefits bestowed are private, not public, and the statute undermines the expressive values of the act.

CTEA does contain a provision beneficial to libraries, section 108(h). It permits a section 108(a)-qualified library or archives or a nonprofit educational institution, during the last 20 years of a published work's term, to reproduce, distribute, display, or perform in either facsimile or digital form, a copy of a work for purposes of preservation, scholarship, or research. The library must determine that the work is not subject to normal commercial exploitation, that a copy cannot be obtained at a reasonable cost, or that the copyright owner has given notice that either of the above conditions apply according to regulations promulgated by the Register of Copyrights. There is little guidance for determining whether a library has conducted a "reasonable investigation" or "noncommercial exploitation." This subsection is broader than other preservation sections in that the work may be reproduced in either digital or analog format; however, it does not permit a library to make up to three copies, but rather "a copy."

Linking

Among the issues raised by the seamless fabric of the World Wide Web is the fundamental question of whether linking to a site with copyright material constitutes copyright infringement. One of the first suits, *Ticketmaster Corp.* v. *Tickets.com,* No. 99-7654, settled. Ticketmaster sought to block a competitor from linking to its internal Web pages. The Central District of California, in a preliminary ruling, stated that hypertext linking does not by itself constitute infringement because no copying is involved.

In *Kelly* v. *Arriba Soft Corp.,*[21] the Ninth Circuit affirmed a ruling by the Central District of California that thumbnail versions of copyrighted images in a visual search engine were a fair use because they served a functional rather than an aesthetic purpose. Arriba did not download images to its own server, but imported them directly from other Web sites. Kelly claimed that Arriba—by allowing the public to view the larger version of a photographer's image on Arriba's site—had created an infringing public display of his works. The court disagreed, finding that Arriba's conduct constituted fair use of Kelly's images.

Creative Commons

The Creative Commons was founded by Lawrence Lessig, now a Stanford law professor, in 2001 with support from the Center for the Public Domain and with the help of the Berkman Center for Internet and Society at Harvard, a nonprofit foundation, to support healthy public domain by programs, grants, partnerships, law, media, technology, and academic research.

Its first project, in December 2002, was the release of a set of copyright licenses[22] free for public use. Through a Web application, the Creative Commons helps people dedicate their works to the public domain or retain copyright while permitting certain uses. The idea is to get artists and scholars to give up some control of their works so that they can be used more freely to create new works.

Peer-to-Peer File Sharing

The strained relationship between copyright owners' exclusive rights and the fair use of digital files, particularly music and movie files, has led owners to seek greater protection in the courts and in Congress. With digital recording devices, users can now make copies of CDs and DVDs without the risk of losing quality. At first, the Internet did not play a large role in consumer copying because audio files were too large. However, with the development of the MPEG-1 Layer-3 (MP3)—a compression format that allows digital music to be played back on a personal computer or other electronic device—and the introduction of high-speed Internet access, users are able to share millions of files. While MP3 by itself is neither illegal nor legal, it—like many new technologies—can be used for both legal and illegal purposes.

Napster and Napster-like software combine "chat" features and a music player, permitting users to share their MP3 collections with each other and to locate other MP3 collections on the Internet. While Napster does not host files on its servers, it does provide a chat program for discussing favorite music, an audio player that allows a musical file to be played inside the Napster system, and a tracking program that allows a user to organize downloaded files. The widespread use of these technologies by consumers uploading and downloading millions of files led the music industry, and later the movie industry, into filing several lawsuits.

In *Recording Industry Association of American* (RIAA) v. *Diamond Multimedia*,[23] RIAA sued Diamond for the proposed distribution of the Rio, a small hand-held device that can receive, store, and replay digital audio files stored on the hard drive of a personal computer. It could not transfer digital musical files to another MP3 player or make copies of any digital audio files. RIAA contended that the Rio did not meet the requirement for "digital audio recording device" as defined by the American Home Recording Act (AHRA),[24] a compromise between the consumer electronics and music industry over the practice of home taping of copyrighted works that recognizes a consumer's right to use, and a retailer's right to sell, all analog and digital audio recording formats. Digital audio recording devices must include a system that prohibits serial copying. The U.S. Court of Appeals for the Ninth Circuit found that because the Rio cannot make copies of digital music recordings, it cannot be considered a digital audio recording device under AHRA.

In *A&M Records, Inc.* v. *Napster*,[25] the federal appeals court upheld an injunction against Napster, an Internet company that made its proprietary Music-Share—a browser software that allows users to share with others logged on to the

Napster system MP3 music files without payment—freely available for Internet users to download. The Napster server maintains a directory and index of file names that users wish to share. When a user requests a file, the server communicates with the requesting user and the "host" user who makes the file available for downloading. Napster terrified the music industry because it showed the potential benefits of digital distribution.

Napster argued that its activities were covered by the section 512(a) of the Digital Millennium Copyright Act[26] "safe harbor" provision that gives service providers protection from direct, vicarious, or contributory infringement subject to limited conditions. The court found that Napster is not covered by the "safe harbor" because it is not a passive conduit. Moreover, the court found Napster guilty of contributory infringement because Napster had actual knowledge of specific infringing uses of the record companies' copyrighted works. The Ninth Circuit recognized, however, that to issue an injunction simply because a computer network allows some users to infringe would violate *Sony Corp. of America* v. *Universal City Studios, Inc.*[27]

The *Sony* court ruled only that when copying equipment is merely "capable of substantial noninfringing uses" such as time-shifting (recording material, such as a television program, for a single later use), then the sale of that equipment does not constitute contributory infringement. All eyes are on the U.S. Supreme Court as this public policy is under review in *Metro-Goldwyn-Mayer Studios* v. *Grokster Ltd.*[28] MGM and more than 30 other companies sued Grokster for infringement by distributing software that enables peer-to peer file sharing of, among other things, their copyrighted works. Grokster does not operate networks, nor does it host a site and facilities. Each user makes files available to other users on the system through individual computers. The software has substantial noninfringing uses such as personal writings, government documents, free songs, and sharing public domain materials. Grokster unquestionably knows that some users will exchange copyrighted files, but defendant's liability cannot be based on a percentage of current use that is infringing. Defendants have no ability to supervise or control file-sharing networks. The Ninth Circuit made clear that any effort to scale back *Sony* was better left to Congress to legislate, not the courts.

Unlike RIAA, movie studios were reluctant to sue individual file-sharers, trying instead to fight the battle with an aggressive education campaign and Movielink, a legitimate movie-download site. These efforts have not caught on, and the Motion Picture Association of America estimates that thousands of films are downloaded illegally each day even though sharing videos requires time and patience. With the advent of faster broadband, downloading movies will become a more significant problem. The industry is watching the Grokster case closely.

Digital Millennium Copyright Act

Among the significant amendments to the Copyright Act was the 1998 Digital Millennium Copyright Act (DMCA),[29] which prohibits the circumvention of antipiracy measures built into computer software and limits the copyright infringement liability of Internet service providers (ISPs). In implementing U.S. obligations under two international agreements concluded at the World Intellectual Property Organization (WIPO), the WIPO Copyright Treaty and the WIPO Performances and Phonograms Treaty, Congress added a new Chapter 12 to the Copyright Act that prohibits the circumvention of technological measures that protect copyrighted works.

The second required rulemaking hearings held in October 2003 (the first round was held in 2000) resulted in adding two classes of works to those exempted from the anticircumvention provisions: (1) "compilations consisting of lists of Web sites blocked by filtering software applications," and (2) "literary works, including computer programs and databases, protected by access control mechanisms that fail to permit access because of malfunction, damage or obsoleteness."

In response to DMCA Section 104 Report, the U.S. Copyright Office recommended against amending DMCA to include digital first sale, and recommended an amendment that would allow for temporary buffer copies incidental to licensed digital transmissions of public performance of sound recordings.[30]

Eight movie studios distributed movies on DVDs protected by encryption called Content Scramble System (CSS) that could be viewed only on players and computers licensed to decrypt. In 1999 a 15-year-old Norwegian wrote "DeCSS" to allow him to copy and play DVDs on his Linux. In *Universal City Studios* v. *Remierdes*,[31] Universal sued to prevent the defendants from posting the explanation on how to use DeCSS or linking to it. The court disagreed with the defendant's argument that section 1201 of DMCA did not apply. Section 1201(a) addresses the right to control access to works whether protected or not, and section 1201(b) provides for anticircumvention for copying. The court said that the anticircumvention provisions were different from copyright and that the defense of fair use was not available. The court said that DeCSS was developed primarily to circumvent the protections placed on the DVDs, and that this was done with full knowledge that the movies could be copied.

In October 2004 the U.S. Supreme Court denied certiorari in *Recording Industry Association of America, Inc.* v. *Verizon Internet Services, Inc.*[32] Section 512(h) of DMCA created a streamlined subpoena process requiring no judicial review, and RIAA used it to obtain contact information of alleged infringers from ISPs. Because music is often shared anonymously online, RIAA wanted the cooperation of ISPs to identify these users. The D.C. Circuit ruled that this provision was not available to RIAA, requiring it to file suit to ask a court to grant a subpoena in order to obtain contact information. The U.S. Circuit Court of Appeals for the Eighth Circuit followed the analysis of the D.C. Circuit and refused to order an ISP to disclose names and addresses.[33]

Landmark Canadian Copyright Case

In 2004 the Supreme Court of Canada addressed the extent to which the fairdealing exception extends to the photocopying practices of the Great Library at Osgoode Hall in Toronto operated by the Law Society of Upper Canada. The society is the self-governing, nonprofit organization that regulates Ontario lawyers in the interest of the public. The court unanimously held that the document delivery activities of the library through its custom photocopy service did not infringe publishers' copyrights but were research bases and fair.[34]

The society promotes access to justice through its Pro Bono Law Ontario program and the Public Legal Education Task Force. Through the library, it provides access to information. In many ways, it is similar to state and county bar associations in the United States. To carry out its mission to meet the research and information needs of the society members, the library offers a variety of services such as reference, access to electronic databases, and legal research seminars, as well as providing a custom photocopy service (CPS) to patrons and self-service photocopy machines. CPS, available on a nonprofit basis to members since 1954, is a document delivery service that provides single copies of published materials for a per-page charge plus a handling fee for up to three items in a single request. For a higher service fee, patrons can receive rush and fax service.

Guidelines for CPS detail the purposes for which the service may be used: research, review, private study, and criticism, as well as use in court and government proceedings. Copies of a single case, statute, or article are generally provided without question; requests for more than 5 percent of a volume may be refused. The society testified that the majority of its copying was Canadian court decisions.

In 1993 CCH Canadian Ltd., Thomson Canada Ltd. (Carswell), and Canada Law Book, Inc. sued the society for copyright infringement. The trial court found that the society had infringed publishers' copyrights in selected works.[35] On appeal to the Federal Court of Appeals, the publishers claimed that all of the works at issue were original and were therefore covered by copyright. The court upheld the publishers' claims, finding that the library infringed when it made copies of these protected materials without a license,[36] but the Supreme Court reversed and ruled for the society.

The library believed that publishers wanted a license fee for any copy of a judicial decision or limited portion of a secondary resource even when the lawyer's purpose in making a copy or requesting a copy was research. The Supreme Court affirmed that research—even research conducted as part of the for-profit practice of law—is nonetheless research to which fair dealing may apply. Such research is not limited to private study, but rather includes research necessary to advise clients, to draft briefs, or prepare cases for argument. The court further recognized the library's mission to provide its patrons access to this important collection of materials and ruled that the library, acting for a user, may rely on fair dealing as a defense to a claim of copyright infringement. Under these circumstances, neither the library nor a lawyer need procure a license to photocopy from publishers.

Moreover, the court recognized the library's good-faith effort to comply with the copyright law by posting a warning notice by the self-service copiers that it would not be responsible for any infringing copies made by users in violation of the law.

The court noted that a publisher's copyright in a judicial decision extended only to the headnotes in the case, but did not extent to the court's written opinion. Thus, a lawyer would need a license to copy headnotes.

To qualify under the exemption of fair dealing, copying must be done only for research and private study and must be in amounts that are "objectively fair." While this case dealt only with photocopies of legal materials, it could be argued that copying by businesses may also be fair dealing within limits. This case is far more expansive than any U.S. case to date.

Digital Media Consumers' Rights Act

The Digital Millennium Copyright Act[37] provided for additional protections for copyright owners in the age of digital copies, but made no provisions for fair use and other exemptions to maintain the balance between copyright owners and users of copyrighted works. Libraries believe that the Digital Media Consumers' Rights Act of 2003[38] (DMCRA) is needed to restore those rights and to promote education and research in the digital age. DMCRA was designated H.R. 107, which is particularly appropriate because section 107 of the Copyright Act addresses fair use. H.R. 107 would allow libraries to unlock technological measures to permit the library to make a preservation copy as formats become obsolete, or permit the library to make a copy for interlibrary loan or electronic reserves. H.R. 107 would allow an educator to bypass a digital lock on an e-book to analyze its contents or to play foreign-produced content on machines purchased in the United States. These examples involve legal copies and uses permitted under the Copyright Act. The exemption allowed libraries in section 1201(d) of DMCA is so narrow as to be meaningless; it would allow a library to look at digitally protected information only to decide whether to purchase it.

This legislation is even more pressing because copyright owners are supporting a variety of bills that would increase protections afforded copyright owners, such as the Inducing Infringement of Copyright Act known as the Induce Act.[39] Introduced by Sen. Orrin Hatch (R-Utah) in June 2004, this legislation was supported by copyright owners but contested by the technology industry, and ISPs worried that the language might make them potentially liable as contributory infringers. This legislation would clearly weaken *Sony*. It appeared likely early in 2005 that similar legislation would be introduced on both sides of the issue in the 109th Congress.

Conclusion

Digital technology has created a fundamental challenge to the copyright system. Now it is up to the parties to find a balance that will both promote the protection of intellectual property and encourage access to the use of copyrighted materials to spur creativity of new works built on the foundation of works that exist.

Notes

1. http:www.cptech.org/ip/wipo/genevadeclaration.html
2. Uniform Computer Information Transactions Act [hereinafter UCITA] at http://www.law.upenn.edu/bll/ulc/ucita/ucita0htm.
3. American Law Institute [hereinafter ALI] at http://www.ali.org.
4. National Conference of Commissioners on Uniform State Laws [hereinafter NCCUSL] at http://www.nccusl.org.

5. ALI, supra note 3.

6. V. Code Ann. §§ 59.1-501.1-59.1-509.2.

7. Md. Code Ann. Com. Law §§ 22-101-22-186 (2001).

8. See Letter from the attorneys general of 24 states to Gene Lebrun, President, National Conference of Commissioners on Uniform State Laws (July 23, 1999) available at http://www.arl.org/info/frn/copy/agoppltr.html.

9. UCITA § 109, supra note 2.

10. UCITA § 304, supra note 2.

11. 533 U.S. 483 (2001).

12. 294, F. Supp.2d 523 (S.D.N.Y. 2003).

13. 244 F.3d 1267 (11th Cir. 2001).

14. *Feist Publications, Inc.* v. *Rural Telephone Service Company, Inc.,* 499 U.S. 340 (1991).

15. The Technology, Education and Copyright Harmonization Act of 2002 [hereinafter TEACH Act], P.L. 107-273, 116 Stat. 1910 (2002).

16. http://www.lib.ncsu.edu/scc/legislative/teachkit (copyright Peggy E. Hoon, Scholarly Communication Librarian, North Carolina State University).

17. http://www.copyright.com/Services/CorporateGuide.

18. Press Release, "Copyright Clearance Center and Innovative Interfaces Partner to Streamline Copyright Compliance for Electronic Reserves" (February 2, 2005), at http://www.copyright.com/ccc/do/viewPage?pageCode=au94.

19. P.L. 105-298, 112 Stat. 2827 (1998).

20. 537 U.S. (2003).

21. 280 F.3d 934 (9th Cir. 2002).

22. http://creativecommons.org

23. 180 F.3d 1072 (9th Cir. 1999).

24. 17 U.S.C.§§ 1001-1010 (1992).

25. 239 F.3d 1004 (9th Cir. 2001).

26. 17 U.S.C. § 512(a).

27. *Sony Corp. of America* v. *Universal City Studios, Inc.,* 464 U.S. 417 (1984).

28. 380 F. 3d 1154, (9th Cir. 2004), cert. granted, 73 U.S.L.W. 3350 (U.S. December 10, 2004).

29. DMCA, P.L. 105-304, 112 Stat. 2863 (1998).

30. http://www.house.gov/judiciary/courts.htm.

31. 111 F. Supp. 2d. 294 (S.D.N.Y. 200) aff'd. sub nom *Universal City Studios* v. *Corley,* 273 F.3d 429 (2d Cir. 2001).

32. 351 F.3d 1229 (D.C. Cir. 2003), cert. denied, 125 S.Ct. 347 (2004).

33. In re Charter Communications Inc., Subpoena Enforcement Matter, 393 F.3d 1171 (8th Circ. 2005).

34. See *CCH Canadian Ltd.* v. *Law Society of Upper Canada,* 236 D.L.R. (4th) 395 (S.C.C. Mar. 04, 2004). Also available at http://www.canlii.org/ca/cas/scc/2004/2004scc13.html.

35. 2 F.C. 451 (Fed. T.D. Nov 09, 1999) and 184 D.L.R. (4th) 186 (Fed. T.D. January 21, 2000).

36. 212 D.L.R. (4th) 385 (Fed. C.A. May 14, 2002).

37. DMCA, supra note 28.

38. H.R. 107, 108th Cong. (2003).

39. S. 2560, 108th Cong. (2004).

Part 2
Legislation, Funding, and Grants

Legislation

Legislation and Regulations
Affecting Libraries in 2004

Emily Sheketoff
Executive Director, Washington Office, American Library Association

Joshua Farrelman
Assistant Director, Office of Government Relations, American Library Association

Library Funding

On February 2, 2004, President Bush announced his $2.4 trillion fiscal year (FY) 2005 budget. With a projected $521 billion deficit forecast, the administration's budget kept non-defense, non-homeland security spending growth to 0.5 percent and reduced spending for 6 of the 15 cabinet departments.

The president requested $220,490,000 for the Library Services and Technology Act (LSTA) administered by the Institute for Museum and Library Services (IMLS), an increase of 11 percent over FY 2004. Within that total was $170,455,000 for Grants to State Library Agencies (an increase of $12.8 million), $23,000,000 for Librarians for the 21st Century program (an increase of $3 million), $16,500,000 for National Leadership Grants for libraries (an increase of $5.2 million), and $3,675,000 for Improving Library Service to Native Americans (an increase of $469,000).

Under the budget request, the Department of Education would have received $53.7 billion in discretionary funding, a $1.7 billion increase or 3 percent over the FY 2004 level. The request included $1.1 billion (an increase of $101 million or 10 percent) for the Reading First State Grants program. The Early Reading First program, an important complement to Reading First, would have received $132 million, an increase of $38 million or 40 percent.

However, despite increases in the overall funding, the president's budget proposed eliminating 38 programs and level-funding nearly 80 others. Among the programs the president proposed eliminating were the Even Start family-literacy program, Star Schools, and the Community Technology Centers program. The Improving Literacy Through School Libraries program, the only federal program exclusively for school libraries, was funded at $19.8 million, the same level as FY 2004.

As part of his Jobs for the 21st Century proposal, President Bush also included $100 million in his budget for the Striving Readers Initiative. This program would make competitive grants available to states and school districts to develop, implement, and evaluate effective reading interventions for middle or high school students reading significantly below grade level.

In September 2004 the House of Representatives and the Senate approved different levels of spending for LSTA and the Improving Literacy Through School Libraries program. The House recommended that LSTA receive $219.9 million and that the Improving Literacy Through School Libraries be level-funded at $19.8 million. The Senate, however, proposed funding LSTA at $223.5 million and allotting $22.8 million for school libraries.

On December 8 President Bush signed the fiscal year 2005 omnibus appropriations bill (H.R. 4818; P.L. 108-447) into law.

The $388.4 billion spending package wrapped up nine separate appropriation bills and included a 0.8 percent across-the-board cut in all non-defense and non-homeland security spending to pay for some program increases. After the across-the-board cut was taken into account, LSTA programs received $205,951,000. This is an increase of $7.7 million over FY 2004, but is $14.5 million below the president's budget request. As a result, the State Grants program received $160,704,000 ($3 million above the previous year and $9.7 million below the president's budget request); the Native American Library Services received $3,472,000 ($266,000 more than the previous year and $203,000 less than the president's request); the National Leadership Grants received $12,301,000 ($1 million above the previous year and $4.2 million below the president's request); and the Librarians for the 21st Century program received $22,816,000 ($2.9 million above the previous year and $184,000 below the president's request).

The omnibus bill funds the Improving Literacy Through School Libraries program at $19,683,264, a $158,736 cut from FY 2004. This level is also more than $3 million below what the Senate had approved in September 2004. At this level, the Department of Education will be able to fund fewer than 100 grants for the approximately 3,000 eligible local education agencies.

Table 1 / Funding for Federal Library and Related Programs, FY 2005
(amounts in thousands)

	Final FY 2004	FY 2005 Budget Request	Final FY 2005
GPO SuDocs	$34,252	$33,033	$31,953
Library of Congress	523,001	602,120	584,871
Institute of Museum and Library Services (IMLS)	262,240	262,240	280,564
Library Services	198,242	220,490	205,951
Museum Programs	31,403	42,000	34,724
National Agricultural Library	21,000	24,000	22,305
National Commission on Libraries and Information Science (NCLIS)	994	1,000	993
National Library of Medicine (includes MLAA)	309,796	325,147	323,346
Library-Related Programs			
Department of Education			
Adult Education and Literacy	590,233	590,233	585,406
Title I, Grants to Local Education Agencies (ESEA)	12,342,309	13,342,309	12,739,571

Even Start (ESEA)	246,910	0	225,095
Educational Technology (ESEA)	691,841	691,841	496,000
Innovative Education Program Strategies (ESEA)	296,549	296,549	198,400
21st Century Community Learning Centers (ESEA)	999,070	999,070	991,077
Star Schools (ESEA)	20,362	0	20,832
Community Technology Centers (ESEA)	9,941	0	4,960
Special Education (IDEA) State Grants	10,068,106	11,068,106	10,589,746
Institute of Education Sciences (formerly OERI)	475,893	449,621	349,198
Educational Research	165,518	185,000	164,194
Educational Statistics	91,664	91,664	91,664
Educational Assessment	94,763	94,832	94,073
Institutional Development (HEA)	399,961	418,800	421,476
College Work Study (HEA)	998,502	998,502	990,257
International Education (HEA)	103,680	103,680	106,819
Postsecondary Education Improvement Fund (HEA)	157,700	32,000	162,604
Inexpensive Book Distribution (RIF)	25,185	25,185	25,296
Improving Literacy Through School Libraries (ESEA)	19,842	19,842	19,683
Reading First State Grants (ESEA)	1,023,923	1,125,000	1,041,600
Early Reading First (ESEA)	94,439	132,000	104,160
Other Government Agencies			
Head Start	6,775,000	6,943,580	6,843,391
NTIA Information Infrastructure Grants (TOP)	14,912	0	0
National Archives and Records Administration	255,185	304,000	264,809
National Endowment for the Arts	120,971	139,400	121,263
National Endowment for the Humanities	137,000	131,000	138,054
National Historical Publications and Records Commission	9,941	3,000	4,960

Workforce Investment Act

Attempts were made in the 108th Congress to reauthorize the Workforce Investment Act (WIA) of 1998, which consolidates, coordinates, and improves employment, training, literacy, and vocational rehabilitation programs. Those attempts failed, despite significant progress in both the House and Senate.

In the House, H.R. 1261 passed in May 2003. A Senate version, S. 1627, passed in November 2003. However, due largely to political considerations, the House did not appoint conferees until June 2004, while the Senate ended the 108th Congress without ever appointing conferees.

S. 1627 included language as part of the National Leadership activities (Sec. 217) that would allow funding to go toward networks, including public libraries, to help them build capacity to meet the performance requirements set forth under the program. Language included in both bills lists libraries as "eligible providers" of adult education and literacy programs and services. This is the same as current law. Reauthorization of WIA was one of the first agenda items in the 109th Congress.

Head Start

The authorization for Head Start, a federal program that has provided comprehensive early childhood development services to millions of low-income children since 1965, expired in FY 2003. Attempts to reauthorize Head Start in the 108th Congress were unsuccessful. In July 2003 the House passed its version (H.R. 2210) of the Head Start reauthorization by a single vote largely along party lines. The Senate's bipartisan version (S. 1940) made it out of the Health, Education, Labor, and Pensions Committee in November 2003, but failed to make it to the full Senate for consideration. Both bills included language urging consultation, collaboration, and outreach to libraries. Reauthorization of Head Start is likely to be among the many measures that the 109th Congress will consider.

National Museum and Library Services Board

On November 20 the U.S. Senate unanimously confirmed seven nominees to the National Museum and Library Services Board: Beverly Allen, Gail Daly, Donald Leslie, Amy Owen, Sandra Pickett, Renee Swartz, and Kim Wang. The 20-member board advises the Institute of Museum and Library Services (IMLS) and makes recommendations for the National Award for Museum and Library Service.

Telecommunications and Universal Service

The American Library Association (ALA) E-rate Task Force sent comments to the Federal Communications Commission (FCC) responding to the latest Notice of Proposed Rulemaking affecting the E-rate program, which provides telecommunications discounts for libraries and K–12 public and private schools. The ALA comments focus on ways to change the poverty formula so that public libraries do not have to rely exclusively on using averaged discount percentages and school lunch eligibility formulas from their local school systems.

Anti-Deficiency Act Holds Up E-Rate Funds

In early August the E-rate administrators stopped all distribution of funds and commitment letters to E-rate award recipients. This action came ostensibly because of a directive from the Office of Management and Budget (OMB) via FCC requiring that the E-rate program comply with government accounting rules even though FCC's Universal Service Program for Schools and Libraries (the parent program of the E-rate) is not a tax. Although the E-rate already complies with standard accounting rules, the OMB requirement prohibits USAC (the Universal Service Administrative Corporation, which administers the E-rate) from sending out commitment letters without all funding for the E-rate program being in the bank at the time the letters are sent. This is rarely possible because universal service contributions are collected from telecommunications carriers on a quarterly basis.

During literally the final minutes of the 108th Congress, the Senate passed H.R. 5419, a bill that provides a one-year fix to the accounting problem. ALA is seeking a permanent solution to this issue in the 109th Congress.

Privacy and Security Concerns

ALA and the librarians it represents continue to be concerned about specific portions of the USA Patriot Act and the effects the act may have on libraries and library users.

There has been strong focus on Section 215 of the act, which allows the FBI to get an order from the secret Foreign Intelligence Surveillance Act (FISA) Court for "any tangible thing" sought "in relation to a foreign intelligence investigation." In response, ALA's Washington Office has been working in coalition with a broad array of civil liberties organizations to promote the Security and Freedom Ensured (SAFE) Act of 2003 (S. 1709/H.R. 3352) and the Freedom to Read Protection Act of 2003 (H.R. 1157).

9/11 Commission Report

The ALA Office of Government Relations was pleased when the National Commission on Terrorist Attacks Upon the United States (the 9/11 Commission) noted that "The Patriot Act vests substantial powers in our federal government. We have seen the government use the immigration laws as a tool in its counter-terrorism effort. Even without the changes we recommend, the American public has vested enormous authority in the U.S. government. . . . Because of concerns regarding the shifting balance of power to the government, we think that a full and informed debate on the Patriot Act would be healthy" (pp. 393–394).

Toward a National ID

The Intelligence Reorganization Act passed in the House on December 7 and the Senate the following day. The act requires creation of national standards for driver's licenses and personal identification cards, basically involving standard fields and standard formats for those fields. The statute does not take the step that an earlier House version of the bill did—creating a federal database of driver's license information. The fact that driver's licenses (or personal identification cards) issued by the states will have standardized fields and, moreover, that only these standardized cards will be accepted as identification by federal agencies, lays the groundwork for a "national ID card" and for expansion of collection of personal information.

Civil Liberties and Privacy Oversight Board

The Intelligence Reorganization Act also creates a Civil Liberties and Privacy Oversight Board within the Executive Office of the President that would ensure that privacy and civil liberties concerns "are appropriately considered" in the implementation of laws, regulations, and executive branch policies relating to efforts to protect the nation against terrorism. The board's responsibilities encompass both oversight and advice and counsel and would include reviewing regulations and policies (including information-sharing guidelines) and providing advice to the president and departments and agencies in the executive branch.

The board would be required to report at least annually to Congress on its major activities. In the Senate version of the bill, this board had subpoena authority; that has been lost. The board is authorized, however, to have access to information from departments and agencies. The board is also authorized to make written requests to persons outside government to produce information, documents, and other evidence.

Privacy Officers

Language requiring every agency to have a "chief privacy officer" was slipped into the Transportation-Treasury Appropriations Act of 2005, one of the nine appropriations bills in the omnibus bill that Congress passed in late November. The chief privacy officer would create policy for privacy and data protection, assuring that technology does not "erode privacy protections relating to the use, collection, and disclosure of information."

WHOIS Database and the Right to Privacy

The Fraudulent Online Identity Sanctions Act (H.R. 3754) establishes harsh penalties for individuals who register an Internet domain using inaccurate content. The act is founded on the theory that people provide inaccurate information in registering a domain name because they intend to use the domain for illegal purposes. In fact, many individuals (particularly those whose sites contain controversial or dissenting speech) provide inaccurate registration information to protect their privacy and freedom of speech.

Domain-name registry has become a controversial topic in technical and political circles. As a result of the collaborative nature of the Internet's beginnings, domain-name registration requires an individual to provide personal information such as names, postal addresses, and personal e-mail addresses. This information is then published in the WHOIS database, freely available to all, despite the fact that data drawn from WHOIS is abused and misused every day by spammers, stalkers, and others.

ALA believes that forcing individuals to provide accurate information on domain-name registries is tantamount to registering printing presses. A writer has the right to publish speech without disclosing his or her physical location; this was upheld by the U.S. Supreme Court in *McIntyre* v. *Ohio Elections Commission,* which overturned an Ohio law requiring name and address disclosure on political pamphlets.

The ALA Washington Office has argued that domain names are a critical part of Internet communications and a type of free speech. U.S. citizens, libraries, and organizations should not be forced to disclose their physical location to the world as a price of obtaining a domain name and participating in the worldwide Internet dialogue. Washington Office staff have met with key House offices about opposing or slowing down this legislation until concerns over these privacy issues can be resolved. Meetings continue to be held on the Hill. Sign-on letters and calls for action are pending.

Data Mining, Security, and Privacy

Data Mining

On May 5, 2004, the Data-Mining Reporting Act of 2004 (H.R. 4290) was introduced by Reps. Jim McDermott (D-Wash.) and William Lacy Clay (D-Mo.). The legislation would require the head of each department or agency of the federal government engaged in any activity using or developing data-mining technology to submit a public report to Congress on all such activities.

In December 2003 the Department of Defense (DOD) Inspector General had released the results of an audit of Terrorism Information Awareness (TIA) conducted as a result of Congressional inquiries. The audit concluded that "although the [Defense Advanced Research Projects Agency (DARPA)] development of TIA-type technologies could prove valuable in combating terrorism," DARPA failed to perform any form of privacy impact assessment, did not involve appropriate privacy and legal experts, and "focused on development of new technology rather than on the policies, procedures, and legal implications associated with the operational use of technology." The report acknowledged that DARPA was sponsoring "research of privacy safeguards and options that would balance security and privacy issues," but found that such measures "were not as comprehensive as a privacy impact assessment would have been in scrutinizing TIA technology."

The final report of the Technology and Privacy Advisory Committee (TAPAC) for the Department of Defense was released on May 24, 2004. TAPAC was created to examine the Terrorism Information Awareness (TIA) program and to develop safeguards "to ensure that the application of this or any like technology developed with DOD is carried out in accordance with U.S. law and American values related to privacy." While calling data mining "a vital tool in the fight against terrorism," the report concludes that TIA and similar government programs need safeguards to adequately protect U.S. citizens' privacy interests and civil liberties and to prevent data mining from becoming "the 21st-century equivalent of general searches, which the authors of the Bill of Rights were so concerned to protect against." The report contains detailed recommendations "intended to help the Secretary of Defense establish the clear rules and policy guidance, educational and technological tools, and appropriate managerial oversight and advisory resources necessary to guide DOD's use of data mining to protect national security without compromising the privacy of U.S. persons."

Peer Review and Information Quality

The Office of Management and Budget (OMB) received 187 comments on its "Proposed Bulletin on Peer Review and Information Quality" (http://www.white house.gov/omb/inforeg/2003iq/iq_list.html). Scientists, academics and individuals submitted the majority (107) of the comments listed in OMB's docket. The second-largest segment of submissions, 49, came from industry representatives (companies, industry associations, and corporate law firms). Twenty-five comments were from the public-interest sector, including ALA, nonprofit organizations, scientific societies, and academic associations. OMB also received six comments from government sources, including state agencies and congressional offices. OMB had not issued the bulletin at the time this report was prepared.

Critical Infrastructure Information

On February 20, 2004, the Department of Homeland Security (DHS) issued an interim final rule for Critical Infrastructure Information Protection. The rule went into effect immediately, but a public comment period was open until May 20 on one specific provision. The department received 64 substantive comments during the public comment period, and some improvements were made to the original draft rule. But despite the fact that almost one third of the comments opposed expanding the program to allow submissions through other federal agencies, DHS plans to do so in the final rule. Other problematic provisions include the fact that submissions are automatically presumed to be made in good faith and that the database tracking the submissions seems to be protected under the program.

Sensitive Homeland Security Information—Proposed Guidelines

Title VIII of the Homeland Security Act, the Homeland Security Information Sharing Act, authorizes the creation of a new and expansive system intended to facilitate the sharing of "sensitive homeland security information" (SHSI) among federal agencies, state and local governments, and law enforcement. According to the act, a loosely defined category of information, "Sensitive but Unclassified" (SBU), is to be expanded to cover SHSI. The act charges the president with issuing a set of regulations that will establish the parameters of the sharing system and the guidelines for participating in it. The president has delegated that responsibility to the DHS secretary. No guidelines have been forthcoming, but there is growing concern that DHS is enacting the requirements through the establishment of closed computer networks, with no opportunity provided for stakeholders outside the government to review or comment on them.

Politics and Science

The House of Representatives Committee on Government Reform, Minority Staff, Special Investigations Division continues to update "Politics and Science in the Bush Administration" (http://www.house.gov/reform/min/politicsand science/pdfs/pdf_politics_and_science_rep.pdf), which reports numerous instances in which the administration has manipulated the scientific process and distorted or suppressed scientific findings.

Flight and Aeronautical Information to Be Removed

According to a November *Federal Register* notice, the National Geospatial-Intelligence Agency (NGA) has announced new withdrawals of unclassified information from the public domain: "The National Geospatial-Intelligence Agency (NGA) intends to remove its Flight Information Publications (FLIP), Digital Aeronautical Flight Information File (DAFIF), and related aeronautical safety of navigation digital and hardcopy publications from public sale and distribution."

The notice states that "This action is taken to accomplish the following objectives: safeguarding the integrity of Department of Defense (DOD) aeronautical navigation data currently available on the public Internet; preventing unfettered access to air facility data by those intending harm to the United States, its interests or allies; upholding terms of bilateral geospatial data-sharing agreements; avoiding competition with commercial interests; and avoiding intellectual property/copyright disputes with foreign agencies that provide host-nation aeronautical data." The *Federal Register* notice is at http://a257.g.akamaitech.net/7/257/2422/06jun20041800/edocket.access.gpo.gov/2004/04-25631.htm. NGA asserts the right to limit disclosure of unclassified satellite imagery based on a statute enacted in 2000 (10 USC 455), which entitles DOD to withhold imagery and related products under certain conditions, independent of their classification status.

Disclosure Prohibition for Satellite Imagery

A proposed prohibition of disclosure under the Freedom of Information Act (FOIA) for much of commercial satellite imagery would have severely restricted public access to a broad swath of unclassified government information. Congressional conferees narrowed the scope of the exemption for certain categories of commercial satellite imagery and related products. As revised, the exemption would apply only to imagery whose sale to non-government customers is already prohibited "for reasons of national security."

The final language in section 914 of the 2005 Defense Authorization Act can be found at http://www.fas.org/sgp/congress/2004/hr4200conf.html#914.

Justice Department Seeks Document Withdrawal

On July 23 it was announced that the Department of Justice (DOJ) had asked the Superintendent of Documents to instruct depository libraries to destroy all copies of five particular documents. The Department of Justice claimed that these were "training materials and other materials that the DOJ staff did not feel were appropriate for external use." On August 2 the Superintendent of Documents notified the Federal Depository Library Program (FDLP) that the Department of Justice had rescinded its request. In the interim, ALA had filed a FOIA request for the documents; this request was withdrawn when DOJ rescinded the destruction request.

On August 24 Sen. Patrick Leahy (D-Vt.), ranking member of the Senate Judiciary Committee, and Rep. John Conyers, Jr. (D-Mich.), ranking member of the House Judiciary Committee, wrote Attorney General John Ashcroft asking him to explain the rationale for the request that the Government Printing Office (GPO) instruct federal depository librarians to withdraw and destroy documents. The ALA Washington Office has been in communication with the congressional offices since the DOJ request.

Leahy and Conyers said about the Justice Department's initial request: "Given the Administration's penchant for secrecy, we fear that this action was yet another attempt to erode the public's right to know." For a copy of the Leahy and Conyers letter, see http://www.house.gov/judiciary_democrats/dojlibrary ltr82404.pdf.

GPO Plans for Future Development

The new Public Printer has publicly indicated his desire to explore all models for sustaining both GPO Access and FDLP, and building on them to ensure an informed public. ALA—through the Committee on Legislation, the Ad Hoc Subcommittee on Government, and the Government Documents Round Table (GODORT)—is in discussion with GPO to ensure a model that retains and enhances no-fee and unfettered public access to government information, including (but not limited to) through federal depository libraries. ALA commented in May 2004 on GPO's proposal for a "collection of last resort," raising concerns about the planning and implementation of this concept (see http://www.ala.org/ala/washoff/ogr/GPOcmts051404.pdf).

With its sister library associations, ALA wrote a letter to the chairman of the Appropriations Subcommittee endorsing GPO's budget request.

Sensitive Homeland Security Information

The Homeland Security Act also requires the promulgation of procedures for "safeguarding" a vaguely defined set of information, "Sensitive Homeland Security Information," and sharing it among firefighters, police officers, public health researchers, and federal, state, and local governments. That responsibility has been given to the Department of Homeland Security (DHS).

On August 26, 2003, 75 organizations representing librarians, journalists, scientists, environmental groups, privacy advocates, and others sent a letter to Homeland Security Secretary Tom Ridge calling on DHS to allow public input on those procedures. DHS had not yet publicly promulgated the procedures at the time this report was prepared.

Removals/Restrictions of Access to Government Information

ALA and others have met with OMB about its plans to issue guidance on the "sensitive but unclassified" (SBU) category presented in a March 19, 2002, memorandum from DOJ and the Information Security Oversight Office (ISOO). It is expected that the DHS guidelines on "sensitive homeland security information" (a subset of SBU) may well serve as the guidance for SBU. ALA and others are continuing to monitor and respond to developments in this area.

Numerous agencies have indicated that they have developed criteria for deciding what materials to restore to public access. These criteria are also applied to decisions on what new materials will be made accessible. The only set of these that have been made available for public comment are from the Federal Geographic Data Committee (FGDC). ALA submitted comments on these proposed guidelines.

Intelligence Budget Secrecy

The 9/11 Commission unanimously recommended that intelligence budget secrecy should be reduced and that individual intelligence agency budget totals should be disclosed annually. As part of the pending intelligence reform bill (S. 2845), the Senate voted 55–37 to require annual disclosure of the total budget request, the total amount authorized, and the total amount appropriated for national intelligence (not purely military or tactical intelligence), beginning in FY 2006 when intelligence funds will be directly appropriated to the new national intelligence director. Opponents said the move would mean nothing less than the destruction of U.S. intelligence, and the CIA and the Justice Department Office of Information and Privacy continue to hold that even 50-year-old intelligence budget figures must not be released.

The Department of Energy (DOE) has decided, however, to do exactly the opposite of what the 9/11 Commission recommended. Until recently, the DOE Office of Intelligence had been one of the 15 members of the U.S. intelligence community whose budget was unclassified (the State Department's Intelligence and Research Bureau is another). But now, for the first time in decades, DOE is withholding all substantive information about its intelligence program and has decided to classify its intelligence budget. More than that, DOE is attempting to retroactively classify budget information that it had previously declassified and published. The reason, according to one official, is that the deputy director of intelligence sent out the word that all budget information was to be treated as classified.

Controlled Unclassified Information

Controlled Unclassified Information (CUI) is yet another category in the growing panoply of government restrictions on unclassified information. According to the Pentagon, CUI "includes, but is not limited to, 'For Official Use Only' information; 'Sensitive But Unclassified' (formerly 'Limited Official Use') information; 'DEA Sensitive Information'; 'DOD Unclassified Controlled Nuclear Information'; 'Sensitive Information', as defined in the Computer Security Act of 1987; and information contained in technical documents."

On September 22, the *Washington Times* reported that the Government Accountability Office (GAO) would investigate methods used by DHS to classify documents. The review was called for by Reps. David R. Obey (D-Wis.), ranking member of the Appropriations Committee, and Martin Sabo (D.-Minn.), ranking member of the Homeland Security Subcommittee.

Less Access to More Information

According to a report issued by the House Government Reform Committee minority, the Bush administration "has repeatedly rewritten laws and changed practices to reduce public and congressional scrutiny of its activities." Announcing the report, Rep. Henry Waxman (D-Calif.) said, "The cumulative effect is an unprecedented assault on the laws that make our government open and accountable." The report provides an exhaustive critique of executive branch secrecy, from various well-known issues such as the secrecy surrounding the vice president's Energy Task Force to numerous less-known measures to block congressional access to agency records. The full text of the September 14, 2004, investigative report on "Secrecy in the Bush Administration" is posted at http://democrats.reform.house.gov/features/secrecy_report/index.asp.

Other New Barriers

New barriers to public access to government information are being thrown up with increasing frequency.

- The Nuclear Regulatory Commission announced in August that "certain security information formerly included in the Reactor Oversight Process will no longer be publicly available, and will no longer be updated on the agency's web site." (See http://www.nrc.gov/reading-rm/doc-collections/news/2004/04-091.html.)
- New controls may be imposed starting October 1 on space surveillance data (orbital elements) that are currently made available on the NASA Web site. (See http://www.celestrak.com/NORAD/elements/notice.shtml.)
- At the request of DHS, FCC agreed to restrict public access to reports of telecommunications disruptions; DHS argued that information about communications outages could create "a roadmap for terrorists."
- On August 4 the *Washington Post* reported that "Nearly 600 times in recent years, a judicial committee acting in private has stripped information from reports intended to alert the public to conflicts of interest involving federal judges," according to a GAO report now itself unavailable on GAO's Web site.

GAO's 'NI' Restriction Category

GAO has a restriction category—NI or non-Internet—for some of its reports. According to staff on one of the congressional oversight committees, the criterion for its application appears to be the request of an agency. Approximately 15 reports have been thus restricted, although they can be requested by fax or in print. The affected reports include

- GAO-04-696NI, "Federal Judiciary: Assessing and Formally Documenting Financial Disclosure Procedures Could Help Ensure Balance Between Judges' Safety and Timely Public Access," published June 30, 2004.
- GAO-04-456RNI, "Capital Power Plant Utility Master Plan," published March 1, 2004.
- GAO-04-15NI, "DOD Excess Property: Risk Assessment Needed on Public Sales of Equipment That Could Be Used to Make Biological Agents," published November 19, 2003.
- GAO-04-80NI, "Combating Terrorism: Improvements Needed in Southern Command's Antiterrorism Approach for In-Transit Forces at Seaports," published October 31, 2003.
- GAO-04-851NI, "Combating Terrorism: Improvements Needed in Pacific Command's Antiterrorism Approach for In-Transit Forces at Seaports," published October 31, 2003.
- GAO-04-81TNI, "DOD Excess Property: Risk Assessment Needed on Public Sales of Equipment That Could Be Used to Make Biological Agents," published October 7, 2003.

- GAO-03-731NI, "Combating Terrorism: Improvements Needed in European Command's Antiterrorism Approach for In-Transit Forces at Seaports," published September 26, 2003.
- GAO-03-995RNI, "Major Management Challenges at SSA," published July 31, 2003.
- GAO-03-896TNI, "Nuclear Security: DOE Faces Security Challenges in the Post September 11, 2001 Environment," published June 24, 2003.
- GAO-03-132NI, "Border Security: Visa Process Should Be Strengthened as an Antiterrorism Tool," published October 21, 2002.
- GAO-02-955TNI, "Combating Terrorism: Preliminary Observations on Weaknesses in Force Protection for DOD Deployments Through Domestic Seaports," published July 23, 2002.
- GAO-02-402RNI, "Space Surveillance Network: Appropriate Controls Needed Over Data Access," published April 22, 2002.
- NSIAD-00-63NI, "Military Capabilities: Focused Attention Needed to Prepare U.S. Forces for Combat in Urban Areas," published February 25, 2000.

There are two other reports bearing the designation NI but GAO will not provide the titles, saying that their release would adversely impact significant property interests or negatively affect public safety.

Access to Presidential Records

On March 28, 2004, Judge Colleen Kollar-Kotelly dismissed a lawsuit brought by a broad coalition of historians and public-interest researchers challenging Executive Order 13233, which significantly increased the authority of current and former presidents to block public requests for unclassified records from prior administrations (see http://www.ala.org/ala/washoff/WOissues/governmentinfo/lessaccessless.htm#exec).

The court ruled that the coalition's complaint was not "justiciable," concluding that the plaintiffs did not have standing and could not demonstrate imminent injury. The executive order, issued in November 2001, went into effect in November 2003. There is currently no movement in Congress to reverse the executive order legislatively.

Judicial Branch

On November 29, 2004, ALA—together with other library, archives, journalists', and public-interest organizations—filed a friends-of-the-court brief with the District of Columbia Circuit Court of Appeals supporting public access to information about the makeup of the National Energy Policy Development Group (NEPDG) convened by Vice President Dick Cheney in 2001. The case was brought by the Sierra Club and Judicial Watch and heard by the U.S. Supreme Court in April 2004. The court, recognizing the importance of the issue and the conflicting principles of separation of powers and public accountability, sent the case back to the District of Columbia Circuit Court of Appeals for adjudication.

The brief argues that the district court should accept the Supreme Court's invitation to develop an innovative procedure for accommodating the competing interests asserted in this case: "When important constitutional principles are on a collision course, as in this case, courts should be wary of any winner-take-all resolution." The friends-of-the-court recommend creating a "Cheney log" following the model of the "Vaughn index," used for many years in FOIA cases. Such an index would identify certain basic information that could be provided by the government without undue burden or compromise of confidentiality; a "Cheney log" would provide information about whether and to what extent non-government persons participated in meetings of NEPDG or its subgroups. That information should provide a sufficient basis for the private parties and the courts to evaluate, thereby triggering Federal Advisory Committee Act (FACA) requirements that protect against the improper influence of special interests on government decision making.

Copyright

Antipiracy and Enforcement Legislation

In 2004 piracy deterrence and punishment were the themes of a number of copyright-related bills that were active in both houses of Congress. Libraries joined in lobbying against many of the bills. ALA supports enforcing existing laws rather than enacting more criminal provisions and opposes the ambiguous and overly broad language characteristics of these bills. It also opposes a controversial bill in the Senate—S. 2560, the Inducing Infringement of Copyright Act—that was aimed at peer-to-peer file-sharing technology. ALA's concern was outlawing a particular technology to the detriment of the development of innovative technology and the ability of libraries to have access to affordable digital technologies.

At the very end of the congressional session, the Senate passed S. 3021, the Family Entertainment and Copyright Act of 2004. The bill was introduced by Sen. Orrin Hatch (R-Utah) on November 20 and was passed on that same day by unanimous consent. The titles of the act included illegally recording movies in theaters, creating an exemption from copyright infringement for devices that permit an individual to skip over content in a motion picture being viewed at home, fostering the preservation of so-called "orphaned" copyrighted works, and tougher anticounterfeiting laws relating to physical goods and fake labels. An amendment by Sen. John McCain (R-Ariz.) was added to the bill—relating not to copyright but to the Professional Boxing Safety Act—and this amendment made the entire bill unacceptable and kept the House from acting on it before adjournment.

Ultimately, the only intellectual-property bill to be enacted was H.R. 3632, the anticounterfeiting measure that was cleared to go to the president on the last day of the session. Bundled with the anticounterfeiting bill was another provision that had passed the House as H.R. 3754, which increases penalties for knowingly submitting false contact information to Internet domain-name registrars when purchasing a Web address.

New Copyright Study by Library of Congress

The Library of Congress is convening a Working Group to re-examine Section 108 of the U.S. Copyright Act. Section 108 is a critical provision concerning reproduction of copyrighted works by libraries and archives, including for preservation and interlibrary loan. The Library of Congress's National Digital Information Infrastructure and Preservation Program (NDIIPP) and the U.S. Copyright Office are forming the Copyright Working Group in response to growing concerns that provisions of the Copyright Act may need revision to address issues arising from use of copyrighted works by libraries and archives in a digital environment. The library has invited Miriam Nisbet, ALA Washington Office legislative counsel, to join the Working Group.

'Broadcast Flag' Rulemaking

On November 4, 2003, FCC issued its rule on a "broadcast flag," which is designed to facilitate the transition to digital television. The rule mandates that a "broadcast flag" copyright-protection scheme be included in all digital television sets, related consumer products, and personal computers to prevent the redistribution of digital content over the Internet. ALA believes the broadcast flag will prevent libraries, educational institutions, and consumers from exercising fair use and other rights under copyright law and will hasten the advent of a world in which the consumer must pay to have access to all digital content. ALA and the other major U.S. library associations (the American Association of Law Libraries, Association of Research Libraries, Medical Library Association, and Special Libraries Association) filed written comments for the rulemaking.

In January 2004 the library associations joined with several other public-interest and consumer organizations to appeal FCC's ruling to the U.S. Court of Appeals for the D.C. Circuit. The petition for review argued that FCC acted both in excess of its statutory authority and contrary to the factual evidence in the record, and asked the court to set aside the FCC order. FCC has filed a motion asking the appeals court to hold the case in abeyance until FCC addresses other matters before it.

UCITA

ALA has worked successfully for five years to fight the enactment by state legislatures of the Uniform Computer Information Transactions Act (UCITA). AFFECT, the anti-UCITA coalition that ALA helped to found and continues to lead, in November published its "12 Principles for Fair Commerce in Software and Other Digital Products." The principles outline 12 fair terms that should be included in shrink-wrap licenses for software and other digital products. The brochure will assist those working with legislators and other policymakers.

Copyright Litigation

In late June ALA and other library and archives associations filed a friends-of-the-court brief in *Faulkner* v. *National Geographic Society,* a case that has major implications for projects that involve retrospective digitization of print versions of scholarly materials and the public's access to those materials. In the brief, the American Association of Law Libraries, ALA, Association of Research Libraries, Medical Library Association, Society of American Archivists, and Special Libraries Association argued that "the decision will . . . have profound consequences for the library and archival communities and those who use collective works."

At stake in the case is whether publishers of collective works and others who may choose to legitimately digitize them can republish those works in a digital format without seeking permission of authors or other contributors. Several freelance photographers, as well as some writers, sued the National Geographic Society (NGS) for copyright infringement because some of their works were included in a CD-ROM produced by NGS. The CD-ROM contains photoscanned images of the entire print version of *National Geographic* magazine from 1888 to 1996 in a searchable format. A lower court found that the publication on CD-ROM was permissible under the Copyright Act. The library and archives associations are asking the U.S. Court of Appeals for the Second Circuit to affirm that decision.

The associations filed the friends-of-the-court brief because of their concern that a reversal of the lower court decision would thwart efforts to digitize selected library collections, thus reducing public access to important resources. The associations support a decision by the U.S. District Court for the Southern District of New York that the Copyright Act permits NGS to reproduce and distribute, through the CD-ROM compilation, the copyrighted materials that appeared in the original issues of the magazine. Judge Lewis A. Kaplan found that as long as digital versions place photographs and articles in the same context as the print original, there is no infringement of copyright. Thus the district court determined that the fact that articles and photographs appeared in a new medium made no difference to the case.

Faulkner v. *National Geographic Society* differs considerably from *New York Times* v. *Tasini,* in which the U.S. Supreme Court affirmed the copyright privileges of freelance writers whose works were originally published in newspapers and periodicals and then licensed by the publishers to commercial electronic databases. The associations believe the Copyright Act permits publishers, libraries, archives, and the public to take advantage of new technologies to preserve and distribute creative works to the public if no changes are made to the original work once republished in a different format.

Legislation and Regulations Affecting Publishing in 2004

Allan Adler

Vice President, Legal and Governmental Affairs
Association of American Publishers
50 F St. N.W., Suite 400
Washington, DC 20001

The Second Session of the 108th Congress was a bitterly partisan election-year period dominated by interparty disputes over the Bush administration's Iraqi war policies and a succession of stalemates between the House and Senate over the congressional appropriations process. However, while gridlock overtook the process of confirming judicial nominees and many of the administration's legislative priorities, a variety of legislative activities of interest to the publishing industry continued to percolate in both the House and Senate.

This report focuses on legislative actions that affect book- and journal-publishing interests, primarily concerning intellectual property protection, freedom of expression, new technologies and "e-commerce," and educational issues. It also reports on significant developments regarding tax and postal matters.

A summary, text, and status report for each piece of referenced legislation, whether enacted or not, can be found online in the Congressional Legislative Reference Service of the Library of Congress at http://thomas.loc.gov. Simply look under the Legislation heading at either Bill Summary or Bill Text, click on the icon labeled 108th Congress, and follow the instructions from there.

For more information, or questions or comments, contact Allan Adler or Emilia Varga-West by telephone at 202-347-3375, by fax at 202-347-3690, or by e-mail at adler@publishers.org or evargawest@publishers.org.

Intellectual Property Issues

Anticounterfeiting Amendments Act

(H.R. 3632; enacted as Title I of the Intellectual Property Protection and Courts Amendments Act, P.L. 108-482, December 23, 2004)

Software companies have increasingly used sophisticated identification features on their packaging to verify the authenticity of their products in the marketplace. Because consumers are now accustomed to looking for these authentication features to guard against purchasing counterfeit goods, legitimate authentication features—such as watermarks and holograms—are increasingly the target for theft by organized criminal enterprises that seek to pass off counterfeit software as authentic.

The Anticounterfeiting Amendments Act expands the scope of provisions in the U.S. code that already criminalize trafficking in counterfeit documentation and packaging for software programs. Earlier stand-alone versions of this legislation proposed to expand the law to include documentation and packaging for phonorecords, motion pictures, and other audiovisual works; add a prohibition for trafficking in illicit "authentication features"; and provide aggrieved parties with a private cause of action against violators of the act. However, these bills would not have added "literary works" (including books) or other kinds of copyrighted works to the existing statute's expanded coverage.

From the beginning of the 108th Congress, AAP has worked with staff for the legislation's lead sponsors, Rep. Lamar Smith (R-Texas) and Sen. Joseph Biden (D-Del.), to include "literary works" within the scope of any amendments to the existing anticounterfeiting statute. AAP argued that these works also deserve anticounterfeiting protection and that there is no legal or policy basis for distinguishing among copyrighted works in making such statutory protection available. However, the library and education communities objected, asserting concerns about potentially becoming the targets of criminal prosecution for unintended violations of the anticounterfeiting prohibitions while engaging in certain routine uses of copyrighted works, such as interlibrary loans and online distance education.

In addition, the question of whether the anticounterfeiting measures protected by such legislation should embrace digital as well as physical measures had been a problem, as opponents of "digital rights management" technology mandates and the anticircumvention provisions in the Digital Millennium Copyright Act (DMCA) claimed that the legislation would provide a "back door" means of strengthening those protections for copyrighted works.

In the end, the enacted legislation avoided that contentious issue by covering only physical anticounterfeiting measures and not goods distributed or sold electronically. It also addressed concerns raised by the "gray market" goods and Internet service provider (ISP) communities about being subjected inadvertently to potential new risks of liability for their otherwise legal actions.

Although book publishers are not yet using such authentication measures for their products, Association of American Publishers (AAP) efforts on this legislation reflect the need to anticipate adoption of such practices by publishers to combat counterfeiting and piracy in the global market. More importantly, AAP's efforts were intended to ensure that "literary works" are not excluded from legal protections afforded by Congress to the products of other copyright-based industries that devote more resources to their government affairs activities in Washington. Given the unfortunate current tendency of lawmakers to narrowly identify copyright as a "special interest" of the motion picture and recording industries, AAP must try to ensure that literary works are regarded no differently than the products of these or other copyright-based industries when Congress considers legislation to improve copyright protection and enforcement.

Fraudulent Online Identity Sanctions Act

(H.R. 3754; enacted as Title II of the Intellectual Property Protection and Courts Amendments Act, P.L. 108-482, December 23, 2004)

As use of the Internet to transact business through commercial Web sites continues to grow, so do the number of cases of online fraud. Unfortunately, the nature of Web sites—through which scams can be conducted in cyberspace—does not afford defrauded consumers any easy or reliable ways of identifying the alleged perpetrators of the fraud for purposes of pursuing redress in the civil or criminal justice systems. In the absence of other reliable ownership or licensing records, consumers must frequently rely on domain-name registration information to identify persons who are responsible for a Web site related to allegedly fraudulent conduct. However, a person who establishes a Web site with the intention of using it to perpetrate fraudulent or otherwise illegal activities may provide false contact information to the domain-name registration authority.

In calling for a sentencing enhancement for criminals who knowingly provide materially false contact information for a Web site that is used in the course of committing a felony, Congress noted that materially false contact information is apparently being used by those who infringe on copyrights and trademarks to hide their identities from their victims. Believing such conduct to be evidence of "willful" infringement deserving additional penalties, Congress amended the copyright and trademark statutes to establish a "rebuttable presumption" of willfulness where an infringer has knowingly provided or caused to be provided "materially false contact information" to a registration authority for a domain name used in connection with the infringement.

In enacting this legislation, Congress did not impose any requirement that all domain-name contact information should be accurate, nor did it restrict the availability and growing use of anonymous but legitimate domain-name registrations where, based on legitimate free speech concerns (e.g., for protest, whistleblower, or dissident Web sites), the registration authority may substitute its own contact information for that of the actual registrant to disguise ownership of the Web site. To protect such interests, Congress made clear that the mere act of providing materially false contact information is not itself a violation of any law.

As in the case of this legislation, which indirectly strengthens copyright protection by easing the copyright owner's burden of proof and enhancing available infringement penalties in certain situations, AAP monitors congressional activity to inform publishers of opportunities to benefit from legislation that is indirectly related to copyright or other publisher interests.

Creation of New Federal Intellectual Property Protection Officials
(H.R. 4818; enacted as part of the Consolidated Appropriations Act, 2005, P.L. 108-447, December 8, 2004)

Apart from providing substantive and procedural statutory protections for copyright interests, Congress recognizes that such interests often can be advanced through the creation of advocacy positions in the federal government with funding for their activities.

While providing fiscal year 2005 funding for various federal agencies in a massive, consolidated appropriations bill shortly before final adjournment, Congress determined to promote the protection of U.S. intellectual property in the global marketplace by establishing two important new federal positions in that part of the legislation (Division B, Title II) that provided appropriations for the Department of Commerce and related agencies.

One position, Chief Negotiator for Intellectual Property Enforcement, was established within the Office of the U.S. Trade Representative (USTR), which plays the lead role in negotiating international agreements on trade and other related matters. The second position, Coordinator for International Intellectual

Property Enforcement, was designated as a presidential appointee to head the National Intellectual Property Law Enforcement Coordination Council (NIPLECC), an interagency body that coordinates domestic and international intellectual property protections and law enforcement among federal and foreign entities. The legislation also provided NIPLECC with $2 million in funding to pursue its responsibilities, which include developing an overall strategy for protecting U.S. intellectual property overseas and overseeing implementation of the policies, objectives, and priorities it is required to establish for agencies with intellectual property protection and law enforcement responsibilities.

AAP works with allied trade associations representing other copyright-based industries to establish advocates within the federal government for the interests of U.S. intellectual property owners, and helps Congress focus on how they should work to advance those interests.

Technical Changes to Special 301 Mechanism of the Trade Act of 1974

(H.R. 1047; enacted as the Miscellaneous Trade and Technical Corrections Act, P.L.108-429, December 3, 2004)

Although global protections for U.S. copyright interests are primarily based on international treaties and agreements negotiated between and among sovereign nations, Congress occasionally has opportunities to advance such protections through domestic legislation affecting the U.S. government's ability to encourage foreign governments to crack down on intellectual property violations in the course of implementing such agreements.

As Congress considered legislation to reduce tariffs for agriculture, textiles, chemicals, pharmaceuticals, electronics, heavy equipment, and food and beverage products, Sen. Orrin Hatch (R-Utah), a strong advocate of intellectual property rights, amended the legislation on the Senate floor to give the U.S. government more tools to protect U.S. intellectual property around the world. Parts of the amendment, later deleted in conference with the House, would have given U.S. companies the ability to ask the U.S. government to suspend certain trade benefits to Caribbean and Central American countries that fail to meet their intellectual property protection and enforcement commitments under certain regional trade agreements, and would have also standardized the criteria for "adequate and effective" intellectual property protection under the Agreement on Trade-Related Aspects of Intellectual Property Rights (TRIPS) of the World Trade Organization (WTO) as a "floor" of minimal protection requirements under several U.S. trade programs.

The enacted legislation did, however, retain a Hatch amendment (Title II, Subtitle C, Section 2201) that gives the U.S. Trade Representative additional time to negotiate with countries prior to bringing alleged failures to provide adequate and effective protection to U.S. intellectual property interests into the WTO dispute-settlement process. More specifically, it reconciles key procedural timetables for the Special 301 provisions of the Trade Act of 1974, as amended, with those for the WTO dispute-settlement process. This will permit USTR to designate a WTO country as a Priority Foreign Country (PFC) under Special 301, while allowing time for remedial negotiations with that country before resorting to a TRIPS case through WTO. Without the amendment, the timing issues deprived USTR of the ability to initiate a TRIPS case within the Special 301 process, where it can benefit from the PFC designation.

As a member of the International Intellectual Property Alliance (IIPA), AAP worked with other copyright-based industry associations to secure enactment of these important provisions. It was expected that Senator Hatch would try again in the new Congress to win enactment of the intellectual property provisions that were dropped from last year's legislation in conference, and AAP will support those efforts through IIPA.

Non-Enacted Legislation

Successive frantic efforts to combine several pending copyright bills into a single legislative "package" for enactment before the end of the 108th Congress (e.g., H.R. 2391, H.R. 4077, and S. 3021) proved unsuccessful, chiefly for procedural reasons having little to do with their substance.

It is likely, however, that many of these measures—left dangling at diverse stages of the legislative process upon final adjournment—will resurface in the new Congress, either individually or in a similar "package" approach. These measures, generally viewed as "pro-copyright" from the perspective of publishers and other copyright-based industries, included bills that would have

- Redressed judicial rulings under which state entities that infringe the rights of patent, trademark, and copyright owners may assert a right of sovereign immunity under the 11th Amendment to avoid the injured party's claims for monetary damages (a result that unfairly allows such entities to protect their own intellectual property rights through damage suits while avoiding damage suits for violating the same statutory rights of others) (see H.R. 2344 and S. 1191)
- Promoted more-active federal criminal and civil law enforcement efforts to combat online copyright infringement by (among other things) (1) creating a pilot program for the Justice Department to send warning letters to ISPs regarding online infringement by their subscribers; (2) establishing an Internet use education program in the attorney general's office; (3) requiring the U.S. Sentencing Commission to consider penalty enhancements for infringement under its sentencing guidelines; (4) authorizing the attorney general to bring civil actions against willful infringers in lieu of criminal prosecutions; (5) creating civil and criminal liability for unauthorized recording of a motion picture during theatrical performance and unauthorized distribution of copyrighted works prior to their commercial release; (6) amending statutory criminal infringement provisions to adapt prosecutorial damage thresholds to the peer-to-peer environment; and (7) allowing courts, in computing statutory damages for infringement, to determine that each part of a compilation is a separate work with independent economic value to be redressed through such damages (see, variously, H.R. 2517, H.R. 2752, H.R. 4077, S. 1932, S. 1933, and S. 2237)
- Established a specific new statutory standard for secondary liability in connection with intentional inducement of copyright infringement, in an

effort to define the liability of persons whose business models promote or facilitate the use of peer-to-peer software or other technologies in ways that support or benefit from the predominant use of such technologies to engage in copyright infringement (S. 2560)

Of course, the final adjournment of the 108th Congress also resolved efforts to advance a number of copyright-related bills that were viewed by publishers and other copyright-based industries as distinctly adverse to their intellectual property interests. Among the pending bills that were opposed by AAP and other copyright interests were measures that would have

- (1) Amended the Digital Millennium Copyright Act (DMCA) to permit the circumvention of technological access and use controls for noninfringing purposes and to legalize tools that would facilitate such circumvention, (2) established a "digital first sale" doctrine for online transmissions of copyrighted works, (3) permitted the making and use of copies of digital works for "archival purposes," (4) permitted private performances or displays of digital works on any digital media device, and (5) made unenforceable any "nonnegotiable license terms" that apply to a digital work that is distributed to the public to the extent that such terms restrict or negate any limitation on the rights of copyright owners under copyright law (see H.R. 107 and H.R. 1066)
- Established a copyright "renewal" process that would strip copyrighted works of their copyright protection and place them in the public domain if the copyright owners failed to renew their rights in compliance with a specified procedure requiring timely payment of a "maintenance fee" within a specific timeframe and every ten years thereafter until the end of the copyright term (H.R. 2601)
- Eliminated copyright protection for "any work produced pursuant to scientific research substantially funded by the Federal Government," and required all federal agencies that fund scientific research through grants, contracts, or cooperative agreements to explicitly state that copyright protection "is not available for any work produced pursuant to such research . . ." (H.R. 2613)
- Required the Federal Trade Commission to issue rules mandating that products that incorporate "digital rights management" technology must be labeled to disclose any related restrictions or limitations that such technology imposes on uses of copyrighted works, including time-shifting, space-shifting, making backup copies, using excerpts, or engaging in second-hand transfer or sale (S. 692)
- Eliminated a copyright owner's ability under DMCA to identify an alleged online infringer by obtaining a subpoena for subscriber information from an ISP through an administrative application that does not require a related pending lawsuit (while making such subpoenas inapplicable to peer-to-peer infringement cases) by barring a "manufacturer of digital media product" from obtaining a subpoena to require an ISP to

identify allegedly infringing subscribers except as authorized under the Federal Rules of Civil Procedure (S. 1621)

These "anti-copyright" measures, or variations on their themes, were also expected to reappear in some form in the new Congress.

Database Protection

Despite a public commitment from the chairmen of two powerful House committees to jointly produce a viable database protection bill for enactment before final adjournment of the 108th Congress, developments in this area in 2004 appear to have only further set back the efforts of proponents of such legislation.

The bill produced by staff of both committees (H.R. 3261) emerged first from the House Judiciary Committee but garnered only lukewarm support from AAP and other supporters of database protection because of its narrow scope and ambiguous elements. Despite its weaknesses, however, even that legislation received an unfavorable report from the House Energy and Commerce Committee, which has historically been hostile to the "misappropriation" framework developed for such legislation and has asserted its jurisdiction primarily on behalf of critics who claim that proponents of database protection legislation are attempting to acquire a copyright-like form of proprietary protection for databases in defiance of the U.S. Supreme Court's *Feist* ruling.

After rejecting the Judiciary Committee's bill, the Commerce Committee reported its own version of database protection legislation (H.R. 3872), which was opposed by AAP and other supporters of database legislation as offering little real protection from misappropriation. The split between the two key House committees assured that no database bill would be considered by the full House during the year.

The resulting House stalemate—combined with a continuing lack of interest in the subject in the Senate—may indicate that a change of tactics or even a period of respite in seeking enactment of database protection legislation is warranted on the part of its supporters in the new Congress.

Regulation of Peer-to-Peer Technologies

Competing legislative proposals to regulate peer-to-peer technologies for reasons unrelated to copyright infringement were much discussed in hearings but, ultimately, not enacted before Congress adjourned. These bills focused on concerns regarding the role of such technologies in exposing children to online pornography (H.R. 2885) and subjecting unwitting consumers to potentially serious invasions of privacy through stealthy installation of "spyware" (H.R. 2929).

Although AAP took no position on this legislation, it will continue to monitor such proposals in the new Congress with respect to their possible utility in dealing with copyright infringement issues associated with such technologies.

Public Access to NIH-Funded Research

A major issue of concern to AAP's Professional and Scholarly (PSP) publishers first came to public attention through the legislative process, although it actually concerned an important matter of agency policy-making more than congressional action.

When the House Appropriations Committee approved proposed appropriations legislation for the Department of Health and Human Services (H.R. 5006) in the summer of 2004, scientific journal publishers learned from the committee report that the National Institutes of Health (NIH)—the federal government's single largest source of funding for biomedical research—had apparently raised concerns in the committee that there was "insufficient public access to reports and data resulting from NIH-funded research" and that the problem was being "exacerbated by the dramatic rise in scientific journal subscription prices." In response, the committee endorsed an NIH proposal to require NIH-funded researchers to electronically submit to PubMed Central—the digital library maintained by the National Library of Medicine—a copy of any resulting report on their research upon its acceptance for publication in any scientific journal so that PubMed Central could make the complete text of such articles "freely and continuously available" to the general public online six months after publication.

Scientific journal publishers, including both commercial publishers and nonprofit societies and university presses, reacted with consternation to the allegation of insufficient public access and protested that the NIH plan would undermine the economic viability of publishers that depend upon subscription revenues to recover their costs and subsidize other activities relating to scientific research. Publishers also questioned whether the plan might adversely affect the peer-review process for scientific journals and force current subscription models to evolve toward an unproven "author pays" model for financing the costs of publication. (Under an author-pays system, a publication charges authors a fee to have their work published online in lieu of charging readers to access articles.)

In late August NIH published a modified version of its proposed "public access" plan for public comment. Supporters commenting on the proposed plan included advocates of "open access" publishing models, library groups that consider copyright to be an obstacle to public access, and "consumer" groups that claim the taxpayer has already paid for the research and shouldn't have to pay again to read the results. Many of the comments critical of the plan, including those filed by various AAP members, focused particularly on the six-month window while more broadly questioning why the government should be intervening in an area of thriving private-sector activity to mandate a "one-size-fits-all" public-access policy that not only fails to consider the diversity of affected interests and practices but also raises a host of issues about inappropriate government control over the dissemination of scientific research reports.

Although the comment period ended in mid-November, the final decision on implementation of the plan had not yet been made when this report was prepared.

Lobbying by AAP and some of its PSP members helped produce language in the Conference Report on the final version of the Health and Human Services appropriations legislation (Division F, Title II of H.R. 4818) that directs NIH to (1) "give full and fair consideration to all comments before publishing its final policy," (2) provide Congress estimated costs of implementing its policy each year, and (3) "continue to work with the publishers of scientific journals to maintain the integrity of the peer review system." AAP will evaluate the final NIH plan upon publication and consider with its members whether further action is warranted.

Freedom of Expression Issues

Intelligence Reform and Terrorism Prevention Act

(S. 2845; enacted as P.L. 108-458, December 17, 2004)

Overreaching by the federal government in classifying materials as "national security information" has always been a matter of serious concern for book publishers, as well as the news media, because it often has the effect of preventing present and even former government officials from fully exploring the details of important national defense and foreign policy matters in their published writings. The ever-present issue of whether important information is being unjustifiably withheld from public disclosure reared its head during congressional consideration of massive intelligence-reform legislation intended to put into effect some of the key recommendations of the National Commission on Terrorist Attacks Upon the United States (the "9/11 Commission").

Early versions of the legislation raised serious concerns that Congress might effectively create a form of "official secrets act" by authorizing the newly created position of Director of National Intelligence to establish a fully autonomous new classification system for intelligence, distinct from the classification system for national security information that is governed by executive order. However, when the Intelligence Reform and Terrorism Prevention Act of 2004 finally emerged from conference, the House and Senate conferees made clear that the legislation "does not expand authority under which information is classified." More hopefully, the legislation even revived the dormant Public Interest Declassification Board, which was established four years ago but never convened, with the specific task of "reviewing" congressional requests for declassification of particular records.

AAP will continue to monitor legislative issues regarding restrictions on public disclosure of information important to understanding the policies and actions of the federal government.

Non-Enacted Legislation

Proposals to Amend the USA Patriot Act

The first half of the 108th Congress saw the introduction of some half-dozen bills designed to revise or repeal Section 215 of the USA Patriot Act, one of the most troubling provisions in the legislation that the prior Congress had enacted to strengthen the ability of law enforcement authorities to investigate and prevent the potential recurrence of the 9/11 terrorist attacks on the United States. The major effort in the second half of the 108th Congress to redress civil liberties concerns about the provision, which expanded the federal government's authority to demand third-party records in connection with terrorism investigations, ultimately failed after political manipulation of a seemingly successful House floor vote left the matter unresolved on a tie vote.

Since its enactment, Section 215 has posed a significant threat to the work of authors and investigative journalists who write about terrorism-related subjects, and has threatened the privacy and First Amendment rights of library patrons and bookstore customers whose reading choices or Internet usage patterns may be subject to demands for disclosure.

Under Section 215, a library or bookstore can be compelled to turn over information about patrons and customers, including borrowing records of a particular individual or a list of individuals who have borrowed or purchased a particular book or visited a particular Web site. Such permissible incursions on First Amendment-protected activities are particularly troubling because the act authorizes search warrants for books, journalists' interview notes, bookstore purchase records, library usage information, and similar materials to be obtained from a secret court, without an adversarial hearing or the need to show "probable cause," and pursuant to "gag orders" that prevent the recipients from even disclosing their receipt. Because they are denied the right to reveal the fact that such a warrant has been received, publishers, librarians, and booksellers are unable to defend their right to disseminate and the right of their patrons to receive constitutionally protected materials.

Although bills to address Section 215 had been introduced in the Senate (S. 1158, S. 1507, and S. 1709), all of the floor actions on such legislation occurred in the House, where a bipartisan group of representatives, led by Rep. Bernie Sanders (I-Vt.), had introduced the first such bill (H.R. 1157) with the intention of exempting libraries and booksellers from Section 215 and allowing law enforcement authorities to obtain records from these sources only with the safeguard of judicially issued warrants. After procedural restrictions thwarted an initial attempt to address the issue by amending an appropriations bill to prohibit the Justice Department from spending any funds for Section 215 searches of library and bookstore records, a successful effort in offering a similar amendment to a different appropriations bill was negated when the provision was later stripped out of the funding bill.

Then, in July 2004, another bipartisan effort was made on the House floor to bar the Justice Department from expending appropriations for the purpose of making any application under Section 215 for an order requiring production of library or bookseller records or customer lists. Although the amendment appeared to have the support of a clear majority of the House when time for voting had expired, the House leadership, aware of the Bush administration's strong opposition to this and other proposals to revise provisions of the USA Patriot Act, held the vote open for more than twice the usual amount of time permitted until it was able to persuade enough members to change their votes so that the amendment failed on a tie vote of 210–210.

With the Bush administration preparing a major lobbying effort in Congress to permanently establish many of the controversial provisions of the USA Patriot Act, AAP will continue to work with other concerned constituencies to press for the repeal or revision of Section 215.

Presidential Records

Not surprisingly, another legislative casualty of the 108th Congress was bipartisan legislation (H.R. 1493) to revoke President Bush's Executive Order 13233, which gave current and past presidents, as well as the current vice president and members of a former president's family, veto power over the release of presidential records. The bill was referred to the House Government Reform Committee, but no further action was taken, in large part because of vehement opposition to the bill from the Bush administration and the partisanship of an election-year session in which the issue of presidential records would have been politically awkward to address.

Recognizing the importance of presidential records to publishers of contemporary works of biography, history, and political science, AAP will support efforts in the present Congress to restore the prior, less-restrictive access policies.

Education Issues

Individuals with Disabilities Education Improvement Act

(H.R. 1350; enacted as P.L. 108-446, December 3, 2004)

For nearly four years, AAP worked with representatives of the major advocacy groups for the blind to draft and secure introduction of a bill to improve the process through which print-disabled students obtain copies of class instructional materials in accessible specialized formats, such as braille or digital text. Shortly before the final adjournment of the 108th Congress, the key provisions of the proposed Instructional Materials Accessibility Act (IMAA) were enacted in modified form as part of legislation reauthorizing the Individuals with Disabilities Education Act (IDEA).

After earlier versions of IMAA had failed to advance in the House and Senate during the previous Congress, the legislation was reintroduced in the House early in the 108th Congress. It was designed to create a national infrastructure so that K–12 grade students who are blind or have other print disabilities could receive accessible versions of core classroom instructional materials in a timely manner. However, continued opposition from the U.S. Department of Education, which rejected the creation of the national file repository proposed in the bill and had additional questions regarding the bill's scope and its preemption of state and local file format requirements, did not bode well for enactment.

In March 2004, however, AAP successfully negotiated an amendment to be included in the House Education Committee's markup of IDEA reauthorization legislation (H.R. 1350) that would require all states and local education agencies, as a condition of receiving IDEA funding, to adopt a national file format for converting print to an accessible format, one of the major objectives of IMAA. Under the amendment, publishers would have two years from the date of enactment to comply with the requirements.

Although AAP and its allies considered the IMAA amendment a huge step forward, they were disappointed about the exclusion of a national repository for publishers' files and hoped to have the opportunity to expand the provision on the Senate side. The House passed H.R. 1350 in April 2004 with the IMAA amendment intact.

AAP and its allies had more success when they took up the same issues with the Senate committee that was overseeing IDEA reauthorization. As the committee developed its own reauthorizing legislation (S. 1248), AAP and its allies were given a chance to improve upon the House-passed IMAA amendment. After weeks of negotiation, the Senate committee in June approved its own IDEA reauthorization bill, which included more of the IMAA provisions addressing the accessibility of print instructional material for students with print disabilities. The key provisions would (1) generally require all states to use the same standardized national electronic file format for the conversion of textbooks and other core instructional materials into accessible formats, (2) mandate that publishers provide such print instructional materials in the form of properly formatted electronic files to a central repository for their timely and convenient distribution to authorized entities for conversion into accessible formats, and (3) establish and authorize funding for a National Instructional Materials Access Center, which would be responsible for cataloging, storing, and distributing the electronic files provided by publishers.

Enactment of the revised IMAA provisions as part of the IDEA reauthorization in December was a coup for AAP, but it does not mark the end of AAP involvement in federal legislation addressing accessibility issues for students with disabilities. On the contrary, AAP expects to work closely with the American Printing House for the Blind, which Congress designated as responsible for establishing and operating the National Instructional Materials Access Center, and to participate in consideration of whether the IMAA measures in this legislation might be adapted to address instructional materials accessibility problems for college students with disabilities.

Higher Education Extension Act

(H.R. 5185; enacted as P.L. 108-366, October 25, 2004)

Theoretically, each of the three major federal laws relating to education programs operates on a staggered schedule of reauthorization so that overlapping deadlines for program expiration will not hinder Congress in giving each reauthorization careful bipartisan consideration. Bipartisanship—along with cooperation between the two houses of Congress—was critical to the successful reauthorization of the Elementary and Secondary Education Act (in the form of the No Child Left Behind Act) early in 2002 and to the reauthorization of the Individuals with Disabilities Education Act in late 2004. These critical elements, however, apparently deserted legislators who struggled unsuccessfully to reach agreements on program reforms while meeting the five-year deadline for reauthorization of the Higher Education Act.

As a result, with a rapidly approaching deadline for the expiration of key funding programs for college students, Congress was only able to vote to maintain the status quo in the programs authorized under the Higher Education Act, and thus simply extended them through the end of fiscal year 2004 (September 30, 2005).

The problem was not a lack of proposals for higher education reform. Key leaders for the House Republican majority had their proposals (H.R. 3311 and H.R. 4283), as did key leaders for the Democratic minority (H.R. 3180, H.R. 3519 and H.R. 5113). However, members could not reach agreement across the aisles on how to address the major issue of college affordability through reforms focused on student grant and loan programs. In addition, House members of both parties criticized their counterparts in the Senate for that body's inaction on higher education reauthorization.

Legislators can be expected to make substantive reform of Higher Education Act programs a priority in the new Congress. AAP will continue to monitor these matters insofar as they may relate to ongoing issues concerning college textbook costs and the Title IV funding that students typically use to cover them.

Non-Enacted Legislation

Cost of College Textbooks

Continuing negative national news coverage regarding the cost of college textbooks spawned a legislative call (H.R. 3567) for an investigation of textbook pricing by the Government Accountability Office (GAO), as well as proposals for tax deductions of up to $1,000 for the cost of such materials (H.R. 4243 and S. 2797). Although none of these bills was enacted, GAO initiated an investigation of textbook pricing at the request of House committee leaders.

The GAO investigation, in which AAP and its members are cooperating, was still pending at the time this report was prepared, and the sponsors of tax deductions for the costs of college textbooks were expected to reintroduce their bills in the new Congress.

Literacy Programs

Creative ways to support literacy programs were also the subject of legislative proposals that did not achieve enactment. One measure (H.R. 126) proposed to establish a grant program through the Secretary of Health and Human Services to promote child literacy and improve children's access to books at home and in early learning and childcare programs, in part through the use of special postage stamps to generate additional funding for children's literacy programs. Another bill (H.R. 2795) would have amended the 1966 Child Nutrition Act to provide vouchers for the purchase of educational books for infants and children participating in the WIC special supplemental nutrition program for women, infants, and children.

AAP will work in the 109th Congress to support legislation that promotes child literacy and improves young children's access to books.

Postal Issues

Non-Enacted Legislation

The 108th Congress started off at high speed with AAP lobbying both the Senate and the House to avert a rate-raising debt crisis at the U.S. Postal Service (USPS) by passing legislation to prevent USPS from continuing to over-fund the Civil Service Retirement System (CSRS) with unnecessary contributions for USPS workers. But efforts to harness this momentum to drive enactment of comprehensive postal reform legislation fell short of the mark.

The Postal Civil Service Retirement System Funding Reform Act of 2003, which had strong bipartisan backing in the key House and Senate committees with jurisdiction over postal affairs, moved quickly through both houses of Congress and was signed into law in April 2003, just over two months after the legislation was first introduced.

The need for the legislation arose out of a financial analysis that the Office of Personnel Management (OPM) conducted at the request of GAO, revealing that USPS had almost fully funded its retirement obligation for postal employees and that additional payments at the current rate would over-fund USPS liability by approximately $71 billion. The new law enacted by Congress in response to this analysis was intended to prevent the overpayment by correcting the statutory formula for the USPS contributions to CSRS, while stipulating that the funds saved are to be used by USPS to (1) pay down its debt to the Treasury Department, (2) maintain current postage rates without any increases until 2006 at the earliest, and (3) fund postal retiree health benefits.

Following this action, attention shifted to efforts to move comprehensive postal-reform legislation. By the end of the first session of the 108th Congress, however, no action had been taken on the proposed Postal Accountability and Enhancement Act (S. 1285), which had been introduced in the Senate in June, more than a month before the President's Commission on Postal Reform released its report. Just as the first session was ending, the Bush administration finally called upon Congress to enact postal reform legislation. The administration's principles for postal reform outlined goals for ensuring that (1) the governing body of USPS can adequately meet the responsibilities and objectives of an organization of its size and scope; (2) USPS costs and performance data are accurately determined and made available to the public; (3) USPS's governing body has the ability and the authority to reduce costs, set rates, and adjust key aspects of its business in order to meet customers' needs; (4) there is an appropriate oversight body that protects consumer welfare and universal mail service; and (5) USPS can operate in a self-sufficient manner to cover all of its obligations.

Leaders on postal matters in the House and Senate responded in the second session of the 108th Congress by introducing similar comprehensive postal reform proposals in each body (H.R. 4341 and S. 2468). Among other things, both bills featured reforms that would (1) shift rate regulation from its current litigation model to one tied to the Consumer Price Index for market-dominant products while permitting flexible market pricing for competitive products, (2) define "postal services" and limit USPS offering of nonpostal products, and (3) give the renamed Postal Regulatory Commission subpoena power and broaden its regulatory and oversight functions.

The respective committees of jurisdiction in the House and Senate gave their approval to this legislation, but neither bill received floor consideration. While this was due, in part, to scheduling problems in an election year plagued by partisan gridlock and a limited calendar, it was also attributable to opposition from major postal unions and continuing concerns of the Bush administration regarding the cost of the legislation. Both bills would have transferred pension cost obligations connected with military service credit for postal employees from USPS to the Treasury, in addition to abolishing the 2006 escrow requirement in order to delay the need for a rate case. The administration also questioned whether the legislation went far enough in providing transparency to prevent cross-subsidization of competitive products with monopoly product revenue, as well as in providing flexibility to reduce high labor costs.

AAP expects that, in an effort to mitigate the likelihood that substantial rate increases will be proposed in 2005, efforts to enact postal-reform legislation will resume in the 109th Congress. AAP will work with legislators in the House and Senate to ensure that reform issues important to AAP and its member publishers are satisfactorily addressed.

Tax Issues

Internet Tax Nondiscrimination Act

(S. 150; enacted as P.L. 108-435, December 3, 2004)

Proponents of a permanent moratorium on multiple and discriminatory taxes over the Internet had to settle for a three-year extension that included significant tinkering with key definitions relating to the pivotal issue of Internet access. Still, this had to be viewed as a better result than had been reached at the end of the first session of the 108th Congress, when the previous two-year extension of the moratorium prohibiting state and local governments from imposing any new Internet-related taxes was allowed to expire in the absence of a consensus on how to extend it.

The Internet Tax Freedom Act of 1998 (ITFA) created a moratorium on multiple and discriminatory taxes and Internet access taxes for three years. ITFA expired in 2001, but was extended by Congress until November 1, 2003. Advocates of a permanent moratorium introduced S. 150 to permanently prohibit taxes on Internet access and multiple and discriminatory taxes on electronic commerce, while phasing out the "grandfather clause" that permitted some state and local governments to continue to collect certain Internet access taxes. It also proposed to change the definition of "Internet access" to cover high-speed DSL, cable modem, wireless, satellite, and dial-up services to ensure that they are covered by the prohibition and exempt from state and local taxation.

But opponents of S. 150 argued that such legislation would constitute an unfunded federal mandate to state and local governments, costing these deficit-ridden governments billions of dollars in desperately needed potential tax revenues. They also claimed that the bill, by altering the definition of "Internet access" to include services that are already being taxed, could further result in a substantial loss of revenue to already struggling states. State and local governments also raised a concern that Internet access providers could begin to "bundle" products and refer to the packages as providing "Internet access" in order to avoid being taxed.

In the enacted compromise, a revised S. 150 changed the definition of access service to exclude telecommunications services, except to the extent that these are used by an Internet access provider to provide Internet access. It also changed the definition of "tax on Internet access" to include any tax on Internet access, regardless of whether it is imposed on a provider or purchaser of such service and regardless of the terminology used to describe the tax.

The legislation extends the ban on state taxation of Internet access and on multiple or discriminatory taxes on electronic commerce until November 1, 2007, while "grandfathering" until that date the Internet-access taxing authority of states that had such a tax prior to the enactment of IFTA in 1998. Similar "grandfathering" through November 1, 2005, is provided for the Internet-access taxing authority of those states that had such a tax prior to the expiration of the moratorium in November 2003, and a separate termination date applies to the ability of states to tax Internet access through a state telecommunications service tax.

AAP took no position on this legislation. However, advocates of a permanent moratorium may seek one during this Congress, and their efforts could implicate the collection of out-of-state sales tax. AAP will continue to monitor Internet tax issues as they arise and inform its members if their interests are likely to be affected.

American Jobs Creation Act of 2004

(H.R. 4520; enacted as P.L. 108-357, October 22, 2004)

Hoping that the second time will be the charm, Congress has once again enacted remedial legislation that it believes should satisfactorily respond to WTO's determination that export-related tax benefits provided to U.S. companies under federal law constitute illegal export subsidies. In the process, however, it came close to denying publishers the benefits of the scheme that it created as an alternative tax incentive for U.S. companies.

In 2000 the European Union (EU) succeeded in having WTO declare the export-related tax deductions under the "foreign sales corporation" (FSC) provisions of U.S. tax law to be a prohibited export subsidy, opening the door to potential retaliatory tariffs by European countries against U.S. industries. The first response from Congress, which replaced the FSC regime with an "extraterritorial income" (ETI) plan, was quickly challenged by EU and was found by WTO in 2002 to constitute a prohibited export subsidy under the relevant trade agreements.

It took more than two years of additional debate for Congress to repeal the ETI plan through a phase-out scheme that it combined with reduction of the existing corporate income tax rate for income attributable to domestic production activities, in order to mitigate the loss to U.S. companies of the deduction for export-related income and make investments in domestic manufacturing facilities more attractive.

Although the House and Senate versions of the legislation each would have provided a deduction for taxable income that is equal to a portion of the taxpayer's qualified production activities income, the Senate bill proposed to define "qualified production property" (for purposes of determining such income attributable to domestic production activities) in a way that would have excluded from this benefit "any film, tape, recording, book, magazine, newspaper or similar property the market for which is primarily topical or otherwise essentially transitory in nature." However, after AAP protested to leaders of the Senate Finance Committee, the legislation emerged from conference without the exclusion of these types of production property.

Despite the inherent difficulties in lobbying on major tax legislation, AAP succeeded in getting the concerns of publishers heard by Congress.

Non-Enacted Legislation

Deduction for Contributions of Book Inventory

When the Senate passed the Charity Aid, Recovery, and Empowerment (CARE) Act by an overwhelming 95–5 vote in April 2003, it looked as though AAP would score another rare victory on tax issues. The CARE Act (S. 476), which was a bipartisan, compromise version of President Bush's Faith-Based and Community Initiative, included a number of amendments to stimulate donations to charitable organizations that were struggling with a decline in contributions coupled with a growing demand for services.

One such provision in the CARE Act was the Contributions of Book Inventory Amendment, sponsored by Senator Hatch. Unfortunately, the House did not take up the Senate-passed version of S. 476 but instead passed its own version of the CARE Act (H.R. 7), which did not include a provision regarding charitable deductions for book inventories.

Originally introduced as a stand-alone bill (S. 680), the Senate amendment would have enhanced the charitable tax deduction incentives under existing law for book publishers to contribute excess book inventory to educational organizations, public libraries, and literacy programs. During the previous Congress, Senator Hatch had made sure that a similar provision was included in the Senate-passed version of the administration's major tax legislation, the RELIEF Act of 2001, but it was dropped with many other provisions from the final version of the tax legislation that the president signed into law. AAP staff worked with Senator Hatch's staff to improve that version of the inventory contributions provisions, and several of the issues raised by AAP resulted in changes in the amendment as introduced and passed in the Senate.

Under current law, a charitable tax deduction for donation of a taxpayer's inventory is limited to the taxpayer's basis (cost) in the inventory. However, a taxpayer may be eligible for an enhanced deduction, which is equal to the lesser of (1) the basis plus one half of an item's appreciated value, or (2) two times the basis, if the items donated are to be used "solely for the care of the ill, the needy, or infants." Unfortunately, book publishers are often prohibited from receiving an enhanced deduction for charitable contributions of their book inventories because of the requirement that the donation be used solely for the care of the ill, the needy, or infants rather than that it be made to charitable organizations that can use the books.

Under the revised Senate-passed amendment, a special rule would have been carved out for book publishers to receive an enhanced deduction for charitable contributions of their book inventories to schools, libraries, and literacy programs for educational purposes. For qualified book contributions, the ceiling on the enhanced deduction for book publishers would have been the amount by which the fair market value of the contributed materials exceeds twice the taxpayer's basis in the materials. A "qualified book contribution" would have referred to a charitable contribution of books to (1) an educational organization that normally maintains a regular faculty and curriculum and normally has a regularly enrolled body of pupils or students in attendance at the place where its educational activities are regularly carried on (schools), (2) a public library, or (3) a 501(c)(3) entity that is organized primarily to make books available to the general public at no cost or to operate a literacy program. "Fair market value" would have been determined by reference to a "bona fide published market price" as determined (1) using the same printing and edition, (2) in the usual market in which the book is customarily sold by the taxpayer, and (3) by the validity of the taxpayer's showing that the taxpayer customarily sold such books in arm's-length transactions within seven years preceding the contribution. In practical terms, this meant that the "bona fide published market price" for contributed books could not be based on the price from the publisher's own price list or catalog, but instead must be an independently verifiable reference to actual sales of those books. Under the amendment, the donee organization would have to (1) use the books consistent with their exempt purpose; (2) not transfer the books in exchange for money, other property, or services; and (3) certify in writing both that the donated books are suitable—in terms of currency, content, and quantity—for use in the organization's educational programs, and that the books will be used in such educational programs.

Unfortunately, the lack of necessary offsets to pay for the costs of new charitable tax deductions in the CARE Act apparently doomed the effort by the bill's lead sponsors, Senators Rick Santorum (R-Pa.) and Joseph Lieberman (D-Conn.), to attach the bill's provisions to the session's only major tax bill, which Congress eventually enacted as the American Jobs Creation Act (see report above).

AAP will work during the 109th Congress to win enactment of the revised charitable tax deduction provisions for donations of book inventories.

Funding Programs and Grant-Making Agencies

National Endowment for the Humanities

1100 Pennsylvania Ave. N.W., Washington, DC 20506
202-606-8400, 800-634-1121
TDD (hearing impaired) 202-606-8282 or 866-372-2930 (toll free)

Thomas C. Phelps

The National Endowment for the Humanities (NEH) is an independent federal agency created in 1965. It is the largest funder of humanities programs in the United States.

Because democracy demands wisdom, NEH serves and strengthens the republic by promoting excellence in the humanities and conveying the lessons of history to all Americans. It accomplishes this mission by providing grants for high-quality humanities projects in four funding areas: preserving and providing access to cultural resources, education, research, and public programs.

NEH grants typically go to cultural institutions, such as museums, archives, libraries, colleges, universities, public television and radio stations, and to individual scholars. The grants

- Strengthen teaching and learning in the humanities in schools and colleges across the nation
- Facilitate research and original scholarship
- Provide opportunities for lifelong learning
- Preserve and provide access to cultural and educational resources
- Strengthen the institutional base of the humanities

Over the past 39 years, the endowment has reached millions of Americans with projects and programs that preserve and study the nation's cultural heritage while providing a foundation for the future.

According to the National Foundation on the Arts and Humanities Act, "The term 'humanities' includes, but is not limited to, the study of the following: language, both modern and classical; linguistics; literature; history; jurisprudence; philosophy; archaeology; comparative religion; ethics; the history, criticism, and theory of the arts; those aspects of social sciences which have humanistic content and employ humanistic methods; and the study and application of the humanities to the human environment with particular attention to reflecting our diverse heritage, traditions, and history and to the relevance of the humanities to the current conditions of national life."

The act, adopted by Congress in 1965, provided for the establishment of the National Foundation on the Arts and the Humanities in order to promote progress and scholarship in the humanities and the arts in the United States. The act included the following findings:

- The arts and the humanities belong to all the people of the United States.
- The encouragement and support of national progress and scholarship in the humanities and the arts, while primarily a matter for private and local initiative, are also appropriate matters of concern to the federal government.
- An advanced civilization must not limit its efforts to science and technology alone, but must give full value and support to the other great branches of scholarly and cultural activity in order to achieve a better understanding of the past, a better analysis of the present, and a better view of the future.
- Democracy demands wisdom and vision in its citizens. It must therefore foster and support a form of education, and access to the arts and the humanities, designed to make people of all backgrounds and wherever located masters of their technology and not its unthinking servants.
- It is necessary and appropriate for the federal government to complement, assist, and add to programs for the advancement of the humanities and the arts by local, state, regional, and private agencies and their organizations. In doing so, the government must be sensitive to the nature of public sponsorship. Public funding of the arts and humanities is subject to the conditions that traditionally govern the use of public money. Such funding should contribute to public support and confidence in the use of taxpayer funds. Public funds provided by the federal government must ultimately serve public purposes Congress defines.
- The arts and the humanities reflect the high place accorded by the American people to the nation's rich cultural heritage and to the fostering of mutual respect for the diverse beliefs and values of all persons and groups.

What NEH Grants Accomplish

Since its founding, NEH has awarded more than 60,000 grants. Following are some facts about NEH grants and their impact.

Interpretive Exhibitions

Interpretive exhibitions provide opportunities for lifelong learning in the humanities for millions of Americans. Since 1967 NEH has made more than 2,400 grants for interpretive exhibitions, catalogs, and public programs, which are among the most highly visible activities supported by the agency. All 50 states and the District of Columbia hosted a total of 134 exhibitions in 2004.

Renewing Teaching

Over the years more than 60,000 high school and college teachers have deepened their knowledge of the humanities through intensive summer study supported by NEH; tens of thousands of students benefit from these better-educated teachers every year.

Reading and Discussion

Since 1982 NEH has supported reading and discussion programs in libraries, encouraging people to discuss works of literature and history. Scholars in the humanities provide thematic direction for the programs. Using well-selected texts and such themes as "Work," "Family," "Diversity," and "Not for Children Only," these programs have attracted more than 1 million Americans to read and talk about what they've read.

Preserving the Nation's Heritage

The United States Newspaper Program is rescuing a piece of history by cataloging and microfilming 67.5 million pages from newspapers dating from the early days of the republic. Another microfilming program has rescued the content of more than 1 million brittle books.

Stimulating Private Support

More than $1.3 billion in humanities support has been generated by NEH's Challenge Grants program, which requires most recipients to raise $3 or $4 in nonfederal funds for every dollar they receive.

Presidential Papers

Ten presidential papers projects are underwritten by NEH, from George Washington to Dwight D. Eisenhower. The Washington and Eisenhower papers have each leveraged more than $1.8 million in nonfederal contributions.

New Scholarship

Endowment grants enable scholars to do in-depth study. Jack Rakove explored the making of the Constitution in his *Original Meanings,* while James McPherson chronicled the Civil War in his *Battle Cry of Freedom.* Both won the Pulitzer Prize, as have 13 other recipients of NEH grants.

History on Screen

Nearly 40 million Americans saw the Ken Burns TV documentary *The Civil War,* and 750,000 people bought the book. Through 340 other NEH-supported films such as *Liberty!, Jazz,* and *The Invisible Man,* and film biographies of Theodore and Franklin Roosevelt, Andrew Carnegie, and Gen. Douglas MacArthur, Americans learn about the events and people that shaped the nation.

Library of America

Millions of books have been sold as part of the Library of America series, a collection of the riches of the nation's literature. Begun with NEH seed money, the more than 170 published volumes include the writings of Henry Adams, Edith Wharton, William James, Eudora Welty, W. E. B. DuBois, and many others.

Science and the Humanities

The scientific past is being preserved with NEH-supported editions of the letters of Charles Darwin, the works of Albert Einstein, and the 14-volume papers of Thomas A. Edison.

Learning Under the Tent

From California to Florida, state humanities councils bring a 21st-century version of Chautauqua to the public, embracing populations of entire towns, cities, even regions. Scholars portray significant figures such as Meriweather Lewis, Sojourner Truth, Willa Cather, Teddy Roosevelt, and Sacagawea, first speaking as the historic character and later giving audiences opportunities to ask questions. The give and take between the scholar/performer and the audiences provides an entertaining, energetic, and thought-provoking exchange about experiences and attitudes in the present and the past.

Technology and the Classroom

NEH's EDSITEment Web site (http://edsitement.neh.gov) assembles the best humanities resources on the Web, drawing up to 170,000 visitors every month. Online lesson plans help teachers use more than 100 Web sites to enhance their teaching. Schools across the country are developing curricula to bring digital resources to the classroom.

Special Initiatives

We the People

We the People is an initiative launched by NEH to encourage the teaching, studying, and understanding of American history and culture. Under this initiative, NEH invites scholars, teachers, filmmakers, curators, librarians, and others to submit grant applications that explore significant events and themes in the nation's history and culture and that advance knowledge of the principles that define the United States.

Proposals responding to the initiative can take the form of

- New scholarship
- Projects to preserve and provide access to documents and artifacts
- Educational projects for every level, from kindergarten through college
- Public programs in libraries, museums, and historical societies, including exhibitions, film, radio, and Internet-based programs

NEH will accept We the People proposals for all programs and all deadlines. Proposals are expected to meet the guidelines of the program that best fits the character of the project. A list of programs and deadlines is available on the NEH Web site.

Proposals will be evaluated through NEH's established review process and will not receive special consideration. The chairman of NEH reserves the right to determine which grants will be designated as We the People projects.

The four main components of We the People are a call for applications to NEH for projects designed to explore significant events and themes in the nation's history; an annual Heroes of History lecture by a scholar on an individual whose heroism has helped to protect America; an Idea of America essay contest for high school juniors; and the We the People Bookshelf, a short list of classic books for young readers to be awarded to schools and libraries for use in local programs.

Plans include expanding We the People through a grant program to support projects that help schools and universities improve their teaching of American history, government, and civics. The Summer Seminar and Institutes program will be expanded to offer teachers more opportunities to study significant texts. Exhibits on the Idea of America essay contest will travel to small and mid-sized communities. NEH will also convene an annual national conference on civics education, the state of historical knowledge, and ways to enhance the teaching of American history.

EDSITEment

EDSITEment, a joint project to share the best humanities Web sites with teachers and students, was launched in 1997. Users of EDSITEment now have access to more than 100 high-quality humanities sites, representing more than 50,000 files searchable through the EDSITEment search engine at www.edsitement.neh.gov.

Federal-State Partnership

The Office of Federal-State Partnership links NEH with the nationwide network of 56 humanities councils, which are located in each state, the District of Columbia, Puerto Rico, the U.S. Virgin Islands, the Northern Mariana Islands, American Samoa, and Guam. Each humanities council funds humanities programs in its jurisdiction. A contact list for all the state councils can be found below:

Directory of State Humanities Councils

Alabama

Alabama Humanities Foundation
1100 Ireland Way, Suite 101
Birmingham, AL 35205-7001
205-558-3980, fax 205-558-3981
http://www.ahf.net
Board Chair Elaine Hughes
Executive Robert Stewart

Alaska

Alaska Humanities Forum
421 W. First Ave., Suite 300
Anchorage, AK 99501
907-272-5341, fax 907-272-3979
http://www.akhf.org
Board Chair Sharon Gagnon
Executive Ira Perman

Arizona

Arizona Humanities Council
Ellis-Shackelford House
1242 N. Central Ave.,
Phoenix, AZ 85004-1887
602-257-0335, fax 602-257-0392
http://www.azhumanities.org
Board Chair Diane Hamilton
Executive Amanda Swain

Arkansas

Arkansas Humanities Council
10800 Financial Centre Pkwy., Suite 465
Little Rock, AR 72211
501-221-0091, fax 501-221-9860
http://www.arkhums.org
Board Chair David Stricklin
Executive Robert E. Bailey

California

California Council for the Humanities
312 Sutter St., Suite 601
San Francisco, CA 94108
415-391-1474, fax 415-391-1312
http://www.calhum.org
Board Chair Charlene L. Simmons
Executive James Quay

Colorado

Colorado Endowment for the Humanities
1490 Lafayette St., Suite 101
Denver, CO 80218
303-894-7951, fax 303-864-9361
http://www.ceh.org
Board Chair Russell F. Ahrens
Executive Margaret A. Coval

Connecticut

Connecticut Humanities Council
955 S. Main St., Suite E
Middletown, CT 06457
860-685-2260, fax 860-704-0429
http://www.ctculture.org
Board Chair Carol Clapp
Executive Bruce Fraser

Delaware

Delaware Humanities Forum
100 W. 10th St., Suite 1009

Wilmington, DE 19801
302-657-0650, fax 302-657-0655
http://www.dhf.org
Board Chair Gene Naomi Danneman
Executive Marilyn Whittington

District of Columbia

Humanities Council of Washington, D.C.
925 U St. N.W.
Washington, DC 20001
202-387-8393, fax 202-387-8149
http://wdchumanities.org
Board Chair Janet Hampton
Executive Joy Austin

Florida

Florida Humanities Council
599 2nd St. S.
St. Petersburg, FL 33701-5005
772-553-3800, fax 772-553-3829
http://www.flahum.org
Board Chair Kathleen Deagan
Executive Janine Farver

Georgia

Georgia Humanities Council
50 Hurt Plaza S.E., Suite 595
Atlanta, GA 30303-2915
404-523-6220, fax 404-523-5702
http://www.georgiahumanities.org
Board Chair Steve Wrigley
Executive Jamil Zainaldin

Hawaii

Hawaii Council for the Humanities
First Hawaiian Bank Bldg.
3599 Waialae Ave., Room 23
Honolulu, HI 96816
808-732-5402, fax 808-732-5402
http://www.hihumanities.org
Board Chair Gail Ainsworth
Executive Robert Buss

Idaho

Idaho Humanities Council
217 W. State St.
Boise, ID 83702
208-345-5346, fax 208-345-5347
http://www.idahohumanities.org

Board Chair Marc Johnson
Executive Rick Ardinger

Illinois

Illinois Humanities Council
203 N. Wabash Ave., Suite 2020
Chicago, IL 60601-2417
312-422-5580, fax 312-422-5588
http://www.prairie.org
Board Chair Arthur Sussman
Executive Kristina Valaitis

Indiana

Indiana Humanities Council
1500 N. Delaware St.
Indianapolis, IN 46202
317-638-1500, fax 317-634-9503
http://www.ihc4u.org
Board Chair Robert S. Kaspar
Executive Scott T. Massey

Iowa

Humanities Iowa
100 Oakdale Campus, Northlawn
University of Iowa
Iowa City, IA 52242-5000
319-335-4153, fax 319-335-4154
http://www.humanitiesiowa.org
Board Chair John C. Fitzpatrick
Executive Christopher Rossi

Kansas

Kansas Humanities Council
112 S.W. Sixth Ave., Suite 210
Topeka, KS 66603
785-357-0359, fax 785-357-1723
http://www.kansashumanities.org
Board Chair Judy Billings
Executive Marion Cott

Kentucky

Kentucky Humanities Council
206 E. Maxwell St.
Lexington, KY 40508
859-257-5932, fax 859-257-5933
http://www.kyhumanities.org
Board Chair James Parker
Executive Virginia Smith

Louisiana

Louisiana Endowment for the Humanities
938 Lafayette St., Suite 300
New Orleans, LA 70113-1027
504-523-4352, fax 504-529-2358
http://www.leh.org
Board Chair R. Lewis McHenry
Executive Michael Sartisky

Maine

Maine Humanities Council
674 Brighton Ave.
Portland, ME 04102-1012
207-773-5051, fax 207-773-2416
http://www.mainehumanities.org
Board Chair Marli Weiner
Executive Dorothy Schwartz

Maryland

Maryland Humanities Council
108 W. Centre St.,
Baltimore, MD 21201-4565
410-665-0095
http://www.mdhc.org
Board Chair Stanley C. Gabor
Executive Margaret Burke

Massachusetts

Massachusetts Foundation for the Humanities
66 Bridge St.
Northampton, MA 01060
413-584-8440, fax 413-584-8454
http://www.mfh.org
Board Chair John Dacey
Executive David Tebaldi

Michigan

Michigan Humanities Council
119 Pere Marquette Drive, Suite 3B
Lansing, MI 48912-1270
517-372-7770, fax 517-372-0027
http://michiganhumanities.org
Board Chair James McConnell
Executive Jan Fedewa

Minnesota

Minnesota Humanities Commission
987 East Ivy Ave.
St. Paul, MN 55106-2046

651-774-0105, fax 651-774-0205
http://www.minnesotahumanities.org
Board Chair Humphrey Doermann
Executive Stanley Romanstein

Mississippi

Mississippi Humanities Council
3825 Ridgewood Rd., Room 311
Jackson, MS 39211
601-432-6752, fax 601-432-6750
http://www.ihl.state.ms.us/mhc
Board Chair Willis Lott
Executive Barbara Carpenter

Missouri

Missouri Humanities Council
543 Hanley Industrial Court, Suite 201
St. Louis, MO 63144-1905
314-781-9660, fax 314-781-9681
http://www.mohumanities.org
Board Chair W. Nicholas Knight
Executive Michael Bouman

Montana

Montana Committee for the Humanities
311 Brantly Hall
University of Montana
Missoula, MT 59812-8214
406-243-6022, fax 406-243-4836
http://www.humanities-mt.org
Board Chair Jean Steele
Executive Mark Sherouse

Nebraska

Nebraska Humanities Council
Lincoln Center Bldg., Suite 500
215 Centennial Mall South
Lincoln, NE 68508
402-474-2131, fax 402-474-4852
http://www.nebraskahumanties.org
Board Chair Kit Dimon
Executive Jane Renner Hood

Nevada

Nevada Humanities Committee
1034 N. Sierra St.
Reno, NV 89507
775-784-6587, fax 775-784-6527
http://www.nevadahumanities.org

Board Chair Belinda Quilici
Executive Judith K. Winzeler

New Hampshire

New Hampshire Humanities Council
19 Pillsbury St.
P.O. Box 2228
Concord, NH 03302-2228
603-224-4071, fax 603-224-4072
http://www.nhhc.org
Board Chair Katherine Muirhead
Executive Deborah Watrous

New Jersey

New Jersey Council for the Humanities
28 W. State St.
Trenton, NJ 08608
609-695-4838, fax 609-695-4929
http://www.njch.org
Board Chair Zachary M. Narrett
Executive Jane Rutkoff

New Mexico

New Mexico Humanities Council
209 Onate Hall
University of New Mexico
Albuquerque, NM 87131
505-277-3705, fax 505-277-6056
http://www.nmeh.org
Board Chair Albert Westwood
Executive Craig Newbill

New York

New York Council for the Humanities
150 Broadway, Suite 1700
New York, NY 10038
212-233-1131, fax 212-233-4607
http://www.nyhumanities.org
Board Chair Donn Rogosin
Executive David Cronin

North Carolina

North Carolina Humanities Council
200 South Elm St., Suite 403
Greensboro, NC 27401
336-334-5325, fax 336-334-5052
http://www.nchumanities.org
Board Chair Lucinda H. MacKethan
Executive Douglas Quin

North Dakota

North Dakota Humanities Council
2900 Broadway East, Suite 3
P.O. Box 2191
Bismarck, ND 58502
701-255-3360, fax 701-223-8724
http://www.nd-humanities.org
Board Chair Lynn Davis
Executive Janet Daley

Ohio

Ohio Humanities Council
471 E. Broad St., Suite 1620
Columbus, OH 43215-3857
614-461-7802, fax 614-461-4651
http://www.ohiohumanities.org
Board Chair Allan Winkler
Executive Gale E. Peterson

Oklahoma

Oklahoma Humanities Council
Festival Plaza
428 W. California, Suite 270
Oklahoma City, OK 73102
405-235-0280, fax 405-235-0289
http://www.okhumanitiescouncil.org
Board Chair Ann Frankland
Executive Anita May

Oregon

Oregon Council for the Humanities
812 S.W. Washington St., Suite 225
Portland, OR 97205
503-241-0543, fax 503-241-0024
http://www.oregonhum.org
Board Chair Gene d'Autremont
Executive Christopher Zinn

Pennsylvania

Pennsylvania Humanities Council
325 Chestnut St., Suite 715
Philadelphia, PA 19106-2607
215-925-1005, fax 215-925-3054
http://www.pahumanities.org
Board Chair Michael A. Tomor
Executive Joseph Kelly

Rhode Island

Rhode Island Council for the Humanities
385 Westminster St., Suite 2
Providence, RI 02903
401-273-2250, fax 401-454-4872
http://www.rihumanities.org
Board Chair Eugene B. Mihaly
Executive Sara Archambault

South Carolina

Humanities Council of South Carolina
2711 Middleburg Drive, Suite 308
P.O. Box 5287
Columbia, SC 29254
803-771-2477, fax 803-771-2487
http://www.schumanities.org
Board Chair Byron E. Gipson
Executive Randy L. Akers

South Dakota

South Dakota Humanities Council
Box 7050, University Station
Brookings, SD 57007
605-688-6113, fax 605-688-4531
http://web.sdstate.edu/humanities
Board Chair John A. Lyons
Executive Donald Simmons

Tennessee

Humanities Tennessee
1003 18th Ave. South
Nashville, TN 37212
615-320-7001, fax 615-321-4586
http://tn-humanities.org
Board Chair Jane Walters
Executive Robert Cheatham

Texas

Texas Council for the Humanities
Banister Place A
3809 S. Second St.
Austin, TX 78704
512-440-1991, fax 512-440-0115
http://www.humanitiestexas.org
Board Chair Maceo C. Dailey, Jr.
Executive Michael Gillette

Utah

Utah Humanities Council
202 W. 300 North
Salt Lake City, UT 84103-1108
801-359-9670, fax 801-531-7869
http://www.utahhumanities.org
Board Chair Phillip Bimstein
Executive Cynthia Buckingham

Vermont

Vermont Humanities Council
11 Loomis St.
Montpelier, VT 05601
802-888-3183, fax 802-888-1236
http://www.vermonthumanities.org
Board Chair William E. Dakin, Jr.
Executive Peter A. Gilbert

Virginia

Virginia Foundation for the Humanities and
    Public Policy
145 Ednam Drive
Charlottesville, VA 22903-4629
434-924-3296, fax 434-296-4714
http://www.virginia.edu/vfh
Board Chair Elizabeth L. Young
Executive Robert C. Vaughan

Washington

Humanities Washington
615 Second Ave., Suite 300
Seattle, WA 98104
206-682-1770, fax 206-682-4158
http://www.humanities.org
Board Chair Maureen Herward
Executive Margaret Ann Bollmeier

West Virginia

West Virginia Humanities Council
1310 Kanawha Blvd. East
Charleston, WV 25301
304-346-8500, fax 304-346-8504
http://www.wvhumanities.org
Board Chair Jill Wilson
Executive Kenneth Sullivan

Wisconsin

Wisconsin Humanities Council
222 South Bedford St., Suite F
Madison, WI 53703-3688
608-262-0706, fax 608-263-7970
http://www.wisconsinhumanities.org
Board Chair Paul Boyer
Executive Dean Bakopoulos

Wyoming

Wyoming Council for the Humanities
1315 E. Lewis St.
Laramie, WY 82072-3459
307-721-9244, fax 307-742-4914
http://www.uwyo.edu/special/wch
Board Chair Audrey Shalinksky
Executive Marcia Britton

American Samoa

Amerika Samoa Humanities Council
P.O. Box 5800
Pago Pago, AS 96799
684-633-4870, fax 684-633-4873
http://www.ashumanities.org
Board Chair Fonoti Savali Vaeao
Executive Niualama Taifane

Guam

Guam Humanities Council
Bank of Guam Headquarters Bldg., Suite 711
111 Chalan Santo Papa
Hagatna, Guam 96910
671-646-4460, fax 671-472-4465
http://www.guamhumanitiescouncil.org
Board Chair Nick Goetzfridt
Executive Jillette Leon-Guerrero

Northern Mariana Islands

Northern Mariana Islands Council for the
    Humanities
P.O. Box 506437
Saipan, MP 96950
670-235-4785, fax 670-235-4786
http://cnmi.humanities.org.mp
Board Chair Elizabeth D. Rechebei
Executive Paz C. Younis

Puerto Rico

Fundación Puertorriqueña de las Humanidades
109 San Jose St., 3rd floor
Box 9023920
San Juan, PR 00902-3920
787-721-2087, fax 787-721-2684
http://www.fprh.org
Board Chair Miquel Rodriguez
Executive Juan M. González Lamela

Virgin Islands

Virgin Islands Humanities Council
1826 Kongens Gade 5-6, Suite 2
St. Thomas, VI 00802
340-776-4044, fax 340-774-3972
http://www.vihumanities.org
Board Chair Roberta Q. Knowles
Executive Mabel J. Maduro

NEH Overview

Division of Preservation and Access

Grants are made for projects that will create, preserve, and increase the availability of resources important for research, education, and public programming in the humanities.

Projects may encompass books, journals, newspapers, manuscript and archival materials, maps, still and moving images, sound recordings, and objects of material culture held by libraries, archives, museums, historical organizations, and other repositories.

Preservation and Access Projects

Support may be sought to preserve the intellectual content and aid bibliographic control of collections; to compile bibliographies, descriptive catalogs, and guides to cultural holdings; to create dictionaries, encyclopedias, databases, and other types of research tools and reference works; and to stabilize material culture collections through the appropriate housing and storing of objects, improved environmental control, and the installation of security, lighting, and fire-prevention systems. Applications may also be submitted for national and regional education and training projects, regional preservation field service programs, and research and demonstration projects that are intended to enhance institutional practice and the use of technology for preservation and access.

Proposals may combine preservation and access activities within a single project. Historically Black Colleges and Universities (HBCUs) with significant institutional collections of primary materials are encouraged to apply.

Eligible applicants: Individuals, nonprofit institutions and cultural organizations, state agencies, and institutional consortia

Application deadlines: May 16, July 1, July 15, and October 3, 2005

Contact: 202-606-8570, e-mail preservation@neh.gov

Division of Public Programs

This division fosters public understanding and appreciation of the humanities by supporting projects that bring significant insights into these disciplines to general audiences of all ages through interpretive exhibitions, radio and television programs, lectures, symposia, multimedia projects, printed materials, and reading and discussion groups.

Grants support consultation with scholars and humanities programming experts to shape an interpretive project; the planning and production of television and radio programs in the humanities intended for general audiences; the planning and implementation of exhibitions, the interpretation of historic sites, and the production of related publications, multimedia components, and educational programs; and the planning and implementation of projects through the use of books, new technologies, and other resources in the collections of libraries and archives in formats such as reading and discussion programs, lectures, symposia, and interpretive exhibitions of books, manuscripts, and other library resources.

Eligible applicants:	Nonprofit institutions and organizations including public television and radio stations and state humanities councils
Application deadlines:	Planning, scripting, implementation, production, February 3, March 22, September 16, and November 3, 2005; Consultation grants, March 22 and September 16, 2005.
Contact:	202-606-8269, e-mail publicpgms@neh.gov

Division of Research Programs

The Division of Research Programs contributes to the creation of knowledge in the humanities through fellowships to individual scholars and grants to support complex, frequently collaborative research.

Fellowships and Stipends

Grants provide support for scholars to undertake full-time independent research and writing in the humanities. Grants are available for a maximum of one year and a minimum of two months of summer study.

Eligible applicants:	Individuals
Application deadlines:	Fellowships, May 1, 2005; Summer Stipends, October 1, 2005
Contact:	202-606-8200 for Fellowships, 202-606-8551 for Summer Stipends, e-mail fellowships@neh.gov, stipends@neh.gov

Research

Grants provide up to three years of support for collaborative research in the preparation for publication of editions, translations, and other important works in the humanities, and in the conduct of large or complex interpretive studies including archaeology projects and humanities studies of science and technology. Grants also support research opportunities offered through independent research centers and international research organizations.

Eligible Applicants:	Individuals, institutions of higher education, non-profit professional associations, scholarly societies, and other nonprofit organizations
Application deadlines:	Collaborative Research, November 1, 2005; Fellowships at Independent Research Institutions, September 1, 2005
Contact:	202-606-8200, e-mail research@neh.gov

Division of Education

Through grants to educational institutions, fellowships to scholars and teachers, and through the support of significant research, this division is designed to strengthen sustained, thoughtful study of the humanities at all levels of education.

Grants support curriculum and materials development efforts; faculty study programs within and among educational institutions; and conferences and networks of institutions. NEH is interested in projects that help teachers use electronic technologies to enhance students' understanding of humanities subjects.

Eligible applicants:	Public and private elementary and secondary schools, school systems, colleges and universities, nonprofit academic associations, and cultural institutions, such as libraries and museums
Application deadlines:	Grants for Teaching and Learning Resources and Curriculum Development, October 3, 2005; Institutional Grants for Historically Black, Hispanic-Serving, and Tribal Colleges and Universities, June 15, 2005; Landmarks of American History: Workshops for School Teachers, August 5, 2005
Contact:	202-606-8500, e-mail education@neh.gov

Seminars and Institutes

Grants support summer seminars and national institutes in the humanities for college and school teachers. These faculty development activities are conducted at colleges and universities across the country. Those wishing to participate in seminars submit their applications to the seminar director.

Eligibility:	Individuals, and institutions of higher learning
Application deadlines:	Participants, March 1, 2005, for summer seminars and institutes in 2005; Directors, March 1, 2005, for summer seminars in 2006
Contact:	202-606-8463, e-mail sem-inst@neh.gov

Office of Challenge Grants

Nonprofit institutions interested in developing new sources of long-term support for educational, scholarly, preservation, and public programs in the humanities can be assisted in these efforts by an NEH Challenge Grant. Grantees are required to raise three or four dollars in new or increased donations for every federal dollar offered. Both federal and nonfederal funds may be used to establish or increase institutional endowments and thus guarantee long-term support for a variety of humanities needs. Funds may also be used for limited direct capital expenditures, where such needs are compelling and clearly related to improvements in the humanities.

Eligible applicants:	Nonprofit postsecondary educational, research, or cultural institutions and organizations working within the humanities
Application deadlines:	February 1, May 2, and November 1, 2005
Contact:	202-606-8309, e-mail challenge@neh.gov

Institute of Museum and Library Services Library Programs

1100 Pennsylvania Ave. N.W., Washington, DC 20506
202-606-5527, fax 202-606-1077
World Wide Web http://www.imls.gov

Robert S. Martin
Director

The Library Services and Technology Act (LSTA), Subchapter II of the Museum and Library Services Act of 1996, changed the federal administration of library programs by moving programs from the U.S. Department of Education to the newly formed Institute of Museum and Library Services (IMLS). The first LSTA grants were made in 1998. A total of $198,243,000 was available for library programs in fiscal year (FY) 2004.

The Museum and Library Services Act was reauthorized in September 2003. The reauthorization updates the purposes of LSTA and makes other technical changes to the law to revise the formula for grants to states and create a National Museum and Library Services Board to provide policy advice to the IMLS director.

The purposes of LSTA are

- To consolidate federal library service programs
- To promote improvement in library services in all types of libraries to better serve the people of the United States
- To facilitate access to resources in all types of libraries
- To cultivate an educated and informed citizenry
- To encourage resource sharing among all types of libraries for the purpose of achieving economical and efficient delivery of library services to the public

Within IMLS, the Office of Library Services is responsible for the administration of LSTA. It comprises the Division of State Programs, which administers the Grants to States program, and the Division of Discretionary Programs, which administers the National Leadership Grants program, the Librarians for the 21st Century program, the Native American Library Services program, and the Native Hawaiian Library Services program. Additionally, annual awards are made to libraries through the National Awards for Museum and Library Service program.

State-Administered Programs

In FY 2004 approximately 80 percent of the annual federal appropriation under LSTA was distributed through the Grants to States program to the state library administrative agencies according to a population-based formula. The formula consists of a minimum amount set by the law plus a supplemental amount based on population. The 2003 reauthorization requires that base allotments of $340,000 to the states and $40,000 to the Pacific Territories be increased to

$680,000 for the states and $60,000 for the Pacific Territories. The new base allotments will be phased in gradually as the total appropriation increases. For 2004 the adjusted base allotment to the states was $478,327; that for the Pacific Territories remained the same.

For 2004 the Grants to States program total appropriation was $157,628,000 (see Table 1). State agencies may use the appropriation for statewide initiatives and services. They may also distribute the funds through competitive subgrants or cooperative agreements to public, academic, research, school, or special libraries. For-profit and federal libraries are not eligible applicants. LSTA State Grant funds have been used to meet the special needs of children, parents, teenagers, the unemployed, senior citizens, and the business community, as well as adult learners. Many libraries have partnered with community organizations to provide a variety of services and programs, including access to electronic databases, computer instruction, homework centers, summer reading programs, digitization of special collections, access to E-books and adaptive technology, bookmobile service, and development of outreach programs to the underserved. The act limits the amount of funds available for administration at the state level to 4 percent and requires a 34 percent match from nonfederal state or local funds.

Grants to the Pacific Territories and Freely Associated States (FAS) are funded under a Special Rule (20 USCA 9131(b)(3)) that authorizes a small competitive grants program in the Pacific. There are six eligible entities in two groups: the Pacific Territories (Insular areas) consisting of Guam, American Samoa, and the Commonwealth of Northern Mariana Islands; and the FAS, which include the Federated States of Micronesia, the Republic of the Marshall Islands, and the Republic of Palau. The funds for this grant program are taken from the allotments for the FAS, but not from the allotments to the territories. The three territories (Guam, American Samoa, and the Commonwealth of Northern Mariana Islands) receive their allotments through the regular program and, in addition, may apply for funds under this program. Five entities (American Samoa, Guam, Commonwealth of Northern Mariana Islands, Federated States of Micronesia, and Republic of the Marshall Islands) received a total of $216,389 in FY 2004. This amount included a set-aside of 5 percent because Pacific Resources for Education and Learning (PREL), based in Hawaii, facilitated the competition. PREL received the set-aside amount to administer parts of the program.

Priorities for funding that support the goals of LSTA are set by the individual state library administrative agencies (SLAAs) based on needs they identify in the five-year plans they are required to submit to IMLS.

Discretionary Programs

In 1998 IMLS began administering the discretionary programs of LSTA. In FY 2004 a total of $40,935,921 was allocated for the National Leadership Grants program, the Librarians for the 21st Century program, the Native American Library Services program, and the Native Hawaiian Library Services program (this figure includes up to $1 million from the IMLS Office of Museum Services to supplement LSTA funding for library and museum collaborations). The total figure includes $6,584,921 in congressionally directed grants.

The FY 2004 congressional appropriation for discretionary programs includes

- National Leadership Grants: $11,263,000
- Librarians for the 21st Century: $19,882,000
- Native American Library Services: $2,726,053
- Native Hawaiian Library Services: $479,947

The National Leadership Grants program provides funding for innovative model programs to enhance the quality of library services nationwide. National Leadership Grants are competitive and intended to produce results useful for the broader library community.

The Librarians for the 21st Century program provides competitive funding to support projects to recruit and educate the next generation of librarians and library leaders, to build institutional capacity in graduate schools of library and information science and develop faculty who will help in this endeavor, and to conduct needed research on the demographics and needs of the profession.

The Native American Library Services program provides opportunities for improved library services for Native American communities, including three types of support to serve Indian tribes and Alaska Native villages.

The Native Hawaiian Library Services program provides opportunities for improved library services to Native Hawaiians.

National Leadership Grants Program

In 2004 IMLS awarded 37 grants totaling $11,913,674 for National Leadership Grants. A total of 154 applications requesting $44,040,052 were received. The projects funded were selected as innovative model projects in the field of library and information science in continuing education and training, library and museum collaborations, preservation and digitization of library resources, and research and demonstration (see Table 2).

The FY 2004 priorities in the four categories of National Leadership Grants funding are described below.

Continuing Education and Training. Supports model programs of continuing education and training in library and information science; includes retention issues as well as intended learning outcomes. Priorities were

- Projects that implement innovative approaches to continuing or specialized education for current librarians and library staff
- Projects that train librarians and library staff to enhance people's ability to find, evaluate, and use information effectively
- Projects that improve the ability of librarians to design and conduct research
- Projects that improve the ability of librarians to create, manage, and preserve digital libraries
- Projects to prepare librarians for professional leadership

Library and Museum Collaborations. Supports innovative projects that model how libraries and museums of all types can work together and with other organizations to expand their services to the public. Priorities were

- Projects that help museums and libraries take a leadership role in building community partnerships to support the development of learning communities
- Projects that develop, document, evaluate, and disseminate model programs of cooperation between libraries and museums
- Research projects that enhance interoperability, integration, and seamless access to digital library and museum resources, particularly projects that are of statewide, regional, thematic, or national scope
- Research projects that develop innovative approaches to the use of broadband technologies for learning
- Research projects that address knowledge integration, digital preservation, or the integration of physical and digital experiences

Preservation or Digitization. Supports model programs to help preserve library resources, to develop model projects and best practices for digitization, and to digitize collections of national value. Priorities were

- Projects that preserve and enhance access to valuable library resources useful to the broader community and that foster the development of learning communities
- Projects that address the challenges of preserving and archiving digital media
- Projects that demonstrate and evaluate the feasibility of collaborative approaches to managing and preserving digital resources, and that are statewide, regional, thematic, or national in scope

Research and Demonstration. Supports research in library science and demonstration projects to test potential solutions to problems. Priorities were

- Projects that conduct research and/or demonstrations to enhance the individual's ability to make more effective use of information resources
- Projects that conduct research and/or demonstrations to enhance library services through the effective and efficient use of new and appropriate technologies
- Collaborative projects that lead to the development of new standards for library services
- Projects that collect data and conduct research on libraries and library services and their effects on users
- Projects that conduct research on users' information needs, expectations, and results, including user studies, usability studies, and outcomes
- Research projects that address knowledge integration, digital preservation, or the integration of physical and digital experiences

Partnership for a Nation of Learners

In September 2004 IMLS and the Corporation for Public Broadcasting created the Partnership for a Nation of Learners, a joint initiative to build and strengthen working relationships among libraries, museums, and public broadcasting licensees that enhance their roles within their communities. The partnership includes a pilot competitive grant program, a professional development curriculum, and a Web site (http://www.partnershipforlearners.org) that will serve as the project's "knowledge commons." Grants ranging from $25,000 to $250,000 will be awarded in 2005 and 2006 to collaborative projects involving a public broadcasting licensee (radio or television) and a museum and/or library.

Librarians for the 21st Century Program

In 2004 IMLS awarded 27 grants totaling $15,784,912 for the Librarians for the 21st Century program using FY 2004 funding (see Table 3). A total of 64 applications requesting $34,218,886 were received.

The FY 2004 priorities for Librarians for the 21st Century grant funding were

- *Priority 1, Master's Level Programs:* Educate the next generation of librarians. In particular, increase the number of students enrolled in nationally accredited graduate library programs preparing for careers of service in libraries.
- *Priority 2, Doctoral Programs:* Develop faculty to educate the next generation of library professionals. In particular, increase the number of students enrolled in doctoral programs that will prepare faculty to teach master's students who will work in school, public, and academic libraries. Develop the next generation of library leaders. In particular, increase the number of students enrolled in doctoral programs that will prepare them to assume positions as library managers and administrators.
- *Priority 3, Pre-Professional Programs:* Recruit future librarians. In particular, attract promising high school and college students to consider careers in librarianship through recruitment strategies that are cost-effective and measurable.
- *Priority 4, Research:* Provide the library community with information needed to support successful recruitment and education of the next generation of librarians. In particular, through funded research, establish baseline data on professional demographics and job availability, and evaluate current programs in library education for their capacity to meet the identified needs.
- *Priority 5, Programs to Build Institutional Capacity:* Develop or enhance curricula within graduate schools of library and information science. In particular, develop new courses and programs in such critical areas as leadership, research methods, and digital librarianship.

Native American Library Services Program

In 2004 IMLS distributed $2,726,053 in grants for American Indian tribes and Alaska Native villages.

The Native American Library Services Program provides opportunities for the improvement of library services to Indian tribes and Alaska Native villages, the latter coming under the definition of eligible Indian tribes as recognized by the secretary of the interior. The program offers three types of support:

- Basic library services grants in the amount of $4,000, which support core library operations on a noncompetitive basis for all eligible Indian tribes and Alaska Native villages that apply for such support. IMLS awarded basic grants to 222 tribes in 26 states in 2004.
- Professional assistance grants in the amount of $2,000, which heighten the level of professional proficiency of tribal library staff. It is a noncompetitive program to support assessments of library services and provide advice for improvement. IMLS awarded professional assistance grants to 59 tribes in 15 states in 2004.
- Enhancement grants, which support new levels of library service for activities specifically identified under LSTA. In 2004 these competitive awards ranged from $21,585 to $150,000. Of the 41 applications received, IMLS awarded 14 enhancement grants for a total of $1,720,053 (see Table 4).

Native Hawaiian Library Services Program

The Native Hawaiian Library Services Program provides opportunities for improved library services for an important part of the nation's community of library users through grants to nonprofit organizations that primarily serve and represent Native Hawaiians, as the term "Native Hawaiian" is defined in section 7207 of the Native Hawaiian Education Act (20 U.S.C. 7517). In 2004 a single Native Hawaiian Library Services Grant was awarded to Alu Like, Inc. of Honolulu in the amount of $479,947.

National Awards for Museum and Library Service

The National Award for Library Service was first awarded in FY 2000. It honors outstanding American libraries that have made a significant and exceptional contribution to their communities. It seeks to recognize libraries that demonstrate extraordinary and innovative approaches to public service; libraries that reach beyond the expected levels of community outreach and core programs generally associated with library services. The principal criterion for selection is evidence of the library's systematic and ongoing commitment to public service through exemplary and innovative programs and community partnerships. Information about the award and upcoming deadlines appear on the IMLS Web site.

The winners received their awards from First Lady Laura Bush at a White House ceremony on January 22, 2004. In addition, for the first time since their inception, the winning institutions also each received $10,000. The winners of the 2003 National Awards for Library and Museum Service were Bozeman (Montana) Public Library; Carnegie Science Center, Pittsburgh; Free Library of Philadelphia; Pocahontas County (West Virginia) Free Libraries; San Angelo (Texas) Museum of Fine Arts; and the *USS Constitution* Museum, Boston.

Evaluation of IMLS Programs

IMLS has taken a leadership role in evaluating the value of its programs through incorporating outcomes-based measurement as a tool to document effectiveness of funded projects. Within the state-administered programs, IMLS continued to provide training in outcomes-based evaluation (OBE). LSTA requires that each state library administrative agency independently evaluate its LSTA activities before the end of the state LSTA five-year plan. In addition, IMLS continues to train all new National Leadership Grants and Librarians for the 21st Century grants recipients in OBE and to present information about evaluation at state, regional, and national professional meetings.

To ensure that it is meeting current public and professional needs in library services, IMLS routinely seeks advice from diverse representatives of the library community, carries out studies of library practice, and evaluates its programs with the assistance of external consultants.

IMLS Conferences and Activities

The 2004 IMLS Web-Wise Conference on Libraries and Museums in the Digital World was held March 3–5 in Chicago. The cohost was the University of Illinois at Chicago, and the theme was Sharing Digital Resources. More than 300 participants representing all types of museums and libraries as well as educators and systems scientists from across the country and the world attended the annual event. Two preconference sessions provided overviews of the Open Archives Initiative Protocol for Metadata Harvesting and of digital preservation. A webcast of conference highlights appears on the IMLS Web site (http://www.imls. gov/pubs/webwise2004/wbws04.htm), and selected conference papers were published in the online peer-reviewed journal *First Monday* (http://www.firstmonday. org/issues/issue9_5).

IMLS hosted a workshop dedicated to defining new relationships and future possibilities for libraries, museums, and K–12 education. The workshop, Charting the Landscape/Mapping New Paths, focused on K–12 education as a foundation for lifelong learning and full participation in family, community, work, and society. Participants in the August 30–31 workshop explored ways in which libraries, museums, schools, and other institutions can work together effectively to fulfill the responsibility for learning that belongs to the entire community. Conference materials are available on the IMLS Web site at http://www.imls. gov/pubs/chartingthelandscape/index.htm.

IMLS participated in the fourth annual National Book Festival, presented in Washington, D.C., by the Library of Congress. The festival took place on the National Mall on October 9. IMLS was a charter sponsor of the event, supporting the Pavilion of the States, which featured representatives from library agencies from the 50 states, the District of Columbia, and U.S. territories.

November 8–10 IMLS presented Learning States, its annual conference for state library administrative agencies (SLAAs). This year's focus was on developing and implementing improved methods for sharing useful information among the SLAAs from all the states and U.S. territories.

IMLS Web Site and Publications

The IMLS Web site provides information on the various grant programs, national awards for library and museum service, and projects funded, along with application forms and staff contacts. The Web site also highlights model projects developed by libraries and museums throughout the country. Through an electronic newsletter, *Primary Source,* IMLS provides timely information on grant deadlines and opportunities. Details on subscribing to the IMLS newsletter are located on the Web site.

The following recent publications are available on the Web site: *2005 Grant and Award Program Brochure*; *Towards Equality of Access: The Role of Public Libraries in Addressing the Digital Divide*; *The Status of Technology and Digitization in the Nation's Museums and Libraries 2002 Report*; and *Sustaining Our Heritage—Commemorating the 25th Anniversary of the Museum Services Act*.

In 2003 IMLS signed a memorandum of understanding with the National Information Standards Organization (NISO) for maintenance of its Framework of Guidance for Building Good Digital Collections, produced by the IMLS Digital Library Forum. The framework, which was updated by NISO in 2004, is also available on the IMLS Web site.

Table 1 / **Library Services and Technology Act, State Allotment Table, FY 2004**
Total Distributed to States: $157,628,000[1]

State	Federal Funds from IMLS (66%)[2]	State Matching Funds (34%)	Total Federal and State Funds
Alabama	$2,507,472	$1,291,728	$3,799,200
Alaska	769,497	396,408	1,165,905
Arizona	2,946,156	1,517,717	4,463,873
Arkansas	1,704,034	877,836	2,581,870
California	16,360,507	8,428,140	24,788,647
Colorado	2,516,533	1,296,396	3,812,929
Connecticut	2,043,433	1,052,678	3,096,111
Delaware	843,489	434,525	1,278,014
Florida	8,037,303	4,140,429	12,177,732
Georgia	4,349,960	2,240,888	6,590,848
Hawaii	1,041,366	536,461	1,577,827
Idaho	1,084,890	558,883	1,643,773
Illinois	6,177,300	3,182,245	9,359,545
Indiana	3,263,933	1,681,420	4,945,353
Iowa	1,806,556	930,650	2,737,206
Kansas	1,706,659	879,188	2,585,847
Kentucky	2,329,448	1,200,019	3,529,467
Louisiana	2,505,725	1,290,828	3,796,553
Maine	1,063,783	548,009	1,611,792
Maryland	2,946,918	1,518,109	4,465,027
Massachusetts	3,385,475	1,744,033	5,129,508
Michigan	5,023,914	2,588,077	7,611,991
Minnesota	2,748,632	1,415,962	4,164,594
Mississippi	1,777,168	915,511	2,692,679
Missouri	3,043,905	1,568,072	4,611,977
Montana	889,652	458,306	1,347,958
Nebraska	1,260,396	649,295	1,909,691

Table 1 / Library Services and Technology Act, State Allotment Table, FY 2004 *(cont.)*

Nevada	1,461,347	752,815	2,214,162
New Hampshire	1,055,006	543,488	1,598,494
New Jersey	4,363,523	2,247,875	6,611,398
New Mexico	1,317,328	678,624	1,995,952
New York	9,142,841	4,709,948	13,852,789
North Carolina	4,241,339	2,184,932	6,426,271
North Dakota	765,120	394,153	1,159,273
Ohio	5,643,905	2,907,466	8,551,371
Oklahoma	2,058,454	1,060,416	3,118,870
Oregon	2,071,028	1,066,893	3,137,921
Pennsylvania	6,057,207	3,120,379	9,177,586
Rhode Island	962,139	495,647	1,457,786
South Carolina	2,335,912	1,203,349	3,539,261
South Dakota	822,538	423,732	1,246,270
Tennessee	3,100,308	1,597,128	4,697,436
Texas	10,328,875	5,320,936	15,649,811
Utah	1,525,917	786,078	2,311,995
Vermont	757,197	390,071	1,147,268
Virginia	3,777,029	1,945,742	5,722,771
Washington	3,223,195	1,660,434	4,883,629
West Virginia	1,293,273	666,232	1,959,505
Wisconsin	2,939,256	1,514,162	4,453,418
Wyoming	703,879	362,604	1,066,483
District of Columbia	736,531	379,425	1,115,956
Puerto Rico	2,235,820	1,151,786	3,387,606
American Samoa	71,777	36,976	108,753
Northern Marianas	76,184	39,246	115,430
Guam	114,146	58,802	172,948
Virgin Islands	96,433	49,678	146,111
Pacific Territories[3]	216,389	111,473	327,862
Total	$157,628,000	$81,202,303	$238,830,303

1 The amount available to states is based on the balance remaining after enacted allocations have been subtracted from the total appropriation as follows:

LIBRARY ALLOCATION, FY 2004	$206,119,000 P.L.108-199
Native Americans	$3,206,000
National Leadership	$39,022,000
Administration	$6,263,000
Total Distributed to States	$157,628,000

2 Calculation is based on the minimum set in the law (P.L. 108-81) and reflects appropriations enacted by P.L. 108-199. Population data are from the Bureau of Census (BOC) estimates. Data used in the state allotment table will be the most current published population estimates available the first day of the fiscal year. Therefore, the population data used in the 2004 table are what was available on the BOC Web site http://eire.census.gov/popest/data/states/tables/ on October 1, 2003.

3 Aggregate allotments (including administrative costs) for Palau, Marshall Islands, and Micronesia are awarded on a competitive basis to eligible applicants, and are administered by Pacific Resources for Education and Learning (PREL).

Table 2 / National Leadership Grants, FY 2004

Education and Training

Cornell University Library $269,630

Cornell will train 12 qualified Native Americans to help establish and maintain preservation programs in institutions within their regions. The program will prepare the interns to train other librarians, archivists, and technicians in preservation basics through workshops, seminars, on-site surveys, simulations, needs assessments, and the establishment of a regional

Table 2 / National Leadership Grants, FY 2004 (cont.)

disaster plan and response capability. This training will enable Native American tribal colleges to greatly extend the life of their cultural heritage materials, to conduct studies of their collections and services, and to prepare viable proposals for external grant funding to support Native American collections.

Illinois State Library $500,000

This program will develop, test, and implement a library leadership program to promote greater understanding and appreciation of the world community in which librarians work. The Illinois State Library will partner with the University of Illinois at Urbana-Champaign's Mortenson Center for International Library Programs to bring together Illinois librarians who have participated in the Illinois State Library's Synergy program and a group of librarians from among the 76 countries with which the Mortenson Center works. They will work together in a two-year leadership training program that includes negotiations, empowerment, fund raising, and advocacy. In a second phase, the Illinois State Library will work with the Mortenson Center to extend the training program to a group of mid-career librarians from Mexico who will interact with librarians from around the United States.

Online Computer Library Center/WebJunction $249,200

The Online Computer Library Center (OCLC) will develop a national clearinghouse for library education and training opportunities, to be hosted and maintained by WebJunction. In this Phase I project, OCLC will develop the technical infrastructure for the clearinghouse, establish procedures for contributing content and maintaining currency, and populate the clearinghouse with course information from American Library Association-accredited library schools. This will provide the infrastructure for later development of a searchable database of information about for-credit and not-for-credit digital courses offered by library schools, as well as library-specific scholarships and continuing education grants; and provide information about digital training modules available through library schools, state library agencies, and OCLC regional networks.

Library and Museum Collaborations

Athens-Clarke County (Georgia) Library $260,030

This library-museum partnership with the Lyndon House Arts Center builds upon each organization's earlier efforts to better serve the local Mexican American community via educational and cultural programs. The project is structured around three main goals: (1) to improve the educational level of the immigrant Mexican population through extensive outreach initiatives (among them establishing a Community Learning Center in conjunction with the Georgia Public Library Service, conducting family literacy programs and language classes, and establishing a distance education program for primary and secondary school diplomas, vocational training, and English instruction); (2) to increase use of library and arts center facilities by the Mexican American community through targeted in-house programming, collection development, and staff training that includes an advisory panel of community resource people to assist with program development and implementation, Spanish-language training for staff, and the improvement of the number of Spanish-language resources; and (3) to provide opportunities for educational and cultural exchange between the new Mexican community and the established community, nurturing understanding by matching Mexican American and Athens families for shared educational and cultural activities through the establishment of a "sister city" relationship with a library and museum in Mexico.

Berkeley (California) Art Museum and Pacific Film Archive $238,787

The Museums and Online Archives Collaboration Community Toolbox will develop a software tool that enables production and sharing of standards-based content and will distribute this tool to cultural organizations through a "community toolbox" Web site. This software tool will allow museums and libraries to produce standards-based data for broad content sharing. The project will also test the effectiveness of the tool for broad content sharing by working with multiple museums to distribute digital content to several national content gateways and will share tools freely with the cultural heritage community.

Table 2 / National Leadership Grants, FY 2004 (cont.)

Boston Public Library $500,000

The Boston Public Library will develop a sustainable partnership with the Museum of Afro-American History, using the upcoming 200th anniversary of the birth of abolitionist William Lloyd Garrison (2005) and the bicentennial of the African Meeting House in Boston (2006) as focal points for exhibits. The goals of "Intersections" are to demonstrate that an overlapping area in collections can lead partners to collaborative programming that will increase the capacity of both institutions to address their missions; to create learning opportunities that illuminate the Abolitionist Movement in New England and to attract audiences to understand it in new ways; and to disseminate information about Intersections that shows how it has addressed current library/museum issues, offers assistance to other museums and libraries in using the project model, and describes a vision for potential change in the field. Major activities include developing and implementing collaborative management, marketing, program evaluation, and plans; mounting three exhibits celebrating William Lloyd Garrison and the African Meeting House; developing, maintaining, and refreshing a Web site that will serve as an online version of the exhibits; and engaging in educational outreach through a downloadable Web-based teacher's guide that is integrated with curriculum standards.

Broome-Tioga BOCES Library Media Services, Binghamton, New York $249,122

Broome-Tioga BOCES Library Media Services' partnership with Roberson Museum and 12 regional school districts will meet the character-education needs curriculum while enhancing standards-based approaches to middle school social studies, literacy, fine arts, and technology integration. Partners will develop and share a middle school character-education curriculum grounded in the region's culture and history; expand learning experiences through use of community resources and technological tools; strengthen curriculum collaboration between area teachers and library/media professionals; increase student commitment to tolerance, acceptance, and respect through participatory learning experiences; and develop a cadre of educational professionals skilled in the integration of character education into core curriculum content areas. Using the New York State Voices and Visions curriculum as a template, a team of classroom teachers, consultants, museum professionals, and library media specialists will shape the focus for older children, integrating core curricular instruction through strategies such as library-based mini-exhibits, performances, Web quests, museum visits, and reflective interpretations to create a national model for a middle school character-education curriculum.

Cleveland Museum of Art $500,000

This application proposes a new model for unleashing the power of the exceptional raw materials held by one museum, the Cleveland Museum of Art, and one library system, the Cuyahoga County (Ohio) Public Library, through a unique partnership. It will create dynamic learning communities, connected by a high-speed public network, that will develop new paradigms for education (both formal and informal), social engagement, and a replicable model for national museum and library collaborations. It will also create "knowledge networks" that access and combine the rich digital media of the institutions and allow them to be blended with the thoughts and resources of the targeted populations, and will use high-resolution video teleconferencing, shared access to intellectual assets such as images and documents, and Web-based community-building software to create a "wrapper of social interactivity" around the resources and communities.

Cornell University Library $499,710

The library, in partnership with Cornell's College of Engineering and the Museum of Science in Boston, will research and develop the use of stereolithographic ("3D printing") technology to create working physical replicas of mechanical artifacts that can then be exchanged electronically between the project partners and manipulated by museum visitors, students, and other users of the collection. The project will integrate an important set of mechanical models from the museum's holdings and create an adaptable program of educational activities and materials to enhance access to the museum's and the library's materials for the general museum public, middle school students, teachers, and university communities. Results will be incorporated into the development of learning standards. The proposed project investi-

Table 2 / National Leadership Grants, FY 2004 *(cont.)*

gates these questions: What are the effects on learning of the integration of digital and physical experiences provided by historical mechanical artifacts, 3D-printed machines, and computer simulation? What different types of learning experiences do users have using printed machines in the museum and classroom settings? Are different types of learning better suited to one or the other of the two distinct contexts? What terminology, descriptive protocols, and asset management practices will enable original artifacts, digital representations, and printed machines to be accurately and appropriately found, accessed, and utilized by users within a library environment?

Eastern Iowa Community College District $247,214

The Advanced Technology Environmental Education Center of the Eastern Iowa Community College District will partner with the Davenport Public Library, the Family Museum of Arts and Science, the Mississippi Bend Area Education Agency, local school districts, MidAmerican Energy Company, and the National Renewable Energy Laboratory to develop a working model of collaboration called "Watts Up with Energy" that will produce learning modules in the area of energy to bring math and science into the hands of elementary students through the study of the environment. It will produce four Web-based learning modules related to energy topics for elementary students. Museum displays will be developed around these modules, and a platform Web site will be developed. Project outcomes and research results will be tested and evaluated.

Fort Worth (Texas) Public Library $233,619

The MUSE project, a collaborative effort of the Fort Worth Public Library, the Forth Worth Public School system, members of the Tarrant County Storyteller's Guild, and the staff of several major arts organizations in Fort Worth (including the National Cowgirl Museum and Hall of Fame, the Log Cabin Village, the Cattle Raisers Museum, and Imagination Celebration) will give local students an introduction to the richness of local history by teaching them how to tell their own stories about the historical objects and art locally available. Student participants will learn about history from library research and observation of museum artifacts. They will receive schoolroom instruction from storytellers-in-residence about how to tell stories and will have the opportunity to present their stories in a public event at the close of the school year. MUSE will foster collaboration among these local institutions by developing a storytelling model that can be used to share the heritage and culture of this community with others. Newspapers in Education, Inc., will produce and distribute a storytelling supplement to 350 area schools.

Green Hill Center for North Carolina Art $224,154

The Green Hill Center for North Carolina Art and the Greensboro Public Library will infuse art into the programming of a 15,000-square-foot new branch in an ethnically diverse community. This will create a branch library where art and literature are seamlessly integrated to promote learning, art appreciation, and opportunities for creative expression. Project activities include active programs for children, art to promote emergent literacy, workshops for daycare workers and parents, a resource center, a teen program, and an artist residency.

Indiana University Libraries $343,437

Indiana University Libraries, with the Indiana State Museum, the Indiana Historical Society, and the Indiana State Library, will create an online sheet music collection showing how museums and libraries with complementary materials can work cooperatively to create shared digital resources. By concentrating initially on the collections of American sheet music owned by each of the partners, it will (1) demonstrate how materials and their attendant metadata—in this case, approximately 10,000 digitized pieces of sheet music and the information used to describe them—can be presented on a single Web site, offering federated searching of all collections or access to one or more selected collections, and (2) show how collaborative digital library development can provide online access to the important regional collections of museums, libraries, and historical societies. These collections may be sheet music; important materials in other formats, such as photographs, maps, and manu-

Table 2 / National Leadership Grants, FY 2004 *(cont.)*

scripts; or artifacts. This project will be the first library/museum partnership to digitize and create metadata for sheet music.

Michigan State University Museum $495,996

Building on a successful pilot phase, this collaboration will develop a Quilt Index as an innovative national model for distributed online management and presentation of thematic collections for museums and libraries. The three main goals, determined through needs assessment, are to (1) create a critical mass of quilt objects and information online; (2) enhance online access to the U.S. quilt and quilt-information collections in museums, libraries, and archives through improved content management and interoperability; and (3) enhance the value, usefulness, and relevance of the index's thematic presentation. The model for distributed collections development around a theme can be applied to many different cultural heritage and natural resource areas, from fossil types to historic toy objects. The index's innovative design pilots a distributed system for entering customized local data that can be replicated locally and shared globally. For libraries, museums, exhibitors, and collections with object-specific focuses, the project will offer a model and a road map for creating an online preservation, management, and presentation system.

Palace of the Governors, Museum of New Mexico, Santa Fe $425,453

The Palace of the Governors—with the New Mexico State Library, Literacy Volunteers of Santa Fe, and other museums, libraries, and archives throughout the state—will present information about the birth of small presses in New Mexico. "Speaking Volumes" will coordinate the efforts of the state museum and state library to strengthen and support collections-based cultural institutions in small, rural, underserved, and low-income communities across the state to achieve the following goals: promote innovation by combining traditional library reading programs with a hands-on book arts component; help museums, libraries, and archives fulfill their potential as partners and sponsors for communities of lifelong learners; expand local programming partnerships among cultural institutions, schools, and community groups; cultivate attendance and participation in cultural activities by new and diverse constituencies; improve public access to New Mexico's literary and technological history and the contributions of the state's diverse cultures; and disseminate historical and cultural information via public programs, print, and digital media.

Plimoth Plantation, Plymouth, Massachusetts $164,163

Plymouth Ancestors, a partnership between the New England Historic Genealogical Society (NEHGS) and the Plimoth Plantation, will offer learners personal experiences of the American past through online services, teaching materials, an annual newsletter, and advanced information technology that deepens the experience of visiting history museums. Learners participate in historical investigation by using basic tools for introductory-level genealogical work. NEHGS and the Plimoth Plantation will place three touch-screen computer kiosks on the grounds of Plimoth Plantation that will offer museum visitors brief biographies of all colonists who arrived in Plymouth between 1620 and 1633; artist renderings of Plymouth Colony and the Wampanoag Homeland for the period 1603–1633; an introduction to genealogy for young visitors; navigational and historical information to acclimate visitors to museum grounds; an introduction to research resources available online and on site at NEHGS; and an opportunity to subscribe to the *Plymouth Ancestors* newsletter. The project will also develop free classroom curriculum materials and links from the Plymouth Ancestors Web site to NEHGS resources.

Simmons College, Boston $272,179

Simmons College Graduate School of Library and Information Science and Northeast Historic Film will create the Moving Image Collections, a tool kit that will let a broad range of museums, libraries, and other institutions with video resources catalog these resources and make them accessible through Web-based digital video libraries. The grantees bring to the project expertise in managing digital documents and creating open-source digital video libraries. National Historic Film, the museum partner, provides video content within the resource limitations common to small museums. The project will be guided by an advisory

Table 2 / National Leadership Grants, FY 2004 *(cont.)*

board with representatives from key digital video-related projects, including the Internet Archive, Open Video, and WGBH-TV.

South Dakota School of Mines and Technology $149,980

The Hands-On Partnership for Science, Literature, and Art in South Dakota (HOP) will increase access to science, literature, and arts experiences by citizens of rural and reservation communities. The South Dakota State Library, Rawlins Municipal Library, Rapid City Arts Council/Dahl Fine Arts Center, South Dakota School of Mines and Technology, and the South Dakota Discovery Center and Aquarium will form 21st Century Learning Communities in a dozen South Dakota communities, with local libraries in a lead role. These communities will host traveling science exhibits and related science, literature, and art programs.

State Library of Louisiana $470,105

The project Louisiana Gumbo will give educators, students, and independent learners across the nation a taste of Louisiana's hidden treasures by digitizing vintage jazz radio broadcasts, interviews and performances, musical instruments, Acadian textiles, costumes, flags, parade bulletins and posters, historical paintings and maps, photographs, documents, and science and technology artifacts held by the State Library of Louisiana, the Louisiana State Museum, and the Historic New Orleans Collection. Digital resources will be accessible via the Louisiana Digital Library Web site. Accompanying standards-based instructional materials will be accessible via the Louisiana Department of Education Web site.

University of California–Los Angeles, Near Eastern Languages and Culture $499,826

Discover Babylon will research and evaluate new approaches for library/museum collaborations to communicate complex concepts using ancient Mesopotamian artifacts in digital form from the Cuneiform Digital Library Initiative and the Walters Art Museum in a collaborative effort of staff members from both institutions and from the Learning Federation Project of the Federation of American Scientists. Participants will walk through a major temple complex, see museum artifacts used by avatars (computer representations of people) in context, and even manipulate artifacts otherwise locked in museum displays. The virtual worlds will be the setting for an educational game in which success depends on an increasingly sophisticated grasp of Babylonian culture.

University of Central Florida Libraries $221,397

Building on the successful pilot project Central Florida Memory (CFM), a consortium of regional historical societies and libraries will provide access to library, museum, historical society, and archival content in Central Florida; create an extensive digital resource for scholars, students, teachers, genealogists, residents, visitors, and the general public; assist museums, historical societies, and libraries in digitizing their collections and becoming forums for sharing expertise and technical knowledge; offer a digital archive for those unable to establish their own digital infrastructure; provide a digital resource for K–12 teachers to bring the region's history into lesson plans; and contribute to the larger body of knowledge of Florida history via access to the CFM Web site through other statewide project sites.

University of Denver $496,963

As an extension of the Colorado Digitization Program's Digital Audio Working Group, the project team will develop an adaptable model project to demonstrate a shared statewide infrastructure available to cultural heritage organizations by digitizing at least 2,000 audio objects to be accessible through catalogs, exhibits, and special indexing. The audio files will be centralized for institutions lacking their own capacity, and central streaming services will be provided. Users will be able to enter a search term, receive a list of audio files containing the search term used in the transcript, and then locate and listen to occurrences of the search term in the audio files. Teacher resources will be created for each collection.

Table 2 / National Leadership Grants, FY 2004 *(cont.)*

Preservation or Digitization

Fondren Library, Rice University $249,959

The Fondren Library will develop the Travelers in the Middle East Archive (TIMEA), a digital archive of narratives documenting travel to the Middle East published between the 18th and early 20th centuries, along with related images and interactive maps. This archive will facilitate defined searching and analysis within and across texts and will integrate images, maps, and text. To make the archive easier and more effective to use in teaching, learning, and research, the project team will employ Connexions, a community-driven approach to authoring, teaching, and learning that seeks to provide free access to a cohesive body of high-quality educational content to anyone in the world.

Free Library of Philadelphia $500,000

The Free Library of Philadelphia will increase access to its significant collection of medieval and Renaissance manuscripts by creating bibliographic records and 3,055 digital images from 1,400 codices and leaves in its Lewis-Widener manuscript collection. The digitized images will be available to the public and scholars through the library's Web site and through the international Digital Scriptorium database of medieval and Renaissance manuscripts, thus unifying in virtual form parts of books scattered throughout the world.

Homer Babbidge Library, University of Connecticut $168,446

The Homer Babbidge Library will create an international metadata-driven, dynamic access tool that will enable users to access and view scanned and geo-referenced images from 1877–1914 Austro-Hungarian topographic maps by querying an easy-to-use digital gazetteer. In addition to being accessible from the university's Web site, the material will be linked to the FamilySearch Web site of the Church of Jesus Christ of Latter-Day Saints. The American Geographic Society Library at the University of Wisconsin–Milwaukee and the New York Public Library are partners in this project; the Bodleian Library at Oxford University and three national libraries in Europe are also participating.

University of North Carolina at Chapel Hill, School of Information and Library Science $95,113

The School of Information and Library Science, in partnership with Folkstreams, Inc., and ibiblio.org, will digitize documentary films on American folk culture and provide global access to them on the Folkstreams.net Web site. The films will be transferred from 16-millimeter film to digital Betacam and, along with the videotapes and digital copies, will be preserved in the Southern Folklife Collection. A multimedia Web site demonstration highlighting the skills required for transfers from 16-millimeter film to digital formats will be created.

University of Tennessee $241,775

The University of Tennessee Library, in partnership with the Arrowmont School of Arts and Crafts and the Pi Beta Phi Elementary School in Gatlinburg, Tennessee, will create a fully searchable online archive of letters, diaries, photographs, and short printed items on the history of the Pi Beta Phi Settlement School. In addition to standard two-dimensional scanning of approximately 2,000 items, the project team will produce 360-degree interactive scans of 50 to 75 artifacts such as ceramics and baskets and will create curriculum packages for students.

Research and Demonstration

Carlsbad (California) City Library $241,705

The Carlsbad City Library—in partnership with the Cerritos Library, Newport Beach Public Library, and San Diego County Public Law Library—will develop a process, documented by a workbook, to create a "library balanced scorecard" with appropriate performance measures for specific libraries. The project will assess the resources required for a library to cre-

Table 2 / National Leadership Grants, FY 2004 *(cont.)*

ate and implement a library scorecard, discover some of the reasons why some people do not use a library, determine if there are unique problems that occur as the size of the library increases, assess the utility of the library scorecard for management as it seeks to communicate the value of a public library, and assess the utility of the library scorecard from the perspective of the library's stakeholders.

Digital Library Federation $292,456

The Digital Library Federation (DLF)—in partnership with Emory University, the University of Illinois at Urbana-Champaign, and the University of Michigan—will research, design, and prototype a "second generation" Open Archives Initiative (OAI) finding system, capitalizing on the lessons learned from the first wave of OAI harvesting and using as its raw material collections drawn from across DLF membership. The aim is to foster better teaching and scholarship through easier, more-relevant discovery of digital resources, and to enhance libraries' ability to build more responsive local services on top of a distributed metadata platform.

Florida International University Libraries $239,602

In this demonstration project, the Florida International University Library Geographic Information System and Remote Sensing Center, Library Latin America and Caribbean Information Center, Environmental Studies Department and Center for Ethnobiology and Natural Products, in partnership with the Docente Escuela Politecnica Nacional of Ecuador, will develop and implement a scalable, highly adaptable, uniform data-management framework and geospatial data collection system that will link geospatial data, diversity collections, charts, and other material on the Andean Amazon region in diverse formats.

General Libraries, Emory University $194,900

Emory University and Virginia Tech will research user quality metrics for metasearch retrieval, conducting a series of studies using production digital library services to determine what criteria underlie the preferences and assumptions of different groups of users regarding metasearch systems.

New Jersey Institute of Technology $498,786

In partnership with the Newark Public Library, the New Jersey Institute of Technology will bring relevant resources directly to library users by providing a sustainable infrastructure for virtually integrating the collections and services of libraries nationwide. The research project will link three commercial databases, the New Jersey Digital Highway, and the online catalog systems at the two test bed libraries.

State University of New York at Buffalo, School of Informatics $266,881

The School of Informatics will conduct a follow-up of a 2000 national baseline survey of public use of the Internet and the public library to document the changes that have occurred in the consumer markets for the Internet and the public library, the impacts of Internet use on the library, and any trends in the data that would suggest how the relationship between the Internet and the public library might be evolving and how public libraries could adjust to these trends. The researchers will also conduct a complementary national survey to investigate why public library users who have Internet access at home continue to use the library for information.

University of California, Berkeley, Electronic Cultural Atlas Initiative $240,162

The Electronic Cultural Atlas Initiative will show how existing and emerging standards and protocols can be used or adapted to create an intermediate infrastructure in support of learners with respect to the questions What? Where? When? and Who? A client interface and links with existing specialized resources will be created and evaluated for two purposes: use by teachers seeking additional resources to supplement textbooks, and use for contextualizing digital objects in library and museum collections by identifying the objects in other collections that are most closely related in terms of place and time of origin and human

Table 2 / National Leadership Grants, FY 2004 *(cont.)*

associations. The researchers will create a prototype demonstrating how the digital environment can be enhanced to advance the educational goals of libraries and museums and will make recommendations for the improvement of standards, protocols, and best practices.

University of North Texas, School of Library and Information Sciences,
Texas Center for Digital Knowledge $233,115

In this research project, the Texas Center for Digital Knowledge will provide empirical evidence to document MARC 21 content designation use, explore the evolution of MARC content designation for patterns of availability and adoption/use level, and investigate a methodological approach to understand the factors contributing to current levels of MARC content designation use and relationships with the cataloging enterprise.

University of Tennessee, School of Information Sciences $446,988

The University of Tennessee School of Information Sciences will provide models to help librarians maximize their use of data about how electronic resources are being used by comparing different methods of data collection and use, including different levels and techniques of usage log data analysis and various kinds of surveys. The Centre for Information Behaviour and the Evaluation of Research (CIBER) of the City University of London will analyze the usage log data, which will be provided by the multilibrary consortium OhioLink and the University of Tennessee.

University of Washington, Information School $492,801

Working with librarians, teachers, and administrators from the Seattle Public Schools, the University of Washington Information School will create, implement, document, evaluate, and disseminate models of exemplary library and information programs in multiplexes of smaller schools.

Table 3 / Librarians for the 21st Century Grants, FY 2004

Priority 1, Master's Level Programs

American Library Association, Office for Diversity $928,142

The Office for Diversity seeks to double the number of under-represented master's degree (MLS) students in its Spectrum Initiative scholarship program, from 105 to 210, while creating and institutionalizing mechanisms to aggregate and disseminate information about diversity recruitment and education initiatives. The office will collaborate with the Association for Library and Information Science Education (ALISE) to hold a national-level dialogue and build an outreach program to enhance the capacities of library schools to attract and matriculate diverse students.

Association of Research Libraries $826,182

The association will collaborate with three partner library schools to recruit and train 45 master's degree students. Activities of these students include a fellowship based on a combination of an ARL position description and learning goals established by fellows, a formal mentorship with a professional in the library hosting the fellowship, and a five-day leadership institute exploring opportunities and challenges facing academic and research libraries. Upon graduation, staff will work with students to identify appropriate positions in research libraries.

Brooklyn (New York) Public Library $516,732

The Brooklyn Public Library will collaborate with Pratt Institute School of Information and Library Science in a pilot training project called PULSE (the Public Urban Library Service Education Project), in which MLS students will experience and become inspired by the many career opportunities at major urban public libraries. The project will also train the students as top librarians with leadership potential and motivate them to commit to public librarianship. Twenty-one students will participate in the work/training program. Emphasis will be placed

Table 3 / Librarians for the 21st Century Grants, FY 2004 *(cont.)*

on recruiting racially, economically, and linguistically diverse students, and they will be offered scholarships based on need. The project will also increase the capacity of the institutions through such activities as establishing a training program and training staff as effective mentors.

Chicago Public Schools, Department of Libraries and Information Services $319,501

The department will partner with Dominican University Graduate School of Library and Information Science to educate 15 students to work as certified school library media specialists in Chicago Public Schools. During the program, a partnership approach will be developed and individuals will be selected to better meet needs within the current student population that are traditionally underserved.

Florida State University, School of Information Studies $679,751

The School of Information Science, along with three partners—Central Florida Library Cooperative, Northeast Florida Library Information Network, and Panhandle Library Access Network—will recruit and educate 30 librarians who will practice in this service area for a minimum of two years after completing their degree. Students will work with five trained mentors, and there will be a special focus on public service, community partnership, and leadership.

Kent State University, School of Library and Information Science $486,621

The school will partner with the Cleveland Municipal School District to recruit and educate 18 school library media specialists and prepare them to perform effectively in urban school districts, especially those implementing smaller learning communities. Their master's degrees will be completed on-site through interactive videoconferencing, and students will receive tuition scholarships.

New York State Library $995,630

The New York State Library, in collaboration with 13 library systems and 6 schools of library and information science, will create "teaching libraries" across the state to provide practical, hands-on experience for librarian recruits from the system's member libraries. Financial support will be provided to 48 master's degree students who represent diverse groups and who will acquire competencies for serving diverse populations.

University of Alabama University Libraries $449,201

The libraries, partnering with the University of Alabama School of Information Studies, will recruit ten students from differing backgrounds and cultures who have completed a graduate degree in another subject to study academic or research librarianship. Practical training and classroom theory will be combined with a mentoring experience to prepare them for careers such as university faculty.

University of Houston–Clear Lake, School of Information and Library Sciences $863,813

The school, in partnership with five school districts and the Harris County Department of Education, will train 30 school librarians while preparing them to serve in schools with large Hispanic populations. Candidates must be Hispanic or have experience working with Hispanic populations. The project will also provide professional development, increase community communication and collaboration, and disseminate information on meeting the needs of Hispanic students.

University of North Texas, School of Library and Information Sciences $790,911

The school will collaborate with ten partner institutions to recruit 20 local bilingual students to complete a master's degree online while serving as "professionals in training" in partner libraries. This program will bring together the need for professional librarians in this region and the need for local graduates to find employment in a professional field.

Table 3 / Librarians for the 21st Century Grants, FY 2004 *(cont.)*

Wayne State University Library System $743,286

The library system will partner with three institutions composed of area museums, libraries, and archives to develop a unique approach to recruiting and educating new digital-projects librarians. Twenty individuals from under-represented groups will be given stipends and placed in a mentoring relationship with senior librarians in the fields of systems, digital-project development, metadata, digital archives, and museum management.

Priority 2, Doctoral Programs

Drexel University, College of Information Science and Technology $478,901

Drexel University College of Information Science and Technology, in collaboration with the Free Library of Philadelphia and the Hagerty Library of Drexel University, will recruit five doctoral students into an interdisciplinary program with a research emphasis on management of digital information. Recruits, drawn from the Philadelphia area, with at least two from a minority population, will be supported with tuition remission and fellowships.

Indiana University, School of Library and Information Science $607,341

The School of Library and Information Science will collaborate with the Curriculum and Instruction Department of the School of Education in Bloomington to prepare five doctoral students in school library media services and provide summer training for another 20 potential doctoral students. Students will engage in formal and situated learning experiences, participate actively in research and policy analysis, and provide service to the community and school library media field.

Syracuse University, School of Information Studies $499,727

The Syracuse University Office of Sponsored Programs will integrate preparation for teaching with targeted library research activities into the doctoral experience to help students successfully make the transition to becoming assistant professors in library science programs by recruiting and enculturating doctoral students. The project will include attracting new doctoral students by providing targeted funding to practicing librarians, providing exposure to research and educational conferences and participation on committees, and promoting active learning through library-oriented research projects and teaching.

University of Missouri–Columbia, School of Information Science and Learning Technologies $446,574

The school will prepare nine students to earn Ph.D.'s and contribute substantively to preparation of future public librarians. Students will be required to take three courses from a department other than the School of Information Science and Learning Technologies, and collaboration between this school and the University of Missouri's Truman School of Public Affairs will offer a unique opportunity to study community decision making, public policy, and public libraries as complex organizations.

University of North Texas, School of Library and Information Science $192,083

The School of Library and Information Sciences will recruit ten diverse doctoral students and provide them with tuition and broadband connectivity for a largely Web-based coursework and socializing graduate experience. This will be combined with faculty and professional mentoring in the area of school media librarianship.

University of Texas at Austin, School of Information $380,822

The school will recruit six doctoral students to study youth librarianship in public and school libraries and the role of youth librarianship in a healthy community. Advanced academic research work will be done with faculty and mentoring professionals, while the doctoral students develop close relationships fostered by library community partnerships and other community resources and development activities found in the Austin area.

Table 3 / Librarians for the 21st Century Grants, FY 2004 *(cont.)*

Priority 3, Pre-Professional Programs

Nebraska Library Commission $343,682

The Nebraska Library Commission will develop a marketing campaign to raise awareness of and identify prospects for library service careers. High school and college students will be recruited, matched with mentors and educational opportunities, and provided with stipends, grants, or scholarships to support the pursuit of pre-professional and professional education. A multimedia campaign and resources will be developed for the project in both English and Spanish to achieve a more diverse cadre of library professionals in Nebraska.

University Libraries, University of Notre Dame $193,911

The University Libraries of Notre Dame and partner institutions in the regional group of Northern Indiana academic libraries will introduce 42 diverse college-bound graduating seniors from area high schools to the profession of academic librarianship through employment as summer student assistants who perform "real" work in various functional units of the participating libraries and through individual mentor services afforded them by academic librarians. These student assistants will be drawn from varied cultural and ethnic backgrounds, and, after the program, their career choices will be tracked.

Priority 4, Research

University of North Carolina at Chapel Hill $994,369

The university will conduct a two-year study that will include an analysis of current and projected U.S. library work force data by state and region, by types of employers, and by functional specializations. It will also assess the likely demand and opportunities for librarians over the next decade, the skills that librarians will need, and incentives for attracting highly qualified individuals to the field. The final report will recommend strategies for the recruitment, education, and retention of future librarians.

University of Wisconsin–Madison, School of Library and Information Studies $347,019

The University of Wisconsin–Madison School of Library and Information Studies and the University of Maryland College of Information Studies and its library partners seek to research supply and demand of subject specialists in research libraries, develop recruiting approaches, and create and test a curricular structure responsive to the future needs of libraries and librarians. The data will be gathered on a national basis.

Priority 5, Programs to Build Institutional Capacity

Indiana University, School of Library and Information Science $939,618

The Indiana University School of Library and Information Science will collaborate with the University of Illinois at Urbana-Champaign to create the first research-based, comprehensive master's-level and post-MLS degree to educate librarians for work in digital library programs in libraries and archives. New internships in digital library projects designed to complement the new concentrations will be added to libraries at both institutions; post-MLS enrollees will be required to complete an internship, and the pilot project will feature paid fellowships for a limited number of students.

Palmer School, Long Island University, C. W. Post Campus $236,575

The school will hasten development of a flexible, collaborative model for providing education for rare books/special collections librarians within the existing framework of an ALA-accredited MLS institutional program. Support will be given to students in an effort to attract trained personnel into a field with grave recruitment concerns and to attract those unaware of opportunities in the special collections/rare book subfield. A portion of the support is specifically designated for students representing diversity, and a portion is reserved for subject specialists holding a Ph.D.

Table 3 / Librarians for the 21st Century Grants, FY 2004 *(cont.)*

Northeast Document Conservation Center $205,500

Northeast Document Conservation Center, in partnership with Simmons College Graduate School of Library and Information Science, seeks to make preservation a basic part of the MLS curriculum through a cooperative project between regional preservation centers and schools of library and information science. The program will provide an opportunity to create consensus about content for a preservation course and create an online curriculum with detailed lesson plans.

Rutgers University, School of Communication, Information, and Library Studies $969,773

The school and its outreach program, Professional Development Studies, will build 22 courses online that will allow students to choose between specialties in school library media services and digital libraries, and will recruit and admit 60 students a year to the online program. Addition of the classes will allow an increased capacity for students of about 50 percent, and six new faculty will be added to support about 20 interactive online classrooms.

Syracuse University, School of Information Studies $713,492

Syracuse will partner with the University of Illinois at Urbana-Champaign and the University of Washington to pilot a collaborative program to offer selected online courses. Collective and individual institutional capacity will be built by providing training for faculty in online pedagogy, allowing the three institutions to focus on areas of strength while students are assured of access to a range of courses.

University of Texas at Austin, School of Information $626,755

The school will build institutional capacity to educate digital librarians by developing future faculty and library managers, as well as recruiting new librarians with a technology-centered digitization curriculum that documents and researches policy and issues related to digital libraries. During the project, a curriculum will be developed and evaluated, a teaching and digitization infrastructure will be created, and research and publications will be initiated that track best practices. By the conclusion of the program, five doctoral students and one master's degree student will be recruited for specialized careers and/or research and teaching in the area of digital libraries.

Table 4 / Native American Library Services Enhancement Grants, FY 2004

Arctic Slope Regional Corporation, Barrow, Alaska $149,999

The objectives of the corporation's digital archive project are to scan onto microfilm and digitize primary source material from the Dr. Rosita Worl collection and other documents from the 1960s and 1970s that are pertinent to the establishment of the North Slope Borough and to the Inupiat culture and language. A full-text index will be generated and mounted on the Internet with links to the scanned images in PDF format. The project will enhance local skills in advanced archival techniques in the environment of a small, remote library by maintaining nationally recognized standards for access to digital collections.

Cheyenne River Sioux Tribe, Eagle Butte, South Dakota $21,585

The Si Tanka University Library Services Enhancement Project will establish an electronic linkage with the South Dakota Library Network that will develop the library's integrated online system and provide expanded electronic resources, increasing the library's presence and effectiveness for the entire Cheyenne River Sioux tribal community.

Confederated Tribes of Warm Springs Reservation of Oregon $150,000

The Warm Springs Community Library Enhancement Project will be a collaborative effort between the Warm Springs Community Library and the Warm Springs Community Action

Table 4 / Native American Library Services Enhancement Grants, FY 2004 *(cont.)*

Team to hire a full-time librarian, increase hours of library operation, coordinate library programs and activities, increase collections, and institute a cataloging and automation system. The library and community action team will initiate a community outreach program to familiarize the community with the local library, to implement a community assessment survey, and to coordinate community volunteers for library programs.

Fort Belknap Indian Community, Harlem, Montana $149,658

This project, Meeting Community Needs Through Expanded Outreach Services, will increase the library's effectiveness by enhancing children's reading activities through after-school and summer reading programs for K–6 children, family reading nights, and storytelling hours with tribal elders, and by increasing the availability of online information resources, upgrading cataloging software, and expanding library holdings in Native American history, culture, and literature.

Hoopa Valley Tribe, Hoopa, California $145,164

The Hooks to Books project will continue the partnership with Humboldt County to provide expanded library services to the Kim Yerton Memorial Library. In support of this partnership, the library plans to improve reading and study space; to increase circulation, computer/Internet usage, and Internet services; and to promote community outreach.

Lummi Tribe, Bellingham, Washington $127,394

This project, Improving Services to Lummi Library Users, will enhance literacy within the Lummi community by hosting holiday literacy events for both children and adults; creating and distributing themed literacy kits to parents, daycare centers, Head Start, and Tribal School students; sponsoring summer reading programs that highlight Native American culture and cultural diversity; and purchasing full-text databases, books, videos, and computer equipment.

Miami Tribe of Oklahoma $146,510

This project, All My Relations, will support the development of an electronic catalog for the Miami Tribal Archives; the enhancement of the library/archives Web site with information of interest to Miami tribal members nationwide, and the improvement of the CHARLIE (Connecting Help and Resources Linking Indians Effectively) Library Network that serves northeast Oklahoma tribes by providing a traveling librarian to mentor and train librarians. It will also implement interlibrary loan services among the eight CHARLIE sites and expand the Roots and Wings program, which distributes books to young tribal members.

Muscogee (Creek) Nation, Okmulgee, Oklahoma $129,562

This project—Muscogee Elders: In Their Own Words, Forever—will establish a partnership between the Muscogee Nation Library and Archives and the Sam Noble Oklahoma Museum of Natural History for digitizing, transcribing, and preserving 27 oral-history interviews with tribal elders. Muscogee library staff will receive training in maintaining archival materials, creating electronic formats, and enhancing accessibility through Internet linkages. Muscogee staff will also learn to conduct oral history interviews with a goal of recording 25 new interviews with elders during this project.

Pueblo of Jemez $146,626

The goals of this New Mexico project, Enhancing the Lives of Our People, are to strengthen the Jemez Library Consortium by sharing library resources and coordinating literacy programs with five local schools; to enhance reading skills of community members of all ages by providing family literacy programs, after-school tutoring, reading clubs, and summer reading; to increase computer literacy and access to information for all community members; and to contribute to the preservation of the Jemez language and culture by providing programs on traditional arts, storytelling, and genealogy.

Table 4 / Native American Library Services Enhancement Grants, FY 2004 *(cont.)*

Pueblo of Santa Clara $150,000

This project will expand the services of the Santa Clara Pueblo Community Library in Espanola, New Mexico, by increasing its technological capabilities; enhancing literacy programs for both its school-aged and elderly populations through elder/grandchild reading programs, tutoring in remedial reading, and reading incentive programs for summer youth workers; and digitizing documents for the tribal language program as well as expanding the tribe's digital archives initiative to include a tribal constitution project that will involve at-risk youth in the preservation of their community's culture.

Red Cliff Band of Lake Superior Chippewa Indians, Bayfield, Wisconsin $75,824

This collaborative project, Mazinaigan Waakaaigan, will enhance library services by sharing the resources of the Red Cliff Library, Red Cliff Even Start Program, and the Red Cliff Language and Historic Preservation Office. It will increase the library's hours and collections, expand academic and technological resources, and improve literacy enrichment programs and language and cultural-preservation initiatives.

Sitka Tribe of Alaska $104,920

This collaborative effort—"the Romaine Hardcastle Photograph Collection, A Model Rural Consortium Project"—will involve the Sitka Tribal Library, the Kettleson Memorial Public Library, Sheldon Jackson College Library, Sitka Historical Society, Isabella Miller Museum, and Sitka National Historical Park. The consortium will work to survey, preserve, and digitize a photograph collection donated by Romaine Hardcastle that spans Sitka tribal history from the 1920s through 1960s as well as to document the photographs by interviewing tribal members who can identify the people and artwork in the collection.

Ysleta del Sur Pueblo of Texas $126,490

This project will support the continuing mission of the Tigua Literacy Program to introduce middle and high school students to strategies for success on standardized tests through peer mentoring and test simulations by building and promoting a collection of biographies and children's nonfiction titles for grades K–8 and by continuing to enhance computer literacy among tribal members.

Zuni Tribe $96,321

The Zuni Public Library Enhancement project will provide for a bookmobile operator and a children's program coordinator in this New Mexico community, as well as collection development for the bookmobile and the main library's children's and adult collections.

Part 3
Library/Information Science Education, Placement, and Salaries

Employment Sources on the Internet

Catherine Barr
Contributing Editor

The library and information science community has always actively shared information about job openings, with individual libraries, professional associations, library schools, and other organizations spreading the word through telephone "joblines" and fax services as well as through advertising in trade journals and use of employment agencies. This activity has naturally progressed to the Internet, and now the World Wide Web and a variety of online listservs and discussion groups have become some of the most useful—and current—resources for library and information professionals seeking jobs within and outside the library profession. Blogs focusing on employment opportunities are a relatively new phenomenon and usually focus on alerting readers to new features on the established sites.

There are now hundreds of job-related sites of interest to library and information professionals. This article makes no attempt to be all-inclusive, but aims instead to point readers to some of the most useful sites.

Many of the sites recommended simply list job openings; however, others also offer advice on searching for jobs, writing résumés, preparing for interviews, and negotiating salaries.

Before spending a lot of time on any Web site, users should check that the site has been updated recently and that out-of-date job listings no longer appear. If a jobseeker has a particular geographic location or specialized field in mind, he or she may find that the Directory of Organizations in Part 6 of this volume will provide a relevant Web address faster than a search of the Web.

Background Information

One particularly useful print resource, *The Information Professional's Guide to Career Development Online* (Information Today, 2001), has a companion Web site at http://www.lisjobs.com/careerdev. Both print and online versions present information on job hunting, networking, and online and continuing education. An article by the same authors—Rachel Singer Gordon and Sarah L. Nesbeitt—titled "Market Yourself Online!" appeared in the October/November 2001 issue of *Marketing Library Services*. The article presents practical advice on promoting yourself and your abilities on the Web; it is available at http://www.infotoday.com/mls/oct01/gordon&nesbeitt.htm.

The Bureau of Labor Statistics of the Department of Labor provides a thorough overview of the work of a librarian, necessary qualifications, and the job and salary outlook at http://www.bls.gov/oco/ocos068.htm. More detailed employment and wage estimates can be found at http://stats.bls.gov/opub/ted/2001/Jan/wk1/art03.htm for librarians; at http://stats.bls.gov/oes/current/oes254010.htm for archivists, curators, and museum technicians; and at http://stats.bls.gov/oes/current/oes254031.htm for library technicians.

An excellent 2002 *American Libraries* feature article by Linda K. Wallace on the breadth of opportunities available to librarians and information professionals—"Places an MLS Can Take You"—is archived at http://www.ala.org/ala/ hrdr/careersinlibraries/al_mls.pdf. A New Jersey-based site called Become a Librarian (http://www.becomealibrarian.org) contains useful material for those considering a career in the field, including a review of distance education courses. The American Library Association (ALA) provides links to information on specific library careers—law librarian, medical librarian, and so forth—on its Careers in Libraries page (http://www.ala.org/ala/hrdr/careersinlibraries/careerslibraries.htm). And How to Apply for a Library Job (http://www.tk421.net/ essays/howto.html) offers thoughtful and practical interview tips.

General Sites/Portals

American Library Association: Human Resource Development and Recruitment
http://www.ala.org/ala/hrdr/humanresource.htm
Maintained by ALA.
A useful source of information on library careers, education and professional development, scholarships, and salaries. There is a special section for library support staff. The Guide to Employment Sources in the Library and Information Professions (http://www.ala.org/ala/hrdr/libraryempresources/2004employmentguide.htm) provides lots of local, national, and international links and gives easy access to library job ads in *American Libraries* (including its Hot Jobs Online, which is updated daily) and in *C&RLNews*. There are also links to ALA's conference placement service and to information about discrimination and unfair employment practices.

Graduate School of Library and Information Science—Resources/Jobs
http://alexia.lis.uiuc.edu/gslis/resources/jobs.html
Maintained by the Graduate School of Library and Information Science at the University of Illinois at Urbana-Champaign.
An excellent, comprehensive site that would be a good starting place for anyone seeking library opportunities. It includes links to sites that have library and information science job postings, dividing them into the following categories: comprehensive, regional, school libraries/media centers, special types of libraries, information technology, and library schools. There are also lists of general employment sites that include library jobs, sources of employment overseas, and library listservs.

Library Job Postings
http://www.libraryjobpostings.org
Compiled by Sarah (Nesbeitt) Johnson of Booth Library, Eastern Illinois University, coauthor of *The Information Professional's Guide to Career Development Online* (Information Today, 2001).
Provides links to library employment sites in the United States and abroad, with easy access by location and by category of job.

LIScareer.com
http://www.liscareer.com
Maintained by Priscilla Shontz, editor of *The Librarian's Career Guidebook* (Scarecrow, 2004).

Subtitled The Library & Information Science Professional's Career Development Center, this helpful site provides no job listings but offers bibliographies of and, when available, links to resources of interest in the areas of career planning, education, job hunting, experience, work/life balance, networking, mentoring, interpersonal skills, leadership, and publishing.

Lisjobs.com—Jobs for Librarians and Information Professionals
http://www.lisjobs.com
Maintained by Rachel Singer Gordon, author of *The Accidental Library Manager* (Information Today, 2005) and coauthor of *The Information Professional's Guide to Career Development Online* (Information Today, 2001).
A searchable database of job listings and guide to online job resources in the United States and abroad. Job seekers can post résumés for a small fee. Also features an advice page and an interesting professional development newsletter, *Info Career Trends.*

The Riley Guide: Employment Opportunities and Job Resources on the Internet
http://www.rileyguide.com
Compiled by Margaret F. Dikel, a private consultant and coauthor with Frances Roehm of *The Guide to Internet Job Searching* (McGraw-Hill, 2002).
A general site rich in advice for the job seeker, from résumé writing and how to target a new employer to tips on networking and interviewing. Links to job sites are organized by discipline; Information Design, Delivery, and Management is found under The Humanities, Social Sciences, and Personal Services.

University of Missouri–Columbia: Library Job Listings
http://www.coe.missouri.edu/~career/library.html
Maintained by Career and Program Support, College of Education, University of Missouri–Columbia.
A no-frills site with links to sites that list library jobs. Includes many state joblines.

Professional Associations

General

Professional Associations in the Information Sciences
http://slisweb.sjsu.edu/resources/orgs.htm
Maintained by San Jose State University's School of Library and Information Science.
An excellent starting place that gives links to a large number of professional associations, from state, regional, and national library associations to specialized groupings. Most are in the United States.

Public

Public library openings can be found at all the general sites/portals listed above. The Public Library Association offers information on public librarianship—from educational requirements and salaries to testimonials from public librarians and the opportunity to participate in Job Shadow Day. The URL is http://www.pla.org/ala/pla/projects/publiclibrecruit/publiclibrarian.htm.

School

School library openings can be found at many of the sites listed above. Sites with interesting material for aspiring school librarians include

AASL: Education and Careers
http://www.ala.org/ala/aasl/aasleducation/educationcareers.htm
The American Association of School Librarians hosts this site.
General education sites usually include school library openings. Among sites with nationwide coverage is

Education America
http://www.educationamerica.net
Library openings can be searched by geographic location.

Special and Academic

AALL Job Placement Hotline
http://www.aallnet.org/hotline/hotline.asp
Maintained by the American Association of Law Librarians.

ALISE: Job Placement
http://www.alise.org/jobplacement/index.html
The Association for Library and Information Science Education posts jobs for deans, directors, program chairs, faculty, visiting and summer faculty, and support positions in the field of library and information science.

ASIS&T Jobline Online
http://www.jobtarget.com/home/index.cfm?site_id=180
Maintained by the American Society for Information Science and Technology.

Association of Research Libraries: Career Resources
http://db.arl.org/careers/index.html
In addition to job listings, there is a database of research library residency and internship programs. ARL's annual salary survey also appears on this site, as does the article "Careers in Research Libraries and Information Science: The Dynamic Role of the Research Librarian."

C&RL News Classified Advertising
http://www.ala.org/ala/acrl/acrlpubs/crlnews/crlcareeropps/careeropportunities.htm
Online access to job postings placed in C&RL News (published by the Association of College and Research Libraries), and to many jobs that can only be found online.

Chronicle of Higher Education
http://chronicle.com/jobs
Access job openings from more than 1,340 institutions. Openings can be browsed by position type or (perhaps more efficiently) by simply searching by keyword such as "library."

EDUCAUSE Job Posting Service
http://www.educause.edu/jobpost
EDUCAUSE member organizations post positions related to technology-based information resources, with a focus on higher education.

HigherEdJobs.com
http://www.higheredjobs.com
Published by Internet Employment Linkage, Inc. Job openings from more than 1,000 institutions can be searched by location, job category, or keyword.

MLANet: Career
http://www.mlanet.org/career/index.html
The Medical Library Association offers much more than job listings here, with brochures on medical librarianship, a mentor program, and a virtual student group.

Special Libraries Association: Career Center
http://www.sla.org/content/jobs/index.cfm
In addition to searchable job listings that are available to all users, SLA provides 24/7 job advice and mentoring to association members.

Government

Library of Congress
http://www.loc.gov/hr/employment

National Archives and Records Administration
http://www.archives.gov/careers/employment/employment.html
Employment, internships, and volunteering.

Miscellaneous

REFORMA Employment
http://www.reforma.org/refoempl.htm
REFORMA (The National Association to Promote Library and Information Services to Latinos and the Spanish-Speaking) collects job postings from list-servs and direct mailings. The page is updated weekly. Knowledge of Spanish is required for some jobs listed here.

Library Periodicals

American Libraries: Career Leads Online
http://www.ala.org/ala/education/empopps/careerleadsb/careerleadsonline.htm
Access ads from previous issues of *American Libraries* as well as new postings that are added daily. "Working Knowledge" is a monthly column about life on the job.

Feliciter
http://www.cla.ca/careers/careeropp.htm
The Canadian Library Association lists openings here; some may have already appeared in the association's publication *Feliciter*.

Library Journal
http://www.libraryjournal.com
Access to online job listings (which may not include all listings in the print edition) is under Tools and Services.

Employment Agencies/Commercial Services

A number of employment agencies and commercial services in the United States and abroad specialize in library-related jobs. Among those that keep up-to-date listings on their Web sites are

ASLIB
http://www.aslib.co.uk/recruitment/index.htm
Lists jobs available in Britain.

Library Associates
http://www.libraryassociates.com/index.php4?page=jobs

TPFL: The Information People
http://www.tfpl.com
Search by area of specialization or by keyword, or choose between Recruitment and Executive Search and Temporary and Contract Recruitment before selecting an area of specialization or specific search term. Jobs around the world are listed, with an emphasis on Europe.

Listservs

Many listservs allow members to post job openings on a casual basis.

LIBJOBS
http://www.ifla.org/II/lists/libjobs.htm
Managed by the International Federation of Library Associations and Institutions (IFLA). Subscribers to this list receive posted job opportunities by e-mail.

NASIGWeb Job Listings
http://www.nasig.org/jobs/list.htm
This site collects serials-related job openings posted on the following listservs: ACQNET, AUTOCAT, COLLIB-L, INNOPAC, LIBJOBS, LITA-L, PACS-L, SERIALST, SLAJOB, STS-L, and ERIL-L.

PUBLIB
http://sunsite.berkeley.edu/PubLib
Public library job openings often appear on this list.

Blogs

Beyond the Job
http://librarycareers.blogspot.com/
Maintained by Sarah Johnson and Rachel Singer Gordon, this blog focuses on job-hunting advice and professional development.

LIScareers News
http://liscareer.blogspot.com/
Posts alerts to new features on LIScareer.com.

Placements and Salaries 2003: Jobs! (Eventually)

Stephanie Maatta

Assistant Professor, University of South Florida
School of Library and Information Science, Tampa

If the economy is rebounding, the library world has yet to feel it. The budget constraints of the last several years showed up in 2003 in salary growth that lagged behind inflation and in job searches that seemed endless and were three times as long, on average, as the previous year.

But here is the good news: In another year of increasingly high unemployment (6 percent) nationwide, *Library Journal*'s annual Placements and Salaries Survey indicated that graduates of American Library Association (ALA)-accredited library and information science (LIS) programs continued to make modest strides in professional positions. The areas of reference and information services and school library media dominated, while offices in administration and management showed healthy growth.

Of the 1,140 graduates who reported full-time placement, 34 percent indicated that they returned to their previous employer as professional staff after graduation. Many of these graduates indicated that they received salary increases and position upgrades upon completion of their master's degree, moving from a paraprofessional or technician position to a professional one. An additional 30 percent of graduates reporting full-time placements indicated they found jobs prior to graduation.

The disappointing news is that in 2003 salaries continued to display sluggish growth for all graduates reporting salary, while salaries for minority graduates decreased significantly, negating the strides made in the previous two years.

Graduates reported an average starting salary of $37,975 in 2003, a 1.39 percent increase over the 2002 average of $37,456, falling below the 2003 national inflation rate of 2.2 percent. The average increases of 4.35 percent seen between 1998 and 2002 seem long gone.

Gender Gap Continues

In 2003 men comprised 20 percent of the graduates reporting a full-time salary and reported starting salaries approximately 7.59 percent higher annually than women. The difference in average salaries between men and women was $3,071, increasing the gap once again ($2,836 or 7.1 percent for 2002). Men continued to receive higher starting salaries in all types of libraries except government facilities.

While men broke the $40,000 barrier, at $40,462, women reporting salaries continued to struggle to reach the levels achieved by their male counterparts in 2000. Between 1998 and 2002, men's starting salaries experienced annual average growth of 4.5 percent while women experienced average growth of 3.73 percent. However, at the upper limits, women continued to dominate the pay scales. A comparison of average high salaries, by schools reporting gender, shows that women received an average of $4,528 (8.57 percent) more than men.

Adapted from *Library Journal*, October 15, 2004.

Women got 90 percent of the reported jobs in school libraries and 86 percent in public libraries, continuing the patterns of previous years. This may account for some of the disparity in pay, with women continuing to find jobs in the more human-service-oriented organizations.

The "other" designation ranges from jobs related to marketing and public relations to those within nonprofit fund-raising and curatorial work. The survey suggests that graduates are finding a broad array of jobs in nontraditional organizations such as corporate and private entities as well as positions connected to traditional libraries in records archives and museums. They also tend to fare well in these jobs. The average starting salaries showed greater parity than 2002, with a difference of 11.6 percent between men and women; in 2002 the salary disparity was 28 percent. Women reporting placement in "other" organizations also reported a 15 percent increase in 2003 starting salaries ($45,376) compared with similar placements in 2002 ($39,413).

Minorities Losing Ground

Approximately 15 percent of the 1,052 who reported full-time salaries identified themselves as members of a minority group. While this shows that more minorities are attaining the LIS degree than in previous years, this group lost significant ground in salary parity in 2003. The average starting salary reported by minority graduates was $36,666 for 2003, 6 percent less than similar placements in 2002 ($38,886), when they exceeded the general average. For the first time since 1999, the average starting salary of minority graduates decreased and is now $680 below the average starting salary.

Lower average salaries for minority graduates may be indicative of the salary decreases experienced in various library types across the board during 2003. Academic (3.09 percent less) and government (12 percent less) libraries showed decreased salaries for all reported full-time placements. Minority graduates made up 18 percent of the reported placements in academic libraries and 10.7 percent in government libraries. The encouraging news, however, is that minority graduates reporting placements in public libraries and with vendors indicated beginning salaries ($35,351) slightly higher than the reported averages of all graduates in that category ($34,901). Also, the average for all placements with vendors during the same period was $38,273, with minority placements reporting average beginning salaries of $38,833.

The largest group of minority graduates (32.48 percent) found jobs in academic libraries, which is somewhat less than in 2002 (40 percent). Placements were down slightly, with 31.85 percent finding positions in public libraries, followed by 17.2 percent in K–12 school media centers (an increase of 3.29 percent from 2002), 6.37 percent in special libraries, and less than 5 percent with vendors, government libraries, and library cooperatives combined. In 2003 minority graduates reporting jobs in "other" organizations (7.01 percent) found the highest average salaries at $46,431, on par with the national average for the "other" category.

The combination of location (Southeast and Southwest) and type of organization may be impacting the salaries of minority graduates. The national average

(text continues on page 392)

Table 1 / Status of 2003 Graduates in Library Professions*

	Number of Schools Reporting	Number of Graduates Responding	Permanent Professional	Temporary Professional	Non-professional	Total	Graduates in Nonlibrary Positions	Unemployed or Status Unreported
Northeast	12	518	330	49	54	433	5	80
Southeast	11	234	165	7	29	201	5	31
Midwest	10	566	383	50	38	471	9	87
Southwest	4	86	62	5	6	73	—	13
West	5	141	80	22	10	112	3	26
Canada	1	17	12	3	1	16	—	1
Total	43	1,562	1,032	136	138	1,306	22	238

* Table based on survey responses from schools and individual graduates. Figures will not necessarily be fully consistent with some of the other data reported that came from individual graduates. Tables do not always add up, individually or collectively, since both schools and individuals omitted data in some cases.

Table 2 / Placements and Full-Time Salaries of 2003 U.S. Graduates/Summary by Region*

Region	Number of Placements	Salaries			Low Salary		High Salary		Average Salary			Median Salary		
		Women	Men	Total	Women	Men	Women	Men	Women	Men	All	Women	Men	All
Northeast	433	283	46	341	$15,000	$12,000	$94,000	$80,000	$38,395	$40,732	$38,618	$36,500	$38,400	$37,000
Southeast	201	138	29	168	10,000	27,300	75,000	61,100	33,686	38,560	34,556	32,282	38,000	34,000
Midwest	471	262	85	349	17,000	10,200	90,000	80,000	37,430	40,468	38,120	36,000	37,967	36,465
Southwest	73	46	15	61	14,000	22,880	70,000	65,000	34,705	38,959	35,751	34,000	37,500	35,000
West	112	65	10	75	17,000	35,000	72,000	70,799	42,738	44,918	43,028	40,000	42,000	40,000
Canada/Intl.**	16	8	5	13	28,310	23,873	40,547	70,000	33,466	36,143	34,496	33,659	28,696	33,659
Combined***	1,290	802	190	1,007	$10,000	$10,200	$94,000	$80,000	$37,391	$40,462	$37,975	$36,000	$38,000	$36,335

* This table represents only salaries reported as full-time. Some data were reported as aggregate without breakdown by gender. Comparison with other tables will show different numbers of placements.
** All international salaries converted to American dollars based on conversion rates for August 16, 2004.
*** U.S. results.

Table 3 / 2003 Total Graduates and Placements by School*

Schools	Graduates			Employed			Unemployed			Students		
	Women	Men	Total	Women	Men	Total	Women	Men	Total	Women	Men	Total
Alabama	64	16	80	9	1	10	2	—	2	1	—	1
Arizona	79	28	107	19	7	26	5	2	7	—	—	—
California (UCLA)	43	5	48	—	—	—	—	1	1	—	—	—
Cal State–Long Beach	16	5	21	9	1	10	—	1	1	—	—	—
Catholic Univ.**	—	—	—	1	—	1	—	—	—	—	—	—
Clarion	56	12	68	14	1	15	2	1	3	—	—	—
Dominican	211	35	246	52	15	67	3	1	4	1	1	2
Drexel	52	25	77	13	1	14	1	1	2	—	—	—
Emporia	—	—	—	32	8	40	3	—	3	1	—	1
Florida State	111	53	164	28	8	36	2	1	3	2	—	2
Hawaii	33	6	39	—	—	—	—	—	—	—	—	—
Illinois	196	43	239	52	11	63	8	1	9	—	—	—
Indiana	165	65	230	18	10	28	2	3	5	—	—	—
Iowa	35	8	43	—	—	—	—	—	—	—	—	—
Kentucky	69	16	85	20	9	29	1	—	1	—	—	—
Long Island	132	20	152	38	4	42	5	1	6	—	—	—
Louisiana State	—	—	—	15	3	18	1	—	1	—	—	—
McGill	—	—	—	11	6	17	—	1	1	—	—	—
Michigan	53	40	93	38	28	66	—	—	—	3	7	10
Missouri–Columbia	95	17	112	36	3	39	3	1	4	—	—	—
N.C. Chapel Hill	64	25	89	24	7	31	3	1	4	—	—	—
N.C. Greensboro	81	9	90	35	1	36	6	—	6	—	—	—
North Texas**	175	28	203	—	—	—	1	—	1	—	—	—

School											
Oklahoma	34	10	44	14	3	17	1	1	2	—	—	—
Pittsburgh	121	36	157	40	5	45	3	4	7	—	—	—
Pratt	77	17	94	23	5	28	5	2	7	—	—	—
Queens College	123	42	165	39	9	48	6	2	8	—	—	—
Rhode Island	—	—	—	12	1	13	3	1	4	1	—	1
Rutgers	102	14	116	32	3	35	3	—	3	—	—	—
San Jose	157	48	205	58	5	63	8	—	8	—	—	—
Simmons	164	35	199	112	25	137	15	4	19	3	—	3
South Carolina	140	22	162	13	2	15	—	—	—	6	1	7
South Florida	113	23	136	13	3	16	2	—	2	—	—	—
Southern Connecticut	53	7	60	21	3	24	3	1	4	—	—	—
Southern Mississippi	32	2	34	5	—	5	1	—	1	—	—	—
Tennessee**	—	—	—	3	—	3	—	—	—	—	—	—
Texas (Austin)	94	14	108	24	6	30	3	—	3	—	—	—
Univ. of Albany**	1	—	1	1	—	1	—	—	—	—	—	—
Univ. of Buffalo	90	30	120	18	5	23	4	3	7	—	—	—
Washington	71	22	93	31	10	41	5	4	9	2	—	2
Wayne State	144	58	202	63	16	79	22	6	28	—	—	—
Wisconsin (Madison)	56	15	71	38	10	48	7	2	9	6	1	7
Wisconsin (Milwaukee)	86	21	107	38	9	47	4	—	4	—	—	—
Total	3,388	872	4,260	1,062	244	1,306	143	45	188	26	10	36

* This table represents reported placements of any kind. Comparison with other tables will show different numbers of placements. Totals are different from gender components as some schools and individuals did not provide gender information.

** For schools that did not fill out the institutional survey, data were taken from graduate surveys, thus there is not full representation of their graduating classes.

Unknown status: 2,158 women, 572 men, for a total of 2,730

Table 4 / Placements by Type of Organization*

Schools	Public		Elementary & Secondary		College & University		Special		Government		Library and Co-op./Network		Vendor		Other		Total		
	Women	Men	Women	Men	Women	Men	Women	Men	Women	Men	Women	Men	Women	Men	Women	Men	Women	Men	Total
Alabama	1	1	3	—	3	—	1	—	—	—	—	—	—	—	—	—	8	1	9
Arizona	6	1	6	1	2	5	3	—	—	—	—	—	—	—	1	—	18	7	25
Cal State–Long Beach	2	—	7	1	—	—	—	—	—	—	—	—	—	—	—	—	9	1	10
Catholic Univ.	1	—	—	—	—	—	—	—	—	—	—	—	—	—	—	—	1	—	1
Clarion	6	—	3	1	2	—	2	—	—	—	1	—	—	—	—	—	14	1	15
Dominican	25	1	9	1	8	9	2	2	—	—	2	—	—	—	5	2	51	15	66
Drexel	2	—	—	—	4	1	4	—	2	—	—	—	—	—	1	—	13	1	14
Emporia State	8	1	12	3	4	2	4	—	2	1	—	—	—	—	2	—	32	8	40
Florida State	9	4	9	—	4	2	—	—	1	—	1	—	1	1	3	1	28	8	36
Illinois	17	1	6	—	22	9	3	—	3	—	—	—	—	—	1	1	52	11	63
Indiana	10	3	3	1	2	4	1	2	—	—	—	—	—	—	2	—	18	10	28
Kentucky	6	2	6	—	5	6	1	—	—	1	1	—	1	—	—	—	20	9	29
Long Island	17	—	14	1	4	1	1	1	—	—	—	—	—	—	2	1	38	4	42
Louisiana State	5	—	1	—	8	3	1	—	—	—	—	—	—	—	—	—	15	3	18
McGill	—	—	1	1	3	2	3	1	—	—	—	—	—	—	3	1	10	5	15
Michigan	4	3	1	—	11	2	2	1	3	1	—	—	—	—	15	14	36	22	58
Missouri–Columbia	9	—	10	—	10	2	4	1	1	—	—	—	1	—	2	—	37	3	40
N.C. Chapel Hill	3	—	3	1	8	2	1	1	3	—	—	—	—	—	6	3	24	7	31
N.C. Greensboro	10	—	16	—	7	1	—	—	1	—	—	—	—	—	—	—	34	1	35

Oklahoma	6	4	—	—	3	3	—	—	—	—	—	—	—	—	1	—	14	3	17
Pittsburgh	12	9	—	—	10	4	6	1	—	—	—	—	1	—	2	—	41	4	45
Pratt	9	1	—	—	3	2	5	—	2	—	—	—	—	—	2	—	23	4	27
Queens College	11	17	2	—	4	—	5	1	2	—	1	—	1	1	2	—	39	9	48
Rhode Island	2	4	—	—	4	1	—	1	1	—	—	—	—	—	1	—	12	1	13
Rutgers	13	9	—	—	5	2	2	—	—	—	—	—	1	—	1	—	32	3	35
San Jose	17	15	3	—	12	1	9	4	2	—	1	—	1	—	4	—	58	5	63
Simmons	28	19	1	—	38	15	15	—	—	—	—	—	1	—	9	1	112	25	137
S. Carolina	4	5	—	—	3	2	—	—	—	—	—	—	—	—	—	—	13	2	15
S. Florida	2	5	1	—	5	2	—	—	—	—	—	—	1	—	—	—	13	3	16
S. Connecticut	9	6	—	—	3	2	1	—	—	—	—	—	1	—	2	—	21	3	24
S. Mississippi	1	2	—	—	2	—	—	—	—	—	—	—	—	—	—	—	5	—	5
Tennessee	2	—	—	—	—	—	—	—	—	—	—	—	1	—	—	—	3	—	3
Texas (Austin)	3	11	1	—	7	3	—	—	1	—	1	—	1	—	2	1	24	6	30
Univ. of Albany	1	—	—	—	—	—	—	—	—	—	—	—	—	—	—	—	1	—	1
Univ. of Buffalo	5	7	2	—	5	2	1	—	1	—	—	—	—	—	4	1	18	5	23
Washington	9	5	1	—	9	4	2	2	2	—	—	—	1	1	1	—	31	10	41
Wayne State	25	12	6	—	16	5	7	1	1	—	—	—	1	—	1	—	63	16	79
Wisc. (Madison)	10	5	1	—	14	4	3	—	3	1	1	—	1	1	1	—	38	11	49
Wisc. (Milwaukee)	19	4	—	—	7	5	6	—	—	2	—	—	—	1	2	—	38	9	47
Total	329	248	42	28	258	108	95	18	26	7	8	1	16	5	77	27	1,057	236	1,293

* This table represents only placements reported by type. Some individuals omitted placement information, rendering some information unusable. Comparison with other tables will show different numbers of placements.

Table 5 / Average Salary Index Starting Library Positions, 1990–2003

Year	Library Schools*	Average Beginning Salary	Dollar Increase in Average Salary	Salary Index	BLS-CPI**
1990	38	$25,306	$725	143.03	130.7
1991	46	25,583	277	144.59	136.2
1992	41	26,666	1,083	150.71	140.5
1993	50	27,116	450	153.26	144.4
1994	43	28,086	970	158.74	148.4
1995	41	28,997	911	163.89	152.5
1996	44	29,480	483	166.62	159.1
1997	43	30,270	790	171.05	161.6
1998	47	31,915	1,645	180.38	164.3
1999	37	33,976	2,061	192.03	168.7
2000	37	34,871	895	197.26	175.1
2001	40	36,818	1,947	208.09	177.1
2002	30	37,456	638	211.70	179.9
2003	43	37,975	519	214.63	184.0

* Includes U.S. schools only
**U.S. Department of Labor, Bureau of Labor Statistics, Consumer Price index, All Urban Consumers (CPI-U), U.S. city average, all items, 1982–1984 = 100. The average beginning professional salary for that period was $17,693.

(continued from page 386)

salaries for minority graduates were exhibiting the effects of a soft economy, with two-thirds of the minority graduates finding placements in organizations that were experiencing reductions or slowed growth in salaries and in areas of the United States with depressed economies.

Where Are the Jobs?

Of the 1,324 graduates (of 1,558) who reported job status, 1,306 (98.6 percent) were employed in some library capacity. This was a positive increase in library employment overall, though graduate responses showed a slight increase in the number of part-time placements compared with 2002, from 12.35 percent to 13.35 percent.

The number of graduates reporting that they were unemployed or reporting no employment status increased to 15.2 percent in 2003, with 216 stating they were unemployed (never got a job and were still looking). However, the number of temporary professional placements remained stable in 2003, with 10.3 percent reporting temporary status compared with 10.5 percent in 2002. Numerous graduates reported holding two part-time jobs in order to obtain a full-time income. This part-time pay ranged from a low of $6.50 per hour to $35 per hour, and many graduates indicated a range of 20 to 24 hours per week of part-time employment. Hiring agencies may be protecting their existing employees and positions by adding temporary and part-time positions to supplement overworked professional staff.

Table 6 / Salaries of Reporting Professionals by Area of Job Assignment*

Assignment	Number	Percent of Total	Low Salary	High Salary	Average Salary	Median Salary
Acquisitions	30	2.70	$23,338	$49,000	$35,067	$35,000
Administration	81	7.28	21,000	73,000	39,400	37,000
Archives	49	4.40	24,000	52,000	34,230	34,000
Automation/Systems	16	1.44	29,120	70,000	42,758	38,500
Cataloging and Classification	57	5.12	22,000	70,000	34,252	33,000
Circulation	32	2.88	18,000	52,000	31,432	32,000
Collection Development	20	1.80	22,450	45,000	35,721	35,000
Database Management	14	1.26	20,800	52,000	39,886	39,000
Digital Services	12	1.08	34,000	51,800	39,433	38,000
Government Documents	7	0.63	34,000	56,000	39,433	38,000
Indexing/Abstracting	3	0.27	30,000	32,500	31,250	31,250
Info. Consultant	7	0.63	37,000	80,000	53,542	49,000
Info. Technology	32	2.88	32,000	90,000	52,935	51,500
Instruction	16	1.44	10,200	49,000	34,663	36,000
Interlibrary Loans	7	0.63	14,000	37,000	26,714	28,000
LAN Manager	1	0.09	32,000	32,000	32,000	32,000
Media Specialist	239	21.47	10,000	88,000	40,828	39,000
Other	29	2.61	17,000	70,000	36,480	36,000
Reference/Info. Services	295	26.50	17,000	80,000	36,738	36,000
Research	5	0.45	30,000	63,000	44,800	40,000
Solo Librarian	57	5.12	15,000	75,000	38,027	36,000
Tech. Services/Serials	8	0.72	12,000	42,000	27,800	26,400
Telecomm.	6	0.54	30,000	42,000	37,457	37,900
Web Services	4	0.36	36,000	94,000	62,500	40,000
Youth Services	86	7.73	23,000	50,123	34,980	35,000
Total	1,113	100.00	$10,000	$94,000	$37,932	$36,000

* This table represents only full-time placements reported by job assignment. Some individuals omitted placement information, rendering some information unusable. Comparison with other tables will show different numbers of placements.

As in previous years, institution type had an impact on the salaries offered to new graduates. Table 7 compares the placements and full-time salaries by type of institution. Public libraries experienced another slight increase (up 2.39 percent compared with 2 percent in 2002) in the overall average beginning salaries, but continued to offer average salaries at the lower level of the scales. However, in 2003, government library placements experienced a serious 12 percent decrease in the beginning average salaries, landing below public libraries. Academic libraries experienced a 3.09 percent decrease in the average beginning salaries to $35,512, down from last year's $36,610, and below the 2001 average of $35,883. Salary decreases may be a symptom of continuing struggles to find public and private funding for library services. LIS schools reported that budget cuts in corporate and government sectors impacted the job search process for their graduates. In many cases, government funds are stretched thin to meet the needs of

(text continues on page 396)

Table 7 / Comparison of Salaries by Type of Organization*

	Total Placements	Salaries		Low Salary		High Salary		Average Salary			Median Salary		
		Women	Men	Women	Men	Women	Men	Women	Men	All	Women	Men	All
Public Libraries													
Northeast	98	80	11	$18,720	$27,000	$52,000	$62,000	$34,369	$40,239	$35,052	$34,000	$39,000	$34,700
Southeast	58	44	9	20,424	24,700	43,000	44,000	31,018	33,744	31,481	30,500	33,000	31,199
Midwest	87	69	8	17,000	29,500	55,000	40,000	34,316	34,188	34,302	34,000	33,000	34,000
Southwest	20	17	2	28,000	33,240	39,520	35,000	32,775	34,120	32,916	31,500	34,120	31,500
West	40	29	9	23,712	10,200	50,000	73,000	40,299	45,850	41,407	39,811	46,800	40,800
All Public	303	239	39	17,000	10,200	55,000	73,000	34,363	38,286	34,901	34,000	36,167	34,000
School Libraries													
Northeast	88	76	4	15,000	34,000	88,000	60,000	41,954	44,706	42,288	40,000	42,413	40,119
Southeast	52	45	1	10,000	35,000	62,000	35,000	34,919	35,000	34,921	35,159	35,000	35,080
Midwest	65	47	12	26,900	30,000	72,000	70,000	39,741	44,583	40,726	38,500	42,000	38,700
Southwest	21	15	2	25,400	40,000	48,000	54,000	34,755	47,000	36,196	35,500	47,000	36,425
West	28	19	4	27,000	38,000	72,000	70,799	47,853	48,619	47,986	42,000	42,839	42,000
Canada/International	4	4	—	21,000	—	38,000	—	32,250	—	32,250	35,000	35,000	35,000
All School	258	206	23	10,000	30,000	88,000	70,799	39,961	45,100	40,574	38,000	42,000	38,500
College/University Libraries													
Northeast	86	51	23	18,000	12,000	58,000	56,000	36,449	39,416	37,299	37,000	41,000	37,800
Southeast	87	52	24	19,000	28,000	43,000	43,000	33,731	37,004	34,729	34,160	37,000	35,000
Midwest	87	57	23	22,000	20,000	50,000	50,028	34,734	36,707	35,297	35,000	37,934	35,000
Southwest	20	12	6	14,000	35,000	49,000	38,000	31,005	36,150	32,720	30,550	35,500	34,500
West	25	19	5	23,338	26,000	52,000	37,000	37,843	32,800	36,793	37,008	35,000	37,000
Canada/International	9	3	3	33,659	23,873	75,000	33,659	47,439	28,766	33,808	33,659	28,766	33,659
All Academic	314	194	84	14,000	12,000	75,000	56,000	35,175	36,363	35,512	35,000	37,000	35,950
Special Libraries													
Northeast	36	28	5	26,000	28,000	55,000	80,000	40,202	44,700	40,863	38,000	37,500	38,000
Southeast	14	12	2	24,000	38,000	50,000	52,000	34,184	45,000	35,729	33,000	45,000	33,500
Midwest	20	15	4	17,000	28,080	75,000	38,000	37,819	33,020	36,809	37,000	33,000	36,941
Southwest	4	4	—	28,500	—	42,000	—	35,000	—	35,000	34,750	—	34,750
West	14	13	1	29,120	29,000	75,000	29,000	46,059	29,000	44,841	44,000	29,000	41,000

Government Libraries, Library Co-ops./Networks, Vendors, Other Organizations

Canada/International	8	5	1	17,000	70,000	51,116	70,000	33,363	70,000	39,470	29,884	70,000	35,196
All Special	96	77	13	17,000	28,000	75,000	80,000	39,094	80,000	39,489	37,000	37,500	37,250
Government Libraries													
Northeast	7	6	1	21,000	33,232	45,000	33,232	34,000	33,232	33,890	37,500	33,232	35,000
Southeast	8	6	2	31,000	34,000	55,000	40,000	38,461	37,000	38,096	36,468	37,000	36,468
Midwest	7	4	3	27,600	24,000	39,000	34,000	33,724	30,193	32,211	34,148	32,580	33,300
Southwest	2	2	—	33,500	—	38,000	—	35,750	—	35,750	35,750	—	35,750
West	3	3	—	29,000	—	33,280	—	30,760	—	30,760	30,000	—	30,000
Canada/International	1	—	1	—	—	—	—	—	—	—	—	—	—
All Government	28	21	7	21,000	24,000	55,000	40,000	34,926	32,473	34,313	34,000	33,232	33,750
Library Co-ops./Networks													
Northeast	2	2	—	34,000	—	41,000	—	37,500	—	37,500	37,500	—	37,500
Southeast	1	1	—	39,000	—	39,000	—	39,000	—	39,000	39,000	—	39,000
Midwest	6	4	1	35,000	35,000	45,000	35,000	40,000	35,000	39,000	40,000	35,000	37,000
All Co-ops./Networks	9	7	1	34,000	35,000	45,000	35,000	39,143	35,000	38,625	39,000	35,000	38,000
Vendors													
Northeast	3	2	1	34,500	32,500	36,000	32,500	35,250	32,500	34,333	35,250	32,500	34,500
Southeast	5	4	1	27,000	61,100	40,000	61,100	33,625	61,100	39,120	33,750	61,100	37,500
Midwest	4	3	1	32,000	43,800	40,000	43,800	36,333	43,800	38,200	37,000	43,800	38,500
West	2	1	1	—	52,000	52,000	52,000	—	52,000	52,000	—	52,000	52,000
Canada/International	1	—	1	—	28,696	28,696	28,696	—	28,696	28,696	—	28,696	28,696
All Vendors	15	10	5	27,000	28,696	40,000	61,100	35,600	43,619	38,273	36,500	43,800	37,000
Other Organizations													
Northeast	28	15	7	20,800	39,000	94,000	80,000	42,693	61,000	47,452	36,500	64,000	42,000
Southeast	13	8	5	32,000	38,000	63,000	45,000	44,118	41,140	42,973	39,000	40,000	40,000
Midwest	29	23	3	25,147	50,000	90,000	63,250	44,006	57,083	45,515	40,000	58,000	42,000
Southwest	8	5	2	40,000	42,500	70,000	65,000	50,555	53,750	51,468	45,976	53,750	45,976
West	8	5	1	39,000	43,000	77,000	43,000	56,600	43,000	54,333	50,000	43,000	48,500
Canada/International	6	1	4	38,558	24,488	38,558	59,000	38,558	39,992	39,649	38,558	38,100	38,558
All Other	92	57	22	20,800	24,488	94,000	80,000	45,376	50,643	46,543	40,000	45,000	43,000

* This table represents only full-time salaries and placements reported by type. Some individuals omitted placement and/or gender information, rendering some information unusable. Comparison with other tables will show different numbers of placements and salaries.

(continued from page 393)

multiple programs and initiatives while grant agencies are becoming more selective in awarding limited funds to an increasing number of applicants.

A Silver Lining

School media centers experienced another modest increase in average salaries of 1.02 percent to $40,574 (compared with $40,161 in 2002). For two years running, school media specialist national average salaries have topped the $40,000 level. Table 6 compares the full-time salaries by area of job assignment. Media specialists are among those who receive the highest salaries, peaking at $88,000, ranking just below placements in Web services ($94,000) and information technology ($90,000). The highly paid media specialists are career-changers. They report they are certified teachers moving from the classroom to the media center with several years (from 6 to 18) of teaching experience. However, this success is not shared by all. Several report having taken full-time placement as media assistants, library aides, or library assistants at very low salaries, reporting in the hope that better positions would become available in their school districts. In some instances this is further exacerbated by location and the type of educational position the graduates obtain. Graduates who got positions in rural areas nationwide and in the Southeast reported annual salaries as low as $10,000 annually as media assistants and as specialized education instructors.

There were shifts in the types of full-time jobs graduates reported for 2003. Administration, digital services, instruction, and media specialist positions were on the rise, while archives, cataloging and classification, and reference and information services jobs were down. Positions in administration and management looked healthy, with 7.28 percent of the total placements compared with 4.42 percent in 2002. Eighteen of the graduates reported job titles of director of the library, branch manager, and department head, and described responsibilities in financial planning and budgeting, policy development, and human resources.

In 2002 fewer than 1 percent of the graduates reported placement in digital services; in 2003, 1.08 percent reported placements related to electronic resources, digitization and preservation, or electronic and digital libraries. While salaries remained relatively constant between 2002 ($39,167) and 2003 ($39,433) for digital services, more graduates identified their positions as related to digital or electronic services.

Academic year 2003 saw a return to graduates reporting positions in instruction. The last time such jobs were reported was 2001, with an average beginning salary of $41,700. In 2003 the total placements in instruction made up 1.44 percent of the placements (up from 0.55 percent in 2001), but with a significantly lower average salary ($34,663). Several graduates reported jobs with such titles as assistant professor or education librarian, indicating that some of these positions held faculty rank within the institution. A number of the graduates reported dual responsibilities in instruction and reference.

Placements in reference and information services (26.5 percent of the total) and media specialists (21.47 percent of the total) continued to dominate job types. In 2003 average salaries for reference and information services ($36,738) fell below the overall average for beginning salaries, down from $37,680 in 2002. Graduates also reported fewer jobs in reference. Some of this may be attributable to reclassification and descriptions of jobs (describing electronic reference librarian as digital services/digital librarian) and the increase in part-time positions.

Outside Libraries

As mentioned, a continuing leader in beginning salaries, the "other" category, offers both variety and generous average salaries. LIS graduates obtaining positions in other organizations reported an average salary of $46,543 (up 2.86 percent from 2002), which is approximately 18 percent higher than the overall average salary. "Other" placements offer challenge and excitement in areas of business analysis, grant-writing and fund raising, and digital initiatives. Graduates describe working in e-commerce, data mining, and data asset management, as well as in community outreach and international relations. Overwhelmingly, graduates noted that "mentoring by influential professors and recognized experts in the field," "value of real client-based projects and portfolios," and "networking and contacts both inside and outside of the profession" were significant in finding and gaining nontraditional jobs. Additionally, extensive experience in areas outside of libraries, such as business and computer sciences, heavily influenced employers in making hiring decisions.

Searching and Searching

For graduates who did not return to an employer or who did not find employment prior to graduation, the job search was challenging. The length of time to find employment ranged from less than one month to more than 19 months. The average job search took 4.5 months after graduation, almost three times as long as the average for the class of 2002. One graduate stated that library jobs were highly competitive with "too few jobs and too many applicants" despite the suggestion of professional staffing shortages. Obtaining jobs in government libraries in particular was a lengthy process, averaging six months. One graduate noted that "the interviewing process can take over a year in some cases" for government positions. On a positive note, one solo librarian advised that "The process of finding a job was grueling, but I didn't give up." The right job turned up in an area where she least expected it would, though her search took eight months. Graduates recommend persistence and perseverance.

Many graduates expressed frustration in not finding salaries that reflect the advanced degree and in not finding professional positions in their regions. For many choosing to complete their degrees through a distance-learning model, it has proven to be a double-edged sword in finding employment. The learning opportunity worked well for placebound students, but the inability to move hampered the job search when jobs were unavailable near home. One graduate indicated that "it was impossible to find a job without relocating outside of the state."

(text continues on page 400)

Table 8 / Placements and Full-Time Salaries of Reporting 2003 Graduates*

Schools	Placements	Salaries Women	Salaries Men	Low Salary Women	Low Salary Men	High Salary Women	High Salary Men	Average Salary Women	Average Salary Men	Average Salary All	Median Salary Women	Median Salary Men	Median Salary All
Alabama	9	7	1	$30,000	$41,000	$48,000	$41,000	$37,454	$41,000	$37,848	$36,107	$41,000	$36,213
Albany	1	1	—	30,000	—	30,000	—	30,000	—	30,000	30,000	—	30,000
Arizona	24	12	6	24,000	22,880	70,000	42,600	38,433	35,247	37,371	35,970	35,500	35,500
Cal State–Long Beach	10	9	1	27,000	70,799	70,000	70,799	47,646	70,799	49,961	42,000	70,799	47,000
Catholic Univ.	1	1	—	40,919	—	40,919	—	40,919	—	40,919	40,919	—	40,919
Clarion	15	14	—	20,800	—	38,000	—	31,974	—	31,974	34,000	—	34,000
Dominican	53	36	10	25,147	30,000	75,000	47,600	38,230	36,204	37,789	36,483	34,500	36,233
Drexel	13	12	1	22,000	51,035	80,000	51,035	36,857	51,035	37,948	34,500	51,035	35,000
Emporia	32	20	8	30,000	36,000	49,980	60,000	35,834	45,188	38,506	35,000	40,000	36,000
Florida State	37	26	7	17,000	27,300	54,000	61,100	34,057	40,300	35,526	33,000	40,000	34,500
Illinois	58	48	9	26,807	31,000	65,000	50,028	37,133	38,948	37,419	36,645	38,000	37,000
Indiana	24	14	10	22,000	20,000	50,000	46,000	34,514	34,682	34,584	34,075	34,370	34,120
Kentucky	26	14	8	22,000	31,500	75,000	43,000	36,955	35,938	36,585	31,250	35,000	34,000
Long Island**	39	28	4	30,940	40,000	64,507	60,000	44,458	47,500	44,579	45,500	45,000	44,500
Louisiana State	17	11	2	27,000	33,000	49,000	36,000	35,696	34,500	35,512	35,159	34,500	35,159
McGill	13	8	5	28,310	23,873	40,547	70,000	33,466	36,143	34,496	33,659	28,696	33,659
Michigan	61	32	16	30,000	36,000	90,000	80,000	45,688	51,516	47,630	41,500	43,500	42,000
Missouri–Columbia	36	29	2	21,000	24,000	48,625	30,000	33,747	27,000	33,311	32,000	27,000	32,000

N.C. Chapel Hill	31	23	8	19,000	35,000	53,946	59,000	34,043	41,738	36,028	36,000	38,100	36,900
N.C. Greensboro	34	28	—	20,424	—	55,000	—	31,060	—	31,060	31,700	—	31,700
Oklahoma	16	11	3	14,000	35,000	39,000	37,900	30,971	35,967	32,041	31,500	35,000	34,000
Pittsburgh**	38	33	3	20,800	30,000	56,000	45,000	35,583	35,860	35,293	36,000	32,580	34,590
Pratt	23	19	4	29,000	28,500	94,000	50,000	40,065	39,500	39,967	36,400	39,750	36,400
Queens College**	47	31	8	27,040	31,199	88,000	80,000	45,489	45,625	44,944	43,900	38,500	43,000
Rhode Island	9	9	—	25,000	—	70,000	—	38,969	—	38,969	34,000	—	34,000
Rutgers	30	27	3	25,000	33,000	75,000	56,000	38,329	41,921	38,688	38,000	36,762	38,000
San Jose	42	34	3	17,000	35,000	72,000	48,000	43,373	41,392	43,212	39,650	41,177	40,000
Simmons	112	85	17	15,000	12,000	56,000	60,000	35,326	39,400	35,971	35,693	39,000	36,000
S. Carolina	13	8	2	10,000	28,000	37,500	40,000	28,038	34,000	29,230	28,500	34,000	28,500
S. Florida	15	12	1	21,840	35,000	62,000	35,000	34,645	35,000	34,672	33,500	35,000	34,000
S. Connecticut	19	17	1	28,000	45,000	67,250	45,000	38,728	45,000	39,076	36,000	45,000	36,250
S. Mississippi	5	5	—	11,000	—	43,000	—	31,780	—	31,780	35,000	—	35,000
Tennessee	3	2	—	30,000	—	31,000	—	30,500	—	30,500	30,500	—	30,500
Texas (Austin)	29	22	6	22,800	29,500	51,800	65,000	34,821	44,167	36,824	34,000	39,500	35,963
Univ. of Albany	1	1	—	30,000	—	30,000	—	30,000	—	30,000	30,000	—	30,000
Univ. of Buffalo	17	10	5	28,000	24,960	50,000	36,325	36,660	32,303	35,208	35,750	33,232	34,714
Washington	30	22	6	28,000	37,000	50,000	52,000	39,748	42,367	40,309	40,000	42,000	40,000
Wayne State	51	34	13	23,924	29,000	72,000	70,000	38,580	38,069	38,438	36,694	35,000	36,000
Wisc. (Madison)	38	22	9	30,000	10,200	55,000	50,000	35,159	36,093	35,430	34,250	37,000	34,500
Wisc. (Milwaukee)	40	28	7	17,000	24,000	48,285	73,000	33,833	40,062	35,079	34,000	37,000	35,000

* This table represents only placements and salaries reported as full time. Some individuals or schools omitted some information, rendering information unusable. Comparisons with other tables will show different numbers of placements and salaries.

** Some individuals reported full-time placements and salaries but not gender

(continued from page 397)

Some of the LIS schools suggested that it was much more difficult for the graduates who were conducting long-distance job searches.

Either as a result of frustration or of active recruitment, a small number of LIS graduates (2.36 percent) had returned to school for additional degrees. Several indicated they are seeking advanced degrees in LIS and other disciplines while a few are working on postgraduate certificates in education. The consensus among those returning for additional degrees was that the master's alone just isn't enough to get the job.

LIS schools reported that the number of job announcements they received for 2003 ranged from fewer than 100 to more than 5000. Many also indicated that with the prevalence of the Internet it is much more difficult to estimate the number of available jobs. Nine schools reported a decrease in the number of job announcements received; in some instances listings dropped by as much as 65 percent.

Both graduates and LIS schools reported greater difficulty placing international students within the United States. Respondents noted that owing to tightened visa laws and regulations, employers were reluctant to sponsor international graduates for full-time employment. The average length of the job search for international students was at the top of the range, with four graduates reporting no employment 18 months after graduation.

Experience Matters

Perhaps in response to the paucity of jobs, graduates were finding out about job opportunities in a variety of ways. Many of the LIS schools indicated they provided access to job announcements by placing them on student bulletin boards and student e-lists. Thirteen of the schools that responded indicated they had formal placement services available. LIS schools also facilitated graduate placement through career workshops and by sponsoring career days. As a result of the myriad tools for communication available, LIS schools reported no major difficulties in placing graduates, with the exception of the international students.

Graduates repeatedly suggested that previous experience in other jobs and networking with local professionals were instrumental in their job search success. One library media specialist summed up the job search by saying, "Prior experience in teaching and technology landed the job!" Many were able to call upon unique skills developed through previous experiences, such as public relations or community service, to complement the more traditional and technological skills they learned in the classroom. A number of graduates also stated that the theoretical and philosophical foundations learned added depth to their understanding of the profession as a whole. Overall, graduates agreed that fieldwork or internships, along with previous experience, had the most impact in obtaining professional placement. And, as in previous years, technological skills and the ability to conduct effective searches were cited as crucial to successfully landing a job.

Accredited Master's Programs in Library and Information Studies

This list of graduate programs accredited by the American Library Association is issued, with additional detail, as a print brochure early in each calendar year by the ALA Office for Accreditation. In addition, regular updates appear on the Office for Accreditation's Web site at http://www.ala.org/alaorg/oa/lisdir.html. More than 200 institutions offering both accredited and nonaccredited programs in librarianship are included in the 57th edition of *American Library Directory* (Information Today, Inc., 2004–2005).

Northeast: Conn., D.C., Md., Mass., N.J., N.Y., Pa., R.I.

Catholic University of America, School of Lib. and Info. Science, 620 Michigan Ave. N.E., Washington, DC 20064. Martha Hale, Dean. Tel. 202-319-5085, fax 202-219-5574, World Wide Web http://slis. cua.edu. Admissions contact: William Turner. Tel. 202-319-5085, e-mail turnerjr @cua.edu.

Clarion University of Pennsylvania, Dept. of Lib. Science, 210 Carlson Lib. Bldg., 840 Wood St., Clarion, PA 16214. Andrea L. Miller, Chair. Tel. 814-393-2271, fax 814-393-2150, World Wide Web http://www. clarion.edu/libsci. Admissions contact: Barbara Reed. Tel. 866-272-5612, e-mail reed@clarion.edu.

Drexel University, College of Info. Science and Technology, 3141 Chestnut St., Philadelphia, PA 19104-2875. David E. Fenske, Dean. Tel. 215-895-2474, fax 215-895-2494, e-mail info@cis.drexel.edu, World Wide Web http://www.cis.drexel.edu. Admissions contact: Matthew Lechtenburg. Tel. 215-895-1951.

Long Island University, Palmer School of Lib. and Info. Science, C. W. Post Campus, 720 Northern Blvd., Brookville, NY 11548-1300. Mary Westermann-Cicio, Acting Dean. Tel. 516-299-2866, fax 516-299-4168, e-mail palmer@cwpost.liu.edu, World Wide Web http://www.liu.edu/ palmer. Admissions contact: Rosemary Chu. Tel. 516-299-2487, e-mail rchu@liu. edu.

Pratt Institute, School of Info. and Lib. Science, 144 W. 14 St., New York, NY 10011.

Tula Giannini, Acting Dean. Tel. 212-647-7682, e-mail infosils@pratt.edu, World Wide Web http://www.pratt.edu/sils. Admissions contact: Virginia Papandrea.

Queens College, City Univ. of New York, Grad. School for Lib. and Info. Studies, 65-30 Kissena Blvd., Flushing, NY 11367-1597. Virgil L. P. Blake, Dir. Tel. 718-997-3790, fax 718-997-3797, e-mail gslis @qcunix1.qc.edu, World Wide Web http:// www.qc.edu/gslis. Admissions contact: Virgil L. P. Blake. E-mail virgil_blake@ qc.edu.

Rutgers University, Dept. of Lib. and Info. Science, School of Communication, Info., and Lib. Studies, 4 Huntington St., New Brunswick, NJ 08903-1071. Nicholas J. Belkin, Dir. Tel. 732-932-7500 ext. 8955, fax 732-932-2644, e-mail scilsmls@scils. rutgers.edu, World Wide Web http://www. scils.rutgers.edu. Admissions contact: Pat Appelbaum.

Saint John's University, Div. of Lib. and Info. Science, 8000 Utopia Pkwy., Jamaica, NY 11439. Elizabeth Pollicino, Assoc. Dir. Tel. 718-990-6200, fax 718-990-2071, e-mail dlis@stjohns.edu, World Wide Web http://www.stjohns.edu/libraryscience. Admissions contact: Joanne Heiser.

Simmons College, Grad. School of Lib. and Info. Science, 300 The Fenway, Boston, MA 02115. Michelle Cloonan, Dean. Tel. 617-521-2800, fax 617-521-3192, e-mail gslis@simmons.edu, World Wide Web http://www.simmons.edu/gslis.

Southern Connecticut State University, School of Communication, Info., and Lib. Science, 501 Crescent St., New Haven, CT

06515. Edward C. Harris, Dean. Tel. 203-392-5781, fax 203-392-5780, e-mail mckay1@southernct.edu, World Wide Web http://www.southernct.edu/departments/ils. Admissions contact: Arlene Bielefield. Tel. 203-392-5708, e-mail bielefielda1@southernct.edu.

Syracuse University, School of Info. Studies, 4-206 Center for Science and Technology, Syracuse, NY 13244-4100. Raymond von Dran, Dean. Tel. 315-443-2911, fax 315-443-5673, e-mail ist@syr.edu, World Wide Web http://www.ist.syr.edu. Admissions contact: Gisela von Dran. Tel. 315-443-2911, e-mail mls@syr.edu.

University at Albany, State Univ. of New York, School of Info. Science and Policy, Draper 113, 135 Western Ave., Albany, NY 12222. Peter Bloniarz, Dean. Tel. 518-442-5110, fax 518-442-5367, e-mail infosci@albany.edu, World Wide Web http://www.albany.edu/sisp. Admissions contact: Frances Reynolds. Tel. 518-442-5110, e-mail reynolds@albany.edu.

University at Buffalo, State Univ. of New York, Dept. of Lib. and Info. Studies, School of Informatics, 534 Baldy Hall, Buffalo, NY 14260. Judith Robinson, Chair. Tel. 716-645-2412, fax 716-645-3775, e-mail ub-lis@buffalo.edu, World Wide Web http://www.informatics.buffalo.edu/lis. Admissions contact: Donna M. King. Tel. 716-645-2412 ext. 1173, e-mail kingd@acsu.buffalo.edu.

University of Maryland, College of Info. Studies, 4105 Hornbake Lib. Bldg., College Park, MD 20742-4345. Bruce Dearstyne, Interim Dean. Tel. 301-405-2033, fax 301-314-9145, World Wide Web http://www.clis.umd.edu. Admissions e-mail lbscgrad@deans.umd.edu, tel. 301-405-2038.

University of Pittsburgh, School of Info. Sciences, 135 N. Bellefield Ave., Pittsburgh, PA 15260. Ronald Larsen, Dean. Tel. 412-624-5142, fax 412-624-5231, e-mail inquiry@mail.sis.pitt.edu, World Wide Web http://www.sis.pitt.edu. Admissions contact: Terry Kizina. Tel. 412-624-5230, e-mail tkizina@mail.sis.pitt.edu.

University of Rhode Island, Grad. School of Lib. and Info. Studies, Rodman Hall, 94 W. Alumni Ave., Kingston, RI 02881. W. Michael Havener, Dir. Tel. 401-874-2947, fax 401-874-4964, e-mail gslis@etal.uri.edu, World Wide Web http://www.uri.edu/artsci/lsc.

Southeast: Ala., Fla., Ga., Ky., La., Miss., N.C., S.C., Tenn., P.R.

Florida State University, School of Info. Studies, Shores Bldg., Tallahassee, FL 32306-2100. Jane B. Robbins, Dean. Tel. 850-644-5772, fax 850-644-9763, e-mail grad@lis.fsu.edu, World Wide Web http://www.lis.fsu.edu.

Louisiana State University, School of Lib. and Info. Science, 267 Coates Hall, Baton Rouge, LA 70803. Beth Paskoff, Dean. Tel. 225-578-3158, fax 225-578-4581, e-mail slis@lsu.edu, World Wide Web http://slis.lsu.edu. Admissions contact: LaToya Coleman Joseph. E-mail lcjoseph@lsu.edu.

North Carolina Central University, School of Lib. and Info. Sciences, 1800 Fayetteville St., Durham, NC 27707. Robert M. Ballard, Interim Dean. Tel. 919-530-6485, fax 919-530-6402, e-mail lsis@nccu.edu, World Wide Web http://www.nccuslis.org. Admissions contact: Timothy Bailey. Tel. 919-530-7320, e-mail tbailey@wpo.nccu.edu.

University of Alabama, School of Lib. and Info. Studies, Box 870252, Tuscaloosa, AL 35487-0252. Elizabeth Aversa, Dir. Tel. 205-348-4610, fax 205-348-3746, e-mail info@slis.ua.edu, World Wide Web http://www.slis.ua.edu.

University of Kentucky, College of Communications and Info. Studies, School of Lib. and Info. Science, 502 King Lib., Lexington, KY 40506-0039. Timothy W. Sineath, Dir. Tel. 859-257-8876, fax 859-257-4205, World Wide Web http://www.uky.edu/CIS/SLIS. Admissions contact: Jane Salsman. Tel. 859-257-3317, e-mail salsman@uky.edu.

University of North Carolina at Chapel Hill, School of Info. and Lib. Science, CB

3360, 100 Manning Hall, Chapel Hill, NC 27599-3360. José-Marie Griffiths, Dean. Tel. 919-962-8366, fax 919-962-8071, e-mail info@ils.unc.edu, World Wide Web http://www.ils.unc.edu. Admissions contact: Betty Dye.

University of North Carolina at Greensboro, Dept. of Lib. and Info. Studies, School of Educ., 349 Curry Bldg., Greensboro, NC 27402-6170. Lee Shiflett, Chair. Tel. 336-334-3477, fax 336-334-5060, e-mail lis@uncg.edu, World Wide Web http://lis.uncg.edu.

University of Puerto Rico, Graduate School of Info. Sciences and Technologies, Box 21906, San Juan, PR 00931-1906. Consuelo Figueras, Dir. Tel. 787-763-6199, fax 787-764-2311, e-mail egcti@rrpac.upr.clu.edu. Admissions contact: Migdalia Dávila. Tel. 787-764-0000 ext. 3530, e-mail mdavila2@rrpac.upr.clu.edu.

University of South Carolina, School of Lib. and Info. Science, Davis College, Columbia, SC 29208. Daniel Barron, Dir. Tel. 803-777-3858, fax 803-777-7938, e-mail ddbarron@gwm.sc.edu, World Wide Web http://www.libsci.sc.edu. Admissions contact: Ruth Roberts. Tel. 800-304-3153, e-mail rroberts@sc.edu.

University of South Florida, School of Lib. and Info. Science, 4202 E. Fowler Ave., CIS 1040, Tampa, FL 33620. Vicki Gregory, Dir. Tel. 813-974-3520, fax 813-974-6840, e-mail lis@cas.usf.edu, World Wide Web http://www.cas.usf.edu/lis. Admissions contact: Mel Pace. Tel. 813-974-7650, e-mail tpace@cas.usf.edu.

University of Southern Mississippi, School of Lib. and Info. Science, 118 College Drive, No. 5146, Hattiesburg, MS 39406-0001. M. J. Norton, Dir. Tel. 601-266-4228, fax 601-266-5774, e-mail slis@usm.edu, World Wide Web http://www.usm.edu/slis. Admissions tel. 601-266-5137, e-mail graduatestudies@usm.edu.

University of Tennessee, School of Info. Sciences, 451 Communications Bldg., 1345 Circle Park Drive, Knoxville, TN 37996-0341. Douglas Raber, Interim Dir. Tel. 865-974-2148, fax 865-974-4967, e-mail sis@utk.edu, World Wide Web http://

www.sis.utk.edu. Admissions contact: Tanya Arnold. Tel. 865-974-2148.

Midwest: Ill., Ind., Iowa, Kan., Mich., Mo., Ohio, Wis.

Dominican University, Grad. School of Lib. and Info. Science, 7900 W. Division St., River Forest, IL 60305. Prudence W. Dalrymple, Dean. Tel. 708-524-6845, fax 708-524-6657, e-mail gslis@dom.edu, World Wide Web http://www.gslis.dom.edu. Admissions contact: Kathleen Swantek. E-mail kswantek@dom.edu.

Emporia State University, School of Lib. and Info. Management, Campus Box 4025, Emporia, KS 66801. Ann L. O'Neill, Dean. Tel. 620-341-5203, fax 620-341-5233, World Wide Web http://slim.emporia.edu. Admissions contact: Candy Boardman. Tel. 620-341-6159, e-mail boardmac@emporia.edu.

Indiana University, School of Lib. and Info. Science, LI 011, 1320 E. 10 St., Bloomington, IN 47405-3907. Blaise Cronin, Dean. Tel. 812-855-2018, fax 812-855-6166, e-mail slis@indiana.edu, World Wide Web http://www.slis.indiana.edu. Admissions contact: Rhonda Spencer.

Kent State University, School of Lib. and Info. Science, Box 5190, Kent, OH 44242-0001. Richard E. Rubin, Dir. Tel. 330-672-2782, fax 330-672-7965, World Wide Web http://www.slis.kent.edu, e-mail inform@slis.kent.edu. Admissions contact: Cheryl Tennant.

University of Illinois at Urbana-Champaign, Grad. School of Lib. and Info. Science, 501 E. Daniel St., Champaign, IL 61820-6211. John Unsworth, Dean. Tel. 217-333-3280, fax 217-244-3302, World Wide Web http://alexia.lis.uiuc.edu. Admissions contact: Carol DeVoss. Tel. 217-333-7197, e-mail apply@alexia.lis.uiuc.edu.

University of Iowa, School of Lib. and Info. Science, 3087 Main Lib., Iowa City, IA 52242-1420. David Eichmann, Dir. Tel. 319-335-5707, fax 319-335-5374, e-mail slis@uiowa.edu, World Wide Web http://www.uiowa.edu/~libsci. Admissions contact: Jane Bradbury. E-mail jane-bradbury @uiowa.edu.

University of Michigan, School of Info., 304 West Hall Bldg., 550 E. University Ave., Ann Arbor, MI 48109-1092. John L. King, Dean. Tel. 734-764-9376, fax 734-764-2475, World Wide Web http://www.si. umich.edu. Admissions contact: Suzanne M. Schuon. Tel. 734-763-2285, e-mail si.admissions@umich.edu.

University of Missouri, College of Educ., School of Info. Science and Learning Technologies, 303 Townsend Hall, Columbia, MO 65211. John Wedman, Dir. Tel. 573-882-4546, fax 573-884-0122, e-mail sislt @missouri.edu, World Wide Web http:// sislt.missouri.edu.

University of Wisconsin–Madison, School of Lib. and Info. Studies, Rm. 4217, Helen C. White Hall, 600 N. Park St., Madison, WI 53706. Louise S. Robbins, Dean. Tel. 608-263-2900, fax 608-263-4849, e-mail uw_ slis@slis.wisc.edu, World Wide Web http://www.slis.wisc.edu. Admissions contact: Barbara J. Arnold. Tel. 608-263-2909, e-mail bjarnold@wisc.edu.

University of Wisconsin–Milwaukee, School of Info. Studies, P.O. Box 413, Milwaukee, WI 53211. Thomas D. Walker, Interim Dean. Tel. 414-229-4707, fax 414-229-6699, e-mail info@sois.uwm.edu, World Wide Web http://www.sois.uwm.edu.

Wayne State University, Lib. and Info. Science Program, 106 Kresge Lib., Detroit, MI 48202. Joseph J. Mika, Dir. Tel. 313-577-1825, fax 313-577-7563, e-mail asklis @wayne.edu, World Wide Web http:// www.lisp.wayne.edu. Admissions contact: Matthew Fredericks. Tel. 313-577-2446, e-mail aj8416@wayne.edu.

Southwest: Ariz., Okla., Texas.

Texas Woman's University, School of Lib. and Info. Studies, P.O. Box 425438, Denton, TX 76204-5438. Ling Hwey Jeng, Dir. Tel. 940-898-2602, fax 940-898-2611, e-mail slis@twu.edu, World Wide Web http://www.twu.edu/cope/slis. Admissions

contact: Patricia Graham. E-mail pgraham @mail.wu.edu.

University of Arizona, School of Info. Resources and Lib. Science, 1515 E. 1 St., Tucson, AZ 85719. Jana Bradley, Dir. Tel. 520-621-3565, fax 520-621-3279, e-mail sirls@u.arizona.edu, World Wide Web http://www.sir.arizona.edu.

University of North Texas, School of Lib. and Info. Sciences, Box 311068, Denton, TX 76203-1068. Samantha K. Hastings, Interim Dean. Tel. 940-565-2731, fax 940-565-3101, e-mail slis@unt.edu, World Wide Web http://www.unt.edu/slis. Admissions contact: Arlita Hallam. Tel. 940-565-2445, e-mail ahallam@lis. admin.unt. edu.

University of Oklahoma, School of Lib. and Info. Studies, 401 W. Brooks, Norman, OK 73019-6032. Danny P. Wallace, Dir. Tel. 405-325-3921, fax 405-325-7648, e-mail slisinfo@ou.edu, World Wide Web http://www.ou.edu/cas/slis. Admissions contact: Maggie Ryan.

University of Texas at Austin, School of Info., 1 University Sta., Austin, TX 78712-0391. Andrew Dillon, Dean. Tel. 512-471-3821, fax 512-471-3971, e-mail info@ ischool.utexas.edu, World Wide Web http:// www.ischool.utexas.edu. Admissions contact: Irene Owens. Tel. 512-471-3624, e-mail iowens@ischool.utexas.edu.

West: Calif., Colo., Hawaii, Wash.

San Jose State University, School of Lib. and Info. Science, 1 Washington Sq., San Jose, CA 95192-0029. Blanche Woolls, Dir. Tel. 408-924-2490, fax 408-924-2476, e-mail office@wahoo.sjsu.edu, World Wide Web http://slisweb.sjsu.edu. Admissions contact: Sharlee Phillips. Tel. 408-924-2417, e-mail sphillip@slis.sjsu.edu.

University of California, Los Angeles, Graduate School of Educ. and Info. Studies, Dept. of Info. Studies, Box 951520, Los Angeles, CA 90095-1520. Virginia A. Walter, Chair. Tel. 310-825-8799, fax

310-206-3076, e-mail info@gseis.ucla. edu, World Wide Web http://is.gseis.ucla. edu. Admissions contact: Susan Abler. Tel. 310-825-5269, e-mail abler@gseis. ucla.edu.

University of Denver, College of Educ., Lib. and Info. Science Program, Wesley Hall, 2153 E. Wesley, Ste. 103, Denver, CO 80208. Deborah S. Grealy, Dir. Tel. 303-871-2747, fax 303-871-3422, World Wide Web http://www.du.edu/lis. Admissions contact: Sandra Snyder-Mondragon. Tel. 303-871-2747, e-mail smondrag@du.edu.

University of Hawaii, Lib. and Info. Science Program, 2550 McCarthy Mall, Honolulu, HI 96822. Rebecca Knuh, Program Chair. Tel. 808-956-7321, fax 808-956-5835, e-mail slis@hawaii.edu, World Wide Web http://www.hawaii.edu/slis. Admissions contact: Gail Morimoto.

University of Washington, The Info. School, Mary Gates Hall, Ste. 370, Box 352840, Seattle, WA 98195-2840. Michael B. Eisenberg, Dean. Tel. 206-685-9937, fax 206-616-3152, e-mail info@ischool. washington.edu, World Wide Web http:// www.ischool.washington.edu. Admissions contact: Lindsay Boswell. Tel. 206-543-1794, e-mail mlis@ischool.washington. edu.

Canada

Dalhousie University, School of Lib. and Info. Studies, 3rd fl., Killam Lib., Halifax, NS B3H 3J5. Fiona Black, Dir. Tel. 902-494-3656, fax 902-494-2451, e-mail slis@ dal.ca, World Wide Web http://www. mgmt.dal.ca/slis. Admissions contact: Judy Dunn.

McGill University, Grad. School of Lib. and Info. Studies, 3459 McTavish St., Montreal, PQ H3A 1Y1. France Bouthillier, Acting Dir. Tel. 514-398-4204, fax 514-398-7193, e-mail gslis@mcgill.ca, World Wide Web http://www.gslis.mcgill.ca. Admissions contact: Kathryn Hubbard.

Université de Montréal, Ecole de Bibliothéconomie et des Sciences de l'Information, C.P. 6128, Succursale Centre-Ville, Montreal, PQ H3C 3J7. Carol Couture, Dir. Tel. 514-343-6400, fax 514-343-5753, e-mail ebsiinfo@ebsi.umontreal.ca, World Wide Web http://www.ebsi.umontreal.ca. Admissions contact: Diane Mayer. E-mail diane.mayer@umontreal.ca.

University of Alberta, School of Lib. and Info. Studies, 3-20 Rutherford S., Edmonton, AB T6G 2J4. Anna Altmann, Dir. Tel. 780-492-4578, fax 780-492-2430, e-mail slis@ualberta.ca, World Wide Web http:// www.slis.ualberta.ca. Admissions contact: Joanne Hilger. Tel. 780-492-4140, e-mail joanne.hilger@ualberta.ca.

University of British Columbia, School of Lib., Archival, and Info. Studies, Ste. 301, 6190 Agronomy Rd., Vancouver, BC V6T 1Z3. Edie Rasmussen, Dir. Tel. 604-822-2404, fax 604-822-6006, e-mail slais@ interchange.ubc.ca, World Wide Web http://www.slais.ubc.ca. Admissions contact: Richard Hopkins. Tel. 604-822-2404, e-mail slaisad@interchange.ubc.ca.

University of Toronto, Faculty of Info. and Media Studies, 140 George St., Rm. 211, Toronto, ON M5S 3G6. Brian Cantwell Smith, Dean. Tel. 416-978-3202, fax 416-978-5762, e-mail inquire@fis.utoronto.ca, World Wide Web http://www.fis.utoronto. ca. Admissions contact: Pamela Hawes. Tel. 416-978-8589, e-mail hawes@fis. utoronto.ca.

University of Western Ontario, Grad. Programs in Lib. and Info. Science, Faculty of Info. and Media Studies, North Campus Bldg., London, ON N6A 5B7. Catherine Ross, Dean. Tel. 519-661-4017, fax 519-661-3506, e-mail mlisinfo@uwo.ca. Admissions contact: Shelley Long.

Library Scholarship Sources

For a more complete list of scholarships, fellowships, and assistantships offered for library study, see *Financial Assistance for Library and Information Studies,* published annually by the American Library Association. The document is also available on the ALA Web site at http://www.ala.org/hrdr/scholarship.html.

American Association of Law Libraries. (1) A varying number of scholarships of a minimum of $1,000 for graduates of an accredited law school who are degree candidates in an ALA-accredited library school; (2) a varying number of scholarships of varying amounts for library school graduates working on a law degree, non-law graduates enrolled in an ALA-accredited library school, and law librarians taking a course related to law librarianship; (3) the George A. Strait Minority Stipend of $3,500 for varying numbers of minority librarians working toward an advanced degree to further a law library career. For information, write to: Scholarship Committee, AALL, 53 W. Jackson Blvd., Suite 940, Chicago, IL 60604.

American Library Association. (1) The Marshall Cavendish Scholarship of $3,000 for a varying number of students who have been admitted to an ALA-accredited library school; (2) the David H. Clift Scholarship of $3,000 for a varying number of students who have been admitted to an ALA-accredited library school; (3) the Tom and Roberta Drewes Scholarship of $3,000 for a varying number of library support staff; (4) the Mary V. Gaver Scholarship of $3,000 for a varying number of individuals specializing in youth services; (5) the Miriam L. Hornback Scholarship of $3,000 for a varying number of ALA or library support staff; (6) the Christopher J. Hoy/ERT Scholarship of $5,000 for a varying number of students who have been admitted to an ALA-accredited library school; (7) the Tony B. Leisner Scholarship of $3,000 for a varying number of library support staff; (8) Spectrum Initiative Scholarships of $6,500 for a varying number of minority students admitted to an ALA-accredited library

school. For information on all ALA scholarships, write to: ALA Scholarship Clearinghouse, 50 E. Huron St., Chicago, IL 60611. Application can also be made online; see http://www.ala.org/hrdr/scholarship.html.

ALA/American Association of School Librarians. The AASL School Librarians Workshop Scholarship of $3,000 for a candidate admitted to a full-time ALA-accredited MLS or school library media program. For information, write to: ALA Scholarship Clearinghouse, 50 E. Huron St., Chicago, IL 60611, or see http://www.ala.org/hrdr/scholarship.html.

ALA/Association for Library Service to Children. (1) The Bound to Stay Bound Books Scholarship of $6,000 each for two students who are U.S. or Canadian citizens, who have been admitted to an ALA-accredited program, and who will work with children in a library for one year after graduation; (2) the Frederic G. Melcher Scholarship of $6,000 each for two U.S. or Canadian citizens admitted to an ALA-accredited library school who will work with children in school or public libraries for one year after graduation. For information, write to: ALA Scholarship Clearinghouse, 50 E. Huron St., Chicago, IL 60611, or see http://www.ala.org/hrdr/scholarship.html.

ALA/Association of College and Research Libraries and the Institute for Scientific Information. (1) The ACRL Doctoral Dissertation Fellowship of $1,500 for a student who has completed all coursework and submitted a dissertation proposal that has been accepted, in the area of academic librarianship; (2) the Samuel Lazerow Fellowship of $1,000 for a research, travel, or writing project in acquisitions or technical services in an academic or research library;

(3) the ACRL and Martinus Nijhoff International West European Specialist Study Grant, which pays travel expenses, room, and board for a ten-day trip to Europe for an ALA member (selection is based on proposal outlining purpose of trip). For information, write to: Megan Bielefeld, ACRL/ALA, 50 E. Huron St., Chicago, IL 60611.

ALA/Association of Specialized and Cooperative Library Agencies. Century Scholarship of up to $2,500 for a varying number of disabled U.S. or Canadian citizens admitted to an ALA-accredited library school. For information, write to: ALA Scholarship Clearinghouse, 50 E. Huron St., Chicago, IL 60611, or see http://www.ala.org/hrdr/scholarship.html.

ALA/International Relations Committee. The Bogle Pratt International Library Travel Fund grant of $1,000 for a varying number of ALA members to attend a first international conference. For information, write to: Michael Dowling, ALA/IRC, 50 E. Huron St., Chicago, IL 60611.

ALA/Library and Information Technology Association. (1) The LITA/Christian Larew Memorial Scholarship of $3,000 for a student who has been admitted to an ALA-accredited program in library automation and information science; (2) the LITA/Sirsi Scholarship in Library and Information Technology of $2,500 for a student who has been admitted to an ALA-accredited program in library automation and information technology; (3) the LITA/OCLC Minority Scholarship in Library and Information Technology of $3,000 for a minority student admitted to an ALA-accredited program; (4) the LITA/LSSI Minority Scholarship of $2,500 for a minority student admitted to an ALA-accredited program. For information, write to: ALA Scholarship Clearinghouse, 50 E. Huron St., Chicago, IL 60611, or see http://www.ala.org/hrdr/scholarship.html.

ALA/Public Library Association. The New Leaders Travel Grant Study Award of up to $1,500 for a varying number of PLA members with MLS degrees and five years' or less experience. For information, write to: PLA Awards Program, PLA/ALA, 50 E. Huron St., Chicago, IL 60611.

American-Scandinavian Foundation. Fellowships and grants for 25 to 30 students, in amounts from $3,000 to $18,000, for advanced study in Denmark, Finland, Iceland, Norway, or Sweden. For information, write to: Exchange Division, American-Scandinavian Foundation, 58 Park Ave., New York, NY 10026.

Association for Library and Information Science Education. A varying number of research grants of up to $2,500 each for members of ALISE. For information, write to: Association for Library and Information Science Education, Box 7640, Arlington, VA 22207.

Association of Jewish Libraries. (1) The AJL Scholarship Fund offers up to two scholarships of $500 each for MLS students who plan to work as Judaica librarians; (2) the Rosalie Katchen Memorial Award of varying amounts for varying numbers of MLS students to enable them to advance in Hebraica or Judaica cataloging. For information, write to: Deborah Stern, Dir., Kaplan Library, Reconstructionist Rabbinical College, 1299 Church Rd., Wyncote, PA 19095, e-mail dstern@rrc.edu.

Association of Seventh-Day Adventist Librarians. The D. Glenn Hilts Scholarship of $1,000 for a member of the Seventh-Day Adventist Church in a graduate library program. For information, write to: Ms. Wisel, Association of Seventh-Day Adventist Librarians, Columbia Union College, 7600 Flower Ave., Takoma Park, MD 20912.

Beta Phi Mu. (1) The Sarah Rebecca Reed Scholarship of $2,000 for a person accepted in an ALA-accredited library program; (2) the Frank B. Sessa Scholarship of $1,250 for a Beta Phi Mu member for continuing education; (3) the Harold Lancour Scholarship of $1,500 for study in a foreign country related to the applicant's work or schooling; (4) the Blanche E. Woolls Scholarship for School Library Media Service of $1,500 for a person accepted in an ALA-accredited library program; (5) the Doctoral Dissertation

Scholarship of $2,000 for a person who has completed course work toward a doctorate; (6) the Eugene Garfield Doctoral Dissertation Scholarship of $3,000 for a person who has approval of a dissertation topic. For information, write to: Wayne Wiegand, Executive Director, Beta Phi Mu, Florida State University, SIS, Tallahassee, FL 32306-2100.

Canadian Association of Law Libraries. The Diana M. Priestly Scholarship of $2,500 for a student with previous law library experience or for entry to an approved Canadian law school or accredited Canadian library school. For information, write to: Ann Rae, Chair, CALL/ACBD Scholarship and Awards Committee, Bora Laskin Law Library, University of Toronto, 78 Queens Park, Toronto, ON M5S 2C5.

Canadian Federation of University Women. (1) The Alice E. Wilson Award of $5,000 for three students enrolled in graduate studies in any field, with special consideration given to candidates returning to study after at least three years; (2) the Margaret McWilliams Pre-Doctoral Fellowship of $11,000 for a full-time student who has completed one full year of study at the doctoral level; (3) the CFUW Memorial Fellowship of $6,500 for a student enrolled in a master's program in science, mathematics, or engineering; (4) the Beverly Jackson Fellowship of $2,000 for a student over age 35 enrolled in graduate work at an Ontario University; (5) the 1989 Polytechnique Commemorative Award of $2,800 for a student enrolled in graduate studies related particularly to women; (6) the Bourse Georgette LeMoyne award of $6,000 for graduate study at a Canadian university where one of the languages of administration and instruction is French; (7) the Dr. Marion Elder Grant Fellowship of $10,000 for a full-time student at the master's or doctoral level (preference will be given to holders of an Acadia University degree); (8) the Margaret Dale Philp Biennial Award of $3,000 for graduate studies in the humanities or social sciences. For information, write to: Fellowships Program Manager, Canadian Federation of University Women, 251

Bank St., Suite 600, Ottawa, ON K2P 1X3, Canada (e-mail cfuwfls@rogers.com, World Wide Web http://www.cfuw.org).

Canadian Library Association. (1) The World Book Graduate Scholarship in Library and Information Science of $2,500; (2) the CLA Dafoe Scholarship of $3,000; and (3) the H. W. Wilson Scholarship of $2,000. Each scholarship is given to a Canadian citizen or landed immigrant to attend an accredited Canadian library school; (4) the Library Research and Development Grant of $1,000 for a member of the Canadian Library Association, in support of theoretical and applied research in library and information science. For information, write to: CLA Membership Services Department, Scholarships and Awards Committee, 328 Frank St., Ottawa, ON K2P 0X8, Canada.

Catholic Library Association. (1) The World Book, Inc., Grant of $1,500 divided among no more than three CLA members for continuing education in children's or school librarianship; (2) the Rev. Andrew L. Bouwhuis Memorial Scholarship of $1,500 for a student accepted into a graduate program in library science. For information, write to: Jean R. Bostley, SSJ, Scholarship Chair, Catholic Library Association, 100 North St., Suite 224, Pittsfield, MA 01201-5109.

Chinese American Librarians Association. (1) The Sally C. Tseng Professional Development Grant offers $1,000 a year to support research by CALA members who are Chinese descendants; (2) the Sheila Suen Lai Scholarship and (3) the C. C. Seetoo/CALA Conference Travel Scholarship each offer $500 to a Chinese descendant who has been accepted in an ALA-accredited program. For information on the Tseng grant, contact Jian Wang, Chair, Sally C. Tseng Professional Development Grant Committee, Branford P. Millar Library, Portland State University, P.O. Box 1151, Portland, OR 97207-1151, e-mail jian@pdx.edu or sctseng888@yahoo.com; for information on the Sheila Suen Lai and C. C. Seetoo scholarships, write to: MengXiong Liu, Clark Library, San

Jose State University, 1 Washington Sq., San Jose, CA 95192-0028.

Church and Synagogue Library Association. The Muriel Fuller Memorial Scholarship of $200 (including texts) for a correspondence course offered by the University of Utah Continuing Education Division. Open to CSLA members only. For information, write to: CSLA, P.O. Box 19357, Portland, OR 97280-0357.

Council on Library and Information Resources. (1) The Rovelstad Scholarship in International Librarianship, to enable a student enrolled in an accredited LIS program to attend the IFLA Annual Conference; (2) the A. R. Zipf Fellowship in Information Management of $8,000, awarded annually to a U.S. citizen enrolled in graduate school who shows exceptional promise for leadership and technical achievement. For more information, write to: Council on Library and Information Resources, 1755 Massachusetts Ave. N.W., Suite 500, Washington, DC 20036.

Sandra Garvie Memorial Fund. A scholarship of $1,000 for a student pursuing a course of study in library and information science. For information, write to: Sandra Garvie Memorial Fund, c/o Director, Legal Resource Centre, Faculty of Extension, University of Alberta, 8303 112th St., Edmonton, AB T6G 2T4, Canada.

Massachusetts Black Librarians' Network. Two scholarships of at least $500 and $1,000 for minority U.S. citizens entering an ALA-accredited master's program in library science, with no more than 12 semester hours toward a degree. For information, write to: Pearl Mosley, Chair, Massachusetts Black Librarians' Network, 27 Beech Glen St., Roxbury, MA 02119.

Medical Library Association. (1) The Cunningham Memorial International Fellowship of $6,000 plus up to $2,000 travel expenses; (2) a scholarship of $5,000 for a person entering an ALA-accredited library program, with no more than one-half of the program yet to be completed; (3) a scholarship of $5,000 for a minority student for graduate study; (4) a varying number of Research, Development and Demonstration Project Grants of $100 to

$1,000 for U.S. or Canadian citizens who are MLA members; (5) the MLA Doctoral Fellowship of $2,000 for doctoral work in medical librarianship or information science; (6) the Rittenhouse Award of $500 for a student enrolled in an ALA-accredited library program or a recent graduate working as a trainee in a library internship program; (7) Continuing Education Grants of $100 to $500 for U.S. or Canadian citizens who are MLA members. For information, write to: Development Department, Medical Library Association, 65 E. Wacker Pl., Suite 1900, Chicago, IL 60601-7298.

Mountain Plains Library Association. (1) A varying number of grants of up to $600 each and (2) a varying number of grants of up to $150 each for MPLA members with at least two years of membership for continuing education. For information, write to: Joseph R. Edelen, Jr., MPLA Executive Secretary, I. D. Weeks Library, University of South Dakota, Vermillion, SD 57069.

REFORMA, the National Association to Promote Library Services to Latinos and the Spanish-Speaking. A varying number of scholarships of $1,000 to $2,000 each for minority students interested in serving the Spanish-speaking community to attend an ALA-accredited school. For information, write to: Ninfa Trejo, Main Library, University of Arizona, 1510 E. University, Tucson, AZ 85721.

Society of American Archivists. The Colonial Dames Awards, two grants of $1,200 each for specific types of repositories and collections. For information, write to: Debra Noland, Society of American Archivists, 521 S. Wells St., 5th fl., Chicago, IL 60607.

Southern Regional Education Board. A varying number of grants of varying amounts to cover in-state tuition for graduate or postgraduate study in an ALA-accredited library school for residents of Louisiana and Delaware (qualifying states vary year by year). For information, write to: Academic Common Market, c/o Southern Regional Education Board, 592 Tenth St. N.W., Atlanta, GA 30318-5790.

Special Libraries Association. (1) Three $6,000 scholarships for students interested in special-library work; (2) the Plenum Scholarship of $1,000 and (3) the ISI Scholarship of $1,000, each also for students interested in special-library work; (4) the Affirmative Action Scholarship of $6,000 for a minority student interested in special-library work; and (5) the Pharmaceutical Division Stipend Award of $1,200 for a student with an undergraduate degree in chemistry, life sciences, or pharmacy entering or enrolled in an ALA-accredited program. For information on the first four scholarships, write to: Scholarship Committee, Special Libraries Association, 1700 18th St. N.W., Washington, DC 20009-2508; for information on the Pharmaceutical Stipend, write to: Susan E. Katz, Awards Chair, Knoll Pharmaceuticals Science Information Center, 30 N. Jefferson St., Whippany, NJ 07981.

Library Scholarship and Award Recipients, 2004

Scholarships and Library awards are listed by organization.

American Association of Law Libraries (AALL)

AALL and West Group George A. Strait Minority Scholarships. *Winners:* Kelly Anders, Helane Davis, Donna Joseph.

AALL Scholarships. *Winners:* (Library Degree for Law School Graduates) Alana Carson, Teresa Kline, Virginia McVarish, Maria Templo, Cindie Leigh; (Library Degree for Non-Law School Graduates) Stephanie Gardner, Michelle Martin-Larsen, Jill Milhorat, Rhodora Bulay; (Law Librarians in Continuing Education Courses) Marianne Alcorn.

James F. Connolly/LexisNexis Academic and Library Solutions Scholarship. *Winner:* Melanie Nelson.

Institute for Court Management Scholarship. *Winner:* Not awarded in 2004.

LexisNexis Grants. *Winners:* Ann T. Davey, Michael VanderHeijden, Courtney L. Selby, Paul Moorman, Jill Milhorat.

LexisNexis John R. Johnson Memorial Scholarships. *Winners:* Not awarded in 2004.

Meira Pimsleur Scholarship. *Sponsor:* Arthur W. Diamond Law Library, Columbia Law School. *Winner:* Not awarded in 2004.

Minority Leadership Development Award. *Winner:* June Kim.

West Group Grants. *Winners:* Amy Rachuba, Virginia A. McVarish, Julia Boxler, Heidi L. Frostestad, Steve Haas, Barbara L. Lah, Nicole Evans, Kathleen Hall.

American Library Association (ALA)

ALA/Information Today Library of the Future Award ($1,500). For a library, consortium, group of librarians, or support organization for innovative planning for, applications of, or development of patron training programs about information technology in a library setting. *Donor:* Information Today, Inc. *Winner:* New Mexico State University Library, Las Cruces for its Border Health Information and Education Network (¡BIEN!).

Hugh C. Atkinson Memorial Award ($2,000). For outstanding achievement (including risk taking) by academic librarians that has contributed significantly to improvements in library automation, management, and/or development or research. *Offered by:* ACRL, ALCTS, LAMA, and LITA divisions. *Winner:* Jerome Yavarkovsky.

Carroll Preston Baber Research Grant (up to $3,000). For innovative research that could lead to an improvement in library services to any specified group(s) of people. *Donor:* Eric R. Baber. *Winner:* Amanda Spink, University of Pittsburgh, for "Multitasking Information Behavior by Public Library Users."

Beta Phi Mu Award ($500). For distinguished service in library education. *Donor:* Beta Phi Mu International Library Science Honorary Society. *Winner:* Linda C. Smith.

Bogle/Pratt International Library Travel Fund Award ($1,000). To ALA member(s) to attend their first international conference. *Donors:* Bogle Memorial Fund and Pratt Institute School of Information and Library Science. *Winner:* Steve Shadle.

W. Y. Boyd Literary Novel Award. See *Literary Prizes, 2004* by Gary Ink.

David H. Clift Scholarship ($3,000). To worthy U.S. or Canadian citizens enrolled in an ALA-accredited program toward an MLS degree. *Winner:* Ann Gunter.

Melvil Dewey Medal. To an individual or group for recent creative professional achievement in library management, training, cataloging and classification, and the tools and techniques of librarianship. *Donor:* OCLC/Forest Press. *Winner:* Sally H. McCallum.

Tom and Roberta Drewes Scholarship ($3,000). To a library support staff member pursuing a master's degree. *Winner:* Heather R. Rhone.

EBSCO/ALA Conference Sponsorship Award ($1,000). To enable ten librarians to attend the ALA Annual Conference. *Donor:* EBSCO Subscription Services. *Winners:* Constance Dickerson, John G. Eye, Rachel Singer Gordon, Virginia Roberts Kinman, Ellen E. Moore, Cassandra E. Osterloh, Samantha Schmehl, Jennifer Smith, Louise Svehla, Sara Wayland.

Equality Award ($500). To an individual or group for an outstanding contribution that promotes equality of women and men in the library profession. *Donor:* Scarecrow Press. *Winner:* Janet B. Wojnaroski.

Freedom to Read Foundation Roll of Honor Award. *Winner:* June Pinnell-Stephens.

Elizabeth Futas Catalyst for Change Award ($1,000). To recognize and honor a librarian who invests time and talent to make positive change in the profession of librarianship. *Donor:* Elizabeth Futas Memorial Fund. *Winner:* John E. Buschman.

Loleta D. Fyan Public Library Research Grant (up to $10,000). For projects in public library development. *Donor:* Fyan Estate. *Winner:* Orange County (Florida) Library System for "Wi-Fi Technology Promotes Customer Service."

Mary V. Gaver Scholarship ($3,000). To a student pursuing an MLS specializing in youth services. *Winner:* Cary Meltzer.

William R. Gordon Spectrum Scholarship. To a designated Spectrum Scholarship recipient. *Winner:* Not awarded in 2004.

Grolier Foundation Award ($1,000). For stimulation and guidance of reading by children and young people. *Donor:* Grolier Publishing. *Winner:* Harley Hamilton.

Ken Haycock Award ($1,000). For significant contribution to public recognition and appreciation of librarianship through professional performance, teaching, or writing. *Winner:* Patricia M. Cavill.

Highsmith Library Literature Award ($500). To an author or coauthors who make an outstanding contribution to library literature issued during the three years preceding the presentation. *Donor:* Highsmith. *Winner:* Not awarded in 2004.

Honorary ALA Membership. Sanford Berman, Norman Horrocks.

Miriam L. Hornback Scholarship ($3,000). To an ALA or library support staff person pursuing a master's degree in library science. *Winner:* Erin Gratz.

Paul Howard Award for Courage ($1,000). To a librarian, library board, library group, or an individual who has exhibited unusual courage for the benefit of library programs or services. *Donor:* Paul Howard Memorial Fund. *Winner:* Not awarded in 2004.

John Ames Humphry/OCLC/Forest Press Award ($1,000). To an individual for significant contributions to international librarianship. *Donor:* OCLC/Forest Press. *Winner:* Nasser Sharify.

Tony B. Leisner Scholarship ($3,000). To a library support staff member pursuing a master's degree program. *Winner:* Fay Ellen Hansen.

Joseph W. Lippincott Award ($1,000). To a librarian for distinguished service to the profession. *Donor:* Joseph W. Lippincott, III. *Winner:* Clifford A. Lynch.

James Madison Award. To recognize efforts to promote government openness. *Winner:* David Sobel, Electronic Privacy Information Center.

Marshall Cavendish Excellence in Library Programing Award ($3,000). Recognizes either a school library or public library that demonstrates excellence in library programming by providing programs that have community impact and respond to community need. *Winner:* Hennepin County (Minnesota) Library.

Marshall Cavendish Scholarship ($3,000). To a worthy U.S. or Canadian citizen to begin an MLS degree in an ALA-accredited program. *Winner:* Patricia H. Fisher.

Schneider Family Book Awards (three awards of $5,000). To authors or illustrators of books that embody artistic expressions of the disability experience of children and adolescent audiences. *Donor:* Katherine Schneider. *Winners:* See *Literary Prizes, 2004* by Gary Ink.

Sirsi Leader in Library Technology Grant ($10,000). To a library organization to encourage and enable continued advancements in quality services for a project that makes creative or groundbreaking use of technology to deliver exceptional services to its community. *Donor:* Sirsi Corporation. *Winners:* Mid-Illinois Talking Book Center, OverDrive, Inc., and Tap Information Services.

Spectrum Initiative Scholarships ($6,500). Presented to minority students admitted to an ALA-accredited library school. *Winners:* Yolanda Alaniz, Alice "Jade" Alburo, Sonia Alcantara, Camille Callison, Duane Carter, Doris Dixon, Vernica Downey, Leigh Esquerra, Barbara Gabaldon, Vi T. Ha, Leigha Jewel Harden, Michael Jara, Patrice Johnson, Juenita Lee, Noreen Ma, Analiza Perez, Amber Prentiss, Randi Robinson, Elizabeth Rush, Carrie Sawyer, Justin Woo, Alicia Yao, Valerie Yazza.

Sullivan Award for Public Library Administrators Supporting Services to Children. To a library supervisor/administrator who has shown exceptional understanding and support of public library services to children. *Donor:* Peggy Sullivan. *Winner:* David W. Singleton.

Howard M. and Gladys B. Teeple Spectrum Scholarship. To a designated Spectrum Scholarship recipient. *Donor:* The Religion and Ethics Institute. *Winner:* Doris Dixon.

Thomson Gale Financial Development Award ($2,500). To a library organization for a financial development project to secure new funding resources for a public or academic library. *Donor:* Gale Group. *Winner:* Worth County School Library, Grant City, Missouri.

Betty J. Turock Spectrum Scholarship. To a designated Spectrum Scholarship recipient. *Donor:* JTBC Foundation. *Winner:* Not awarded in 2004.

H. W. Wilson Library Staff Development Award ($3,500). To a library organization for a program to further its staff development goals and objectives. *Donor:* H. W. Wilson Company. *Winner:* J. Edgar and Louise S. Monroe Library, Loyola University, New Orleans.

World Book–ALA Goal Grant (up to $10,000). To ALA units for the advancement of public, academic, or school library service and librarianship through support of programs that implement the goals and priorities of ALA. *Donor:* Scott Fetzer Foundation, World Book. *Winner:* Carol Brey-Casiano Presidential Committee, Association for Library Trustees and Advocates, Chapter Relations Office, Public Information Office, and Washington Office for advocacy institutes.

American Association of School Librarians (AASL)

AASL ABC/CLIO Leadership Grant (up to $1,750). For planning and implementing leadership programs at state, regional, or local levels to be given to school library associations that are affiliates of AASL. *Donor:* ABC/CLIO. *Winner:* Colorado Association of School Librarians.

AASL/Baker & Taylor Distinguished Service Award ($3,000). For outstanding contributions to librarianship and school library development. *Donor:* Baker & Taylor Books. *Winner:* M. Ellen Jay.

AASL Collaborative School Library Media Award ($2,500). For expanding the role of the library in elementary and/or secondary school education. *Donor:* Sagebrush Corporation. *Winner:* Margaret Lincoln.

AASL Crystal Apple Award. To an individual or group that has had significant impact on school libraries and students. *Winner:* Bound to Stay Bound Books, Inc.

AASL/Frances Henne Award ($1,250). To a school library media specialist with five or fewer years in the profession to attend an AASL regional conference or ALA Annual Conference for the first time. *Donor:* Greenwood Publishing Group. *Winner:* Cynthia Welsh.

AASL/Highsmith Research Grant (up to $5,000). To conduct innovative research aimed at measuring and evaluating the impact of school library media programs on learning and education. *Donor:* Highsmith, Inc. *Winners:* Robyn Young, Kathy Latrobe, Rhonda Taylor.

AASL School Librarian's Workshop Scholarship ($3,000). To a full-time student preparing to become a school library media specialist at the preschool, elementary, or secondary level. *Donor:* Jay W.

Toor, president, Library Learning Resources. *Winner:* Deborah Goetjen.

Distinguished School Administrators Award ($2,000). For expanding the role of the library in elementary and/or secondary school education. *Donor:* ProQuest. *Winner:* William Harner, principal, Greenville County (South Carolina) School District.

Information Technology Pathfinder Award ($1,000 to the specialist and $500 to the library). To library media specialists for innovative approaches to microcomputer applications in the school library media center. *Donor:* Follett Software Company. *Winners:* (Secondary) Rebecca Perkins; (Elementary) not awarded in 2004.

Intellectual Freedom Award ($2,000, and $1,000 to media center of recipient's choice). To a school library media specialist who has upheld the principles of intellectual freedom. *Donor:* ProQuest. *Winner:* Not awarded in 2004.

National School Library Media Program of the Year Award ($10,000 each in three categories). To school districts and a single school for excellence and innovation in outstanding library media programs. *Donor:* AASL and Follett Library Resources. *Winners:* (Single School) Lois Lenski Elementary School, Littleton, Colorado; (Large School District) Northside Independent School District, San Antonio; (Small School District) Boston Arts Academy/Fenway High School, Boston.

Association for Library Collections and Technical Services (ALCTS)

Hugh C. Atkinson Memorial Award. *See under* American Library Association.

Paul Banks and Carolyn Harris Preservation Award ($1,500). To recognize the contribution of a professional preservation specialist who has been active in the field of preservation and/or conservation for library and/or archival materials. *Donor:* Preservation Technologies. *Winner:* Jan Merrill-Oldham.

Best of *LRTS* Award ($250). To the author(s) of the best paper published each year in the division's official journal. *Winner:* Amy Weiss for "Proliferating Guidelines:

A History and Analysis of the Cataloging of Electronic Resources."

Blackwell's Scholarship Award ($2,000 scholarship to the U.S. or Canadian library school of the recipient's choice). To honor the author(s) of the year's outstanding monograph, article, or original paper in the field of acquisitions, collection development, and related areas of resource development in libraries. *Donor:* Blackwell's. *Winners:* Katharine Treptow Farrell and Marc Truittt for "The Case for Standards in the Integrated Library System" (*LRTS*, 2003).

Bowker/Ulrich's Serials Librarianship Award ($1,500). For leadership in serials-related activities. *Donor:* R. R. Bowker. *Winner:* Pamela Bluh.

First Step Award (Wiley Professional Development Grant) ($1,500). For librarians new to the serials field to attend ALA's Annual Conference. *Donor:* John Wiley & Sons. *Winner:* Vickie Melicher.

Leadership in Library Acquisitions Award ($1,500). For significant contributions by an outstanding leader in the field of library acquisitions. *Donor:* Harrassowitz. *Winner:* Kent Mulliner.

Margaret Mann Citation (and $2,000 to the U.S. or Canadian library school of the winning author's choice). To a cataloger or classifier for achievement in the areas of cataloging or classification. *Donor:* Online Computer Library Center. *Winner:* Barbara Tillett.

Esther J. Piercy Award ($1,500). To a librarian with no more than ten years experience for contributions and leadership in the field of library collections and technical services. *Donor:* YBP Library Services. *Winner:* Not awarded in 2004.

Association for Library Service to Children (ALSC)

ALSC/BWI Summer Reading Program Grant ($3,000). To an ALSC member for implementation of an outstanding public library summer reading program for children. *Donor:* BWI. *Winner:* Long Beach (California) Public Library and Information Center.

ALSC/Sagebrush Education Resources Literature Program Award ($1,000 toward ALA Annual Conference attendance). To an ALSC member for the development of an outstanding literature program for children. *Donor:* Sagebrush Corporation. *Winner:* Nancy J. Keane.

May Hill Arbuthnot Honor Lectureship. To an author, critic, librarian, historian, or teacher of children's literature who prepares a paper considered to be a significant contribution to the field of children's literature. *Winner:* Richard Jackson.

Mildred L. Batchelder Award. See *Literary Prizes, 2004* by Gary Ink.

Louise Seaman Bechtel Fellowship ($4,000). For librarians with 12 or more years of professional-level work in children's library collections, to read and study at the Baldwin Library/George Smathers Libraries, University of Florida (must be an ALSC member with an MLS from an ALA-accredited program). *Donor:* Bechtel Fund. *Winners:* Jean Hatfield, Joyce Laiosa.

Pura Belpré Award. See *Literary Prizes, 2004* by Gary Ink.

Bound to Stay Bound Books Scholarships (scholarships of $6,500 each). For men and women who intend to pursue an MLS or advanced degree and who plan to work in the area of library service to children. *Donor:* Bound to Stay Bound Books. *Winners:* Anita Coley, Corinne Hatcher, Jeanette Moore, Virginia Rassaei.

Caldecott Medal. See *Literary Prizes, 2004* by Gary Ink.

Andrew Carnegie Medal. To the U.S. producer of the most distinguished video for children in the previous year. *Donor:* Carnegie Corporation of New York. *Winners:* Paul Gagne and Melissa Reilly (Weston Woods Studios) for *Giggle Giggle Quack*.

Carnegie-Whitney Awards (up to $5,000). For the publication of bibliographic aids for research. *Donor:* James Lyman Whitney and Andrew Carnegie Funds. *Winners:* Association for Library Service to Children, ALA, for *Building a Home Library*; Jacob Gapko for *Children and Young Adults With Muscular Dystrophy: An Annotated Bibliography*; Cynthia Hsieh for *Everything You Want to Know About Asian American Youth: An Annotated Bibliography and Resources Guide*; Sylvia Ortiz for *Bilingual Guide to Border Health Information: For Promotoras, Librarians, Health Educators, the Public, Students and Researchers*.

Distinguished Service to ALSC Award ($1,000). To recognize significant contributions to, and an impact on, library services to children and/or ALSC. *Winner:* Virginia Walter.

Frederic G. Melcher Scholarship ($6,000). To two students entering the field of library service to children for graduate work in an ALA-accredited program. *Winners:* Lauren Anduri, Carolann MacMaster.

John Newbery Medal. See *Literary Prizes, 2004* by Gary Ink.

Penguin Young Readers Group Awards ($600). To children's librarians in school or public libraries with ten or fewer years of experience to attend the ALA Annual Conference for the first time. Must be a member of ALSC. *Donor:* Penguin Young Readers Group. *Winners:* Kathy Clair, Kimberly DeStefano, Nicole Sparling, Terry W. Warner.

Robert F. Sibert Medal. To the author of the most distinguished informational book for children published during the preceding year. *Donor:* Bound to Stay Bound Books. *Winner:* Jim Murphy for *The True and Terrifying Story of the Yellow Fever Epidemic of 1793* (Clarion).

Laura Ingalls Wilder Medal. To an author or illustrator whose works have made a lasting contribution to children's literature. *Winner:* Not awarded in 2004.

Association for Library Trustees and Advocates (ALTA)

ALA Trustee Citations. To recognize public library trustees for individual service to library development on the local, state, regional, or national level. *Winner:* Alma Dennis.

ALTA/Gale Outstanding Trustee Conference Grant Award ($750). *Donor:* Gale Research. *Winners:* Karen Dyer, Joel Hondorp.

ALTA Literacy Award (citation). To a library trustee or an individual who, in a volunteer capacity, has made a significant contribution to addressing the illiteracy problem in the United States. *Winner:* William H. Wilson.

ALTA Major Benefactors Honor Award (citation). To individuals, families, or corporate bodies that have made major benefactions to public libraries. *Winners:* John and Peter Clements, Bank of Southside Virginia.

Association of College and Research Libraries (ACRL)

ACRL Academic/Research Librarian of the Year Award ($3,000). For outstanding contribution to academic and research librarianship and library development. *Donor:* YBP Library Services. *Winner:* Tom Kirk.

ACRL Distinguished Education and Behavioral Sciences Librarian Award ($1,000). To an academic librarian who has made an outstanding contribution as an education and/or behavioral sciences librarian through accomplishments and service to the profession. *Donor:* John Wiley & Sons. *Winner:* Laurene E. Zaporozhetz.

ACRL Doctoral Dissertation Fellowship ($1,500). To a doctoral student in the field of academic librarianship whose research has potential significance in the field. *Donor:* Thomson Scientific. *Winner:* Judy Jeng.

ACRL Women's Studies Section Awards for Achievement (two awards of $1,000). To recognize achievements in women's studies librarianship. *Donors:* Greenwood Publishing Group and Routledge. *Winners:* Phyllis Holman Weisbard, Donna Roe.

Hugh C. Atkinson Memorial Award. *See under* American Library Association.

Coutts Nijhoff International West European Specialist Study Grant (up to 4,500 euros). Supports research pertaining to West European studies, librarianship, or the book trade. *Sponsor:* Coutts Nijhoff International. *Winner:* Helene S. Baumann.

Miriam Dudley Instruction Librarian Award ($1,000). For contribution to the advancement of bibliographic instruction in a college or research institution. *Donor:* Elsevier Science. *Winner:* William Miller.

EBSCO Community College Learning Resources Achievement and Leadership Awards ($500). *Donor:* EBSCO Information Services. *Winners:* Carolyn Norman, Janice Peyton, Lonna Beers.

Excellence in Academic Libraries Awards ($3,000 plus travel expenses). To recognize an outstanding community college, college, and university library. *Donor:* Blackwell's Book Services. *Winners:* (Community College) Richland College (Dallas); (College) Hope College, Holland, Michigan; (University) University of Washington, Seattle.

Haworth Press Distance Learning Librarian Conference Sponsorship Award ($1,200). To an ACRL member working in distance-learning librarianship in higher education. *Winner:* Susan S. Lowe

Innovation in Instruction Award ($3,000). Recognizes and honors librarians who have developed and implemented innovative approaches to instruction within their institution in the preceding two years. *Donor:* LexisNexis. *Winner:* Not awarded in 2004.

Marta Lange/*Congressional Quarterly* Award ($1,000). Recognizes an academic or law librarian for contributions to bibliography and information service in law or political science. *Donor:* CQ Press. *Winner:* Lucia Snowhill.

Samuel Lazerow Fellowship for Research in Acquisitions or Technical Services ($1,000). To foster advances in acquisitions or technical services by providing librarians a fellowship for travel or writing in those fields. *Sponsor:* Thomson Scientific. *Winners:* Karen M. Letarte, Jacqueline P. Samples.

Katharine Kyes Leab and Daniel J. Leab Exhibition Catalog Awards (citations). For the best catalogs published by American or Canadian institutions in conjunction with exhibitions of books and/or manuscripts. *Winners:* (Division I–Expensive) Georgianna Ziegler, Folger Shakespeare Library, Washington, D.C., *Elizabeth I: Then and Now;* (Division II–Moderately Expensive)

Michael O'Driscoll, Bruce Peel Special Collections Library, University of Alberta, *First Impressions: The Fledgling Years of the Black Sparrow Press 1966–1970;* (Division III–Inexpensive) Anne H. Hoy and Kimball Higgs, Grolier Club of New York, *The Auroral Light: Photographs by Women from Grolier Club Member Collections;* (Division IV–Brochures) Getty Research Institute, Los Angeles, *Robert Motherswell: A la Pintura (To Painting);* (Division V, Electronic Exhibitions) Bancroft Library, University of California at Berkeley, *The California Grizzly at the Bancroft Library.*

Oberly Award for Bibliography in the Agricultural Sciences ($350). Biennially, for the best English-language bibliography in the field of agriculture or a related science in the preceding two-year period. *Donor:* Eunice Rockwood Oberly Memorial Fund. *Winner:* Not awarded in 2004.

Publication of the Year Award (citation). Recognizes an outstanding publication or publications related to instruction in a library environment published in the preceding two years. *Winners: Information Literacy Instruction: Theory and Practice* by Esther Stampfer Grassian and Joan Kaplowitz (Information Literacy Sourcebooks, 2001), and "A Discipline-Based Approach to Information Literacy" by Ann J. Grafstein (*Journal of Academic Librarianship,* July 2002).

Association of Specialized and Cooperative Library Agencies (ASCLA)

ASCLA Century Scholarship (up to $2,500). For a library school student or students with disabilities admitted to an ALA-accredited library school. *Winner:* Jeffrey Thompson.

ASCLA Exceptional Service Award. *Winner:* Miami-Dade (Florida) Public Library System.

ASCLA Leadership Achievement Award. To recognize leadership and achievement in the areas of consulting, multitype library cooperation, and state library development. *Winner:* Valerie Wilford.

ASCLA/National Organization on Disability Award for Library Service to People with Disabilities ($1,000). To a library organization to recognize an innovative project to benefit people with disabilities. *Donor:* Keystone Systems. *Winner:* Ward M. Canaday Center for Special Collections, University of Toledo (Ohio).

ASCLA Professional Achievement Award. To recognize professional achievement within the areas of consulting, networking, statewide service, and programs. *Winner:* Amy Owen, former Utah state librarian.

ASCLA Service Award (citation). For outstanding service and leadership to the division. *Winner:* Sara Laughlin.

Francis Joseph Campbell Citation. For a contribution of recognized importance to library service for the blind and physically handicapped. *Winner:* Canadian National Institute for the Blind Library, Toronto.

Ethnic and Multicultural Information and Exchange Round Table

David Cohen/EMIERT Multicultural Award ($300). To recognize articles of significant research and publication that increase understanding and promote multiculturalism in North American libraries. *Donor:* Routledge. *Winner:* Plummer Alston Jones, Jr.

Gale/EMIERT Multicultural Award ($1,000). For outstanding achievement and leadership in serving the multicultural/multiethnic community. *Donor:* Gale Research. *Winner:* Not awarded in 2004.

Exhibits Round Table

Friendly Booth Award (citation). *Winner:* Not awarded in 2004.

Christopher J. Hoy/ERT Scholarship ($5,000). To an individual or individuals who will work toward an MLS degree in an ALA-accredited program. *Donor:* Family of Christopher Hoy. *Winner:* Angelica Guerrero.

Kohlstedt Exhibit Award (citation). To companies or organizations for the best single, multiple, and island booth displays at the ALA Annual Conference. *Winners:* Not awarded in 2004.

Federal and Armed Forces Librarians Round Table (FAFLRT)

FAFLRT Achievement Award. *Winner:* Susan Tarr.

Adelaide del Frate Conference Sponsor Award ($1,000). To encourage library school students to become familiar with federal librarianship and ultimately seek work in federal libraries; for attendance at ALA Annual Conference and activities of the Federal and Armed Forces Librarians Round Table. *Winner:* Rebecca Pernell.

Distinguished Service Award (citation). To honor a FAFLRT member for outstanding and sustained contributions to the association and to federal librarianship. *Winner:* Carol Bursik.

Gay, Lesbian, Bisexual, and Transgendered Round Table (GLBT)

Stonewall Book Awards. See *Literary Prizes, 2004* by Gary Ink.

Government Documents Round Table (GODORT)

James Bennett Childs Award. To a librarian or other individual for distinguished lifetime contributions to documents librarianship. *Winner:* Robert A. Walter.

Bernadine Abbott Hoduski Founders Award (plaque). To recognize documents librarians who may not be known at the national level but who have made significant contributions to the field of state, international, local, or federal documents. *Winner:* Melody S. Kelly.

LexisNexis/GODORT/ALA Documents to the People Award ($2,000). To an individual, library, organization, or noncommercial group that most effectively encourages or enhances the use of government documents in library services. *Winner:* Counting California, a service of the University of California Libraries.

Newsbank/Readex/GODORT/ALA Catharine J. Reynolds Award ($2,000). Grants to documents librarians for travel and/or study in the field of documents librarianship or area of study benefiting performance as documents librarians. *Donor:*

Newsbank and Readex Corporation. *Winner:* Kristin R. Eschenfelder.

W. David Rozkuszka Scholarship ($3,000). To provide financial assistance to an individual who is currently working with government documents in a library while completing a master's program in library science. *Winner:* Mark Phillips.

Intellectual Freedom Round Table (IFRT)

John Phillip Immroth Memorial Award for Intellectual Freedom ($500). For notable contribution to intellectual freedom fueled by personal courage. *Winner:* Nolan T. Yelich, state librarian of Virginia.

Eli M. Oboler Memorial Award ($500). Biennially, to an author of a published work in English or in English translation dealing with issues, events, questions, or controversies in the area of intellectual freedom. *Winners:* Wendell Berry and David James Duncan for *Citizens Dissent: Security, Morality, and Leadership in an Age of Terror* (Orion Society, 2003).

SIRS-ProQuest State and Regional Achievement Award ($1,000). To an innovative and effective intellectual freedom project covering a state or region during the calendar year. *Donor:* Social Issues Resource Series (SIRS)-ProQuest. *Winner:* Colorado Association of Libraries Intellectual Freedom Committee.

Library Administration and Management Association (LAMA)

Hugh C. Atkinson Memorial Award. *See under* American Library Association.

Diana V. Braddom Fundraising and Financial Development Section Scholarship ($1,000). To enable attendance at the ALA Annual Conference. *Donor:* Diana V. Braddom. *Winners:* Patricia Linville, Margot J. Durbin.

John Cotton Dana Library Public Relations Awards. To libraries or library organizations of all types for public relations programs or special projects ended during the preceding year. *Donor:* H. W. Wilson Company. *Winners:* Barrington (Illinois) Area Library; Halifax (Nova Scotia) Public Libraries; Dr. Martin Luther King, Jr. Library, San Jose, California; Las Vegas–Clark County (Nevada) Library District; Edmon Low Library, Oklahoma State University; Orange County (California) Public Library; Pioneer Library System, Norman Oklahoma.

LAMA/AIA Library Buildings Award (citation). Biennial awards to recognize excellence in the architectural design and planning of libraries. *Sponsors:* American Institute of Architects and LAMA. *Winners:* Not awarded in 2004.

LAMA Cultural Diversity Grant ($1,000). To support creation and dissemination of resources that will assist library administrators and managers in developing a vision and commitment to diversity. *Winner:* Jill Keally, University of Tennessee Libraries.

LAMA Group Achievement Award. To honor LAMA committees or task forces, recognizing outstanding teamwork supporting the goals of LAMA. *Winner:* Not awarded in 2004.

LAMA Leadership Award. *Winner:* Rodney Henshaw.

LAMA President's Award. *Winner:* Not awarded in 2004.

LAMA/YBP Student Writing and Development Award ($1,000 grant to attend the ALA Annual Conference). *Donor:* YBP Library Services. *Winner:* Melanie Boyd.

Library and Information Technology Association (LITA)

Hugh C. Atkinson Memorial Award. *See under* American Library Association.

LITA/Brett Butler Entrepreneurship Award ($5,000). To recognize a librarian or library for demonstrating exemplary entrepreneurship by providing innovative products or services. *Donor:* Thomson Gale Group. *Winner:* Susan McGlamery, Metropolitan Cooperative Library System, Pasadena, California.

LITA/Christian Larew Memorial Scholarship ($3,000). To encourage the entry of qualified persons into the library and information technology field. *Sponsor:* Informata.com. *Winner:* Rachel Howard.

LITA/Endeavor Student Writing Award ($1,000). For the best unpublished manuscript on a topic in the area of libraries and information technology written by a student or students enrolled in an ALA-accredited library and information studies graduate program. *Donor:* Endeavor Information Systems. *Winner:* Judy Jeng.

LITA/Gaylord Award for Achievement in Library and Information Technology ($1,000). *Donor:* Gaylord Bros., Inc. *Winner:* Discontinued in 2003.

LITA/Library Hi Tech Award ($1,000). To an individual or institution for a work that shows outstanding communication for continuing education in library and information technology. *Donor:* Emerald Press. *Winner:* Eric Lease Morgan.

LITA/LSSI Minority Scholarship in Library and Information Science ($2,500). To encourage a qualified member of a principal minority group to work toward an MLS degree in an ALA-accredited program with emphasis on library automation. *Donor:* Library Systems and Services, Inc. *Winner:* Sandra D'Souza.

LITA/OCLC Frederick G. Kilgour Award for Research in Library and Information Technology ($2,000 and expense-paid attendance at ALA Annual Conference). To bring attention to research relevant to the development of information technologies. *Donor:* OCLC. *Winner:* Carl Lagoze.

LITA/OCLC Minority Scholarship in Library and Information Technology ($3,000). To encourage a qualified member of a principal minority group to work toward an MLS degree in an ALA-accredited program with emphasis on library automation. *Donor:* OCLC. *Winner:* Robin Mae White.

LITA/Sirsi Scholarship in Library and Information Technology ($2,500). To encourage the entry of qualified persons into the library automation field who demonstrate a strong commitment to the use of automated systems in libraries. *Donor:* Sirsi, Inc. *Winner:* Kelly Jean Sattler.

Library History Round Table (LHRT)

Phyllis Dain Library History Dissertation Award ($500). To the author of a dissertation treating the history of books, libraries, librarianship, or information science. *Winner:* Not awarded in 2004.

Donald G. Davis Article Award (certificate). For the best article written in English in the field of U.S. and Canadian library history. *Winner:* Virgil Blake for "James Forging the Anglo-American Cataloging Alliance: Descriptive Cataloging, 1830–1908."

Justin Winsor Prize Essay ($500). To an author of an outstanding essay embodying original historical research on a significant subject of library history. *Winner:* Joyce M. Latham.

Eliza Atkins Gleason Book Award. Presented every third year to the author of the best book in English in the field of library history. *Winner:* Louise S. Robbins for *The Dismissal of Miss Ruth Brown: Civil Rights, Censorship, and the American Library* (University of Oklahoma).

Library Research Round Table (LRRT)

Jesse H. Shera Award for Distinguished Published Research ($500). For a research article on library and information studies published in English during the calendar year. *Winners:* Jeffrey D. Kushkowski, Kathy A. Parsons, and William H. Wiese for "Master's and Doctoral Thesis Citations: Analysis and Trends of a Longitudinal Study" (*portal: Libraries and the Academy,* 3 (3), 2003).

Jesse H. Shera Award for Support of Dissertation Research ($500). To recognize and support dissertation research employing exemplary research design and methods. *Winner:* Not awarded in 2004.

Map and Geography Round Table (MAGERT)

MAGERT Honors Award. To recognize lifetime achievement and contributions to map and geography librarianship. *Winner:* David Yehling Allen.

New Members Round Table (NMRT)

NMRT/Student Chapter of the Year Award. To an ALA student chapter for outstanding contributions to ALA. *Winner:* University of California at Los Angeles Department of Information Studies.

NMRT/3M Professional Development Grant. To NMRT members to encourage professional development and participation in national ALA and NMRT activities. *Donor:* 3M. *Winners:* Tiffani Conner, Sarah Robbins, Nanette E. Wargo.

Shirley Olofson Memorial Award ($1,000): To an individual to help defray costs of attending the ALA Annual Conference. *Winner:* Genevieve Gallagher.

Office for Diversity

Achievement in Diversity Research Honor. To an ALA member who has made significant contributions to diversity research in the profession. *Winner:* Kathleen de la Peña McCook.

Diversity Research Grants ($2,500): To the authors of research proposals that address critical gaps in the knowledge of diversity issues within library and information science. *Winners:* Elizabeth L. Marcoux, Jane Karp, Kyung-Sun Kim.

Office for Intellectual Freedom

Freedom to Read Foundation Roll of Honor (citation): To recognize individuals who have contributed substantially to the foundation. *Winner:* June Pinnell-Stephens.

Office for Literacy and Outreach Services

Jean E. Coleman Library Outreach Lecture. *Winner:* Richard Chabran.

Estela and Raúl Mora Award ($1,000 and plaque) For the most exemplary program celebrating *Día de Los Niños/Día de Los Libros.* *Winner:* Providence (Rhode Island) Public Library.

Public Information Office

Scholastic Library/Grolier National Library Week Grant ($5,000). To libraries or library associations of all types for a public awareness campaign in connection with National Library Week in the year the grant is awarded. *Sponsor:* Scholastic

Library Publishing. *Winner:* St. Mary Parish Library, Franklin, Louisiana.

Public Library Association (PLA)

Advancement of Literacy Award (plaque). To a publisher, bookseller, hardware and/or software dealer, foundation, or similar group that has made a significant contribution to the advancement of adult literacy. *Donor: Library Journal. Winners:* Tom Brokaw (anchor) and Elizabeth Fischer and Subrata De (producers) of NBC "Dateline" for "A Loss for Words."

Baker & Taylor Entertainment Audio Music/ Video Product Grant ($2,500 worth of audio music or video products). To help a public library to build or expand a collection of either or both formats. *Donor:* Baker & Taylor Entertainment. *Winner:* Petersburg (Alaska) Public Library.

Demco Creative Merchandising Grant ($1,000 and $2,000 in display merchandise). To a public library proposing a project for the creative display and merchandising of materials either in the library or in the community. *Donor:* Demco, Inc. *Winner:* Clifton (New Jersey) Public Library.

EBSCO Excellence in Small and/or Rural Public Service Award ($1,000). Honors a library serving a population of 10,000 or less that demonstrates excellence of service to its community as exemplified by an overall service program or a special program of significant accomplishment. *Donor:* EBSCO Subscription Services. *Winner:* Tecumseh (Oklahoma) Public Library.

Highsmith Library Innovation Award ($2,000). Recognizes a public library's innovative achievement in planning and implementing a creative community service program. *Donor:* Highsmith. *Winner:* Maricopa County (Arizona) Library District.

Allie Beth Martin Award ($3,000). Honors a public librarian who has demonstrated extraordinary range and depth of knowledge about books or other library materials and has distinguished ability to share that knowledge. *Donor:* Baker & Taylor. *Winner:* Jean D. Trebbi.

New Leaders Travel Grants (up to $1,500). To enhance the professional development and improve the expertise of public librarians by making possible their attendance at major professional development activities. *Winners:* Polly Bonnett, Tracy Lynn Cline, Kathryn Crouse, Christina L. Jones, Rebecca Lynn.

Public Libraries Magazine Feature Writing Awards ($500 and $300). To public library employees for feature-length articles published during the preceding year. *Winners:* Solina Kasten Marquis, Michael Sullivan.

Charlie Robinson Award ($1,000). Honors a public library director who, over a period of seven years, has been a risk taker, an innovator, and/or a change agent in a public library. *Donor:* Baker & Taylor. *Winner:* Jane Light.

Leonard Wertheimer Award ($1,000). To a person, group, or organization for work that enhances and promotes multilingual public library service. *Donor:* NTC Publishing Group. *Winner:* Not awarded in 2004.

Women's National Book Association/Ann Heidbreder Eastman Grant ($750). To a librarian to take a course or participate in an institute devoted to aspects of publishing as a profession or to provide reimbursement for such study completed within the past year. *Winner:* Kimberley Kowal.

Reference and User Services Association (RUSA)

Virginia Boucher-OCLC Distinguished ILL Librarian Award ($2,000). To a librarian for outstanding professional achievement, leadership, and contributions to interlibrary loan and document delivery. *Winner:* Joan Stein.

Dartmouth Medal. For creating current reference works of outstanding quality and significance. *Donor:* Dartmouth College. *Winner:* Charles Scribner's Sons/Thomson Gale for *The Encyclopedia of Food and Culture* (2003).

Dun & Bradstreet Award for Outstanding Service to Minority Business Communities (BRASS) ($2,000). *Donor:* Dun & Bradstreet. *Winner:* Nettie Seaberry.

Dun & Bradstreet Public Librarian Support Award (BRASS) ($1,000). To support the attendance at the ALA Annual Conference of a public librarian who has performed outstanding business reference service. *Donor:* Dun & Bradstreet. *Winner:* Kay Cormier.

Gale Group Award for Excellence in Business Librarianship (BRASS) ($3,000). To an individual for distinguished activities in the field of business librarianship. *Donor:* Gale Group. *Winner:* Michael Madden.

Genealogical Publishing Company/History Section Award ($1,500). To encourage and commend professional achievement in historical reference and research librarianship. *Donor:* Genealogical Publishing Company. *Winner:* Samuel J. Boldrick.

Margaret E. Monroe Library Adult Services Award (citation). To a librarian for impact on library service to adults. *Winner:* Cynthia Orr.

Bessie Boehm Moore/Thorndike Press Award ($1,000). To a library organization that has developed an outstanding and creative program for library service to the aging. *Winner:* Discontinued in 2003.

Isadore Gilbert Mudge–R. R. Bowker Award ($5,000). For distinguished contributions to reference librarianship. *Donor:* R. R. Bowker. *Winner:* Robert Balay.

Reference Service Press Award ($2,500). To the author or authors of the most outstanding article published in *RUSQ* during the preceding two volume years. *Donor:* Reference Service Press. *Winner:* Tim Spindler.

John Sessions Memorial Award (plaque). To a library or library system in recognition of work with the labor community. *Donor:* AFL/CIO. *Winner:* Ruth A. Haas Library, Western Connecticut State University.

Louis Shores–Greenwood Publishing Group Award ($3,000). To an individual, team, or organization to recognize excellence in reviewing of books and other materials for libraries. *Donor:* Greenwood Publishing Group. *Winner:* Nancy Pearl.

Thomson Financial Student Travel Award (BRASS) ($1,000). For a student enrolled in an ALA-accredited master's degree program to attend the ALA Annual Conference. *Donor:* Thomson Financial. *Winner:* Naaznin Adatia.

Thomson Gale Award for Excellence in Reference and Adult Services ($3,000). To a library or library system for developing an imaginative and unique library resource to meet patrons' reference needs. *Donor:* Thomson Gale. *Winner:* North Carolina State University Libraries.

Social Responsibilities Round Table (SRRT)

Jackie Eubanks Memorial Award ($500). To honor outstanding achievement in promoting the acquisition and use of alternative media in libraries. *Donor:* AIP Task Force. *Winner:* Not awarded in 2004.

Coretta Scott King Awards. See *Literary Prizes, 2004* by Gary Ink.

Young Adult Library Services Association (YALSA)

Alex Awards. To the authors of ten books published for adults that have high potential appeal to teenagers. *Winners:* Amanda Davis for *Wonder When You'll Miss Me* (William Morrow/HarperCollins); Mark Haddon for *The Curious Incident of the Dog in the Night-Time* (Doubleday); Khaled Hosseini for *The Kite Runner* (Riverhead); Audrey Niffenegger for *The Time Traveler's Wife* (MacAdam Cage); Z. Z. Packer for *Drinking Coffee Elsewhere* (Riverhead); Mary Roach for *Stiff* (Norton); Mark Salzman for *True Notebooks* (Knopf); Marjane Satrapi for *Persepolis* (Pantheon); Jacquline Winspear for *Maisie Dobbs* (Soho); Bart Yates for *Leave Myself Behind* (Kensington).

Baker & Taylor/YALSA Conference Grants ($1,000). To young adult librarians in public or school libraries to attend an ALA Annual Conference for the first time. *Donor:* Baker & Taylor. *Winners:* Robin Brenner, Cathy Nelson.

Book Wholesalers, Inc./YALSA Collection Development Grant ($1,000). To YALSA members who represent a public library and work directly with young adults, for collection development materials for young adults. *Winners:* Judith Isaacs, Alison A. O'Reilly.

Margaret A. Edwards Award ($2,000). To an author whose book or books have provided young adults with a window through which they can view their world and which will help them to grow and to understand themselves and their role in society. *Donor: School Library Journal. Winner:* Ursula K. Le Guin for *A Wizard of Earthsea* (Bantam Spectra); *The Tombs of Atuan, The Farthest Shore,* and *Tehanu* (Simon and Schuster); *The Left Hand of Darkness* (Penguin); and *The Beginning Place* (Tor).

Great Book Giveaway (books, videos, CDs, and audio cassettes valued at a total of $25,000). *Winner:* Tri-Community Library, Prairie Lea, Texas.

Frances Henne/YALSA/VOYA Research Grant ($500 minimum). To provide seed money to an individual, institution, or group for a project to encourage research on library service to young adults. *Donor:* Scarecrow Press. *Winners:* Amy Alessio, Nick Burton.

Michael L. Printz Award. See *Literary Prizes, 2004* by Gary Ink.

YALSA/Sagebrush Award ($1,000). For an exemplary young adult reading or literature program. *Donor:* Sagebrush Corporation. *Winner:* Diane P. Tuccillo.

American Society for Information Science and Technology (ASIS&T)

ASIS&T Award of Merit. For an outstanding contribution to the field of information science. *Winner:* Howard White.

ASIS&T Best Information Science Book. *Winners:* Charles Bourne and Trudi Bellardo Hahn for *A History of Online Information Services 1963–1976* (MIT Press).

ASIS&T/ISI Outstanding Information Science Teacher Award ($500). *Winner:* Donald Cleveland.

ASIS&T Proquest Doctoral Dissertation Award ($1,000 plus expense-paid attendance at ASIS&T Annual Meeting). *Winner:* Lennart Björneborn.

ASIS&T/ISI Doctoral Dissertation Proposal Scholarship. *Winner:* Meng Yang.

ASIS&T Research Award. For a systematic program of research in a single area at a level beyond the single study, recognizing contributions in the field of information science. *Winner:* Boyd Rayward.

ASIS&T Special Award. To recognize long-term contributions to the advancement of information science and technology and enhancement of public access to information and discovery of mechanisms for improved transfer and utilization of knowledge. *Winner:* Tim Berners Lee.

ASIS&T/UMI Doctoral Dissertation Award. *Winner:* Not awarded in 2004.

James M. Cretsos Leadership Award. *Winners:* Stacy Surla and Tom Terrell.

Watson Davis Award. *Winner:* Joseph Busch.

ISI Citation Analysis Research Grant. *Winner:* David Hubbard.

ISI Doctoral Dissertation Proposal Scholarship ($1,500). *Winner:* Lennart Björneborn.

Pratt Severn Best Student Research Paper. *Winner:* Tori Orr.

John Wiley & Sons Best *JASIST* Paper Award. *Winner:* Cecilia Brown for "The Role of Electronic Preprints in Chemical Communication: Analysis of Citation, Usage, and Acceptance in the Journal Literature."

Art Libraries Society of North America (ARLIS/NA)

ARLIS/NA Conference Attendance Award. *Winners:* Heather Ball, Polly McCord.

ARLIS/NA Internship Award. Provides financial support for students preparing for a career in art librarianship or visual resource librarianship. *Winner:* Cathy Billings.

John Benjamins Award. To recognize research and publication in the study and analysis of periodicals in the fields of the fine arts, literature, and cross-disciplinary studies. *Winner:* Not awarded in 2004.

Andrew Cahan Photography Award. To encourage conference participation of art information professionals in the field of photography. *Winner:* Tom Beck.

Distinguished Service Award. To honor an individual whose exemplary service in art librarianship, visual resources curatorship, or a related field has made an outstanding national or international contribution to art information and/or art librarianship. *Winner:* Angela Giral.

Melva J. Dwyer Award. To the creators of exceptional reference or research tools relating to Canadian art and architecture. *Winners:* Barbara Fischer and Fern Bayer for *General Idea Editions: 1967–1995* (Blackwood Gallery, University of Toronto at Mississauga).

Howard and Beverly Joy Karno Award. To provide financial assistance to a professional art librarian in Latin America through interaction with ARLIS/NA members and conference participation. *Winner:* Jorge Orlando Melo.

David Mirvish Books/Books on Art Travel Award (C$500). To encourage art librarianship in Canada. *Winner:* Not awarded in 2004.

Gerd Muehsam Award. To one or more graduate students in library science programs to recognize excellence in a graduate paper or project. *Winner:* Ann C. Shincovich for "An Examination of Copyright Issues Related to the Creation of a Digital Resource for the Artists' Books Collection at the Frick Fine Arts Library, University of Pittsburgh."

Salander O'Reilly Student Travel Award. To promote participation in ARLIS/NA by supporting travel for a student considering a career in art librarianship. *Winner:* Sandra Cowan.

Puvill Libros Award. To encourage professional development of European art librarians through interaction with ARLIS/NA colleagues and conference participation. *Winner:* Eila Ramo.

Research Libraries Group Asia/Oceania Award. To encourage professional development of art information professionals who reside in Asia/Oceania through interaction with ARLIS/NA colleagues and conference participation. *Winner:* Joye Volker.

Research Libraries Group Award. To promote participation in ARLIS/NA by supporting conference travel for an individual who has not attended an ARLIS/NA Annual Conference. *Winner:* Nicole Gjertsen.

H. W. Wilson Foundation Research Grant. To support research activities by ARLIS/NA members in the fields of librarianship, visual resources curatorship, and the arts. *Winners:* Ruth Wallach for "Public Art and City Transportation: Los Angeles, New York, Washington, D.C."; Margaret Culbertson for "House-Family Portrait Photographs of the Nineteenth Century."

George Wittenborn Memorial Book Award. For outstanding publications in the visual arts and architecture. *Winner: A Private Passion: 19th Century Paintings and Drawings from the Grenville L. Winthrop Collection, Harvard University,* edited by Stephan Wolohojian and Anne Tahinci (Yale University Press and the Metropolitan Museum of Art).

Worldwide Book Award for Publications. *Winners:* Joan Bennedett for "Managing the Small Art Museum Library"; Sarah McCleskey for "Staffing Standards and Core Competencies in Academic Art and Architecture Departmental Libraries: A Preliminary Study."

Association for Library and Information Science Education (ALISE)

ALISE Award for Teaching Excellence in the Field of Library and Information Science Education. *Winner:* Connie Van Fleet.

ALISE Methodology Paper Competition ($500). *Winner:* Not awarded in 2004.

ALISE Pratt-Severn Faculty Innovation Award ($1,000). *Winner:* Not awarded in 2004.

ALISE Professional Contribution to Library and Information Science Education Award. *Winner:* Carol Collier Kuhlthau.

ALISE Research Grant Awards (one or more grants totaling $5,000): *Winners:* Cathy M. Perley and Rebecca Miller for "Performance Characteristics Required of Information Professionals Working in Competitive Business Environments."

ALISE Service Award. *Winner:* Not awarded in 2004.

ALISE Bohdan S. Wynar Research Paper Competition. For a research paper concerning any aspect of librarianship or information studies by a member of ALISE. *Winner:* Not awarded in 2004.

Doctoral Students to ALISE Award ($400 toward attendance at the ALISE Annual Conference). *Winners:* Philip Edwards, Jianqiang Wang.

Eugene Garfield/ALISE Doctoral Dissertation Awards ($500). *Winners:* Samuel E. Trosow for "Information for Society: Towards a Critical Theory of Intellectual Property Policy"; Kalpana Shankar for "Scientists, Records, and the Practical Politics of Infrastructure."

OCLC/ALISE Library and Information Science Research Grants (up to $15,000). *Winners:* Corinne Jorgensen, Feili Tu and Nancy Zimmerman, Elizabeth Yakel.

Beta Phi Mu

Beta Phi Mu Award. *See under* American Library Association.

Doctoral Dissertation Scholarship. *Winner:* Arif Dagli.

Eugene Garfield Doctoral Dissertation Fellowships ($3,000). *Winners:* Arif Dagli, Bin Li, Mia Liza A. Lustria, Jianquiang Wang, Xiaojun Yuan, Jinwon Ho.

Harold Lancour Scholarship for Foreign Study ($1,500). For graduate study in a foreign country related to the applicant's work or schooling. *Winner:* Akbar Williams.

Sarah Rebecca Reed Scholarship ($2,000). For study at an ALA-accredited library school. *Winner:* Barbara Gabaldon.

Frank B. Sessa Scholarship for Continuing Professional Education ($1,250). For continuing education for a Beta Phi Mu member. *Winner:* Kris Donovan.

Blanche E. Woolls Scholarship ($1,500). For a beginning student in school library media services. *Winner:* Ann M. Preczewski.

Bibliographical Society of America (BSA)

BSA Fellowships (up to $2,000 a month for two months). For scholars involved in bib-

liographical inquiry and research in the history of the book trades and in publishing history. *Winners:* Daisy A. Aaronian, Tatjana T. Chorney, Gerald W. Cloud, David R. Como, Aileen Fyfe, Scott H. Husby, Coleman Hutchison, Philip M. Oldfield, Patricia J. Osmond de Martino, Anna Lisa Taylor.

William L. Mitchell Prize for Research on Early British Serials ($1,000). For the best single work published between January 1, 2002, and September 1, 2005. To be awarded in January 2006.

Justin G. Schiller Prize for Bibliographical Work on Pre-20th-Century Children's Books ($2,000). To encourage scholarship in the bibliography of historical childen's books. *Winner:* To be awarded in January 2007 and every three years thereafter.

Canadian Library Association (CLA)

Olga B. Bishop Award ($200). To a library school student for the best paper on government information or publications. *Winner:* Rhonda Miller.

CLA Award for the Advancement of Intellectual Freedom in Canada. *Winner:* Monique Désormeaux.

CLA Elizabeth Dafoe Scholarship ($3,000). *Winner:* Melanie Sellar.

CLA/Information Today Award for Innovative Technology. *Donor:* Information Today, Inc. *Winner:* Windsor (Ontario) Public Library.

CLA Outstanding Service to Librarianship Award. *Donor:* R. R. Bowker. *Winner:* Wendy Newman.

CLA Research and Development Grant ($1,000). *Winner:* Ross Gordon.

CLA Student Article Award. *Winner:* Jannah McCarville for "Balancing Access and Privacy in Archives."

CLA/3M Award for Achievement in Technical Services ($1,000). *Winner:* Metadata Service of Library and Archives Canada.

W. Kaye Lamb Award for Service to Seniors. *Winner:* Toronto Public Library.

H. W. Wilson Scholarship ($2,000). *Winner:* Kenneth Gariepy.

World Book Graduate Scholarship in Library Science ($2,500). *Winner:* Rumi Graham.

Canadian Association for School Libraries (CASL)

CASL Margaret B. Scott Award of Merit. For the development of school libraries in Canada. *Winners:* Lillian Carefoot and Gloria Hersak.

CASL National Book Service Teacher-Librarian of the Year Award. *Winner:* Lois Barranoik.

Canadian Association of College and University Libraries (CACUL)

CACUL Conference Grants. *Winners:* Georgina R. Z. Saranchuk, Rand Walker, Anna Stoute, Susan Atkey.

CACUL/Miles Blackwell Award for Outstanding Academic Librarian. *Sponsor:* Blackwell's. *Winner:* Doug Poff.

CACUL Innovation Achievement Award ($1,500). *Sponsor:* Micromedia ProQuest. *Winner:* Groupe de Travail sur le Traitment de la Documentation du Sous-Comite des Bibliothèques (CREPUQ).

CTCL Award for Outstanding College Librarian. *Winner:* Janice Hayes.

CTCL Innovation Achievement Award. *Sponsor:* Micromedia ProQuest. *Winners:* Medicine Hat College, Holland College

Canadian Association of Public Libraries (CAPL)

CAPL/Brodart Outstanding Public Library Service Award. *Winner:* Linda Cook.

Canadian Association of Special Libraries and Information Services (CASLIS)

CASLIS Award for Special Librarianship in Canada. *Winner:* Not awarded in 2004.

Canadian Library Trustees Association (CLTA)

CLTA/Stan Heath Achievement in Literacy Award. For an innovative literacy program by a public library board. *Donor:* ABC Canada. *Winner:* Not awarded in 2004.

CLTA Merit Award for Distinguished Service as a Public Library Trustee. *Winner:* Isabelle Butters.

Chinese-American Librarians Association (CALA)

CALA Distinguished Service Award. To a librarian who has been a mentor, role model, and leader in the fields of library and information science. *Winner:* Linna Chien Yu.

CALA President's Recognition Award. *Winners:* Zhijia Shen, Liana Zhou, Karen Wei.

Sheila Suen Lai Scholarship ($500). *Winner:* Iva Seto.

C. C. Seetoo/CALA Conference Travel Scholarship ($500). For a student to attend the ALA Annual Conference and CALA program. *Winner:* Justina Huang.

Sally T. Tseng Professional Development Grant. *Winners:* Yunshan Ye, Lisa Zhao and Li Fu (joint application).

Huang Tso-ping and Wu Yao-yu Scholarship Memorial Research Grants (total $1,000). *Winners:* Qing Fang, Yaolin Zhou, Cuibo Wang, Carrie Fang.

Church and Synagogue Library Association (CSLA)

CSLA Award for Outstanding Congregational Librarian. For distinguished service to the congregation and/or community through devotion to the congregational library. *Winner:* Not awarded in 2004.

CSLA Award for Outstanding Congregational Library. For responding in creative and innovative ways to the library's mission of reaching and serving the congregation and/or the wider community. *Winner:* Not awarded in 2004.

CSLA Award for Outstanding Contribution to Congregational Libraries. For providing inspiration, guidance, leadership, or resources to enrich the field of church or synagogue librarianship. *Winner:* Joyce Kight.

Muriel Fuller Scholarship Award. *Winner:* Jan Philipson.

Helen Keating Ott Award for Outstanding Contribution to Children's Literature. *Winner:* Not awarded in 2004.

Pat Tabler Memorial Scholarship Award. *Winner:* Not awarded in 2004.

Coalition for Networked Information

Paul Evan Peters Award. To recognize notable and lasting international achievements related to high-performance networks and the creation and use of information resources and services that advance scholarship and intellectual productivity. *Winner:* Brewster Kahle.

Paul Evan Peters Fellowship ($2,500 a year for two years). To a student pursuing a graduate degree in librarianship or the information sciences. *Winner:* Phillip M. Edwards.

Council on Library and Information Resources

Rovelstad Scholarship in International Librarianship. To enable a student enrolled in an accredited LIS program to attend the IFLA Annual Conference. *Winner:* Kathleen Marie Smith.

A. R. Zipf Fellowship in Information Management ($5,000). To a student enrolled in graduate school who shows exceptional promise for leadership and technical achievement. *Winner:* Joan A. Smith.

International Federation of Library Associations and Institutions (IFLA)

Hans-Peter Geh Grant. To enable a librarian from the former Soviet Union to attend a conference in Germany or elsewhere. *Winner:* Not awarded in 2004.

IFLA/3M International Marketing Awards. To organizations that promote library service and generate widespread visibility and support for libraries through their strategic approach to marketing communi-

cations. *Winners:* Australian Islamic College, Kewdale, Western Australia; Krasheninnikov Regional Research Library, Kamchatka, Russia; African Rice Center in Abidjan, Ivory Coast.

Frederic Thorpe Award (£15,000 total). To librarians working in libraries for the blind. *Donor:* Ulverscroft Foundation. *Winners:* Wendy Patricia Ling, Ademike Olorundore, Sarah Home.

Medical Library Association (MLA)

Estelle Brodman Award for the Academic Medical Librarian of the Year. To honor significant achievement, potential for leadership, and continuing excellence at mid-career in the area of academic health sciences librarianship. *Winner:* Kathryn "Katy" Nesbit (awarded posthumously).

Lois Ann Colaianni Award for Excellence and Achievement in Hospital Librarianship. To a member of MLA who has made significant contributions to the profession in the area of overall distinction or leadership in hospital librarianship. *Winner:* Christine Chastain-Warheit.

Cunningham Memorial International Fellowship ($6,000). A six-month grant and travel expenses in the United States and Canada for a foreign librarian. *Winner:* Raphael E. Euppah, Nairobi (Kenya) Hospital.

Louise Darling Medal. For distinguished achievement in collection development in the health sciences. *Winner:* Gayle Willard.

Janet Doe Lectureship. *Winner:* Fred W. Roper.

EBSCO/MLA Annual Meeting Grant (up to $1,000). *Winners:* Jon Crossno, Anne Heimann, Misa Mi, Lin Wu.

Ida and George Eliot Prize. For an essay published in any journal in the preceding calendar year that has been judged most effective in furthering medical librarianship. *Donor:* Login Brothers Books. *Winners:* Eileen Abels, Keith Cogdill, and Lisl Zach, for "The Contributions of Library and Information Services to Hospitals and Academic Health Sciences Centers: A Preliminary Taxonomy."

Murray Gottlieb Prize. For the best unpublished essay submitted by a medical librarian on the history of some aspect of health sciences or a detailed description of a library exhibit. *Donors:* Ralph and Jo Grimes. *Winner:* Beth Wagner for "History of Tumor Measurement Using Radiographs."

Hospital Libraries Section/MLA Professional Development Grants. *Winners:* Lisa Blackwell, Pamela Barnard.

David A. Kronick Traveling Fellowship ($2,000). *Sponsor:* Bowden-Massey Foundation. *Winner:* Ellen T. Crumley.

Joseph Leiter NLM/MLA Lectureship. *Winner:* Donald Henderson. *Topic:* "Surveillance for Disease, Detection, Eradication and Biodefense."

Donald A. B. Lindberg Research Fellowship. *Winner:* Timothy B. Patrick.

Lucretia W. McClure Excellence in Education Award. To an outstanding eduator in the field of health sciences librarianship and informatics. *Winners:* Janis Glover, Kathryn "Katy" Nesbit (awarded posthumously).

John P. McGovern Award Lectureship. *Winner:* Not awarded in 2004.

Majors/MLA Chapter Project of the Year Award. *Sponsor:* Majors Scientific Books. *Winner:* Pacific Northwest Chapter of MLA.

Medical Informatics Section/MLA Career Development Grant ($1,500). For up to two individuals to support a career development activity that will contribute to advancement in the field of medical informatics. *Winners:* Margaret Gorman, Sara Anne Hook.

MLA Award for Distinguished Public Service. *Winner:* U.S. Sen. Arlen Specter (R-Pa.).

MLA Continuing Education Grant ($100–$500). *Winner:* Bette Sydelko.

MLA Fellowships. *Winners:* Thomas G. Basler, Carole M. Gilbert, Henry L. Lemkau, Faith A. Meakin, Diane G. Schwartz.

MLA/NLM Spectrum Scholarship ($5,000). To support a minority student intending to become a health sciences information professional. *Winner:* Leigh Esquirra.

MLA President's Award. *Winners:* Martha R. Fishel and Betsy L. Humphreys.

MLA Research, Development, and Demonstration Project Grant ($100 to $1,000). *Winner:* Ellen T. Crumley.

MLA Scholarship (up to $5,000). For graduate study at an ALA-accredited library school. *Winner:* Amanda Biggins.

MLA Scholarship for Minority Students (up to $5,000). For graduate study at an ALA-accredited library school. *Winner:* Rebecca Davies-Venn.

Marcia C. Noyes Award. For an outstanding contribution to medical librarianship. The award is the highest professional distinction of MLA. *Winner:* Nancy M. Lorenzi.

Rittenhouse Award. For the best unpublished paper on medical librarianship submitted by a student enrolled in, or having been enrolled in, a course for credit in an ALA-accredited library school or a trainee in an internship program in medical librarianship. *Donor:* Rittenhouse Medical Bookstore. *Winner:* Derek Hansen for "Adolescent Health Information Seeking on the Web: A Multidisciplinary Review."

Thomson ISI/Frank Bradway Rogers Information Advancement Award ($500). For an outstanding contribution to knowledge of health science information delivery. *Winners:* Joyce E. B. Backus, Paula Kitendaugh, Lori J. Klein, Eve-Marie Lacroix, Wei Ma, Jennifer Marill, and Naomi Miller, National Library of Medicine.

REFORMA (National Association to Promote Library and Information Services to Latinos and the Spanish-Speaking)

REFORMA scholarships ($1,500). To students who qualify for graduate study in library science and who are citizens or permanent residents of the United States. *Winners:* Gonzalo A. Garcia, Marisa H. Grijalva, Maricela A. Leon, Annabelle V. Nuñez, Marisa L. Ramirez.

K. G. Saur (Munich, Germany)

K. G. Saur Award for Best *LIBRI* Student Paper ($500). To author(s) to recognize the most outstanding article published in *LIBRI* during the preceding year. *Donor:* K. G. Saur Publishing. *Winner:* Sue Beer for "Information Flow and Peripherality in Remote Island Areas of Scotland" (vol. 54, 148–157).

Society of American Archivists (SAA)

C. F. W. Coker Award for Description. *Winner:* RLG Encoded Archival Description Advisory Group.

Colonial Dames of America Scholarships (up to $1,200). To enable new archivists to attend the Modern Archives Institute of the National Archives and Records Administration. *Winners:* Shugana Campbell, Ann T. Boltin, Luciana M. Spracher.

Council Exemplary Service Award. To recognize outstanding service and exemplary contribution to the profession. *Winner:* John Carlin.

Fellows' Posner Prize. For an outstanding essay dealing with a facet of archival administration, history, theory, or methodology, published in *American Archivist*. *Winners:* James O'Toole for "Democracy—and Documents—in America" and George Bolotenko for "Frost on the Walls in Winter: Russian and Ukrainian Archives Since the Great Dislocation (1991–1999)."

Philip M. Hamer–Elizabeth Hamer Kegan Award. For individuals and/or institutions that have increased public awareness of a specific body of documents. *Winner:* Pennsylvania Historical and Museum Commission for *Documenting Pennsylvania's Past: The First Century of the Pennsylvania State Archives.*

Oliver Wendell Holmes Award. To enable overseas archivists already in the United States or Canada for training to attend the SAA annual meeting. *Winner:* Bart Ballaux.

J. Franklin Jameson Award. For individuals and/or organizations that promote greater public awareness of archival activities and programs. *Winner:* Not awarded in 2004.

Sister M. Claude Lane Award. For a significant contribution to the field of religious archives. *Winner:* John Treanor.

Waldo Gifford Leland Prize. For writing of superior excellence and usefulness in the field of archival history, theory, or practice. *Winner:* Gregory S. Hunter for *Developing and Maintaining Practical Archives: A How-To-Do-It Manual,* 2nd edition (Neal-Schuman).

Theodore Calvin Pease Award. For the best student paper. Catherine O'Sullivan for "Diaries, Online Diaries, and the Future Loss to Archives; or, Blogs and the Blogging Bloggers Who Blog Them."

Harold T. Pinkett Minority Student Award. To encourage minority students to consider careers in the archival profession and promote minority participation in SAA. *Winner:* Josué Hurtado.

Preservation Publication Award. To recognize an outstanding work published in North America that advances the theory or the practice of preservation in archival institutions. *Winners:* Anne R. Kenney and Nancy Y. McGovern for their Web-based tutorial "Digital Preservation Management: Implementing Short-term Strategies for Long-term Problems."

SAA Fellows. Highest individual distinction awarded to a limited number of members for their outstanding contribution to the archival profession. *Honored:* Sara S. Hodson, Gregory S. Hunter, Karen Jefferson, Alden Monroe, Daniel Pitti.

Special Libraries Association (SLA)

Mary Adeline Connor Professional Development Scholarship ($6,000). *Winner:* Susan E. Randolph.

John Cotton Dana Award. For exceptional support and encouragement of special librarianship. *Winners:* Donna Scheeder, Barbara Semonche.

Diversity Leadership Development Award. *Winners:* Innocent A. Awasom, Praveen Kumar Jain, Paiki Muswazi, Akram Sadeghi Pari, Cassandra M. Shieh.

Factiva Leadership Award ($2,000). To an SLA member who exemplifies leadership as a special librarian through excellence in personal and professional competencies. *Winner:* SLA Special Committee on Competencies (Dee Magnoni, Eileen Abels, Joanne Gard Marshall, John R. Latham, Rebecca Jones).

Steven I. Goldspiel Memorial Research Grant. *Winners:* Not awarded in 2004.

Hall of Fame Award. To a member or members of the association at or near the end of an active professional career for an extended and sustained period of distinguished service to the association. *Winners:* Ellen Miller, Wilda Newman, Ruth Seidman.

SLA Affirmative Action Scholarship. *Winner:* Florante P. Ibanez.

SLA Fellows. *Honored:* Susan DiMattia, Richard Geiger, Karen Kreizman Reczek, Agnes Mattis, Lyle Minter.

SLA Membership Achievement Award. *Winner:* Kenlee Ray.

SLA President's Award. *Winner:* SLA Executive Director Selection Committee (Tamika Barnes, Lynn Berard, Richard Hulser, Mary Lee Kennedy, Dottie Moon).

SLA Professional Award. *Winners:* T. N. Prakash, Elton B. Stephens.

SLA Student Scholarships. For graduate study in librarianship leading to a master's degree in library or information science. *Winners:* Roberta Craig, Dawn R. Pottinger, Margaret A. Smith.

Rose L. Vormelker Award. *Winners:* Anne Caputo, Doris Helfer.

H. W. Wilson Company Award ($500). For the most outstanding article in the past year's *Information Outlook. Donor:* H. W. Wilson Company. *Winners:* Jill Konieczko, Cynthia Powell.

Part 4
Research and Statistics

Library Research and Statistics

Research and Statistics on Libraries and Librarianship in 2004

Denise M. Davis
Director, Office for Research and Statistics, American Library Association

The times are changing, but many things remain surprisingly the same.

Surveys of libraries of all types show similar results—funding is "strained," staffing figures are flat, library "use" is rising, materials acquisition costs continue to rise, and materials acquisitions (in counts) are flat. We know that public libraries have been struggling with the question of filtering on public and staff computers, with decisions by governing boards determining whether a library receives federal funding for many technology-related purchases and services. We also know that school librarians and their support staff have lost jobs because of economic downturns, may not be rehired, or may be replaced with volunteers—this despite research that correlates student performance with the presence of a library and professional staffing.

Achievements and Concerns

Digital Virtual Reference

Digital virtual reference (VR) projects have sprouted all over the country and are no longer limited to larger libraries, cooperatives, or statewide initiatives. Effective analysis is being conducted at state libraries, by statewide VR programs, and by research libraries. Early figures indicate very high levels of accuracy in reference interactions. The results of evaluation and assessment of VR are expected to appear more prominently in the literature in 2005.

Journal Pricing

Academic libraries continue to feel the journal-pricing pinch and unlikely voices are being heard on this topic—from the editorial boards of scientific journals. The resignation of the entire editorial board of the *Journal of Algorithms* on December 31, 2003, was reported by both the *Chronicle of Higher Education* and *Library Journal*. In late January 2004 a proposal to create a new journal on algorithms was approved by the ACM (Association for Computing Machinery) Publications Board.

The Association of Research Libraries (ARL) highlighted in its *ARL Bimonthly Report 234* (June 2004) that serials prices continue to rise. In an article titled "Serials Trends Reflected in the ARL Statistics 2002–03," Martha Kyrillidou, director of ARL's Statistics and Measurement Program, reported that serials unit costs had increased 215 percent over the previous 17 years (full data are available in *ARL Statistics 2002–03*). It was further reported in *ARL Bimonthly Report 235* (August 2004) that its members spent, on average, 26 percent of materials budgets on electronic collections in 2001–2002 and that electronic journals represented 92 percent of that expenditure. ARL further reported that journal pricing increased for its members by 712 percent between 1994 and 2002. It very likely will not be long before this proportion increases as humanities titles go the way of science, technology, and medicine titles. Total expenditures on library materials represented 40 percent of total operating budgets in 2002–2003 for ARL libraries.

LIS Study

Library and information science (LIS) programs throughout the country continue to grow. Many LIS deans have reported record enrollment in the master's-level programs, in large part a result of distance education. But although enrollment figures are rising, it is not entirely clear whether the graduates are finding employment in libraries. A work force study funded by the Institute of Museum and Library Services (IMLS) will be conducted under the direction of José-Marie Griffiths, dean of the School of Information and Library Science, University of North Carolina, Chapel Hill. This is a two-year research study on the future of librarians in the work force and began in fall 2004.

Publication Delays

Research relevant—even critical—to decision making and planning continues to be delayed years before publication, leaving us wondering about other mechanisms for getting this valuable information out to the library community. The American Library Association (ALA) has reported publication delays of as much as two years; scholarly publications cite even longer gaps. Thomas Nisonger of the Indiana University School of Library and Information Science has revised the study on LIS deans' and ARL directors' perception of library journals and found that delays in publication have affected perceptions. Some groups are investigating leveraging institutes, conferences, and other public forums more effectively as venues for presenting research findings and compensating for the publication delays. Unfortunately, if these forums do not publish their proceedings, the attempt may not result in a solution to the publication-pipeline clogs.

Deaths During 2004

The library research community saw the loss of many in 2004. Among the most notable were Anne Grodzins Lipow and William A. Katz. Lipow, who died September 9, was founder and director of Library Solutions Institute and Press and a long-time trainer and advocate of innovative reference techniques including digital virtual reference. For more information about her contributions, visit http://

www.library-solutions.com. Katz, who died September 12, was retired from the faculty of the School of Information Science and Policy, State University of New York at Albany. He is best known for his books on reference sources and services, including the two-volume *Introduction to Reference Work*. For more information, visit http://www.albany.edu/sisp/news/katz.htm.

Research Relevant to All Libraries

Colorado Staff Study

One of the more significant studies to be completed in 2004 was "Retirement, Retention, and Recruitment: The Future of Librarianship in Colorado" by Nicolle Steffen, Keith Curry Lance, Becky Russell, and Zeth Lietzau of the Library Research Service (LRS), Colorado Department of Education (September 2004). The study was sponsored by the Management and Administration Division of the Colorado Association of Libraries (MADCAL) and funded by the Colorado State Library. Of the estimated 4,520 people employed by Colorado's academic, public, and school libraries, 1,159 (26 percent) responded to the survey. The study revealed that of the 1,241 total respondents to the survey (including special library respondents), 216, or 17 percent, indicated that they plan to retire in the next five years. Nearly three quarters (71 percent) of librarians who reported planning to retire within five years were 55 or older. Remaining librarian retirees were between 45 and 54 (29 percent) and none were younger than 45. Of these, 47 percent were in school libraries. This study provides a wealth of information about why individuals did not pursue credentialed library careers, whether a poor economy has affected career plans, and many other factors. Not surprising was that 66 percent of those responding indicated that low salaries kept them from pursuing an MLS degree. [See "Retirement, Retention, and Recruitment: The Future of Librarianship in Colorado" later in Part 4—*Ed.*]

The Colorado study findings are similar to those of Mary Jo Lynch, Stephen Tordella, and Thomas Godfrey in their report "Retirement and Recruitment: A Deeper Look" (*America Libraries,* January 2005; available at http://www.ala.org/ala/ors/reports). This report updates a March 2002 study analyzing the profession using the 2000 census as the base and looking at occupational groups. Findings show that the ten-year period beginning in 2010 will see 45 percent of today's librarians reach age 65—the early wave of "baby boomer" librarians. This study also confirms the Colorado finding that many librarians come to the profession as a second career choice.

Salary Survey

ALA continues its annual salary survey. The survey is a random stratified sample of university, college, two-year academic, and public libraries throughout the United States. All public libraries serving populations of 500,000 or more are included each year. The 2004 findings show a modest increase (2.3 percent) in mean salaries across all libraries sampled; the national average was 2.5 percent. Salaries reported ranged from a low of $13,878 to a high of $241,280, with a mean of $52,188 and a median of $48,792. The most significant improvement was for beginning librarians, with an increase of 7.5 percent over salaries reported in 2003. More information about the study is available at http://www.ala. org/ala/ors/reports/salsursumart04.htm. Supplemental questions about position titles were also included in the 2004 survey and will be used to develop and conduct a support staff salary survey in 2005. ALA will administer the 2005 surveys of professional and support staff for the Office on Research and the ALA Allied Professional Association.

Florida Studies 'Taxpayer Return'

The State Library and Archives of Florida undertook a year-long study resulting in the report "Taxpayer Return on Investment in Florida Public Libraries: Summary Report September 2004." The project director was José-Marie Griffiths. Its purposes included understanding individual libraries' economic impact compared with that of other types of organizations. The project used standard models of economic values, notably the model developed by Regional Economic Models and the Contingent Valuation Method. Some interesting findings from the study:

- Every dollar invested in public libraries yielded a return of $6.54 to the economy.
- The economic benefit of public libraries to individuals ranged from $7.10 for recreational use of the library to $143.86 for work-related use.
- The educational contribution of public libraries was valued at $2.1 billion.

Additional information about the project and a copy of the final report are available at http://dlis.dos.state.fl.us/bld/roi/finalreport.cfm.

CLIR Eyes Nonsubscription Periodicals

The Council on Library and Information Resources (CLIR) released a study in June by Eileen Fenton, Donald W. King, Ann Okerson, and Roger C. Schonfeld titled "The Nonsubscription Side of Periodicals: Changes in Library Operations and Costs Between Print and Electronic Formats." Although it focuses on research and academic libraries, the study is invaluable in understanding the life-cycle costs to an organization as well as expenditures for a dual-format collection and the costs associated with managing the transition away from subscription-based collections. The research team surveyed 11 academic libraries—four small, three medium, and four large—during the first half of 2003 and recommend formulas for determining life-cycle values for print and electronic titles. The report is available for purchase, and can be accesssed online at http://www.clir.org/ pubs/abstract/pub127abst.html.

Academic Libraries

The academic library research agenda seemed to be less focused in 2004 than in the previous year. The three most significant areas of research were funding and expenditures, electronic services, and marketing.

ACRL Studies Library PR

ALA's Association of College and Research Libraries (ACRL) released *Marketing and Public Relations Practices in College Libraries,* compiled by Anita Rothwell Lindsay and issued as CLIP Note No. 34. The book summarizes the results of a marketing and public relations survey with responses from more than 175 college libraries. The survey determined that although 52.5 percent of responding academic libraries agreed that fulfilling part of their mission included marketing and public relations activities, only 4.1 percent had formal marketing plans or strategies. In fact, 66.4 percent of respondents did not plan to develop a marketing plan or other formal policies to coordinate marketing and public relations activities. The findings further indicate that for those libraries developing marketing materials and so forth, the majority of staff assigned to these activities had no prior experience in the area, nor had they been trained in communications, marketing, or public relations. The report includes samples of marketing and public relations materials to assist libraries in planning efforts, as well as a selected bibliography. More information about the report is at http://www.ala.org/ala/acrlbucket/nonserialtitles/clip34.htm.

ARL Upgrades Survey

ARL decided to include questions on electronic resources metrics and emerging digital library operations in the supplement of its base survey beginning in July 2004. This is the first "universe" survey—one that surveys all possible respondents—to formally incorporate electronic metrics. Although the National Center for Education Statistics (NCES) has introduced electronic metrics into its surveys of public, state, and academic libraries, reporting those data has been problematic. More information about this change is available at http://www.arl.org/stats/arlstat/changes.html.

ARL Reports

The ARL Office of Leadership and Management Services published two notable SPEC Kits in 2004. The first was *SPEC Kit 280, Library User Surveys* by Tom Diamond, head of Reference Services at Louisiana State University. ARL members completed the survey on library user surveys, reporting on current activities and updating Elaine Brekke's 1994 findings published in *SPEC Kit 205, User Surveys in ARL Libraries.* With 54 percent of members responding, the current data indicate that Web-based forms are the predominant method for administering surveys. "The responding libraries confirmed that the survey data was highly valuable for meeting the top three survey goals of assessing library service strengths and weaknesses, assessing user perceptions, and assessing the access of library services and resources." The results clearly link marketing value and issues of customer awareness of library services.

The second was *SPEC Kit 282, Managing Electronic Resources* by Vicki Grahame, head of the Catalog Department at the University of California–Irvine. Released in August, the report focuses on organizational and staffing issues. The survey gathered information about staff training, processing activities, and use of committees or teams to manage electronic resources. Of the 123 ARL member libraries responding, 87 percent reported making personnel or organizational changes to accommodate processing and management of electronic resources, especially in the area of cross-functional personnel changes. For more information about these and other ARL SPEC Kits, go to http://www.arl.org/spec/complete.html.

Following on the early work on LibQual+ and performance measures, ARL noted in *ARL Bimonthly Report 236* (October 2004) that LibQual+ reported a record number of libraries and consortia participating and that more than 112,000 individuals responded. More than 550 libraries in seven countries have used the tool since the pilot project began in 2000. For more information, see http://www.arl.org/newsltr/236/lq2004.html. In addition, ARL will launch an interactive data analysis tool for LibQual+ data. This tool will add further value to the data collected by ARL member libraries by providing a mechanism for creating categories for analysis.

NCES Academic Libraries Survey

The National Center for Education Statistics (NCES) has launched its third interactive Web-based survey of 3,700 U.S. academic libraries. The academic library survey began in 1966, was part of the Integrated Postsecondary Education System (IPEDS) until 2000, and occurs biennially in even-numbered years. The survey collected several new items in 2004, including the question "Is the library collection entirely electronic?" as well as seeking more specific information about electronic reference sources and aggregation services. It also added a new section on information literacy. NCES continues to experience delays in getting reported data back out to the library community. The Office of Management and Budget (OMB) instituted new requirements that have delayed the release of the 2002 final data and report. In addition, NCES has new standards that add another layer of review before final data and reports can be released. The good news is that data are released to the Peer Tools as soon after submission and preliminary editing as possible.

Public Libraries

NCLIS Analysis

One of the more valuable, and critical, accomplishments of 2004 was the release by Robert E. Molyneux, director, Statistics and Surveys, at the U.S. National Commission on Libraries and Information Science (NCLIS) of comparative data files from the NCES Federal State Cooperative System for Public Library Data (FSCS). *Public Libraries in the United States, a Statistical Portrait* analyzed data sets from 1987 to 2001 and ranked states against 20 characteristics for the period 1991–2001. These data were first released to the NCLIS Web site in fall 2004 and followed by an article in the January 2005 issue of *American Libraries*. To review the data files and ranking tables, see http://www.nclis.gov/statsurv/NCES/stateranks/index.html.

Deep Web

Kathleen R. Murray and William E. Moen report on deep Web searching improvements and apply them to the Library of Texas project. Their article, *The Deep Web: Resource Discovery in the Library of Texas,* appeared in the spring 2004 issue of *Texas Library Journal* (80(1):16–24). The concept of data mining, or deep searching, is not new to the library information field. What is noteworthy of Moen's work is the application of deep Web searching analysis within a meta search tool and a controlled multitype content environment of freely accessible Web resources and commercial aggregated content. Of particular interest in this research is the use of Web log analysis to understand user behavior while in a meta search tool.

E-Metrics Help

Florida State University's Information Use Management and Policy Institute is again at the forefront of electronic measures, more commonly referred to as e-metrics. This time it is with a National Leadership Grant from IMLS to develop an E-Metrics Instructional System (EMIS), a Web-based, interactive instructional system designed to help librarians understand selected e-metrics, how to collect these e-metrics, and how to use these e-metrics for decision making and communication purposes (especially to external stakeholder groups). The step-by-step training modules include a "how-to" section and a range of e-metrics such as virtual reference and user training. Of special note is an interactive annual report tool developed by a consultant to the project, Joe Ryan. John Carlo Bertot and Charles R. McClure direct the project. Additional information is available at http://www.ii.fsu.edu/emis.

GIS-Aided Research

Geographic Information Systems (GISs) continue to be employed by public libraries to analyze service areas. JaNae Kinikin of Weber State University reported on a study completed for Weber County (Utah) Library System in an article titled "Applying Geographic Information Systems to the Weber County Library System" (*Information Technology and Libraries,* September 2004). Kinikin studied current patron use of library branches and demographic characteristics of income and ethnicity. The study revealed that a majority (61 percent) of Weber County Library System patrons resided within a three-mile radius of a branch. Although some registered borrowers could not be plotted because of such factors as having a post office box address, the study helped library staff understand patron income and ethnicity so that collections and services could be more accurately targeted by branch.

Gates Foundation Studies

The Bill and Melinda Gates Foundation continues its work to improve access to technology in public libraries and to assess the impact of its philanthropy. Among the studies released in 2004 was a report titled *Toward Equality of*

Access: The Role of Public Libraries in Addressing the Digital Divide. The report found that public libraries have helped narrow the digital divide by providing free public access to computers and the Internet, and that there continue to be disparities in Internet use. Reported in this study were data from the U.S. Department of Commerce from 2002 noting disparities by race, age, and income level. The report provides a useful overview of the policy issues, pulling together information from a variety of studies. The report is available at http://www.imls.gov/pubs/pdf/equality.pdf.

The Gates Foundation also launched an impact study with the Information Use Management and Policy Institute at Florida State University to look at status and impact of public-access computers in public libraries. The award was to support two national surveys, in 2004 and 2006, of public libraries' use of technology in providing network-based services and resources, and their ability to affect their communities through technology and network-based services and resources. ALA's Washington Office is also supporting the study. More information is available at http://www.ii.fsu.edu/getann.cfm?pageID=5&annID=16.

ULC Studies Revenue, Governance

The Urban Libraries Council (ULC) released a study titled "Governance and Revenue Structures: New Field Data on Metropolitan Public Libraries." Among the findings were that more libraries experienced increases in general operating revenues in 2002–2003 than did not, and that local funding continued to be the primary source of revenue for public libraries. And, as the economy declined in many areas of the country, ULC members reported exploration of new revenue sources including "entrepreneurial ventures such as bookstores, coffee shops, and event space leasing." Library foundations continued to play a significant role in fund raising. The report is available at http://www.urbanlibraries.org/governance revenuereport.html.

School Libraries

AASL Study on Media Specialists

Issues concerning closing of school media centers have long been a focus of research for the American Association of School Librarians (AASL). In the 2004 edition of *School Library Media Research,* an online refereed journal of AASL, a study done by Donna Shannon, associate professor and coordinator, School Media Program, University of South Carolina School of Library and Information Science in Columbia, presents valuable information about the importance of curriculum for school librarians and media specialists, and discusses employment opportunities for students graduating with a specialization in school librarianship. The study, "Preparation of School Library Media Specialists in the United States," surveyed accredited and nonaccredited programs in six areas: schools, program(s), and faculty; student enrollment; certification requirements; internship requirements; distance education; and recruitment. Shannon reported that there were 48 accredited and 151 nonaccredited programs at the time of the study (1999–2000), and that three of the accredited programs planned to close at the end of the 1999–2000 academic year. Not surprisingly, distance education was viewed as a highly significant method for encouraging study of school librarianship. The study findings show that only 65 of the 117 responding institutions reported offering any form of distance education in this curriculum area. The article is available online at http://www.ala.org/ala/aasl/aaslpubsandjournals/slmrb/slmrcontents/volume72004/shannon.htm.

NCES High School Survey

NCES has been involved in a longitudinal study to monitor the transitions of a national sample of high school students as they progress from 10th to 12th grades and eventually to the work world. The Education Longitudinal Study of 2002 (ELS:2002) will obtain information not only from students and their school records, but also from students' parents, their teachers, their librarians, and the administrators of their schools. For the first time, libraries and their use by students is being studied as part of a longitudinal study. Findings about the library studies of 10th graders have been published as an E.D. Tab, *School Library Media Centers: Selected Results from the Education Longitudinal Study of 2002 (ELS:2002)* (NCES 2005-302), available at http://www.nces.ed.gov/surveys/els2002. More information about ELS:2002, including the study questionnaires, is available at http://www.nces.ed.gov/surveys/els2002/questionnaires.asp. Additional information about NCES longitudinal studies is available in an article published in *Education Statistics Quarterly,* "Studying Education as a Lifelong Process," in 2000. The article is available at http://www.nces.ed.gov/programs/quarterly/vol_2/2_1/1-esq21-a.asp.

Technology in Education

Technology in education was the featured topic of the summer 2004 issue of *Education Statistics Quarterly.* Articles included "Computer and Internet Use by Children and Adolescents in 2001" by Matthew DeBell and Chris Chapman, "Internet Access in U.S. Public Schools and Classrooms: 1994–2002" by Anne Kleiner and Laurie Lewis, "Participation in Technology-Based Postcompulsory Education" by Lisa Hudson and Linda Shafer, and "Invited Commentary: Children, Schools, Computers, and the Internet: The Impact of Continued Investment in Educational Technology Under NCLB" by Susan Patrick, director, Office of Educational Technology, U.S. Department of Education. The issue is online at http://www.nces.ed.gov/programs/quarterly/vol_5/5_4.

Other Research Benefiting the Profession

Report on Digital Reference

R. David Lankes, in his article "The Digital Reference Research Agenda" (*Journal of the American Society for Information Science and Technology* 55(4) [2004]), focuses on the output of a symposium held at Harvard in August 2002 to present a research agenda for the study of digital reference. Digital reference is defined in this agenda as ". . . the use of human intermediation to answer questions in a digital environment." The agenda questions digital reference in six areas: digital libraries, information retrieval, reference and library science, computer mediated communication, systems theory, and education. Lankes asks a further question regarding the role of human expertise in an information-systems environment to respond to patron inquiries. The result is a nicely developed research inquiry model. The article also is available on Lankes's Web site at http://quartz.syr.edu/rdlankes/tiki-list_file_gallery.php?galleryId=1.

Networked Reference Standard

The National Information Standards Organization (NISO) continues its work to develop a Networked Reference Standard. Sally H. McCallum of the Library of Congress chairs NISO Standards Committee AZ. For more information about the work of this committee, visit http://www.niso.org/committees/committee_az.html.

Search and Retrieve Web (SRW) and Metadata

William E. Moen, University of North Texas School of Library and Information Sciences, has written extensively in the areas of metadata analysis, the application of Z39.50 standard in a search and retrieval Web environment, and generally about Z39.50. The following is a sampling of Moen's work: "A Web Services Approach to Search and Retrieve: The Next Generation Z39.50," "Metadata Interaction, Integration, and Interoperability," and "The Dublin Core Metadata Initiative: Cross-Domain Resource Description and Resource Discovery." Each his presentations is available online at http://www.unt.edu/wmoen/presentations.htm.

Digital Collections

NISO and IMLS released a revision of *A Framework of Guidance for Building Good Digital Collections.* IMLS transferred maintenance of the framework to NISO in September 2003; the update represents the work of NISO's advisory group formed to contribute to the document's further development. The framework outlines high-level principles for identifying and organizing digital resources. It includes guidelines relating to quality and provides a list of supporting resources. A copy of the revised framework is available at http://www.niso.org/framework/forumframework.html.

IMLS began a second technology and digitization survey of libraries and museums. The first study formed the baseline data set, and the second survey's goals include updating the data set and identifying information on developments and trends since 2001. The second study should produce a report in 2005. The baseline study is available online at http://www.imls.gov/reports/techreports/intro02.htm.

Library Statistics Standard Revision

ANSI/NISO Z39.7-2004, "Information Services and Use: Metrics and Statistics for Libraries and Information Providers—Data Dictionary" was approved in October 2004. Z39.7 is an interactive Web-based utility for identifying standard definitions, methods, and practices relevant to library statistics activities in the

United States. Like the previous editions of Z39.7, the aim of the standard remains to assist librarians and researchers (now defined as "the information community") by indicating and defining useful, quantifiable information to measure the resources and performance of libraries and to provide a body of valid and comparable data on American libraries. A maintenance agency had not been identified for the standard at the time of this report. The standard is available online at http://www.niso.org/emetrics.

Project COUNTER

Project COUNTER (Counting Online Usage of NeTworked Electronic Resources) released a revision to its code of practice in April 2004 and plans code development for e-books and e-reference works. The changes to the code include a more comprehensive list of definitions and terms used, a clarification of the definition for number of successful full-text requests in HTML and PDF, a consolidation of protocols for recording intermediary aggregator or gateway usage to a table, and a new appendix for auditing standards and procedures for vendors and publishers. Discussion of "turnaways"—rejected sessions or unsuccessful log-ins—continued Additional information about COUNTER is available at http://www.project counter.org.

Awards and Grants that Honor and Support Excellent Research

The professional library associations offer many awards and grants to recognize and encourage research. The 2004 awards and grants here are listed under the name of the sponsoring association, and in the case of ALA by the awarding division, in alphabetical order. More-detailed information about the prizes and prizewinners can be found at the association Web sites.

The Mary Jo Lynch Award for Library and Information (LIS) Students, a new award to honor the contributions of long-time ALA Office for Research and Statistics Director Mary Jo Lynch, will be given in 2005. The award—intended to encourage library school student statistical research using public library data collected at the state and national level—is sponsored by ALA, NCES, NCLIS, and FSCS. The award will be announced at the FSCS Annual Conference held each December.

American Library Association

http://www.ala.org

Carroll Preston Baber Research Grant
Winner: Amanda Spink, University of Pittsburgh, for "Multitasking Information Behavior by Public Library Users."

Jesse H. Shera Award for Excellence in Published Research
Winners: Jeffrey D. Kushkowski, Kathy A. Parsons, and William H. Wiese for "Master's and Doctoral Thesis Citations: Analysis and Trends of a Longitudinal Study," *portal: Libraries and the Academy,* 3 (3): 459–479, 2003.

American Association of School Librarians (AASL)

http://www.ala.org/aasl

AASL/Highsmith Research Grant
Winners: Robyn Young for "More than Just Comics: Graphic Novels and Their Effect on Student Achievement," and Kathy Latrobe and Rhonda Taylor for "Survey of LMS's Attributes for Ongoing Program Assessment."

Association of College and Research Libraries (ACRL)

http://www.ala.org/acrl

Doctoral Dissertation Fellowship
Winner: Judy Jeng for "Usability of Digital Library: An Evaluation Model."

Samuel Lazerow Fellowship for Research in Collections and Technical Services in Academic and Research Libraries
Winners: Karen M. Letarte and Jacqueline P. Samples for "Looking at FRBR Through Users' Eyes: Toward Improved Catalog Displays for Electronic Serials."

Coutts Nijhoff International West European Specialist Study Grant
Winner: Helene S. Baumann for translation from German to English of the subject thesaurus of the Pictorial Archive of the German Colonial Society (Bildarchiv der Deutschen Kolonialgesellschaft).

IS Publication Award
Winners: Esther Stampfer Grassian and Joan Kaplowitz for *Information Literacy Instruction: Theory and Practice* (Information Literacy Sourcebooks, 2001), and Ann J. Grafstein for "A Discipline-Based Approach to Information Literacy" (*Journal of Academic Librarianship*, July 2002).

Library and Information Technology Association/OCLC

http://www.ala.org/lita

Frederick G. Kilgour Award for Research in Library and Information Technology
Winner: Carl Lagoze.

American Society for Information Science and Technology

http://www.asis.org

ASIS&T Research Award
Winner: Boyd Rayward.

ASIS&T ProQuest Doctoral Dissertation Award
Winner: Lennart Björneborn.

ASIS&T/ISI Doctoral Dissertation Proposal Scholarship
Winner: Meng Yang.

ISI/ Citation Analysis Research Grant
Winner: David Hubbard.

John Wiley & Sons Best *JASIST* Paper Award
Winner: Cecilia Brown for "The Role of Electronic Preprints in Chemical Communication: Analysis of Citation, Usage, and Acceptance in the Journal Literature."

ASIS&T Best Information Science Book
Winners: Charles Bourne and Trudi Bellardo Hahn for *A History of Online Information Services 1963–1976* (MIT Press).

Association for Library and Information Science Education

http://www.alise.org

Eugene Garfield/ALISE Doctoral Dissertation Award
Winners: Samuel E. Trosow for "Information for Society: Towards a Critical Theory of Intellectual Property Policy," Kalpana Shankar for "Scientists, Records, and the Practical Politics of Infrastructure."

Research Grant Award
Winners: Cathy M. Perley and Rebecca Miller for "Performance Characteristics Required of Information Professionals Working in Competitive Business Environments."

Medical Library Association

http://www.mlanet.org

Donald A. B. Lindberg Research Fellowship
Winner: Timothy B. Patrick for "Evidence-Based Information Retrieval in Bioinformatics." Patrick is assistant professor of health informatics, Health Management and Informatics, School of Medicine, University of Missouri–Columbia, and the second individual to receive this research fellowship. Focusing on postgenomic medicine, the research project will address the crucial need for evidence-based medicine to ensure high-quality health care, thus furthering understanding of the information retrieval partnership between health sciences information professionals and bioinformatics researchers.

President's Award
Winners: Martha Fishel and Betsy Humphreys, in recognition of their work in transferring MLA's scholarly publication, the *Bulletin of the Medical Library Association* (*BMLA*), now known as the *Journal of the Medical Library Association* (*JMLA*), into digital format from 1911.

Ida and George Eliot Prize
Winners: Eileen Abels, Keith Cogdill, and Lisl Zach for "The Contributions of Library and Information Services to Hospitals and Academic Health Sciences Centers: A Preliminary Taxonomy."

Retirement, Retention, and Recruitment: The Future of Librarianship in Colorado

Keith Curry Lance

Library Research Service

In Colorado as throughout the nation, librarianship is being—or is about to be—transformed by a generational wave of retirements. These losses raise related issues of retention and recruitment. The majority of the retirees have been in key leadership positions for 20 years or more, so their departures over at least the next five years will create dozens of openings for new library directors, department heads, association officers, and library educators and trainers. Many of these high-profile positions have not been vacant—or, at least, open to up-and-coming librarians—for decades. Who will take the places of these retirees? As library directorships and other senior positions become vacant, staff in the middle echelons are likely to move up, creating vacancies at middle-management levels. (Some vacant positions may, of course, simply be eliminated.) When staff openings exist, replacements may be hard to find. What will persuade individuals to choose librarianship as a career? What can be done to tempt existing librarians to remain in a field whose losses to retirement are only exacerbated by further losses to other fields?

Decision-makers for libraries must examine the patterns that can be discerned in the growing wave of retirements for lessons that will help to inform their efforts to shape the future of the profession through recruiting and retention efforts. It is not just a matter of how to recruit new librarians or how to retain incumbents generally; it is a matter of repopulating the library community's leadership.

A statewide online survey of Colorado library workers was conducted between October 15 and November 30, 2003. A total of 1,241 responses were received from both credentialed and non-credentialed library workers, as well as library and information science (LIS) students, at all types of libraries. Of the estimated 4,520 workers employed in Colorado's academic, public, and school libraries, 1,159 (26 percent) responded to the survey. Credentialed librarians and public library workers were somewhat over-represented relative to their proportions in the known universe of academic, public, and school library workers. (The size of the special library work force in Colorado, as in the nation, is unknown.)

Librarians and paraprofessionals planning to retire within the next five years were asked, among other things, to report that fact and to identify factors influencing their decision to retire. Incumbent paraprofessionals and current LIS students were asked questions relating to recruitment, such as what factors most encourage or discourage them from choosing librarianship as a profession. Incumbent librarians and paraprofessionals were asked questions about what would influence them to remain in the field. Those considering leaving the field were asked what other fields appear attractive and why. While the survey generated a lot of data, it did not capture all of the data one might wish. For instance, data was not captured from librarians who have already retired or about positions that may be vacant and whose fates may not yet be determined. Still, the answers to the questions asked shed considerable light on the status of librarianship in Colorado.

Retirements over the next five years are likely to be numerous, but they will not be restricted to those reaching the traditional retirement age of 65. Neither are retirements likely to be evenly distributed among library types, geographic areas, or specialties. Those who are retiring also tend to be among the state's most active library leaders—people who preside over professional organizations, chair committees, make presentations, and write books and articles. This wave of librarian retirements, which has already begun—and which will continue through at least the next five years—will affect some parts of the profession more than others, and the imbalances apt to result will require thoughtful care and attention.

Thus, the relationship between these three Rs—retirement, recruitment, and retention—is one that calls for a comprehensive statewide strategy to ensure that users of libraries of all types in all parts of the state receive equitable, high-quality services from credentialed librarians. Specific recommendations for action by various key players in the state's library leadership, which are justified by the findings of this study, are offered.

Retirement

As noted, Colorado librarians are retiring at a dramatic rate. To address the high incidence of retirements during the next five years, decision-makers for libraries will need to know which types of librarians are retiring, and why they are retiring, what their loss means for the professional community as well as the positions they are vacating, and where to look for their successors.

How many librarians are retiring? More than 20 percent (22 percent) of responding Colorado librarians expect to retire within the next five years. Of all responding school librarians, almost half (47 percent) indicate plans to retire within five years—more than twice the percentage for special librarians, more than three times the percentage for public librarians, and almost five times the percentage for academic librarians. This is likely explained by the fact that the percentage of school librarian respondents age 55 or over was also dramatically higher than for other types of librarians.

Who are these retirees? Many librarians are not waiting until age 65 to retire. Almost 30 percent of those who expect to retire within the next five years are ages 45 to 54. These retirees will take with them enormous amounts of experience. Nearly 9 out of 10 responding librarians who are retirement candidates have more than 10 years of library experience, and 3 out of 5 have more than 20 years of experience.

How have librarian retirements been affected by the recent economic downturn? The downturn has affected many librarians' retirement plans. Of responding prospective retirees from librarian positions, 1 out of 5 now plans to retire later than originally planned. Another 1 out of 5 now plans to retire earlier.

What human capital is being lost to retirement? Retiring librarians will also take with them substantial administrative skills. Of responding prospective retirees, 3 out of 4 are supervisors, 2 out of 5 are generalists, and 1 out of 5 is an administrator. In addition to losing leadership skills in the workplace, librarianship is also losing such skills in the professional community. Four out of 5 retiring librarians who responded to this survey have served in one or more leadership roles in the profession, compared with only about half of all responding library workers. Considering what we know about current LIS students, librarian retirements may lead to shortages in the following areas: school librarianship, information technology, cataloging, reference, and digital resources.

What is happening to retirees and their jobs? Retiring librarians who participated in this study are not optimistic about the future of their positions. Many expect their jobs to be downgraded, combined with other jobs, or eliminated. Of responding prospective retirees, almost 1 out of 5 expects his or her job to be combined with another or eliminated. Almost 1 out of 5 expects to be succeeded by someone with less education. Fortunately, these retirees are not abandoning the profession altogether. More than half of them plan to continue working part-time or on-call. More than 2 out of 5 also plan to volunteer in libraries.

Where do we find their replacements? To find some of the likeliest candidates to fill librarian vacancies due to retirement, we do not need to look very far. Four out of 5 retiring librarians said they worked or volunteered in a library or school before becoming librarians. This suggests that current paraprofessionals and volunteers may be good candidates for recruitment into librarianship.

Retention

Because of the high number of librarian retirements, it will not be enough to recruit more people into the profession. Decision-makers must also formulate policies, develop workplace environments, and structure librarians' jobs in ways that encourage those already in the profession not to abandon it, whether to early retirement or to another profession that they perceive to be more lucrative or fulfilling.

What do incumbent librarians identify as factors that make librarianship most attractive or most discourage the choice of a library career? Echoing LIS students and paraprofessionals, incumbent librarians identify low financial compensation (78 percent) and misconceptions about the field (58 percent) as leading factors discouraging recruitment of new librarians. Interestingly, however, they believe that service to others (57 percent) and intellectual challenge (53 percent) outrank love of books or reading (45 percent) as factors that make librarianship an attractive career option.

What are incumbent librarians doing on the job? To what other fields are those leaving librarianship going? The traditional conception of libraries as places to obtain books appears to be most prevalent among public librarians. Academic, school, and special librarians who replied to this survey are more likely to specialize in digital resources than their public librarian counterparts and are, therefore, less book-focused.

Those who are tempted to leave librarianship do not venture far. Academic librarians are most likely to move to other higher education jobs. School librarians reported being most likely to move to other K–12 education jobs. Special librarians say they are likeliest to move to either academia or business. The lone exception is public librarians, who say they are most likely to move to jobs in the business world.

What does the future of librarianship—and of their own careers—look like to incumbent librarians? Librarians, especially beyond the state's major cities and their suburbs, are not optimistic about the profession's ability to maintain adequate educational requirements for librarian positions. Librarians responding from non-metropolitan areas are almost four times more likely than their metropolitan counterparts to expect that their successors will have less education. This concern is particularly acute in school libraries. Responding school librarians are five times more likely than other librarian types to expect that their successors will have less education.

Worst of all, Eastern Plains librarians feel that the very existence of their positions will be threatened when they leave their jobs. Respondents from this region are most likely to expect that their jobs may be eliminated altogether.

Public, school, and special librarians tend to have stronger professional and/ or family ties to Colorado. Responding academic librarians expect that they will have to be more mobile to advance professionally. Most likely, this is because of the limited number of colleges and universities in Colorado and draconian budget cuts to higher education. Responding librarians from this sector are least likely to limit themselves to jobs in Colorado when compared with other librarian types.

Who is staying in librarianship and why? Who is not? Many librarians responding from Colorado's high country find the location of their jobs an incentive to stay at their libraries. Librarians in the Mountains/Western Slope region are more likely than their counterparts from other regions to identify their location as a reason for remaining in their current organization.

Older librarians stay in their jobs not because they are ambitious, but rather because they enjoy their work and rely on the fringe benefits that accompany their salaries. With age, librarian respondents choose to remain in their current organizations less because of perceived advancement opportunities and more because of the variety of work and the adequacy of benefits.

For academic librarian respondents and, to a lesser extent, their special librarian counterparts, collegiality in the workplace was perceived as a very important reason to remain with their current organizations. Collegiality was less important to most participants from public and school libraries—particularly in non-metropolitan areas—possibly because they are much less likely to work with other librarians.

Librarians in their 30s and early 40s are sometimes tempted away from the library profession by the appeal of other fields. Librarian respondents ages 30 to 44 are the most likely of all age groups (16 percent vs. 5 percent to 9 percent) to consider leaving librarianship.

Recruitment

In view of the high number of retiring librarians, decision-makers need to be aware of the foreseeable supply of librarians to meet a growing demand. They also need to be prepared to position librarianship as a profession vis-à-vis other information- and education-related professions with which we compete for the "best and brightest." Achieving that end will depend on the extent to which they understand the factors that encourage and discourage individuals from choosing a career in librarianship. In particular, it will depend on understanding why more of those already working in libraries do not opt to become credentialed librarians.

Who is pursuing library education and where? The ages of LIS students involved in this study suggest that librarianship is often a second career. Of responding students, 4 out of 5 are ages 30 to 54. Only 16 percent are under age 30. LIS students tend to be attracted to the field after gaining some actual work experience in a library setting. Of the students who replied to this survey, 3 out of 4 have at least some library work experience. A quarter have more than five years of library experience.

Prospective librarians are earning graduate degrees via a variety of options. Over half of responding students are enrolled at the University of Denver, attending the only MLIS program based at a Colorado university. In addition, 1 out of 5 participates in the Kansas-based Emporia in the Rockies extension program, 1 out of 7 participates in an out-of-state program online, and 1 out of 12 is enrolled at either the University of Colorado, Denver, or the University of Northern Colorado programs for school librarians. In addition to LIS students in these school-specific programs, some prospective school librarians may be pursuing master's degrees in library and information science from the University of Denver, Emporia in the Rockies, or another program based outside Colorado.

With which fields does library and information science compete? Library and information science competes most frequently for prospective recruits with other professions that connect inquiring minds with information and help them to apply that information in their own lives or the lives of others. Like incumbent librarians, LIS students who returned this survey are most tempted away from librarianship by education (K–12 or higher), computer technology, and business.

What encourages and discourages students and paraprofessionals to choose a career in librarianship? Generally, students and paraprofessionals agree that a love of books and reading is the factor that most encourages choosing a career in librarianship (61 percent and 65 percent, respectively). For students, second and third place go to intellectual challenge (46 percent) and service to others (42 percent). For paraprofessionals, that order is reversed: service to others (56 percent) and intellectual challenge (39 percent). Students and paraprofessionals agree, rather resoundingly, that the factor they believe most discourages choosing a library career is low financial compensation (81 percent and 63 percent, respectively). They also agree on a distant second: misconceptions about librarianship (48 percent and 39 percent, respectively).

Surprisingly, paraprofessionals responding from the Mountains/Western Slope region are more likely to consider pursuing library degrees than their Front Range counterparts. Paraprofessionals responding from the Eastern Plains are least likely to consider pursuing a library degree. These inclinations are probably based on accurate assessments of the library job markets in different regions of the state. For instance, many public libraries in the Mountains/Western Slope region are library districts, whose budgets can or will afford the ability to create more librarian jobs. But many public libraries on the Eastern Plains may not be able to afford credentialed librarian salaries.

Paraprofessional respondents are most encouraged to pursue librarianship if financial aid is available and if several interrelated logistical issues are addressed. These issues include class location and schedule, availability of online classes, and flexible work schedule.

How do student expectations about school librarianship differ from reality? Those planning to become school librarians may not have realistic expectations about the nature of the work. Only 8 percent of LIS students who said they plan to be school librarians expect to work with digital resources, but 39 percent of incumbent school librarians claim this specialty.

There is a market for graduate library education beyond the state's few major metropolitan areas. Three out of four non-metropolitan paraprofessionals report that access to online courses would encourage them to pursue LIS degrees or other credentials. Almost half of that group would be discouraged by inconveniently located educational institutions.

Why aren't more of those who already work in libraries pursuing library education? Of paraprofessional study participants not considering pursuing LIS credentials, over half believe a degree is not necessary to do their job and more than 2 out of 5 feel constrained financially from academic pursuits. Public and school library workers, in particular, report feeling discouraged by concerns about family obligations. Responding academic library paraprofessionals are most discouraged by a perceived lack of employer support. Reflecting the concern of all library workers that librarianship is not a well-paid profession, a third of all paraprofessionals do not believe a degree would improve their compensation.

Conclusion

To sum up the major findings of this Colorado study, many librarians are retiring, but far more from the school library sector than any other. The factors that make librarianship attractive to incumbent librarians are service to others, intellectual challenge, and love of books and reading. The most powerful factors that discourage choosing librarianship as a profession are clear to them. By far, the most discouraging factor is low financial compensation, followed by public misconceptions about the field. Recruits to librarianship tend to be those in their middle years seeking second careers. The "competition" for these individuals comes from education (both K–12 and higher), computer technology, and business. Incentives they believe would encourage more people to pursue LIS education include financial aid, flexible work schedules, more conveniently located class sites, and online courses.

The full report on this study, "Retirement, Retention, and Recruitment: The Future of Librarianship in Colorado," and related documents are available at http://www.LRS.org. In addition to providing full documentation of the study and its findings, the report offers recommendations for action to state leadership organizations, library decision-makers and individual libraries, library educators, librarians, and library job-seekers. (See http://www.lrs.org/documents/closer_look/RRR_web.pdf.) Accompanying the report is a trifold mini-brochure, "Quotable Facts About the Future of Librarianship in Colorado," which summarizes the major findings. (See http://www.lrs.org/documents/quotable/QF_Future_Librarianship.pdf.) Related issues of FAST FACTS: Recent Statistics from the Library Research Service are also posted on the LRS Web site. (See http://www.lrs.org/fastfacts/ff2005.asp.)

Number of Libraries in the United States and Canada

Statistics are from *American Library Directory (ALD) 2004–2005* (Information Today Inc., 2004). Data are exclusive of elementary and secondary school libraries.

Libraries in the United States

Public Libraries	16,811 *
Public libraries, excluding branches	9,603 †
Main public libraries that have branches	1,831
Public library branches	7,208
Academic Libraries	3,617 *
Junior college	1,118
Departmental	177
Medical	5
Religious	8
University and college	2,499
Departmental	1,449
Law	174
Medical	242
Religious	207
Armed Forces Libraries	312 *
Air Force	87
Medical	11
Army	142
Medical	29
Navy	68
Law	1
Medical	14
Government Libraries	1,249 *
Law	410
Medical	183
Special Libraries (excluding public, academic, armed forces, and government)	8,497 *
Law	999
Medical	1,693
Religious	596

Note: Numbers followed by an asterisk are added to find "Total libraries counted" for each of the three geographic areas (United States, U.S.-administered regions, and Canada). The sum of the three totals is the "Grand total of libraries listed" in *ALD*. For details on the count of libraries, see the preface to the 57th edition of *ALD*—*Ed.*
† Federal, state, and other statistical sources use this figure (libraries *excluding* branches) as the total for public libraries.

Total Special Libraries (including public, academic, armed forces, and government)	9,781
Total law	1,584
Total medical	2,177
Total religious	1,106
Total Libraries Counted(*)	30,486

Libraries in Regions Administered by the United States

Public Libraries	28 *
Public libraries, excluding branches	10 †
Main public libraries that have branches	3
Public library branches	18
Academic Libraries	36 *
Junior college	6
Departmental	3
Medical	0
University and college	30
Departmental	22
Law	3
Medical	1
Religious	1
Armed Forces Libraries	2 *
Air Force	1
Army	1
Navy	0
Government Libraries	7 *
Law	2
Medical	2
Special Libraries (excluding public, academic, armed forces, and government)	12 *
Law	4
Medical	2
Religious	
Total Special Libraries (including public, academic, armed forces, and government)	21
Total law	9
Total medical	5
Total religious	2
Total Libraries Counted(*)	85

Libraries in Canada

Public Libraries	2,104*
Public libraries, excluding branches	829†
Main public libraries that have branches	141
Public library branches	1,275
Academic Libraries	357*
Junior college	92
Departmental	16
Medical	0
Religious	4
University and college	265
Departmental	191
Law	16
Medical	23
Religious	33
Government Libraries	318*
Law	25
Medical	5
Special Libraries (excluding public, academic, armed forces, and government)	1,075*
Law	115
Medical	197
Religious	28
Total Special Libraries (including public, academic, and government)	1,181
Total law	156
Total medical	225
Total religious	100
Total Libraries Counted(*)	3,854

Summary

Total U.S. Libraries	30,486
Total Libraries Administered by the United States	85
Total Canadian Libraries	3,854
Grand Total of Libraries Listed	34,425

Highlights of NCES Surveys

Public Libraries

The following are highlights from the E.D. Tab publication *Public Libraries in the United States: Fiscal Year 2001,* released in July 2003. The data were collected by the National Center for Education Statistics (NCES). For more information on NCES surveys, see the article "National Center for Education Statistics Library Statistics Program" in Part 1.

Number of Public Libraries and Population of Legal Service Area

- There were 9,129 public libraries (administrative entities) in the 50 states and the District of Columbia in fiscal year (FY) 2001. (Of the 9,129 public libraries, 7,352 were single-outlet libraries, 1,776 were multiple-outlet libraries, and 1 had 0 public-service outlets, providing only books-by-mail service.)
- Public libraries served 97 percent of the total population of the states and the District of Columbia, either in legally established geographic service areas or in areas under contract.
- Eleven percent of the public libraries served 72 percent of the population of legally served areas in the United States; each of these public libraries had a legal service area population of 50,000 or more.

Service Outlets

- In FY 2001, 81 percent of public libraries had one single direct service outlet (an outlet that provides service directly to the public). Nineteen percent had more than one direct service outlet. Types of direct service outlets include central library outlets, branch library outlets, and bookmobile outlets.
- A total of 1,528 public libraries (17 percent) had one or more branch library outlets, with a total of 7,450 branch outlets. The total number of central library outlets was 8,971. The total number of stationary outlets (central library outlets and branch library outlets) was 16,421. Eight percent of public libraries had one or more bookmobile outlets, with a total of 879 bookmobiles.

Legal Basis and Interlibrary Relationships

- In FY 2001, 55 percent of public libraries were part of a municipal government, 11 percent were part of a county/parish, 15 percent were nonprofit association libraries or agency libraries, 9 percent were separate government units known as library districts, 5 percent had multijurisdictional legal basis under an intergovernmental agreement, 3 percent were part of a school district, 1 percent were part of a city/county, and 2 percent reported their legal basis as "other."

- Seventy-six percent of public libraries were members of a system, federation, or cooperative service, while 23 percent were not. Two percent served as the headquarters of a system, federation, or cooperative service.

Collections

- Nationwide, public libraries had 767.1 million books and serial volumes in their collections, or 2.8 volumes per capita, in FY 2001. By state, the number of volumes per capita ranged from 1.7 to 5.0.
- Public libraries nationwide had 34.3 million audio materials and 25.2 million video materials in their collections).
- Nationwide, public libraries provided 8.5 materials in electronic format per 1,000 population (e.g., CD-ROMs, magnetic tapes, and magnetic disks).

Library Services

Children's Services

- Nationwide, circulation of children's materials was 653.9 million, or 37 percent of total circulation, in FY 2001. Attendance at children's programs was 51.8 million.

Internet Access and Electronic Services

- Nationwide, 96 percent of public libraries had access to the Internet. Ninety-one percent of all public libraries made the Internet available to patrons directly or through a staff intermediary, 4 percent of public libraries made the Internet available to patrons through a staff intermediary only, and 1 percent of public libraries made the Internet available only to library staff.
- Internet terminals available for public use in public libraries nationwide numbered 123,000, or 2.2 per 5,000 population. The average number of Internet terminals available for public use per stationary outlet was 7.5.
- Ninety-nine percent of the unduplicated population of legal service areas had access to the Internet through their local public library.
- Nationwide, 90 percent of public libraries provided access to electronic services.

Other Services

- Total nationwide circulation of public library materials was 1.8 billion, or 6.5 materials circulated per capita. By state, the highest circulation per capita was 13.8, and the lowest was 2.1.
- Nationwide, 19.5 million library materials were loaned by public libraries to other libraries.
- Nationwide, reference transactions in public libraries totaled 296.2 million, or 1.1 reference transactions per capita.

- Nationwide, library visits in public libraries totaled 1.2 billion, or 4.3 library visits per capita.

Staff

- Public libraries had a total of 133,000 paid full-time-equivalent (FTE) staff in FY 2001, or 12.18 paid FTE staff per 25,000 population. Of the total FTE staff, 23 percent, or 2.75 per 25,000 population, had master's degrees from programs of library and information studies accredited by the American Library Association (ALA-MLS degrees); 11 percent were librarians by title but did not have an ALA-MLS degree; and 67 percent were in other positions.
- Forty-five percent of all public libraries, or 4,072 libraries, had librarians with ALA-MLS degrees.

Operating Income and Expenditures

Operating Income

- In FY 2001, 77 percent of public libraries' total operating income of about $8.2 billion came from local sources, 13 percent from state sources, 1 percent from federal sources, and 9 percent from other sources, such as monetary gifts and donations, interest, library fines, and fees.
- Nationwide, the average total per capital1 operating income for public libraries was $30.02. Of that, $23.20 was from local sources, $3.82 from state sources, $.17 from federal sources, and $2.82 from other sources.
- Per capita operating income from local sources was under $3 for 9 percent of public libraries, $3 to $14.99 for 36 percent of libraries, $15 to $29.99 for 33 percent of libraries, and $30 or more for 22 percent of libraries.

Operating Expenditures

- Total operating expenditures for public libraries were $7.6 billion in FY 2001. Of this, 64 percent was expended for paid staff and 15 percent for the library collection.
- Thirty-one percent of public libraries had operating expenditures of less than $50,000, 41 percent spent $50,000 to $399,999, and 28 percent spent $400,000 or more.
- Nationwide, the average per capita operating expenditure for public libraries was $27.64. By state, the highest average per capita operating expenditure was $51.58, and the lowest was $12.28.
- Expenditures for library collection materials in electronic format were 1 percent of total operating expenditures for public libraries. Expenditures for electronic access were 3 percent of total operating expenditures.

State Library Agencies

The following are highlights taken from the E.D. Tab publication *State Library Agencies: Fiscal Year 2002*, released in March 2004.

Governance

- Nearly all state library agencies (48 states and the District of Columbia) are located in the executive branch of government. In two states (Arizona and Tennessee), the state library agency is located in the legislative branch. Sixteen state libraries are independent agencies within the executive branch.

- Of the state library agencies located in the executive branch, approximately two-thirds (33 states) are part of a larger agency.

- The state libraries of Louisiana, New Hampshire, New Mexico, and North Carolina are part of the Department of Cultural Resources. The Delaware, Florida, Illinois, Missouri, and Washington state library agencies are part of their department of state. In 12 states, the agency is located in the department of education.

Allied and Other Special Operations

- Allied operations are those for which state libraries provide services not ordinarily considered a state library agency function. These special operations may include maintaining state archives, managing state records, conducting legislative research for the state, or operating a museum or art gallery.

- Fifteen state library agencies reported having one or more allied operations.

- State library agencies in 15 states contracted with public or academic libraries in their states to serve as state resource centers or reference/information service centers. State library agencies in 27 states hosted or provided funding for a state Center for the Book.

- In nine states (Alaska, Arizona, Connecticut, Florida, Kentucky, Nevada, Oklahoma, Texas, and Virginia), state library agencies serve as the state archives and provide state records management services. The Tennessee state library agency also serves as the state archives, and Kansas state records are managed by the state library agency. In four states (Arizona, California, Kansas, and Oklahoma), state library agencies serve as the primary state legislative research organization. The state history museum or art gallery is an allied operation of the Alaska, Arizona, and Connecticut state library agencies.

- Thirteen state library agencies reported expenditures for allied operations. These expenditures totaled $24.2 million. Of states reporting such expenditures, Virginia reported the highest expenditure ($4.7 million) and the lowest expenditure for allied operations was West Virginia with $3,000. The State Libraries Survey requests information about state library expenditures for allied operations. The Alaska and New Hampshire state library agencies have allied operations, but expenditures for those operations are not from the state library agency budget.

Electronic Services and Information

Electronic Networks, Databases, and Catalogs

- Most state library agencies (46 states and the District of Columbia) planned or monitored the development of electronic networks. State library agencies in 38 states and the District of Columbia operated electronic networks. State library agencies in 46 states and the District of Columbia supported the development of bibliographic databases via electronic networks, and state library agencies in 45 states and the District of Columbia supported the development of full-text or data files via electronic networks.

- All 50 states provided or facilitated library access to online databases through subscription, lease, license, consortial membership, or agreement.

- With the exceptions of Idaho and Washington State, all state library agencies facilitated or subsidized electronic access to a union catalog, a list of titles of works, usually periodicals, in physically separate library collections. The union catalog includes location data that indicate libraries in which a given item can be found in the holdings of other libraries in the state. Most state library agencies provided access to the holdings of other libraries in the state via a Web-based union catalog (47 agencies). Twenty-one state libraries offered union catalog access via a Telnet gateway. Seven state libraries provided access on CD-ROMs, and 12 states provided electronic access to the union catalog in some other way.

- Forty-seven state library agencies reported combined expenditures for statewide database licensing for a total of $53.2 million. Of these states, Texas had the highest expenditure ($9.2 million) among states that reported expenditures for statewide database licensing, while three states (Alaska, North Dakota, and Rhode Island) spent less than $20,000. All state library agencies with such expenditures provided statewide database licensing services to public libraries in their states. At least two-thirds of state library agencies provided statewide database licensing services to the following user groups: academic, school, and special libraries; and other state agencies.

- For ten state libraries, 100 percent of their statewide database licensing expenditures came from federal sources. State funds accounted for 100 percent of 14 agencies' statewide database licensing expenditures.

Internet Access

- All state library agencies facilitated library access to the Internet in one or more of the following ways: providing Internet training or consulting to state or local library staff or state library end users; providing a subsidy to libraries for Internet participation; providing equipment to libraries to access the Internet; providing access to directories, databases, or online catalogs; and managing gopher/Web sites, file servers, bulletin boards, or listservs.

- Nearly all state library agencies (48 states) had Internet workstations available for public use, ranging in number from 1 to 4 (12 agencies); 5 to

9 (16 agencies); 10 to 19 (10 agencies); 20 to 29 (4 agencies); 30 to 39 (3 agencies); and 40 or more (3 agencies). Louisiana reported the largest number of public-use Internet terminals (49). Of 48 state libraries' Internet workstations available for public use, 567 were owned by the state library agency and 63 were placed in the library by other agencies or groups.

- The fastest Internet connection at most state libraries is the T1 line at 27 library agencies, followed by 15 states and the District of Columbia accessing the Internet using T3 lines. The fastest Internet connections in the Arizona, Idaho, and Oklahoma state libraries operate at 100 million bits per second (mbps). The Arkansas state library's fastest connection transmits data at 90–135 mbps and New Mexico's state library is connected to the Internet at a speed of 10 mbps. The Pennsylvania state library agency's fastest Internet connection uses DS-3 lines, which transmit at 5–10 mbps.

- State library agencies for 32 states and the District of Columbia were applicants to the Universal Service (E-rate discount), program established by the Federal Communications Commission (FCC) under the Telecommunications Act of 1996 (P.L. 104-104).

Library Development Services

Services to Public Libraries

- Public libraries serve all residents of a given community, district, or region, and typically receive financial support, in whole or part, from public funds.
- All state library agencies provided the following types of services to public libraries: administration of LSTA grants; collection of library statistics; continuing education programs; and library planning, evaluation, and research. Nearly all state library agencies (47 to 50 agencies) provided consulting services, interlibrary loan referral services, library legislation preparation or review, and review of technology plans for the E-rate discount program.
- Services to public libraries provided by 40 to 45 state library agencies were administration of state aid, literacy program support, reference referral services, state standards or guidelines, statewide public relations or library promotion campaigns, and summer reading program support. Two-thirds of state library agencies (34 agencies) provided union list development.
- Thirteen state library agencies reported accreditation of public libraries, and 24 state library agencies reported certification of public librarians.

Services to Academic Libraries

- Academic libraries are integral parts of colleges, universities, or other academic institutions for postsecondary education, organized and administered to meet the needs of students, faculty, and affiliated staff.
- More than two-thirds of state library agencies (36 to 43 agencies) provided the following services to academic libraries: administration of LSTA

grants, continuing education, interlibrary loan referral services, or reference referral services. The state library agencies for California, Illinois, Montana, and New York administered state aid to academic libraries.

- Thirty-one state library agencies provided consulting services, 26 states and the District of Columbia provided union list development, and 23 states and the District of Columbia provided statewide public relations/ library promotion campaigns to academic libraries.

- No state library agency accredits academic libraries. The state library agencies in Indiana, Massachusetts, New Mexico, and Washington reported certification of academic librarians.

Services to School Library Media Centers

- School library media centers (LMCs) are integral parts of the educational program of elementary and secondary schools, with materials and services that meet the curricular, information, and recreational needs of students, teachers, and administrators.

- At least two-thirds of state library agencies (35 to 42) provided administration of LSTA grants, continuing education, interlibrary loan referral services, or reference referral services to LMCs.

- Thirty-one agencies provided consulting services, and 25 agencies provided library planning/evaluation research or statewide public relations/ library promotions campaigns to LMCs.

- The state library agencies for California, Colorado, Illinois, and Montana administered state aid to school LMCs.

- No state library agency reported accreditation of school library media centers, but Indiana and Massachusetts reported certification of library media specialists.

Services to Special Libraries

- Special libraries are located in business firms, professional associations, government agencies, or other organized groups. A special library may be maintained by a parent organization to serve a specialized clientele; or an independent library may provide materials or services, or both, to the public, a segment of the public, or other libraries. Special libraries include libraries in state institutions. The scope of special library collections and services is limited to the subject interests of the host or parent institution. Over two-thirds of state library agencies (38 to 44 agencies) served special libraries through administration of LSTA grants, continuing education, interlibrary loan referral, and reference referral services.

- Thirty-one state library agencies provided consulting services to special libraries, and 26 agencies provided union list development or library planning, evaluation, and research. Thirty-eight state agencies provided reference referral services to special libraries.

- The state library agencies for California, Colorado, Illinois, Montana, New York, Oklahoma, Rhode Island, and Washington administered state aid to special libraries.

- The Oklahoma state library agency accredits special libraries, and the library agencies for Indiana, Massachusetts, Oklahoma, and Washington State reported certification of librarians of special libraries.

Services to Systems

- Systems are groups of autonomous libraries joined together by formal or informal agreements to perform various services cooperatively, such as resource sharing or communications. Systems include multitype library systems and public library systems, but not multiple outlets under the same administration.
- Two-thirds of state library agencies administered LSTA grants to library systems.
- Furthermore, at least half of state library agencies (26 to 31 agencies) provided the following services to library systems: consulting services; continuing education; interlibrary loan referral; library legislation preparation or review; library planning; evaluation and research; administration of state aid; collection of library statistics; reference referral; and review of technology plans for the E-rate discount program.
- Six state library agencies reported library system accreditation, and seven agencies reported certification of librarians of library systems.

Service Outlets

- State library service outlets have regular hours of service in which state library staff are present to serve users. The state library, as part of its regular operation, pays the staff and all service costs. The main or central outlet is a single unit library where the principal collections are located and handled. Other outlets have separate quarters, a permanent basic collection of books and/or other materials, permanent paid staff, and a regular schedule of hours open to users.
- State library agencies reported a total of 137 service outlets—47 main or central outlets, 70 other outlets (excluding bookmobiles), and 20 bookmobiles. The user groups receiving library services through these outlets, and the number of outlets serving them, included the general public (99 outlets); state government employees (91 outlets); blind and physically handicapped individuals (57 outlets); residents of state correctional institutions (34 outlets); and residents of other state institutions (25 outlets).

Collections

- The number of book and serial volumes held by state library agencies totaled 22.6 million. Two state library agencies each had book and serial volumes over 2 million: New York had 2.5 million and Michigan had 2.3 million volumes. The number of books and serial volumes in the Connecticut, New Jersey, and Texas state libraries exceeded 1 million. The state library agencies for Hawaii, Maryland, and the District of Columbia do not maintain collections.

- Forty-one state library agencies held a total of 29.5 million uncataloged government documents. The states with the largest collections of uncataloged government documents were California (4.3 million) and Illinois (3.3 million). Three other state library agencies had a collection that exceeded two million uncataloged government documents: Arkansas (2.1 million), Ohio (2.5 million), and Oklahoma (2.6 million).

Staff

- The total number of budgeted full-time-equivalent (FTE) positions in state library agencies was 3,832. Librarians with ALA-MLS degrees accounted for 1,201 positions, or 31 percent of total FTE positions; other professionals accounted for 20 percent of total FTE positions; and other paid staff accounted for 49 percent. Rhode Island reported the largest percentage (63 percent) of ALA-MLS librarians, and Virginia reported the smallest (12 percent).
- Most of the budgeted FTE positions (55 percent) were in library services; 19 percent were in library development; 12 percent were in administration; and 15 percent were in other services, such as allied operations. Some two-thirds of the library development positions were for public library development.

Income

- Sources of state library income or revenue are the federal government, the state government, and other sources, such as local, regional, or multijurisdictional sources. State library agencies may also receive income from private sources, such as foundations, corporations, friends-of-libraries groups, and individuals. State libraries may also generate revenue through fees for service or fines.
- State library agencies reported a total income or revenue of close to $1.2 billion in FY 2002. Most income was from state sources (84 percent), followed by federal sources (13 percent) and other sources (3 percent).
- Federal income totaled approximately $150.0 million, with 95 percent, or $142.0 million, from LSTA grants.
- State library agency income from state sources totaled $971.1 million, with two-thirds ($648 million) designated for state aid to libraries. In 13 states, more than 75 percent of the state library agency income from state sources was designated for state aid to libraries, with Massachusetts having the largest percentage (96 percent). Five states (Hawaii, New Hampshire, South Dakota, Vermont, and Wyoming) and the District of Columbia did not target state funds for aid to libraries.
- The District of Columbia Public Library functions as a state library agency and is eligible for federal LSTA funds in this capacity. The state library agency for Hawaii is associated with the Hawaii State Public Library System and operates all public libraries within its jurisdiction. The state funds for aid to libraries for these two agencies This includes staff

not reported under administration, library development, or library services, such as staff in allied operations.

• Three states (Hawaii, New Hampshire, and South Dakota) and the District of Columbia targeted 100 percent of their state income on state library agency operations.

Expenditures

• State library agencies reported total expenditures of over $1.1 billion in FY 2002. Over four-fifths (85 percent) of these expenditures were from state funds, followed by federal funds (13 percent) and funds from other sources (2 percent).

• The state library agencies with the highest total expenditures per capita were those for the District of Columbia with $47.99, Hawaii with $20.22, and Delaware with $11.88. The agencies with total expenditures of less than $2 per capita were those for Arizona, Indiana, Iowa, Texas, and Washington.

• Operating expenditures are the current and recurrent costs necessary for the provision of services by the state library agencies. Operating expenditures include LSTA expenditures for statewide services conducted directly by the state library and administration of the LSTA funds. Not included are the LSTA expenditures for grants and other funds distributed to libraries. Seventy-five percent of state library operating expenditures are from state sources, and 22 percent are from federal sources.

• The state libraries with the highest per capita operating expenditures were Connecticut ($5.58), Alaska ($4.67), Vermont ($4.37), Wyoming ($3.56), and Montana and South Dakota ($3.40). Eighteen states reported total per capita operating expenditures under $1.

• Financial assistance to libraries accounted for 70 percent of total expenditures of state library agencies. Fifty-one percent of such expenditures were targeted to individual public libraries, and 21 percent went to public library systems.

Public Policy Issues

• Thirty-six state library agencies had a combined total of $27.1 million in grant and contract expenditures to assist public libraries with state or federal education reform initiatives. The area of adult literacy and family literacy accounted for 87 percent of such expenditures, and pre-kindergarten learning accounted for 13 percent.

Academic Libraries

The following are highlights taken from the E.D. Tab publication *Academic Libraries: 2000,* released in November 2003.

Services

- In FY 2000, of the 3,923 two-year and four-year degree-granting postsecondary institutions in the United States, 3,527 reported in the NCES-sponsored Academic Libraries Survey that they had their own academic library. Of these 3,527 libraries, 87 percent responded to the Academic Libraries Survey.
- In FY 2000 academic libraries at degree-granting postsecondary institutions in the United States reported a total of about 194 million circulation transactions, including reserves.
- In FY 2000 academic libraries provided a total of about 9.5 million interlibrary loans to other libraries (both academic libraries and other types of libraries) and received about 7.7 million loans.
- Twenty-five libraries reported that they were open 168 hours a week (24 hours a day, 7 days a week). Overall, the largest percentage of academic libraries (44 percent) reported providing 60 to 79 hours of public service per typical week in fall 2000. In addition, 40 percent provided 80 or more public-service hours per typical week. The percentage of institutions providing 80 or more public-service hours ranged from 6 percent in less-than-four-year institutions to 81 percent in doctorate-granting institutions.
- In total, academic libraries reported a gate count of about 16.5 million visitors per typical week in fall 2000 (about 1.6 visits per total full-time equivalent [FTE] enrollment).
- About 1.6 million reference transactions were reported in a typical week in fall 2000 by all academic libraries.
- In FY 2000 academic libraries reported about 432,000 presentations to groups serving about 7.5 million.

Collections

- All together, the nation's 3,527 academic libraries at degree-granting postsecondary institutions reported inventories totaling 913.5 million paper volumes (books, bound serials, and government documents) at the end of FY 2000.
- Of the total paper volumes held at the end of FY 2000, 43 percent (396.8 million) were held by 4 percent (126) of the institutions, which are those categorized under the Carnegie Classification as Research I or Research II institutions. Fifty-five percent of the volumes were at those institutions classified as either Research or Doctoral in the Carnegie Classification.
- The median number of paper volumes held per FTE student was 53.2 volumes. Median volumes held ranged from 18.1 per FTE in less-than-four-year institutions to 116 in doctorate-granting institutions.
- In FY 2000 the median number of paper volumes added to collections per FTE student was 1.5. The median number added ranged from 0.7 per FTE student in less-than-four-year institutions to 2.7 in doctorate-granting institutions.

Staff

- There was a total of 95,665 FTE staff working in academic libraries in FY 2000. Of these, 31,016 (32 percent) were librarians or other professional staff; 37,899 (40 percent) were other paid staff; 229 (less than 0.5 percent) were contributed services staff; and 26,521 (28 percent) were student assistants.
- Excluding student assistants, the median number of academic library FTE staff per 1,000 FTE students was 5.6. The median ranged from 3.7 in less-than-four-year institutions to 8.5 in doctorate-granting institutions.

Expenditures

- In FY 2000 total expenditures for the 3,527 libraries at degree-granting postsecondary institutions were $5 billion. The three largest expenditure items for all academic libraries were salaries and wages at $2.5 billion (50 percent), current paper and electronic serial subscriptions at $1.1 billion (23 percent), and paper books and bound serials at $552.1 million (11 percent).
- The 568 libraries at doctorate-granting institutions (16 percent of the total institutions) accounted for $3.3 billion, or 65 percent of the total expenditure dollars at all academic libraries at degree-granting postsecondary institutions.
- In FY 2000 the median amount for total operating expenditures per FTE student was $326.46, and the median for information resource expenditures was $90.91.

Electronic Services

- In FY 2000, 94 percent of degree-granting postsecondary institutions with an academic library had access from within the library to an electronic catalog of the library's holdings, 99 percent had Internet access within the library, 73 percent had library reference service by e-mail within the library, and 72 percent had access to library reference service by e-mail from elsewhere on campus. Ninety-eight percent had instruction by library staff on the use of Internet resources within the library.
- In FY 2000, 58 percent of academic libraries had technology within the library to assist persons with disabilities, and 49 percent had access to this service from elsewhere on campus. Ninety-four percent provided services to distance-education students.
- More than four-fifths (82 percent) of academic libraries had computers not dedicated to library functions for patron use inside the library. Less than one-fifth (18 percent) had video/desktop conferencing by or for the library within the library, and about one-fourth (26 percent) had access from elsewhere on campus. Twenty-one percent had satellite broadcasting by or for the library within the library, and 29 percent had access from elsewhere on campus.
- Nearly one-half (49 percent) of academic libraries provided electronic document delivery to patrons' accounts.

Library Acquisition Expenditures, 2003–2004: U.S. Public, Academic, Special, and Government Libraries

The information in these tables is taken from *American Library Directory* (*ALD*) *2004–2005* (Information Today, Inc., 2004). The tables report acquisition expenditures by public, academic, special, and government libraries.

The total number of libraries in the United States and in regions administered by the United States listed in this 57th edition of *ALD* is 30,571, including 16,839 public libraries, 3,653 academic libraries, 8,509 special libraries, 314 armed forces libraries, and 1,256 government libraries.

Understanding the Tables

Number of libraries includes only those U.S. libraries in *ALD* that reported annual acquisition expenditures (3,521 public libraries, 1,581 academic libraries, 382 special libraries, 143 government libraries). Libraries that reported annual income but not expenditures are not included in the count. Academic libraries include university, college, and junior college libraries. Special academic libraries, such as law and medical libraries, that reported acquisition expenditures separately from the institution's main library are counted as independent libraries.

The amount in the *total acquisition expenditures* column for a given state is generally greater than the sum of the categories of expenditures. This is because the total acquisition expenditures amount also includes the expenditures of libraries that did not itemize by category.

Figures in *categories of expenditure* columns represent only those libraries that itemized expenditures. Libraries that reported a total acquisition expenditure amount but did not itemize are only represented in the total acquisition expenditures column.

Table 1 / Public Library Acquisition Expenditures

State	Number of Libraries	Total Acquisition Expenditures	Books	Other Print Materials	Periodicals/ Serials	Manuscripts & Archives	AV Equipment	AV Materials	Microforms	Electronic Reference	Preservation
Alabama	54	9,319,351	3,744,065	25,624	290,117	0	226,960	433,906	192,073	178,745	3,094
Alaska	16	1,091,522	533,242	9,800	147,531	0	5,000	58,237	3,500	61,628	2,420
Arizona	37	16,923,355	9,498,837	995,783	1,508,472	0	71,833	1,668,962	63,697	1,682,026	55,350
Arkansas	29	5,797,106	3,014,630	12,200	220,248	0	3,061	146,855	38,534	908,375	8,900
California	128	96,503,275	43,393,253	1,218,193	6,531,231	151,790	1,331,709	6,142,801	722,087	6,807,049	299,859
Colorado	33	14,224,494	8,729,454	50,360	785,148	0	2,200	771,638	20,700	1,188,640	4,100
Connecticut	110	17,789,931	6,106,062	41,329	1,528,907	2,000	112,253	666,807	163,427	1,149,666	35,566
Delaware	9	1,003,518	565,093	5,000	67,889	2,000	1,000	72,466	17,500	3,500	3,500
District of Columbia	1	2,599,996	0	0	0	0	0	0	0	0	0
Florida	69	54,838,737	28,581,206	484,888	4,307,047	40,164	1,550,166	2,312,483	248,005	2,902,976	34,250
Georgia	34	18,548,184	8,010,144	0	403,016	720	189,274	743,054	65,271	568,960	24,731
Hawaii	1	2,369,146	1,782,806	0	508,716	0	0	0	77,624	0	0
Idaho	36	2,798,057	1,183,111	31,000	91,233	0	61,150	139,359	17,200	598,536	11,300
Illinois	231	47,370,094	19,055,356	88,801	1,772,137	13,800	286,003	3,834,068	182,393	4,306,437	64,394
Indiana	112	29,237,801	11,365,667	57,061	1,300,532	0	408,753	2,218,489	171,940	1,681,006	179,457
Iowa	173	13,344,116	4,417,988	129,435	529,601	1,430	59,973	920,385	18,097	386,505	12,917
Kansas	91	9,970,146	4,912,000	584,227	1,280,748	450	66,040	684,012	48,815	1,143,010	2,141
Kentucky	60	11,402,252	3,331,023	46,779	145,045	0	59,166	719,718	10,089	320,817	8,346
Louisiana	29	10,245,391	4,058,696	55,696	607,734	0	58,400	442,459	27,694	115,439	13,300
Maine	61	2,072,185	1,251,464	6,961	233,395	950	82,233	86,237	18,600	77,024	4,645
Maryland	18	15,008,404	11,627,209	134,807	202,274	0	94,400	743,978	0	689,731	500
Massachusetts	171	23,287,808	14,700,077	95,880	2,197,166	6,085	244,248	1,261,904	153,297	726,559	16,509
Michigan	180	43,745,208	13,924,762	38,074	1,830,156	2,700	280,959	2,951,737	125,754	2,335,214	121,872
Minnesota	68	17,983,382	7,941,379	2,086	519,105	–	23,250	1,491,293	3,194	632,717	359
Mississippi	24	4,409,828	1,621,146	79,798	171,349	0	1,200	225,347	19,736	1,222,487	2,798

Missouri	57	22,847,365	12,816,059	56,049	1,390,118	0	300,036	2,294,649	414,185	3,379,191	29,125
Montana	31	1,782,462	938,423	2,253	109,928	6,700	50	20,750	3,047	109,665	52,282
Nebraska	64	5,263,867	1,922,836	1,000	225,915	200	21,813	301,717	42,981	1,066,868	6,795
Nevada	9	9,054,867	483,183	73,313	154,907	0	11,000	34,426	61,804	232,737	3,000
New Hampshire	101	4,027,798	1,746,357	30,918	194,196	717	11,254	288,719	36,682	119,373	16,718
New Jersey	128	31,246,968	18,733,057	154,776	2,332,692	0	232,647	1,957,295	205,764	1,506,282	25,665
New Mexico	17	3,490,037	2,410,320	22,476	45,638	875	8,214	478,268	6,794	192,201	3,500
New York	259	178,120,364	27,875,328	510,349	6,451,366	9,500	531,330	4,011,894	432,313	3,474,759	118,500
North Carolina	60	14,739,792	5,087,666	14,935	387,768	2,402	40,530	538,627	76,066	293,880	3,544
North Dakota	17	1,143,572	468,129	5,085	136,665	0	6,500	48,794	7,760	62,839	1,500
Ohio	116	98,869,160	35,771,141	337,482	7,766,916	2,000	1,892,856	9,170,374	547,826	4,569,176	886,806
Oklahoma	22	6,024,487	3,552,815	44,329	1,186,109	0	48,585	310,578	4,777	169,996	5,472
Oregon	68	14,662,638	6,939,404	24,141	1,366,383	7,000	77,290	2,020,664	16,728	1,067,314	49,726
Pennsylvania	161	50,622,043	6,535,487	25,590	893,082	250	39,914	1,049,384	142,930	803,173	135,667
Rhode Island	23	3,748,320	1,204,284	43,040	139,491	750	0	172,442	13,764	330,563	5,129
South Carolina	30	12,248,660	7,688,970	7,007	1,071,048	1,000	383,941	1,151,606	167,653	914,325	25,599
South Dakota	26	2,095,436	1,194,488	48,298	248,054	530	14,800	223,591	25,050	97,290	2,146
Tennessee	47	13,075,252	9,856,437	44,403	772,960	14,000	49,481	445,523	19,334	1,195,372	85,621
Texas	180	31,895,587	17,430,943	232,216	3,179,419	0	249,921	1,760,529	266,242	1,586,781	35,494
Utah	17	16,618,818	6,799,894	218,137	678,230	0	0	2,429,324	21,462	571,204	16,213
Vermont	58	1,139,793	723,121	18,987	83,680	120	2,500	82,169	2,100	60,861	1,610
Virginia	53	15,385,695	8,531,454	41,572	1,227,829	52,256	99,544	1,194,838	192,922	859,006	591,559
Washington	34	17,058,907	7,097,146	81,237	548,746	0	1,000	1,753,427	11,500	871,585	0
West Virginia	20	3,046,654	910,133	17,314	92,987	0	12,853	130,231	4,880	50,698	3,383
Wisconsin	130	17,794,443	8,524,778	152,318	2,276,368	0	425,766	1,530,503	99,678	452,514	216,218
Wyoming	17	1,233,232	420,617	409	52,857	60	0	44,328	245	97,316	2,800
U.S. Virgin Islands	1	8,000	7,000	0	1,000	0	0	0	0	0	0
Total	3,521	1,049,127,504	409,018,140	6,401,416	60,193,149	320,449	9,681,056	62,180,845	5,233,714	53,822,016	3,234,380
Estimated % of Acquisition Expenditures			38.99	0.61	5.74	0.03	0.92	5.93	0.50	5.13	0.31

Table 2 / Academic Library Acquisition Expenditures

State	Number of Libraries	Total Acquisition Expenditures	Books	Other Print Materials	Periodicals/ Serials	Manuscripts & Archives	AV Equipment	AV Materials	Microforms	Electronic Reference	Preservation
Alabama	30	21,926,305	5,081,461	98,218	13,779,024	3,000	35,493	123,718	179,997	1,089,818	216,364
Alaska	4	1,711,384	485,184	29,885	633,289	0	15,705	375	74,421	327,612	84,526
Arizona	19	16,003,051	1,720,757	79,184	2,855,596	22,834	20,967	109,395	210,102	1,376,412	55,387
Arkansas	15	9,667,488	1,405,309	81,903	6,242,825	2,600	12,937	84,496	148,237	785,891	147,275
California	108	90,236,072	20,135,029	516,867	35,056,399	0	477,560	773,115	1,636,535	10,226,552	1,312,936
Colorado	22	18,194,925	2,979,489	34,691	9,682,237	5,000	5,641	29,938	88,876	645,724	67,428
Connecticut	25	47,368,237	14,456,330	55,365	16,099,238	500	28,453	218,174	187,291	6,023,570	881,235
Delaware	4	498,637	154,000	16,000	89,386	0	14,476	0	17,901	55,000	0
District of Columbia	11	21,386,727	2,955,640	224,601	6,887,964	4,725	26,300	6,164	79,442	676,559	127,685
Florida	49	43,873,100	10,445,513	553,629	20,535,468	0	182,824	450,954	690,280	5,989,092	503,219
Georgia	43	45,202,209	6,968,436	255,480	18,468,954	1,000	74,615	92,574	589,910	3,027,734	977,513
Hawaii	7	2,432,349	357,739	204	994,253	0	3,000	18,516	47,432	277,423	25,014
Idaho	6	7,901,539	1,623,166	107,705	4,995,806	500	0	5,929	34,278	924,431	212,714
Illinois	63	86,583,338	17,806,042	1,533,731	34,126,763	4,395	230,273	476,255	420,577	7,392,793	2,219,014
Indiana	33	33,916,618	8,375,690	5,400	17,675,603	46,000	106,093	196,396	206,640	3,117,349	228,254
Iowa	36	20,377,076	4,537,699	339,839	12,285,720	275	69,435	111,580	334,035	1,330,476	176,495
Kansas	32	6,889,479	1,979,325	9,582	2,677,804	2,000	15,059	95,616	68,182	822,057	101,560
Kentucky	26	28,085,971	4,425,461	23,375	15,045,849	31,225	5,188	193,379	307,338	2,299,667	404,233
Louisiana	20	18,675,494	2,278,634	185,586	7,238,156	3,070	16,084	16,976	105,785	852,421	93,296
Maine	11	9,630,334	2,149,520	0	5,631,210	200	1,287	39,678	219,425	1,319,998	233,146
Maryland	35	29,574,894	5,656,398	78,688	9,858,669	1,704	97,732	137,168	417,263	2,298,206	366,838
Massachusetts	55	82,234,614	10,488,813	962,962	32,437,826	2,000	347,672	300,152	1,140,273	4,964,727	831,005
Michigan	48	39,951,018	10,558,465	98,626	22,054,034	2,100	88,949	120,736	464,127	3,845,753	319,328
Minnesota	30	27,325,075	4,204,571	515,252	4,983,537	0	77,172	218,992	198,322	1,627,400	172,514
Mississippi	14	9,911,369	823,697	0	3,491,623	1,600	179,040	21,226	129,217	898,729	119,004
Missouri	42	34,218,757	5,549,964	1,375,484	18,909,334	2,312	59,430	207,305	197,325	2,867,374	379,745

Montana	13	5,980,782	1,259,619	0	4,466,824	0	40,121	17,495	0	123,225	54,199
Nebraska	19	12,655,167	1,588,312	95,691	3,911,680	100	64,800	85,638	109,536	602,824	111,522
Nevada	3	3,966,798	132,158	0	97,644	0	0	0	0	46,616	0
New Hampshire	11	7,725,082	1,617,470	43,833	3,206,699	0	14,686	34,149	30,438	765,613	78,698
New Jersey	27	33,759,356	7,524,097	512,763	7,816,342	318,913	50,304	76,015	964,474	1,534,042	1,070,849
New Mexico	16	11,081,912	3,018,196	146,625	6,056,615	0	26,277	30,586	139,095	981,976	227,932
New York	115	134,405,672	14,202,183	1,651,764	33,895,807	36,440	364,877	532,245	1,322,720	10,683,178	1,045,861
North Carolina	58	44,162,567	8,318,458	41,064	21,621,483	4,500	336,676	263,356	828,542	3,848,079	376,816
North Dakota	11	5,273,911	621,273	29,173	2,669,620	0	5,545	62,077	52,854	611,706	63,632
Ohio	54	45,318,837	7,976,699	107,281	14,872,914	4,635	194,582	375,273	512,863	3,655,328	611,640
Oklahoma	24	18,071,891	1,667,853	203,126	4,983,609	4,100	19,807	31,673	187,928	2,991,509	76,522
Oregon	33	21,620,488	3,496,895	199,506	7,064,458	0	120,316	195,764	134,457	2,161,958	254,502
Pennsylvania	76	82,054,463	14,563,344	3,720,505	26,746,885	22,298	243,864	551,662	911,038	15,697,169	702,593
Rhode Island	9	10,988,419	2,607,128	331,344	6,927,492	8,500	48,000	50,923	297,150	332,170	299,055
South Carolina	25	14,138,534	1,210,595	9,295	2,155,643	25,000	110,560	54,547	241,476	680,855	110,291
South Dakota	11	4,072,978	703,925	0	2,026,807	680	6,500	9,119	60,664	728,884	55,724
Tennessee	38	29,965,855	3,973,907	113,297	12,965,971	2,614	13,600	125,748	334,637	2,156,757	161,109
Texas	84	82,600,280	14,377,109	255,362	26,649,491	75,668	390,657	338,631	864,580	6,599,660	594,601
Utah	10	11,210,025	3,920,634	2,329	6,292,482	55,808	41,841	125,891	45,030	534,731	191,279
Vermont	14	8,020,316	1,922,322	21,040	3,264,427	3,000	15,093	98,177	69,993	1,618,680	140,247
Virginia	37	35,420,522	7,513,122	361,841	20,203,305	18,524	155,632	301,217	478,755	3,506,834	273,983
Washington	28	16,818,207	3,771,273	126,168	9,642,623	2,990	107,000	155,614	362,259	1,142,512	120,819
West Virginia	21	4,119,333	822,434	165,800	1,470,908	8,598	43,957	42,102	128,547	994,908	22,587
Wisconsin	39	21,707,575	5,690,764	40,408	8,776,965	27,432	87,440	278,425	420,029	2,511,196	272,232
Wyoming	4	3,685,602	376,747	1,000	2,805,498	0	9,845	57,335	293	374,104	60,780
American Samoa	1	5,000	1,000	0	3,000	0	0	1,000	0	0	0
Guam	1	9,000	0	0	0	0	0	0	0	0	0
Puerto Rico	10	6,948,328	893,173	5,911	2,849,000	500	43,000	28,925	14,111	572,394	6,900
U.S. Virgin Islands	1	230,045	0	0	0	0	0	0	0	0	0
Total	1,581	1,429,793,005	261,373,022	15,367,283	566,180,759	757,340	4,746,365	7,972,394	16,704,680	130,519,676	17,240,391
Estimated % of Acquisition Expenditures			18.28	1.07	39.60	0.05	0.33	1.41	1.17	9.13	1.21

Table 3 / Special Library Acquisition Expenditures

State	Number of Libraries	Total Acquisition Expenditures	Books	Other Print Materials	Periodicals/ Serials	Manuscripts & Archives	AV Equipment	AV Materials	Microforms	Electronic Reference	Preservation
								Categories of Expenditure (in U.S. dollars)			
Alabama	2	2,250	1,600	0	650	0	0	0	0	0	0
Alaska	0	0	0	0	0	0	0	0	0	0	0
Arizona	15	185,511	36,588	0	35,322	2,150	0	5,000	50	3,000	13,700
Arkansas	0	0	0	0	0	0	0	0	0	0	0
California	36	2,171,946	412,063	32,500	384,190	900	20,800	21,500	16,000	91,000	214,625
Colorado	5	26,103	17,350	0	4,398	0	1,855	2,000	0	0	0
Connecticut	7	109,573	63,463	383	6,550	19,431	702	0	1,000	3,000	9,894
Delaware	0	0	0	0	0	0	0	0	0	0	0
District of Columbia	7	1,574,314	191,225	35,000	190,025	18,000	0	0	25,000	625,000	300,000
Florida	18	421,243	132,591	4,250	99,635	1,250	7,000	4,000	1,700	11,500	11,663
Georgia	2	79,300	8,300	0	71,000	0	0	0	0	0	0
Hawaii	5	123,800	54,500	2,500	61,000	200	1,000	0	0	0	4,600
Idaho	3	124,100	21,000	0	20,500	500	1,000	500	0	80,000	500
Illinois	32	4,520,722	484,875	60,160	1,925,045	47,400	15,300	17,250	23,501	619,180	27,900
Indiana	6	333,490	39,799	0	3,500	0	525	1,000	3,350	1,000	1,000
Iowa	4	242,700	1,000	0	0	0	3,000	0	0	1,000	1,000
Kansas	6	86,617	27,127	0	43,990	100	0	0	7,000	4,800	850
Kentucky	4	43,901	14,836	0	8,679	0	0	0	0	0	962
Louisiana	1	1,600	0	0	0	0	0	0	0	0	0
Maine	2	4,297	2,673	0	1,500	0	0	0	0	0	124
Maryland	10	378,269	42,731	2,000	124,836	50	1,000	0	0	49,992	550
Massachusetts	16	1,555,853	508,242	5,100	226,770	5,500	0	16,500	500	369,400	50,880
Michigan	4	115,625	28,000	0	11,000	0	0	0	0	0	0
Minnesota	7	157,580	16,080	0	8,900	2,000	500	5,000	1,500	5,000	2,600
Mississippi	2	116,150	10,100	0	106,050	0	0	0	0	0	0

Missouri	9	3,330,174	253,880	2,000	2,909,091	300	4,028	0	200	54,061	92,624
Montana	5	103,800	17,300	3,000	59,000	4,000	0	0	16,000	3,000	0
Nebraska	5	24,678	14,026	500	5,300	2,000	0	0	2,102	0	0
Nevada	1	1,000	0	0	0	0	0	0	0	0	0
New Hampshire	4	254,925	0	0	0	0	0	0	0	0	0
New Jersey	12	453,780	29,900	4,000	62,250	2,000	7,050	6,500	100	24,200	6,000
New Mexico	4	35,500	10,900	4,000	3,900	0	300	200	500	1,100	2,800
New York	46	3,283,791	876,267	8,475	1,937,477	46,200	5,992	79,479	8,400	72,275	39,125
North Carolina	1	14,000	0	0	0	0	0	0	0	0	0
North Dakota	1	10,347	5,848	0	3,999	0	0	0	0	0	500
Ohio	21	1,535,661	270,247	18,630	911,143	3,800	3,150	12,272	4,639	199,546	12,234
Oklahoma	3	467,100	3,500	0	2,100	2,500	15,000	0	0	0	0
Oregon	6	17,300	12,400	100	4,750	0	0	0	50	126,425	16,128
Pennsylvania	18	1,256,904	181,199	56,663	265,946	29,357	528	4,566	1,800		10,200
Rhode Island	2	51,145	32,695	0	8,000	0	0	0	0	0	0
South Carolina	5	385,600	75,800	0	30,600	0	0	0	0	0	0
South Dakota	0	0	0	0	0	0	0	0	0	0	0
Tennessee	5	40,610	17,479	2,500	12,349	0	500	2,073	0	5,009	0
Texas	12	1,336,539	151,757	38,984	117,810	750	1,105	795	3,500	91,700	2,500
Utah	1	1,000	0	0	0	0	0	0	0	0	0
Vermont	2	8,209	856	0	153	0	0	0	0	0	0
Virginia	15	572,704	127,505	32,900	48,511	22,350	41,470	3,135	3,000	41,734	101,160
Washington	3	15,000	2,500	0	650	7,500	0	0	0	2,000	200
West Virginia	1	10,000	2,500	0	7,000	0	0	500	0	0	0
Wisconsin	6	173,245	62,550	0	89,000	0	1,595	1,000	0	18,900	0
Wyoming	0	0	0	0	0	0	0	0	0	0	0
Total	382	25,757,956	4,263,252	313,645	9,812,569	218,238	133,400	183,270	119,892	2,502,822	924,319
Estimated % of Acquisition Expenditures			16.55	1.22	38.10	0.85	0.52	0.71	0.47	9.72	3.59

Table 4 / Government Library Acquisition Expenditures

State	Number of Libraries	Total Acquisition Expenditures	Books	Other Print Materials	Periodicals/ Serials	Manuscripts & Archives	AV Equipment	AV Materials	Microforms	Electronic Reference	Preservation
										Categories of Expenditure (in U.S. dollars)	
Alabama	3	680,169	370,233	0	22,770	6,000	21,244	218	11,880	210,788	21,166
Alaska	0	0	0	0	0	0	0	0	0	0	0
Arizona	1	11,697	5,000	3,000	3,697	0	0	0	0	0	0
Arkansas	1	45,000	35,000	0	10,000	0	0	0	0	0	0
California	25	5,248,462	1,102,805	712,499	756,110	0	14,357	28,682	108,098	138,601	21,056
Colorado	3	166,300	51,000	4,000	23,500	0	0	0	0	7,800	0
Connecticut	0	0	0	0	0	0	0	0	0	0	0
Delaware	0	0	0	0	0	0	0	0	0	0	0
District of Columbia	3	3,122,784	36,000	0	20,000	0	0	0	0	23,000	5,000
Florida	5	409,500	105,500	0	208,500	1,000	0	32,000	52,000	48,000	500
Georgia	0	0	0	0	0	0	0	0	0	0	0
Hawaii	2	1,139,106	382,746	0	753,360	0	0	0	3,000	0	0
Idaho	1	57,500	13,000	0	40,000	0	0	2,000	0	2,500	0
Illinois	2	26,100	0	0	0	0	0	0	0	0	0
Indiana	0	0	0	0	0	0	0	0	0	0	0
Iowa	1	195,342	181,342	0	14,000	0	0	0	0	0	0
Kansas	2	667,572	305,477	197,768	118,029	0	0	0	0	35,444	10,854
Kentucky	0	0	0	0	0	0	0	0	0	0	0
Louisiana	6	4,449,593	5,745	0	143,425	0	0	0	0	12,045	0
Maine	2	374,866	4,000	0	75,000	0	0	0	0	6,000	0
Maryland	8	6,426,500	585,000	8,000	2,683,500	0	5,000	0	0	1,350,000	72,000
Massachusetts	8	3,326,485	268,072	0	45,000	0	0	0	0	42,000	7,500
Michigan	2	58,383	25,311	5,000	22,815	0	0	4,807	0	450	0
Minnesota	5	1,196,414	21,000	0	61,500	0	0	0	0	52,000	0

State											
Mississippi	1	2,500	0	0	0	0	0	0	0	0	0
Missouri	2	456,546	300,000	0	0	0	0	0	0	60,000	0
Montana	4	531,192	21,850	0	229,538	0	0	0	985	6,819	12,000
Nebraska	0	0	0	0	0	0	0	0	0	0	0
Nevada	3	954,753	698,785	0	69,230	0	2,414	0	4,662	133,949	0
New Hampshire	0	0	0	0	0	0	0	0	0	0	0
New Jersey	0	0	0	0	0	0	0	0	0	0	0
New Mexico	1	633,000	25,000	240,000	121,000	0	0	0	2,000	230,000	15,000
New York	9	2,409,523	1,165,070	0	225,300	0	2,630	6,000	1,000	57,324	13,300
North Carolina	5	512,560	419,410	3,300	22,620	0	5,000	29,000	7,700	7,300	11,230
North Dakota	1	43,000	8,000	0	30,000	0	0	0	0	5,000	0
Ohio	3	193,798	49,000	0	13,000	0	0	0	0	17,500	0
Oklahoma	1	28,950	1,630	205	14,520	0	0	0	0	11,625	970
Oregon	4	169,567	48,400	0	78,167	500	1,000	0	0	0	0
Pennsylvania	10	1,579,060	1,165,375	0	4,500	0	3,500	10,000	0	156,750	8,000
Rhode Island	2	897,000	663,827	0	66,087	0	0	669	4,000	162,417	0
South Carolina	2	55,915	13,839	0	36,801	0	0	0	0	5,275	0
South Dakota	0	0	0	0	0	0	0	0	0	0	0
Tennessee	3	253,693	94,410	4,531	19,351	0	0	11,401	0	0	0
Texas	2	203,054	154,439	0	34,174	0	0	12,941	0	1,500	0
Utah	2	269,700	30,200	0	231,500	0	0	0	0	2,000	6,000
Vermont	0	0	0	0	0	0	0	0	0	0	0
Virginia	3	101,295	50,350	0	30,233	0	0	4,663	0	5,400	109
Washington	1	4,000	2,000	0	2,000	0	0	0	0	0	0
West Virginia	0	0	0	0	0	0	0	0	0	0	0
Wisconsin	3	202,100	34,100	0	83,000	0	0	0	0	46,000	1,000
Wyoming	1	229,000	190,000	0	24,000	0	0	0	10,000	0	5,000
Total	143	37,331,979	8,632,916	1,178,303	6,336,227	7,500	55,145	142381	219,325	2,837,487	210,685
Estimated % of Acquisition Expenditures			23.12	3.16	16.97	0.02	0.15	0.38	0.59	7.60	0.56

LJ Budget Report: Tipping Point

Norman Oder
Senior News Editor, *Library Journal*

After several years of budget sluggishness, libraries report a definite uptick in fiscal support and one that's expected to continue healthily.

Overall library budgets are projected to grow over the next year, according to the 484 libraries responding to the *Library Journal* (*LJ*) Budget Survey 2005, regardless of library size, with an average rise of 5 percent (see Table 1). Materials budgets are expected to go up 4.7 percent, while salaries budgets should rise 5.2 percent. The statistics are relatively consistent regardless of size of library. Libraries spend an average of 14 percent of their budgets on materials and 61 percent on personnel. While each situation is different, libraries overall appear to be reaping the ripple effects of better state budgets. Reported the National Council of State Legislatures in December, "Budget overruns are less severe than in recent years. And budget gaps are practically nonexistent." Still, the group warned that 22 states expected significant budget challenges for fiscal year (FY) 2006.

Libraries are hardly losing pace with the public, since per capita circulation rose from 8.46 to 8.78 in FY 2004, an increase of 3.8 percent. Still, that does not necessarily translate into robust service increases. In fact, responding libraries reported that hours actually decreased 1 percent from the previous year. The mean number of weekly opening hours for a system's largest library was 59.

Moreover, statistics over five years suggest some divergences. As total budgets have gone up 25 percent from FY 1999 to FY 2004, salaries budgets have risen 32 percent and materials budgets have risen 16 percent. Specifically, 63.4 percent of libraries reported increases in materials funding, while a not-insubstantial 25.7 percent of libraries reported decreases. As for salaries budgets, 87.6 percent reported increases while only 7.1 percent reported decreases. Numerous libraries reported facing increasing nonsalary personnel costs, notably health insurance.

Some libraries, especially in growing communities with increasing property tax revenues, project a sunny future. However, several states have clouds on the

Table 1 / Library Budget Trends

Population Served	Total Budget 2005	Change in 2005	Materials Budget 2005	Change in 2005	Salaries Budget 2005	Change in 2005
Total Sample	$6,401,000	+5.0%	$898,000	+4.7%	$3,936,000	+5.2%
Under 10,000	192,000	4.5	33,000	2.5	123,000	4.9
10,000–24,999	636,000	2.2	85,000	1.5	369,000	3.7
25,000–49,999	1,451,000	4.2	179,000	3.5	901,000	4.3
50,000–99,999	2,323,000	4.2	300,000	2.5	1,432,000	4.5
100,000–499,999	8,132,000	4.9	1,155,000	6.1	4,917,000	4.5
500,000–999,999	24,866,000	6.9	3,686,000	6.5	15,840,000	5.0
1 million or more	57,218,000	3.9	7,594,000	2.0	33,706,000	7.2

Source: *LJ* Budget Survey 2005

Adapted from *Library Journal,* January 2005.

Table 2 / Use of Grant/Outside Funding
Expenditure of grants or other additional funding
by category

Department/Category	Percent
Books/Materials	51
Children's Services	50
Programming	47
Technology/Automation	31
YA/Teen Services	30
Adult services	24
Internet Access (hardware, etc.)	20
Staff development	14
Database subscriptions	10
Outreach/bookmobile	10
Staff hours	9
Marketing	8

Source: *LJ* Budget Survey 2005

horizon. In Ohio, traditionally the home of substantial state support, libraries expect no increase, so they will rely more on local tax levies. In Pennsylvania, libraries have felt the sting of state library cuts. Facilities in California have been hurt—some hugely—by the ripple effect of state budget cuts to municipalities. In both Washington and Missouri, library funding increases are hampered by state tax caps.

Per Capita Funding Tops $34

Responding libraries projected their FY 2005 (or FY 2005–2006) per capita funding at $34.40, an increase of nearly 4 percent over the previous year, which saw an increase of 3.1 percent. Seventy-four percent reported an increase in per capita funding, while 14 percent reported a decrease and 13 percent said it would remain the same.

As for the source of funding, 79 percent comes from local taxes, 13 percent from other levels of government, and 9 percent from all other sources.

Respondents reported an overall 0.1 percent increase in staffing in the past year, with 21 percent of total staff holding an MLS or equivalent. The ratio of MLS to non-MLS staff is holding steady except at the largest libraries, where the percentage holding master's degrees is rising slightly.

About one-quarter of libraries (26 percent) have launched entrepreneurial activities to raise funds. Of those, 59 percent have opened bookstores and 37 percent have opened cafes. Libraries reported some decreases in fund raising, from $279,999 in 1999—when the economy was more flush—to $213,000 in 2004. Libraries devoted 54 percent of fund-raising dollars to operating budgets and 26 percent to capital projects.

Internet and Remote Access

Any library visitor knows that demand for public-access computers is often high; indeed, libraries reported an overall increase in Internet usage of 24.7 percent, with 81 percent noting increases. Libraries reported an overall increase in use of remote computer access of 23.8 percent. Some 45 percent of respondents reported increases, while 43 percent said they don't measure such use.

As for the Children's Internet Protection Act (CIPA), which ties receipt of E-rate discounts to filtering the Internet, 59.5 percent of respondents said they complied. A slightly larger percentage (65 percent) said they filter at least some Internet terminals.

It was predicted that smaller libraries might not choose to comply with CIPA, given the limited savings; also, it is believed people in smaller, close-knit communities are less likely to flout rules of acceptable Internet usage. Indeed, only 44 percent of the smallest libraries (serving fewer than 10,000 people) filter any terminals, compared with more than three-quarters of libraries serving more than 100,000.

Of those responding, 62 percent apply for E-rate discounts. Some 85 percent of libraries serving more than 500,000 people apply for discounts.

Local Progress Reports

Here is a fiscal snapshot of how public libraries expect to fare nationwide. Dollars represent projected budgets for FY 2005 or FY 2005–2006.

Note: These figures do not include grants or donations, which raise funding significantly at some libraries.

Serving fewer than 10,000

Britton Public Library, SD
$75,000 (up 1.4%)

With a projected $40 in per capita spending, this library is open 55 hours a week. Funded only by the town, the library must find a way to tax or charge users from surrounding areas.

Cambridge Community Library, ID
$34,536 (up 2.4%)

The library has seen its budget increase only 12 percent in five years. "We are able to provide basic services but have limited open hours and staff," the director reports. Per capita spending is $20.

Pretty Prairie Public Library, KS
$5200 (up 8.3%)

Though the per capita budget is under $7, this library nevertheless posts circulation figures of over 17 per capita. "Money is tight," but "we love our work," the director reports.

Robert R. Jones Public Library District, IL
$204,000 (up 1.5%)

This library spends nearly 25 percent of its budget on materials and 40 percent on personnel. A new building, friends group, and growing tax base presage a bright future. Per capita: $43.

Sherburne Public Library, NY
$150,264 (up 11.1%)

Its budget has risen by 40 percent in five years, but the rise in fuel costs and the addition of a full-time manager stretched available funds at this library. Per capita: $38.

Serving 10,000–24,999

Homewood Public Library, IL
$1,850,000 (up 2.8%)

With a funding of $94 and circulation of 17 per capita, this library may seem to be riding high, but its total budget has increased only 4 percent in five years because of county tax caps.

Stuttgart Public Library, AR
$224,700 (up 5%)

This library has seen its budget rise only 19 percent in five years. Population losses and a drop in state funding keep per capita spending under $11.

Waynesboro Public Library, VA
$887,831 (up 1.4%)

Despite per capita funding of $45, the materials budget has shrunk by 5 percent over five years, and local and state cuts mean the "nonsalary budget is very tight."

Western Allegheny Community Library, PA
$283,400 (up 8.3%)

The total budget has increased by 69 percent in five years, but the library's per capita support remains under $15. Cuts in state aid last year limited collections and programming.

Serving 25,000–49,999

Carnegie Public Library, Washington Court House, OH
$1,165,430 (up 4.2%)

State tax support for libraries has been frozen since 2000, but this library has three more years of cash reserves available to maintain services. Per capita: more than $37.

Dover Public Library, NH
$1,200,000 (up 9.1%)

The total budget has increased 53 percent in five years, but a lack of state funding and property tax resistance threatens growth. Per capita: $40.

Juneau Public Libraries, AK
$1,799,200 (up 4.1%)

Per capita spending tops $57, but the library will use only about 7 percent of its budget for materials. The state has eliminated municipal revenue sharing, and the cost of health insurance and pensions has skyrocketed.

Owatonna Public Library, MN
$1,120,347 (up 6%)

The library's budget increase of 21 percent over five years has all been absorbed by personnel costs, especially health insurance. The library has used dwindling trust funds for materials. Per capita tops $32.

Princeton Public Library, NJ
$4,158,642 (up 11.7%)

With a per capita at $129, the library has seen its budget rise 57 percent in five years, thanks to a new library and enthusiastic supporters.

Serving 50,000–99,999

Bowling Green Public Library, KY
$2,190,774 (up 4%)

Though its per capita is under $23, the library spends 14.6 percent of its budget on materials. The library serves both city and county, but relies mostly on city funding.

Elkhart Public Library, IN
$5,422,000 (down 1.4%)

Despite the decline, per capita spending tops $60. The legislature last year reduced libraries' capacity to increase annual tax receipts from 5 percent annually to 4.4 percent.

Laurens County Library, SC
$850,191 (unchanged)

Major local job losses prevent budget growth, and per capita is just under $12. This two-branch system spends more than 25 percent of the value of its E-rate discounts on filtering and outside Internet maintenance.

Riverside Regional Library, MO
$844,225 (down 0.4%)

With per capita over $13, this six-branch system struggles under a state tax cap. Inflation, especially in the cost of employee medical insurance, hurts, the director says.

Serving 100,000–499,999

Blount County Public Library, TN
$1,850,000 (up 5.8%)

While the library's budget has risen 79 percent in five years, in part because of a new library, the materials budget has declined 5.5 percent. Cafe and meeting space revenues may help. Per capita: $16.50.

Butte County Library, CA
$2,000,000 (up 2.3%)

Facing cuts caused by a state squeeze on local government, the library chose to axe its materials budget completely and depend on donations. Per capita: $9.

Fort Vancouver Regional Library District, WA
$15,371,092 (up 0.4%)

The library's budget has increased 9.2 percent over five years, as Initiative 747, passed in 2001, limits public entities to an annual revenue increase of only 1 percent. Per capita: nearly $38.

Lee County Library System, FL
$27,205,653 (up 8.1%)

The total budget has risen 94 percent in five years—with materials up 64 percent. The recent rollback of the library's tax rate may slow growth. Per capita: over $50.

Montgomery City-County Public Library, AL
$3,685,249 (up 3.6%)

Struggling for increases, the library has earmarked nearly all its budget increase for personnel. Per capita: over $16.

Serving 500,000–999,999

Baltimore County Public Library, MD
$33,546,537 (up 8%)

With steady but small increases, the library nudges toward $44 per capita. State budget problems may cause a decrease.

Boston Public Library, MA $39,000,000 (up 1.9%)

Though per capita is still above $62, the library has seen its budget cut 5 percent over five years. Continued level funding is anticipated.

El Paso Public Library, TX
$8,836,390 (up 10%)

While the total budget has increased only 13 percent over five years, the materials budget has doubled. The library recently cut hours at most facilities, but expects better news in FY 2005–2006. Per capita: under $15.

Milwaukee Public Library, WI
$20,627,107 (down 2.5%)

The library faces cuts in branch hours at five of 12 branches and a 34 percent materials cut. Per capita: about $35.

Serving 1,000,000 or more

Brooklyn Public Library, NY
$88,569,272 (up 9.5%)

While the library's budget went up 25 percent over five years, its materials budget remained static. Still, there's a 21.7 percent jump for FY 2005. Per capita: nearing $36.

Carnegie Library of Pittsburgh, PA
$21,915,800 (up 0.6%)

Over five years, the library has increased its materials budget by 51 percent but trimmed the salary budget by 1 percent. Declines in state funding hurt. Per capita: over $16.

Fairfax County Public Library, VA
$27,922,447 (up 2.6%)

In five years, the salary budget has risen 35 percent, but the materials budget has declined 39 percent. County budget cuts may presage reduced hours. Per capita: nearing $27.

Harris County Public Library, TX
$23,765,865 (up 14.1%)

The total budget has nearly doubled in five years. Still, finances are so tight that computers are on a seven-year replacement schedule rather than four-year. Per capita: nearing $20.

Los Angeles Public Library, CA
$107,033,243 (down 2.2%)

Though funding has risen by 42 percent over five years, the library may be threatened by a large projected shortfall in city funds. Per capita: over $27.

Public Library State Rankings, Preliminary Data for 2002

	Library Visits per Capita*	Reference Trans- actions per Capita	Circulation Trans- actions per Capita	Book and Serial Volumes per Capita	Audio Materials per 1,000 Population	Video Materials per 1,000 Population
Alabama	48	41	49	42	44	44
Alaska	29	48	32	20	24	6
Arizona	38	30	24	51	33	35
Arkansas	50	47	45	38	51	50
California	32	19	38	44	41	39
Colorado	7	10	7	32	35	11
Connecticut	2	12	12	11	16	5
Delaware	37	45	29	46	37	37
District of Columbia**	40	1	51	7	28	51
Florida	34	5	39	49	34	30
Georgia	44	17	42	48	50	47
Hawaii	26	23	31	34	6	46
Idaho	6	33	17	24	29	26
Illinois	13	6	16	17	4	12
Indiana	3	9	4	12	3	2
Iowa	15	43	11	15	15	7
Kansas	8	11	5	4	12	3
Kentucky	39	49	37	41	40	43
Louisiana	49	14	47	35	48	36
Maine	22	35	23	1	30	19
Maryland	18	8	10	25	14	29
Massachusetts	14	28	20	3	20	14
Michigan	32	31	33	23	17	27
Minnesota	16	18	8	22	18	22
Mississippi	51	50	50	39	49	42
Missouri	27	27	19	19	21	24
Montana	35	51	34	25	36	34
Nebraska	19	32	13	9	13	10
Nevada	31	44	35	45	32	28
New Hampshire	24	42	22	8	22	9
New Jersey	20	25	28	17	25	23
New Mexico	45	46	41	33	43	49
New York	11	3	25	12	2	18
North Carolina	36	24	36	43	47	48
North Dakota	30	37	21	14	26	25
Ohio	1	2	1	10	1	1
Oklahoma	25	39	30	37	45	31
Oregon	4	20	2	28	7	13
Pennsylvania	42	35	40	36	8	32
Rhode Island	10	28	26	16	31	20
South Carolina	41	16	43	39	42	41
South Dakota	5	20	15	6	23	16
Tennessee	46	40	48	50	46	45

	Library Visits per Capita*	Reference Trans- actions per Capita	Circulation Trans- actions per Capita	Book and Serial Volumes per Capita	Audio Materials per 1,000 Population	Video Materials per 1,000 Population
Texas	47	15	44	46	39	40
Utah	21	6	3	31	5	17
Vermont	17	33	27	4	19	15
Virginia	28	13	14	30	27	38
Washington	23	4	6	27	11	21
West Virginia	43	38	46	29	38	33
Wisconsin	9	20	8	21	10	4
Wyoming	12	26	18	2	9	8

	Paid FTE Staff per 25,000 Population	Paid FTE Librarians per 25,000 Population	ALA-MLS Librarians per 25,000 Population	Other Paid FTE Staff per 25,000 Population	Total per Capita Operating Income	State per Capita Operating Income
Alabama	43	35	42	46	47	27
Alaska	26	24	20	22	13	21
Arizona	41	44	27	36	36	45
Arkansas	51	49	51	43	48	36
California	46	46	25	38	27	15
Colorado	14	28	15	11	7	34
Connecticut	4	8	1	4	6	35
Delaware	50	43	43	47	37	8
District of Columbia**	5	10	2	3	3	49
Florida	36	42	24	31	30	16
Georgia	44	50	28	33	42	7
Hawaii	33	39	10	26	40	2
Idaho	24	33	45	16	35	31
Illinois	7	12	9	8	2	10
Indiana	2	13	8	2	5	9
Iowa	21	4	30	37	29	30
Kansas	6	7	21	5	14	29
Kentucky	34	20	48	45	38	25
Louisiana	29	19	31	30	28	19
Maine	13	9	17	23	31	44
Maryland	12	14	14	15	15	6
Massachusetts	9	6	5	18	12	11
Michigan	28	26	13	25	17	22
Minnesota	25	30	23	18	19	18
Mississippi	31	32	46	29	51	14
Missouri	16	29	36	12	20	26
Montana	42	22	49	50	39	37
Nebraska	18	5	34	32	25	39
Nevada	37	48	35	28	22	32
New Hampshire	15	1	12	39	21	46
New Jersey	11	25	5	7	9	23
New Mexico	40	34	40	44	44	40
New York	8	18	4	6	4	13

	Paid FTE Staff per 25,000 Population	Paid FTE Librarians per 25,000 Population	ALA-MLS Librarians per 25,000 Population	Other Paid FTE Staff per 25,000 Population	Total per Capita Operating Income	State per Capita Operating Income
North Carolina	47	51	33	34	43	17
North Dakota	39	21	50	49	46	24
Ohio	1	11	7	1	1	1
Oklahoma	35	26	38	41	34	32
Oregon	17	31	16	14	10	43
Pennsylvania	32	36	22	27	32	3
Rhode Island	10	17	3	13	11	4
South Carolina	38	41	26	35	41	20
South Dakota	22	15	41	24	24	49
Tennessee	49	47	46	42	50	49
Texas	48	45	32	40	45	41
Utah	30	40	37	20	26	38
Vermont	23	3	29	48	33	47
Virginia	27	38	19	17	23	12
Washington	19	37	11	10	8	42
West Virginia	44	23	44	51	49	5
Wisconsin	20	16	18	21	18	28
Wyoming	3	2	38	9	16	48

	Local per Capita Operating Income	Other per Capita Operating Income	Total Operating Expenditures per Capita	Total Collection Expenditures per Capita	Total Staff Expenditures per Capita	Salaries and Wages Expenditures per Capita
Alabama	45	41	47	47	46	45
Alaska	10	34	11	18	15	17
Arizona	28	51	35	30	34	34
Arkansas	43	43	50	48	50	50
California	25	31	27	36	25	28
Colorado	5	15	10	3	10	11
Connecticut	8	4	6	10	4	3
Delaware	39	18	38	34	41	41
District of Columbia**	1	17	2	17	1	1
Florida	29	44	33	28	35	36
Georgia	42	48	40	45	38	38
Hawaii	51	32	37	42	33	22
Idaho	31	19	34	40	31	32
Illinois	2	11	5	5	7	6
Indiana	3	24	4	2	9	9
Iowa	26	25	26	24	28	26
Kansas	12	9	12	9	17	15
Kentucky	33	29	41	38	44	44
Louisiana	24	35	32	39	36	35
Maine	34	6	30	35	29	23
Maryland	22	7	15	6	13	12
Massachusetts	13	12	13	4	12	5
Michigan	13	20	19	25	21	21

	Local per Capita Operating Income	Other per Capita Operating Income	Total Operating Expenditures per Capita	Total Collection Expenditures per Capita	Total Staff Expenditures per Capita	Salaries and Wages Expenditures per Capita
Minnesota	16	29	17	21	16	16
Mississippi	49	45	51	51	51	51
Missouri	17	16	23	11	27	25
Montana	40	10	45	48	45	46
Nebraska	19	37	25	13	24	24
Nevada	31	2	24	16	23	27
New Hampshire	18	14	20	22	19	18
New Jersey	6	28	8	15	5	8
New Mexico	37	49	42	41	42	42
New York	7	3	3	8	3	4
North Carolina	41	39	43	43	40	40
North Dakota	47	22	46	37	47	47
Ohio	48	8	1	1	2	2
Oklahoma	30	38	36	31	37	37
Oregon	9	21	9	14	8	13
Pennsylvania	44	13	31	27	32	33
Rhode Island	27	1	14	20	11	10
South Carolina	35	46	39	31	39	39
South Dakota	20	23	28	26	26	29
Tennessee	46	46	48	50	48	48
Texas	38	50	44	44	43	43
Utah	21	40	22	7	22	30
Vermont	36	5	29	28	30	31
Virginia	23	36	21	19	20	20
Washington	4	33	7	12	6	7
West Virginia	50	42	49	46	49	49
Wisconsin	15	27	18	23	18	19
Wyoming	11	26	16	33	14	14

FTE=Full-time equivalent

* Per capita is based on the unduplicated population of legal service areas.

** The District of Columbia, while not a state, is included in the state rankings; special care should be using in comparing its data to state data.

Source: Compiled by Robert E. Molyneux, U.S. National Commission on Libraries and Information Science, using FY 2002 data from the U.S. National Center for Education Statistics made available in 2004 (http://www.nclis.gov/statsurv/NCES/stateranks/index.html).

Library Buildings 2004:
Projects Top $1.2 Billion Nationally

Bette-Lee Fox

Managing Editor, *Library Journal*

People look at a billion dollars in one of two ways: if it is the result of the long, hard effort of years of fund raising, they rejoice; if it signifies an astronomical budget deficit, they cringe. How, then, should we respond to reaching the $1 billion mark ($1,242,436,438, to be exact) in this year's spending for public library construction? One would suppose with a bit of both—elation at the availability of such wealth and trembling at the enormous cost of building today.

The 203 public library projects completed between July 1, 2003, and June 30, 2004, share features beyond the soaring prices we face in the 21st century. Two of the largest buildings (the combined San Jose Public Library/San Jose State University in California, and the Seattle Public Library Central Library) alone account for 27 percent of expenditures. Several facilities (among them Winter Haven Public Library in Florida and Oak Park Public Library in Illinois) incorporate public spaces, especially parks, into their design, while a number of structures are shared between communities and school districts (Pacific Park Branch, Glendale, California; Oak Lawn Public Library, Fresno, California).

Still others, like San Jose, merge public and academic facilities (Seminole Community Library at St. Petersburg College in Florida; Jackson County Central Library/Rogue Community College Library, Medford, Oregon). Joint-use with community services continues unabated this year, even handcuffing libraries to police stations (e.g., Curtiss e-Library, Hialeah, Florida).

Better Late Than Never?

Two public projects came to fruition after years of trying. The B. B. Comer Memorial Library in Sylacauga, Alabama, raised funds through a foundation over 12 years, and the Cary Memorial Library in Lexington, Massachusetts, took nine years to bring a 1909 structure into the information age. Not wanting to wait that long, veterans of Spring Valley, Illinois, American Legion Post 182 contributed $200,000 to the Richard A. Mautino Memorial Library on the condition that it be finished in 2004 so they could start enjoying it.

The 36 academic projects include the other half of those joint-use facilities, plus a number of specialized schools of law, music, science, and hotel management. The $40 million addition/renovation at Marquette University in Milwaukee encompasses 226,813 square feet.

This year's architectural picture remains bright, even if one does get a bit glassy-eyed when looking at the dollars involved. But technological adaptability, teen centers, high-tech systems, and expanded community service have their price. Now that these buildings are completed, with all that glorious innovation, people will rejoice and come to the library.

Adapted from *Library Journal*, December 2004.

Table 1 / New Academic Library Buildings, 2004

Name of Institution	Project Cost	Gross Area (Sq. Ft.)	Sq. Ft. Cost	Construction Cost	Equipment Cost	Book Capacity	Architect
Dr. Martin Luther King Jr. Library, San Jose State University, CA*	$167,502,700	492,603	$216.14	$106,470,000	$10,326,700	2,000,000	Carrier Johnson
Kellogg Library, California State University, San Marcos	48,610,000	200,530	182.31	36,558,044	7,431,000	499,120+	Carrier Johnson; Gunnar Birkerts
Student Learning Center, University of Georgia, Athens	40,000,000	204,000	159.93	32,625,000	100,000	5,000	Cooper Carry
Marian Gould Gallagher Law Lib., University of Washington School of Law, Seattle**	37,427,750	98,000	270.41	26,500,000	10,927,750	560,502	Mahlum Architects, in assoc. w/ Kohn Pederson Fox
Digital Library and Learning Resource Center, Riverside Community College District, CA	25,320,000	111,300	167.12	18,600,000	4,034,000	120,000	tBP/Architecture
Library and Learning Center, Metropolitan State University, St. Paul	20,944,000	86,400	232.64	20,100,000	290,000	80,000	Meyer, Scherer & Rockcastle
Marnie and John Burke Memorial Library, Spring Hill College, Mobile, AL	17,700,000	71,015	158.67	11,268,000	596,500	350,000	Shepley Bulfinch Richardson...
Jean Gray Hargrove Music Library, University of California–Berkeley	13,720,408	28,775	341.93	9,839,016	1,011,408	237,080	Mack Scogin Merrill Elam
San Bernardino Valley College Library, CA	13,700,000	41,000	234.15	9,600,000	600,000	130,000	Ehrlich Archs.; Blurock Archs.
George I. Alden Library and Learning Center, Quinsigamond Community College, Worcester, MA	11,700,000	56,000	178.57	10,000,000	1,700,000	90,000	Einhorn Yaffee Prescott

Project						
Dennis L. Jones Seminole Community Library, St. Petersburg College, Seminole, FL	9,204,000	52,000	146.15	7,600,000	1,144,000	Harvard Jolly
Columbia College Library, Sonora, CA	8,200,000	13,000	584.62	7,600,000	600,000	Grothe & Smith
Library and Science Building, Sussex County Community College, Newton, NJ	8,000,000	27,000	222.22	6,000,000	600,000	RJF Fletcher Thompson
Learning Resource Center, Barstow College, CA	7,540,000	28,000	222.86	6,240,000	1,300,000	Addington Partnership
Learning Resource Center, Northwestern Connecticut Community College, Winsted	6,800,000	24,000	212.5	5,100,000	271,430	Tai Soo Kim Partners
Westminster Law Library, University of Denver, Sturm College of Law**	6,264,300	36,000	134.61	4,845,837	325,567	Univ. of Denver; H& L Arch. Shepley Bulfinch Richardson...
Stratton Taylor Library, Rogers State University, Claremore, OK	4,500,000	45,000	93.33	4,200,000	98,965	Graber and Imel Architects
Joe Dini Jr. Library and Student Center, Western Nevada Community College, Carson City	3,656,614	22,464	138.47	3,110,814	545,800	Hershenow + Klippenstein
Universal Orlando Foundation Library at Rosen College, University of Central Florida/Rosen College of Hospitality Management, Orlando***	1,626,289	9,235	126	1,163,610	280,000	Helman Hurley Charvat Peacock
McMillen Library, Indiana Institute of Technology (Indiana Tech), Fort Wayne	1,140,600	7,880	135	1,063,800	76,800	Moake Park Group

* Joint academic/public project; ** Libraries part of larger law school building projects; *** Library part of larger Rosen College project.

Table 2 / Academic Library Buildings, Additions and Renovations, 2004

Name of Institution	Status	Project Cost	Gross Area (Sq. Ft.)	Sq. Ft. Cost	Construction Cost	Equipment Cost	Book Capacity	Architect
John P. Raymor, S.J., Library, Marquette University, Milwaukee	Total	$40,000,000	226,813	$127.86	$29,000,000	$6,000,000	1,845,000	Shepley Bulfinch Richardson...
	New	32,000,000	126,813	189.26	24,000,000	4,000,000	225,000	Opus North
	Renovated	8,000,000	100,000	50	5,000,000	2,000,000	1,620,000	
John M. Olin Library, Washington University, St. Louis	Total	36,950,631	193,147	n.a.	n.a.	n.a.	1,755,000	Kallman McKinnell & Wood
	New	n.a.	17,000	n.a.	n.a.	n.a.	n.a.	
	Renovated	n.a.	176,147	n.a.	n.a.	n.a.	n.a.	
Santa Monica College Library, CA	Total	25,850,000	98,146	238.75	23,432,000	2,418,000	172,800	Anshen + Allen
	New	n.a.	41,309	n.a.	n.a.	1,659,066	76,320	
	Renovated	n.a.	56,837	n.a.	n.a.	758,934	96,480	
Marquand Library of Art and Archaeology, Princeton University, NJ	Total	20,000,000	49,000	306.12	15,000,000	1,000,000	400,000	Shepley Bulfinch Richardson...
	New	n.a.	19,000	n.a.	n.a.	n.a.	n.a.	
	Renovated	n.a.	30,000	n.a.	n.a.	n.a.	n.a.	
Asa Griggs Candler Library, Emory University, Atlanta	Total	17,000,000	64,000	n.a.	n.a.	n.a.	n.a.	S/L/A/M Collaborative
	New	n.a.	10,000	n.a.	n.a.	n.a.	n.a.	
	Renovated	n.a.	54,000	n.a.	n.a.	n.a.	n.a.	
College of St. Catherine Library, St. Paul	Total	n.a.	80,748	104.65	8,450,000	450,000	380,520	Shepley Bulfinch Richardson...; Hammel, Green & Abrahamson
	New	n.a.	25,000	126	3,150,000	n.a.	40,740	
	Renovated	n.a.	55,748	95.07	5,300,000	n.a.	339,780	
Porter Henderson Library, Angelo State University, San Angelo, TX	Total	5,601,325	119,926	43.6	5,228,325	373,000	n.a.	DMS Architects
	New	5,001,000	41,000	112.88	4,628,000	373,000	n.a.	
	Renovated	600,325	78,926	7.61	600,325	0	n.a.	
Rice-Aron Library, Marlboro College, VT	Total	2,826,253	22,500	117.45	2,642,578	183,675	167,508	Daniel V. Scully
	New	n.a.	12,000	191.67	2,300,000	n.a.	66,957	
	Renovated	n.a.	10,500	32.63	342,578	n.a.	100,551	

n.a. = not available

Table 3 / Academic Library Buildings, Renovations Only, 2004

Name of Institution	Project Cost	Gross Area (Sq. Ft.)	Sq. Ft. Cost	Construction Cost	Equipment Cost	Book Capacity	Architect
John K. Mullen of Denver Memorial Library, Catholic University of America, Washington, DC	$6,000,000	27,359	$137.55	$3,763,249	$306,988	99,153	Smith Group
W. E. B. DuBois Library, University of Massachusetts, Amherst	853,000	40,000	15	600,000	40,000	306,312	not reported
Lougheed Library, St. Thomas Aquinas College, Sparkill, NY	809,000	14,500	41.38	600,000	125,000	124,860	Arcari & Iovino
Smith Music Library, Hardin-Simmons University, Abilene, TX	655,000	4,300	134.88	580,000	75,000	30,000	Rick Weatherl
Mount Holyoke College Library, S. Hadley, MA	335,300	5,000	61.4	307,000	0	0	Hill-Engineers, Architects
E. H. Butler Library, Buffalo State College, NY	311,000	5,500	34.64	190,500	95,500	0	Hamilton Houston Lownie
Lourdes Library, Gwynedd-Mercy College, Gwynedd Valley, PA	220,000	5,400	n.a.	n.a.	40,000	10,500	none
Lewis J. Ort Library, Frostburg State University, MD	52,620	12,700	2.28	29,000	23,620	n.a.	none

n.a. = not available

489

Table 4 / New Public Library Buildings, 2004

Community	Pop. ('000)	Code	Project Cost	Const. Cost	Gross Sq. Ft.	Sq. Ft. Cost	Equip. Cost	Site Cost	Other Costs	Volumes	Federal Funds	State Funds	Local Funds	Gift Funds	Architect
Arkansas															
Benton	88	MS	$6,313,780	$4,485,904	33,861	$132.48	$658,456	$785,000	$384,420	150,000	$0	$0	$5,518,780	$795,000	Purifoy & Grisham
California															
Canoga Park	68	B	6,158,014	3,930,000	12,500	314.40	221,755	1,683,260	322,999	50,000	0	0	6,158,014	0	Carde Ten Archs.
Creston	1	B	154,612	140,321	960	146.17	4,538	Leased	9,753	3,750	0	0	107,612	47,000	Avalon Design
Fresno	53	B	6,946,821	5,056,321	22,050	229.31	300,000	653,900	936,600	75,000	0	0	5,039,001	1,907,820	DKSJ
Glendale	30	B	4,753,694	2,187,623	10,463	209.08	814,318	1,371,616	380,137	n.a.	1,283,497	332,759	3,137,438	2,775	Siegel; Liedenfrost
Livermore	79	M	26,300,000	20,000,000	53,000	377.36	2,400,000	Owned	3,900,000	200,000	0	0	26,300,000	0	George Miers
Los Angeles	58	B	4,857,651	3,500,000	10,500	333.33	186,193	761,458	410,000	40,000	0	0	4,857,651	0	City of Los Angeles
Los Angeles	32	B	7,699,230	4,005,000	12,500	320.40	225,218	3,132,212	336,800	50,000	0	0	7,699,230	0	Barton Phelps Assocs.
Los Angeles	36	B	5,629,451	3,815,000	12,500	305.20	235,620	1,172,318	406,513	50,000	0	0	5,629,451	0	M2A Milofsky & Michali
Los Angeles	26	B	7,234,076	3,920,000	12,500	313.60	195,285	2,772,411	346,380	50,000	0	0	7,234,076	0	Killefer Flammang
Los Angeles	46	B	4,606,463	3,570,000	10,500	340.00	215,683	480,780	340,000	40,000	0	0	4,606,463	0	Thirtieth St. Architects
N. Hollywood	81	B	4,330,502	3,894,888	10,500	370.94	172,487	Owned	263,127	40,000	0	0	4,330,502	0	Fremer/Savel
Northridge	55	B	4,499,302	3,447,951	12,500	275.84	202,275	528,326	320,750	50,000	0	0	4,499,302	0	Tetra Design Inc.
Oak Park	13	B	3,775,944	2,421,954	10,000	242.20	261,700	Leased	1,092,290	35,000	0	396,000	3,359,944	20,000	Fields Devereaux
Playa Vista	26	B	3,775,491	3,304,714	10,500	314.73	198,010	n.a.	272,767	40,000	0	0	3,775,491	n.a.	Johnson Fain
San Jose	1,025	MS	167,502,700	106,470,000	492,603	216.14	10,326,700	Owned	50,706,000	2,000,000	91,000,000	1,000,000	66,502,700	10,000,000	Carrier Johnson
San Jose	55	B	9,083,000	6,848,000	24,200	282.98	315,000	Owned	1,920,000	120,000	0	0	9,083,000	0	Field Paoli
Santa Clara	107	M	41,313,363	30,353,063	80,000	379.41	2,648,118	Owned	8,312,182	385,000	0	0	41,313,363	0	Group 4 Architecture
Sun Valley	77	B	4,454,883	3,648,321	12,500	291.87	199,464	327,958	279,140	50,000	300,000	0	4,154,883	0	Fields Devereaux
Colorado															
Aurora	290	B	4,848,779	2,930,629	16,900	173.41	240,000	Owned	1,678,150	27,250	0	0	4,848,779	0	Brendle Library
Aurora	290	B	6,505,116	4,707,031	28,100	167.51	875,000	n.a.	923,085	64,821	0	0	6,407,830	97,286	Brendle Library
Dolores	8	M	1,085,384	930,000	6,500	143.08	54,706	Owned	100,678	25,000	0	250,000	350,000	485,384	Humphries Poli
Florissant	3	B	1,631,852	1,094,362	6,700	163.34	155,871	100,000	281,619	10,000	0	1,790	1,540,869	89,193	Pinnacle; Frye Gillan…
Westminster	n.a.	B	3,900,000	3,300,000	15,000	220.00	300,000	Owned	300,000	70,000	0	0	3,875,000	25,000	Bennett Wagner…
Woodland Park	20	M	5,647,855	3,996,957	30,818	129.70	464,723	250,000	936,175	80,000	0	8,210	5,240,813	398,832	Pinnacle; Frye Gillan…
Florida															
Clearwater	110	MS	20,247,000	14,532,915	90,000	161.48	2,700,000	Owned	3,014,085	275,000	0	0	17,572,000	2,675,000	Stern; Harvard Jolly
Parkland	22	M	1,679,000	1,300,000	12,000	108.33	285,000	Owned	94,000	40,000	0	0	1,679,000	0	Schenkel Shultz

Symbol Code: B=Branch Library; BS=Branch and System Headquarters; M=Main Library; MS=Main and System Headquarters; S=System Headquarters; n.a.=not available

Location	No.	Symbol												Architect
Seminole	52	M	9,204,000	7,600,000	52,000	146.15	1,144,000	Owned	460,000	85,000	300,000	8,904,000	0	Harvard Jolly
St. Augustine	35	BS	4,425,000	2,682,274	25,000	107.29	1,054,338	255,185	433,203	100,000	300,000	4,125,000	0	CRG Architects
Tamarac	140	B	7,769,277	4,427,004	30,000	147.57	875,543	1,051,230	1,415,500	80,000	0	6,718,047	1,051,230	Cartaya & Assocs.
Winter Haven	27	M	4,667,000	3,190,842	31,500	101.30	799,000	349,985	327,173	110,000	500,000	3,963,000	204,000	Architects in Assn.
Illinois														
Chicago	37	B	4,936,659	4,223,755	14,000	301.70	198,539	Owned	514,365	75,000	1,200,000	3,736,659	0	Jackson Architects
Coal Valley	5	M	895,505	615,837	7,540	81.68	79,000	100,000	100,668	55,000	350,000	395,505	150,000	Kelly & Assocs.
Elgin	120	M	29,800,000	23,900,000	139,980	170.74	1,000,000	2,300,000	2,600,000	460,000	2,275,000	29,500,000	300,000	Frye Gillan Molinaro
Elmhurst	43	M	23,360,000	17,600,000	90,000	195.55	2,900,000	Owned	2,860,000	425,000	250,000	20,900,000	185,000	Lohan Caprile...
Mt. Olive	2	M	790,000	702,000	4,180	167.94	30,000	Owned	58,000	60,000	250,000	536,000	4,000	Gary Olson & Assocs.
Summit	10	M	5,757,478	4,495,285	18,190	247.13	135,182	97,000	1,030,011	59,676	0	5,757,478	0	Frye Gillan Molinaro
Indiana														
Monroeville	7	B	1,548,122	1,224,509	7,300	167.74	83,072	87,667	152,874	34,000	0	1,548,122	0	Schenkel Schultz
New Haven	20	B	2,053,328	1,470,929	10,500	140.08	116,742	294,989	170,668	51,000	0	2,053,328	0	Martin Riley Mock
Woodburn	7	B	1,443,959	1,203,010	8,200	146.71	89,110	28,405	123,434	46,500	0	1,443,959	0	Morrison Kattman...
Kentucky														
Frenchburg	7	M	1,712,505	1,311,568	9,575	136.98	111,423	118,808	170,706	25,000	1,712,505	0	0	Mayes, Sudderth...
Somerset	10	B	288,118	190,530	2,300	82.84	51,425	10,000	36,163	12,000	100,000	178,118	10,000	Design Management
Williamstown	24	M	2,370,541	1,552,362	12,500	124.19	205,781	175,000	437,398	63,000	1,607,760	587,791	175,000	Sherman•Carter...
Louisiana														
Abbeville	51	BS	4,949,063	4,039,824	26,800	150.74	300,000	211,936	397,303	121,500	0	4,949,063	0	Hidell...; Sellers Grp.
Lydia	2	B	610,217	468,529	5,000	93.71	68,040	Owned	73,648	20,700	0	610,217	0	Paul Allain
Shreveport	12	B	1,876,960	1,333,612	8,500	156.90	210,340	180,000	153,008	24,793	0	1,876,960	0	Byron J. Stewart
Shreveport	10	B	1,773,948	1,382,723	8,500	162.67	189,125	130,680	71,420	28,321	0	1,773,948	0	Newman Partnership
Vacherie	11	B	1,838,522	1,500,000	8,427	178.00	135,000	Owned	203,522	58,049	0	1,838,522	0	Greg G. Gardiol
Zachary	16	B	4,395,518	3,182,028	18,000	176.78	434,675	355,795	423,020	89,430	0	4,324,637	70,881	Cockfield•Jackson
Maryland														
Abingdon	40	B	8,750,000	5,075,000	36,000	140.97	575,000	n.a.	3,100,000	200,000	0	8,750,000	n.a.	Morris & Ritchie
St.Michaels	3	B	1,532,720	1,332,796	8,000	166.60	115,544	32,000	52,380	3643 l.f.	0	750,000	782,720	Pamela P. Gardner
Massachusetts														
Blackstone	9	M	4,774,185	3,909,281	16,897	231.36	407,015	Owned	457,889	57,800	1,918,676	2,855,509	0	J. Stewart Roberts
Chicopee	55	MS	9,189,163	6,960,188	31,600	220.26	537,300	360,000	1,331,675	175,000	2,779,341	4,119,822	2,290,000	Caolo & Bieniek
Merrimac	6	M	4,035,000	2,930,000	16,000	183.13	300,000	300,000	805,000	55,000	1,673,741	2,351,259	10,000	Amsler Woodhouse...
Rowley	6	M	3,222,480	2,237,559	13,644	164.00	314,633	130,000	540,288	50,453	1,302,480	1,740,000	180,000	Burt Hill Kosar...
Sunderland	4	M	2,477,322	2,103,597	9,400	223.79	141,819	Owned	231,906	36,000	1,079,272	1,186,350	211,700	J. Stewart Roberts

Symbol Code: B=Branch Library; BS=Branch and System Headquarters; M=Main Library; MS=Main and System Headquarters; S=System Headquarters; n.a.=not available

Table 4 / New Public Library Buildings, 2004 (cont.)

Community	Pop. ('000)	Code	Project Cost	Const. Cost	Gross Sq. Ft.	Sq. Ft. Cost	Equip. Cost	Site Cost	Other Costs	Volumes	Federal Funds	State Funds	Local Funds	Gift Funds	Architect
Michigan															
Clinton Twp.	142	M	$21,954,359	$14,273,776	84,000	$169.93	$3,925,970	$500,000	$3,254,613	500,000	$0	$0	$21,341,109	$613,250	TMP Assocs.
Ida	1	B	763,669	531,057	7,686	69.09	106,918	Owned	125,694	15,000	0	0	598,062	165,607	David Arthur
Nebraska															
Seward	6	M	4,080,394	3,178,921	25,775	123.33	225,110	232,085	444,278	51,000	23,057	0	395,208	3,662,129	Clark Enersen
New Jersey															
Hasbrouck Hgts.	12	M	2,185,000	1,635,000	14,000	116.78	250,000	Owned	300,000	68,250	250,000	750,000	1,185,000	0	Arcari & Iovino
Newton	8	M	3,008,510	2,395,000	12,400	193.15	200,000	228,650	184,860	67,260	0	431,123	2,577,387	0	Arcari & Iovino
Princeton	30	M	18,021,069	11,666,989	61,283	190.38	2,705,645	125,000	3,523,435	175,000	100,000	2,199,190	6,000,000	9,721,879	Hillier Architecture
New Mexico															
Farmington	114	M	11,564,849	7,305,211	52,000	140.48	1,684,630	1,389,628	1,185,380	258,000	0	0	11,462,647	102,202	Hidell & Assocs.
New York															
Mahopac	27	M	8,535,417	6,737,974	35,818	188.12	635,273	Owned	1,162,170	225,000	0	73,794	7,900,000	561,623	Michael Esmay
North Carolina															
Winterville	25	B	1,051,782	876,650	6,200	141.40	105,000	Owned	70,132	20,000	1,025,782	0	0	26,000	JFK Architecture
Ohio															
McClure	29	B	454,420	379,533	2,600	145.97	15,347	18,000	41,540	15,000	0	0	454,420	n.a.	Lee Short
New Albany	55	B	4,196,381	3,138,671	21,053	149.08	377,410	425,000	255,300	140,709	0	2,098,190	2,098,191	0	Acock Assocs.
New Richmond	2	B	1,834,596	1,573,166	10,000	157.32	97,102	Owned	164,328	37,735	0	0	1,834,596	0	Moody Nolan
North Olmsted	34	B	6,797,295	5,772,295	36,000	160.34	500,000	Owned	525,000	n.a.	0	0	6,797,295	0	CBLH Design
Strongville	44	B	7,352,000	6,300,000	36,000	175.00	252,000	Owned	800,000	91,400	0	0	7,352,000	0	RCU Architects
Willoughby Hills	67	B	949,915	556,000	4,100	135.61	168,023	200,000	25,892	20,000	0	0	949,915	0	David Holzheimer
Oklahoma															
Choctaw	9	B	2,133,595	1,434,263	9,000	159.36	195,133	99,163	405,036	60,000	0	0	1,933,519	200,076	Elliott + Assocs.
Grove	18	B	879,420	788,287	10,250	76.90	39,895	Owned	51,238	67,511	49,000	0	571,295	259,125	Glover Architects
Oklahoma City	660	BS	24,003,651	20,249,871	114,130	177.43	1,750,000	Owned	2,003,780	200,000	0	0	24,003,651	0	Beck Assocs.
Oregon															
Independence	8	M	1,932,132	1,232,909	7,400	166.60	105,907	353,300	240,016	40,000	300,000	400,000	674,221	569,291	Crow/Clay & Assocs.
Medford	82	MS	19,804,334	13,842,089	83,191	166.39	1,020,014	1,686,220	3,256,011	240,000	0	0	19,495,150	309,184	Fletcher Farr Ayotte

Symbol Code: B=Branch Library; BS=Branch and System Headquarters; M=Main Library; MS=Main and System Headquarters; S=System Headquarters; n.a.=not available

Location	#	Code													Architect
Portland	n.a.	B	7,000,000	5,200,000	24,000	216.67	600,000	Owned	1,200,000	75,000	0	0	7,000,000	0	Thomas Hacker
Pennsylvania															
Shrewsbury	13	M	1,477,014	949,921	10,000	94.99	407,654	Leased	119,439	53,100	0	300,000	50,000	1,127,014	Slonaker-McCall
Stewartstown	13	B	1,524,000	1,200,000	10,000	120.00	105,000	101,000	118,000	40,000	0	230,000	531,415	762,585	Murphy & Dittenhafer
South Carolina															
Florence	128	MS	16,500,000	13,000,000	83,000	156.63	2,000,000	Owned	1,500,000	235,000	0	0	6,000,000	10,500,000	Craig Gaulden Davis
Greenville	28	B	1,905,880	1,200,831	11,306	106.21	205,273	376,166	123,610	5232 l.f.	0	0	1,493,021	412,859	DesignStrategies, LLC
Myrtle Beach	32	B	2,664,911	1,999,313	22,640	88.31	258,652	270,000	136,946	100,000	0	0	2,604,911	60,000	Pike-McFarland-Hall
Tennessee															
Knoxville	29	B	2,684,094	2,013,073	14,000	143.79	187,886	322,091	161,044	53,000	0	0	2,684,094	0	Lewis Group
Union City	32	M	5,853,432	4,190,003	30,000	139.67	468,132	545,000	650,297	107,500	0	0	106,859	5,746,573	Anderson Vaughan
Texas															
Austin	43	B	4,775,616	2,800,567	16,000	175.04	400,150	944,899	630,000	70,000	0	0	4,775,616	0	Stanley Architects
Carrollton	115	M	10,996,600	6,850,000	42,512	161.12	1,145,000	1,125,000	1,876,400	187,500	0	0	9,871,600	1,125,000	F & S Partners
Crowley	8	M	1,452,953	1,029,855	10,000	102.99	162,786	124,933	85,379	40,000	0	0	1,363,808	89,145	Magee Architects
El Paso	93	B	4,645,216	3,349,651	22,000	152.26	605,000	Owned	690,565	95,000	0	0	4,625,216	20,000	Perspectiva Arch.
Houston	150	B	8,089,880	5,145,589	42,000	122.51	1,189,880	Owned	1,754,411	185,000	0	0	8,089,880	101,743	Gant Architects
Richmond	90	B	7,147,400	4,177,500	33,500	124.70	1,800,000	750,000	419,900	125,000	0	0	6,247,400	900,000	Hermes Architects
Uvalde	25	MS	4,900,542	3,935,542	35,000	112.44	445,000	100,000	420,000	140,000	336,000	0	0	4,564,542	Hidell & Assocs.
Whitesboro	4	M	2,250,000	1,000,000	6,100	163.93	80,000	20,000	1,150,000	50,000	0	0	40,000	2,210,000	not reported
Utah															
St. George	38	B	4,188,434	2,943,080	16,700	176.23	361,459	Owned	883,895	83,100	0	0	4,188,434	0	Cooper Roberts…
Syracuse	35	B	1,832,106	1,147,602	8,100	141.68	215,762	Leased	468,742	70,000	27,275	0	1,804,831	0	Cooper Roberts…
Virginia															
Bealeton	n.a.	B	2,283,420	1,607,989	10,600	151.70	196,099	174,200	305,132	60,000	0	0	2,109,220	174,200	Lukmire Partnership
Washington															
Dupont	4	B	570,180	423,304	3,608	117.32	113,071	Leased	33,805	15,280	0	0	564,980	5,200	BCRA Architects
Seattle	1779	MS	162,737,000	124,621,000	362,987	343.32	9,423,000	Owned	28,693,000	1,400,000	0	0	135,758,000	26,979,000	Metro Arch; LMN
Seattle	13	B	3,407,056	1,752,240	7,200	243.37	208,365	475,547	970,904	27,700	0	0	3,393,056	14,000	Miller Hayashi
West Virginia															
Green Bank	4923	B	257,096	220,591	4,200	52.52	26,505	Owned	10,000	20,000	0	26,446	25,000	205,650	Clayton L. Carter

Symbol Code: B=Branch Library; BS=Branch and System Headquarters; M=Main Library; MS=Main and System Headquarters; S=System Headquarters; n.a.=not available

493

Table 5 / Public Library Buildings, Additions and Renovations, 2004

Community	Pop. ('000)	Code	Project Cost	Const. Cost	Gross Sq. Ft.	Sq. Ft. Cost	Equip. Cost	Site Cost	Other Costs	Volumes	Federal Funds	State Funds	Local Funds	Gift Funds	Architect
Alabama															
Birmingham	48	B	$2,600,000	$1,992,840	28,700	$69.43	$407,841	Owned	$199,319	85,000	$0	$0	$2,600,000	$0	William Pantsari
Sylacauga	25	M	3,300,000	2,796,472	39,000	71.70	97,167	165,000	241,361	100,000	0	0	1,691,545	1,608,455	Evan Terry Assocs.
Arkansas															
Russellville	55	B	58,193	53,842	1,150	46.82	0	Owned	4,351	n.a.	0	13,333	44,860	0	Crafton, Tull
California															
Big Sur	2	B	62,405	43,545	363	119.96	15,660	Leased	3,200	3,040	0	0	1,800	60,605	Pacific Mobile
Fairfield	131	BS	4,506,335	2,358,745	39,065	60.38	787,250	Owned	1,360,340	145,000	0	0	4,506,335	0	Kaplan-McLaughlin...
Imperial	9	M	925,626	808,048	4,196	192.58	52,784	Owned	64,794	40,000	0	0	925,626	0	Jim Duggins
Laton	2	B	620,445	428,900	1,632	262.81	31,145	1	160,399	7,000	0	0	618,215	2,230	James Oakes
Colorado															
Aurora	290	B	1,677,000	1,301,855	20,140	64.64	178,000	Owned	197,145	63,260	0	0	1,677,000	0	Gifford Spurck
Pueblo	142	M	23,785,000	17,760,000	108,000	164.44	686,000	1,594,000	3,745,000	500,000	0	0	18,730,000	5,055,000	Antoine Predock
Florida															
Davie	38	B	514,951	248,896	10,000	24.89	222,055	Owned	44,000	30,000	0	0	514,951	0	Frimet Design
Deerfield Beach	32	B	323,634	214,260	15,120	14.17	90,479	Leased	18,895	40,000	0	0	323,634	0	Tamara Peacock
Hallandale	58	B	701,827	371,785	14,700	25.29	281,342	Leased	48,700	40,000	0	0	701,827	0	Synalovski Gutierrez
Hialeah	11	B	607,575	485,000	4,908	98.82	53,285	Owned	69,290	2,500	75,990	0	531,585	0	Angel H. Lamela
Immokalee	18	B	739,164	497,645	8,035	61.93	93,488	Owned	148,031	50,000	0	340,000	343,638	55,526	Barany Schmitt...
Jacksonville	35	B	360,179	256,616	7,300	35.15	71,260	Owned	32,303	58,000	0	0	360,179	0	Junck & Walker
Jupiter	64	B	3,039,957	2,392,254	22,000	108.74	433,305	Owned	214,398	110,000	0	0	3,039,957	0	BEA International
Lake City	20	B	245,516	120,126	7,000	17.16	120,390	Leased	5,000	77,500	0	101,940	120,126	23,450	none
Lutz	23	B	1,074,096	769,585	4,900	157.06	215,784	Owned	88,727	58,000	0	0	1,074,096	0	URS Corp. Southern
Orlando	941	MS	1,388,173	1,043,682	26,000	40.14	228,785	Owned	115,706	92,200	0	0	1,388,173	0	HKS Architects
Pompano Beach	92	B	1,958,272	1,396,729	16,584	84.22	392,674	Owned	168,869	30,000	0	0	469,084	1,489,188	Joseph Middlebrooks
Tampa	14	B	1,977,293	1,370,516	7,100	193.03	161,381	199,798	245,598	30,000	0	580,000	1,397,293	0	FleischmanGarcia
Georgia															
Vidalia	53	B	571,500	261,200	5,200	50.23	26,500	275,000	8,800	60,000	0	258,800	11,200	301,500	Van Page & Assocs.

Symbol Code: B=Branch Library; BS=Branch and System Headquarters; M=Main Library; MS=Main and System Headquarters; S=System Headquarters; n.a.=not available

Location	No.	Code												Architect
Illinois														
Arlington Heights	76	M	727,000	538,000	24,000	22.42	85,000	Owned	104,000	456,165	0	727,000	0	Frye Gillan Molinaro Johnson;
LaSalle	10	M	2,851,532	2,330,341	13,900	167.75	199,930	132,000	189,261	55,000	382,000	2,393,532	76,000	apaceDesign
Oak Lawn	55	M	6,282,404	5,727,404	45,000	127.28	180,000	Owned	375,000	350,000	29,500	6,202,904	50,000	Gilfillan/Callahan. arch
Spring Valley	6	M	1,190,061	959,699	11,300	84.93	63,101	Owned	167,261	36,000	250,000	479,722	460,339	apaceDesign
Indiana														
Fort Wayne	21	B	704,254	534,309	11,900	44.90	109,786	Owned	60,159	59,000	0	704,254	0	Cole & Cole
Fort Wayne	22	B	941,719	749,849	11,200	66.95	126,298	Owned	65,572	82,000	0	941,719	0	Vintage Archonics
Iowa														
Iowa City	63	M	18,374,114	13,165,544	107,000	123.04	1,601,478	1,330,298	2,276,794	320,000	0	17,374,114	1,000,000	Engberg Anderson
Sioux City	20	B	69,110	55,192	1,860	29.67	13,918	Leased	n.a.	14,000	5,898	32,451	30,761	Matthew J. Basye
W. Des Moines	46	M	950,000	380,000	30,000	12.67	375,000	Owned	195,000	220,000	0	950,000	17,000	Renaissance Design
Kansas														
Hays	20	M	3,673,758	3,251,036	29,949	108.55	159,918	Owned	262,804	200,000	0	3,173,758	500,000	Stecklein & Brungardt
Louisiana														
Oak Grove	12	MS	43,000	35,800	5,855	6.11	7,200	Owned	0	40,000	0	43,000	0	none
Maryland														
Eldersburg	40	B	1,088,211	959,000	22,500	42.62	33,391	Owned	95,820	108,656	0	1,088,211	3,500	Meyers & Affiliates
Massachusetts														
Canton	21	M	9,446,000	7,439,000	35,553	209.23	788,000	Owned	1,219,000	153,000	2,505,569	6,500,316	440,115	Burt Hill Kosar...
E. Longmeadow	15	M	4,836,260	3,221,296	19,981	161.22	507,295	Owned	1,107,669	93,344	1,496,607	2,096,953	1,242,700	J. Stewart Roberts
Fall River	92	M	4,420,354	3,634,833	29,979	121.25	392,962	Owned	392,559	175,000	767,784	3,226,968	425,602	Archs Design; Wise...
Lexington	30	M	15,500,000	12,700,000	62,500	203.20	906,919	Owned	1,893,081	225,000	3,011,541	7,488,459	5,000,000	Stephen Hale
Michigan														
Detroit	951	B	8,900,000	7,034,000	28,000	251.21	666,000	Owned	1,200,000	100,000	0	3,900,000	5,000,000	Smith Group
Mount Clemons	22	B	718,990	533,600	11,000	48.51	113,000	Owned	72,390	140,000	0	708,990	25,000	David Milling
Waterford	73	M	2,149,898	1,761,000	27,321	64.46	112,359	Owned	276,539	131,000	0	2,146,898	3,000	David Milling
Minnesota														
Brooklyn Center	160	MS	17,818,855	10,888,000	65,765	165.56	3,715,235	233,000	2,982,620	n.a.	0	17,723,855	95,000	Buetow; Abraham
Mississippi														
Biloxi	45	B	806,200	660,000	7,500	88.00	100,000	Owned	46,200	40,000	300,000	506,200	0	Gary Lamas

Symbol Code: B=Branch Library; BS=Branch and System Headquarters; M=Main Library; MS=Main and System Headquarters; S=System Headquarters; n.a.=not available

Table 5 / Public Library Buildings, Additions and Renovations, 2004 (cont.)

Community	Pop. ('000)	Code	Project Cost	Const. Cost	Gross Sq. Ft.	Sq. Ft. Cost	Equip. Cost	Site Cost	Other Costs	Volumes	Federal Funds	State Funds	Local Funds	Gift Funds	Architect
Missouri															
Fredericktown	12	B	$349,334	$59,563	7,130	$8.35	$88,136	$188,000	$13,635	24,650	$0	$53,607	$280,927	$14,800	Randall Pierce
Kansas City	240	MS	39,600,000	24,400,000	175,000	139.43	3,200,000	3,500,000	8,500,000	836,000	5,200,000	6,000,000	11,500,000	16,900,000	HNTB; Gould Evans
Springfield	240	B	4,510,857	2,212,780	36,000	61.47	752,195	1,350,000	195,882	120,000	0	0	4,295,857	215,000	Sapp Design
New Hampshire															
Conway	8	M	1,807,745	1,482,858	15,912	93.19	134,200	Owned	190,687	61,000	0	0	1,178,250	629,495	Tennant/Wallace
Plainfield	2	M	904,067	738,931	5,900	125.24	27,635	45,750	91,751	22,000	0	0	513,000	438,848	Weller & Michal
New Jersey															
Bound Brook	10	M	56,000	48,800	5,162	9.45	0	Owned	7,200	56,100	0	0	56,000	0	Arcari & Iovino
Franklin Lakes	10	M	3,600,000	3,000,000	19,000	157.89	360,000	Owned	240,000	85,000	153,876	709,760	2,334,364	402,000	Buell Kratzer Powell
Phillipsburg	32	M	1,596,679	1,417,819	21,000	67.51	32,474	Owned	146,386	150,000	0	367,000	1,189,554	40,125	Architectural Studio
Tenafly	14	M	58,750	53,250	600	88.75	0	Owned	5,500	79,230	0	0	58,750	0	Arcari & Iovino
Waldrick	10	M	905,057	643,267	7,783	82.65	144,507	Owned	117,283	60,000	0	103,000	552,057	250,000	Arcari & Iovino
Warren	15	M	1,761,046	1,556,046	20,334	76.52	80,000	Owned	125,000	61,680	0	430,759	1,330,287	0	Arcari & Iovino
West Caldwell	11	M	900,000	510,000	13,000	39.23	300,000	Owned	90,000	64,625	0	180,000	420,000	300,000	Adalbert Albu
New Mexico															
Albuquerque	556	B	3,090,000	2,500,000	15,227	164.18	300,000	Owned	290,000	120,000	0	200,000	2,890,000	0	Cherry/See Archs.
New York															
Centereach	61	M	8,800,000	6,700,000	77,000	87.01	400,000	Leased	1,700,000	500,000	0	48,000	8,500,000	255,000	Holzman Moss
College Point	26	B	2,645,000	2,090,000	8,000	261.25	230,000	Owned	325,000	42,900	0	65,982	2,579,018	0	Schuman, Lichtenstein
New York	51	B	1,754,000	1,468,000	10,280	142.80	101,000	Owned	185,000	20,580	0	0	1,754,000	0	Guggenheimer Archs.
New York	43	B	6,224,069	5,387,741	19,000	283.57	221,916	Owned	614,412	40,000	0	0	5,724,069	500,000	Hom + Goldman
Richmond Hill	73	B	178,250	51,450	3,000	17.15	126,800	Owned	0	96,600	0	0	178,250	0	Peter Magnani
Selden	61	B	5,400,000	4,400,000	30,000	146.67	150,000	Leased	850,000	56,659	0	0	5,400,000	0	Holzman Moss
North Carolina															
Asheville	25	B	709,978	591,978	7,837	75.53	78,000	Owned	40,000	40,000	0	0	659,978	50,000	Keith Hargrove
Goldston	1	B	392,844	238,148	3,300	72.16	32,086	90,000	32,610	12,000	0	0	247,844	145,000	Alley, Williams...
Swansboro	7	B	651,141	553,679	5,489	100.87	11,233	Owned	86,229	30,530	0	0	651,141	0	Angerio Design

Symbol Code: B=Branch Library; BS=Branch and System Headquarters; M=Main Library; MS=Main and System Headquarters; S=System Headquarters; n.a.=not available

Location	No.	Code													Architect
Ohio															
Beavercreek	40	B	627,000	387,000	6,000	64.50	170,000	Leased	70,000	20,000	0	0	473,000	154,000	Architect Group
Columbiana	7	M	1,734,717	1,065,143	6,588	161.68	90,321	383,560	195,693	73,000	0	0	1,731,317	3,400	Ziska Architects
Delaware	76	M	1,041,044	810,673	33,000	24.56	162,392	Owned	6,979	220,000	1,041,044	0		0	Triad Architects
Elyria	56	B	48,690	42,502	12,573	3.38		Owned	6,188	n.a.	0	0	48,690	0	none
Sandusky	48	M	10,847,222	7,296,618	62,817	116.16	1,268,015	1,219,513	1,063,076	200,000	0	0	7,783,628	3,063,594	David Holzheimer
Shreve	5	B	1,234,897	739,819	7,717	95.86	225,585	64,658	204,835	31,703	0	0	1,234,897	0	Van Dyke Architects
Toledo	7	B	806,460	666,851	6,752	98.76	55,314	Owned	84,295	33,800	0	0	806,460	25,000	The Collaborative
Twinsburg	22	M	2,665,366	2,267,487	15,400	147.24	161,657	Owned	236,222	50,000	0	0	2,605,391	59,975	CBLH
Oklahoma															
Tulsa	37	B	1,454,449	1,204,174	20,244	59.48	182,196	Owned	68,079	40,000	0	0	1,436,129	18,320	Olsen-Coffey
Oregon															
Haines	1	B	436,000	314,000	2,400	130.83	8,000	80,000	34,000	12,000	0	0	348,000	88,000	HDN Architects
Halfway	1	B	234,000	146,000	2,500	58.40	11,000	50,000	27,000	15,000	0	0	208,000	26,000	HDN Architects
Richland	1	B	62,000	46,000	1,200	38.33	7,000	n.a.	9,000	8,000	0	0	48,000	14,000	HDN Architects
Pennsylvania															
Feasterville	19	M	2,852,438	1,723,999	13,150	131.10	226,000	655,000	247,439	75,000	275,000	0	2,577,438	0	George J. Donovan
Philadelphia	26	B	3,967,887	3,535,205	12,000	294.60	194,679	Owned	238,003	60,000	0	0	3,924,887	43,000	Buell Kratzer Powell
Rhode Island															
East Greenwich	12	M	2,150,000	1,765,566	11,800	149.62	87,557	Owned	296,877	55,618	936,000	0	541,000	673,000	Prout Robert & Elias
Hope	10	M	444,663	352,644	1,776	198.56	50,187	Owned	41,832	15,945	144,800	0	177,863	122,000	Prout Robert & Elias
Middletown	17	M	1,698,926	1,289,399	13,000	99.18	69,709	138,985	200,833	84,000	750,050	0	405,218	543,658	Robinson Green...
Providence	15	B	3,128,807	2,386,009	6,850	348.32	184,362	101,021	457,415	26,000	992,795	655,113	612,370	868,529	Ann Beha Architects
Providence	45	B	4,932,792	3,787,537	16,920	223.85	287,952	220,733	636,570	50,000	2,098,921	0	618,369	2,215,502	Ann Beha Architects
South Carolina															
Bamberg	7	B	790,767	622,265	7,003	88.86	132,000	Owned	36,502	21,900	450,000	23,000	217,767	100,000	James, DuRant...
South Dakota															
De Smet	3	M	94,109	94,109	1,440	65.35	0	Owned	0	n.a.	0	94,109	0	0	none
Tennessee															
Jackson	94	M	446,355	396,069	4,200	94.30	19,794	Owned	30,492	n.a.	0	0	400,000	46,355	Anderson Vaughan
Texas															
Dallas	68	B	2,851,494	1,903,645	17,353	109.70	750,924	Owned	196,925	70,000	0	0	2,851,494	0	dsgn associates
Dallas	28	B	1,947,373	1,292,128	16,605	77.82	467,000	Owned	188,245	70,000	0	0	1,947,373	0	dsgn associates
Denton	106	B	6,472,342	3,313,688	32,801	101.02	698,225	1,250,000	1,210,429	106,797	0	0	6,472,342	0	H.H. Meyer; Sherer...
Medina	2	M	272,500	219,359	2,409	91.06	15,601	Owned	37,540	1,800	0	0	0	272,500	Jim Rather

Symbol Code: B=Branch Library; BS=Branch and System Headquarters; M=Main Library; MS=Main and System Headquarters; S=System Headquarters; n.a.=not available

Table 5 / Public Library Buildings, Additions and Renovations, 2004 *(cont.)*

Community	Pop. ('000)	Code	Project Cost	Const. Cost	Gross Sq. Ft.	Sq. Ft. Cost	Equip. Cost	Site Cost	Other Costs	Volumes	Federal Funds	State Funds	Local Funds	Gift Funds	Architect
Utah															
St. George	9	B	$2,261,742	$1,464,178	14,356	$101.99	$286,996	Owned	$510,568	49,944	$0	$0	$2,261,742	$0	Cooper, Roberts...
W. Valley City	109	B	1,023,935	891,989	14,019	63.63	60,233	Owned	71,713	90,000	0	0	1,023,935	0	Cooper, Roberts...
Washington															
Ellensburg	16	M	2,130,000	1,058,000	19,500	54.25	350,000	Owned	722,000	100,000	0	0	1,905,000	225,000	Lewis Architecture
Seattle Kane	27	B	2,537,664	1,864,785	8,970	207.89	93,024	Owned	579,855	45,000	0	0	2,326,000	211,664	Snyder Hartung
Seattle Kane	23	B	1,262,780	840,180	8,090	103.85	98,686	Owned	323,914	39,500	0	0	1,201,116	61,664	Snyder Hartung
Seattle	20	B	3,137,000	2,316,152	15,000	154.41	251,502	Owned	569,346	66,700	0	0	60,000	3,077,000	Streeter & Assocs.
Seattle	39	B	4,884,276	3,549,533	15,000	236.64	374,998	Owned	959,745	66,700	0	0	4,859,276	25,000	Miller/Hull Partnership
Wisconsin															
Fond du Lac	69	M	5,550,000	4,376,499	58,000	75.46	450,000	Owned	723,501	200,000	0	0	4,050,000	1,500,000	Durrant Group
Kenosha	93	B	5,103,792	3,935,355	42,300	93.03	594,271	100,000	474,166	165,000	0	0	5,103,792	0	Durrant Group
Madison	17	B	936,759	618,082	9,300	66.46	227,864	Leased	90,813	32,000	0	0	723,154	213,605	Frye Gillan Molinaro
Menasha	24	M	4,654,372	3,973,779	42,600	93.28	258,223	Owned	422,370	134,700	0	0	3,488,515	1,165,857	Durrant Group
Middleton	25	M	1,062,000	851,714	10,000	85.17	125,600	Owned	84,686	n.a.	0	0	781,100	280,900	Strang
Random Lake	6	M	199,971	166,134	5,500	30.21	18,025	Owned	15,812	n.a.	0	0	0	199,971	LJM Architects

Symbol Code: B=Branch Library; BS=Branch and System Headquarters; M=Main Library; MS=Main and System Headquarters; S=System Headquarters; n.a.=not available

Table 6 / Public Library Buildings, Six-Year Cost Summary

	Fiscal 1999	Fiscal 2000	Fiscal 2001	Fiscal 2002	Fiscal 2003	Fiscal 2004
Number of new buildings	77	114	80	101	103	99
Number of ARRs*	118	127	132	111	92	104
Sq. ft. new buildings	1,555,583	1,752,395	1,924,548	2,144,185	2,340,374	3,178,027
Sq. ft. ARRs	2,188,221	2,272,684	2,215,702	2,351,100	1,725,902	2,096,243
New Buildings						
Construction cost	$192,319,192	$232,832,870	$275,404,635	$303,284,460	$420,486,065	$655,261,309
Equipment cost	25,382,314	36,127,111	51,445,962	44,985,041	51,738,413	72,422,017
Site cost	22,634,855	28,655,584	33,375,676	28,523,513	30,095,454	30,873,801
Other cost	43,631,263	39,878,940	39,511,803	48,115,515	69,981,113	157,419,044
Total—Project cost	283,967,624	331,345,167	400,838,076	429,787,571	573,531,535	916,026,171
ARRs—Project cost	280,604,091	301,200,950	285,583,407	358,658,087	263,624,575	326,410,267
New and ARR Project cost	$564,571,715	$632,546,117	$686,421,483	$788,445,658	$837,156,110	$1,242,436,438
Fund Sources						
Federal, new buildings	$7,655,690	$7,598,492	$2,687,151	$5,395,598	$9,106,615	$3,765,492
Federal, ARRs	9,268,183	2,600,334	6,959,013	5,197,596	6,482,225	6,202,088
Federal, total	$16,923,873	$10,198,826	$9,646,164	$10,593,194	$15,588,840	$9,967,580
State, new buildings	$17,122,988	$12,456,471	$6,696,211	$13,745,400	$18,465,123	$115,846,277
State, ARRs	21,677,529	36,982,165	19,396,775	18,874,053	16,090,024	24,889,690
State, total	$38,800,517	$49,438,636	$26,092,986	$32,619,453	$34,555,147	$140,735,967
Local, new buildings	$226,616,333	$287,118,370	$356,563,114	$363,288,508	$507,445,956	$703,245,493
Local, ARRs	201,166,513	220,776,786	211,059,513	312,253,572	207,977,217	237,027,037
Local, total	$427,782,846	$507,895,156	567,622,627	675,542,080	715,423,173	940,272,530
Gift, new buildings	$32,563,613	$26,544,144	$34,923,118	$39,257,565	$39,094,374	$93,284,817
Gift, ARRs	48,614,252	33,309,803	43,344,138	20,795,667	31,972,475	58,402,733
Gift, total	$81,177,865	$59,853,947	$78,267,256	$60,053,232	$71,066,849	$151,687,550
Total funds used	$564,685,101	$627,386,565	$681,629,033	$778,807,959	$836,634,009	$1,242,663,627

* Additions, remodelings, and renovations.

Book Trade Research and Statistics

Prices of U.S. and Foreign Published Materials

Janet B. Belanger

Editor, ALA ALCTS Library Materials Price Index Group

The Library Materials Price Index (LMPI) Group of the American Library Association's Association for Library Collections and Technical Services' Publications Committee continues to monitor library prices for a range of library materials from sources within North America and from other key publishing centers around the world. During 2003 price increases for library materials were mixed, with three categories underperforming the U.S. Consumer Price Index (CPI), though not to the extreme seen in 2002. Preliminary data for 2004 show an increase in the CPI but less significant increases in periodicals for the first time in several years. CPI data are obtained from the Bureau of Labor Statistics Web site at http://www.bls.gov/cpi.

Some indexes have not been updated and are repeated from last year. Several factors have hampered index preparation in recent years. These include mergers and acquisitions in the publishing and distribution world that make it more difficult to determine what is published in a foreign country by "multinational" firms; the conversion of several key countries to the euro; and migrations by vendors to new internal systems.

	Percent Change				
Index	2000	2001	2002	2003	2004
CPI	3.4*	1.6	2.4	1.9	3.3
Periodicals	9.2	8.6	7.6	8.2	6.5
Serial services	5.3	5.8	5.1	7.2	7.1
Hardcover books	-2.4	15.1	-10.3	0.8	n.a.
Academic books	2.0*	0.4*	2.0	1.3	n.a.
College books	2.3	1.9	n.a.	n.a.	n.a.
Mass market paperbacks	2.3	9.4	1.3	-0.3	n.a.
Trade paperbacks	-5.7	22.9	-18.0	4.9	n.a.
Newspapers	2.0	2.9	3.6	3.5	2.1

* Correction/update of data appearing in last year's publication.
n.a. = not available

U.S. Published Materials

Tables 1 through 8B indicate average prices and price indexes for library materials published primarily in the United States. These indexes are U.S. Periodicals (Table 1), U.S. Serial Services (Table 2), U.S. Hardcover Books (Table 3), North American Academic Books (Table 4), U.S. College Books (Table 5), U.S. Mass Market Paperback Books (Table 6), U.S. Paperbacks (Excluding Mass Market) (Table 7), and U.S. Daily Newspapers and International Newspapers (Tables 8A and 8B). A table on U.S. Nonprint Media is no longer included.

Periodical and Serial Prices

The LMPI Group and Swets Information Services jointly produce the U.S. Periodical Price Index (Table 1). The subscription prices shown are publishers' list prices, excluding publisher discount or vendor service charges. This report includes 2003, 2004, and 2005 data indexed to the base year of 1984.

Compiled by Brenda Dingley, this table shows that U.S. periodical prices, excluding Russian translations, increased by 6.5 percent from 2004 to 2005. This figure represents a 1.7 percent decrease in the overall rate of inflation from the 8.2 percent figure posted from 2003 to 2004. Including the Russian translations category, the single-year increase was slightly higher, at 7.0 percent for 2005. This figure is 0.9 percent lower than the rate of 7.9 percent for the entire sample in 2004. The 2005 prices show the overall greatest price increases in the social sciences. However, unlike in 2004 when three subject categories (Agriculture, Sociology and Anthropology, and Labor and Industrial Relations) showed double-digit increases, with the highest increase at 16 percent, no subject category in 2005 showed comparable increases. The Psychology category posted the highest percentage price increase this year (at 9.1 percent), while Education posted the second-highest increase (at 8.7 percent) and Physical Education and Recreation posted the third-highest increase at 8.6 percent. Children's Periodicals showed the lowest increase, at 1.4 percent.

More extensive reports from the periodical price index were published annually in the April 15 issue of *Library Journal* through 1992, in the May issue of *American Libraries* from 1993 through 2002, and in the October 2003 issue of *Library Resources and Technical Services*. All subsequent reports are available on the ALCTS Web site at http://www.ala.org/ala/alcts/alctspubs/pubsresources/resources.htm. Future editions of the U.S. Periodical Price Index will also be posted on the ALCTS Web site as they are completed.

The U.S. Serial Services Index (Table 2) has been updated through 2004. Compiler Nancy Chaffin noted that titles continued to experience migration from print to electronic format. As the index is built only of printed products, the e-only titles were dropped from the various subject indexes. As this trend continues, it becomes more difficult to identify new titles that are print subscriptions.

All areas of serial services saw increases in prices for 2004, with the highest a tie between General and Humanities and U.S. Documents (both at 11.3 percent) and the lowest (5.2 percent) in Science and Technology. The average increase was 7.1 percent for all subject categories. More extensive reports on serial ser-

(text continues on page 513)

Table 1 / U.S. Periodicals: Average Prices and Price Indexes, 2003–2005

Index Base: 1984 = 100

Subject Area	1984 Average Price	2003 Average Price	2003 Index	2004 Average Price	2004 Index	2005 Average Price	2005 Index
U.S. periodicals excluding Russian translations	$54.97	$303.96	552.9	$328.47	597.5	$349.79	636.3
U.S. periodicals including Russian translations	72.47	389.45	537.4	420.14	579.8	449.69	620.5
Agriculture	24.06	115.67	480.8	134.15	557.6	141.46	587.9
Business and economics	38.87	178.40	459.0	196.04	504.4	205.85	529.6
Chemistry and physics	228.90	1,626.47	710.6	1,765.20	771.2	1,879.56	821.1
Children's periodicals	12.21	26.67	218.4	28.23	231.2	28.62	234.4
Education	34.01	159.39	468.7	175.10	514.9	190.32	559.6
Engineering	78.70	471.29	598.8	509.73	647.7	552.02	701.4
Fine and applied arts	26.90	64.79	240.9	68.77	255.6	70.93	263.7
General interest periodicals	27.90	50.38	180.6	52.32	187.5	54.47	195.2
History	23.68	79.33	335.0	85.09	359.3	89.65	378.6
Home economics	37.15	145.62	392.0	159.40	388.4	171.03	416.7
Industrial arts	30.40	128.55	422.9	140.28	461.5	144.97	476.9
Journalism and communications	39.25	139.61	355.7	149.77	381.6	160.88	409.9
Labor and industrial relations	29.87	147.69	494.4	163.80	548.4	168.73	564.9
Law	31.31	109.31	349.1	115.91	370.2	120.95	386.3
Library and information sciences	38.85	129.79	334.1	127.07	327.1	136.99	352.6
Literature and language	23.02	71.43	310.3	76.16	330.8	80.39	349.2
Mathematics, botany, geology, general science	106.56	647.10	607.3	704.12	660.8	729.15	684.3
Medicine	125.57	847.76	675.1	895.72	713.3	962.83	766.8
Philosophy and religion	21.94	72.18	329.0	77.16	351.7	81.11	369.7
Physical education and recreation	20.54	59.33	288.8	64.25	312.8	69.77	339.7
Political science	32.43	161.24	497.2	176.12	543.1	189.87	585.5
Psychology	69.74	419.39	601.4	454.84	652.2	496.41	711.8
Russian translations	381.86	2,112.70	553.3	2,288.20	599.2	2,496.09	653.7
Sociology and anthropology	43.87	235.83	537.6	261.86	596.9	284.18	647.8
Zoology	78.35	591.06	754.4	632.61	807.4	680.81	868.9
Total number of periodicals							
Excluding Russian translations	3,731	3,729		3,729		3,728	
Including Russian translations	3,942	3,914		3,912		3,910	

Compiled by Brenda Dingley, University of Missouri, Kansas City, based on subscription information supplied by Swets Information Services. For further comments, see the October 2003 issue of *Library Resources and Technical Services* and the ALCTS Web site: http://www.ala.org/ala/alctscontent/alctspubsbucket/ alctsresources/general/periodicalsindex/2004-PPI.pdf.

Table 2 / U.S. Serial Services: Average Price and Price Indexes 2002–2004

Index Base: 1984 = 100

Subject Area	1984	2002		2003			2004		
	Average Price	Average Price	Index	Average Price	Percent Increase	Index	Average Price	Percent Increase	Index
U.S. serial services*	$295.13	$747.16	253.2	$800.74	7.2	271.3	$857.96	7.1	290.7
Business	437.07	849.65	194.4	911.89	7.3	208.6	975.45	7.0	223.2
General and humanities	196.55	569.02	289.5	596.50	4.8	303.5	663.75	11.3	337.7
Law	275.23	839.65	305.1	916.06	9.1	332.8	975.82	6.5	354.5
Science and technology	295.36	975.49	330.3	1,054.03	8.1	356.9	1,108.86	5.2	375.4
Social sciences	283.82	656.54	231.3	698.13	6.3	246.0	768.44	10.1	270.7
U.S. documents	97.37	202.60	208.1	189.05	-6.7	194.2	210.39	11.3	216.1
Total number of services	1,537	1,311		1,310			1,326		

Compiled by Nancy J. Chaffin, Arizona State University (West) from data supplied by the Faxon Company, publishers' list prices, and library acquisitions records.

The definition of a serial service has been taken from American National Standard for Library and Information Services and Related Publishing Practices–Library Materials–Criteria for Price Indexes (ANSI Z39.20 - 1983).

*Excludes Wilson Index; excludes Russian translations as of 1988.

Table 3 / U.S. Hardcover Books: Average Prices and Price Indexes, 2002–2004
Index Base: 1997 = 100

Category	1997 Average Price	2002 Final			2003 Final			2004 Preliminary		
		Volumes	Average Price	Index	Volumes	Average Price	Index	Volumes	Average Price	Index
Agriculture	$63.70	455	$65.87	103.4	615	$55.50	87.1	512	$61.47	96.5
Arts	55.99	2,481	60.87	108.7	3,094	50.97	91.0	3,178	53.91	96.3
Biography	54.78	2,476	50.13	91.5	4,849	78.82	143.9	2,876	48.74	89.0
Business	99.34	1,988	99.71	100.4	2,050	99.61	100.3	1,896	95.14	95.8
Education	85.74	1,439	62.24	72.6	2,566	82.58	96.3	1,393	63.18	73.7
Fiction	24.97	5,289	30.35	121.5	5,728	27.46	110.0	5,941	25.84	103.5
General works	108.87	775	157.12	144.3	832	142.96	131.3	847	230.06	211.3
History	62.81	3,594	57.43	91.4	4,361	73.27	116.7	4,207	52.93	84.3
Home economics	36.79	926	32.28	87.7	1,393	29.78	80.9	1,360	29.25	79.5
Juveniles	19.25	7,489	22.56	117.2	15,316	28.11	146.0	13,522	27.17	141.1
Language	71.90	1,013	70.71	98.3	2,766	86.56	120.4	1,190	73.01	101.5
Law	109.95	1,250	97.32	88.5	1,289	102.92	93.6	1,319	107.26	97.6
Literature	62.07	2,253	66.95	107.9	2,231	73.64	118.6	2,074	62.55	100.8
Medicine	111.88	2,755	101.61	90.8	3,440	93.84	83.9	2,780	95.35	85.2
Music	57.87	631	53.04	91.7	985	51.05	88.2	1,029	42.98	74.3
Philosophy, psychology	59.87	2,494	65.61	109.6	2,871	57.15	95.5	2,728	55.42	92.6
Poetry, drama	46.99	945	44.87	95.5	1,198	48.42	103.0	1,193	41.00	87.3
Religion	54.32	2,812	45.74	84.2	4,043	45.43	83.6	5,497	39.46	72.6
Science	103.54	4,458	106.51	102.9	5,052	110.00	106.2	4,356	109.72	106.0
Sociology, economics	79.32	7,153	70.27	88.6	8,727	75.53	95.2	7,958	70.03	88.3
Sports, recreation	46.97	1,395	41.68	88.7	1,677	42.39	90.2	1,813	39.78	84.7
Technology	133.58	3,128	95.95	71.8	3,541	93.35	69.9	3,103	111.96	83.8
Travel	44.87	586	38.70	86.2	779	49.78	110.9	961	37.70	84.0
Totals	$72.67	57,785	$62.84	86.5	79,403	$63.33	87.1	71,733	$58.06	79.9

Compiled by Catherine Barr from data supplied by the R. R. Bowker Company's Books in Print database.
Final data for each year include items listed between January of that year and June of the following year with an imprint date of the specified year.

Table 4 / North American Academic Books: Average Prices and Price Indexes 2001–2003
Index Base: 1989 = 100

Subject Area	LC Class	1989		2001		2002		2003			
		No. of Titles	Average Price	No. of Titles	Average Price	No. of Titles	Average Price	No. of Titles	Average Price	% Change 2002–2003	Index
Agriculture	S	897	$45.13	1,158	$66.65	1,194	$72.28	1,072	$63.80	-11.7	141.4
Anthropology	GN	406	32.81	524	44.15	573	50.87	530	49.25	-3.2	150.1
Botany	QK	251	69.02	196	89.83	225	80.54	189	87.20	8.3	126.3
Business and economics	H	5,979	41.67	5,833	57.93	6,047	58.93	6,050	62.30	5.7	149.5
Chemistry	QD	577	110.61	478	133.49	458	147.20	470	152.78	3.8	138.1
Education	L	1,685	29.61	2,233	41.82	2,390	42.30	2,643	45.08	6.6	152.2
Engineering and technology	T	4,569	64.94	5,573	89.54	5,688	88.12	5,650	94.08	6.8	144.9
Fine and applied arts	M-N	3,040	40.72	5,116	51.11	5,274	58.19	4,839	58.61	0.7	143.9
General works	A	333	134.65	63	50.52	85	69.17	68	56.87	-17.8	42.2
Geography	G	396	47.34	693	58.14	772	64.91	741	64.51	-0.6	136.3
Geology	QE	303	63.49	237	76.38	237	69.20	225	75.74	9.5	119.3
History	C-D-E-F	5,549	31.34	7,151	39.46	7,771	40.68	7,957	42.04	3.3	134.1
Home economics	TX	535	27.10	593	31.87	665	31.85	631	30.38	-4.6	112.1
Industrial arts	TT	175	23.89	189	28.84	229	30.02	221	28.69	-4.4	120.1
Law	K	1,252	51.10	1,694	66.83	2,047	71.12	2,029	75.40	6.0	147.6
Library and information science	Z	857	44.51	557	54.43	575	60.37	529	79.71	32.0	179.1
Literature and language	P	10,812	24.99	12,189	34.07	12,645	35.83	15,695	32.48	-9.4	130.0

Subject	LC Class	No. titles	Avg. price	No. titles	Avg. price	No. titles	Avg. price	No. titles	Avg. price	% change	Index
Mathematics and computer science	QA	2,707	44.68	4,069	67.75	4,206	66.47	3,894	72.15	8.5	161.5
Medicine	R	5,028	58.38	5,782	73.13	5,682	72.04	7,940	75.06	4.2	128.6
Military and naval science	U-V	715	33.57	527	52.86	579	56.26	502	62.19	10.5	185.3
Philosophy and religion	B	3,518	29.06	4,631	44.29	5,091	45.02	5,230	46.12	2.4	158.7
Physical education and recreation	GV	814	20.38	944	28.54	1,028	28.58	1,052	29.37	2.8	144.1
Physics and astronomy	QB	1,219	64.59	1,181	89.20	1,219	88.94	1,221	90.38	1.6	139.9
Political science	J	1,650	36.76	1,654	51.02	1,771	50.83	1,803	52.09	2.5	141.7
Psychology	BF	890	31.97	1,045	43.94	1,008	44.85	982	50.79	13.2	158.9
Science (general)	Q	433	56.10	358	82.31	400	86.72	372	80.97	-6.6	144.3
Sociology	HM	2,742	29.36	3,798	45.77	4,030	45.84	4,059	47.76	4.2	162.7
Zoology	QH,L,P,R	1,967	71.28	2,106	80.99	2,280	81.91	2,029	81.58	-0.4	114.5
Average for all subjects		59,299	$41.69	70,572	$54.81	74,169	$55.90	78,623	$56.62	1.3	135.8

Compiled by Stephen Bosch, University of Arizona, from electronic data provided by Baker and Taylor, Blackwell North America, and Yankee Book Peddler. The data represent all titles (hardcover, trade, and paperback books, as well as annuals) treated for all approval plan customers serviced by the three vendors. Due to the merger between Yankee and Baker and Taylor, Baker and Taylor no longer services approval accounts so the B&T data represent imprints in their database. This table covers titles published or distributed in the United States and Canada during the calendar years listed.

This index does not include paperback editions. The overall average price of materials is lower than if the index consisted only of hardbound editions.

Table 5 / U.S. College Books: Average Prices and Price Indexes, 1999–2001

(Index base for all years: 1983=100. 2000 also indexed to 1999; 2001 also indexed to 2000)

Choice Subject Categories	1983		1999			2000				2001			
	No. of Titles	Avg. Price Per Title	No. of Titles	Avg. Price Per Title	Prices Indexed to 1983	No. of Titles	Avg. Price Per Title	Prices Indexed to 1983	Prices Indexed to 1999	No. of Titles	Avg. Price Per Title	Prices Indexed to 1983	Prices Indexed to 2000
General	11	$24.91	23	$50.75	203.7	—	—	—	—	—	—	—	—
Humanities	40	$24.53	36	$45.73	186.4	43	$49.57	202.1	108.4	41	$48.69	198.5	98.2
Art and architecture	372	40.31	373	53.21	132.0	123	52.61	130.5	98.9	130	49.73	123.4	94.5
Communication	51	22.22	82	47.38	213.2	60	46.12	207.5	97.3	63	49.90	224.6	108.2
Language and literature	109	23.39	88	45.40	194.1	102	49.05	209.7	108.0	98	51.23	219.0	104.4
African and Middle Eastern [4]	—	—	26	37.94	—	25	51.31	—	135.2	30	44.89	—	87.5
Asian and Oceanian [4]	—	—	29	41.02	—	28	49.21	—	120.0	23	42.26	—	85.9
Classical	19	28.68	25	48.06	167.6	16	48.33	168.5	100.6	20	51.94	181.1	107.5
English and American	579	23.47	512	46.48	198.0	515	45.60	194.3	98.1	530	47.06	200.5	103.2
Germanic	53	20.45	41	42.90	209.8	25	50.51	247.0	117.8	42	46.39	226.8	91.8
Romance	93	20.47	89	42.43	207.3	106	46.61	227.7	109.9	86	46.80	228.6	100.4
Slavic	35	23.09	31	52.81	228.7	25	49.26	213.3	93.3	22	52.00	225.2	105.6
Performing arts	19	24.32	22	42.73	175.7	15	39.22	161.3	91.8	15	44.75	184.0	114.1
Film	67	24.81	79	48.72	196.4	110	47.60	191.8	97.7	90	50.46	203.4	106.0
Music	106	25.09	119	46.56	185.6	80	51.21	204.1	110.0	115	50.67	202.0	99.0
Theater and Dance [5]	51	23.18	43	45.01	194.2	50	47.63	205.5	105.8	53	50.94	219.8	107.0
Philosophy	155	26.27	177	47.83	182.1	155	46.43	176.7	97.1	158	45.80	174.3	98.6
Religion	196	19.33	209	38.95	201.5	149	40.37	208.9	103.6	222	37.94	196.3	94.0
Total Humanities [6]	2,038	$26.26	1,981	$46.74	178.0	1,932	$48.32	184.0	103.4	1,988	$48.05	183.0	99.4
Science/technology	159	$36.11	88	$39.94	110.6	63	$38.50	106.6	96.4	55	$43.14	119.5	112.0
History of science/technology	56	28.45	79	46.32	162.8	70	41.25	145.0	89.0	75	47.06	165.4	114.1
Astronautics/astronomy	18	27.78	34	41.74	150.2	56	35.94	129.4	86.1	57	43.96	158.3	122.3
Biology	145	39.28	103	52.95	134.8	113	55.49	141.3	104.8	129	46.98	119.6	84.7
Botany	23	31.78	86	50.75	159.7	82	59.13	186.1	116.5	75	59.21	186.3	100.1
Zoology	38	44.21	79	47.10	106.5	70	53.93	122.0	114.5	71	56.62	128.1	105.0
Chemistry	30	48.57	64	99.32	204.5	35	109.93	226.3	110.7	47	82.99	170.9	75.5
Earth science	42	35.43	63	58.86	166.1	55	66.09	186.5	112.3	59	72.64	205.0	109.9
Engineering	154	44.88	70	76.12	169.6	78	82.37	183.5	108.2	70	77.66	173.0	94.3
Health sciences	121	24.45	124	41.91	171.4	124	53.09	217.1	126.7	138	49.67	203.1	93.6
Information/computer science	63	29.48	40	43.15	146.4	35	42.53	144.3	98.6	35	53.12	180.2	124.9
Mathematics	44	32.82	70	59.17	180.3	101	59.57	181.5	100.7	84	55.91	170.4	93.9
Physics	38	34.13	38	58.97	172.8	45	47.02	137.8	79.7	57	47.71	139.8	101.5
Sports/physical education	61	18.67	53	35.98	192.7	55	37.89	202.9	105.3	47	37.73	202.1	99.6
Total Science/technology	992	$34.77	991	$53.22	153.1	982	$55.41	159.4	104.1	999	$54.51	156.8	98.4

Social/behavioral sciences	173	$24.24	66	43.50	179.4	54	$41.11	169.6	94.5	86	52.42	216.2	127.5
Anthropology	98	26.68	162	51.33	192.4	147	50.91	190.8	99.2	152	50.52	189.4	99.2
Business management/labor	156	25.01	146	41.23	164.8	153	44.19	176.7	107.2	140	44.37	177.4	100.4
Economics	315	27.60	245	48.86	177.0	260	53.92	195.4	110.3	256	50.00	181.2	92.7
Education	120	20.23	204	43.74	216.2	153	43.25	213.8	98.9	162	47.61	235.3	110.1
History, geography/area studies	92	25.58	48	48.43	189.3	50	45.24	176.8	93.4	88	44.85	175.3	99.1
Africa	17	26.94	31	48.75	180.9	32	51.90	192.7	106.5	23	56.62	210.2	109.1
Ancient history	46	31.80	39	53.58	168.5	42	65.94	207.3	123.1	26	48.23	151.7	73.1
Asia and Oceania	58	25.55	61	49.95	195.5	65	49.60	194.1	99.3	80	49.27	192.8	99.3
Central and Eastern Europe [3]	—	—	44	50.76	—	54	51.21	—	100.9	61	46.41	—	90.6
Latin America and Caribbean	25	24.72	47	49.35	199.6	64	50.85	205.7	103.0	49	47.76	193.2	93.9
Middle East and North Africa	33	28.42	34	52.69	185.4	40	48.34	170.1	91.8	39	51.94	182.8	107.4
North America	274	24.42	430	39.76	162.8	431	38.11	156.1	95.8	364	40.33	165.2	105.8
United Kingdom [3]	—	—	124	52.90	—	113	53.60	—	101.3	104	55.81	—	104.1
Western Europe [3]	—	—	128	49.73	213.8	124	53.32	187.7	107.2	156	48.71	193.5	91.4
Political science	439	25.00	24	53.44	—	19	46.93	—	87.8	31	48.37	—	103.1
Comparative politics [2]	—	—	202	52.57	—	197	53.10	—	101.0	170	51.12	—	96.3
International relations [2]	—	—	137	50.28	—	142	50.74	—	100.9	160	50.78	—	100.1
Political theory [2]	—	—	59	40.08	—	50	50.78	—	126.7	55	48.90	—	96.3
U.S. politics [2]	—	—	166	42.78	—	183	45.05	—	105.3	146	42.43	—	94.2
Psychology	162	26.57	141	45.92	172.8	116	39.86	150.0	86.8	106	49.65	186.9	124.6
Sociology	244	24.38	132	47.02	192.9	156	45.63	187.2	97.0	193	50.61	207.6	110.9
Total Social/behavioral sciences	2,537	$25.81	2,670	$46.58	180.5	2,645	$47.31	183.3	101.6	2,647	$47.93	185.7	101.3
Total General, Humanities, Science/technology, Social/behavioral sciences (excl. Reference) [6]	5,578	$27.57	5,665	$47.81	173.4	5,559	$49.10	178.1	102.7	5,634	$49.14	178.2	100.1
Reference	506	$44.75	—	—	—	—	—	—	—	—	—	—	—
General [1]	—	—	64	$88.00	—	93	$73.74	—	83.8	109	$84.57	—	114.7
Humanities [1]	—	—	185	97.60	—	199	89.33	—	91.5	177	94.47	—	105.8
Science/technology [1]	—	—	73	97.50	—	91	85.67	—	87.9	82	103.90	—	121.3
Social/behavioral [1]	—	—	236	94.03	—	243	97.96	—	104.2	266	107.83	—	110.1
Total Reference	506	$44.75	558	$94.98	212.2	626	$89.83	200.7	94.6	634	$99.59	222.6	110.9
Grand Total (incl. Reference) [6]	6,084	$29.00	6,223	$52.04	179.5	6,185	$53.22	183.5	102.3	6,268	$54.24	187.0	101.9

1 Began appearing as separate sections in July 1997.
2 Began appearing as separate sections in March 1988
3 Began appearing as separate sections, replacing Europe, in July 1997.
4 Began appearing as separate sections in September 1995.
5 Separate sections for Theater and Dance combined in September 1995.
6 1983 totals include Linguistics (incorporated into Language and Literature in 1985). Non-European/Other (replaced by African and Middle Eastern and Asian and Oceanian in September 1995), and Europe (replaced by Central and Eastern Europe, United Kingdom and Western Europe in July 1997).

Compiled by Donna Alsbury, Florida Center for Library Automation.

Table 6 / U.S. Mass Market Paperbacks: Average Per-Volume Prices, 2002–2004
Index Base: 1997 = 100

Category	1997 Average Prices	2002 Final Volumes	2002 Final Average Prices	2002 Final Index	2003 Final Volumes	2003 Final Average Prices	2003 Final Index	2004 Preliminary Volumes	2004 Preliminary Average Prices	2004 Preliminary Index
Agriculture	$7.50	2	$7.95	106.0	1	$7.95	106.0	0	n.a.	n.a.
Arts	6.54	20	8.61	131.7	4	7.86	120.2	6	7.65	117.0
Biography	6.46	74	6.70	103.7	44	7.39	114.4	39	7.59	117.5
Business	6.51	5	7.57	116.3	9	8.96	137.6	3	9.63	147.9
Education	7.32	62	5.34	73.0	25	6.86	93.7	12	7.40	101.1
Fiction	5.40	2,186	6.71	124.3	2,348	6.72	124.4	2,330	6.80	125.9
General works	7.48	19	8.53	114.0	13	7.90	105.6	9	8.37	111.9
History	6.13	47	6.52	106.4	38	7.13	116.3	41	7.55	123.2
Home economics	6.89	24	7.63	110.7	25	7.62	110.6	17	7.80	113.2
Juveniles	4.69	2,246	5.73	122.2	2,054	5.60	119.4	2,081	5.75	122.6
Language	5.92	59	6.54	110.5	53	4.01	67.7	27	5.81	98.1
Law	6.69	2	7.99	119.4	3	7.48	111.8	3	8.96	133.9
Literature	6.72	70	7.68	114.3	71	7.58	112.8	43	7.22	107.4
Medicine	6.53	33	6.99	107.0	19	7.54	115.5	26	7.10	108.7
Music	7.97	8	7.41	93.0	7	6.77	84.9	4	7.48	93.9
Philosophy, psychology	6.52	137	7.17	110.0	111	7.69	117.9	100	8.27	126.8
Poetry, drama	6.41	18	7.18	112.0	27	7.30	113.9	14	6.54	102.0
Religion	6.99	122	8.20	117.3	166	8.10	115.9	108	7.86	112.4
Science	5.17	59	6.23	120.5	29	6.04	116.8	13	6.74	130.4
Sociology, economics	6.76	73	7.48	110.7	74	7.67	113.5	56	7.95	117.6
Sports, recreation	6.43	46	7.69	119.6	44	7.34	114.2	38	7.51	116.8
Technology	6.87	17	7.63	111.1	11	6.66	96.9	3	8.31	121.0
Travel	8.75	17	9.25	105.7	1	5.99	68.5	2	7.97	91.1
Totals	$5.36	5,346	$6.39	119.2	5,177	$6.37	118.8	4,975	$6.46	120.5

Table 7 / U.S. Paperbacks (Excluding Mass Market): Average Prices and Price Indexes, 2002–2004
Index Base: 1997 = 100

Category	1997 Average Price	2002 Final			2003 Final			2004 Preliminary		
		Volumes	Average Price	Index	Volumes	Average Price	Index	Volumes	Average Price	Index
Agriculture	$28.50	464	$26.69	93.7	562	$26.73	93.8	439	$27.19	95.4
Arts	27.78	2,606	27.87	100.3	3,447	29.48	106.1	2,745	32.62	117.4
Biography	19.83	2,758	24.42	123.2	2,824	21.86	110.2	2,940	23.51	118.6
Business	128.45	3,033	56.23	43.8	3,354	59.21	46.1	2,905	57.33	44.6
Education	27.41	3,223	35.06	127.9	3,640	35.88	130.9	2,561	30.21	110.2
Fiction	16.22	9,832	18.10	111.6	9,547	18.42	113.6	11,125	18.63	114.9
General works	199.57	850	46.98	23.5	1,096	48.04	24.1	2,540	183.03	91.7
History	26.24	4,294	26.05	99.3	6,459	29.03	110.6	4,376	33.77	128.7
Home economics	25.16	1,234	19.35	76.9	1,639	20.78	82.6	1,608	20.07	79.8
Juveniles	19.26	1,479	19.33	100.4	2,855	26.17	135.9	4,894	26.15	135.8
Language	28.98	12,381	29.68	102.4	2,460	34.20	118.0	2,002	34.40	118.7
Law	44.78	1,469	50.17	112.0	1,801	51.21	114.4	1,475	55.86	124.7
Literature	20.98	2,287	27.38	130.5	2,625	26.05	124.2	2,048	26.37	125.7
Medicine	47.25	3,791	44.47	94.1	4,044	41.77	88.4	3,641	40.29	85.3
Music	22.18	1,282	21.87	98.6	1,688	26.14	117.9	1,557	22.58	101.8
Philosophy, psychology	23.72	4,034	25.08	105.7	4,200	24.64	103.9	4,102	24.33	102.6
Poetry, drama	17.00	2,366	16.95	99.7	3,185	19.04	112.0	3,388	17.15	100.9
Religion	20.03	4,505	19.58	97.8	6,203	22.73	113.5	6,033	21.11	105.4
Science	48.57	3,295	49.21	101.3	4,458	40.04	82.4	3,098	43.55	89.7
Sociology, economics	31.23	8,113	32.76	104.9	9,974	39.51	126.5	8,230	37.89	121.3
Sports, recreation	23.56	2,645	21.27	90.3	3,002	22.13	93.9	2,576	21.58	91.6
Technology	69.52	6,103	59.16	85.1	5,721	65.04	93.6	4,386	57.23	82.3
Travel	20.13	2,012	19.90	98.9	2,074	22.76	113.1	2,237	21.46	106.6
Totals	$38.45	84,056	$31.33	81.5	86,858	$32.85	85.4	80,906	$35.45	92.2

Compiled by Catherine Barr from data supplied by the R. R. Bowker Company's Books in Print database.
Final data for each year include items listed between January of that year and June of the following year with an imprint date of the specified year.

Table 8A / U.S. Daily Newspapers:
Average Prices and Price Indexes, 1990–2005
Index Base: 1990 = 100

Year	No. Titles	Average Price	Percent Increase	Index
1990	165	$189.58	0.0	100.0
1991	166	198.13	4.5	104.5
1992	167	222.68	12.4	117.5
1993	171	229.92	3.3	121.3
1994	171	261.91	13.9	138.2
1995	172	270.22	3.2	142.5
1996	166	300.21	11.1	158.4
1997	165	311.77	3.9	164.5
1998	163	316.60	1.5	167.0
1999	162	318.44	0.6	168.0
2000	162	324.26	1.8	171.0
2001	160	330.78	2.0	174.5
2002	158	340.38	2.9	179.5
2003	156	352.65	3.6	186.0
2004	154	364.97	3.5	192.5
2005	154	372.64	2.1	196.6

Table 8B / International Newspapers:
Average Prices and Price Indexes, 1993–2005
Index Base: 1993 = 100

Year	No. Titles	Average Price	Percent Change	Index
1993	46	$806.91	0.0	100.0
1994	46	842.01	4.3	104.3
1995	49	942.13	11.9	116.3
1996	50	992.78	5.4	123.0
1997	53	1,029.49	3.7	127.6
1998	52	1,046.72	1.7	129.7
1999	50	1,049.13	0.2	130.0
2000	50	1,050.88	0.2	130.2
2001	50	1,038.26	-1.2	128.7
2002	49	1,052.69	1.4	130.5
2003	46	1,223.31	16.2	151.6
2004	43	1,301.71	6.4	161.3
2005	47	1,352.23	3.9	167.6

Compiled by Genevieve S. Owens, Williamsburg Regional Library, and Wilba Swearingen, Louisiana State University Health Sciences Center Library, New Orleans, from data supplied by EBSCO Information Services. We thank Kathleen Born of EBSCO for her assistance with this project.

(text continued from page 502)

vices pricing are available on the ALCTS Web site at http://www.ala.org/ala/alcts/alctspubs/pubsresources/resources.htm.

Book Prices

Average book prices continued to be mixed across categories and formats in 2003. Hardcover books (Table 3) showed a slight (0.78 percent) increase, but preliminary figures for 2004 indicate that the decreasing trend seen the previous year is likely to continue.

The average price of North American Academic Books in 2003 (Table 4) increased by a very modest 1.3 percent in contrast to preceding years, which showed 2.0 percent and 0.4 percent increases in pricing. The data used for this index is derived from titles treated by Blackwell's Book Services and Yankee Book Peddler in their approval plans during the calendar years listed and titles treated by Baker and Taylor through all order types during the calendar years listed. The index does include paperback editions as supplied by these vendors and the recent increases in the number of paperbacks distributed as part of the approval plans has clearly influenced the prices reflected in the index figures. Blackwell's showed an increase in the number of paperbacks during the past several years, and they now constitute 33 percent of the titles listed by Blackwell's. In 2003–2004 the number of paperbacks treated in the approval plan increased 6 percent and the number of hardbacks decreased 2 percent. Other vendors are showing similar impacts from the growth of paperback publishing. Paperbacks will continue to be a part of this index, as they are included in the approval plan data and represent a viable part of the North American book market. The direct impact on inflation caused by hardback/paperback pricing continues to be unquantifiable, but it is clear that the modest increases in overall price inflation for academic books during the past few years seems to correlate to increases in paperback numbers.

Other factors are also certainly at work as larger numbers of titles are being treated on approval plans, but the overall average price isn't seeing steep increases. Analysis of the data as it is processed shows that the overlap titles that are excluded from the index tend to be more expensive than the unique titles processed by each vendor. This fact will tend to hold down the average price and increases in the index. In all cases the average price of a book for each vendor is 4 percent to 6 percent higher than the aggregate average price. This shows that when the titles are combined in the aggregate index the unique titles each vendor handles tend to be cheaper than the titles that overlap. This makes sense, since publications from small publishers tend to be cheaper than those from mainstream publishers and the small publishers will tend to make up more of the unique titles handled by each vendor. The vendors are all going to carry the full title list from Macmillan or Oxford University Press, but a small regional press may not be carried by all three vendors. Publishers seem to be willing to bring more titles to press, yet keep overall price increases in the low single digits. Current trends reported by vendors indicate that increases are going to grow in 2004, but, with the exchange rate going south, all bets are off.

Price changes vary, as always, among subject areas. This year there were a few double-digit increases in subject areas and several areas saw prices decrease. Price increases in the areas of science, technology, and medicine (STM) no longer continue to dominate other non-STM areas, although the overall average price for STM books remains high. There were actually no STM areas that showed double-digit increases. Chemistry, normally an area with significant increases, only went up 3.8 percent, but even that increase—on an average price of $152.78—has a large impact. Areas that did see double-digit increases were Psychology (13.2 percent), Military and Naval Science (10.5 percent—no publishers cashing in on current interest here!), and Library Science (32.0 percent).

It is good to remember that price indexes become less accurate at describing price changes the smaller the sample becomes. The Library Science area showed a 32 percent increase in prices, but to then conclude that all books in the area increased 32 percent is not correct. This area has a small sample size of only 529 books, and, since it also includes the class Z area, the presence of just a few large expensive bibliographic sets can have a major impact on prices for the category. Many areas in the social sciences showed large increases, so overall the area did consistently display higher price inflation and has become the top area for increases in book prices. The humanities were spared large increases as the Fine Arts area, and Literature showed either a minimal increase or an actual decrease. General Works has a relatively small number of titles but large numbers of expensive encyclopedic sets, so prices in this category will always be volatile. A handful of titles can result in large increases or large decreases. The General Works category dropped 17 percent after a 36 percent increase the year before.

U.S. College Books (Table 5) repeats data published earlier, giving information based on titles reviewed during 2000 in *Choice* magazine, a publication of the Association of College and Research Libraries. This index will be updated next year; due to a change in compiler and revisions in the preparation of the index, it was not possible to complete it in time for publication this year. The table shows a modest increase of only 1.9 percent across all categories. However, almost the entire increase came from the Reference category, which rose 10.9 percent. With the exception of Reference books, the average price remained almost flat.

Prices of mass market paperback books (Table 6) recorded a small decrease (0.31 percent) between 2002 and 2003, but trade and other paperback prices (Table 7) rose 4.85 percent, reversing the 17.99 percent decline registered between 2001 and 2002.

Newspaper Prices

The indexes for U.S. (Table 8A) and international (Table 8B) newspapers compiled by Genevieve Owens and Wilba Swearingen show lower percentage price increases than last year. The U.S. newspaper price increase of 2.1 percent is below inflation and is the largest drop (from 3.5 percent) since 1996. This reflects a market that may be starting to stabilize as newspaper publishers begin to find their way in an electronic environment. The slight increase is due to higher postage rates. The increase for international newspapers of 3.9 percent, while far lower than the 6.4 percent of last year, may still reflect the continued weakness of the U.S. dollar against most other major currencies, possibly combined with slight increases in postage rates. The high average costs of this material reflect the high frequency of publication and cost of timely shipment in the area of international newspapers. The figures reflect an increase of four international newspapers. These titles were not included last year due to their publication status. Data are provided with the assistance of EBSCO Subscription Services.

Prices of Other Media

The U.S. nonprint media index (former Table 9) does not appear this year. Those wishing historical information can find data for 1997 and 1998, indexed to a base of 1980, in the 2001 edition of the *Bowker Annual*. The database, compiled in previous years by Dana Alessi, collects information from titles reviewed in *Booklist, Library Journal, School Library Journal,* and *Video Librarian.*

The CD-ROM price inventory that formerly appeared as Table 10 has also been discontinued. As with U.S. Serial Services, many of the titles that were published in CD-ROM format have migrated to Web editions. Additionally, the changes from single workstation pricing to network pricing or site licenses made tracking of the prices for this category of material difficult to obtain.

Efforts to develop a price index for electronic journals are still under discussion, but many factors have hindered progress in this area, not the least of which are the continued volatility of pricing models, consortial pricing, and institution-specific package deals. The Association of Research Libraries is also considering ways to gather this important economic data for libraries.

Foreign Prices

Exchange rates were closely watched during 2004 and the dollar's weakness continued to negatively impact acquisition of materials from Great Britain and the euro zone countries.

Dates	12/31/99	12/31/00	12/31/01	12/31/02	12/31/03	12/31/04
Canada	1.5375	1.5219*	1.5925*	1.5592*	1.2958*	1.1880**
Euro	0.9871	1.0666*	1.1322*	0.9414*	0.7913*	0.7530**
U.K.	0.6014	0.6836*	0.6938*	0.6182*	0.5478*	0.5240**
Japan	102.16	112.22	127.59*	121.89*	106.27*	103.1100**

* Data from the regional Federal Reserve Bank of St. Louis (http://www.stls.frb.org/fred/data/exchange.html).
**Data from Financial Management Services. U.S. Treasury Department (http://fms.treas.gov/intn.html). The change is due to the Federal Reserve Bank of St. Louis no longer reporting Euro to U.S. and U.K. to U.S. rates.

The foreign price indexes that follow are British Academic Books (Table 9) and Latin American Periodicals (Tables 10A and 10B). Tables showing prices for German academic books, German academic periodicals, and Dutch English-language periodicals have not been updated and are not included in this volume. Please refer to earlier editions of the *Bowker Annual* for historical information.

Table 9 / British Academic Books: Average Prices and Price Indexes, 2002–2004

Index Base: 1985 = 100; prices listed are pounds sterling

Subject Area	1985 No. of Titles	1985 Average Price	2002 No. of Titles	2002 Average Price	2002 Index	2003 No. of Titles	2003 Average Price	2003 Index	2004 No. of Titles	2004 Average Price	2004 Index
General works	29	£30.54	30	£30.91	101.2	32	£42.20	138.2	33	£28.22	92.4
Fine arts	329	21.70	480	33.64	155.0	490	31.14	143.5	518	32.41	149.4
Architecture	97	20.68	170	37.27	180.2	153	35.74	172.8	143	39.85	192.7
Music	136	17.01	147	35.73	210.1	137	37.59	221.0	142	36.78	216.2
Performing arts except music	110	13.30	243	30.29	227.7	208	33.35	250.8	225	29.98	225.4
Archaeology	146	18.80	109	42.14	224.1	100	44.84	238.5	104	42.88	228.1
Geography	60	22.74	35	50.50	222.1	38	60.51	266.1	46	43.66	192.0
History	1,123	16.92	1,241	31.53	186.3	1,041	34.30	202.7	1,164	32.87	194.3
Philosophy	127	18.41	333	45.14	245.2	306	42.87	232.9	303	40.19	218.3
Religion	328	10.40	738	35.18	338.3	579	38.35	368.8	691	34.23	329.1
Language	135	19.37	252	47.15	243.4	210	48.60	250.9	228	42.87	221.3
Miscellaneous humanities	59	21.71	23	30.21	139.2	33	33.49	154.3	29	31.56	145.4
Literary texts (excluding fiction)	570	9.31	997	14.23	152.8	976	14.68	157.7	1,292	13.64	146.5
Literary criticism	438	14.82	582	36.94	249.3	485	39.22	264.6	533	39.76	268.3
Law	188	24.64	639	58.07	235.7	552	55.97	227.2	580	55.19	224.0
Library science and book trade	78	18.69	57	37.00	198.0	62	36.88	197.3	70	47.01	251.5
Mass communications	38	14.20	150	34.25	241.2	113	35.51	250.1	137	39.25	276.4
Anthropology and ethnology	42	20.71	95	47.32	228.5	52	49.68	239.9	58	48.64	234.9
Sociology	136	15.24	238	42.55	279.2	205	47.07	308.9	209	41.35	271.3
Psychology	107	19.25	146	41.44	215.3	131	44.63	231.8	156	42.41	220.3
Economics	334	20.48	548	52.84	258.0	556	56.20	274.4	520	55.54	271.2
Political science, international relations	314	15.54	780	40.30	259.3	724	41.33	266.0	744	42.57	273.9
Miscellaneous social sciences	20	26.84	38	49.62	184.9	31	44.53	165.9	44	55.33	206.1
Military science	83	17.69	81	31.69	179.1	62	38.66	218.5	80	36.35	205.5
Sports and recreation	44	11.23	68	38.43	342.2	79	32.75	291.6	105	41.69	371.2
Social service	56	12.17	97	32.02	263.1	83	32.04	263.3	88	33.52	275.4
Education	295	12.22	386	35.78	292.8	369	39.14	320.3	376	41.76	341.7
Management and business administration	427	19.55	969	39.91	204.1	849	42.67	218.3	781	44.79	229.1
Miscellaneous applied social sciences	13	9.58	25	42.23	440.8	25	55.07	574.8	29	45.79	478.0
Criminology	45	11.45	98	35.04	306.0	128	33.55	293.0	119	35.44	309.5

Applied interdisciplinary social sciences	254	14.17	564	43.21	304.9	528	42.86	302.5	517	45.54	321.4
General science	43	13.73	47	44.97	327.5	46	37.55	273.5	37	40.95	298.2
Botany	55	30.54	32	62.00	203.0	21	61.71	202.1	25	69.77	228.5
Zoology	85	25.67	62	55.41	215.9	40	51.99	202.5	42	53.30	207.6
Human biology	35	28.91	52	54.23	187.6	32	52.76	182.5	24	56.43	195.2
Biochemistry	26	33.57	28	75.16	223.9	13	57.23	170.5	27	70.82	211.0
Miscellaneous biological sciences	152	26.64	132	59.22	222.3	110	52.13	195.7	118	56.36	211.6
Chemistry	109	48.84	95	80.43	164.7	72	72.41	148.3	71	78.59	160.9
Earth sciences	87	28.94	88	65.94	227.9	76	64.19	221.8	72	61.57	212.8
Astronomy	43	20.36	81	49.67	244.0	59	50.33	247.2	54	51.99	255.4
Physics	76	26.58	173	63.79	240.0	184	61.89	232.8	179	61.85	232.7
Mathematics	123	20.20	213	50.87	251.8	224	50.87	251.8	192	48.75	241.3
Computer sciences	150	20.14	241	37.96	188.5	138	39.66	196.9	139	42.51	211.1
Interdisciplinary technical fields	38	26.14	54	50.77	194.2	42	50.12	191.7	45	57.20	218.8
Civil engineering	134	28.68	149	77.93	271.7	73	72.71	253.5	103	83.35	290.6
Mechanical engineering	27	31.73	35	74.52	234.9	38	89.25	281.3	30	83.34	262.7
Electrical and electronic engineering	100	33.12	113	59.58	179.9	107	62.41	188.4	106	58.01	175.2
Materials science	54	37.93	44	80.24	211.5	42	82.24	216.8	48	89.62	236.3
Chemical engineering	24	40.48	36	83.20	205.5	5	77.89	192.4	21	64.21	158.6
Miscellaneous technology	217	36.33	240	59.31	163.3	239	52.82	145.4	223	55.15	151.8
Food and domestic science	38	23.75	44	47.70	200.8	33	51.08	215.1	38	46.72	196.7
Non-clinical medicine	97	18.19	203	39.90	219.4	169	37.11	204.0	183	43.09	236.9
General medicine	73	21.03	74	59.32	282.1	63	46.04	218.9	61	46.34	220.4
Internal medicine	163	27.30	168	57.08	209.1	178	55.26	202.4	152	56.35	206.4
Psychiatry and mental disorders	71	17.97	178	35.38	196.9	199	30.50	169.7	211	33.21	184.8
Surgery	50	29.37	37	64.41	219.3	41	63.20	215.2	43	71.39	243.1
Miscellaneous medicine	292	22.08	241	53.15	240.7	276	50.24	227.5	254	45.74	207.2
Dentistry	20	19.39	8	37.35	192.6	22	40.30	207.8	20	37.61	194.0
Pharmacy*	n.a.	n.a.	13	61.45	n.a.	16	48.52	n.a.	7	36.42	n.a.
Nursing	71	8.00	53	26.30	328.8	82	25.08	313.5	79	24.43	305.4
Agriculture and forestry	78	23.69	61	60.40	255.0	68	59.97	253.1	7	56.00	236.4
Animal husbandry and veterinary medicine	34	20.92	40	47.48	227.0	35	50.34	240.6	46	54.92	262.5
Natural resources and conservation	58	22.88	74	60.78	265.6	60	49.44	216.1	57	52.57	229.8
Total, all books	9,049	£19.07	13,473	£41.51	217.7	12,145	£41.62	218.2	12,825	£40.85	214.2

Compiled by Curt Holleman, Southern Methodist University, from data supplied by B. H. Blackwell and the Library and Information Statistics Unit at Loughborough University.
* New category introduced in 2001.

Table 10A / Latin American Periodical Price Index, 2002–2003
Country and Region Index

	Total Titles	Mean w/o newspapers	Index (1992 = 100)	Weighted mean w/o newspapers	Index (1992 = 100)
Country					
Argentina	149	$103.14	107	$85.32	104
Bolivia	5	42.16	69	32.84	29
Brazil	301	41.81	81	37.54	82
Caribbean	29	40.80	96	41.60	98
Chile	33	162.30	85	60.89	82
Colombia	57	84.28	107	109.24	105
Costa Rica	23	42.83	104	51.36	100
Cuba	15	61.93	114	46.46	87
Ecuador	18	73.78	111	79.81	99
El Salvador	8	57.38	106	54.51	85
Guatemala	12	141.67	101	178.88	102
Honduras	n.a.	n.a.	n.a.	n.a.	n.a.
Jamaica	12	43.08	93	68.85	122
Mexico	210	117.05	97	93.75	105
Nicaragua	7	28.58	116	32.37	136
Panama	11	38.77	108	39.46	113
Paraguay	7	19.33	95	30.85	101
Peru	50	131.59	106	117.98	109
Uruguay	22	84.13	98	56.82	94
Venezuela	37	100.49	95	80.59	82
Region					
Caribbean	56	46.23	98	48.13	100
Central America	63	59.93	103	78.85	105
South America	676	76.26	107	77.60	110
Mexico	210	117.05	97	93.75	105
Latin America	1,005	82.52	99	79.53	110

Subscription information provided by Blackwell North America, Library of Congress Rio Office, and the University of Texas. Index based on 1992 LAPPI mean prices. The 2001/2002 subscription prices were included in this year's index if a new subscription price was not available.
Compiled by Scott Van Jacob, University of Notre Dame.
n.a. = fewer than five subscription prices were found

Table 10B / Latin American Periodical Price Index, 2002–2003: Subject Index

Subjects	Mean	Index (1992 = 100)	Weighted mean	Index (1992 = 100)
Social sciences	$87.96	99	$81.33	104
Humanities	46.11	88	51.80	117
Science/technology	66.44	89	94.10	118
General	108.51	79	84.00	80
Law	111.15	101	137.32	153
Newspapers	678.33	144	763.27	197
Totals w/o newspapers	82.52	96	79.53	104
Total with newspapers	117.44	115	98.42	120
Total titles w/o newspapers = 1,005				
Total titles with newspapers = 1,070				

British Prices

The price index for British academic books (Table 9) is compiled by Curt Holleman from information supplied by Blackwell's Book Services. The average price in pounds of a British book went from £41.62 in 2003 to £40.85 in 2004, a decrease of 1.9 percent. However, the dollar fell 12.1 percent compared to the pound during the same period, and the number of books identified as possible academic purchases went up 5.6 percent. Therefore, the actual cost for libraries in the United States of keeping up with British publishing in 2004 experienced a double-digit increase in spite of the slight decrease of the average price of British books in pounds.

Latin American Prices

Scott Van Jacobs compiles the Latin American Periodicals indexes (Tables 10A and 10B, former Tables 14A and 14B) with prices provided by Blackwell's Book Services, the Library of Congress's Rio Office and the University of Texas, Austin.

Due to loss of the vendor providing data, the Latin American Periodical Price Index will not be updated this year and the 2002–2003 index is repeated. Based on that data, the weighted overall mean for Latin American periodicals including newspapers rose 13.8 percent in 2002–2003, a significant increase from the 3.7 percent of the previous period. When newspapers are not included, the increase was 9.5 percent, again much higher than the 1.6 percent of the previous period. However, increases varied widely by region and especially by country. Currency fluctuations may well account for much of this variation.

The most recent Latin American book price index was published in 1997. A new index based on data provided by Latin American book vendors is expected to replace that index, but is not yet available.

Using the Price Indexes

Librarians are encouraged to monitor trends in the publishing industry and changes in economic conditions when preparing budget forecasts and projections. The ALA ALCTS Library Materials Price Index Group endeavors to make information on publishing trends readily available by sponsoring the annual compilation and publication of price data contained in Tables 1 to 10B. The indexes cover newly published library materials and document prices and rates of percentage changes at the national and international level. They are useful benchmarks against which local costs can be compared, but because they reflect retail prices in the aggregate, they are not a substitute for cost data that reflect the collecting patterns of individual libraries, and they are not a substitute for specific cost studies.

Differences between local prices and those found in national indexes arise partially because these indexes exclude discounts, service charges, shipping and handling fees, and other costs that the library might incur. Discrepancies may also relate to a library's subject coverage; mix of titles purchased, including both current and backfiles; and the proportion of the library's budget expended on domestic or foreign materials. These variables can affect the average price paid by an individual library, although the individual library's rate of increase may not differ greatly from the national indexes.

LMPI is interested in pursuing studies that would correlate a particular library's costs with the national prices. The group welcomes interested parties to its meetings at ALA Annual Conference and Midwinter Meeting.

The current Library Materials Price Index Group consists of compilers Catherine Barr, Ajaye Bloomstone, Stephen Bosch, Nancy Chaffin, Brenda Dingley, Virginia Gilbert, Curt Holleman, Frederick Lynden, Genevieve Owens, Wilba Swearingen, Steven Thompson, and Scott van Jacob, and editor Janet Belanger.

Book Title Output and Average Prices: 2003 Final and 2004 Preliminary Figures

Andrew Grabois

Senior Director for Publisher Relations and Content Development, R. R. Bowker

American book title output reached another all-time high of 171,061 titles in 2003, according to figures compiled by R. R. Bowker. This final total represents a staggering increase of 23,941 new titles and editions, or 16.27 percent, over the 147,120 titles reported in 2002. Fueled by an 80.11 percent increase in new juvenile titles and editions, the 2003 total follows the modest 3.83 percent increase reported in 2002. Based on preliminary figures, we can project a final title output of 185,000 for 2004, an increase of 8.15 percent over 2003, and—once again—the highest national total ever recorded. With the preliminary 2004 figure for juvenile titles already eclipsing the record-breaking total for that category in 2003, it will not be long before U.S. title output exceeds the once-unimaginable total of 200,000 new titles and editions.

As explained in the 2000 edition of the *Bowker Annual*, the title output and average price figures are now compiled from Bowker's *Books In Print* database, resulting in a more accurate and comprehensive picture of American book publishing.

Table 1 / American Book Production, 2001–2004

Category	2001 Final	2002 Final	2003 Final	2004 Preliminary
Agriculture	1,195	921	1,174	948
Arts	5,324	5,107	6,541	5,927
Biography	4,887	5,306	7,706	5,861
Business	5,023	5,028	5,399	4,782
Education	3,914	4,723	6,213	3,969
Fiction	17,349	17,303	17,599	19,426
General works	1,553	1,644	1,996	3,394
History	9,028	7,929	10,824	8,588
Home economics	2,430	2,183	3,059	2,982
Juveniles	9,582	11,208	20,187	20,497
Language	2,954	13,452	5,284	3,221
Law	3,266	2,715	3,109	2,784
Literature	6,009	4,609	4,948	4,159
Medicine	7,080	6,574	7,483	6,430
Music	3,098	1,920	2,574	2,589
Philosophy, psychology	6,320	6,663	7,187	6,920
Poetry, drama	2,924	3,328	4,391	4,603
Religion	8,015	7,436	10,343	11,658
Science	8,928	7,804	9,512	7,508
Sociology, economics	16,555	15,327	18,701	16,120
Sports, recreation	3,789	4,086	4,718	4,418
Technology	9,359	9,239	9,253	7,444
Travel	3,121	2,615	2,860	3,203
Totals	141,703	147,120	171,061	157,431

Output by Format and by Category

Book title output for 2003 showed significant increases for the hardcover and trade and other paperback formats, while mass market continued its steady decline. Hardcover output (Table 2) increased by an astonishing 21,618 titles (37.41 percent); other paperbacks, including trade paperbacks (Table 5) increased by 2,802 (3.33 percent); and mass market paperback output (Table 4) declined by 169 titles (3.16 percent).

All nonfiction subject categories showed increases in title output between 2002 and 2003. The nonfiction categories that experienced the largest year-over-year increases in new titles were biography with an increase of 2,400 titles (45.23 percent), religion with an increase of 2,907 titles (39.09 percent), history with an increase of 2,895 titles (36.51 percent), and education with an increase of 1,490 titles (31.55 percent). The Language category decreased by 8,168 (60.72 percent), reflecting the one-time introduction of some 10,000 Yiddish-language print-on-demand titles that distorted the total for that category in 2002.

Fiction, a traditional measure of the overall health of the publishing industry, experienced an increase of 296 titles (1.71 percent) between 2002 and 2003, following a decline of 46 titles (0.27 percent) in 2002. The increases registered by hardcover and mass market formats in this category were offset by a decline in

Table 2 / Hardcover Average Per-Volume Prices, 2002–2004

Category	2002 Prices	2003 Final			2004 Preliminary		
		Vols.	$ Total	Prices	Vols.	$ Total	Prices
Agriculture	$65.87	615	$34,130.88	$55.50	512	$31,474.37	$61.47
Arts	60.87	3,094	157,685.80	50.97	3,178	171,339.28	53.91
Biography	50.13	4,849	382,212.62	78.82	2,876	140,169.54	48.74
Business	99.71	2,050	204,191.83	99.61	1,896	180,376.82	95.14
Education	62.24	2,566	211,895.71	82.58	1,393	88,011.60	63.18
Fiction	30.35	5,728	157,297.69	27.46	5,941	153,490.98	25.84
General works	157.12	832	118,944.64	142.96	847	194,864.95	230.06
History	57.43	4,361	319,511.29	73.27	4,207	222,687.90	52.93
Home economics	32.28	1,393	41,488.71	29.78	1,360	39,784.45	29.25
Juveniles	22.56	15,316	430,590.23	28.11	13,522	367,454.90	27.17
Language	70.71	2,766	239,421.81	86.56	1,190	86,884.45	73.01
Law	97.32	1,289	132,669.58	102.92	1,319	141,469.81	107.26
Literature	66.95	2,231	164,299.18	73.64	2,074	129,723.76	62.55
Medicine	101.61	3,440	322,823.30	93.84	2,780	265,065.89	95.35
Music	53.04	985	50,280.24	51.05	1,029	44,227.01	42.98
Philosophy, psychology	65.61	2,871	164,084.51	57.15	2,728	151,194.77	55.42
Poetry, drama	44.87	1,198	58,002.57	48.42	1,193	48,914.91	41.00
Religion	45.74	4,043	183,667.31	45.43	5,497	216,918.60	39.46
Science	106.51	5,052	555,730.89	110.00	4,356	477,961.57	109.72
Sociology, economics	70.27	8,727	659,127.92	75.53	7,958	557,307.55	70.03
Sports, recreation	41.68	1,677	71,083.00	42.39	1,813	72,126.40	39.78
Technology	95.95	3,541	330,548.31	93.35	3,103	347,399.18	111.96
Travel	38.70	779	38,781.19	49.78	961	36,225.42	37.70
Totals	$62.84	79,403	$5,028,469.21	$63.33	71,733	$4,165,074.11	$58.06

trade and other paperbacks. The preliminary 2004 figures for Fiction show significant increases in all formats. The Juveniles category (children's and young adult titles), also seen by the publishing industry as a bellwether category, registered a historic increase of 8,979 titles (80.11 percent) between 2002 and 2003, following an increase of 1,626 titles (16.97 percent) between 2001 and 2002. Preliminary figures for 2004 already show 20,497 new juvenile titles and editions, which is an increase of 310 titles (1.54 percent) over 2003 and the highest total ever recorded. This guarantees a second consecutive year exceeding 20,000 new titles and editions.

Average Book Prices

As in 2002, average book prices were mixed in 2003, with some subject categories showing price increases and others recording decreases. The overall average book price for hardcover books (Table 2) increased by a negligible $0.49 (0.78 percent) between 2002 and 2003, following a decrease of $7.21 (10.30 percent) between 2001 and 2002. Preliminary figures for 2004 point to further decreases in this format. Hardcovers priced at less than $81 (Table 3), which constitute 77 percent of all hardcovers, experienced similar price volatility. The

Table 3 / Hardcover Average Per-Volume Prices, Less Than $81, 2002–2004

Category	2002 Prices	2003 Final			2004 Preliminary		
		Vols.	$ Total	Prices	Vols.	$ Total	Prices
Agriculture	$36.47	499	$17,288.22	$34.65	399	$14,403.01	$36.10
Arts	40.44	2,728	104,685.54	38.37	2,839	108,099.20	38.08
Biography	32.77	2,693	99,700.39	37.02	2,582	79,956.34	30.97
Business	43.18	1,328	53,341.37	40.17	1,256	49,035.54	39.04
Education	44.26	1,780	71,693.13	40.28	1,094	45,053.78	41.18
Fiction	26.86	5,647	144,293.09	25.55	5,904	147,261.06	24.94
General works	42.93	471	19,484.64	41.37	489	18,275.49	37.37
History	40.43	3,315	130,610.50	39.40	3,617	138,093.31	38.18
Home economics	27.28	1,354	35,223.61	26.01	1,327	33,963.70	25.59
Juveniles	18.91	14,788	291,979.55	19.74	13,106	264,444.46	20.18
Language	44.63	2,015	71,443.66	35.46	815	34,176.55	41.93
Law	53.26	677	32,711.77	48.32	688	32,700.16	47.53
Literature	40.99	1,688	70,095.22	41.53	1,697	70,375.96	41.47
Medicine	45.37	1,938	79,598.73	41.07	1,624	66,468.57	40.93
Music	37.15	834	29,841.64	35.78	918	27,999.71	30.50
Philosophy, psychology	41.48	2,270	87,302.58	38.46	2,225	82,816.22	37.22
Poetry, drama	34.58	1,018	35,675.12	35.04	1,081	33,251.73	30.76
Religion	32.65	3,491	105,712.43	30.28	5,036	143,225.57	28.44
Science	41.89	2,569	99,807.34	38.85	2,145	88,252.22	41.14
Sociology, economics	47.43	6,115	266,896.06	43.65	6,015	261,285.96	43.44
Sports, recreation	34.50	1,565	52,200.45	33.35	1,709	53,974.60	31.58
Technology	46.30	1,981	86,843.10	43.84	1,557	69,621.78	44.72
Travel	30.03	677	21,073.94	31.13	888	24,703.80	27.82
Totals	$35.74	61,441	$2,007,502.08	$32.67	59,011	$1,887,438.72	$31.98

average price for these selected hardcovers decreased by $3.07 (8.59 percent) in 2003, following a decrease of 74 cents (2.02 percent) in 2002. This downward trend looks likely to continue in 2004.

The overall average price for mass market paperback books (Table 4) recorded a decrease of 2 cents (0.31 percent) between 2002 and 2003, following an increase of 8 cents (1.27 percent) between 2001 and 2002. Paperbacks other than mass market (Table 5) registered an increase of $1.52 (4.85 percent), reversing the decrease of $6.87 (17.99 percent) recorded between 2001 and 2002.

The average book prices for fiction titles, usually considered a bellwether for book prices in the trade, were mixed in 2003. Hardcover fiction titles decreased $2.89 (9.52 percent), reversing the increase of $1.51 (5.24 percent) recorded in 2002. Mass market increased 1 cent (0.09 percent), while trade and other paperbacks increased 32 cents (1.77 percent). The preliminary figures for 2004 again show only mass market titles increasing in price.

Hardcover children's books (Juveniles) increased $5.55 (24.6 percent) in 2003, reversing a decrease of $1.29 (5.41 percent) recorded in 2002. Children's mass market paperbacks decreased 13 cents (2.19 percent), reversing the increase of 24 cents (4.40 percent) reported in 2002, while trade and other paperback children's titles increased $6.84 (35.39 percent), following an increase of $1.06 (5.83 percent) reported in 2002.

Table 4 / Mass Market Paperbacks Average Per-Volume Prices, 2002–2004

Category	2002 Prices	2003 Final			2004 Preliminary		
		Vols.	$ Total	Prices	Vols.	$ Total	Prices
Agriculture	$7.95	1	$7.95	$7.95	0	0.00	0.00
Arts	8.61	4	31.43	7.86	6	45.92	7.65
Biography	6.70	44	325.29	7.39	39	296.09	7.59
Business	7.57	9	80.68	8.96	3	28.89	9.63
Education	5.34	25	171.46	6.86	12	88.76	7.40
Fiction	6.71	2,348	15,769.89	6.72	2,330	15,846.37	6.80
General works	8.53	13	102.66	7.90	9	75.34	8.37
History	6.52	38	271.05	7.13	41	309.43	7.55
Home economics	7.63	25	190.49	7.62	17	132.63	7.80
Juveniles	5.73	2,054	11,511.93	5.60	2,081	11,957.99	5.75
Language	6.54	53	212.46	4.01	27	156.88	5.81
Law	7.99	3	22.44	7.48	3	26.89	8.96
Literature	7.68	71	538.03	7.58	43	310.40	7.22
Medicine	6.99	19	143.24	7.54	26	184.70	7.10
Music	7.41	7	47.42	6.77	4	29.92	7.48
Philosophy, psychology	7.17	111	854.14	7.69	100	826.75	8.27
Poetry, drama	7.18	27	197.05	7.30	14	91.53	6.54
Religion	8.20	166	1,344.91	8.10	108	848.47	7.86
Science	6.23	29	175.22	6.04	13	87.67	6.74
Sociology, economics	7.48	74	567.43	7.67	56	444.99	7.95
Sports, recreation	7.69	44	322.74	7.34	38	285.31	7.51
Technology	7.63	11	73.31	6.66	3	24.93	8.31
Travel	9.25	1	5.99	5.99	2	15.94	7.97
Totals	$6.39	5,177	$32,967.21	$6.37	4,975	$32,115.80	$6.46

Most of the other subject categories recorded mixed average prices in 2003, with many categories showing year-to-year price increases and decreases, varying by format. Philosophy/psychology, for example, shows an average price decrease of $8.46 (12.9 percent) for hardcover titles, an increase of 52 cents (7.25 percent) for mass market paperback titles, and a decrease of 44 cents (1.75 percent) for trade and other paperback titles. Religion recorded an average price decrease of 32 cents (0.7 percent) for hardcover titles, a decrease of 10 cents (1.22 percent) for mass market paperback titles, and an increase of $3.15 (16.09 percent) for trade and other paperback titles.

Each of the 23 standard subject groups used here represents one or more specific Dewey Decimal Classification numbers, as follows: Agriculture, 630–699, 712–719; Art, 700–711, 720–779; Biography, 920–929; Business, 650–659; Education, 370–379; Fiction; General Works, 000–099; History, 900–909, 930–999; Home Economics, 640–649; Juveniles; Language, 400–499; Law, 340–349; Literature, 800–810, 813–820, 823–899; Medicine, 610–619; Music, 780–789; Philosophy, Psychology, 100–199; Poetry, Drama, 811, 812, 821, 822; Religion, 200–299; Science, 500–599; Sociology, Economics, 300–339, 350–369, 380–389; Sports, Recreation, 790–799; Technology, 600–609, 620–629, 660–699; Travel, 910–919.

Table 5 / Other Paperbacks Average Per-Volume Prices, 2002–2004

Category	2002 Prices	2003 Final			2004 Preliminary		
		Vols.	$ Total	Prices	Vols.	$ Total	Prices
Agriculture	$26.69	562	$15,019.61	$26.73	439	$11,937.76	$27.19
Arts	27.87	3,447	101,634.15	29.48	2,745	89,535.97	32.62
Biography	24.42	2,824	61,726.48	21.86	2,940	69,121.21	23.51
Business	56.23	3,354	198,591.27	59.21	2,905	166,536.50	57.33
Education	35.06	3,640	130,600.16	35.88	2,561	77,372.64	30.21
Fiction	18.10	9,547	175,898.72	18.42	11,125	207,270.00	18.63
General works	46.98	1,096	52,653.35	48.04	2,540	464,899.41	183.03
History	26.05	6,459	187,507.51	29.03	4,376	147,792.18	33.77
Home economics	19.35	1,639	34,059.52	20.78	1,608	32,271.26	20.07
Juveniles	19.33	2,855	74,707.66	26.17	4,894	127,967.12	26.15
Language	29.68	2,460	84,141.25	34.20	2,002	68,864.29	34.40
Law	50.17	1,801	92,237.30	51.21	1,475	82,387.55	55.86
Literature	27.38	2,625	68,375.86	26.05	2,048	54,004.45	26.37
Medicine	44.47	4,044	168,910.82	41.77	3,641	146,699.53	40.29
Music	21.87	1,688	44,122.15	26.14	1,557	35,157.41	22.58
Philosophy, psychology	25.08	4,200	103,483.40	24.64	4,102	99,817.07	24.33
Poetry, drama	16.95	3,185	60,657.27	19.04	3,388	58,091.68	17.15
Religion	19.58	6,203	140,995.24	22.73	6,033	127,339.20	21.11
Science	49.21	4,458	178,497.93	40.04	3,098	134,918.62	43.55
Sociology, economics	32.76	9,974	394,029.45	39.51	8,230	311,844.45	37.89
Sports, recreation	21.27	3,002	66,435.70	22.13	2,576	55,600.30	21.58
Technology	59.16	5,721	372,070.39	65.04	4,386	251,029.64	57.23
Travel	19.90	2,074	47,200.81	22.76	2,237	48,010.97	21.46
Totals	$31.33	86,858	$2,853,556.00	$32.85	80,906	$2,868,469.21	$35.45

Book Sales Statistics, 2004:
AAP Preliminary Estimates

Association of American Publishers

Net sales for the entire United States publishing industry are estimated to have increased by 1.3 percent from 2003 to 2004 to a grand total of $23.72 billion, according to figures compiled by the Association of American Publishers (AAP). Overall, trade sales rose 1.9 percent to $5.16 billion. Adult trade hardbound gained 6.3 percent ($2.61 billion); paperbound sales rose 2.8 percent ($1.51 billion). Juvenile hardbound sales were down 16.7 percent ($581 million), but paperbound sales were up 3.8 percent with sales of $465.6 million.

El-hi (elementary/high school) sales were up 0.1 percent ($4.30 billion) and higher education sales rose 1.8 percent, with sales of $3.45 billion. Standardized test sales grew by 12.4 percent ($923.9 million).

Sales of professional and scholarly books were up 2 percent in 2004, with sales of $4.06 billion. Book club and mail order publications (down 8.9 percent, with sales of $1.18 billion) and mass market paperback sales (down 8.9 percent, with sales of $1.11 billion) all lost ground in 2004. Publishing sales of religious books (which include many self-help texts) grew 5.6 percent in 2004, totaling $1.33 billion. "Other" book publishing sales were up 5 percent ($2.20 billion), emphasizing the overall growth in publishing sales through this catchall designation.

Table 1 gives complete details. Please note that the table is not directly comparable with those in editions of the *Bowker Annual* previous to 2004 because of a change by AAP in the way in which the statistics are analyzed and reported; AAP decided last year that the size of the market had been overstated since 1997. The updated statistics also changed some reporting segments. The book club and mail order segments have been combined, the subscription reference category eliminated, and the "all other" segment significantly expanded.

The sales figures were prepared for AAP by Management Practice, Inc., based on year-to-date data in the AAP 2004 December Monthly Sales Report, the U.S. Department of Commerce's Census of Manufacturers, and other statistical data.

For more information, contact Kathryn Blough, AAP New York (telephone 212-255-0200 ext. 263, e-mail kblough@publishers.org).

Table 1 / Estimated Book Publishing Industry Sales, 1992, 1997, 2002–2004
(figures in thousands of dollars)

	1992 Census	1997 Census	2002	% Change from 2001	2003	% Change from 2002	2004	% Change from 2003	Compound Growth Rate 1992–2004	1997–2004
Trade (total)	$2,214,425	$4,227,878	$5,002,325	10.2	$5,063,813	1.2	$5,159,791	1.9	7.3	2.9
Adult hardbound	1,204,438	2,254,632	2,512,135	12.8	2,451,844	-2.4	2,606,310	6.3	6.6	2.1
Adult paperbound	531,641	1,175,442	1,474,219	12.9	1,465,374	-0.6	1,506,404	2.8	9.1	3.6
Juvenile hardbound	369,673	547,803	542,767	2.7	697,999	28.6	581,433	-16.7	3.8	0.9
Juvenile paperbound	108,673	250,001	473,204	-0.6	448,597	-5.2	465,644	3.8	12.9	9.3
Book clubs and mail order		1,982,213	1,422,821	-9.0	1,294,767	-9.0	1,179,533	-8.9		-7.1
Mass market paperback	927,543	878,436	1,239,100	18.6	1,218,035	-1.7	1,109,630	-8.9	1.5	3.4
Religious	262,291	753,968	840,112	-3.3	1,261,848	50.2	1,332,511	5.6	14.5	8.5
Professional	2,360,903	3,107,362	3,840,440	8.9	3,978,696	3.6	4,058,269	2.0	4.6	3.9
El-hi (K–12 education)	1,833,540	2,457,828	4,185,718	-5.0	4,290,361	2.5	4,294,651	0.1	7.4	8.3
Higher education	1,653,702	2,602,882	3,273,115	12.9	3,390,947	3.6	3,451,984	1.8	6.3	4.1
Standardized tests	210,982	356,281	731,287	13.1	821,967	12.4	923,891	12.4	13.1	14.6
All other	853,862		1,862,155	19.2	2,100,142	12.8	2,205,150	5.0		14.5
Total	$9,463,386	$17,220,710	$22,397,072	6.4	$23,420,576	4.6	$23,715,410	1.3	8.0	4.7

Source: Association of American Publishers

U.S. Book Exports and Imports, 2004

Albert N. Greco

Senior Researcher
The Institute for Publishing Research
angreco@aol.com

In 2004 the United States posted a record $665.9 billion international trade deficit, and the book industry contributed $193.9 million to that imbalance. But while the book industry's 2004 record is certainly alarming, the emergence of a "weak" dollar against many foreign currencies (especially the euro) is a harbinger that exports of U.S. books may improve and the value of imports lessen in 2005.

For many U.S. publishers, book exports were once a growing and lucrative market. Sales revenues increased 196.7 percent between 1970 and 1980, and the performance in subsequent years was equally impressive—up another 172.7 percent between 1980 and 1990. Yet few publishers, it seems, grasped the fact that slippage was taking place in the export market. Between 1990 and 2000 exports increased a modest 32.6 percent, and between 2000 and 2004 they declined 7.3 percent. Book imports, on the other hand, were growing, generating revenues for foreign publishers and printers eager to penetrate the financially appealing U.S. market. Between 1970 and 1980 the value of book imports into the United States increased at a torrid pace of 233.2 percent, easily surpassing the percentage change in exports. This surge in book imports was replicated between 1980 and 1990 (up 178.9 percent). While the percentage change slowed between 1990 and 2000 (up 86 percent), imports continued to outperform exports, and between 2000 and 2004 imports posted a respectable 21.6 percent growth rate, again outperforming exports.

One useful way to gauge the shift in trade is to evaluate a basic export-import ratio. In 1970 this ratio stood at 1.90. By 2000 the export share had eroded to 1.18, declining further to 0.90 by 2004. Table 1 outlines these developments.

Still another substantive statistical tool is to compare total exports to total book shipments. Drawing on data released by the U.S. Department of Commerce's International Trade Administration as well as various issues of the Book Industry Study Group's *Book Industry Trends,* one can determine exports as a percentage of total shipments. In 1970 exports accounted for 7.2 percent of all book shipments (which includes both domestic and export sales). By 1995 this total stood at an impressive 9.1 percent. In the following years erosion was evident, and the percentage slipped to 7.6 percent in 2000 and 6.6 percent by 2004 (Book Industry Study Group, 2005).

This meant that U.S. publishers were unable to tap into the important, and growing, international market for books, posing a serious problem for publishers facing sagging domestic sales. Table 2 outlines in detail these developments.

The Market for U.S. Book Exports in 2004

A review of the data covering the years 1996–2004 reveals only a few modest changes and some dangerous slippage. Exports sagged over that period to Japan

(text continues on page 531)

Table 1 / U.S. Trade in Books: 1970–2004
($ million)

Year	U.S. Book Exports	U.S. Book Imports	Ratio of Exports to Imports
1970	$174.9	$92.0	1.90
1975	269.3	147.6	1.82
1980	518.9	306.5	1.69
1985	591.2	564.2	1.05
1990	1,415.1	855.1	1.65
1995	1,779.5	1,184.5	1.50
1996	1,775.6	1,240.1	1.43
1997	1,896.6	1,297.5	1.46
1998	1,841.8	1,383.7	1.33
1999	1,871.1	1,441.4	1.30
2000	1,877.0	1,590.5	1.18
2001	1,712.3	1,627.8	1.05
2002	1,681.2	1,661.2	1.01
2003	1,693.6	1,755.9	0.96
2004	1,740.5	1,934.4	0.90

Source: U.S. Department of Commerce, International Trade Administration. All totals are rounded off to one decimal point. Data for individual categories may not add to totals due to statistical rounding. Due to changes in the classification of "U.S. traded products" and what constitutes products classified as "books," data prior to 1990 are not strictly comparable to data beginning in 1990.

Table 2 / U.S. Book Industry Shipments Compared to U.S. Book Exports: 1970–2004
($ million)

Year	Total Shipments	U.S. Book Exports	Exports as a Percent of Total Shipments
1970	$2,434.2	$174.9	7.2%
1975	3,536.5	269.3	7.6
1980	6,114.4	518.9	8.5
1985	10,165.7	591.2	5.8
1990	14,982.6	1,415.1	9.4
1995	19,471.0	1,779.5	9.1
1996	20,285.7	1,775.6	8.8
1997	21,131.9	1,896.6	9.0
1998	22,507.0	1,841.8	8.2
1999	23,926.9	1,871.1	7.8
2000	24,749.0	1,877.0	7.6
2001	24,742.6	1,712.3	6.9
2002	25,270.2	1,681.2	6.7
2003	25,998.5	1,693.6	6.5
2004	26,450.9	1,740.5	6.6

Source: U.S. Department of Commerce, International Trade Administration; and the Book Industry Study Group, Inc. (BISG). BISG's totals were used for shipments beginning in 1985 through 2004. Commerce totals were used for 1970–1980. Due to changes in the classification of U.S. traded products and what constitutes products classified as "books," data prior to 1990 are not strictly comparable to data beginning in 1990. All totals are rounded off to one decimal point. Data for individual categories may not add to totals due to statistical rounding.

Table 3 / Top Ten Export Destinations for U.S. Books: 1996–2004
($'000)

Country	1996	1997	1998	1999	2000	2001	2002	2003	2004	Percent Change 1996–2004
Canada	$740,393	$823,614	$807,583	$807,541	$756,667	$727,698	$742,619	$776,441	$812,833	9.8
United Kingdom	226,309	254,441	237,062	253,646	264,230	250,031	270,622	274,596	289,196	27.8
Japan	129,515	120,262	133,281	101,146	123,100	129,316	100,804	95,835	98,436	-24.0
Australia	118,076	138,070	157,928	139,588	116,302	66,010	70,806	76,067	78,549	-33.5
Mexico	62,011	58,239	58,770	65,599	73,886	63,804	64,938	68,132	66,087	6.6
Singapore	36,024	36,851	26,536	41,135	60,669	48,985	49,570	48,358	57,974	60.9
Germany	42,365	48,847	40,671	43,134	34,341	34,007	29,081	34,128	27,174	-35.9
South Korea	33,978	29,196	16,106	24,627	36,793	35,499	29,131	24,698	26,670	-21.5
Hong Kong	21,949	23,923	21,292	20,667	32,492	29,409	31,559	19,234	22,936	4.5
India	14,599	17,838	12,286	11,954	14,430	15,992	19,513	16,807	18,967	29.9

Source: U.S. Department of Commerce, International Trade Administration.

Note: Individual shipments are excluded from the foreign trade data if valued under $2,500. All totals are rounded off to one decimal point. Data for individual categories may not add to totals due to statistical rounding.

(text continued from page 528)

(down 24 percent), Australia (down 33.5 percent), Germany (down 35.9 percent), and South Korea (down 21.5 percent). Exports to NAFTA partners Canada and Mexico posted single-digit increases—Canada 9.8 percent and Mexico 6.6 percent. Significant increases were recorded by only three nations: the United Kingdom (up 27.8 percent), Singapore (up 60.9 percent), and India (up 29.9 percent). Table 3 outlines changes between 1996 and 2004.

As for events in 2004, data on the top 25 export destinations revealed some important business patterns. This cluster of nations accounted for $1.65 billion, 94.7 percent of total U.S. book exports. Overall, exports increased a modest 2.9

Table 4 / U.S. Book Exports to 25 Principal Countries: 2004

Country	Value ($'000)	Percent Change 2003–2004
Canada	$812,833	4.7
United Kingdom	289,196	5.3
Japan	98,436	2.7
Australia	78,549	3.3
Mexico	66,087	-3.0
Singapore	57,974	19.9
Germany	27,174	-20.4
South Korea	26,670	8.0
Hong Kong	22,936	19.2
India	18,967	12.9
China	18,110	16.9
South Africa	17,966	19.7
Taiwan	15,966	-22.9
Netherlands	15,877	-18.2
Philippines	13,395	16.9
New Zealand	10,643	15.7
Brazil	8,930	-11.5
France	8,168	-33.0
Belgium	6,619	-53.5
Malaysia	6,463	-15.4
Nigeria	6,371	23.3
Thailand	6,065	-14.8
Switzerland	5,286	-48.6
Italy	4,556	2.9
Spain	4,523	0.8
Total, Top 25 Countries	$1,647,758	2.9
All Others	$92,761	0.4
Grand Total	$1,740,519	2.8

Source: U.S. Department of Commerce, International Trade Administration. Note: Individual shipments are excluded from the foreign trade data if valued under $2,500. All totals are rounded off to one decimal point. Data for individual categories may not add to totals due to statistical rounding.

percent to these 25 nations. While the developing nations in the Asian-Pacific Rim recorded impressive increases in exports (notably Singapore, Hong Kong, India, China, the Philippines, and New Zealand), the industrialized nations of Europe as well as our long-standing trading partner Canada generated far smaller increases and in some instances saw declines (the Netherlands, France, Belgium). Clearly, the imbalance between the U.S. dollar and the euro adversely affected sales to Europe. This trend needs to be evaluated by the U.S. book industry to determine what, if anything, can be done to invigorate sales to these nations. Table 4 lists data on these 25 nations.

A review of book categories sheds some light on this export situation. As could be expected, sharp declines were recorded in total export revenues in the beleaguered dictionaries and encyclopedias categories (which are also experiencing deep declines in the U.S. market). Art and pictorial books also dipped sharply. The only bright spots were the performance of hardbound books (an eclectic category) and religious books. Mass market paperbacks, suffering declining sales in the United States, generated a solid 9.6 percent increase in value. Overall, revenues inched up 2.8 percent while units were off a dramatic 18.1 percent. Table 5 contains data on revenues and units.

Table 5 / U.S. Exports of Books: 2004

Category	Value ($'000)	Percent Change 2003–2004	Units ('000)	Percent Change 2003–2004
Dictionaries and thesauruses	$2,953	-7.4	618	3.0
Encyclopedias	8,292	-21.1	1,574	-24.2
Textbooks	402,057	13.2	65,254	22.4
Religious books	86,352	19.7	64,291	-19.5
Technical, scientific, and professional	391,532	5.5	75,641	-3.0
Art and pictorial books	11,113	-47.0	5,612	-9.9
Hardcover books, n.e.s.	146,608	28.5	34,568	20.9
Mass market paperbacks	228,901	9.6	137,405	10.6
Total, All books	$1,740,519	2.8	825,201	-18.1

Source: U.S. Department of Commerce, International Trade Administration.

Note: Individual shipments are excluded from the foreign trade data if valued under $2,500. All totals are rounded off to one decimal point. Data for individual categories may not add to totals due to statistical rounding.

n.e.s = not elsewhere specified

The U.S, Department of Commerce released detailed data sets on exports by book category to the top ten destinations. The overall performance of mass market paperbacks was impressive, with strong growth rates to the Philippines, the United Kingdom, Singapore, and the Netherlands. China, one of the leading sources of book imports, recorded a surprising decline of 9.9 percent as an export market. Table 6 outlines these trends.

Technical, scientific, and professional books, traditionally one of the best book export categories, posted good increases in revenues; as for units, this category experienced four respectable increases (Australia, Singapore, Germany, and China) plus five exceptionally disappointing declines (Canada, the United King-

Table 6 / U.S. Exports of Mass Market Paperbacks (Rack Size):
Top Ten Markets 2004

Country	Value ($'000)	Percent Change 2003–2004	Units ('000)	Percent Change 2003–2004
Canada	$123,375	9.9	76,638	11.0
United Kingdom	32,130	22.7	18,853	32.1
Japan	14,547	3.0	11,238	4.0
South Africa	9,381	11.4	2,821	14.9
Australia	6,106	-26.6	4,027	-30.6
Philippines	5,404	224.4	2,626	270.2
Germany	4,623	-10.1	3,655	-10.8
Singapore	4,509	-9.6	2,686	43.9
China	2,816	-2.3	1,553	-9.9
Netherlands	2,576	20.9	729	43.9

Source: U.S. Department of Commerce, International Trade Administration. Note: All totals are rounded off to one decimal point. Data for individual categories may not add to totals due to statistical rounding.

Table 7 / U.S. Exports of Technical, Scientific, and Professional Books:
Top Ten Markets 2004

Country	Value ($'000)	Percent Change 2003–2004	Units ('000)	Percent Change 2003–2004
Canada	$137,688	22.4	14,785	-5.4
United Kingdom	70,628	8.0	6,966	-31.4
Japan	42,630	2.0	3,262	-14.8
Australia	19,358	16.2	5,820	22.0
Mexico	15,435	-17.0	22,255	-8.8
Singapore	13,537	2.8	3,206	17.6
Germany	12,690	4.6	1,495	15.3
China	7,499	90.9	1,172	23.9
South Korea	6,886	48.8	705	-19.3
India	6,548	19.3	6,153	718.8

Source: U.S. Department of Commerce, International Trade Administration. Note: All totals are rounded off to one decimal point. Data for individual categories may not add to totals due to statistical rounding.

dom, Japan, Mexico, and South Korea). India, on the other hand, generated an impressive 718.8 percent increase in units and a 19.3 percent increase in revenues. Overall, this category should have had better results; English is the international language of the technical and scientific community, and the United States has long been one of the major sources of cutting-edge research. Table 7 covers this category.

The export market for textbooks was robust in 2004, up 13.2 percent in revenues and a sharp 22.4 percent in units. Although el-hi books are included, college textbooks are the dominant sector in this category. Superb sales in terms of dollars and units were recorded for Singapore, Japan, the United Kingdom, and India. The prognosis is for continued growth in this category for the next few years. Table 8 lists the growth recorded by textbooks.

Table 8 / U.S. Exports of Textbooks: Top Ten Markets 2004

Country	Value ($'000)	Percent Change 2003–2004	Units ('000)	Percent Change 2003–2004
United Kingdom	$112,331	12.8	20,950	21.7
Canada	74,125	3.8	7,266	21.9
Singapore	36,474	86.1	6,461	94.7
Japan	32,422	91.3	3,216	73.8
Australia	28,220	-6.5	4,332	-11.1
South Korea	16,379	9.9	3,615	27.2
Mexico	14,832	-34.3	3,409	44.0
Netherlands	9,266	4.5	3,252	-16.7
Hong Kong	7,539	8.9	1,359	48.5
India	5,931	147.4	1,056	112.9

Source: U.S. Department of Commerce, International Trade Administration. Note: All totals are rounded off to one decimal point. Data for individual categories may not add to totals due to statistical rounding.

Religious books posted record sales in the United States in 2004 because of the broad appeal of a cluster of books, many published by Evangelical Christian publishers. Religious books include Bibles, hymnals, testaments, prayer books, and the ubiquitous "other religious" category (composed of histories, biographies, the important religious fiction category, and so forth). The domestic performance carried over into the international market in terms of revenues (up 19.7 percent); units, however, sagged (down 19.5 percent). The United Kingdom retained its position as the primary export market for religious books in revenue terms, but trade with South Africa and Australia was impressive. Units sales among the top ten nations remained uneven, with deep declines posted by nations outside the top ten circle. Table 9 outlines the strength of this category.

Table 9 / U.S. Exports of Religious Books: Top Ten Markets 2004

Country	Value ($'000)	Percent Change 2003–2004	Units ('000)	Percent Change 2003–2004
United Kingdom	$21,546	47.8	10,094	-65.9
Canada	12,949	21.7	4,236	63.9
Australia	7,934	73.5	3,332	31.0
Mexico	6,986	-7.2	3,750	25.6
Nigeria	5,553	25.8	3,497	31.2
South Africa	2,268	145.4	1,732	178.1
Philippines	2,078	38.1	1,411	-2.1
Jamaica	1,830	6.9	1,287	-2.0
Ghana	1,671	30.7	2,292	37.0
Argentina	1,632	-15.0	1,789	36.5

Source: U.S. Department of Commerce, International Trade Administration. Note: All totals are rounded off to one decimal point. Data for individual categories may not add to totals due to statistical rounding.

Americans read bestsellers, primarily new frontlist books. While there is ebb and flow in the publication of new blockbuster bestsellers (basically triggered by John Grisham, Mary Higgins Clark, and a cluster of other "big book" authors), the export market for hardbound books surged 28.5 percent in revenues with a slightly more modest 20.9 percent increase in units. While Canada retained its leading share of U.S. hardbound book exports, impressive dollar tallies were generated by the United Kingdom (up 118.6 percent), India (up 568.9 percent), the Philippines (up 500.9 percent), and Singapore (up 345.2 percent). A review of new books scheduled for publication in 2005 contains a number of major authors with "big book" potential, although this list seems a bit "thinner" than the 2004 list; still, any new Harry Potter hardbound book provokes optimism even among skeptics. Table 10 lists information about hardbound sales for 2004.

Table 10 / U.S. Exports of Hardbound Books: Top Ten Markets 2004

Country	Value ($'000)	Percent Change 2003–2004	Units ('000)	Percent Change 2003–2004
Canada	$91,086	16.0	17,966	28.8
United Kingdom	24,433	118.6	5,964	-5.9
Australia	9,457	34.0	2,060	17.7
India	4,291	568.9	1,710	541.6
New Zealand	3,094	34.8	431	45.3
Philippines	2,087	500.9	1,597	395.0
Japan	1,490	-70.9	593	-65.2
Taiwan	1,031	14.0	263	38.1
Singapore	967	345.2	270	231.1
Germany	819	47.0	416	163.7

Source: U.S. Department of Commerce, International Trade Administration. Note: All totals are rounded off to one decimal point. Data for individual categories may not add to totals due to statistical rounding.

For the past few years, there have been three underperforming book export categories: encyclopedias, dictionaries, and art and pictorial books. Domestically, the availability of spell-check and grammar-check capabilities on computers undermined dictionaries, which had been an active book category. And of course the emergence of the Internet (in particular the rise of Google and other search engines) made the traditional 24-volume hardbound encyclopedia an anachronism—or a decorative door jam. The market also seems to have leveled off somewhat for beautifully illustrated four-color art and pictorial books.

Export totals for these three categories were depressing in 2004. Dictionaries dipped 7.4 percent in revenues (although they were up 3 percent in unit sales); encyclopedia revenues declined 21.1 percent (with a corresponding 24.2 percent decrease in units); and art and pictorial books faced a staggering 47 percent drop in revenue (and a 9.9 percent decline in units).

The day may come, probably sooner rather than later, when data on these three clusters will become marginalized, and dropped from our analysis. For this year, however, detailed information can be found in Table 11 for encyclopedias, Table 12 for dictionaries, and Table 13 for art and pictorial books.

Table 11 / U.S. Exports of Encyclopedias and Serial Installments:
Top Ten Markets 2004

Country	Value ($'000)	Percent Change 2003–2004	Units ('000)	Percent Change 2003–2004
Mexico	$2,014	-25.8	467	-21.2
Canada	1,912	31.7	424	51.6
Japan	1,085	0.4	156	-17.0
South Africa	513	0.1	53	-9.1
Australia	487	-16.9	80	-15.9
Colombia	313	45.7	69	53.9
Philippines	213	-51.4	38	-71.5
Venezuela	156	-48.1	n.a.	n.a.
Switzerland	115	-87.7	24	-87.9
Pakistan	107	n.a.	15	n.a.

Source: U.S. Department of Commerce, International Trade Administration. Note: All totals are rounded off to one decimal point. Data for individual categories may not add to totals due to statistical rounding.
n.a. = no data available.

The Market for U.S. Book Imports, 2004

In 1996 China was an insignificant source of printed books. By 2004 it held the top ranking, an impressive 27.58 percent share by value of total book imports. The increase in value of its imports into the United States between 1996 and 2004 was 829.5 percent. The United Kingdom, traditionally the primary source of U.S. book imports, languished in second place (up 9 percent between 1996 and 2004), not far ahead of Canada (up 98.2 percent between 1996 and 2004).

By the end of 2005, China—even if it generates only half the percentage increases it recorded in 2004—will emerge as the largest source of printed books in almost every book category.

Other major sources of books during these nine years included Hong Kong (down 16.2 percent in value), Singapore (up 18.5 percent), and Italy (down 13.9 percent). Rounding out the top ten nations were Germany (up 5.9 percent), Spain (up 57.2 percent), Japan (down 26.2 percent), and Korea (up 117.9 percent).

Continued declines in the U.S. dollar against major foreign currencies are likely to have a dampening effect on imports, possibly in 2005. Table 14 lists data on these nations between 1996 and 2004.

Data on the top 25 nations sending books into the United States revealed that they accounted for an overwhelming 97.9 percent of all book imports. Aside from China, other nations posting strong increases in 2004 included a number in Asia or the Pacific Rim, including Indonesia (up 152.9 percent), India (up 34.6 percent), South Korea (up 18.4 percent), and Singapore (up 10.2 percent).

Table 12 / U.S. Exports of Dictionaries (Including Thesauruses): Top Ten Markets 2004

Country	Value ($'000)	Percent Change 2003–2004	Units ('000)	Percent Change 2003–2004
Canada	$1,226	54.2	308	55.4
Mexico	611	-36.2	102	-42.9
Australia	395	62.4	71	238.4
Switzerland	166	n.a.	43	n.a.
United Kingdom	150	-11.4	27	-13.1
Micronesia	51	n.a.	13	n.a.
Singapore	44	430.7	3	535.3
Hong Kong	37	n.a.	6	n.a.
Philippines	33	-71.5	8	-70.3
Japan	32	-70.5	6	-45.0

Source: U.S. Department of Commerce, International Trade Administration. Note: All totals are rounded off to one decimal point. Data for individual categories may not add to totals due to statistical rounding.
n.a. = no data available.

Table 13 / U.S. Exports of Art and Pictorial Books 2004: Top Ten Markets

Country	Value ($'000)	Percent Change 2003–2004	Units ('000)	Percent Change 2003–2004
United Kingdom	$2,939	-18.9	1,317	-28.6
Canada	1,646	-3.1	224	-11.8
Australia	930	73.7	521	95.8
Japan	717	-92.7	382	-70.7
Germany	691	173.2	381	236.7
France	469	-67.7	233	-34.3
Taiwan	435	26.9	254	23.5
Mexico	426	-8.4	625	197.5
Netherlands	303	153.2	190	241.1
South Korea	291	-52.0	198	-33.2

Source: U.S. Department of Commerce, International Trade Administration. Note: All totals are rounded off to one decimal point. Data for individual categories may not add to totals due to statistical rounding.

Developing nations in the Western Hemisphere also penetrated the U.S. market, including Brazil (up 37.3 percent) and Mexico (up 3.7 percent), and several European nations were rather active (Switzerland, up 97.1 percent, and France, up 19.5 percent). Table 15 lists this data.

Table 14 / Top Ten Import Sources of Books: 1996–2004
($'000)

Country	1996	1997	1998	1999	2000	2001	2002	2003	2004	Percent Change 1996–2004
China	$57,402	$73,310	$101,012	$142,459	$220,895	$267,582	$338,489	$413,065	$533,524	829.5
United Kingdom	279,532	283,380	314,290	278,252	317,660	303,897	267,853	287,972	304,619	9.0
Canada	146,009	189,413	215,825	221,462	229,045	243,689	251,085	275,053	289,423	98.2
Hong Kong	221,894	203,243	200,242	229,293	224,834	229,719	223,452	189,783	185,963	-16.2
Singapore	96,124	92,134	94,672	89,000	86,630	96,325	100,610	103,383	113,900	18.5
Italy	91,268	85,514	102,525	100,475	94,983	87,779	83,360	84,167	78,567	-13.9
Germany	54,147	57,536	63,066	57,082	57,345	53,092	55,993	52,055	57,353	5.9
Spain	31,375	36,673	37,596	46,590	55,506	50,474	50,994	48,407	49,330	57.2
Japan	66,034	66,281	58,775	55,087	59,268	49,956	47,198	45,277	48,726	-26.2
South Korea	21,229	17,544	25,816	29,728	29,430	35,559	40,459	39,083	46,265	117.9

Source: U.S. Department of Commerce, International Trade Administration. Note: All totals are rounded off to one decimal point. Data for individual categories may not add to totals due to statistical rounding.

Table 15 / U.S. Book Imports from 25 Principal Countries: 2004

Country	Value ($'000)	Percent Change 2003–2004
China	$533,524	29.2
United Kingdom	304,619	5.8
Canada	289,423	5.2
Hong Kong	185,963	-2.0
Singapore	113,900	10.2
Italy	78,567	-6.7
Germany	57,353	10.2
Spain	49,330	1.9
Japan	48,726	7.6
South Korea	46,265	18.4
France	24,508	19.5
Mexico	22,627	3.7
Belgium	19,912	-5.1
Colombia	16,860	-15.4
Israel	14,508	1.5
Netherlands	13,483	-26.6
Malaysia	10,800	-4.3
Australia	10,545	21.4
Thailand	9,953	-14.5
Taiwan	7,469	-15.9
India	8,222	34.6
United Arab Emirates	7,142	5.7
Switzerland	7,013	97.1
Brazil	6,703	37.3
Indonesia	5,839	152.9
Total: Top 25 Countries	$1,893,256	10.2
All Others:	$41,095	9.2
Grand Total	$1,934,350	10.2

Source: U.S. Department of Commerce, International Trade Administration. Note: All totals are rounded off to one decimal point. Data for individual categories may not add to totals due to statistical rounding. Individual shipments are excluded from the foreign trade data if valued under $2,500.

While some of this business activity involved importing published books into the United States, a significant amount involved the offshore printing of books by U.S. publishers (in China, Indonesia, and India, for example). Starting in the late 1990s, the price of printing, paper, and binding declined in the United States because of overcapacity (the U.S. lithographic printing sector sustained some deep business declines in the 1990s). But even when time-sensitive deliveries were factored into the business model, the price of offshore printing still significantly undercut American printing costs. Recent reports (as of March 2005) indicated that U.S. printing overcapacity had diminished because of the influx of orders for el-hi books, a revving up of catalog and direct-mail pieces (the "do not call" law cut deeply into telephone solicitations, prompting a reliance on printed solicitation materials), and projected "big books" (again Harry Potter hovers over the publishing landscape with a projected 10 million print run).

As for specific book categories, imported mass market paperbacks led the way with revenues up 53.8 percent. Foreign dictionaries and thesauruses posted a solid 33.1 percent gain, perhaps a sign that foreign-language training in the United States is not as bleak as has been suggested. Other strong niches included religious books, always a popular book format (up 18.9 percent), and technical and professional books (up 17.6 percent). Hardcover imports were up 3.9 percent. Table 16 provides data on these major categories.

Table 16 / U.S. Imports of Books: 2004

Category	Value ($'000)	Percent Change 2003–2004
Dictionaries and thesauruses	$15,407	33.1
Encyclopedias	6,458	-49.6
Textbooks	217,413	10.3
Religious books	99,478	18.9
Technical, scientific, and professional	265,561	17.6
Hardcover books, n.e.s.	577,274	3.9
Mass market paperbacks	128,727	53.8
Total, All books	$1,934,350	10.2

Source: U.S. Department of Commerce, International Trade Administration. Note: All totals are rounded off to one decimal point. Data for individual categories may not add to totals due to statistical rounding. Individual shipments are excluded from the foreign trade data if valued under $2,500.

n.e.s = not elsewhere specified

A review of the major categories illuminated the emergence of China as the principal source of printed books. While the United Kingdom again dominated textbook imports, its revenues dipped 10.4 percent while units declined 25.1 percent. China, on the other hand, generated an impressive 85.5 percent increase in revenues and a staggering increase of 95.6 percent in units. If it maintains this pace, China will become the largest source of printed textbooks by the end of 2005.

Singapore was the only other trading partner with very strong results (up 130.9 percent in revenues, 50.6 percent in units). A total of six nations sustained declines in revenues or units, with Spain experiencing a precipitous decline (down 42.6 percent in revenues, 42.7 percent in units).

Some U.S. publishers invested in electronic versions of textbooks, primarily online versions. To date, it appears that students have been very reluctant to buy (or, in one instance, rent) access to electronic textbooks even though the price (or rent) is generally about half of the suggested retail price. While it is possible that electronic textbooks will replace printed texts, it is highly unlikely that this transformation will take place in this decade. Table 17 outlines these revenue and unit developments.

Table 17 / U.S. Imports of Textbooks: Top Ten Markets 2004

Country	Value ($'000)	Percent Change 2003–2004	Units ('000)	Percent Change 2003–2004
United Kingdom	$74,378	-10.4	5,482	-25.1
China	52,025	85.5	12,631	95.6
Canada	28,904	21.5	5,793	11.9
Hong Kong	15,428	-17.7	6,470	6.5
Singapore	10,910	130.9	2,186	50.6
Italy	4,214	-17.8	1,207	-30.3
Mexico	4,185	-0.6	622	-7.6
Colombia	3,279	-26.2	1,881	-11.9
Spain	3,206	-42.6	621	-42.7
Germany	2,546	21.8	213	-4.8

Source: U.S. Department of Commerce, International Trade Administration. Note: All totals are rounded off to one decimal point. Data for individual categories may not add to totals due to statistical rounding.

South Korea and China dominated the religious book category, and their results were extraordinary both in revenues (South Korea up 50 percent, China up 78.2 percent) and units (South Korea up 263.2 percent, China up 104.3 percent). It is highly likely China will emerge as the primary source of printed religious books in 2005.

Italy's performance was odd, up 174.8 percent in revenues and down 19.6 percent in units. The only other nation with double-digit gains was Colombia (up 20.8 percent in revenues though down 5 percent in units).

Some attempts have been made in the United States to offer electronic versions of religious books, notably Bibles and commentaries. To date, this initiative has been lackluster, and it is unlikely that electronic religious books will become a dominant format in the next decade or two, if ever. See Table 18 for details.

Table 18 / U.S. Imports of Bibles, Testaments, Prayer Books, and Other Religious Books: Top Ten Markets 2004

Country	Value ($'000)	Percent Change 2003–2004	Units ('000)	Percent Change 2003–2004
South Korea	$17,981	50.0	18,384	263.2
China	17,371	78.2	10,424	104.3
Israel	12,948	4.2	3,563	9.3
Belgium	8,683	5.6	2,542	-5.0
Colombia	7,543	20.8	6,763	-5.0
United Kingdom	4,474	-16.5	989	-39.2
Hong Kong	3,735	7.3	3,959	69.7
Italy	3,481	174.8	573	-19.6
Spain	3,167	-12.2	1,017	-19.3
France	2,659	-14.9	5,365	43.0

Source: U.S. Department of Commerce, International Trade Administration. Note: All totals are rounded off to one decimal point. Data for individual categories may not add to totals due to statistical rounding.

While Canada and the United Kingdom dominated the technical and professional book categories for decades, China's performance in 2004 was spectacular (up 231 percent in revenues, 89 percent in units). Canada and the United Kingdom both sustained declines in units (Canada down 22.3 percent and the United Kingdom down 16.2 percent), with Canada also experiencing an erosion in revenues (down 11.9 percent). If China is able to replicate its pace in this category in 2005, it will easily surpass both the United Kingdom and Canada; China's revenues were up 231 percent and units up 89 percent.

Italy, Japan, and Mexico also increased their profile in this niche in 2005, with Italy's strong showing in both revenues (up 69.1 percent) and units (up 124.8 percent) setting a torrid pace.

However, the real future of technical and professional books is cloudy. The emergence of viable electronic distribution systems casts a shadow over the long-term future of printed professional and technical books. While some erosion in print is anticipated in 2005–2006, the real transformation is likely to become evident by the end of the decade, leading ultimately to a marginalization of this vibrant printed-book category. Table 19 lists data on this niche.

Table 19 / U.S. Imports of Technical, Scientific, and Professional Books: Top Ten Markets 2004

Country	Value ($'000)	Percent Change 2003–2004	Units ('000)	Percent Change 2003–2004
Canada	$66,706	-11.9	39,398	-22.3
United Kingdom	66,389	25.8	5,579	-16.2
China	33,727	231.0	7,632	89.0
Germany	25,828	6.4	2,077	-19.2
Mexico	8,550	44.4	11,467	238.8
Japan	8,242	16.1	1,173	22.6
Netherlands	7,659	-29.5	663	5.5
Hong Kong	7,372	2.0	2,167	-20.6
Belgium	5,021	19.6	152	115.3
Italy	4,557	69.1	1,329	124.8

Source: U.S. Department of Commerce, International Trade Administration. Note: All totals are rounded off to one decimal point. Data for individual categories may not add to totals due to statistical rounding.

China totally dominated the hardbound import business, generating more revenues (up 32.7 percent) than the next three nations combined: Hong Kong (down 3.8 percent), the United Kingdom (down 23.7 percent), and Singapore (down 2.2 percent). China's unit statistics were also strong (up 37.2 percent at 101,686,000 units).

Germany's revenues were up (by 28.6 percent), and France's tallies were uniformly impressive, up 113.9 percent in revenues and 162.2 percent in units. A number of other nations suffered declines in revenues, notably Italy (down 27.7 percent) and Japan (down 0.3 percent).

While e-books continue to receive a great deal of attention in the United States, sales remain small (estimated at about $10 million in 2004), and it is highly unlikely that printed hardbound books will be replaced by electronic versions in the foreseeable future (and certainly not before 2015). Table 20 outlines developments in the hardbound books category.

Table 20 / U.S. Imports of Hardbound Books: Top Ten Markets 2004

Country	Value ($'000)	Percent Change 2003–2004	Units ('000)	Percent Change 2003–2004
China	$217,715	32.7	101,686	37.2
Hong Kong	80,045	-3.8	35,311	-11.4
United Kingdom	71,436	-23.7	11,453	-24.0
Singapore	48,171	-2.2	22,012	13.3
Canada	33,081	2.6	9,391	20.0
Italy	32,293	-27.7	8,230	-21.9
Spain	19,504	14.2	3,315	-19.6
Japan	15,858	-0.3	3,011	2.8
France	8,673	113.9	1,202	162.2
Germany	7,849	28.6	1,229	-15.1

Source: U.S. Department of Commerce, International Trade Administration. Note: All totals are rounded off to one decimal point. Data for individual categories may not add to totals due to statistical rounding.

Mass market paperback sales declined in the United States in 2004, and many industry observers wondered about the economic vitality of this important genre. A review of the import data revealed that relatively small amounts of mass market paperbacks were imported, with China again leading all nations in revenues (up 136.4 percent) and units (up 129 percent). It appears that unit manufacturing costs for mass market books still makes U.S. printers competitive in this area. See Table 21.

Table 21 / U.S. Imports of Mass Market Paperbacks (Rack Size): Top Ten Markets 2004

Country	Value ($'000)	Percent Change 2003–2004	Units ('000)	Percent Change 2003–2004
China	$34,833	136.4	33,592	129.0
United Kingdom	22,182	14.9	4,031	-8.1
Canada	17,283	48.8	17,272	137.0
Singapore	12,332	124.9	8,616	139.0
Italy	12,192	129.8	4,332	41.3
Hong Kong	10,358	-9.0	5,955	-31.4
Spain	5,003	67.2	2,559	20.1
Japan	1,575	13.2	207	87.5
Australia	1,510	537.2	542	169.0
Mexico	1,483	13.4	425	10.6

Source: U.S. Department of Commerce, International Trade Administration. Note: All totals are rounded off to one decimal point. Data for individual categories may not add to totals due to statistical rounding.

Encyclopedias and dictionaries remain small, almost insignificant import categories (see Tables 22 and 23 for details). It is likely these two categories will be deleted from later studies.

Table 22 / U.S. Imports of Encyclopedias and Serial Installments:
Top Ten Markets 2004

Country	Value ($'000)	Percent Change 2003–2004	Units ('000)	Percent Change 2003–2004
China	$1,162	0.1	386	5.3
United Kingdom	866	-79.8	158	-70.3
Canada	796	-28.5	72	-26.8
Hong Kong	791	-49.1	125	-56.3
Mexico	690	17.9	123	10.0
Spain	552	-6.6	26	-72.2
Netherlands	459	n.a.	130	n.a.
Slovak Republic	203	n.a.	30	n.a.
Italy	191	-64.9	49	-62.5
United Arab Emirates	159	42.3	34	230.2

Source: U.S. Department of Commerce, International Trade Administration. Note: All totals are rounded off to one decimal point. Data for individual categories may not add to totals due to statistical rounding. Calculations used two decimal points because of the size of the totals.
n.a. = no data available for previous year.

Table 23 / U.S. Imports of Dictionaries (Including Thesauruses):
Top Ten Markets 2004

Country	Value ($'000)	Percent Change 2003–2004	Units ('000)	Percent Change 2003–2004
United Kingdom	$3,160	106.6	496	8.7
China	2,570	56.9	910	10.3
France	2,450	-22.3	324	-18.8
Italy	2,257	627.3	365	139.3
Germany	1,849	7.3	439	-17.8
Singapore	805	72.4	246	59.0
Spain	504	-12.6	163	-11.0
Canada	381	-11.7	617	57.5
Poland	309	333.2	168	1388.2
Colombia	197	19.2	70	-7.7

Source: U.S. Department of Commerce, International Trade Administration. Note: All totals are rounded off to one decimal point. Data for individual categories may not add to totals due to statistical rounding.

Conclusions and Recommendations

A number of conclusions and recommendations emerged after my review of the export and import statistical data and a series of discussions with publishing executives.

1 Exports are very important to the bottom line of publishers since exports reduce dependency on the flat domestic U.S. market for books (Greco, 2005).

2 The inherent limitations of globalization pose a serious problem for publishers since a single global book market does not exist (and may never exist) for books.

3 Carefully planned foreign rights policies must coexist with book export offices, and increased attention needs to be paid to foreign rights to capitalize on this revenue stream.

4 The distribution of books from the United States to foreign markets is often hampered by inefficient export operations. More attention needs to be paid to what has emerged as a serious bottleneck.

5 Titles are printed abroad by U.S. book publishers and imported into this country because unit manufacturing costs for certain classes of books are lower abroad. With increasing levels of the international piracy of books all too evident, topping the $500 million mark in 2004 (International Intellectual Property Alliance, 2005), some attention needs to be paid to the security of digital versions of books in the hands of foreign printers.

6 The U.S. book industry needs to create a central office monitoring—on a monthly basis—export sales, changes in book category imports, and the daily impact of currency changes on the bottom line.

U.S. publishing is a cultural endeavor, and it has been since the first press was established in what is now Massachusetts in 1639. But it is also a commercial endeavor, generating billions of dollars in net publishers' revenues and employing more than 95,000 people. More attention—indeed, far more attention—needs to be paid to collecting and analyzing basic yet critical econometric data so that the U.S. book publishing industry can remain in business for another 366 years.

References

Book Industry Study Group, Inc. (2005). *Book Industry Trends 2004.* Book Industry Study Group, Inc.

Greco, A. N. (2005). *The Book Publishing Industry.* Lawrence Erlbaum Associates.

International Intellectual Property Alliance (2005). "Appendix A: IIPA Special 301 Recommendations; International Intellectual Property Alliance 2005 Special 301 Report—Appendix B: Methodology" (http://www.iipa.org).

Number of Book Outlets in the United States and Canada

The *American Book Trade Directory* (Information Today, Inc.) has been published since 1915. Revised annually, it features lists of booksellers, wholesalers, periodicals, reference tools, and other information about the U.S. and Canadian book markets. The data shown in Table 1, the most current available, are from the 2004–2005 edition of the directory.

The 25,243 stores of various types shown are located throughout the United States, Canada, and regions administered by the United States. "General" bookstores stock trade books and children's books in a general variety of subjects. "College" stores carry college-level textbooks. "Educational" outlets handle school textbooks up to and including the high school level. "Mail order" outlets sell general trade books by mail and are not book clubs; all others operating by mail are classified according to the kinds of books carried. "Antiquarian" dealers sell old and rare books. Stores handling secondhand books are classified as "used." "Paperback" stores have more than 80 percent of their stock in paperbound books. Stores with paperback departments are listed under the appropriate major classification ("general," "department store," "stationer," etc.). Bookstores with at least 50 percent of their stock on a particular subject are classified by subject.

Table 1 / Bookstores in the United States and Canada, 2003

Category	United States	Canada
Antiquarian General	1,103	88
Antiquarian Mail Order	414	12
Antiquarian Specialized	201	6
Art Supply Store	84	1
College General	3,226	181
College Specialized	122	10
Comics	210	23
Computer Software	1,347	0
Cooking	276	4
Department Store	1,673	2
Educational*	188	36
Federal Sites†	249	1
Foreign Language*	34	3
General	5,238	735
Gift Shop	153	14
Juvenile*	183	24
Mail Order General	204	16
Mail Order Specialized	524	24
Metaphysics, New Age, and Occult	206	26
Museum Store and Art Gallery	539	37
Nature and Natural History	158	7
Newsdealer	65	4
Office Supply	24	4
Other‡	2,330	294
Paperback§	180	8

Religious*	2,812	229
Self Help/Development	27	10
Stationer	7	7
Toy Store	41	20
Used*	503	96
Totals	22,321	1,922

* Includes Mail Order Shops for this topic, which are not counted elsewhere in this survey.

† National Historic Sites, National Monuments, and National Parks.

‡ Stores specializing in subjects or services other than those covered in this survey.

§ Includes Mail Order. Excludes used paperback bookstores, stationers, drugstores, or wholesalers handling paperbacks.

Review Media Statistics

Compiled by the staff of the *Bowker Annual*

Number of Books and Other Media Reviewed by Major Reviewing Publications, 2003–2004

	Adult		Juvenile		Young Adult		Total	
	2003	2004	2003	2004	2003	2004	2003	2004
Booklist[1]	5,078	5,218	3,651	3,456	—	—	8,729	8,674
BookPage[2]	n.a.	765	n.a.	132	n.a.	31	n.a.	928
Bulletin of the Center for Children's Books[3]	—	—	847	840	—	—	847	840
Chicago Sun Times	500	550	85	80	—	—	585	585
Chicago Tribune Sunday Book Section	600	600	275	275	25	25	900	900
Choice[4]	6,520	6,666	—	—	—	—	6,520	7,538
Horn Book Guide	—	—	4,728	4,429	—	—	4,728	4,429
Horn Book Magazine	9	5	259	306	101	107	369	418
Kirkus Reviews[5]	2,692	2,474	1,405	1,590	—	—	4,097	4,064
Library Journal[6]	6,205	6,210	—	—	—	—	6,205	6,210
Los Angeles Times	1,500	1,200	—	—	—	—	1,500	1,200
New York Times Sunday Book Review[5]	1,058	1,060	138	130	—	—	1,196	1,190
Publishers Weekly[7]	6,455	6,160	2,600	2,143	—	—	9,055	8,303
School Library Journal[6]	300	387	4,193	4,339	—	—	4,493	4,726
Washington Post Book World	1,500	1,500	150	150	50	50	1,700	1,700

n.a.=not available

1 All figures are for a 12-month period from September 1, 2003 to August 31, 2004 (vol. 100). YA books are included in the juvenile total. *Booklist* also reviewed 679 other media.

2 BookPage also reviewed 60 audiobooks.

3 All figures are for 12-month period beginning September and ending July/August. YA books are included in the juvenile total. The *Bulletin* also reviewed 13 professional books.

4 All materials reviewed in *Choice* are scholarly publications intended for undergraduate libraries. Total includes 858 Internet sites and 14 CD-ROMs.

5 YA books are included in the juvenile total.

6 In addition *LJ* reviewed 323 audiobooks, 399 videos/DVDs, 55 magazines, 282 books in "Collection Development," 199 online databases and CD-ROMs, 46 Web sites, and previewed 998 books and audiobooks in "Prepub Alert," "Prepub Mystery," and "Prepub Audio."

7 Adult figure includes about 60 notes; juvenile figure includes 514 notes and 386 reprint notices.

Part 5
Reference Information

Bibliographies

The Librarian's Bookshelf

Cathleen Bourdon, MLS

Executive Director, Reference and User Services Association, American Library Association

Most of the books on this selective bibliography have been published since 2002; a few earlier titles are retained because of their continuing importance.

General Works

American Library Directory, 2005–2006. 2 vols. Information Today, 2005. $299.

Annual Review of Information Science and Technology (ARIST). Vol. 39. Ed. by Blaise Cronin. Information Today, 2004. $99.95.

The Bowker Annual Library and Book Trade Almanac, 2005. Information Today, 2005. $199.

Encyclopedia of Library and Information Science. 2nd ed. Ed. by Miriam A. Drake. Marcel Dekker, 2003. $1,500.

Indexing and Abstraction in Theory and Practice. 3rd ed. By F. W. Lancaster. University of Illinois, Urbana-Champaign, GSLIS, 2003. $57.50.

International Encyclopedia of Information and Library Science. Ed. by John Feather and Paul Sturges. Routledge, 2003. $195.

International Yearbook of Library and Information Management, 2003–2004. Ed. by G. E. Gorman. Scarecrow Press, 2004. $75.

Library Literature and Information Science Index. H. W. Wilson, 1921–. Also available online, 1984–.

Academic Libraries

ARL Statistics. Association of Research Libraries. Annual. 1964–. $120.

Academic Library Trends and Statistics, 2003. Association of College and Research Libraries/American Library Association, 2004. 3 vols. $240.

CLIP (College Library Information Packet) *Notes.* Association of College and Research Libraries/American Library Association, 1980–. Most recent volume is No. 34, 2004. $28.

Digital Resources and Librarians: Case Studies in Innovation, Invention, and Implementation. Ed. by Patricia O'Brien Libutti. Association of College and Research Libraries/American Library Association, 2004. Paper $35.50.

Leadership, Higher Education, and the Information Age: A New Era for Information Technology and Libraries. Ed. by Carrie E. Regenstein and Barbara I. Dewey. Neal-Schuman, 2003. Paper $75.

Marketing and Public Relations Practices in College Libraries (CLIP Note No. 34). Comp. by Anita Rothwell Lindsay. Association of College and Research Libraries/

American Library Association, 2004. Paper $28.

SPEC Kits. Association of Research Libraries. 1973–. 10/yr. $260.

Survey of the State of Audio Collections in Academic Libraries. By Abby Smith, David Randal Allen, and Karen Allen. Council on Library and Information Resources, 2004. Paper $20.

Administration and Personnel

Access in the Future Tense. Council on Library and Information Resources, 2004. Paper $20.

The Accidental Library Manager. By Rachel Singer Gordon. Information Today, 2004. Paper $29.50.

Advances in Library Administration and Organization. Most recent volume is No. 21. Ed. by Edward D. Garten and Delmus E. Williams. Elsevier Science, 2004. $90.

Beyond the Basics: The Management Guide for Library and Information Professionals. By G. Edward Evans and Patricia Layzell Ward. Neal-Schuman, 2003. Paper $59.95.

Business Planning for Cultural Heritage Institutions. By Liz Bishoff and Nancy Allen. Council on Library and Information Resources, 2004. Paper $20.

Human Resource Management in Today's Academic Library: Meeting Challenges and Creating Opportunities. By Janice Simmons-Welburn and Beth McNeil. Libraries Unlimited, 2004. $45.

Information Security and Ethics: Social and Organizational Issues. Ed. by Marian Quigley. IRM Press, 2004. Paper $64.95.

Libraries, Mission and Marketing: Writing Mission Statements That Work. By Linda K. Wallace. American Library Association, 2003. Paper $27.

The Library as Place: Symposium on Building and Revitalizing Health Sciences Libraries in the Digital Age. National Library of Medicine and the Association of Academic Health Sciences Libraries (AAHSL), 2004. DVD $10 or free download from www.aahsl.org/building.

The Library Compensation Handbook: A Guide for Administrators, Librarians and Staff. By David A. Baldwin. Libraries Unlimited, 2003. $47.50.

The Library's Crisis Communications Planner: A PR Guide for Handling Every Emergency. By Jan Thenell. American Library Association, 2004. Paper $25.

Library Marketing That Works! By Suzanne Walters. Neal-Schuman, 2004. Paper and CD-ROM $65.

Managing Outsourcing in Library and Information Services. By Sheila Pantry and Peter Griffiths. Facet Publishing, 2004. Paper $75.

The Practical Library Manager. By Bruce E. Massis. Haworth Press, 2003. Paper $24.95.

RFID in Libraries. Library Video Network, 2004. DVD or VHS $75.

Training Skills for Staff. By Barbara Allan and Barbara Moran. Scarecrow Press, 2003. Paper $47.50.

Transitioning from Librarian to Middle Manager. By Pixey Ann Mosley. Libraries Unlimited, 2004. Paper $40.

The 2003 OCLC Environmental Scan: Pattern Recognition. By Cathy De Rosa, Lorcan Dempsey, and Alane Wilson. OCLC, 2004. Paper $15.

Advocacy

The Essential Friends of Libraries: Fast Facts, Forms and Tips. By Sandy Dolnick. American Library Association, 2004. Paper and CD-ROM $42.

Lobbying for Libraries and the Public's Access to Government Information: An Insider's View. By Bernadine E. Abbott-Hoduski. Scarecrow Press, 2003. $39.95.

Lobbying for Public and School Libraries: A History and Political Playbook. By Richard S. Halsey. Scarecrow Press, 2003. Paper $36.

Making Our Voices Heard: Citizens Speak Out for Libraries. By Sally Gardner Reed and Beth Nawalinski. Friends of Libraries U.S.A., 2004. Notebook and CD-ROM $30.

101+ Great Ideas for Libraries and Friends. By Sally Gardner Reed, Beth Nawalinski, and Alexander Peterson. Neal-Schuman, 2004. Paper $65.

Partnering with Purpose: A Guide to Strategic Partnership Development for Libraries and Other Organizations. By Janet L. Crowther and Barry Trott. Libraries Unlimited, 2004. Paper $32.

Political Advocacy for School Librarians: You Have the Power! By Sandy Schuckett. Linworth Publishing, 2004. Paper $39.95.

The Successful Library Trustee Handbook. By Mary Y. Moore. American Library Association, 2004. Paper $32.

Visible Librarian: Asserting Your Value with Marketing and Advocacy. By Judith A. Siess. American Library Association, 2003. Paper $34.

Bibliographic Instruction/Information Literacy

Dimensions and Use of the Scholarly Information Environment: Introduction to a Data Set Assembled by the Digital Library Federation and Outsell, Inc. By Amy Friedlander. Council on Library and Information Resources, 2002. Paper $40.

Hands-On Information Literacy Activities. By Jane Birks and Fiona Hunt. Neal Schuman, 2002. Paper and CD-ROM $75.

The Handy 5: Planning and Assessing Integrated Information Skills Instruction. Ed. by Robert Grover, Carol Fox, and Jacqueline McMahon Lakin. Scarecrow Press, 2002. Paper $22.50.

Information Literacy: Essential Skills for the Information Age. 2nd ed. By Michael B. Eisenberg, Carrie A. Lowe, and Kathleen L. Spitzer. Libraries Unlimited, 2004. Paper $48.

Integrating Information Literacy into the Higher Education Curriculum: Practical Models for Transformation. By Ilene F. Rockman. Jossey-Bass, 2004. $36.

Internet Workshops: 10 Ready-to-Go Workshops for K–12 Educators. By Beverley E. Crane. Neal-Schuman, 2002. Paper and CD-ROM $59.95.

Learning About Books and Libraries 2. By Carol K. Lee and Janet Langford. Upstart Books, 2003. Paper $17.95.

Library Anxiety: Theory, Research, and Application. By Anthony J. Onwuegbuzie, Qun G. Jiao, and Sharon L. Bostick. Scarecrow Press, 2004. Paper $39.50.

Media Literacy: Activities for Understanding the Scripted World. By Roberta S. Endich. Linworth Publishing, 2004. Paper $29.95.

Music Library Instruction. Ed. by Deborah Campana. Scarecrow Press, 2004. Paper $34.95.

Teaching Information Literacy: 35 Practical Standards-Based Exercises for College Students. By Joanne M. Burkhardt, Mary C. MacDonald, and Andrée J. Rathemacher. Association of College and Research Libraries/American Library Association, 2003. Paper $35.

Teaching Information Skills: Theory and Practice. By Jo Webb and Chris Powis. Facet Publishing, 2004. $99.95.

Teaching with Computers: Strategies That Work in Grades K–6. By M. Ellen Jay and Hilda L. Jay. Neal-Schuman, 2003. Paper $59.95.

Cataloging and Classification

Anglo-American Cataloging Rules. 2nd ed. By Canadian Library Association, American Library Association, and the Chartered Institute of Library and Information Professionals. American Library Association, 2002. Loose-leaf and binder $87.

Cataloging the Web: Metadata, AACR and MARC 21. Ed. by Wayne Jones, Judith R. Ahronheim, and Josephine Crawford. Scarecrow Press, 2002. Paper $39.50.

Cataloging with AACR2 and MARC21: For Books, Electronic Resources, Sound Recordings, Videorecordings, and Serials. 2nd ed. By Deborah A. Fritz. American Library Association, 2004. Loose-leaf $68.

The Concise AACR2. 4th ed. By Michael Gorman. American Library Association, 2004. Paper $40.

Education for Cataloging and the Organization of Information: Pitfalls and the Pendulum. Ed. by Janet Swan Hill. Haworth Press, 2003. Paper $49.95.

Electronic Cataloging: AACR2 and Metadata for Serials and Monographs. Ed. by Sheila S. Intner, Sally C. Tseng, and Mary Lynette Larsgaard. Haworth Press, 2003. Paper $29.95.

Essential Cataloguing. By J. H. Bowman. Facet Publishing, 2003. Paper $55.

MARC21 for Everyone: A Practical Guide. By Deborah A. Fritz and Richard J. Fritz. American Library Association, 2003. Paper $48.

Maxwell's Handbook for AACR2: Explaining and Illustrating the Anglo-American Cataloguing Rules Through the 2003 Update. 4th ed. By Robert L. Maxwell. American Library Association, 2004. Paper $65.

Metadata Fundamentals for All Librarians. By Priscilla Caplan. American Library Association, 2003. Paper $42.

Metadata in Practice. Ed. by Diane I. Hillman and Elaine L. Westbrooks. American Library Association, 2004. Paper $50.

Small Library Cataloging. 3rd ed. By Herbert Hoffman. Scarecrow Press, 2002. $35.

Understanding Metadata. National Information Standards Organization (NISO), 2004. Free PDF download file from http://www.niso.org.

Wynar's Introduction to Cataloging and Classification. Revised 9th ed. By Arlene G. Taylor. Libraries Unlimited, 2004. $49.50.

Children's and Young Adult Services and Materials

Books in Bloom: Creative Patterns and Props That Bring Stories to Life. By Kimberly K. Faurot. American Library Association, 2003. Paper $38.

Cool Story Programs for the School-Age Crowd. By Rob Reid. American Library Association, 2004. Paper $32.

Hooking Teens with the Net. By Linda W. Braun. Neal-Schuman, 2003. Paper $45.

Neal-Schuman Guide to Celebrations and Holidays Around the World: The Best Books, Media, and Multicultural Learning Activities. By Kathryn I. Matthew and Joy L. Lowe. Neal-Schuman, 2004. Paper $65.

The Newbery and Caldecott Awards: A Guide to the Medal and Honor Books. By the Association for Library Service to Children (ALSC). American Library Association, 2004. Paper $19.

Newbery and Caldecott Awards: A Subject Index. By Denise Goetting, Susan Marshall Richard, Sheryl Moore Curry, and Betsy Bryan Miguez. Linworth Publishing, 2004, Paper $39.95.

One-Person Puppetry Streamlined and Simplified: With 38 Folk-Tale Scripts. By Yvonne Amar Frey. American Library Association, 2004. Paper $38.

Rhyming, Writing, and Role-Play: Quick and Easy Lessons for Beginning Readers. By Mary A. Lombardo. Linworth Publishing, 2004. Paper $15.95.

Storytimers: Changing the World One Child at a Time. Library Video Network, 2003. Video, $130.

Technically Involved: Technology-Based Youth Participation Activities for Your Library. By Linda W. Braun. American Library Association, 2003. Paper $34.

Teens and Libraries: Getting It Right. By Virginia A. Walter and Elaine Meyers. American Library Association, 2003. Paper $32.

Totally Tubeys! 24 Storytimes with Tube Crafts. By Priscella Morrow. Upstart Books, 2003. Paper $16.95.

Twenty Tellable Tales: Audience Participation Folktales for the Beginning Storyteller. By Margaret Read MacDonald. American Library Association, 2004. Paper $28.

Youth Development and Public Libraries: Tools for Success. Ed. by Kurstin Finch Gnehm. Urban Libraries Council, 2002. $20.

Collection Development

Choice's Outstanding Academic Titles, 1998–2002: Reviews of Scholarly Titles That Every Library Should Own. Ed. by Rebecca Ann Bartlett. Association of College and Research Libraries/American Library Association, 2003. $90.

The Core Business Web: A Guide to Key Information Resources. Ed. by Gary W. White. Haworth Press, 2003. Paper $29.95.

The Coretta Scott King Awards: 1970–2004. 3rd ed. Ed. by Henrietta M. Smith. American Library Association, 2004. Paper $35.

Electronic Theses and Dissertations: A Sourcebook for Educators, Students and Librarians. By Edward A. Fox, Shahrooz Feizabadi, Joseph M. Moxley, and Christian R. Weisser. Marcel Dekker, 2004. $79.75.

From A to Zine: Building a Winning Zine Collection in Your Library. By Julie Bartel. American Library Association, 2004. Paper $35.

Graphic Novels in Your Media Center: A Definitive Guide. By Allison A. W. Lyga and Barry Lyga. Libraries Unlimited, 2004. Paper $35.

Help Wanted: Job and Career Information Resources. Ed. by Gary W. White. Reference and User Services Association/American Library Association, 2003. Paper $25.

The Kovacs Guide to Electronic Library Collection Development: Essential Core Subject Collections, Selection Criteria, and Guidelines. By Diane Kovacs and Kara L. Robinson. Neal-Schuman, 2004. Paper $125.

Reference Collection Development: A Manual. Ed. by Alice J. Perez. Reference and User Services Association/American Library Association, 2004. Paper $27.

Scholarly Publishing: Books, Journals, Publishers, and Libraries in the Twentieth Century. Ed. by Richard E. Abel, Lyman W. Newlin, Katrina Strauch, and Bruce Strauch. Wiley, 2002. $29.95.

Copyright

Complete Copyright: An Everyday Guide for Librarians. By Carrie Russell. American Library Association, 2004. Paper $50.

Copyright for Teachers and Librarians. By Rebecca P. Butler. Neal-Schuman, 2004. Paper $59.95.

Copyright Issues Relevant to the Creation of a Digital Archive: A Preliminary Assessment. By June M. Besek. Council on Library and Information Resources, 2003. Paper $15.

Intellectual Property Rights in a Networked World: Theory and Practice. Ed. by Richard A. Spinello and Herman T. Tavani. Information Science Publishing, 2004. Paper $76.46.

The Librarian's Copyright Companion. By James S. Heller. William S. Hein, 2004. Paper $45.

Customer Service

Creating the Customer-Driven Library: Building on the Bookstore Model. By Jeannette Woodward. American Library Association, 2004. Paper $38.

Face It! Using Your Face to Sell Your Message. By Arch Lustberg. Library Video Network, 2002. Video $75.

High Tech, High Touch: Library Customer Service Through Technology. By Lynn Jurewicz and Todd Cutler. American Library Association, 2003. Paper $38.

Distance Education

Attracting, Educating, and Serving Remote Users Through the Web: A How-to-Do-It Manual for Librarians. Ed. by Donnelyn Curtis. Neal-Schuman, 2002. Paper $55.

Libraries Without Walls 5: The Distributed Delivery of Library and Information Services. Ed. by Peter Brophy, Shelagh Fisher, and Jenny Craven. Facet Publishing, 2004. $125.

Library Services for Business Students in Distance Education: Issues and Trends. Ed. by Shari Buxbaum. Haworth Press, 2002. Paper $34.95.

The Electronic Library

Building an Electronic Resource Collection: A Practical Guide. By Stuart D. Lee and Frances Boyle. Facet Publishing, 2004. Paper $75.

The Changing Landscape for Electronic Resources: Content, Access, Delivery, and Legal Issues. Ed. by Yem S. Fong and Suzanne M. Ward. Haworth Press, 2004. Paper $29.95.

Diffuse Libraries: Emergent Roles for the Research Library in the Digital Age. By

Wendy Pratt Lougee. Council on Library and Information Resources, 2002. Paper $15.

Digital Futures: Strategies for the Information Age. By Marilyn Deegan and Simon Tanner. Neal-Schuman, 2002. Paper $55.

E-Book Functionality: What Libraries and Their Patrons Want and Expect from Electronic Books. By Susan Gibbons, Thomas A. Peters, and Robin Bryan. Library and Information Technology Association/ American Library Association, 2003. Paper $34.99.

The Information Commons: A Public Policy Report. By Nancy Kranich. Brennan Center for Justice, New York University of Law, 2004. Free PDF download from http://brennancenter.org/resources/books.html.

Virtual Inequality: Beyond the Digital Divide. By Karen Mossberger, Caroline J. Tolbert, and Mary Stansbury. Georgetown University Press, 2003. Paper $19.95.

Evaluation of Library Services

How Libraries and Librarians Help: A Guide to Identifying User-Centered Outcomes. By Joan C. Durrance and Karen E. Fisher. American Library Association, 2004. Paper $42.

Libraries Act on Their LibQUAL+ Findings: From Data to Action. Ed. by Fred M. Heath, Martha Kyrillidou, and Consuella A. Askew. Haworth Press, 2004. Paper $29.95.

Library Collection Assessment Through Statistical Sampling. By Brian J. Baird. Scarecrow Press, 2004. Paper $29.95.

The Library's Continuous Improvement Fieldbook: 29 Ready-to-Use Tools. By Sara Laughlin, Denise Sisco Shockley, and Ray Wilson. American Library Association, 2003. Paper $35.

Measuring for Results: The Dimensions of Public Library Effectiveness. By Joseph R. Matthews. Libraries Unlimited, 2004. Paper $40.

Outcomes Assessment in Higher Education: Views and Perspectives. Ed. by Peter Hernon and Robert E. Dugan. Libraries Unlimited, 2004. Paper $50.

Usage and Usability Assessment: Library Practices and Concerns. By Denise Troll Covey. Council on Library and Information Resources, 2002. Paper $20.

Fund-Raising

Big Book of Library Grant Money, 2004–2005. American Library Association, 2004. Paper $275.

Fundraising for Libraries: 25 Proven Ways to Get More Money for Your Library. By James Swan. Neal-Schuman, 2002. Paper $69.95.

Grants for School Libraries. By Sylvia D. Hall-Ellis and Ann Jerabek. Libraries Unlimited, 2003. Paper $35.

Made Possible: Succeeding with Sponsorships. By Patricia Martin. Jossey-Bass, 2003. Paper $30.

Information Science

Emerging Frameworks and Methods: Proceedings of the Fourth International Conference on Conceptions of Library and Information Science. Ed. by Harry Bruce, Raya Fidel, Peter Ingwersen, and Pertti Vakkari. Libraries Unlimited, 2002. Paper $40.

Introduction to Modern Information Retrieval. 2nd ed. By G. G. Chowdhury. Facet Publishing, 2004. Paper $89.95.

Understanding Information Systems: What They Do and Why We Need Them. By Lee Ratzan. American Library Association, 2004. Paper $58.

Intellectual Freedom

Banned Books Resource Guide. Office for Intellectual Freedom/American Library Association, 2004. Paper $35.

Banned in the U.S.A.: A Reference Guide to Book Censorship in Schools and Public Libraries. By Herbert N. Foerstel. Greenwood, 2002. $54.95.

IFLA/FAIFE World Report on Libraries and Intellectual Freedom. IFLA/FAIFE, 2003. Paper 27 euros.

Intellectual Freedom Manual. 6th ed. ALA Office for Intellectual Freedom/American Library Association, 2002. Paper $45.

Libricide: The Regime-Sponsored Destruction of Books and Libraries in the Twentieth Century. By Rebecca Knuth. Praeger, 2003. $39.95.

Refuge of a Scoundrel: The Patriot Act in Libraries. By Herbert N. Foerstel. Libraries Unlimited, 2004. $35.

Safeguarding Our Patrons' Privacy: What Every Librarian Needs to Know About the USA Patriot Act and Related Anti-Terrorism Measures. Association of Research Libraries, 2003. Video and manual $35.

Saving Our Children from the First Amendment. By Kevin W. Saunders. New York University Press, 2004. $48.

Interlibrary Loan, Document Delivery, and Resource Sharing

Interlibrary Loan and Document Delivery in the Larger Academic Library: A Guide for University, Research, and Larger Public Libraries. By Lee Andrew Hilyer. Haworth Press, 2002. Paper $24.95.

Interlibrary Loan Policies Directory. 7th ed. Ed. by Leslie R. Morris. Neal-Schuman, 2002. Paper $199.95.

Legal Solutions in Electronic Reserves and the Electronic Delivery of Interlibrary Loan. By Janet Brennan Croft. Haworth Press, 2004. Paper $19.95.

The Internet/Web

The Accidental Webmaster. By Julie M. Still. Information Today, 2003. Paper $29.50.

Internet and Personal Computing Fads. By Mary Ann Bell, Mary Ann Berry, and James L. Van Roekel. Haworth Press, 2004. Paper $15.95.

The Internet Under the Hood: An Introduction to Network Technologies for Information Professionals. By Robert E. Molyneux. Libraries Unlimited, 2003. Paper $40.

The Librarian's Internet Survival Guide. By Irene E. McDermott. Information Today, 2002. Paper $29.50.

Library Web Sites: Creating Online Collections and Services. By A. Paula Wilson. American Library Association, 2004. Paper $35.

Net Effects: How Librarians Can Manage the Unintended Consequences of the Internet. Ed. by Marylaine Block. Information Today, 2003. $39.50.

The Web Library: Building a World Class Personal Library with Free Web Resources. By Nicholas G. Tomaiuolo. Information Today, 2004. Paper $29.95.

Web Site Design with the Patron in Mind: A Step-by-Step Guide for Libraries. By Susanna Davidsen and Everyl Yankee. American Library Association, 2004. Paper $40.

XML: A Guide for Librarians. By Ron Gilmour. Library and Information Technology Association/American Library Association, 2003. Paper $29.

XML in Libraries. Ed. by Roy Tennant. Neal-Schuman, 2002. Paper $75.

Knowledge Management

Knowledge Management Lessons Learned: What Works and What Doesn't. By Michael E. D. Koenig and T. Kanti Srikantaiah. Information Today, 2004. $44.50.

Knowledge Management: Libraries and Librarians Taking Up the Challenge. Ed. by Hans-Christoph Hobohm. K. G. Saur, 2004. 74 euros.

Librarians and Librarianship

The ALA Survey of Librarian Salaries 2004. Ed. by Diane LaBarbera. American Library Association, 2004. Paper $70.

ARL Annual Salary Survey, 2003–2004. Association of Research Libraries, 2004. Paper $130.

Back Talk with Dr. Alan Sokoloff. By Alan Sokoloff. Library Video Network, 2002. Video $130.

Careers in Music Librarianship II: Traditions and Transitions. Ed. by Paula Elliot and Linda Blair. Scarecrow Press, 2004. Paper $29.95.

Dewey Need to Get Organized? A Time Management and Organization Guide for School Librarians. By J'aimé L. Foust. Linworth Publishing, 2003. Paper $39.95.

Dismantling the Public Sphere: Situating and Sustaining Librarianship in the Age of the New Public Philosophy. By John E. Buschman. Libraries Unlimited, 2003. Paper $60.

Ethics and Librarianship. By Robert Hauptman. McFarland, 2002. Paper $35.

Expectations of Librarians in the 21st Century. Ed. by Karl Bridges. Greenwood, 2003. $67.95.

First Have Something to Say: Writing for the Profession. By Walt Crawford. American Library Association, 2003. Paper $29.

Getting Libraries the Credit They Deserve: A Festschrift in Honor of Marvin H. Scilken. Ed. by Loriene Roy and Antony Cherian. Scarecrow Press, 2002. Paper $26.50.

The Image and Role of the Librarian. Ed. by Wendi Arant and Candace R. Benefiel. Haworth Press, 2003. Paper $24.95.

Jeremiad Jottings. By Blaise Cronin. Scarecrow Press, 2004. Paper $24.95.

Jump Start Your Career in Library and Information Science. By Priscilla K. Shontz. Scarecrow Press, 2002. Paper $22.50.

The Librarian's Guide to Writing for Publication. By Rachel Singer Gordon. Scarecrow Press, 2004. Paper $34.95.

Our Own Selves: More Meditations for Librarians. By Michael Gorman. American Library Association, 2004. Paper $28.

Public Speaking Handbook for Librarians and Information Professionals. By Sarah R. Statz. McFarland, 2003. Paper $39.95.

Reflecting on Leadership. By Karin Wittenborg, Chris Ferguson, and Michael Keller. Council on Library and Information Resources, 2004. Paper $15.

Straight from the Stacks: A Firsthand Guide to Careers in Library and Information Science. By Laura Townsend Kane. American Library Association, 2003. Paper $34.

Time Management, Planning and Prioritization for Librarians. By Judith A. Siess. Scarecrow Press, 2002. Paper $29.95.

Women's Issues at IFLA: Equality, Gender and Information on Agenda: Papers from the Programs of the Round Table on Women's Issues at IFLA Annual Conferences, 1993–2002. Ed. by Leena Siitonen. K. G. Saur, 2004. $78.

Library Automation

The Accidental Systems Librarian. By Rachel Singer Gordon. Information Today, 2002. Paper $29.50.

Directory of Library Automation Software, Systems, and Services. Ed. by Pamela Cibbarelli. Information Today, 2004. Paper $89. Published biennially.

Neal-Schuman Directory of Management Software for Public Access Computers. By Michael P. Sauers and Louise E. Alcorn. Neal-Schuman, 2003. Paper $99.95.

Library Buildings and Space Planning

Energy Management Strategies in Public Libraries. By Edward Dean. Libris Design, 2002. Paper $35.

Libraries Designed for Users: A 21st Century Guide. By Nolan Lushington. Neal-Schuman, 2002. Paper $99.95.

The Most Beautiful Libraries in the World. By Jacques Bosser. Abrams, 2003. $50.

Library History

A Brief History of the Future of Libraries. By Gregg Sapp. Scarecrow Press, 2003. $65.

Carnegie. By Peter Krass. Wiley, 2002. $35.

A History of the Farmington Plan. By Ralph D. Wagner. Scarecrow Press, 2002. $69.50.

JSTOR: A History. By Roger C. Schonfeld. Princeton University Press, 2003. $29.95.

Library: An Unquiet History. By Matthew Battles. W. W. Norton, 2003. $24.95.

The Road Home: My Life and Times. By Vartan Gregorian. Simon & Schuster, 2003. $29.95.

Winsor, Dewey, and Putnam: The Boston Experience. By Donald G. Davis, Jr., Kenneth E. Carpenter, Wayne A. Wiegand, and Jane Aikin. GLIS Publications Office, University of Illinois, 2002. Paper $8.

Wrestling with the Muse: Dudley Randall and the Broadside Press. By Melba Joyce Boyd. Columbia University Press, 2004. $29.50.

Museums/Archives

Developing and Maintaining Practical Archives: A How-to-Do-It Manual for Archivists and Librarians. 2nd ed. By Gregory S. Hunter. Neal-Schuman, 2003. Paper $65.

Libraries, Museums and Archives: Legal Issues and Ethical Challenges in the New Information Era. Ed. by Thomas A. Lipinski. Scarecrow Press, 2002. $59.95.

Moving Archives: The Experience of Eleven Archivists. Ed. by John Newman and Walter Jones. Scarecrow Press, 2003. $35.

Thirty Years of Electronic Records. Ed. by Bruce I. Ambacher. Scarecrow Press, 2003. Paper $42.

Preservation

Assessing Preservation Needs: A Self-Survey Guide. By Beth Patkus. Northeast Document Conservation Center, 2003. Paper $15.

Developing Print Repositories: Models for Shared Preservation and Access. By Bernard Reilly, Jr. Council on Library and Information Resources, 2003. Paper $20.

National Digital Preservation Initiatives: An Overview of Developments in Australia, France, the Netherlands, and the United Kingdom and of Related International Activity. By Neil Beagrie. Council on Library and Information Resources, 2003. Paper $20.

An Ounce of Prevention: Integrated Disaster Planning for Archives, Libraries, and Record Centers. 2nd ed. By Johanna Wellheiser and Jude Scott. Scarecrow Press, 2002. Paper $30.

Protecting Your Library's Digital Sources: The Essential Guide to Planning and Preservation. By Miriam B. Kahn. American Library Association, 2004. Paper $40.

The State of Digital Preservation: An International Perspective. Council on Library

and Information Resources, 2002. Paper $20.

To Preserve and Protect: The Strategic Stewardship of Cultural Resources. Library of Congress Symposium. Superintendent of Documents, 2002. Paper $23.

Vandals in the Stacks? A Response to Nicholson Baker's Assault on Libraries. By Richard J. Cox. Greenwood, 2002. $64.95.

Public Libraries

Author Day Adventures: Bringing Literacy to Life with an Author Visit. By Helen Foster James. Scarecrow Press, 2003. Paper $19.95.

Consumer Health Information for Public Librarians. By Lynda M. Baker and Virginia Manbeck. Scarecrow Press, 2002. $45.

Creating Policies for Results: From Chaos to Clarity. By Sandra Nelson and June Garcia. American Library Association, 2003. Paper $50.

Exemplary Public Libraries: Lessons in Leadership, Management and Service. By Joy M. Greiner. Libraries Unlimited, 2004. $45.

Free and Public: One Hundred and Fifty Years at the Public Library of Cincinnati and Hamilton County, 1853–2003. By John Fleischman. Orange Frazer Press, 2003. $34.95.

Hennen's Public Library Planner: A Manual and Interactive CD-ROM. By Thomas J. Hennen, Jr. Neal-Schuman, 2004. Paper and CD-ROM $125.

Introduction to Public Librarianship. By Kathleen de la Peña McCook. Neal-Schuman, 2004. Paper $59.95.

The Public Library Manager's Forms, Policies and Procedures Handbook with CD-ROM. By Rebecca Brumley. Neal-Schuman, 2004. Paper with CD-ROM $125.

Public Library Data Service Statistical Report. Public Library Association/American Library Association, 2004. Paper $80.

The Public Library Start-Up Guide. By Christine Lind Hage. American Library Association, 2003. Paper $42.

The Responsive Public Library: How to Develop and Market a Winning Collection.

2nd ed. By Sharon L. Baker and Karen L. Wallace. Libraries Unlimited, 2002. Paper $46.

Small Libraries: A Handbook for Successful Management. 2nd ed. By Sally Gardner Reed. McFarland, 2002. Paper $35.

Readers' Advisory

ALA's Guide to Best Reading. American Library Association, 2004. Kit $34.95. Camera-ready lists of the year's best books for children, teens, and adults.

The Booktalker's Bible: How to Talk About the Books You Love to Any Audience. By Chapple Langemack. Libraries Unlimited, 2003. Paper $30.

Booktalks and More: Motivating Teens to Read. By Lucy Schall. Libraries Unlimited, 2003. Paper $35.

Christian Fiction: A Guide to the Genre. By John Mort. Libraries Unlimited, 2002. $55.

Connecting Boys with Books: What Libraries Can Do. By Michael Sullivan. American Library Association, 2003. Paper $32.

The Horror Readers' Advisory: The Librarian's Guide to Vampires, Killer Tomatoes, and Haunted Houses. By Becky Siegel Spratford and Tammy Hennigh Clausen. American Library Association, 2004. Paper $36.

Readers' Advisor's Companion. Ed. by Kenneth D. Shearer and Robert Burgin. Libraries Unlimited, 2002. Paper $37.50.

Reading and Reader Development: The Pleasure of Reading. By Judith Elkin, Briony Train, and Debbi Denham. Facet Publishing, 2003. $85.

Reference Services

Conducting the Reference Interview. Library Video Network, 2004. VHS or DVD $99.

The Digital Reference Research Agenda. Ed. by R. David Lankes, Scott Nicholson, and Abby Goodrum. Association of College and Research Libraries/American Library Association, 2003. Paper $24.

Digital Reference Services. Ed. by Bill Katz. Haworth Press, 2004. Paper $34.95.

Digital Versus Non-Digital Reference: Ask a Librarian Online and Offline. Ed. by Jessamyn West. Haworth Press, 2004. Paper $29.95.

Doing the Work of Reference: Practical Tips for Excelling as a Reference Librarian. Ed. by Celia Hales Mabry. Haworth Press, 2002. Paper $44.95.

Going Live: Starting and Running a Virtual Reference Service. By Steve Coffman. American Library Association, 2003. Paper $42.

Introduction to Reference Work in the Digital Age. By Joseph Janes. Neal-Schuman, 2003. Paper $59.95.

The Librarian's Guide to Genealogical Services and Research. By James Swan. Neal-Schuman, 2004. Paper $75.

Puzzles and Essays from "The Exchange": Tricky Reference Questions. By Charles R. Anderson. Haworth Press, 2003. Paper $14.95.

Reading and the Reference Librarian: The Importance to Library Service of Staff Reading Habits. By Juris Dilevko and Lisa Gottlieb. McFarland, 2004. Paper $45.

The Virtual Reference Experience: Integrating Theory into Practice. Ed. by David Lankes, Joseph Janes, Linda C. Smith, and Christina M. Finneran. Neal-Schuman, 2004. Paper $75.

Virtual Reference Services: Issues and Trends. Ed. by Stacey Kimmel and Jennifer Heise. Haworth Press, 2003. Paper $29.95.

Virtual Reference Training: The Complete Guide to Providing Anytime, Anywhere Answers. By Buff Hirko and Mary Bucher Ross. American Library Association, 2004. Paper $42.

School Libraries/Media Centers

Center Stage: Library Programs that Inspire Middle School Patrons. By Patricia Potter Wilson and Roger Leslie. Libraries Unlimited, 2002. Paper $35.

Helping Teachers Teach: A School Library Media Specialist's Role. 3rd ed. By Philip M. Turner and Ann Marlow Riedling. Libraries Unlimited, 2003. Paper $40.

Learning Right from Wrong in the Digital Age: An Ethics Guide for Parents, Teach-

ers, *Librarians and Others Who Care About Computer-Using Young People.* Linworth Publishing, 2003. Paper $44.95.

Lesson Plans for the Busy Librarian: A Standards-Based Approach for the Elementary Library Media Center. By Joyce Keeling. Libraries Unlimited, 2002. Paper $30.

The Power of Reading: Insights from the Research. 2nd. ed. By Stephen D. Krashen. Libraries Unlimited, 2004. Paper $25.

Power Tools Recharged: 125+ Essential Forms and Presentations for Your School Library Information Program. By Joyce Kasman Valenza. American Library Association, 2004. Loose-leaf with CD-ROM $55.

Redefining Literacy for the 21st Century. By David F. Warlick. Linworth Publishing, 2004. Paper $44.95.

Still Talking That Book! Booktalks to Promote Reading Grades 3–12, Volume IV. By Cathlyn Thomas and Carol Littlejohn. Linworth Publishing, 2003. Paper $36.95.

Technologies for Education: A Practical Guide. 4th ed. By Ann E. Barron, Gary W. Orwig, Karen S. Ivers, and Nick Lilavois. Libraries Unlimited, 2002. Paper $48.

Serials

Do We Want to Keep Our Newspapers? Ed. by David McKitterick. King's College London, 2003. Paper £15.

E-Serials Cataloging: Access to Continuing and Integrating Resources Via the Catalog and the Web. Ed. by Jim Cole and Wayne Jones. Haworth Press, 2002. Paper $39.95.

E-Serials: Publishers, Libraries, Users and Standards. 2nd ed. Ed. by Wayne Jones. Haworth Press, 2002. Paper $39.95.

Introduction to Serials Work for Library Technicians. By Scott Millard. Haworth Press, 2004. $39.95.

Journals of the Century. Ed. by Tony Stankus. Haworth Press, 2002. Paper $29.95.

Serials in the Park. Ed. by Patricia Sheldahl French and Richard L. Worthing. Haworth Press, 2004. Paper $34.95.

The Nonsubscription Side of Periodicals: Changes in Library Operations and Costs Between Print and Electronic Formats. By Roger C. Schonfeld, Donald W. King, Ann

Okerson, and Eileen Gifford Fenton. Council on Library and Information Resources, 2004. Paper $20.

Services for Special Groups

Bridging the Digital Divide in the Spanish Speaking Community. Colorado Sate Library. Library Video Network, 2004. DVD $40.

5-Star Programming and Services for Your 55+ Customers. By Barbara T. Mates. American Library Association, 2003. Paper $42.

From Outreach to Equity: Innovative Models of Library Policy and Practice. Ed. by Robin Osborne. American Library Association, 2004. Paper $32.

Libraries to the People: Histories of Outreach. Ed. by Robert S. Freeman and David M. Hovde. McFarland, 2002. Paper $39.95.

Serving Seniors: A How-to-Do-It Manual for Librarians. By RoseMary Honnold and Saralyn A. Mesaros. Neal-Schuman, 2004. Paper $59.95.

Technical Services

The Complete Guide to Acquisitions Management. By Frances C. Wilkinson and Linda K. Lewis. Libraries Unlimited, 2003. Paper $45.

Guide to Out-of-Print Materials (ALCTS Acquisitions Guides Series #12). By Narda Tafuri, Anna Seaberg, and Gary Handman. Scarecrow Press, 2004. Paper $18.50.

Innovative Redesign and Reorganization of Library Technical Services: Paths for the Future and Case Studies. Ed. by Bradford Lee Eden. Libraries Unlimited, 2004. Paper $45.

Periodicals and Periodical Indexes

Acquisitions Librarian
Advanced Technology Libraries
Against the Grain
American Archivist

American Libraries
Behavioral and Social Sciences Librarian
Book Links
Booklist
Bookmobile and Outreach Services
The Bottom Line
Cataloging and Classification Quarterly
Catholic Library World
Children and Libraries: The Journal of the
  Association for Library Services to Chil-
  dren
CHOICE
Collection Management
College and Research Libraries
College and Undergraduate Libraries
Community and Junior College Libraries
Computers in Libraries
Criticas
DTTP: Documents to the People
The Electronic Library
Information Technology and Libraries
Information Outlook (formerly Special Li-
  braries)
Interface
Journal of Academic Librarianship
Journal of Education for Library and Infor-
  mation Science
Journal of Information Ethics
Journal of Interlibrary Loan, Document
  Delivery and Information Supply
Journal of Library Administration
Journal of the American Society for Informa-
  tion Science and Technology
Journal of the Medical Library Association
Knowledge Quest
Law Library Journal
Legal Reference Services Quarterly
Libraries & Culture
Library Administration and Management
Library and Archival Security
Library and Information Science Research
  (LIBRES)

Library Hi-Tech News
Library Hotline
Library Issues: Briefings for Faculty and
  Academic Administrators
Library Journal
Library Media Connection (formerly Book
  Report and Library Talk
Library Mosaics
The Library Quarterly
Library Resources and Technical Services
Library Technology Reports
Library Trends
Medical Reference Services Quarterly
MultiMedia Schools
Music Library Association Notes
Music Reference Services Quarterly
Net Connect
The One-Person Library
portal: Libraries and the Academy
Progressive Librarian
Public Libraries
Public Library Quarterly
RBM: A Journal of Rare Books, Manuscripts,
  and Cultural Heritage
Reference and User Services Quarterly (for-
  merly RQ)
Reference Librarian
Resource Sharing & Information Networks
RSR: Reference Services Review
Rural Libraries
School Library Journal
Science & Technology Libraries
Searcher
Serials Librarian
Serials Review
Technical Services Quarterly
Technicalities
Unabashed Librarian
Video Librarian
Voice of Youth Advocates (VOYA)
World Libraries
Young Adult Library Services

Ready Reference

How to Obtain an ISBN

Doreen Gravesande
Director
United States ISBN/SAN Agency

The International Standard Book Numbering (ISBN) system was introduced into the United Kingdom by J. Whitaker & Sons Ltd. in 1967 and into the United States in 1968 by R. R. Bowker. The Technical Committee on Documentation of the International Organization for Standardization (ISO TC 46) is responsible for the international standard.

The purpose of this standard is to "establish the specifications for the International Standard Book Number (ISBN) as a unique international identification system for each product form or edition of a monographic publication published or produced by a specific publisher." The standard specifies the construction of an ISBN, the rules for assignment and use of an ISBN, and all metadata associated with the allocation of an ISBN.

Types of monographic publications to which an ISBN may be assigned include printed books and pamphlets (in various product formats); electronic publications (either on the Internet or on physical carriers such as CD-ROMs or diskettes); educational/instructional films, videos and transparencies; educational/instructional software; audio books on cassettes or CD or DVD; braille publications; and microform publications.

Serial publications, printed music, and musical sound recordings are excluded from the ISBN standard as they are covered by other identification systems.

The ISBN is used by publishers, distributors, wholesalers, bookstores, and libraries, among others, in 217 countries and territories as an ordering and inventory system. It expedites the collection of data on new and forthcoming editions of monographic publications for print and electronic directories used by the book trade. Its use also facilitates rights management and the monitoring of sales data for the publishing industry.

The current ISBN consists of 10 digits. On January 1, 2007, a revised ISBN standard will change the ISBN to a 13-digit identifier that will substantially increase the numbering capacity of the worldwide ISBN system.

All existing 10-digit ISBNs at that time will be converted to a 13-digit ISBN by the addition of the Bookland EAN prefix 978 (as is currently done when a 10-digit ISBN is converted to a 13-digit bar code).

Once all 10-digit ISBNs have been exhausted by national ISBN agencies, the International ISBN Agency will begin allocating new complete 13-digit ISBNs with the EAN prefix 979.

Construction of an ISBN

An ISBN currently consists of 10 digits separated into the following parts:

1 Group identifier: national, regional, or geographic area
2 Publisher or producer identifier
3 Title identifier
4 Check digit

When an ISBN is written or printed, it should be preceded by the letters ISBN, and each part should be separated by a space or hyphen. In the United States, the hyphen is used for separation, as in the following example: ISBN 1-879500-01-9. In this example, 1 is the group identifier, 879500 is the publisher identifier, 01 is the title identifier, and 9 is the check digit. The group of English-speaking countries, which includes the United States, Australia, Canada, New Zealand, and the United Kingdom, uses the group identifiers 0 and 1.

The ISBN Organization

The administration of the ISBN system is carried out at three levels—through the International ISBN Agency in Berlin, through the national agencies, and through the publishing houses themselves. The International ISBN Agency in Berlin, which is responsible for assigning country prefixes and for coordinating the worldwide implementation of the system, has an advisory panel that represents the International Organization for Standardization (ISO), publishers, and libraries. The International ISBN Agency publishes the *Publishers International ISBN Directory,* which is a listing of all national agencies' publishers with their assigned ISBN publisher prefixes. R. R. Bowker, as the publisher of *Books In Print* with its extensive and varied database of publishers' addresses, was the obvious place to initiate the ISBN system and to provide the service to the U.S. publishing industry. To date, the U.S. ISBN Agency has entered more than 160,000 publishers into the system.

ISBN Assignment Procedure

Assignment of ISBNs is a shared endeavor between the U.S. ISBN Agency and the publisher. Publishers can make online application through the ISBN Agency's Web site, or by phone or fax. After an application is received and processed by the agency, an ISBN Publisher Prefix is assigned, along with a computer generated block of ISBNs that is mailed or e-mailed to the publisher. The publisher then has the responsibility to assign an ISBN to each title, keep an accurate record of each number assigned, and register each title in the *Books In Print* database at http://www.bowkerlink.com. It is the responsibility of the ISBN Agency to validate assigned ISBNs and keep a record of all ISBN publisher prefixes in circulation.

ISBN implementation is very much market-driven. Major distributors, wholesalers, retailers, and so forth recognize the necessity of the ISBN system and request that publishers register with the ISBN Agency. Also, the ISBN is a mandatory bibliographic element in the International Standard Bibliographical Description (ISBD). The Library of Congress Cataloging in Publication (CIP) Division directs publishers to the agency to obtain their ISBN prefixes.

Location and Display of the ISBN

On books, pamphlets, and other printed material, the ISBN shall be printed on the verso of the title leaf or, if this is not possible, at the foot of the title leaf itself. It should also appear on the outside back cover or on the back of the jacket if the book has one (the lower right-hand corner is recommended). The ISBN shall also appear on any accompanying promotional materials following the provisions for location according to the format of the material.

On other monographic publications, the ISBN shall appear on the title or credit frames and any labels permanently affixed to the publication. If the publication is issued in a container that is an integral part of the publication, the ISBN shall be displayed on the label. If it is not possible to place the ISBN on the item or its label, then the number should be displayed on the bottom or the back of the container, box, sleeve, or frame. It should also appear on any accompanying material, including each component of a multi-type publication.

Printing of ISBN in Machine-Readable Coding

All books should carry ISBNs in Bookland EAN bar code machine-readable format. All ISBN Bookland EAN bar codes start with the EAN prefix 978 for books (see Figure 1).

The 978 ISBN Bookland/EAN prefix is followed by the first nine digits of the ISBN. The check digit of the ISBN is dropped and replaced by a check digit calculated according to the EAN rules.

Figure 1 / Printing the ISBN in Bookland/EAN Symbology

ISBN 1-879500-01-9

9 781879 500013

The following is an example of the conversion of the ISBN to ISBN Bookland/EAN:

ISBN	1-879500-01-9
ISBN without check digit	1-879500-01
Adding EAN flag	978187950001
EAN with EAN check digit	9781879500013

After January 1, 2007, publishers with existing 10-digit ISBNs will need to convert them to a 13-digit ISBN by the addition of the EAN prefix 978 (see Figure 1 above).

A new 13-digit ISBN beginning with the EAN prefix 979 and issued by the International ISBN Agency will not require conversion.

Five-Digit Add-On Code

In the United States, a five-digit add-on code is used for additional information. In the publishing industry, this code is used for price information. The lead digit of the five-digit add-on has been designated a currency identifier, when the add-on is used for price. Number 5 is the code for the U.S. dollar; 6 denotes the Canadian dollar; 1 the British pound; 3 the Australian dollar; and 4 the New Zealand dollar. Publishers that do not want to indicate price in the add-on should print the code 90000 (see Figure 2).

Figure 2 / Printing the ISBN Bookland/EAN Number in Bar Code with the Five-Digit Add-On Code

978 = ISBN Bookland/EAN prefix
5 + Code for U.S. $
0995 = $9.95

90000 means no information
in the add-on code

Reporting the Title and the ISBN

After the publisher reports a title to the ISBN Agency, the number is validated and the title is listed in the many R. R. Bowker hard-copy and electronic publications, including *Books in Print, Forthcoming Books, Paperbound Books in Print, Books in Print Supplement, Books Out of Print, Books in Print Online, Books in Print Plus-CD ROM, Children's Books in Print, Subject Guide to Children's Books in Print, Books Out Loud: Bowker's Guide to AudioBooks; Bowker's Complete Video Directory, The Software Encyclopedia, Software for Schools,* and other specialized publications.

For ISBN application and information, visit the ISBN Agency Web site at http://www.isbn.org, call the toll free number 877-310-7333, fax 908-219-0188, or write to the United States ISBN Agency, 630 Central Ave., New Providence, NJ 07974.

How to Obtain an ISSN

National Serials Data Program
Library of Congress

In the early 1970s the rapid increase in the production and dissemination of information and an intensified desire to exchange information about serials in computerized form among different systems and organizations made it increasingly clear that a means to identify serial publications at an international level was needed. The International Standard Serial Number (ISSN) was developed and has become the internationally accepted code for identifying serial publications.

The number itself has no significance other than as a brief, unique, and unambiguous identifier. It is an international standard, ISO 3297, as well as a U.S. standard, ANSI/NISO Z39.9. The ISSN consists of eight digits in Arabic numerals 0 to 9, except for the last, or check, digit, which can be an X. The numbers appear as two groups of four digits separated by a hyphen and preceded by the letters ISSN—for example, ISSN 1234-5679.

The ISSN is not self-assigned by publishers. Administration of the ISSN is coordinated through the ISSN Network, an intergovernmental organization within the UNESCO/UNISIST program. The network consists of national and regional centers, coordinated by the ISSN International Centre, located in Paris. Centers have the responsibility to register serials published in their respective countries.

Because serials are generally known and cited by title, assignment of the ISSN is inseparably linked to the key title, a standardized form of the title derived from information in the serial issue. Only one ISSN can be assigned to a title; if the title changes, a new ISSN must be assigned. Centers responsible for assigning ISSNs also construct the key title and create an associated bibliographic record.

The ISSN International Centre handles ISSN assignments for international organizations and for countries that do not have a national center. It also maintains and distributes the collective ISSN database that contains bibliographic records corresponding to each ISSN assignment as reported by the rest of the network. The database contains more than 1 million ISSNs.

In the United States, the National Serials Data Program at the Library of Congress is responsible for assigning and maintaining the ISSNs for all U.S. serial titles. Publishers wishing to have an ISSN assigned should request an application form from the program, or download one from the program's Web site, and ask for an assignment. Assignment of the ISSN is free, and there is no charge for its use.

The ISSN is used all over the world by serial publishers to distinguish similar titles from each other. It is used by subscription services and libraries to manage files for orders, claims, and back issues. It is used in automated check-in systems by libraries that wish to process receipts more quickly. Copyright centers use the ISSN as a means to collect and disseminate royalties. It is also used as an identification code by postal services and legal deposit services. The ISSN is included as a verification element in interlibrary lending activities and for union catalogs as a collocating device. In recent years, the ISSN has been incorporated into bar codes for optical recognition of serial publications and into the standards for the identification of issues and articles in serial publications. Another recent use for the ISSN is as a linking mechanism in online systems where the ISSN can serve to connect catalog records or citations in abstracting and indexing databases with full-text journal content via OpenURL resolvers or reference linking services.

For further information about the ISSN or the ISSN Network, U.S. libraries and publishers should contact the National Serials Data Program, Library of Congress, Washington, DC 20540-4160; 202-707-6452; fax 202-707-6333; e-mail issn@loc.gov. ISSN application forms and instructions for obtaining an ISSN are also available via the Library of Congress World Wide Web site, http://lcweb.loc.gov/issn.

Non-U.S. parties should contact the ISSN International Centre, 20 rue Bachaumont, 75002 Paris, France; telephone 33-1-44-88-22-20; fax 33-1-40-26-32-43; e-mail issnic@issn.org; World Wide Web http://www.ISSN.org.

How to Obtain an SAN

Doreen Gravesande

Director
United States ISBN/SAN Agency

SAN stands for Standard Address Number. It is a unique identification code for addresses of organizations that are involved in or served by the book industry, and that engage in repeated transactions with other members within this group. It is recognized as the identification code for electronic communication within the industry.

For purposes of this standard, the book industry includes book publishers, book wholesalers, book distributors, book retailers, college bookstores, libraries, library binders, and serial vendors. Schools, school systems, technical institutes, and colleges and universities are not members of this industry, but are served by it and therefore included in the SAN system.

The purpose of SAN is to facilitate communications among these organizations, of which there are several hundreds of thousands, that engage in a large volume of separate transactions with one another. These transactions include purchases of books by book dealers, wholesalers, schools, colleges, and libraries from publishers and wholesalers; payments for all such purchases; and other communications between participants. The objective of this standard is to establish an identification code system by assigning each address within the industry a unique code to be used for positive identification for all book and serial buying and selling transactions.

Many organizations have similar names and multiple addresses, making identification of the correct contact point difficult and subject to error. In many cases, the physical movement of materials takes place between addresses that differ from the addresses to be used for the financial transactions. In such instances, there is ample opportunity for confusion and errors. Without identification by SAN, a complex record-keeping system would have to be instituted to avoid introducing errors. In addition, problems with the current numbering system—such as errors in billing, shipping, payments, and returns—are significantly reduced by using the SAN system. SAN will also eliminate one step in the order fulfillment process: the "look-up procedure" used to assign account numbers. Previously a store or library dealing with 50 different publishers was assigned a different account number by each of the suppliers. SAN solved this problem. If a publisher indicates its SAN on its stationery and ordering documents, vendors to whom it sends transactions do not have to look up the account number, but can proceed immediately to process orders by SAN.

Libraries are involved in many of the same transactions as book dealers, such as ordering and paying for books and charging and paying for various services to other libraries. Keeping records of transactions, whether these involve buying, selling, lending, or donations, entails similar operations that require an SAN. Having the SAN on all stationery will speed up order fulfillment and eliminate errors in shipping, billing, and crediting; this, in turn, means savings in both time and money.

History

Development of the Standard Address Number began in 1968 when Russell Reynolds, general manager of the National Association of College Stores (NACS), approached R. R. Bowker and suggested that a "Standard Account Number" system be implemented in the book industry. The first draft of a standard was prepared by an American National Standards Institute (ANSI) Committee Z39 subcommittee, which was co-chaired by Russell Reynolds and Emery Koltay of Bowker. After Z39 members proposed changes, the current version of the standard was approved by NACS on December 17, 1979.

Format

The SAN consists of six digits plus a seventh *Modulus 11* check digit; a hyphen follows the third digit (XXX-XXXX) to facilitate transcription. The hyphen is to be used in print form, but need not be entered or retained in computer systems. Printed on documents, the Standard Address Number should be preceded by the identifier "SAN" to avoid confusion with other numerical codes (SAN XXXXXXX).

Check Digit Calculation

The check digit is based on *Modulus 11,* and can be derived as follows:

1. Write the digits of the basic number.

   2 3 4 5 6 7
2. Write the constant weighting factors associated with each position by the basic number.

   7 6 5 4 3 2
3. Multiply each digit by its associated weighting factor.

   14 18 20 20 18 14
4. Add the products of the multiplications. $14 + 18 + 20 + 20 + 18 + 14 = 104$
5. Divide the sum by *Modulus 11* to find the remainder. $104 \div 11 = 9$ plus a remainder of 5
6. Subtract the remainder from the *Modulus 11* to generate the required check digit. If there is no remainder, generate a check digit of zero. If the check digit is 10, generate a check digit of X to represent 10, since the use of 10 would require an extra digit. $11 - 5 = 6$
7. Append the check digit to create the standard seven-digit Standard Address Number.

   SAN 234-5676

SAN Assignment

R. R. Bowker accepted responsibility for being the central administrative agency for SAN, and in that capacity assigns SANs to identify uniquely the addresses of organizations. No SANs can be reassigned; in the event that an organization should cease to exist, for example, its SAN would cease to be in circulation entirely. If an organization using an SAN should move or change its name with no change in ownership, its SAN would remain the same, and only the name or address would be updated to reflect the change.

The SAN should be used in all transactions; it is recommended that the SAN be imprinted on stationery, letterheads, order and invoice forms, checks, and all other documents used in executing various book transactions. The SAN should always be printed on a separate line above the name and address of the organization, preferably in the upper left-hand corner of the stationery to avoid confusion with other numerical codes pertaining to the organization, such as telephone number, zip code, and the like.

SAN Functions

The SAN is strictly a Standard Address Number, becoming functional only in applications determined by the user; these may include activities such as purchasing, billing, shipping, receiving, paying, crediting, and refunding. It is the system used by Pubnet, a leading publishing industry e-commerce exchange, and is required in all electronic data interchange communications using the Book Industry Systems Advisory Committee (BISAC) EDI formats. Every department that has an independent function within an organization could have a SAN for its own identification.

For additional information or suggestions, write to Paula Kurdi, ISBN/SAN Agency, R. R. Bowker, LLC, 630 Central Ave., New Providence, NJ 07974, call 908-219-0283, or fax 908-219-0188. The e-mail address is ISBN-SAN@bowker.com. The SAN Web site for online applications is at http://www.isbn.org.

Distinguished Books

Notable Books of 2004

The Notable Books Council of the Reference and User Services Association, a division of the American Library Association, selected these titles for their significant contribution to the expansion of knowledge or for the pleasure they can provide to adult readers.

Fiction

Barnes, Julian. *The Lemon Table.* Knopf (1-4000-4214-3).

Christensen, Lars Saabye. *The Half Brother.* Arcade (1-55970-715-1).

De Bernières, Louis. *Birds Without Wings.* Knopf (1-4000-4341-7)

Dybek, Stuart. *I Sailed with Magellan.* Farrar (0-374-17407-5).

Khadra, Yasmina. *The Swallows of Kabul.* Doubleday (0-385-51001-2).

Mda, Zakes. *The Madonna of Excelsior.* Farrar (0-374-20008-4).

Mitchell, David. *Cloud Atlas.* Random (0-375-50725-6).

Munro, Alice. *Runaway.* Knopf (1-4000-4281-X).

Niemi, Mikael. *Popular Music from Vittula.* Seven Stories (1-58322-523-4).

Roth, Philip. *The Plot against America.* Houghton (0-618-50928-3).

Wolff, Tobias. *Old School.* Knopf (0-375-40146-6).

Nonfiction

Chernow, Ron. *Alexander Hamilton.* Penguin (1-59420-009-2).

Ehrlich, Paul R., and Anne E. Ehrlich. *One with Nineveh: Politics, Consumption, and the Human Future.* Island (1-55963-879-6).

Fischer, David Hackett. *Washington's Crossing.* Oxford (0-19-517034-2).

Henig, Robin Marantz. *Pandora's Baby: How the First Test Tube Babies Sparked the Reproductive Revolution.* Houghton (0-618-22415-7).

Hersh, Seymour M. *Chain of Command: The Road from 9/11 to Abu Ghraib.* HarperCollins (0-06-019591-6).

Hughes, Robert. *Goya.* Knopf (0-394-58028-1).

Kurlansky, Mark. *1968: The Year That Rocked the World.* Ballantine (0-345-45581-9).

Lansky, Aaron. *Outwitting History: How One Man Rescued a Million Books and Saved a Civilization.* Algonquin (1-56512-429-4).

Moats, David. *Civil Wars: A Battle for Gay Marriage.* Harcourt (0-15-101017-X).

National Commission on Terrorist Attacks upon the United States. *The 9/11 Commission Report: Final Report of the National Commission on Terrorists Attacks upon the United States.* Authorized ed. Norton (0-393-32671-3).

Philbrick, Nathaniel. *Sea of Glory: America's Voyage of Discovery: The U.S. Exploring Expedition, 1838–1842.* Viking (0-670-03231-X).

Sokolove, Michael. *The Ticket Out: Darryl Strawberry and the Boys of Crenshaw.* Simon & Schuster (0-7432-2673-9).

Vine, Phyllis. *One Man's Castle: Clarence Darrow in Defense of the American Dream.* HarperCollins (0-06-621415-7).

Poetry

Giovanni, Nikki. *The Collected Poetry of Nikki Giovanni, 1968–1998.* HarperCollins (0-06-054133-4).

Kooser, Ted. *Delights and Shadows.* Copper Canyon (1-55659-201-9).

Best Books for Young Adults

Each year a committee of the Young Adult Library Services Association (YALSA), a division of the American Library Association, compiles a list of the best fiction and nonfiction appropriate for young adults ages 12 to 18. Selected on the basis of each book's proven or potential appeal and value to young adults, the titles span a variety of subjects as well as a broad range of reading levels.

Aidinoff, Elsie V. *The Garden.* Harper-Collins (0-06-055605-6.)

Allen, Thomas B. *George Washington, Spymaster: How the Americans Outspied the British and Won the Revolutionary War.* National Geographic (0-7922-5126-1.)

Almond, David. *Fire-Eaters.* Random (0-385-73170-1).

Bass, L. G. *Sign of the Qin: Outlaws of Moonshadow Marsh, No. 1.* Hyperion (0-7868-1918-9).

Bausum, Ann. *With Courage and Cloth: Winning the Fight for a Woman's Right to Vote.* Simon & Schuster (0-7922-7647-7).

Bolden, Tonya. *Wake Up Our Souls: A Celebration of Black American Artists.* Harry N. Abrams (0-8109-4527-4).

Braff, Joshua. *The Unthinkable Thoughts of Jacob Green.* Workman (1-56512-420-0).

Burgess, Melvin. *Doing It.* Henry Holt (0-8050-7565-8).

Choldenko, Gennifer. *Al Capone Does My Shirts: A Novel.* Putnam (0-399-23861-1).

Chotjewitz, David. *Daniel Half Human and the Good Nazi.* Doris Orgel, trans. Simon & Schuster (0-689-85747-0).

Corrigan, Eireann. *Splintering.* Scholastic (0-439-53597-2).

Curtis, Christopher Paul. *Bucking the Sarge.* Random (0-385-32307-7).

de Lint, Charles. *The Blue Girl.* Penguin (0-670-05924-2).

Dr. Ernest Drake's Dragonology: The Complete Book of Dragons. Dugald Steer, ed. Candlewick (0-7636-2329-6).

Dunkle, Clare B. *The Hollow Kingdom.* Henry Holt (0-8050-7390-6).

Farmer, Nancy. *The Sea of Trolls.* Simon & Schuster (0-689-86744-1).

Fisher, Catherine. *The Oracle Betrayed.* HarperCollins (0-06-057157-8).

Flake, Sharon. *Who Am I Without Him? Short Stories About Girls and the Boys in Their Lives.* Hyperion (0-7868-0693-1).

Flinn, Alex. *Nothing to Lose.* HarperCollins (0-06-051750-6).

Freedman, Russell. *The Voice That Challenged a Nation: Marian Anderson and the Struggle for Equal Rights.* Houghton (0-618-15976-2).

Fusco, Kimberly Newton. *Tending to Grace.* Random (0-375-82862-1).

Gothic: Ten Original Dark Tales Deborah Noyes, ed. Candlewick (0-7636-2243-5).

Greenberg, Jan, and Sandra Jordan. *Andy Warhol: Prince of Pop.* Random (0-385-73056-X).

Halpin, Brendan. *Donorboy.* Random (1-4000-6277-2).

Hautman, Pete. *Godless.* Simon & Schuster (0-689-86278-4).

Hoose, Phillip M. *The Race to Save the Lord God Bird.* Farrar (0-374-36173-8).

Horowitz, Anthony. *Eagle Strike: An Alex Rider Adventure.* Putnam (0-399-23979-0).

Janeczko, Paul B. *Worlds Afire: The Hartford Circus Fire of 1944.* Candlewick (0-7636-2235-4).

Jocelyn, Marthe. *Mable Riley: A Reliable Record of Humdrum, Peril, and Romance.* Candlewick (0-7636-2120-X).

Johnson, Angela. *Bird.* Penguin (0-8037-2847-6).

Johnson, Kathleen Jeffrie. *A Fast and Brutal Wing.* Henry Holt (0-59643-013-3).

Johnson, Maureen. *The Key to the Golden Firebird.* HarperCollins (0-06-054138-5).

Koertge, Ron. *Margaux with an X.* Candlewick (0-7636-2401-2.)

Koja, Kathe. *The Blue Mirror.* Farrar (0-374-30849-7).

Konigsburg, E. L. *The Outcasts of 19 Schuyler Place.* Simon & Schuster (0-689-86636-4).

Kubert, Joe. *Yossel, April 19, 1943: A Story of the Warsaw Ghetto Uprising.* Simon & Schuster (0-7434-7516-X).

Lawrence, Michael. *A Crack in the Line.* HarperCollins (0-06-072477-3).

Lawrence, Iain. *B for Buster.* Random (0-385-73086-1).

Leavitt, Martine. *Heck, Superhero.* Front Street (1-886910-94-4.)

Levithan, David. *The Realm of Possibility.* Random (0-375-82845-1).

McKinley, Robin. *Sunshine.* Berkley (0-425-19178-8).

McNaughton, Janet. *An Earthly Knight.* HarperCollins (0-06-008992-X).

McWhorter, Diane. *A Dream of Freedom: The Civil Rights Movement from 1954 to 1968.* Scholastic (0-439-57678-4).

Marchetta, Melina. *Saving Francesca.* Random (0-375-82982-2).

Meyer, L. A. *Curse of the Blue Tattoo: Being an Account of the Misadventures of Jacky Faber, Midshipman and Fine Lady.* Harcourt (0-15-205115-5).

Morgan, Nicola. *Fleshmarket.* Random (0-385-73154-X).

Moriarty, Jaclyn. *The Year of Secret Assignments.* Scholastic (0-439-49881-3).

Morpurgo, Michael. *Private Peaceful.* Scholastic (0-439-63648-5).

Myers, Walter Dean. *Here in Harlem: Poems in Many Voices.* Holiday House (0-8234-1853-7).

Napoli, Donna Jo. *Bound.* Simon & Schuster (0-689-86175-3).

Nelson, Blake. *Rock Star, Susperstar.* Penguin (0-670-05933-1).

Oppel, Kenneth. *Airborn.* HarperCollins (0-06-053180-0).

Peck, Richard. *The Teacher's Funeral: A Comedy in Three Parts.* Penguin (0-8037-2736-4).

Peters, Julie Anne. *Luna: A Novel.* Little, Brown (0-316-73369-5).

Pratchett, Terry. *A Hat Full of Sky.* HarperCollins (0-06-058660-5).

Rapp, Adam. *Under the Wolf, Under the Dog.* Candlewick (0-7636-1818-7).

Reeve, Philip. *Predator's Gold: A Novel.* HarperCollins (0-06-072193-6).

Robinson, Sharon. *Promises to Keep: How Jackie Robinson Changed America.* Scholastic (0-439-42592-1).

Rosoff, Meg. *How I Live Now.* Random (0-385-74677-6).

Saenz, Benjamin Alire. *Sammy and Juliana in Hollywood.* Cinco Puntos (0-938317-81-4).

Satrapi, Marjane. *Persepolis 2: The Story of a Return.* Random (0-375-42288-9).

Schmidt, Gary D. *Lizzie Bright and the Buckminster Boy.* Houghton (0-618-43929-3).

Seagle, Steven T. *It's a Bird.* DC Comics (1-40120-109-1).

Shinn, Sharon. *The Safe-Keeper's Secret.* Penguin (0-670-05910-2).

Shusterman, Neal. *The Schwa Was Here.* Penguin (0-525-47182-0).

Silverstein, Ken. *The Radioactive Boy Scout: The True Story of a Boy and His Backyard Nuclear Reactor.* Random (0-375-50351-X).

Sones, Sonya. *One of Those Hideous Books Where the Mother Dies.* Simon & Schuster (0-689-85820-5).

Strasser, Todd. *Can't Get There from Here.* Simon & Schuster (0-689-84169-8).

Stratton, Allan. *Chanda's Secrets.* Firefly (1-55037-835-X).

Stroud, Jonathan. *The Golem's Eye: The Bartimaeus Trilogy, Book Two.* Hyperion (0-7868-1860-3).

Tocher, Timothy. *Chief Sunrise, John McGraw, and Me.* Cricket (0-8126-2711-3).

Townley, Roderick. *Sky: A Novel in 3 Sets and an Encore.* Simon & Schuster (0-689-85712-8).

Turnbull, Ann. *No Shame, No Fear.* Candlewick (0-7636-2505-1).

Unger, Zac. *Working Fire: The Making of an Accidental Fireman.* Penguin (1-59420-001-7).

Updale, Eleanor. *Montmorency: Thief, Liar, Gentleman?* Scholastic (0-439-58035-8).

Van der Vat, Dan. *D-Day: The Greatest Invasion—A People's History.* St. Martin's (1-58234-314-4).

Weeks, Sarah. *So B. It: A Novel.* HarperCollins (0-06-623622-3).

Werlin, Nancy. *Double Helix.* Penguin (0-8037-2606-6).

Westerfeld, Scott. *So Yesterday.* Penguin (1-59514-000-X).

Whedon, Joss. *Fray.* Dark Horse Comics (1-56971-751-6).

Whitney, Kim Ablon. *See You Down the Road: A Novel.* Random (0-375-82467-7).

Williams-Garcia, Rita. *No Laughter Here.* HarperCollins (0-688-16247-9).

Wolf, Allan. *New Found Land: Lewis and Clark's Voyage of Discovery.* Candlewick (0-7636-2113-7).

Wooding, Chris. *The Haunting of Alaizabel Cray.* Orchard (0-439-54656-7).

Woodson, Jacqueline. *Behind You.* Penguin (0-399-23988-X).

Yolen, Jane, and Robert J. Harris. *Prince Across the Water.* Penguin (0-399-23897-2).

Quick Picks for Reluctant Young Adult Readers

The Young Adult Library Services Association, a division of the American Library Association, annually chooses a list of outstanding titles that will stimulate the interest of reluctant teen readers. This list is intended to attract teens who, for whatever reason, choose not to read.

The list, compiled by a 12-member committee, includes titles published from late 2003 through 2004, both fiction and nonfiction.

Abbott, Hailey. *Summer Boys.* Scholastic (0-439-54020-8).

Brisick, Jamie. *Have Board, Will Travel.* HarperCollins (0-06-056359-1).

Burnham, Niki. *Royally Jacked.* Simon & Schuster (0-689-86668-2).

Coker, Cheo Hodari. *Unbelievable: The Life, Death and Afterlife of the Notorious B.I.G.* Three Rivers (0-609-80835-4).

Choyce, Lesley. *Thunderbowl.* Orca (1-55143-277-3).

CosmoGirl Quiz Book: All About You. Sterling/Hearst (1-58816-381-4).

Davidson, Dana. *Jason and Kyra.* Hyperion (0-7868-1851-4).

De La Cruz, Melissa. *The Au Pairs.* Simon & Schuster (0-689-87066-3).

Dr. Ernest Drake's Dragonology. Candlewick (0-7363-2329-6).

Ehrenhaft, Daniel. *Ten Things to Do Before I Die.* Random (0-385-73007-1).

Flake, Sharon. *Who Am I Without Him? A Short Story Collection About Girls and the Boys in Their Lives.* Hyperion (0-7868-0693-1).

Flinn, Alex. *Nothing to Lose.* HarperCollins (0-06-051751-4).

Giles, Gail. *Playing in Traffic.* Roaring Brook (1-59643-005-2).

Gottlieb, Andrew. *In the Paint: Tattoos of the NBA and the Stories Behind Them.* Hyperion (0-7868-8868-7).

Grandits, John. *Technically, It's Not My Fault: Concrete Poems.* Clarion (0-618-42833-X).

Hareas, John. *NBA's Greatest.* Dorling Kindersley (0-7894-9977-0).

Harrison, Lisi. *The Clique.* Little, Brown (0-316-70129-7).

Hartinger, Brent. *Last Chance Texaco.* HarperCollins (0-06-050912-0).

Heimberg, Jason, and Justin Heimberg. *The Official Movie Plot Generator: 27,000 Hilarious Movie Plot Combinations.* Brothers Heimberg (0-9740439-1-5).

Heneghan, James. *Hit Squad.* Orca (1-55143-269-2).

Hirano, Kohta. Hellsing series, vols. 1–4. Dark Horse Comics (1-59307-056-X, 1-59307-057-8, 1-59307-202-3, 1-59307-259-7).

Hobbs, Valerie. *Letting Go of Bobby James, or How I Found My Self of Steam.* Farrar (0-374-34384-5).

The Homer Book. HarperCollins (0-06-073884-7).

Hopkins, Cathy. Truth or Dare series. *The Princess of Pop* (0-689-87002-7), *Teen Queens and Has-Beens* (0-689-87129-5), *White Lies and Barefaced Truths* (0-689-87003-5). Simon & Schuster.

Hopkins, Ellen. *Crank.* Simon & Schuster (0-689-86519-8).

Horowitz, Anthony. *Eagle Strike.* Penguin (0-399-23979-0).

Hrdlitschka, Shelley. *Kat's Fall.* Orca (1-55143-312-5).

Jacobs, Thomas. *They Broke the Law; You Be the Judge: True Cases of Teen Crime.* Free Spirit (1-57542-134-8).

Johns, Geoff. *Teen Titans: A Kid's Game.* DC Comics (1-4012-0308-6).

Jones, Patrick. *Things Change.* Walker (0-8027-8901-3).

Kenner, Rob, and George Pitts. *VX: 10 Years of Vibe Photography.* Abrams (0-8109-4546-0).

Klancher, Lee. *Monster Garage: How to Customize Damn Near Everything.* Motorbooks (0-7603-1748-8).

Kool Moe Dee. *There's a God on the Mic: The True 50 Greatest MCs.* Thunder's Mouth (1-56025-533-1).

Leiker, Ken. *Unscripted.* Simon & Schuster (0-7434-7761-8).

Lynch, Clam. *Ruby Gloom's Keys to Happiness.* Abrams (0-8109-5036-7).

McGrath, Jeremy. *Wide Open: A Life in Supercross.* Harper (0-06-053727-2).

Mackler, Carolyn. *Vegan Virgin Valentine.* Candlewick (0-7636-2155-2).

McManners, Hugh. *Ultimate Special Forces.* Dorling Kindersley (0-7894-9973-8).

Manning, Sarra. *Guitar Girl.* Dutton (0-525-47234-7).

Miller, Timothy, and Steve Milton. *NASCAR Now.* Firefly (1-55297-829-X).

Milner-Halls, Kelly. *Albino Animals.* Darby Creek (1-58196-012-3).

Minter, J. *The Insiders.* Bloomsbury (1-58234-895-2).

Morgan, David Lee. *LeBron James: The Rise of a Star.* Gray (1-886228-74-4).

Myers, Walter Dean. *Shooter.* HarperCollins (0-06-029519-8).

Myracle, Lauren. *ttyl.* Abrams (0-8109-4821-4).

Nagatomo, Haruno. *Draw Your Own Manga: All the Basics.* Kodansha America (4-7700-2951-9).

Nash, Naomi. *You Are So Cursed.* Dorchester (0-8439-5310-1).

Naylor, Caroline. *Beauty Trix for Cool Chix: Easy-to-Make Lotions, Potions, and Spells to Bring Out a Beautiful You.* Watson-Guptill (0-8230-6957-5).

Nelson, Blake. *Rock Star, Superstar.* Viking (0-670-05933-1).

O'Connell, Tyne. *Pulling Princes.* Bloomsbury (1-58234-957-6).

Oppell, Kenneth. *Airborn.* HarperCollins (0-06-053181-9).

Parker, Daniel, and Lee Miller. Watching Alice series. *Break the Surface* (1-59514-001-8), *Walk On Water* (1-59514-002-6). Penguin.

Perez. Marlene. *Unexpected Development.* Roaring Brook (1-59643-006-0).

Rabb, M. E. The Missing Persons series. *The Chocolate Lover* (0-14-250042-9), *The Rose Queen* (0-14-250041-0), *The Unsuspecting Gourmet* (0-14-250044-5), *The Venetian Policeman* (0-14-250043-7). Penguin.

Riley, Andy. *The Book of Bunny Suicides.* Penguin (0-452-28518-6).

Ripley's Believe It or Not. Mint (1-893951-73-1).

Rohrer, Russ. *Ten Days in the Dirt: Spectacle of Off-Road Motorcycling.* Motorbooks (0-7603-1803-4).

Rothbart, Davy. *Found: The Best Lost, Tossed and Forgotten Items from Around the World.* Simon & Schuster (0-7432-5114-8).

Seate, Mike. *Choppers: Heavy Metal.* Motorbooks (0-7603-2053-5).

Shaw, Maria. *Maria Shaw's Star Gazer: Your Soul Searching, Dream Seeking, Make Something Happen Guide to the Future.* Llewellyn (0-7387-0422-9).

Shaw, Tucker. *Confessions of a Backup Dancer.* Simon & Schuster (0-689-87075-2).

Sleator, William. *The Boy Who Couldn't Die.* Abrams (0-81094-824-9).

Sones, Sonya. *One of Those Hideous Books Where the Mother Dies.* Simon & Schuster (0-689-85820-5).

So What? The Good, the Mad and the Ugly: The Official Metallica Illustrated Chronicles. Broadway (0-7679-1881-9).

Stephens, J. B. The Big Empty series. *The Big Empty* (1-59514-006-9), *Paradise City* (1-59514-007-7). Penguin.

Stolarz, Laurie F. *Blue Is for Nightmares.* Llewellyn (0-73-870391-5).

Strasser, Todd. *Can't Get There From Here.* Simon & Schuster (0-8118-4033-6).

Sweeney, Joyce. *Takedown.* Marshall Cavendish (0-7614-5175-7).

Takaya, Natsuki. Fruits Basket series, vols. 1–5 (1-59182-603-9, 1-59182-604-7, 1-59182-605-5, 1-59182-606-3, 1-59182-607-1). Tokyopop.

Thomson, Celia. The Nine Lives of Chloe King series. *The Fallen* (0-689-86658-5), *The Stolen* (0-689-86659-3). Simon & Schuster.

Thorley, Joe. *Avril Lavigne: The Unofficial Book.* Virgin (1-85227-0497).

Vizzini, Ned. *Be More Chill.* Hyperion (0-7868-0995-7).

Walters, Eric. *Overdrive.* Orca (1-55143-318-4).

Westerfeld, Scott. *The Secret Hour.* HarperCollins (0-06-051951-7).

Weyn, Suzanne. *Bar Code Tattoo.* Scholastic (0-439-39562-3).

Whedon, Joss. *Fray.* Dark Horse Comics (1-56971-751-6).

Woods, Brenda. *Emako Blue.* Penguin (0-399-24006-3).

Woodson, Jacqueline. *Behind You.* Penguin (0-399-23988-X).

YM The Best of (Say Anything). Random (0-553-37601-2).

Audiobooks for Young Adults

Each year a committee of the Young Adult Library Services Association, a division of the American Library Association, compiles a list of the best audiobooks for young adults ages 12 to 18. The titles are selected for their teen appeal and recording quality, and because they enhance the audience's appreciation of any written work on which the recordings may be based. While the list as a whole addresses the interests and needs of young adults, individual titles need not appeal to this entire age range but rather to parts of it.

Abomination, by Robert Swindells, narrated by Amanda Hulme. Bolinda, 3 discs, 3 hours and 30 minutes (1-7403-0909-X).

Al Capone Does My Shirts: A Novel, by Gennifer Choldenko, narrated by Johnny Heller. Recorded Books, 5 cassettes, 5 hours and 45 minutes (1-4025-6409-0).

Aleutian Sparrow, by Karen Hesse, narrated by Sarah Jones. Listening Library, 1 cassette, 1 hour and 45 minutes (0-8072-7961-3).

Battle of Jericho, by Sharon M. Draper, narrated by J. D. Jackson. Recorded Books, 6 cassettes, 8 hours and 15 minutes (1-4025-6485-6).

Becoming Naomi León, by Pam Muñoz Ryan, narrated by Annie Kozuch. Listening Library, 3 cassettes, 4 hours and 15 minutes (1-4000-9088-1).

Blind Beauty, by K. M. Peyton, narrated by Nicki Praull. Bolinda, 6 cassettes, 9 hours (1-7409-4250-8).

The Cat Ate My Gymsuit, by Paula Danziger, narrated by Caitlin Brodnick and the Full Cast Audio Family. Full Cast Audio, 3 discs, 2 hours and 45 minutes (1-9320-7656-5).

The Dons, by Archimede Fusillo, narrated by Dino Marnika. Bolinda, 4 discs, 4 hours (1-7409-3125-4).

Fault Line, by Janet Tashjian, narrated by Clara Bryant and Jason Harris. Listening Library, 3 cassettes, 4 hours (0-8072-2082-5).

First Part Last, by Angela Johnson, narrated by Khalipa Oldjohn and Kole Kristi. Listening Library, 1 cassette, 1 hour and 45 minutes (1-4000-9066-0).

Flipped, by Wendelin Van Draanen, narrated by Andy Paris and Carine Montertrand. Recorded Books, 5 cassettes, 7 hours and 15 minutes (1-4025-7307-3).

Girl Underground, by Morris Gleitzman, narrated by Mary-Anne Fahey. Bolinda, 3 discs, 3 hours and 30 minutes (1-7409-3526-8).

Golem's Eye, by Jonathan Stroud, narrated by Simon Jones. Listening Library, 10 cassettes, 16 hours and 30 minutes (0-8072-1979-7).

The Grand Canyon, by Donald Davis. August House, 1 disc, 49 minutes (0-8748-3739-1).

Jennifer Government, by Max Barry, narrated by Michael Kramer. Books on Tape, 6 cassettes, 9 hours (0-7366-9102-4).

Keesha's House, by Helen Frost, narrated by multiple readers. Recorded Books, 2 cassettes, 2 hours and 15 minutes (1-4025-9930-7).

Keys to the Kingdom series, by Garth Nix, narrated by Allan Corduner. Listening Library. *Mister Monday,* 5 cassettes, 8 hours (0-8072-1657-7), *Grim Tuesday,* 4 cassettes, 7 hours (0-8072-1728-X).

Kite Rider, by Geraldine McCaughrean, narrated by Cynthia Bishop and the Full Cast Audio Family. Full Cast Audio, 6 discs, 6 hours and 45 minutes (1-9320-7638-7).

Life of Pi, by Yann Martel, narrated by Jeff Woodman. HighBridge Audio, 7 cassettes, 11 hours and 30 minutes (1-5651-1779-4).

Montmorency: Thief, Liar, Gentleman? by Eleanor Updale, narrated by Stephen Fry. Listening Library, 3 cassettes, 5 hours and 15 minutes (0-8072-2370-0).

No Time Like Show Time, by Michael Hoeye, narrated by Campbell Scott. Listening Library (0-8072-0887-6).

Peter and the Starcatchers, by Dave Barry and Ridley Pearson, narrated by Jim Dale. Brilliance Audio, 7 discs, 9 hours (1-5935-5979-8).

Pirates, by Celia Rees, narrated by Jennifer Wiltsie. Listening Library, 6 cassettes, 9 hours (0-8072-2073-6).

Pool Boy, by Michael Simmons, narrated by Chad Lowe. Listening Library, 3 cassettes, 3 hours and 30 minutes (0-8072-2323-9).

The River Between Us, by Richard Peck, narrated by Lina Patel with Daniel Passer. Listening Library, 3 cassettes, 4 hours (1-4000-8626-4).

Ruby in the Smoke, by Phillip Pullman, narrated by Anton Lesser. Listening Library, 4 cassettes, 6 hours and 30 minutes (1-4000-8512-8).

The Shadow in the North, by Philip Pullman, read by Anton Lesser. Listening Library, 6 cassettes, 9 hours and 30 minutes (1-4000-8971-9).

Shooter, by Walter Dean Myers, narrated by Chad Coleman, Bernie McInerny, and Michelle Santopietro. Recorded Books, 3 discs, 3 hours and 45 minutes (1-4025-8492-X).

The Three Documents That Made America: The Declaration of Independence, the Constitution of the U.S.A. and the Bill of Rights, by Sam Fink, read by Sam Fink and Terry Bregy. Audio Bookshelf, 2 discs, 1 hour 30 minutes (0-9741711-2-3).

Walking the Choctaw Road, by Tim Tingle. Cinco Puntos (0-9383-1782-2).

The Wee Free Men, by Terry Pratchett, narrated by Stephen Briggs. HarperCollins Audio, 7 cassettes, 9 hours (0-06-056625-6).

A Hat Full of Sky, by Terry Pratchett, narrated by Stephen Briggs. HarperCollins Audio, 8 discs, 9 hours (0-06-074768-4).

Notable Children's Books

A list of notable children's books is selected each year by the Notable Children's Books Committee of the Association for Library Service to Children, a division of the American Library Association. Recommended titles are selected by children's librarians and educators based on originality, creativity, and suitability for children. [See "Literary Prizes, 2004" later in Part 5 for Caldecott, Newbery, and other award winners—*Ed.*]

Books for Younger Readers

Baker, Jeannie. *Home.* Illus. Greenwillow (0-06-623935-4).

Beaumont, Karen. *Baby Danced the Polka.* Illus. by Jennifer Plecas. Dial (0-8037-2587-6).

Brown, Don. *Odd Boy Out: Young Albert Einstein.* Illus. Houghton (0-618-49298-4).

Chen, Chih-Yuan. *Guji Guji.* Illus. Kane/Miller (1-929132-67-0).

Crews, Nina. *The Neighborhood Mother Goose.* Illus. Greenwillow (0-06-051573-2).

English, Karen. *Hot Day on Abbott Avenue.* Illus. by Javaka Steptoe. Clarion (0-395-98527-7).

Ernst, Lisa Campbell. *The Turn-Around, Upside-Down Alphabet Book.* Illus. Simon & Schuster (0-689-85685-7).

Fleischman, Paul. *Sidewalk Circus.* Illus. by Kevin Hawkes. Candlewick (0-7636-1107-7).

Fox, Mem. *Where Is the Green Sheep?* Illus. by Judy Horacek. Harcourt (0-15-204907-X).

Henkes, Kevin. *Kitten's First Full Moon.* Illus. Greenwillow (0-06-058828-4).

Hopkinson, Deborah. *Apples to Oregon: Being the (Slightly) True Narrative of How a Brave Pioneer Father Brought Apples, Peaches, Pears, Plums, Grapes, and Cherries (and Children) Across the Plains.* Illus. by Nancy Carpenter. Simon & Schuster (0-689-84769-6).

Knutson, Barbara. *Love and Roast Chicken: A Trickster Tale from the Andes Mountains.* Illus. Carolrhoda (1-57505-657-7).

Lehman, Barbara. *The Red Book.* Illus. Houghton (0-618-42858-5).

Look, Lenore. *Ruby Lu, Brave and True.* Illus. by Anne Wilsdorf. Simon & Schuster (0-689-84907-9).

Neubecker, Robert. *Wow! City!* Illus. Hyperion (0-7868-0951-5).

Prelutsky, Jack. *If Not for the Cat.* Illus. by Ted Rand. Greenwillow (0-06-059677-5).

Ravishankar, Anushka. *Tiger on a Tree.* Illus. by Pulak Biswas. Farrar (0-374-37555-0).

Seeger, Laura Vaccaro. *Lemons Are Not Red.* Illus. Roaring Brook (1-59643-008-7).

Sierra, Judy. *Wild About Books.* Illus. by Marc Brown. Knopf (0-375-82538-X).

Thompson, Lauren. *Polar Bear Night.* Illus. by Stephen Savage. Scholastic (0-439-49524-5).

Willems, Mo. *Knuffle Bunny: A Cautionary Tale.* Illus. Hyperion (0-7868-1870-0).

Wormell, Christopher. *Teeth, Tails, & Tentacles: An Animal Counting Book. Illus.* Running Press (0-7624-2100-2).

Books for Middle Readers

Bang, Molly. *My Light.* Illus. Scholastic (0-439-48961-X).

Bernier-Grand, Carmen T. *César: ¡Sí, Se Puede! = Yes, We Can!* Illus. by David Diaz. Marshall Cavendish (0-7614-5172-2).

Bredsdorff, Bodil. *The Crow-Girl.* Transalted by Faith Ingwersen. Farrar (0-374-31247-8).

Coman, Carolyn. *The Big House.* Illus. by Rob Shepperson. Front Street (1-932425-09-8).

Cottrell Boyce, Frank. *Millions.* Harper-Collins (0-06-073330-6).

Gelman, Rita Golden. *Doodler Doodling.* Illus. by Paul O. Zelinsky. Greenwillow (0-688-16645-8).

Grandits, John. *Technically, It's Not My Fault: Concrete Poems.* Illus. Clarion (0-618-42833-X).

Grimes, Nikki. *What Is Goodbye?* Illus. by Raúl Colón. Hyperion (0-7868-0778-4).

Hamilton, Virginia. *The People Could Fly: The Picture Book.* Illus. by Leo and Diane Dillon. Knopf (0-375-82405-7).

Hesse, Karen. *The Cats in Krasinski Square.* Illus. by Wendy Watson. Scholastic (0-439-43540-4).

Hodges, Margaret. *Merlin and the Making of the King.* Illus. by Trina Schart Hyman. Holiday (0-8234-1647-X).

Ibbotson, Eva. *The Star of Kazan.* Illus. by Kevin Hawkes. Dutton (0-525-47347-5).

Jocelyn, Marthe. *Mable Riley: A Reliable Record of Humdrum, Peril, and Romance.* Candlewick (0-7636-2120-X).

Kerley, Barbara. *Walt Whitman: Words for America.* Illus. by Brian Selznick. Scholastic (0-439-35791-8).

Landowne, Youme. *Sélavi, That Is Life: A Haitian Story of Hope.* Illus. Cinco Puntos (0-938317-84-9).

Matthews, L. S. *Fish.* Delacorte (0-385-73180-9).

Montgomery, Sy. *The Tarantula Scientist.* Photos by Nic Bishop. Houghton (0-618-14799-3).

Morrison, Toni. *Remember: The Journey to School Integration.* Illus. Houghton (0-618-39740-X).

Moss, Marissa. *Mighty Jackie: The Strike-Out Queen.* Illus. by C. F. Payne. Simon & Schuster (0-689-86329-2).

Pearce, Philippa. *The Little Gentleman.* Illus. by Tom Pohrt. Greenwillow (0-06-073160-5).

Rogers, Gregory. *The Boy, the Bear, the Baron, the Bard.* Illus. Roaring Brook (1-59643-009-5).

Rumford, James. *Sequoyah: The Cherokee Man Who Gave His People Writing.* Illus. Houghton (0-618-36947-3).

Schanzer, Rosalyn. *George vs. George: The American Revolution as Seen from Both Sides.* Illus. National Geographic (0-7922-7349-4).

Scieszka, Jon. *Science Verse.* Illus. by Lane Smith. Viking (0-670-91057-0).

Shange, Ntozake. *Ellington Was Not a Street.* Illus. by Kadir Nelson. Simon & Schuster (0-689-82884-5).

Sís, Peter. *The Train of States.* Illus. Greenwillow (0-06-057838-6).

Woodson, Jacqueline. *Coming on Home Soon.* Illus. by E. B. Lewis. Putnam (0-399-23748-8).

Books for Older Readers

Almond, David. *The Fire-Eaters.* Delacorte (0-385-73170-1).

Bausum, Ann. *With Courage and Cloth: Winning the Fight for a Woman's Right to Vote.* National Geographic (0-7922-7647-7).

Choldenko, Gennifer. *Al Capone Does My Shirts: A Novel.* Putnam (0-399-23861-1).

Chotjewitz, David. *Daniel, Half Human: And the Good Nazi.* Translated by Doris Orgel. Simon & Schuster (0-689-85747-0).

Curtis, Christopher Paul. *Bucking the Sarge.* Random (0-385-32307-7).

Doyle, Brian. *Boy O'Boy.* Douglas & McIntyre (0-375-82401-4).

Drez, Ronald J. *Remember D-Day: The Plan, the Invasion, Survivor Stories.* Illus. National Geographic (0-7922-6666-8).

Farmer, Nancy. *The Sea of Trolls.* Simon & Schuster (0-689-86744-1).

Fisher, Catherine. *The Oracle Betrayed.* Greenwillow (0-06-057157-8).

Freedman, Russell. *The Voice That Challenged a Nation: Marian Anderson and the Struggle for Equal Rights.* Clarion (0-618-15976-2).

Hoose, Phillip M. *The Race to Save the Lord God Bird.* Farrar (0-374-36173-8).

Is This Forever, or What? Poems & Paintings from Texas. Ed. by Naomi Shihab Nye. Greenwillow (0-06-051178-8).

Johnson, Angela. *Bird.* Dial (0-8037-2847-6).

Kadohata, Cynthia. *Kira-Kira.* Simon & Schuster (0-689-85639-3).

Konigsburg, E. L. *The Outcasts of 19 Schuyler Place.* Simon & Schuster (0-689-86636-4).

Leavitt, Martine. *Heck Superhero.* Front Street (1-886910-94-4).

McKay, Hilary. *Indigo's Star*. Simon & Schuster (0-689-86563-5).

McWhorter, Diane. *A Dream of Freedom: The Civil Rights Movement from 1954 to 1968*. Illus. Scholastic (0-439-57678-4).

Myers, Walter Dean. *Here in Harlem: Poems in Many Voices*. Holiday (0-8234-1853-7).

Nelson, Marilyn. *Fortune's Bones: The Manumission Requiem*. Front Street (1-932425-12-8).

Oppel, Kenneth. *Airborn*. HarperCollins (0-06-053180-0).

Peck, Richard. *The Teacher's Funeral: A Comedy in Three Parts*. Dial (0-8037-2736-4).

Pratchett, Terry. *A Hat Full of Sky*. HarperCollins (0-06-058660-5).

Ryan, Pam Muñoz. *Becoming Naomi León*. Scholastic (0-439-26969-5).

Schmidt, Gary D. *Lizzie Bright and the Buck-minster Boy*. Clarion (0-618-43929-3).

Shusterman, Neal. *The Schwa Was Here*. Dutton (0-525-47182-0).

Stolz, Joëlle. *The Shadows of Ghadames*. Translated by Catherine Temerson. Delacorte (0-385-73104-3).

Weeks, Sarah. *So B. It*. HarperCollins (0-06-623622-3).

Books for All Ages

Thomas, Dylan. *A Child's Christmas in Wales*. Illus. by Chris Raschka. Candlewick (0-7636-2161-7).

Under the Spell of the Moon: Art for Children from the World's Great Illustrators. Ed. By Patricia Aldana, translated by Stan Dragland. Douglas & McIntyre (0-88899-559-8).

Notable Children's Videos

These titles are selected by a committee of the Association for Library Service to Children, a division of the American Library Association. Recommendations are based on originality, creativity, and suitability for young children. The members select materials that respect both children's intelligence and imagination, exhibit venturesome creativity, and encourage the interest of users.

Diary of a Worm. 10 mins. Weston Woods. Ages 5–9.

The Dot. 9 mins. Weston Woods. Ages 5–10.

Duck for President. 16 mins. Weston Woods. Ages 5–8.

The ErlKing. 6 mins. National Film Board of Canada. Ages 12–14.

Fireboat: The Heroic Adventures of the John J. Harvey. 13 mins. Spoken Arts. Ages 5–8.

I Stink! 9 mins. Weston Woods. Ages 2–8.

Journey of the Loggerhead. 30 mins. Environmental Media. Ages 8–14.

Let's Get Real. 35 mins. New Day Films. Ages 12–14.

Liberty's Kids Series. 60 mins (2 episodes). WHYY-TV/PBS. Ages 5–10.

Life on the Edge: A Guide to Pacific Coastal Habitats. 35 mins. Earthwise Media. Ages 8–12.

Pollyanna. 100 mins. WGBH Boston Video. Ages 8–12.

The Pot That Juan Built. 17 mins. Weston Woods. Ages 6–12.

Science, Please. 40 mins. National Film Board of Canada. Ages 5–14.

Thank You, Sarah: The Woman Who Saved Thanksgiving. 11 mins. Spoken Arts. Ages 6–10.

This Is the House That Jack Built. 7 mins. Weston Woods. Ages 3–7.

Through My Thick Glasses. 13 mins. Pravda and National Film Board of Canada. Ages 13–14.

The Wheels on the Bus. 6 mins. Weston Woods. Ages 2–6.

Notable Recordings for Children

This list of notable recordings for children was selected by the Association for Library Service to Children, a division of the American Library Association. Recommended titles, many of which are recorded books, are chosen by children's librarians and educators on the basis of their originality, creativity, and suitability.

"Al Capone Does My Shirts." 5 hrs. and 45 mins., 5 cassettes. Recorded Books. Grades 4 and up. A humorous story set on Alcatraz Island in 1935.

"Beethoven's Wig 2: More Sing-Along Symphonies." 40 mins., 1 CD. Rounder Kids. All ages. Humorous renditions of classic melodies.

"Bucking the Sarge." 6 hrs. and 10 mins., 4 cassettes or 5 CDs. Listening Library. Grades 6 and up. Read by Michael Boatman.

"Dragon Rider." 11 hrs. and 35 mins., 7 cassettes or 10 CDs. Listening Library. Grades 4 and up. Brendan Fraser reads Cornelia Funke's fantasy.

"Duck for President." 14 mins., cassette only, cassette and hardcover book, CD only, CD and hardcover book, or Spanish-language cassette or cassette and book. Weston Woods. Preschool and up. Randy Travis presents another installment of Doreen Cronin's farm saga. The Spanish version is read by Jorge Pupo.

"Fireboat: The Heroic Adventures of the John J. Harvey." 15 mins., cassette or CD and hardcover book. Live Oak Media. All ages. Judd Hirsch reads Maira Kalman's story of the contribution to 9/11 heroism of an almost scrapped fireboat and its crew.

"Flipped." 7 hrs. and 15 mins., 5 cassettes. Recorded Books. Grades 5 and up. Andy Paris and Carine Montbertrand portray the characters in Wendelin Van Draanen's coming-of-age story.

"Heartbeat." 1 hr. and 30 mins., 2 cassettes or 2 CDs. Harper Children's Audio. Grades 4–8. Mandy Siegfried reads Sharon Creech's story-in-poems.

"A House of Tailors." 3 hrs. and 29 mins., 2 cassettes or 3 CDs. Listening Library. Grades 3–8. Patricia Reilly Giff's story about German immigrants in the 1870s is read by Blair Brown.

"I Lost My Bear." 9 mins., cassette only, cassette and hardcover, cassette and paperback, CD only, CD and hardcover, or CD and paperback. Weston Woods. Preschool–Grade 2. Kristen Hahn reads Jules Feiffer's story about a young girl's anguished search for her bear.

"I Stink!" 7 mins., cassette or CD alone or with hardcover book. Weston Woods. Preschool–Grade 2. Andy Richter is the voice of a city garbage truck in this story based on Kate and Jim McMullan's picture book.

"Ida B. . . . and Her Plans to Maximize Fun, Avoid Disaster, and (Possibly) Save the World." 3 hrs. and 14 mins., 2 cassettes or 3 CDs. Listening Library. Grades 3–8. Katherine Hannigan's lighthearted novel is read by Lili Taylor.

"The Last Holiday Concert." 3 hrs., 1 min., 2 cassettes or 3 CDs. Listening Library. Grades 3–7. Fred Berman narrates Andrew Clements's humorous story.

"Mike Mulligan and His Steam Shovel: A New Work for Narrator and Symphony Orchestra." 51 mins., 1 CD. Simon & Schuster. All ages. A musically extended version of Virginia Lee Burton's classic children's story.

"More Perfect Than the Moon." 1 hr., 1 CD. Harper Children's Audio. Grades 2–6. Glenn Close reads Patricia MacLachlan's fourth book about Sarah and her family.

"Muncha! Muncha! Muncha!" 11 mins., cassette or CD and hardcover book. Live Oak Media. Preschool–Grade 2. William Dufris reads the tale about three young bunnies and the farmer they outwit.

"No More Nasty." 3 hrs. and 45 mins., 3 cassettes. Recorded Books. Grades 3–6. Amy

MacDonald's humorous story is read by Johnny Heller.

"Pincus and the Pig: A Klezmer Tale." 45 mins., 1 CD. Tzadik. All ages. Maurice Sendak narrates his Yiddish retelling of "Peter and the Wolf" with musical accompaniment by the Shirim Klezmer Orchestra.

"The Pot That Juan Built." 13 mins., cassette or CD alone or with hardcover book. Weston Woods. All ages. With music and sound effects, Alfred Molina reads this poem telling the story of artist Juan Quezada.

"Princess in Pink: The Princess Diaries, Volume V." 7 hrs. and 31 mins., 6 cassettes or 7 CDs. Listening Library. Grades 6 and up. Clea Lewis reads Meg Cabot's fifth book about the adventures of Princess Mia.

"Rhinoceros Tap." 42 mins., CD and hardcover book. Workman Publishing. All ages. Adam Bryant invites listeners to sing along to 16 silly songs.

"The Ruby in the Smoke." 6 hrs. and 26 mins., 4 cassettes. Listening Library. Grades 6 and up. Philip Pullman's tale of Sally Lockhart's quest to unravel the mystery of her father's death in 1870s London is read by Anton Lesser.

"Sing Along with Putumayo." 39 mins., CD. Putumayo Kids. All ages. Singers perform folk and blues classics.

"The Teacher's Funeral." 4 hrs. and 42 mins., 3 cassettes or 5 CDs. Listening Library. Grades 4 and up. Dylan Baker reads Richard Peck's comic account of rural life in the early 1900s.

"When Marian Sang." 29 mins., cassette or CD and hardcover book. Live Oak Media. All ages. Gail Nelson's reading and the sound of Marian Anderson's voice tell an inspiring story.

Notable Software and Online Subscription Services for Children

This list is chosen by a committee of the Association for Library Service to Children, a division of the American Library Association. Titles are chosen on the basis of their originality, creativity, and suitability for young children.

Software

Spy Spooky Mansion Deluxe. Scholastic. Ages 6 and up. Fifteen picture puzzles must be solved before a skeleton guides the player out of a haunted house. Once out, the skeleton invites the player back in for a new round of games and clues. Windows/Macintosh.

Learn to Play Chess with Fritz and Chesster 2: Chess in the Black Castle. Viva Media. Ages 8 and up. This Fritz and Chesster adventure focuses on strategy. Bianca and Fritz enter the creepy Black Castle to rescue their mentor, Chesster the Rat, who is being held hostage. Only by increasing their chess skills do they stand a chance of outwitting the nefarious King Black. A free year's subscription to playchess.com is included with purchase. Windows.

Photo Puzzle Builder. APTE. Ages 6 and up. Users can create anagrams, crosswords, word searches, photo-scrambles, and photo jigsaws using personal digital photos and graphics. Puzzles can be edited and the final results can be saved, printed, exported, and posted on a Web site. Windows/Macintosh.

Starry Night: Complete Space and Astronomy Pack. Imaginova. Ages 9 and up. With this realistic planetarium program, young astronomers can see the sky from any point on Earth, controlling time, location, elevation, and more, and can pilot the Deep Space Explorer up to 700 million light years from Earth for stunning views of the universe. Includes Sky-Theatre, a full-length documentary on DVD, and an accompanying text, *Starry Night Companion.* Windows/Macintosh.

Subscription Services

Digital Curriculum. AIMS Multimedia. Ages 7 and up. This comprehensive interactive learning resource integrates full-length videos, video clips, still images, encyclopedia content, teacher guides, lesson plans, and online assessments and assignments. Users can supplement learning at home and school with more than 90,000 educational multimedia components for every subject. Includes correlations to state and national standards.

Bestsellers of 2004

Hardcover Bestsellers: No Room at the Top

Daisy Maryles
Executive Editor, *Publishers Weekly*

Laurele Riippa
Editor, Adult Announcements, *Publishers Weekly*

In real estate, it's location, location, location. For bestsellers, it's name, name, name. While debut novelists do get on the charts (six did so in 2004) and there are some formerly unknowns on the nonfiction side, these are the exceptions. More than 90 percent of the fiction authors on our 2004 end-of-the-year list have been there before. In nonfiction, when it is a first book, name recognition generally comes from the author's day job. The operative word for nonfiction is platform—authors need to be famous in another field; they need to be experts in the subject they are writing on; they need access to the media or, even better, to *be* the media. The 2004 nonfiction top sellers bear this out.

In fact, the 2004 list of top bestsellers strongly resembles the 2003 list. In fiction, the same two books lead—Dan Brown's *The Da Vinci Code* and Mitch Albom's *The Five People You Meet in Heaven*. Brown's book sold more than 4.2 million copies in 2004 and, to date, has sold well over 10 million copies. A $35 illustrated edition of *Da Vinci*, printed in time for holiday sales, sold more than 900,000 copies. Albom's book sold more than 3.2 million copies in 2004 and has more than seven million in print. In nonfiction, too, No. 1 and No. 2 are repeaters. Rick Warren's *The Purpose-Driven Life* sold more than 11 million copies in 2004; total in print has passed the 22-million mark. Arthur Agatston's *The South Beach Diet* sold more than 3 million in 2004, with total sales of about 7,429,000.

Brown led the fiction charts for 31 of the 51 weeks (*Publishers Weekly* skips the last week of the year) in 2004; Albom took that spot for two weeks. That doesn't leave much for the rest of the high rollers. Things were a little more open in nonfiction, where *The South Beach Diet* commandeered the No. 1 slot for 16 weeks. That's twice as long as the fourth nonfiction bestseller, Jon Stewart's *America (The Book)*, which sold more than 1.5 million copies in 2004.

Million-Copy Babies

Sixteen 2004 bestsellers went over the 1-million mark—eight in fiction and eight in nonfiction. That's two more than in 2003, but one short of the record set 10 years ago, in 1994. Among them was Dan Brown's *Angels & Demons,* the fifth-bestselling novel of the year. The other seven-figure novelists are regulars on these bestseller charts, including John Grisham, Tim LaHaye and Jerry B. Jenkins, Michael Crichton, and Patricia Cornwell—all familiar names on these end-of-year charts. Crichton wasn't on in 2003, but only because he didn't have a new book that year.

Adapted from *Publishers Weekly,* March 28, 2005.

Publishers Weekly 2004 Bestsellers

FICTION

1. **The Da Vinci Code** by Dan Brown. Doubleday (3/03) **4,290,000
2. **The Five People You Meet in Heaven** by Mitch Albom. Hyperion (9/03) 3,287,722
3. **The Last Juror** by John Grisham. Doubleday (2/04)**2,290,000
4. **Glorious Appearing** by Tim LaHaye and Jerry B. Jenkins. Tyndale (3/04) 1,600,318
5. **Angels & Demons** by Dan Brown. Atria (5/00) **1,285,000
6. **State of Fear** by Michael Crichton. HarperCollins (12/04) 1,249,277
7. **London Bridges** by James Patterson. Little, Brown (11/04) 1,064,378
8. **Trace** by Patricia Cornwell. Putnam (9/04) 1,033,573
9. **The Rule of Four** by Ian Caldwell and Dustin Thomason. Dial (5/04) **945,000
10. **The Da Vinci Code: Special Illustrated Collector's Edition** by Dan Brown. Doubleday (11/04) **905,000
11. **I Am Charlotte Simmons** by Tom Wolfe. Farrar, Straus & Giroux (11/04) 775,829
12. **Night Fall** by Nelson De Mille. Warner (11/04) 748,775
13. **A Salty Piece of Land** by Jimmy Buffett. Little, Brown (11/04) 698,675
14. **Ten Big Ones** by Janet Evanovich. St. Martin's (6/04) 688,978
15. **Black Wind** by Clive Cussler and Dirk Cussler. Putnam (11/04) 653,381

NONFICTION

1. **The Purpose-Driven Life** by Rick Warren. Zondervan (10/02) 7,340,000
2. **The South Beach Diet** by Arthur Agatston, M.D. Rodale (4/03) 3,002,597
3. **My Life** by Bill Clinton. Knopf (6/04) 2,000,000
4. **America (The Book)** by Jon Stewart and the "Daily Show" writers. Warner (9/04) 1,519,027
5. **The South Beach Diet Cookbook** by Arthur Agatston, M.D. Rodale (4/04) 1,490,898
6. **Family First** by Dr. Phil McGraw. Free Press (9/04) **1,355,000
7. **He's Just Not That into You** by Greg Behrendt and Liz Tuccillo. Simon Spotlight Entertainment (9/04) 1,261,055
8. **Eats, Shoots & Leaves** by Lynne Truss. Gotham (4/04) 1,092,128
9. **Your Best Life Now** by Joel Osteen. Warner Faith (9/04) 974,645
10. **Guinness World Records 2005** by Guinness World Records Ltd. Guinness Publishing (8/04) 970,000
11. **Unfit for Command** by John O'Neill and Jerome R. Corsi. Regnery (8/04) 814,015
12. **The Automatic Millionaire** by David Bach. Broadway (12/03) **735,000
13. **The Proper Care and Feeding of Husbands** by Dr. Laura Schlessinger. HarperCollins (1/04) 724,330
14. **The Family** by Kitty Kelley. Doubleday (9/04) **715,000
15. **Plan of Attack** by Bob Woodward. Simon & Schuster (4/04) **675,000

Note: Rankings are determined by sales figures provided by publishers; the numbers generally reflect reports of copies "shipped and billed" in calendar year 2004 and publishers were instructed to adjust sales figures to include returns through February 1, 2005. Publishers did not at that time know what their total returns would be—indeed, the majority of returns occur after that cut-off date—so none of these figures should be regarded as final net sales. (Dates in parentheses indicate month and year of publication.)

* All sales figures reflect books sold only in calendar year 2004.

**Sales figures were submitted to *PW* in confidence, for use in placing titles on the lists. Numbers shown are rounded down to indicate relationship to sales figures of other titles.

In nonfiction, Agatston scored another million-unit bestseller with *The South Beach Diet Cookbook*, the No. 5 hardcover nonfiction bestseller for the year, with sales of more than 1,490,000. His *South Beach Diet* led the charts for 16 weeks and the cookbook topped the list for one. The runner-up for most times in the lead spot was Stewart's *America*; it topped the list eight times.

Bill Clinton's *My Life* beat out Hillary Clinton's *Living History*, both in sales and end-of-the-year ranking. His book sold 2 million copies last year, almost 500,000 more than his wife's 2003 sales figure. His was the No. 3 best-selling nonfiction book in 2004; hers was No. 5 in 2003.

There are two new faces on the list of nonfiction titles that surpassed the 1 million mark—one with TV connections, the other an unusual British import. The first, *He's Just Not That into You: The No-Excuses Truth to Understanding Guys*, is written by Greg Behrendt and Liz Tuccillo, consultant and executive story editor, respectively, for HBO's "Sex and the City." The book launched the Simon Spotlight Entertainment imprint and a one-hour "Oprah" launched the book into numbers heaven. Its sales of more than 1,260,000 had a lot to do with Simon & Schuster's 2004 robust bottom line. What may be the first grammar book to hit the big time, *Eats, Shoots & Leaves: The Zero Tolerance Approach to Punctuation* by Lynne Truss, is No. 8 on the 2004 charts, with sales of more than 1 million copies. Gotham's first printing was about 133,000—an aggressive figure for a book wherein a comma plays a key role.

The Three Faces of the List

Bestsellers last year could be summarized in three words: Brown, politics and religion. It was an election year, the country was polarized, and there were plenty of media celebs and political pundits penning rhetoric about what's wrong and/or right in governmental circles. Five of the top 15 books are political—*My Life*, *America*, *Unfit for Command*, *The Family* and *Plan of Attack*. The latter rounds off the top 15 with sales of about 675,000. At least 30 more political titles appeared on the 2004 bestseller lists, a record for this category.

Religion is perhaps the only publishing segment that has enjoyed growth in each of the last 10 years. It has also placed more titles each year on these lists. Books by two pastors are among the top 15—Warren, of course, and Joel Osteen, whose *Your Best Life Now* has sold close to 975,000 copies and is still high on the weekly charts. He's an author with a very substantial platform—he's pastor of Lakewood Church in Houston, Texas, the largest church in America, with more than 25,000 people attending each weekend; and his syndicated weekly TV broadcast was rated by Nielsen Media Research as the No. 1 inspirational program nationally. Check the titles on these pages, and you will find about 20 more nonfiction bestsellers in the religion and inspiration category.

Cookbooks are always popular, no matter what your politics or religion. That was very evident throughout the year, with many cookbooks, often driven by the influence of the Food TV Network, appearing on our weekly charts. In 2004, 11 new cookbooks sold more than 100,000 copies, compared to 4 that reached that level in 2003.

FICTION: Who's on First?

How *Publishers Weekly*'s bestsellers compared with the rankings in major chains, independents and wholesalers

	Sales Outlets*									
PW Rankings	**BN/BN.C**	**W**	**B**	**I**	**BT**	**O**	**TC**	**S**	**K**	**AM.C**
1. The Da Vinci Code	1	2	1	3	2	1	1	1	1	1
2. The Five People You Meet . . .	2	1	2	1	3	3	2	2	5	2
3. The Last Juror	5	3	5	8	6	20	—	4	32	5
4. Glorious Appearing	21	11	17	—	24	—	—	—	—	—
5. Angels & Demons	3	8	3	6	10	—	14	41	—	11
6. State of Fear	7	10	7	2	39	35	15	7	22	10
7. London Bridges	8	5	12	16	11	—	—	24	—	14
8. Trace	12	16	15	17	9	—	—	16	—	16
9. The Rule of Four	4	14	4	5	5	4	4	3	3	3
10. The Da Vinci Code: Illustrated	—	4	6	22	—	—	21	32	—	28
11. I Am Charlotte Simmons	20	39	18	28	—	8	16	22	15	9
12. Night Fall	9	22	19	19	32	—	43	26	—	15
13. A Salty Piece of Land	11	7	9	4	20	—	28	33	—	17
14. Ten Big Ones	18	21	20	—	8	2	—	20	—	13
15. Black Wind	23	20	30	34	—	—	9	—	—	—

NONFICTION: What's on Second?

How *Publishers Weekly*'s bestsellers compared with the rankings in major chains, independents and wholesalers

	Sales Outlets*									
PW Rankings	**BN/BN.C**	**W**	**B**	**I**	**O**	**TC**	**DK**	**S**	**K**	**AM.C**
1. The Purpose-Driven Life	3	3	3	1	23	48	8	14	51	8
2. The South Beach Diet	1	1	1	6	7	5	2	2	3	3
3. My Life	4	4	4	5	4	1	6	13	—	4
4. America (The Book)	2	2	2	4	2	3	13	3	2	1
5. The South Beach Diet Cookbook	9	11	8	—	—	29	33	20	—	15
6. Family First	25	13	27	43	—	—	—	45	—	34
7. He's Just Not That into You	5	5	5	3	34	6	11	9	28	7
8. Eats, Shoots & Leaves	7	18	6	2	1	2	3	6	1	5
9. Your Best Life Now	6	6	16	7	—	—	—	—	—	42
10. Guinness World Records 2005	49	36	—	40	—	—	—	100	—	—
11. Unfit for Command	13	10	19	—	—	42	26	27	—	6
12. The Automatic Millionaire	14	14	9	21	—	—	—	66	—	18
13. The Proper Care and Feeding . . .	8	7	7	10	—	—	—	—	17	16
14. The Family	43	—	—	—	26	—	—	55	—	—
15. Plan of Attack	10	17	10	—	8	14	19	12	8	12

*BN/BN.C = Barnes & Noble and B&N.com   **W** = Waldenbooks
B = Borders   **I** = Ingram
BT = Baker & Taylor   **O** = Olsson's
TC = Tattered Cover   **DK** = Davis Kidd
S = Harry W. Schwartz   **K** = Kepler's
AM.C = Amazon.com

Missing in Action

Thirteen of the hardcover novels that sold more than 100,000 copies in 2004 have yet to land on one of *PW*'s weekly charts; in nonfiction, 42 never landed on the weekly charts. In total, 131 fiction and 132 nonfiction books published in the last two years sold more than 100,000 copies. In 2004 a record 96 nonfiction hardcovers made *Publishers Weekly*'s weekly lists—so even strong sales isn't enough to guarantee chart placement. Still, it's sometimes hard to understand how sales of 200,000 and more for books like Jimmy Carter's *Sharing Good Times*, *Now Discover Your Strengths* by Marcus Buckingham and Donald O. Clifton, and the pope's *Rise, Let Us Be on Our Way* can reach those numbers and not have any bestseller presence.

As always, all our calculations are based on shipped-and-billed figures supplied by publishers for new books released in 2003 and 2004 (a few books published earlier that continued their tenures on our 2004 weekly lists and/or our monthly religion lists are included). These figures reflect only 2004 sales, and publishers were instructed not to include book club and overseas transactions. We also asked publishers to take into account returns through February 1. Sales figures on these pages should not be considered final. For many of these books, especially those published in the final third of the year, returns are not yet calculated.

All books listed below with a pound sign (#) were submitted to *Publishers Weekly* in confidence, for use in placing titles on the lists. Numbers shown are rounded down to indicate relationship to sales figures of other titles.

The Fiction Runners-Up

16. *R Is for Ricochet.* Sue Grafton. Putnam (650,627)
17. *Echoes.* Danielle Steel. Delacorte (#645,000)
18. *Second Chance.* Danielle Steel. Delacorte (#645,000)
19. *3rd Degree.* James Patterson and Andrew Gross. Little, Brown (632,919)
20. *The Dark Tower VII: The Dark Tower.* Stephen King. Scribner (#630,000)
21. *Ransom.* Danielle Steel. Delacorte (#615, 000)
22. *Sam's Letters to Jennifer.* James Patterson. Little, Brown (614,425)
23. *Hour Game.* David Baldacci. Warner (593,772)
24. *The Dark Tower VI: Song of Susannah.* Stephen King. Scribner (#585,000)
25. *Metro Girl.* Janet Evanovich. HarperCollins (574,645)
26. *Northern Lights.* Nora Roberts. Putnam (570,000)
27. *New Spring.* Robert Jordan. Tor (548,937)
28. *Life Expectancy.* Dean Koontz. Bantam (#530,000)
29. *The Gift.* Nora Roberts. Silhouette (507,000)
30. *The Christmas Thief.* Mary Higgins Clark and Carol Higgins Clark. Simon & Schuster/Scribner (#496,000)

400,000+

Night Time Is My Time. Mary Higgins Clark. Simon & Schuster (#495,000)

Hidden Prey. John Sandford. Putnam (474,534)

Whiteout. Ken Follett. Dutton (426,155)

Night of Rain and Stars. Maeve Binchy. Dutton (405,000)

Are You Afraid of the Dark? Sidney Sheldon. Morrow (401,638)

300,000+

The Godfather Returns. Mark Winegardner. Random House (392,191)

Skinny Dip. Carl Hiaasen. Knopf (389,010)

Lost City. Clive Cussler with Paul Kemprecos. Putnam (386,994)

Jonathan Strange & Mr. Norrell. Susanna Clarke. Bloomsbury. (366,233)

The Plot Against America. Philip Roth. Houghton Mifflin (357,932)

Shopaholic & Sister. Sophie Kinsella. Delacorte (#350,000)

The Bourne Legacy. Eric Van Lustbader. St. Martin's (326,862)

Skeleton Man. Tony Hillerman. HarperCollins (324,811)

Emma's Secret. Barbara Taylor Bradford. St. Martin's (324,567)

Blowout. Catherine Coulter. Putnam (320,407)

Divided in Death. J. D. Robb. Putnam (318,000)

The Taking. Dean Koontz. Bantam (#310,000)

200,000+

Twisted. Jonathan Kellerman. Ballantine (287,814)

Visions in Death. J. D. Robb. Putnam (287,000)

A Redbird Christmas. Fannie Flagg. Random House (281,708)

Can You Keep a Secret? Sophie Kinsella. Delacorte (#270,000)

The Narrows. Michael Connelly. Little, Brown (266,992)

Light on Snow. Anita Shreve. Little, Brown (253,802)

Babylon Rising: The Secret of Ararat. Tim LaHaye and Bob Phillips. Bantam (#245,000)

White Hot. Sandra Brown. Simon & Schuster (#235,000)

By Order of the President. W. E. B. Griffin. Putnam (232,700)

Kill the Messenger. Tami Hoag. Bantam (#225,000)

Just One Look. Harlan Coben. Dutton (218,483)

Bergdorf Blondes. Plum Sykes. Miramax (214,000)

Blind Alley. Iris Johansen. Bantam (#205,000)

The Jane Austen Book Club. Karen Fowler. Putnam (202,906)

The Case for a Creator. Lee Strobel. Zondervan (202,330)

Incubus Dreams. Laurell K. Hamilton. Berkley (201,287)

150,000+

Murder List. Julie Garwood. Ballantine (196,766)

Therapy. Jonathan Kellerman. Ballantine (190,853)

Double Homicide. Faye Kellerman and Jonathan Kellerman. Warner (188,442)

Olivia Joules and the Overactive Imagination. Helen Fielding. Viking (187,224)

The Princes of Ireland. Edward Rutherfurd. Doubleday (#185,000)

Firestorm. Iris Johansen. Bantam (#185,000)

The Amateur Marriage. Anne Tyler. Knopf (181,294)

Bad Business. Robert B. Parker. Putnam (179,992)

Memorial Day. Vince Flynn. Atria (#178,000)

Reckless Abandon. Stuart Woods. Putnam (176,705)

Absolute Friends. John le Carré. Little, Brown (173,387)

The Cat Who Talked Turkey. Lilian Jackson Braun. Putnam (170,825)

Christmas Blessing. Donna Van Liere. St. Martin's (170,421)

The Time Traveler's Wife. Audrey Niffenegger. MacAdam/Cage (170,000)

The Sunday Philosophy Club. Alexander McCall Smith. Pantheon (169,581)

Shem Creek. Dorothea Benton Frank. Berkley (166,411)

Little Earthquakes. Jennifer Weiner. Atria (#160,000)

The Birth of Venus. Sarah Dunant. Random House (159,433)

The Virgin's Lover. Philippa Gregory. Touchstone (158,350)

When Christmas Comes. Debbie Macomber. Mira (158,00)

Dark Justice. Jack Higgins. Putnam (157,568)

Savannah. John Jakes. Dutton (157,558)

One False Move. Alex Kava. Mira (157,000)

The Prince of Beverly Hills. Stuart Woods. Putnam (155,449)

The Two Swords: The Hunter's Blades Trilogy Book III. R. A. Salvatore. Wizards of the Coast/Forgotten Realms (151,232)

125,000+

The Full Cupboard of Life. Alexander McCall Smith. Pantheon (149,958)

A Death in Vienna. Daniel Silva. Putnam (149,424)

My Sister's Keeper. Jodi Picoult. Atria (#145,000)

Paranoia. Joseph Finder. St. Martin's (142,045)

The Zero Game. Brad Meltzer. Warner (138,098)

Islands. Anne Rivers Siddons. HarperCollins (137,942)

The Cat Who Went Bananas. Lilian Jackson Braun. Putnam (137,653)

Bet Me. Jennifer Crusie. St. Martin's (136,782)

To the Last Man. Jeffrey Shaara. Ballantine (135,597)

Falling Awake. Jayne Ann Krentz. Putnam (134,340)

Melancholy Baby. Robert B. Parker. Putnam (128,976)

The Second Chair. John Lescroart. Dutton (126,669)

Grant Comes East. Newt Gingrich and William R. Forstchen. St. Martin's (125,502)

100,000+

Drive Me Crazy. Eric Jerome Dickey. Dutton (122,509)

Body Double. Tess Gerritsen. Ballantine (122,215)

Playing with Boys. Alisa Valdes-Rodriguez. St. Martin's (121,231)

Double Play. Robert B. Parker. Putnam (117,462)

The Exile. Allan Folsom. Forge (117,446)

The Collected Stories of Louis L'Amour, Vol. II. Louis L'Amour. Bantam (#117,300)

The Winds of Change. Martha Grimes. Viking (117,161)

Good Grief. Lolly Winston. Warner (116,114)

Liars and Thieves. Stephen Coonts. St. Martin's (113,251)

Renegade. Diana Palmer. HQN Books (111,000)

High Druid of Shannara: Tanequil. Terry Brooks. Del Rey (110,365)

Tears for Water. Alicia Keys. Putnam (109,983)

Double Shot. Diane Mott Davidson. Morrow (109,000)

The Shop on Blossom Street. Debbie Macomber. Mira (109,000)

Kiss Me While I Sleep. Linda Howard. Ballantine (108,900)

Little Children. Tom Perrotta. St. Martin's (108,568)

The Paid Companion. Amanda Quick. Putnam (107,414)

The Summer I Dared. Barbara Delinsky. Scribner (#106,800)

A Good Year. Peter Mayle. Knopf (106,574)

Seduced by Moonlight. Laurell K. Hamilton. Ballantine (106,396)

See Jane Die. Erica Spindler. Mira (106,000)

Gilead. Marilynne Robinson. Farrar, Straus & Giroux (105,746)

Hunter Fear. Kay Hooper. Bantam (#103,500)

Bait. Karen Robards. Putnam (103,021)

Runaway. Alice Munro. Knopf (102,777)

The Color of Death. Elizabeth Lowell. Morrow (101,000)

Dune: The Battle of Corrin. Brian Herbert and Kevin J. Anderson. Tor (100,769)

The Runes of the Earth. Steven Donaldson. Putnam (100,430)

Killer Smile. Lisa Scottoline. HarperCollins (100,337)

Hot Target. Suzanne Brockmann. Ballantine (100,207)

The Nonfiction Runners-Up

16. *American Soldier.* Tommy R. Franks. ReganBooks (660,648)
17. *Good to Great.* Jim Collins. CollinsBusiness (654,382)
18. *The Perricone Promise.* Nicholas Perricone. Warner (591,447)
19. *The Passion.* Photographs by Ken Duncan and Philippe Antonello. Tyndale (579,931)
20. *Dress Your Family in Corduroy and Denim.* David Sedaris. Little, Brown (569,474)
21. *Against All Enemies.* Richard A. Clarke. Free Press (#540,000)
22. *Deliver Us from Evil.* Sean Hannity. ReganBooks (527,364)
23. *Faithful.* Stewart O'Nan and Stephen King. Scribner (#510,000)
24. *The Power of Intention.* Wayne W. Dyer. Hay House (496,264)
25. *The Present.* Spencer Johnson. Doubleday (#471,500)
26. *When Will Jesus Bring the Porkchops?* George Carlin. Hyperion (471,399)
27. *Chronicles: Volume One.* Bob Dylan. Simon & Schuster (#456,000)
28. *The Sexy Years.* Suzanne Somers. Crown (455,882)
29. *How to Talk to a Liberal (if You Must).* Ann Coulter. Crown (445,792)
30. *Big Russ and Me.* Tim Russert. Miramax (445,000)

400,000+

His Excellency: George Washington. Joseph J. Ellis. Knopf (436,698)
Battle Ready. Tom Clancy with Tony Zinni and Tony Koltz. Putnam (423,713)
The 8th Habit. Stephen R. Covey. Free Press (#400.000)

300,000+

Trump: How to Get Rich. Donald J. Trump. Random House (381,756)
Alexander Hamilton. Ron Chernow. Penguin Press (374,953)
The Ultimate Weight Solution. Dr. Phil McGraw. Free Press (#360,000)
Barefoot in Paris. Ina Garten. Clarkson Potter (350,793)
Atkins for Life Low-Carb Cookbook. Veronica Atkins with Stephanie Nathanson. St. Martin's (338,045)
Three Weeks with My Brother. Nicholas Sparks and Micah Sparks. Warner (337,451)
The Gourmet Cookbook. Edited by Ruth Reichl. Houghton Mifflin (326,139)
Trump: Billionaire. Donald J. Trump. Random House (323,584)

Ten Minutes from Normal. Karen Hughes. Viking (321,709)
Jan Karon's Mitford Cookbook and Kitchen Reader. Jan Karon. Viking (316,534)
Eating for Life. Bill Phillips. High Point Media (304,428)

200,000+

Come Thirsty. Max Lucado. W Publishing (293,206)
Bushworld. Maureen Dowd. Putnam (282,794)
The Abs Diet. David Zinczenko with Ted Spiker. Rodale (268,574)
Shadow Divers. Robert Kurson. Random House (268,189)
The Price of Loyalty. Ron Suskind. Simon & Schuster (#260,000)
The Last Season. Phil Jackson. Penguin Press (256,538)
Father Joe. Tony Hendra. Random House (255,712)
Learning to Sing. Clay Aiken. Random House (253,540)
Live Like You Were Dying. Tim Nichols and Craig Wiseman. Rutledge Hill (250,339)
Miracle. Anne Geddes and Celine Dion. Andrews McMeel (249,000)

Will They Ever Trust Us Again? Michael Moore. Simon & Schuster (#235,000)

Rise, Let Us Be on Our Way. Pope John Paul II. Warner (232,597)

Sharing Good Times. Jimmy Carter. Simon & Schuster (#225,000)

Between a Rock and a Hard Place. Aron Ralston. Atria (#222,000)

The Book for People Who Do Too Much. Bradley Trevor Greive. Andrews McMeel (222,000)

Founding Mothers. Cokie Roberts. Morrow (219,811)

Now, Discover Your Strengths. Marcus Buckingham and Donald O. Clifton. Free Press (#215,000)

Imperial Hubris. Anonymous. Brassey's (210,000)

Emeril's Potluck. Emeril Lagasse. Morrow (205,161)

The Case for a Creator. Lee Strobel. Zondervan (202,330)

150,000+

Friends to the End. Bradley Trevor Greive. Andrews McMeel (198,000)

The Complete Cartoons of the New Yorker. Edited by Bob Mankoff. Black Dog & Leventhal (190,000)

Diana. Ros Coward and PQ Publishers. Andrews McMeel (189,000)

Prophecy. Sylvia Browne. Dutton (188,519)

The Games Do Count. Brian Kilmeade. ReganBooks (187,560)

Hallelujah! The Welcome Table. Maya Angelou. Random House (187,095)

What's the Matter with Kansas? Thomas Frank. Holt/Metropolitan (187,000)

The World According to Mister Rogers. Fred Rogers. Hyperion (184,458)

Millionaire Women Next Door. Thomas J. Stanley. Andrews McMeel (182,000)

Ending Your Day Right. Joyce Meyer. Warner Faith (177,244)

On the Down Low. J. L. King. Broadway (#174,888)

Queer Eye for the Straight Guy. Ted Allen, Kyan Douglas, Thom Filicia, Carson Kressley, and Jai Rodriguez. Clarkson Potter (173,343)

He-Motions. T. D. Jakes. Putnam (171,606)

Super Foods RX. Steven G. Pratt. Morrow (170,260)

Worse Than Watergate. John Dean. Little, Brown (169,547)

American Dynasty. Kevin Phillips. Viking (168,581)

Seven Things That Steal Your Joy. Joyce Meyer. Warner Faith (168,029)

Green River, Running Red. Ann Rule. Free Press (#167,500)

Give Me a Break. John Stossel. HarperCollins (167,463)

Magical Thinking. Augusten Burroughs. St. Martin's (165,755)

Humor Me. Barbara Johnson. W Publishing (164,887)

The Sinatra Treasures. Charles Pignone. Bulfinch (163,157)

In Pursuit of Peace. Joyce Meyer. Warner Faith (157,631)

Walk Away the Pounds. Leslie Sansone. Warner Faith/Center Street (156,779)

Woman Power. Dr. Laura Schlessinger. HarperCollins (155,278)

Getting in the Gap. Wayne W. Dyer. Hay House (154,397)

A Man of Faith. David Aikman. W Publishing (152,413)

Epic. John Eldredge. Nelson (152,362)

The Faith of George W. Bush. Stephen Mansfield. Tarcher (151,524)

Skywriting. Jane Pauley. Random House (150,732)

Breaking the Da Vinci Code. Darrell L. Bock. Nelson (150,304)

125,000+

The Fabric of the Cosmos. Brian Greene. Knopf (148,486)

The New Strong-Willed Child. James Dobson. Tyndale (145,113)

Straight Talk. Joyce Meyer. Warner Faith (142,881)

The Fred Factor. Mark Sanborn. Doubleday (#140,000)

How to Make Love Like a Porn Star. Jenna Jameson. ReganBooks (137,383)

In the Shadow of No Towers. Art Spiegelman. Pantheon (134,562)

Caddy for Life. John Feinstein. Little, Brown (133,488)

Bringing Tuscany Home. Frances Mayes. Broadway (#133,000)

Confronting Reality. Larry Bossidy and Ram Charan. Crown Business (133,398)

100,000+

Belly Laughs. Jenny McCarthy. DaCapo (122,146)

Confessions of an Heiress. Paris Hilton. Fireside (121,855)

Funny Cide. Sally Jenkins. Putnam (120,173)

How Clean Is Your House? Aggie MacKenzie and Kim Woodburn. Dutton (117,176)

Blue Blood. Edward Conlon. Riverhead (117,024)

Will in the World. Stephen Greenblatt. W. W. Norton (#117,000)

The Gift of Change. Marianne Williamson. Harper San Francisco (116,216)

Ric Flair: To Be the Man. Ric Flair with Keith Elliot Greenberg, edited by Mark Madden. Pocket (115,000)

A Brother's Journey. Richard Pelzer. Warner (114,380)

Farewell, Jackie. Edward Klein. Viking (112,927)

Waking the Dead. John Eldredge. Nelson (111,752)

Chain of Command. Seymour M. Hersh.

HarperCollins (111,049)

Ted Williams. Leigh Montville. Doubleday (#110,500)

Nice Girls Don't Get the Corner Office. Lois Frankel. Warner (110,331)

The Happiest Toddler on the Block. Harvey Karp, M.D. Bantam (#109,000)

Hippie. Barry Miles. Sterling (108,501)

Rewriting History. Dick Morris. ReganBooks (106,242)

Michael Moore Is a Big Fat Stupid White Man. David T. Hardy. ReganBooks (105,450)

Let Me Tell You a Story. Red Auerbach and John Feinstein. Little, Brown (103,558)

Why Courage Matters. John McCain. Random House (103,444)

Sylvia Browne's Lessons for Life. Sylvia Browne. Hay House (103,372)

The Bible Answer Book. Hank Hanegraaff. J. Countryman (103,342)

Wolfgang Puck Makes It Easy. Wolfgang Puck. Rutledge Hill (102,616)

Homegrown Democrat. Garrison Keillor. Viking (102,600)

QBQ! The Question Behind the Question. John Miller. Putnam (101,505)

Carolyn 101. Carolyn Kepcher. Fireside (100,825)

The DNA of Relationships. Gary Smalley. Tyndale (100,499)

Paperback Bestsellers: Everything All Over Again

Dermot McEvoy

Senior Editor, *Publishers Weekly*

Daisy Maryles

Executive Editor, *Publishers Weekly*

Let's talk about Dan Brown's phenomenal performance on the charts one more time, and then we'll move on to the rest of the top bestsellers of 2004. Brown is the first author ever to place all his backlist titles (*Angels & Demons, Deception Point* and *Digital Fortress*) on the mass market charts while his new book (you've heard of *The Da Vinci Code*?) is leading the hardcover charts. Those three paperbacks enjoyed a combined run of 152 weeks on the 2004 charts, with *Angels* commanding the No. 1 spot for 34 of the 51 weeks. And, yes, the three are among the top 10 mass market bestsellers of 2004.

There is also the annual Nora Roberts bestseller count—she's the author with the most bestsellers on the weekly lists. Some are reissues of older titles, but many are new books. Her 2004 paperback tally is 17 mass market titles and 3 trade paperbacks. That's higher then her 2003 numbers: 11 in mass market and 5 in trade paper.

First Fiction Triumphs

In a repeat of 2003, more than half of the trade paperbacks that sold more than 100,000 copies in 2004 are novels. And this group includes a large number of debuts—18 of the 25 trade paper titles with sales of 500,000 or more are fiction; 9 of them are debuts. Most enjoyed long runs on the 2004 weekly charts and, in fact, 7 of these books were among the longest-running bestsellers last year. The bestselling trade paperback fiction in both 2003 and 2004, *The Secret Life of Bees*, didn't miss a single week on the charts last year. So far, it's been on the trade paper list for 110 weeks, 31 of those weeks in the No. 1 spot. It's a good example of the quality fiction titles that shine on the trade paper list (many of them had brief sojourns on the hardcover list). The second bestselling trade fiction title, *The Lovely Bones*, was on the paperback list for 24 weeks and on the hardcover fiction charts for an impressive 65 weeks.

The Oprah Touch

Four of the fiction titles in the top 25 were picked for Oprah's on-air classics book club. The 2004 group included the 1932 Pulitzer Prize novel, *The Good Earth* by Pearl S. Buck, with sales of more than 740,000 copies last year. Selling even better was Leo Tolstoy's *Anna Karenina*, with more than 900,000 copies. Carson McCullers's *The Heart Is a Lonely Hunter* was a debut novel published in 1940, when the author was 23. The book had sold more than a million copies before Oprah, and it tallied an additional 735,000 in 2004. Oprah's first classics pick was *One Hundred Years of Solitude* by Gabriel García Márquez. It was first published in Spanish in 1967 and has gone on to sell more than 30 million copies in 37 languages; last year alone, it sold about 850,000 copies.

Paper Politics

Politics was a hot subject last year, and our trade paper list had quite a few titles in that category. Judging by the numbers, the most successful was *The 9/11 Commission Report*, with sales of about 1,430,000. Hillary Clinton's *Living History* was another strong title, selling more than 310,000 copies. Barack Obama's memoir, *Dreams from My Father*, first published in 1995 to modest sales, took flight after his keynote speech at the Democratic Convention in July; 2004 sales were about 298,000.

Tie-ins Reap Sales

While most of the bestsellers listed in these pages were published in 2003 and 2004, there are some books released earlier. A good many of these are movie or television tie-ins, and this year we even have Broadway musical tie-ins, specifically Gregory Maguire's *Wicked* (the prequel to *The Wizard of Oz*). The most successful tie-in in 2004 was *The Notebook* by Nicholas Sparks—it showed up on both the trade (590,000 sold) and mass market charts (1,875,000).

Mass Market Numbers High

Over the last decade, mass market numbers have fallen, while the numbers for hardcover bestsellers continue to rise. The type of books that appear on these end-of-year lists has also remained steady—mass market is the home of genre fiction. The only nonfiction topic that sells more than 500,000 copies thse days is diet. In 2004 two Atkins titles were still selling in the beginning of the year, but they dropped off the list in mid-spring. The only other nonfiction title, also a diet book, was *The Ultimate Weight Solution Food Guide* by Dr. Phil McGraw.

Genre fiction and bestselling reprints are what fill the slots on the mass market charts. It's pretty much romance and women's fiction vs. mystery and suspense, with the former a bit ahead in number of titles. Popular commercial titles rule this list, while more literary fiction and strong narratives command the trade paperback category. No new trend here, just more of the same.

Rules for Inclusion

Listed on the following pages are trade paperbacks and mass market titles published in 2003 and 2004; the rankings are based only on 2004 sales. To qualify, trade paperbacks had to have sold more than 100,000 copies in 2004; for mass markets, sales of more than 500,000 were required. A single asterisk (*) indicates the book was published in 2003; a double asterisk (**) means the book was published earlier but either remained or reappeared on *Publishers Weekly*'s bestseller charts in 2004. These reappearances are most often movie tie-ins. A pound symbol (#) indicates that the shipped-and-billed figure was rounded down to the nearest 5,000 to indicate the book's sales relationship to other titles; the actual figures were given to *Publishers Weekly* in confidence for use only in placing titles on these lists.

Trade Paperbacks

One Million+

The South Beach Diet Good Fats/Good Carbs Guide. Arthur Agatston. Orig. Rodale (2,419,332)

The 9/11 Commission Report. The 9/11 Commission. Norton. Orig. (1,430,000)

*The Secret Life of Bees. Sue Monk Kidd. Rep. Penguin (1,175,291)

The Lovely Bones. Alice Sebold. Rep. Little, Brown (1,117,738)

750,000+

The Wedding. Nicholas Sparks. Rep. Warner (965,338)

Anna Karenina. Leo Tolstoy. Reissue. Oprah Pick. Penguin (937,408)

**Reading Lolita in Tehran.* Azar Nafisi. Rep. Random (883,715)

**1,000 Places to See Before You Die.* Patricia Schultz. Orig. Workman (873,797)

One Hundred Years of Solitude. Gabriel García Márquez. Rep. Oprah. Perennial (849,337)

The Curious Incident of the Dog in the Night-Time. Mark Haddon. Rep. Vintage (834,790)

The Kite Runner. Khaled Hosseini. Rep. Riverhead (808,391)

Atkins for Life. Robert C. Atkins, M.D. Rep. St. Martin's/Griffin (760,000)

500,000+

#**The Good Earth.* Pearl S. Buck. Reissue. Oprah Pick. Washington Square (740,000)

***The Heart Is a Lonely Hunter.* Carson McCullers. Rep. Oprah Pick. Mariner (735,618)

The Devil in the White City. Erik Larson. Rep. Vintage (621,234)

**Life of Pi.* Yann Martel. Rep. Harvest (618,599)

The Devil Wears Prada. Lauren Weisberger. Rep. Broadway (598,869)

The Time Traveler's Wife. Audrey Niffenegger. Rep. Harvest (595,332)

***The Notebook.* Nicholas Sparks. Movie tie-in. Warner (594,147)

***Tuesdays with Morrie.* Mitch Albom. Rep. Broadway (582,668)

***No. 1 Ladies' Detective Agency.* Alexander McCall Smith. Rep. Anchor (582,140)

The Case for Easter. Lee Strobel. Orig. Zondervan (572,123)

All He Ever Wanted. Anita Shreve. Rep. Little, Brown (557,225)

#*The Ultimate Weight Solution.* Dr. Phil McGraw. Rep. Free Press (530,000)

***Rich Dad, Poor Dad.* Robert T. Kiyosaki and Sharon L. Lechter. Orig. Warner (512,464)

**Middlesex.* Jeffrey Eugenides. Rep. Picador (500,000)

300,000+

Sacred Stone. Clive Cussler. Rep. Berkley (470,031)

**Three Junes.* Julia Glass. Rep. Anchor (463,109)

Shepherds Abiding. Jan Karon. Rep. Penguin (451,522)

Lies. Al Franken. Rep. Plume (410,190)

Glorious Appearing. Tim LaHaye and Jerry B. Jenkins. Rep. Tyndale (410,000)

Bad Cat. Jim Edgar. Orig. Workman (403,000)

The Known World. Edward P. Jones. Rep. Amistad (400,000)

The Kalahari Typing School for Men. Alexander McCall Smith. Rep. Anchor (390,437)

The Dante Club. Matthew Pearl. Rep. Random (388,488)

**Cold Mountain.* Charles Frazier. Movie tie-in. Vintage (381,067)

Angry Housewives Eating Bon Bons. Lorna Landvik. Rep. Ballantine (369,509)

***Wicked.* Gregory Maguire. Broadway tie-in. ReganBooks (363,696)

Bridget Jones: The Edge of Reason. Helen Fielding. Movie tie-in. Penguin (352,328)

Friday Night Lights. H.G. Bissinger. Movie tie-in. Da Capo (350,110)

The Red Hat Society. Sue Ellen Cooper. Orig. Warner (331,487)

Dude, Where's My Country? Michael Moore. Rep. Warner (324,619)

#*Living History.* Hillary Clinton. Rep. Scribner (311,857)

**Running with Scissors.* Augusten Burroughs. Rep. Picador (310,000)

30-Minute Meals 2. Rachael Ray. Orig. Lake Isle (300,000)

250,000+

Dreams from My Father. Barack Obama. Orig. Crown (298,028)

Under the Banner of Heaven. Jon Krakauer. Rep. Anchor (294,016)

Flyboys. James Bradley. Rep. Little, Brown (282,479)

Cooking 'Round the Clock. Rachael Ray. Orig. Lake Isle (280,000)

#**Bringing Down the House.* Ben Mezrich. Rep. Free Press (275,000)

Stupid White Men. Michael Moore. Rep. ReganBooks (273,572)

Moneyball. Michael Lewis. Rep. Norton (273,000)

Experiencing the Passion of Jesus. Lee Strobel and Garry Poole. Orig. Zondervan (267,587)

The Prodigal: Abram's Daughters #4. Beverly Lewis. Orig. Bethany (266,994)

A Short History of Nearly Everything. Bill Bryson. Rep. Broadway (261,623)

*Atonement. Ian McEwan. Rep. Anchor (255,064)

*Girl with a Pearl Earring. Tracy Chevalier. Movie tie-in. Plume (253,703)

Robert Ludlum's The Lazarus Vendetta. Patrick Larkin. Orig. St. Martin's/Griffin (250,000)

200,000+

**Mere Christianity. C. S. Lewis. Rep. Harper San Francisco (245,000)

*Revenge of the Middle-Aged Woman. Elizabeth Buchan. Rep. Penguin (231,631)

#Queen's Fool. Philippa Gregory. Rep. Touchstone (230,100)

The Namesake. Jhumpa Lahiri. Rep. Mariner (226,212)

Trading Up. Candace Bushnell. Rep. Hyperion (220,000)

Lovers and Dreamers 3-in-1. Nora Roberts. Rep. Berkley (216,123)

The Sacrifice: Abram's Daughters #3. Beverly Lewis. Orig. Bethany (209,199)

The Perricone Prescription. Nicholas Perricone. Rep. HarperCollins (208,987)

**Dr. Atkins' New Carbohydrate Gram Counter. Robert C. Atkins. M.D. Orig. M. Evans (206,409)

*What Not to Wear. Susannah Constantine. Rep. Riverhead (204,618)

The Dirty Girls Social Club. Alisa Valdes-Rodriguez. Rep. St. Martin's/Griffin (200,000)

150,000+

Stiff. Mary Roach. Rep. Norton (199,990)

Finally. Boston Globe. Orig. Triumph (195,000)

The Dogs of Babel. Carolyn Parkhurst. Rep. Little, Brown (187,793)

The Amateur Marriage. Anne Tyler. Rep. Ballantine (187,636)

The Savage Nation. Michael Savage. Rep. Plume (185,596)

The Birth of Venus. Sarah Dunant. Rep. Random (184,958)

*Father to Daughter. Harry H. Harrison, Jr. Orig. Workman (183,793)

#The 7 Habits of Highly Effective People. Stephen R. Covey. Revised. Free Press (182,587)

*Chicken Soup for the Mother & Daughter Soul. Canfield, Hansen. Orig. HCI (176,674)

**A Raisin in the Sun. Lorraine Hansberry. Broadway tie-in. Vintage (174,974)

Chicken Soup for the Teenage Soul IV. Canfield, Hansen. Orig. HCI (173,849)

*Play Poker Like the Pros. Phil Hellmuth. Orig. HarperCollins (173,753)

Chicken Soup for the Girlfriend's Soul. Canfield, Hansen. Orig. HCI (171,526)

**The Tipping Point. Malcolm Gladwell. Rep. Little, Brown (169,589)

**It's Not About the Bike. Lance Armstrong. Rep. Berkley (167,395)

#Benjamin Franklin. Walter Isaacson. Rep. S&S (161,378)

Hidden Riches. Nora Roberts. Rep. Berkley (160,866)

Diary. Chuck Palahniuk. Rep. Anchor (155,557)

Dry. Augusten Burroughs. Rep. Picador (155,000)

The Faith of George W. Bush. Stephen Mansfield. Rep. Tarcher (154,000)

Under God. Toby Mac and Michael Tait. Orig. Bethany (153,641)

*Big Fish. Daniel Wallace. Movie tie-in. Penguin (153,285)

The Lady and the Unicorn. Tracy Chevalier. Rep. Plume (152,346)

The Privilege of Youth. Dave Pelzer. Rep. Plume (151,744)

#*Shopaholic Ties the Knot. Sophie Kinsella. Orig. Delta (151,501)

The Murder Room. P. D. James. Rep. Vintage (151,010)

Sex and the City: Kiss and Tell. Amy Sohn. Rep. Pocket (150,000)

125,000+

Wicked Musical Tie-In Edition. Gregory Maguire. Broadway tie-in. ReganBooks (148,262)

Who's Looking Out for You? Bill O'Reilly. Rep. Broadway (148,151)

Chicken Soup Life Lessons for Women. Canfield, Hansen. Orig. HCI (148,082)

The Bush Survival Bible. Gene Stone. Orig. Random (147,404)

Chicken Soup for the African American Soul. Canfield, Hansen. Orig. HCI (147,266)

**Smart Couples Finish Rich.* David Bach. Rep. Broadway (146,975)

Absolute Friends. John le Carré. Rep. Little, Brown (146,623)

Chicken Soup for the PreTeen Soul 2. Canfield, Hansen. Orig. HCI (146,352)

#*In Her Shoes.* Jennifer Weiner. Rep. Washington Square (144,892)

Chicken Soup for the Bride's Soul. Canfield, Hansen. Orig. HCI (143,705)

Every Storm. Lori Wick. Orig. Harvest (143,000)

Rich Dad's Who Took My Money? Robert T. Kiyosaki and Sharon L. Lechter, C.P.A. Orig. Warner (142,636)

#*Brick Lane.* Monica Ali. Rep. Scribner (141,983)

The Sweet Potato Queens' Field Guide to Men. Jill Conner Browne. Orig. Crown (139,311)

The Step Diet Book. James O. Hill, John C. Peters and Bonnie T. Jortberg. Orig. Workman (139,000)

#*The Hornet's Nest.* Jimmy Carter. Rep. S&S (138,460)

Rejoice. Karen Kingsbury with Gary Smalley. Orig. Tyndale (137,334)

Don't Think of an Elephant. George Lakoff. Orig. Chelsea Green (136,694)

Franklin and Winston. Jon Meacham. Rep. Random (135,967)

#*Villa Incognito.* Tom Robbins. Rep. Bantam (135,896)

Pope Bottle Science. Lynn Brunelle. Orig. Workman (135,000)

Let Freedom Ring. Sean Hannity. Rep. Regan (134,494)

The Voice of Knowledge. Don Miguel Ruiz. Orig. Amber-Allen (133,993)

Every Second Counts. Lance Armstrong. Rep. Broadway (133,698)

Pattern Recognition. William Gibson. Rep. Berkley (131,653)

Kate Remembered. A. Scott Berg. Rep. Berkley (128,492)

What Not to Wear: For Every Occasion. Trinny Woodall. Rep. Riverhead (128,230)

The Essential 55. Ron Clark. Rep. Hyperion (128,000)

Reunion. Karen Kingsbury with Gary Smalley. Orig. Tyndale (127,686)

One Tuesday Morning. Karen Kingsbury. Orig. Zondervan (126,325)

100,000+

Monster Careers. Jeffrey Taylor. Orig. Penguin (124,546)

Woman, Thou Art Loosed! T. D. Jakes. Rep. Berkley (123,984)

Curves. Gary Heavin. Rep. Perigee (122,596)

#*Holy Blood, Holy Grail.* Michael Baigent, Richard Leight and Henry Lincoln. Rep. Delta (122,472)

Confessions of an Ugly Stepsister. Gregory Maguire. Rep. ReganBooks (121,270)

The Abs Diet Eat Right Every Time Guide. David Zinczenko. Orig. Rodale (120,248)

Bucky Katt's Big Book of Fun. Darby Conley. Orig. Andrews McMeel (119,500)

#*The Official Fahrenheit 9/11 Reader.* Michael Moore. Orig. S&S (118,000)

The Pleasure of My Company. Steve Martin. Rep. Hyperion (118,000)

Oryx & Crake. Margaret Atwood. Rep. Anchor (117,318)

Uniform Justice. Donna Leon. Rep. Penguin (117,187)

#*Nervous.* Zane. Rep. Atria (116,800)

Nights in Rodanthe. Nicholas Sparks. Rep. Warner (116,308)

#*The Funny Thing Is . . .* Ellen DeGeneres. Rep. S&S (116,000)

Our Lady of the Forest. David Guterson. Rep. Vintage (116,000)

Lucia Lucia. Adriana Trigiani. Rep. Ballantine (115,688)

Get Togethers. Rachael Ray. Orig. Lake Isle (115,000)

Positively Fifth Street. James McManus. Rep. Picador (115,000)

#*The Happiest Baby on the Block. Harvey Karp, M.D. Rep. Bantam (114,500)
**The Elegant Universe. Brian Greene. TV tie-in. Vintage (114,391)
Treason. Ann Coulter. Rep. Crown (113,734)
Everyday Grace. Marianne Williamson. Rep. Riverhead (113,257)
Lost in a Good Book. Jasper Fforde. Rep. Penguin (112,572)
Garfield Tips the Scales. Jim Davis. Orig. Ballantine (112,520)
*The Dinner Doctor. Anne Byrn. Orig. Workman (112,057)
Babyville. Jane Green. Rep. Broadway (108,122)
The Other Woman. Eric Dickey. Rep. NAL (106,693)
#Holly. Jude Deveraux. Rep. Atria (106,500)
*The Virgin Blue. Tracy Chevalier. Rep. Plume (106,498)
Chicken Soup to Inspire a Woman's Soul. Canfield, Hansen. Orig. HCI (106,102)
The Darwin Awards III. Wendy Northcutt. Rep. (104,041)
Haley's Cleaning Hints. Rosemary Haley. Rep. NAL (104,010)
Chicken Soup for the Fisherman's Soul. Canfield, Hansen. Orig. HCI (103,980)
*Queen Bees and Wannabes. Rosalind Wiseman. Movie tie-in. Crown (103,923)
*Michelangelo and the Pope's Ceiling. Ross King. Rep. Penguin (103,359)
Stitch 'N Bitch Nation. Debbie Stoller. Orig. Workman (103,126)
*East of Eden. John Steinbeck. Rep. Oprah Pick. Penguin (102,779)
Sea of Glory. Nathaniel Philbrick. Rep. Penguin (102,632)
Grits (Girls Raised in the South) Guide to Life. Deborah Ford. Rep. Plume (102,501)
The Probable Future. Alice Hoffman. Rep. Ballantine (102,327)
Naughty or Nice. Eric Dickey. Rep. NAL (101,891)
The Coffee Trader. David Liss. Rep. Ballantine (101,874)
Oceans Apart. Karen Kingsbury. Orig. Zondervan (101,016)
**Plainsong. Kent Haruf. TV tie-in. Vintage (100,113)
The Good Wife Strikes Back. Elizabeth Buchan. Rep. Penguin (100,000)

The Great Fire. Shirley Hazzard. Rep. Picador (100,000)
#Girls Night In. Meg Cabot et al. Orig. Red Dress Ink (100,000)
#Born O'Hurley. Nora Roberts. Reissue. Silhouette (100,000)
#Devin & Shane. Nora Roberts. Reissue. Silhouette (100,000)
#Rafe & Jared. Nora Roberts. Reissue. Silhouette (100,000)

Almanacs, Atlases and Annuals

The World Almanac and Book of Facts, 2005. Edited by Ken Park. Annual. World Almanac (400,000)
J. K. Lasser's Your Income Tax 2005. J. K. Lasser. Annual Wiley (316,931)
*The World Almanac and Book of Facts, 2004. Annual. World Almanac (250,000)
The 2005 Old Farmer's Almanac. Annual. Yankee (245,844)
AAA Europe TravelBook, 5th Edition. Annual. AAA (196,707)
2005 AAA North American Road Atlas. Annual. AAA (178,568)
What Color Is Your Parachute? 2005. Richard Nelson Bolles. Orig. Ten Speed (107,000)

Mass Market

Two Million+

**Angels & Demons. Dan Brown. Rep. Pocket (3,800,000) 2004
#Bleachers. John Grisham. Rep. Dell (2,850,000)
#The Last Juror. John Grisham. Rep. Dell (3,792,483)
**Deception Point. Dan Brown. Rep. Pocket (2,500,000)
#Skipping Christmas. John Grisham. Movie tie-in. Dell (2,400,000)
#Safe Harbour. Danielle Steel. Rep. Dell (2,250,000)
Blue Dahlia. Nora Roberts. Rep. Jove (2,177,030)
Digital Fortress. Dan Brown. Rep. St. Martin's (2,000,000)

One Million+

**Dr. Atkins New Diet Revolution.* Robert C. Atkins, M.D. Revised. Avon (1,900,000)

***The Notebook.* Nicholas Sparks. Movie tie-in. Warner (1,875,589)

The Guardian. Nicholas Sparks. Rep. Warner (1,780,816)

**Prey.* Michael Crichton. Rep. Avon (1,750,000)

Birthright. Nora Roberts. Rep. Jove (1,735,936)

Blow Fly. Patricia Cornwell. Rep. Berkley (1,727,676)

The Big Bad Wolf. James Patterson. Rep. Warner (1,682,504)

Chesapeake Blue. Nora Roberts. Rep. Jove (1,600,294)

The Teeth of the Tiger. Tom Clancy. Rep. Berkley (1,582,497)

The Second Time Around. Mary Higgins Clark. Rep. Pocket (1,555,000)

The Lake House. James Patterson. Rep. Warner (1,552,317)

The Jester. James Patterson. Rep. Warner (1,511,234)

Split Second. David Baldacci. Rep. Warner (1,344,354)

Blindside. Catherine Coulter. Rep. Jove (1,338,199)

#*Odd Thomas.* Dean Koontz. Rep. Bantam (1,326,206)

Remember When. Nora Roberts. Rep. Berkley (1,325,239)

Nights in Rodanthe. Nicholas Sparks. Rep. Warner (1,306,303)

A Little Fate. Nora Roberts. Rep. Jove (1,253,031)

A Little Magic. Nora Roberts. Rep. Jove (1,249,207)

To the Nines. Janet Evanovich. Rep. St. Martin's (1,200,000)

**The Atkins Essentials.* Robert C. Atkins, M.D. Orig. Avon (1,200,000)

Hello, Darkness. Sandra Brown. Rep. Pocket Star (1,200,000)

#*The Face.* Dean Koontz. Rep. Bantam (1,167,889)

Naked Prey. John Sandford. Rep. Berkley (1,119,611)

Conspiracy Club. Jonathan Kellerman. Rep. Ballantine (1,109,961)

Full Blast. Janet Evanovich. Orig. St. Martin's (1,100,000)

The Ultimate Weight Solution Food Guide. Dr. Phil. Orig. Pocket (1,100,000)

Trojan Odyssey. Clive Cussler. Rep. Berkley (1,070,000)

#*Dance with Me.* Luanne Rice. Rep. Bantam (1,050,000)

#*Dark Horse.* Tami Hoag. Rep. Bantam (1,030,000)

#*Dating Game.* Danielle Steel. Rep. Dell (1,025,000)

Wild Orchids. Jude Deveraux. Rep. Pocket (1,000,000)

750,000+

Divided in Death. J. D. Robb. Rep. Berkley (996,121)

White Death. Clive Cussler. Rep. Berkley (992,932)

The Sherbrooke Twins. Catherine Coulter. Rep. Jove (985,609)

Late Bloomer. Fern Michaels. Rep. Pocket Star (975,000)

Always. Jude Deveraux. Orig. Pocket (900,000)

Flirting with Pete. Barbara Delinsky. Rep. Pocket (900,000)

The Vanished Man. Jeffery Deaver. Rep. Pocket (900,000)

#*Beach Girls.* Luanne Rice. Orig. Bantam (942,546)

Lost Light. Michael Connelly. Rep. Warner (941,929)

#*Dead Aim.* Iris Johansen. Rep. Bantam (934,313)

The Christmas Train. David Baldacci. Rep. Warner (932,112)

#*The Bourne Supremacy.* Robert Ludlum. Movie tie-in. Bantam (882,953)

Capital Crimes. Stuart Woods. Rep. Signet (859,304)

The Hanged Man's Song. John Sandford. Rep. Berkley (858,316)

Emma's Secret. Barbara Taylor Bradford. Rep. St. Martin's (850,000)

The Tristan Betrayal. Robert Ludlum. Rep. St. Martin's (850,000)

A Man to Call My Own. Johanna Lindsey. Rep. Pocket Star (850,000)

#*The Killing Hour.* Lisa Gardner. Rep. Bantam (821,652)

Robert Ludlum's The Altman Code. Gayle Lynds. Rep. St. Martin's (800,000)

Tom Clancy's Splinter Cell. David Michaels. Rep. Berkley (788,864)

#*The Secret Hour.* Luanne Rice. Rep. Bantam (787,655)

#*Johnny Angel.* Danielle Steel. Rep. Dell (786,747)

Op-Center 11: Call to Treason. Jeff Rovin. Rep. Berkley (783,416)

To Die For. Linda Howard. Orig. Ballantine (770,508)

Street Dreams. Faye Kellerman. Rep. Warner (752,815)

500,000+

The Real Deal. Fern Michaels. Orig. Pocket (730,000)

The Footprints of God. Greg Iles. Rep. Pocket Star (725,000)

No Second Chance. Harlan Coben. Rep. Signet (688,496)

Liberty. Stephen Coonts. Rep. St. Martin's (675,000)

#*The Sight of the Stars.* Danielle Steel. Rep. Dell (667,659)

Heart Full of Lies. Ann Rule. Rep. Pocket (625,000)

Executive Power. Vince Flynn. Rep. Pocket Star (610,000)

The Avenger. Fredrick Forsyth. Rep. St. Martin's (600,000)

Nowhere to Run. Mary Jane Clark. Rep. St. Martin's (600,000)

Kiss Me, Kill Me. Ann Rule. Orig. Pocket Star (600,000)

Blacklist. Sara Paretsky. Rep. Signet (594,866)

Seizure. Robin Cook. Rep. Berkley (592,544)

Bare Bones. Kathy Reichs. Rep. Pocket Star (580,000)

Isle of Palms. Dorothea Frank. Rep. Berkley (577,720)

#*Sense of Evil.* Kay Hooper. Rep. Bantam (571,731)

Power Plays #8: Wild Card. Jerome Preisler. Rep. Berkley (571,206)

Midnight. Dean Koontz. Rep. Berkley (565,299)

Twisted. Jeffery Deaver. Rep. Pocket (560,000)

The Price. Joan Johnston. Rep. Pocket Star (560,000)

Celeste. V. C. Andrews. Orig. Pocket Star (560,000)

The Rocky Road to Romance. Janet Evanovich. Revision. HarperTorch (550,000)

The Reluctant Suitor. Kathleen E. Woodiwiss. Rep. Avon (550,000)

Reckless Abandon. Stuart Woods. Rep. Signet (547,005)

The Second Chair. John Lescroart. Rep. Signet (544,178)

Black Cat. V. C. Andrews. Rep. Pocket Star (535,000)

Secret Window. Stephen King. Rep. Signet (533,629)

#*Babylon Rising.* Tim LaHaye with Greg Dinallo. Rep. Dell (532,806)

The Passions of Chelsea Kane. Barbara Delinsky. Reissue. HarperTorch (530,000)

The Sinister Pig. Tony Hillerman. Rep. HarperTorch (523,000)

Not Even for Love. Sandra Brown. Rep. Warner (521,774)

The Rivals. Joan Johnston. Orig. Pocket (510,000)

Beachcomber. Karen Robards. Rep. Pocket Star (510,000)

The Sinner. Tess Gerritsen. Rep. Ballantine (507,916)

Truth or Dare. Jayne Anne Krentz. Rep. Jove (506,021)

Flashpoint. Suzanne Brockmann. Rep. Ballantine (501,322)

Shutter Island. Dennis Lehane. Rep. HarperTorch (501,000)

In Her Shoes. Jennifer Weiner. Rep. Pocket Star (500,000)

Die in Plain Sight. Elizabeth Lowell. Rep. Avon (500,000)

Exit Wounds. J. A. Jance. Rep. Avon (500,000)

When He Was Wicked. Julia Quinn. Orig. Avon (500,000)

#*Hot Stuff.* Carly Phillips. Orig. HQN (500,000)

#*Missing.* Sharon Sala. Orig. Mira (500,000)

#*44 Cranberry Point.* Debbie Macomber. Orig. Mira (500,000)

#*Changing Habits.* Debbie Macomber. Orig. Mira (500,000)

#*In Silence.* Erica Spindler. Rep. Mira (500,000)

#*On a Snowy Night.* Debbie Macomber. Reissue. Mira (500,000)

#Captivated. Nora Roberts. Reissue. Silhouette (500,000)

#With Open Arms. Nora Roberts. Reissue. Silhouette (500,000)

#Charmed & Enchanted. Nora Roberts. Reissue. Silhouette (500,000)

#Winner Takes All. Nora Roberts. Reissue. Silhouette (500,000)

#Reunion. Nora Roberts. Reissue. Silhouette (500,000)

* Published in 2003.
** Published prior to 2003.
# Sales figures were submitted to *Publishers Weekly* in confidence, for use in placing titles on the lists. Numbers shown are rounded down to the nearest 25,000 to indicate relationship to sales figures of other titles.

Children's Bestsellers: Hollywood Comes Calling

Diane Roback

Senior Editor, Children's Books, *Publishers Weekly*

Last year was a strong one for children's books: in hardcover, 238 titles sold more than 75,000 copies; in paperback, 310 books sold more than 100,000 copies. Numbers-wise, however, the year belonged to Lemony Snicket.

The Series of Unfortunate Events began in 1999, with a 20,000-copy first printing for the first volume, *The Bad Beginning*. By the end of 2003 the series had already sold 13 million copies worldwide. But with last November's release of the Paramount film, sales catapulted into the stratosphere. The 11 titles in the series, plus six movie tie-in editions, sold 8.1 million copies in total (3 million frontlist and 5.1 million backlist) in 2004.

There were only 9 picture books in the top 25 slots for hardcover frontlist last year, further proof of the predominance of fiction these days. Several picture books by longtime favorites could be found near the top of the charts: Eric Carle, Jan Brett, Robert Sabuda, and the team of Jamie Lee Curtis and Laura Cornell. And a handful of celebrities made their marks on the list as well, including Billy Crystal, Katie Couric, Maria Shriver, and Madonna.

Fiction series in particular were big: Lemony Snicket of course, but also Magic Tree House, Junie B. Jones, the Spiderwick Chronicles, the Princess Diaries. One-off hits, almost exclusively in the fantasy genre, included *Dragon Rider, Peter and the Starcatchers, Shadowmancer, The Supernaturalist, The Golem's Eye,* and *Charlie Bone and the Invisible Boy.*

In hardcover backlist, 10 of the top 12 titles were Lemony Snicket books. But at the top of the list was another movie tie-in, *The Polar Express.* Chris Van Allsburg's 1985 picture book is a reliable bestseller each Christmas season (202,000 sold in 2002 and 235,000 in 2003), but the holiday movie, which had a domestic gross of $162.7 million, helped the original hardcover sell 1.3 million copies last year (plus another million copies of four movie tie-ins). In other highlights, a 2003 fantasy hit was still going strong a year later: *Eragon* by Christopher Paolini sold three-quarters of a million copies. Kate DiCamillo's *The Tale of Despereaux* saw sales of nearly 300,000 in the year it won the Newbery

Medal. Jamie Lee Curtis's four backlist picture books sold just under 1 million copies combined. And two novelties, *My Granny's Purse* and *Tails*, proved backlist stalwarts, each selling more than 300,000 copies.

The biggest news in paperback frontlist was the release of a Harry Potter reprint, *Harry Potter and the Order of the Phoenix*, with almost 1.5 million copies sold, nearly double that of the next contender on the list. Paperback movie tie-ins abounded for a raft of kids' films, including *The Incredibles, Spider-Man 2, The Polar Express, Shark Tale,* and *Shrek 2*. Big standalone fiction reprints were *Hoot, The Sisterhood of the Traveling Pants,* and the student edition of *Life of Pi*. And in series, those aimed at preteen girls ruled the roost: The New Adventures of Mary-Kate and Ashley, W.I.T.C.H., and Lizzie McGuire.

Louis Sachar's *Holes*, which garnered widespread critical and commercial success (and was the basis for a hit movie), commanded the top spot in our paperback backlist list, selling just under 500,000 copies in multiple editions. The next two slots went to classics *The Giver* and *The Outsiders*, each selling in excess of 400,000 copies. The Magic Tree House series sold more than 5 million copies in backlist (and an additional 643,000 copies in frontlist). And Junie B. Jones sold nearly 3.4 million copies (plus another 465,000 in frontlist). Clearly, those two series have evergreen appeal for each new crop of emerging readers. Sales for the Harry Potter backlist, however, have dropped off: 900,000 copies of the first four Harry Potter titles sold last year, compared to almost 1.9 million copies in 2003.

Hardcover Frontlist

300,000+

1. *The Grim Grotto (A Series of Unfortunate Events #11)*. Lemony Snicket, illus. by Brett Helquist. HarperCollins (1,404,367)

2. *santaKid*. James Patterson, illus. by Michael Garland. Little, Brown (431,638)

3. *Mister Seahorse*. Eric Carle. Philomel (426,014)

4. *Summer of the Serpent (Magic Tree House #31)*. Mary Pope Osborne, illus. by Sal Murdocca. Random (368,182)

5. *A Series of Unfortunate Events: The Bad Beginning* (movie tie-in). Lemony Snicket, illus. by Brett Helquist. HarperKidsEntertainment (323,608)

6. *It's Hard to Be Five*. Jamie Lee Curtis, illus. by Laura Cornell. HarperCollins/Cotler (319,651)

7. *I Already Know I Love You*. Billy Crystal, illus. by Elizabeth Sayles. HarperCollins (313,405)

8. *The O'Reilly Factor for Kids*. Bill O'Reilly and Charles Flowers. HarperEntertainment (305,000)

9. *Peter and the Starcatchers*. Ridley Pearson and Dave Barry. Disney (300,000)

200,000+

10. *Dragon Rider.* Cornelia Funke. Scholastic/Chicken House (293,194)

11. *The Wrath of Mulgarath (The Spiderwick Chronicles #5).* Tony DiTerlizzi and Holly Black. S&S (292,390)

12. The Ironwood Tree (The Spiderwick Chronicles #4). Tony DiTerlizzi and Holly Black. S&S (283,302)

13. *Winter of the Ice Wizard (Magic Tree House #32).* Mary Pope Osborne, illus. by Sal Murdocca. Random (275,026)

14. *Where the Sidewalk Ends (30th Anniversary Edition).* Shel Silverstein. HarperCollins (265,832)

15. *The Umbrella.* Jan Brett. Putnam (258,821)

16. *Shadowmancer.* G. P. Taylor. Putnam (255,276)

17. *Junie B., First Grader: Shipwrecked.* Barbara Park, illus. by Denise Brunkus. Random (241,440)

18. *Junie B., First Grader: Boo . . . and I MEAN It!* Barbara Park, illus. by Denise Brunkus. Random (223,421)

19. *A Series of Unfortunate Events: The Reptile Room* (movie tie-in). Lemony Snicket, illus. by Brett Helquist. HarperKidsEntertainment (218,963)

20. *A Series of Unfortunate Events: The Wide Window* (movie tie-in). Lemony Snicket, illus. by Brett Helquist. HarperKidsEntertainment (204,302)

21. *The Princess Diaries, Vol. V: Princess in Pink.* Meg Cabot. HarperCollins (203,830)

100,000+

22. *Yakov and the Seven Thieves.* Madonna, illus. by Gennady Spirin. Callaway/Penguin (198,441)

23. *Disney Princess Music Player Storybook.* Reader's Digest (193,754)

24. *America the Beautiful.* Adapted and illus. by Robert Sabuda. S&S (193,408)

25. *Walter the Farting Dog: Trouble at the Yard Sale.* William Kotzwinkle and Glenn Murray, illus. by Audrey Colman. Dutton (184,685)

26. *Duck for President.* Doreen Cronin, illus. by Betsy Lewin. S&S (181,809)

27. *Lost in the Woods.* by Carl R. Sams II and Jean Stoick. Carl R. Sams II Photography (179,251)

28. *The Supernaturalist.* Eoin Colfer. Hyperion/Miramax (175,000)

29. *Egypotology.* Emily Sands, illus. by Nick Harris, Ian Andrew and Helen Ward. Candlewick (171,035)

30. *Thanks & Giving: All Year Long.* Edited by Marlo Thomas and Christopher Cerf. S&S (170,742)

31. *The Blue Ribbon Day.* Katie Couric, illus. by Marjorie Priceman. Doubleday (169,776)

32. *What's Happening to Grandpa?* Maria Shriver, illus. by Sandra Speidel. Little, Brown (167,883)

33. *Emeril's There's a Chef in My Family!* Emeril Lagasse, illus. by Charles Yuen. HarperCollins (165,568)

34. *Disney Princess: Happily Ever After Stories.* Disney (150,000)

35. *The Golem's Eye (Bartimaeus Trilogy #2).* Jonathan Stroud. Hyperion/Miramax (150,000)

36. *Hop on Pop* (board book). Dr. Seuss. Random (149,944)

37. *Charlie Bone and the Invisible Boy.* Jenny Nimmo. Scholastic/Orchard (147,444)

38. *Disney's Home on the Range.* Golden/Disney (146,982)

39. *Travel Team.* Mike Lupica. Philomel (142,139)

40. *Sleeping Beauty.* Michael Teitelbaum. Golden/Disney (141,965)

41. *Old MacDonald* (board book). Illus. by Michelle Berg. Scholastic/Cartwheel (140,904)

42. *Care Bears: Storybook Treasury.* Scholastic/Cartwheel (139,847)

43. *Wild About Books.* Judy Sierra, illus. by Marc Brown. Knopf (138,683)

44. *The World of Dick & Jane and Friends.* Grosset & Dunlap (134,595)

45. *Your Favorite Seuss.* Dr. Seuss. Random (134,075)

46. *Shrek 2: Movie Storybook.* Tom Mason and Dan Danko, illus. by Peter Bollinger. Scholastic/Cartwheel (131,761)

47. *Wormwood.* G. P. Taylor. Putnam (128,810)

48. *Beyond the Deepwoods (The Edge Chronicles #1).* Paul Stewart and Chris Riddell. Random/Fickling (128,435)

49. *The Artemis Fowl Files.* Eoin Colfer. Hyperion/Miramax (125,000)

50. *When Washington Crossed the Delaware.* Lynne Cheney, illus. by Peter M. Fiore. S&S (122,870)

51. *Science Verse.* Jon Scieszka, illus. by Lane Smith. Viking (121,028)

52. *Away Laughing on a Fast Camel.* Louise Rennison. HarperTempest (119,595)

53. *Chasing Vermeer.* Blue Balliett, illus. by Brett Helquist. Scholastic Press (117,477)

54. *Disney/Pixar's Finding Nemo.* Random/Disney (117,122)

55. *The Polar Express, The Movie: Shadowbook.* Houghton Mifflin (115,142)

56. *Teen Idol.* Meg Cabot. HarperCollins (115,009)

57. *This Little Piggy* (board book). Illus. by Michelle Berg. Scholastic/Cartwheel (107,845)

58. *Cars, Trucks, Planes, and Trains.* Reader's Digest (107,275)

59. *Rakkety Tam.* Brian Jacques. Philomel (105,795)

60. *Disney Pixar: Amazing Adventures Movie Theater Storybook & Movie Projector.* Reader's Digest (105,673)

61. *The Adventures of Abdi.* Madonna, illus. by Andrej and Olga Dugin. Callaway/ Penguin (104,532)

62. *The Velveteen Rabbit* (board book). Margery Williams, illus. by Thea Kliros. HarperFestival (103,364)

63. *Midnight over Sanctaphrax (The Edge Chronicles #2)*. Paul Stewart and Chris Riddell. Random/Fickling (101,430)

64. *SpongeBob SpookyPants*. Lauryn Silverhardt. Simon Spotlight (100,696)

65. *Numbers and Shapes Discovery Cards (Baby Einstein)*. Julie Aigner-Clark. Hyperion (100,000)

75,000+

66. *Disney's Aladdin*. Golden (96,504)

67. *The Princess Present: A Princess Diaries Book*. Meg Cabot. HarperCollins (96,134)

68. *The Girl Who Loved Tom Gordon: A Pop-Up Book*. Stephen King, illus. by Alan Dingman, adapted by Peter Abrahams. Little Simon (94,744)

69. *Trickster's Queen*. Tamora Pierce. Random (93,226)

70. *Stormchaster (The Edge Chronicles #3)*. Paul Stewart and Chris Riddell. Random/Fickling (93,183)

71. *My First Taggies Book: I Love You* (board book). Illus. by Kaori Wantanabe. Scholastic/Cartwheel (93,071)

72. *Kitten's First Full Moon*. Kevin Henkes. Greenwillow (92,487)

73. *Little Cricket's Song*. Joanne Barkas, illus. by Claudine Gevry. Reader's Digest (91,964)

74. *Rhinoceros Tap*. Sandra Boynton. Workman (91,763)

75. *The Giving Tree (40th Anniversary Edition Book with CD)*. Shel Silverstein. HarperCollins (91,115)

76. *Nickelodeon Movie Theater Storybook & Movie Projector*. Reader's Digest (90,786)

77. *Barbie: Swan Lake*. Sue Kassirer. Golden (86,925)

78. *Bear Stays Up for Christmas*. Karma Wilson, illus. by Jane Chapman. S&S/McElderry (86,520)

79. *Buried Treasure: Tales from Bikini Bottom*. Simon Spotlight (86,505)

80. *The Train of States*. Peter Sís. Greenwillow (84,770)

81. *How Do Dinosaurs Clean Their Rooms?* Jane Yolen, illus. by Mark Teague. Scholastic/Blue Sky (84,204)

82. *Disney's Beauty and the Beast*. Teddy Slater, illus. by Ric Gonzalez and Ron Dias. Golden (83,868)

83. *ttyl*. Lauren Myracle. Abrams/Amulet (82,234)

84. *Hop-Along Bunny* (board book). A. S. Retore. Scholastic/Cartwheel (82,148)

85. *Dora's Favorite Fairy Tales*. Adapted by Leslie Goldman. Simon Spotlight (81,267)

86. *The Best Halloween Ever*. Barbara Robinson. HarperCollins/Cotler (81,091)

87. *Who Let the Ghosts Out? (Mostly Ghostly #1).* R. L. Stine. Delacorte (80,846)

88. *Shrek 2: Shrek's Opposites* (board book). Scholastic (80,084)

89. *Abarat: Days of Magic, Nights of War.* Clive Barker. HarperCollins/Cotler (79,564)

90. *Buzz-Buzz, Busy Bees.* Dawn Bentley, illus. by Heather Cahoon. Little Simon (79,331)

91. *Santa Claus Is Comin' to Town.* J. Fred Coots, illus. by Steven Kellogg. HarperCollins (79,239)

92. *You're All My Favorites.* Sam McBratney, illus. by Anita Jeram. Candlewick (78,809)

93. *Olivia* (board book). Ian Falconer. Atheneum/Schwartz (76,545)

94. *Barbie: Make Your Own Little Golden Book.* Golden (75,855)

95. *Ida B: . . . and Her Plans to Maximize Fun, Avoid Disaster, and (Possibly) Save the World.* Katherine Hannigan. Greenwillow (75,161)

96. *Chicka, Chicka, 1, 2, 3.* Bill Martin, Jr. and Michael Sampson, illus. by Lois Ehlert. S&S (75,113)

Hardcover Backlist

300,000+

1. *The Polar Express.* Chris Van Allsburg. Houghton Mifflin, 1985 (1,305,367)

2. *The Bad Beginning (A Series of Unfortunate Events #1).* Lemony Snicket, illus. by Brett Helquist. HarperCollins, 1999 (986,085)

3. *The Reptile Room (A Series of Unfortunate Events #2).* Lemony Snicket, illus. by Brett Helquist. HarperCollins, 1999 (753,693)

4. *Eragon* (regular and deluxe edition). Christopher Paolini. Knopf, 2003 (753,002)

5. *The Wide Window (A Series of Unfortunate Events #3).* Lemony Snicket, illus. by Brett Helquist. HarperCollins, 2000 (642,627)

6. *Goodnight Moon* (board book). Margaret Wise Brown, illus. by Clement Hurd. HarperFestival, 1991 (616,414)

7. *Green Eggs & Ham.* Dr. Seuss. Random, 1960 (560,573)

8. *Oh, the Places You'll Go!* Dr. Seuss. Random, 1990 (483,064)

9. *The Miserable Mill (A Series of Unfortunate Events #4).* Lemony Snicket, illus. by Brett Helquist. HarperCollins, 2000 (473,241)

10. *The Very Hungry Caterpillar* (board book). Eric Carle, Philomel, 1994 (456,764)

11. *One Fish, Two Fish, Red Fish, Blue Fish.* Dr. Seuss. Random, 1960 (433,648)

12. *Storybook Treasury of Dick & Jane and Friends.* Grosset & Dunlap, 2003 (432,428)

13. *The Cat in the Hat.* Dr. Seuss. Random, 1957 (420,309)

14. *The Austere Academy (A Series of Unfortunate Events #5)*. Lemony Snick-et, illus. by Brett Helquist. HarperCollins, 2000 (419,958)

15. *Guess How Much I Love You* (board book). Sam McBratney, illus. by Anita Jeram. Candlewick, 1996 (413,515)

16. *The Ersatz Elevator (A Series of Unfortunate Events #6)*. Lemony Snicket, illus. by Brett Helquist. HarperCollins, 2001 (387,102)

17. *The Slippery Slope (A Series of Unfortunate Events #10)*. Lemony Snicket, illus. by Brett Helquist. HarperCollins, 2003 (366,057)

18. *The Vile Village (A Series of Unfortunate Events #7)*. Lemony Snicket, illus. by Brett Helquist. HarperCollins, 2001 (355,286)

19. *The Carnivorous Carnival (A Series of Unfortunate Events #9)*. Lemony Snicket, illus. by Brett Helquist. HarperCollins, 2002 (338,766)

20. *The Hostile Hospital (A Series of Unfortunate Events #8)*. Lemony Snicket, illus. by Brett Helquist. HarperCollins, 2001 (333,038)

21. *My Granny's Purse*. P. H. Hanson. Workman, 2003 (330,784)

22. *Mr. Brown Can Moo, Can You?* (board book). Dr. Seuss. Random, 1996 (314,750)

23. *Are You My Mother?* P. D. Eastman. Random, 1960 (307,508)

24. *Tails*. Matthew Van Fleet. Harcourt/Red Wagon, 2003 (301,775)

200,000+

25. *The Tale of Despereaux*. Kate DiCamillo, illus. by Timothy Basil Ering. Candlewick, 2003 (297,667)

26. *I'm Gonna Like Me*. Jamie Lee Curtis, illus. by Laura Cornell. HarperCollins/Cotler, 2002 (288,606)

27. *Hop on Pop*. Dr. Seuss. Random, 1963 (284,811)

28. *Dr. Seuss's ABC* (board book). Dr. Seuss. Random, 1996 (282,882)

29. *Dr. Seuss's ABC*. Dr. Seuss. Random, 1960 (280,167)

30. *Snuggle Puppy* (board book). Sandra Boynton. Workman, 2003 (279,457)

31. *Dragonology*. Ernest Drake, illus. by Helen Ward, Wayne Anderson and Douglas Carrel. Candlewick, 2003 (277,066)

32. *The Poky Little Puppy*. Jane Sebring Lowrey. Golden, 2001 (266,577)

33. *Today I Feel Silly & Other Moods That Make My Day*. Jamie Lee Curtis, illus. by Laura Cornell. HarperCollins/ Cotler, 1998 (266,418)

34. *Dora's Storytime Collection*. Simon Spotlight, 2003 (256,856)

35. *Go, Dog. Go!* P. D. Eastman. Random, 1961 (251,540)

36. *The Giving Tree*. Shel Silverstein. HarperCollins, 1964 (248,119)

37. *The Field Guide (The Spiderwick Chronicles #1)*. Tony DiTerlizzi and Holly Black. S&S, 2003 (235,739)

38. *The Foot Book* (board book). Dr. Seuss. Random, 1996 (228,644)

39. *Disney/Pixar's Finding Nemo*. Golden, 2003 (225,941)

40. *Where Do Balloons Go?* Jamie Lee Curtis, illus. by Laura Cornell. Harper-Collins/Cotler, 2000 (215,808)

41. *When I Was Little.* Jamie Lee Curtis, illus. by Laura Cornell. Harper-Collins/ Cotler, 1993 (203,285)

42. *Disney Storybook Collection.* Disney, 1998 (200,000)

43. *Disney's Princess Collection.* Sarah Heller. Disney, 1999 (200,000)

100,000+

44. *There's a Wocket in My Pocket!* (board book). Dr. Seuss. Random, 1996 (197,667)

45. *The Little Red Hen.* J. P. Miller. Golden, 2001 (196,832)

46. *I'm a Big Sister.* Joanna Cole, illus. by Maxie Chambliss. HarperCollins, 1997 (195,198)

47. *Fox in Socks.* Dr. Seuss. Random, 1965 (193,035)

48. *The Seeing Stone (The Spiderwick Chronicles #2).* Tony DiTerlizzi and Holly Black. S&S, 2003 (190,785)

49. *I'm a Big Brother.* Joanna Cole, illus. by Maxie Chambliss. HarperCollins, 1997 (186,507)

50. *Clap Your Hands.* Random, 2002 (183,166)

51. *Barnyard Dance!* (board book). Sandra Boynton. Workman, 1993 (180,454)

52. *Lucinda's Secret (The Spiderwick Chronicles #3).* Tony DiTerlizzi and Holly Black. S&S, 2003 (176,528)

53. *My First Taggies Book: Sweet Dreams* (board book). Illus. by Kaori Watanabe. Scholastic/Cartwheel, 2003 (176,171)

54. *Mirror Me! (Baby Einstein).* Julie Aigner-Clark. Hyperion, 2002 (175,000)

55. *The Cat in the Hat Comes Back.* Dr. Seuss. Random, 1958 (174,832)

56. *The Going-to-Bed Book* (board book). Sandra Boynton. Little Simon, 1982 (172,475)

57. *I Can Read with My Eyes Shut!* Dr. Seuss. Random, 1978 (163,475)

58. *The Shy Little Kitten.* Cathleen Schurr. Golden, 1999 (161,987)

59. *Neighborhood Animals (Baby Einstein).* Marilyn Singer, illus. by Nadeem Zaidi. Hyperion, 2001 (160,000)

60. *Fish in a Box (Friendship Box).* Random/Disney, 2003 (159,345)

61. *How the Grinch Stole Christmas.* Dr. Seuss. Random, 1957 (158,210)

62. *The Runaway Bunny* (board book). Margaret Wise Brown, illus. by Clement Hurd. HarperFestival, 1991 (155,562)

63. *Put Me in the Zoo.* Robert Lopshire. Random, 1960 (154,781)

64. *Haunted Castle on Hallow's Eve (Magic Tree House #30).* Mary Pope Osborne, illus. by Sal Murdocca. Random, 2003 (153,189)

65. *My Little Golden Book About God.* Eloise Wilkin. Golden, 2000 (153,030)

66. *Christmas in Camelot (Magic Tree House #29).* Mary Pope Osborne, illus. by Sal Murdocca. Random, 2001 (152,387)
67. *Disney Princess Movie Theater Storybook & Movie Projector.* Reader's Digest, 2002 (147,653)
68. *I Am Not Going to Get Up Today!* Dr. Seuss, illus. by James Stevenson. Random, 1987 (140,987)
69. *Are You My Mother?* (board book). P. D. Eastman. Random, 1998 (140,968)
70. *Count with Dora.* Phoebe Beinstein, illus. by Thompson Bros. Simon Spotlight, 2002 (139,694)
71. *Go, Dog. Go!* (board book). P. D. Eastman. Random, 1997 (137,781)
72. *Ten Apples Up on Top!* Theo. LeSieg, illus. by Roy McKie. Random, 1961 (135,003)
73. *The Second Summer of the Sisterhood.* Ann Brashares. Delacorte, 2003 (129,803)
74. *The Little Engine That Could.* Watty Piper. Platt & Munk, 2003 (129,280)
75. *The Man Who Walked Between the Towers.* Mordicai Gerstein. Roaring Brook, 2004 (128,762)
76. *My Little People Farm.* Reader's Digest, 1997 (127,546)
77. *Thomas and Friends: Thomas and the Big Big Bridge.* Rev. W. Awdry. Golden, 2003 (125,500)
78. *Animal Discovery Cards (Baby Einstein).* Julie Aigner-Clark. Hyperion, 2003 (125,000)
79. *Don't Let the Pigeon Drive the Bus!* Mo Willems. Hyperion, 2003 (125,000)
80. *Disney's Princess Music Box.* Disney, 2002 (125,000)
81. *Language Discovery Cards (Baby Einstein).* Julie Aigner-Clark. Hyperion, 2003 (125,000)
82. *How I Became a Pirate.* Melinda Long, illus. by David Shannon. Harcourt, 2003 (124,605)
83. *Stranger in the Woods.* Carl R. Sams II and Jean Stoick. Carl R. Sams II Photography, 2000 (122,763)
84. *Scholastic Children's Dictionary* (updated). Scholastic Reference, 2002 (121,369)
85. *How Do You Know It's Christmas?* Golden, 2002 (121,192)
86. *A Light in the Attic.* Shel Silverstein. HarperCollins, 1981 (120,581)
87. *So Big!* Anna Jane Hays, illus. by Christopher Moroney. Random, 2003 (120,496)
88. *Where the Wild Things Are.* Maurice Sendak. HarperCollins, 1963 (118,718)
89. *Diary of a Worm.* Doreen Cronin, illus. by Harry Bliss. HarperCollins/Cotler, 2003 (118,419)
90. *Put Me in the Zoo* (board book). Robert Lopshire. Random, 2001 (118,300)
91. *Oh, the Thinks You Can Think!* Dr. Seuss. Random, 1975 (117,550)
92. *Pajama Time!* (board book). Sandra Boynton. Workman, 2000 (117,174)
93. *I Love You, Mommy.* Edie Evans. Golden, 1999 (114,402)

94. *Dora's Color Adventure.* Phoebe Beinstein, illus. by Susan Hall. Simon Spotlight, 2002 (113,980)

95. *I Love You, Daddy.* Edie Evans. Golden, 2001 (113,894)

96. *Moo Baa La La La* (board book). Sandra Boynton. Little Simon, 1982 (110,628)

97. *If You Give a Mouse a Cookie.* Laura Joffe Numeroff, illus. by Felicia Bond. HarperCollins/Geringer, 1985 (109,197)

98. *The Hidden Staircase (Nancy Drew #2).* Carolyn Keene. Grosset & Dunlap, 1930 (107,745)

99. *A Fish Out of Water.* Helen Palmer. Random, 1961 (106,135)

100. *The Secret of the Old Clock (Nancy Drew #1).* Carolyn Keene, Grosset & Dunlap, 1930 (105,537)

101. *Good Night, Sweet Butterflies.* Dawn Bentley, illus. by Heather Cahoon. Little Simon, 2003 (104,728)

102. *The Alphabet Book* (board book). P. D. Eastman. Random, 2000 (102,667)

103. *Time for Bed* (board book). Mem Fox, illus. by Jane Dyer. Harcourt/Red Wagon, 1993 (101,523)

104. *Peekaboo Kisses.* Barney Saltzberg. Harcourt/Red Wagon, 2002 (101,010)

105. *Disney's Storybook Collection Volume 2.* Disney, 2002 (100,000)

106. *See & Spy Shapes (Baby Einstein).* Julie Aigner-Clark, illus. by Nadeem Zaidi. Hyperion, 2001 (100,000)

107. *Jane's Animal Expedition (Baby Einstein).* Julie Aigner-Clark. Hyperion, 2002 (100,000)

108. *Walt Disney's Classic Storybook.* Disney, 2001 (100,000)

75,000+

109. *Hand, Hand, Fingers, Thumb* (board book). Al Perkins. Random, 1998 (99,472)

110. *The Very Lonely Firefly* (board book). Eric Carle. Philomel, 1999 (96,466)

111. *The Night Before Christmas.* Clement C. Moore, illus. by Christian Birmingham. Running Press/Courage, 1995 (91,846)

112. *Alice's Adventures in Wonderland.* Adapted and illus. by Robert Sabuda. Little Simon, 2003 (91,477)

113. *A Fly Went By.* Mike McClintock. Random, 1958 (90,680)

114. *Ten Apples Up on Top* (board book). Dr. Seuss. Random, 1998 (89,675)

115. *The Bungalow Mystery (Nancy Drew #3).* Carolyn Keene. Grosset & Dunlap, 1930 (86,800)

116. *Good Night, Gorilla* (board book). Peggy Rathmann. Putnam, 1996 (86,690)

117. *Wonderful Wizard of Oz.* Adapted and illus. by Robert Sabuda. Little Simon, 2000 (86,309)

118. *Elmo's Big Lift and Look Book.* Anna Ross. Random, 1994 (86,294)

119. *From Head to Toe* (board book). Eric Carle. HarperFestival, 1999 (86,131)

120. *Caterpillar Spring, Butterfly Summer.* Susan Hood, illus. by Claudine Gevry. Reader's Digest, 2003 (85,302)
121. *Christmastime Is Here!* Reader's Digest, 2002 (83,906)
122. *The Tower Treasure (Hardy Boys #1).* Franklin Dixon. Grosset & Dunlap, 1927 (83,174)
123. *Inkheart.* Cornelia Funke. Scholastic/ Chicken House, 2003 (81,412)
124. *If You Take a Mouse to School.* Laura Joffe Numeroff, illus. by Felicia Bond. HarperCollins/Geringer, 2002 (80,991)
125. *Falling Up.* Shel Silverstein. HarperCollins, 1996 (80,686)
126. *The Very Busy Spider* (board book). Eric Carle. Philomel, 1995 (80,505)
127. *The Mystery at Lilac Inn (Nancy Drew #4).* Carolyn Keene. Grosset & Dunlap, 1930 (79,747)
128. *The Secret of Shadow Ranch (Nancy Drew #5).* Carolyn Keene. Grosset & Dunlap, 1930 (79,166)
129. *Dora's Book of Words/Libro de Palabras de Dora.* Phoebe Beinstein, illus. by the Thompson Bros. Simon Spotlight, 2003 (78,343)
130. *The Very Quiet Cricket* (board book). Eric Carle. Philomel, 1997 (78,191)
131. *Midnight for Charlie Bone.* Jenny Nimmo. Scholastic/Orchard, 2003 (78,073)
132. *Click, Clack Moo: Cows That Type.* Doreen Cronin, illus. by Betsy Lewin. S&S, 2000 (77,892)
133. *Mommy's Best Kisses.* Margaret Anastas, illus. by Susan Winter. Harper-Collins, 2003 (77,797)
134. *Philadelphia Chickens.* Sandra Boynton. Workman, 2002 (76,948)
135. *Where Is Baby's Belly Button?* Karen Katz. Little Simon, 2000 (76,731)
136. *The Secret of Red Gate Farm (Nancy Drew #6).* Carolyn Keene. Grosset & Dunlap, 1931 (75,937)
137. *The Very Hungry Caterpillar.* Eric Carle. Philomel, 1969 (75,169)
138. *Snowmen at Night.* Mark and Caralyn Buehner. Dial, 2002 (75,137)

Paperback Frontlist

300,000+

1. *Harry Potter and the Order of the Phoenix.* J. K. Rowling. Scholastic (1,488,503)
2. *Disney/Pixar's The Incredibles* (movie novelization). Irene Trimble. Random/Disney (1,122,281)
3. *Spider-Man 2: Spider-Man Versus Doc Ock.* Acton Figueroa, illus. by Jesus Redondo. HarperFestival (666,010)
4. *Shark Tale: The Movie Novel.* Louise Gikow. Scholastic (596,983)
5. *My Little Pony: Pony Party.* Kate Egan, illus. by Carlo LoRaso. Harper-Festival (490,837)

6. *Spider-Man 2: Everyday Hero.* Acton Figueroa, illus. by Ivan Vasquez. HarperFestival (430,208)

7. *Spider-Man 2: Doc Around the Clock.* Jacob Ben Gunter. HarperFestival (379,276)

8. *The Sisterhood of the Traveling Pants* (trade paper and mass market). Ann Brashares. Dell (356,211)

9. *The Polar Express, The Movie: The Journey Begins.* Kitty Richards. Houghton Mifflin (332,757)

10. *The Polar Express, The Movie: The Magic Journey.* Tracy West. Houghton Mifflin (325,306)

200,000+

11. *Junie B., First Grader: Cheater Pants (Junie B. Jones #21).* Barbara Park, illus. by Denise Brunkus. Random (292,539)

12. *A Series of Unfortunate Events: The Pessimistic Posters.* Lemony Snicket. HarperKidsEntertainment (290,714)

13. *A Series of Unfortunate Events: The Puzzling Puzzles.* Lemony Snicket. HarperKidsEntertainment (290,393)

14. *Sparkly Boohball (Boohbah).* Dawn Sawyer, illus. by Jeff Albrecht. Scholastic (281,653)

15. *Hoot.* Carl Hiaasen. Knopf (258,395)

16. *Case of the Clue at the Zoo (New Adventures of Mary-Kate and Ashley #39).* HarperEntertainment (256,896)

17. *The Polar Express, The Movie: Trip to the North Pole.* Ellen Weiss. Houghton Mifflin (252,878)

18. *Spider-Man 2: The Daily Bugle Stories.* Jacob Ben Gunter. HarperFestival (248,261)

19. *Dora's Book of Manners.* Christine Ricci, illus. by Susan Hall. Simon Spotlight (247,130)

20. *Shrek 2: Ogre Hunter.* Janet Halfmann, illus. by Linda Karl. Scholastic (244,194)

21. *Spider-Man 2: Friends and Foes.* Michael Teitelbaum. HarperFestival (229,769)

22. *The Case of the Dog Show Mystery (The New Adventures of Mary-Kate and Ashley #41).* HarperEntertainment (227,092)

23. *A Series of Unfortunate Events: Behind the Scenes with Count Olaf.* Lemony Snicket. HarperKidsEntertainment (225,224)

24. *Harry Potter and the Prisoner of Azkaban* (mass market). J. K. Rowling. Scholastic (221,500)

25. *My Little Pony: Fun at the Fair.* Kate Egan, illus. by Ken Edwards. HarperFestival (218,779)

26. *SpongeBob SquarePants Movie Novelization.* Adapted by Marc Cerasini. Simon Spotlight (218,027)

27. *Return of the Supers! (Disney/Pixar's The Incredibles).* Random/Disney (212,101)
28. *Spider-Man 2: Hurry Up, Spider-Man!* Kate Egan, illus. by Bob Ostrom. HarperFestival (207,891)
29. *Dora Loves Boots.* Alison Inches, illus. by Zina Saunders. Simon Spotlight (205,668)
30. *My Little Pony: Fashion Fun.* Ann Marie Capalija, illus. by Ken Edwards. HarperFestival (203,467)

100,000+

31. *I Like It Like That (Gossip Girl #5).* Cecily Von Ziegesar. Little, Brown (197,156)
32. *Shrek 2: The Potion Plan.* Gail Herman, illus. by Isidre Mones and Marc Mones. Scholastic (197,122)
33. *Spider-Man 2: Hands Off, Doc Ock!* Kate Egan, illus. by Isidre Mones. HarperFestival (188,503)
34. *Life of Pi* (student edition). Yann Martel. Harcourt/Harvest (182,397)
35. *The Princess Diaries, Vol. IV: Princess in Waiting.* Meg Cabot. Harper-Trophy (181,972)
36. *Shark Tale: Don't Surf on My Turf.* Janet Halfmann, illus. by Jim Durk. Scholastic (178,876)
37. *Ella Enchanted* (mass market). Gail Carson Levine. Avon (177,868)
38. *Shrek 2: Cat Attack!* David and Bobbi Weiss. Scholastic (177,349)
39. *Ice-Cream Dreams.* Adapted by Nancy Krulik, illus. by Heather Martinez. Simon Spotlight (174,329)
40. *Chicken Soup for the Teenage Soul IV.* HCI (173,000)
41. *New York Minute.* HarperEntertainment (172,139)
42. *Trouble at the Krusty Krab!* Adapted by Steven Banks, illus. by Zina Saunders. Simon Spotlight (168,598)
43. *Shark Tale: Hip Hop 'Til You Flop.* Janet Halfmann, illus. by Ken Edwards. Scholastic (167,647)
44. *The Incredible Dash (Disney/Pixar's The Incredibles).* Random/Disney (164,491)
45. *Bubble Blowers, Beware!* Adapted by David Lewman, illus. by Barry Goldberg. Simon Spotlight (164,347)
46. *You're the One I Want (Gossip Girl #6).* Cecily Von Ziegesar. Little, Brown (164, 296)
47. *The Second Summer of the Sisterhood.* Ann Brashares. Delacorte (155,034)
48. *Barbie: The Princess and the Pauper.* Golden (153,937)
49. *Showdown!* Random/Disney (152,842)
50. *Dora's Fairy-Tale Adventure.* Adapted by Christine Ricci, illustrated by Susan Hall. Simon Spotlight (151,512)

51. *The Case of the Cheerleading Mystery (New Adventures of Mary-Kate and Ashley #42).* HarperEntertainment (150,965)
52. *The Power of Five (W.I.T.C.H. #1).* Disney/Volo (150,000)
53. *Artemis Fowl: The Eternity Code.* Eoin Colfer. Hyperion/Miramax (150,000)
54. *The Amulet of Samarkand (Bartimaeus Trilogy #1).* Jonathan Stroud. Hyperion/Miramax (150,000)
55. *Best Dressed (Lizzie McGuire #13).* Jasmine Jones. Disney/Volo (150,000)
56. *Head over Heels (Lizzie McGuire #12).* Jasmine Jones. Disney/Volo (150,000)
57. *The Disappearance (W.I.T.C.H. #2).* Disney/Volo (150,000)
58. *Barney: Play Time!* Scholastic (148,524)
59. *Junie B., First Grader: One-Man Band (Junie B. Jones #22).* Barbara Park, illus. by Denise Brunkus. Random (148,363)
60. *Road Trip.* Adam Beechen, illus. by Heather Martinez. Simon Spotlight (145,905)
61. *Strawberry Shortcake Goes Camping.* Grosset & Dunlap (144,581)
62. *Shark Tale: Workin' at the Whale Wash.* Dennis Shealy. Scholastic (144,377)
63. *Disney's Lion King 1-½.* Random/ Disney (141,372)
64. *Spider-Man 2: The Movie Storybook.* Kate Egan. HarperFestival (139,246)
65. *The Halloween Cat.* Christine Ricci, illus. by Zina Saunders. Simon Spotlight (138,349)
66. *New York Minute: There's Something About Roxy.* HarperEntertainment (134,003)
67. *Chicken Soup for the Preteen Soul 2.* HCI (134,000)
68. *Dora Goes to School.* Adapted by Leslie Valders, illus. by Robert Roper. Simon Spotlight (131,937)
69. *My Little Pony: Belle of the Ball.* Ruth Benjamin, illus. by Ken Edwards. HarperFestival (129,594)
70. *Shrek 2: Play-Along Stickerbook.* Sonia Sander. Scholastic (129,512)
71. *My Little Pony: The Big Balloon Race.* Jennifer Frantz. HarperFestival (128,084)
72. *Lost Treasure of the Emerald Eye.* Geronimo Stilton. Scholastic (127,188)
73. *Dick & Jane: Play Time.* Grosset & Dunlap (126,409)
74. *Shrek 2: The Movie Novel.* Jesse Leon McCann. Scholastic (125,105)
75. *The Fire of Friendship (W.I.T.C.H. #4).* Disney/Volo (125,000)
76. *Dick & Jane: We Play.* Grosset & Dunlap (124,116)
77. *Shrek 2 Mad Libs.* Price Stern Sloan (123,676)
78. *The City of Ember.* Jeanne DuPrau. Random (122,939)
79. *Because of Winn-Dixie* (movie tie-in). Kate DiCamillo. Candlewick (122,061)

80. *The House of the Scorpion.* Nancy Farmer. Aladdin (120,961)
81. *Fun with Dick & Jane.* Grosset & Dunlap (120,668)
82. *The Incredibles: The Movie Storybook (Disney/Pixar's The Incredibles).* Random Disney (120,332)
83. *Mystery of Metru Nui (Bionicle Adventures #1).* Greg Farshtey. Scholastic (119,487)
84. *Crispin: The Cross of Lead.* Avi. Hyperion (117,000)
85. *Finding Meridian (W.I.T.C.H. #3).* Disney/Volo (117,000)
86. *Camp SpongeBob.* Kim Ostrow and Molly Reisner, illus. by Heather Martinez. Simon Spotlight (115,386)
87. *Pop Bottle Science.* Lynn Brunelle, illus. by Paul Meisel. Workman (115,371)
88. *Thomas and Friends: James Goes Buzz Buzz.* Rev. W. Awdry, illus. by Richard Courtney. Random (114,428)
89. *Dick & Jane: Up and Away.* Grosset & Dunlap (114,065)
90. *Judy Moody Saves the World!* Megan McDonald, illus. by Peter H. Reynolds. Candlewick (111,241)
91. *Zombie Butts from Uranus.* Andy Griffiths. Scholastic (106,833)
92. *Care Bears: Special Delivery.* Quinlan B. Lee, illus. by Jay Johnson. Cartwheel/ Scholastic (106,262)
93. *Shark Tale: Lenny's Fishy Fib.* Gail Herman, illus. by Carlo Loraso. Scholastic (105,959)
94. *Dick & Jane: We See.* Grosset & Dunlap (105,431)
95. *Dick & Jane: Away We Go.* Grosset & Dunlap (105,325)
96. *Shark Tale: Movie Storybook.* Sara Pennypacker, illus. by Barry Gott. Scholastic (104,623)
97. *Black Water (Pendragon #4).* D.J. MacHale. Aladdin (104,604)
98. *Girls on Film (The A-List #2).* Zoey Dean. Little, Brown (103,211)
99. *Rudolph, the Red-Nosed Reindeer.* Golden (103,103)
100. *Say "Cheese!"* Christine Ricci, illus. by Steven Savitsky. Simon Spotlight (103,094)
101. *A Cinderella Story* (movie novelization). Robin Wasserman. Scholastic (103,018)
102. *Molly Moon's Incredible Book of Hypnotism.* Georgia Byng. HarperTrophy (102,589)
103. *My Little Pony: Wishes Do Come True!* Ann Marie Capalija, illus. by Lyn Fletcher. HarperFestival (102,226)
104. *Surviving the Applewhites.* Stephanie S. Tolan. HarperTrophy (102,167)
105. *Barbie: Fashion Show Fun!* Mary Man-Kong. Golden (101,303)
106. *A Week in the Woods.* Andrew Clements. Aladdin (100,253)

Paperback Backlist

300,000+

1. *Holes* (multiple editions). Louis Sachar. Dell, 2000 (489,887)
2. *The Giver* (multiple editions). Lois Lowry. Dell, 1994 (450,892)
3. *The Outsiders.* S. E. Hinton. Puffin, 1997 (407,954)
4. *Dinosaurs Before Dark (Magic Tree House #1).* Mary Pope Osborne, illus. by Sal Murdocca. Random, 1992 (407,854)
5. *The Knight at Dawn (Magic Tree House #2).* Mary Pope Osborne, illus. by Sal Murdocca. Random, 1993 (329,638)
6. *Mummies in the Morning (Magic Tree House #3).* Mary Pope Osborne, illus. by Sal Murdocca. Random, 1993 (329,600)
7. *The Lion, the Witch and the Wardrobe.* C. S. Lewis, illus. by Pauline Baynes. HarperTrophy, 1994 (325,598)
8. *Because of Winn-Dixie.* Kate DiCamillo. Candlewick, 2001 (307,678)
9. *Junie B. Jones and the Stupid Smelly Bus (Junie B. Jones #11).* Barbara Park, illus. by Denise Brunkus. Random, 1992 (304,317)

200,000+

10. *Pirates Past Noon (Magic Tree House #4).* Mary Pope Osborne, illus. by Sal Murdocca. Random, 1994 (297,015)
11. *Harry Potter and the Goblet of Fire.* J. K. Rowling. Scholastic, 2002 (274,629)
12. *Night of the Ninjas (Magic Tree House #5).* Mary Pope Osborne, illus. by Sal Murdocca. Random, 1995 (259,791)
13. *Harry Potter and the Sorcerer's Stone.* J. K. Rowling. Scholastic, 1999 (258,029)
14. *Dr. Seuss's The Cat in the Hat* (movie novelization). Random, 2003 (256,250)
15. *Junie B. Jones and a Little Monkey Business (Junie B. Jones #12).* Barbara Park, illus. by Denise Brunkus. Random, 1993 (253,753)
16. *Junie B. Jones and Some Sneaky Peeky Spying (Junie B. Jones #14).* Barbara Park, illus. by Denise Brunkus. Random, 1994 (251,608)
17. *Junie B. Jones and Her Big Fat Mouth (Junie B. Jones #13).* Barbara Park, illus. by Denise Brunkus. Random, 1993 (251,381)
18. *A Wrinkle in Time* (digest and mass market). Madeleine L'Engle. Dell, 1998 (248,443)
19. *Afternoon on the Amazon (Magic Tree House #6).* Mary Pope Osborne, illus. by Sal Murdocca. Random, 1995 (244,062)
20. *Harry Potter and the Prisoner of Azkaban.* J. K. Rowling. Scholastic, 2001 (244,010)

21. *Midnight on the Moon (Magic Tree House #8).* Mary Pope Osborne, illus. by Sal Murdocca. Random, 1996 (241,320)

22. *Speak.* Laurie Halse Anderson. Puffin, 2001 (238,039)

23. *Disney Princess: Beauties in Bloom.* Random/Disney, 2003 (237,833)

24. *High Tide in Hawaii (Magic Tree House #28).* Mary Pope Osborne, illus. by Sal Murdocca. Random, 2003 (237,537)

25. *Charlie and the Chocolate Factory.* Roald Dahl. Puffin, 1988 (229,610)

26. *Dolphins at Daybreak (Magic Tree House #9).* Mary Pope Osborne, illus. by Sal Murdocca. Random, 1997 (229,267)

27. *Where the Wild Things Are.* Maurice Sendak. HarperTrophy, 1988 (222,039)

28. *Junie B., First Grader: Toothless Wonder (Junie B. Jones #20).* Barbara Park, illus. by Denise Brunkus. Random, 2003 (216,391)

29. *Dora's Easter Basket.* Sarah Willson, illus. by Susan Hall. Simon Spotlight, 2003 (216,195)

30. *Sunset of the Sabertooth (Magic Tree House #7).* Mary Pope Osborne, illus. by Sal Murdocca. Random, 1996 (214,355)

31. *Maniac Magee.* Jerry Spinelli. Little, Brown, 1999 (212,887)

32. *The Magician's Nephew.* C. S. Lewis, illus. by Pauline Baynes. HarperTrophy, 1994 (212,326)

33. *Ella Enchanted.* Gail Carson Levine. HarperTrophy, 1998 (211,468)

34. *The Care and Keeping of You: The Body Book for Girls.* Valorie Schaefer, illus. by Norm Bendel. Pleasant Company, 1998 (209,649)

35. *Roll of Thunder, Hear My Cry.* Mildred Taylor. Puffin, 1991 (207,702)

36. *Number the Stars.* Lois Lowry. Dell/Yearling, 1990 (207,024)

37. *Junie B. Jones Has a Monster Under Her Bed (Junie B. Jones #18).* Barbara Park, illus. by Denise Brunkus. Random, 1997 (202,829)

38. *Junie B. Jones Is a Party Animal (Junie B. Jones #10).* Barbara Park, illus. by Denise Brunkus. Random, 1997 (202,254)

39. *Junie B. Jones Is (Almost) a Flower Girl (Junie B. Jones #13).* Barbara Park, illus. by Denise Brunkus. Random, 1999 (201,803)

100,000+

40. *Junie B. Jones and the Mushy Gushy Valentine (Junie B. Jones #14).* Barbara Park, illus. by Denise Brunkus. Random, 1999 (199,944)

41. *Junie B. Jones Has a Peep in Her Pocket (Junie B. Jones #15).* Barbara Park, illus. by Denise Brunkus. Random, 2000 (197,493)

42. *Frog and Toad Are Friends.* Arnold Lobel. HarperTrophy, 1979 (195,704)

43. *Junie B. Jones Loves Handsome Warren (Junie B. Jones #17).* Barbara Park, illus. by Denise Brunkus. Random, 1996 (192,408)

44. *Polar Bears Past Bedtime (Magic Tree House #12).* Mary Pope Osborne; illus. by Sal Murdocca. Random, 1998 (189,338)

45. *Junie B. Jones and the Yucky Blucky Fruitcake (Junie B. Jones #5)*. Barbara Park, illus. by Denise Brunkus. Random, 1995 (188,716)

46. *Best Dad in the Sea (Disney/Pixar's Finding Nemo)*. Random/Disney, 2003 (187,582)

47. *Pat the Bunny*. Dorothy Kunhardt. Golden, 2001 (186,231)

48. *Junie B. Jones Is Not a Crook (Junie B. Jones #19)*. Barbara Park, illus. by Denise Brunkus. Random, 1997 (185,587)

49. *Are You There God? It's Me, Margaret* (digest and mass market). Judy Blume. Dell/Yearling, 1971 (184,811)

50. *Bridge to Terabithia*. Katherine Paterson, illus. by Donna Diamond. HarperTrophy, 1987 (183,949)

51. *Junie B. Jones Is a Beauty Shop Guy (Junie B. Jones #11)*. Barbara Park, illus. by Denise Brunkus. Random, 1998 (182,453)

52. *Thomas & Friends: Little Engines Can Do Big Things*. Illus. by Ted Gadecki. Random, 2000 (180,638)

53. *Charlotte's Web*. E. B. White, illus. by Garth Williams. HarperTrophy, 1974 (178,779)

54. *The Wiggles and Friends*. Grosset & Dunlap, 2003 (176,910)

55. *Junie B. Jones and That Meanie Jim's Birthday (Junie B. Jones #16)*. Barbara Park, illus. by Denise Brunkus. Random, 1996 (175,133)

56. *Just Me and My Dad*. Mercer Mayer. Golden, 2001 (174,796)

57. *Tales of a Fourth Grade Nothing*. Judy Blume. Puffin, 2003 (172,406)

58. *Tonight on the Titanic (Magic Tree House #17)*. Mary Pope Osborne, illus. by Sal Murdocca. Random, 1999 (170,812)

59. *Thomas and Friends: Catch Me, Catch Me!* Rev. W. Awdry, illus. by Owain Bell. Random, 1990 (169,875)

60. *Bug Stew!* Random/Disney, 2003 (168,421)

61. *Amelia Bedelia*. Peggy Parish, illus. by Fritz Siebel. HarperTrophy, 1992 (165,649)

62. *Just Me and My Mom*. Mercer Mayer. Golden, 2001 (163,676)

63. *Monster*. Walter Dean Myers. HarperTempest, 2001 (162,904)

64. *Junie B. Jones Is a Graduation Girl (Junie B. Jones #17)*. Barbara Park, illus. by Denise Brunkus. Random, 2001 (162,443)

65. *Junie B., First Grader: Boss of Lunch (Junie B. Jones #19)*. Barbara Park, illus. by Denise Brunkus. Random, 2003 (162,062)

66. *Junie B. Jones Smells Something Fishy (Junie B. Jones #12)*. Barbara Park, illus. by Denise Brunkus. Random, 1998 (161,370)

67. *Ghost Town at Sundown (Magic Tree House #10)*. Mary Pope Osborne. Random, 1997 (160,922)

68. *Oh Yuck!* Joy Masoff, illus. by Terry Sirrell. Workman, 2000 (160,077)

69. *My Little Pony: Pinkie's Pie's Spooky Dream*. Jodi Huelin, illus. by Ken Edwards. HarperFestival, 2003 (159,728)

70. *Dora's Backpack.* Sarah Willson, illus. by Robert Roper. Simon Spotlight, 2002 (158,038)

71. *Lions at Lunchtime (Magic Tree House #11).* Mary Pope Osborne, illus. by Sal Murdocca. Random, 1998 (156,972)

72. *Bud, Not Buddy* (digest and mass market). Christopher Paul Curtis. Dell, 2002 (154,733)

73. *Junie B., First Grader: At Last! (Junie B. Jones #18).* Barbara Park, illus. by Denise Brunkus. Random, 2002 (154,024)

74. *The Watsons Go to Birmingham—1963* (digest and mass market). Christopher Paul Curtis. Dell, 1997 (151,611)

75. *Vacation Fun Mad Libs.* Roger Price. Price Stern Sloan, 1987 (150,833)

76. *Danny and the Dinosaur.* Syd Hoff. HarperTrophy, 1992 (150,800)

77. *Artemis Fowl.* Eoin Colfer. Hyperion/Miramax, 2002 (150,000)

78. *Lizzie Goes Wild (Lizzie McGuire #3).* Kirsten Larson. Disney/Volo, 2002 (150,000)

79. *Picture This! (Lizzie McGuire #5).* Jasmine Jones. Disney/Volo, 2003 (150,000)

80. *New Kid in School (Lizzie McGuire #6).* Kirsten Larson. Disney/Volo, 2003 (150,000)

81. *Broken Hearts (Lizzie McGuire #7).* Kirsten Larson. Disney/Volo, 2003 (150,000)

82. *Junie B. Jones Is Captain Field Day (Junie B. Jones #16).* Barbara Park, illus. by Denise Brunkus. Random, 2001 (148,802)

83. *The Thief Lord.* Cornelia Funke, illus. by Christian Burmingham. Scholastic/ Chicken House, 2003 (144,504)

84. *Biscuit.* Alyssa Satin Capucilli, illus. by Pat Schories. HarperTrophy, 1997 (143,388)

85. *Vacation Under the Volcano (Magic Tree House #13).* Mary Pope Osborne, illus. by Sal Murdocca. Random, 1998 (142,532)

86. *Mad Libs on the Road.* Roger Price. Price Stern Sloan, 1999 (140,690)

87. *Dora in the Deep Sea.* Christine Ricci, illus. by Robert Roper. Simon Spotlight, 2003 (139,810)

88. *Disney Princess: A Pony for a Princess.* Andrea Posner-Sanchez, illus. by Francesc Mateu. Random/Disney, 2002 (138,197)

89. *Revolutionary War on Wednesday (Magic Tree House #22).* Mary Pope Osborne, illus. by Sal Murdocca. Random, 2000 (138,189)

90. *Meet Diego!* Leslie Valdes, illus. by Susan Hall. Simon Spotlight, 2003 (138,022)

91. *Original Mad Libs #1.* Roger Price. Price Stern Sloan, 1958 (137,595)

92. *Frindle.* Andrew Clements. Aladdin, 1996 (136,143)

93. *Earthquake in the Early Morning (Magic Tree House #24).* Mary Pope Osborne, illus. by Sal Murdocca. Random, 2001 (134,907)

94. *Hatchet.* Gary Paulsen. Aladdin, 1996 (134,712)

95. *The Horse and His Boy.* C. S. Lewis, illus. by Pauline Baynes. HarperTrophy, 1994 (134,712)

96. *Thomas and Friends: Diesel 10 Means Trouble.* Illus. by Richard Courtney. Random, 2000 (133,146)

97. *Go Ask Alice.* Anonymous. Aladdin, 1971 (132,156)

98. *Hour of the Olympics (Magic Tree House #16).* Mary Pope Osborne, illus. by Sal Murdocca. Random, 1998 (131,245)

99. *Good Morning, Gorillas (Magic Tree House #26).* Mary Pope Osborne, illus. by Sal Murdocca. Random, 2002 (130,426)

100. *Tigers at Twilight (Magic Tree House #19).* Mary Pope Osborne, illus. by Sal Murdocca. Random, 1999 (130,269)

101. *My Little Pony: A Pony's Tale.* Jodi Huelin, illus. by Ken Edwards. HarperFestival, 2003 (130,113)

102. *The Berrylicious Bake-Off.* Monique Stephens. Grosset & Dunlap, 2003 (130,091)

103. *Hungry, Hungry Sharks.* Joanna Cole. Random, 1986 (129,767)

104. *The Great Race.* Kerry Milliron, illus. by Eric Binder and Tom LaPadua. Random, 2000 (129,001)

105. *Brain Quest: 1st Grade.* Chris Welles Feder, illus. by Kimble Mead. Workman, 1999 (128,643)

106. *Chicken Soup for the Teenage Soul on Tough Stuff.* HCI, 2001 (128,000)

107. *Stargirl.* Jerry Spinelli. Knopf, 2002 (125,597)

108. *Twister on Tuesday (Magic Tree House #23).* Mary Pope Osborne, illus. by Sal Murdocca. Random, 2001 (125,352)

109. *When Moms Attack (Lizzie McGuire #1).* Kim Ostrow. Disney/Volo, 2002 (125,000)

110. *The Rise and Fall of the Kate Empire (Lizzie McGuire #4).* Kirsten Larson. Disney/Volo, 2002 (125,000)

111. *Totally Crushed (Lizzie McGuire #2).* Kiki Thorpe. Disney/Volo, 2002 (125,000)

112. *James and the Giant Peach.* Roald Dahl. Puffin, 1988 (124,553)

113. *The Princess Diaries.* Meg Cabot. HarperTrophy, 2001 (124,496)

114. *Stage Fright on a Summer Night (Magic Tree House #25).* Mary Pope Osborne, illus. by Sal Murdocca. Random, 2002 (124,261)

115. *Gossip Girl #1.* Cecily Von Ziegesar. Little, Brown, 2002 (123,963)

116. *Where the Red Fern Grows.* Wilson Rawls. Dell/Laurel-Leaf, 1997 (123,704)

117. *Harry Potter and the Chamber of Secrets.* J. K. Rowling. Scholastic, 2000 (123,415)

118. *Chicken Soup for the Teenage Soul on Love and Friendship.* HCI, 2002 (123,000)

119. *The Day My Butt Went Psycho.* Andy Griffiths. Scholastic, 2003 (122,456)

120. *Dingoes at Dinnertime (Magic Tree House #20).* Mary Pope Osborne, illus. by Sal Murdocca. Random, 2000 (122,242)

121. *The Pigman.* Paul Zindel. Random/ Starfire, 1983 (121,469)

122. *Brain Quest: 2nd Grade.* Chris Welles Feder, illus. by Kimble Mead. Workman, 1999 (121,446)

123. *Freak the Mighty.* Rodman Philbrick. Scholastic, 2001 (121,066)

124. *I Like Bugs.* Margaret Wise Brown. Random, 1999 (120,784)

125. *Prince Caspian.* C. S. Lewis, illus. by Pauline Baynes. HarperTrophy, 1994 (119,865)

126. *Dinosaur Babies.* Lucille Recht Penner. Random, 1991 (119,580)

127. *Because I'm Worth It (Gossip Girl #4).* Cecily Von Ziegesar. Little, Brown, 2003 (119,284)

128. *Good Night, Dora!* Christine Ricci, illus. by Susan Hall. Simon Spotlight, 2002 (119,059)

129. *Read with Dick & Jane Vol. 1: We Look.* Grosset & Dunlap, 2003 (118,737)

130. *Read with Dick & Jane Vol. 3: Jump and Run.* Grosset & Dunlap, 2003 (118,675)

131. *The Amazing SpongeBobini.* Steven Banks, illus. by Heather Martinez. Simon Spotlight, 2003 (118,498)

132. *Day of the Dragon King (Magic Tree House #14).* Mary Pope Osborne, illus. by Sal Murdocca. Random, 1998 (118,341)

133. *The Chronicles of Narnia.* C. S. Lewis, illus. by Pauline Baynes. Harper-Trophy, 2001 (118,028)

134. *The Adventures of Captain Underpants.* Dav Pilkey. Scholastic, 1997 (117,498)

135. *All-American Girl.* Meg Cabot. HarperTrophy, 2003 (117,437)

136. *Little Bear.* Else Holmelund Minarik, illus. by Maurice Sendak. Harper-Trophy, 1978 (117,268)

137. *Captain Underpants and the Wrath of the Wicked Wedgie Woman.* Dav Pilkey. Scholastic, 2001 (117,186)

138. *The A-List.* Zoey Dean. Little, Brown, 2003 (117,002)

139. *Island of the Blue Dolphins.* Scott O'Dell. Dell/Yearling, 1971 (115,836)

140. *Esperanza Rising.* Pam Muñoz Ryan. Scholastic, 2002 (115,643)

141. *Dinosaur Days (Step into Reading).* Joyce Milton. Random, 1985 (115,551)

142. *The Voyage of the Dawn Treader.* C. S. Lewis, illus. by Pauline Baynes. HarperTrophy, 1994 (114,943)

143. *Thomas and Friends: Down at the Docks.* Rev. W. Awdry, illus. by Richard Courtney. Random, 2003 (114,857)

144. *Toy Story 2.* Random/Disney, 2003 (114,813)

145. *Captain Underpants and the Attack of the Talking Toilets.* Dav Pilkey. Scholastic, 1999 (114,389)

146. *The Westing Game.* Ellen Raskin. Puffin, 1992 (114,339)

147. *Read with Dick & Jane Vol. 6: Go, Go, Go.* Grosset & Dunlap, 2003 (114,288)

148. *Read with Dick & Jane Vol. 4: Guess Who?* Grosset & Dunlap, 2003 (114,233)

149. *Loser.* Jerry Spinelli. HarperCollins/ Cotler, 2003 (113,549)

150. *What's Growing, Strawberry Shortcake?* Grosset & Dunlap, 2003 (113,000)

151. *Freckle Juice.* Judy Blume. Dell/Yearling, 1978 (112,394)

152. *Spider-Man: I Am Spider-Man.* Acton Figueroa. HarperFestival, 2002 (112,801)

153. *Walk Two Moons.* Sharon Creech. HarperTrophy, 1996 (112,366)

154. *The Silver Chair.* C. S. Lewis, illus. by Pauline Baynes. HarperTrophy, 1994 (111,695)

155. *Judy Moody.* Megan McDonald, illus. by Peter H. Reynolds. Candlewick, 2002 (111,469)

156. *The Boxcar Children (The Boxcar Children Mysteries, #1).* Gertrude Chandler Warner, illus. by L. Kate Deal. Albert Whitman, 1942 (111,000)

157. *Blubber.* Judy Blume. Dell/Yearling, 1976 (110,933)

158. *The Princess Diaries, Vol. III: Princess in Love.* Meg Cabot. Harper-Trophy, 2003 (110,724)

159. *The Princess Diaries, Vol. II: Princess in the Spotlight.* Meg Cabot. HarperTrophy, 2002 (110,619)

160. *Captain Underpants and the Perilous Plot of Professor Poopypants.* Dav Pilkey. Scholastic, 2000 (110,481)

161. *Biscuit Finds a Friend.* Alyssa Satin Capucilli, illus. by Pat Schories. HarperTrophy, 1998 (110,111)

162. *Goodnight Moon.* Margaret Wise Brown, illus. by Clement Hurd. Harper-Trophy, 1977 (109,368)

163. *Strawberry Shortcake Goes to School.* Emily Sollinger. Grosset & Dunlap, 2003 (109,229)

164. *The Last Battle.* C. S. Lewis, illus. by Pauline Baynes. HarperTrophy, 1994 (109,197)

165. *Thanksgiving on Thursday (Magic Tree House #27).* Mary Pope Osborne, illus. by Sal Murdocca. Random, 2002 (109,152)

166. *Brain Quest: 3rd Grade.* Chris Welles Feder, illus. by Kimble Mead. Workman, 1999 (108,603)

167. *Dolphins.* Sharon Bokoske. Random, 1993 (107,996)

168. *Brain Quest: Kindergarten.* Chris Welles Feder, illus. by Kimble Mead. Workman, 1999 (107,983)

169. *The Sign of the Beaver.* Elizabeth George Speare. Dell/Yearling, 1984 (107,977)

170. *Frog and Toad Together.* Arnold Lobel. HarperTrophy, 1979 (107,880)

171. *Sarah, Plain and Tall.* Patricia MacLachlan. HarperTrophy, 1987 (107,770)

172. *Frog and Toad All Year.* Arnold Lobel. HarperTrophy, 1984 (107,558)

173. *Superfudge.* Judy Blume. Puffin, 2003 (107,206)

174. *Ahoy, Captain Feathersword!* Grosset & Dunlap, 2003 (107,006)

175. *Chicken Soup for the Preteen Soul.* HCI, 2000 (107,000)

176. *Cinderella's Countdown.* Random/Disney, 2002 (106,847)

177. *The Night Before Kindergarten.* Natasha Wing, illus. by Julie Durrell. Grosset & Dunlap, 2001 (106,297)

178. *Joey Pigza Swallowed the Key.* Jack Gantos. HarperTrophy, 2000 (106,067)

179. *Viking Ships at Sunrise (Magic Tree House #15).* Mary Pope Osborne, illus. by Sal Murdocca. Random, 1998 (105,672)

180. *You Know You Love Me (Gossip Girl #2).* Cecily Von Ziegesar. Little, Brown, 2002 (105,453)

181. *Thomas's ABC Book.* Rev. W. Awdry. Random, 1998 (105,337)

182. *Civil War on Sunday (Magic Tree House #21).* Mary Pope Osborne, illus. by Sal Murdocca. Random, 2000 (105,249)

183. *Read with Dick & Jane Vol. 2: Something Funny.* Grosset & Dunlap, 2003 (104,861)

184. *Read with Dick & Jane Vol. 5: Go Away Spot.* Grosset & Dunlap, 2003 (104,294)

185. *Captain Underpants and the Invasion of the Incredibly Naughty Cafeteria Ladies.* Dav Pilkey. Scholastic, 1999 (104,198)

186. *It's a Strawberry World.* Grosset & Dunlap, 2003 (103,834)

187. *Follow Those Feet!* Christine Ricci, illus. by Susan Hall. Simon Spotlight, 2003 (103,254)

188. *Among the Hidden.* Margaret Peterson Haddix. Aladdin, 1998 (102,291)

189. *Fever 1793.* Laurie Halse Anderson. Aladdin, 2002 (102,043)

190. *Tuck Everlasting.* Natalie Babbitt. FSG/Sunburst, 1985 (102,011)

191. *Double Fudge.* Judy Blume. Puffin, 2003 (101,815)

192. *From the Mixed-Up Files of Mrs. Basil E. Frankweiler.* E. L. Konigsburg. Aladdin, 1998 (101,713)

193. *Christmas Carol Mad Libs.* Leonard Stern. Price Stern Sloan, 2003 (101,667)

194. *All I Want Is Everything (Gossip Girl #3).* Cecily Von Ziegesar. Little, Brown, 2003 (101,513)

195. *All by Myself.* Mercer Mayer. Golden, 2001 (101,447)

196. *The Best Christmas Pageant Ever.* Barbara Robinson. HarperTrophy, 1988 (101,326)

197. *Gathering Blue.* Lois Lowry. Dell/ Laurel-Leaf, 2002 (101,315)

198. *Out of the Dust.* Karen Hesse. Scholastic, 1999 (101,150)

199. *The Phantom Tollbooth*. Norton Juster. Dell/Yearling, 1988 (101,023)
200. *Buffalo Before Breakfast (Magic Tree House #18)*. Mary Pope Osborne, illus. by Sal Murdocca. Random, 1999 (100,918)
201. *Farewell to Manzanar*. Jeanne Houston. Dell/Laurel-Leaf, 1983 (100,753)
202. *Flat Stanley (40th Anniversary Edition)*. Jeff Brown, illus. by Scott Nash. HarperTrophy, 2003 (100,440)
203. *Stone Fox*. John Reynolds Gardiner, illus. by Greg Hargreaves. HarperTrophy, 1983 (100,325)
204. *Fudge-a-Mania*. Judy Blume. Puffin, 2003 (100,166)

Literary Prizes, 2004

Gary Ink

Research Librarian, *Publishers Weekly*

Academy of American Poets Academy Fellowship. For distinguished poetic achievement. *Offered by:* Academy of American Poets. *Winner:* Li-Young Lee.

Ambassador Book Awards. To honor an exceptional contribution to the interpretation of life and culture in the United States. *Offered by:* English-Speaking Union. *Winners:* (poetry) Frank Bidart and David Gewanter for *Robert Lowell's Collected Poems* (Farrar, Straus & Giroux); (fiction) Richard Powers for *The Time of Our Singing* (Farrar, Straus & Giroux); (American studies) David Maraniss for *They Marched Into Sunlight* (Simon & Schuster).

American Academy of Arts and Letters Award of Merit for Poetry. To an outstanding U.S. poet. *Offered by:* American Academy of Arts and Letters. *Winner:* Rosanna Warren.

American Academy of Arts and Letters Awards in Literature. To honor writers of exceptional achievement. *Offered by:* American Academy of Arts and Letters. *Winners:* (poetry) Henri Cole, Marilyn Hacker, Greg Williamson; (fiction) Arnost Lustig, Joe Ashby Porter; (creative nonfiction) Samuel Hynes, Louis Rubin.

American Academy of Arts and Letters Rome Fellowships. For a one-year residency at the American Academy in Rome by young writers of promise. *Offered by:* American Academy of Arts and Letters. *Winners:* Lisa Williams, Anthony Doerr.

American Book Awards. For literary achievement by people of various ethnic backgrounds. *Offered by:* Before Columbus Foundation. *Winners:* (fiction) Diana Abu-Jaber for *Crescent* (Norton); Kristin Lattany for *Breaking Away* (One World); Ruth Ozeki for *All Over Creation* (Viking); Michael Walsh for *And All the Saints* (Warner Books); (poetry) Diane Sher Lutovich for *What I Stole* (Sixteen Rivers).

Hans Christian Andersen Awards. To an author and an illustrator whose body of work has made an important and lasting contribution to children's literature. *Offered by:* International Board on Books for Young People (IBBY). *Winners:* (author) Martin Waddell; (illustrator) Max Velthuijs.

Bancroft Prizes. For books of exceptional merit and distinction in American history, American diplomacy, and the international relations of the United States. *Offered by:* Columbia University. *Winners:* Edward L. Ayers for *In the Presence of Mine Enemies* (Norton); Steven Hahn for *A Nation Under Our Feet* (Belknap Press); George M. Marsden for *Jonathan Edwards: A Life* (Yale University).

Barnes & Noble Discover Great New Writers Awards. To honor a first novel and a first work of nonfiction by American authors. *Offered by:* Barnes & Noble, Inc. *Winners:* (fiction) Monica Ali for *Brick Lane* (Scribner); (nonfiction) Jay Griffiths for *A Sideways Look at Time* (Tarcher).

Mildred L. Batchelder Award. For an American publisher of a children's book originally published in a foreign country and subsequently published in English in the United States. *Offered by:* American Library Association, Association for Library Service to Children. *Winner:* Walter Lorraine Books/Houghton Mifflin for *Run, Boy, Run* by Uri Orlev, translated from Hebrew by Hillel Halkin.

Pura Belpré Awards. To a Latino/Latina writer and illustrator whose work portrays, affirms, and celebrates the Latino cultural experience in an outstanding work of literature for children and youth. *Offered by:* American Library Association, Association for Library Service to Children. *Winners:* (author) Julia Alvarez for *Before We Were Free* (Knopf); (illustrator) Yuyi Morales for *Just a Minute: A Trickster Tale and Counting Book* (Chronicle Books).

Curtis Benjamin Award for Creative Publishing. *Offered by:* Association of American Publishers. *Winner:* Jean Feiwel.

Helen B. Bernstein Award. For excellence in journalism. *Offered by:* New York Public Library. *Winner:* Dana Priest for *The Mission* (Norton).

Book Sense Book of the Year Awards. To honor titles that member stores have most enjoyed handselling during the past year. *Offered by:* American Booksellers Association. *Winners:* (fiction) Dan Brown for *The Da Vinci Code* (Doubleday); (nonfiction) Azar Nafisi for *Reading Lolita in Tehran* (Random House); (children's literature) Christopher Paolini for *The Inheritance, Book I* (Knopf); (children's illustrated) David Shannon for *How I Became a Pirate,* text by Melinda Long (Harcourt); (paperback) Sue Monk Kidd for *The Secret Life of Bees* (Penguin).

Boston Globe/Horn Book Awards. For excellence in children's literature. *Offered by: Boston Globe* and *Horn Book Magazine. Winners:* (fiction) David Almond for *The Fire-Eaters* (Delacorte); (nonfiction) Jim Murphy for *An American Plague* (Clarion); (picture book) Mordicai Gerstein for *The Man Who Walked Between the Towers* (Roaring Brook).

W. Y. Boyd Literary Novel Award. To an author for a military novel that honors the service of American veterans during a time of war. *Donor:* William Young Boyd. *Offered by:* American Library Association. *Winner:* James Nelson for *Glory in the Name* (Morrow).

Michael Braude Award. For light verse. *Offered by:* American Academy of Arts and Letters. *Winner:* R. S. Gwynn.

Randolph Caldecott Medal. For the artist of the most distinguished picture book. *Offered by:* American Library Association, Association for Library Service to Children. *Winner:* Mordicai Gerstein for *The Man Who Walked Between the Towers* (Roaring Brook).

California Book Awards. To California residents to honor books of fiction and poetry published in the previous year. *Offered by:* Commonwealth Club of California. *Winners:* (Gold Medal for Poetry) August

Kleinzahler for *The Strange Hours Travelers Keep* (Farrar, Straus & Giroux); (Gold Medal for Fiction) Marianne Wiggins for *Evidence of Things Unseen* (Simon & Schuster).

John W. Campbell Memorial Award. For science fiction writing. *Offered by:* Center for the Study of Science Fiction. *Winner:* Jack McDevitt for *Omega* (Ace).

Carnegie Medal (United Kingdom). For the outstanding children's book of the year. *Offered by:* The Library Association. *Winner:* Jennifer Donnelly for *A Gathering Light* (Bloomsbury).

Chicago Tribune Literary Prize. For a lifetime of literary achievement by an author whose body of work has had great impact on American society. *Offered by: Chicago Tribune. Winner:* August Wilson.

Chicago Tribune Young Adult Fiction Prize. For a fiction work of high literary merit that addresses themes especially relevant to adolescents and speaks to their role and significance in society. *Offered by: Chicago Tribune. Winner:* Blue Balliett for *Chasing Vermeer* (Scholastic).

Arthur C. Clarke Award (United Kingdom). For the best science fiction novel published in the United Kingdom. *Offered by:* British Science Fiction Association. *Winner:* Neal Stephenson for *Quicksilver* (Heinemann).

Philip K. Dick Award. For a distinguished science fiction paperback original published in the United States. *Offered by:* Norwescon. *Winner:* Richard K. Morgan for *Altered Carbon* (Del Rey).

Draine-Taylor Biography Prize (Canada). To a Canadian author of a biography, autobiography, or memoir. *Offered by:* Claire Draine Taylor and Nathan A. Taylor. *Winner:* Geoffrey Stevens for *The Player: The Life and Times of Dalton Camp* (Key Porter).

Margaret A. Edwards Award. For lifetime contribution to writing for young adults. *Offered by:* American Library Association, Young Adult Library Services Association. *Winner:* Ursula K. Le Guin.

Marian Engel Award (Canada). To a female Canadian author in mid-career for a body of work. *Offered by:* Hilary M. Weston. *Winner:* Elisabeth Harver.

E. M. Forster Award. To a young writer from England, Ireland, Scotland, or Wales for a stay in the United States. *Offered by:* American Academy of Arts and Letters. *Winner:* Robin Robertson.

Forward Prize (United Kingdom). For poetry. *Offered by: The Forward. Winners:* (best collection) Kathleen Jamie for *The Tree House* (Picador); (best first collection) Leontia Flynn for *These Days* (Jonathan Cape).

Frost Medal. To recognize achievement in poetry over a lifetime. *Offered by:* Poetry Society of America. *Winner:* Richard Howard.

Giller Prize (Canada). For the best novel or short story collection written in English. *Offered by:* Giller Prize Foundation. *Winner:* Alice Munro for *Runaway* (Knopf).

Golden Kite Awards. For children's books. *Offered by:* Society of Children's Book Writers and Illustrators. *Winners:* (picture book text) Amy Timberlake for *The Dirty Cowboy,* illus. by Adam Rex (Farrar, Straus & Giroux); (picture book illustration) Loren Long for *I Dream of Trains,* text by Angela Johnson (Simon & Schuster); (fiction) Jerry Spinelli for *Milkweed* (Knopf); (nonfiction) Robert Byrd for *Leonardo* (Dutton).

Kate Greenaway Medal (United Kingdom). For children's book illustration. *Offered by:* The Library Association. *Winner:* Shirley Hughes for *Ella's Big Chance* (Bodley Head).

Gryphon Award. To the author of the best book for kindergarten through fourth-grade readers. *Offered by:* Center for Children's Books, University of Illinois. *Winner:* Douglas Florian for *It's Raining Cats and Dogs* (Harcourt).

Guardian First Book Award (United Kingdom). For recognition of a first book. *Offered by: The Guardian. Winner:* Armand Marie Leroi for *Mutants* (Harper-Collins).

O. B. Hardison, Jr. Poetry Prize. To a U.S. poet who has published at least one book in the past five years, and has made important contributions as a teacher, and is com-mitted to furthering the understanding of poetry. *Offered by:* Folger Shakespeare Library. *Winner:* Reginald Gibbons.

Heartland Prizes. To recognize an outstanding work of fiction and an outstanding work of nonfiction, each about people and places in America's heartland. *Offered by: Chicago Tribune. Winners:* (fiction) Ward Just for *An Unfinished Season* (Houghton Mifflin); (nonfiction) Ann Patchett for *Truth & Beauty* (HarperCollins).

Ernest Hemingway Foundation Award. For a distinguished work of first fiction by an American. *Offered by:* PEN New England. *Winner:* Jennifer Haigh for *Mrs. Kimble* (Morrow).

Hugo Awards. For outstanding science fiction writing. *Offered by:* World Science Fiction Convention. *Winners:* (best novel) Lois McMaster Bujold for *Paladin of Souls* (Eos); (best related book) John Grant and others for *The Chesley Awards for Science Fiction and Fantasy Art: A Retrospective* (AAPPL); (best editor) Gardner Dozois; (best artist) Bob Eggleton.

Hurston/Wright Legacy Awards. To writers of African American descent for a book of fiction, a book of first fiction, and a book of nonfiction. *Offered by:* Hurston/Wright Foundation and Borders Books. *Winners:* (fiction) Zakes Mda for *The Heart of Redness* (Farrar, Straus & Giroux); (first fiction) Tayari Jones for *Leaving Atlanta*; (nonfiction) Wil Haygood for *In Black and White: The Life of Sammy Davis, Jr.* (Knopf).

IMPAC Dublin Literary Award (Ireland). For a book of high literary merit, written in English or translated into English. *Offered by:* IMPAC Corp. and the city of Dublin. *Winner:* Tahar Ben Jelloun for *This Blinding Absence of Light* (New Press).

Rona Jaffe Writers' Awards. To identify and support women writers of exceptional talent in the early stages of their careers. *Offered by:* Rona Jaffe Foundation. *Winners:* (fiction) Carin Clevidence, Ann Harleman; (poetry) Dana Levin, Tracy Smith, Sharan Strange; (creative nonfiction) Michele Morano.

Jerusalem Prize (Israel). To a writer whose works best express the theme of freedom of the individual in society. *Offered by:* Jerusalem International Book Fair. *Winner:* Antonio Lobo Antunes.

Samuel Johnson Prize for Nonfiction (United Kingdom). For an outstanding work of nonfiction. *Offered by:* British Broadcasting Corporation. *Winner:* Anna Funder for *Stasiland: Stories from Behind the Berlin Wall* (Granta).

Sue Kaufman Prize for First Fiction. For a first novel or collection of short stories. *Offered by:* American Academy of Arts and Letters. *Winner:* Nell Freudenberger for *Lucky Girls* (Ecco).

Ezra Jack Keats Awards. For children's picture books. *Offered by:* New York Public Library and the Ezra Jack Keats Foundation. *Winners:* (new writer award) Jeron Ashford for *Yesterday I Had the Blues* (illus. by R. Gregory Christie) (Tricycle Press); (new illustrator award) Gabi Swaitkowska for *My Name Is Yoon,* text by Helen Recorvits (Farrar, Straus & Giroux).

Coretta Scott King Awards. For works that promote the cause of peace and brotherhood *Offered by:* American Library Association, Social Responsibilities Round Table. *Winners:* (author) Angela Johnson for *The First Part Last* (Simon & Schuster); (illustrator) Ashley Bryan for *Beautiful Blackbird* (Atheneum)

Coretta Scott King/John Steptoe Awards for New Talent. For an outstanding book designed to bring visibility to a black writer or artist at the beginning of his or her career. *Offered by:* American Library Association, Social Responsibilities Round Table. *Winner:* (author) Hope Anita Smith for *The Way a Door Closes,* illus. by Shane Evans (Holt); (illustrator) Elbrite Brown for *My Family Plays Music,* text by Judy Cox (Holiday House).

Kiriyama Pacific Rim Book Prizes. For a book of fiction and a book of nonfiction that best contribute to a fuller understanding among the nations and peoples of the Pacific Rim. *Offered by:* Kiriyama Pacific Rim Institute. *Winners:* (fiction) Shan Sa for *The Girl Who Played Go* (Knopf); (nonfiction) Inga Cunningham for *Dancing With Strangers* (Text Publishing).

Robert Kirsch Award. To a living author whose residence or focus is the American West, and whose contributions to American letters clearly merit body-of-work recognition. *Offered by: Los Angeles Times. Winner:* Ishmael Reed.

Koret Jewish Book Awards. To underline the centrality of books in Jewish culture and to encourage serious readers to seek the best in Jewish books. *Offered by:* Koret Foundation. *Winners:* (fiction) Barbara Honigmann for *A Love Made Out of Nothing* and *Zohara's Journey,* translated from German by John Barrett (Godine); Aharon Megged for *Foiglman,* translated from Hebrew by Marganit Weinberger-Rotman (Toby Press); (biography/autobiography) Benjamin Harshav for *Marc Chagall and His Times* (Stanford); (history) Shmuel Feiner for *The Jewish Enlightenment,* translated from Hebrew by Chaya Naor (University of Pennsylvania); (philosophy/thought) Daniel Matt for *The Zohar,* Pritzker Edition, Volumes I and II (Stanford); (young writer on Jewish themes) Rachel Kadish.

Harold Morton Landon Translation Award. For a book of verse translated into English by a single translator. *Offered by:* Academy of American Poets. *Winners:* Anselm Hollo for *Pentti Saarikoski's Trilogy* (La Alameda Press); Charles Martin for Ovid's *Metamorphoses* (Norton).

Lannan Foundation Literary Awards. To recognize writers who have made significant contributions to English-language literature. *Offered by:* Lannan Foundation. *Winners:* (fiction) Rikki Ducornet; (nonfiction) Luis Alberto Urrea; (poetry) W. S. Merwin.

Lannan Foundation Literary Fellowships. To recognize young and mid-career writers of distinctive literary merit who demonstrate potential for continued outstanding work. *Offered by:* Lannan Foundation. *Winners:* Edwidge Danticat, Thomas Frank, Mavis Gallant, Micheline Aharonian Marcom, Rebecca Seiferle.

James Laughlin Award. To commend and support a second book of poetry. *Offered by:* Academy of American Poets. *Winner:* Jeff Clark for *Music and Suicide* (Farrar, Straus & Giroux).

Ruth Lilly Poetry Fellowships. To help aspiring writers to continue their study and practice of poetry. *Offered by:* The Poetry Association. *Winners:* Nathan Bartel, Emily Moore.

Ruth Lilly Poetry Prize. To a U.S. poet whose accomplishments warrant extraordinary recognition. *Offered by:* The Poetry Association. *Winner:* Kay Ryan.

Astrid Lindgren Award (Sweden). In memory of Astrid Lindgren to honor outstanding children's book writing. *Offered by:* Swedish Government. *Winner:* Lygia Bojunga.

Locus Awards. For science fiction writing. *Offered by:* Locus Publications. *Winners:* (best novel) Dan Simmons for *Ilium* (Eos); (best first novel) Cory Doctorow for *Down and Out in the Magic Kingdom* (Tor); (best fantasy novel) Lois McMaster Bujold for *Paladin of Souls* (Eos); (best young adult) Terry Pratchett for *The Wee Free Men* (HarperCollins); (best anthology) *The Year's Best Science Fiction: Twentieth Annual Collection,* Gardner Dozois, ed. (St. Martin's); (best collection) Ursula K. Le Guin for *Changing Planes* (Harcourt); (best nonfiction/art book) Neil Gaiman and others for *The Sandman: Endless Nights* (Vertigo); (best editor) Gardner Dozois; (best book publisher) Tor.

Los Angeles Times Book Prizes. To honor literary excellence. *Offered by: Los Angeles Times. Winners:* (fiction) Pete Dexter for *Train* (Doubleday); (biography) Neil Smith for *American Empire* (University of California); (current interest) Ross Terrill for *The New Chinese Empire* (Basic Books); (history) Henry Weincek for *An Imperfect God* (Farrar, Straus & Giroux); (poetry) Anthony Hecht for *Collected Later Poems* (Knopf); (science and technology) Philip J. Hilts for *Protecting America's Health* (Knopf); (mystery/thriller) George P. Pelecanos for *Soul Circus* (Little, Brown); (young adult fiction) Jennifer Donnelly for *A Northern Light* (Harcourt); (Art Seidenbaum Award for first fiction) Mark Haddon for *The Curious Incident of the Dog in the Night-Time* (Doubleday).

Man Booker Prize (United Kingdom). For the best novel written in English by a Commonwealth author. *Offered by:* Booktrust and the Man Group. *Winner:* Alan Hollinghurst for *The Line of Beauty* (Picador).

Lenore Marshall Poetry Prize. For an outstanding book of poems published in the United States. *Offered by:* Academy of American Poets. *Winner:* Eamon Grennan for *Still Life with Waterfall* (Graywolf).

Vicky Metcalf Award for Children's Literature (Canada). To a Canadian author of children's literature for a body of work. *Offered by:* George Cedric Metcalf Foundation. *Winner:* Roslyn Schwartz.

National Arts Club Medal of Honor for Literature. *Offered by:* National Arts Club. *Winner:* Shirley Hazzard.

National Book Awards. For the best books of the year published in the United States. *Offered by:* National Book Foundation. *Winners:* (fiction) Lily Tuck for *The News from Paraguay* (HarperCollins); (nonfiction) Kevin Boyle for *Arc of Justice* (Holt); (poetry) Jean Valentine for *Door in the Mountain* (Wesleyan University Press); (young people's literature) Pete Hautman for *Godless* (Simon & Schuster).

National Book Critics Circle Awards. For literary excellence. *Offered by:* National Book Critics Circle. *Winners:* (fiction) Edward P. Jones for *The Known World* (Amistad Press); (nonfiction) Paul Hendrickson for *Sons of Mississippi* (Knopf); (biography/autobiography) William Taubman for *Khrushchev: The Man and His Era* (Norton); (criticism) Rebecca Solnit for *River of Shadows* (Viking); (poetry) Susan Stewart for *Columbarium* (University of Chicago); (lifetime achievement award) Studs Terkel.

National Book Foundation Medal for Distinguished Contribution to American Letters. To a person who has enriched the nation's literary heritage over a life of service or a corpus of work. *Offered by:* National Book Foundation. *Winner:* Judy Blume.

Nebula Awards. For science fiction writing. *Offered by:* Science Fiction and Fantasy Writers of America. *Winners:* (best novel) Elizabeth Moon for *The Speed of Dark* (Ballantine); (Grand Master) Robert Silverberg.

John Newbery Medal. For the most distinguished contribution to literature for children. *Offered by:* American Library Association, Association for Library Service to Children. *Winner:* Kate DiCamillo for *The Tale of Despereaux* (Candlewick).

Nobel Prize in Literature (Sweden). For the total literary output of a distinguished career. *Offered by:* Swedish Academy. *Winner:* Elfriede Jelinek.

Flannery O'Connor Awards for Short Fiction. For collections of short fiction. *Offered by:* PEN American Center. *Winners:* Gary Fincke for *Sorry I Worried You* (University of Georgia); Barbara Sutton for *The Send-Away Girl* (University of Georgia).

Scott O'Dell Award. For historical fiction. *Offered by: Bulletin of the Center for Children's Books,* University of Chicago. *Winner:* Richard Peck for *The River Between Us* (Dial).

Orange Prize for Fiction (United Kingdom). For the best novel written by a woman and published in the United Kingdom. *Offered by:* Orange Plc. *Winner:* Andrea Levy for *Small Island* (Review).

Pearson Writers' Trust Nonfiction Prize (Canada). To a Canadian author of a non-fiction book. *Offered by:* Pearson Canada. *Winner:* Brian Fawcett for *Virtual Clearcut* (Thomas Allen).

Pegasus Awards: Mark Twain Poetry Award. To honor an American poet for his or her contribution to humor in verse. *Offered by:* The Poetry Foundation. *Winner:* Billy Collins.

Pegasus Awards: Neglected Masters Award. To bring attention to an underappreciated U.S. poet. *Offered by:* The Poetry Foundation. *Winner:* Samuel Menashe.

PEN Award for Poetry in Translation. For a book-length translation of poetry from any language into English and published in the United States. *Offered by:* PEN American Center. *Winner:* Peter Cole for *J'Accuse* by Aharon Shabtai (New Directions).

PEN Award for the Art of the Essay. For an outstanding book of essays by an American writer. *Offered by:* PEN American Center. *Winner:* Stewart Justman for *Seeds of Mortality* (Ivan R. Dee).

PEN/Martha Albrand Award for the Art of the Memoir. To honor a U.S. author's first book-length memoir. *Offered by:* PEN American Center. *Winner:* Anthony Swofford for *Jarhead* (Scribner).

PEN/Robert Bingham Fellowships. To writers whose first novels or story collections, published in the two previous years, represent distinguished literary achievement and suggest great promise. *Offered by:* PEN American Center. *Winners:* Jonathan Safran Foer, Monique Truong, Will Heinrich.

PEN/Book-of-the-Month Club Translation Award. For a book-length literary translation from any language into English. *Offered by:* PEN American Center. *Winner:* Margaret Sayers Peden for *Sepharad* by Antonio Munoz Molina (Harcourt).

PEN/Faulkner Award for Fiction. To honor the best work of fiction published by an American. *Offered by:* PEN American Center. *Winner:* John Updike for *The Early Stories: 1953–1975* (Knopf).

PEN/Malamud Award. To an author who has demonstrated long-term excellence in short fiction. *Offered by:* PEN American Center. *Winners:* Barry Hannah, Melie Meloy.

PEN/Nabokov Award. To celebrate the accomplishments of a living author whose body of work, either written in or translated into English, represents achievement in a variety of literary genres. *Offered by:* PEN American Center. *Winner:* Mavis Gallant.

PEN/Voelcker Award for Poetry. To an American poet at the height of his or her powers. *Offered by:* PEN American Center. *Winner:* Robert Pinsky.

Edgar Allan Poe Awards. For outstanding mystery, suspense, and crime writing. *Offered by:* Mystery Writers of America. *Winners:* (novel) Ian Rankin for *Resurrection Men* (Little, Brown); (first novel) Rebecca Pawel for *Death of a Nationalist* (Soho Press); (paperback original) Sylvia Maultash for *Find Me Again* (Dundurn Group); (fact crime) Erik Larson for *The Devil in the White City* (Crown); (Grand Master Award) Joseph Wambaugh.

Katherine Anne Porter Award. To a prose writer of demonstrated achievement.

Offered by: American Academy of Arts and Letters. *Winner:* Nicholson Baker.

Michael L. Printz Award. For excellence in literature for young adults. *Offered by:* American Library Association, Association of Library Service to Children. *Winner:* Angela Johnson for *The First Part Last* (Simon & Schuster).

Pulitzer Prizes in Letters. To honor distinguished work by American writers, dealing preferably with American themes. *Offered by:* Columbia University Graduate School of Journalism. *Winners:* (fiction) Edward P. Jones for *The Known World* (Amistad Press); (biography) William Taubman for *Khrushchev* (Norton); (history) Steven Hahn for *A Nation Under Our Feet* (Belknap Press); (general nonfiction) Anne Applebaum for *Gulag* (Doubleday); (poetry) Franz Wright for *Walking to Martha's Vineyard* (Knopf).

Quality Paperback Book Club New Visions Award. For the most distinct and promising work of nonfiction by a new writer *Offered by:* Quality Paperback Book Club. *Winner:* Dan Rhodes for *Timoleon Vieta Comes Home* (Canongate).

Quality Paperback Book Club New Voices Award. For the most distinct and promising work of fiction by a new writer *Offered by:* Quality Paperback Book Club. *Winner:* Nicole LeBlanc for *Random Family* (Scribner).

Raiziss/De Palchi Translation Award. For a translation into English of a significant work of modern Italian poetry by a living translator. *Offered by:* Academy of American Poets. *Winner:* Andrew Frisardi for *The Selected Poems of Giuseppe Ungaretti* (Farrar, Straus & Giroux).

Rea Award for the Short Story. To honor a living writer who has made a significant contribution to the short story as an art form. *Offered by:* Dungannon Foundation. *Winner:* Antonya Nelson.

Rita Awards. *Offered by:* Romance Writers of America. *Winners:* (best traditional romance) Marion Lennox for *Her Royal Baby* (Harlequin Mills & Boon); (best regency romance) Nancy Butler for *Prospero's Daughter* (Signet); (best long contemporary series) Kathleen Creighton for *The Top Gun's Return* (Harlequin); (best short contemporary series) Nicole Burnham for *The Knight's Kiss* (Silhouette Books); (best short historical romance) Lisa Kleypas for *Worth Any Price* (Avon); (best long historical romance) Kathleen Givens for *The Destiny* (Warner Books); (best paranormal romance) Linda Fallon for *Shades of Midnight* (Kensington); (best romantic suspense) Nora Roberts for *Remember When—Part 1* (Putnam); (best inspirational romance) Gayle Roper for *Autumn Dreams* (Multnomah); (best contemporary single title) Nora Roberts for *Birthright* (Putnam); (best romantic novella) Gayle Wilson for "Prisoner of the Tower" in *The Wedding Chase* (Harlequin); (best novel with strong romantic elements) Kristin Hannah for *Between Sisters* (Ballantine); (best first book) Susan Crandall for *Back Roads* (Warner Books).

Rogers Writers' Trust Fiction Prize (Canada). To a Canadian author of a novel or short story collection. *Offered by:* Rogers Communications. *Winner:* Kevin Patterson for *Country of Cold* (Vintage).

Richard and Hinda Rosenthal Foundation Award. For a work of fiction that is a considerable literary achievement though not necessarily a commercial success. *Offered by:* American Academy of Arts and Letters. *Winner:* Olympia Vernon for *Eden* (Grove Press).

Juan Rulfo International Latin American and Caribbean Prize (Mexico). To honor the lifetime achievement of a native of Latin America or the Caribbean, writing in Spanish, Portuguese, or English, or a native of Spain or Portugal writing in Spanish or Portuguese. *Offered by:* Juan Rulfo Awards Committee. *Winner:* Juan Goytisolo.

Schneider Family Book Awards. To honor authors and illustrators for books that embody artistic expressions of the disability experience of children and adolescents. *Offered by:* American Library Association. *Winners:* (ages 0–10) Glenna Lang for *Looking Out for Sarah* (Charlesbridge); (ages 11–13) Wendy Mass for *A Mango-Shaped Space* (Little, Brown); (ages 13–18) Andrew Clements for *Things Not Seen* (Turtleback Books).

Shelley Memorial Award. To a poet living in the United States who is chosen on the basis of genius and need. *Offered by:* Poetry Society of America. *Winner:* Yusef Komunyakaa.

Robert F. Sibert Award. For the most distinguished informational book for children. *Offered by:* American Library Association, Association for Library Service to Children. *Winner:* Jim Murphy for *An American Plague* (Clarion).

Smarties Book Prizes (United Kingdom). To encourage high standards and to stimulate interest in books for children. *Offered by:* Nestlé Rowntree. *Winners:* (9–11 years) Sally Grindley for *Spilled Water* (Bloomsbury); (6–8 years) Paul Stewart and Chris Riddell for *Fergus Crane* (Doubleday); (5 and younger) Mini Grey for *Biscuit Bear* (Cape); (Special Award) Paul Stewart and Chris Riddell for *Fergus Crane.*

W. H. Smith Literary Awards (United Kingdom). For the best books of the year as selected by the British public. *Offered by:* W. H. Smith, Ltd. *Winners:* (fiction) J. K. Rowling for *Harry Potter and the Order of the Phoenix* (Bloomsbury); (literary fiction) Richard Powers for *The Time of Our Singing* (Vintage); (first fiction) Monica Ali for *Brick Lane* (Doubleday).

Spur Awards. *Offered by:* Western Writers of America. *Winners:* (best first novel) Miles Hood Swarthout for *The Sergeant's Lady* (Forge); (best drama script) for *And Starring Pancho Villa as Himself;* (best western novel) Brian Hall for *I Should Be Extremely Happy in Your Company* (Viking); (novel under 90,000 words) Win Blevins for *So Wild a Dream* (Forge); (original paperback novel) Barbara Wright for *Plain Language* (Touchstone); (nonfiction biography) Ernest Haycox, Jr. for *On a Silver Desert: The Life of Ernest Haycox* (University of Oklahoma Press); (nonfiction, contemporary) Rebecca Solnit for *River of Shadows: Eadweard Muybridge and the Technological Wild West* (Viking); (nonfiction, historical) Colin G. Calloway for *One Vast Winter Count: The Native American West Before Lewis and Clark* (University of Nebraska Press); (short fiction) Andrew Geyer for "Second Coming"

in *Whispers in Dust and Bone* (Texas Tech University Press); (short nonfiction) Elliott West for *Reconstructing Race* (*Western Historical Quarterly,* spring 2003); (juvenile fiction) E. Cody Kimmel for *In the Eye of the Storm: The Adventures of Young Buffalo Bill* (HarperCollins); (juvenile nonfiction) Ginger Wadsworth for *Words West: Voices of Young Pioneers* (Clarion Books); (documentary) Paul Andrew Hutton for "Carson and Cody: The Hunter Heroes" (Gary L. Foreman/Native Sun Productions, the History Channel); (poetry) Paul Zarzyski for *Wolf Tracks on the Welcome Mat* (Oreana Books); (illustrated children's book) S. D. Nelson for *The Star People: A Lakota Story* (Abrams).

Wallace Stevens Award. To recognize outstanding and proven mastery in the art of poetry. *Offered by:* Academy of American Poets. *Winner:* Richard Wilbur.

Stonewall Book Awards. *Offered by:* Gay, Lesbian, Bisexual, and Transgendered Round Table, American Library Association. *Winners:* (Barbara Gittings Literature Award) Monique Truong for *The Book of Salt* (Houghton Mifflin); (Israel Fishman Nonfiction Award) John D'Emilio for *Lost Prophet: The Life and Times of Bayard Rustin* (Free Press).

Charles Taylor Prize for Literary Nonfiction (Canada). To honor a book of creative nonfiction widely available in Canada and written by a Canadian citizen or landed immigrant. *Offered by:* Charles Taylor Foundation. *Winner:* Isabel Huggan for *Belonging: Home Away from Home* (Knopf).

Sydney Taylor Children's Book Awards. For a distinguished contribution to Jewish children's literature. *Offered by:* Association of Jewish Libraries. *Winners:* (older readers) Nancy Patz for *Who Was the Woman Who Wore the Hat?* (Dutton); (younger readers) Aubrey Davis for *Bagels from Benny,* illus. by Dusan Petricic (Kids Can Press).

Templeton Prize for Progress Toward Research or Discoveries About Spiritual Realities. To honor a person judged to have contributed special insights to religion and spirituality. *Offered by:* Templeton Foundation. *Winner:* George F. R. Ellis.

Kate Frost Tufts Discovery Award. For a first or very early book of poetry by an emerging poet. *Offered by:* Claremont Graduate School. *Winner:* Adrian Blevins for *The Brass Girl Brouhaha* (Ausable Press).

Kingsley Tufts Poetry Award. For a book of poetry by a mid-career poet. *Offered by:* Claremont Graduate School. *Winner:* Henri Cole for *Middle Earth* (Farrar, Straus & Giroux).

Whitbread Literary Awards (United Kingdom). For literature of merit that is readable on a wide scale. *Offered by:* Booksellers Association of Great Britain. *Winners:* (first novel) Susan Fletcher for *Eve Green* (Fourth Estate); (children's) Geraldine McCaughrean for *Not the End of the World* (Oxford); (novel) Andrea Levy for *Small Island* (Review); (biography) John Guy for *My Heart Is My Own* (Fourth Estate); (poetry) Michael Symmons Roberts for *Corpus* (Cape); (book of the year) Andrea Levy for *Small Island* (Review).

Whiting Writers' Awards. For emerging writers of exceptional talent and promise. *Offered by:* Mrs. Giles Whiting Foundation. *Winners:* (poetry) Catherine Barnett, Dan Chiasson, A. Van Jordan; (fiction) Daniel Alarcon, Kirsten Bakis, Victor La Valle; (nonfiction) Allison Glock, John Jeremiah Sullivan.

Walt Whitman Award. To a U.S. poet who has not published a book of poems in a standard edition. *Offered by:* Academy of American Poets. *Winner:* Geri Doran.

Robert H. Winner Memorial Award. To a mid-career poet over 40 who has published no more than one book of poetry. *Offered by:* Poetry Society of America. *Winner:* John McKernan.

L. L. Winship Award. For a book of poetry, fiction, or creative nonfiction with a New England subject or written by a New England author. *Offered by:* PEN New England. *Winners:* Carlo Rotella for *An Education at the Fights* (Houghton Mifflin),

Joan Leegant for *An Hour in Paradise* (Norton).

Thomas Wolfe Award. For significant literary achievement. *Offered by:* Thomas Wolfe Society and the University of North Carolina at Chapel Hill. *Winner:* Ellen Gilchrist.

Helen and Kurt Wolff Translator's Prize. For an outstanding translation from German into English, published in the United States. *Offered by:* Goethe Institut Inter Nationes Chicago. *Winner:* Breon Mitchell for *Morenga* by Uwe Timm (New Directions).

World Fantasy Convention Awards. For outstanding fantasy writing. *Offered by:* World Fantasy Convention. *Winners:* (novel) Jo Walton for *Tooth and Claw* (Tor); (anthology) Rosalie Parker, ed., for *Strange Tales* (Tartarus Press); (collection) Elizabeth Hand for *Bibliomancy* (PS Publishing); (lifetime achievement) Stephen King, Gahan Wilson.

Writers' Trust of Canada/Matt Cohen Award (Canada). To a Canadian author whose life has been dedicated to writing as a primary pursuit, for a body of work. *Offered by:* Writers' Trust of Canada. *Winner:* Audrey Thomas.

Writers' Trust of Canada/Timothy Findley Award (Canada). To a male Canadian author in mid-career for a body of work. *Offered by:* Writers' Trust of Canada. *Winner:* Guy Vanderhaeghe.

Writers' Trust of Canada/McClelland & Stewart Journey Prize (Canada). To a new, developing Canadian author for a short story or an excerpt from a novel-in-progress. *Offered by:* McClelland & Stewart and James A. Michener. *Winner:* Jessica Grant for *My Husband's Jump* (work-in-progress).

Young Lions Fiction Award. For a novel or collection of short stories by an American under the age of 35. *Offered by:* Young Lions of the New York Public Library. *Winner:* Monique Truong for *The Book of Salt* (Houghton Mifflin).

Part 6
Directory of Organizations

Directory of Library and Related Organizations

Networks, Consortia, and Other Cooperative Library Organizations

United States

Alabama

Alabama Health Libraries Assn., Inc. (ALHeLa), Univ. of S. Alabama, Baugh Medical Libs., Mobile 36617. SAN 372-8218. Tel. 251-471-7855, fax 251-471-7857. *Dir.* Tom Williams.

Jefferson County Hospital Librarians Assn., Brookwood Medical Center, Birmingham 35209. SAN 371-2168. Tel. 205-877-1131, fax 205-877-1189.

Library Management Network, Inc. (LMN), 110 Johnston St. S.E., Decatur 35601. SAN 322-3906. Tel. 256-308-2529, fax 256-308-2533. *System Coord.* Charlotte Moncrief.

Marine Environmental Sciences Consortium, Dauphin Island Sea Lab, Dauphin Island 36528. SAN 322-0001. Tel. 251-861-2141, fax 251-861-4646, e-mail disl@disl.org. *Dir.* George Crozier.

Network of Alabama Academic Libraries, c/o Alabama Commission on Higher Education, Montgomery 36130-2000. SAN 322-4570. Tel. 334-242-2164, fax 334-242-0270. *Dir.* Sue O. Medina.

Alaska

Alaska Library Network (ALN), 344 W. 3rd Ave., Ste. 125, Anchorage 99501. SAN 371-0688. Tel. 907-269-6570, fax 907-269-6580, e-mail aslanc@eed.state.ak.us.

Arizona

Maricopa County Community College District/Lib. Technical Services, 2411 W. 14th St., Tempe 85281-6942. SAN 322-0060. Tel. 480-731-8774, fax 480-731-8787. *Head, Technical Services.* Vince Jenkins.

Arkansas

Arkansas Area Health Education Center Consortium (AHEC), Sparks Regional Medical Center, Fort Smith 72901-4992. SAN 329-3734. Tel. 479-441-5337, fax 479-441-5339. *Dir.* Grace Anderson.

Arkansas Independent Colleges and Universities, 1 Riverfront Pl., Ste. 610, North Little Rock 72114. SAN 322-0079. Tel. 501-378-0843, fax 501-374-1523. *Pres.* Kearney E. Dietz.

Northeast Arkansas Hospital Library Consortium, 223 E. Jackson, Jonesboro 72401. SAN 329-529X. Tel. 870-972-1290, fax 870-931-0839. *Dir.* Karen Crosser.

South Arkansas Film Coop., c/o Malvern-Hot Spring County Lib., Malvern 72104. SAN 321-5938. Tel. 501-332-5441, fax 501-332-6679, e-mail hotspringcountylibrary@yahoo.com.

California

Bay Area Library and Information Network (BAYNET), 672 Prentiss St., San Francisco 94110-6130. SAN 371-0610. Tel. 415-826-2464, e-mail infobay@baynetlibs.org.

Central Assn. of Libraries (CAL), 605 N. El Dorado St., Stockton 95202-1999. SAN 322-0125. Tel. 209-937-8649, fax 209-937-8292, e-mail 4999@ci.stockton.ca.us. *Dir.* Darla Gunning.

Consortium for Open Learning, 333 Sunrise Ave., No. 229, Roseville 95661-3479. SAN 329-4412. Tel. 916-788-0660, fax 916-788-0696, e-mail cdl@calweb.com. *Mgr.* Sandra Scott-Smith.

Consortium of Foundation Libraries, c/o Packard Foundation, Los Altos 94022. SAN 322-2462. Tel. 650-917-7116. *Chair* Michelle Butler.

Consumer Health Information Program and Services (CHIPS), County of Los Angeles Public Lib., Carson 90745. SAN 372-8110. Tel. 310-830-0909, fax 310-834-4097, e-mail chips@colopl.org. *Libn.* Scott A. Willis.

Dialog Corporation, 2440 W. El Camino Real, Mountain View 94040. SAN 322-0176. Tel. 650-254-7000, fax 650-254-8093.

Gold Coast Library Network, 4882 McGrath St., Ste. 230, Ventura 93003-7721. Tel. 805-650-7732, fax 805-642-9095, e-mail goldcln@rain.org. *Dir.* Vincent Schmidt.

Hewlett-Packard Library Information Network, 1501 Page Mill Rd., Palo Alto 94304. SAN 375-0019. Tel. 650-857-3091, fax 650-852-8187. *Dir.* Eugenie Prime.

Kaiser Permanente Library System–Southern California Region (KPLS), Health Sciences Lib., Riverside 92505. SAN 372-8153. Tel. 951-353-3659, fax 951-353-3262. *Dir.* William Paringer.

Metropolitan Cooperative Library System (MCLS), 3675 E. Huntington Dr., Ste. 100, Pasadena 91107. SAN 371-3865. Tel. 626-683-8244, fax 626-683-8097, e-mail mclshq@mcls.org. *Exec. Dir.* Barbara Custen.

National Network of Libraries of Medicine–Pacific Southwest Region (NN-LM PSRML), Louise M. Darling Biomedical Lib., Los Angeles 90095-1798. SAN 372-8234. Tel. 310-825-1200, fax 310-825-5389, e-mail psr-nnlm@library.ucla.edu. *Dir.* Judy Consales.

Nevada Medical Library Group (NMLG), Barton Memorial Hospital Lib., South Lake Tahoe 96150. SAN 370-0445. Tel. 530-542-3000 ext. 2903, fax 530-541-4697. *In Charge* Laurie Anton.

Northern California Assn. of Law Libraries (NOCALL), PMB 336, San Francisco 94105. SAN 323-5777. E-mail admin@nocall.org. *Pres.* Tina Dumas.

Northern California Consortium of Psychology Libraries (NCCPL), Saybrook Graduate School and Research Center, San Francisco 94133. SAN 371-9006. Tel. 415-394-5062, fax 415-433-9271, e-mail nccpl-d@jfku.edu. *Dir., Lib. Services.* Annemarie Welteke.

OCLC Western Service Center, 3281 E. Guasti Rd., Ste. 560, Ontario 91761. SAN 370-0747. Tel. 909-937-3300, fax 909-937-3384. *Dir.* Pamela Bailey.

Peninsula Libraries Automated Network (PLAN), 2471 Flores St., San Mateo 94403-4000. SAN 371-5035. Tel. 650-358-6714, fax 650-358-6715. *Database Mgr.* Susan Yasar.

Research Libraries Group, Inc. (RLG), 2029 Stierlin Ct., Ste. 100, Mountain View 94043-4684. SAN 322-0206. Fax 650-964-0943, e-mail ric@notes.rlg.org. *Pres.* James Michalko.

San Bernardino, Inyo, Riverside Counties United Library Services (SIRCULS), 3581 Mission Inn Ave., Riverside 92501-3377. SAN 322-0222. Tel. 909-369-7995, fax 909-784-1158, e-mail sirculs@inlandlib.org. *Exec. Dir.* Kathleen F. Aaron.

San Francisco Biomedical Lib. Network (SFBLN), H. M. Fishbon Memorial Lib., San Francisco 94115. SAN 371-2125. Tel. 415-885-7378, e-mail fishbon@itsa.ucfs.edu.

Santa Clarita Interlibrary Network (SCIL-NET), Powell Lib., Santa Clarita 91321. SAN 371-8964. Tel. 661-259-3540, fax 661-222-9159. *Libn.* John Stone.

Serra Cooperative Library System, 820 E. St., San Diego 92101. SAN 372-8129. Tel. 619-232-1225, fax 619-696-8649, e-mail serral@sbcglobal.net. *System Coord.* Susan Swisher.

Substance Abuse Librarians and Information Specialists (SALIS), P.O. Box 9513, Berkeley 94709-0513. SAN 372-4042. Tel. 510-642-5208, fax 510-642-7175, e-mail salis @arg.org. *Chair* Stephanie Asteriadis.

Colorado

Arkansas Valley Regional Library Service System (AVRLSS), 635 W. Corona, Ste. 113, Pueblo 81004. SAN 371-5094. Tel. 719-542-2156, fax 719-542-3155. *Chair* Dorothy Cowgill.

Bi-State Academic Libraries (BI-SAL), c/o Marycrest International Univ., Denver 80236-2711. SAN 322-1393. Tel. 563-326-9254, fax 563-326-9250. *Libn.* Mary Edwards.

Bibliographical Center for Research, Rocky Mountain Region, Inc. (BCR), 14394 E. Evans Ave., Aurora 80014-1478. SAN 322-0338. Tel. 303-751-6277, fax 303-751-9787, e-mail admin@bcr.org. *Exec. Dir.* David H. Brunell.

Central Colorado Library System (CCLS), 9255 W. Alameda Ave., Ste. C, Lakewood 80226-2802. SAN 371-3970. Tel. 303-422-1150, fax 303-431-9752. *Dir.* Gordon C. Barhydt.

Colorado Alliance of Research Libraries, 3801 E. Florida Ave., Ste. 515, Denver 80210. SAN 322-3760. Tel. 303-759-3399, fax 303-759-3363.

Colorado Assn. of Law Libraries, P.O. Box 13363, Denver 80201. SAN 322-4325. Tel. 303-492-7312, fax 303-713-6218. *Pres.* Holly Kulikowski.

Colorado Council of Medical Librarians (CCML), P.O. Box 101058, Denver 80210-1058. SAN 370-0755. Tel. 303-837-7375, fax 303-837-7977. *Pres.* Lynne Fox.

Peaks and Valleys Library Consortium, c/o Arkansas Valley Regional Lib. Services System, Pueblo 81004. SAN 328-8684. Tel. 719-542-2156, fax 719-542-3155. *Dir.* Donna Jones Morris.

Connecticut

Capital Area Health Consortium, 270 Farmington Ave., Ste. 352, Farmington 06032-1994. SAN 322-0370. Tel. 860-676-1110, fax 860-676-1303, e-mail info@cahc.org. *Pres.* Karen Goodman.

Connecticut Library Consortium, 2911 Dixwell Ave., Ste. 201, Hamden 06518-3130. SAN 322-0389. Tel. 203-288-5757, fax 203-287-0757. *Exec. Dir.* Bradley Christine.

Council of State Library Agencies in the Northeast (COSLINE), Connecticut State Lib., Hartford 06106. SAN 322-0451. Tel. 860-757-6510, fax 860-757-6503.

CTW Library Consortium, Olin Memorial Lib., Middletown 06459-6065. SAN 329-4587. Tel. 860-685-3889, fax 860-685-2661. *System Libn.* Alan E. Hagyard.

Hartford Consortium for Higher Education, 950 Main St., Ste. 314, Hartford 06103. SAN 322-0443. Tel. 860-906-5016, fax 860-906-5118. *Exec. Dir.* Rosanne Druckman.

LEAP, 110 Washington Ave., North Haven 06473. SAN 322-4082. Tel. 203-239-1411, fax 203-239-9458. *Exec. Dir.* Diana Sellers.

Libraries Online, Inc. (LION), 100 Riverview Center, Ste. 252, Middletown 06457. SAN 322-3922. Tel. 860-347-1704, fax 860-346-3707. *Exec. Dir.* Joan Gillespie.

Library Connection, Inc., 599 Matianuck Ave., Windsor 06095-3567. Tel. 860-298-5322, fax 860-298-5328. *Exec. Dir.* George Christian.

North Atlantic Health Sciences Libraries, Inc. (NAHSL), Medial Lib. CB-3, Hartford 06102. SAN 371-0599. Tel. 508-856-6099, fax 508-856-5899. *Chair* Edward Donnald.

Delaware

Central Delaware Library Consortium, Dover Public Lib., Dover 19901. SAN 329-3696. Tel. 302-736-7030, fax 302-736-5087. *Dir.* Sheila B. Anderson.

Delaware Library Consortium (DLC), Delaware Academy of Medicine, Wilmington 19806. SAN 329-3718. Tel. 302-656-6398, fax 302-656-0470, e-mail library@ delamed.org. *In Charge.* Gail P. Gill.

District of Columbia

Council for Christian Colleges and Universities, 321 8th St. N.E., Washington 20002. SAN 322-0524. Tel. 202-546-8713, fax

202-546-8913, e-mail council@cccu.org. *Pres.* Robert C. Andringa.

District of Columbia Area Health Science Libraries (DCAHSL), American College of Obstetrics and Gynecology Resource Center, Washington 20024. SAN 323-9918. Tel. 202-863-2518, fax 202-484-1595, e-mail resources@acog.org. *Dir.* Mary Hyde.

EDUCAUSE, c/o 1150 18th St. N.W., Ste. 1010, Washington 20036. SAN 371-487X. Tel. 202-872-4200, fax 202-872-4318. *Pres.* Brian Hawkins.

FEDLINK/Federal Lib. and Info. Network, c/o Federal Lib. and Info. Center Committee, Washington 20540-4935. SAN 322-0761. Tel. 202-707-4800, fax 202-707-4818, e-mail flicc@loc.gov. *Exec. Dir.* Susan M. Tarr.

Library of Congress, National Lib. Service for the Blind and Physically Handicapped (NLS), 1291 Taylor St. N.W., Washington 20542. SAN 370-5870. Tel. 202-707-5100, fax 202-707-0712, e-mail nls@loc.gov. *Dir.* Frank Kurt Cylke.

OCLC CAPCON Service Center, 1990 M St. N.W., Ste. 200, Washington 20036-3430. SAN 321-5954. Tel. 202-331-5771, fax 202-331-5788, e-mail capcon@oclc.org. *Exec. Dir.* Katherine Blauer.

Transportation Research Board, 500 5th St. N.W., Washington 20001. SAN 370-582X. Tel. 202-334-2990, fax 202-334-2527. *Dir.* Barbara Post.

Veterans Affairs Library Network (VAL-NET), Lib. Programs Office 19E, Washington 20420. SAN 322-0834. Tel. 202-273-8523, fax 202-273-9386. *Network Services.* Ginny DuPont.

Washington Theological Consortium, 487 Michigan Ave. N.E., Washington 20017-1585. SAN 322-0842. Tel. 202-832-2675, fax 202-526-0818, e-mail wtconsort@aol.com. *Dir.* John Crossin.

Florida

Central Florida Library Cooperative (CFLC), 431 E. Horatio Ave., Ste. 230, Maitland 32751. SAN 371-9014. Tel. 407-644-9050, fax 407-644-7023. *Exec. Dir.* Marta Westall.

Florida Library Information Network, State Lib. and Archives of Florida, Tallahassee 32399-0250. SAN 322-0869. Tel. 850-245-6600, fax 850-245-6744, e-mail library@dos.state.fl.us.

Miami Health Sciences Library Consortium (MHSLC), KBI/IDM (142D), Miami 33125-1673. SAN 371-0734. Tel. 786-596-6506, fax 786-596-5910. *Pres.* Devica Samsundar.

Palm Beach Health Sciences Library Consortium (PBHSLC), c/o Good Samaritan Medical Center Medical Lib., West Palm Beach 33402. SAN 370-0380. Tel. 561-650-6315, fax 561-650-6417.

Panhandle Library Access Network (PLAN), 5 Miracle Strip Loop, Ste. 8, Panama City Beach 32407-3850. SAN 370-047X. Tel. 850-233-9051, fax 850-235-2286. *Exec. Dir.* William P. Conniff.

Southeast Florida Library Information Network, Inc. (SEFLIN), 100 S. Andrews Ave., Fort Lauderdale 33301. SAN 370-0666. Tel. 954-334-1280, fax 954-334-1295. *Pres.* William Miller.

Southwest Florida Library Network, Bldg III, Unit 7, Fort Myers 33913. Tel. 239-225-4225, fax 239-225-4229. *Exec. Dir.* Barbara J. Stites.

Tampa Bay Library Consortium, Inc., 1202 Tech Blvd., Ste. 202, Tampa 33619. SAN 322-371X. Tel. 813-740-3963, fax 813-628-4425.

Tampa Bay Medical Library Network (TABAMLN), Orlando Regional Health Care-Health Sciences Lib., Orlando 32806-2134. SAN 322-0885. Tel. 321-841-5878, fax 407-237-6349.

Georgia

Assn. of Southeastern Research Libraries (ASERL), c/o SOLINET, Atlanta 30309-2955. SAN 322-1555. Tel. 404-892-0943, fax 404-892-7879. *Exec. Dir.* John Burger.

Atlanta Health Science Libraries Consortium, Sauls Memorial Lib., Atlanta 30309. SAN 322-0893. Tel. 404-605-2306, fax 404-609-6641. *Pres.* Amy Harkness.

Atlanta Regional Consortium for Higher Education, 50 Hurt Plaza, Ste. 735, Atlanta 30303-2923. SAN 322-0990. Tel. 404-651-

2668, fax 404-651-1797, e-mail arche@ atlantahighered.org. *Pres.* Michael Gerber.

Georgia Interactive Network for Medical Information (GAIN), c/o Medical Lib., School of Medicine, Mercer Univ., Macon 31207. SAN 370-0577. Tel. 478-301-2515, fax 478-301-2051. *Dir.* Jan H. LaBeause.

Georgia Online Database (GOLD), c/o Public Lib. Services, Atlanta 30345-4304. SAN 322-094X. Tel. 404-982-3560, fax 404-982-3563.

Metro Atlanta Library Assn. (MALA), c/o Atlanta Fulton Public Lib.-ILC, Atlanta 30303-1089. SAN 378-2549. Tel. 404-730-1733, fax 404-730-1988. *Pres.* Rick L. Wright.

Southeastern Library Network (SOLINET), 1438 W. Peachtree St. N.W., Ste. 200, Atlanta 30309-2955. SAN 322-0974. Tel. 404-892-0943, fax 404-892-7879. *Exec. Dir.* Kate Nevins.

SWGHSLC, Colquitt Regional Medical Center Health Sciences Lib., Moultrie 31776. SAN 372-8072. Tel. 229-890-3460, fax 229-891-9345. *Libn.* Susan Leik.

Hawaii

Hawaii-Pacific Chapter of the Medical Library Assn. (HPC-MLA), 1221 Punchbowl St., Honolulu 96813. SAN 371-3946. Tel. 808-536-9302, fax 808-524-6956. *Chair* Alice Witkowski.

Idaho

Canyon Owyhee Library Group, 203 E. Idaho Ave., Homedale 83628. Tel. 208-337-4613, fax 208-337-4933. *Media Specialist* Sherry Thomas.

Catalyst, c/o Boise State Univ., Albertsons Lib., Boise 83725-1430. SAN 375-0078. Tel. 208-426-1234, 208-426-4231, 208-426-4024, fax 208-426-1885.

Cooperative Information Network (CIN), 8385 N. Government Way, Hayden 83835-9280. SAN 323-7656. Tel. 208-772-5612, fax 208-772-2498. *In Charge* John W. Hartung.

Gooding County Library Consortium, c/o Gooding High School, Gooding 83330.

SAN 375-0094. Tel. 208-934-4831, fax 208-934-4347. *Head Libn.* Cora Caldwell.

Grangeville Cooperative Network, c/o Grangeville Centennial Lib., Grangeville 83530-1729. SAN 375-0108. Tel. 208-983-0951, fax 208-983-2336, e-mail library@grangeville.us.

Idaho Health Information Assn. (IHIA), Kootenai Medical Center, W. T. Wood Medical Lib., Coeur d'Alene 83814. SAN 371-5078. Tel. 208-666-3498, fax 208-666-2854. *Dir.* Marcie Horner.

Library Consortium of Eastern Idaho, 457 Broadway, Idaho Falls 83402. SAN 323-7699. Tel. 208-612-8450, fax 208-529-1467. *System Admin.* Roger Evans.

Lynx, c/o Boise Public Lib., Boise 83702-7195. SAN 375-0086. Tel. 208-384-4238, fax 208-384-4025. *Dir.* Stephen Cottrell.

VALNet, Lewis-Clark State College Lib., Lewiston 83501. SAN 323-7672. Tel. 208-792-2227, fax 208-792-2831.

Illinois

Alliance Library System, 600 High Point Lane, East Peoria 61611. SAN 371-0637. Tel. 309-694-9200, fax 309-694-9200. *Exec. Dir.* Kitty Pope.

American Theological Library Assn. (ATLA), 250 S. Wacker Dr., Ste. 1600, Chicago 60606-5889. SAN 371-9022. Tel. 312-454-5100, fax 312-454-5505, e-mail atla@atla.com. *Exec. Dir.* Dennis A. Norlin.

Areawide Hospital Library Consortium of Southwestern Illinois (AHLC), c/o St. Elizabeth Hosp. Health Sciences Lib., Belleville 62222. SAN 322-1016. Tel. 618-234-2120 ext. 1181, fax 618-222-4620. *Coord.* Michael Campese.

Assn. of Chicago Theological Schools, Catholic Theological Union, Paul Bechtold Lib., Chicago 60615-5698. SAN 370-0658. Tel. 773-753-5322, fax 773-753-5340. *Dir.* Kenneth O'Malley.

Capital Area Consortium, Decatur Memorial Hospital Health Science Lib., Decatur 62526. Tel. 217-876-2940, fax 217-876-2945. *Coord.* Karen Stoner.

Center for Research Libraries, 6050 S. Kenwood, Chicago 60637-2804. SAN 322-1032. Tel. 773-955-4545, fax 773-955-4339. *Pres.* Bernard F. Reilly.

Chicago and South Consortium, Governors State Univ. Lib., University Park 60466. SAN 322-1067. Tel. 708-534-5000 ext. 5142, fax 708-534-8454.

Consortium of Museum Libraries in the Chicago Area, c/o Morton Arboretum, Sterling Morton Lib., Lisle 60532-1293. SAN 371-392X. Tel. 630-719-7932, fax 630-719-7950. *Chair* Michael T. Stieber.

Council of Directors of State University Libraries in Illinois (CODSULI), Univ. of Illinois at Springfield, Springfield 62794. SAN 322-1083. Tel. 217-206-6597, fax 217-206-6354.

East Central Illinois Consortium, Carle Foundation Hospital Lib., Urbana 61801. SAN 322-1040. Tel. 217-383-3456, fax 217-383-3452. *Mgr.* Gerald Dewitt.

Fox Valley Health Science Library Consortium, Provena St. Joseph Hospital Medical Lib., Elgin 60123. SAN 329-3831. Tel. 847-695-3200, fax 847-888-3532, e-mail fuhslc@uic.edu.

Heart of Illinois Library Consortium, 210 W. Walnut St., Canton 61520. SAN 322-1113. *Chair* Michelle Quinones.

Illinois Library and Information Network (ILLINET), c/o Illinois State Lib., Springfield 62701-1796. SAN 322-1148. Tel. 217-782-2994, fax 217-785-4326. *Dir.* Jean Wilkins.

Illinois Library Computer Systems Organization (ILCSO), Univ. of Illinois, Lib. and Info. Science Bldg., Ste. 228, Champaign 61820-6211. SAN 322-3736. Tel. 217-244-7593, fax 217-244-7596, e-mail oncall @listserv.ilcso.uiuc.edu. *Dir.* Kristine Hammerstrand.

Illinois Office of Educational Services, 2450 Foundation Dr., Ste. 100, Springfield 62703-5464. SAN 371-5108. Tel. 217-786-3010, fax 217-786-3020, e-mail oesiscc@ siu.edu.

LIBRAS, Inc., North Central College, Naperville 60540. SAN 322-1172. Tel. 630-637-5709, fax 630-637-5716. *Pres.* Ted Schwitzner.

Metropolitan Consortium of Chicago, Chicago School of Professional Psychology, Chicago 60605. SAN 322-1180. Tel. 312-913-6742, fax 312-786-9611. *Coord.* Margaret White.

National Network of Libraries of Medicine–Greater Midwest Region (NN-LM GMR), c/o Lib. of Health Sciences, Univ. of Illinois at Chicago, Chicago 60612-4330. SAN 322-1202. Tel. 312-996-2464, fax 312-996-2226, e-mail gmr@uic.edu. *Dir.* Susan Jacobson.

Private Academic Libraries of Illinois (PALI), c/o Wheaton College Lib., Franklin and Irving, Wheaton 60187. SAN 370-050X. E-mail crflatzkehr@curf.edu. *Pres.* P. Paul Snezek.

Quad Cities Libraries in Cooperation (Quad-LINC.), 220 W. 23 Ave., Coal Valley 61240. SAN 373-093X. Tel. 309-799-3155 ext. 3254, fax 309-799-7916. *Asst. Dir., Technical Services and Automation* Mary-Anne Stewart.

River Bend Library System (RBLS), 220 W. 23 Ave., Coal Valley 61240-9624. SAN 371-0653. Tel. 309-799-3155, fax 309-799-7916.

Sangamon Valley Academic Library Consortium, MacMurray College, Henry Pfeiffer Lib., Jacksonville 62650. SAN 322-4406. Tel. 217-479-7110, fax 217-245-5214.

Indiana

American Zoo and Aquarium Assn. (AZA-LSIG), Indianapolis Zoo, Indianapolis 46222. SAN 373-0891. Tel. 317-630-5110, fax 317-630-5114. *Mgr. Lib. Services.* Susan Braun.

Central Indiana Health Science Libraries Consortium, Indiana University School of Medicine Lib., Indianapolis 46202. SAN 322-1245. Tel. 317-274-8358, fax 317-274-4056. *Pres.* Elaine Skopelja.

Collegiate Consortium of Western Indiana, c/o Cunningham Memorial Lib., Terre Haute 47809. SAN 329-4439. Tel. 812-237-3700, fax 812-237-3376.

Evansville Area Library Consortium, 3700 Washington Ave., Evansville 47750. SAN 322-1261. Tel. 812-485-4151, fax 812-485-7564. *Coord.* Jane Saltzman.

Indiana Cooperative Library Services Authority (INCOLSA), 6202 Morenci Trail, Indianapolis 46268-2536. SAN 322-1296. Tel. 317-298-6570, fax 317-328-2380.

Indiana State Data Center, Indiana State Lib., Indianapolis 46204-2296. SAN 322-1318.

Tel. 317-232-3733, fax 317-232-3728. *Coord.* Frank H. Wilmot.

Northeast Indiana Health Science Libraries Consortium (NEIHSL), Univ. of Saint Francis Health Sciences Lib., Fort Wayne 46808. SAN 373-1383. Tel. 260-434-7691, fax 260-434-7695. *Coord.* Lauralee Aven.

Northwest Indiana Health Science Library Consortium, c/o N.W. Center for Medical Education, Gary 46408-1197. SAN 322-1350. Tel. 219-980-6852, 219-980-6709, fax 219-980-6524, 219-980-6566. *Libn.* Felicia A. Young.

Iowa

Consortium of College and University Media Centers (CCUMC), Instructional Technology Center, Iowa State Univ., Ames 50011-3243. SAN 322-1091. Tel. 515-294-1811, fax 515-294-8089, e-mail ccumc@ccumc. org. *Exec. Dir.* Don A. Rieck.

Dubuque Area Library Information Consortium, c/o N.E. Iowa Community College, Burton Payne Lib., Peosta 52068. Tel. 563-556-5110 ext. 269, fax 563-557-0340. *Pres.* Deb Seiffert.

Iowa Private Academic Library Consortium (IPAL), c/o Buena Vista University Lib., Storm Lake 50588. SAN 329-5311. Tel. 712-749-2127, 712-749-2203, fax 712-749-2059, e-mail library@bvu.edu. *Univ. Libn.* Jim Kennedy.

Linn County Library Consortium, Hiawatha Public Lib., Hiawatha 52233. SAN 322-4597. Tel. 319-393-1414, fax 319-393-6005. *Pres.* Jeaneal Weeks.

Polk County Biomedical Consortium, c/o Des Moines Area Community College, Ankeny Campus, Ankeny 50021. SAN 322-1431. Tel. 515-964-6573, fax 515-965-7126. *In Charge* Diane Messersmith.

Quad City Area Biomedical Consortium, Great River Medical Center Lib., West Burlington 52655. SAN 322-435X. Tel. 319-768-4075, fax 319-768-4080. *Coord.* Judy Hawk.

Sioux City Library Cooperative (SCLC), c/o Sioux City Public Lib., Sioux City 51101-1203. SAN 329-4722. Tel. 712-255-2933 ext. 251, fax 712-279-6432. *Chair* Peg Brady.

State of Iowa Libraries Online (SILO), State Lib. of Iowa, Des Moines 50319. SAN 322-1415. Tel. 515-281-4105, fax 515-281-6191. *State Libn.* Mary Wegner.

Kansas

Associated Colleges of Central Kansas, 210 S. Main St., McPherson 67460. SAN 322-1474. Tel. 620-241-5150, fax 620-241-5153.

Dodge City Library Consortium, c/o Central Elementary School, Dodge City 67801. SAN 322-4368. Tel. 620-227-1601, fax 620-227-1721. *Chair* Linda Zupancic.

Kansas Library Network Board, 300 S.W. Tenth Ave., Rm. 343N, Topeka 66612-1593. SAN 329-5621. Tel. 785-296-3875, fax 785-296-6650. *Exec. Dir.* Eric Hansen.

Kentucky

Assn. of Independent Kentucky Colleges and Universities, 484 Chenault Rd., Frankfort 40601. SAN 322-1490. Tel. 502-695-5007, fax 502-695-5057. *Pres.* Gary S. Cox.

Eastern Kentucky Health Science Information Network (EKHSIN), c/o Camden-Carroll Lib., Morehead 40351. SAN 370-0631. Tel. 606-783-6860, fax 606-783-2799. *Dir.* Larry VeSant.

Kentuckiana Metroversity, Inc., 200 W. Broadway, Ste. 700, Louisville 40202. SAN 322-1504. Tel. 502-897-3374, fax 502-895-1647.

Kentucky Health Science Libraries Consortium, VA Medical Center, Lib. Services 142D, Louisville 40206-1499. SAN 370-0623. Tel. 502-894-6240, fax 502-894-6134. *Head Libn.* Gene M. Haynes.

Theological Education Assn. of Mid America (TEAM-A), c/o Southern Baptist Theological Seminary, Louisville 40280-0294. SAN 322-1547. Tel. 502-897-4807, fax 502-897-4600. *Libn.* Bruce Keisling.

Louisiana

Central Louisiana Medical Center Library Consortium (CLMLC), VA Medical Center 142D, Alexandria 71306. Tel. 318-619-

9102, fax 318-619-9144, e-mail clmlc@ yahoo.com. *Coord.* Miriam J. Brown.

Health Sciences Library Assn. of Louisiana (HSLAL), Tulane Health Sciences Lib., New Orleans 70112-2632. SAN 375-0035. Tel. 504-584-2404, fax 504-587-7417. *Chair* Susan Dorsey.

Loan SHARK, State Lib. of Louisiana, Baton Rouge 70802. SAN 371-6880. Tel. 225-342-4918, 225-342-4920, fax 225-219-4725. *Coord.* Virginia R. Smith.

Louisiana Government Information Network (LaGIN), c/o State Lib. of Louisiana, Baton Rouge 70802. SAN 329-5036. Tel. 225-342-4920, e-mail lagin@pelican.state.lib.la.us. *Coord.* Virginia Smith.

New Orleans Educational Telecommunications Consortium, 2 Canal St., Ste. 2038, New Orleans 70130. SAN 329-5214. Tel. 504-524-0350, fax 504-524-0327, e-mail noetc_Inc.@excite.com. *Exec. Dir.* Michael Adler.

Maine

Health Science Library Information Consortium (HSLIC), 211 Marginal Way, No. 245, Portland 04101. SAN 322-1601. Tel. 207-871-4081. *Chair* John Hutchinson.

Maryland

ERIC Processing and Reference Facility, 4483-A Forbes Blvd., Lanham 20706. SAN 322-161X. Tel. 301-552-4200, fax 301-552-4700, e-mail info@ericfac.piccard.csc.com. *Dir.* Donald Frank.

Library Video Network (LVN), 320 York Rd., Towson 21204. SAN 375-5320. Tel. 410-887-2090, fax 410-887-2091, e-mail lvn@bcpl.net. *Mgr.* Carl Birkmeyer.

Maryland Interlibrary Loan Organization (MILO), c/o Enoch Pratt Free Lib., Baltimore 21201-4484. SAN 343-8600. Tel. 410-396-5498, fax 410-396-5837, e-mail milo@epfl.net. *Mgr.* Emma E. Beaven.

National Network of Libraries of Medicine (NN-LM), National Lib. of Medicine, Bethesda 20894. SAN 373-0905. Tel. 301-496-4777, fax 301-480-1467. *Dir.* Angela Ruffin.

National Network of Libraries of Medicine–Southeastern Atlantic Region (NNLM

SEA), Univ. of Maryland Health Sciences and Human Services Lib., Baltimore 21201-1512. SAN 322-1644. Tel. 410-706-2855, fax 410-706-0099. *Exec. Dir.* M. J. Tooey.

Regional Alcohol and Drug Abuse Resource Network (RADAR), National Clearinghouse for Alcohol and Drug Information, Rockville 20852. SAN 377-5569. Tel. 301-468-2600, fax 301-468-6433, e-mail info@health.org. *Coord.* Marion Pierce.

U.S. National Library of Medicine (NLM), 8600 Rockville Pike, Bethesda 20894. SAN 322-1652. Tel. 301-594-5983, fax 301-402-1384, e-mail custserv@nlm.nih.gov.

Washington Research Library Consortium (WRLC), 901 Commerce Dr., Upper Marlboro 20774. SAN 373-0883. Tel. 301-390-2031, fax 301-390-2020. *Exec. Dir.* Lizanne Payne.

Massachusetts

Boston Biomedical Library Consortium (BBLC), c/o Percy R. Howe Memorial Lib., Boston 02115. SAN 322-1725. Tel. 617-262-5200 ext. 244, fax 617-262-4021.

Boston Library Consortium, 700 Boylston St., Rm. 317, Boston 02117. SAN 322-1733. Tel. 617-262-0380, fax 617-262-0163. *Exec. Dir.* Barbara G. Preece.

Boston Theological Institute Library Program, 45 Francis Ave., Cambridge 02138. SAN 322-1741. Tel. 617-349-3602 ext. 315, fax 617-496-4111. *Coord.* Patricia Glaspie.

Cape Libraries Automated Materials Sharing (CLAMS), 270 Communication Way, Unit 4E-4F, Hyannis 02601. SAN 370-579X. Tel. 508-790-4399, fax 508-771-4533. *Exec. Dir.* Monica Grace.

Catholic Library Assn., 100 North St., Ste. 224, Pittsfield 01201-5109. SAN 329-1030. Tel. 413-443-2252, fax 413-442-2252, e-mail cla@cathla.org. *Exec. Dir.* Jean R. Bostley, SSJ.

Central and Western Massachusetts Automated Resource Sharing (C/W Mars), 1 Sunset Lane, Paxton 01612-1197. SAN 322-3973. Tel. 508-755-3323, fax 508-755-3721. *Exec. Dir.* Joan Kuklinski.

Consortium for Information Resources, Emerson Hospital, John Cuming Bldg., 3rd fl., Concord 01742. SAN 322-4503. Tel. 978-287-3090, fax 978-287-3651.

Cooperating Libraries of Greater Springfield (CLIC), Springfield College, Springfield 01109. SAN 322-1768. Tel. 413-748-3502, fax 413-748-3631. *Acting Dir.* Andrea Taupier.

Fenway Libraries Online (FLO), c/o Wentworth Institute of Technology, Boston 02115. SAN 373-9112. Tel. 617-442-2384, fax 617-442-1519. *Dir.* Jamie Ingram.

Fenway Library Consortium, Simmons College, Beatly Lib., Boston 02115. SAN 327-9766. Tel. 617-521-2741, 617-573-8536, fax 617-521-3093. *Dir.* Robert E. Dugan.

Massachusetts Health Sciences Libraries Network (MAHSLIN), South Shore Hospital, South Weymouth 02190. SAN 372-8293. Tel. 781-340-8528, fax 781-331-0834. *Pres.* Kathy McCarthy.

Merrimack Valley Library Consortium, 123 Tewksbury St., Andover 01810. SAN 322-4384. Tel. 978-475-7632, fax 978-475-7179. *Exec. Dir.* Lawrence Rungren.

Metrowest Massachusetts Regional Library System (METROWEST), 135 Beaver St., Waltham 02452. Tel. 781-398-1819, fax 781-398-1821. *Admin.* Sondra H. Vandermark.

Minuteman Library Network, Ten Strathmore Rd., Natick 01760-2419. SAN 322-4252. Tel. 508-655-8008, fax 508-655-1507. *Exec. Dir.* Carol B. Caro.

National Network of Libraries of Medicine–New England Region (NN-LM NER), Univ. of Massachusetts Medical School, Shrewsbury 01545. SAN 372-5448. Tel. 508-856-5979, fax 508-856-5977. *Dir.* Elaine Martin.

NELINET, Inc., 153 Cordaville Rd., Southborough 01772. SAN 322-1822. Tel. 508-460-7700 ext. 1934, fax 508-460-9455. *Exec. Dir.* Arnold Hirshon.

North of Boston Library Exchange, Inc./NOBLE, 26 Cherry Hill Dr., Danvers 01923. SAN 322-4023. Tel. 978-777-8844, fax 978-750-8472. *Exec. Dir.* Ronald A. Gagnon.

Northeast Consortium of Colleges and Universities in Massachusetts (NECCUM), Northern Essex Community College, Haverhill 01830. SAN 371-0602. Tel. 978-556-3400, fax 978-556-3738. *Dir.* Linda Hummel-Shea.

Northeastern Consortium for Health Information (NECHI), Lowell General Hospital Health Science Lib., Lowell 01854. SAN 322-1857. Tel. 978-937-6247, fax 978-937-6855. *Libn.* Donna Beales.

SAILS, Inc., 547 W. Groves St., Ste. 4, Middleboro 02346. SAN 378-0058. Tel. 508-946-8600, fax 508-946-8605. *Pres.* Carole Julius.

Southeastern Massachusetts Consortium of Health Science Libraries (SEMCO), South Shore Hospital, South Weymouth 02190. SAN 322-1873. Tel. 781-340-8528, fax 781-331-0834. *Dir.* Kathy McCarthy.

Southeastern Massachusetts Regional Library System (SEMLS), Ten Riverside Dr., Lakeville 02347. Tel. 508-923-3531, fax 508-923-3539, e-mail semls@semls.org. *Admin.* Cynthia A. Roach.

West of Boston Network/WEBNET, Horn Lib., Babson College, Babson Park 02457. SAN 371-5019. Tel. 781-239-4308, fax 781-239-5226. *Pres.* Sheila Ekman.

Western Massachusetts Health Information Consortium, Baystate Medical Center Health Sciences Lib., Springfield 01199. SAN 329-4579. Tel. 413-794-1291, fax 413-794-1978. *Pres.* Karen Dorval.

Michigan

Berrien Library Consortium, c/o William Hessel Lib., Lake Michigan College, Benton Harbor 49022-1899. SAN 322-4678. Tel. 269-927-8605, fax 269-927-6656. *Pres.* Diane Baker.

Detroit Area Consortium of Catholic Colleges, c/o Sacred Heart Seminary, Detroit 48206. SAN 329-482X. Tel. 313-883-8500, fax 313-868-6440. *Dir.* Karen Mchaffey.

Kalamazoo Consortium for Higher Education (KCHE), Kalamazoo College, Kalamazoo 49006. SAN 329-4994. Tel. 269-337-7220, fax 269-337-7219. *Pres.* James F. Jones.

Lakeland Library Cooperative, 4138 Three Mile Rd. N.W., Grand Rapids 49544. SAN

308-132X. Tel. 616-559-5253, fax 616-559-4329. *Dir.* Daniel J. Siebersma.

Michigan Assn. of Consumer Health Information Specialists (MACHIS), Bronson Methodist Hospital, Kalamazoo 49007. SAN 375-0043. Tel. 269-341-8627, fax 269-341-8828. *Dir.* Marge Kars.

Michigan Health Sciences Libraries Assn. (MHSLA), William Beaumont Hospital Medical Lib., Royal Oak 48073. SAN 323-987X. Tel. 248-551-1747, fax 248-551-1060. *Pres.* Joan Emahiser.

Michigan Library Consortium (MLC), 1407 Rensen St., Ste. 1, Lansing 48910-3657. SAN 322-192X. Tel. 517-394-2420, fax 517-394-2096, e-mail reception@mlcnet.org. *Purchasing* Diana Mitchell.

Northland Interlibrary System (NILS), 316 E. Chisholm St., Alpena 49707. SAN 329-4773. Tel. 989-356-1622, fax 989-354-3939. *Interim Dir.* Christine Johnson.

Southeastern Michigan League of Libraries (SEMLOL), Lawrence Technological Univ., Southfield 48075. SAN 322-4481. Tel. 248-204-3000, fax 248-204-3005. *Officer* Gary Cocozzoli.

Southwest Michigan Library Cooperative (SMLC), 305 Oak St., Paw Paw 49079. SAN 371-5027. Tel. 616-657-4698, fax 616-657-4494. *Dir.* Alida L. Geppert.

Suburban Library Cooperative (SLC), 16480 Hall Rd., Clinton Township 48038. SAN 373-9082. Tel. 586-286-5750, fax 586-286-8951. *Dir.* Tammy L. Turgeon.

The Library Network (TLN), 13331 Reeck Rd., Southgate 48195-3054. SAN 370-596X. Tel. 734-281-3830, fax 734-281-1817, 734-281-1905. *Dir.* A. Michael Deller.

Upper Peninsula of Michigan Health Science Library Consortium, c/o Marquette Health System Hospital, Marquette 49855. SAN 329-4803. Tel. 906-225-3429, fax 906-225-3524. *In Charge* Janis Lubenow.

Upper Peninsula Region of Library Cooperation, Inc., 1615 Presque Isle Ave., Marquette 49855. SAN 329-5540. Tel. 906-228-7697, fax 906-228-5627. *In Charge* Suzanne Dees.

Valley Library Consortium, 3210 Davenport Ave., Saginaw 48602-3495. Tel. 989-497-0925, fax 989-497-0918. *Exec. Dir.* Karl R. Steiner.

Minnesota

Arrowhead Health Sciences Library Network, Univ. of Minnesota–Duluth Lib., Duluth 55812. SAN 322-1954. Tel. 218-726-8104, fax 218-726-6205. *Coord.* Adele Krusz.

Capital Area Library Consortium (CALCO), c/o Minnesota Dept. of Transportation, Lib. MS155, Saint Paul 55155. SAN 374-6127. Tel. 651-296-5272, fax 651-297-2354. *Libn.* Shirley Sherkow.

Central Minnesota Libraries Exchange (CMLE), Miller Center, Rm. 130-D, Saint Cloud 56301-4498. SAN 322-3779. Tel. 320-255-2950, fax 320-654-5131, e-mail cmle@stcloudstate.edu. *Dir.* Patricia A. Post.

Community Health Science Library, c/o Saint Francis Medical Center, Breckenridge 56520. SAN 370-0585. Tel. 218-643-7542, fax 218-643-7452. *Dir.* Karla Lovaasen.

Cooperating Libraries in Consortium (CLIC), 1619 Dayton Ave., Ste. 204, Saint Paul 55104. SAN 322-1970. Tel. 651-644-3878, fax 651-644-6258. *Exec. Dir.* Chris Olson.

Metronet, 1619 Dayton Ave., Ste. 314, Saint Paul 55104. SAN 322-1989. Tel. 651-646-0475, fax 651-649-3169, e-mail info@metronet.lib.mn.us. *Exec. Dir.* Susan Baxter.

Metropolitan Library Service Agency (MELSA), 1619 Dayton Ave., No. 314, Saint Paul 55104-6206. SAN 371-5124. Tel. 651-645-5731, fax 651-649-3169, e-mail melsa@melsa.org. *Exec. Dir.* Marlene Moulton Janssen.

MINITEX Library Information Network, Univ. of Minnesota–Twin Cities, 15 Andersen Lib., Minneapolis 55455-0439. SAN 322-1997. Tel. 612-624-4002, fax 612-624-4508. *Dir.* William DeJohn.

Minnesota Theological Library Assn. (MTLA), c/o Bethel Seminary Lib., Saint Paul 55112. SAN 322-1962. Tel. 651-641-3202, fax 651-638-6006. *Pres.* Sandy Oslund.

North Country Library Cooperative, 5528 Emerald Ave., Mountain Iron 55768-2069.

SAN 322-3795. Tel. 218-741-1907, fax 218-741-1908. *Dir.* Linda J. Wadman.

Northern Lights Library Network, 103 Graystone Plaza, Detroit Lakes 56501-3041. SAN 322-2004. Tel. 218-847-2825, fax 218-847-1461, e-mail nloffice@nlln.org. *Dir.* Ruth Solie.

SMILE (Southcentral Minnesota Inter-Library Exchange), 1400 Madison Ave., No. 622, Mankato 56001. SAN 321-3358. Tel. 507-625-7555, fax 507-625-4049, e-mail smile@tds.lib.mn.us. *Dir.* Nancy K. Steele.

Southeastern Libraries Cooperating (SELCO), 2600 19th St. N.W., Rochester 55901-0767. SAN 308-7417. Tel. 507-288-5513, fax 507-288-8697. *Exec. Dir.* Ann B. Hutton.

Southwest Area Multicounty Multitype Interlibrary Exchange (SAMMIE), 109 S. 5th St., Ste. 30, Marshall 56258. SAN 322-2039. Tel. 507-532-9013, fax 507-532-2039, e-mail sammie@starpoint.net. *Dir.* Robin Chaney.

Twin Cities Biomedical Consortium (TCBC), c/o Fairview Univ. Medical Center, Minneapolis 55455. SAN 322-2055. Tel. 612-273-6595, fax 612-273-2675. *Chair* Michael Scott.

Valley Medical Network, Lake Region Hospital Lib., Fergus Falls 56537. SAN 329-4730. Tel. 218-736-8158, fax 218-736-8731. *Dir.* Connie Schulz.

Waseca Interlibrary Resource Exchange (WIRE), c/o Waseca High School Media Center, Waseca 56093. SAN 370-0593. Tel. 507-835-5470 ext. 218, fax 507-835-1724, e-mail tlol@waseca.k12.mn.us.

West, P.O. Box 64526, Saint Paul 55164-0526. SAN 322-4031. Tel. 651-687-7000, fax 651-687-5614, e-mail west.customer.service@thomson.com.

Mississippi

Central Mississippi Library Council (CMLC), c/o Millsaps College Lib., Jackson 39210. SAN 372-8250. Tel. 601-974-1070, fax 601-974-1082. *Admin.* Tom Henderson.

Mississippi Biomedical Library Consortium, c/o College of Veterinary Medicine, Mississippi State Univ., Mississippi State 39762. SAN 371-070X. Tel. 662-325-

1240, fax 662-325-1141, e-mail library@cvm.msstate.edu.

Missouri

Health Sciences Library Network of Kansas City, Inc. (HSLNKC), Univ. of Missouri Health Sciences Lib., Kansas City 64108-2792. SAN 322-2098. Tel. 816-235-1880, fax 816-235-5194.

Kansas City Metropolitan Library and Information Network, 15624 E. 24 Hwy., Independence 64050. SAN 322-2101. Tel. 816-521-7257, fax 816-461-0966. *Exec. Dir.* Susan Burton.

Kansas City Regional Council for Higher Education, Park Univ., Parkville 64152-3795. SAN 322-211X. Tel. 816-741-2816, fax 816-741-1296, e-mail kcrche@kcrche.com. *Dir.* Gloria Brady.

Library Systems Service, Bernard Becker Medical Lib., Saint Louis 63110. SAN 322-2187. Tel. 314-362-2778, fax 314-362-0190. *Mgr.* Russ Monika.

Missouri Library Network Corporation, 8045 Big Bend Blvd., Ste. 202, Saint Louis 63119-2714. SAN 322-466X. Tel. 314-918-7222, fax 314-918-7727. *Acting Dir.* Tracy Byerly.

Saint Louis Regional Library Network, 341 Sappington Rd., Saint Louis 63122. SAN 322-2209. Tel. 314-965-1305, fax 314-965-4443.

Nebraska

Lincoln Health Sciences Library Group (LHSLG), Univ. of Nebraska-Lincoln, Lincoln 68588-4100. SAN 329-5001. Tel. 402-472-2554, fax 402-472-5131.

NEBASE, c/o Nebraska Lib. Commission, Lincoln 68508-2023. SAN 322-2268. Tel. 402-471-2045, fax 402-471-2083.

Southeast Nebraska Library System, 5730 R St., Ste. C-1, Lincoln 68505. SAN 322-4732. Tel. 402-467-6188, fax 402-467-6196.

Nevada

Information Nevada, Interlibrary Loan Dept., Nevada State Lib. and Archives, Carson City 89701-4285. SAN 322-2276. Tel.

775-684-3326, fax 775-684-3330. *Head of ILL* Mona Reno.

New Hampshire

Carroll County Library Cooperative, c/o Madison Lib., Madison 03849. SAN 371-8999. Tel. 603-367-8545, e-mail librarian @madison.lib.nh.us.

Health Science Libraries of New Hampshire and Vermont, Lakes Region General Hospital, Laconia 03246. SAN 371-6864. Tel. 603-527-2837, fax 603-527-7197.

Hillstown Cooperative, 3 Meetinghouse Rd., Bedford 03110. SAN 371-3873. Tel. 603-472-2300, fax 603-472-2978.

Librarians of the Upper Valley Cooperative (LUV Coop), 1173 U.S. Rte. 4, Canaan 03741. SAN 371-6856. Tel. 603-523-9650, e-mail canaantownlibrary@hotmail. com. *In Charge* Amy Thurber.

Merri-Hill-Rock Library Cooperative, c/o Sandown Public Lib., Sandown 03873-0580. SAN 329-5338. Tel. 603-887-3428, fax 603-887-0590, e-mail sandownlibrary @gsinet.net. *Chair* Diane Heer.

New England Law Library Consortium, Inc. (NELLCO), 9 Drummer Rd., Keene 03431. SAN 322-4244. Tel. 603-357-3385, fax 603-357-2075. *Exec. Dir.* Tracy L. Thompson.

New Hampshire College and University Council, 3 Barrell Ct., Ste. 100, Concord 03301-8543. SAN 322-2322. Tel. 603-225-4199, fax 603-225-8108. *Exec. Dir.* Thomas R. Horgan.

Nubanusit Library Cooperative, c/o Peterborough Town Lib., Peterborough 03458. SAN 322-4600. Tel. 603-924-8040, fax 603-924-8041.

Scrooge and Marley Cooperative, 695 Main St., Laconia 03246. SAN 329-515X. Tel. 603-524-4775. *Chair* Randy Brough.

Seacoast Cooperative Libraries, North Hampton Public Lib., North Hampton 03862. SAN 322-4619. Tel. 603-964-6326, fax 603-964-1107, e-mail coop@hampton.lib. nh.us. *Dir.* Pamela Schwotzer.

New Jersey

Basic Health Sciences Library Network (BHSL), Mountainside Hospital Health Science Lib., Montclair 07042. SAN 371-4888. Tel. 973-429-6240, fax 973-680-7850. *Coord.* Pat Regenberg.

Bergen Passaic Health Sciences Library Consortium, c/o Englewood Hospital and Medical Center, Health Sciences Lib., Englewood 07631. SAN 371-0904. Tel. 201-894-3069, fax 201-894-9049, e-mail lia.sabbagh@ehmc.com.

Central New Jersey Health Science Libraries Consortium (CJHSLA), Saint Francis Medical Center Medical Lib., Trenton 08629. SAN 370-0712. Tel. 609-599-5068, fax 609-599-5773. *Libn.* Donna Barlow.

Central New Jersey Regional Library Cooperative, 4400 Rte. 9 S., Ste. 3400, Freehold 07728-1383. SAN 370-5102. Tel. 732-409-6484, fax 732-409-6492. *Dir.* Connie S. Paul.

Cosmopolitan Biomedical Library Consortium, Overlook Hospital Medical Lib., Summit 07902. SAN 322-4414. Tel. 908-522-2699. *In Charge* Vicki Sciuk.

Health Sciences Library Assn. of New Jersey (HSLANJ), Saint Michaels Medical Center, Newark 07102. SAN 370-0488. Tel. 973-877-5471, fax 973-877-5378. *Dir.* Larry Dormer.

Highlands Regional Library Cooperative, 66 Ford Rd., Ste. 124, Denville 07834. SAN 329-4609. Tel. 973-664-1776, fax 973-664-1780. *Exec. Dir.* Joanne P. Roukens.

INFOLINK/Eastern New Jersey Regional Library Cooperative, Inc., 44 Stelton Rd., Ste. 330, Piscataway 08854. SAN 371-5116. Tel. 732-752-7720, fax 732-752-7785. *Exec. Dir.* Cheryl O'Connor.

Integrated Information Solutions, 600 Mountain Ave., Rm. 6A-200, Murray Hill 07974. SAN 329-5400. Tel. 908-582-4840, fax 908-582-3146, e-mail libnet@library. lucent.com. *Mgr.* M. E. Brennan.

Libraries of Middlesex Automation Consortium (LMxAC), 1030 Saint George, Ste. 203, Avenel 07001. SAN 329-448X. Tel. 732-750-2525, fax 732-750-9392.

Monmouth-Ocean Biomedical Information Consortium (MOBIC), Community Medical Center, Toms River 08755. SAN 329-5389. Tel. 732-557-8117, fax 732-557-8354. *Libn.* Reina Reisler.

Morris Automated Information Network (MAIN), c/o Morris County Lib., 30 East Hanover Ave., Whippany 07981. SAN 322-4058. Tel. 973-631-5353, fax 973-631-5366. *Network Admin.* Ellen L. Sleeter.

Morris-Union Federation, 214 Main St., Chatham 07928. SAN 310-2629. Tel. 973-635-0603, fax 973-635-7827.

New Jersey Health Sciences Library Network (NJHSN), Mountainside Hospital, Montclair 07042. SAN 371-4829. Tel. 973-429-6240, fax 973-680-7850, e-mail pat. regenberg@ahsys.org.

New Jersey Library Network, Lib. Development Bureau, Trenton 08625. SAN 372-8161. Tel. 609-984-3293, fax 609-633-3963.

South Jersey Regional Library Cooperative, Paint Works Corporate Center, Gibbsboro 08026. SAN 329-4625. Tel. 856-346-1222, fax 856-346-2839. *Exec. Dir.* Karen Hyman.

Virtual Academic Library Environment (VALE), William Paterson Univ. Lib., Wayne 07470-2103. Tel. 973-720-3179, fax 973-720-3171. *Chair* Marianne Gaunt.

New Mexico

Alliance for Innovation in Science and Technology Information (AISTI), 369 Montezuma Ave., No. 156, Santa Fe 87501. Fax 505-466-2196. *Exec. Dir.* Corinne Machado.

New Mexico Consortium of Academic Libraries, Dean's Office, Albuquerque 87131-1466. SAN 371-6872. Tel. 505-277-5057, fax 505-277-6019, 505-277-7288. *Dean* Camila Alire.

New Mexico Consortium of Biomedical and Hospital Libraries, Albuquerque Regional Medical Center/Lib., Albuquerque 87102. SAN 322-449X. Tel. 505-727-8291, fax 505-727-8190, e-mail medicall@sjhs.org. *Libn.* Marian Frear.

New York

Academic Libraries of Brooklyn, Long Island University Lib.–LLC 517, Brooklyn 11201. SAN 322-2411. Tel. 718-488-1081, fax 715-780-4057. *Dean* Constance Woo.

American Film and Video Assn./Resource Center, Cornell Cooperative Extension, Ithaca 14853. SAN 377-5860. Tel. 607-255-2080, fax 607-255-9946, e-mail rescenter@cornell.edu. *Marketing* Sich Andrew.

Associated Colleges of the Saint Lawrence Valley, State Univ. of New York College at Potsdam, Potsdam 13676-2299. SAN 322-242X. Tel. 315-267-3331, fax 315-267-2389. *Exec. Dir.* Anneke J. Larrance.

Brooklyn-Queens-Staten Island Health Sciences Librarians (BQSI), Saint John's Episcopal Hospital, South Shore Div. Medical Lib., Brooklyn 11201. SAN 370-0828. Tel. 718-869-7699, fax 718-250-6428. *Pres.* Narciso Rodriguez.

Capital District Library Council for Reference and Research Resources, 28 Essex St., Albany 12206. SAN 322-2446. Tel. 518-438-2500, fax 518-438-2872. *Exec. Dir.* Jean K. Sheviak.

Central New York Library Resources Council (CLRC), 6493 Ridings Rd., Syracuse 13206-1195. SAN 322-2454. Tel. 315-446-5446, fax 315-446-5590, e-mail mclane@clrc.org. *Exec. Dir.* Michael J. McLane.

Council of Archives and Research Libraries in Jewish Studies (CARLJS), 330 7th Ave., 21st fl., New York 10001. SAN 371-053X. Tel. 212-629-0500, fax 212-629-0508, e-mail nfjc@jewishculture.org. *Assoc. Dir.* Dana Schneider.

Library Consortium of Health Institutions in Buffalo (LCHIB), 155 Abbott Hall, SUNY at Buffalo, Buffalo 14214. SAN 329-367X. Tel. 716-829-3900 ext. 143, fax 716-829-2211. *Exec. Dir.* Martin E. Mutka.

Long Island Library Resources Council (LILRC), Melville Lib. Bldg., Ste. E5310, Stony Brook 11794-3399. SAN 322-2489. Tel. 631-632-6650, fax 631-632-6662. *Dir.* Herbert Biblo.

Manhattan-Bronx Health Sciences Libraries Group, c/o KPR Medical Lib., New York 10016. SAN 322-4465. Tel. 212-856-8743, fax 212-856-8892. *Research* Ilene Somin.

Medical and Scientific Libraries of Long Island (MEDLI), c/o Palmer School of Lib. and Info. Science, Brookville 11548.

SAN 322-4309. Tel. 516-299-2866, 516-299-4110, fax 516-299-4168. *Pres.* Mary Westermann-Cicio.

Medical Library Center of New York, 220 5th Ave., 7th fl., New York 10001-7708. SAN 322-3957. Tel. 212-427-1630, fax 212-876-6697. *Dir.* William Self.

Metropolitan New York Library Council (METRO), 57 E. 11 St., 4th fl., New York 10003-4605. SAN 322-2500. Tel. 212-228-2320 ext. 10, fax 212-228-2598. *Exec. Dir.* Dottie Hiebing.

National Network of Libraries of Medicine-Middle Atlantic Region (NN-LM MAR), New York Academy of Medicine, New York 10029-5293. Tel. 212-822-7396, fax 212-534-7042, e-mail rml1@nyam.org. *Assoc. Dir.* Naomi Adelman.

Northeast Foreign Law Libraries Cooperative Group, Columbia Univ. Lib., New York 10027. SAN 375-0000. Tel. 212-854-1411, fax 212-854-3295. *Coord.* Silke Sahl.

Northern New York Library Network, 6721 U.S. Hwy. 11, Potsdam 13676. SAN 322-2527. Tel. 315-265-1119, fax 315-265-1881, e-mail info@nnyln.org. *Exec. Dir.* John J. Hammond.

Nylink, 74 N. Pearl St., 5th fl., Albany 12207. SAN 322-256X. Tel. 518-443-5444, fax 518-432-4346, e-mail nylink@nylink.suny.edu. *Exec. Dir.* Mary-Alice Lynch.

Research Library Assn. of South Manhattan, New York Univ. Bobst Lib., New York 10012. SAN 372-8080. Tel. 212-998-2477, fax 212-995-4366. *Dean of Lib.* Carol Mandel.

Rochester Regional Library Council, 390 Packetts Landing, Fairport 14450. SAN 322-2535. Tel. 585-223-7570, fax 585-223-7712, e-mail rrlc@rrlc.org. *Exec. Dir.* Kathleen M. Miller.

South Central Regional Library Council, 215 N. Cayuga St., Ithaca 14850. SAN 322-2543. Tel. 607-273-9106, fax 607-272-0740, e-mail scrlc@lakenet.org. *Exec. Dir.* Jean Currie.

Southeastern New York Library Resources Council (SENYLRC), 220 Rte. 299, Highland 12528. SAN 322-2551. Tel. 845-691-2734, fax 845-691-6987. *Exec. Dir.* John L. Shaloiko.

United Nations System Electronic Information Acquisitions Consortium (UNSEIAC), c/o Dag Hammarskjold Lib., Rm. L-166A, New York 10017. SAN 377-855X. Tel. 212-963-7440, fax 212-963-2608. *Head Libn.* Linda Stoddart.

Western New York Library Resources Council, 4455 Genesee St., Buffalo 14225. SAN 322-2578. Tel. 716-633-0705, fax 716-633-1736. *Exec. Dir.* Gail M. Staines.

North Carolina

Cape Fear Health Sciences Information Consortium, Southeastern Regional Medical Center, Lumberton 28358. SAN 322-3930. Tel. 910-671-5000, fax 910-671-4143.

Consortium of Southeastern Law Libraries (COSELL), Kathrine R. Everett Law Lib., Chapel Hill 27599. SAN 372-8277. Tel. 919-962-6202, fax 919-962-1193.

Microcomputer Users Group for Libraries in North Carolina (MUGLNC), Catawba College, Salisbury 28144. Fax 704-637-4304. *Dir.* John Harer.

North Carolina Area Health Education Centers, Univ. of North Carolina Health Sciences Lib., CB 7585, Chapel Hill 27599-7585. SAN 323-9950. Tel. 919-962-0700, fax 919-966-5592. *In Charge* Diana McDuffee.

North Carolina Community College System, 200 W. Jones St., Raleigh 27603-1379. SAN 322-2594. Tel. 919-733-7051, fax 919-733-0680. *Admin. Dir.* Phil Albano.

North Carolina Library and Information Network, State Lib. of North Carolina, Raleigh 27699-4640. SAN 329-3092. Tel. 919-807-7400, fax 919-733-8748. *State Libn.* Sandra M. Cooper.

Northwest AHEC Library at Hickory, Valley Regional Medical Center, Hickory 28602. SAN 322-4708. Tel. 828-326-3662, fax 828-326-3484. *Dir.* Stephen Johnson.

Northwest AHEC Library at Salisbury, c/o Rowan Regional Medical Center, Salisbury 28144. SAN 322-4589. Tel. 704-210-5069, fax 704-636-5050.

Northwest AHEC Library Information Network, Wake Forest Univ. School of Medicine, Winston-Salem 27157-1049. SAN

322-4716. Tel. 336-713-7009, fax 336-713-7028. *Senior Libn.* Julie Richardson.

Triangle Research Libraries Network, Wilson Lib., Chapel Hill 27514-8890. SAN 329-5362. Tel. 919-962-8022, fax 919-962-4452.

Western North Carolina Library Network (WNCLN), Univ. of North Carolina at Asheville, Asheville 28804-3299. SAN 376-7205. Tel. 828-232-5095, fax 828-232-5137. *Dir.* Mark A. Stoffan.

North Dakota

Dakota West Cooperating Libraries (DWCL), c/o Mandan Public Lib., Mandan 58554-3149. SAN 373-1391. *Dir.* Kelly Steckler.

Mid-America Law School Library Consortium (MALSLC), Univ. of North Dakota School of Law, Grand Forks 58202. SAN 371-6813. Tel. 701-777-2535, fax 701-777-2219. *Chair* Gary Gott.

Tri-College University Libraries Consortium, 650 NP Ave., Fargo 58102. SAN 322-2047. Tel. 701-231-8170, fax 701-231-7205.

Ohio

Central Ohio Hospital Library Consortium, Mount Carmel, Columbus 43222-1560. SAN 371-084X. Tel. 614-234-5214, fax 614-234-1257. *Dir.* Rebecca Ayers.

Cleveland Area Metropolitan Library System (CAMLS), 20600 Chagrin Blvd., Ste. 500, Shaker Heights 44122-5334. SAN 322-2632. Tel. 216-921-3900, fax 216-921-7220. *Exec. Dir.* Michael G. Snyder.

Columbus Area Library and Information Council of Ohio (CALICO), c/o Westerville Public Lib., Westerville 43081. SAN 371-683X. Tel. 614-882-7277, fax 614-882-5369.

Consortium of Popular Culture Collections in the Midwest (CPCCM), c/o Popular Culture Lib., Bowling Green 43403-0600. SAN 370-5811. Tel. 419-372-2450, fax 419-372-7996. *Chair* Peter Berg.

Greater Cincinnati Library Consortium, 2181 Victory Pkwy., Ste. 214, Cincinnati 45206-2855. SAN 322-2675. Tel. 513-751-4422, fax 513-751-0463, e-mail gclc@gclc-lib.org. *Exec. Dir.* Michael R. McCoy.

Molo Regional Library System, 123 N. Bridge St., Newcomerstown 43832-1093. SAN 322-2705. Tel. 330-364-8535, fax 330-364-8537, e-mail molo@molorls.org.

NEOUCOM Council of Associated Hospital Librarians, Oliver Ocasek Regional Medical Info. Center, Rootstown 44272. SAN 370-0526. Tel. 330-325-6616, 330-325-6600, fax 330-325-0522. *Dir.* Thomas C. Atwood.

NOLA Regional Library System, 4445 Mahoning Ave. N.W., Warren 44483. SAN 322-2713. Tel. 330-847-7744, fax 330-847-7704, e-mail nola@nolanet.org. *Dir.* Paul Pormen.

Northwest Library District (NORWELD), 181½ S. Main St., Bowling Green 43402. SAN 322-273X. Tel. 419-352-2903, fax 419-353-8310. *Dir.* Allan Gray.

OCLC Online Computer Library Center, Inc., 6565 Frantz Rd., Dublin 43017-3395. SAN 322-2748. Tel. 614-764-6000, fax 614-718-1017, e-mail oclc@oclc.org. *Pres., CEO.* Jay Jordan.

Ohio Library and Information Network (Ohio-LINK), 2455 N. Star Rd., Ste. 300, Columbus 43221. SAN 374-8014. Tel. 614-728-3600, fax 614-728-3610, e-mail info @ohiolink.edu. *Exec. Dir.* Thomas J. Sanville.

Ohio Network of American History Research Centers, Ohio Historical Society Archives-Lib., Columbus 43211-2497. SAN 323-9624. Tel. 614-297-2510, fax 614-297-2546, e-mail ohsref@ohiohistory.org. *Research* Louise Jones.

Ohio Valley Area Libraries, 252 W. 13 St., Wellston 45692. SAN 322-2756. Tel. 740-384-2103, fax 740-384-2106, e-mail ovalrls @oplin.lib.oh.us; oval@oplin.lib.oh.us. *Dir.* Marion J. Cochran.

OHIONET, 1500 W. Lane Ave., Columbus 43221-3975. SAN 322-2764. Tel. 614-486-2966, fax 614-486-1527. *Exec. Dir., CEO* Michael P. Butler.

Southwestern Ohio Council for Higher Education, 3155 Research Blvd., Ste. 204, Dayton 45420-4015. SAN 322-2659. Tel. 937-258-8890, fax 937-258-8899, e-mail soche@soche.org.

State Assisted Academic Library Council of Kentucky (SAALCK), c/o GCLC, Cincinnati 45206. SAN 371-2222. Fax 513 751-0463, e-mail saalck@saalck.org. *Exec. Dir.* Michael McCoy.

Oklahoma

Greater Oklahoma Area Health Sciences Library Consortium (GOAL), Mercy Memorial Health Center-Resource Center, Ardmore 73401. SAN 329-3858. Tel. 580-220-6625, fax 580-220-6599. *Pres.* Catherine Ice.

Oklahoma Health Sciences Library Assn. (OHSLA), University of Oklahoma-HSC Bird Health Science Lib., Oklahoma City 73190. SAN 375-0051. Tel. 405-271-2285 ext. 48755, fax 405-271-3297. *Dir.* Clinton M. Thompson.

Oregon

Chemeketa Cooperative Regional Library Service, c/o Chemeketa Community College, Salem 97305-1453. SAN 322-2837. Tel. 503-399-5105, fax 503-399-7316, e-mail cocl@chemeketa.edu. *Coord.* Linda Cochrane.

Coos County Library Service District, Extended Service Office, Tioga 104, 1988 Newmark, Coos Bay 97420. SAN 322-4279. Tel. 541-888-7260, fax 541-888-7285. *Dir.* Mary Jane Fisher.

Library Information Network of Clackamas County, 16239 SE McLoughlin Blvd., Ste. 208, Oak Grove 97267-4654. SAN 322-2845. Tel. 503-723-4888, fax 503-794-8238.

Orbis Cascade Alliance, 1501 Kincaid, No. 4, Eugene 97401-4540. SAN 377-8096. Tel. 541-346-1832, fax 541-346-1968, e-mail orbcas@uoregon.edu. *Chair* Kelley Patricia.

Oregon Health Sciences Libraries Assn. (OHSLA), Oregon Health and Science Univ. Lib., Portland 97239-3098. SAN 371-2176. Tel. 503-494-3462, fax 503-494-3322, e-mail lib@ohsu.edu. *Dir.* James Morgan.

Southern Oregon Library Federation, c/o Klamath County Lib., Klamath Falls 97601. SAN 322-2861. Tel. 541-882-8894, fax 541-882-6166. *Dir.* Andy Swanson.

Southern Oregon Library Information System (SOLIS), 724 S. Central Ave., Ste. 112, Medford 97501. Tel. 541-772-2141, fax 541-772-2144, e-mail solis97501@yahoo.com. *Asst. Admin.* Sylvia Lee.

Washington County Cooperative Library Services, 111 N.E. Lincoln St., MS No. 58, Hillsboro 97124-3036. SAN 322-287X. Tel. 503-846-3222, fax 503-846-3220. *Mgr.* Eva Calcagno.

Pennsylvania

Associated College Libraries of Central Pennsylvania, c/o Commonwealth Libs., Harrisburg 17126-1745. Tel. 717-783-5968, fax 717-783-2070. *Pres.* Janet Hurlbert.

Berks County Library Assn. (BCLA), Albright College Lib., Reading 19612-5234. SAN 371-0866. Tel. 610-921-7212. *Pres.* Joan King.

Central Pennsylvania Consortium, Dickinson College, Carlisle 17013-2896. SAN 322-2896. Tel. 717-245-1515, fax 717-245-1807, e-mail cpc@dickinson.edu.

Central Pennsylvania Health Sciences Library Assn. (CPHSLA), Education Resource Center, Chambersburg Hospital, Chambersburg 17201. SAN 375-5290. Tel. 717-267-4886, fax 717-267-6383. *Pres.* Debra Miller.

Consortium for Health Information and Library Services, 1 Medical Center Blvd., Upland 19013-3995. SAN 322-290X. Tel. 610-447-6163, fax 610-447-6164, e-mail chi@hslc.org.

Cooperating Hospital Libraries of the Lehigh Valley Area, Saint Luke's Hospital, Estes Lib., Bethlehem 18015. SAN 371-0858. Tel. 610-954-3407, fax 610-954-4651. *Chair* Sharon Hrabina.

Delaware Valley Information Consortium (DEVIC), St. Mary Medical Center Medical Lib., Langhorne 19047. Tel. 215-710-2012, fax 215-710-4638. *Dir.* Ann B. Laliotes.

Eastern Mennonite Associated Libraries and Archives (EMALA), 2215 Millstream Rd., Lancaster 17602. SAN 372-8226. Tel. 717-393-9745, fax 717-393-8751. *Chair* Edsel Burdge.

Erie Area Health Information Library Cooperative (EAHILC), UPMC Northwest Medical Lib., Franklin 16323. SAN 371-0564. Tel. 814-437-7000 ext. 5331, fax 814-437-4538, e-mail nwmc@mail.cosmosbbs.com. *Chair* Ann L. Lucas.

Greater Philadelphia Law Library Assn. (GPLLA), P.O. Box 335, Philadelphia 19105-0335. SAN 373-1375. E-mail gplla-l@hslc.org. *Pres.* Jeffrey W. Kreiling.

Health Sciences Libraries Consortium, 3600 Market St., Ste. 550, Philadelphia 19104-2646. SAN 323-9780. Tel. 215-222-1532, fax 215-222-0416, e-mail support@hslc.org. *Exec. Dir.* Joseph C. Scorza.

Interlibrary Delivery Service of Pennsylvania (IDS), c/o Bucks County IU, No. 22, Doylestown 18901. SAN 322-2942. Tel. 215-348-2940 ext. 1620, fax 215-348-8315, e-mail ids@bucksiu.org. *Admin. Dir.* Beverly J. Carey.

Keystone Library Network, Educational Resources Group, Harrisburg 17110-1201. Tel. 717-720-4088, fax 717-720-4453. *Coord.* Mary Lou Sowden.

Laurel Highlands Health Science Library Consortium, 116 Luna Lane, Johnstown 15904. SAN 322-2950. Tel. 814-341-0242, fax 814-266-8230. *Dir.* Heather W. Brice.

Lehigh Valley Assn. of Independent Colleges, 130 W. Greenwich St., Bethlehem 18018. SAN 322-2969. Tel. 610-625-7888, fax 610-625-7891. *Exec. Dir.* Tom A. Tenges.

Northeastern Pennsylvania Library Network, c/o Marywood Univ. Lib., Scranton 18509-1598. SAN 322-2993. Tel. 570-348-6260, fax 570-961-4769. *Dir.* Catherine H. Schappert.

Northwest Interlibrary Cooperative of Pennsylvania (NICOP), Edinboro Univ. of Pennsylvania, Edinboro 16444. SAN 370-5862. Tel. 814-732-1534, fax 814-732-2883. *Chair* Christine Troutman.

PALINET, 3000 Market St., Ste. 200, Philadelphia 19104-2801. SAN 322-3000. Tel. 215-382-7031, fax 215-382-0022, e-mail palinet@palinet.org. *Exec. Dir.* Catherine C. Wilt.

Pennsylvania Library Assn., 220 Cumberland Pkwy., Ste. 10, Mechanicsburg 17055.

Tel. 717-766-7663, fax 717-766-5440. *Exec. Dir.* Glenn R. Miller.

Philadelphia Area Consortium of Special Collections Libraries (PACSCL), Historical Society of Pennsylvania, Philadelphia 19107. SAN 370-7504. Tel. 215-985-1445, fax 215-985-1446, e-mail info@pacscl.org. *Chair* David Moltke-Hansen.

Southeastern Pennsylvania Theological Library Assn. (SEPTLA), c/o Lancaster Theological Seminary, Lancaster 17603. SAN 371-0793. Tel. 717-290-8755. *Chair* Marsha Blake.

State System of Higher Education Library Cooperative (SSHELCO), c/o Bailey Lib., Slippery Rock 16057. Tel. 724-738-2630, fax 724-738-2661.

Susquehanna Library Cooperative (SLC), Harvey A. Andruss Lib., Bloomsburg Univ., Bloomsburg 17815-1301. SAN 322-3051. Tel. 570-389-4224. *Chair* John B. Pitcher.

Tri-State College Library Cooperative (TCLC), c/o Rosemont College Lib., Rosemont 19010-1699. SAN 322-3078. Tel. 610-525-0796, fax 610-525-1939, e-mail tclc@hslc.org. *Coord.* Ellen Gasiewski.

Rhode Island

Cooperating Libraries Automated Network (CLAN), 600 Sandy Lane, Warwick 02886. SAN 329-4560. Tel. 401-738-2200, fax 401-736-8949. *Chair* Susan Reed.

Library of Rhode Island (LORI), c/o Office of Lib. and Info. Services, Providence 02908-5870. SAN 371-6821. Tel. 401-222-2726, fax 401-222-4195. *Coord. of Lib. Services* Anne Parent.

South Carolina

Charleston Academic Libraries Consortium (CALC), Trident Technical College, Charleston 29423. SAN 371-0769. Tel. 843-574-6088, fax 843-574-6484. *Chair* Drucie Raines.

Columbia Area Medical Librarians' Assn. (CAMLA), Professional Lib., Columbia 29201. SAN 372-9400. Tel. 803-898-1735, fax 803-898-1712. *Coord.* Neeta N. Shah.

South Carolina AHEC, c/o Medical Univ. of SC, Charleston 29403. SAN 329-3998. Tel. 843-792-4431, fax 843-792-4430. *Exec. Dir.* David Garr.

South Carolina State Library/South Carolina Lib. Network, 1430 and 1500 Senate St., Columbia 29201. SAN 322-4198. Tel. 803-734-8666, fax 803-734-8676, e-mail webadm@leo.scsl.state.sc.us. *Dir.* James B. Johnson.

South Dakota

South Dakota Library Network (SDLN), 1200 University, Unit 9672, Spearfish 57799-9672. SAN 371-2117. Tel. 605-642-6835, fax 605-642-6472. *Dir.* Gary Johnson.

Tennessee

Assn. of Memphis Area Health Science Libraries (AMAHSL), c/o Methodist Healthcare Nursing Lib., Memphis 38104. SAN 323-9802. Tel. 901-726-8862, fax 901-726-8807. *Libn.* Denise Fesmire.

Consortium of Southern Biomedical Libraries (CONBLS), Meharry Medical College, Nashville 37208. SAN 370-7717. Tel. 615-327-6728, fax 615-327-6448. *Acting Dir.* Marvelyn E. Thompson.

Knoxville Area Health Sciences Library Consortium (KAHSLC), Univ. of Tennessee Medical Center, Knoxville 37920. SAN 371-0556. Tel. 865-544-9525. *In Charge* Doris Prichard.

Mid-Tennessee Health Science Librarians Assn., VA Medical Center, Nashville 37212. SAN 329-5028. Tel. 615-327-4751 ext. 5523, fax 615-321-6336.

Tennessee Health Science Library Assn. (THeSLA), Holston Valley Medical Center Health Sciences Lib., Kingsport 37660. SAN 371-0726. Tel. 423-224-6870, fax 423-224-6014, e-mail sharon_m_brown@wellmont.org.

Tri-Cities Area Health Sciences Libraries Consortium, East Tennessee State Univ., James H. Quillen College of Medicine, Johnson City 37614. SAN 329-4099. Tel. 423-439-6252, fax 423-439-7025. *Dir.* Biddanda Ponnappa.

West Tennessee Academic Library Consortium, Lambuth Univ. Lib., Jackson 38301. SAN 322-3175. Tel. 731-425-3479, fax 731-425-3200. *Dir.* Pamela R. Dennis.

Texas

Abilene Library Consortium, 241 Pine St., Ste. 15C, Abilene 79601. SAN 322-4694. Tel. 325-672-7081, fax 325-672-7084. *Exec. Dir.* Robert Gillette.

Amigos Library Services, Inc., 14400 Midway Rd., Dallas 75244-3509. SAN 322-3191. Tel. 972-851-8000, fax 972-991-6061, e-mail amigos@amigos.org. *Exec. Dir.* Bonnie Juergens.

Council of Research and Academic Libraries (CORAL), P.O. Box 290236, San Antonio 78280-1636. SAN 322-3213.

Del Norte Biosciences Library Consortium, El Paso Community College, El Paso 79998. SAN 322-3302. Tel. 915-831-4149, fax 915-831-4639. *Coord.* Becky Perales.

Harrington Library Consortium, 2201 Washington, Amarillo 79109. SAN 329-546X. Tel. 806-371-5135, fax 806-371-5119. *Mgr.* Roseann Perez.

Health Libraries Information Network (Health LINE), UT Southwestern Medical Center Lib., Dallas 75390-9049. SAN 322-3299. Tel. 214-648-2626, fax 214-648-2826. *In Charge* Brian Bunnett.

Houston Area Research Library Consortium (HARLiC), c/o Moody Medical Lib., Galveston 77555-1035. SAN 322-3329. Tel. 409-772-2371, fax 409-762-9782. *Pres.* Brett Kirkpatrick.

National Network of Libraries of Medicine-South Central Region (NNLM SCR), c/o HAM-TMC Library, Houston 77030-2809. SAN 322-3353. Tel. 713-799-7880, fax 713-790-7030, e-mail nnlmscr@library.tmc.edu. *Assoc. Dir.* Renee Bougard.

Northeast Texas Library System (NETLS), 625 Austin, Garland 75040-6365. SAN 370-5943. Tel. 972-205-2566, fax 972-205-2767. *Dir.* Claire Bausch.

Piasano Consortium, Victoria College, Univ. of Houston, Victoria Lib., Victoria 77901-5699. SAN 329-4943. Tel. 361-570-4150, 361-570-4848, fax 361-570-4155. *Coord.* Joe F. Dahlstrom.

South Central Academic Medical Libraries Consortium (SCAMeL), c/o Lewis Lib., UNTHSC, Fort Worth 76107. SAN 372-8269. Tel. 817-735-2380, fax 817-735-5158.

Texas Council of State University Librarians, Texas Lib. Assn., Austin 78746-6763. SAN 322-337X. *Pres.* Kathy Hoffman.

Texnet, P.O. Box 12927, Austin 78711. SAN 322-3396. Tel. 512-463-5406, fax 512-936-2306, e-mail ill<@>tsl.state.tx.us.

Utah

Forest Service Library Network, Rocky Mountain Research Sta., Ogden 84401. SAN 322-032X. Tel. 801-625-5445, fax 801-625-5129, e-mail rmrs_library@fs.fed.us.

National Network of Libraries of Medicine–MidContinental Region (NN-LM MCR), Univ. of Utah, Spencer S. Eccles Health Sciences Lib., Salt Lake City 84112-5890. SAN 322-225X. Tel. 801-587-3412, fax 801-581-3632. *Dir.* Wayne J. Peay.

Utah Academic Library Consortium (UALC), Brigham Young Univ., Provo 84602-8000. SAN 322-3418. Tel. 801-422-2905, fax 801-422-0466, e-mail ualcmail@library.utah.edu. *Chair* Constance Lundberg.

Utah Health Sciences Library Consortium, c/o Univ. of Utah, Spencer S. Eccles Health Science Lib., Salt Lake City 84112. SAN 376-2246. Tel. 801-401-7518, fax 801-581-3632.

Vermont

Vermont Resource Sharing Network, c/o Vermont Dept. of Libs., Montpelier 05609-0601. SAN 322-3426. Tel. 802-828-3261, fax 802-828-2199. *Dir., Lib. Services* Marjorie Zunder.

Virgin Islands

VILINET (Virgin Islands Library and Information Network), c/o Division of Libs., Museums and Archives, Saint Thomas 00802. SAN 322-3639. Tel. 340-774-3407, fax 340-775-1887. *Dir.* Sharlene Harris.

Virginia

American Indian Higher Education Consortium (AIHEC), 121 Oronoco St., Alexandria 22314. SAN 329-4056. Tel. 703-838-0400, fax 703-838-0388, e-mail aihec@aihec.org. *Pres.* James Shanley.

Defense Technical Information Center, 8725 John J. Kingman Rd, Ste. 1948, Fort Belvoir 22060-6218. SAN 322-3442. Tel. 703-767-9100, fax 703-767-9183. *Acting Admin.* Paul Ryan.

Lynchburg Area Library Cooperative, Randolph Macon Woman's College, Lynchburg 24503. SAN 322-3450. Tel. 434-947-8133, fax 434-947-8134.

Lynchburg Information Online Network (LION), 2315 Memorial Ave., Lynchburg 24503. SAN 374-6097. Tel. 434-381-6311, fax 434-381-6173. *Dir.* John G. Jaffe.

NASA Libraries Information System, NASA Galaxie/NASA Langley Research Center Technical Lib., NASA Langley Research Center, MS 185-Technical Lib., Hampton 23681-2199. SAN 322-0788. Tel. 757-864-2356, fax 757-864-2375, e-mail tech-library@larc.nasa.gov. *Branch Mgr.* Carolyn L. Helmetsie.

Richmond Academic Library Consortium (RALC), Virginia Commonwealth Lib., Richmond 23284-2033. SAN 322-3469. Tel. 804-828-1107, fax 804-862-6125. *Pres.* John E. Ulmschneider.

Southside Virginia Library Network (SVLN), Longwood Univ., Farmville 23909-1897. SAN 372-8242. Tel. 434-395-2633, fax 434-395-2453. *Dir.* Calvin J. Boyer.

Southwestern Virginia Health Information Librarians (SWVAHILI), Carilion Health Sciences Lib., Roanoke 24033. SAN 323-9527. Tel. 540-981-8039, fax 540-981-8666, e-mail kdillon@carilion.com. *Chair* Kelly Near.

United States Army Training and Doctrine Command (TRADOC)/Lib. Program Office, U.S. Army HQ TRADOC, Fort Monroe 23651-5000. SAN 322-418X. Tel. 757-788-5524, fax 757-788-5941. *Dir.* Janet Scheitle.

Virginia Independent College and University Library Assn., c/o Mary Helen Cochran Lib., Sweet Briar 24595. SAN 374-6089.

Tel. 434-381-6138, fax 434-381-6173. *Dir.* John Jaffee.

Virginia Tidewater Consortium for Higher Education, 1417 43rd St., Norfolk 23529-0293. SAN 329-5486. Tel. 757-683-3183, fax 757-683-4515, e-mail lgdotolo@aol.com. *Pres.* Lawrence G. Dotolo.

Virtual Library of Virginia (VIVA), George Mason Univ., Fairfax 22030. Tel. 703-993-4652, fax 703-993-4662. *Chair* Ralph Alberico.

Washington

Cooperating Libraries in Olympia (CLIO), Evergreen State College Lib. L2300, Olympia 98505. SAN 329-4528. Tel. 360-866-6000 ext. 6260, fax 360-867-6790. *Dean* Lee Lyttle.

Inland NorthWest Health Sciences Libraries (INWHSL), P.O. Box 10283, Spokane 99209-0283. SAN 370-5099. Tel. 509-324-7344, fax 509-324-7349. *Business* Robert Pringle.

National Network of Libraries of Medicine-Pacific Northwest Region (NN-LM PNR), Univ. of Washington, Seattle 98195-7155. SAN 322-3485. Tel. 206-543-8262, fax 206-543-2469, e-mail nnlm@u.washington.edu. *Dir.* Sherrilynne S. Fuller.

OCLC/Lacey Office, Bldg. 3, 4224 6th Ave. S.E., Lacey 98503. SAN 322-3507. Tel. 360-923-4056, 360-923-4000 ext. 4056, fax 360-923-4009. *Collection Management* Glenda Lammers.

Palouse Area Library Information Services (PALIS), c/o Neill Public Lib., Pullman 99163. SAN 375-0132. Tel. 509-334-3595, fax 509-334-6051. *Dir.* Mike Pollastro.

Washington Idaho Network (WIN), Foley Center Lib., Spokane 99258. Tel. 509-323-6545, fax 509-324-5398, e-mail winsupport@gonzaga.edu. *Pres.* Eileen Bell-Garrison.

West Virginia

Huntington Health Science Library Consortium, Marshall Univ. Health Science Libs., Huntington 25701-3655. SAN 322-4295. Tel. 304-691-1753, fax 304-691-1766. *Dir.* Edward Dzierzak.

Mid-Atlantic Law Library Cooperative (MALLCO), College of Law Lib., Morgantown 26506. SAN 371-0645. Tel. 304-293-7641, 304-293-7775, fax 304-293-6020. *In Charge* Camille M. Riley.

Wisconsin

Fox River Valley Area Library Consortium, Moraine Park Technical College, Fond Du Lac 54935. SAN 322-3531. Tel. 920-924-3112, 920-922-8611, fax 920-924-3117. *In Charge* Charlene Pettit.

Fox Valley Library Council, c/o OWLS, Appleton 54911. SAN 323-9640. Tel. 920-832-6190, fax 920-832-6422. *Pres.* Ken Hall.

Library Council of Southeastern Wisconsin, Inc., 814 W. Wisconsin Ave., Milwaukee 53233-2309. SAN 322-354X. Tel. 414-271-8470, fax 414-286-2798, e-mail lcomm@execpc.com. *Exec. Dir.* Susie M. Just.

North East Wisconsin Intertype Libraries, Inc. (NEWIL), 515 Pine St., Green Bay 54301. SAN 322-3574. Tel. 920-448-4412, fax 920-448-4420. *Coord.* Terrie Howe.

Northwestern Wisconsin Health Science Library Consortium, Wausau Hospital, Dr. Joseph F. Smith Medical Lib., Wausau 54401. Tel. 715-847-2121, 715-847-2184, fax 715-847-2183. *In Charge* Jan Kraus.

South Central Wisconsin Health Science Library Consortium, c/o Fort Healthcare Medical Lib., Fort Atkinson 53538. SAN 322-4686. Tel. 920-568-5194, fax 920-568-5195. *Coord.* Carrie Garity.

Southeastern Wisconsin Health Science Library Consortium, Veteran's Admin. Center Medical Lib., Milwaukee 53295. SAN 322-3582. Tel. 414-384-2000 ext. 42342, fax 414-447-2128. *Dir.* Janice Curnes.

Southeastern Wisconsin Information Technology Exchange, Inc. (SWITCH), 6801 N. Yates Rd., Milwaukee 53217-3985. SAN 371-3962. Tel. 414-351-2423, fax 414-228-4146. *Coord.* William A. Topritzhofer.

University of Wisconsin System School Library Education Consortium (UWSSLEC), Graduate and Continuing Educ., Univ. of

Wisconsin–Whitewater, Whitewater 53190. Tel. 262-472-1463, 262-472-5208, fax 262-472-5210, e-mail lenchoc@uww.edu. *Co-Dir.* E. Anne Zarinnia.

Wisconsin Area Research Center Network/ ARC Network, Wisconsin Historical Society, Madison 53706. SAN 373-0875. Tel. 608-264-6477, fax 608-264-6486. *Head of Public Services* Richard Pifer.

Wisconsin Library Services (WILS), 728 State St., Rm. 464, Madison 53706-1494. SAN 322-3612. Tel. 608-263-4981, 608-263-4962, fax 608-262-6067, 608-263-3684. *Dir.* Kathryn Schneider Michaelis.

Wisconsin Valley Library Service (WVLS), 300 N. 1st St., Wausau 54403. SAN 371-3911. Tel. 715-261-7250, fax 715-261-7259. *Dir.* Heather Ann Eldred.

WISPALS Library Consortium, c/o Gateway Technical College, Kenosha 53144-1690. Tel. 262-564-2602, fax 262-564-2787. *Coord.* Ellen J. Pedraza.

Wyoming

University of Wyoming Information Network Plus (UWIN Plus), Coe Lib., Rm. 104A, Laramie 82071. SAN 371-4861. Tel. 307-766-5379, fax 307-766-5368, e-mail uwin-plus@uwyo.edu. *Coord.* Jenny Garcia.

Western Council of State Libraries, Inc., Supreme Court and State Lib. Bldg, Cheyenne 82002. SAN 322-2314. Tel. 307-777-5911. *Pres.* Lesley Boughton.

WYLD Network, c/o Wyoming State Lib., Cheyenne 82002-0060. SAN 371-0661. Tel. 307-777-6339, fax 307-777-6289. *Automation System Coord., Mgr.* Brian A. Greene.

Canada

Alberta

Alberta Assn. of College Librarians (AACL), Lakeland College Learning Resources Centre, Vermillion T9X 1K5. SAN 370-0763. Tel. 780-853-8468, fax 780-853-8662. *Acting Dir.* Greg Michaud.

Northern Alberta Health Libraries Assn. (NAHLA), Inst. of Health Economics Lib., Edmonton T5J 3N4. SAN 370-5951. Tel. 780-448-4881, e-mail nahla@freenet. edmonton.ab.ca. *Pres.* Janice Varney.

Quicklaw Inc./Calgary Branch, 505 3rd St. S.W., Ste. 1010, Calgary T2P 3E6. SAN 322-3817. Tel. 403-262-6505, fax 403-264-7193, e-mail twozny@quicklaw.com.

Quicklaw Inc./Edmonton Branch, 1805, 9835 113th St., Edmonton T5K 1N4. SAN 378-200X. Tel. 780-488-1732, fax 780-482-2353. *Mgr.* David Carlson.

British Columbia

BC Electronic Library Network (ELN), Simon Fraser Univ., Burnaby V5A IS6. Tel. 604-268-7003, fax 604-291-3023, e-mail eln@ola.bc.ca; office@eln.bc.ca. *Mgr.* Anita Cocchia.

British Columbia College and Institute Library Services, Langara College Lib., Vancouver V5Y 2Z6. SAN 329-6970. Tel. 604-323-5237, fax 604-323-5544, e-mail cils@langara.bc.ca. *Dir.* Mary Anne Epp.

Quicklaw Inc./Vancouver Branch, 355 Burrard St., Ste. 920, Vancouver V6C 2G8. SAN 322-3841. Tel. 604-684-1462, fax 604-684-5581. *In Charge* Jeff Purkiss.

Manitoba

Manitoba Government Libraries Council (MGLC), c/o Instructional Resources Unit Education Lib., Winnipeg R3G 0T3. SAN 371-6848. Tel. 204-945-7833, fax 204-945-8756. *Chair* John Tooth.

Manitoba Library Consortium, Inc. (MLCI), c/o Lib. Admin., Univ. of Winnipeg, Winnipeg R3B 2E9. SAN 372-820X. Tel. 204-786-9801, fax 204-783-8910. *Chair* Mark Leggott.

Quicklaw Inc./Winnipeg Branch, 388 Donald St., Ste. 110, Winnipeg R3B 2J4. SAN 378-2042. Tel. 204-942-4959, fax 204-956-0064. *In Charge* J. LaBossiere.

New Brunswick

Maritimes Health Libraries Assn. (MHLA-ABSM), c/o Region 7 Hospital Corp., Miramich E1V 3G5. SAN 370-0836. Tel. 506-623-3215, fax 506-623-3280. *Libn.* Nancy McAllister.

Nova Scotia

NOVANET, 1550 Bedford Hwy., No. 501, Bedford B4A 1E6. SAN 372-4050. Tel. 902-453-2461, fax 902-453-2369. *Dir.* Lennard Tan.

Quicklaw Inc./Halifax Branch, 5162 Duke St., Ste. 300, Halifax B3J 1N7. SAN 325-4194. Tel. 902-420-1666, fax 902-422-3016. *Vice Pres.* Ruth Rintoul.

Ontario

Bibliocentre, 80 Cowdray Ct., Scarborough M1S 4N1. SAN 322-3663. Tel. 416-289-5151, fax 416-299-4841. *Exec. Dir.* Janice Hayes.

Canadian Assn. of Research Libraries (Assn. des Bibliothèques de Recherche du Canada), Morisset Hall, Rm. 239, Ottawa K1N 9A5. SAN 323-9721. Tel. 613-562-5385, fax 613-562-5195, e-mail carladm@ uottawa.ca. *Exec. Dir.* Timothy Mark.

Canadian Health Libraries Assn. (CHLA-ABSC), 39 River St., Toronto M5A 3P1. SAN 370-0720. Tel. 416-646-1600, fax 416-646-9460, e-mail info@chla-absc.ca. *Pres.* Penny Logan.

Hamilton and District Health Library Network, c/o St. Joseph's Hospital, Hamilton L8N 4A6. SAN 370-5846. Tel. 905-522-1155 ext. 3410. *Coord.* Jean Maragno.

Health Science Information Consortium of Toronto, c/o Gerstein Science Info. Center, Univ. of Toronto, Toronto M5S 1A5. SAN 370-5080. Tel. 416-978-6359, fax 416-971-2637. *Exec. Dir.* Laurie Scott.

Ontario Health Libraries Assn. (OHLA), c/o Lakeridge Health, Oshawa L1G 2B9. SAN 370-0739. Tel. 905-576-8711 ext. 3334, fax 905-721-4759.

Ontario Library Consortium (OLC), Owen Sound and North Grey Union Public Lib., Owen Sound N4K 4K4. *Pres.* Judy Armstrong.

Quicklaw Inc., 275 Sparks St., Ste. 901, Ottawa K1R 7X9. SAN 322-368X. Tel. 613-238-3499, fax 613-238-7597, e-mail adingle@quicklaw.com.

Quicklaw Inc./Ottawa Branch, 901 Saint Andrews Tower, Ottawa K1R 7X9. SAN 322-3825. Tel. 613-238-3499, fax 613-238-7597. *Vice Pres.* Alan Dingle.

Quicklaw Inc./Toronto Branch, 1 First Canadian Pl., Ste. 930, Toronto M5X 1C8. SAN 322-3833. Tel. 416-862-7656, fax 416-862-8073. *Vice Pres.* Patrick McNeill.

Shared Library Services (SLS), South Huron Hospital, Shared Lib. Services, Exeter N0M 1S2. SAN 323-9500. Tel. 519-235-4002 ext. 249, fax 519-235-4476, e-mail shha.sls@hphp.org. *Libn.* Linda Wilcox.

Toronto Health Libraries Assn. (THLA), 3324 Yonge St., Toronto M4N 3R1. SAN 323-9853. Tel. 416-485-0377, fax 416-485-6877, e-mail medinfoserv@rogers.com.

Toronto School of Theology, 47 Queen's Park Crescent E, Toronto M5S 2C3. SAN 322-452X. Tel. 416-978-4039, fax 416-978-7821. *Chair* Noel S. McFerran.

Prince Edward Island

Quicklaw Inc./Charlottetown Branch, 52 Water St., Ste. 301, Charlottetown C1A 1A4. Tel. 902-894-1459, fax 902-894-3109. *Mgr.* Mike Ives.

Quebec

Assn. des Bibliothèques de la Santé Affiliées à l'Université de Montréal (ABSAUM), c/o Health Lib., Univ. of Montreal, Montreal H3C 3J7. SAN 370-5838. Tel. 514-343-6826, fax 514-343-2350. *Dir.* Diane Raymond.

Canadian Heritage Information Network (CHIN), 15 Eddy St., 4th fl., Gatineau K1A 0M5. SAN 329-3076. Tel. 819-994-1200, fax 819-994-9555, e-mail service@ chin.gc.ca. *Mgr.* Patricia Young.

Quicklaw Inc./Montreal Branch, 215 St.-Jacques St., Ste. 1111, Montreal H2Y 1M6. SAN 378-2026. Tel. 514-287-0339, fax 514-287-0350.

National Library and Information-Industry Associations, United States and Canada

American Association of Law Libraries

Executive Director, Susan E. Fox
53 W. Jackson Blvd., Ste. 940, Chicago, IL 60604
312-939-4764, fax 312-431-1097
World Wide Web http://www.aallnet.org

Object

The American Association of Law Libraries (AALL) is established for educational and scientific purposes. It shall be conducted as a nonprofit corporation to promote and enhance the value of law libraries to the public, the legal community, and the world; to foster the profession of law librarianship; to provide leadership in the field of legal information; and to foster a spirit of cooperation among the members of the profession. Established 1906.

Membership

Memb. 5,000+. Persons officially connected with a law library or with a law section of a state or general library, separately maintained. Associate membership available for others. Dues (Indiv., Indiv. Assoc., and Inst.) $145; (Inst. Assoc.) $256 times the number of members; (Retired) $36; (Student) $36; (SIS Memb.) $12 each per year. Year. July 1–June 30.

Officers

Pres. Victoria K. Trotta; *V.P.* Claire M. Germain; *Secy.* Catherine Lemann; *Treas.* Joyce Manna Janto.

Executive Board

Kathy Carlson, Ann T. Fessenden, Janis L. Johnston, Anne K. Meyers, Nina Platt, Merle J. Slyhoff, Kathie J. Sullivan.

Committees

AALL Archives Policy Review (Special).
AALL Centennial Celebration (Special).
AALL LexisNexis Call for Papers Committee.
AALLNET (Advisory).
ABA Standards for Academic Law Libraries (Task Force).
Access to Electronic Legal Information.
Annual Meeting Local (Advisory).
Annual Meeting Program.
Awards.
Bylaws.
Career Development (Task Force).
Cataloging and Intranet Access to Electronic Resources (Special).
Citation Formats.
Copyright.
Council of Chapter Presidents.
Council of Newsletter Editors.
Council of SIS Chairs.
CRIV (Relations with Information Vendors).
Diversity.
Economic Status of Law Librarianship.
Executive Board Finance and Budget.
Executive Board Governance.
Executive Board Strategic Planning.
Fair Business Practices Implementation Task Force.
Funding Advocacy Initiatives (Special).
Gen X Gen Y Task Force.
George Strait Fund-Raising.
Government Relations.
Graduate Education for Law Librarianship.
Grants.
Index to Foreign Legal Periodicals (Advisory).
Indexing of Periodical Literature (Advisory).

Licensing Principles for Electronic Resources (Special).
LLJ and AALL Spectrum Editorial Board (Advisory).
Membership and Retention.
Membership Publications (Special).
Mentoring.
Nominations.
Open Access Task Force.

Placement.
Planned Giving (Special).
Price Index for Legal Publications (Advisory).
Public Relations.
Publications.
Recruitment to Law Librarianship.
Research.
Scholarships.

American Library Association

Executive Director, Keith Michael Fiels
50 E. Huron St., Chicago, IL 60611
800-545-2433, 312-280-1392, fax 312-440-9374
World Wide Web http://www.ala.org

Object

The mission of the American Library Association (ALA) is to provide leadership for the development, promotion, and improvement of library and information services and the profession of librarianship in order to enhance learning and ensure access to information for all. Founded 1876.

Membership

Memb. (Indiv.) 59,752; (Inst.) 4,237; (Corporate) 233; (Total) 64,222 (as of July 31, 2004). Any person, library, or other organization interested in library service and librarians. Dues (Indiv.) 1st year, $50; 2nd year, $75, 3rd year and later, $100; (Trustee and Assoc. Memb.) $45; (Student) $25; (Foreign Indiv.) $60; (Other) $35; (Inst.) $110 and up, depending on operating expenses of institution.

Officers (2004–2005)

Pres. Carol Brey-Casiano, Dir. of Libs., El Paso Public Lib.,501 N. Oregon St., El Paso, TX 79901. Tel. 410-396-5395, fax 410-396-1321, e-mail breycx@elpasotexas.gov; *Pres.-Elect* Michael Gorman, Dean of Lib. Services, CSU-Fresno, 5200 N. Barton, Fresno, CA 93740-0001. Tel. 559-278-2403, fax 559-278-6952, email michaelg@csufresno.edu; *Immediate Past Pres.* Carla D. Hayden, Dir., Enoch Pratt Free Lib., 400 Cathedral St., Baltimore, MD. Tel. 410-396-5395, e-mail chayden@epfl.net; *Treas.* Teri R. Switzer, Asst. Dir., J.R./Budget, Auraria Lib., Univ. of Colorado, 1100 Lawrence St., Denver, CO 80204-2041. Tel. 303-556-3523, fax 303-556-3528, e-mail teri.switzer@cudenver.edu; *Exec. Dir.* Keith Michael Fiels, ALA Headquarters, 50 E. Huron St., Chicago, IL 60611. Tel. 312-280-1392, fax 312-944-3897, e-mail kfiels@ala.org.

Executive Board

Kathleen E. Bethel (2005), Nancy Davenport (2005), Michael A. Golrick (2006), Janet Swan Hill (2007), Nann Blaine Hilyard (2007), James R. Rettig (2006), Barbara K. Stripling (2005), Patricia M. Wong (2005).

Endowment Trustees

Robert R. Newlen, Rick J. Schwieterman, Carla J. Stoffle; *Exec. Board Liaison* Teri R. Switzer; *Staff Liaison* Gregory L. Calloway.

Divisions

See the separate entries that follow: American Assn. of School Libns.; Assn. for Lib. Collections and Technical Services; Assn. for Lib. Service to Children; Assn. for Lib. Trustees and Advocates; Assn. of College and Research Libs.; Assn. of Specialized and Cooperative Lib. Agencies; Lib. Admin. and Management Assn.; Lib. and Info. Technology Assn.; Public Lib. Assn.; Reference and User Services Assn.; Young Adult Lib. Services Assn.

Publications

ALA Handbook of Organization (ann.).
American Libraries (11 a year; memb.; organizations $60; foreign $70; single copy $6).
Book Links (6 a year; U.S. $28.95; foreign $36; single copy $6).
Booklist (22 a year; U.S. and possessions $79.95; foreign $95; single copy $6).

Round Table Chairpersons

(ALA staff liaison is given in parentheses.)
Continuing Library Education Network and Exchange. Jasmine Y. Posey (Lorelle R. Swader).
Ethnic and Multicultural Information Exchange. Victor Lynn Schill (Tanga Morris).
Exhibits. Amy Rosenbaum (Deidre Ross).
Federal and Armed Forces Libraries. Linda M. Resler (Reginald Scott).
Gay, Lesbian, Bisexual, Transgendered. Anne L. Moore, Stephen E. Stratton (Satia Orange).
Government Documents. John H. Moran (Reginald Scott).
Intellectual Freedom. Barbara M. Jones (Nanette Perez).
International Relations. Nancy M. Bolt (Michael Dowling, Delin Guerra).
Library History. Jean L. Preer (Denise M. Davis).

Library Instruction. Cynthia M. Akers (Lorelle R. Swader).
Library Research. Stephen E. Wiberley, Jr. (Denise M. Davis).
Library Support Staff Interests. James L. Hill (Lorelle R. Swader).
Map and Geography. Susan M. Moore (Danielle M. Alderson).
New Members. Sally Gibson (Kimberly Sanders).
Social Responsibilities. Rory Litwin (Satia Orange).
Staff Organizations. Virginia L. Fore (Lorelle R. Swader).
Video. Nell J. Chenault (Danielle M. Alderson).

Committee Chairpersons

(ALA staff liaison is given in parentheses.)
Accreditation (Standing). Robert Wedgeworth (Karen L. O'Brien).
American Libraries Advisory (Standing). Hector Escobar (Leonard Kniffel).
Appointments (Standing). Michael Gorman (Lois Ann Gregory-Wood).
Awards (Standing). Timothy P. Grimes (Cheryl Malden).
Budget Analysis and Review (Standing). Patricia H. Smith (Gregory Calloway).
Chapter Relations (Standing). Ling Hwey Jeng (Michael Dowling).
Committee on Committees (Elected Council Committee). Michael Gorman (Lois Ann Gregory-Wood).
Conference Committee (Standing). Joseph M. Eagan (Deidre Ross).
Conference Program Coordinating Team. Susan Logue (Deidre Ross).
Constitution and Bylaws (Standing). Norman Horrocks (JoAnne Kempf).
Council Orientation (Standing). Charles E. Kratz, Jr. (Lois Ann Gregory-Wood).
Diversity (Standing). Michael J. Miller (Gwendolyn Prellwitz).
Education (Standing). Loriene Roy (Lorelle R. Swader).
Election (Standing). Peggy Sullivan (Al Companio).

Human Resource Development and Recruitment (Standing). Julie Brewer (Lorelle R. Swader).

Information Technology Policy Advisory. Alice M. Calabrese-Berry (Frederick Weingarten).

Intellectual Freedom (Standing). Kenton Oliver (Judith F. Krug).

International Relations (Standing). John W. Berry (Michael Dowling).

Legislation (Standing). Jan W. Sanders (Lynne E. Bradley).

Literacy (Standing). Vivian Wynn (Dale P. Lipschultz).

Literacy and Outreach Services Advisory (Standing). Victor Lynn Schill (Satia Orange).

Membership (Standing). Marcia L. Boosinger (Gerald G. Hodges).

Organization (Standing). Melora Ranney Norman (Lois Ann Gregory-Wood).

Orientation, Training, and Leadership Development. Donna O. Dziedzic (Dorothy H. Ragsdale).

Pay Equity (Standing). Marva L. DeLoach (Lorelle R. Swader).

Policy Monitoring (Standing). Stephen L. Matthews (Lois Ann Gregory-Wood).

Professional Ethics (Standing). Sarah M. Pritchard (Beverley Becker, Judith F. Krug).

Public Awareness Advisory (Standing). Sally Gardner Reed (Mark R. Gould).

Publishing (Standing). Anders Dahlgren (Donald Chatham).

Research and Statistics (Standing). Daniel O. O'Connor (Denise M. Davis).

Resolutions. James Casey (Lois Ann Gregory-Wood).

Status of Women in Librarianship (Standing). Myra Michele Brown (Lorelle R. Swader).

Web Advisory. Michelle E. Frisque (Sherri Vanyek).

Joint Committee Chairpersons

American Federation of Labor/Congress of Industrial Organizations–ALA, Library Service to Labor Groups, RUSA. Dan D. Golodner (ALA); Anthony Sarmiento (AFL/CIO).

Association of American Publishers–ALA. Carol Brey-Casiano (ALA); to be appointed (AAP).

Association of American Publishers–ALCTS. Sheryl J. Nichin-Keith (ALCTS); Athena S. Michael (AAP).

Children's Book Council–ALA. Ginny Moore Kruse (ALA); Jeanne McDermott (CBC).

Society of American Archivists–American Association of Museums–ALA (Joint Committee on Library-Archives Relationships). Kathleen Bethel (ALA); William K. Barnett (SAA); To be appointed (AAM).

American Library Association
American Association of School Librarians

Executive Director, Julie A. Walker
50 E. Huron St., Chicago, IL 60611
312-280-4382, 800-545-2433 ext. 4382, fax 312-664-7459
E-mail aasl@ala.org, World Wide Web http://www.ala.org/aasl

Object

The American Association of School Librarians (AASL) is interested in the general improvement and extension of library media services for children and young people. AASL has specific responsibility for planning a program of study and service for the improvement and extension of library media services in elementary and secondary schools as a means of strengthening the educational program; evaluation, selection, interpretation, and utilization of media as they are used in the context of the school program; stimulation of continuous study and research in the library field and establishing criteria of evaluation; synthesis of the activities of all units of the American Library Association in areas of mutual concern; representation and interpretation of the need for the function of school libraries to other educational and lay groups; stimulation of professional growth, improvement of the status of school librarians, and encouragement of participation by members in appropriate type-of-activity divisions; conducting activities and projects for improvement and extension of service in the school library when such projects are beyond the scope of type-of-activity divisions, after specific approval by the ALA Council.

Established in 1951 as a separate division of ALA.

Membership

Memb. 9,900+. Open to all libraries, school library media specialists, interested individuals, and business firms with requisite membership in ALA.

Officers (2004–2005)

Pres. Dawn P. Vaughn; *Pres.-Elect* J. Linda Williams; *Treas./Financial Officer* to be announced; *Past Pres.* Frances R. Roscello.

Board of Directors

Officers; Cassandra G. Barnett, Kathleen V. Ellis, Dolores D. Gwaltney, Elizabeth Haynes, Sara Kelly Johns, Melissa P. Johnston, Jo Ellen Priest Misakian, Terri G. Kirk, Kathy Latrobe, Ann M. Martin, Claudia M. Myers, Sylvia K. Norton, Joanne M. Proctor, A. Elaine Twogood, Jan Weber, Julie A. Walker (ex officio).

Publications

Knowledge Quest (5 a year; memb.; non-memb. $40). *Ed.* Debbie Abilock. E-mail kq@abilockl.net.

School Library Media Research (nonsubscription electronic publication available to memb. and nonmemb. at http://www.ala.org/aasl/slmr). *Ed.* Daniel Callison, School of Lib. and Info. Sciences, 10th and Jordan, Indiana Univ., Bloomington, IN 47405. E-mail callison@indiana.edu.

AASL Hotlinks (monthly electronic newsletter automatically sent to members)

Committee Chairpersons

AASL @ your library Special Committee. Deborah D. Levitov.

AASL/ACRL Joint Information Literacy Committee. Allison Kaplan, Adis Beesting.

AASL/ELMS Executive Committee. Mary A. Berry.

AASL/Highsmith Research Grant. Carol A. Doll.

AASL/ISS Executive Committee. Susan G. Williamson.

AASL/SPVS Executive Committee. Doug Johnson.

ABC/CLIO Leadership Grant. Mary Frances Long.

Affiliate Assembly. Rosina R. Alaimo.

Alliance for Association Excellence. To be announced.

American Univ. Press Book Selection. Toni Negro.

Annual Conference. Vicki Emery, Hilda K. Weisburg.

Appointments. M. Veanna Baxter.

Awards. Elizabeth L. Marcoux.

Bylaws and Organization. Carolyn Cain.

Collaborative School Library Media Award. Karen R. Lemmons.

Distinguished School Administrator Award. Veronica C. Pastecki.

Distinguished Service Award. Katherine A. Bassett.

Frances Henne Award. Jan Weber.

ICONnect Online Courses for Professionals and Families. To be announced.

Information Technology Pathfinder Award. Cara Cavin.

Intellectual Freedom. Judith E. Rodgers.

Intellectual Freedom Award. Kimberly A. Grimes.

International Relations Committee. Ross Todd.

Knowledge Quest Editorial Board. Debbie Abilock.

Leadership Forum Planning. Sara Kelly Johns.

Legislation. Dennis J. LeLoup, Claudia M. Myers.

National Conference, 2005. Rosina Alaimo, Mary K. Biagini.

National Institute Planning. Carol A. Gordon.

National School Library Media Program of the Year Award. Jo Ann Carr.

NBPTS Special. Sallie H. Barringer.

NCATE Coordinating Committee. Judi Repman.

New Member Mentoring Task Force. Gene Hainer.

Nominating 2005. Bonnie J. Grimble.

Publications. Nancy A. Miller.

Reading for Understanding Special Committee. Sharon Coatney.

Recruitment for the Profession Task Force. Nancy Everhart.

Research/Statistics. Keith Curry Lance.

School Librarians Workshop Scholarship. Elizabeth B. Day.

SLMR Electronic Editorial Board. Daniel J. Callison.

Teaching for Learning Committee. Catherine Marriott.

Web Advisory. Constance J. Champlin.

Web Site Resource Guides Editorial Board. To be announced.

American Library Association
Association for Library Collections and Technical Services

Executive Director, Charles Wilt
50 E. Huron St., Chicago, IL 60611
800-545-2433 ext. 5030, fax 312-280-5033
E-mail cwilt@ala.org
World Wide Web http://www.ala.org/alcts

Object

The Association for Library Collections and Technical Services (ALCTS) envisions an environment in which traditional library roles are evolving. New technologies are making information more fluid and raising expectations. The public needs quality information anytime, anyplace. ALCTS provides frameworks to meet these information needs.

ALCTS provides leadership to the library and information communities in developing principles, standards, and best practices for creating, collecting, organizing, delivering, and preserving information resources in all forms. It provides this leadership through its members by fostering educational, research, and professional service opportunities. ALCTS is committed to quality information, universal access, collaboration, and life-long learning.

Standards: Develop, evaluate, revise, and promote standards for creating, collecting, organizing, delivering, and preserving information resources in all forms.

Best practices: Research, develop, evaluate, and implement best practices for creating, collecting, organizing, delivering, and preserving information resources in all forms.

Education: Assess the need for, sponsor, develop, administer, and promote educational programs and resources for life-long learning.

Professional development: Provide opportunities for professional development through research, scholarship, publication, and professional service.

Interaction and information exchange: Create opportunities to interact and exchange information with others in the library and information communities.

Association operations: Ensure efficient use of association resources and effective delivery of member services.

Established 1957; renamed 1988.

Membership

Memb. 4,865. Any member of the American Library Association may elect membership in this division according to the provisions of the bylaws.

Officers (2004–2005)

Pres. Carol Pitts Diedrichs, Univ. of Kentucky Lib., 1-85 William T. Young Lib., Lexington, KY 40506-0456. Tel. 859-257-0500 ext. 2087, fax 859-257-8379, e-mail diedrichs@uky.edu; *Pres.-Elect* Rosann V. Bazirjian, Walter Clinton Jackson Lib., Univ. of North Carolina–Greensboro, 1000 Spring Garden St., Greensboro, NC 27402. Tel. 336-334-5880, fax 336-334-5399, e-mail rvbazirj @uncg.edu; *Past Pres.* Brian E. C. Schottlaender, Univ. of California at San Diego Lib., 9500 Gilman Dr., 0175G, La Jolla, CA 92093-0175. Tel. 858-534-3060, fax 858-534-6193, e-mail becs@ucsd.edu; *Councilor* Bruce Chr. Johnson, Cataloging Distribution Service, Lib. of Congress, Washington, DC 20540-0001. Tel. 202-707-1652, fax 202-707-3959, e-mail bjoh@loc.gov.

Address correspondence to the executive director.

Board of Directors

Larry P. Alford, Rosann V. Bazirjian, Yvonne A. Carignan, Mary Case, Cynthia D. Clark, Lauren Corbett, Karen D. Darling, Carol Pitts Diedrichs, John Duke, Barbara Berger Eden, Lisa B. German, Bruce Chr. Johnson, Sara Shatford Layne, Miriam W. Palm, Helen Reed, Brian E. C. Schottlaender, Katherine L. Walter, Charles Wilt.

Publications

ALCTS Newsletter Online (q.; free). *Ed.* Miriam W. Palm, 2185 Waverley St., Palo Alto, CA 94301. Tel./fax 650-327-8989, e-mail miriam.palm@stanford.edu. Posted to http://www.ala.org/alcts.

Library Resources & Technical Services (q.; memb.; nonmemb. $75). *Ed.* Peggy Johnson, Univ. of Minnesota Lib., 499 Wilson Lib., 309 19th Ave. S., Minneapolis, MN 55455. Tel. 612-624-2312, fax 612-626-9353, e-mail m-john@tc.umn.edu.

Section Chairpersons

Acquisitions. Lisa B. German.
Cataloging and Classification. Sara Shatford Layne.
Collection Management and Development. Larry P. Alford.
Preservation and Reformatting. Yvonne A. Carignan.
Serials. Lauren Corbett.

Committee Chairpersons

Hugh C. Atkinson Memorial Award (ALCTS/ACRL/LAMA/LITA). James L. Mullins.
Association of American Publishers/ALCTS Joint Committee. Karolyn Anderson, Sheryl Nichin-Keith.
Paul Banks and Carolyn Harris Preservation Award Jury. Andrew S. Hart.
Best of *LRTS* Award Jury. Cynthia Shelton.

Blackwell's Scholarship Award Jury. Joyce G. McDonough.
Budget and Finance. Kay Walter.
Education. Karen M. Letarte.
Fund Raising. Jennifer F. Paustenbaugh.
International Relations. D. E. Perushek.
Leadership Development. Dina Giambi.
LRTS Editorial Board. Peggy Johnson.
MARBI. Adam L. Schiff.
Membership. Sheila A. Smyth.
Nominating. Olivia M. A. Madison.
Organization and Bylaws. Barbara Berger Eden.
Esther J. Piercy Award Jury. Julia A. Gammon.
Planning. Helen Reed.
Program. Genevieve Owens.
Publications. Narda Tafuri.

Discussion Groups

Authority Control in the Online Environment (ALCTS/LITA). Manon Theroux.
Automated Acquisitions/In-Process Control Systems. Lynne C. Branche-Brown.
Creative Ideas in Technical Services. Jack Hall, Kalyani Parthasarathy.
Electronic Resources. Jina Choi Wakimoto.
MARC Formats (ALCTS/LITA). Karen J. Davis, Helen E. Gbala, Marc Truitt.
Newspapers. Jessica Beth Albano, Sharon E. Clark.
Out of Print. Lia S. Hemphill.
Pre-Order and Pre-Catalog Searching. Susan L. Seiler.
Role of the Professional in Academic Research Technical Service Departments. Michael Wright.
Scholarly Communications. Carolyn K. Coates.
Technical Services Administrators of Medium-Sized Research Libraries. JoAnne Deeken.
Technical Services Directors of Large Research Libraries. Robert A. Wolven.
Technical Services Workstations (ALCTS/LITA). Birong A. Ho.

American Library Association
Association for Library Service to Children

Executive Director, Malore I. Brown
50 E. Huron St., Chicago, IL 60611
312-280-2162, 800-545-2433 ext. 2162
E-mail mbrown@ala.org
World Wide Web http://www.ala.org/alsc

Object

Interested in the improvement and extension of library services to children in all types of libraries. Responsible for the evaluation and selection of book and nonbook materials for, and the improvement of techniques of, library services to children from preschool through eighth grade or junior high school age, when such materials or techniques are intended for use in more than one type of library. Founded 1901.

Membership

Memb. 3,712. Open to anyone interested in library services to children. For information on dues, see ALA entry.

Address correspondence to the executive director.

Officers

Pres. Gretchen Wronka; *V.P./Pres.-Elect* Ellen Fader; *Past Pres.* Cynthia K. Richey.

Directors

Floyd Dickman, Carol Edwards, Jean Gaffney, Molly S. Kinney, Debra McLeod, Jane Marino, Judith O'Malley, Kathy Toon, Rose Trevino.

Publications

Children and Libraries: The Journal of the Association for Library Service to Children (JOYS) (q.; memb.; nonmemb. $40; foreign $50).

Committee Chairpersons

Priority Group I: Child Advocacy

Consultant. Marge Loch-Wouters.
Early Childhood Programs and Services.
Intellectual Freedom.
International Relations.
Legislation.
Library Service to Special Population Children and their Caregivers.
Preschool Services Discussion Group.
School-Age Programs and Service.
Social Issues Discussion Group.

Priority Group II: Evaluation of Media

Consultant. Leslie Molnar.
Great Web Sites.
Notable Children's Books.
Notable Children's Recordings.
Notable Children's Videos.
Notable Computer Software for Children.

Priority Group III: Professional Awards and Scholarships

Consultant. Linda Ward-Callaghan.
ALSC/BWI Summer Reading Program Grant.
ALSC/Sagebrush Education Resources Literature Program Grant.
Arbuthnot Honor Lecture.
Louise Seaman Bechtel Fellowship.
Distinguished Service Award.
Penguin Young Readers Group Awards.
Scholarships: Melcher and Bound to Stay Bound.

Priority Group IV: Organizational Support

Consultant. Kathleen Simonetta.
Local Arrangements.
Membership.
Nominating.

Organization and Bylaws.
Planning and Budget.
Preconference Planning.

Priority Group V: Projects and Research

Consultant. Hedra Packman.
Collections of Children's Books for Adult Research (Discussion Group).
National Planning of Special Collections.
Oral History.
Publications.
Research and Development.

Priority Group VI: Award Committees

Consultant. Dudley Carlson.
Mildred L. Batchelder Award Selection.
Pura Belpré Award.
Randolph Caldecott Award.
Andrew Carnegie Award.
Theodor Seuss Geisel Award.
John Newbery Award.

Sibert Informational Book Award.
Laura Ingalls Wilder Award.

Priority Group VII: Partnerships

Consultant. Alan Bern.
Liaison with National Organizations Serving Children and Youth.
Public Library-School Partnerships Discussion Group.
Quicklists Consulting Committee.

Priority Group VIII: Professional Development

Consultant. Marie Orlando.
Children and Technology.
Children's Book Discussion Group.
Education.
Managing Children's Services.
Managing Children's Services Discussion Group.
Storytelling Discussion Group.

American Library Association
Association for Library Trustees and Advocates

Executive Director, Kerry Ward
50 E. Huron St., Chicago, IL 60611-2795
312-280-2160, 800-545-2433 ext. 2161, fax 312-280-3256
E-mail kward@ala.org
World Wide Web http://www.ala.org/alta

Object

The Association for Library Trustees and Advocates (ALTA) is interested in the development of effective library service for all people in all types of communities and in all types of libraries; it follows that its members are concerned, as policymakers, with organizational patterns of service, with the development of competent personnel, the provision of adequate financing, the passage of suitable legislation, and the encouragement of citizen support for libraries.

ALTA recognizes that responsibility for professional action in these fields has been assigned to other divisions of ALA; its spe-

cific responsibilities as a division, therefore, are

1. A continuing and comprehensive educational program to enable library trustees to discharge their grave responsibilities in a manner best fitted to benefit the public and the libraries they represent
2. Continuous study and review of the activities of library trustees
3. Cooperation with other units within ALA concerning their activities relating to trustees
4. Encouraging participation of trustees

in other appropriate divisions of ALA

5. Representation and interpretation of the activities of library trustees in contacts outside the library profession, particularly with national organizations and governmental agencies

6. Promotion of strong state and regional trustee organizations

7. Efforts to secure and support adequate library funding

8. Promulgation and dissemination of recommended library policy

9. Assuring equal access of information to all segments of the population

10. Encouraging participation of trustees in trustee/library activities, at local, state, regional, and national levels

Organized 1890. Became an ALA division in 1961.

Membership

Memb. 1,200. Open to all interested persons and organizations. For dues and membership year, see ALA entry.

Officers (2004–2005)

Pres. Marguerite E. Ritchey. E-mail margueritemr@hotmail.com; *1st V.P./Pres.-Elect* Jane Rowland. E-mail jrowland@calumetcitypl.org; *2nd V.P.* Anne D. Sterling. E-mail nimbleleap@aol.com; *Councilor* Donald Roalkvam. E-mail droalkva@allstate.com; *Past Pres.* Shirley Bruursema. E-mail libsabsarg@aol.com.

Publication

The Voice (q.; memb.).

American Library Association
Association of College and Research Libraries

Executive Director, Mary Ellen K. Davis
50 E. Huron St., Chicago, IL 60611-2795
312-280-2523, 800-545-2433 ext. 2523, fax 312-280-2520
E-mail mdavis@ala.org
World Wide Web http://www.ala.org/acrl

Object

The Association of College and Research Libraries (ACRL) provides leadership for development, promotion, and improvement of academic and research library resources and services to facilitate learning, research, and the scholarly communication process. ACRL promotes the highest level of professional excellence for librarians and library personnel in order to serve the users of academic and research libraries. Founded 1938.

Membership

Memb. 12,343. For information on dues, see ALA entry.

Officers

Pres. Frances J. Maloy, Div. Leader, Access Services, Emory Univ., 540 Asbury Circle, Atlanta, GA 30322. Tel. 404-727-0126. fax 404-727-0827, e-mail libfm@emory.edu; *Pres.-Elect* Camila Alire, Lib. Dean, Univ. of New Mexico, General Lib. MSC 05 3020, Albuquerque, NM 87131. Tel. 505-277-2678, e-mail calire@unm.edu; *Past Pres.* Tyrone Cannon, Lib. Dean, Univ. of San Francisco, 2130 Fulton St., San Francisco, CA 94117. Tel. 415-422-6167, fax 314-422-5949, e-mail cannont@usfca.edu; *Budget and Finance Chair* Susan M. Allen, Chief Libn., Getty Research Lib./Getty Research Inst., 1200 Getty Center, Los Angeles, CA 90049-1688. Tel. 310-440-7611, fax 310-440-7781, e-mail sallen@getty.edu; *ACRL Councilor* Elaine Didier, Professor, Oakland Univ., Kresge Lib., Rochester, MI 48309-4484. Tel. 248-370-2499, e-mail didier@oakland.edu.

Board of Directors

Officers; Nancy H. Allen, Lori A. Goetsch, Rita Jones, Lynne King, Patricia Kreitz, W. Bede Mitchell, Pamela Snelson, Dorothy A. Washington.

Publications

Choice (11 a year; $280; foreign $330). *Ed.* Irving Rockwood.
Choice Reviews-on-Cards ($360; foreign $420).
ChoiceReviews.online ($310).
College & Research Libraries (6 a year; memb.; nonmemb. $65). *Ed.* William Gray Potter.
College & Research Libraries News (11 a year; memb.; nonmemb. $44). *Ed.* Stephanie D. Orphan.
Publications in Librarianship (formerly *ACRL Monograph Series*) (occasional). *Ed.* Charles Schwartz.
RBM: A Journal of Rare Books, Manuscripts, and Cultural Heritage (2 a year; $40). *Ed.* Richard Clement.
List of other publications and rates available through the ACRL office.

Committee and Task Force Chairpersons

AASL/ACRL Information Literacy (interdivisisional). Adis C. Beesting, Allison G. Kaplan.
Academic/Research Librarian of the Year Award Selection. Edward Warro.
ACRL/Harvard Leadership Institute Advisory. John William Collins III.
Appointments. Janice Simmons-Welburn.
Hugh C. Atkinson Memorial Award. Jim Mullins.
Budget and Finance. Susan M. Allen.

Bylaws. Michelle M. Reid.
Choice Editorial Board. Joan L. Heath.
Colleagues. Charles Lowry, James Williams.
College & Research Libraries Editorial Board. William Gray Potter.
College & Research Libraries News Editorial Board. Brian E. Coutts.
Standards and Accreditation. Paul J. Beavers.
Conference Program Planning, Chicago (2005). Frances Maloy.
Copyright. Thomas Deardorff.
Council of Liaisons. Julie B. Todaro.
Doctoral Dissertation Fellowship. Dolores Fidishun.
Effective Practices Review Committee. Priscilla Finley.
Ethics. Douglas Archer.
Excellence in Academic Libraries Award (Nominations). Trevor Dawes.
Excellence in Academic Libraries Award (Selection). Helen Spalding.
First Year Experience. Jane A. Carlin.
Friends Fund. John Popko.
Government Relations. Janice A. Fryer.
Information Literacy Advisory. Keith Gresham.
Institute for Information Literacy Executive. Loanne L. Snavely.
Intellectual Freedom. Robert P. Holley.
International Relations. Kara J. Malenfant.
Samuel Lazerow Fellowship. Anne Moore.
Long-Term Investment Fund. Erika C. Linke.
Marketing Academic and Research Libraries. Frank D'Andraia.
Membership. John H. Pollitz.
National Conference Executive Committee, Minneapolis 2005. Camila A. Alire.
New Publications Advisory. Jan Kemp.
Nominations. Lori Goetsch.
President's Program Planning Committee, Chicago, 2005. Victoria A. Hanawalt, Jane Treadwell.
President's Program Planning Committee, New Orleans, 2006. Louise Sherby, Lynn Connaway.
Professional Development. Patricia A. Promis.
Publications. Jamie W. Gill.
Publications in Librarianship Editorial Board. Charles A. Schwartz.
Racial and Ethnic Diversity. Hector Escobar, Jr.

RBM: A Journal of Rare Books, Manuscripts, and Cultural Heritage Editorial Board. Richard W. Clement.

Research. Mary K. Sellen.

Review and Revision of the Guidelines for the Preparation of Policies on Library Access. C. Denise Stephens.

Scholarly Communications. Ray English.

Spectrum Scholars Mentor. Theresa S. Byrd.

Standards and Accreditation. Paul J. Beavers.

Statistics. Leslie A. Manning.

Status of Academic Librarians. Sharon McCaslin.

Virtual Meetings. Norice Lee.

Discussion Group Chairpersons

Academic Library Outreach. Stephanie R. Davis-Kahl.

Alliances for New Directions in Teaching/Learning. Mark Horan.

Australian-Canadian-New Zealand Studies. Faye Christenberry.

Consumer and Family Studies. Priscilla C. Geahigan.

Electronic Reserves. Laureen Esser.

Electronic Text Centers. Robert H. Scott.

Fee-Based Information Service Centers in Academic Libraries. Steve Coffman.

Heads of Public Services. Amy Knapp.

Libraries and Information Science. Susan Searing.

Library Development. Barton Lessin.

Media Resources. Diane Kachmar.

MLA International Bibliography. Kathleen Kluegel.

Personnel Administrators and Staff Development Officers. Susan Marks, Judy Anne Sackett.

Philosophical, Religious, and Theological Studies. Celestina Wroth.

Popular Cultures. Paul A. Kauppila.

Regional Campus Libraries. Darby Syrkin.

Scholarly Communications. Richard Fyffe.

Sports and Recreation. Mila C. Su.

Team-Based Organizations. Robert Patrick Mitchell.

Section Chairpersons

African-American Studies Librarians. Myrtis Cochran.

Anthropology and Sociology. Wade Kotter.

Arts. Sandra Mooney.

Asian, African, and Middle Eastern. Majed Khader.

College Libraries. Damon Hickey.

Community and Junior College Libraries. Mary Carr.

Distance Learning. Steven Dew.

Education and Behavioral Sciences. Judith Walker.

Instruction. Elizabeth DuPuis.

Law and Political Science. Lynne Rudasill.

Literatures in English. Jennifer Stevens.

Rare Books and Manuscripts. Elaine Smyth.

Science and Technology. Jeanne Davidson.

Slavic and East European. Janke Pilch.

University Libraries. Carol Ann Hughes.

Western European Studies. Thomas Izbicki.

Woman's Studies. Ruth Dickstein.

American Library Association
Association of Specialized and Cooperative Library Agencies

Executive Director, Cathleen Bourdon
50 E. Huron St., Chicago, IL 60611-2795
312-280-4398, 800-545-2433 ext. 4398, fax 312-944-8085
World Wide Web http://www.ala.org/ascla

Object

Represents state library agencies, specialized library agencies, multitype library cooperatives, and independent librarians. Within the interests of these types of library organizations, the Association of Specialized and Cooperative Library Agencies (ASCLA) has specific responsibility for

1. Development and evaluation of goals and plans for state library agencies, specialized library agencies, and multitype library cooperatives to facilitate the implementation, improvement, and extension of library activities designed to foster improved user services, coordinating such activities with other appropriate ALA units

2. Representation and interpretation of the role, functions, and services of state library agencies, specialized library agencies, multitype library cooperatives, and independent librarians within and outside the profession, including contact with national organizations and government agencies

3. Development of policies, studies, and activities in matters affecting state library agencies, specialized library agencies, multitype library cooperatives and independent librarians relating to (a) state and local library legislation, (b) state grants-in-aid and appropriations, and (c) relationships among state, federal, regional, and local governments, coordinating such activities with other appropriate ALA units

4. Establishment, evaluation, and promotion of standards and service guidelines relating to the concerns of this association

5. Identifying the interests and needs of all persons, encouraging the creation of services to meet these needs within the areas of concern of the association, and promoting the use of these services provided by state library agencies, specialized library agencies, multitype library cooperatives, and independent librarians

6. Stimulating the professional growth and promoting the specialized training and continuing education of library personnel at all levels in the areas of concern of this association and encouraging membership participation in appropriate type-of-activity divisions within ALA

7. Assisting in the coordination of activities of other units within ALA that have a bearing on the concerns of this association

8. Granting recognition for outstanding library service within the areas of concern of this association

9. Acting as a clearinghouse for the exchange of information and encouraging the development of materials, publications, and research within the areas of concern of this association

Membership

Memb. 917.

Board of Directors (2004–2005)

Pres. Peggy D. Rudd; *Pres.-Elect* Diana M. Paque; *Past Pres.* Tom W. Sloan; *Dirs.-at-Large* Greg Carlson, Sarah E. Hamrick, Stephen Prine, Jeanette Smithee; *Div. Councilor* Cynthia Roach; *Newsletter Editor* Sara

G. Laughlin; *Section Reps.* Susanne Bjorner, Ruth J. Nussbaum, Gregory Pronevitz, Rahye L. Puckett, Kendall French Wiggin.

Executive Staff

Exec. Dir. Cathleen Bourdon; *Deputy Exec. Dir.* Lillian Lewis.

Publications

Interface (q.; memb.; single copies $7). *Ed.* Sara G. Laughlin, 1616 Treadwell La., Bloomington, IN 47408. Tel. 812-334-8485.

Committee Chairpersons

Accessibility Assembly. Rhea Joyce Rubin.
American Correctional Association/ASCLA Joint Committee on Institution Libraries. Jean Clancy Botta.
Awards. Barratt Wilkins.
Conference Program Coordination. Jeanette P. Smithee.
Legislation. Barbara H. Will.
Membership Promotion. Ronald P. Leonard.
Planning and Budget. Diana M. Paque, Tom W. Sloan.
Publications. William J. Wilson.
Standards Review. Rod Wagner.

American Library Association
Library Administration and Management Association

Executive Director, Lorraine Olley
50 E. Huron St., Chicago, IL 60611
312-280-5036, 800-545-2433 ext. 5036, fax 312-280-5033
E-mail lolley@ala.org
World Wide Web http://www.ala.org/lama

Object

The Library Administration and Management Association (LAMA) provides an organizational framework for encouraging the study of administrative theory, for improving the practice of administration in libraries, and for identifying and fostering administrative skill. Toward these ends, the division is responsible for all elements of general administration that are common to more than one type of library. These may include organizational structure, financial administration, personnel management and training, buildings and equipment, and public relations. LAMA meets this responsibility in the following ways:

1. Study and review of activities assigned to the division with due regard for changing developments in these activities
2. Initiating and overseeing activities and projects appropriate to the division, including activities involving bibliography compilation, publication, study, and review of professional literature within the scope of the division
3. Synthesizing the activities of other ALA units that have a bearing upon the responsibilities or work of the division
4. Representing and interpreting library administrative activities in contacts outside the library profession
5. Aiding the professional development of librarians engaged in administration and encouraging their participation in appropriate type-of-library divisions
6. Planning and developing programs of study and research in library administrative problems that are most needed by the profession

Established 1957.

Membership

Memb. 4,800.

Officers (July 2004–June 2005)

Pres. Virginia Steel; *Pres.-Elect* Catherine Murray-Rust; *Past Pres.* Paul M. Anderson; *Dirs.-at-Large* Kathryn Hammell Carpenter, Melissa Carr; *Div. Councilor* Charles E. Kratz; *COLA Chair* Mary Ellen Chijioke; *Budget and Finance Chair* Rod MacNeil; *Section Chairs* Philip Tramdack (BES), Peter Pearson (FRFDS), Kerry Ransel (HRS), Patricia Kelley (LOMS), Deborah Nolan (MAES), Amy Shaw (PRMS), Emily Bergman (SASS); *Ex officio* Bonnie Allen, Susan Anthes, Drew Harrington, Michele Russo, Eric Shoaf, Elizabeth Titus, Jeanne Voyles, Joan R. Giesecke, Marta Deyrup, Gregg Sapp.

Address correspondence to the executive director.

Publications

Library Administration and Management (q.; memb.; nonmemb. $65; foreign $75). *Ed.* Marta Deyrup; *Assoc. Ed.* Gregg Sapp.

LEADS from LAMA (approx. biweekly; free through Internet). *Ed.* Lorraine Olley. To subscribe, send to listproc@ala.org the message *subscribe lamaleads [first name last name]*.

Committee Chairpersons

Budget and Finance. Roderick MacNeil.
Council of LAMA Affiliates. Mary Ellen Chijioke.
Cultural Diversity. Joyce Taylor.
Editorial Advisory Board. Amy K. Weiss.
Education. Tracy Bicknell-Holmes.
Financial Advancement. Arne J. Almquist.

Governmental Affairs. Elena Rosenfeld.
Leadership Development. Janice D. Simmons-Welburn.
Membership. Susan Mueller.
Nominating, 2005 Elections. June Koelker.
Organization. Joan R. Giesecke.
President's Program 2005. Cathy Miesse, Kathryn Deiss.
Program. George Lupone.
Publications. Stephen B. Van Buren.
Recognition of Achievement. Marilyn G. Genther.
Research. Harold Carter.
Special Conferences and Programs. Barbara G. Preece.
Strategic Planning Implementation. Michele C. Russo.

Section Chairpersons

Buildings and Equipment. Philip Tramdack.
Fund Raising and Financial Development. Peter Pearson.
Human Resources. Kerry Ransel.
Library Organization and Management. Patricia Kelley.
Measurement, Assessment, and Evaluation. Deborah Nolan.
Public Relations and Marketing. Amy Shaw.
Systems and Services. Emily Bergman.

Discussion Group Chairpersons

Assistants-to-the-Director. Robert E. Withers.
Dialogue with Directors. Brian Gray.
Diversity Officers. Laura K. Blessing, Laura Bayard.
Library Storage. Lori Driscoll, Deborah Slingluff.
Middle Management. Sarah Lynn McIntyre, Tricia Segal.
Women Administrators. Meg K. Scharf.

American Library Association
Library and Information Technology Association

Executive Director, Mary C. Taylor
50 E. Huron St., Chicago, IL 60611
312-280-4270, 800-545-2433
E-mail mtaylor@ala.org
World Wide Web http://www.lita.org

Object

The Library and Information Technology Association (LITA) envisions a world in which the complete spectrum of information technology is available to everyone—in libraries, at work, and at home. To move toward this goal, LITA provides a forum for discussion, an environment for learning, and a program for actions on many aspects of information technology for both practitioners and managers.

LITA educates, serves, and reaches out to its members, other ALA members and divisions, and the entire library and information community through its publications, programs, and other activities designed to promote, develop, and aid in the implementation of library and information technology. LITA is concerned with the planning, development, design, application, and integration of technologies within the library and information environment, with the impact of emerging technologies on library service, and with the effect of automated technologies on people.

Membership

Memb. 4,800.

Officers (2004–2005)

Pres. Colby Mariva Riggs; *V.P./Pres.-Elect* Patrick J. Mullin; *Past Pres.* Thomas C. Wilson.

Directors

Officers; Kristin A. Antelman, Mark A. Beatty, David C. Dorman, Jennie L. McKee, Andrew K. Pace, Bonnie S. Postlethwaite, Flo J. Wilson; *Councilor* Karen G. Schneider; *Bylaws and Organization* Colleen Cuddy; *Exec. Dir.* Mary C. Taylor.

Publication

Information Technology and Libraries (ITAL) (q.; memb.; nonmemb. $55; single copy $20). *Ed.* John P. Webb. For information or to send manuscripts, contact the editor.

Committee Chairpersons

Budget Review. Thomas C. Wilson.
Bylaws and Organization. Colleen Cuddy.
Committee Chair Coordinator. Jonathan Rothman.
Education. Catherine L. Wilkinson.
Executive. Colby Mariva Riggs.
International Relations. David J. Nutty.
ITAL Editorial Board. John P. Webb.
Legislation and Regulation. Eulalia A. Roel.
LITA/Brett Butler Entrepreneurship Award. Donald Russell Bailey.
LITA/Endeavor Student Writing Award. Dan Marmion.
LITA/Library Hi Tech Award. Ronald A. Peterson.
LITA/LSSI and LITA/OCLC Minority Scholarships. Adriene I. Lim.
LITA National Forum 2005. Thomas P. Dowling.
LITA National Forum 2006. Dale Poulter.
LITA/OCLC Kilgour Award. Heidi E. Hanson.
LITA/Sirsi and LITA/Christian Larew Scholarships. Flo Wilson.
Membership Development. Navjit K. Brar.
Nominating. Pat Ensor.
Program Planning. David W. Bretthauer.

Publications. Nancy N. Colyar.
Regional Institutes. Peter Murray.
Technology and Access. Aimee Fifarek.
Top Technology Trends. David Ward.
TER Board. Sharon Rankin.
Web Coordinating. Michelle L. Frisque.

Interest Group Chairpersons

Interest Group Coordinator. Lorre Smith.
Authority Control in the Online Environment (LITA/ALCTS). Leah Manon Theroux.
Digital Library Technologies. Holley Whitehurst Long.
Distance Learning. Cindy Kristof.
Electronic Publishing/Electronic Journals.

Lloyd Davidson.
Emerging Technologies. Maurice York.
Heads of Library Technology. Byron Mayes.
Human/Machine Interface. Lisa Martincik.
Imagineering. Catherine Wagner.
Internet Portals. Harrison Dekker.
Internet Resources. Matthew M. Calsada.
MARC Formats (LITA/ALCTS). Mark Truitt.
Open Source Systems. Kyle Fenton.
Personal Computing. Florence Ye Tang.
Secure Systems and Services. George J. Harmon.
Standards. Nathan D. M. Robertson.
Technical Services Workstations (LITA/ALCTS). Birong Ho.
Technology and the Arts. Nancy Friedland.

American Library Association
Public Library Association

Executive Director, Greta K. Southard
50 E. Huron St., Chicago, IL 60611
312-280-5752, 800-545-2433 ext. 5752, fax 312-280-5029
E-mail pla@ala.org
World Wide Web http://www.pla.org

Object

The Public Library Association (PLA) has specific responsibility for

1. Conducting and sponsoring research about how the public library can respond to changing social needs and technical developments
2. Developing and disseminating materials useful to public libraries in interpreting public library services and needs
3. Conducting continuing education for public librarians by programming at national and regional conferences, by publications such as the newsletter, and by other delivery means
4. Establishing, evaluating, and promoting goals, guidelines, and standards for public libraries

5. Maintaining liaison with relevant national agencies and organizations engaged in public administration and human services, such as the National Association of Counties, the Municipal League, and the Commission on Post-Secondary Education
6. Maintaining liaison with other divisions and units of ALA and other library organizations, such as the Association of American Library Schools and the Urban Libraries Council
7. Defining the role of the public library in service to a wide range of user and potential user groups
8. Promoting and interpreting the public library to a changing society through legislative programs and other appropriate means

9. Identifying legislation to improve and to equalize support of public libraries

PLA enhances the development and effectiveness of public librarians and public library services. This mission positions PLA to

- Focus its efforts on serving the needs of its members
- Address issues that affect public libraries
- Commit to quality public library services that benefit the general public

The goals of PLA are

Advocacy and recognition. Public libraries will be recognized as the destination for a wide variety of valuable services and their funding will be a community priority.

A literate nation. PLA will be a valued partner of public library initiatives to create a nation of readers.

Staffing and recruitment. Public libraries will be recognized as exciting places to work and will be staffed by skilled professionals who are recognized as the information experts, are competitively paid, and reflect the demographics of their communities.

Training and knowledge transfer. PLA will be nationally recognized as the leading source for continuing education opportunities for public library staff and trustees.

Membership

Memb. 10,000+. Open to all ALA members interested in the improvement and expansion of public library services to all ages in various types of communities.

Officers (2004–2005)

Pres. Clara Nalli Bohrer, West Bloomfield Township Public Lib., 4600 Walnut Lake Rd., West Bloomfield, MI 48323-2557. Tel. 248-682-2120, fax 248-232-2333, e-mail bohrercn@wblib.org; *Pres.-Elect* Daniel Walters, Las Vegas-Clark County Lib. Dist., 833 Las Vegas Blvd. North, Las Vegas, NV

89101-2030. Tel. 702-507-3611, fax 702-507-3609, e-mail waltersd@lvccld.org; *Past-Pres.* Luis Herrera, Pasadena Public Lib., 285 E. Walnut St., Pasadena, CA 91101. E-mail lherrera@ci.pasadena.ca.us.

Publication

Public Libraries (bi-m.; memb.; nonmemb. $50; foreign $60; single copy $10). *Managing Ed.* Kathleen Hughes, PLA, 50 E. Huron St., Chicago, IL 60611.

Cluster Chairpersons

Issues and Concerns Steering Committee. Donna Joy Press.
Library Development Steering Committee. Sylvia Sprinkle-Hamlin.
Library Services Steering Committee. Carol Simmons.

Committee Chairs

Issues and Concerns Cluster

Intellectual Freedom. Penelope Jeffrey.
International Relations. Kathleen Imhoff.
Legislation. Mark Smith.
Library Confidentialty Task Force. Catherine O'Connell.
Public Policy in Public Libraries. Joan Clark.
Recruitment of Public Librarians. Larry Neal.
Research and Statistics. Rochelle Logan.
Workload Measures and Staffing Patterns. Regina Cooper.

Library Development Cluster

Branch Libraries. Cheryl Smith.
Marketing Public Libraries. Mary Fran Bennett.
Metropolitan Libraries. Therese Bigelow.
Practical Applications of Technology in Public Libraries. Ross McLachlan.
Public Library Systems. Juliet Machie.
Rural Library Services. Dwight Emlyn McInvaill.
Small and Medium-Sized Libraries. Laurel Best.

Technology in Public Libraries. Charles McMorran.

Library Services Cluster

Adult Continuing and Independent Learning Services. Kathleen Degyansky.
Audiovisual. Jana Prock.
Basic Education and Literarcy Services. Robin Osborne.
Career and Business Services. Barbara Spruill.
Cataloging Needs of Public Libraries. Vivian Bordeaux.
Collection Management Committee. Mary Wallace.
Community Information Services. Timothy Rogers.
Reader's Advisory. Teresa A. Beck.
Services to Elementary-School-Age Children and Their Caregivers. Allison L. Grant.
Services to Multicultural Populations. Mary Louise Daneri.
Services to Preschool Children and Their Caregivers. Pamela A. Martin-Diaz.
Services to Teenagers and Their Caregivers. Bill Stack.

Business Committees

@ your library Campaign Task Force. Kathleen S. Reif.
2005 Annual Conference Coordinating Committee. Kathy Coster.
2005 Leadership Development. Joan Clark.
2006 Annual Conference Coordinating Committee. Bruce Schauer.
2006 National Conference. Toni Garvey.
2006 National Conference (Program). Sandra Nelson.
Assessing for Results Book Review Committee. Sandra Nelson.
Awards. Christine Lind Hage.
Budget and Finance. Eva Poole.
Bylaws and Organization. Claudia Sumler.
Leadership Development 2005. Joan L. Clark.
Leadership Development 2006. William Knott.
Membership. Albert Tovar.
PLA Partners. David Paynter.
President's Events 2005. Marilyn Boria.
President's Events 2006. Rivkah Sass.
Publications, Electronic Communications Advisory. Pauline Baughman.
Publications, PLA Monographs. Margaret Smith.
Publications, *Public Libraries* Advisory. Isabel Dale Silver.
Publications, *Statistical Report* Advisory. Irene Blalock.
Publications, University Press Books for Public Libraries. Saul Amdursky.
State Relations. Thomas Hehman.
Task Force on Preschool Literacy Initiatives (joint with ALSC). Harriet Henderson, Elaine Meyers.

American Library Association
Reference and User Services Association

Executive Director, Cathleen Bourdon
50 E. Huron St., Chicago, IL 60611-2795
312-280-4398, 800-545-2433 ext. 4398, fax 312-944-8085
E-mail rusa@ala.org
World Wide Web http://www.ala.org/rusa

Object

The Reference and User Services Association (RUSA) is responsible for stimulating and supporting in every type of library the delivery of reference/information services to all groups, regardless of age, and of general library services and materials to adults. This involves facilitating the development and conduct of direct service to library users, the development of programs and guidelines for service to meet the needs of these users, and assisting libraries in reaching potential users.

The specific responsibilities of RUSA are

1. Conduct of activities and projects within the association's areas of responsibility
2. Encouragement of the development of librarians engaged in these activities, and stimulation of participation by members of appropriate type-of-library divisions
3. Synthesis of the activities of all units within the American Library Association that have a bearing on the type of activities represented by the association
4. Representation and interpretation of the association's activities in contacts outside the profession
5. Planning and development of programs of study and research in these areas for the total profession
6. Continuous study and review of the association's activities

Membership

Memb. 4,900.

Officers (July 2004–June 2005)

Pres. Gwen Arthur; *Pres.-Elect* Diane M. Zabel; *Past Pres.* Nancy Huling; *Secy.* Danise Gianneschi Hoover.

Directors-at-Large

Denise Beaubien Bennett, Carla Rickerson, Pamela C. Sieving, Cathleen Alice Towey, Amy Tracy Wells, Carol Z. Womack; *Councilor* Neal Wyatt; *Eds.* Connie J. Van Fleet, Danny P. Wallace; *Ex Officio* Suzanne Sweeney; *Exec. Dir.* Cathleen Bourdon.

Publication

RUSQ (q.; memb. $50, foreign memb. $60, single copies $15). *Eds.* Connie J. Van Fleet, Danny P. Wallace.

Section Chairpersons

Business Reference and Services. Stacey A. Marien.
Collection Development and Evaluation. Betty A. Gard.
History. Louis A. Vyhananek.
Machine-Assisted Reference. Doris Ann Sweet.
Reference Services. Maira I. Liriano.
Sharing and Transforming Access to Resources. Mary Allison Hollerich.

Committee Chairpersons

Access to Information. Janet These O'Keefe.
AFL/CIO Joint Committee on Library Services to Labor Groups. Mary M. D. Parker, Anthony R. Sarmiento.

Awards Coordinating. Neal Wyatt.
Conference Program. Robert H. Kieft.
Conference Program Coordinating. Corinne M. Hill.
Membership. Rebecca L. Johnson, Lori S. Thornton.
Margaret E. Monroe Library Adult Services Award. Jon J. Kadus.
Isadore Gilbert Mudge/R. R. Bowker Award. Jerilyn A. Marshall.
Nominating 2005. David A. Tyckoson.
Organization. Michael Gutierrez.
Planning and Finance. Nancy Huling.

Professional Development. Bobray J. Bordelon.
Publications. Joseph E. Straw.
Reference Services Press Award. Susan J. Beck.
John Sessions Memorial Award. Dan D. Golodner.
Standards and Guidelines. Tracy Hull.
Thomson Gale Research Award for Excellence in Reference and Adult Services. Teresa A. Beck, Lori S. Thornton.
Web Policies (subcommittee). Joseph E. Straw.

American Library Association
Young Adult Library Services Association

Executive Director, Beth Yoke
50 E. Huron St., Chicago, IL 60611
312-280-4390, 800-545-2433 ext. 4390, fax 312-664-7459
E-mail yalsa@ala.org, World Wide Web http://www.ala.org/yalsa

Object

In every library in the nation, quality library service to young adults is provided by a staff that understands and respects the unique informational, educational, and recreational needs of teenagers.

Equal access to information, services, and materials is recognized as a right, not a privilege. Young adults are actively involved in the library decision-making process. The library staff collaborates and cooperates with other youth-serving agencies to provide a holistic, community-wide network of activities and services that support healthy youth development. To ensure that this vision becomes a reality, the Young Adult Library Services Association (YALSA)

1. Advocates extensive and developmentally appropriate library and information services for young adults, ages 12 to 18

2. Promotes reading and supports the literacy movement

3. Advocates the use of information and communications technologies to provide effective library service

4. Supports equality of access to the full range of library materials and services, including existing and emerging information and communications technologies, for young adults

5. Provides education and professional development to enable its members to serve as effective advocates for young people

6. Fosters collaboration and partnerships among its individual members with the library community and other groups involved in providing library and information services to young adults

7. Influences public policy by demonstrating the importance of providing library and information services that meet the unique needs and interests of young adults

8. Encourages research and is in the vanguard of new thinking concerning the provision of library and information services for youth

Membership

Memb. 4,089. Open to anyone interested in library services and materials for young adults. For information on dues, see ALA entry.

Officers (July 2004–June 2005)

Pres. David C. Mowery, Brooklyn (New York) Public Lib. Tel. 718-230-2753, e-mail d.mowery@brooklynpubliclibrary.org; *V.P./ Pres.-Elect* Pam Spencer Holley, 757-824-3233, e-mail pamsholley@aol.com; *Past Pres.* Audra Caplan, Harford County (Maryland) Public Lib. Tel. 410-273-5600, e-mail caplan@hcplonline.info; *Div. Councilor* Catherine Clancy, Boston (Massachusetts) Public Lib. Tel. 617-787-6313, e-mail cclancy@bpl.org; *Fiscal Officer* C. Allen Nichols, Wadsworth-Ella M. Everhard Public Lib., Wadsworth, Ohio. Tel. 330-335-1299, e-mail allen@wadsworth.lib.oh.us.

Directors

Officers; Linda Braun (2005), Sarah Cornish (2007), Sarah Flowers (2007), Francisca Goldsmith (2006), Jessica Mize (2006), Kevin Scanlon (2005); *Chair, Organization and Bylaws* Donald J. Kenney; *Chair, Strategic Planning* Ranae Pierce.

Publication

Young Adult Library Services (quarterly) (memb.; nonmemb. $40; foreign $50). *Ed.* Jana Fine.

Committee Chairpersons

Alex Awards. Kimberley Hrivnak.
Audio Books and Media Exploration. Amy E. Spaulding.
Best Books for Young Adults. Angelina Benedetti.
Division and Membership Promotion. Sarajo S. Wentling.
Margaret A. Edwards Award 2005. Cindy Dobrez.
Margaret A. Edwards Award 2006. Mary Arnold.
Graphic Novels Task Force. Katharine Louise Kan.
Intellectual Freedom. Paula Brehm-Heeger.
Local Arrangements. Amy Alessio and Gail Tobin.
Legislation. Laurel Sandor.
Nominating. Betty Acerra.
Organization and Bylaws. Donald Kenney.
Outreach to Young Adults with Special Needs. Kristin Fletcher-Spear.
Partnerships Advocating for Teens. Sandra Payne.
Popular Paperbacks for Young Adults. Sally Leahey.
Preconference Planning 2005—Best of the Best Selection. Michael Cart.
President's Program 2005 Planning. Jana Fine.
Michael L. Printz Award 2005. Betty B. Carter.
Michael L. Printz Award 2006. Michael Cart.
Professional Development. Mary Lee Hastler.
Program Planning Clearinghouse and Evaluation. Carol Marlowe.
Publications. Donald J. Kenney.
Publishers Liaison. Jody Sharp.
Quick Picks for Reluctant Young Adult Readers. Maureen Hartman.
Research. Sarah O'Neal.
Selected DVDs and Videos for Young Adults. Shauna Yusko.
Serving Young Adults in Large Urban Populations Discussion Group. Sandra Payne.
Strategic Planning. Ranae Pierce.
Teaching Young Adult Literature Discussion Group. Teri Lesesne.
Technology for Young Adults. Cathy Delneo.
Teen Advisory Groups Committee. Tracey Firestone.
Teen Read Week. Nicholas Buron.
YA Galley. Diane Monnier.
Youth Participation. Gretchen Dombrock.

American Merchant Marine Library Association

(An affiliate of United Seamen's Service)
Executive Director, Roger T. Korner
20 Exchange Place, Ste. 2901, New York, NY 10005
212-269-0711, e-mail ussammla@ix.netcom.com
World Wide Web http://uss-ammla.com

Object

Provides ship and shore library service for American-flag merchant vessels, the Military Sealift Command, the U.S. Coast Guard, and other waterborne operations of the U.S. government. Established 1921.

Officers (2004–2005)

Pres. Talmage E. Simpkins; *Chair, Executive Committee* Edward R. Morgan; *V.P.s* John M. Bowers, Capt. Timothy A. Brown, James Capo, David Cockroft, Ron Davis, Capt. Remo Di Fiore, John Halas, Sakae Idemoto, Rene Lioeanjie, Michael R. McKay, George E. Murphy, Capt. Gregorio Oca, Michael Sacco, John J. Sweeney; *Secy.* Donald E. Kadlac; *Treas.* William D. Potts; *Gen. Counsel* John L. DeGurse, Jr.; *Exec. Dir.* Roger T. Korner.

American Society for Information Science and Technology

Executive Director, Richard B. Hill
1320 Fenwick Lane, Ste. 510, Silver Spring, MD 20910
301-495-0900, fax 301-495-0810, e-mail asis@asis.org
World Wide Web http://www.asis.org

Object

The American Society for Information Science and Technology (ASIS&T) provides a forum for the discussion, publication, and critical analysis of work dealing with the design, management, and use of information, information systems, and information technology.

Officers

Pres. Nicholas J. Belkin, Rutgers Univ.; *Pres.-Elect* Michael Leach, Harvard Univ.; *Treas.* June Lester, Oklahoma Univ.; *Past Pres.* Samantha Hastings, Univ. of North Texas.

Address correspondence to the executive director.

Membership

Memb. (Indiv.) 3,500; (Student) 800; (Inst.) 250. Dues (Indiv.) $140; (Student) $40; (Inst.) $650 and $800.

Board of Directors

Dirs.-at-Large Marianne Afifi, Allison Brueckner, Donald Case, Beverly Colby, Vicki Gregory, Gail Hodge, Beata Panagopoulos, Dietmar Wolfram; *Deputy Dirs.* Pascal Calarco, Amy Wallace; *Exec. Dir.* Richard B. Hill.

Publications

Advances in Classification Research, vols. 1–10. Available from Information Today, Inc., 143 Old Marlton Pike, Medford, NJ 08055.

Annual Review of Information Science and Technology. Available from Information Today, Inc.

ASIS Thesaurus of Information Science and Librarianship. Available from Information Today, Inc.

Bulletin of the American Society for Information Science and Technology. Available from ASIS&T.

Editorial Peer Review: Its Strengths and Weaknesses by Ann C. Weller. Available from Information Today, Inc.

Electronic Publishing: Applications and Implications. Eds. Elisabeth Logan and Myke Gluck. Available from Information Today, Inc.

Evaluating Networked Information Services: Techniques, Policy and Issues by Charles R. McClure and John Carlo Bertot. Available from Information Today, Inc.

From Print to Electronic: The Transformation of Scientific Communication. Susan Y. Crawford, Julie M. Hurd, and Ann C. Weller. Available from Information Today, Inc.

Historical Studies in Information Science. Eds. Trudi Bellardo Hahn and Michael Buckland. Available from Information Today, Inc.

Information Management for the Intelligent Organization: The Art of Environmental Scanning, 2nd edition, by Chun Wei Choo, Univ. of Toronto. Available from Information Today, Inc.

Intelligent Technologies in Library and Information Service Applications by F. W. Lancaster and Amy Warner. Available from Information Today, Inc.

Introductory Concepts in Information Science by Melanie J. Norton. Available from Information Today, Inc.

Journal of the American Society for Information Science and Technology. Available from John Wiley and Sons, 605 Third Ave., New York, NY 10016.

Knowledge Management for the Information Professional. Eds. T. Kanti Srikantaiah and Michael Koenig. Available from Information Today, Inc.

Knowledge Management: The Bibliography. Compiled by Paul Burden. Available from Information Today, Inc.

Proceedings of ASIS&T Annual Meetings. Available from Information Today, Inc.

Scholarly Publishing: The Electronic Frontier. Eds. Robin P. Peek and Gregory B. Newby. Available from MIT Press, Cambridge, Massachusetts.

Statistical Methods for the Information Professional by Liwen Vaughan. Available from Information Today, Inc.

Studies in Multimedia. Eds. Susan Stone and Michael Buckland. Based on the Proceedings of the 1991 ASIS Mid-Year Meeting. Available from Information Today, Inc.

The Web of Knowledge: A Festschrift in Honor of Eugene Garfield. Eds. Blaise Cronin and Helen Barsky Atkins. Available from Information Today, Inc.

Committee Chairpersons

Awards and Honors. Stephanie Wright.

Budget and Finance. June Lester.

Constitution and Bylaws. Julian Warner.

Education. Thomas Terrell.

Leadership Development. Penny O'Connor.

Membership. Kris Liberman.

Nominations. Samantha Hastings.

Standards. Gail hornburg.

American Theological Library Association

250 S. Wacker Dr., Ste. 1600, Chicago, IL 60606-5889
Tel. 888-665-2852, 312-454-5100, fax 312-454-5505
E-mail atla@atla.com
World Wide Web http://www.atla.com/atlahome.html

Mission Statement

The mission of the American Theological Library Association (ATLA) is to foster the study of theology and religion by enhancing the development of theological and religious libraries and librarianship. In pursuit of this mission, the association undertakes

- To foster the professional growth of its members, and to enhance their ability to serve their constituencies as administrators and librarians
- To advance the profession of theological librarianship, and to assist theological librarians in defining and interpreting the proper role and function of libraries in theological education
- To promote quality library and information services in support of teaching, learning, and research in theology, religion, and related disciplines and to create such tools and aids (including publications) as may be helpful in accomplishing this
- To stimulate purposeful collaboration among librarians of theological libraries and religious studies collections; and to develop programmatic solutions to information-related problems common to those librarians and collections

Membership

(Inst) 265; (International Inst.) 5; (Indiv.) 632; (affiliates) 62.

Officers (2004–2005)

Pres. Paul F. Stuehrenberg, Divinity Libn., Yale Univ. Divinity School, 409 Prospect St., New Haven, CT 06511. Tel. 203-432-5292, fax 203-432-3906, e-mail paul.stuehrenberg@yale.edu; *V.P.* Christine Wenderoth, Dir., JKM Lib., 1100 E. 55 St., Chicago, IL 60615. Tel. 773-256-0735, fax 773-256-0737, e-mail cwendero@lstc.edu; *Secy.* Anne Womack, Assoc. Dir./Collections Libn., Vanderbilt Univ. Divinity Lib., 419 21st Ave. S., Nashville, TN 37240-0007. Tel. 615-322-2865, fax 615-343-2918, e-mail anne.womack@vanderbilt.edu; *Past Pres.* Paul Schrodt, Libn., John W. Dickhaut Lib., Methodist Theological School in Ohio, 3081 Columbus Pike, Delaware, OH 43015-8004. Tel. 740-362-3435, fax 740-362-3456, e-mail pschrodt@mtso.edu; *Exec. Dir.* Dennis A. Norlin, American Theological Lib. Assn., 250 S. Wacker Drive, Ste. 1600, Chicago, IL 60606-5889. Tel. 312-454-5100, fax 312-454-5505, e-mail dnorlin@atla.com.

Board of Directors

Officers; William B. Badke, Assoc. Canadian Theological Schools Lib.; Duane Harbin, Southern Methodist Univ.; Paula Hayden Hamilton, Sanctuary for Sacred Arts; Timothy D. Lincoln, Austin Presbyterian Theological Seminary; Sara J. Myers, Union Theological Seminary; James C. Pakala, Covenant Theological Seminary; Herman A. Peterson; Sacred Heart Major Seminary; Roberta Schaafsma, Duke Univ. Divinity School Lib.; Sharon A. Taylor, Andover Newton Theological School.

Publications

ATLA Indexes in MARC Format (2 a year).
ATLA Religion Database on CD-ROM, 1949–.
ATLA Religion Database: Ten Year Subset on CD-ROM, 1993–.
Biblical Studies on CD-ROM (ann.).
Catholic Periodical and Literature Index on CD-ROM (ann.).
Index to Book Reviews in Religion (ann.).
Newsletter (q.; memb.; nonmemb. $50). *Ed.* Jonathan West.
Old Testment Abstracts on CD-ROM (ann.).
Proceedings (ann.; memb.; nonmemb. $50). *Ed.* Jonathan West.
Religion Index One: Periodicals (2 a year).
Research in Ministry: An Index to Doctor of Ministry Project Reports (ann.), and online.

Archivists and Librarians in the History of the Health Sciences

President, Lilla Vekerdy
Rare Book Librarian, Bernard Becker Medical Library, Washington University School of Medicine, 660 S. Euclid Ave., St. Louis, MO 63110
314-362-4235, e-mail vekerdyl@wustl.edu
World Wide Web http://www.library.ucla.edu/libraries/biomed/alhhs

Object

This association was established exclusively for educational purposes to serve the professional interests of librarians, archivists, and other specialists actively engaged in the librarianship of the history of the health sciences by promoting the exchange of information and by improving the standards of service.

Membership

Memb. 170. Dues $15 (Americas), $21 (other countries).

Officers (May 2004–May 2005)

Pres. Lilla Vekerdy; *Secy.-Treas.* Micaela Sullivan-Fowler, Libn./Curator, Health Sci-ences Lib., Univ. of Wisconsin, 1305 Linden Dr., Madison, WI 53706. Tel. 608-262-2402, fax 608-262-4732, e-mail micaela@library.wisc.edu; *Past Pres.* Jodi Koste, Archivist, Tompkins-McCaw Lib., Box 980582, Rich-mond, VA 23298-0582. Tel. 804-828-9898, fax 804-828-6089, e-mail jlkoste@vcu.edu.

Publication

The Watermark (q.; memb.). *Co-Eds.* Linda Lohr, History of Medicine Collection, Health Sciences Lib., Univ. of Buffalo, B5 Abbott Hall, 3455 Main St., Buffalo, NY 14214-3002. Tel. 716-829-3900 ext. 136, fax 716-829-2211, e-mail lalohr@buffalo.edu; Eric v.d. Luft, SUNY Upstate Medical Univ., Health Sciences Lib., 766 Irving Ave. Syra-cuse, NY 13210. Tel. 315-464-4585, e-mail lifte@upstate.edu.

ARMA International–The Association for Information Management Professionals

Executive Director/CEO, Peter R. Hermann
13725 W. 109 St., Ste. 101, Lenexa, KS 66215
800-422-2762, 913-341-3808, fax 913-341-3742
E-mail hq@arma.org, World Wide Web http://www.arma.org

Object

To advance the practice of records and information management as a discipline and a profession; to organize and promote programs of research, education, training, and networking within that profession; to support the enhancement of professionalism of the membership; and to promote cooperative endeavors with related professional groups.

Membership

Annual dues $150 for international affiliation. Chapter dues vary. Membership categories are Chapter Member ($150 plus chapter dues), Student Member ($15), and Unaffiliated Member ($150).

Officers (July 2004–June 2005)

Pres. David P. McDermott, J. R. Simplot Co., 5369 Irving St., Boise, ID 83706-1211. Tel. 208-327-3209, fax 208-327-3212, e-mail dave.mcdermott@simplot.com; *Pres.-Elect* Cheryl L. Pederson, Cargill, Inc., Box 5716, Minneapolis, MN 55440-5716. Tel. 952-742-6363, fax 952-742-4467, e-mail cheryl_pederson@cargill.com; *Immediate Past Pres. and Board Chair* Gisele L. Crawford, City of Edmonton, Corp. Records, City Hall, 1 Sir Winston Churchill Sq., Edmonton, AB T5J 2R7, Canada. Tel. 780-496-8001, fax 780-496-7817, e-mail gisele.crawford@edmonton.ca; *Treas.* Fred A. Pulzello, Morgan Stanley, 1633 Broadway, 20th fl., New York, NY 10019. Tel. 212-537-2164, fax 212-507-6979, e-mail fred.pulzello@morganstanley.com; *Dirs.* Sonia A. Black, Carol E. B. Choksy, Patrick Cunningham, William S. Gaskill, Steven Gray, Dianne Hagan, John T. Phillips, Roberta Shaffer, Mary-Ellyn Strauser, Judy Tyler, Richard Weinholdt, Susan B. Whitmire.

Publication

Information Management Journal. Ed. Nikki Swartz.

Art Libraries Society of North America (ARLIS/NA)

Executive Director, Elizabeth Clarke
329 March Rd., Ste. 232, Box 11, Ottawa, ON K2K 2E1, Canada
800-817-0621, fax 613-599-7027
E-mail eclarke@igs.net
World Wide Web http://www.arlisna.org

Object

To foster excellence in art librarianship and visual resources curatorship for the advancement of the visual arts. Established 1972.

Membership

Memb. 1,100. Dues (Inst./Business Affiliate) $145; (Indiv.) $85; (Student) $45; (Retired/Unemployed) $45; (Sustaining) $250; (Sponsor) $500; (Overseas) $65. Year. Jan. 1–Dec. 31. Membership is open to all those interested in visual librarianship, whether they be professional librarians, students, library assistants, art book publishers, art book dealers, art historians, archivists, architects, slide and photograph curators, or retired associates in these fields.

Officers

Pres. Jeanne M. Brown, Head, Architecture Studies Lib., Univ. of Nevada, Las Vegas, Box 45-4049, Las Vegas, NV 89154. Tel. 702-895-4369, fax 702-895-1975, e-mail jbrown@ccmail.nevada.edu; *V.P./Pres.-Elect* Margaret Webster, Dir., Knight Visual Resources Facility, B-56 Sibley Hall, Cornell Univ., Ithaca, NY 14853. Tel. 607-255-3300, fax 607-255-1900, e-mail mnw3@cornell.edu; *Secy.* Judith Herschman, Art Libn., UCLA Arts Lib., 1400 Public Policy, Los Angeles, CA 90095. Tel. 310-206-5426, fax 310-825-1301, e-mail jherschm@library.ucla.edu; *Treas.* Lynda White, Assoc. Dir. of Management Info. Services, Alderman Lib., Univ. of Virginia, P.O. Box 400114, Charlottesville, VA 22904-4114. Tel. 434-924-3240, fax 434-924-1431, e-mail lsw6y@virginia.edu; *Past Pres.* Allen Townsend, Libn., Amon Carter Museum, 3501 Camp Bowie Blvd., Fort Worth, TX 76106. Tel. 817-989-5073, fax 817-989 5079, e-mail allen.townsend@cartermuseum.org; *Assoc. Admin.* Vicky Roper, ARLIS/NA, 329 March Rd., Ste. 232, Box 11, Ottawa, ON K2K 2E1, Canada. Tel. 800-817-0621, fax 613-599-7027, e-mail vicky@mcphersonclarke.com.

Address correspondence to the executive director.

Publications

ARLIS/NA Update (bi-m.; memb.).
Art Documentation (2 a year; memb., subscription).
Handbook and List of Members (ann.; memb.).
Occasional Papers (price varies).
Miscellaneous others (request current list from headquarters).

Committee Chairpersons

AWS Advisory. Lorna Corbetta Noyes.
ARLIS/NA and VRA Joint Summer Educational Institution Implementation. Maureen Burns, Trudy Jacoby.
Awards. Clayton Kirking.
Cataloging (Advisory). Elizabeth O'Keefe.
Development. Kim Collins.
Distinguished Service Award. Lamia Doumato.
Diversity. Miguel Juarez, Shannon Van Kirk.
Finance. Phil Heagy.
International Relations. Daniel Starr.
Membership. Janine Henri.
Gerd Muehsam Award. Jeff Ross.
Nominating. Betsy Peck Learned.
Professional Development. Heather Ball.
Public Policy. D. Vanessa Kam, Cara List.
Publications. Jack Robertson.
Research Awards. Polly Trump, Eric Schwab.

Standards. Ann Whiteside.
Strategic Planning. Leslie Abrams, Lucie Stylianopoulos.
Travel Awards. Kitty Chibnik, Nensi Brailo.

Visual Resources Advisory. Mary S. Wasserman.
George Wittenborn Award. Paula Epstein, Claire Eike.

Asian/Pacific American Librarians Association (APALA)

Executive Director, Ling Hwey Jeng
Professor and Director, School of Library and Information Studies
Texas Woman's University, Denton, Texas
E-mail LingHwey@yahoo.com
World Wide Web http://www.apalaweb.org

Object

To provide a forum for discussing problems and concerns of Asian/Pacific American librarians; to provide a forum for the exchange of ideas by Asian/Pacific American librarians and other librarians; to support and encourage library services to Asian/Pacific American communities; to recruit and support Asian/Pacific American librarians in the library/information science professions; to seek funding for scholarships in library/information science programs for Asian/Pacific Americans; and to provide a vehicle whereby Asian/Pacific American librarians can cooperate with other associations and organizations having similar or allied interests. Founded 1980; incorporated 1981; affiliated with American Library Association 1982.

Membership

Open to all librarians and information specialists of Asian/Pacific descent working in U.S. libraries and information centers and other related organizations, and to others who support the goals and purposes of APALA. Asian/Pacific Americans are defined as those who consider themselves Asian/Pacific Americans. They may be Americans of Asian/Pacific descent, Asian/Pacific people with the status of permanent residency, or Asian/Pacific people living in the United States. Dues (Inst.) $50; (Indiv.) $20; (Students/Unemployed Librarians) $10.

Officers (July 2004–June 2005)

Pres. Heawon Paick. E-mail hwpaick@netscape.net; *V.P./Pres.-Elect* Ganga Dakshinamurti. E-mail ganga_dakshinamurti@umanitoba.ca; *Secy.* Joy Chase. E-mail joy.chase@evc.edu; *Treas.* Buenaventura ("Ven") Basco. E-mail bbasco@mail.ucf.edu; *Past Pres.* Yvonne Chen. E-mail ychen@direcway.com.

Publication

APALA Newsletter (q.). *Ed.* Kenneth Yamashita, Lib. Div. Mgr., Stockton-San Joaquin City Public Lib., 1209 W. Downs St., Stockton, CA 95207.

Committee Chairs

Awards Committee. Dora Ho, Cathy Lu.
Constitution and Bylaws. Thaddeus Bejnar.
Finance. Buenaventura Basco.
Membership and Recruitment. Mohoko Hosoi.
Newsletter and Publications. Kenneth Yamashita.
Nomination. Gary Colmenar.
Program. Heawon Paick.
Publicity. Smiti Gandhi.
Scholarship. Sandy Wee.
Web. May Chang.

AIIM—The Enterprise Content Management Association

President, John F. Mancini
1100 Wayne Ave., Ste. 1100, Silver Spring, MD 20910
800-477-2446, 301-587-8202, fax 301-587-2711
E-mail aiim@aiim.org, World Wide Web http://www.aiim.org
European Office: The IT Centre, 8 Canalside, Lowesmoor Wharf, Worcester WR1 2RR,
England. Tel. 44-1905-727600, fax 44-1905-727609, e-mail info@aiim.org.uk.

Object

AIIM is an international authority on enterprise content management, the tools and technologies that capture, manage, store, preserve, and deliver content in support of business processes. Founded 1943 as the Association for Information and Image Management.

Officers

Chair A. J. Hyland, Hyland Software; *V. Chair* Larry Wischerth, TIAA-CREF; *Treas.* Don McMahan, Fujitsu Computer Products of America; *Past Chair* Martyn Christian, Filenet Corp.

Publication

e-doc Magazine (bi-m.; memb.).

Association for Library and Information Science Education

Executive Director, Deborah York
1009 Commerce Park Drive, Ste. 150, Oak Ridge, TN 37839
Tel. 865-425-0155, fax 865-481-0390, e-mail contact@alise.org
World Wide Web http://www.alise.org

Object

The Association for Library and Information Science Education (ALISE) is devoted to the advancement of knowledge and learning in the interdisciplinary field of information studies. Established 1915.

Membership

Memb. 500. Any library/information science school with a program accredited by the ALA Committee on Accreditation may become an institutional member. Any school that offers a graduate degree in librarianship or a cognate field but whose program is not accredited by the ALA Committee on Accreditation may become an institutional member at a lower rate. Any school outside the United States and Canada offering a program comparable to that of institutional membership may become an international affiliate institutional member. Any organizational entity wishing to support LIS education may become an associate institutional member. Any faculty member, administrator, librarian, researcher, or other individual employed full time may become a personal member. Any retired or part-time faculty member, student, or other individual employed less than full time may become a personal member. Any student may become a member at a lower rate.

Officers (2005–2006)

Pres. Ken Haycock, Univ. of British Columbia. E-mail ken@kenhaycock.com; *Pres.-Elect* John Budd, Univ. of Missouri–Columbia. E-mail buddj@missouri.edu; *Secy.-Treas.* James A. Benson, St. John's

Univ. E-mail bensonj@stjohns.edu; *Past Pres.* Louise S. Robbins, Univ. of Wisconsin–Madison. E-mail lrobbins@slis.wisc.edu.

Directors

Officers; Linda C. Smith, Univ. of Illinois, Urbana-Champaign; Gloria Leckie, Univ. of Western Ontario; Heidi Julian, Univ. of Alberta.

Publications

ALISE Library and Information Science Education Statistical Report (ann.; $65).
Journal of Education for Library and Information Science (4 a year; $150; foreign $175).
Membership Directory (ann.; $25).

Committee Chairpersons

Awards and Honors. Alvin Schrader.
Budget and Finance. James Benson.
Conference Planning. Connie Van Fleet, Julie Hersberger.
Governance. Louise Robbins.
Government Relations. David Fenske.
International Relations. Prudence Dalrymple.
Membership. Sydney Pierce.
Nominating. Stephen Bajjlay.
Publications. Christine Pawley.
Recruitment. Lorna Peterson.
Research. Lynne McKechnie.

Association of Academic Health Sciences Libraries

Executive Director, Shirley Bishop
2150 N. 107 St., Ste. 205, Seattle, WA 98133
206-367-8704, fax 206-367-8777
E-mail aahsl@shirleybishopinc.com.
World Wide Web http://www.aahsl.org

Object

The Association of Academic Health Sciences Libraries (AAHSL) is composed of the directors of libraries of more than 140 accredited U.S. and Canadian medical schools belonging to the Association of American Medical Colleges. Its goals are to promote excellence in academic health science libraries and to ensure that the next generation of health practitioners is trained in information-seeking skills that enhance the quality of healthcare delivery, education, and research. Founded 1977.

Membership

Memb. 140+. Regular membership is available to nonprofit educational institutions operating a school of health sciences that has full or provisional accreditation by the Association of American Medical Colleges. Regular members shall be represented by the chief administrative officer of the member institution's health sciences library. Associate membership (and nonvoting representation) is available at $600 to organizations having an interest in the purposes and activities of the association.

Officers (2004–2005)

Pres. J. Michael Homan, Mayo Medical Lib., Mayo Foundation; *Pres.-Elect* Logan Ludwig, Medical Center Lib., Loyola Univ.; *Secy.-Treas.* Ruth Riley, School of Medicine Lib., Univ. of South Carolina; *Past Pres.* J. Roger Guard, Medical Center Academic Info. Technology and Libs., Univ. of Cincinnati.

Association of Independent Information Professionals (AIIP)

8550 United Plaza Blvd., Ste. 1001, Baton Rouge, LA 70809
225-408-4400, fax 225-922-4611, e-mail info@aiip.org
World Wide Web http://www.aiip.org

Object

AIIP's members are owners of firms providing such information-related services as online and manual research, document delivery, database design, library support, consulting, writing, and publishing. The objectives of the association are

- To advance the knowledge and understanding of the information profession
- To promote and maintain high professional and ethical standards among its members
- To encourage independent information professionals to assemble to discuss common issues
- To promote the interchange of information among independent information professionals and various organizations
- To keep the public informed of the profession and of the responsibilities of the information professional

Membership

Memb. 700+.

Officers (2004–2005)

Pres. Mary Ellen Bates, Bates Information Services. Tel. 303-444-0506, e-mail mbates @BatesInfo.com; *Pres.-Elect* Jodi Gregory, Access Information Services. Tel. 937-439-0418, e-mail access@access-inform.com; *Secy.* Debbie Wynot, Library Consultants. Tel. 504-885-5926; *Treas.* Theresa Buiel, ThinkLink. Tel. 781-963-2251; *Past Pres.* Cindy Shamel, Shamel Information Services. Tel. 858-673-467 e-mail cshamel@shamel info.com.

Publications

Connections (q.).
Membership Directory (ann.).
Professional Paper series.

Association of Jewish Libraries (AJL)

c/o NFJC, 330 Seventh Ave., 21st fl., New York, NY 10001
212-725-5359, e-mail ajlibs@osu.edu
World Wide Web http://www.jewishlibraries.org

Object

Mission

The Association of Jewish Libraries promotes Jewish literacy through enhancement of libraries and library resources and through leadership for the profession and practitioners of Judaica librarianship. The association fosters access to information, learning, teaching, and research relating to Jews, Judaism, the Jewish experience, and Israel.

Goals

• Maintain high professional standards for Judaica librarians and recruit qualified individuals into the profession

• Facilitate communication and exchange of information on a global scale

• Encourage quality publication in the field in all formats and media

• Stimulate publication of high-quality children's literature

• Facilitate and encourage establishment of Judaica library collections

• Enhance information access for all through application of advanced technologies

• Publicize the organization and its activities in all relevant venues

• Stimulate awareness of Judaica library services among the public at large

• Promote recognition of Judaica librarianship within the wider library profession

• Encourage recognition of Judaica library services by other organizations and related professions

• Ensure continuity of the association through sound management, financial security, effective governance, and a dedicated and active membership

Membership

Memb. 1,400. Dues $50; (Student/Retired) $30. Year. July 1–June 30.

Officers (June 2004–June 2006)

Pres. Ronda Rose, Kosofsky Lib., Temple Emanuel, Beverly Hills; *V.P./Pres.-Elect* Laurel Wolfson, Hebrew Union College; *V.P. Memb.* Joseph Galron, Ohio State Univ., Columbus; *V.P. Publications* Elana Gensler, Hebrew Academy of Long Beach (New York); *Treas.* Schlomit Schwartzer, Univ. of Miami; *Recording Secy.* Susan Dubin, Off-the-Shelf Lib. Services; *Corresponding Secy.* Noreen Wachs, Ramaz Middle School, New York; *Past Pres.* Pearl Berger, Yeshiva Univ. Libs., New York.

Address correspondence to the association.

Publications

AJL Newsletter (q.). *Eds.* Libby K. White. Baltimore Hebrew Univ., 5800 Park Heights Ave., Baltimore, MD 21215

Judaica Librarianship (irreg.). *Ed.* Zachary M. Baker, Area Studies Resource Group, Green Lib., Stanford Univ., 557 Escondido Mall, Stanford, CA 94305.

Division Presidents

Research and Special Library. Peggy Pearlstein, Lib. of Congress.

Synagogue, School, and Center Libraries. Linda R. Silver, Jewish Education Center of Cleveland.

Association of Research Libraries

Executive Director, Duane E. Webster
21 Dupont Circle N.W., Ste. 800, Washington, DC 20036
202-296-2296, fax 202-872-0884
E-mail arlhq@arl.org, World Wide Web http://www.arl.org

Object

The mission of the Association of Research Libraries (ARL) is to shape and influence forces affecting the future of research libraries in the process of scholarly communication. ARL's programs and services promote equitable access to and effective use of recorded knowledge in support of teaching, research, scholarship, and community service. The association articulates the concerns of research libraries and their institutions, forges coalitions, influences information policy development, and supports innovation and improvement in research library operations. ARL is a not-for-profit membership organization comprising the libraries of North American research institutions and operates as a forum for the exchange of ideas and as an agent for collective action.

Membership

Memb. 123. Membership is institutional. Dues $20,150 for 2005.

Officers

Pres. Ann Wolpert, MIT; *V.P./Pres.-Elect* Brian E. C. Schottlaender, Univ. of California–San Diego; *Past Pres.* Sarah Thomas, Cornell.

Board of Directors

Camila Alire, Univ. of New Mexico; Joyce Garnett, Univ. of Western Ontario; Marianne Gaunt, Rutgers Univ.; Fred Heath, Univ. of Texas; Tom Leonard, Univ. of California–Berkeley; Rush Miller, Univ. of Pittsburgh; Sherrie Schmidt, Arizona State Univ.; Brian Schottlaender, Univ. of California–San Diego; Sarah Thomas, Cornell; Suzanne Thorin, Indiana Univ.; Paul Willis, Univ. of South Carolina; Betsy Wilson, Univ. of Washington; Ann Wolpert, MIT.

Publications

ARL: A Bimonthly Report on Research Libraries Issues and Actions from ARL, CNI, and SPARC (bi-m.).
ARL Academic Law and Medical Library Statistics (ann.).
ARL Annual Salary Survey (ann.).
ARL Preservation Statistics (ann.).
ARL Statistics (ann.).
ARL Supplementary Statistics (ann.).
SPEC Kits (6 a year).

Committee and Work Group Chairpersons

AAU/ARL Global Resources Program Advisory Committee. Barbara Allen, CIC.
Collections and Access Issues. Alice Prochaska, Yale.
Diversity. Barbara Dewey, Tennessee.
Finance. Fred Heath, Texas at Austin.
Information Policies. Lance Query, Tulane.
Intellectual Property and Copyright. Winston Tabb, Johns Hopkins.
Membership. Paula Kaufman, Illinois at Urbana-Champaign.
Preservation of Research Library Materials. William Gosling, Michigan.
Research Library Leadership and Management. Camila Alire, New Mexico.
Scholarly Communication. Carol Mandel, New York.
SPARC Steering Committee. James Neal, Columbia.
Special Collections Task Force. Joe Hewitt, Univ. of North Carolina.

Statistics and Measurement. Brinley Franklin, Univ. of Connecticut.

Working Group on Digitizing Government Document Collections. Kenneth Frazier, Wisconsin–Madison.

ARL Membership

Nonuniversity Libraries

Boston Public Lib., Canada Inst. for Scientific and Technical Info., Center for Research Libs., Lib. of Congress, National Agricultural Lib., National Lib. of Canada, National Lib. of Medicine, New York Public Lib., New York State Lib., Smithsonian Institution Libs.

University Libraries

Alabama, Alberta, Arizona, Arizona State, Auburn, Boston College, Boston Univ., Brigham Young, British Columbia, Brown, California–Berkeley, California–Davis, California–Irvine, California–Los Angeles, California–Riverside, California–San Diego, California–Santa Barbara, Case Western Reserve, Chicago, Cincinnati, Colorado, Colorado State, Columbia, Connecticut, Cornell, Dartmouth, Delaware, Duke, Emory, Florida, Florida State, George Washington, Georgetown, Georgia, Georgia Inst. of Technology, Guelph, Harvard, Hawaii, Houston, Howard, Illinois–Chicago, Illinois–Urbana-Champaign, Indiana, Iowa, Iowa State, Johns Hopkins, Kansas, Kent State, Kentucky, Laval, Louisiana State, Louisville, McGill, McMaster, Manitoba, Maryland, Massachusetts, Massachusetts Inst. of Technology, Miami (Florida), Michigan, Michigan State, Minnesota, Missouri, Montreal, Nebraska–Lincoln, New Mexico, New York, North Carolina, North Carolina State, Northwestern, Notre Dame, Ohio, Ohio State, Oklahoma, Oklahoma State, Oregon, Pennsylvania, Pennsylvania State, Pittsburgh, Princeton, Purdue, Queen's (Kingston, Ontario, Canada), Rice, Rochester, Rutgers, Saskatchewan, South Carolina, Southern California, Southern Illinois, SUNY–Albany, SUNY–Buffalo, SUNY–Stony Brook, Syracuse, Temple, Tennessee, Texas, Texas A&M, Texas Tech, Toronto, Tulane, Utah, Vanderbilt, Virginia, Virginia Tech, Washington, Washington (Saint Louis, Missouri), Washington State, Waterloo, Wayne State, Western Ontario, Wisconsin, Yale, York.

Association of Vision Science Librarians

Chair 2004–2005, Elaine Wells
SUNY College of Optometry, Harold Kohn Vision Lib.,
33 W. 42 St., New York, NY 10036-8003
Tel. 212-780-5086, e-mail ewells@sunyopt.edu
World Wide Web http://spectacle.berkeley.edu/~library/AVSL.HTM

Object

To foster collective and individual acquisition and dissemination of vision science information, to improve services for all persons seeking such information, and to develop standards for libraries to which members are attached. Founded 1968.

Membership

Memb. (U.S.) 85; (Foreign) 35.

Publications

Core List of Audio-Visual Related Serials.
Guidelines for Vision Science Libraries.

Opening Day Book, Journal and AV Collection—Visual Science.
Ph.D. Theses in Physiological Optics (irreg.).
Publication Considerations in the Age of Electronic Opportunities.
Standards for Vision Science Libraries.
Union List of Vision-Related Serials (irreg.).

Meetings

Annual meeting held in December in connection with the American Academy of Optometry; midyear mini-meeting with the Medical Library Association.

Beta Phi Mu
(International Library and Information Studies Honor Society)

Executive Director, Wayne Wiegand
College of Information, Florida State University, Tallahassee, FL 32306-2100
850-644-3907, fax 850-644-9763
E-mail beta_phi_mu@lis.fsu.edu
World Wide Web http://www.beta-phi-mu.org

Object

To recognize and encourage scholastic achievement among library and information studies students and to sponsor appropriate professional and scholarly projects. Founded at the University of Illinois in 1948.

Membership

Memb. 23,000. Open to graduates of library school programs accredited by the American Library Association who fulfill the following requirements: complete the course requirements leading to a fifth year or other advanced degree in librarianship with a scholastic average of 3.75 where A equals 4 points (this provision shall also apply to planned programs of advanced study beyond the fifth year that do not culminate in a degree but that require full-time study for one or more academic years) and in the top 25 percent of their class; receive a letter of recommendation from their respective library schools attesting to their demonstrated fitness for successful professional careers.

Officers

Pres. Michael Havener, Graduate School of Lib. and Info. Studies, Rodman Hall, Univ. of Rhode Island, 94 W. Alumni Ave., Ste. 2, Kingston, RI 02881. Tel. 401-874-4641, fax 401-874-4964, e-mail mhavener@uri.edu; *V.P./Pres.-Elect* Anna Perrault, Univ. of South Florida, 4202 Fowler Ave. E., CIS 1040, Tampa, FL 33620-7800; *Treas.* Robin Gault, College of Law Lib., Florida State Univ., Tallahassee, FL 32306-1600. Tel. 850-644-7487, fax 850-644-5216, e-mail rgault@law.fsu.edu; *Exec. Dir.* Wayne Wiegand, College of Information, Florida State Univ., Tallahassee, FL 32306-2100. Tel. 850-644-3907, fax 850-644-9763, e-mail beta_phi_mu@lis.fsu.edu.

Directors

Susan M. Agent, Nicholas C. Burckel, Michael Carpenter, Timothy Sineath, Sue Stroyan, Danny P. Wallace, Blanche Woolls.

Publications

Beta Phi Mu Monograph Series. Book-length scholarly works based on original research in subjects of interest to library and information professionals. Available from Greenwood Press, 88 Post Rd. W., Box 5007, Westport, CT 06881-9990.

Chapbook Series. Limited editions on topics of interest to information professionals. Call Beta Phi Mu for availability.

Newsletter. (2 a year). *Ed.* Lynne Barrett.

Chapters

Alpha. Univ. of Illinois, Grad. School of Lib. and Info. Science; *Beta.* (Inactive). Univ. of Southern California, School of Lib. Science; *Gamma.* Florida State Univ., School of Lib. and Info. Studies; *Delta* (Inactive). Loughborough College of Further Educ., School of Libnship., Loughborough, England; *Epsilon.* Univ. of North Carolina, School of Lib. Science; *Zeta.* Atlanta Univ., School of Lib. and Info. Studies; *Theta.* Pratt Inst., Grad. School of Lib. and Info. Science; *Iota.* Catholic Univ. of America, School of Lib. and Info. Science; Univ. of Maryland, College of Lib. and Info. Services; *Kappa.* (Inactive). Western Michigan Univ., School of Libnship.; *Lambda.* Univ. of Oklahoma, School of Lib. Science; *Mu.* Univ. of Michigan, School of Lib. Science; *Xi.* Univ. of Hawaii, Grad. School of Lib. Studies; *Omicron.* Rutgers Univ., Grad. School of Lib. and Info. Studies; *Pi.* Univ. of Pittsburgh, School of Lib. and Info. Science; *Rho.* Kent State Univ., School of Lib. Science; *Sigma.* Drexel Univ., School of Lib. and Info. Science; *Tau.* (Inactive). State Univ. of New York at Genesee, School of Lib. and Info. Science; *Upsilon.* (Inactive). Univ. of Kentucky, College of Lib. Science; *Phi.* Univ. of Denver, Grad. School of Libnship. and Info. Mgt.; *Chi.* Indiana Univ., School of Lib. and Info. Science; *Psi.* Univ. of Missouri at Columbia, School of Lib. and Info. Sciences; *Omega.* (Inactive). San Jose State Univ., Div. of Lib. Science; *Beta Alpha.* Queens College, City College of New York, Grad. School of Lib. and Info. Studies; *Beta. Simmons College, Grad. School of Lib. and Info. Science; *Beta Delta.* State Univ. of New York at Buffalo, School of Info. and Lib. Studies; *Beta Epsilon.* Emporia State Univ., School of Lib. Science; *Beta Zeta.* Louisiana State Univ., Grad. School of Lib. Science; *Beta Eta.* Univ. of Texas at Austin, Grad. School of Lib. and Info. Science; *Beta Theta.* (Inactive). Brigham Young Univ., School of Lib. and Info. Science; *Beta Iota.* Univ. of Rhode Island, Grad. Lib. School; *Beta Kappa.* Univ. of Alabama, Grad. School of Lib. Service; *Beta Lambda.* North Texas State Univ., School of Lib. and Info. Science; Texas Woman's Univ., School of Lib. Science; *Beta Mu.* Long Island Univ., Palmer Grad. Lib. School; *Beta Nu.* Saint John's Univ., Div. of Lib. and Info. Science; *Beta Xi.* North Carolina Central Univ., School of Lib. Science; *Beta Omicron.* (Inactive). Univ. of Tennessee at Knoxville, Grad. School of Lib. and Info. Science; *Beta Pi.* Univ. of Arizona, Grad. Lib. School; *Beta Rho.* Univ. of Wisconsin at Milwaukee, School of Lib. Science; *Beta Sigma.* (Inactive). Clarion State College, School of Lib. Science; *Beta Tau.* Wayne State Univ., Div. of Lib. Science; *Beta Upsilon.* (Inactive). Alabama A&M Univ., School of Lib. Media; *Beta Phi.* Univ. of South Florida, Grad. Dept. of Lib., Media, and Info. Studies; *Beta Psi.* Univ. of Southern Mississippi, School of Lib. Service; *Beta Omega.* Univ. of South Carolina, College of Libnship.; *Beta Beta Alpha.* Univ. of California at Los Angeles, Grad. School of Lib. and Info. Science; *Beta Beta Gamma.* Rosary College, Grad. School of Lib. and Info. Science; *Beta Beta Delta.* Univ. of Cologne, Germany; *Beta Beta Epsilon.* Univ. of Wisconsin at Madison, Lib. School; *Beta Beta Zeta.* Univ. of North Carolina at Greensboro, Dept. of Lib. Science and Educational Technology; *Beta Beta Theta.* Univ. of Iowa, School of Lib. and Info. Science; *Beta Beta Iota.* State Univ. of New York, Univ. at Albany, School of Info. Science and Policy; *Beta Beta Kappa.* Univ. of Puerto Rico Grad. School of Info. Sciences and Technologies; *Pi Lambda Sigma.* Syracuse Univ., School of Info. Studies.

Bibliographical Society of America

Executive Secretary, Michele E. Randall
Box 1537, Lenox Hill Station, New York, NY 10021
212-452-2710 (tel./fax), e-mail bsa@bibsocamer.org
World Wide Web http://www.bibsocamer.org

Object

To promote bibliographical research and to issue bibliographical publications. Organized 1904.

Membership

Memb. 1,200. Dues $65. Year. Jan.–Dec.

Officers

Pres. John Bidwell. E-mail jbidwell@morgan library.org; *V.P.* Irene Tichenor. E-mail itichenor@earthlink.net; *Treas.* R. Dyke Benjamin. E-mail dyke.benjamin@lazard.com; *Secy.* Christine A. Ruggere. E-mail ruggere@jhmi.edu.

Council

(2005) William Baker, Patricia Fleming, James May, Deirdre C. Stam; (2006) Susan M. Allen, John N. Hoover, Mark S. Lasner, Bruce Whiteman; (2007) Eric Holzenberg, Hope Mayo, Justin G. Schiller, Arthur L. Schwarz.

Publication

Papers of the Bibliographical Society of America (q.; memb.). *Ed.* Trevor Howard-Hill, Thomas Cooper Lib., Univ. of South Carolina, Columbia, SC 29208. Tel./fax 803-777-7046, e-mail RalphCrane@msn.com.

Canadian Association for Information Science (CAIS) (Association Canadienne des Sciences de l'Information)

Dalhousie University, School of Lib. and Info. Studies
Halifax, NS B3H 3J5, Canada
902-494-2473, fax 902-494-2451

Object

To promote the advancement of information science in Canada and encourage and facilitate the exchange of information relating to the use, access, retrieval, organization, management, and dissemination of information.

Membership

Institutions and individuals interested in information science and involved in the gathering, organization, and dissemination of information (such as information scientists, archivists, librarians, computer scientists, documentalists, economists, educators, journalists, and psychologists) who support CAIS's objectives can become association members.

Dues (Inst.) $165; (Personal) $75; (Senior) $40; (Student) $25.

Directors

Pres. Louise Spiteri, Dalhousie Univ.; *V.P.*
Lynne Howarth, Univ. of Toronto; *Past Pres.*
France Bouthillier, McGill Univ.; *Treas.*
Donna Chan, Univ. of Western Ontario; *Dir.,*
Communications Haidar Moukdad, Dalhousie
Univ.; *Dir., Membership* Rick Kopak, Univ.

of British Columbia; *Secy.* Kimiz Dalkir,
McGill Univ.

Publication

Canadian Journal of Information and Library
Science

Canadian Library Association (CLA)

Executive Director, Don Butcher
328 Frank St., Ottawa, ON K2P 0X8
613-232-9625 ext. 306, fax 613-563-9895
E-mail dbutcher@cla.ca, World Wide Web http://cla.ca

Object

To promote, develop, and support library and
information services in Canada and to work
in cooperation with all who share our values
in order to present a unified voice on issues
of mutual concern. The association represents
the Canadian library and information community to the federal government and related
commissions, carries on international liaison
with other library associations, offers professional development programs, and supports
library services and intellectual freedom.
Founded in 1946, CLA is a nonprofit voluntary organization governed by an elected
executive council.

Membership

Memb. (Indiv.) 2,200; (Inst.) 450. Open to
individuals, institutions, and groups interested in librarianship and in library and information services.

Officers

Pres. Stephen Abram, V.P., Corporate Devel-
opment, Sirsi Corp.; *V.P./Pres.-Elect* Barbara
Clubb, Chief Libn., Ottawa Public Lib.;
Treas. A. A. "Sandy" Cameron, Dir., Regina
Public Lib.

Publication

Feliciter: Linking Canada's Information Pro-
fessionals (6 a year; newsletter).

Divisions

Canadian Association of College and Univer-
sity Libraries (CACUL).
Canadian Association of Public Libraries
(CAPL).
Canadian Association of Special Libraries
and Information Services (CASLIS).
Canadian Library Trustees' Association
(CLTA).
Canadian Assn. for School Libs. (CASL).

Catholic Library Association

Executive Director, Jean R. Bostley, SSJ
100 North St., Ste. 224, Pittsfield, MA 01201-5109
413-443-2252, fax 413-442-2252, e-mail cla@cathla.org
World Wide Web http://www.cathla.org

Object

The promotion and encouragement of Catholic literature and library work through cooperation, publications, education, and information. Founded 1921.

Membership

Memb. 1,000. Dues $45–$300. Year. July–June.

Officers (2003–2005)

Pres. M. Dorothy Neuhofer, OSB, St. Leo Univ., Box 6665 MC 2128, Saint Leo, FL 33574-6665. Tel. 352-588-8260, fax 352-588-8484, e-mail dorothy.neuhofer@saint leo.edu; *V.P./Pres.-Elect* Kenneth O'Malley, CP, Paul Bechtold Lib., Catholic Theological Union, 5401 S. Cornell Ave., Chicago, IL 60615-5698. Tel. 772-753-5322, fax 773-753-5440, e-mail omalleyk@ctu.lib.il.us; *Past Pres.* Sally Anne Thompson, Pope John XXIII Catholic School Community, 16235 N. 60 St., Scottsdale, AZ 85254-7323. Tel. 480-905-0939, fax 480-905-0955, e-mail desertsat @aol.com.

Address correspondence to the executive director.

Executive Board

Officers; Kathy C. Born, 1120 Hickory Lake Dr., Cincinnati, OH 45233. E-mail kathyborn @peoplepc.com; John R. Edson, Hamburg Public Lib., 102 Buffalo St., Hamburg, NY 14075; Anne LeVeque, U.S. Conference of Catholic Bishops, 3211 4th St. N.E., Washington, DC 20017. E-mail aleveque@usccb. org; Maxine C. Lucas, St. Mel School, 20874 Ventura Blvd., Woodland Hills, CA 91364. E-mail maxine.lucas@gte.net; Nancy K. Schmidtmann, 174 Theodore Dr., Coram, NY 11727. E-mail natopolo@yahoo.com; Cecil R. White, St. Patrick's Seminary, 320 Middlefield Rd., Menlo Park, CA 94025. E-mail stpats@ix.netcom.com.

Publications

Catholic Library World (q.; memb.; nonmemb. $60). *General Ed.* Mary E. Gallagher, SSJ; *Production Ed.* Allen Gruenke.
Catholic Periodical and Literature Index (*CLPI*) (q.; $400 calendar year; abridged ed., $125 calendar year; *CPLI* on CD-ROM, inquire). *Ed.* Kathleen Spaltro.

Chief Officers of State Library Agencies (COSLA)

167 W. Main St., Ste. 600, Lexington, KY 40507
859-231-1925, fax 859-231-1928, e-mail ttucker@amrinc.net

Object

To provide a means of cooperative action among its state and territorial members, to strengthen the work of the respective state and territorial agencies, and to provide a continuing mechanism for dealing with the problems faced by the heads of these agencies, which are responsible for state and territorial library development.

Membership

COSLA is an independent organization of the men and women who head the state and territorial agencies responsible for library development. Its membership consists solely of the top library officers of the 50 states, the District of Columbia, and the territories, variously designated as state librarian, director, commissioner, or executive secretary.

Officers (2004–2006)

Pres. GladysAnn Wells, Dir., State Lib. of Arizona, State Capitol, 1700 W. Washington, Rm. 200, Phoenix, AZ 85007. Tel. 602-542-4035, fax 602-542-4972, e-mail gawells@lib.az.us; *V.P./Pres.-Elect* J. Gary Nichols, State Libn., Maine State Lib., 64 State House Sta., Augusta, ME 04333. Tel. 207-287-5600, fax 207-287-5615, e-mail gary.nichols@state.me.us; *Secy.* Michael York, State Libn., New Hampshire State Lib., 20 Park St., Concord, NH 03301-6316. Tel. 603-271-2392, fax 603-271-6826, e-mail myork@library.state.nh.us; *Treas.* Peggy D Rudd, Dir. and Libn., Texas Lib. and Archives Commission, P.O. Box 12927, Austin, TX 78711-2927. Tel. 512-463-5460, fax 512-463-5436, e-mail prudd@tsl.state.tx.us; *Past Pres.* Karen Crane, Dir., Alaska Libs., Archives and Museums, Box 110571, Juneau, AK 99811-0571. Tel. 907-465-2910, fax 907-465-2151, e-mail karen_crane@eed.state.ak.us; *Dirs.* Christie Pearson Brandau, State Libn., State of Michigan, P.O. Box 30007, Lansing, MI 48909-7507. Tel. 517-373-5504, fax 517-373-4480, e-mail cbrandau@michigan.gov; Susan McVey, Dir., State of Oklahoma Dept. of Libs., 200 N.E. 18 St., Oklahoma City, OK 73105-3298. Tel. 405-521-3173, fax 405-525-7804, e-mail smcvey@oltn.odl.state.ok.us.

Chinese American Librarians Association (CALA)

Executive Director, Sally C. Tseng
949-552-5615, fax 949-857-1988, e-mail sctseng888@yahoo.com
World Wide Web http://www.cala-web.org

Object

To enhance communications among Chinese American librarians as well as between Chinese American librarians and other librarians; to serve as a forum for discussion of mutual problems and professional concerns among Chinese American librarians; to promote Sino-American librarianship and library services; and to provide a vehicle whereby Chinese American librarians may cooperate with other associations and organizations having similar or allied interests.

Membership

Memb. 770. Open to anyone who is interested in the association's goals and activities. Dues (regular) $30; (international/student/nonsalaried) $15; (inst.) $100; (life) $400.

Officers

Pres. Shixing Wen. E-mail shwen@umich. edu; *V.P./Pres.-Elect* Diana Wu. E-mail diana.wu@sjsu.edu; *Treas.* Dora Ho. E-mail doraho@yahoo.com; *Past Pres.* Amy Tsiang. E-mail ctsiang@library.ucla.edu; *Exec. Dir.* Sally C. Tseng. E-mail sctseng888@yahoo. com.

Publications

Journal of Library and Information Science (2 a year; memb.; nonmemb. $15). *Ed.* Zhijia Shen. E-mail shen@colorado.edu.

Membership Directory (memb.).
Newsletter (3 a year; memb.; nonmemb. $10). *Ed.* Jian Liu. E-mail jiliu@Indiana. edu.

Committee Chairpersons

Awards. Ying Zhang.
Conference Program Committee. Diana Wu.
Conference Local Arrangements. Connie Qing Kong Haley.
Constitution and Bylaws. Xiaoyin Zhang.
Finance. Esther Lee.
International Relations. Guoqing Li.
Joint Conference of Librarians of Color (JCLC). Liana Hong Zhou, Linna Yu.
Membership. Jian Anna Xiong.
Mentorship Task Force. Vickie Doll.
Nominating. Amy Tsiang.
Public Relations and Fund Raising. Lisa Zhao.
Publications. Haipeng Li.
Scholarships. Shali Zhang.
Sally C. Tseng Professional Development Grant. Manuel Urrizola, Ying Xu.
Webmaster. Shixing Wen.

Chapter Presidents

California. Diane Lai.
Florida. Dongmei Cao.
Greater Mid-Atlantic. Anna Ho.
Midwest. Xudong Jin.
Northeast. Chi-chun Hsieh.
Southwest. Peyyi Wann.

Church and Synagogue Library Association (CSLA)

Box 19357, Portland, OR 97280-0357
503-244-6919, 800-542-2752, fax 503-977-3734
E-mail CSLA@worldaccessnet.com
World Wide Web http://www.worldaccessnet.com/~CSLA

Object

To act as a unifying core for the many existing church and synagogue libraries; to provide the opportunity for a mutual sharing of practices and problems; to inspire and encourage a sense of purpose and mission among church and synagogue librarians; to study and guide the development of church and synagogue librarianship toward recognition as a formal branch of the library profession. Founded 1967.

Membership

Memb. 1,800. Dues (Inst.) $175; (Affiliated) $70; (Church/Synagogue) $45 ($50 foreign); (Indiv.) $25 ($30 foreign). Year. Jan.–Dec.

Officers (July 2004–July 2005)

Pres. Rod McClendon; *Pres.-Elect* Evelyn Pockrass; *2nd V.P.* Craig Kubic; *Treas.* Warren Livingston; *Admin.* Judith Janzen; *Past Pres.* Naomi Kauffman; *Ed., Church and Synagogue Libraries* Karen Bota, 490 N. Fox Hills Dr., No. 7, Bloomfield Hills, MI 48304; *Book Review Ed.* Monica Tenney, 399 Blenheim Rd., Columbus, OH 43214-3219. E-mail motenney@aol.com.

Executive Board

Officers; committee chairpersons.

Publications

Bibliographies (1–5; price varies).
Church and Synagogue Libraries (bi-mo.; memb.; nonmemb. $35; Canada $45).
CSLA Guides (1–20; price varies).

Committee Chairpersons

Awards. Curtis Howard.
Conference. Naomi Kauffman, Rod McClendon.
Library Services. Judy Livingston.
Nominations and Elections. Marjorie Smink.
Publications. Alice Hamilton.

Coalition for Networked Information

Executive Director, Clifford A. Lynch
21 Dupont Circle, Ste. 800, Washington, DC 20036
202-296-5098, fax 202-872-0884
E-mail info@cni.org, World Wide Web http://www.cni.org

Mission

The Coalition for Networked Information (CNI) is an organization to advance the transformative promise of networked information technology for the advancement of scholarly communication and the enrichment of intellectual productivity.

Membership

Memb. 203. Membership is institutional. Dues $5,800. Year. July–June.

Officers (July 2004–June 2005)

Duane Webster, Exec. Dir., Association of Research Libraries; Brian L. Hawkins, Pres., EDUCAUSE.

Steering Committee

Richard P. West, California State Univ. (*Chair*); Daniel E. Atkins, Univ. of Michigan; Nancy Eaton, Pennsylvania State Univ.; Brian L. Hawkins, EDUCAUSE; Vace Kundakci, Columbia Univ.; Clifford Lynch, CNI; Susan Lane Perry, Andrew W. Mellon Foundation and Council on Lib. and Info. Resources; Donald J. Waters, Andrew W. Mellon Foundation; Duane Webster, ARL; Ann J. Wolpert, MIT.

Publication

CNI-Announce (subscribe by e-mail to cni-announce-subscribe@cni.org).

Council on Library and Information Resources

1755 Massachusetts Ave. N.W., Ste. 500, Washington, DC 20036-2124
202-939-4750, fax 202-939-4765
World Wide Web http://www.clir.org

Object

In 1997 the Council on Library Resources (CLR) and the Commission on Preservation and Access (CPA) merged and became the Council on Library and Information Resources (CLIR). CLIR's mission is to expand access to information, however recorded and preserved, as a public good. CLIR is an independent, nonprofit organization. CLIR identifies and defines the key emerging issues related to the welfare of libraries and the constituencies they serve, convenes the leaders who can influence change, and promotes collaboration among the institutions and organizations that can achieve change. The council's interests embrace the entire range of information resources and services from traditional library and archival materials to emerging digital formats. It assumes a particular interest in helping institutions cope with the accelerating pace of change associated with the transition into the digital environment.

CLIR is an independent nonprofit organization. While maintaining appropriate collaboration and liaison with other institutions and organizations, the council operates independently of any particular institutional or vested interests.

Through the composition of its board, it brings the broadest possible perspective to bear upon defining and establishing the priority of the issues with which it is concerned.

Board

CLIR's Board of Directors currently has 16 members.

Officers

Chair Charles Phelps; *Pres.* Nancy A. Davenport. E-mail ndavenport@CLIR.org; *Treas.* Herman Pabbruwe.

Address correspondence to headquarters.

Publications

Annual Report.
CLIR Issues (bi-mo.).
Technical reports.

Federal Library and Information Center Committee

Executive Director, Susan M. Tarr
Library of Congress, Washington, DC 20540-4935
202-707-4800
World Wide Web http://www.loc.gov/flicc

Object

The Federal Library and Information Center Committee (FLICC) makes recommendations on federal library and information policies, programs, and procedures to federal agencies and to others concerned with libraries and information centers. The committee coordinates cooperative activities and services among federal libraries and information centers and serves as a forum to consider issues and policies that affect federal libraries and information centers, needs and priorities in providing information services to the government and to the nation at large, and efficient and cost-effective use of federal library and information resources and services. Furthermore, the committee promotes improved access to information, continued development and use of the Federal Library and Information Network (FEDLINK), research and development in the application of new technologies to federal libraries and information centers, improvements in the management of federal libraries and information centers, and relevant education opportunities. Founded 1965.

Membership

Libn. of Congress, Dir. of the National Agricultural Lib., Dir. of the National Lib. of Medicine, Dir. of the National Lib. of Educ., representatives of each of the cabinet-level executive departments, and representatives of each of the following agencies: National Aeronautics and Space Admin., National Science Foundation, Smithsonian Institution, U.S. Supreme Court, National Archives and Records Admin., Admin. Offices of the U.S. Courts, Defense Technical Info. Center, Government Printing Office, National Technical Info. Service (Dept. of Commerce), Office of Scientific and Technical Info. (Dept. of Energy), Exec. Office of the President, Dept. of the Army, Dept. of the Navy, Dept. of the Air Force, and chair of the FEDLINK Advisory Council. Fifteen additional voting member agencies shall be selected on a rotating basis by the voting members of FEDLINK. These rotating members will serve a three-year term. One representative of each of the following agencies is invited as an observer to committee meetings: Government Accountability Office, General Services Admin.,

Joint Committee on Printing, National Commission on Libs. and Info. Science, Office of Mgt. and Budget, Office of Personnel Mgt., and U.S. Copyright Office.

Officers

Chair James H. Billington, Libn. of Congress; *Chair Designate* Deanna Marcum, Assoc. Libn. for Lib. Services, Lib. of Congress; *Exec. Dir.* Susan M. Tarr.

Address correspondence to the executive director.

Publications

FEDLINK Technical Notes (every other month).
FLICC Newsletter (q.).

Federal Publishers Committee

Chair, Glenn W. King
Bureau of the Census, Washington, DC 20233
301-763-4176, fax 301-457-4707
E-mail glenn.w.king@census.gov

Object

To foster and promote effective management of data development and dissemination in the federal government through exchange of information, and to act as a focal point for federal agency publishing.

Membership

Memb. 500. Membership is available to persons involved in publishing and dissemination in federal government departments, agencies, and corporations, as well as independent organizations concerned with federal government publishing and dissemination. Some key federal government organizations represented are the Joint Committee on Printing, Government Printing Office, National Technical Info. Service, National Commission on Libs. and Info. Science, and the Lib. of Congress.

Officers

Chair Glenn W. King; *V. Chair, Programs* Sandra Smith; *Dirs.* John Ward, Leslie M. Greenberg.

Publication

Guide to Federal Publishing (occasional).

Friends of Libraries U.S.A. (FOLUSA)

Executive Director, Sally G. Reed
1420 Walnut St., Ste. 450, Philadelphia, PA 19102-4017
800-936-5872, 215-790-1674, fax 215-545-3821
E-mail folusa@folusa.org, World Wide Web http://www.folusa.org

Object

Friends of Libraries U.S.A. (FOLUSA) is a national nonprofit organization providing networking opportunities and educational support for local friends-of-libraries groups across the country. More than 2,000 friends groups, libraries, and individuals are members of FOLUSA, representing hundreds of thousands of library supporters.

Established in 1979 as a committee of the Library Administration and Management Association (LAMA) of the American Library Association, FOLUSA is a national leader in library support and advocacy. Its mission is to motivate and support local friends groups in their efforts to preserve and strengthen libraries, and to create awareness and appreciation of library services by

- Assisting in developing friends groups in order to generate local and state support
- Providing guidance, education, and counsel throughout the friends network
- Promoting the development of strong library advocacy programs
- Serving as a clearinghouse of information and expertise
- Promoting early-childhood literacy in partnership with friends groups

Through publications, online resources, consulting services, and support, FOLUSA works with local and state friends groups to enhance their efforts as advocates, volunteers, program and community-outreach catalysts, and as fund-raisers in support of their local and state libraries.

Since 1989 FOLUSA has presented an annual public service award to a member of Congress who has shown leadership and support of library issues. The award presentation is part of Library Legislative Day in Washington, D.C. Awards for friends groups annually total more than $15,000 and recognize outstanding community and volunteer involvement.

Membership

Membership is open to all friends of libraries groups, libraries, and individuals who support libraries. Dues (indiv.) $35 up; (small libraries, budgets under $1 million) $50; (large libraries, budgets over $1 million) $100; (small friends groups, fewer than 100 members) $40; (medium friends groups, 100 to 499 members) $65; (large friends groups, 500+ members) $100.

Officers (2004–2005)

Pres. Susan Schmidt; *V.P./Pres.-Elect* Doug Roesemann; *Secy.* Margaret Schuster; *Treas.* Bette Kozlowski; *Past Pres.* Lana Porter.

Directors

Jeff Bantly, Peggy Barber, John Barnes, John Carson, Martin Covert, Mary Dodge, Tim Fusco, Martin Gomez, William Gordon, Barbara Hoffert, Cherine Janzen, Stephen Klein, Mary D. Lankford, Don Leslie, Deborah Loeding, Margaret Murray, Veronda Pitchford, Julia Ratliff, Kay Runge, Rocco Staino, Virginia Stanley, Michael Utasi, David Warren.

Publications

NewsUpdate, (bi-mo.)
Making Our Voices Heard: Citizens Speak Out for Libraries

Getting Grants in Your Community
101+ Great Ideas for Libraries and Friends

Services

Literary Landmarks—a national register of places commemorating important Ameri-can authors

Books for Babies, a turnkey program for distributing reading kits and babies' first books to new parents

Consulting services, training, and workshops at the regional, state, and national levels focusing on developing friends groups, fund raising, and advocacy

National Church Library Association

Executive Director, Susan Benish
275 S. 3rd St., Ste. 101A, Stillwater, MN 55082
651-430-0770, e-mail info@churchlibraries.org
World Wide Web http://www.churchlibraries.org

Object

The National Church Library Association (NCLA, formerly the Lutheran Church Library Association) is a nonprofit organization that serves the unique needs of congregational libraries and those who manage them. NCLA provides inspiration, solutions, and support to church librarians in the form of printed manuals and guidelines, booklists, a quarterly journal (*Libraries ALIVE*), national conferences, a mentoring program, online support, and personal advice. Regional chapters operate throughout the country.

Membership

Memb. 800 churches, 100 personal. Dues $35, $50. Year. Jan.–Jan.

Officers

Pres. Barbara Livdahl; *V.P.* Karen Gieseke; *Secy..* Brenda Langerud; *Treas.* Esther Bunch; *Past Pres.* Bonnie McLellan.

Address correspondence to the executive director.

Directors

Betty Bender, Gerrie Buzard, Sandra Cully, Rev. James Ketcham, Una Lamb, Rachel Riensche, Violet Russell.

Publication

Libraries ALIVE (q.; memb.).

Committee Chairpersons

Advisory. Mary Jordan.
Librarian Resources. Marlys Johnson.

Medical Library Association

Executive Director, Carla Funk
65 E. Wacker Place, Ste. 1900, Chicago, IL 60601-7298
312-419-9094, fax 312-419-8950
E-mail info@mlahq.org, World Wide Web http://www.mlanet.org

Object

The Medical Library Association (MLA), a nonprofit educational organization, is comprised of health sciences information professionals with more than 4,700 members worldwide. Through its programs and services, MLA provides lifelong educational opportunities, supports a knowledge base of health information research, and works with a global network of partners to promote the importance of quality information for improved health to the healthcare community and the public.

Membership

Memb. (Inst.) 884; (Indiv.) 3,664. Institutional members are medical and allied scientific libraries. Individual members are people who are (or were at the time membership was established) engaged in professional library or bibliographic work in medical and allied scientific libraries or people who are interested in medical or allied scientific libraries. Dues (Student) $35; (Emeritus) $55; (International) $100; (Indiv.) $150; and (Inst.) $235–$545, based on the number of the library's periodical subscriptions. Members may be affiliated with one or more of MLA's 23 special-interest sections and 14 regional chapters.

Officers

Pres. Joanne G. Marshall, Univ. of North Carolina at Chapel Hill, Chapel Hill, NC 27514-3360; *Pres.-Elect* Mary Joan ("M.J.") Tooey, Univ. of Maryland, Health Sciences and Human Services Lib., 601 W. Lombard St., Baltimore, MD 21201; *Past Pres.* Patricia Thibodeau, Duke Univ. Medical Center Lib., Box 3702, DUMC, 103 Seeley G. Mudd Bldg., Durham, NC 277102.

Directors

Nancy W. Clemmons (2006), Norma F. Funkhouser (2004), Sarah H. Gable (2007), Dixie A. Jones (2007), Rosalind K. Lett (2006), Michelynn McKnight (2005), Faith Meakin (2007), Gerald J. Perry (2005), Neil Rambo (2005).

Publications

Journal of the Medical Library Association (q.; $163).

MLA News (10 a year; $58).

Miscellaneous (request current list from association headquarters).

Music Library Association

8551 Research Way, Ste. 180, Middleton, WI 53562
608-836-5825
World Wide Web http://www.musiclibraryassoc.org

Object

To promote the establishment, growth, and use of music libraries; to encourage the collection of music and musical literature in libraries; to further studies in musical bibliography; to increase efficiency in music library service and administration; and to promote the profession of music librarianship. Founded 1931.

Membership

Memb. 1,177. Dues (Inst.) $125; (Indiv.) $90; (Retired) $60; (Student) $35. Year. July 1–June 30.

Officers

Pres. Bonna J. Boettcher, Music Lib. and Sound Recordings Archives, William T. Jerome Lib., 3rd fl., Bowling Green State Univ., Bowling Green, OH 43403-0179. Tel. 419-372-9929, fax 419-372-2499, e-mail bboettc@bgnet.bgsu.edu; *Rec. Secy.* Michael Colby, Catalog Dept., Shields Lib., 100 N. West Quad, Univ. of California–Davis, Davis, CA 95616-5292. Tel. 530-752-0931, fax 530-754-8785, e-mail mdcolby@ucdavis. edu; *Treas./Exec. Secy.* Nancy B. Nuzzo, Music Lib., Univ. at Buffalo, 112 Baird Hall, Buffalo, NY 14260-4750. Tel. 716-645-2924, fax 716-645-3906, e-mail nuzzo@buffalo.edu.

Members-at-Large

Linda Blair, Eastman School of Music; Pamela Bristah, Wellesley College; Paul Cauthen, Univ. of Cincinnati; Ruthan Boles McTyre, Univ. of Iowa; Amanda Maple, Penn State Univ.; Matthew Wise, New York Univ.

Special Officers

Advertising Mgr. Susan Dearborn, 1572 Massachusetts Ave., No. 57, Cambridge, MA 02138. Tel. 617-876-0934; *Business Mgr.* Jim Zychowicz, 8551 Research Way, Ste. 180, Middleton, WI 53562. Tel. 608-836-5825; *Asst. Convention Mgr.* Gordon Rowley, Box 395, Bailey's Harbor, WI 54202. Tel. 920-839-2444, e-mail baileysbreeze@ itol.com; *Convention Mgr.* Annie Thompson, 435 S. Gulfstream Ave., Apt. 506, Sarasota, FL 34326. Tel. 941-955-5014, fax 941-316-0468, e-mail figarotu@msn.com; *Placement* Jennifer Ottervik, Univ. of South Carolina Music Lib., 813 Assembly St., Columbia, SC 29208. Tel. 803-777-5425, fax 803-777-1426, e-mail ottervikj@gwm.sc.edu; *Publicity* Kenneth Calkins, Music Lib., Univ. of California, San Diego, 9500 Gilman Dr., No 0175Q, La Jolla, CA 92093. Tel. 858-534-1267, fax 858-534-0189, e-mail kcalkins@ ucsd.edu.

Publications

MLA Index and Bibliography Series (irreg.; price varies).
MLA Newsletter (q.; memb.).
MLA Technical Reports (irreg.; price varies).
Music Cataloging Bulletin (mo.; $25).
Notes (q.; indiv. $85; inst. $100).

Committee and Roundtable Chairpersons

Administration. Robert Acker, DePaul Univ.
Bibliographic Control. Nancy Lorimer, Stanford Univ.
Development. Allie Wise Goudy, Western Illinois Univ.
Education. Deborah Pierce, Univ. of Washington.

Finance. Pamela Bristah, Wellesley College. Legislation. Lenore Coral, Cornell Univ. Membership. Michael Rogan, Tufts Univ. Preservation. Alice Carli, Eastman School of Music. Public Libraries. Steven Landstreet, Free Lib. of Philadelphia. Publications. Karen Little, Univ. of Louisville. Reference and Public Service. Martin Jenkins, Wright State Univ. Resource Sharing and Collection Development. Brian Doherty, Arizona State Univ.

National Association of Government Archives and Records Administrators (NAGARA)

48 Howard St., Albany, NY 12207
518-463-8644, fax 518-463-8656
E-mail nagara@caphill.com
World Wide Web http://www.nagara.org

Object

Founded in 1984, NAGARA is a growing nationwide association of local, state, and federal archivists and records administrators, and others interested in improved care and management of government records. NAGARA promotes public awareness of government records and archives management programs, encourages interchange of information among government archives and records management agencies, develops and implements professional standards of government records and archival administration, and encourages study and research into records management problems and issues.

Membership

Most NAGARA members are federal, state, and local archival and records management agencies.

Officers

Pres. Timothy A. Slavin, Delaware Public Archives, 121 Duke of York St., Dover, DE 19901. Tel. 302-739-5318, fax 302-739-2578, e-mail timothy.slavin@state.de.us; *V.P.* Preston Huff, National Archives and Records Admin., Southwest Region, 501 W. Felix St., Bldg. 1, Fort Worth, TX 76115. Tel. 817-831-5627, e-mail preston.huff@

nara.gov; *Secy.* Caryn Wojcik, Michigan Records Mgt. Services, Michigan Historical Center, 3405 N. Martin Luther King, Jr. Blvd., Lansing, MI 48909. Tel. 517-335-8222, fax 517-335-9418, e-mail wojcikc@michigan.gov; *Treas.* John Stewart, National Archives and Records Admin., Great Lakes Region, 7358 S. Pulaski Rd., Chicago, IL 60629-5898. Tel. 773-581-7816, fax 312-886-7883, e-mail john.stewart@nara.gov.

Directors

Paul Bergeron, City of Nashua (New Hampshire); Terry B. Ellis, County Records Mgr., Salt Lake County Records Mgt. and Archives; Nancy Fortna, National Archives and Records Admin., Washington, D.C.; Mary Beth Herkert, Oregon State Archives; Richard Hite, Rhode Island State Archives; Kay Lanning Minchew, Troup County (Georgia) Archives; Barbara Voss, National Archives and Records Admin., Rocky Mountain Region.

Publications

Clearinghouse (q.; memb.).
Crossroads (q.; memb.).
Government Records Issues (series).
Preservation Needs in State Archives (report).
Program Reporting Guidelines for Government Records Programs.

NFAIS

Executive Director, Bonnie Lawlor
1518 Walnut St., Ste. 1004, Philadelphia, PA 19102
215-893-1561, fax 215-893-1564
E-mail nfais@nfais.org
World Wide Web http://www.nfais.org

Object

NFAIS (formerly the National Federation of Abstracting and Information Services) is an international nonprofit membership organization composed of leading information providers. Its membership includes government agencies, nonprofit scholarly societies, and private sector businesses. NFAIS serves groups that aggregate, organize, or facilitate access to information. To improve members' capabilities and to contribute to their ongoing success, NFAIS provides a forum to address common interests through education and advocacy. Founded 1958.

Membership

Memb. 50+. Full members: regular and government organizations that provide information services, primarily through organizing, compiling, and providing access to original or source materials. Examples of full members: organizations that assemble tables of contents, produce abstract and indexing services, provide library cataloging services, or generate numeric or factual compilations. Associate members: organizations that operate or manage online information services, networks, in-house information centers, and libraries; undertake research and development in information science or systems; are otherwise involved in the generation, promotion, or distribution of information products under contract; or publish original information sources. Corporate affiliated members: another member of the corporation or government agency must already be a NFAIS member paying full dues.

Officers (2004–2005)

Pres. Linda Sacks; *Pres.-Elect* Lucian Parziale; *Treas.* Kevin Bouley; *Secy.* Terence Ford; *Past Pres.* Marjorie Hlava.

Directors

Barbara Bauldock, Linda Beebe, David Brown, Matt Dunie, Walter Finch, Janice Mears, John Regazzi.

Staff

Exec. Dir. Bonnie Lawlor. E-mail blawlor@nfais.org; *Dir., Planning and Communications* Jill O'Neill. E-mail jilloneill@nfais.org; *Customer Service* Margaret Manson. E-mail mmanson@nfais.org.

Publications

NFAIS Newsletter (mo.; North America $120; elsewhere $135).

For a detailed list of NFAIS publications, see the NFAIS Web site (http://www.nfais.org).

National Information Standards Organization

Executive Director, Patricia R. Harris
4733 Bethesda Ave., Ste. 300, Bethesda, MD 20814
301-654-2512, fax 301-654-1721
E-mail nisohq@niso.org, World Wide Web http://www.niso.org

Object

NISO, the National Information Standards Organization, a nonprofit association accredited by the American National Standards Institute (ANSI), identifies, develops, maintains, and publishes technical standards to manage information in our changing and ever-more-digital environment. NISO standards apply both traditional and new technologies to the full range of information-related needs, including retrieval, repurposing, storage, metadata, and preservation.

Experts from their respective fields volunteer to lend their expertise in the development of NISO standards. The standards are approved by the consensus body of NISO's voting membership, which consists of more than 80 voting members representing libraries, government, associations, and private businesses and organizations. NISO is supported by its membership and corporate grants. Formerly a committee of the American National Standards Institute (ANSI), NISO, formed in 1939, was incorporated in 1983 as a nonprofit educational organization. NISO is accredited by ANSI and serves as the U.S. Technical Advisory Group to ISO/TC 46.

Membership

Memb. 80+. Open to any organization, association, government agency, or company willing to participate in and having substantial concern for the development of NISO standards.

Officers

Chair Jan Peterson, V.P., Content Development, Infotrieve, Los Angeles; *V. Chair/ Chair-Elect* Carl Grant, Pres. and COO, VTLS, Inc., Blacksburg, Virginia; *Secy.* Patricia R. Harris, NISO, Bethesda, Maryland; *Treas.* Michael J. Mellinger, Davandy LLC, St. Louis; *Past Chair* Beverly P. Lynch, Univ. of California, Los Angeles.

Publications

Information Standards Quarterly (U.S $89/ year, foreign $130).

For additional NISO publications, see the article "National Information Standards Organization (NISO) Standards" later in Part 6.

NISO published standards are available free of charge as downloadable PDF files from the NISO Web site (http://www.niso.org). Standards in hard copy are available for sale on the Web site. The *NISO Annual Report* is available on request.

REFORMA (National Association to Promote Library and Information Services to Latinos and the Spanish-Speaking)

President, José Ruiz-Alvarez
World Wide Web http://www.reforma.org

Object

Promoting library services to the Spanish-speaking for more than 30 years, REFORMA, an affiliate of the American Library Association, works in a number of areas: to promote the development of library collections to include Spanish-language and Latino-oriented materials; the recruitment of more bilingual and bicultural professionals and support staff; the development of library services and programs that meet the needs of the Latino community; the establishment of a national network among individuals who share our goals; the education of the U.S. Latino population in regard to the availability and types of library services; and lobbying efforts to preserve existing library resource centers serving the interest of Latinos.

Membership

Memb. 800+. Any person who is supportive of the goals and objectives of REFORMA.

Officers

Pres. José Ruiz-Alvarez, Arlington (Texas) Public Lib. Tel. 817-459-6395, e-mail jruiz@pub-lib.ci.arlington.tx.us; *Pres.-Elect* Ana Elba Pavón, San Francisco Public Lib. Tel. 415-355-5739, e-mail apavon@sfpl.org; *Past Pres.* Linda Chavez Doyle, County of Los Angeles Public Lib. Tel. 310-830-0231, fax 310-834-4097, e-mail lcdoyle@lhqsmpt.colapl.org; *Treas.* Ramona Grijalva, Tucson (Arizona) Lib. Tel. 520-791-4791, e-mail rgrijal1@ci.tucson.az.us; *Secy.* Delores Carlito, Mervyn H. Sterne Lib., Univ. of Alabama. Tel. 205-934-6364, e-mail delo@uab.edu; *Archivist* Sal Güereña. Tel. 805-893-8563, e-mail guerena@library.ucsb.edu; *Office Mgr.* Sandra Rios Balderrama, P.O. Box 25963, Scottsdale, AZ 85255-0116. Tel. 480-471-7452, fax 480-471-7442, e-mail reformaoffice @riosbalderrama.com.

Publication

REFORMA Newsletter (q.; memb.).

Committees

Pura Belpré Award. Rose Treviño.
Children's and Young Adult Services. Rose Treviño.
Education. Sonia Ramirez-Wohlmuth.
Finance. Linda Chavez Doyle.
Fund-raising. Lucía González.
Information Technology. Francisco Garcia.
International Relations. Hector Marino.
Joint Ethnic Caucus Conference. John Ayala, Toni Bissessar.
Legislative. Mario A. Ascencio.
Librarian of the Year. Loida Garcia-Febo.
Member at Large. Cal Zunt.
Membership. Diana Morales.
Mentoring Committee. Gwen Gregory, Patricia Tarin.
Mora Award. Jon Sundell.
Nominations. Ina Rimpau.
Organizational Development. Patricia Clark.
Program Committee. Ana Elba Pavón.
Public Relations. Selina Beloz.
Scholarship. José Aguiñaga.

Meetings

General membership and board meetings take place at the American Library Association's Midwinter Meeting and Annual Conference.

RLG

Manager of Corporate Communications, Jennifer Hartzell
2029 Stierlin Court, Ste. 100, Mountain View, CA 94043-4684
Tel. 650-691-2207, fax 650-964-0943
E-mail jlh@notes.rlg.org, World Wide Web http://www.rlg.org

Object

Founded as the Research Libraries Group in 1974, RLG is a not-for-profit membership corporation of libraries, archives, museums, and other memory institutions with remarkable collections for research and learning. RLG and its members collaborate on standards and specific projects to bring these collections online, help deliver them around the world, and support their preservation in digital form. As part of this work, RLG offers Internet-based services to institutions and individuals for improving information discovery and use. RLG's main classes of information, available on the Internet, are international union catalogs (e.g., RedLightGreen, RLG Union Catalog, Hand Press Books); article- and chapter-level indexes to journals and books (e.g., Anthropology Plus and Avery Index to Architectural Periodicals); *RLG Archival Resources*: full-text finding aids and archival collections cataloging); and RLG Cultural Materials: a digitized objects database, plus Trove.net for image licensing and the AMICO Library of high-quality art multimedia and descriptions. RLIN21 includes a Web interface to find and download cataloging copy from RLG catalogs, as well as a PC-based client to create and maintain records in these catalogs. *RLG's ILL Manager* is peer-to-peer PC-based software for handling an institution's interlibrary loan traffic. CJK, Eureka, Marcadia, and RLIN21 are RLG trademarks.

Membership

Memb. 160+. Membership is open to any nonprofit institution with an educational, cultural, or scientific mission. All members have equal access to RLG activities and service discounts. Annual dues, based on the size of institutional operating budget, support RLG member programs and projects. Membership is not a requirement to use RLG services.

Directors

RLG is governed by a board of up to 19 directors: 12 elected from and by RLG's member institutions, up to six at-large directors elected by the board itself, and the president. Theirs is the overall responsibility for the organization's governance and for ensuring that it fulfills its purpose and goals. Annual board elections are held in the spring. In 2005 the board's chair is James G. Neal, vice president for information services and university librarian, Columbia University. For a current list of directors, see http://www.rlg.org/en/page.php?Page_ID=122.

Staff

Pres. and CEO James Michalko; *Chief Operating Officer* Molly Singer; *Dir., Member Programs and Initiatives* Linda West; *Dir., Integrated Information Services* Susan Yoder; *Dir., Computer Development* David Richards; *Dir., Customer and Operations Support* Jack Grantham; *Financial Controller* Marc Israel.

Publications

RLG regularly issues Web-based informational, research, and user publications. See http://www.rlg.org/en/page.php?Page_ID=5 or contact RLG for more information. RLG newsletters include *RLG DigiNews* (bi-m.; Web-based newsletter to help keep pace with preservation uses of digitization).

RLG Focus (bi-m.; Web-based user-services newsletter).

RLG News (2 a year; 20-page magazine).

Scholarly Publishing and Academic Resources Coalition (SPARC)

Enterprise Director, Richard Johnson
21 Dupont Circle, Ste. 800, Washington, DC 20036
202-296-2296, fax 202-872-0884
E-mail sparc@arl.org
World Wide Web http://www.arl.org/sparc

Mission

SPARC is an initiative developed by the Association of Research Libraries to correct market dysfunctions in the scholarly publishing system. These dysfunctions have driven the cost of scholarly journals (especially in science, technology, and medicine) to insupportably high levels that inhibit the advancement of scholarship and are at odds with fundamental needs of scholars and the academic enterprise.

SPARC is a catalyst for action. Its pragmatic agenda stimulates the emergence of new scholarly communication models that expand dissemination of scholarly research and reduce financial pressures on libraries. Action by SPARC in concert with other stakeholders unleashes the promise of the networked digital environment to serve scholarship.

Strategy

SPARC strategy seeks to reduce the economic barriers to access, sharing, and use of scholarship and, in particular, scientific research. Since 2002 SPARC's highest priority has been on advancing the goal of "open access." As a practical matter, SPARC program activity also recognizes that, in some areas, the interests of academe may be best served in the near term by affordable subscription-supported publishing solutions.

Its focus on science—though not to the exclusion of the social sciences and humanities—is motivated by the crippling impact of high and rising STM journal prices on library operations and the readily demonstrable impact of scientific research on achieving public policy aims.

Underlying SPARC's strategy is a recognition that

• The central functions of scholarly publishing, traditionally aggregated in printed journals, can become increasingly disaggregated in the digital networked environment, enabling the performance of the functions to be distributed among multiple agents.

• Standards or conventions can ensure that information about the fulfillment of the functions can be shared and correlated across the network—for example via technical standards (e.g., OAI Metadata Harvesting Protocol) or legal instruments (e.g., Creative Commons licenses).

This process of disaggregation and distributed integration of the functions of scholarly publication offers the possibility of breaking the monopoly control on unique articles that is the source of much of the dysfunction in the system.

SPARC's role in stimulating change focuses on

• Educating stakeholders about the problems facing scholarly communication and the opportunities for change

• Advocating policy changes that advance the potential of the digital networked environment to advance scholarly communication and recognize that dissemination is an essential, inseparable component of the scientific research process

• Incubating real-world demonstrations of business and publishing models that advance changes benefiting scholarship and academe

With SPARC's encouragement the disaggregation process is playing out today, for example with the emergence of NIH's Pub-

Med Central as a supplemental access channel to research that is certified and published in traditional (albeit digital in most cases) journals.

While SPARC recognizes that licensed scholarly resources will continue to play a significant part in library operations for the foreseeable future, its concentration is on building new models rather than optimizing the efficiency of traditional models. SPARC does not discount the importance of extracting cost savings on existing resources, but believes that the need for best practices, training, and exercise of consortial buying power in these areas is better served by other organizations.

SPARC Priorities

SPARC actions will, foremost, aim to advance the viability and acceptance of open-access publishing models. Nonetheless, SPARC recognizes that change will play out differently in individual fields of science and scholarship. Its program therefore aims at building a broader understanding of the opportunities for change in all fields.

Membership

SPARC and SPARC Europe are supported by a membership of more than 300 libraries. Several major library organizations around the world are SPARC affiliate members. Membership is institutional. Full North American member dues are $5,000 a year, with a $7,500 purchase commitment. Other membership categories are available. SPARC Europe members are listed at http://www.sparceurope.org.

Publications

SPARC Open-Access Newsletter (http://www.earlham.edu/~peters/fos)
SPARC e-news (subscribe by sending name, title, organization and e-mail address to sparc@arl.org)
Create Change: A Resource for Faculty and Librarian Action to Reclaim Scholarly Communication (http://www.createchange.org)
See http://www.arl.org/sparc/pubs/index.html for a complete list of SPARC publications.

Society for Scholarly Publishing

Executive Directors, Francine Butler, Jerry Bowman
10200 W. 44 Ave., Ste. 304, Wheat Ridge, CO 80033
303-422-3914, fax 303-422-8894
E-mail ssp@resourcenter.com
World Wide Web http://www.sspnet.org

Object

To draw together individuals involved in the process of scholarly publishing. This process requires successful interaction of the many functions performed within the scholarly community. The Society for Scholarly Publishing (SSP) provides the leadership for such interaction by creating opportunities for the exchange of information and opinions among scholars, editors, publishers, librarians, printers, booksellers, and all others engaged in scholarly publishing.

Membership

Memb. 800. Open to all with an interest in the scholarly publishing process and dissemination of information. Dues (Indiv.) $115; (Supporting) $1,100; (Sustaining) $2,750. Year. Jan. 1–Dec. 31.

Executive Committee (July 1, 2004–June 30, 2005)

Pres. Heather Joseph, BioOne; *Pres.-Elect* Norman Frankel, American Medical Assn.; *Past Pres.* Margaret Reich, American Physiological Society; *Secy.-Treas.* Ray Fastiggi, Rockefeller Univ. Press.

Meetings

An annual meeting is conducted in late May/June; the location changes each year. Additionally, SSP conducts several seminars throughout the year and a Top Management Roundtable each fall.

Society of American Archivists

Executive Director, Nancy Perkin Beaumont
527 S. Wells St., Fifth Floor, Chicago, IL 60607
312-922-0140, fax 312-347-1452
World Wide Web http://www.archivists.org

Object

Provides leadership to ensure the identification, preservation, and use of records of historical value. Founded 1936.

Membership

Memb. 4,000. Dues (Indiv.) $70–$180, graduated according to salary; (Assoc.) $70, domestic; (Student) $40; (Inst.) $225; (Sustaining) $440.

Officers (2004–2005)

Pres. Rand Jimerson; *V.P.* Richard Pearce-Moses; *Treas.* Fynnette Eaton.

Council

Frank Boles, Mark Duffy, Elaine Engst, Aimee Felker, Peter Gottlieb, Kathryn Neal, Christopher Paton, Peter Wosh, Joel Wurl.

Staff

Exec. Dir. Nancy Perkin Beaumont; *Memb. Services Coord.* Jeanette Spears; *Publishing Dir.* Teresa Brinati; *Educ. Dir.* Solveig DeSutter; *Webmaster and Graphic Designer* Brian Doyle; *Meetings Program Coord.* Carlos Salgado; *Educ. Program Coord.* Jodie Strickland.

Publications

American Archivist (q.; $85; foreign $90). *Ed.* Philip Eppard, *Managing Ed.* Teresa Brinati. Books for review and related correspondence should be addressed to the managing editor.
Archival Outlook (bi-m.; memb.). *Ed.* Teresa Brinati.

Software and Information Industry Association (SIIA)

1090 Vermont Ave. N.W., Washington, DC 20005
Tel. 202-289-7442, fax 202-289-7097
World Wide Web http://www.siia.net

Membership

Memb. 600 companies. Formed January 1, 1999, through the merger of the Software Publishers Association (SPA) and the Information Industry Association (IIA). Open to companies involved in the creation, distribution, and use of software, information products, services, and technologies. For details on membership and dues, see the SIIA Web site.

Staff

Pres. Kenneth Wasch. E-mail kwasch@siia. net.

Officers

Chair Steve Manzo, Reed Elsevier; *V. Chair* Mark H. Webbink, Red Hat; *Treas.* Stuart Udell, Kaplan K–12; *Secy.* Jessica Perry, Dow Jones.

Board of Directors

Officers; Cindy Braddon, McGraw-Hill; John Brigden, Veritas; Piper Cole, Sun Microsystems; Daniel Cooperman, Oracle Corp.; Clare Hart, Factiva; Doug Kemp, Bloomberg; Edward S. Knight, NASDAQ; Bernard McKay, Intuit; Robert W. Merry, Congressional Quarterly; Sylvia Metayer, Houghton Mifflin; Jessica Perry, Dow Jones; Gail Elizabeth Pierson, Riverdeep Interactive Learning; Jason Stewart, Thomson Corp.; Ken Wasch, SIIA.

Special Libraries Association (SLA)

Executive Director, Janice R. Lachance
331 South Patrick Street, Alexandria, VA 22314
703-647-4900, fax 703-647-4901
E-mail sla@sla.org, World Wide Web http://www.sla.org

Mission

To advance the leadership role of our members in putting knowledge to work for the benefit of decision-makers in corporations, government, the professions, and society; to shape the destiny of our information- and knowledge-based society.

Membership

Memb. 12,000. Dues (Organizational) $500; (Indiv.) $125; (Student) $35.

Officers (July 2004–June 2005)

Pres. Ethel Salonen; *Pres.-Elect* Pamela Rollo; *Past Pres.* Cynthia Hill; *Treas.* Gloria Zamora; *Chapter Cabinet Chair* Jacquelyn Knuckle; *Chapter Cabinet Chair-Elect* Patricia Cia; *Div. Cabinet Chair* Brent Mai; *Div. Chapter Chair-Elect* Trudy Katz.

Directors

Officers; Susan Klopper, Jesus Lau, Lynn McCay, Renee Massoud, Barbara Spiegelman, Dan Trefethen.

Publication

Information Outlook (mo.) (memb., nonmemb. $125/yr.)

Committee Chairpersons

Association Office Operations. Ethel Salonen.
Awards and Honors. William Fisher.
Bylaws. Lyle Minter.
Cataloging. Dorothy McGarry.
Committees. Richard Wallace.
Conference Planning (2005). Juanita Richardson.

Diversity Leadership Development. Debbie Jan.
Finance. Gloria Zamora.
Nominating. Carol Ginsburg.
Professional Development. Sylvia Piggott.
Public Policy. Pat Wilson.
Public Relations. Cindy Romaine.
Research. Eileen Abels.
SLA Endowment Fund Grants. Susan DiMattia.
SLA Scholarship. Linda Morgan Davis.
Strategic Planning. Renee Massoud.
Student and Academic Relations. Rebecca Vargha.
Technical Standards. Foster Zhang.

Theatre Library Association (TLA)

c/o The New York Public Library for the Performing Arts, 40 Lincoln Center Plaza, New York, NY 10023
212-944-3895, fax 212-944-4139
World Wide Web http://tla.library.unt.edu

Object

To further the interests of collecting, preserving, and using theater, cinema, and performing-arts materials in libraries, museums, and private collections. Founded 1937.

Membership

Memb. 375. Dues (Indiv./Inst.) $30. Year. Jan. 1–Dec. 31.

Officers

Pres. Martha S. LoMonaco, Fairfield Univ.; *V.P.* Kenneth Schlesinger, LaGuardia Community College/CUNY; *Exec. Secy.* Nancy Friedland, Columbia Univ.; *Treas.* Paul Newman, private collector.

Executive Board

Pamela Bloom, Susan Brady, Maryann Chach, Annette Fern, Mark Maniak, Judith S. Mar-

kowitz, Julian Mates, Robert W. Melton, Tobin Nellhaus, Louis Rachow, Jason Rubin, Don B. Wilmeth; *Honorary* Paul Myers, Marian Seldes; *Historian* Louis A. Rachow; *Legal Counsel* Madeleine Nichols.

Publications

Broadside (q.; memb.). *Ed.* Ellen Truax.
Performing Arts Resources (occasional; memb.).
Membership Directory. Ed. Maryann Chach.

Committee Chairpersons

Finance. Paul Newman.
Membership. Paul Newman, Maryann Chach, Kenneth Schlesinger.
Nominating. Bob Taylor.
Professional Award. Nena Couch, Camille Croce Dee.
Programs. Kevin Winkler.
Strategic Planning. Kenneth Schlesinger.
TLA/Freedley Awards. Richard Wall.

Urban Libraries Council (ULC)

President, Martín Gómez
1603 Orrington Ave., Ste. 1080, Evanston, IL 60201
847-866-9999, fax 847-866-9989
E-mail info@urbanlibraries.org
World Wide Web http://www.urbanlibraries.org

Object

To identify and make known the opportunities for urban libraries serving cities of 100,000 or more individuals, located in a Standard Metropolitan Statistical Area; to provide information on state and federal legislation affecting urban library programs and systems; to facilitate the exchange of ideas and programs of member libraries and other libraries; to develop programs that enable libraries to act as a focus of community development and to supply the informational needs of the new urban populations; to conduct research and educational programs that will benefit urban libraries and to solicit and accept grants, contributions, and donations essential to their implementation.

ULC currently receives core funding from membership dues. Current major projects supported by grant funding from a variety of sources include: Librarians for America's Neighborhoods (funded by a grant from the Institute for Museum and Library Services), and Learning in Libraries (funded by the Wallace Foundation). ULC is a 501(c)(3) not-for-profit corporation based in the state of Illinois.

Membership

Membership is open to public libraries serving populations of 100,000 or more located in a Standard Metropolitan Statistical Area and to corporations specializing in library-related materials and services. Annual dues are based on the size of the library's operating budget, according to the following schedule

(to be revised for the 2006 financial year): under $2 million to $10 million, $3,000; over $10 million, $5,000. In addition, ULC member libraries may choose Sustaining or Contributing status (Sustaining, $12,000; Contributing, $7,000). Corporate membership dues are $5,000.

Officers (2004–2005)

Chair Donna Nicely, Dir., Nashville Public Lib., 615 Church St., Nashville, TN 37219-2314. Tel. 615-862-5760; *V. Chair/Chair-Elect* Jane Light, Dir., San Jose Public Lib., 150 E. San Fernando St., San Jose, CA 95112. Tel. 408-808-2150; *Secy./Treas.* Mary Dempsey, Commissioner, Chicago Public Lib., 400 S. State St., Chicago, IL 60605. Tel. 312-747-4090; *Past Chair* Duncan Highsmith, Chairman, Highsmith, Inc., W5527 State Rd. 106, P.O. Box 800, fort Atkinson, WI 53538-0800. Tel. 920-563-9571.

Officers serve one-year terms, members of the executive board two-year terms. New officers are elected and take office at the summer annual meeting of the council.

Executive Board

Marie Harris Aldridge. E-mail maldridge1@prodigy.net; Ginnie Cooper. E-mail g.cooper@brooklynpubliclibrary.org; Mary Dempsey. E-mail mdempsey@chipublib.org; Herb Elish. E-mail elishh@carnegielibrary.org; Diane Frankel. E-mail dfrankel@museum-management.com; Duncan Highsmith. E-mail dhighsmith@highsmith.com; Charles Higueras. E-mail chigueras@ghcp.com; John Kretzmann. E-mail j-kretzmann@northwestern.edu; Patricia Lasher. E-mail pjl@fullenweider.com; Wai-Fong Lee. E-mail wflee@sccd.ctc.edu; Jane Light. E-mail jane.light@sjlibrary.org; Rosalind McGee. E-mail rozmcgee@xmission.com; Michael Morand. E-mail michael.morand@yale.edu; Donna Nicely. E-mail donna.nicely@nashville.gov; Clement Price. E-mail caprice@andromeda.rutgers.edu; Raymond Santiago. E-mail santiagor@mdpls.org.

Key Staff

Pres. Martín Gómez; *Senior V.P., Admin./Member Services* Bridget A. Bradley; *V.P., Program/Development* Danielle Milam.

State, Provincial, and Regional Library Associations

The associations in this section are organized under three headings: United States, Canada, and Regional. Both the United States and Canada are represented under Regional associations.

United States

Alabama

Memb. 1,200. Term of Office. Apr. 2004–Apr. 2005. Publication. *The Alabama Librarian* (q.).

Pres. Tim Dodge, Auburn Univ. Libs., 213 Mell St., Auburn Univ., Auburn 36849-5606. Tel. 334-844-1729, fax 334-844-4461, e-mail dodgeti@auburn.edu; *Pres.-Elect* Jane Garrett, Baldwin Middle Magnet School, Montgomery 36102. Tel. 334-279-0022, e-mail jgarrett@alalinc.net or rjgarrett_1991@yahoo.com; *Past Pres.* Juanita Owes, Montgomery City-County Public Lib., P.O. Box 1950, Montgomery 36102. Tel. 334-240-4300, fax 334-240-4977, e-mail jowes@mccpl.lib.al.us; *Secy.* Kelyn Ralya, Alabama Public Lib. Service, 6030 Monticello Dr., Montgomery 36130. Tel. 800-723-8459 ext. 976, e-mail kralya@apls.state.al.us; *Treas.* Vivian B. White, Montgomery City-County Public Library, P.O. Box 1950, Montgomery, AL 36102. Tel. 334-240-4300, fax 334-240-4977; *Exec. Dir.* Virginia Lott, Bailey Building, 400 S. Union St., Ste. 395, Montgomery 36104. Tel. 877-563-5146 (toll-free), 334-263-1272, fax 334-265-1281, fax 334-265-1281, e-mail psgllc@bellsouth.net.

Address correspondence to the executive director.

World Wide Web http://allanet.org.

Alaska

Memb. 460+. Publication. *Newspoke* (bi-mo.).

Pres. Judith Anglin. E-mail juditha@first citylibraries.org; *Co-V.P./Committees* Judith Green. E-mail afjfg@uaa.alaska.edu; *Co-V.P./Committees* Colleen Tyrrell. E-mail Ctyrrell@chartercollege.edu; *V.P./Conference* Freya Anderson. E-mail freya_anderson @eed.state.ak.us; *Secy.* Jennifer Brown. E-mail jfjdb@uas.alaska.edu; *Treas.* Diane Ruess. E-mail ffder@uaf.edu; *Past Pres.* Michael Catoggio. E-mail afmlc@uaa.alaska. edu; *Exec. Officer* Mary Jennings. E-mail maryj@gci.net.

Address correspondence to the secretary, Alaska Lib. Assn., Box 81084, Fairbanks 99708. Fax 877-863-1401, e-mail akla@akla. org.

World Wide Web http://www.akla.org.

Arizona

Memb. 1,000. Term of Office. Nov. 2004–Nov. 2005. Publication. *AzLA Newsletter* (mo.).

Pres. Thomas Sullivan, Tucson-Pima Public Lib. Tel. 520-791-4391, e-mail laura. sullivan@tucsonaz.gov; *Pres.-Elect* Deborah Tasnadi, Peoria Public Lib. Tel. 623-773-7555, e-mail taznphx@yahoo.com; *Secy.* Louisa Aikin, Mustang Lib. Tel. 480-312-6035, e-mail laikin@scottsdaleaz.gov; *Treas.* Denise Keller, Pinal County Lib. Tel. 520-866-6457, e-mail denise.keller@co.pinal.az. us; *Past Pres.* Betsy Stunz-Hall, Tucson-Pima Public Lib. Tel. 520-791-4391, fax 520-791-3213, e-mail betsy.stunz-hall@tucsonaz. gov; *Admin. Asst.* Courtney Gilstrap. Tel. 602-712-9822, fax 602-252-5265, e-mail azla.admin@gilstrapmottacole.com.

Address correspondence to the administrative assistant, AzLA, 2302 N. 3 St., Ste. F, Phoenix 86004.

World Wide Web http://www.azla. affiniscape.com.

Arkansas

Memb. 600. Term of Office. Jan.–Dec. 2005. Publication. *Arkansas Libraries* (bi-mo.).

Pres. Art Lichtenstein, Torreyson Lib., Univ. of Central Arkansas, 201 Donaghey Ave., Conway 72035. Tel. 501-450-5203, e-mail artl@uca.edu; *V.P.* Diane Hughes, Lake

Hamilton Junior H.S., 281 Wolf St., Pearcy 71964. Tel. 501-767-2731, fax 501-767-1711, e-mail diane.hughes@lh.dsc.k12.ar.us; *Secy.-Treas.* Jamie Melson, Main Lib., Central Arkansas Lib. System, 100 Rock St., Little Rock 72201. Tel. 501-918-3074, fax 501-376-1830, e-mail jamiem@cals.lib.ar.us; *Past Pres.* Loretta Edwards, Univ. of Arkansas for Medical Sciences, 4301 W. Markham, Slot 586, Little Rock 72205. Tel. 501-686-6752, fax 501-686-6745, e-mail edwards lorettaj@uams.edu; *Exec. Dir.* Jennifer Coleman, Arkansas Lib. Assn., 9 Shackleford Plaza, Ste. 1, Little Rock 72211. Tel. 501-228-0775, fax 501-228-5535, e-mail arl association@aol.com.

Address correspondence to the executive director.

World Wide Web http://www.arlib.org.

California

Memb. 2,500. Publication. *California Libraries* (bi-mo., print and online).

Pres. Danis Kreimeier, Yorba Linda Public Lib. Tel. 714-777-2873 ext. 121, e-mail danisk@ylpl.lib.ca.us; *V.P./Pres.-Elect* Margaret Miles, Plumas County Lib. Tel. 530-283-6269, e-mail margaretmiles@countyof plumas.com; *Treas.* Annette Milliron DeBacker, North Bay Cooperative Lib. System. Tel. 707-544-0142, e-mail annetnbc@sonic. net; *Past Pres.* Les Kong, CSU–San Bernardino. Tel. 909-880-5111, e-mail lkong@ csusb.edu; *Exec. Dir./Secy.* Susan Negreen, California Lib. Assn., 717 20th St., Ste. 200, Sacramento 95814. Tel. 916-447-8541, fax 916-447-8394, e-mail snegreen@cla-net.org.

Address correspondence to the executive director.

World Wide Web http://www.cla-net.org.

Colorado

Memb. 1,100. Term of Office. Oct. 2004–Oct. 2005. Publication. *Colorado Libraries* (q.). *Co-Eds.* Janet Lee, Dayton Memorial Lib., Regis Univ., 3333 Regis Blvd., D-20, Denver 80221. Tel. 303-458-3552, fax 303-964-5143, e-mail jlee@regis.edu; Eileen Dumas, Aurora Public Lib., 14949 E. Alameda Pkwy., Aurora 80012. Tel. 303-739-6637, fax 303-739-6579, e-mail edumas@ci.aurora. co.us.

Pres. Ellen Greenblatt, Auraria Lib., 1100 Lawrence St., Denver 80204. Tel. 303-556-6704, e-mail ellen.greenblatt@cudenver.edu; *V.P./Pres.-Elect* Judy Barnett, Wasson H.S., 2115 Afton Way, Colorado Springs 80909. Tel. 719-328-2024, e-mail barnejm@d11. org.; *Secy.* To be announced; *Treas.* Shannon Cruthers, Auraria Lib., 1100 Lawrence St., Denver 80204. Tel. 303-556-6701, e-mail scruther@carbon.cudenver.edu; *Past Pres.* Paul Paladino, Montrose Lib. Dist., 320 S. 2 St., Montrose 81401. Tel. 970-249-9656, fax 970-240-1901, e-mail ppaladin@colosys.net; *Exec. Dir.* Kathleen Sagee Noland, Colorado Association of Libs., 12081 W. Alameda Pkwy., No. 427, Lakewood, CO 80228. Tel. 303-463-6400, e-mail kathleen@cal-webs. org.

Address correspondence to the executive director.

World Wide Web http://www.cal-webs. org.

Connecticut

Memb. 1,100. Term of Office. July 2004–June 2005. Publication. *Connecticut Libraries* (11 a year). *Ed.* David Kapp, 4 Llynwood Dr., Bolton 06040. Tel. 203-647-0697.

Pres. Chris Bradley, Connecticut Lib. Consortium, 2911 Dixwell Ave., Hamden 06518-3130. Tel. 203-288-5757; *V.P./Pres.-Elect* Alice Knapp, Ferguson Lib., Stamford 06904. Tel. 203-964-1000; *Treas.* Jan Fisher, Bridgeport Public Lib., Bridgeport 06604. Tel. 203-576-7777; *Past Pres.* Les Kozerowitz, Norwalk Public Lib., 1 Belden Ave., Norwalk 06850. Tel. 203-899-2780; *Admin.* Karen Zoller, Connecticut Lib. Assn., Box 85, Willimantic 06226-0085. Tel. 860-465-5006, e-mail cla@ctlibrarians.libct.org.

Address correspondence to the administrator.

World Wide Web http://cla.uconn.edu.

Delaware

Memb. 300. Term of Office. Apr. 2004–Apr. 2005. Publication. *DLA Online Bulletin* (electronic only at http://www.dla.lib.de.us/ bulletin.shtml).

Pres. Margaret Prouse, Delaware Tech, Terry Campus, 100 Campus Dr., Dover 19904. Tel. 302-857-1060, fax 302-857-1099, e-mail mprouse@college.dtec.edu; *V.P.* Hilary Welliver, Dover Public Lib. 45 State St., Dover 19901. Tel. 302-736-7034, fax 302-736-5087, e-mail hwell@lib.de. us; *Treas.* Michael Gutierrez, Univ. of Delaware Lib., Newark 19717-5267. Tel. 302-832-0234, fax 302-831-1046, e-mail mgutierrez@udel.edu; *Secy.* Tamatha Lambert, Laurel Public Lib., 101 E. 4 St., Laurel 19956. Tel. 302-875-3184, e-mail tlambert@lib.de.us. Address correspondence to the association, Box 816, Dover 19903-0816. E-mail dla@dla.lib.de.us.

World Wide Web http://www.dla.lib.de.us.

District of Columbia

Memb. 300+. Term of Office. July 2004– June 2005. Publication. *Intercom* (mo.).

Pres. Noel Rutherford, District of Columbia Public Lib. Tel. 202-282-0213, fax 202-282-2326, e-mail nrutherf@yahoo.com; *V.P./Pres.-Elect* Kathryn Ray. Tel. 202-885-3238, e-mail kcrdlb@verizon.net; *Secy.* Mykie Howard. Tel. 202-994-1321, fax 202-994-5154, e-mail mhowa3@gwu.edu; *Treas.* Sara Striner. Tel. 202-707-2957, e-mail sstr@loc.gov; *Past Pres.* Jean Craigwell. Tel. 202-458-6172, fax 202-458 3914, e-mail jcwell@juno.com.

Address correspondence to the association, Box 14177, Benjamin Franklin Sta., Washington, DC 20044. Tel. 202-872-1112.

World Wide Web http://www.dcla.org.

Florida

Memb. (Indiv.) 1,400+. Term of Office. April 2004–March 2005. Publication. *Florida Libraries* (s. ann.). *Ed.* Gloria Colvin, Strozier Lib., Florida State Univ., Tallahassee 32306. Tel. 850-644-5211, fax 850-644-5016, e-mail gcolvin@mailer.fsu.edu.

Pres. Derrie Perez, USF Lib. System, 4202 E. Fowler St., Lib. 122, Tampa 33620-5400. Tel. 813-974-1642, fax 813-974-5153, e-mail dperez@lib.usf.edu; *Pres.-Elect* Nancy Pike, Sarasota County Lib. System, 6700 Clark Rd., Sarasota 34241. Tel. 941-861-9842, fax 941-861-9855, e-mail nmpike@scgov.net;

Secy. Faye C. Roberts, State Lib. and Archives of Florida, R. A. Gray Bldg., 500 S. Bronough St., Tallahassee 32399. Tel. 850-245-6637, fax 850-245-6643, e-mail fcroberts@dos.state.fl.us; *Treas.* Shannon Bennett-Manross, M. M. Bennett Lib., Gibbs Campus, St. Petersburg College, 6605 5th Ave. N., St. Petersburg 33781. Tel. 727-341-3517, fax 727-341-4654, e-mail manross.shannon@spcollege.edu; *Past Pres.*John Szabo, Clearwater Public Lib., 100 N. Osceola Ave., Clearwater 33755. Tel. 727-462-6800, fax 727-462-6420, e-mail jszabo@clearwater-fl.com; *Exec. Secy.* Marjorie Cook, Florida Lib. Assn., 1133 W. Morse Blvd., Winter Park 32789. Tel. 407-647-8839, fax 407-629-2502, e-mail mjs@crowsegal.com.

Address correspondence to the executive secretary.

World Wide Web http://www.flalib.org.

Georgia

Memb. 1,080. Term of Office. Dec. 2004– Dec. 2005. Publication. *Georgia Library Quarterly. Ed.* Susan Cooley, Sara Hightower Regional Lib., 205 Riverside Pkwy., Rome 30161. Tel. 706-236-4621, fax 706-236-4631, e-mail cooleys@mail.floyd.public.lib.ga.us.

Pres. Julie Walker, Georgia Public Lib. Services, 1800 Century Place, Ste. 150, Atlanta 30345. Tel. 303-982-3578, fax 404-982-3563, e-mail jwalker@georgialibraries.org; *1st V.P./Pres.-Elect* Robert E. Fox, Jr., Clayton College and State Univ. Lib., P.O. Box 285, Morrow 30260. Tel. 770-961-3520, e-mail bobfox@mail.clayton.edu; *2nd V.P.* Patty Phipps, Georgia Institute of Technology Lib., 704 Cherry St., Atlanta 30332-0900. Tel. 404-385-4816, e-mail patty.phipps@library.gatech.edu; *Secy.* Laura Burtie, Univ. Lib., Georgia State Univ., 100 Decatur St., Atlanta 30303. Tel. 404-463-9945; *Treas.* Carol Stanley, Athens Technical College, 1317 Athens Hwy., Elberton 30635. Tel. 706-213-2116; *ALA Councillor* Ann Hamilton, Henderson Lib., Georgia Southern Univ., Box 8074, Statesboro 30460-8074. Tel. 912-681-5115, e-mail ahamilton@georgiasouthern.edu; *Past Pres.* George Gaumond,

Odum Lib., Valdosta State Univ., Valdosta 31698. Tel. 229-333-5860, fax 229-259-5055, e-mail ggaumond@valdosta.edu.

Address correspondence to the president, c/o Georgia Lib. Assn., Box 793, Rex 30273-0793

World Wide Web http://wwwlib.gsu.edu/gla.

Hawaii

Memb. 320. Publication. *HLA Newsletter* (3 a year).

Pres. A. Lee Adams, Univ. of Hawaii at Manoa. E-mail president@hlaweb.org; *V.P.* Carol Kellett, Univ. of Hawaii at Manoa. E-mail vicepresident@hlaweb.org; *Secy.* Nancy Sack, Univ. of Hawaii at Manoa. E-mail secretary@hlaweb.org; *Co-Treas.* Kuang-Tien ("KT") Yao, Xin Li. E-mail treasurer@hlaweb.org; *Past Pres.* Catherine Hamer. E-mail pastpresident@hlaweb.org.

Address correspondence to the president. World Wide Web http://www.hlaweb.org.

Idaho

Memb. 500. Term of Office. Oct. 2004–Oct. 2005.

Pres. Barbara Greever, Univ. of Idaho Lib., Box 442350, Moscow 83844-2350. Tel. 208-885-2510, e-mail bgreever@uidaho.edu; *V.P./Pres.-Elect* Val Fenske, 4288 N. La-Fontana Way, Boise 83702. Tel. 208-332-6967, e-mail vfenske@sde.state.id.us; *Secy.* Lynn Baird, Univ. of Idaho Lib., Box 442350, Moscow 83844-2350. Tel. 208-885-6713, e-mail lbaird@uidaho.edu; *Treas.* Pam Bradshaw, Idaho State Lib., 325 W. State St., Boise 82702. Tel. 208-334-2150, e-mail pbradsha@isl.state.id.us; *Past Pres.* Vicki Kreimeyer, Boise Public Lib., 715 S. Capitol Blvd., Boise 83702. Tel. 208-384-4341, e-mail vkreimeyer@cityofboise.org.

Address correspondence to the president. World Wide Web http://www.idaho libraries.org.

Illinois

Memb. 3,000. Term of Office. July 2004–July 2005. Publication. *ILA Reporter* (bi-mo.).

Pres. Allen Lanham, Booth Lib., Eastern Illinois Univ., 600 Lincoln Ave., Charleston 61920; *V.P./Pres.-Elect* Dianne C. Harmon, Joliet Public Lib., Black Road Branch, 3395 Black Rd., Joliet 60431; *Treas.* Christopher Bowen, Downers Grove Public Lib., 1050 Curtiss, Downers Grove 60515-4606; *Past Pres.* Nancy M. Gillfillan, Fondulac District Lib., 140 E. Washington St., East Peoria 61611-2526; *Exec. Dir.* Robert P. Doyle, 33 W. Grand Ave., Ste. 301, Chicago 60610-4306. Tel. 312-644-1896, fax 312-644-1899, e-mail ila@ila.org.

Address correspondence to the executive director.

World Wide Web http://www.ila.org.

Indiana

Memb. 3,000+. Term of Office. March 2004–April 2005. Publications. *Focus on Indiana Libraries* (11 a year), *Indiana Libraries* (s. ann.). *Ed.* Crissy Gallion.

Pres. John Robson. Tel. 812-877-8365, fax 812-877-8175, e-mail john.m.robson@rose-hulman.edu; *1st V.P.* Wendy Phillips. Tel. 317-814-3901, fax 317-571-4285, e-mail wphillips@carmel.lib.in.us; *2nd V.P.* Sara Laughlin. Tel. 812-334-8485, fax 812-336-2215, e-mail laughlin@bluemarble.net; *Secy.* Nancy Wootton Colborn. Tel. 574-237-4321, fax 574-237-4472, e-mail ncolborn@iusb.edu; *Treas.* Faye Terry. Tel. 317-232-1938, fax 317-232-0002, e-mail fterry@statelib.in.us; *Past Pres.* Nancy McGriff. Tel. 219-767-2263 ext. 389, e-mail nmcgriff@scentral.k12.in.us; *Exec. Dir.* Linda Kolb. E-mail lkolb@ilfonline.org.

Address correspondence to Indiana Lib. Federation, 941 E. 86 St., Ste. 260, Indianapolis 46240. Tel. 317-257-2040, fax 317-257-1389, e-mail ilf@indy.net.

World Wide Web http://www.ilfonline.org.

Iowa

Memb. 1,700. Term of Office. Jan.–Dec. Publication. *The Catalyst* (bi-mo.). *Ed.* Laurie Hews.

Pres. Katherine F. Martin, Rod Lib., Univ. of Northern Iowa, Cedar Falls 50613-3675. Tel. 319-273-7255, fax 319-273-2913, e-mail katherine.martin@uni.edu; *V.P./Pres.-Elect*

Susan Craig, Iowa City Public Lib., 123 S. Linn St., Iowa City 52240. Tel. 319-356-5200 ext. 153, fax 319-365-5495, e-mail scraig@icpl.org; *Secy.* Marilyn Murphy, Busse Center Lib., Mt. Mercy College, 1330 Elmhurst Dr. N.E., Cedar Rapids 52402. Tel. 319-363-8213 ext. 1244, fax 319-363-9060, e-mail marilyn@mmc.mtmercy.edu; *Past Pres.* Kay Weiss, Burlington Public Lib., 501 N. 4th St., Burlington 52601-5279. Tel. 319-753-1647, e-mail kweiss@aea16.k12.ia.us; *Exec. Dir.* Laurie Hews. Tel. 515-273-5322, fax 515-309-4576, e-mail ialibrary@mcleod usa.net.

Address correspondence to the association, 3636 Westown Pkwy., Ste. 202, West Des Moines 50266.

World Wide Web http://www.iowalibrary association.org.

Kansas

Memb. 1,500. Term of Office. July 2004–June 2005. Publication. *KLA Newsletter* (q.).

Pres. Patti Butcher, NEKLS, 3300 Clinton Pkwy., No. 100, Lawrence 66047. Tel. 785-838-4090, fax 785-838-3989, e-mail pbutcher @nekls.org; *1st V.P.* Tim Rogers, Johnson County Lib., Box 2933, Shawnee Mission 66201, e-mail rogers@jocolibrary.org; *Secy.* Kristen Becker, Liberal Memorial Lib., 509 N. Kansas, Liberal 67901; *Past Pres.* Bob Walter, Axe Lib., Pittsburg State Univ., Pittsburg 66762; *Exec. Dir.* Rosanne Siemens, Kansas Lib. Assn., 1020 Washburn, Topeka 66604. Tel. 866-552-4636, 785-235-1383, fax 785-235-1383, e-mail kansaslibrary association@yahoo.com.

Address correspondence to the executive director.

World Wide Web http://skyways.lib.ks.us/ KLA.

Kentucky

Memb. 1,900. Term of Office. Oct. 2004–Oct. 2005. Publication. *Kentucky Libraries* (q.).

Pres. Linda Kompanik, Logan County Public Lib., 201 W. 6th St., Russellville 42276. Tel. 270-726-6129, fax 270-726-6127, e-mail lindak@loganlibrary.org; *V.P./ Pres.-Elect* Christine McIntosh, Bernheim

Middle School, 700 Audubon Dr., Shepherdsville 40165. Tel. 502-543-7614, fax 502-543-8295, e-mail cmcintosh@bullitt. k12.ky.us; *Secy.* Laura Whayne, Kentucky Transportation Center, Univ. of Kentucky, 176 Raymond Bldg., Lexington 40506-0281. Tel. 859-257-4513 ext. 234, fax 859-257-1815, e-mail lwhayne@engr.uky.edu; *Past Pres.* Carol Nutter, Camden-Carroll Lib., Morehead State Univ., Morehead 40351. Tel. 606-783-5110, fax 606-783-2799, e-mail c.nutter@moreheadstate.edu; *Exec. Secy.* Tom Underwood, 1501 Twilight Trail, Frankfort 40601. Tel. 502-223-5322, fax 502-223-4937, e-mail kylibasn@mis.net.

Address correspondence to the executive secretary.

World Wide Web http://www.kylibasn.org.

Louisiana

Memb. (Indiv.) 1,170; (Inst.) 56. Term of Office. July 2004–June 2005. Publication. *Louisiana Libraries* (q.).

Pres. Terry Thibodeaux. Tel./fax 225-621-8281, e-mail thibodeaux@cox.net; *1st V.P./ Pres.-Elect* Jackie Choate. Tel. 337-893-2655, fax 337-898-0526, e-mail jchoate@ state.lib.la.us; *2nd V.P.* Christy Reeves. Tel. 225-219-9501, e-mail creeves@state.lib.la. us; *Secy.* Catherine Brooks. Tel. 225-343-4941, fax 225-387-3324, e-mail cbrooks 54@cox.net; *Past Pres.* Charlene Cain. Tel. 225-578-4957, fax 225-578-5773, e-mail llcain@lsu.edu.

Address correspondence to Louisiana Lib. Assn., 421 S. 4 St., Eunice 70535. Tel. 337-550-7890, fax 337-550-7846, e-mail office@ llaonline.org.

Maine

Memb. 950. Term of Office. (Pres., V.P.) July 2004–July 2005. Publication. *Maine Memo* (mo.).

Pres. Steve Norman, Belfast Free Lib., 106 High St., Belfast 04915. Tel. 207-338-3884, e-mail snorman@belfastlibrary.org; *V.P.* Pam Turner, Baxter Memorial Lib., 71 South St., Gorham 04038. Tel. 207-839-5031, e-mail pturner@baxter-memorial.lib. me.us; *Secy.* Janet Morgan, Wiscasset Public Lib., Box 367, 21 High St., Wiscasset 04578-

0367. Tel. 207-882-7161, fax 207-882-6698, e-mail jmorgan@wiscasset.lib.me.us; *Treas.* Nikki Maounis, Rockland Public Lib., 80 Union St., Rockland 04841-2925. Tel. 207-594-0310, e-mail nmaounis@ci.rockland.me; *Past Pres.* Anne Davis, Gardiner Public Lib., 152 Water St., Gardiner 04345. Tel. 207-582-3312, e-mail annedavis@gpl.lib.me.us.

Address correspondence to the association, 60 Community Dr., Augusta 04330. Tel. 207-623-8428, fax 207-626-5947. World Wide Web http://mainelibraries.org.

Maryland

Memb. 1,000. Term of Office. July 2004–July 2005. Publications. *Happenings* (mo.), *The Crab* (q.).

Pres. Raineyl Coiro, Eastern Shore Regional Lib., 122–126 S. Division St., Salisbury 21801. Tel. 410-742-1537, fax 410-548-5807; *1st V.P./Pres.-Elect* Kay Bowman, Davis Community Lib.; *2nd V.P.* Lee Wisel, Weis Lib., Columbia Union College; *Secy.* Monica McAbee, PGCMLS, Central; *Treas.* Beth Pelle, Frederick County Public Libs.; *Past Pres.* Daraka Cook, Community College Baltimore County–Catonsville; *Exec. Dir.* Margaret Carty.

Address correspondence to the association, 1401 Hollins St., Baltimore 21223. Tel. 410-947-5090, fax 410-947-5089, e-mail mla@mdlib.org.

World Wide Web http://mdlib.org.

Massachusetts

Memb. (Indiv.) 950; (Inst.) 100. Term of Office. July 2004–June 2005. Publication. *Bay State Libraries* (10 a year).

Pres. Carolyn Noah. Tel. 508-757-4110 ext. 305, fax 508-757-4370, e-mail cnoah@cmrls.org; *V.P./Pres.-Elect* Kathleen Baxter. Tel. 781-320-7230, fax 781-320-7230, e-mail Katie_Baxter-fac@nobles.edu; *Secy.* Marnie Warner. Tel. 617-878-0338, fax 617-723-8821, e-mail Warner_m@jud.state.ma.us; *Treas.* Deborah Abraham. Tel. 617-394-2303, fax 617-389-1230, e-mail abraham@noblenet.org; *Past Pres.* Barbara Flaherty. Tel. 978-671-0949 ext. 101, fax 978-670-9493, e-mail bflaherty@mailserv.mvlc.lib.ma.us; *Exec. Mgr.* Diane Klaiber, Massachu-

setts Lib. Assn., P.O. Box 1445, Marstons Mills 02648. Tel. 508-428-5865, fax 508-428-5865, e-mail malibraries@comcast.net.

Address correspondence to the executive manager.

World Wide Web http://www.masslib.org.

Michigan

Memb. (Indiv.) 1,850; (Inst.) 375. Term of Office. July 2004–June 2005 Publications. *Michigan Librarian Newsletter* (6 a year), *Michigan Library Association Forum* e-journal (2 a year).

Pres. Linda Farynk, Saginaw Valley State Univ., 415 W. Main St., Midland 48640. Tel. 989-964-4236, fax 989-964-2003, e-mail lfarynk@svsu.edu; *Pres.-Elect* Michael McGuire, Traverse Area District Lib., 610 Woodmere Ave., Traverse City 49686. Tel. 616-932-8500, fax 616-932-8538, e-mail mike@tcnet.org; *V.P.* Cindy Lou Poquette, Indian River Area Lib., P.O. Box 160, Indian River 49749. Tel. 231-238-8581, fax 231-238-9494, e-mail indriv1@northland.lib.mi.us; *Secy.* Sheryl Vanderwagen, Lakeland Lib. Cooperative, 4138 Three Mile Rd., Grand Rapids 49544. Tel. 616-559-5253, fax 616-559-4329, e-mail sheryl@llcoop.org; *Treas.* Faye Backie, Michigan State Univ., 227 Clarendon Rd., East Lansing 48823. Tel. 517-432-6123, fax 517-432-0487, e-mail backie@msu.edu; *Past Pres.* Marcia Warner, Public Libs. of Saginaw. E-mail m.warner@saginawlibrary.org.

Address correspondence to Michigan Lib. Assn., 1407 Rensen St., Ste. 2, Lansing 48910. Tel. 517-394-2774, fax 517-394-2675, e-mail mla@mlcnet.org.

World Wide Web http://www.mla.lib.mi.us.

Minnesota

Memb. 1,200. Term of Office. (Pres., Pres.-Elect) Jan.–Dec. 2005. Publication. *MLA Newsletter* (6 a year).

Pres. Marlene Moulton Janssen. Tel. 651-645-5731, fax 651-649-3169, e-mail marlene@melsa.org; *Pres.-Elect* Audrey Betcher. Tel. 507-285-8011, fax 507-287-1910, e-mail audrey@rochester.lib.mn.us; *Secy.* Michele McGraw. Tel. 952-847-5931, e-mail mmcgraw@hclib.org; *Treas.* Bescye Burnett.

Tel. 320-650-2512, fax 320-650-2501, e-mail bescyeb@grrl.lib.mn.us; *Past Pres.* Bill Sozanski. Tel. 218-726-8102, fax 218-726-8019, e-mail bsozansk@d.umn.edu; *Exec. Dir.* Alison Schaub, Minnesota Lib. Assn., 1619 Dayton Ave., Ste. 314, Saint Paul 55104. Tel. 651-641-0982, fax 651-641-3169, e-mail alison@mnlibraryassociation.org.

Address correspondence to the executive director.

World Wide Web http://www.mnlibrary association.org.

Mississippi

Memb. 600. Term of Office. Jan.–Dec. 2005. Publication. *Mississippi Libraries* (q.).

Pres. Susan S. Cassagne, Natchez Adams Wilkinson Lib. Service. Tel. 601-445-8862, fax 601-446-7795, e-mail scassagne@naw.lib.ms.us; *V.P./Pres.-Elect* Catherine A. Nathan, First Regional Lib. System. Tel. 662-429-4439, e-mail cnathan@first.lib.ms.us; *Secy.* Linda Milner, Mid Mississippi Lib. System. Tel. 662-289-5151, e-mail asst director@midmissregional.lib.ms.us; *Treas.* Carol D. Green, Univ. of Southern Mississippi. Tel. 601-266-4476, e-mail carol.green@usm.edu; *Past Pres.* Juanita Flanders, Hinds Community College, Box 1100, Raymond 39154-1100. Tel. 601-857-3380, fax 601-857-3293, e-mail hjflanders@hinds.cc.ms.us; *Exec. Secy.* Mary Julia Anderson, Box 20448, Jackson 39289-1448. Tel. 601-352-3917, fax 601-352-4240, e-mail mla@meta3.net.

Address correspondence to the executive secretary.

World Wide Web http://www.lib.usm.edu/~mla/org/main.html.

Missouri

Memb. 825. Term of Office. Jan.–Dec. 2005. Publication. *MO INFO* (bi-mo.). *Ed.* Margaret Booker.

Pres. Ann Campion Riley, Lovejoy Lib., Southern Illinois Univ.–Edwardsville, 14140 Cross Trails Dr., Chesterfield 63017-3309. Tel. 618-650-2779, e-mail anriley@siue.edu; *Pres.-Elect* Wicky Sleight, Kirkwood Public Lib., 140 E. Jefferson Ave., Kirkwood 63122. Tel. 314-821-5770, fax 314-822-3755, e-mail

jtz005@mail.connect.more.net; *Secy.* Marie Concannon, 106B Ellis Lib., Columbia 65201. Tel. 573-882-0748, e-mail concannonm @missouri.edu; *Treas.* Catherine Craven, Health Management and Information–UMC, P.O. Box 7702, Columbia 65205. Tel. 573-882-1542, e-mail ckcraven@earthlink.net; *Past Pres.* Victor Gragg, Trustee, Mid-Continent Public Lib., 15616 E. 24 Hwy., Independence 64050. Tel. 816-796-4408, fax 816-521-7253, e-mail vgragg@juno.com; *Exec. Dir.* Margaret Booker. Tel. 573-449-4627, fax 573-449-4655, e-mail mla@kinetic.more.net.

Address correspondence to the executive director.

World Wide Web http://www.molib.org.

Montana

Memb. 600. Term of Office. July 2004–June 2005. Publication. *Montana Library Focus* (bi-mo.).

Pres. Richard Wojtowicz, MSU Libs., Box 173320, Bozeman 59717-3320. Tel. 406-994-1873, fax 406-994-2851, e-mail richw@montana.edu; *V.P./Pres.-Elect* Milla L. Cummins, Livingston-Park County Public Lib., 228 W. Callender St., Livingston 59047-2618. Tel. 406-222-0862, fax 406-222-6522, e-mail mcummins@ycsi.net; *Secy./Treas.* Debbi Kramer, Judith Basin County Lib., P.O. Box 486, Standford 59479. Tel. 406-566-2277 ext. 123, e-mail spclk@3rivers.net; *Past Pres.* John Finn, Great Falls Public Lib., 301 2nd Ave. N., Great Falls 59401-2593. Tel. 406-453-0349, fax 406-453-0181, e-mail jfinn@mtlib.org; *Exec. Dir.* Karen A. Hatcher, 510 Arbor St., Missoula 59802-3126. Tel. 406-721-3347, fax 406-243-2060, e-mail hatcher@montana.com.

Address correspondence to the executive director.

World Wide Web http://www.mtlib.org.

Nevada

Memb. 450. Term of Office. Jan.–Dec. 2005. Publication. *Nevada Libraries* (q.).

Pres. Ian Campbell, Washoe County Lib. System. E-mail idcampbe@mail.co.washoe.nv.us; *V.P./Pres.-Elect* Kim Clanton-Green, Las Vegas-Clark County Lib. Dist., Sahara

West Lib. E-mail clanton-green@lvccld.org; *Treas.* Joanne Ross, Las Vegas-Clark County Lib. Dist., Spring Valley Lib. E-mail rossj@lvccld.org; *Past Pres.* Felton Thomas, Jr., Las Vegas/Clark County Lib. Dist. E-mail thomasf@lvccld.org; *Exec. Secy.* Patrick Dunn, Elko-Lander-Eureka Counties Lib., 720 Court St., Elko 89801. Tel. 775-738-3066, fax 775-738-8262, e-mail pfdunn@clan.lib.nv.us.

Address correspondence to the executive secretary.

World Wide Web http://www.nevada libraries.org.

New Hampshire

Memb. 700. Publication. *NHLA News* (q.).

Pres. Catherine Redden, Lane Memorial Lib., 2 Academy Ave., Hampton 03842. Tel. 603-926-3368, e-mail director@hampton.lib.nh.us; *V.P.* Doris Mitton, Dalton Public Lib., 741 Dalton Rd., Unit 2, Dalton 03598. Tel. 603-837-2751, e-mail daltonpl@ncia.net; *Secy.* Jennifer Bone, Keene Public Lib., 60 Winter St., Keene 03431. Tel. 603-352-0157 e-mail jbone@ci.keene.nh.us; *Past Pres.* Andrea Thorpe, Richards Free Lib., 58 N. Main St., Newport 03773. Tel. 603-863-3430, e-mail athorpe@newport.lib.nh.us.

Address correspondence to the association, Box 2332, Concord 03302.

World Wide Web http://webster.state.nh.us/nhla.

New Jersey

Memb. 1,700. Term of Office. July 2004–June 2005. Publication. *New Jersey Libraries Newsletter* (mo.).

Pres. Carol Phillips, East Brunswick Public Lib., 2 Jean Walling Civic Center, East Brunswick 08816. Tel. 732-390-6789, fax 732-390-6796, e-mail cphillips@ebpl.org; *V.P.* April Judge, West Caldwell Public Lib., 30 Clinton Rd., West Caldwell 07006. Tel. 973-226-5441, fax 973-228-7578, e-mail bookdirector@yahoo.com; *2nd V.P.* Michele Reutty, Hasbrouck Heights Lib., 320 Boulevard, Hasbrouck Heights 07604. Tel. 201-288-0484, fax 201-288-6653, e-mail reutty@bccls.org; *Secy.* Margery Kirby Cyr, Old Bridge Public Lib., 1 Old Bridge Plaza, Old Bridge 08857. Tel. 732-721-5600 ext. 5014, fax 732-679-0556, e-mail mcyr@lmxac.org; *Treas.* Keith McCoy, Roselle Free Public Lib., 104 W. 4 Ave., Roselle 07203. Tel. 908-245-5809, fax 908-298-8881, e-mail wkmccoy@lmxac.org; *Past Pres.* Patricia Ann Hannon, Emerson Public Lib., 20 Palisade Ave., Emerson 07630. Tel. 201-261-5569, fax 201-262-7999, e-mail pahannon@verizon.net; *Exec. Dir.* Patricia Tumulty, NJLA, Box 1534, Trenton 08607. Tel. 609-394-8032, fax 609-394-8164, e-mail ptumulty@njla.org.

Address correspondence to the executive director.

World Wide Web http://www.njla.org.

New Mexico

Memb. 550. Term of Office. Apr. 2004–Apr. 2005. Publication. *New Mexico Library Association Newsletter* (6 a year). *Ed.* Pam Mackellar. E-mail pmackellar@earthlink.net.

Pres. Heather Gallegos-Rex. E-mail hgallego@stlib.st.nm.us; *V.P.* Kathy Matter. E-mail Matterkathy@aol.com; *Secy.* Julia Clarke. E-mail jckarke@cabq.gov; *Treas.* Kathyrn Albrecht. E-mail kalbrecht@admin.nmt.edu; *Past Pres.* Eileen Longsworth. E-mail elongsworth@cabq.gov.

Address correspondence to the association, Box 26074, Albuquerque 87125. Tel. 505-400-7309, fax 505-899-7600, e-mail nmla@worldnet.att.net.

World Wide Web http://www.nmla.org.

New York

Memb. 3,000. Term of Office. Oct. 2004–Nov. 2005. Publication. *NYLA Bulletin* (6 a year). *Ed.* David Titus.

Pres. Rocco Staino. Tel. 914-669-5414, e-mail stainor@northsalem.k12.ny.us; *Pres.-Elect* Jennifer Morris. Tel. 585-394-8260, e-mail jmorris@pls-net.org; *Treas.* Christine McDonald. Tel. 518-92-6508, e-mail mcdonald@crandalllibrary.org; *Past Pres.* Arthur Friedman. Tel. 516-572-7883, e-mail friedma@sunynassau.edu; *Exec. Dir.* Michael J. Borges. E-mail director@nyla.org.

Address correspondence to the executive director, New York Lib. Assn., 252 Hudson Ave., Albany 12210. Tel. 800-252-6952 or

518-432-6952, fax 518-427-1697, e-mail info@nyla.org.

World Wide Web http://www.nyla.org.

North Carolina

Memb. 1,100. Term of Office. Oct. 2003–Oct. 2005. Publication. *North Carolina Libraries* (q.). *Ed.* Plummer Alston Jones, Jr., Assoc. Professor, Dept. of Libnship., Educ. Technology, and Distance Learning, East Carolina Univ., 122 Joyner E., Greenville 27858-4353. Tel. 252-328-6803, fax 252-328-4368, e-mail jonesp@mail.ecu.edu.

Pres. Pauletta Brown Bracy, North Carolina Central Univ., SLIS, Box 19586, Durham 27707. Tel. 919-560-6401, fax 919-560-6402, e-mail pbracy@wpo.nccu.edu; *V.P./Pres.-Elect* Robert Burgin, North Carolina Central Univ., 307 Swiss Lake Dr., Cary 27513. Tel. 919-380-8074, e-mail rburgin@mindspring.com; *Secy.* Connie Keller, Technical Services, Elon Univ., Box 187, Elon 27244. Tel. 336-278-6578, e-mail keller@elon.edu; *Treas.* Diane Kester, Dept. of Libnship., Educ. Technology, and Distance Learning, East Carolina Univ., 122 Joyner E., Greenville 27858-4353. Tel. 252-328-6621, e-mail kester@soe.ecu.edu; *Past Pres.* Ross Holt, Randolph County Public Lib., 201 Worth St., Asheboro 27203. Tel. 336-318-6806, fax 336-318-6823, e-mail rholt@ncsl.dcr.state.nc.us; *Admin. Asst.* Kim Parrott, North Carolina Lib. Assn., 1811 Capital Blvd., Raleigh 27604. Tel. 919-839-6252, fax 919-839-6253, e-mail nclaonline@ibiblio.org.

Address correspondence to the administrative assistant.

World Wide Web http://www.nclaonline.org.

North Dakota

Memb. (Indiv.) 400; (Inst.) 18. Term of Office. Sept. 2004–Sept. 2005. Publication. *The Good Stuff* (q.). *Ed.* Marlene Anderson, Bismarck State College Lib., Box 5587, Bismarck 58506-5587. Tel. 701-224-5578.

Pres. Marlene Anderson, Bismarck State College Lib., Box 5587, Bismarck 58506-5587. Tel. 701-224-5578, fax 701-224-5551, e-mail marlene.anderson@bsc.nodak.edu;

Pres.-Elect Jeanne Narum, Minot Public Lib., 516 2nd Ave. S.W., Minot 58701. Tel. 701-852-1045, fax 701-852-2595, e-mail jnarum@ndak.net; *Treas.* Michael Safratowich, Harley French Lib. of the Health Sciences, Univ. of North Dakota, Box 9002, Grand Forks 58202-9002. Tel. 701-777-2602, fax 701-777-4790, e-mail msafrat@medicine.nodak.edu; *Past Pres.* Pamela K. Drayson, North Dakota State Univ. Lib., Box 5599, Fargo 58105-5599 Tel. 701-231-8352, fax 701-231-6128, e-mail pamela.drayson@ndsu.nodak.edu.

Address correspondence to the president.

World Wide Web http://ndsl.lib.state.nd.us/ndla.

Ohio

Memb. 3,400+. Term of Office. Jan.–Dec. 2005. Publications. *Access* (mo.), *Ohio Libraries* (q.).

Pres. Pam Hickson-Stevenson, Portage County Dist. Lib., Garrettsville; *V.P./Pres.-Elect* J. Craig Miller, Holmes County District Public Lib., Millersburg; *Secy.-Treas.* Cindy Lombardo, Tuscaraws County Public Lib., New Philadelphia; *Past Pres.* Tom Adkins, Garnet A. Wilson Public Lib. of Pike County, Waverly; *Exec. Dir.* Douglas S. Evans.

Address correspondence to the executive director, OLC, 2 Easton Oval, Ste. 525, Columbus 43219-7008. Tel. 614-416-2258, fax 614-416-2270, e-mail olc@olc.org.

World Wide Web http://www.olc.org.

Oklahoma

Memb. (Indiv.) 1,050; (Inst.) 60. Term of Office. July 2004–June 2005. Publication. *Oklahoma Librarian* (bi-mo.). *Ed.* Christine Detlaff. E-mail dettlaffc@redlandscc.edu.

Pres. Lynn McIntosh. E-mail crlsdir@oltn.odl.state.ok.us; *V.P./Pres.-Elect* Jeanie Johnson. E-mail jeanie_johnson@sde.state.ok.us; *Secy.* Lynda Reynolds. E-mail libdirector@stillwater.org; *Treas.* Deborah Willis. E-mail dwillis@mls.lib.ok.us; *Past Pres.* Anne Prestamo. E-mail prestamo@cox.net; *Exec. Dir.* Kay Boies, 300 Hardy Dr., Edmond 73013. Tel. 405-348-0506, fax 405-348-1629, e-mail kboies@coxinet.net.

Address correspondence to the executive director.

World Wide Web http://www.oklibs.org.

Oregon

Memb. (Indiv.) 1,000+. Publications. *OLA Hotline* (bi-w.), *OLA Quarterly*.

Pres. Mo Cole, Northwest Christian College. Tel. 541-684-7237, e-mail mcole@nwcc.edu; *V.P./Pres.-Elect* Leah Griffith, Newberg Public Lib. Tel. 503-538-1256, e-mail leahg@ccrls.org; *Secy.* Marsha Richmond, Oregon Trail Lib. Dist. Tel. 541-481-3365, e-mail otld@hotmail.com; *Treas.* Suzanne Sager, Portland State Univ. Tel. 503-725-8169, e-mail sagers@pdx.edu; *Past Pres.* Faye Chadwell, Univ. of Oregon Libs. Tel. 541-346-1819, e-mail chadwelf@uoregon.edu.

Address correspondence to Oregon Library Association, P.O. Box 2042, Salem 97308. E-mail ola@olaweb.org.

World Wide Web http://www.olaweb.org.

Pennsylvania

Memb. 1,800. Term of Office. Jan.–Dec. 2005. Publication. *PaLA Bulletin* (10 a year).

Pres. Catherine Alloway, Public Services Dir., Dauphin County Lib. System, 101 Walnut St., Harrisburg 17101. Tel. 717-234-4961, fax 717-234-7479, e-mail calloway@dcls.org; *1st V.P.* Evelyn Minick, Univ. Libn., St. Joseph's Univ. E-mail minick@sju.edu; *2nd V.P.* Sue Erdman, Joseph T. Simpson Public Lib. E-mail serdman@ccpa.net; *Treas.* Catherine Schappert, Dir. of Lib. Services, Marywood Univ. E-mail chs@marywood.edu; *Past Pres.* Jonelle Prether Darr, Cumberland County Lib. System. Tel. 717-240-6175, fax 717-240-7770, e-mail jdarr@ccpa.net; *Exec. Dir.* Glenn R. Miller, Pennsylvania Lib. Assn., 220 Cumberland Pkwy., Ste. 10, Mechanicsburg 17055. Tel. 717-766-7663, fax 717-766-5440, e-mail glenn@palibraries.org.

Address correspondence to the executive director.

World Wide Web http://www.palibraries.org.

Rhode Island

Memb. (Indiv.) 350+; (Inst.) 50+. Term of Office. June 2003–June 2005. Publication. *Rhode Island Library Association Bulletin.* Ed. Leslie McDonough.

Pres. Derryl R. Johnson, 10 Midway St., North Scituate 02857. Tel. 401-258-7443, e-mail dejohnson2@earthlink.net; *V.P./Pres.-Elect* Cindy Lunghofer, East Providence Public Lib., 41 Grove Ave., East Providence 02914. Tel. 401-434-2453, e-mail book_n@yahoo.com; *Secy.* Joyce May, East Providence Public Lib., 41 Grove Ave., East Providence 02914. Tel. 401-434-2453, e-mail joycemy@lori.state.ri.us; *Treas.* Janet A. Levesque, Cumberland Public Lib., 1464 Diamond Hill Rd., Cumberland 02864. Tel. 401-333-2552 ext. 5, e-mail jlevesque@cumberlandlibrary.org; *Past Pres.* David Macksam, Cranston Public Lib., 140 Sockanosset Cross Rd., Cranston 02920. Tel. 401-943-9080, fax 401-946-5079, e-mail davidmm@lori.state.ri.us.

World Wide Web http://www.uri.edu/library/rila/rila.html.

South Carolina

Memb. 550+. Term of Office. Jan.–Dec. 2005. Publication. *News and Views.*

Pres. Elizabeth Shuping, Horry County Memorial Lib., 1603 4th Ave., Conway 29526. Tel. 843-248-1550, fax 843-248-1549. e-mail eshuping@excite.com; *1st V.P./Pres.-Elect* Joyce Durant, Rogers Lib., Francis Marion Univ., P.O. Box 100547, Florence 29501. Tel. 843-661-1304, fax 843-661-1309, e-mail jdurant@fmarion.edu; *2nd V.P. for Membership* Quincy Pugh, Richland County Public Lib., 1431 Assembly St., Columbia 29201. Tel. 803-929-3449, fax 803-929-3448, e-mail qpugh@richland.lib.sc.us; *Secy.* Kathy Mitchell, Beaufort County Lib., 311 Scott St., Beaufort 29902. Tel. 843-525-4060, fax 843-525-4055, e-mail kathym@mail.co.beaufort.sc.us; *Treas.* Camille McCutcheon, USC Spartanburg Lib., 800 University Way, Spartanburg 29303. Tel. 864-503-5612, fax 864-503-5601, e-mail cmccutcheon@uscs.edu; *Past Pres.* Marilyn Tisirigotis, Harvin Clarendon County Lib.,

215 N. Brooks St., Clarendon 29102. Tel. 803-435-8633, fax 803-435-8101, e-mail marilynt@infoave.net; *Exec. Secy.* Bree Amerson, P.O. Box 1763, Columbia 29202. Tel. 803-252-1087, fax 803-252-0580, e-mail bamerson@capconsc.com.

Address correspondence to the executive secretary.

World Wide Web http://www.scla.org.

South Dakota

Memb. (Indiv.) 497; (Inst.) 54. Term of Office. Oct. 2004–Oct. 2005. Publication. *Book Marks* (bi-mo.). *Ed.* Lisa Brunick, Augustana College. E-mail lisa_brunick@augie.edu.

Pres. Deb Hagemeier, Augustana College. E-mail deb_hagemeier@augie.edu; *V.P./Pres.-Elect* Kevin Kenkel, Dakota Wesleyan Univ. E-mail kekenkel@dwu.edu; *Secy.* LaVera Rose, South Dakota State Lib., Pierre. E-mail lavera.rose@state.sd.us; *Exec. Secy./Treas.* Brenda Hemmelman, Rapid City Public Lib. E-mail bkstand@rap.midco.net; *Past Pres.* Dennis Nath, Mitchell School Dist. E-mail denny.nath@k12.sd.us.

Address correspondence to the executive secretary, SDLA, Box 1212, Rapid City 57709-1212. Tel. 605-394-3169 ext. 501, e-mail bkstand@rap.midco.net.

World Wide Web http://www.usd.edu/sdla.

Tennessee

Memb. 725. Term of Office. July 2004–June 2005. Publications. *Tennessee Librarian* (q.), *TLA Newsletter* (bi-mo.) (both electronic only at http://www.tnla.org).

Pres. Kay Due, Memphis/Shelby County Public Lib. and Info. Center, Memphis 38111. E-mail duek@memphis.lib.tn.us; *V.P./Pres.-Elect* Cathy Taylor, White County Public Lib., 144 S. Main St., Sparta 32583-2299. E-mail cathymt@charter.net; *Recording Secy.* Francis Adams-O'Brien, Municipal Technical Advisory Service, 120 Conference Center, Knoxville 37996-4105. E-mail frances.adams-obrien@tennessee.edu; *Past Pres.* Kathy Pagles, Blount County Public Lib., Maryville 37804. E-mail kpagles@blounttn.org; *Exec. Dir.* Annelle R. Huggins, Tennessee Lib. Assn., Box 241074, Memphis 38124. Tel. 901-485-6952, e-mail ahuggins@midsouth.rr.com.

Address correspondence to the executive director.

World Wide Web http://tnla.org.

Texas

Memb. 7,300. Term of Office. Apr. 2004–Apr. 2005. Publications. *Texas Library Journal* (q.), *TLACast* (9 a year).

Pres. Dana C. Rooks, Univ. of Houston, 114 Univ. Libs., Houston 77204-2000. Tel. 713-743-9795, fax 713-743-9811, e-mail drooks@uh.edu; *Pres.-Elect* Gretchen McCord Hoffmann. E-mail ghoffmann@fulbright.com; *Treas.* S. Joe McCord. E-mail mccord@cl.uh.edu; *Past Pres.* Eva Poole, Denton Public Lib. System, 502 Oakland St., Denton 76201-3102. Tel. 940-349-7735, fax 940-349-8260, e-mail eva.poole@cityofdenton.com; *Exec. Dir.* Patricia H. Smith, 3355 Bee Cave Rd., Ste. 401, Austin 78746-6763. Tel. 512-328-1518, fax 512-328-8852, e-mail pats@txla.org.

Address correspondence to the executive director.

World Wide Web http://www.txla.org.

Utah

Memb. 650. Term of Office. May 2004–May 2005. Publication. *UTAH Libraries News* (bi-mo.) (electronic at http://www.ula.org/newsletter).

Pres. Gene Nelson, Provo City Lib., 550 N. University Ave., Provo 84601-1618. Tel. 801-852-6663, e-mail genen@provo.lib.ut.us; *Treas./Exec. Secy.* Christopher Anderson.

Address correspondence to the executive secretary, 2150 South 1300 East, Ste. 500 MS 55, Salt Lake City 84106. Tel. 801-273-8150, e-mail admin.ula@xmission.com.

World Wide Web http://www.ula.org.

Vermont

Memb. 400. Publication. *VLA News* (6 a year).

Pres. David Clark, Ilsley Public Lib., 75 Main St., Middlebury 05753. Tel. 802-388-

4095, fax 802-388-4367, e-mail dclark@myriad.middlebury.edu; *V.P./Pres.-Elect* Daisy Benson, Bailey/Howe Lib., Univ. of Vermont, Burlington 05405. Tel. 802-656-0636, fax 802-656-4038, e-mail daisy.benson@uvm.edu; *Secy.* Mary Kasamatsu, Waterbury Public Lib., 28 N. Main St., Waterbury 05676. Tel. 802-244-7036, e-mail waterbury publiclibrary@hotmail.com; *Treas.* Donna Edwards, Samuel Read Hall Lib., Lyndon State College, P.O. Box 919, Lyndonville 05851. Tel. 802-626-6447, fax 802-626-6331, e-mail donna.edwards@lsc.vsc.edu; *Past Pres.* Ellen F. Hall, Kreitzberg Lib., Norwich Univ., 23 Harmon Dr., Northfield 05663. Tel. 802-485-2169, e-mail ehall@norwich.edu.

Address correspondence to VLA, Box 803, Burlington 05402.

World Wide Web http://www.vermont libraries.org.

Virginia

Memb. 1,100+. Term of Office. Oct. 2004–Oct. 2005. Publications. *Virginia Libraries* (q.). *Co.-Eds.* Cy Dillon. Tel. 540-365-4428, e-mail cdillon@ferrum.edu; Carolyn Gardner. Tel. 757-727-1218, e-mail cgardner@hampton.gov; *VLA Newsletter* (10 a year). *Ed.* Kevin Tapp. Tel. 540-231-4073, e-mail ktapp@vt.edu.

Pres. Ruth Kifer, George Mason Univ., 4400 University Dr., Mail Stop 1A6, Fairfax 22030. Tel. 703-993-9050, e-mail rkifer@gmu.edu; *Pres.-Elect* Ruth Arnold, Staunton Public Lib., 1 Churchville Ave., Staunton 24401. Tel. 540-332-3902, e-mail arnoldr@ci.staunton.va.us; *Secy.* Lydia Williams, Longwood Univ. Lib., Redfore and Pine Sts., Farmville 23909. Tel. 434-395-2432, e-mail lwilliam@longwood.edu; *Treas.* Steve Preston, Amherst County Public Lib., P.O. Box 370, Amherst 24521. Tel. 434-946-9388, e-mail spreston@acpl.us; *Past Pres.* Morel Fry, Perry Lib., Old Dominion Univ., Norfolk 23529-0256. Tel. 757-683-4143, e-mail mfry@odu.edu; *Exec. Dir.* Linda Hahne, Box 8277, Norfolk 23503-0277. Tel. 757-583-0041, e-mail lhahne@coastalnet.com.

Address correspondence to the executive director.

World Wide Web http://www.vla.org.

Washington

Memb. 1,200. Term of Office. Apr. 2003–Apr. 2005. Publication. *ALKI* (3 a year).

Pres. John Sheller, Federal Way 320th/KCLS, 848 S. 320, Federal Way 98003. Tel. 253-839-0257, fax 206-296-5053, e-mail jsheller@wla.org; *V.P./Pres.-Elect* Carolynne Myall, John F. Kennedy Lib., Eastern Washington Univ., 816 F St., Cheney 99004. Tel. 509-359-6967, fax 509-359-2476, e-mail cmyall@ewu.edu; *Secy.* Nancy Slote, Fairwood Lib./KCLS, 17009 140th S.E., Renton 98058. Tel. 425-226-0522, e-mail nslote@kcls.org; *Treas.* Wayne Suggs, Richland Public Lib., 955 Northgate Dr., Richland 99352, e-mail wsuggs@richland.lib.wa.us; *Assn. Coord.* Gail E. Willis.

Address correspondence to the association office, 4016 1st Ave. N.E., Seattle 98105-6502. Tel. 206-545-1529, fax 206-545-1543, e-mail washla@wla.org.

World Wide Web http://www.wla.org.

West Virginia

Memb. 650+. Term of Office. Dec. 2004–Nov. 2005. Publication. *West Virginia Libraries* (6 a year). *Ed.* Pamela Coyle, Martinsburg Public Lib., 101 W. King St., Martinsburg 25401 Tel. 304-267-8933, e-mail pcoyle@martin.lib.wv.us.

Pres. Penny Pugh, West Virginia Univ. Libs., P.O. Box 6069, West Virginia Univ., Morgantown 26506. Tel. 304-293-4040 ext. 4043, e-mail ppugh@wvu.edu; *1st V.P./Pres.-Elect* Martha C. Yancey, Evansdale Lib., West Virginia Univ. Libs., P.O. Box 6105, Morgantown 26505. Tel. 304-293-5039 ext. 5118, e-mail myancey@wvu.edu; *2nd V.P.* Olivia L. Bravo, Kanawha County Public Lib., 123 Capitol St., Charleston 25301; *Secy.* Margaret Smith, Hamlin Lincoln County Public Lib.; *Treas.* Thelma Hutchins, Fairmont State Univ.; *Past Pres.* Charley Hively, Parkersburg/Wood County Public Lib. E-mail hivelyc@park.lib.wv.us.

Address correspondence to the president.

World Wide Web http://www.wvla.org.

Wisconsin

Memb. 1,800. Term of Office. Jan.–Dec. 2005. Publication. *WLA Newsletter* (q.).

Pres. Terry Dawson, Appleton Public Lib., 225 N. Oneida St., Appleton 54911-4780. Tel. 920-832-6170, fax 920-832-6182, e-mail tdawson@apl.org; *Pres.-Elect* David Weinhold, Eastern Shores Llb. System, 4632 S. Taylor Dr., Sheboygan 53081. E-mail weinhold@esls.lib.wi.us; *Secy.* Genevieve Foskett, Highsmith Corporate Lib., P.O. Box 800, Fort Atkinson 53538-0800. E-mail gfoskett@highscmith.com; *Treas.* Gayle Falk, Burlington Public Lib., 166 E. Jefferson St., Burlington 53105-1491. Tel. 262-763-7623, fax 262-763-1938, e-mail gafalk@burlington.lib.wi.us; *Past Pres.* Nancy A. McClements, Memorial Lib., UW–Madison, 728 State St., Madison 53706. Tel. 608-262-8271, fax 608-262-8569, e-mail nmcclements@library.wisc.edu; *Exec. Dir.* Lisa Strand. Tel. 608-245-3640, fax 608-245-3646, e-mail strand@scls.lib.wi.us.

Address correspondence to the association, 5250 E. Terrace Dr., Ste. A1, Madison 53718-8345.

World Wide Web http://www.wla.lib.wi.us.

Wyoming

Memb. 450+. Term of Office. Oct. 2004–Oct. 2005.

Pres. Deb Schlinger. E-mail dschling@will.state.wy.us; *V.P./Pres.-Elect* Erin Kinney; *Past Pres.* Carey Hartmann; *Exec. Secy.* Laura Grott, Box 1387, Cheyenne 82003. Tel. 307-632-7622, fax 307-638-3469, e-mail grottski@aol.com.

Address correspondence to the executive secretary.

World Wide Web http://www.wyla.org.

Canada

Alberta

Memb. 500. Term of Office. May 2004–Apr. 2005. Publication. *Letter of the LAA* (5 a year).

Pres. Pam Ryan, Univ. of Alberta Libs., 5-02 Cameron Lib., Edmonton T6G 2J8. Tel. 780-492-7324, fax 780-492-8302, e-mail pam.ryan@ualberta.ca; *1st V.P.* Judy Moore, Centre for Reading and the Arts, Edmonton Public Lib., 7 Sir Winston Churchill Sq., Edmonton T5J 2V4. Tel. 780-496-7062, fax 780-944-7570, e-mail jmoore@epl.ca; *2nd V.P.* Connie Forst, RR 1, Willingdon T0B 0R0. Tel. 780-459-1681, fax 780-458-5772, e-mail cforst@nlls.ab.ca; *Treas.* Rachel Sarjeant-Jenkins, Medicine Hat Public Lib., 352 1st St. S.E., Medicine Hat T1A 0A6. Tel. 403-502-8528, fax 403-502-8529, e-mail racsar@medicinehat.ca; *Past Pres.* Michael Perry, Univ. of Lethbridge, 4401 University Dr., Lethbridge T1K 3M4. Tel. 403-329-2272, fax 403-329-2022, e-mail mike.perry@uleth.ca; *Exec. Dir.* Christine Sheppard, 80 Baker Crescent N.W., Calgary T2L 1R4. Tel. 403-284-5818, fax 403-282-6646, e-mail christine.sheppard@shaw.ca.

Address correspondence to the executive director.

World Wide Web http://www.laa.ab.ca.

British Columbia

Memb. 750. Term of Office. June 2004–April 2005. Publication. *BCLA Reporter.* Ed. Ted Benson.

Pres. Diana Guinn, Port Moody Public Lib., 100 Newport Dr., Port Moody V3H 3E1. Tel. 604-469-4580, fax 604-469-4576, e-mail diana.guinn@cityofportmoody.com; *V.P./Pres.-Elect* Melanie Houlden, Surrey Public Lib., 13742 72nd Ave., Surrey V3W 2P4. Tel. 604-572-8269, fax 604-596-8523, e-mail mghoulden@city.surrey.bc.ca; *Past Pres.* Alison Nussbaumer, Univ. of Northern British Columbia, 3333 University Way, Prince George V2N 4Z9. Tel. 250-960-6612, fax 604-960-6610, e-mail alison@unbc.ca; *Treas.* Tanya Thiessen, Surrey Public Lib., Guildford Branch, 15105 105th Ave., Surrey V3R 7G9. E-mail tthiessen@shaw.ca; *Exec. Dir.* Michael Burris.

Address correspondence to the association, 900 Howe St., Ste. 150, Vancouver V6Z 2M4. Tel. 604-683-5354, fax 604-609-0707, e-mail office@bcla.bc.ca.

World Wide Web http://www.bcla.bc.ca.

Manitoba

Memb. 500+. Term of Office. May 2004–May 2005. Publication. *Newsline* (mo.).

Pres. Linwood DeLong, Univ. of Winnipeg Lib., 515 Portage Ave., Winnipeg R3B 2E9. Tel. 204-786-9124, fax 204-786-1824, e-mail l.delong@uwinnipeg.ca; *V.P.* Michael Hohner, Univ. of Winnipeg Lib., 515 Portage Ave., Winnipeg R3B 2E9. Tel. 204-786-9812, fax 204-786-1824, e-mail m.honner@uwinnipeg.ca; *Secy.* Patricia Barrett, 219 Elizabeth Dafoe Lib., Univ. of Manitoba, Winnipeg R3T 2N2. Tel. 204-474-7435, fax 204-474-7583, e-mail p_barrett@umanitoba.ca; *Treas.* Larry Laliberte, Elizabeth Dafoe Lib., Univ. of Manitoba, Winnipeg R3T 2N2. Tel. 204-480-1439, fax 204-989-8476, e-mail laliber@cc.umanitoba.ca; *Past Pres.* Theresa Lomas, Sir William Stephenson Lib., 765 Keewatin St., Winnipeg R2X 3B9. Tel. 204-986-7156, fax 204-986-7201, e-mail tlomas@winnipeg.ca.

Address correspondence to the association, 606-100 Arthur St., Winnipeg R3B 1H3. Tel. 204-943-4567, fax 204-942-1555, e-mail mla@uwinnipeg.ca.

World Wide Web http://www.mla.mb.ca.

Ontario

Memb. 4,200. Term of Office. Jan. 2005–Jan. 2006. Publications. *Access* (q.), *Teaching Librarian* (q.).

Pres. Cynthia Archer, York Univ. Lib. E-mail carcher@yorku.ca; *V.P./Pres.-Elect* Janet Kaufman, Univ. of Guelph. E-mail jkaufman@uoguelph.ca; *Treas.* Roderick McLean. E-mail rodm@vianet.on.ca; *Past Pres.* Ken Roberts, Hamilton Public Lib. Tel. 905-546-3215, fax 905-546-3202, e-mail kroberts@hpl.ca; *Exec. Dir.* Larry Moore. E-mail lmoore@accessola.com.

Address correspondence to the association, 100 Lombard St., Ste. 303, Toronto M5C 1M3. Tel. 416-363-3388, fax 416-941-9581, e-mail info@accessola.com.

World Wide Web http://www.accessola.com.

Quebec

Memb. (Indiv.) 125; (Inst.) 13; (Commercial) 2. Term of Office. June 2004–May 2005. Publication. *ABQ/QLA Bulletin* (3 a year).

Pres. Ann Moffat. E-mail amoffat@westmount.org; *V.P.* Wendy Wayling. E-mail wwayling@westmount.org; *Treas.* Kay Turner. E-mail kturner@emsb.qc.ca; *Past Pres.* Sonia Djevalikian. E-mail sdjevalikian@ville.kirkland.qc.ca; *Exec. Secy.* Janet Ilavsky, Box 1095, Pointe-Claire H9S 4H9. Tel. 514-421-7541, e-mail abqla@abqla.qc.ca.

Address correspondence to the executive secretary.

World Wide Web http://www.abqla.qc.ca.

Saskatchewan

Memb. 225. Term of Office. June 2004–May 2005. Publication. *Forum* (5 a year).

Pres. Michael Keaschuk, Chinook Regional Lib., 1240 Chaplin St. W., Swift Current S9H 0G8. Tel. 306-773-3186, fax 306-773-0434, e-mail mkeaschuk@chinook.lib.sk.ca; *V.P.* Colleen Murphy, Dr. John Archer Lib., Univ. of Regina, Regina S4S 0A2. Tel. 306-585-4028, fax 306-585-4493, e-mail colleen.murphy@uregina.ca; *Treas.* Rosemary Loeffler, La Ronge Public Lib., Box 5680, La Ronge S0J 1L0. Tel. 306-425-2160, fax 306-425-3883, e-mail r.loeffler.sla@pnls.lib.sk.ca; *Past Pres.* Gregory Salmers, Estevan Public Lib., 701 Souris Ave., Estevan S4A 2T1. Tel. 306-636-1621, 306-634-5830, e-mail greg@southeast.lib.sk.ca; *Exec. Dir.* Judith Silverthorne, 2010 7th Ave., No. 15, Regina S4R 1C2. Tel. 306-780-9413, fax 306-780-9447, e-mail slaexdir@sasktel.net.

Address correspondence to the executive director.

World Wide Web http://www.lib.sk.ca/sla.

Regional

Atlantic Provinces: N.B., N.L., N.S., P.E.

Memb. (Indiv.) 219; (Inst.) 26. Term of Office. May 2004–May 2005. Publications.

APLA Bulletin (bi-mo.), *Membership Directory* (ann.).

Pres. Allan Groen, Provincial Libn., Province of Prince Edward Island, Box 7500, Morell, PE C0A 1S0. Tel. 902-961-7316, fax 902-961-7322, e-mail ajgroen@gov.pe.ca; *V.P./Pres.-Elect* Jennifer Richard, Vaughan Memorial Lib., Acadia Univ., Wolfville, NS. Tel. 902-585-1403, fax 902-585-1748, e-mail jennifer.richard@acadiau.ca; *Secy.* Gillian Byrne, Queen Elizabeth II Lib., Memorial Univ. of Newfoundland, St. John's, NL A1B 3Y1. Tel. 709-737-7427, fax 709-737-2153, e-mail gbyrne@mun.ca; *Treas.* Denise Corey-Fancy. E-mail dcorey@ns.sympatico.ca; *Past Pres.* Laurette Mackey, York Lib. Region, New Brunswick Public Lib. Service, 4 Carleton, Fredericton, NB E3B 5P4. Tel. 506-453-5380, fax 506-457-4878, e-mail laurette.mackey@gnb.ca.

Address correspondence to Atlantic Provinces Lib. Assn., c/o School of Lib. and Info. Studies, Dalhousie Univ., Halifax, NS B3H 3J5.

World Wide Web http://www.apla.ca.

Mountain Plains: Ariz., Colo., Kan., Mont., Neb., Nev., N.Dak., N.M., Okla., S.Dak., Utah, Wyo.

Memb. 820. Publications. *MPLA Newsletter* (bi-mo.), *Ed. and Adv. Mgr.* Lisa Mecklenberg Jackson, Montana Legislative Reference Center, Box 201706, Helena, MT 59620-1706. Tel. 406-444-2957, e-mail ljackson@state.mt.us.

Pres. Beth Avery, Leslie J. Savage Lib., Western State College, Gunnison, CO 81231. Tel. 970-943-2898, fax 970-943-2042, e-mail bavery@western.edu; *V.P./Pres.-Elect* Sharon Osenga, Meridian Lib. System, Kearney, NE 68847. Tel. 308-234-2087, fax 308-234-4040, e-mail sosenga@frontiernet.net; *Past Pres.* Carol Hammond, Thunderbird: The American Graduate School of International Mgt., Glendale, AZ 85306, e-mail hammondc @t-bird.edu; *Exec. Secy.* Joe Edelen, I. D. Weeks Lib., 414 E. Clark St., Univ. of South Dakota, Vermillion, SD 57069. Tel. 605-677-6082, fax 605-677-5488, e-mail jedelen@usd.edu.

Address correspondence to the executive secretary, Mountain Plains Lib. Assn.

World Wide Web http://www.usd.edu/mpla.

New England: Conn., Maine, Mass., N.H., R.I., Vt.

Memb. (Indiv.) 1,300; (Inst.) 100. Term of Office. Nov. 2004–Oct. 2005. Publication. *New England Libraries* (bi-mo.). *Ed.* David Bryan. E-mail newslettereditor@nelib.org.

Pres. Joanne Lamothe, Tufts Lib., 46 Broad St., Weymouth, MA 02188. Tel. 781-337-1402, fax 781-682-6123, e-mail president @nelib.org; *V.P./Pres.-Elect* Janice Wilbur, d'Alzon Lib., Assumption College, 500 Salisbury St., Worcester, MA 01609. Tel. 508-767-7271, fax 508-767-7374, e-mail vice president@nelib.org; *Secy.* Kathleen Boyd, Salve Regina Univ. Lib., 100 Ochre Point Ave., Newport, RI 02840-4192. Tel. 401-341-2374, fax 401-341-2951, e-mail secretary @nelib.org; *Treas.* Mary Anne Golda, U.S. Coast Guard Academy Lib., 35 Mohegan Ave., New London, CT 06320. Tel. 860-444-8519, e-mail treasurer@nelib.org; *Past Pres.* John Barrett, 1 Mooreland Ave., Concord, NH 03301. Tel. 603-226-0846, e-mail past president@nelib.org.

Address correspondence to New England Lib. Assn., 14 Pleasant St., Gloucester, MA 01930. Tel. 972-282-0787, fax 978-282-1304, e-mail info@nelib.org.

World Wide Web http://www.nelib.org.

Pacific Northwest: Alaska, Idaho, Mont., Ore., Wash., Alberta, B.C.

Memb. (Active) 550; (Subscribers) 100. Term of Office. Aug. 2004–Aug. 2005. Publication. *PNLA Quarterly.*

Pres. Jan Zauha, Montana State Univ.–Bozeman, Box 173320, Bozeman, MT 59717-3320. Tel. 406-994-6554, fax 406-994-2851, e-mail alijz@montana.edu; *1st V.P./Pres.-Elect* Charlotte Glover, Ketchikan Public Lib., 629 Dock St., Ketchikan, AK 99904. Tel. 907-225-0370, fax 907-225-0153, e-mail charg@firstcitylibraries.org; *2nd V.P.* Christine Sheppard, Lib. Assn. of Alberta, 80 Baker Crescent N.W., Calgary, AB T2L 1R4. Tel. 403-284-5818, e-mail christine.sheppard @shaw.ca; *Secy.* Marg Anderson, SAIT, Lib. and Info. Technology Program, 1301 16th

Ave. N.W., Calgary, AB T2M 0L4. Tel. 403-284-7016, fax 403-284-7127, e-mail marg. anderson@sait.ca; *Treas.* Kay Vynanek, Holland/New Lib., Rm. 101, Washington State Univ., Pullman, WA 99164-5610. Tel. 509-335-5517, fax 509-335-0934, e-mail kayv@wsu.edu; *Past Pres.* Mary DeWalt, Ada Community Lib., 10664 W. Victory Rd., Boise, ID 83709. Tel. 208-362-0181, fax 208-362-0303, e-mail adewalt@adalib.org.

Address correspondence to the president, Pacific Northwest Lib. Assn.

World Wide Web http://www.pnla.org.

Southeastern: Ala., Ark., Fla., Ga., Ky., La., Miss., N.C., S.C., Tenn., Va., W.Va.

Memb. 500. Term of Office. Nov. 2004–Oct. 2005. Publication. *The Southeastern Librarian* (q.).

Pres. Judith A. Gibbons, Field Services Dir., Kentucky Dept. for Libs. and Archives, P.O. Box 537, Frankfort, KY 40602. Tel. 502-564-8300, fax 502-564-5773, e-mail judith.gibbons@ky.gov; *1st V.P./Pres.-Elect* Faith A. Line, Dir., Sumter County Lib., 111 N. Harvin St., Sumter, SC 29150. Tel. 803-773-7273, fax 803-773-4875, e-mail linef@infoave.net; *Secy.* Carol S. Brinkman, Head, Kersey Lib., Univ. of Louisville, 3426 Warner Ave., Louisville, KY 40207. Tel. 502-852-1008, fax 502-852-0020, e-mail csbrin01@gwise.louisville.edu; *Treas.* William N. Nelson, Augusta State Univ. Lib., 3317 Sugar Mill Rd., Augusta, GA 30907. Tel. 706-737-1745, fax 706-667-4415, e-mail wnelson@aug.edu.

Address correspondence to Gordon N. Baker, Southeastern Library Association, Administrative Services, P.O. Box 950, Rex, GA 30273-0950. Tel. 770-961-3520, fax 770-961-3712, e-mail gordonbaker@mail.clayton.edu.

State and Provincial Library Agencies

The state library administrative agency in each of the U.S. states will have the latest information on its state plan for the use of federal funds under the Library Services and Technology Act (LSTA). The directors and addresses of these state agencies are listed below.

Alabama

Rebecca Mitchell, Dir., Alabama Public Lib. Service, 6030 Monticello Dr., Montgomery 36130. Tel. 334-213-3902, fax 334-213-3993, e-mail rmitchell@apls.state.al.us.

Alaska

George Smith, Acting Dir., Div. of Libs., Archives, and Museums, Box 110571, Juneau 99811-0571. Tel. 907-465-2911, fax 907-465-2151, e-mail george_smith@eed.state.ak.us.

Arizona

GladysAnn Wells, State Libn., Arizona State Lib., Archives and Public Records, Ste. 200, 1700 W. Washington, Phoenix 85007-2896. Tel. 602-542-4035, fax 602-542-4972, e-mail gawells@lib.az.us.

Arkansas

Jack C. Mulkey, State Libn., Arkansas State Lib., 1 Capitol Mall, 5th fl., Little Rock 72201. Tel. 501-682-1526, fax 501-682-1899, e-mail jmulkey@asl.lib.ar.us.

California

Susan Hildreth, State Libn., California State Lib., Box 942837, Sacramento 94237. Tel. 916-654-0174, fax 916-654-0064, e-mail shildreth@library.ca.gov.

Colorado

Nancy M. Bolt, State Libn. and Asst. Commissioner, Dept. of Educ., State Lib., Rm. 309, 201 E. Colfax Ave., Denver 80203. Tel. 303-866-6900, fax 303-866-6940, e-mail nancybolt@earthlink.net.

Connecticut

Kendall F. Wiggin, State Libn., Connecticut State Lib., 231 Capitol Ave., Hartford 06106. Tel. 860-757-6510, fax 860-757-6503, e-mail kwiggin@cslib.org.

Delaware

Anne Norman, Dir. and State Libn., Div. of Libs., State Lib., 43 S. DuPont Hwy., Dover 19901. Tel. 302-739-4748 ext. 126, fax 302-739-6787, e-mail norman@lib.de.us.

District of Columbia

Richard L. Jackson, Interim Dir., District of Columbia Public Lib., 901 G St. N.W., Ste. 400, Washington 20001. Tel. 202-727-1101, fax 202-727-1129, e-mail richardlee.jackson@dc.gov.

Florida

Judith Ring, State Libn., Div. of Lib. and Info., R. A. Gray Bldg., 500 S. Bronough St., Tallahassee 32399-0250. Tel. 850-245-6600, fax 850-245-6735, e-mail jring@dos.state.fl.us.

Georgia

Lamar Veatch, State Libn., Georgia Public Lib. Service, 1800 Century Place, Ste. 150, Atlanta 30345. Tel. 404-982-3560, fax 404-982-3563, e-mail lveatch@georgialibraries.org.

Hawaii

Jo Ann Schindler, State Libn., Hawaii State Public Lib. System, 44 Merchant St., Honolulu 96813. Tel. 808-586-3704, fax 808-586-3715, e-mail joann@librarieshawaii.org.

Idaho

Charles Bolles, State Libn., Idaho State Lib., 325 W. State St., Boise 83702. Tel. 208-334-2150, fax 208-334-4016, e-mail cbolles@isl.state.id.us.

Illinois

Jean Wilkins, Dir., Illinois State Lib., 300 S. 2 St., Springfield 62701-1796. Tel. 217-782-2994, fax 217-785-4326, e-mail jwilkins@ilsos.net.

Indiana

Barbara Maxwell, Dir., Indiana State Lib., 140 N. Senate Ave., Indianapolis 46204. Tel. 317-232-3692, fax 317-232-0002, e-mail bmaxwell@statelib.lib.in.us.

Iowa

Mary Wegner, State Libn., State Lib. of Iowa, 1112 E. Grand Ave., Des Moines 50319. Tel. 515-281-4105, fax 515.281.6191, e-mail mary.wegner@lib.state.ia.us.

Kansas

Mark Galbreath, Acting State Libn., Kansas State Lib., State Capitol, 3rd fl., Topeka 66612. Tel. 785-296-3296, fax 785-296-6650, e-mail markg@kslib.info.

Kentucky

Jim Nelson, State Libn./Commissioner, Kentucky Dept. for Libs. and Archives, 300 Coffee Tree Rd., Frankfort 40601. Tel. 502-564-8300 ext. 312, fax 502-564-5773, e-mail jim.nelson@ky.gov.

Louisiana

Thomas F. Jaques, State Libn., State Lib. of Louisiana, P.O. Box 131, Baton Rouge 70821-0131. Tel. 225-342-4923, fax 225-219-4804, e-mail tjaques@pelican.state.lib.la.us.

Maine

J. Gary Nichols, State Libn., Maine State Lib., 64 State House Sta., Augusta 04333. Tel. 207-287-5600, fax 207-287-5615, e-mail gary.nichols@maine.gov.

Maryland

Irene Padilla, Asst. State Superintendent for Lib. Development and Services, Maryland State Dept. of Educ., 200 W. Baltimore St., Baltimore 21201. Tel. 410-767-0435, fax 410-333-2507, e-mail ipadilla@msde.state.md.us.

Massachusetts

Robert C. Maier, Dir., Massachusetts Board of Lib. Commissioners, 648 Beacon St., Boston 02215. Tel. 617-267-9400, fax 617-421-9833, e-mail robert.maier@state.ma.us.

Michigan

Christie Pearson Brandau, State Libn., Lib. of Michigan, 702 W. Kalamazoo, P.O. Box 30007, Lansing 48909-7507. Tel. 517-373-7513, fax 517-373-5815, e-mail cbrandau@michigan.gov.

Minnesota

Suzanne Miller, Dir., Lib. Development and Services, Minnesota Dept. of Educ., 1500 Hwy. 36 West, Roseville 55113-4266. Tel. 651-582-8722, fax 651-582-8897, e-mail suzanne.miller@state.mn.us.

Mississippi

Sharman Bridges Smith, Exec. Dir., Mississippi Lib. Commission, 1221 Ellis Ave., Jackson 39289-0700. Tel. 601-961-4039, fax 601-354-6713, e-mail sharman@mlc.lib.ms.us.

Missouri

Sara Parker, State Libn., Secy. of State's Office, Kirkpatrick State Info. Center, 600 W. Main, P.O. Box 387, Jefferson City 65102-0387. Tel. 573-751-2751, fax 573-751-3612, e-mail sara.parker@sos.mo.gov.

Montana

Darlene Staffeldt, State Libn., Montana State Lib., 1515 E. 6 Ave., P.O. Box 201800, Helena 59620-1800. Tel. 406-444-3115, fax 406-444-0266, e-mail dstaffeldt@state.mt.us.

Nebraska

Rod Wagner, Dir., Nebraska Lib. Commission, 1200 N St., Ste. 120, Lincoln 68508. Tel. 402-471-4001, fax 402-471-2083, e-mail rwagner@neon.nlc.state.ne.us.

Nevada

Sara Jones, Admin., Nevada State Lib. and Archives, 100 N. Stewart St., Carson City 89710. Tel. 775-684-3315, fax 775-684-3311, e-mail sfjones@clan.lib.nv.us.

New Hampshire

Michael York, State Libn., New Hampshire State Lib., 20 Park St., Concord 03301-6314. Tel. 603-271-2392, fax 603-271-6826, e-mail myork@library.state.nh.us.

New Jersey

Norma E. Blake, State Libn., New Jersey State Lib., 185 W. State St., Trenton 08625-0520. Tel. 609-292-6201, fax 609-292-2746, e-mail rpallante@njstatelib.org.

New Mexico

Richard Akeroyd, State Libn., New Mexico State Lib., 1209 Camino Carlos Rey, Santa Fe 87505. Tel. 505-476-9762, fax 505-476-9761, e-mail rakeroyd@stlib.state.nm.us.

New York

Janet M. Welch, State Libn./Asst. Commissioner for Libs., New York State Lib., 10C34 Cultural Educ. Center, Albany 12230. Tel. 518-474-5930, fax 518-486-6880, e-mail jwelch2@mail.nysed.gov.

North Carolina

Sandy Cooper, State Libn., State Lib. of North Carolina, 4640 Mail Service Center, 109 E. Jones St., Raleigh 27699-4640. Tel. 919-733-2570, fax 919-733-8748, e-mail scooper@library.dcr.state.nc.us.

North Dakota

Doris Ott, State Libn., North Dakota State Lib., 604 E. Boulevard, Bismarck 58505-0800. Tel. 701-328-2492, fax 701-328-2040, e-mail dott@state.nd.us.

Ohio

Joanne Budler, State Libn., State Lib. of Ohio, 274 E. 1 Ave., Columbus 43201. Tel. 614-644-7061, fax 614-466-3584, e-mail jbudler@sloma.state.ohio.us.

Oklahoma

Susan McVey, Dir., Oklahoma Dept. of Libs., 200 N.E. 18 St., Oklahoma City 73105. Tel. 405-521-2502, fax 405-525-7804, e-mail smcvey@oltn.odl.state.ok.us.

Pennsylvania

Mary Clare Zales, Deputy Secy. of Educ. for Commonwealth Libs. and Commissioner for Libs., Office of Commonwealth Libs., 333 Market St., Harrisburg 17126-1745. Tel. 717-787-2646, fax 717-772-3265, e-mail mzales @state.pa.us.

Rhode Island

Anne T. Parent, Chief of Lib. Services, Office of Lib. and Info. Services, 1 Capitol Hill, Providence 02908-5870. Tel. 401-222-5763, fax 401-222-4260, e-mail annept@gw.doa.state.ri.us.

South Carolina

James B. Johnson, Jr., Dir., South Carolina State Lib., P.O. Box 11469, Columbia 29211. Tel. 803-734-8656, fax 803-734-8676, e-mail jim@leo.scsl.state.sc.us.

South Dakota

Dorothy Liegl, Acting State Libn., South Dakota State Lib., Mercedes MacKay Bldg., 800 Governors Dr., Pierre 57501-2294. Tel. 605-773-3131, fax 605-773-4950, e-mail dorothy.liegl@state.sd.us.

Tennessee

Edwin S. Gleaves, State Libn. and Archivist, Tennessee State Lib. and Archives, 403 Seventh Ave. N., Nashville 37243-0312. Tel. 615-741-7996, fax 615-532-9293, e-mail edwin.gleaves@state.tn.us.

Texas

Peggy D. Rudd, Dir./Libn., Texas State Lib. and Archives Commission, P.O. Box 12927, Austin 78711-2927. Tel. 512-463-5460, fax 512-463-5436, e-mail peggy.rudd@tsl.state.tx.us.

Utah

Donna Jones Morris, Dir., Utah State Lib. Div., 250 N. 1950 W., Salt Lake City 84115-7901. Tel. 801-715-6770, fax 801-715-6767, e-mail dmorris@utah.gov.

Vermont

Sybil Brigham McShane, State Libn., Vermont Dept. of Libs., Pavillion Office Bldg., 109 State St., Montpelier 05609. Tel. 802-828-3265, fax 802-828-2199, e-mail sybil.mcshane@dol.state.vt.us.

Virginia

Nolan T. Yelich, Libn. of Virginia, Lib. of Virginia, 800 E. Broad St., Richmond 23219. Tel. 804-692-3535, fax 804-692-3594, e-mail nyelich@lva.lib.va.us.

Washington

Jan Walsh, State Libn., Washington State Lib. Div., Office of the Secy. of State, 6880 Capitol Blvd., Tumwater 98501. Tel. 360-704-5253, fax 360-586-7575, e-mail jwalsh@secstate.wa.gov.

West Virginia

James D. Waggoner, Secy., West Virginia Lib. Commission, 1900 Kanawha Blvd. E., Charleston 25305. Tel. 304-558-2041, fax 304-558-2044, e-mail waggoner@wvlc.lib.wv.us.

Wisconsin

Richard Grobschmidt, Asst. Superintendent, Div. for Libs., Technology and Community Learning, Wisconsin Dept. of Public Instruction, P.O. Box 7841, Madison 53707-7841. Tel. 608-266-2205, fax 608-267-1052, e-mail richard.grobschmidt@dpi.state.wi.us.

Wyoming

Lesley Boughton, State Libn., Wyoming State Lib., 2301 Capitol Ave., Cheyenne 82002. Tel. 307-777-5911, fax 307-777-6289, e-mail lbough@state.wy.us.

American Samoa

Cheryl Morales, Territorial Libn., Feleti Barstow Public Lib., Box 997687, Pago Pago, AS 96799. Tel. 11-684-633-5816, fax 11-684-633-5213, e-mail feletibarstow@yahoo.com.

Federated States of Micronesia

Eliuel K. Pretrict, Secy., Dept. of Health, Educ., and Social Affairs, FSM Div. of Educ., P.O. Box PS 70, Palikir Sta., Pohnpei, FM 96941. Tel. 11-691-320-2619, fax 11-691-320-5500, e-mail fsmhealth@mail.fm.

Guam

(Position vacant) Dir./Territorial Libn., Guam Public Lib. System, 254 Martyr St., Agana 96910-0254. Tel. 671-475-4753, fax 671-477-9777.

Northern Mariana Islands

Kevin Latham, Dir., Commonwealth Public Lib., Box 501092, Saipan 96950. Tel. 670-235-7322, fax 670-235-7550, e-mail kclatham@gmail.com.

Palau

Mario Katosang, Minister of Educ., Republic of Palau, Box 7080, Koror, PW 96940. Tel. 11-680-488-2973, fax 11-680-488-2930.

Puerto Rico

Cesar Rey Hernandez, Secy. of Educ., Puerto Rico Dept. of Educ./Public Lib. Programs, Box 190759, San Juan, PR 00919-0759. Tel. 787-759-2004, fax 787-250-0275, e-mail rey_ce@de.gobierno.pr.

Republic of the Marshall Islands

Lenest Lanki, Secy., Internal Affairs, Marshall Islands, Box 629, Majuro, MH 96960. Tel. 11-692-625-5024, fax 11-692-625-5353, e-mail ltlanki@hotmail.com.

Virgin Islands

Claudette C. Lewis, Exec. Assistant Commissioner, Div. of Libs., Archives, and Museums, Cyril E. King Airport Terminal Bldg., St. Thomas, VI 00802. Tel. 340-774-3320, fax 809-775-5706.

Canada

Alberta

Bonnie Gray, Mgr., Public Lib. Services, Alberta Community Development, 803 Standard Life Centre, 10405 Jasper Ave., Edmonton T5J 4R7. Tel. 780-415-0295, fax 780-415-8594, e-mail bonnie.gray@gov.ab.ca.

British Columbia

Maureen Woods, Dir., Public Lib. Services Branch, Ministry of Community, Aboriginal and Women's Services, Box 9490, Sta. Provincial Govt., Victoria V8W 9N7. Tel. 250-356-1791, fax 250-953-3225, e-mail maureen.woods@gems8.gov.bc.ca.

Manitoba

Christine Moore, Acting Dir., Public Library Services, Manitoba Dept. of Culture, Heritage and Tourism, Unit 200, 1525 1st St., Brandon R7A 7A1. Tel. 204-726-6864, fax 204-726-6868, e-mail cmoore@gov.mb.ca.

New Brunswick

Sylvie Nadeau, Exec. Dir., New Brunswick Public Lib. Service, 250 King St., Place 6000, Fredericton E3B 9M9. Tel. 506-453-2354, fax 506-444-4064, e-mail sylvie.nadeau@gnb.ca. World Wide Web http://www.gnb.ca/publiclibraries.

Newfoundland and Labrador

Shawn Tetford, Exec. Dir., Provincial Info. and Lib. Resources Board of Newfoundland and Labrador, 48 St. George's Ave., Stephenville A2N 1K9. Tel. 709-643-0900, fax 709-643-0925, e-mail shawntetford@nlpublic libraries.ca, World Wide Web http://www.nl publiclibraries.ca.

Northwest Territories

A. J. "Sandy" MacDonald, Territorial Libn., Northwest Territories Public Lib. Services, 75 Woodland Dr., Hay River X0E 1G1. Tel. 867-874-6531, fax 867-874-3321, e-mail sandy_macdonald@gov.nt.ca. World Wide Web http://www.nwtpls.gov.nt.ca.

Nova Scotia

Elizabeth Armstrong, Dir., Nova Scotia Provincial Lib., 3770 Kempt Rd., Halifax B3K 4X8. Tel. 902-424-2455, fax 902-424-0633, e-mail armstreh@gov.ns.ca.

Nunavut

Robin Brown, Mgr., Lib. Policy, Baker Lake Headquarters, Nunavut Public Lib. Services, Box 270, Baker Lake X0C 0A0. Tel. 867-793-3326, fax 867-793-3332, e-mail rbrown2@gov.nu.ca.

Ontario

Rita Scagnetti, Dir., Heritage and Libs. Branch, Ontario Government Ministry of Culture, 400 University Ave., 4th fl., Toronto M7A 2R9. Tel. 416-314-7342, fax 416-314-7635, e-mail rita.scagnetti@mcl.gov.on.ca.

Prince Edward Island

Allan Groen, Provincial Libn., Province of Prince Edward Island, P.O. Box 7500, Morell C0A 1S0. TeL 902-961-7316, fax 902-961-7322, e-mail ajgroen@gov.pe.ca.

Quebec

André Couture, Dir., Direction des Politiques et de la Coordination des Programmes, 225 Grande Allée Est, RC-C, Quebec G1R 5G5. Tel. 418-644-0485, fax 418-643-4080, e-mail andre.couture@mcc.gouv.qc.ca.

Saskatchewan

Joylene Campbell, Provincial Libn., Saskatchewan Learning, 1945 Hamilton St., Regina S4P 2C8. Tel. 306-787-2972, fax 306-787-2029, e-mail jccampbell@library.gov.sk.ca.

Yukon Territory

Julie Ourom, Mgr., Public Libs., Dept. of Community Services, Box 2703, Whitehorse Y1A 2C6. Tel. 867-667-5447, fax 867-393-3663, e-mail julie.ourom@gov.yk.ca.

State School Library Media Associations

Alabama

Children's and School Libns. Div., Alabama Lib. Assn. Memb. 650. Publication. *The Alabama Librarian* (q.).

Chair Christine Bowman, Alabama Public Lib. Service, 6030 Monticello Dr., Montgomery 36130. Tel. 800-723-8459 ext. 978, e-mail cbowman@apls.state.al.us; *Exec. Dir.* Virginia Lott, ALLA, 400 S. Union St., Ste. 395, Montgomery 36104. Tel. 334-263-1272, fax 334-262-5255, e-mail psgllc@bellsouth.net.

Address correspondence to the executive director.

World Wide Web http://allanet.org.

Alabama Instructional Media Assn. Memb. 400. Term of Office. July 2004–June 2005.

Pres. Sharon Allen, Head Elementary. Tel. 334-260-1054, e-mail sharon.allen@mps.k12.al.us; *V.P./Pres.-Elect* Lisa Hathcock, Weaver Elementary. Tel. 256-741-7105; *Secy.* Lisa Boyd, Bottenfield Junior H.S. Tel. 205-379-2571, e-mail lboyd@jefcoed.com; *Treas.* Tywanna Burton, Vestavia Hills Elementary West. Tel. 205-402-5159; *Past Pres.* Linda Parker, Shades Valley H.S. Tel. 205-956-3482, e-mail lkparker6250@yahoo.com.

Address correspondence to Tywanna Burton, Vestavia Hills Elementary West, 1965 Merryvale Rd., Westavia Hills 35216.

World Wide Web http://www.fayette.k12.al.us/fes/aima.

Alaska

Alaska Assn. of School Libns. Memb. 200+. Term of Office. Mar. 2005–Mar. 2006. Publication. *Puffin* (3 a year).

Pres. Valerie Oliver. E-mail oliver_valerie@asd.k12.org; *Pres.-Elect* Barb Bryson. E-mail barb_bryson@valdez.cc; *Secy.* Tiki Levinson. E-mail tlevinson@dgsd.k12.ak.us; *Treas.* Barb Kreher. E-mail kreherb@mail.jsd.k12.ak.us; *Past Pres.* Karen J. Davis. E-mail kjdavis@edulynx.com; *School Lib. Coord. for Alaska State Lib.* Sue Sherif. E-mail sue_sherif@eed.state.ak.us.

World Wide Web http://www.akla.org/akasl.

Arizona

Teacher-Librarian Div., Arizona Lib. Assn. Memb. 1,000. Term of Office. Dec. 2004–Dec. 2006. Publication. *AZLA Newsletter.*

Chair Ann Dutton Ewbank, Cholla Middle School. Tel. 602-896-5409, e-mail adutton@ch.wesd.k12.az.us.

Address correspondence to the chairperson.

World Wide Web http://www.azla.affiniscape.com.

Arkansas

Arkansas Assn. of Instructional Media. Term of Office. Jan.–Dec. 2005.

Pres. Djuna Dudeck. E-mail ddudeck@yahoo.com; *Pres.-Elect* Rachel Shankles. E-mail shankles@cablelynx.com; *Secy.* Sandra Elliot. E-mail elliots@mboro.dsc.k12.ar.us; *Treas.* Pat McDonald. E-mail pmcdona@aol.com; *Past Pres.* Sara Dickey. E-mail sarad@rsc.k12.ar.us.

Address correspondence to the president.

World Wide Web http://aaim.k12.ar.us.

California

California School Lib. Assn. Memb. 2,200. Publication. *CSLA Journal* (2 a year). *Ed.* Lesley Farmer.

Pres. Ann H. Wick, 28266 Twin Ponds Rd., Clovis 93611. Tel. 559-855-2709, e-mail awick@sierra.k12.ca.us; *Pres.-Elect* Kathryn Matlock, 1336 La Loma Dr., Redlands 92373. Tel. 909-792-0895, e-mail kmatlock@rialto.k12.ca.us; *Secy.* Marianne Newman, 352 N. California St., Los Angeles 91775-2309. Tel. 626-309-9112, e-mail msnewm@aol.com; *Treas.* Mary Helen Fischer, 4302 Boles Rd., Placerville 95326. Tel. 530-626-1846, e-mail mfischer@directcon.net; *Past Pres.* Susan Maass, Chaffey Joint Union H.S. Dist., 11801 Lark Dr., Rancho Cucamonga 91701. Tel. 909-989-1600 ext. 2065, e-mail susan_ maass@cjuhsd.k12.ca.us; *Office Mgr.* Sue Dalrymple, 717 K St., Ste. 515, Sacramento 95814. Tel. 916-447-2684, fax 916-447-2695, e-mail csla@pacbell.net; *Exec. Dir.* Penny Kastanis. E-mail pkastanis@pacbell.net. World Wide Web http://www.schoolibrary.org.

Address correspondence to the office manager.

Colorado

Colorado Assn. of School Libns. Memb. 500. Term of Office. Oct. 2004–Oct. 2005. Publication. *Newsletter* (5 a year).

Pres. Kim Meyer, Marshdale Elementary, 26663 N. Turkey Creek Rd., Evergreen 80439. Tel. 303-982-5188, fax 303-982-5187, e-mail kmeyer@jeffco.k12.co.us; *V.P./Pres.-Elect* Gwen Giddens, Colorado Springs School Dist. 11, 711 San Rafael, Colorado Springs 80903. Tel. 719-520-2254, e-mail giddegb@d11.org; *Secy.* Sherry Crow, Midland International Elementary, 2110 W. Broadway, Colorado Springs 80904. Tel. 719-328-4524, e-mail crowsr@d11.org; *Exec. Dir.* Kathleen Sagee Noland, Colorado Assn. of Libs., 12081 W. Alameda Pkwy., No. 427, Lakewood 80228. Tel. 303-463-6400, fax 303-798-2485, e-mail kathleen@cal-webs.org. World Wide Web http://www.cal-webs.org.

Connecticut

Connecticut Educational Media Assn. Memb. 550. Term of Office. July 2004–June 2005. Publications. *CEMA Update* (q.); *CEMA Gram* (mo.).

Pres. Jerilyn Van Leer, 213 Cotton Hill Rd., New Hartford 06057. Tel. 860-489-3767, e-mail jeri_vanleer@whps.org; *V.P.* Diane Kimball, 42 Carriage Dr., Meriden 06450. Tel. 203-639-7578, e-mail dkimball @wallingford.k12.ct.us; *Secy.* Christopher Barlow, 38 Highgate Rd., Trumbull 06611. Tel. 203-268-6946, e-mail christophbarlow @sbcglobal.net; *Treas.* Sewell Pruchnik, 85 Benson Rd., Bridgewater 06752. Tel. 860-355-2693, e-mail spruchnik@snet.net; *Past Pres.* Rebecca Cochrane, 1261 Washington St., Unit 14, Middletown 06457. E-mail bukgrl @yahoo.com; *Admin. Secy.* Anne Weimann,

25 Elmwood Ave., Trumbull 06611. Tel. 203-372-2260, e-mail aweimann@snet.net. Address correspondence to the administrative secretary. World Wide Web http://www.ctcema.org.

Delaware

Delaware School Lib. Media Assn., Div. of Delaware Lib. Assn. Memb. 100+. Term of Office. Apr. 2004–Apr. 2005. Publications. *DSLMA Newsletter* (electronic; irreg.); column in *DLA Bulletin* (3 a year) (electronic at http://www.dla.lib.de.us/bulletin.shtml).

Pres. Janet Shaw, Shue-Medill Middle School, 1500 Capitol Trail, Newark 19711. Tel. 302-454-2171 ext. 112, e-mail shawj@ christina.k12.de.us; *V.P.* Gina Baumgartner, North Dover Elementary School, 855 State College Rd., Dover 19904. Tel. 302-672-1980, e-mail gbaumgartner@capital.k12.de.us; *Secy.* Christine Kutcher, Olive B. Loss Elementary School, 200 Brennan Blvd., Bear 19701. Tel. 302-832-1343, e-mail cakutcher @yahoo.com; *Past Pres.* Barbara Ruszkowski, Padua Academy, 905 N. Broom St., Wilmington 19806-4544. Tel. 302-421-3739, e-mail brusz@aol.com.

Address correspondence to the president. World Wide Web http://www.udel.edu/educ/slms/dslma.html.

District of Columbia

District of Columbia Assn. of School Libns. Memb. 35. Publication. *Newsletter* (4 a year).

Pres. André Maria Taylor. E-mail diva librarian2@aol.com; *V.P./Pres.-Elect* Ora Hall. E-mail ceorahall@aol.com.

Florida

Florida Assn. for Media in Education. Memb. 1,450. Term of Office. Nov. 2004–Oct. 2005. Publication. *Florida Media Quarterly.* Ed. Nancy Pelser-Borowicz.

Pres. James Carey. E-mail president@ floridamedia.org; *Pres.-Elect* Sandra Dunnavant; *V.P.* Sandra McMichael; *Secy.* Pat Dedicos; *Treas.* Sherie Bargar; *Exec. Dir.* Londra Mead. Tel. 407-275-3777, fax 407-275-3667, e-mail info@floridamedia.org. Address correspondence to the Executive

Director, FAME, P.O. Box 560787, Orlando 32856-0787.

World Wide Web http://www.florida media.org.

Georgia

Georgia Lib. Assn., School Lib. Media Division.

Chair Richard Horah. Tel. 912-961-3046, e-mail horahric@mail.armstrong.edu.

Georgia Lib. Media Assn. Memb. 701. Term of Office. Jan. 2005–Jan. 2006.

Pres. Cawood Cornelius. E-mail ccornelius @gcbe.org; *Pres.-Elect* Donna Milner. E-mail donnamilner@yahoo.com; *Secy.* Rosalind L. Dennis. E-mail rosalind_l_dennis@ fc.dekalb.k12.ga.us; *Treas.* Rebecca Amerson. E-mail rebecca.amerson@cherokee. k12.ga.us; *Past Pres.* Millicent Drake Norman. E-mail mdnorman@atlanta.k12.ga.us.

World Wide Web http://www.glma-inc. org.

Hawaii

Hawaii Assn. of School Libns. Memb. 200+. Term of Office. June 2004–May 2005. Publication. *HASL Newsletter* (4 a year).

Pres. Loraine Hotoke, Liholiho Elementary. E-mail loraine_hotoke@notes.k12.hi.us; *Co-V.P.s, Programming* Lynette Kam. E-mail kamw009@hawaii.rr.com; Karen Muronaga, Lincoln Elementary. E-mail karen_ muronaga@notes.k12.hi.us; *V.P., Membership* Sandy Pak. E-mail sandra_pak@notes. k12.hi.us; *Recording Secy.* Deb Peterson, Punahou (Cooke Lib.). E-mail dpeterson@ punahou.edu; *Corresponding Secy.* Elissa Pickard, Dole Middle School. E-mail elissa_ pickard@notes.k12.hi.us; *Treas.* Linda Marks, Kalihi Uka Elementary. E-mail flcadiz@ aol.com; *Past Pres.* Jo-An Goss. E-mail gossj002@hawaii.rr.com.

Address correspondence to the association, Box 235019, Honolulu 96823.

World Wide Web http://www.k12.hi.us/ ~hasl.

Idaho

Educational Media Div., Idaho Lib. Assn. Memb. 86. Term of Office. Oct. 2003–Oct.

2005. Publication. Column in *The Idaho Librarian* (q.).

Chair Norma Jean Sprouffske, Caldwell School Dist. 132, 1101 Cleveland Blvd., Caldwell 83605. Tel. 208-455-3305, e-mail njsprouffske@earthlink.net; *Past Chair* Penni Cyr, Moscow Senior H.S., Moscow 83843. Tel. 208-882-2591, e-mail cpenni@ SD281.k12.id.us.

Address correspondence to the chairperson.

Illinois

Illinois School Lib. Media Assn. Memb. 1,100. Term of Office. July 2004–June 2005. Publications. *ISLMA News* (4 a year); *ISLMA Membership Directory* (ann.).

Pres. Lou Ann Jacobs, Pontiac Twp. H.S., Pontiac 61764. Tel. 815-844-6113, fax 815-844-6116, e-mail ljacobs363@aol.com; *Pres.-Elect* Leslie Forsman, Triopia CUSD No. 27, 2204 Concord-Arenzville Rd., Concord 62631. Tel. 217-457-2284 or 217-457-2281, fax 217-457-2277, e-mail lforsman@ hotmail.com; *Exec. Secy.* Kay Maynard, ISLMA, P.O. Box 598, Canton 61520. Tel. 390-649-0911, e-mail islma@islma.org.

World Wide Web http://www.islma.org.

Indiana

Assn. for Indiana Media Educators. Term of Office. May 2004–Apr. 2005. Publications. *FOCUS on Indiana Libraries* (mo.); *Indiana Libraries* (q.).

Pres. Carl A. Harvey II, North Elementary School, Noblesville 46060-2099. Tel. 317-773-0482 ext. 140, fax 317-776-6274, e-mail carl_harvey@mail.nobl.k12.in.us; *Pres.-Elect* Rick A. Jones, Eastbrook H.S., Marion 46953. Tel. 765-664-1214 ext. 104, fax 765-664-1216, e-mail rajones@eastbrook.k12.in.us; *Secy.* Kimberly Carr, Monroe Central H.S., Parker City 47368. Tel. 765-468-7545, fax 765-468-8878, e-mail kimc@monroec.k12. in.us; *Treas.* Sue Jones, Tecumseh Middle School, Lafayette 47905-2096. Tel. 765-772-4750, fax 765-772-4763, e-mail sjones@lsc. k12.in.us.

Address correspondence to the association, 941 E. 86 St., Ste. 260, Indianapolis 46240. Tel. 317-257-2040, fax 317-257-1389, e-mail ilf@indy.net.

World Wide Web http://www.ilfonline. org/Units/Associations/aime/index.htm.

Iowa

Iowa Assn. of School Libns. Memb. 300. Term of Office. Jan. 2004–Jan. 2005. Publication. *The Advocate* (electronic, 4 a year). *Ed.* Becky Stover Johnson. E-mail bcjohnson @cr.k12.ia.us.

Pres. Jill Hofmockel. E-mail jhofmockel @ccs.k12.ia.us; *V.P./Pres.-Elect* Kristin Stein Graeber. E-mail steingraeberk@aea15. k12.ia.us; *Secy./Treas.* Debra Dorzweiler. E-mail ddorzweiler@west-branch.k12.ia.us; *Past Pres.* Dale Vande Haar. E-mail dale. vandehaar@dmps.k12.ia.us; *Exec. Dir., Iowa Lib. Assn.* Laurie Hews, 3636 Westown Pkwy., West Des Moines 50266. Tel. 800-452-5507, e-mail ialib@mcleoudusa.net.

Address correspondence to the executive director.

World Wide Web http://www.iowalibrary association.org and http://www.iema-ia.org.

Kansas

Kansas Assn. of School Libns. Memb. 700. Term of Office. Aug. 2004–July 2005. Publication. *KASL Newsletter* (s. ann.).

Pres. Ann Schuster. Tel. 913-239-6010, e-mail aschuster@bv229.k12.ks.us; *Pres.-Elect* Linda Roberts. Tel. 620-347-4115, e-mail lroberts@usd246.org; *Secy.* Nora Jones. Tel. 620-241-9560, e-mail nora.jones@mcpherson. com; *Treas.* Teresa MacKay. Tel. 316-747-3356, e-mail tmackay@usd396.net; *Past Pres.* Susan Ryan. Tel. 785-379-5950, e-mail ryans@snh450.k12.ks.us; *Exec. Secy.* Judith Eller, 8517 W. Northridge, Wichita 67205. Tel. 316-773-6723, e-mail judy.eller@ wichita.edu.

Address correspondence to the executive secretary.

World Wide Web http://skyways.lib.ks.us/ kasl.

Kentucky

Kentucky School Media Assn. Memb. 620. Term of Office. Oct. 2004–Oct. 2005. Publication. *KSMA Newsletter* (q.).

Chair Lisa Hughes, Heath H.S., 4330 Metropolis Lake Rd., West Paducah 42086.

Tel. 270-538-4104, fax 270-538-4091, e-mail lhughes@mccracken.k12.ky.us; *Chair-Elect* Angie Hawkins, South Heights Elementary School, 1199 Madison St., Henderson 42420. Tel. 270-831-5080, fax 270-831-5082, e-mail ahawkins@henderson.k12.ky.us.

Address correspondence to the chairperson.

World Wide Web http://www.kysma.org.

Louisiana

Louisiana Assn. of School Libns. Memb. 300+. Term of Office. July 2004–June 2005.

Pres. Linda Holmes. E-mail holmesl@ wfpsb.org; *1st V.P./Pres.-Elect* Kathryn Arrington. E-mail karrington@ebrschools. org; *2nd V.P.* Susan Cheshire. E-mail dcheshir @bellsouth.net; *Secy.* Anne Maverick. E-mail amaverick@ebrschools.org.

Address correspondence to the association, c/o Louisiana Lib. Assn., 421 S. 4 St., Eunice 70535. Tel. 337-550-7890, fax 337-550-7846, e-mail office@llaonline.org.

World Wide Web http://www.llaonline. org/sig/lasl.

Maine

Maine School Lib. Assn. Memb. 350. Term of Office. May 2003–May 2005. Publication. *Maine Entry* (with the Maine Lib. Assn.; q.).

Pres. Gretchen Asam, Presque Isle H.S. E-mail asamg1@yahoo.com; *1st V.P.* Terri Caouette, Lincoln Middle School. E-mail tcaouette@yahoo.com; *2nd V.P.* Donna Chale, Warsaw Middle School. E-mail dchale @warsaw-ms.sad53.k12.me.us; *Secy.* Margaret McNamee, Biddeford H.S. E-mail margaretmc@lamere.net; *Treas.* Pam Goucher, Freeport Middle School. E-mail pam_ goucher@coconetme.org; *Exec. Secy.* Edna Comstock.

Address correspondence to the president.

World Wide Web http://www.maslibraries. org.

Maryland

Maryland Educational Media Organization. Term of Office. July 2004–June 2005.

Pres. Dorothy P. D'Ascanio, Jackson Road Elementary School, Montgomery County Public Schools, 900 Jackson Rd., Silver

Spring 20904. E-mail dorothy_p._d'ascanio @fc.mcps.k12.md.us; *Secy.* Patricia Goff, Kenwood H.S., Baltimore County. E-mail pgoff@bcps.org; *Treas.* Sandra Bicksler, Professional Lib., Anne Arundel County. E-mail sbicksler@aacps.org; *Past Pres.* Jay Bansbach, Severn Elementary School, Severn 21144. E-mail cjbansbach@yahoo.com.

Address correspondence to the association, Box 21127, Baltimore 21228.

World Wide Web http://mdedmedia.org.

Massachusetts

Massachusetts School Lib. Media Assn. Memb. 700. Term of Office. June 2004–May 2005. Publication. *Media Forum* (q.).

Pres. Ann Perham, Needham H.S. Tel. 781-455-0800 ext. 1708, e-mail ann_ perham@needham.k12.ma.us; *Pres.-Elect* Kathy Lowe, Boston Arts Academy, Fenway H.S., Boston. Tel. 617-635-6470 ext. 236, fax 617-635-9204, e-mail kathylowe@ verizon.net; *Secy.* Phyllis Robinson, East Middle School, Braintree. Tel. 781-380-0170 ext. 1112, e-mail phyllis_robinson@braintree schools.org; *Treas.* Barbara Andrews. E-mail andrews2mmrls@yahoo.com; *Exec. Dir.* Doris Smith, MSLMA, P.O. Box 505, Bedford 01730. Tel. 781-275-2551, e-mail dsmith @mslma.org.

Address correspondence to the executive director.

World Wide Web http://www.mslma.org.

Michigan

Michigan Assn. for Media in Education. Memb. 1,400. Term of Office. Jan.–Dec. 2005. Publications. *Media Spectrum* (3 a year); *MAME Newsletter* (4 a year).

Pres. Joanne Steckling, Clarkston Community Schools, Sashabaw Middle School, 5565 Pine Knob Lane, Clarkston 48346. Tel. 248-623-4261, fax 248-623-4262, e-mail joanne@jsteckling.com; *Secy.* Sue Taylor, Birmingham School Dist., Derby Middle School, 1300 Derby Rd., Birmingham 48009. Tel. 248-203-5052, e-mail st03bps@ birmingham.k12.mi.us; *Treas.* Bruce Popejoy, East Jackson Community Schools, 4340 Walz Rd., Jackson 49201. Tel. 517-764-6010, fax 517-764-6081, e-mail mame

exhibits@aol.com; *Past Pres.* Diane Nye, St. Joseph Public Schools, 2214 S. State St., St. Joseph 49085. Tel. 269-982-4626, fax 269-982-4663, e-mail dnye@remc11.k12.mi.us; *Exec. Dir.* Roger Ashley, MAME, 1407 Rensen, Ste. 3, Lansing 48910. Tel. 517-394-2808, fax 517-394-2096, e-mail ashleymame @aol.com.

Address correspondence to the executive director.

World Wide Web http://www.mame.gen. mi.us.

Minnesota

Minnesota Educational Media Organization. Memb. 600. Term of Office. July 2004–July 2005. Publications. *Minnesota Media*; *ImME-DIAte*; *MEMOrandom*; *MTNews.*

Pres. Jane Prestebak, Robbinsdale Area Learning Center, 3730 Toledo Ave., Rm. 108, Robbinsdale 55422. Tel. 763-504-4921, e-mail jane_prestebak@rdale.k12.mn.us; *Co-Pres.-Elect* Mary Garlie, Park Rapids Area H.S., 401 Huntsinger, Park Rapids 56470. Tel. 218-237-6499, e-mail mgarlie@park rapids.k12.mn.us; Laurie Conzemius, Pine Meadow Elementary, 1029 5th St. N., Sartell 56377. Tel. 320-656-3701 ext. 811, e-mail conzemius@sartell.k12.mn.us; *Secy.* Leslie Yoder, SPPS, 1930 Como Ave., St. Paul 55108. Tel. 651-603-4923, e-mail leslie.yoder @spps.org; *Treas.* Margaret Meyer, 4371 107th Ave., Clear Lake 55319. Tel. 763-261-6324, e-mail mmeyer@becker.k12.mn.us; *Past Pres.* Doug Johnson, 46813 Cape Horn Rd., Cleveland 56017. Tel. 507-387-7698 ext. 473, 507-931-0077, e-mail djohns1@ isd77.k12.mn.us; *Admin. Asst.* Deanna Sylte, P.O. Box 130555, Roseville 55113. Tel./fax 651-771-8672, e-mail dsylte@tcq.net.

World Wide Web http://memoweb.org.

Mississippi

School Section, Mississippi Lib. Assn. Memb. 1,300.

Chair Bettie Cox, Mississippi School of the Arts. Tel. 601-823-9356, fax 601-823-9257, e-mail betcox@mde.K12.ms.us; *V. Chair* Diane B. Willard, Franklin Junior H.S. Tel. 601-384-2441, e-mail dwillard@fcsd.

k12.ms.us; *Exec. Dir., MLA* Mary Julia Anderson.

Address correspondence to School Section, Mississippi Lib. Assn., Box 20448, Jackson 39289-1448. Tel. 601-352-3917, fax 601-352-4240, e-mail mla@meta3.net.

World Wide Web http://www.misslib.org

Missouri

Missouri Assn. of School Libns. Memb. 1,100. Term of Office. June 2004–May 2005. Publications. *Media Horizons* (ann.); *Connections* (q.).

Pres. Patricia Bibler; *1st V.P./Pres.-Elect* Susan Rundel; *2nd V.P.* Linda Weatherspoon; *Secy.*Sandy Peitzman; *Treas.* Kathy Lawson; *Past Pres.* Cheryl Hoemann.

Address correspondence to the association, 15 Fawn Meadows Dr., Eureka 63025-1207. Tel. 636-938-6477, fax 636-938-5887, e-mail masloffice@charter.net.

World Wide Web http://maslonline.org.

Montana

Montana School Lib. Media Div., Montana Lib. Assn. Memb. 200+. Term of Office. July 2004–June 2005. Publication. *FOCUS* (published by Montana Lib. Assn.) (q.).

Chair Yvette Majerus, Moore Public Schools, 509 Highland Ave., Moore 59464. Tel. 406-374-2231, e-mail ymajerus@moore. k12.mt.us; *Exec. Dir., Montana Lib. Assn.* Karen A. Hatcher, 510 Arbor St., Missoula 59802. E-mail hatcher@montana.com.

World Wide Web http://www.mtlib.org/slmd/slmd.html.

Nebraska

Nebraska Educational Media Assn. Memb. 370. Term of Office. July 2004–June 2005. Publication. *NEMA News* (q.).

Pres. Gail Formanack. E-mail gail. formanack@ops.org; *Pres.-Elect* Donna Helvering. E-mail dhelveri@mpsomaha.org; *Secy.* Jayne Engel Hlavac. E-mail jengel@ esu7.org; *Treas.* Mary Reiman. E-mail mreiman@lps.org; *Past Pres.* Deb Grove. E-mail dgrove@paplv.esu3.org; *Exec. Secy.* Trudy Pedley. E-mail trpedley@ellipse.net.

Address correspondence to the executive secretary.

World Wide Web http://nema.k12.ne.us.

Nevada

Nevada School and Children's Libs. Section, Nevada Lib. Assn. Memb. 120.

Chair Linda Rauenbuehler, Henderson Dist. Public Lib. E-mail llrauenbuehler@ hdpl.org; *Exec. Secy.* Arnie Maurins. E-mail amaurins@mail.co.washoe.nv.us.

Address correspondence to the executive secretary.

New Hampshire

New Hampshire Educational Media Assn., Box 418, Concord 03302-0418. Memb. 265. Term of Office. June 2004–June 2005. Publication. *Online* (irreg., electronic only).

Pres. Linda Sherouse, North Hampton School, 201 Atlantic Ave., North Hampton 03862. Tel. 603-964-5501 ext. 230, fax 603-964-9018, e-mail lsherouse@sau21.k12.nh. us; *Pres.-Elect* Dorothy Grazier, Winnacunnet H.S., 1 Alumni Dr., Hampton 03842. Tel. 603-926-3395, e-mail dgrazier@winnacunnet. k12.nh.us; *V.P.-Elect* Diane Beaman, Belmont H.S., 255 Seavey Rd., Belmont 03220. Tel. 603-267-6525, e-mail dbeaman@shaker. k12.nh.us; *Recording Secy.* Mimi Crowley, Amherst St. School, 71 Amherst St., Nashua 03064. E-mail crowleym@nashua.edu; *Treas.* Jeff Kent, Dewey School, 38 Liberty St., Concord 03301. Tel. 603-225-0833, e-mail jkent@csd.k12.nh.us; *Past Pres.* Becky Albert, Tilton School, 30 School St., Tilton 03276. Tel. 603-286-1752, e-mail balbert@ tiltonschool.org.

Address correspondence to the president.

World Wide Web http://www.nhema.net.

New Jersey

Educational Media Assn. of New Jersey. Memb. 1,100. Term of Office. Aug. 2004–July 2005. Publication. *Bookmark* (mo.).

Pres. Mary Lewis, David Brearley Middle/H.S., 401 Monroe Ave., Kenilworth 07033. Tel. 908-931-9696 ext. 319, fax 908-931-1618, e-mail maryklewis@optonline.net; *Pres.-Elect* LaDawna Harrington, Avenel

Middle School, 85 Woodbine Ave., Avenel 07001. Tel. 732-396-7028, e-mail ladawna. harrington@woodbridge.k12.nj.us; *V.P.* Mary Moyer, Delsea H.S., Box 405, Fries Mill Rd., Franklinville 08322. Tel. 856-694-0100 ext. 239, fax 856-694-3146, e-mail mmoyerlib@comcast.net; *Corresponding Secy.* Pat Massey, South Plainfield H.S., 200 Lake St., South Plainfield 07080. Tel. 908-754-4620 ext. 286, fax 908-756-7659, e-mail pmassey@spnet.k12.nj.us or pmassey6@ yahoo.com; *Past Pres.* Cathie Miller, Princeton Day School, Box 75, Great Rd., Princeton 08542. Tel. 609-924-6700 ext. 242, e-mail cmiller@pds.org.

Address correspondence to the president-elect.

Association office, Box 610, Trenton 08607. Tel. 609-394-8032.

World Wide Web http://www.emanj.org.

New York

School Lib. Media Section, New York Lib. Assn., 252 Hudson St., Albany 12210. Tel. 518-432-6952. Memb. 880. Term of Office. Oct. 2004–Oct. 2005. Publications. *SLMS-Gram* (q.); participates in *NYLA Bulletin* (mo. except July and Aug.).

Pres. Patricia Shanley. Tel. 845-783-9574, e-mail pshanley@frontiernet.net; *Pres.-Elect* Marcia Eggleston; *V.P., Communications* Ellen Rubin; *V.P., Conferences* Bev Rovelli; *Secy.* Anne Hegel; *Treas.* Sally Daniels; *Past Pres.* Rosina Alaimo.

Address correspondence to the president.

World Wide Web http://www.nyla.org

North Carolina

North Carolina School Lib. Media Assn. Memb. 1,115. Term of Office. Oct. 2004–Oct. 2005.

Pres. Karen Lowe, Northwest RESA, 201 Curtis Bridge Rd., Wilkesboro 28697. Tel. 336-667-1754, fax 336-667-0503, e-mail lowekr@charter.net; *V.P./Pres.-Elect* Sandra D. Andrews, Rowan Salisbury Schools, 1636 Parkview Circle, Salisbury 28144. Tel. 704-639-3013, fax 704-639-3015, e-mail andrewsd @rss.k12.nc.us; *Secy.* Corine Warren, J. W. Coon Elementary School, 905 Hope Mills Rd., Fayetteville 28304. Tel. 910-425-6141,

fax 910-425-0878, e-mail corinewarren@ guilford.k12.nc.us; *Treas.* Libby Oxenfeld, Guilford County Schools, 120 Franklin Blvd. Greensboro 27401. Tel. 336-370-2310, fax 336-370-2363, e-mail oxenfee@guilford.k12. nc.us; *Past Pres.* Edna Cogdell, Cumberland County Public Schools, 2465 Gillespie St., Fayetteville 28301. Tel. 910-678-2614, fax 910-678-2641, e-mail ednac@ccs.k12.nc.us.

Address correspondence to the president.

World Wide Web http://www.ncslma.org.

North Dakota

School Lib. and Youth Services Section, North Dakota Lib. Assn. Memb. 100. Term of Office. Sept. 2004–Sept. 2005. Publication. *The Good Stuff* (q).

Chair Debbie K. Job, Bismarck Public Schools, 810 N. 1 St., Bismarck 58501-3630. Tel. 701-221-3404, e-mail deb_job@educ8. org.

Address correspondence to the chairperson.

Ohio

Ohio Educational Lib. Media Assn. Memb. 1,000. Term of Office. Jan.–Dec. 2005. Publication. *Ohio Media Spectrum* (q.).

Pres. Christine Findlay. E-mail christine. findlay@centerville.k12.oh.us; *V.P.* Carla Southers. E-mail csouthers@yahoo.com; *Treas.* Elaine Ezell. E-mail eezell@bgnet. bgsu.edu; *Past Pres.* Joanna McNally. E-mail joanna.mcnally@lnoca.org; *Dir. of Services* Kate Brunswick, 17 S. High St., Ste. 200, Columbus 43215. Tel. 614-221-1900, fax 614-221-1989, e-mail oelma@mecdc.org.

Address correspondence to the director of services.

World Wide Web http://www.oelma.org.

Oklahoma

Oklahoma Assn. of School Lib. Media Specialists. Memb. 300+. Term of Office. July 2004–June 2005. Publication. *Oklahoma Librarian.*

Pres. Margo Canaday. E-mail mcanaday@ bps.k12.ok.us; *Pres.-Elect* Deborah Maehs; *Secy.* Connie Wise; *Treas.* Yvonne Grady; *Past Pres.* Ellen Duecker.

Address correspondence to the president, c/o Oklahoma Lib. Assn., 300 Hardy Dr., Edmond 73013. Tel. 405-348-0506. World Wide Web http://www.oklibs.org/oaslms.

Oregon

Oregon Educational Media Assn. Memb. 600. Term of Office. July 2004–June 2005. Publication. *OEMA Newsletter* (electronic).

Pres. Martha Decherd. E-mail martha_decherd@ddouglas.k12.or.us; *Pres.-Elect* Jim Tindall. E-mail tindallj@nwasco.k12.or.us; *Secy.* Jenny Takeda. E-mail jenny_takeda@beavton.k12.or.us; *Treas.* Merrie Olson. E-mail molson@epud.net; *Past Pres.* Linda Ague. E-mail ague@4j.lane.edu; *Exec. Dir.* Jim Hayden, Box 277, Terrebonne 97760. Tel./fax 541-923-0675, e-mail jhayden@bendnet.com.

Address correspondence to the executive director.

World Wide Web http://www.oema.net.

Pennsylvania

Pennsylvania School Libns. Assn. Memb. 1,500+. Term of Office. July 2004–June 2006. Publication. *Learning and Media* (q.).

Pres. Anita Vance. E-mail alv@lion.crsd.k12.pa.us; *V.P./Pres.-Elect* Andrea Miller. E-mail amiller@clarion.edu; *Secy.* Carolyn Walsh. E-mail cwalsh6946@aol.com; *Treas.* Connie Roupp. E-mail croupp@stny.rr.com; *Past Pres.* Geneva Reeder. E-mail greeder@dejazzd.com.

Address correspondence to the president. World Wide Web http://www.psla.org.

Rhode Island

Rhode Island Educational Media Assn. Memb. 398. Term of Office. June 2004–May 2005.

Pres. Phyllis Humphrey. E-mail rid04893@ride.ri.net; *V.P.* Beth Sinwell. E-mail ehsin@chariho.k12.ri.us; *Secy.* Sue Fleisig. E-mail suefleisig@aol.com; *Treas.* Judi O'Brien. E-mail obrienj@ride.ri.net; *Past Pres.* Holly Barton. E-mail bartonh@ride.ri.net.

Address correspondence to the association, Box 470, East Greenwich 02818. World Wide Web http://www.ri.net/RIEMA.

South Carolina

South Carolina Assn. of School Libns. Memb. 1,100. Term of Office. June 2004–May 2005. Publication. *Media Center Messenger* (4 a year).

Pres. Robbie Van Pelt. E-mail robbie vanpelt@aol.com; *V.P./Pres.-Elect* Lawren Hammond. E-mail lmhammond3@comcast.net; *Secy.* Kitt Lisenby. E-mail kittlisenby@yahoo.com; *Treas.* Stephen Reed. E-mail screed3103@aol.com; *Past Pres.* Martha Taylor. E-mail martha_taylor@charter.net.

Address correspondence to the president. World Wide Web http://www.scasl.net.

South Dakota

South Dakota School Lib. Media Assn., Section of the South Dakota Lib. Assn. and South Dakota Education Assn. Memb. 140+. Term of Office. Oct. 2004–Oct. 2005.

Chair Carol Riswold, Sioux Falls Lincoln H.S. E-mail riswocar@sf.k12.sd.us.

Tennessee

Tennessee Assn. of School Libns. Memb. 450. Term of Office. Jan.–Dec. 2005. Publication. *Footnotes* (q.).

Pres. Allison Roberts, Barger Academy of Fine Arts, 4808 Brainerd Rd., Chattanooga 37411. Tel. 423-493-0348, e-mail roberts_allison@hcde.org; *V.P./Pres.-Elect* Brenda Moriarty, Lincoln Elementary School, 610 Summer St., Kingsport 37664. Tel. 423-378-2367, e-mail bmoriarty@k12.tn.com; *Secy.* Judy McCready, McConnell Elementary School, 8609 Columbus Rd., Hixson 37343. E-mail judith_mccready@hcde.org; *Treas.* Lynn Caruthers, Joseph Brown Elementary School, 301 Cord Dr., Columbia 38401. Tel. 931-388-3601, e-mail lcaruth@charter.net; *Past Pres.* Diane Chen, Hickman Elementary School, 112 Stewart's Ferry Park, Nashville 37214. E-mail chend@k12.tn.net.

Address correspondence to the president.

World Wide Web http://www.korrnet.org/tasl.

Texas

Texas Assn. of School Libns. (Div. of Texas Lib. Assn.). Memb. 4,051. Term of Office. Apr. 2004–Apr. 2005. Publication. *Media Matters* (3 a year).

Chair Tanya Tullos, Sherwood Elementary, 1700 Sherwood Forest Dr., Houston 77043. Tel. 713-365-4800, fax 325-365-4808, e-mail tullost@springbranchisd.com; *Chair-Elect* Jack Strawn, O'Connor H.S., 7722 Cascade Oak Dr., San Antonio 78249. Tel. 210-695-4800 ext. 2230, fax 210-695-4804, e-mail e028015@nisd.net; *Secy.* Charlyn Trussell, Mission CISD, 2207 Clinton St., Mission 78572. Tel. 956-580-5605; *Past Chair* Janice Richardson, Leander Middle School, 18215 Lura Lane, Jonestown 78645. Tel. 512-434-7840, fax 512-434-7805, e-mail janice.richardson@leanderisd.org.

Address correspondence to the Texas Library Association, 3355 Bee Cave Rd., Ste. 401, Austin 78746. Tel. 512-328-1518, fax 512-328-8852, e-mail tla@txla.org.

World Wide Web http://www.txla.org/groups/tasl/index.html.

Utah

Utah Educational Lib. Media Assn. Memb. 390. Term of Office. Mar. 2004–Feb. 2005. Publication. *UELMA Newsletter* (4 a year).

Pres. Fawn Morgan, Layton H.S., 440 Lancer Lane, Layton 84041. Tel. 801-402-4996, fax 801-402-4801, e-mail fmorgan@dsdmail.net; *Pres.-Elect* Nan Allsen. E-mail nan@nsanpete.k12.ut.us; *Secy.* Elayne Finlinson. E-mail efinlinson@dsdmail.net; *Past Pres.* Burke Belknap, Snow Canyon H.S., 1385 N. Lava Flow Dr., St. George 84770. Tel. 435-634-1967, fax 435-634-1130, e-mail burke@m.schs.wash.k12.org; *Exec. Dir.* Larry Jeppesen, Cedar Ridge Middle School, 65 N. 200 W., Hyde Park 84318. Tel. 435-563-6229, fax 435-563-3914, e-mail larry.jeppesen@cache.k12.ut.us.

Address correspondence to the executive director.

World Wide Web http://www.uelma.org.

Vermont

Vermont Educational Media Assn. Memb. 226. Term of Office. May 2004–May 2005. Publication. *VEMA News* (q.).

Pres. Angel Harris, Alburg Community Educ. Center. E-mail angharr@gisu.org; *Pres.-Elect* Dan Greene, U32 Junior-Senior H.S., Montpelier. E-mail dgreen@u32.org; *Secy.* Marsha Middleton, North Country Union H.S., Newport. E-mail mmiddleton@ncuhs.org; *Treas.* Donna Smyth, Proctor Elementary School. E-mail dsmyth@proctorelem.org; *Past Pres.* Rebecca Brown, Morrisville Schools. E-mail rebecca.brown@morrisville.org.

Address correspondence to the president.

World Wide Web http://www.vema-online.org.

Virginia

Virginia Educational Media Assn. Memb. 1,450. Term of Office. (Pres., Pres.-Elect) Nov. 2004–Nov. 2005; (other offices 2 years in alternating years). Publication. *Mediagram* (q.).

Pres. Kathy Lehman, Thomas Dale H.S., Chesterfield County. E-mail kathy_lehman@ccpsnet.net; *Pres.-Elect* Dee Griffith, Mountain View Elementary, Loudoun County. E-mail dgriffit@loudoun.k12.va.us; *Secy.* Patty Kline, Ladysmith Elementary School, Caroline County. E-mail pkline@caroline.k12.va.us; *Treas.* Betty Lynn Darden, C. Vernon Spratley Middle School, Hampton. E-mail bldarden@cox.net; *Past Pres.* Betsy Davis, Norfolk Public Schools. E-mail bdavis@nps.k12.va.us; *Exec. Dir.* Jean Remler. Tel./fax 703-764-0719, e-mail jremler@pen.k12.va.us.

Address correspondence to the association, Box 2743, Fairfax 22031-0743.

World Wide Web http://vema.gen.va.us.

Washington

Washington Lib. Media Assn. Memb. 1,466. Term of Office. Oct. 2004–Oct. 2005. Publications. *The Medium* (3 a year); *The Message* (2 a year).

Pres. Kay Evey. E-mail eveyk@tukwila. wednet.edu; *Pres.-Elect* Sarah Applegate. E-mail sapplegate@nthurston.k12.wa.us; *V.P.* Marianne Hunter. E-mail mhunter@ nthurston.k12.wa.us; *Secy.* Terry McCausland. E-mail tmccausland @nsd.org; *Treas.* Kathy Kugler. E-mail kkugler@mindspring. com.

Address correspondence to the association, Box 50194, Bellevue 98015-0194. E-mail wlma@wlma.org.

World Wide Web http://www.wlma.org.

West Virginia

School Library Division, West Virginia Lib. Assn. Memb. 50. Term of Office. Nov. 2004–Nov. 2005. Publication. *WVLA School Library News* (5 a year).

Chair Ginny Frank. E-mail vfrank@ access.k12.wv.us; *Chair-Elect* Pat Ramsburg. E-mail pramsbur@access.k12.wv.us; *Secy.* Kathy Bargeloh. E-mail kbargelo@access. k12.wv.us; *Past Chair* Vicky Davis. E-mail vldavis@access.k12.wv.us.

Address correspondence to the chairperson.

World Wide Web http://www.fscwv.edu/ users/bstefanowicz/index.htm.

Wisconsin

Wisconsin Educational Media Assn. Memb. 1,100+. Term of Office. Apr. 2004–Apr. 2005. Publication. *Dispatch* (7 a year).

Pres. Kate Bugher. E-mail kbugher@ madison.k12.wi.us; *Pres.-Elect* Annette Smith. E-mail smitha@mail.milton.k12.wi. us; *Secy.* Kathy Boguszewski. E-mail kboguszewski@janesville.k12.wi.us; *Treas.* Mike Weber. E-mail weber@hartfordjt1. k12.wi.us; *Past Pres.* Mary Lou Zuege. E-mail zuegmar@sdmf.k12.wi.us.

Address correspondence to the president or the secretary.

World Wide Web http://www.wema online.org.

Wyoming

Section of School Library Media Personnel, Wyoming Lib. Assn. Memb. 90+. Term of Office. Oct. 2004–Oct. 2005. Publications. *WLA Newsletter*; *SSLMP Newsletter*.

Chair Mary Jayne Jordan, Sundance H.S. E-mail jordanmj@hms.crooknet.k12.wy.us; *Chair-Elect* Jan Segerstrom, Jackson Hole H.S. E-mail jasegerstrom@teton1.k12.wy.us; *Secy.* Deb Lanthier. E-mail deb_lanthier@ hotmail.com. Address correspondence to the chairperson.

International Library Associations

International Association of Agricultural Information Specialists (IAALD)

c/o Pamela Q. Andre, Acting President
Box 218, 5863 Lilac Circle
St. Leonard, MD 20685
410-586-1274
E-mail pamandre@hotmail.com
World Wide Web http://www.iaald.org

Object

The association facilitates professional development of and communication among members of the agricultural information community worldwide. Its goal is to enhance access to and use of agriculture-related information resources. To further this mission, IAALD will promote the agricultural information profession, support professional development activities, foster collaboration, and provide a platform for information exchange. Founded 1955.

Membership

Memb. 300+. Dues (Inst.) US$95; (Indiv.) $45.

Officers

Acting Pres. Pamela Q. Andre, Box 218, 5863 Lilac Circle, St. Leonard, MD 20685. Tel. 410-586-1274, e-mail pamandre@ hotmail.com; *Secy.-Treas.* Margot Bellamy, 14 Queen St., Dorchester-on-Thames, Wallingford, Oxon OX10 7HR, England. Tel. 44-1865-340054, e-mail margot.bellamy@ fritillary.demon.co.uk.

Publications

Quarterly Bulletin of the IAALD (memb.).
World Directory of Agricultural Information Resource Centres.

International Association of Law Libraries (IALL)

Box 5709, Washington, DC 20016-1309
Tel. 804-924-3384, fax 804-924-7239
World Wide Web http://www.iall.org

Object

IALL is a worldwide organization of librarians, libraries, and other persons or institutions concerned with the acquisition and use of legal information emanating from sources other than their jurisdictions, and from multinational and international organizations.

IALL's basic purpose is to facilitate the work of librarians who must acquire, process, organize, and provide access to foreign legal materials. IALL has no local chapters but maintains liaison with national law library associations in many countries and regions of the world.

Membership

More than 800 members in more than 50 countries on five continents.

Officers (2004–2005)

Pres. Jules Winterton (Great Britain); *1st V.P.* Richard A. Danner (USA); *2nd V.P.* Jarmila Looks (Switzerland); *Secy.* Ann Morrison (Canada); *Treas.* Gloria F. Chao (USA); *Past Pres.* Holger Knudsen (Germany).

Board Members

Jennefer Aston (Ireland); Amanda Barratt (South Africa); Marie-Louise H. Bernal (USA); James Butler (Australia); Mark D. Engsberg (USA); Giina Kaskla (Belgium); Petal Kinder (Australia); Halvor Kongshavn (Norway); Bettina Picone-Maxion (Italy); Silke A. Sahl (USA).

Publication

International Journal of Legal Information (3 a year; US$65 for individuals; $95 for institutions).

International Association of Music Libraries, Archives and Documentation Centres (IAML)

c/o Roger Flury, IAML Secretary General
Music Room, National Library of New Zealand
Box 1467, Wellington, New Zealand
Tel. 64-4-474-3039, fax 64-4-474-3035, e-mail roger.flury@natlib.govt.nz
World Wide Web http://www.iaml.info

Object

To promote the activities of music libraries, archives, and documentation centers and to strengthen the cooperation among them; to promote the availability of all publications and documents relating to music and further their bibliographical control; to encourage the development of standards in all areas that concern the association; and to support the protection and preservation of musical documents of the past and the present.

Membership

Memb. 2,000.

Board Members

Pres. Massimo Gentili-Tedeschi, Biblioteca Nazionale Braidense, Ufficio Ricerca Fondi Musicali, via Conservatorio, 12, I-20122 Milano, Italy. Tel. 39-02-7601-1822, fax 39-02-7600-3097, e-mail gentili@icil64.cilea.it; *Past Pres.* John H. Roberts, Music Lib., 240 Morrison Hall, Univ. of California, Berkeley, CA 94720. Tel. 510-642-2428, fax 510-642-8237, e-mail jroberts@library.berkeley.edu; *V.P.s* James P. Cassaro, Theodore M. Finney Music Lib., Univ. of Pittsburgh, B28 Music Bldg., Pittsburgh, PA 15260. Tel. 412-624-4130, fax 412-624-4180, e-mail cassaro@pitt.edu; Dominique Hausfater, Mediathèque Hector Berlioz, Conservatoire National Supérieur de Musique et de Danse de Paris, 209 Ave. Jean-Jaurès, F-75019 Paris, France. Tel. 33-1-40-40-46-28, fax 33-1-40-40-45-34, e-mail dhausfater@cnsmdp.fr; Ruth Hellen, Audio Visual Services, Enfield Libs., Town Hall, Green Lane, London N13 4XD, England. Tel. 44-208-379-2760, fax 44-208-379-2761, e-mail r-hellen@enfield.gov.uk; Federica Riva, Bibliotecario del Conservatorio Sezione Musicale della Biblioteca Palatina, Nel Conservatorio di Musica Arrigo Boito, via Conservatorio 27/a, I-43100 Parma, Italy. Tel. 39-0521-381-958, fax 39-0521-200-398, e-mail f.riva@agora.it; *Treas.* Martie Severt, MCO Muziekbibliotheek, Postbus 125, NL-1200 AC Hilversum, Netherlands. E-mail m.severt@mco.nl.

Publication

Fontes Artis Musicae (4 a year; memb.). *Ed.* John Wagstaff, Music Faculty Lib., Oxford Univ., St. Aldate's, Oxford OX1 1DB, England.

Professional Branches

Archives and Documentation Centres. Judy Tsou, Univ. of Washington, Seattle, WA 98145.
Broadcasting and Orchestra Libraries. Jutta Lambrecht, Westdeutscher Rundfunk, Dokumentation und Archive, Appellhofplatz 1, D-50667 Köln, Germany.
Libraries in Music Teaching Institutions. Anne Le Lay, Bibliothèque du CNR,' 22 rue de la Belle Feuille, F-92100 Boulogne-Billancourt, France.
Public Libraries. Kirsten Husted, Biblioteket for Vejle By og Amt, Willy Sørensen Plads 1, Vejle, Denmark.
Research Libraries. Joachim Jaenecke, Staatsbibliothek zu Berlin, 10102 Berlin, Germany.

International Association of School Librarianship (IASL)

Penny Moore, Executive Director
P.O. Box 83, Zillmere, Qld. 4034, Australia
Fax 617-3633-0570, e-mail iasl@kb.com.au
World Wide Web http://www.iasl-slo.org

Object

The objectives of the International Association of School Librarianship are to advocate the development of school libraries throughout all countries; to encourage the integration of school library programs into the instructional and curriculum development of the school; to promote the professional preparation and continuing education of school library personnel; to foster a sense of community among school librarians in all parts of the world; to foster and extend relationships between school librarians and other professionals connected with children and youth; to foster research in the field of school librarianship and the integration of its conclusions with pertinent knowledge from related fields; to promote the publication and dissemination of information about successful advocacy and program initiatives in school librarianship; to share information about programs and materials for children and youth throughout the international community; and to initiate and coordinate activities, conferences, and other projects in the field of school librarianship and information services. Founded 1971.

Membership

Memb. 850.

Officers and Executive Board

Pres. Peter Genco, USA; *V.P.s* James Henri, Hong Kong; Judy O'Connell, Australia; Dilgit Singh, Malaysia; *Financial Officer* Anne Lockwood, Australia; *Dirs.* Margaret Balfour-Awuah, Africa–Sub-Sahara; Lourense Das, Europe; Rose Dotten, Canada; Eleanor Howe, USA; Elizabeth Greef, Oceania; Sandra Lee, East Asia; Colleen MacDonell, International Schools; Constanza Mekis, Latin America; Gail Parr, Asia; John Royce, North Africa/Middle East.

Publications

Selected Papers from Proceedings of Annual Conferences (all $25).
21st Annual Conference, 1992, Belfast, Northern Ireland. Toward the 21st Century: Books and Media for the Millennium.
22nd Annual Conference, 1993, Adelaide, Australia. Dreams and Dynamics.

23rd Annual Conference, 1994, Pittsburgh. Literacy: Traditions, Cultures, Technology.
24th Annual Conference, 1995, Worcester,

England. Sustaining the Vision.
25th Annual Conference, 1996, Ocho Rios, Jamaica. School Libraries Imperatives for the 21st Century.

International Association of Technological University Libraries (IATUL)

c/o President, Gaynor Austen, Library, Queensland University of Technology, GPO Box 2434, Brisbane, Qld. 4001, Australia
Tel. 61-7-3864-2560, fax 61-7-3864-1823, e-mail g.austen@qut.edu.au
World Wide Web http://www.iatul.org

Object

To provide a forum where library directors can meet to exchange views on matters of current significance in the libraries of universities of science and technology. Research projects identified as being of sufficient interest may be followed through by working parties or study groups.

Membership

Ordinary, associate, sustaining, and honorary. Membership fee is 107 euros a year, sustaining membership 500 euros a year. Memb. 232 (in 42 countries).

Officers and Executives

Pres. Gaynor Austen, Queensland Univ. of Technology, GPO Box 2434, Brisbane, Qld. 4001, Australia. Tel. 61-7-3864-2560, fax 61-7-3864-1823, e-mail g.austen@qut.edu. au; *1st V.P.* C. Lee Jones, Linda Hall Lib., 5109 Cherry St., Kansas City, MO 64110. Tel. 816-926-8742, fax 816-926-8790, e-mail leejones@lindahall.org; *2nd V.P.* Marianne Norlander, Linköping Univ. Lib., 581 83 Linköping, Sweden. E-mail marno@bibl.liu. se; *Secy.* Judith Palmer, Radcliffe Science

Lib., Oxford Univ., Parks Rd., Oxford OX1 3QP, England. E-mail judith.palmer@bodley. ox.ac.uk; *Treas.* Maria Heijne, Delft Univ. of Technology Lib., Postbus 98, 2600 MG Delft, Netherlands. Tel. 31-15-278-56-56, fax 31-15-257-20-60, e-mail m.a.m.heijne@ library.tudelft.nl; *Membs.* Ana Azevedo, Biblioteca Faculdade de Engenharia da Universidade do Porto, R. Roberto Frias 4200-465, Porto, Portugal. E-mail ana@fe.up.pt; Murray Shepherd, Waterloo, ON N2L 3G1, Canada. E-mail mcshephe@sympatico.ca; Catherine J. Matthews, Lib., Ryerson Polytechnic Univ., 340 Victoria St., Toronto, ON M5B 2K3, Canada. E-mail cmatthew@acs. ryerson.ca; Arja-Riitta Haarala, Tempere Univ. of Technology Lib., Tempere, Finland. E-mail arja-riitta.haarala@tut.fi; Paul Sheehan, Dublin City Univ. Lib., Dublin, Ireland. E-mail paul.sheehan@dcu.ie; Reiner Kallenborn, Munich Technical Univ. Lib., Munich, Germany. E-mail kallenborn@ub.tum.de; *Past Pres.* Michael Breaks, Heriot-Watt Univ. Lib., Edinburgh EH14 4AS, Scotland. Tel. 44-131-451-3570, fax 44-131-451-3164, e-mail m.l.breaks@hw.ac.uk.

Publication

IATUL Proceedings on CD-ROM (ann.).

International Council on Archives (ICA)

Joan van Albada, Secretary-General
60 Rue des Francs-Bourgeois, F-75003 Paris, France
Tel. 33-1-40-27-63-06, fax 33-1-42-72-20-65, e-mail ica@ica.org
World Wide Web http://www.ica.org

Object

To establish, maintain, and strengthen relations among archivists of all lands, and among all professional and other agencies or institutions concerned with the custody, organization, or administration of archives, public or private, wherever located. Established 1948.

Membership

Memb. c. 1,700 (representing c. 180 countries and territories).

Officers

Secy.-Gen. Joan van Albada; *Deputy Secy.-* *Gens.* Perrine Canavaggio, Marcel Caya; *Office Mgr.* Annick Carteret.

Publications

Comma (memb.).

Flash (3 a year; memb.).

Guide to the Sources of the History of Nations (Latin American Series, 11 vols. pub.; Africa South of the Sahara Series, 20 vols. pub.; North Africa, Asia, and Oceania Series: 15 vols. pub.).

Guide to the Sources of Asian History (English-language series [India, Indonesia, Korea, Nepal, Pakistan, Singapore], 14 vols. pub.; National Language Series [Indonesia, Korea, Malaysia, Nepal, Thailand], 6 vols. pub.; other guides, 3 vols. pub.).

International Federation of Film Archives (FIAF)

Secretariat, 1 Rue Defacqz, B-1000 Brussels, Belgium
Tel. 32-2-538-3065, fax 32-2-534-4774, e-mail info@fiafnet.org
World Wide Web http://www.fiafnet.org

Object

Founded in 1938, FIAF brings together institutions dedicated to rescuing films both as cultural heritage and as historical documents. FIAF is a collaborative association of the world's leading film archives whose purpose has always been to ensure the proper preservation and showing of motion pictures. A total of 126 archives in more than 60 countries collect, restore, and exhibit films and cinema documentation spanning the entire history of film.

FIAF seeks to promote film culture and facilitate historical research, to help create new archives around the world, to foster training and expertise in film preservation, to encourage the collection and preservation of documents and other cinema-related materials, to develop cooperation between archives, and to ensure the international availability of films and cinema documents.

Officers

Pres. Eva Orbanz; *Secy.-Gen.* Meg Labrum; *Treas.* Karl Griep; *Membs.* Magdalena Acosta, Claude Bertemes, Jan-Erik Billinger, Hong-Teak Chung, Stefan Droessler, Sylvia

Naves, Hisashi Okajima, Susan Oxtoby, Roger Smither, Boris Todorovitch, Paolo Cherchi Usai.

Address correspondence to Christian Dimitriu, Senior Administrator, c/o the Secretariat. E-mail info@fiafnet.org.

Publications

Journal of Film Preservation.
International Filmarchive CD-ROM.
For other FIAF publications, see the Web site http://www.fiafnet.org.

International Federation of Library Associations and Institutions (IFLA)

Box 95312, 2509 CH The Hague, Netherlands
Tel. 31-70-314-0884, fax 31-70-383-4827
E-mail ifla@ifla.org, World Wide Web http://www.ifla.org

Object

To promote international understanding, cooperation, discussion, research, and development in all fields of library activity, including bibliography, information services, and the education of library personnel, and to provide a body through which librarianship can be represented in matters of international interest. Founded 1927.

Officers and Governing Board

Pres. Kay Raseroka, Univ. Lib. of Botswana, Gaborone, Botswana; *Pres.-Elect* Alex Byrne, Univ. of Technology, Sydney, Australia; *Treas.* Ingrid Parent, National Lib. of Canada, Ottawa; *Governing Board* Nancy E. Gwinn, Smithsonian Inst. Lib., Chevy Chase, Maryland; Torny Kjekstad, Baerum Public Lib., Bekkestua, Norway; Marian Koren, Netherlands Public Lib. Assn., The Hague, Netherlands; Evgeniy Kuzmin, Ministry of Culture of the Russian Federation, Moscow, Russia; Claudia Lux, Zentral- und Landesbibliothek, Berlin, Germany; Ia McIlwaine, School of Lib., Archive, and Info. Studies, London, England; John Meriton, National Art Lib., Victoria and Albert Museum, London, England; Sissel Nilsen, National Lib. of Norway, Oslo, Norway; Vinyet Panyella, Biblioteca de Catalunya, Barcelona, Spain; Cristobal Pasadas Urena, Universidad de Granada Biblioteca, Granada, Spain; Shawky Salem, ACML–Egypt, Alexandria, Egypt; Edward

Swanson, MINITEX Lib. Info. Network, Minneapolis, Minnesota; Barbara Tillet, Lib. of Congress, Washington, D.C.; Ellen Tise, Univ. of the Western Cape, Bellville, South Africa; Tiiu Valm, National Lib. of Estonia, Tallinn, Estonia; Jacinta Were, Univ. of Nairobi Lib., Nairobi, Kenya; Jianzhong Wu, Shanghai Lib., Shanghai, China; Ana Maria Peruchena Zimmermann, ABGRA, Buenos Aires, Argentina; *Secy.-Gen.* Peter J. Lor; *Coord. Professional Activities* Sjoerd M. J. Koopman.

Publications

IFLA Annual Report.
IFLA Directory (bienn.).
IFLA Journal (4 a year).
IFLA Professional Reports.
IFLA Publications Series.
International Cataloguing and Bibliographic Control (q.).
International Preservation News.

American Membership

American Assn. of Law Libs.; American Lib. Assn.; Art Libs. Society of North America; Assn. for Lib. and Info. Science Educ.; Assn. of Research Libs.; International Assn. of Law Libs.; International Assn. of School Libns.; Medical Lib. Assn.; Special Libs. Assn. *Institutional Membs.* There are 139 libraries and related institutions that are institutional members or consultative bodies and sponsors of IFLA in the United States (out of a total of 1,715), and 154 personal affiliates (out of a total of 410).

International Organization for Standardization (ISO)

ISO Central Secretariat, 1 rue de Varembé, Case Postale 56, CH-1211
Geneva 20, Switzerland
41-22-749-0111, fax 41-22-733-3430, e-mail central@iso.org
World Wide Web http://www.iso.org

Object

A worldwide federation of national standards bodies, founded in 1947, at present comprising some 145 members, one in each country. The object of ISO is to promote the development of standardization and related activities in the world with a view to facilitating international exchange of goods and services, and to developing cooperation in the spheres of intellectual, scientific, technological, and economic activity. The scope of ISO covers international standardization in all fields except electrical and electronic engineering standardization, which is the responsibility of the International Electrotechnical Commission (IEC). The results of ISO technical work are published as International Standards.

Officers

Pres. Masami Tanaka, Japan; *V.P. (Policy)* Torsten Bahke, Germany; *V.P. (Technical Management)* Ziva Patir, Israel; *Secy.-Gen.* Alan Bryden; *Past Pres.* Oliver R. Smoot, USA.

Technical Work

The technical work of ISO is carried out by some 190 technical committees. These include:

ISO/TC 46–Information and documentation (Secretariat, Association Française de Normalization, 11 Ave. Francis de Pressensé, 93571 Saint-Denis La Plaine, Cedex, France). Scope: Standardization of practices relating to libraries, documentation and information centers, indexing and abstracting services, archives, information science, and publishing.

ISO/TC 37–Terminology and other language resources (Secretariat, INFOTERM, Aichholzgasse 6/12, 1120, Vienna, Austria, on behalf of Österreichisches Normungsinstitut). Scope: Standardization of principles, methods, and applications relating to terminology and other language resources.

ISO/IEC JTC 1–Information technology (Secretariat, American National Standards Institute, 25 W. 43 St., 4th fl., New York, NY 10036). Scope: Standardization in the field of information technology.

Publications

ISO Annual Report.
ISO Focus (11 a year).
ISO CataloguePlus on CD-ROM (combined catalog of published standards and technical work program) (ann.).
ISO International Standards.
ISO Management Systems (bi-mo.).
ISO Memento (ann.).
ISO Online information service on World Wide Web (http://www.iso.org).

Foreign Library Associations

The following is a list of regional and national library associations around the world. A more complete list can be found in *International Literary Market Place* (Information Today, Inc.).

Regional

Africa

Standing Conference of Eastern, Central, and Southern African Lib. and Info. Assns., c/o Uganda Lib. Assn., P.O. Box 5894, Kampala, Uganda. E-mail library@imul.com, World Wide Web http://www.ou.edu/cas/slis/ULA/ula_index.htm.

The Americas

Asociación de Bibliotecas Universitarias, de Investigación e Institucionales del Caribe (Assn. of Caribbean Univ., Research, and Institutional Libs.), Box 23317, UPR Sta., San Juan, PR 00931-3317. Tel. 787-790-8054, 787-764-0000, e-mail acuril@rrpac. upr.clu.edu, World Wide Web http://acuril. rrp.upr.edu. *Pres.* Shamin Renwick; *Exec. Secy.* Oneida Rivera de Ortiz.

Seminar on the Acquisition of Latin American Lib. Materials, c/o *Exec. Secy.* Laura Gutiérrez-Witt, SALALM Secretariat, Benson Latin American Collection, Sid Richardson Hall 1.109, Univ. of Texas, Austin, TX 78713. Tel. 512-495-4471, fax 512-495-4488, e-mail sandyl@mail. utexas.edu, World Wide Web http://www. lib.utexas.edu/benson/secretariat.

Asia

Congress of Southeast Asian Libns. (CONSAL), c/o *Secy.-Gen.* Tay Ai Cheng, c/o National Lib. Board, 3 Temasek Ave., 07-00 Centennial Tower, Singapore 039190. Tel. 65-633-21785, fax 65-633-21781, e-mail aicheng@nlb.gov.sg, World Wide Web http://www.consal.org.sg.

The Commonwealth

Commonwealth Lib. Assn., P.O. Box 144, Mona, Kingston 7, Jamaica. Tel. 809-927-2123, fax 809-927-1926, e-mail nkpodo @uwimona.edu.jm. *Pres.* Elizabeth Watson; *Exec. Secy.* Norma Amenu-Kpodo.

Standing Conference on Lib. Materials on Africa, Commonwealth Secretariat, Marlborough House, Pall Mall, London SW1Y 5HX, England. Tel. 020-7747-6253, fax 020-7747-6168, e-mail scolma@hotmail. com, World Wide Web http://www.lse.ac. uk/library/scolma. *Chair* Sheila Allcock; *Secy.* David Blake.

Europe

Ligue des Bibliothèques Européennes de Recherche (LIBER) (Assn. of European Research Libs.), c/o Erland Kolding Nielsen, Dir.-Gen., Royal Lib., Box 2149, DK-1016 Copenhagen, Denmark. Tel. 45-33-47-4301, fax 45-33-32-98-46, e-mail ekn@kb.dk, World Wide Web http://www. kb.dk/guests/intl/liber.

National

Argentina

Asociación de Bibliotecarios Graduados de la República Argentina (ABGRA) (Assn. of Graduate Libns. of Argentina), Tucuman 1424, 8 piso D, C1050AAB Buenos Aires. Tel./fax 11-4371-5269, e-mail info@ abgra.org.ar, World Wide Web http:// www.abgra.org.ar. *Pres.* Ana Maria Peruchena Zimmermann; *Exec. Secy.* Rosa Emma Monfasani.

Australia

Australian Lib. and Info. Assn., Box 6335, Kingston, ACT 2604. Tel. 2-6215-8222, fax 2-6282-2249, e-mail enquiry@alia.org. au, World Wide Web http://www.alia.org. au. *Pres.* Christine Mackenzie; *Exec. Dir.* Jennifer Nicholson.

Australian Society of Archivists, c/o Queensland State Archives, Box 1397, Sunnybank Hills, Qld. 4109. E-mail qsa@iie.qld.gov.au or, World Wide Web http://www.archives.qld.gov.au. *Pres.* Kathryn Dan; *Secy.* Fiona Burn.

Council of Australian State Libs., c/o State Lib. of Victoria, 328 Swanston St., Melbourne, Vic. 3000. Tel. 3-8664-7512, fax 3-9639-4737, e-mail casl@slv.vic.gov.au, World Wide Web http://www.casl.org.au. *Chief Exec. Officer* Frances Awcock.

Austria

Österreichische Gesellschaft für Dokumentation und Information (Austrian Society for Documentation and Info.), Lustkandlgasse 4/29, 1090 Vienna. E-mail office@oegdi.at, World Wide Web http://www.oegdi.at. *Pres.* Gerhard Richter.

Vereinigung Österreichischer Bibliothekarinnen und Bibliothekare (Assn. of Austrian Libns.), Voralberger Federal State Lib., Fluherstr. 4, 6900 Bregenz. E-mail voeb@uibk.ac.at, World Wide Web http://voeb.uibk.ac.at. *Pres.* Harald Weigel; *Secy.* Werner Schlacher.

Bangladesh

Lib. Assn. of Bangladesh, c/o Inst. of Lib. and Info. Science, Bangladesh Central Public Lib. Bldg., Shahbagh, Dacca 1000. Tel. 2-504-269, e-mail msik@icddrb.org. *Pres.* M. Shamsul Islam Khan; *Gen. Secy.* Kh. Fazlur Rahman.

Barbados

Lib. Assn. of Barbados, Box 827E, Bridgetown. *Pres.* Shirley Yearwood; *Secy.* Hazelyn Devonish.

Belgium

Archives et Bibliothèques de Belgique/Archief- en Bibliotheekwezen in België (Archives and Libs. of Belgium), Ruisbroekstr. 2-10, B-1000 Brussels. Tel. 2-519-5351, fax 2-519-5533, e-mail wim.devos@kbr.be. *Gen. Secy.* Wim De Vos.

Association Belge de Documentation/Belgische Vereniging voor Documentatie (Belgian Assn. for Documentation), chaussée de Wavre 1683, Waversesteenweg, B-1160 Brussels. Tel. 2-675-58-62, fax 2-672-74-46, e-mail info@abd-bvd.be, World Wide Web http://www.abd-bvd.be. *Pres.* Philippe Laurent.

Association Professionnelle des Bibliothécaires et Documentalistes (Assn. of Libns. and Documentation Specialists), 30 rue Rêve d'Or, 7100 La Louvière. Tel. 064-22-18-34, fax 064-21-28-50, e-mail biblio.hainaut@skynet.be, World Wide Web http://www.apbd.be. *Pres.* Laurence Boulanger; *Secy.* Laurence Hennaux.

Vlaamse Vereniging voor Bibliotheek-, Archief-, en Documentatiewezen (Flemish Assn. of Libns., Archivists, and Documentalists), Statiestraat 179, B-2600 Berchem, Antwerp. Tel. 3-281-4457, fax 3-218-8077, e-mail vvbad@vvbad.be, World Wide Web http://www.vvbad.be. *Pres.* Geert Puype; *Exec. Dir.* Marc Storms.

Belize

Belize Lib. Assn., c/o Central Lib., Bliss Inst., Box 287, Belize City. Tel. 2-7267, fax 2-34246. *Pres.* H. W. Young; *Secy.* Robert Hulse.

Bolivia

Asociación Boliviana de Bibliotecarios (Bolivian Lib. Assn.), c/o Biblioteca y Archivo Nacional, Calle Bolivar, Sucre. *Dir.* Gunnar Mendoza.

Bosnia and Herzegovina

Drustvo Bibliotekara Bosne i Hercegovine (Libns. Society of Bosnia and Herzegovina), Zmaja od Bosne 8B, 71000 Sarajevo. Tel. 33-275-312, fax 33-218-431, e-mail nubbih@nub.ba, World Wide Web http://www.nub.ba. *Pres.* Nevenka Hajdarovic.

Botswana

Botswana Lib. Assn., Box 1310, Gaborone. Tel. 31-355-2295, fax 31-357-291. *Chair* Bobana Badisang; *Secy.* Peter Tshukudu.

Brazil

Associação dos Arquivistas Brasileiros (Assn. of Brazilian Archivists), Av. Presidente Vargas 1733, Sala 903, 20210-030 Rio de Janiero RJ. Tel. 21-2507-2239, fax 21-3852-2541, e-mail aab@aab.org.br, World Wide Web http://www.aab.org.br. *Pres.* Lia Temporal Malcher; *Secy.* Laura Regina Xavier.

Brunei Darussalam

Persatuan Perpustakaan Kebangsaan Negara Brunei (National Lib. Assn. of Brunei), Perpustakaan Universiti Brunei Darussalam, Jalan Tungku Link Gadong BE 1410. Tel. 2-223-060. *Pres.* Puan Nellie bte Dato Paduka Haji Sunny.

Cameroon

Association des Bibliothécaires, Archivistes, Documentalistes et Muséographes du Cameroun (Assn. of Libns., Archivists, Documentalists, and Museum Curators of Cameroon), B.P. 4609, Yaoundé, Nlongkak. Tel. 222-6362, fax 222-4785, e-mail abadcam@yahoo.fr. *Pres.* Hilaire Omokolo.

Canada

Bibliographical Society of Canada/La Société Bibliographique du Canada, Box 575, Postal Sta. P, Toronto, ON M5S 2T1. E-mail mcgaughe@yorku.ca, World Wide Web http://www.library.utoronto.ca/bsc. *Pres.* Carl Spadoni; *Secy.* Anne McGaughey.

Canadian Assn. for Info. Science/Association Canadienne des Sciences de l'Information, c/o Louise Spiteri, School of Lib. and Info. Studies, Faculty of Management, Dalhousie Univ., 6225 University Ave., Rm. 3621, Halifax, NS B3H 3J5. Tel. 902-494-2473, fax 902-494-2451, e-mail louise.spiteri@dal.ca. *Pres.* Louise Spiteri. World Wide Web http://www.cais-acsi.ca.

Canadian Assn. for School Libraries (CASL), c/o Marlene Asselin, Assoc. Professor, Faculty of Educ., Dept. of Language and Literacy, Univ. of British Columbia, 2034 Lower Mall, Vancouver, BC V6T 1Z2.

Tel. 604-822-5733, fax 604-822-3154. *Co-Pres.* Marlene Asselin, Gloria Hersak. World Wide Web http://www.caslibraries.ca.

Canadian Assn. of Research Libraries/Association des Bibliothèques de Recherche du Canada (CARL/ABRC), Univ. of Ottawa, 65 University St., Rm. 239, Ottawa, ON K1N 9A5. Tel. 613-562-5385, fax 613-562-5195, World Wide Web http://www.uottawa.ca/library/carl.

Canadian Lib. Assn., c/o *Exec. Dir.* Don Butcher, 328 Frank St., Ottawa, ON K2P 0X8. Tel. 613-232-9625, fax 613-563-9895, e-mail dbutcher@cla.ca. (For detailed information on the Canadian Lib. Assn. and its divisions, see "Canadian Library Association" in Part 1 and "National Library and Information-Industry Associations, United States and Canada" earlier in Part 6. For information on the library associations of the provinces of Canada, see "State, Provincial, and Regional Library Associations.")

Chile

Colegio de Bibliotecarios de Chile AG (Chilean Lib. Assn.), Paraguay 383, Torre 11, Oficina 122, 6510017 Santiago. Tel. 2-222-5652, fax 2-635-5023, e-mail cbc@uplink.cl, World Wide Web http://www.bibliotecarios.cl. *Pres.* Marcia Marinovic Simunovic; *Secy.* Ana Maria Pino Yanez.

China

China Society for Lib. Science, 33 Zhongguancum (S), Beijing 100081. Tel. 10-6841-9270, fax 10-6841-9271, e-mail ztxhmsc@pulicf.nls.cov.cn. *Secy.-Gen.* Gulian Li; *Pres.* Liu Deyou.

Colombia

Asociación Colombiana de Bibliotecarios y Documentalistas (Colombian Assn. of Libns. and Documentalists), Carrera 50, 27-70, Modulo 1 Nivel 4, Bloque C, Colceincias, Bogotá. Tel. 1-360-3977 ext. 326, World Wide Web http://www.biblio.ucaldas.edu.co. *Pres.* Jaime Vasquez Restrepo.

Congo, Democratic Republic

Association Zaïroise des Archivistes, Bibliothécaires et Documentalistes (Zaire Association of Archivists, Librarians, and Documentalists), BP 805, Kinshasa X1. Tel. 012-30123. *Exec. Secy.* E. Kabeba-Bangasa.

Costa Rica

Asociación Costarricense de Bibliotecarios (Costa Rican Assn. of Libns.), Apdo. 3308, San José. *Secy.-Gen.* Nelly Kopper.

Côte d'Ivoire

Association pour le Développement de la Documentation, des Bibliothèques et Archives de la Côte d'Ivoire, c/o Bibliothèque Nationale, BPV 180, Abidjan. Tel. 32-38-72. *Secy.-Gen.* Cangah Guy; *Dir.* Ambroise Agnero.

Croatia

Hrvatsko Knjiznicarsko Drustvo (Croatian Lib. Assn.), Ulica Hrvatske bratske zajednice 4, 10 000 Zagreb. Tel. 1-615-93-20, fax 1-616-41-86, e-mail hbd@nsk.hr, World Wide Web http://pubwww.srce.hr./hkd. *Pres.* Dubravka Stancin-Rosic; *Secy.* Dunja Marie Gabriel.

Cuba

Lib. Assn. of Cuba, c/o Direccion de Relaciones Internacionales, Ministerio de Cultura, Calle 4 e/m 11y13, Vedado, Havana. Tel. 7-55-2244, fax 7-66-2053. *Dir.* Marta Terry González.

Cyprus

Kypriakos Synthesmos Vivliothicarion (Lib. Assn. of Cyprus), Box 1039, 1434 Nicosia. Tel. 22-404-849. *Pres.* Costas D. Stephanov; *Secy.* Paris G. Rossos.

Czech Republic

Svaz Knihovniku Informachnich Pracovniku Ceske Republiky (Assn. of Lib. and Info. Professionals of the Czech Republic), National Lib., Klementinum 190, 11001 Prague. Tel. 2-2166-3111, fax 2-2166-3261, e-mail vit.richter@nkp.cz, World Wide Web http://www.nkp.cz. *Pres.* Vit Richter.

Denmark

Arkivforeningen (Archives Society), c/o Landsarkivet for Sjaelland, jagtvej 10, 22 Copenhagen N. Tel. 31-39-35-20, fax 33-15-32-39. *Pres.* Tyge Krogh; *Secy.* Charlotte Steinmark.

Danmarks Biblioteksforening (Danish Lib. Assn.), Vesterbrogade 20/5, 1620 Copenhagen V. Tel. 33-25-09-35, fax 33-25-79-00, World Wide Web http://www.dbf.dk. *Dir.* Winnie Vitzansky.

Danmarks Forskningsbiblioteksforening (Danish Research Lib. Assn.), c/o Statsbiblioteket, Universitetsparken 8000, Århus C. Tel. 45-89-46-22-07, fax 45-89-46-22-20, e-mail df@statsbiblioteket.dk, World Wide Web http://www.dfdf.dk. *Pres.* Erland Kolding; *Secy.* Hanne Dahl.

Kommunernes Skolebiblioteksforening (formerly Danmarks Skolebiblioteksforening) (Assn. of Danish School Libs.), Krimsveg 29B 1, DK-2300 Copenhagen S. Tel. 33-11-13-91, fax 33-11-13-90, e-mail komskolbib@ksbf.dk, World Wide Web http://www.ksbf.dk. *Chief Exec.* Paul Erik Sorensen.

Dominican Republic

Asociación Dominicana de Bibliotecarios (Dominican Assn. of Libns.), c/o Biblioteca Nacional, Plaza de la Cultura, Cesar Nicolás Penson 91, Santo Domingo. Tel. 809-688-4086, e-mail biblioteca.nacional @dominicana.com. *Pres.* Prospero J. Mella-Chavier; *Secy.-Gen.* V. Regús.

Ecuador

Asociación Ecuatoriana de Bibliotecarios (Ecuadoran Lib. Assn.), c/o Casa de la Cultura Ecuatoriana Benjamin Carrión, Ave. 12 de Octubre 555, Quito. Tel. 2-528-840, fax 2-223-391, e-mail asoebfp@hotmail.com, World Wide Web http://www.eicyt.org.ec/aeb. *Pres.* Wilson Vega.

Egypt

Egyptian Assn. for Lib. and Info. Science, c/o Dept. of Archives, Libnship., and Info. Science, Faculty of Arts, Univ. of Cairo, Cairo. Tel. 2-567-6365, fax 2-572-9659. *Pres.* S. Khalifa; *Secy.* Hosam El-Din.

El Salvador

Asociación de Bibliotecarios de El Salvador (El Salvador Lib. Assn.), c/o Biblioteca Nacional, 8A Avda. Norte y Calle Delgado, San Salvador. Tel. 216-312, World Wide Web http://ues.edu.sv/abes/informacion.htm. *Pres.* Olinda Estela Gomez Moran.

Asociación General de Archivistas de El Salvador (Assn. of Archivists of El Salvador), Archivo General de la Nación, Direccion Nacional de Patrimonio Cultural, Palacio Nacional, San Salvador. Tel. 222-94-18, fax 281-58-60, e-mail agnes@agn.gob.sv, World Wide Web http://www.agn.gob.sv.

Ethiopia

Ye Ethiopia Betemetshaft Serategnoch Mahber (Ethiopian Lib. and Info. Assn.), Box 30530, Addis Ababa. Tel. 1-511-344, fax 1-552-544. *Pres.* Mulugeta Hunde; *Secy.* Girma Makonnen.

Finland

Suomen Kirjastoseura (Finnish Lib. Assn.), Kansakoulukatu 10 A 19, FIN-00100 Helsinki. Tel. 9-694-1858, fax 9-694-1859, e-mail fla@fla.fi, World Wide Web http://www.kaapeli.fi/~fla/presentation.html. *Pres.* Mirja Ryynanen; *Secy.-Gen.* Tuula Haavisto.

France

Association des Archivistes Français (Assn. of French Archivists), 9 rue Montcalm, F-75018 Paris. Tel. 1-46-06-39-44, fax 1-46-06-39-52, e-mail secretariat@archivistes.org, World Wide Web http://www.archivistes.org. *Pres.* Henri Zuber; *Secy.* Agnès Dejob.

Association des Bibliothécaires Français (Assn. of French Libns.), 31 rue de Chab-rol, F-75010 Paris. Tel. 1-55-33-10-30, fax 1-55-30-10-31, e-mail abf@abf.asso.fr, World Wide Web http://www.abf.asso.fr. *Pres.* Gérard Briand; *Gen. Secy.* Jean-François Jacques.

Association des Professionnels de l'Information et de la Documentation (Assn. of Info. and Documentation Professionals), 25 rue Claude Tillier, F-75012 Paris. Tel. 1-43-72-25-25, fax 1-43-72-30-41, e-mail adbs @adbs.fr, World Wide Web http://www.adbs.fr. *Pres.* Florence Wilhelm.

Germany

Arbeitsgemeinschaft der Spezialbibliotheken (Assn. of Special Libs.), c/o Forschungs-zentrum, Jülich GmbH, Zentralbibliothek, 52426 Jülich. Tel. 2461-61-2907, fax 2461-61-6103, World Wide Web http://www.aspb.de. *Chair* Rafael Ball.

Berufsverband Information Bibliothek (Assn. of Info. and Lib. Professionals), Gartenstr. 18, 72764 Reutlingen. Tel. 7121-3491-0, fax 7121-300-433, e-mail mail@bib-info.de, World Wide Web http://www.bib-info.de. *Pres.* Klaus Peter Boettger; *Secy.* Katharina Boulanger.

Deutsche Gesellschaft für Informationswissenschaft und Informationspraxis eV (German Society for Info. Science and Practice), Ostbahnhofstr. 13, 60314 Frankfurt-am-Main 1. Tel. 69-43-03-13, fax 69-49-09-09-6, e-mail mail@dgi-info.de, World Wide Web http://www.dgd.de. *Pres.* Gabriele Beger.

Deutscher Bibliotheksverband eV (German Lib. Assn.), Strasse des 17 Juni 114, 10623 Berlin. Tel. 30-39-00-14-80, fax 30-39-00-14-84, e-mail dbv@bibliotheksverband.de, World Wide Web http://www.bibliotheksverband.de. *Pres.* Brigitte Scherer.

VdA—Verband Deutscher Archivarinnen und Archivare (Assn. of German Archivists), Postfach 2119, 99402 Weimar. Tel. 03643-870-235, fax 03643-870-164, e-mail info@vda.archiv.net, World Wide Web http://www.vda.archiv.net. *Chair* Volker Wahl.

Verein der Diplom-Bibliothekare an Wissenschaftlichen Bibliotheken (Assn. of

Certified Libns. at Academic Libs.), c/o Stadtbuecherei Muelheim an der Ruhr, Friedrich-Ebert Str. 47, 45468 Muelheim an der Ruhr. Tel. 221-574-7161, fax 221-574-7110, World Wide Web http://www.bibliothek.uni-regensburg.de/vddb. *Chair* Klaus-Peter Boettger.
Verein Deutsche Bibliothekare (Assn. of German Libns.), Unter den Linden 8, 10117 Berlin. Tel. 30-266-1728, fax 30-266-1717, e-mail elsmann@uni-bremen.de. *Pres.* Daniela Luelfing; *Secy.* Thomas Elsmann.

Ghana

Ghana Lib. Assn., Box 4105, Accra. Tel. 2-668-731. *Pres.* E. S. Asiedo; *Secy.* A. W. K. Insaidoo.

Greece

Enosis Hellinon Bibliothekarion (Greek Lib. Assn.), 4 Skoulenion St., 10561 Athens. Tel. 1-3226-625. *Pres.* K. Xatzopoulou; *Gen. Secy.* E. Kalogeraky.

Guyana

Guyana Lib. Assn., c/o National Lib., 76-77 Church and Main Sts., Georgetown. Tel. 226-2690, fax 227-4053, e-mail natlib@sdnp.org.gy, World Wide Web http://www.natlib.gov.gy. *Pres.* Ivor Rodriguez; *Secy.* Gwyneth George.

Honduras

Asociación de Bibliotecarios y Archiveros de Honduras (Assn. of Libns. and Archivists of Honduras), 11a Calle, 1a y 2a Avdas., No. 105, Comayagüela DC, Tegucigalpa. *Pres.* Fransisca de Escoto Espinoza; *Secy.-Gen.* Juan Angel R. Ayes.

Hong Kong

Hong Kong Lib. Assn., GPO 10095, Hong Kong. E-mail hklib@hklib.org.hk, World Wide Web http://www.hklib.org.hk. *Pres.* Tommy Yeung.

Hungary

Magyar Könyvtárosok Egyesülete (Assn. of Hungarian Libns.), Hold u 6, H-1054 Budapest. Tel./fax 1-311-8634, e-mail mke@oszk.hu, World Wide Web http://www.mke.oszk.hu. *Pres.* Bakos Klara; *Gen. Secy.* Katalin Haraszti.

Iceland

Upplysing—Felag bokasafns-og upplysingafraeoa (Information—the Icelandic Library and Information Science Assn.), Lagmuli 7, 108 Reykjavik. Tel. 553-7290, fax 588-9239, e-mail upplysing@bokis.is, World Wide Web http://www.bokis.is. *Pres.* H. A. Hardarson; *Secy.* A. Agnarsdottir.

India

Indian Assn. of Academic Libns., c/o Jawaharlal Nehru Univ. Lib., New Mehrauli Rd., New Delhi 110067. Tel. 11-683-1717. *Secy.* M. M. Kashyap.
Indian Assn. of Special Libs. and Info. Centres, P-291, CIT Scheme 6M, Kankurgachi, Calcutta 700054. Tel. 33-2352-9651, e-mail iaslic@vsnl.net, World Wide Web http://www.iaslic.org. *Publisher* J. M. Das.
Indian Lib. Assn., A/40-41, Flat 201, Ansal Bldg., Mukerjee Nagar, Delhi 110009. Tel. 11-326-4748, e-mail ilanet1@nda.vsnl.net.in. *Pres.* Kalpana Dasgsupta.

Indonesia

Ikatan Pustakawan Indonesia (Indonesian Lib. Assn.), Jalan Merdeka Selatan No. 11, 10110 Jakarta, Pusat. Tel. 21-375-718, fax 21-345-5611. *Pres.* S. Kartosdono.

Iraq

Iraq Archivists Institute, c/o National Centre of Archives, National Lib. Bldg., Bab-Al-Muaddum, Baghdad. Tel. 1-416-8440. *Dir.* Salim Al-Alousi.

Ireland

Cumann Leabharlann Na h-Eireann (Lib. Assn. of Ireland), 53 Upper Mount St., Dublin. Tel. 1-6120-2193, fax 1-6121-3090, e-mail president@libraryassociation. ie, World Wide Web http://www.library association.ie. *Pres.* Gobnait O'Riordan; *Hon. Secy.* Denise Murphy.

Israel

Israel Libns. and Info. Specialists Assn., 9 Beit Hadfus St., Givaat Shaul, Jerusalem. Tel. 2-6589515, fax 2-6251628, e-mail icl@icl.org.il, World Wide Web http:// www.icl.org.il. *Pres.* Benjamin Schachter.

Israel Society of Libs. and Info. Centers, P.O. Box 28273, 91282 Jerusalem. Tel./fax 2-624-9421, e-mail asmi@asmi.org.il, World Wide Web http://www.asmi.org.il. *Chair* Shoshana Langerman.

Italy

Associazione Italiana Biblioteche (Italian Lib. Assn.), C.P. 2461, 00100 Rome. Tel. 6-446-3532, fax 6-444-1139, e-mail aib@ aib.it, World Wide Web http://www.aib.it. *Pres.* Miriam Scarabo; *Secy.* Marco Cupellaro.

Jamaica

Jamaica Lib. Assn., P.O. Box 125, Kingston 5. Tel./fax 876-927-1614, e-mail liaja president@yahoo.com, World Wide Web http://www.liaja.org.jm. *Pres.* Byron Palmer; *Secy.* F. Salmon.

Japan

Joho Kagaku Gijutsu Kyokai (Info. Science and Technology Assn.), Sasaki Bldg., 2-5-7 Koisikawa, Bunkyo-ku, Tokyo 112-0002. Tel. 3-3813-3791, fax 3-3813-3793, e-mail infosta@infosta.or.jp, World Wide Web http://www.infosta.or.jp. *Pres.* T. Gondoh; *Gen. Mgr.* Yukio Ichikawa.

Nihon Toshokan Kyokai (Japan Lib. Assn.), 1-11-14 Shinkawa, Chuo-ku, Tokyo 104 0033. Tel. 3-3523-0811, fax 3-3523-0841, e-mail info@jla.or.jp, World Wide Web http://www.jla.or.jp. *Secy.-Gen.* Reiko Sakagawa.

Senmon Toshokan Kyogikai (Japan Special Libs. Assn.), c/o Japan Lib. Assn., Bldg. F6, 1-11-14 Shinkawa, Chuo-ku, Tokyo 104-0033. Tel. 3-3537-8335, fax 3-3537-8336, e-mail jsla@jsla.or.jp, World Wide Web http://www.jsla.or.jp. *Pres.* Kousaku Inaba; *Exec. Dir.* Fumihisa Nakagawa.

Jordan

Jordan Lib. Assn., P.O. Box 6289, Amman. Tel./fax 6-462-9412. *Pres.* Anwar Akroush; *Secy.* Yousra Abu Ajamieh.

Kenya

Kenya Lib. Assn., Box 46031, Nairobi. Tel. 2-334-244, fax 2-336-885, e-mail jwere@ ken.healthnet.org. *Chair* Jacinta Were; *Secy.* Alice Bulogosi.

Korea (Republic of)

Korean Lib. Assn., 1-KA, Hoehyun-Dong, Choong-ku, Seoul 100-177. Tel. 02-535-4868, fax 2-535-5616, e-mail klanet@ hitel.net, World Wide Web http://korla.or. kr. *Pres.* Ki Nam Shin; *Exec. Dir.* Won Ho Jo.

Laos

Association des Bibliothécaires Laotiens (Assn. of Laotian Libns.), c/o Direction de la Bibliothèque Nationale, Ministry of Info. and Culture, B.P. 122, Vientiane. Tel. 21-212-452, fax 21-213-408, e-mail pfd-mill@pan.laos.net.la.

Latvia

Lib. Assn. of Latvia, Latvian National Lib., Kr. Barona 14, 2 Stavs, 205 telpa, 1423 Riga. Tel. 371-728-7620, fax 371-728-0851, e-mail lnb@lbi.lnb.lv, World Wide Web http://www.lnb.lv. *Pres.* Aldis Abele.

Lebanon

Lebanese Lib. Assn., c/o American Univ. of Beirut, Univ. Lib./Serials Dept., Box 11-0236, Beirut. Tel. 1-350-000, fax 1-340-460, World Wide Web http://www.aub.edu.lb. *Pres.* Fawz Abdalleh; *Exec. Secy.* Rudaynah Shoujah.

Lesotho

Lesotho Lib. Assn., Private Bag A26, Maseru. Tel./fax 340-601, e-mail mmc@doc.isas.nul.ls, World Wide Web http://www.sn.apc.org. *Chair* S. M. Mohai; *Secy.* N. Taole.

Lithuania

Lithuanian Libns. Assn., Sv. Ignoto 6-108, LT-2600, Vilnius. Tel./fax 2-750-340, e-mail lbd@vpu.lt, World Wide Web http://www.lbd.lt.

Macedonia

Bibliotekarsko Drustvo na Makedonija (Union of Libns.' Assns. of Macedonia), Box 566, 91000 Skopje. Tel. 91-226-846, fax 91-232-649, e-mail mile@nubsk.edu.mk or bmile47@yahoo.com. *Pres.* Mile Boseki; *Secy.* Poliksena Matkovska.

Malawi

Malawi Lib. Assn., Box 429, Zomba. Tel. 50-522-222, fax 50-523-225. *Chair* Joseph J. Uta; *Secy.* Vote D. Somba.

Malaysia

Persatuan Perpustakaan Malaysia (Lib. Assn. of Malaysia), 232 Jalan Tun Razak, 50572 Kuala Lumpur. Tel. 3-2687-1700, fax 3-2692-7082, e-mail pnmweb@pnm.my, World Wide Web http://www.pnm.my. *Pres.* Chew Wing Foong; *Secy.* Leni Abdul Latif.

Mali

Association Malienne des Bibliothécaires, Archivistes, et Documentalistes (Mali Assn. of Libns., Archivists, and Documentalists), Rue Kasse Keita, Bamako. Tel. 22-49-63. *Dir.* Mamadou Konoba Keita.

Malta

Malta Lib. and Info. Assn. (MaLIA), c/o Univ. of Malta Lib., Tal-Qroqq, Msida MSD 06. Tel. 2132-2054, e-mail mpar1@lib.um.edu.mt, World Wide Web http://www.malia-malta.org. *Chair* Robert Mizzi.

Mauritania

Association Mauritanienne des Bibliothécaires, Archivistes et Documentalistes (Mauritanian Assn. of Libns., Archivists, and Documentalists), c/o Bibliothèque Nationale, B.P. 20, Nouakchott. *Pres.* O. Diouwara; *Secy.* Sid'Ahmed Fall dit Dah.

Mauritius

Mauritius Lib. Assn., c/o The British Council, Royal Rd., P.O. Box 111, Rose Hill. Tel. 454-9550, fax 454-9553, e-mail ielts @mu.britishcouncil.org, World Wide Web http://www.britishcouncil.org/mauritius. *Pres.* K. Appadoo; *Secy.* S. Rughoo.

Mexico

Asociación Mexicana de Bibliotecarios (Mexican Assn. of Libns.), Apdo. 80-065, Administracion de Correos 80, 06001 México D.F. 06760. Tel. 55-55-75-33-96, fax 55-55-75-11-35, e-mail correo@ambac.org.mx, World Wide Web http://www.ambac.org.mx. *Secy.* Graciela Tecuatt Quechol.

Myanmar

Myanmar Lib. Assn., c/o National Lib., Strand Rd., Yangon. *Chief Libn.* U Khin Maung Tin.

Nepal

Nepal Lib. Assn., Box 2773, Kathmandu. Tel. 1-331-316, fax 1-483-720. *Contact* Rudra Prasad Dulal.

The Netherlands

Nederlandse Vereniging voor Beroepsbeoefenaren in de Bibliotheek-Informatie-en Kennissector (Netherlands Assn. of Libns., Documentalists, and Info. Specialists), NVB-Nieuwegracht 15, 3512 LC Utrecht. Tel. 30-231-1263, fax 30-231-1830, e-mail info@nvbonline.nl, World Wide Web http://www.nvb-online.nl. *Pres.* J. S. M. Savenije.

New Zealand

Lib. and Info. Assn. of New Zealand, Old Wool House, Level 6, 139-141 Featherston St., Box 12-212, Wellington 6038. Tel. 4-473-5834, fax 4-499-1480, e-mail office@lianza.org.nz, World Wide Web http://www.lianza.org.nz. *Pres.* Mirla Edmundson.

Nicaragua

Asociación Nicaraguense de Bibliotecarios y Profesionales a Fines (Nicaraguan Assn. of Libns.), Apdo. 3257, Managua. *Exec. Secy.* Susana Morales Hernández.

Nigeria

Nigerian Lib. Assn., c/o Kwara College of Technology, Ilorin. Tel. 1-236-047, fax 1-263-1716, e-mail nln@nlbn.org. *Pres.* A. O. Banjo; *Secy.* D. D. Bwayili.

Norway

Arkivarforeningen (Assn. of Archivists), Postboks 4015, Ulleval Sta., 0806 Oslo. Tel. 22-022-657, fax 22-237-489, e-mail synne.stavheim@riksarkivaren.dep.no.
Norsk Bibliotekforening (Norwegian Lib. Assn.), Malerhaugveien 20, N-0661 Oslo. Tel. 2324-3430, fax 2267-2368, e-mail nbf@norskbibliotekforening.no, World Wide Web http://www.norskbibliotekforening.no. *Dir.* Berit Aaker.

Pakistan

Pakistan Lib. Assn., c/o Pakistan Inst. of Development Economics, Univ. Campus, Box 1091, Islamabad 44000. Tel. 51-921-4523, fax 51-922-1375, e-mail nlpiba@ishpaknet.com.pk, World Wide Web http://www.nlp.gov.pk. *Pres.* Sain Malik; *Secy.-Gen.* Atta Ullah.

Panama

Asociación Panameña de Bibliotecarios (Panama Lib. Assn.), c/o Biblioteca Interamericana Simón Bolivar, Estafeta Universitaria, Panama City. *Pres.* Bexie Rodriguez de León.

Paraguay

Asociación de Bibliotecarios del Paraguay (Assn. of Paraguayan Libns.), c/o Yoshiko M. de Freundorfer, Escuela de Bibliocolegia, Universidad Nacional de Asunción, Casilla 910, 2064 Asunción. *Pres.* Gloria Ondina Ortiz; *Secy.* Celia Villamayor de Diaz.

Peru

Asociación de Archiveros del Perú (Peruvian Assn. of Archivists), Archivo Central Salaverry, 2020 Jesús Mario, Universidad del Pacifico, Lima 11. Tel. 1-471-2277, fax 1-265-0958, e-mail dri@u8p.edu.pe. *Pres.* José Luis Abanto Arrelucea.
Asociación Peruana de Bibliotecarios (Peruvian Assn. of Libns.), Bellavista 561 Miraflores, Apdo. 995, Lima 18. Tel. 1-474-869. *Pres.* Martha Fernandez de Lopez; *Secy.* Luzmila Tello de Medina.

Philippines

Assn. of Special Libs. of the Philippines, Rm. 301, National Lib. Bldg., T. M. Kalaw St., 1100 Ermita, Manila. Tel./fax 2-893-9590, fax 2-893-9589, e-mail vvtl26_ph@yahoo.com. *Pres.* Valentina Tolentino; *Secy.* Socorro G. Elevera.
Bibliographical Society of the Philippines, National Lib. of the Philippines, T. M. Kalaw St., 1000 Ermita, Manila. Tel. 2-525-3196, fax 2-524-2324, e-mail amb@nlp.gov.ph, World Wide Web http://www.nlp.gov.ph. *Chief* Leticia D. A. Tominez.
Philippine Libns. Assn., c/o National Lib. of the Philippines, Rm. 301, T. M. Kalaw St.,

Manila. Tel. 2-523-0068, e-mail libfamv@ mail.dlsu.edu.ph, World Wide Web http:// www.dlsu.eduph/library/plai. *Pres.* Fe Angelo Verosa; *Secy.* Shirley L. Nava.

Poland

Stowarzyszenie Bibliotekarzy Polskich (Polish Libns. Assn.), al. Niepodleglosci 213, 02-086 Warsaw. Tel. 22-608-2256, fax 22-825-9157, e-mail biurozgsbp@wp.pl, World Wide Web http://ebib.oss.wroc.pl/ sbp. *Chair* Jan Wolosz; *Secy.-Gen.* Elzbieta Stefanczyk.

Portugal

Associação Portuguesa de Bibliotecários, Arquivistas e Documentalistas (Portuguese Assn. of Libns., Archivists, and Documentalists), R. Morais Soares, 43C-1 DTD, 1900-341 Lisbon. Tel. 21-816-1980, fax 21-815-4508, e-mail apbad@apbad.pt, World Wide Web http://www.apbad.pt. *Pres.* Ernestina de Castro.

Puerto Rico

Sociedad de Bibliotecarios de Puerto Rico (Society of Libns. of Puerto Rico), P.O. Box 22898, Universidad de Puerto Rico, San Juan 00931. Tel. 787-764-0000 ext. 5205, fax 787-763-0000 ext. 5204, e-mail vtorres@upracd.upr.clu.edu. *Pres.* Victor Federico Torres; *Secy.* Doris E. Rivera Marrero.

Russia

Rossiiskaya Bibliotechnaya Assotsiatsiya (Russian Lib. Assn.), 18 Sadovaya St., St. Petersburg 191069. Tel. 812-118-85-36, fax 812-110-58-61, e-mail rba@nlr.ru, World Wide Web http://www.rba.ru. *Exec. Secy.* Maya Shaparneva.

Senegal

Association Sénégalaise des Bibliothécaires, Archivistes et Documentalistes (Senegalese Assn. of Libns., Archivists, and Documentalists), BP 3252, Dakar. Tel. 221-864-2773, fax 221-824-2379, e-mail ebad@ebad.ucad.sn, World Wide Web http://www.ebad.ucad.sn. *Pres.* Ndiaye Djibril.

Serbia and Montenegro

Jugoslovenski Bibliografsko Informacijski Institut, Terazije 26 11000 Belgrade. Tel. 11-687-836, fax 11-687-760, e-mail suzana @jbi.bg.ac.yu, World Wide Web http:// www.jbi.bg.ac.yu/yubinold/index.html. *Dir.* Radomir Glavicki.

Sierra Leone

Sierra Leone Assn. of Archivists, Libns., and Info. Scientists, c/o COMAHS Lib. Board, New England, Freetown. Tel. 22-22-0758. *Pres.* Deanna Thomas.

Singapore

Lib. Assn. of Singapore, Geyland East Community Lib., 50 Geyland East Ave. 1, 3rd fl., Singapore 389777. Tel. 6749-7990, fax 6749-7480, World Wide Web http://www. las.org.sg.

Slovenia

Zveza Bibliotekarskih Druötev Slovenije (Union of Assns. of Slovene Libns.), Turjaöka 1, 1000 Ljubljana. Tel. 01-20-01-193, fax 01-42-57-293, World Wide Web http:// www.zbds-zveza.si. *Pres.* Melita Ambrožič. E-mail melita.ambrozic@nuk.uni-lj.si.

South Africa

Lib. and Info. Assn. of South Africa (formerly African Lib. Assn. of South Africa), c/o P.O. Box 1598, Pretoria 0001. Tel. 12-481-2870, fax 12-481-2873, e-mail liasa @liasa.org.za, World Wide Web http:// www.liasa.org.za. *Exec. Dir.* Gwenda Thomas.

Spain

Asociación Española de Archiveros, Bibliotecarios, Museólogos y Documentalistas (Spanish Assn. of Archivists, Libns., Curators, and Documentalists), Recoletos 5, 28001 Madrid. Tel. 91-575-1727, fax 91-

578-1615, e-mail anabad@anabad.org, World Wide Web http://www.anabad.org. *Pres.* Julia M. Rodriguez Barrero.

Sri Lanka

Sri Lanka Lib. Assn., Professional Center, 275/75 Bauddhaloka Mawatha, Colombo 7. Tel./fax 1-258-9103, e-mail slla@operamail.com, World Wide Web http://www.naresa.ac.lk/slla. *Pres.* N. U. Yapa.

Swaziland

Swaziland Lib. Assn., Box 2309, Mbabane. Tel. 404-2633, fax 404-3863, e-mail sd nationalarchives@realnet.co.sz, World Wide Web http://www.swala.sz. *Chair* Nomsa Mkhwanazi; *Secy.* Sibongile Nxumaloi.

Sweden

Svensk Biblioteksförening (Swedish Lib. Assn.), Saltmätargatan 3A, Box 3127, S-10362 Stockholm. Tel. 8-545-132-30, fax 8-545-132-31, e-mail info@biblioteks foreningen.org, World Wide Web http://www.sab.se. *Secy.-Gen.* Niclas Lindberg.

Svenska Arkivsamfundet (Swedish Assn. of Archivists), c/o Landsarkivet i Lund, Anna-Christina Ulfsparre, Box 2016, S-22002 Lund. Tel. 46-197-000, fax 46-197-070, e-mail info@arkivsamfundet.org, World Wide Web http://www.arkivsamfundet.org. *Pres.* Berndt Fredriksson; *Secy.* Julia Aslund.

Switzerland

Association des Bibliothèques et Bibliothécaires Suisses/Vereinigung Schweizerischer Bibliothekare/Associazione dei Bibliotecari Svizzeri (Assn. of Swiss Libs. and Libns.), Hallestr. 58, CH-3012 Bern. Tel. 31-382-4240, fax 31-382-4648, e-mail bbs@bbs.ch, World Wide Web http://www.bbs.ch. *Gen. Secy.* Barbara Krauchi.

Schweizerische Vereinigung für Dokumentation/Association Suisse de Documentation (Swiss Assn. of Documentation), Schmidgasse 4, Postfach 601, CH-6301 Zug. Tel. 41-726-45-05, fax 41-726-45-09, e-mail svd-asd@hispeed.ch, World Wide Web http://www.svd-asd.org. *Pres.* Urs Naegeli, *Secy.* Harald Schwenk.

Verein Schweizerischer Archivarinnen und Archivare (Assn. of Swiss Archivists), Schweizerisches Bundesarchiv, Archivstr. 24, 3003 Bern. Tel. 31-322-89-89, e-mail andreas.kellerhals@bar.admin.ch, World Wide Web http://www.staluzern.ch/vsa. *Pres.* Andreas Kellerhals.

Taiwan

Lib. Assn. of China, c/o National Central Lib., 20 Chungshan S. Rd., Taipei 100-01. Tel. 2-2331-2675, fax 2-2370-0899, e-mail lac@msg.ncl.edu.tw, World Wide Web http://www.lac.ncl.edu.tw. *Pres.* Huang Shih-wson; *Secy.-Gen.* Teresa Wang Chang.

Tanzania

Tanzania Lib. Assn., P.O. Box 3433, Dar es Salaam. Tel. 22-277-5411, e-mail tla_tanzania@yahoo.com, World Wide Web http://www.tlatz.org. *Chair* Alli Mcharazo.

Thailand

Thai Lib. Assn., 1346 Akarnsongkrau Rd. 5, Klongchan, Bangkapi, 10240 Bangkok. Tel. 2-734-8022, fax 2-734-8024, World Wide Web http://tla.tiac.or.th. *Pres.* Khunying Maenmas Chawalit; *Exec. Secy.* Vorrarat Srinamngern.

Trinidad and Tobago

Lib. Assn. of Trinidad and Tobago, Box 1275, Port of Spain. Tel. 868-687-0194, e-mail secretary@latt.org.tt, World Wide Web http://www.latt.org.tt/cms. *Pres.* Ernesta Greenidge; *Secy.* Sheryl Washington.

Tunisia

Association Tunisienne des Documentalistes, Bibliothécaires et Archivistes (Tunisian Assn. of Documentalists, Libns., and Archivists), Centre de Documentation Nationale Rue 8004, Rue Sidi El Benna R P, 1000 Tunis. Tel. 651-924. *Pres.* Ahmed Ksibi.

Turkey

Türk Küüphaneciler Dernegi (Turkish Libns. Assn.), Elgün Sok-8/8, 06440 Kizilay/Ankara. Tel. 312-230-13-25, fax 312-232-04-53. *Pres.* A. Berberoglu; *Secy.* A. Kaygusuz.

Uganda

Uganda Lib. Assn., Box 5894, Kampala. Tel. 141-285-001 ext. 4, fax 141-347-625, e-mail library@imzul.com. *Chair* Magara Elisam; *Secy.* Charles Batembyze.

Ukraine

Ukrainian Lib. Assn., 14 Chigorina St., Kiev 252042. Tel./fax 380-44-268-05-33, e-mail pashkova@uba.kiev.ua, World Wide Web http://www.uba.org.ua. *Pres.* Valentyna S. Pashkova.

United Kingdom

ASLIB (Assn. for Info. Management), Temple Chambers, 3–7 Temple Ave., London EC4Y 0HP, England. Tel. 20-7583-8900, fax 20-7583-8401, e-mail aslib@aslib. com, World Wide Web http://www.aslib. co.uk. *Dir.* R. B. Bowes.

Bibliographical Society, Institute of English Studies, Senate House, Rm. 304, Malet St., London WC1E 7HU, England. Tel. 20-7611-7244, fax 20-7611-8703, e-mail secretary@bibsoc.org.uk, World Wide Web http://www.bibsoc.org.uk/bibsoc. htm. *Hon. Secy.* David Pearson.

Chartered Inst. of Lib. and Info. Professionals (formerly the Lib. Assn.), 7 Ridgmount St., London WC1E 7AE, England. Tel. 20-7255-0500, fax 20-7255-0501, e-mail info@cilip.org.uk, World Wide Web http://www.cilip.org.uk. *Chief Exec.* Bob McKee.

School Lib. Assn., Unit 2, Lotmead Business Village, Lotmead Farm, Wanborough, Swindon, Wilts. SN4 0UY, England. Tel. 1793-791-787, fax 1793-791-786, e-mail info@sla.org.uk, World Wide Web http://

www.sla.org.uk. *Pres.* Aidan Chambers; *Chief Exec.* Kathy Lemaire.

Scottish Lib. Assn., 1st fl., Bldg. C, Brandon Gate, Leechlee Rd., Hamilton ML3 6AU, Scotland. Tel. 1698-458-888, fax 1698-283-170, e-mail sla@slainte.org.uk, World Wide Web http://www.slainte.org.uk. *Dir.* Elaine Fulton.

Society of Archivists, Prioryfield House, 20 Canon St., Taunton, Somerset TA1 1SW, England. Tel. 1823-327-030, fax 1823-371-719, e-mail offman@archives.org.uk, World Wide Web http://www.archives. org.uk. *Exec. Secy.* Patrick S. Cleary.

Society of College, National, and Univ. Libs (SCONUL) (formerly Standing Conference of National and Univ. Libs.), 102 Euston St., London NW1 2HA, England. Tel. 20-7387-0317, fax 20-7383-3197, e-mail info@sconul.ac.uk, World Wide Web http://www.sconul.ac.uk. *Exec. Secy.* A. J. C. Bainton.

Welsh Lib. Assn., c/o Publications Office, Dept. of Info. and Lib. Studies, Llanbadarn Fawr, Aberystwyth, Dyfed SY23 3AS, Wales. Tel. 1970-622-174, fax 1970-622-190, e-mail hle@aber.ac.uk, World Wide Web http://www.dil.aber.ac.uk/holi/wla/ wla.htm. *Pres.* Andrew Green.

Uruguay

Agrupación Bibliotecológica del Uruguay (Uruguayan Lib. and Archive Science Assn.), Cerro Largo 1666, 11200 Montevideo. Tel. 2-400-57-40. *Pres.* Luis Alberto Musso.

Asociación de Bibliotecólogos del Uruguay, Eduardo V. Haedo 2255, Box 1315, 11000 Montevideo. Tel./fax 2-499-989, e-mail abu@adinet.com.uy. *Pres.* Eduardo Correa.

Vatican City

Biblioteca Apostolica Vaticana, Cortile del Belvedere, 00120 Vatican City, Rome. Tel. 6-6987-9402, fax 6-6988-4795, e-mail bav@librs6k.vatlib.it. *Prefect* Don Raffaele Farina.

Venezuela

Colegio de Bibliotecólogos y Archivólogos de Venezuela (Venezuelan Lib. and Archives Assn.), Apdo. 6283, Caracas. Tel. 2-572-1858. *Pres.* Elsi Jimenez de Diaz.

Vietnam

Hôi Thu-Vien Viet Nam (Vietnamese Lib. Assn.), National Lib. of Vietnam, 31 Trang Thi, 10000 Hanoi. Tel. 4-824-8051, fax 4-825-3357, e-mail info@nlv.gov.vn, World Wide Web http://www.nlv.gov.vn.

Zambia

Zambia Lib. Assn., Box 38636, Lusaka. *Chair* Benson Njobvu. E-mail bensonnjobvu @hotmail.com.

Zimbabwe

Zimbabwe Lib. Assn., Box 3133, Harare. *Chair* Driden Kunaka; *Hon. Secy.* Albert Masheka.

Directory of Book Trade and Related Organizations

Book Trade Associations, United States and Canada

For more extensive information on the associations listed in this section, see the annual edition of *Literary Market Place* (Information Today, Inc.).

AIGA (American Institute of Graphic Arts), 164 Fifth Ave., New York, NY 10010. Tel. 212-807-1990, fax 212-807-1799, e-mail info@aiga.org, World Wide Web http://www.aiga.org. *Exec. Dir.* Richard Grefe. E-mail grefe@aiga.org.

American Booksellers Assn., 828 S. Broadway, Tarrytown, NY 10591. Tel. 800-637-0037, 914-591-2665, fax 914-591-2724, World Wide Web http://www.bookweb. org. *Pres.* Mitchell Kaplan, Books & Books, 265 Aragon Ave., Coral Gables, FL 33134-5009. Tel. 305-442-4408, fax 305-444-9751, e-mail kaplan296@aol. com; *V.P./Secy.* Suzanne Staubach, UConn Co-op, 2075 Hillside Rd., Storrs, CT 06269-2019. Tel. 860-486-5027, fax 860-486-4318, e-mail staubach@uconn.edu or suzannestaubach@rcn.com; *Chief Exec. Officer* Avin Mark Domnitz. E-mail avin @bookweb.org.

American Literary Translators Assn. (ALTA), Univ. of Texas–Dallas, MC35, Box 830688, Richardson, TX 75083-0688. Tel. 972-883-2093, fax 972-883-6303, e-mail jdickey @utdallas.edu, World Wide Web http:// www.literarytranslators.org. *Pres.* David Ball; *Contact* Jessie Dickey.

American Medical Publishers Assn. (AMPA), 308 E. Lancaster Ave., Ste. 110, Wynnewood, PA 19096. Tel. 610-642-2810, fax 610-642-0628, e-mail ampa@association-cba.org, World Wide Web http://www. ampaonline.org. *Exec. Dir.* Christine Boylan.

American Printing History Assn., Box 4519, Grand Central Sta., New York, NY 10163-4519. World Wide Web http://www. printinghistory.org. *Pres.* Martin Antonetti; *Exec. Secy.* Stephen Crook. E-mail sgcrook@printinghistory.org.

American Society of Indexers, 10200 W. 44 Ave., Ste. 304, Wheat Ridge, CO 80033. Tel. 303-463-2887, fax 303-422-8894, e-mail info@asindexing.org, World Wide Web http://www.asindexing.org/site. *Pres.* Enid Zafran; *V.P.* Maria Coughlin; *Exec. Dirs.* Francine Butler, Jerry Bowman.

American Society of Journalists and Authors, 1501 Broadway, Ste. 302, New York, NY 10036. Tel. 212-997-0947, fax 212-768-7414, e-mail execdir@asja.org, World Wide Web http://www.asja.org. *Pres.* Lisa Collier Cool; *Exec. Dir.* Brett Harvey.

American Society of Magazine Editors, 810 Seventh Ave., 24th fl., New York, NY 10019. Tel. 212-872-3700, fax 212-906-0128, e-mail asme@magazine.org. *Exec. Dir.* Marlene Kahan.

American Society of Media Photographers, 150 N. 2 St., Philadelphia, PA 19106. Tel. 215-451-2767, fax 215-451-0880, e-mail mopsik@asmp.org, World Wide Web http://www.asmp.org. *Pres.* Susan Carr; *Exec. Dir.* Eugene Mopsik.

American Society of Picture Professionals, 409 S. Washington St., Alexandria, VA

22314. Tel. 703-299-0219, fax 703-299-0219, e-mail cathy@aspp.com, World Wide Web http://www.aspp.com. *Pres.* Eileen Flanagan; *Exec. Dir.* Cathy D.-P. Sachs.

American Translators Assn., 225 Reinekers Lane, Ste. 590, Alexandria, VA 22314. Tel. 703-683-6100, fax 703-683-6122, e-mail ata@atanet.org, World Wide Web http://www.atanet.org. *Pres.* Scott Brennan; *Pres.-Elect* Marian S. Greenfield; *Secy.* Alan K. Melby; *Treas.* Jiri Stejskal; *Exec. Dir.* Walter W. Bacak, Jr. E-mail walter@atanet.org.

Antiquarian Booksellers Assn. of America, 20 W. 44 St., 4th fl., New York, NY 10036-6604. Tel. 212-944-8291, fax 212-944-8293, e-mail inquiries@abaa.org, World Wide Web http://www.abaa.org. *Pres.* John Crichton, Brick Row Book Shop; *V.P.* Forrest Proper, Joslin Hall Rare Books; *Exec. Dir.* Liane Thomas Wade. E-mail hq@abaa.org.

Assn. of American Publishers, 71 Fifth Ave., New York, NY 10003. Tel. 212-255-0200, fax 212-255-7007. *Washington Office* 50 F St. N.W., Washington, DC 20001-1564. Tel. 202-347-3375, fax 202-347-3690. *Pres./CEO* Patricia S. Schroeder; *V.P.s* Allan Adler, Kathryn Blough, Barbara Meredith; *Dir., Communications and Public Affairs* Judith Platt; *Exec. Dir., School Div.* Stephen D. Driesler; *Exec. Dir., Higher Education* Bruce Hildebrand; *Chair* Jane Friedman, HarperCollins; *V. Chair* Anthony Lucki, Houghton Mifflin.

Assn. of American Univ. Presses, 71 W. 23 St., Ste. 901, New York, NY 10010. Tel. 212-989-1010, e-mail info@aaupnet.org, World Wide Web http://aaupnet.org. *Pres.* Douglas Armato; *Exec. Dir.* Peter Givler. Address correspondence to the executive director.

Assn. of Authors' Representatives, Box 237201, Ansonia Sta., New York, NY 10023. E-mail info@aar-online.org, World Wide Web http://aar-online.org.

Assn. of Canadian Publishers, 161 Eglinton Ave. E., Ste. 702, Toronto, ON M4P 1J5. Tel. 416-487-6116, fax 416-487-8815, e-mail admin@canbook.org, World Wide Web http://www.publishers.ca. *Pres.* Kirk Howard, Dundurn Press. Tel. 416-214-5544, e-mail jkh@dundurn.com; *V.P.* Bob Tyrrell, Orca Book Publishers. Tel. 250-380-1229, e-mail tyrrell@orcabook.com; *Exec. Dir.* Margaret Eaton.

Assn. of Educational Publishers (AEP), 510 Heron Dr., Ste. 201, Logan Township, NJ 08085. Tel. 856-241-7772, fax 856-241-0709, e-mail mail@edpress.org, World Wide Web http://www.edpress.org. *Pres.* Hugh Roome; *Pres.-Elect* Keith Garton; *V.P.* Jo-Ann McDevitt; *Treas.* Thomas Mason; *Past Pres.* Robert W. Harper; *Exec. Dir.* Charlene F. Gaynor. E-mail cgaynor@edpress.org.

Assn. of Graphic Communications, 330 Seventh Ave., 9th fl., New York, NY 10001-5010. Tel. 212-279-2100, fax 212-279-5381, World Wide Web http://www.agcomm.org. *Pres.* Susan Greenwood. E-mail susie@agcomm.org.

Book Industry Study Group, 19 W. 21 St., Ste. 905, New York, NY 10010. Tel. 646-336-7141, fax 646-336-6214, e-mail info@bisg.org, World Wide Web http://www.bisg.org. *Chair* Joseph Gonnella, Barnes & Noble; *V. Chair* Andrew Weber, Random House; *Secy.* Deborah E. Wiley, John Wiley & Sons; *Treas.* Jan Nathan, Publishers Marketing Assn.; *Exec. Dir.* Jeff Abraham. E-mail jeff@bisg.org.

Book Manufacturers Institute, 65 William St., Ste. 300, Wellesley, MA 02481-3800. Tel. 781-239-0103, fax 781-239-0106, e-mail info@bmibook.com, World Wide Web http://www.bmibook.org. *Pres.* David N. Mead, Banta Book Group; *V.P./Pres.-Elect* William L. Upton, Malloy Inc.; *Treas.* John J. Edwards, Edwards Brothers, Inc.; *Exec. V.P./Secy.* Bruce W. Smith. Address correspondence to the executive vice president.

Bookbuilders of Boston, 44 Highland Circle, Halifax, MA 02338. Tel. 781-293-8600, fax 866-820-0469, e-mail office@bbboston.org, World Wide Web http://www.bbboston.org. *Pres.* Victor Curran, DS Graphics; *1st V.P.* Marty Rabinowitz, Addison-Wesley Professional; *2nd V.P.* Carol Heston, Victor Graphics; *Treas.* Larry Bisso, Bradford & Bigelow; *Secy.* Kelly Bower, Pearson Technology Group.

Bookbuilders West, Box 2277, Benicia, CA 94510. Tel. 707-746-8668, e-mail president @bookbuilders.org, World Wide Web http://www.bookbuilders.org. *Pres.* Ramona Beville, Von Hoffmann; *1st V.P.* Elise Gochberg, Coral Graphics; *Secy.* Nancy Tabor, CMP; *Treas.* Michael O'Brien, TechBooks/GTS.

Canadian Booksellers Assn., 789 Don Mills Rd., Ste. 700, Toronto, ON M3C 1T5. Tel. 866-788-0790 (toll free) or 416-467-7883, fax 416-467-7886, e-mail enquiries@cbabook.org, World Wide Web http://www.cbabook.org. *Pres.* Pat Joas, Univ. of New Brunswick Bookstore, Saint John, NB. E-mail joas@unbsj.ca; *V.P.* Paul McNally, McNally Robinson Booksellers Ltd. E-mail paul@grant.mcnallyrobinson.ca; *Exec. Dir.* Susan Dayus. E-mail sdayus @cbabook.org.

Canadian ISBN Agency, c/o Published Heritage, Library and Archives Canada, 395 Wellington St., Ottawa, ON K1A 0N4. Tel. 866-578-7777 (toll free) or 819-994-6872, fax 819-997-7517, e-mail isbn@lac-bac.gc.ca.

Canadian Printing Industries Association, 75 Albert St., Ste. 906, Ottawa, ON K1P 5E7. Tel. 613-236-7208, fax 613-236-8169, e-mail pboucher@cpia-aci.ca, World Wide Web http://www.cpia-aci.ca. *Pres.* Pierre Boucher; *Chair* Jeff Ekstein.

Catholic Book Publishers Assn., 8404 Jamesport Dr., Rockford, IL 61108. Tel. 815-332-3245, e-mail cbpa3@aol.com, World Wide Web http://cbpa.org. *Pres.* John D. Wright; *V.P.* Kay Weiss; *Secy.* Jean Larkin; *Treas.* Therese Brown; *Exec. Dir.* Terry Wessels.

Chicago Book Clinic, 5443 N. Broadway, Ste. 101, Chicago, IL 60640. Tel. 773-561-4150, fax 773-561-1343, e-mail kgboyer@ix.netcom.com, World Wide Web http://www.chicagobookclinic.org. *Pres.* Tammy Levy, McGraw-Hill, 130 E. Randolph, Ste. 400, Chicago, IL 60601. Tel. 312-233-7804, fax 312-233-6763, e-mail tammy_levy@mcgraw-hill.com; *V.P.* Jen Thomas, FiberMark, 916 Asot Dr., Elgin, IL 60123. Tel. 847-630-0244, e-mail jthomas@fibermark.com; *Admin.* Kevin G. Boyer.

Children's Book Council, 12 W. 37 St., 2nd fl., New York, NY 10018-7480. Tel. 212-966-1990, fax 212-966-2073, World Wide Web http://www.cbcbooks.org. *Chair* Lori Benton; *V. Chair/Chair-Elect* Simon Boughton; *Secy.* Andrew Smith; *Treas.* Virginia Duncan.

Copyright Society of the USA. *Pres.* Barry Slotnick; *V.P./Pres.-Elect* Helene Blue; *Secy.* Jay Kogan; *Treas.* Gloria Phares; *Admin.* Amy Nickerson. E-mail amy@csusa.org, World Wide Web http://www.csusa.org.

Council of Literary Magazines and Presses, 154 Christopher St., Ste. 3C, New York, NY 10014. Tel. 212-741-9110, fax 212-741-9112, e-mail info@clmp.org, World Wide Web http://www.clmp.org. *Pres.* Ira Silverberg; *Exec. Dir.* Jeffrey Lependorf. E-mail jlependorf@clmp.org.

Educational Paperback Assn., Box 1399, East Hampton, NY 11937. Tel. 631-329-3315, e-mail edupaperback@aol.com, World Wide Web http://www.edupaperback.org. *Pres.* Dick Tinder; *V.P.* Jean Srnecz; *Treas.* Anne Sterling; *Exec. Secy.* Marilyn Abel.

Evangelical Christian Publishers Assn., 4816 S. Ash Ave., Ste. 101, Tempe, AZ 85282. Tel. 480-966-3998, fax 480-966-1944, e-mail mkuyper@ecpa.org, World Wide Web http://www.ecpa.org. *Pres./CEO* Mark W. Kuyper; *Chair* Mark D. Taylor, Tyndale House Publishers; *V. Chair* Randy Scott, Standard Publishing; *Secy.* Robert Fryling, InterVarsity Press; *Treas.* John Howard, Howard Publishers; *Memb.-at-Large* Kent R. Wilson, NavPress.

Graphic Artists Guild, 90 John St., Ste. 403, New York, NY 10038. Tel. 212-791-3400, fax 212-792-0333, e-mail admin@gag.org, World Wide Web http://www.gag.org. *Pres.* John Schmelzer. E-mail president@gag.org; *V.P.* Christine Labate. E-mail vicepresident@gag.org; *Admin. Dir.* Patricia McKiernan. E-mail admin@gag.org.

Great Lakes Booksellers Assn., c/o *Exec. Dir.* Jim Dana, Box 901, 208 Franklin St., Grand Haven, MI 49417. Tel. 616-847-2460, fax 616-842-0051, e-mail glb@books-glba.org, World Wide Web http://www.books-glba.org. *Pres.* Sue Boucher,

Lake Forest Book Store, Lake Forest, IL. E-mail lfbooks@aol.com; *V.P.* Nicola Rooney, Nicola's Books, Ann Arbor, MI. E-mail nicolasbooks@sbcglobal.net.

Guild of Book Workers, 521 Fifth Ave., New York, NY 10175. Tel. 212-292-4444, e-mail publicity@guildofbookworkers.allmail.net, World Wide Web http://palimpsest.stanford. edu/byorg/gbw. *Pres.* Betsy Palmer Eldridge; *V.P.* Mark Andersson; *Memb. Secy.* Cris Clair Takacs. E-mail membership@ guildofbookworkers.allmail.net.

Horror Writers Assn., Box 50577, Palo Alto, CA 94303. E-mail hwa@horror.org, World Wide Web http://www.horror.org. *Pres.* Joseph Nassise; *V.P.* Gary Braunbeck; *Secy.* Patricia Lee Macomber; *Treas.* Nancy Etchemendy.

International Assn. of Printing House Craftsmen (IAPHC), 7042 Brooklyn Blvd., Minneapolis, MN 55429. Tel. 800-466-4274, 763-560-1620, fax 763-560-1350, World Wide Web http://www.iaphc.org. *Chair* Norm Belanger; *V. Chair* John Leininger; *Pres./CEO* Kevin Keane. E-mail kkeane 1069@aol.com.

International Standard Book Numbering U.S. Agency, 630 Central Ave., New Providence, NJ 07974. Tel. 877-310-7333, fax 908-219-0188, e-mail isbn-san@bowker. com, World Wide Web http://www.isbn. org. *Chair* Michael Cairns; *Dir.* Doreen Gravesande; *ISBN/SAN Managing Ed.* Paula Kurdi.

Jewish Book Council, 15 E. 26 St., 10th fl., New York, NY 10010. Tel. 212-532-4949 ext. 297, fax 212-481-4174, World Wide Web http://www.jewishbookcouncil.org. *Exec. Dir.* Carolyn Starman Hessel.

Library Binding Institute, 14 Bay Tree Lane, Tequesta, FL 33469. Tel. 561-745-6821, fax 561-745-6813, e-mail info@lbibinders. org, World Wide Web http://www. lbibinders.org. *Exec. Dir.* Debra Nolan. E-mail dnolan@lbibinders.org.

Magazine Publishers of America, 810 Seventh Ave., 24th fl., New York, NY 10019. Tel. 212-872-3700, e-mail mpa@magazine. org, World Wide Web http://www. magazine.org. *Pres./CEO* Nina B. Link. Tel. 212-872-3710, e-mail president@

magazine.org; *Exec. V.P./General Mgr.* Michael Pashby. Tel. 212-872-3750.

Midwest Independent Publishers Assn., Box 581432, Minneapolis, MN 55458-1432. Tel. 651-917-0021, World Wide Web http://www.mipa.org. *Pres.* Sybil Smith. E-mail smitheprs@aol.com; *V.P. Memb.* Pat Bell. E-mail mipa1981@aol.com.

Miniature Book Society, c/o *Pres.* Neale Albert, 815 Park Ave., New York, NY 10021. Tel. 212-861-9093, fax 212-772-9905, e-mail nalbert@paulweiss.com. *V.P.* Jon Mayo, Box 74, North Clarendon, VT 05759. Tel. 802-773-9695, fax 802-773-1493, e-mail microbib@sover.net; *Secy.* Patricia Pistner; *Treas.* Kathy King; *Exec. Secy.* Mark Palcovic, 620 Clinton Springs Ave., Cincinnati, OH 45229-1325. Tel. 513-861-3554, fax 513-556-2113, World Wide Web http://www.mbs.org.

Minnesota Book Publishers Roundtable. *Pres.* Hilary Reeves, Milkweed Editions, 1011 Washington Ave. S., Ste. 300, Minneapolis 55415. Tel. 612-332-2535, fax 612-215-2550, e-mail hilary_reeves@ milkweed.org, World Wide Web http:// www.publishersroundtable.org. *Secy.* Susan Doerr, Consortium Book Sales and Distribution, 1045 Westgate Dr., St. Paul 55114. Tel. 651-379-5333, fax 651-917-6406, e-mail sdoerr@csbd.com; *Treas.* Ann Regan, Minnesota Historical Society and Borealis Books, 345 Kellogg Blvd. W., St. Paul 55102. Tel. 651-297-4457, fax 651-297-1345, e-mail ann.regan@ mnhs.org. Address correspondence to the president.

Mountains and Plains Booksellers Assn., 19 Old Town Sq., Ste. 238, Fort Collins, CO 80524. Tel. 970-484-5856, fax 970-407-1479, e-mail info@mountainsplains.org, World Wide Web http://www.mountains plains.org.

National Assn. for Printing Leadership, 75 W. Century Rd., Paramus, NJ 07652. Tel. 800-642-6275 or 201-634-9600, fax 201-986-2976, e-mail info@napl.org, World Wide Web http://www.napl.org. *Pres./ CEO* Joseph P. Truncale.

National Assn. of College Stores, 500 E. Lorain St., Oberlin, OH 44074-1294. Tel. 800-622-7498, 440-775-7777, fax 440-

775-4769, e-mail info@nacs.org, World Wide Web http://www.nacs.org. *CEO* Brian Cartier.

National Assn. of Independent Publishers, Box 430, Highland City, FL 33846-0430. Tel./fax 813-648-4420, e-mail naip@aol. com, World Wide Web http://www.loc. gov/loc/cfbook/coborg/nai.html. *Exec. Dir.* Betsy Lampe.

National Coalition Against Censorship (NCAC), 275 Seventh Ave., New York, NY 10001. Tel. 212-807-6222, fax 212-807-6245, e-mail ncac@ncac.org, World Wide Web http://www.ncac.org. *Exec. Dir.* Joan E. Bertin; *Communications Coord.* Max Cartagena.

New Atlantic Independent Booksellers Assn. (NAIBA), 2667 Hyacinth St., Westbury, NY 11590. Tel. 516-333-0681, fax 516-333-0689, e-mail info@naiba.com. *Pres.* Lynn Gonchar, Tudor Bookshop and Cafe, 651 Wyoming Ave., Kingston, PA 18704. Tel. 570-288-9697, fax 570-288-9601; *Exec. Dir.* Eileen Dengler.

New England Booksellers Assn., 1770 Massachusetts Ave., Ste. 332, Cambridge, MA 02140. Tel. 800-466-8711, 617-576-3070, fax 617-576-3091, e-mail rusty@neba.org, World Wide Web http://www.newengland books.org. *Pres.* Linda Ramsdell; *V.P.* Susan Novotny; *Treas.* Peter Sevenair; *Exec. Dir.* Wayne A. Drugan, Jr.

North American Bookdealers Exchange, Box 606, Cottage Grove, OR 97424. Tel./fax 541-942-7455, e-mail nabe@bookmarketing profits.com, World Wide Web http://book marketingprofits.com. *Dir.* Al Galasso.

Northern California Independent Booksellers Assn., The Presidio, 37 Graham St., Ste. 210, Box 29169, San Francisco, CA 94129. Tel. 415-561-7686, fax 415-561-7685, e-mail office@nciba.com, World Wide Web http://www.nciba.com. *Pres.* Alzada Knickerbocker; *V.P.* Nick Setka; *Exec. Dir.* Hut Landon.

Pacific Northwest Booksellers Assn., 317 W. Broadway, Ste. 214, Eugene, OR 97401-2890. Tel. 541-683-4363, fax 541-683-3910, e-mail info@pnba.org. *Pres.* Pat Rutledge, A Book for All Seasons, 703 Hwy. 2, Leavenworth, WA 98826-1354. Tel. 509-548-1451, fax 509-548-2062, e-

mail abookfor@earthlink.net; *Exec. Dir.* Thom Chambliss.

PEN American Center, Div. of International PEN, 568 Broadway, New York, NY 10012. Tel. 212-334-1660, fax 212-334-2181, e-mail pen@pen.org, World Wide Web http://www.pen.org. *Pres.* Salman Rushdie; *V.P.s* Peter Carey, Francine Prose; *Treas.* Honor Moore; *Secy.* Rick Moody.

Periodical and Book Assn. of America, 481 Eighth Ave., Ste. 826, New York, NY 10001. Tel. 212-563-6502, fax 212-563-4098, e-mail info@pbaa.net, World Wide Web http://www.pbaa.net. *Pres.* Robert Kerekes. E-mail bob.kerekes@ingram periodicals.com; *Board Chair* William Michalopoulos. E-mail william_michalopoulos @businessweek.com; *Exec. Dir.* Lisa W. Scott. E-mail lscott@pbaa.net.

Publishers Marketing Assn., 627 Aviation Way, Manhattan Beach, CA 90266. Tel. 310-372-2732, fax 310-374-3342, e-mail info@pma-online.org, World Wide Web http://www.pma-online.org. *Pres.* Kent Sturgis; *Exec. Dir.* Jan Nathan.

Research and Engineering Council of the Graphic Arts Industry, Box 1086, White Stone, VA 22578. Tel. 800-642-6275 ext. 1397, e-mail recouncil@rivnet.net, World Wide Web http://www.recouncil.org. *Pres.* Jeffrey L. White. E-mail jwhite@printcafe. com; *Pres.-Elect* Lynn R. Poretta. E-mail lporet1@hallmark.com; *Managing Dir.* Ronald L. Mihills. E-mail recouncil@ rivnet.net.

Romance Writers of America, 16000 Stuebner Airline Dr., Ste. 140, Spring, TX 77379. Tel. 832-717-5200, fax 832-717-5201, e-mail info@rwanational.com, World Wide Web http://www.rwanational.com. *Pres.* Tara Taylor Quinn; *Pres.-Elect* Gayle Wilson.

Science Fiction and Fantasy Writers of America, P.O. Box 877, Chestertown, MD 21620. E-mail execdir@sfwa.org, World Wide Web http://www.sfwa.org. *Pres.* Catherine Asaro; *V.P.* Andrew Burt; *Treas.* Justin Stanchfield; *Secy.* Deborah J. Ross; *Exec. Dir.* Jane Jewell.

Small Press Center for Independent Publishing, 20 W. 44 St., New York, NY 10036.

Tel. 212-764-7021, fax 212-354-5365, World Wide Web http://www.smallpress. org. *Exec. Dir.* Karin Taylor.

Small Publishers Assn. of North America (SPAN), Box 1306-W, Buena Vista, CO 81211-1306. Tel. 719-395-4790, fax 719-395-8374, e-mail span@spannet.org, World Wide Web http://www.spannet.org. *Exec. Dir.* Scott Flora.

Society of Children's Book Writers and Illustrators (SCBWI), 8271 Beverly Blvd., Los Angeles, CA 90048. Tel. 323-782-1010, fax 323-782-1892, World Wide Web http://www.scbwi.org. *Pres.* Stephen Mooser. E-mail stephenmooser@scbwi.org; *Exec. Dir.* Lin Oliver.

Society of Illustrators (SI), 128 E. 63 St., New York, NY 10021. Tel. 212-838-2560, fax 212-838-2561, e-mail info@society illustrators.org, World Wide Web http://www.societyillustrators.org.

Society of National Association Publications (SNAP), 8405 Greensboro Dr., Ste. 800, McLean, VA 22102. Tel. 703-506-3285, fax 703-506-3266, e-mail snapinfo@snap online.org, World Wide Web http://www. snaponline.org. *Pres.* Peter Banks. E-mail pbanks@diabetes.org; *V.P.* Larry Price. E-mail lprice@aba.com; *Treas.* Robert Fromberg. E-mail rfromberg@hfma.org.

Technical Assn. of the Pulp and Paper Industry, 15 Technology Pkwy., South Norcross, GA 30092 (P.O. Box 105113, Atlanta, GA 30348). Tel. 770-446-1400, fax 770-446-6947, World Wide Web http://www.tappi.

org. *Pres.* Kathleen M. Bennett, Georgia-Pacific; *V.P.* Willis J. Potts, Inland Paperboard and Packaging; *Exec. Dir.* W. H. Gross.

Western Writers of America, c/o *Secy./Treas.* James Crutchfield, 1012 Fair St., Franklin, TN 37064. E-mail tncrutch@aol.com. World Wide Web http://www.western writers.org. *Pres.* Rita Cleary; *V.P.* Cotton Smith.

Women's National Book Assn., c/o Susannah Greenberg Public Relations, 2166 Broadway, Ste. 9-E, New York, NY 10024. Tel./fax 212-208-4629, e-mail publicity @bookbuzz.com, World Wide Web http://www.wnba-books.org. *Pres.* Jill A. Tardiff, Bamboo River Assocs., 625 Madison St., Unit B, Hoboken, NJ 07030. Tel. 201-656-7220, fax 201-792-0254, e-mail jtardiff-wnbanyc@worldnet.att.net; *V.P./Pres.-Elect* Laurie Beckelman, Prentice Associates, Inc., 160 Tea Rock Lane, Marshfield, MA 02050. Tel. 781-834-8002, e-mail lbeckelman@aol.com; *Secy.* Michele Leber, 1805 Crystal Dr., No. 911, Arlington, VA 22202-4420. Tel. 703-920-2010, fax 703-979-6372, e-mail michele. leber@comcast.net; *Treas.* Amy Barden, 3101 Ravensworth, Alexandria, VA 22302. Tel. 703-578-4023, e-mail amyb3cat@ yahoo.com; *Past Pres.* Margaret E. Auer, Dean of Univ. Libs., Univ. of Detroit Mercy, Box 19900, Detroit, MI 48219-0900. Tel. 313-993-1090, fax 313-993-1780, e-mail auerme@udmercy.edu.

International and Foreign Book Trade Associations

For Canadian book trade associations, see the preceding section, "Book Trade Associations, United States and Canada." For a more extensive list of book trade organizations outside the United States and Canada, with more detailed information, consult *International Literary Market Place* (Information Today, Inc.), which also provides extensive lists of major bookstores and publishers in each country.

International

African Publishers' Network, BP 3429, Abidjan 01, Côte d'Ivoire. Tel. 04-20-21-18-01, fax 04-20-21-18-03, e-mail apnetes@yahoo.com, World Wide Web http://www.freewebs.com/africanpublishers. *Chair* Mamadou Aliou Sow; *Exec. Secy.* Akin Fasemore.

Afro-Asian Book Council, 4835/24 Ansari Rd., Daryaganj, New Delhi 110002, India. Tel. 11-326-1487, fax 11-326-7437, e-mail sdas@ubspd.com. *Secy.-Gen.* Sukumar Das; *Dir.* Abul Hasan.

Centre Régional pour la Promotion du Livre en Afrique (Regional Center for Book Promotion in Africa), P.O. Box 1646, Yaoundé, Cameroon. Tel. 22-4782. *Secy.* William Moutchia.

Centro Régional para el Fomento del Libro en América Latina y el Caribe (CERLALC) (Regional Center for Book Promotion in Latin America and the Caribbean), Calle 70, No. 9-52, Apdo. Aéreo 57348, Santafé de Bogotá 2, Colombia. Tel. 1-212-6056, fax 1-255-4614, e-mail libro@cerlalc.com, World Wide Web http://www.cerlalc.com. *Dir.* Carmen Barvo.

Federation of European Publishers, Ave. de Tervueren 204, B-1150 Brussels, Belgium. Tel. 2-770-11-10, fax 2-771-20-71, e-mail fep.alemann@brutele.be, World Wide Web http://www.fep-fee.be. *Pres.* J. Arne Bach; *Dir.-Gen.* Anne Bergman-Tahon.

International Assn. of Scientific, Technical and Medical Publishers (STM), POB 90407, NL-2509 LK The Hague, Netherlands. Tel. 70-314-09-30, fax 70-314-09-40, e-mail info@stm-assoc.org, World Wide Web http://www.stm-assoc.org. *Chair* Eric Swanson; *Secy.* Lex Lefebvre.

International Board on Books for Young People (IBBY), Nonnenweg 12, CH-4055 Basel, Switzerland. Tel. 61-272-2917, fax 61-272-2757, e-mail ibby@ibby.org; *Exec. Dir.* Kimete Basha; *Admin. Dir.* Elizabeth Page.

International Booksellers Federation, Chaussée de Charleroi 51b, Boîte 1, 1060 Brussels, Belgium. Tel. 2-223-4940, fax 2-223-4938, e-mail ibf.booksellers@skynet.be, World Wide Web http://www.ibf-booksellers.org. *Pres.* Yvonne Steinberger; *Dir.* Françoise Dubruille.

International League of Antiquarian Booksellers, 400 Summit Ave., Saint Paul, MN 55102. Tel. 800-441-0076, 612-290-0700, fax 612-290-0646, e-mail info@ilab-lila.com, World Wide Web http://www.ilab.org. *Secy.-Gen.* Steven Temple.

International Publishers Assn. (Union Internationale des Editeurs), Ave. Miremont 3, CH-1206 Geneva, Switzerland. Tel. 22-346-3018, fax 22-347-5717, e-mail secretariat@ipa-uie.org, World Wide Web http://www.ipa-uie.org. *Pres.* Ana Maria Cabanellas; *Secy.-Gen.* Jens Bammel.

National

Argentina

Cámara Argentina del Libro (Argentine Book Assn.), Avda. Belgrano 1580, 4 piso, 1093 Buenos Aires. Tel. 1-4381-8383, fax 1-4381-9253, e-mail cal@editores.com, World Wide Web http://www.editores.com. *Dir.* Norberto J. Pou.

Fundación El Libro (Book Foundation), Hipolito Yrigoyen 1628, 5 piso, 1344 Buenos Aires. Tel. 11-4374-3288, fax 11-4375-0268, e-mail fundacion@el-libro.

com.ar, World Wide Web http://www. el-libro.com.ar. *Pres.* Carlos Alberto Pazos; *Dir.* Marta V. Diaz.

Australia

Australian and New Zealand Assn. of Antiquarian Booksellers, 604 High St., Prahran, Vic. 3181. Tel. 3-9525-1649, e-mail admin@anzaab.com, World Wide Web http://www.anzaab.com.au. *Pres.* Barbara Hince.

Australian Booksellers Assn., 828 High St., Unit 9, Kew East, Vic. 3102, Australia. Tel. 3-9859-7322, fax 3-9859-7344, e-mail mail@aba.org.au, World Wide Web http://www.aba.org.au. *Pres.*Tim Peach; *Exec. Dir.* Celia Pollock.

Australian Publishers Assn., Ste. 60, 89 Jones St., Ultimo, NSW 2007. Tel. 2-9281-9788, fax 2-9281-1073, e-mail apa@publishers. asn.au, World Wide Web http://www. publishers.asn.au. *Chief Exec.* Susan Bridge.

Austria

Hauptverband des Österreichischen Buchhandels (Austrian Publishers and Booksellers Assn.), Grünangergasse 4, A-1010 Vienna. Tel. 1-512-15-35, fax 1-512-84-82, e-mail hvb@buecher.at, World Wide Web http://www.buecher.at. *Pres.* Anton C. Hilscher.

Verband der Antiquare Österreichs (Austrian Antiquarian Booksellers Assn.), Grünangergasse 4, A-1010 Vienna. Tel. 1-512-15-35, fax 1-512-84-82, e-mail sekretariat @hvb.at, World Wide Web http://www. antiquare.at. *Pres.* Norbert Donhofer.

Belarus

National Book Chamber of Belarus, 11 Masherow Ave., 220600 Minsk, Belarus. Tel. 172-235-839, fax 172-235-825, e-mail palata@palata.belpak.minsk.by. *Contact* Anatoli Voronko.

Belgium

Vlaamse Boekverkopersbond (Flemish Booksellers Assn.), Hof ter Schriecklaan 17, 2600 Berchem/Antwerp. Tel. 3-230-89-23, fax 3-281-22-40, e-mail info@boek.be,

World Wide Web http://www.boek.be. *Gen. Secy.* Luc Tessens.

Bolivia

Cámara Boliviana del Libro (Bolivian Booksellers Assn.), Casilla 682, Calle Capitan Ravelo No. 2116, La Paz. Tel. 2-44-4339, fax 2-44-1523, e-mail cabolib@ceibo. entelnet.bo. *Pres.* Rolando Condori Salinas; *Secy.* Teresa G. de Alvarez.

Brazil

Cámara Brasileira do Livro (Brazilian Book Assn.), Cristiano Viana 91, 05411-000 Sao Paulo-SP. Tel. /fax 11-3069-1300, e-mail cbl@cbl.org.br, World Wide Web http:// www.cbl.org.br. *Pres.* Oswaldo Siciliano; *Gen. Mgr.* Aloysio T. Costa.

Sindicato Nacional dos Editores de Livros (Brazilian Publishers Assn.), Av. Rio Branco 37, Sala 1.504 , 20090-003 Rio de Janeiro-RJ. Tel. 21-2233-6481, fax 21-2253-8502, e-mail snel@snel.org.br, World Wide Web http://www.snel.org.br. *Pres.* Paulo Roberto Rocco.

Chile

Cámara Chilena del Libro AG (Chilean Assn. of Publishers, Distributors, and Booksellers), Av. Libertador Bernardo O'Higgins 1370, Oficina 501, Santiago de Chile. Tel. 56-2-698-9519, fax 56-2-698-9226, e-mail prolibro@tie.cl, World Wide Web http://www.camlibro.cl. *Pres.* Eduardo Castillo Garcia.

Colombia

Cámara Colombiana del Libro (Colombian Book Assn.), Carrera 17A, No. 37-27, Bogotá DC. Tel. 1-288-6188, fax 1-287-3320, e-mail camlibro@camlibro.com.co, World Wide Web http://www.camlibro. com.co.

Czech Republic

Svaz českých knihkupců a nakladatelů (Czech Publishers and Booksellers Assn.), Jana Masaryka 56, 120 00 Prague 2. Tel. 2-224-219-944, fax 2-224-219-942, e-mail sckn

@sckn.cz, World Wide Web http://www. sckn.cz. *Chair* Jitka Undeova.

Denmark

Danske Boghandlerforening (Danish Booksellers Assn.), Siljangade 6.3, DK 2300 Copenhagen S. Tel. 3254-2255, fax 3254-0041, e-mail ddb@bogpost.dk, World Wide Web http://www.bogguide.dk. *Pres.* Jesper Moller.

Danske Forlaeggerforening (Danish Publishers Assn.), 18/1 Kompagnistr. 1208, Copenhagen K. Tel. 3315-6688, fax 3315-6588, e-mail publassn@webpartner.dk. *Dir.* Tune Olsen.

Ecuador

Cámara Ecuatoriana del Libro, Núcleo de Pichincha, Avda. Eloy Alfaro No. 355, piso 9, Casilla 17-01, Quito. Tel. 2-553-311, fax 2-222-150, e-mail celnp@hoy.net, World Wide Web http://celibro.org.ec. *Pres.* Luis Mora Ortega.

Egypt

General Egyptian Book Organization, Corniche el-Nil—Ramlet Boulac, Cairo 11221. Tel. 2-5775-228, fax 2-5765-058, e-mail info@egyptianbook.org, World Wide Web http://www.egyptianbook.org. *Chair* Mostago Esmat el Sarha.

Estonia

Estonian Publishers Assn., Roosikrantsi 6, 10119 Tallinn. Tel. 2-644-9836, fax 2-641-1443, e-mail astat@eki.ee. *Dir.* A. Trummal.

Finland

Kirjakauppaliitto Ry (Booksellers Assn. of Finland), Eerikinkatu 15-17 D 43-44, FIN-00100 Helsinki. Tel. 9-6859-9110, fax 9-6859-9119, e-mail toimisto@kirjakauppaliitto.fi, World Wide Web http://www.kirjakauppaliitto.fi. *Dir.* Olli Erakivi.

Suomen Kustannusyhdistys (Finnish Book Publishers Assn.), Box 177, FIN-00121 Helsinki. Tel. 9-228-77-250, fax 9-612-1226, e-mail veikko.sonninen@skyry.net,

World Wide Web http://www.skyry.net. *Dir.* Veikko Sonninen.

France

Cercle de la Librairie (Circle of Professionals of the Book Trade), 35 Rue Grégoire-de-Tours, F-75006 Paris. Tel. 1-44-41-28-00, fax 1-44-41-28-65, e-mail commercial@electre.com, World Wide Web http://www.electre.com. *Pres.* Charles Henri Flammarion.

Fédération Française des Syndicats de Libraires (FFSL) (French Booksellers Assn.), 43 Rue de Châteaudun, F-75009 Paris. Tel. 1-42-82-00-03, fax 1-42-82-10-51. *Pres.* Jean-Luc Dewas.

France Edition, 115 Blvd. Saint-Germain, F-75006 Paris. Tel. 1-44-41-13-13, fax 1-46-34-63-83, e-mail info@franceedition.org, World Wide Web http://www.franceedition.org. *Pres.* Liana Levi. *New York Branch* French Publishers Agency, 853 Broadway, Ste. 1509, New York, NY 10003-4703. Tel. 212-254-4540, fax 212-979-6229, World Wide Web http://frenchpubagency.com.

Syndicat National de la Librairie Ancienne et Moderne (National Assn. of Antiquarians and Modern Booksellers), 4 Rue Gît-le-Coeur, F-75006 Paris. Tel. 1-43-29-46-38, fax 1-43-25-41-63, e-mail slam-livre@wanadoo.fr, World Wide Web http://www.slam-livre.fr. *Pres.* Frédéric Castaing.

Syndicat National de l'Edition (National Union of Publishers), 115 Blvd. Saint-Germain, F-75006 Paris. Tel. 1-44-41-40-50, fax 1-44-41-40-77, World Wide Web http://www.snedition.fr. *Pres.* Serge Eyrolles.

Union des Libraires de France (Union of French Booksellers), 40 Rue Grégoire-de-Tours, F-75006 Paris. Tel./fax 1-43-29-88-79. *Pres.* Eric Hardin; *Gen. Delegate* Marie-Dominique Doumenc.

Germany

Börsenverein des Deutschen Buchhandels e.V. (Stock Exchange of German Booksellers), Grosser Hirschgraben 17-21, 60313 Frankfurt-am-Main. Tel. 69-1306-291, fax 69-1306-294, e-mail emmerling

@boev.de, World Wide Web http://www.
boersenverein.de. *Gen. Mgr.* Harald Heker.
Verband Deutscher Antiquare e.V. (German
Antiquarian Booksellers Assn.), Ge-
schaftsstelle, Herr Norbert Munsch, See-
blick 1, 56459 Elbingen. Tel. 6535-909-
147, fax 6435-909-148, e-mail buch@
antiquare.de, World Wide Web http://
www.antiquare.de. *Pres.* Joechen Granier.

Ghana

University Bookshop (formerly West African
University Booksellers Assn.), Univ. of
Ghana, P.O. Box 25, Legon. Tel./fax 21-
500-398, unibks@ug.gn.apc.org. *Mgr.*
Emmanuel K. H. Tonyigah.

Greece

Hellenic Federation of Publishers and Booksellers, Themistocleous 73, 10683 Athens.
Tel. 1-33-00-924, fax 1-33-01-617, e-mail
poev@otenet.gr. *Pres.* Georgios Dardanos.

Hungary

Magyar Könyvkiadók és Könyvterjesztök
Egyesülése (Assn. of Hungarian Publish-
ers and Booksellers), Kertesz u 41, 1073
Budapest. Tel. 1-343-25-40, fax 1-343-25-
41, e-mail mkke@mkke.hu, World Wide
Web http://www.mkke.hu. *Pres.* István
Bart; *Secy.-Gen.* Péter Zentai.

Iceland

Félag Islenskra Bókaútgefenda (Icelandic
Publishers Assn.), Baronsstig 5, 101 Reykjavik. Tel. 511-8020, fax 511-5020, e-mail
baekur@mmedia.is. *Chair* Sigurdur Sva-
varsson; *Gen. Mgr.* Vilborg Hardardóttir.

India

Federation of Indian Publishers, Federation
House, 18/1-C Institutional Area, JNU
Rd., Aruna Asaf Ali Marg, New Delhi
110067. Tel. 11-2696-4847, 11-2685-
2263, fax 11-2686-4054, e-mail fip1@
satyam.net.in, World Wide Web http://
www.fiponweb.com. *Pres.* Shri Anand
Bhushan.

Indonesia

Ikatan Penerbit Indonesia (Assn. of Indonesian Book Publishers), Jl. Kalipasir 32,
Jakarta 10330. Tel. 21-314-1907, fax 21-
314-6050, e-mail sekretariat@ikapi.or.id,
World Wide Web http://www.ikapi.or.id.
Pres. Arselan Harahap; *Secy.-Gen.* Robinson Rusdi.

Ireland

CLE: The Irish Book Publishers Assn., 43/44
Temple Bar, Dublin 2. Tel. 1-670-7393,
fax 1-670-7642, e-mail info@publishing
ireland.com, World Wide Web http://
www.publishingireland.com. *Contact* Orla
Martin.

Israel

Book and Printing Center, Israel Export Institute, 29 Hamered St., P.O. Box 50084, Tel
Aviv 68125. Tel. 3-514-2830, fax 3-514-
2902, e-mail export-institute@export.gov.
il or pama@export.gov.il, World Wide
Web http://www.export.gov.il. *Dir.-Gen.*
Yechiel Assia.

Book Publishers Assn. of Israel, Box 20123,
Tel Aviv 61201. Tel. 3-561-4121, fax 3-
561-1996, e-mail info@tbpai.co.il, World
Wide Web http://www.tbpai.co.il. *Manag-
ing Dir.* Amnon Ben-Shmuel; *Chair* Shay
Hausman.

Italy

Associazione Italiana Editori (Italian Publishers Assn.), Via delle Erbe 2, 20121 Milan.
Tel. 2-86-46-3091, fax 2-89-01-0863,
e-mail aie@aie.it, World Wide Web http://
www.aie.it. *Dir.* Ivan Cecchini.

Associazione Librai Antiquari d'Italia (Antiquarian Booksellers Assn. of Italy), Via
del Parione, 11, 50123 Florence. Tel. 55-
282-635, fax 55-214-831, e-mail alai@
alai.it, World Wide Web http://www.alai.
it. *Pres.* Francesco Chellini.

Jamaica

Booksellers' Assn. of Jamaica, c/o Novelty
Trading Co. Ltd., Box 80, Kingston. Tel.

876-922-5883, fax 876-922-4743. *Pres.* Keith Shervington.

Japan

Japan Assn. of International Publications (formerly Japan Book Importers Assn.), Chiyoda Kaikan 21-4, Nihonbashi 1-chome, Chuo-ku, Tokyo 103-0027. Tel. 3-3271-6901, fax 3-3271-6920, e-mail jaip@ poppy.ocn.ne.jp, World Wide Web http:// www.jaip.gr.jp. *Chair* Seishiro Murata; *Secy.-Gen.* Hiroshi Takahashi.

Japan Book Publishers Assn., 6 Fukuro-machi, Shinjuku-ku, Tokyo 162-0828. Tel. 3-3268-1301, fax 3-3268-1196, e-mail rd@jbpa.or.jp, World Wide Web http:// www.jbpa.or.jp. *Pres.* Kunizo Asakura; *Exec. Dir.* Tadashi Yamashita.

Kenya

Kenya Publishers Assn., P.O. Box 42767, Nairobi 00100. Tel. 20-375-2344, fax 20-375-4076, e-mail kenyapublishers@ wananchi.com, World Wide Web http:// www.kenyabooks.org. *Exec. Secy.* Lynnette Kariuki.

Korea (Republic of)

Korean Publishers Assn., 105-2 Sagan-dong, Jongro-gu, Seoul 110-190. Tel. 2-735-2701, fax 2-738-5414, e-mail kpa@kpa21. or.kr, World Wide Web http://www. kpa21.or.kr. *Pres.* Choon Ho Na; *Secy.-Gen.* Jong Jin Jung.

Latvia

Latvian Publishers Assn., Kr. Barona iela 36-4, 1011 Riga. Tel. 371-728-2392, fax 371-728-0549, e-mail lga@gramatizdeveji.lv, World Wide Web http://www.gramatiz deveji.lv. *Exec. Dir.* Dace Pugaca.

Lithuania

Lithuanian Publishers Assn., K Sirbydo 6, 2600 Vilnius. Tel./fax 5-261-7740, e-mail lla@centras.lt, World Wide Web http:// www.lla.lt. *Pres.* Aleksandras Krasnovas.

Malaysia

Malaysian Book Publishers' Assn., No. 39 Jln Nilam 1-2, Subang Sq., Subang High-Tech Industrial Park Batutiga, 40000 Shah Alam, Selangor. Tel. 3-5637-9044, fax 3-5637-9043, e-mail inquiry@cerdik.com. my, World Wide Web http://www. mabopa.com.my. *Pres.* Ng Tieh Chuan.

Mexico

Cámara Nacional de la Industria Editorial Mexicana (Mexican Publishers' Assn.), Holanda No. 13, CP 04120, Mexico 21. Tel. 55-5688-24-34, fax 55-5604-43-47, e-mail cepromex@caniem.com, World Wide Web http://www.caniem.com. *Co-Pres.* A. H. Gayosso, J. C. Cramerez.

The Netherlands

KVB (formerly Koninklijke Vereeniging ter Bevordering van de Belangen des Boekhandels) (Royal Dutch Book Trade Assn.), Postbus 15007, 1001 MA Amsterdam. Tel. 20-624-02-12, fax 20-620-88-71, e-mail info@kvb.nl, World Wide Web http:// www.kvb.nl. *Exec. Dir.* C. Verberne.

Nederlands Uitgeversverbond (Royal Dutch Publishers Assn.), Postbus 12040, 1100 AA Amsterdam. Tel. 20-43-09-150, fax 20-43-09-179, e-mail info@nuv.nl, World Wide Web http://www.nuv.nl. *Pres.* Henk J. L. Vonhoff.

Nederlandsche Vereeniging van Antiquaren (Netherlands Assn. of Antiquarian Booksellers), Postbus 364, 3500 AJ Utrecht. Tel. 30-231-92-86, fax 30-234-33-62, e-mail bestbook@wxs.nl, World Wide Web http://nvva.nl. *Pres.* Ton Kok.

Nederlandse Boekverkopersbond (Dutch Booksellers Assn.), Prins Hendriklaan 72, 3721 AT Bilthoven. Tel. 30-228-79-56, fax 030-228-45-66, e-mail nbb@boek bond.nl, World Wide Web http://www. boekbond.nl. *Pres.* W. Karssen; *Exec. Secy.* A. C. Doeser.

New Zealand

Booksellers New Zealand, Box 13-248, Wellington. Tel. 4-478-5511, fax 4-478-

5519, e-mail enquiries@booksellers.co.nz,
World Wide Web http://www.booksellers.
co.nz. *Chair* Tony Moores, *Chief Exec.*
Alice Heather

Nigeria

Nigerian Publishers Assn., GPO Box 2541,
Ibadan. Tel. 2-241-4427, fax 2-241-3396,
e-mail nigpa@skannet.com or nigpa@
steineng.net. *Pres.* V. Nwankwo.

Norway

Norske Bokhandlerforening (Norwegian
Booksellers Assn.), Øvre Vollgate 15,
0158 Oslo 1. Tel. 22-00-75-80, fax 22-33-
38-30, e-mail firmapost@bokhandler
foreningen.no, World Wide Web http://
www.bokhandlerforeningen.no. *Dir.* Randi
Øgrey.

Norske Forleggerforening (Norwegian Publishers Assn.), Øvre Vollgate 15, 0158
Oslo 1. Tel. 22-00-75-80, fax 22-33-38-30,
e-mail dnf@forleggerforeningen.no,
World Wide Web http://www.forlegger
foreningen.no. *Dir.* Per Christian Opsahl.

Peru

Cámara Peruana del Libro (Peruvian Publishers Assn.), Av. Cuba 427, Jesús Maria.
Apartado 10253, Lima 11. Tel. 511-472-
9516, fax 511-265-0735, e-mail cp-libro@
amauta.rcp.net.pe, World Wide Web
http://www.cpl.org.pe/Camara/clpagpri.ht
m. *Pres.* Carlos Augusto Benavides Aqui-
je; *Secy.* Emilio Presentación Malpartida.

Philippines

Philippine Educational Publishers Assn., 84
P. Florentino St., 3008 Quezon City. Tel.
2-712-4106, fax 2-731-3448, e-mail
dbuhain@cnl.net. *Pres.* Dominador D.
Buhain.

Poland

Polskie Towarzystwo Wydawców Ksiazek
(Polish Society of Book Editors), ul.
Mazowiecka 2/4, 00048 Warsaw. Tel. 22-
826-7271, fax 22-826-0735. *Pres.* Janusz

Fogler; *Gen. Secy.* Donat Chruscicki.
Stowarzyszenie Ksiegarzy Polskich (Assn. of
Polish Booksellers), ul. Mokotowska 4/6,
00641 Warsaw. Tel. 22-252-874, World
Wide Web http://www.bookweb.org/orgs/
1322.html. *Pres.* Tadeusz Hussak.

Portugal

Associação Portuguesa de Editores e
Livreiros (Portuguese Assn. of Publishers
and Booksellers), Av. dos Estados Unidas
da America 97, 6 Esq., 1700-167 Lisbon.
Tel. 21-843-51-80, fax 21-848-93-77, e-
mail geral@apel.pt, World Wide Web
http://www.apel.pt. *Pres.* Graca Didier.

Russia

Publishers Assn., B. Nikitskaya St. 44,
121069 Moscow. Tel. 95-202-1174, fax
95-202-3989. *Contact* I. Laptev.
Russian Book Chamber, Kremlevskaja nab
1/9, 119019 Moscow. Tel. 95-203-4653,
fax 95-298-2576, e-mail chamber@aha.ru,
World Wide Web http://www.bookchamber.
ru. *Dir.-Gen.* Boris Lenski.

Serbia and Montenegro

Assn. of Yugoslav Publishers and Booksellers, POB 570, 11000 Belgrade. Tel. 11-
642-248, fax 11-646-339, e-mail ognjenl
@eunet.yu, World Wide Web http://www.
beobookfair.co.yu. *Gen. Dir.* Ognjen Laki-
cevic.

Singapore

Singapore Book Publishers Assn., c/o Cannon International, 86 Marine Parade Centre, No. 03-213, Singapore 440086. Tel.
65-344-7801, fax 65-447-0897, e-mail
twcsbpa@singnet.com.sg. *Pres.* K. P.
Siram.

Slovenia

Zdruzenie Zaloznikov in Knjigotrzcev Slov-
enije Gospodarska Zbornica Slovenije
(Assn. of Publishers and Booksellers of
Slovenia), Dimiceva 13, 1504 Ljubljana.
Tel. 1-5898-474, fax 1-5898-100, e-mail

info@gzs.si, World Wide Web http://www.gzs.si. *Pres.* Milan Matos.

South Africa

Publishers Assn. of South Africa, Box 22640, Fish Hoek, Cape Town 7974. Tel. 21-782-7677, fax 21-782-7679, e-mail pasa@publishsa.co.za, World Wide Web http://www.publishsa.co.za. *Admin.* Desiree Murdoch.

South African Booksellers Assn. (formerly Associated Booksellers of Southern Africa), P.O. Box 870, Bellville 7530. Tel. 21-918-8616, fax 21-951-4903, e-mail fnel@naspers.com, World Wide Web http://sabooksellers.com. *Pres.* Guru Redhi; *Secy.* Peter Adams.

Spain

Federación de Gremios de Editores de España (Federation of Spanish Publishers Assns.), Cea Bermúdez 44-2 Dcha, 28003 Madrid. Tel. 91-534-5195, fax 91-535-2625, e-mail fgee@fge.es, World Wide Web http://www.federacioneditores.org. *Pres.* D. Emiliano Martinez; *Exec. Dir.* Antonio Ma Avila.

Sri Lanka

Sri Lanka Assn. of Publishers, 112 S. Mahinda Mawatha, Colombo 10. Tel. 1-695-773, fax 1-696-653, e-mail dayawansajay@hotmail.com. *Gen. Secy.* Gamini Wijesuriya.

Sudan

Sudanese Publishers Assn., c/o Institute of African and Asian Studies, Khartoum Univ., Box 321, Khartoum 11115. Tel. 249-11-778-0031, fax 249-11-770-358, e-mail makkawi@sudanmail.net. *Dir.* Abel Rahim Makkawi.

Sweden

Svenska Förläggareföreningen (Swedish Publishers Assn.), Drottninggatan 97, S-11360 Stockholm. Tel. 8-736-19-40, fax 8-736-19-44, e-mail info@forlaggareforeningen, World Wide Web http://www.forlaggare foreningen.se. *Dir.* Kristina Ahlinder.

Switzerland

Schweizerischer Buchhandler- und Verleger-Verband (Swiss German-Language Book-sellers and Publishers Assn.), Alderstr. 40, 8034 Zurich. Tel. 1-421-28-00, fax 1-421-28-18, e-mail sbvv@swissbooks.ch, World Wide Web http://www.swissbooks.ch. *Exec. Dir.* Martin Jann.

Association Suisse des Éditeurs de Langue Française (ASELF) (Swiss Assn. of English-Language Publishers), 2 Ave. Agassiz, 1001 Lausanne. Tel. 21-319-71-11, fax 21-319-79-10, World Wide Web http://www.culturactif.ch/editions/asef1.htm. *Pres.* Francine Bouchet.

Thailand

Publishers and Booksellers Assn. of Thailand, 947/158-159 Moo 12, Bang Na-Trad Rd., Bang Na, Bangkok 10260. Tel. 2-954-9560-4, fax 2-954-9565-6, e-mail info@pubat.or.th, World Wide Web http://www.pubat.or.th.

Uganda

Uganda Publishers and Booksellers Assn., Box 7732, Kampala. Tel. 41-259-163, fax 41-251-160, e-mail mbd@infocom.co.ug. *Contact* Martin Okia.

United Kingdom

Antiquarian Booksellers Assn., Sackville House, 40 Piccadilly, London W1J 0DR, England. Tel. 20-7439-3118, fax 20-7439-3119, e-mail info@aba.org.uk, World Wide Web http://www.aba.org.uk. *Pres.* Jonathan Potter.

Assn. of Learned and Professional Society Publishers, South House, The Street, Clapham, Worthing, West Sussex BN13 3UU, England. Tel. 1903-871-686, fax 1903-871-457, e-mail chief-exec@alpsp.org, World Wide Web http://www.alpsp.org. *Secy.-Gen.* Sally Morris.

Booktrust, 45 East Hill, Wandsworth, London SW18 2QZ, England. Tel. 20-8516-2977, fax 20-8516-2978, World Wide Web http://www.booktrust.org.uk.

Educational Publishers Council, 29B Montague St., London WC1B 5BH, England. Tel. 20-7691-9191, fax 20-7691-9199, e-mail mail@publishers.org.uk, World Wide Web http://www.publishers.org.uk. Chair Philip Walters; Dir. Graham Taylor.

Publishers Assn., 29B Montague St., London WC1B 5BH, England. Tel. 20-7691-9191, fax 20-7691-9199, e-mail mail@publishers.org.uk, World Wide Web http://www.publishers.org.uk. Pres. Anthony Forbes-Watson; Chief Exec. Ronnie Williams.

Scottish Book Trust, Sandeman House, Trunks Close, 55 High St., Edinburgh EH1 1SR, Scotland. Tel. 131-524-0160, fax 131-228-4293, e-mail info@scottishbooktrust.com, World Wide Web http://www.scottishbooktrust.com.

Scottish Publishers Assn., Scottish Book Centre, 137 Dundee St., Edinburgh EH11 1BG, Scotland. Tel. 131-228-6866, fax 131-228-3220, e-mail info@scottishbooks.org, World Wide Web http://www.scottishbooks.org. Dir. Lorraine Fannin; Chair Timothy Wright.

Welsh Books Council (Cyngor Llyfrau Cymru), Castell Brychan, Aberystwyth, Ceredigion SY23 2JB, Wales. Tel. 1970-624-151, fax 1970-625-385, e-mail castelbrychan@wbc.org.uk, World Wide Web http://www.cllc.org.uk. Dir. Gwerfyl Pierce Jones.

Uruguay

Cámara Uruguaya del Libro (Uruguayan Publishers Assn.), Juan D. Jackson 1118, 11200 Montevideo. Tel. 82-41-57-32, fax 82-41-18-60, e-mail camurlib@adinet.com.uy. Pres. Ernesto Sanjines.

Venezuela

Cámara Venezolana del Libro (Venezuelan Publishers Assn.), Av. Andrés Bello, Torre Oeste 11, piso 11, Of. 112-0, Apdo. 51858, Caracas 1050-A. Tel. 212-793-1347, fax 212-793-1368, e-mail cavelibro@cantv.net. Dir. M. P. Vargas.

Zambia

Booksellers and Publishers Assn. of Zambia, Box 31838, Lusaka. Tel./fax 1-255-166, e-mail bpaz@zamnet.zm, World Wide Web http://africanpublishers.org. Exec. Dir. Basil Mbewe.

Zimbabwe

Zimbabwe Book Publishers Assn., P.O. Box 3041, Harare. Tel 4-754-256, fax 4-754-256, e-mail engelbert@collegepress.co.zw.

National Information Standards Organization (NISO) Standards

Information Retrieval

Z39.2-1994 (R 2001) Information Interchange Format
Z39.47-1993   Extended Latin Alphabet Coded Character Set for
                      Bibliographic Use (ANSEL)
Z39.50-2003   Information Retrieval (Z39.50) Application Service
                      Definition and Protocol Specification
Z39.53-2001   Codes for the Representation of Languages for
                      Information Interchange
Z39.64-1989 (R 2002) East Asian Character Code for Bibliographic Use
Z39.76-1996 (R 2002) Data Elements for Binding Library Materials
Z39.84-2000   Syntax for the Digital Object Identifier
Z39.89-2003   The U.S. National Z39.50 Profile for Library Applications

Library Management

Z39.7-2005   Information Services and Use: Metrics and Statistics for
                      Libraries and Information Providers—Data Dictionary
Z39.20-1999   Criteria for Price Indexes for Print Library Materials
Z39.71-1999   Holdings Statements for Bibliographic Items
Z39.73-1994 (R 2001) Single-Tier Steel Bracket Library Shelving
Z39.83-2002   Part 2: Protocol Implementation

Preservation and Storage

Z39.32-1996 (R 2002) Information on Microfiche Headers
Z39.48-1992 (R 2002) Permanence of Paper for Publications and Documents in
                      Libraries and Archives
Z39.62-2000   Eye-Legible Information on Microfilm Leaders and
                      Trailers and on Containers of Processed Microfilm on
                      Open Reels
Z39.74-1996 (R 2002) Guides to Accompany Microform Sets
Z39.77-2001   Guidelines for Information About Preservation Products
Z39.78-2000   Library Binding
Z39.79-2001   Environmental Conditions for Exhibiting Library and
                      Archival Materials

Publishing and Information Management

Z39.9-1992 (R 2001) International Standard Serial Numbering (ISSN)
Z39.14-1997 (R 2002) Guidelines for Abstracts
Z39.18-1995   Scientific and Technical Reports—Elements,
                     Organization, and Design
Z39.19-1993 (R 2003) Guidelines for the Construction, Format, and Management
                     of Monolingual Thesauri
Z39.23-1997 (R 2002) Standard Technical Report Number Format and Creation
Z39.26-1997 (R 2002) Micropublishing Product Information
Z39.41-1997 (R 2002) Printed Information on Spines
Z39.43-1993 (R 2001) Standard Address Number (SAN) for the Publishing
                     Industry
Z39.56-1996 (R 2002) Serial Item and Contribution Identifier (SICI)
NISO/ANSI/ISO   Electronic Manuscript Preparation and Markup
  12083 (R 2002)
Z39.82-2001   Title Pages for Conference Publications
Z39.85-2001   Dublin Core Metadata Element Set
ANSI/NISO   Specifications for the Digital Talking Book
  Z39.86-2002

In Development/NISO Initiatives

Z39.19 revision—Developing the Next Generation of Standards for Controlled
  Vocabularies and Thesauri
Z39.18 revision—Scientific and Technical Reports—Preparation, Presentation,
  and Preservation
Z39.29 revision—Bibliographic References
Metasearch Initiative—Access Management, Collection Description, and Search/
  Retrieve
Networked Reference Services (Draft standard for Trial Use through April 2005)
Technical Metadata for Digital Still Images
OpenURL Framework for Context-Sensitive Services
Serials JWP—partnering with EDItEUR to support the use of ONIX for Serials
  to communicate information about serial products and subscriptions.
ISBN revision—13-digit ISBN approved for transition by January 1, 2007.

NISO is continually examining emerging areas for standardization. These
initiatives support our ongoing standards development program. Some of the topics NISO is exploring are

- Electronic Resource Management
- Digital Reference Services
- Performance Measures and Statistics for Libraries
- Reference Linking
- Controlled Vocabularies, Interoperability, and Thesauri
- Electronic Journals—Best Practices

- Scientific and Technical Reports: Spanning the New Technology
- Archiving Electronic Publications

NISO Technical Reports and Other Publications

Environmental Guidelines for the Storage of Paper Records (TR-01-1995)
Guidelines for Indexes and Related Information Retrieval Devices (TR-02-1997)
Guidelines to Alphanumeric Arrangement and Sorting of Numerals and Other Symbols (TR-03-1999)
Information Standards Quarterly (*ISQ*) (NISO quarterly newsletter)
Metadata Demystified: A Guide for Publishers
The RFP Writer's Guide to Standards for Library Systems
Understanding Metadata
Up and Running: Implementing Z39.50—Proceedings of a Symposium Sponsored by the State Library of Iowa
Z39.50: A Primer on the Protocol
Z39.50 Implementation Experiences

Workshop reports and white papers are available on the NISO Web site at http://www.niso.org/standards/std_resources.html.

For more information, contact NISO, 4733 Bethesda Ave., Suite 300, Bethesda, MD 20814. Tel. 301-654-2512, fax 301-654-1721, e-mail nisohq@niso.org, World Wide Web http://www.niso.org.

Calendar, 2005–2014

The list below contains information on association meetings or promotional events that are, for the most part, national or international in scope. State and regional library association meetings are also included. To confirm the starting or ending date of a meeting, which may change after the *Bowker Annual* has gone to press, contact the association directly. Addresses of library and book trade associations are listed in Part 6 of this volume. For information on additional book trade and promotional events, see *Literary Market Place* and *International Literary Market Place*, published by Information Today, Inc., and other library and book trade publications such as *Library Journal, School Library Journal,* and *Publishers Weekly.* An Information Today events calendar can be found at http://www.infotoday.com/calendar.shtml.

2005

June

1–2	Search Engine Strategies	London, England
2–3	Rhode Island Library Assn.	Newport
2–5	Antiquarian Booksellers Assn.	London, England
3–5	BookExpo America	New York
4–9	Special Libraries Assn.	Toronto
9–11	Assn. of Canadian Archivists	Saskatoon
15–18	American Theological Library Assn.	Austin
15–18	Canadian Library Assn. Annual Conference	Calgary
17–20	North American Serials Interest Group	Minneapolis
23–29	American Library Assn. Annual Conference	Chicago
24–27	BookExpo Canada	Toronto
27–30	National Educational Computing Conference	Philadelphia
29–7/3	International Assn. of Technological University Libraries	Quebec City

July

1–3	National Education Association Expo	Los Angeles
7–10	Tokyo International Book Fair	Tokyo
8–10	Society of Indexers	Exeter, England
10–15	International Assn. of Music Libraries, Archives, and Documentation Centers	Warsaw, Poland
16–21	American Assn. of Law Libraries	San Antonio

July 2005 *(cont.)*

20–25	Hong Kong Book Fair	Hong Kong

August

3–6	Pacific Northwest Library Assn.	Sitka, Alaska
8–11	Search Engine Strategies 2005	San Jose
13–21	Society of American Archivists	New Orleans
14–18	World Library and Information Conference	
	(IFLA General Conference)	Oslo, Norway

September

1–5	Beijing International Book Fair	Beijing, China
14–17	Kentucky Library Assn.	Louisville
18–21	ARMA International	Chicago
20–23	North Carolina Library Assn.	Winston-Salem
21–23	Minnesota Library Assn.	Minneapolis
21–23	North Dakota Library Assn.	Grand Forks
28–30	Nebraska Library Assn.	Lincoln
30–10/2	Library and Information Technology Assn.	
	National Forum	San Jose

October

1–4	Arkansas Library Assn.	Little Rock
3–4	West Virginia Library Assn.	Shepherdstown
5–7	Ohio Library Council	Columbus
5–7	South Dakota Library Assn.	Pierre
5–9	American Assn. of School Librarians	Pittsburgh
6–7	Idaho Library Assn.	Pocatello
6–8	Washington Library Media Assn.	Yakima
11–13	Arizona Library Assn.	Mesa
11–15	Illinois Library Assn.	Peoria
12–15	Wyoming Library Assn./Mountain Plains	
	Library Assn.	Jackson Hole
16–18	New England Library Assn.	Worcester, MA
18–21	EDUCAUSE	Orlando
19–21	Iowa Library Assn.	Dubuque
19–22	Nevada Library Assn.	Reno
19–24	Frankfurt Book Fair	Frankfurt, Germany
20–21	Virginia Library Assn.	Williamsburg
22–26	Medical Informatics Assn.	Washington, DC
23–25	OCLC Members Council Meeting	Dublin, OH
24–26	Internet Librarian	Monterey
25–28	Michigan Library Assn.	Grand Rapids
25–28	Mississippi Library Assn.	Vicksburg
25–28	Wisconsin Library Assn.	Lacrosse

26–28	Missouri Library Assn.	Kansas City
26–29	Michigan Assn. for Media in Education	Detroit
26–29	New York Library Assn.	Buffalo
27–29	Illinois School Library Media Assn.	Decatur
27–29	Educational Media Assn. of New Jersey	Cherry Hill
28–30	U.S. Board on Books for Young People	Callaway Gardens, GA
28–11/2	American Society for Information Science and Technology	Charlotte, NC

November

| 4–7 | California Library Assn. | Pasadena |
| 10–13 | Colorado Assn. of Libraries | Denver |

2006

January

| 16–19 | Assn. for Library and Information Science Education | San Antonio |
| 20–25 | American Library Assn. Midwinter Meeting | San Antonio |

February

| 2–4 | Ontario Library Assn. | Toronto |
| 20–26 | Music Library Assn. | Memphis |

March

3–5	Michigan Assn. for Media in Education	Petoskey
20–25	Public Library Assn.	Boston
29–31	Oklahoma Library Assn.	Tulsa

April

2–8	National Library Week	
3–5	United Kingdom Serials Group	Warwick, England
5–7	Tennessee Library Assn./Southeastern Library Assn.	Memphis
17–21	Florida Library Assn.	Orlando
19–22	Washington Library Assn.	Tacoma
25–28	Texas Library Assn.	Houston

May

2–7	Montana Library Assn.	Missoula
3–5	Wisconsin Assn. of Public Libraries	Wisconsin Rapids
19–24	Medical Library Assn.	Phoenix
23–24	Vermont Library Assn.	Burlington

June 2006

1–3	Canadian Assn. for Information Science	Toronto
10–15	Special Libraries Assn.	Baltimore
14–17	Canadian Library Assn.	Ottawa
15–17	Assn. of Canadian Archivists	St. John's, NL
18–23	International Assn. of Music Libraries, Archives, and Documentation Centers	Gothenburg, Sweden
21–24	American Theological Library Assn.	Chicago
22–28	American Library Assn. Annual Conference	New Orleans

July

15–20	American Assn. of Law Libraries	St. Louis
31–8/6	Society of American Archivists	Washington, DC

August

4–6	Americas Conference on Information Systems	Acapulco
TBA	World Library and Information Conference (IFLA General Conference)	Seoul

September

27–29	Minnesota Library Assn.	St. Cloud

October

2–4	West Virginia Library Assn.	Huntington
4–5	Idaho Library Assn.	Moscow
4–9	Frankfurt Book Fair	Frankfurt, Germany
10–13	EDUCAUSE	Dallas
11–13	Iowa Library Assn.	Council Bluffs
12–15	REFORMA/Black Caucus of the American Library Assn./American Indian Library Assn.	Dallas
22–24	New England Library Assn.	Burlington, VT
22–25	ARMA International	San Antonio
26–29	Library and Information Technology Assn. (LITA) National Forum	Nashville

November

1–4	New York Library Assn.	Saratoga Springs
3–9	American Society for Information Science and Technology	Austin
11–15	American Medical Informatics Assn.	Washington, DC

2007

January

16–19	Assn. for Library and Information Science Education	Seattle

| 19–24 | American Library Assn. Midwinter Meeting | Seattle |

February

| 1–3 | Ontario Library Assn. | Toronto |

March

7–9	Tennessee Library Assn.	Nashville
12–17	Texas Library Assn.	San Antonio
29–4/1	ACRL National Conference	Baltimore

April

| 11–13 | Kansas Library Assn. | Topeka |

May

| 18–23 | Medical Library Assn. | Philadelphia |

June

| 2–7 | Special Libraries Assn. | Denver |
| 21–27 | American Library Assn. Annual Conference | Washington, DC |

July

| 14–18 | American Assn. of Law Libraries | New Orleans |

August

| 27–9/2 | Society of American Archivists | Chicago |

October

3–5	West Virginia Library Assn.	Morgantown
6–10	Arkansas Library Assn.	Little Rock
7–10	ARMA International	Baltimore
14–16	New England Library Assn.	Sturbridge, MA

November

| 10–14 | American Medical Informatics Assn. | Chicago |

2008

January

| 11–16 | American Library Assn. Midwinter Meeting | Philadelphia |

March

| 25–29 | Public Library Assn. | Minneapolis |

April 2008

7–12	Texas Library Assn.	Dallas
9–11	Kansas Library Assn.	Wichita

May

16–21	Medical Library Assn.	Chicago

June

2–4	Canadian Assn. for Information Science	Vancouver
26–2/7	American Library Assn. Annual Conference	Anaheim

July

12–16	American Assn. of Law Libraries	Portland
26–31	Special Libraries Assn.	Seattle

August

23–31	Society of American Archivists	San Francisco

October

3–4	Arkansas Library Assn.	Little Rock
20–23	ARMA International	Las Vegas

December

3–5	West Virginia Library Assn.	White Sulphur Springs

2009

January

23–28	American Library Assn. Midwinter Meeting	Denver

April

1–3	Kansas Library Assn.	Overland Park
20–25	Texas Library Assn.	Houston

June

13–18	Special Libraries Assn.	Washington, DC

July

9–15	American Library Assn. Annual Conference	Chicago

2010

January

15–20	American Library Assn. Midwinter Meeting	Boston

April

12–16   Texas Library Assn.   San Antonio

June

24–30   American Library Assn. Annual Conference   Orlando

2011
January

28–2/2   American Library Assn. Midwinter Meeting   Chicago

June

23–29   American Library Assn. Annual Conference   New Orleans

2012
January

20–25   American Library Assn. Midwinter Meeting   San Antonio

June

21–27   American Library Assn. Annual Conference   Anaheim

2013
January

25–30   American Library Assn. Midwinter Meeting   Seattle

June

20–26   American Library Assn. Annual Conference   Washington, DC

2014
January

24–29   American Library Assn. Midwinter Meeting   Philadelphia

June

26 –2/7   American Library Assn. Annual Conference   Las Vegas

Acronyms

CRIA. Canadian Recording Industry
Association
CRL. Center for Research Libraries
CRS. Congressional Research Service
CSLA. Church and Synagogue Library
Association
CTEA. Copyright Term Extension Act
CUI. Security measures, Controlled
Unclassified Information

D

DLF. Digital Library Federation
DMCA. Digital Millennium Copyright Act
DMCRA. Digital Media Consumers' Rights
Act
DOE. Education, U.S. Department of
DRM. Digital rights management
DTB. Digital talking book (DTB) technology
DTIC. Defense Technical Information Center

E

EAR. National Technical Information
Service, Export Administration
Regulations
eCFR. National Archives and Records
Administration, Electronic Code of
Federal Regulations
EDB. Energy, Science and Technology
Database
EMIERT. American Library Association,
Ethnic and Multicultural Information and
Exchange Round Table
ERIC. Educational Resources Information
Center
ERM. Electronic resources, Electronic
Resource Management
ERMI. Council on Library Information
Resources, E-Resources Management
Initiative
ETS. Educational Testing Service

F

FAFLRT. American Library Association,
Federal and Armed Forces Librarians
Round Table
FBI. Federal Bureau of Investigation
FCC. Federal Communications Commission

FDLP. Government Printing Office, Federal
Depository Library Program
FEDRIP. National Technical Information
Service, FEDRIP (Federal Research in
Progress Database)
FIAF. International Federation of Film
Archives
FLICC. Federal Library and Information
Center Committee
FOLUSA. Friends of Libraries U.S.A.
FPC. Federal Publishers Committee

G

GAO. Government Accountability Office
GLBT. American Library Association, Gay,
Lesbian, Bisexual, and Transgendered
Round Table
GODORT. American Library Association,
Government Documents Round Table
GPO. Government Printing Office
GRC. National Technical Information
Service, GOV.Research Center

I

IAALD. International Association of
Agricultural Information Specialists
IACs. Defense Technical Information Center,
Information Analysis Centers
IALL. International Association of Law
Libraries
IAML. International Association of Music
Libraries, Archives and Documentation
Centres
IASL. International Association of School
Librarianship
IATUL. International Association of
Technological University Libraries
ICBS. International Committee of the Blue
Shield
IDLH. Databases, Immediately Dangerous to
Life or Health Concentrations Database
IEEPA. International Emergency Economic
Powers Act
IFLA. International Federation of Library
Associations and Institutions
IFRT. American Library Association,
Intellectual Freedom Round Table
ILL/DD. Interlibrary loan/document delivery

IMAA. Instructional Materials Accessibility Act

IMLS. Institute of Museum and Library Services

IR. Institutional repositories

ISBN. International Standard Book Number

ISO. International Organization for Standardization

ISSN. International Standard Serial Number

J

JAMA. Journal of the American Medical Association

L

LAMA. Library Administration and Management Association

LHRT. American Library Association, Library History Round Table

LIS. Library/information science

LITA. Library and Information Technology Association

LOCKSS. Government Printing Office, LOCKSS (Lots of Copies Keep Stuff Safe)

LRRT. American Library Association, Library Research Round Table

LSP. National Center for Education Statistics, Library Statistics Program

LSTA. Library Services and Technology Act

M

MAGERT. American Library Association, Map and Geography Round Table

MLA. Medical Library Association; Music Library Association

N

NAGARA. National Association of Government Archives and Records Administrators

NAL. National Agricultural Library

NARA. National Archives and Records Administration

NCBI. National Center for Biotechnology Information

NCES. National Center for Education Statistics

NCLA. National Church Library Association

NCLB. No Child Left Behind

NCLIS. National Commission on Libraries and Information Science

NCLSP. Canada, National Core Library Statistics Program

NDIIPP. National Digital Information Infrastructure and Preservation Program

NEH. National Endowment for the Humanities

NFAIS. NFAIS (National Federation of Abstracting and Information Services)

NIH. National Institutes of Health

NIOSH. National Institute for Occupational Safety and Health

NISO. National Information Standards Organization

NLE. National Library of Education

NLM. National Library of Medicine

NMRT. American Library Association, New Members Round Table

NPG. National Institute for Occupational Safety and Health, NIOSH Pocket Guide to Chemical Hazards (NPG)

NTIS. National Technical Information Service

O

OAI. Open Archives Initiative

OECD. Organization for Economic Cooperation and Development

P

PLA. Public Library Association

R

RIAA. Recording Industry Association of America

RUSA. Reference and User Services Association

S

SAA. Society of American Archivists

SAN. Standard Address Number

SIIA. Software and Information Industry
  Association
SLA. Special Libraries Association
SNOMED CT. National Library of Medicine,
  Systematized Nomenclature of
  Medicine—Clinical Terms
SPARC. Scholarly Publishing and Academic
  Resources Coalition
SRIM. National Technical Information
  Service, Selected Research in Microfiche
SRRT. American Library Association, Social
  Responsibilities Round Table
SSP. Society for Scholarly Publishing
STINET. Scientific and Technical
  Information Network
StLA. State libraries and library agencies,
  NCES State Library Agencies survey

T

TLA. Theatre Library Association

U

UCITA. Uniform Computer Information
  Transactions Act

ULC. Urban Libraries Council
UMLS. National Library of Medicine,
  Unified Medical Language System
USPS. Postal Service, U.S.

V

VR. Digital reference, virtual reference

W

WIPO. World Intellectual Property
  Organization
WISER. National Library of Medicine,
  Wireless Information System for
  Emergency Responders
WNC. World News Connection

Y

YALSA. Young Adult Library Services
  Association
YPG. Association of American Publishers,
  Young to Publishing Group

Index of Organizations

Please note that many cross-references refer to entries in the Subject Index.

A

A&M Records, Inc., 297–298
AGRICOLA (Agricultural OnLine Access),
  58, 81
Agriculture Network Information Center
  (AgNIC), 58–59
Agriculture, U.S. Department of (USDA), *see*
  National Agricultural Library
AGRIS (Agricultural Science and Technolo-
  gy database), 81
Amazon.com, 14
American Association of Law Libraries
  (AALL), 661–662
  awards, 411
American Association of School Librarians
  (AASL), 9, 665–666
  advocacy, 11–12
  awards, 413–414
  grants, 444
  Information Literacy Standards for Student
    Learning, 262
  media specialists, study on, 440–441
American Booksellers Association (ABA),
  19, 162–165
  Book Buyer's Handbook, 162–163
  Book Sense, 163–164
  Web site, 162
American Booksellers Foundation for Free
  Expression (ABFFE), 164–165
American Folklife Center, 30–31, 37
American Library Association (ALA),
  125–138, 662–683
  accreditation policies, 138, 401–405
  advocacy, 126
  at your library, 130
  author poster series, 135
  awards, 136–137, 153, 411–423
  Banned Books Week, 128–129, 153
  Careers in Libraries, 380

celebrity READ poster campaign, 135
Complete Copyright . . ., 127
conferences, 10, 132–134, 224
copyright-related activities, 318
Diversity, Office for, 420
divisions, 125–126
E-rate program, 308
Ethnic and Multicultural Information and
  Exchange Round Table (EMIERT)
  awards, 417
Exhibits Round Table awards, 417
fair-use campaign, 126–127
Federal and Armed Forces Librarians
  Round Table (FAFLRT) awards, 418
Gay, Lesbian, Bisexual, and Transgendered
  Round Table (GLBT), 418
Government Documents Round Table
  (GODORT) awards, 418
grants, 136, 443
highlights, 126–130
Human Resource Development and
  Recruitment, 380
information, access to, 127–128
information literacy, 261–264
Intellectual Freedom Round Table (IFRT),
  418, 420
Lawyers for Libraries, 129
leadership, 135–136
Library History Round Table (LHRT)
  awards, 419–420
Library Research Round Table (LRRT)
  awards, 420
Licensing Digital Content . . ., 225
literacy, 129–130, 420
Map and Geography Round Table
  (MAGERT); awards, 420
members, honorary, 137–138
National Library Legislative Day, 128
New Members Round Table (NMRT)
  awards, 420

Subject Index

Please note that many cross-references refer to entries in the Index of Organizations.

A

A&M Records, Inc. v. *Napster,* 297–298
Abdul-Jabbar, Kareem, 36
Academic books, 239, 333
  copyright practices, 251–252, 253
  electronic resources, 227
  prices and price indexes
    British averages, 516–517(table), 519
    North American, 506–507(table)
    U.S. college books, 508–509(table)
  See also Association of American Publishers, Professional/Scholarly Publishing; Society for Scholarly Publishing; Textbooks
Academic libraries, *see* College and research libraries
Academic publishing, 148–150, 179, 249
Access, open, 232–236
  alternative to, 247
  cost considerations, 233–235
  funding, 243
  NEH grants, 349
Accreditation, 138, 282, 401–405
Acquisitions
  electronic, 222
  expenditures, 467–475
    academic libraries, 470–471(table)
    government libraries, 474–475(table)
    public libraries, 468–469(table)
    special libraries, 472–473(table)
  Library of Congress, 27–28
  See also specific types of libraries, e.g., Public libraries
Adults, services for
  NCES Fast Response Survey System, 98
  readers' advisory, bibliography for librarians, 560
  See also Literacy programs; Reference and User Services Association

Advocacy; bibliography for librarians, 552–553
Agatston, Arthur, 586, 588
Agencies, library, *see* Library associations and agencies
Agricultural libraries, *see* International Association of Agricultural Information Specialists; National Agricultural Library
Alabama
  humanities councils, 343
  library associations, 724
  networks and cooperative library organizations, 639
  school library media associations, 746
Alaska
  humanities councils, 343
  library associations, 724
  networks and cooperative library organizations, 639
  school library media associations, 746
Albom, Mitch, 20, 586
Almanacs, bestselling, 601
America (The Book) (Stewart), 14, 21, 586, 588
American Home Recording Act (AHRA), 297
American Jobs Creation Act, 336–337
American Samoa, humanities council, 348
Angels and Demons (Brown), 20, 586, 595
Anna Karenina (Tolstoy), 596
Anticounterfeiting Amendment Act, 321–322
Archives, 226
  acquisition expenditures
    academic libraries, 470–471(table)
    government libraries, 474–475(table)
    public libraries, 468–469(table)
    special libraries, 472–473(table)
  bibliography for librarians, 559

B